D0926967

EXPLORATIONS
IN GENERAL THEORY
IN SOCIAL SCIENCE

EXPLORATIONS IN GENERAL THEORY IN SOCIAL SCIENCE

Essays in Honor of Talcott Parsons

Edited by

Jan J. Loubser
Rainer C. Baum
Andrew Effrat
Victor Meyer Lidz

VOLUME TWO

THE FREE PRESS
A Division of Macmillan Publishing Co., Inc.
NEW YORK
Collier Macmillan Publishers
LONDON

Copyright © 1976 by The Free Press
A Division of Macmillan Publishing Co., Inc.

All rights reserved. No part of this book may be reproduced
or transmitted in any form or by any means, electronic or
mechanical, including photocopying, recording, or by any
information storage and retrieval system, without permission
in writing from the Publishers.

The Free Press
A Division of Macmillan Publishing Co., Inc.
866 Third Avenue, New York, N.Y. 10022

Collier Macmillan Canada, Ltd.

Library of Congress Catalog Card Number: 75–8427

Printed in the United States of America

printing number

1 2 3 4 5 6 7 8 9 10

Library of Congress Cataloging in Publication Data
Main entry under title:

Explorations in general theory in social science.

    Includes bibliographical references and index.
    1. Sociology--Methodology--Addresses, essays, lectures.
2. Parsons, Talcott, 1902-   --Addresses, essays,
lectures. I. Parsons, Talcott, 1902-   II. Loubser, Jan J.
HM24.E87   301'.01   75-8427
ISBN 0-02-919370-2 (v. 1)
ISBN 0-02-919381-8

301.01
E96
v.2

COPYRIGHT ACKNOWLEDGMENTS

Quotations from the following titles are reprinted with the permission of The Free Press, A Division of Macmillan Publishing Co., Inc.:

Talcott Parsons, *The Structure of Social Action* (1937, 1965); Allen & Unwin, Ltd.

Talcott Parsons, *Essays in Sociological Theory* (1949, 1954)

Talcott Parsons, *The Social System* (1951)

Talcott Parsons, *Structure and Process in Modern Societies* (1960)

Talcott Parsons, *Social Structure and Personality* (1964)

Talcott Parsons, *Sociological Theory and Modern Society* (1967)

Talcott Parsons, *Politics and Social Structure* (1969)

Talcott Parsons and Robert F. Bales, *Family, Socialization and Interaction Process* (1955); Routledge & Kegan-Paul, Ltd.

Talcott Parsons, Robert F. Bales, and Edward A. Shils, *Working Papers in the Theory of Action* (1953)

Talcott Parsons and Alexander M. Henderson (trans.), *Max Weber: The Theory of Social and Economic Organization* (1954)

Talcott Parsons, Edward Shils, Kaspar D. Naegele, and Jesse R. Pitts, *Theories of Society* (1961)

Talcott Parsons and Neil J. Smelser, *Economy and Society* (1956); Routledge & Kegan-Paul, Ltd.

CONTENTS

Volume Two

PART VI: ORGANIZATIONAL ANALYSIS

VOLUME ONE
The Companion Volume

GENERAL INTRODUCTION *Jan J. Loubser*

PART I: META-THEORY

PART II: GENERAL ACTION ANALYSIS

PART III: SOCIALIZATION

PREFACE

This tribute to Talcott Parsons has been long in coming into print. First conceived in 1968, contributions were invited in 1969 and most were completed and edited before the end of 1971. Successive appropriate target dates for publication—1972, coinciding with Parsons' seventieth birthday; 1973, when he retired from Harvard—came and passed without the end in sight. Perhaps the best *ex post facto* rationale for the date achieved is the twenty-fifth anniversary of *The Social System* or the American bicentennial! But *any* year is appropriate for a tribute to Talcott Parsons, which The Free Press, the publisher of most of his books, well realized as it met every contingency with ingenuity and efficiency.

The inspiration and object of dedication of this book is Talcott Parsons, a social scientist of rare distinction. A professed "incurable theorist," he is equally well known for some lasting empirical insights and analyses. A highly productive researcher, he is also remembered vividly as a splendid teacher by those who have had the privilege of studying with him, as have each of the editors and most of the contributors. His work, more than that of any other contemporary figure, has profoundly influenced the intellectual bases of modern social science in several disciplines. This compendium is the second to appear in his honor and is unlikely to be the last.*

This is a book by students of the theory of action, as Parsons' theoretical corpus has become known. Some of the contributors have not been students of Talcott Parsons in the personal sense but students of his work, the theory of action. These "explorations" are intended to illustrate, if not prove, the usefulness of the maps of a master "cartographer" even in territory not before charted in detail. If some of the contributions question some of the most basic aspects of the theory of action, they do so in the intellectual tradition and inquiring spirit of Talcott Parsons. As such, they are tributes to him of no less magnitude than those reflecting a more direct acceptance of his formulations. They equally demonstrate the vitality of the theory of action and the dynamics of theoretical action or action oriented to theory. The extraordinary diversity of these contributions reflects the active interest of a new generation of social scientists in sustaining a high level of discourse on and investigation of the basic issues that Talcott Parsons has articulated with greater theoretical sophistication than was possible before the theory of action.**

The usual observation that "this book would not have been possible without the help and co-operation of so and so" would sound even more pedantic in this case. But special thanks are in order: The contributors showed great patience with our editorial prescriptions and suggestions as well as with the inordinate but inevitable delays in publication. The fact that most of their contributions were completed by the end of 1971 does not in any way detract from their importance. However, the reader should be aware of this obvious explanation for the lack of references to relevant works published since 1971.

We honor the memory of Thomas O'Dea, who did not live to see the publication of the book.

At The Free Press we had the good fortune to work with James Cron in the early stages and with

---

*The first was Alex Inkeles and Bernard Barber (eds.), *Stability and Social Change* (Boston: Little, Brown, 1973).

**For the most up-to-date bibliography of Talcott Parsons, see Talcott Parsons and Charles Martel, *Dialogues with Parsons* (New York: The Free Press, forthcoming).

Charlie Smith in the final, critical stages. Both of them were most supportive in what even to them as seasoned editors was an undertaking of unusual proportions. The production editor, Bob Harrington, guided us through the various editing stages with great skill and perseverance.

Victor Meyer Lidz wishes to acknowledge the support of the Department of Sociology of the University of Chicago and especially its chairman at the time, Morris Janowitz, in arranging for time free of teaching obligations that greatly facilitated his participation in the editorial tasks.

J.J.L.
R.C.B.
A.E.
V.M.L.

ABOUT THE EDITORS

Loubser, Jan J. Born in South Africa in 1932, he is Director of the Social Science Research Council of Canada since 1974. He was Professor of Sociology, University of Cape Town, South Africa, and taught at the University of Toronto and the Ontario Institute for Studies in Education. He is a former President of the Canadian Sociology and Anthropology Association. He is author of *The Impact of Industrial Conversion and Workers' Attitudes to Change* and *The York County Board: A Study in Educational Innovation,* as well as of articles on moral action, values, and social change.

Baum, Rainer C. Born in Breslau, then Germany, in 1934, he is Associate Professor of Sociology at the University of Pittsburgh having previously been associated with the University of Toronto and the University of British Columbia. A general sociologist with interests in theory, comparative nation-building, and stratification, he is currently engaged in cross-national comparative research on modernization problems. He is the author or coauthor of articles in *Sociological Inquiry, The Indian Journal of Social Research,* and *Aging and Human Development* (1975) and in books edited by Edward Harvey, Walter Gerson, and Stanton Wheeler.

Effrat, Andrew Born in New York City in 1939, he is Associate Professor of Sociology in Education at the Ontario Institute for Studies in Education in Toronto and has also taught at Harvard and at Haverford College. He is Editor of *Sociological Inquiry* and has edited special issues of the journal on *Applications of Parsonian Theory, Perspectives in Political Sociology,* and *Critiques of Modern Culture and Consciousness.* He is also Editor of *Interchange: A Journal of Educational Studies.*

Lidz, Victor Meyer Born in Baltimore, Maryland, in 1941, he is currently Lecturer in the Department of Sociology of the University of Pennsylvania. Previously, he served as an Instructor in Sociology and the Collegiate Division of the Social Sciences at the University of Chicago. As an undergraduate and graduate student at Harvard University, he began study of the theory of action in Talcott Parsons' courses. His publications include contributions to the journal, *Sociological Inquiry,* "The Gift of Life and Its Reciprocation" (with Talcott Parsons and Renée C. Fox) in *Social Research,* and *Readings on Premodern Societies* (coeditor with Talcott Parsons).

ABOUT THE CONTRIBUTORS

Ben-David, Joseph   Born in Gyor, Hungary, he is Professor of Sociology at the Hebrew University, Jerusalem, and Research Associate at the Department of Sociology, University of Chicago. He is a foreign honorary member of the American Academy of Art and Sciences and a foreign associate of the National Academy of Education (U.S.). He has served as visiting professor at the University of California, Berkeley, and was a fellow of the Center of Advanced Study in the Behavioral Sciences, Palo Alto. He is past President of the Israeli Sociology Association. Among his publications are *The Scientist's Role in Society* and *American Higher Education, Directions Old and New*.

Bidwell, Charles E.   Born in Chicago in 1932, he is Professor of Sociology and Education at the University of Chicago. Among his publications are *Administrative Relationships;* "The School as a Formal Organization"; and "School District Organization and Student Achievement." He is a former Editor of *Sociology of Education* and is currently Editor of the *American Journal of Sociology*.

Bourricaud, François   Born in 1922, he is Professor at the Université René Descartes, Paris. A Rockefeller Fellowship allowed him to study under Talcott Parsons from 1950 to 1952. Since then, he has taught sociology in various capacities in France and abroad. He has worked extensively and many times in Latin America, notably in Peru. He has been a fellow at the Center for Advanced Study in the Behavioral Sciences, Palo Alto. His main publications are *Eléments pour une sociologie de l'action* (selection and translation of some of Parsons' essays); *Esquisse d'une théorie de l'autorité; Pouvoir et société dans le Pérou contemporain;* and *Université à la dérive*.

Cartwright, Bliss C.   Born in Sheboygan, Wisconsin, in 1941, he is Assistant Professor of Sociology, State University of New York at Buffalo. Currently, he is engaged in research on state supreme court litigation (1870–1970) and is the author of articles in *American Sociological Review, Law and Society Review,* and *Psychological Bulletin*.

Dreeben, Robert   Born in New York City in 1930, he is Professor of Education at the University of Chicago, having previously taught at Harvard University in the Department of Social Relations and in the Graduate School of Education. He is the author of *On What Is Learned in School, The Nature of Teaching* and "American Schooling" in Barber and Inkeles (eds.), *Stability and Social Change*.

Eisenstadt, S. N.   Born in Warsaw in 1922, he is Professor of Sociology at the Hebrew University in Jerusalem and has been visiting professor at Harvard, M.I.T., Oslo, Chicago, and other universities. He has been a fellow at the Centre for Advanced Study in the Behavioral Studies, Wassenaar. He is a member of the Israeli Academy of Sciences and Humanities, a foreign honorary member of the American Academy of Arts and Sciences, an honorary fellow of the London School of Economics, and a fellow, N.I.A.S. His books include *The Absorption of*

Immigrants; From Generation to Generation; Social Differentiation and Stratification; Israeli Society; The Political Systems of Empires; and *Modernization: Protest and Change.* He has also edited a number of collections of contributions to comparative analysis, such as *The Protestant Ethic and Modernization,* and large volumes of readings in *Political Sociology; Israeli Society; Intellectuals and Traditions;* and *Post-Traditional Societies.*

Fox, Renée C.   Born in New York City in 1928, she is Professor and Chairman in the Department of Sociology at the University of Pennsylvania. She is also Professor of Sociology in the Department of Medicine and in the Department of Psychiatry. She has taught at Barnard College, Harvard University, the Official University of the Congo in Lubumbashi, and Sir George Williams University in Montreal. She has also served as Scientific Advisor to the Centre de Recherches Sociologiques in Kinshasa. She is the author of *Experiment Perilous; The Emerging Physician: A Sociological Approach to the Development of a Congolese Medical Profession* (with Willy de Craemer): and *The Courage to Fail: A Social View of Organ Transplants and Dialysis* (with Judith P. Swazey).

Gould, Mark   Born in 1945, he teaches sociology at Haverford College. He is currently completing his doctoral dissertation on *Revolution and the Development of Capitalism.*

Hills, R. Jean   Born in Oacoma, South Dakota, in 1929, he is Professor of Educational Administration, Centre for the Study of Administration in Education, at the University of British Columbia, He is the author of *Toward a Science of Organization, The Concept of System,* and of articles appearing in *Administrative Science Quarterly, Educational Administration Quarterly, School Review, Administrator's Notebook, Journal of Educational Administration,* and *Elementary School Journal.*

Johnson, Harry M.   Born in Cambridge, Massachusetts, in 1917, he is Professor of Sociology at the University of Illinois, Urbana. He is the author of *Sociology: A Systematic Introduction* and of various articles. He is especially interested in ethnic-group relations.

Luhmann, Niklas   Born in Lüneburg, Germany, in 1927, he is Professor of Sociology at the University of Bielefeld, Germany, and member of the Rheinisch-Westfälische Akademie der Wissenschaften, Düsseldorf. His books include *Functionen und Folgen formaler Organisation; Vertrauen; Zweckbegriff und Systemrationalität; Legitimation durch Verfahren; Soziologische Aufklärung; Politische Planung; Theorie der Gesellschaft oder Sozialtechnologie—Was leistet die Systemforschung?* (with Jürgen Habermas); *Rechtssoziologie; Personal im öffentlichen Dienst: Eintritt und Karrieren* (with Renate Mayntz); *Rechtssystem und Rechtsdogmatik;* and *Macht.*

Rueschemeyer, Dietrich   Born in Berlin, Germany, in 1930, he is Professor of Sociology at Brown University. He has formerly taught at the University of Cologne, Dartmouth College, the University of Toronto and, as a visitor, at the Hebrew University of Jerusalem. He has edited a collection of essays by Talcott Parsons in German translation and is author of *Lawyers and Their Society: A Comparative Study of the Legal Profession in Germany and in the United States.*

Robertson, Roland   Born in Norwich, England, in 1938, he is Professor of Sociology at the University of Pittsburgh, having previously taught at the University of Leeds, the University of

Essex, and the University of York (England), where he was Chairman of the Department of Sociology. He is the author of *The Sociological Interpretation of Religion* and *Meaning and Change* and coauthor of *International Systems and the Modernization of Societies* and *Deviance, Crime and Socio-Legal Control*. He is also Editor of *The Sociology of Religion*.

Tominaga, Ken'ichi   Born in Tokyo, Japan, in 1931, he is Associate Professor of Sociology at the University of Tokyo. He has served as visiting research associate at the University of Illinois, at Harvard, and as visiting fellow at the Australian National University. He is the author of *Shakaihendō no Riron* (A Theory of Social Change) and *Sangyōshakai no Dōtai* (Dynamics of Industrial Society) and the editor of *Keiei to Shakai* (Business Organization and Society) and *Keizai-shakaigaku* (Economic Sociology).

Warner, R. Stephen   Born in 1941 in Oakland, California, he is Assistant Professor of Sociology at Yale University. He has also taught at Sonoma State College and at the University of California, Berkeley. He is the author of *Sociological Theory in Historical Context* and of several essays on sociological theory, including the works of Marx and Weber. During 1974–75, he was recipient of a Guggenheim Fellowship for a study of values and consensus in sociological theory and empirical research.

IV

GENERALIZED MEDIA
IN ACTION

INTRODUCTION

Rainer C. Baum

The conception of generalized media of interchange probably constitutes Parsons' most significant theoretical effort during the sixties. The significance—it seems to me—lies far more at the abstract than at the concrete level. This does not deny that interesting questions can be raised about the similarities and differences between money and, for example, power in relatively concrete terms. But I take it that the conceptions of *generalized medium, functional specialization,* and *indirectly mediated contingent action* constitute the major advances. Their import lies in improving our grasp of the functional requisites of complex systems.

So far (1971), Parsons has presented two sets of generalized media of interchange. One, developed in some though far from sufficient detail, covers the non-economic money analogues of value-commitments, influence, and power. Together with money, they are all operative at the level of the societal system.[1] Another set, rather more cryptic and only extant in outline form, covers "definition of the situation," "affect," "performance capacity," and "intelligence," all operative at the level of the general action system.[2] As Lidz and Lidz (this volume) have recently presented four types of functionally specialized intelligence as media for the organism, "rounding out" this schema for action theory calls for the development of media relevant for the analysis of culture and personality. One might think of a medium conception of "pure reason," "practical reason," "aesthetic reason," or the like for culture and of the mechanisms of defense and those of adjustment for personality.

However, incompleteness of the types of media is only one of the remaining lacunae. Another has to do with the preliminary stage of formulation of the kinds of media proposed to date. Here there are two sources to conceptual underdevelopment. First, for the general action media the categories of interchange cover only special forms of the media

and not the respectively variable forms of the "intrinsic valuables" they control. This differential emphasis is also apparent for the societal media, though less so. Second, only suggestive labels have been supplied for the different forms of the media at each level. Satisfactory definitions of forms of money, power, influence, and value-commitments are still outstanding. Relative to the very concept of medium rather than its special forms, this applies to the general action media as well. For example, just what exactly "intelligence" or "performance capacity" cover has remained rather fuzzy.

Furthermore, the earlier developed set of societal media has not been left alone. Parsons changed his mind about the security base of influence. He shifted this from general solidarity bonds to "certain types of knowledge"[3] without specifying what types he had in mind. He also reallocated one code component of a societal medium, using it for a general action medium by designating "success" as the coordinating standard of performance capacity.[4] Apparently he substituted "sovereignty" as the coordinating standard of power.[5] He uses "sovereignty" in a special sense. It refers to a collectivity's capacity to maintain independence in its power supply-expenditure balance on the basis of a Schumpeterian circular flow, as well as on power credit creation through leadership influence, *but not* on the basis of a change in the structure of broader value-commitments. The latter case always involves a loss, however temporary, of independence and the need to rely on supports themselves contingent on de-differentiation. This strikes me as a far superior formulation of the coordinating standard of power than the original "success" standard which tempted one to think of the special case of charismatic authority. Yet the whole point of the conception of power as a medium makes best sense for the case of rational-legal authority. The problem is, later publications of the original power paper have not shown change in this respect. According to what is in print, one does not know whether Parsons changed his mind towards sovereignty or not. Fortunately, print is not the sole basis here. It seems that the unexpurgated republication of the original power paper was an unfortunate oversight.[6]

Thus relative lateness and remaining incompleteness characterize this aspect of action theory. The former is probably due to the joint impact of two growing concerns emerging most clearly also during the sixties, the latter to the inevitable complexity of an interdisciplinary social science paradigm.

One of the growing concerns has been an attempt to build a neo-evolutionary theory of change.[7] Another has been a growing treatment of the four-function paradigm as a set of system-environment relations. This set comprises (1) higher complexity and higher instability of components of the environment relative to those of the system, (2) a system boundary previous to the outside, (3) boundary maintenance through control of interchanges "aiming" to maintain the inside-outside difference in complexity and stability, and (4) contingency of the system on environment(s) which can be maintained in the form of *relative* system autonomy to the extent that special mechanisms select from environment(s) what the system "wants" to be dependent on. In short, the four-function paradigm was viewed from a system-environment *relations* perspective that poses essentially comparable problems for all living systems. Further, because systems face multiple environments posing different problems of adaptation they tend to "respond" to this need for differentiated system-environment relations by internal differentiation.[8] The basic view here is that a growth of coping ability with more and more external variety on the part of a system comes about through creation of greater internal variety. Then, finally, as boundary maintenance involves mediated interchanges, processes for which communication is the basic model, the need for media rises with internal differentiation into subsystems.

This general answer to the query "Why media?" seems to me more pertinent than Parsons' occasional remarks tracing their history to experiences derived from the analysis of the relations between economy and "society".[9] There can be no doubt that economics did play the major role in conceptualizing media. However, Parsons tries to use economic theory as a special case of a more general social theory, and hence money, the principle economic medium, as merely one function-specific medium among a family of four in all. This does involve "generalization from" economic theory and the economic case but not in the simple form of taking economics as the master template right away. Rather it demands seeing economic theory as a special variant of social theory first, and then generalizing pertinent findings to other subsystems in society. Yet as the changes and inconsistencies just indicated illustrate, there is a danger in starting the whole enterprise of media theorizing at the societal level. Like most other concepts in the complex edifice that is action theory, media are interdependent. Starting the development of this aspect of the theory at any level other than the general action level constitutes a problem. One cannot go into extensive detail mapping of the components unless one has the general action media worked out. In the reverse case, as for instance starting with the societal level, which actually happened, there is the danger of premature detail specification. This is one of the rare examples where Parsons did not start at the top and work his way "down," and that choice is our fate.

The attempt is quite clearly to develop a conception of media of interchange adequate for a generalized social science paradigm, not just for better understanding highly differentiated social systems. I think this relates both to relative lateness and remaining incompleteness in this part of action theory. There is a double constraint that characterizes Parsons' work as a whole. He has always refused to sacrifice to greater precision anything of the inevitable complexity and generality which such a paradigm requires. He has never been that kind of logical fetishist quite willing to abandon what he "knew" to be true and relevant in the service of mere elegance. Then also he has always maintained and practiced a commitment to cumulative theory-building to a degree rarely found elsewhere in the social sciences. That does not mean that he refused to change his mind when necessary; but it does make it notoriously difficult to understand any given piece of writing with all its implications entirely on the ground of its own statements. The occasional opinion to be heard that "his applied essays are marvelous and have—thank God—nothing to do with his theorizing" illustrate the point. As to comprehensiveness in standing on its own feet, however, there is a very notable exception. This is a paper incongruously titled "Some Problems in General Theory in Sociology,"[10] which is anything but sociological in the traditional sense. It is the most comprehensive and concise statement of the theory of action I know. This is also the place where he spelled out the general action media, rudimentary as they are. In fact, they are so rudimentary that they cannot serve as a model for introducing the reader to media theorizing. Very important media components such as an operative code, security base, and intrinsic satisfiers, or "the real things" symbolically represented by media, have not been formulated to a degree of precision sufficient for introductory purposes.

In light of these facts it was decided to let the societal media serve as an introduction to the why and whence of media theory in the theory of action. This demanded, however, using a somewhat unorthodox format so far as introductions go. If the case of the societal media is to serve at all adequately in giving the reader a general overview as to the general role of media, a fairly extensive presentation seems necessary. This means covering what is in print, but scattered over a fairly wide terrain, and therefore presenting a systematic overview. On the other hand, it also demands a departure from the more usual format of an introduction to a set of contributions in the sense of not addressing oneself in any greater detail to what the contributors have to say. The reason is simple: Our space is not unlimited. But this is not too serious an issue, for the usual in introductions is frequently not at all the ideal. In part this is a matter of taste; and for clarity's sake, I have to state mine. Having left the nursery for quite some time, I find little use in premastication of what I can chew myself. Unless, therefore, a set of contributions are manifestly on their own terms so far apart as to require a Herculean effort to sense any connections, introductory "discussions" of what they say are simply not called for. The contributions in this section are not that far apart. Therefore, I shall confine myself to a brief reference to these essays at the relevant points in presenting an outline of the societal media. Indicating what issues they treat rather than covering what they say should be quite sufficient. This should rationalize my effort. The first part of it will deal with supplying an answer to the question "Why media?" The second part will render an outline of the principal components of the societal media.

SELECTED BACKGROUND CHARACTERISTICS OF MEDIA THEORIZING

"We would like to reformulate the process of rationalization as the tendency of social systems to develop progressively higher levels of structural differentiation under the pressure of adaptive agencies."[11] For present purposes this quote is doubly important. It locates an intellectual effort in a tradition, and it appears towards the end of a book dealing with the subject matter of its assertion. Thus one has as aim the provision of greater specification to Max Weber's abiding concern with the increasing rationalization of social action. The fact that it appears so late in the first major systematic macrosociological effort seems to be symptomatic of two usages of the concept of differentiation. The first usage, usually appearing in adjectival form, as in "highly differentiated society," involves a state description of a system. More precisely, it denotes a given level of organized complexity in functional specialization of a society. As a state description its main service is to define critical problems of analysis and provide the conceptual scaffolding necessary for the level of complex societal organization envisaged. As usual in social science the "problems" are not just those of the scientist. They partly overlap and intermesh with those of the observed, the subject-matter. In the present instance there is an empirical picture of modern man valiantly struggling with universal problems in an increasingly rational manner of organization and thereby generating additional problems, those peculiar to coping with rationality itself.

The second usage, usually appearing in noun form as "differentiation," forms one of four critical components of a model concerning a specific type of social change deemed evolutionary because it results in society's increased capacity in rational problem solving. Developed somewhat later and in far greater detail by Smelser,[12] it is a model of structural and processual change in society below the level of values. Media are necessary conceptual complements both for state descriptions of different levels of differentiation and for the model of evolutionary structural change. However, their systematic application has been far more characteristic of the former. This does not mean that media have not been already one part of the study of evolutionary development. The reason is simple. One can study broad-gauged evolutionary development without using a theory of processes of change. A comparative and sequential ordering of structural types of society can yield interesting results. Here such media as money and power play an important role in sequential ordering.[13] Given the more systematic development of media as conceptual tools in the analysis of structural types of society with given levels of internal differentiation, this account will be largely restricted accordingly. The role of media in Smelser's model of structural change will only receive secondary and marginal attention.

Turning then to the construction of a model of a society characterized by a high level of internal functional differentiation, Parsons and Smelser[14] first decided to treat "the economy" as only one of a family of four such function-specific structural sets. This view derived of course from applying the general action four-function paradigm of adaptation, goal-attainment, integration, and pattern maintenance to the most comprehensive social system, the "society." At this societal level then, four-function structural differentiation refers to four sub-systems: economy, polity, societal community, and pattern maintenance-and-modification, in the AGIL functional sense respectively. Given the over-all objective of rendering greater specification to Max Weber's concern with growing rationality in action, they chose the economy as paradigmatic and attempted to generalize to other functional subsystems.

As a strategy for theory construction this signals a return to the basic approach of Pareto for Parsons.[15] This seems to me symptomatic both: (1) of the interim characterized by a primary preoccupation with elaborating Durkheim's insight concerning order rather than randomness of ends in action with Freud, and (2) of the more recent attempts to conceive of *Wertbeziehungen* as more subject to dynamic process as articulated through a medium value-commitments. It also (3) signals a renewed attempt to make economic theory proper continuous with other social theories, an endeavour whose feasibility was explicitly denied in the interim.[16]

Two facts recommended starting with economic action as an instance of rational action from which one could learn about other types. Empirically, economic action appears as that area of human conduct where rational decision-making in the pursuit of fairly clearly delineated special objectives has been most securely institutionalized. Also, economic theory had a conceptual category, "price," quite efficacious for the analysis of rational choice, which had no convincing parallel in sociological theory. Yet clearly, participation in the economy as commonly understood was social action. Therefore, price should be a special case of a more general concept useful for the analysis of all social relational action as defined in a voluntarist framework. This program seemed to require at least three departures from common sense: (1) not treating a subsystem as a concrete social structure, (2) a conception of action as a resultant of a combinatorial process, and (3) a search for function-specific analogues in the other three subsystems for "value in exchange" which underlies "economizing about utilities" in order to supersede the limitations inherent in the kinds of interest reductions often associated with utilitarian exchange theorists.

As to the first of the three departures from common sense, one cannot treat any subsystem in concrete terms. Parsons usually uses the term "collectivity" or "individual-in-role" when making references to concrete living people, rarely function, structure, system or subsystem. A differentiated subsystem of society, as for example the economy, therefore does not refer to something concrete as the sum of all firms. Differentiated function-specific subsystems always refer to "aspects" of social action. Some concrete collectivity or relations between them can have "primary" aspects, as for example having "primarily" economic functional significance for society. Originally some rather commonsense reasons were given for insisting on this distinction and its anticommonsense message. In one sense practically all concrete units of society are part of the economy as buyer or seller, producer or consumer. "Thus households, universities, hospitals, units of government, churches, etc., are *in* the economy. But *no* concrete unit participates *only* in the economy."[17] The same holds of course for the other societal subsystems. As subjects, supporters, and consumers of governmental authority and services we are all individually and collectively in the polity. But none participate only in the polity. Again, as speakers of a common language, beings who can agree most of the time on the meaning of traffic signals and on the rule that $2 + 2 = 4$, all of us are in the pattern maintenance and modification subsystem. But none participate exclusively in it. All of us are in some social class, are subject to law, live in some community, hence participate in the societal community. But many of us "belong" to organization such as a church, a professional association, or sports clubs that exist across societal boundaries. And again, most of us participate not only in the societal community but also in the polity, the economy, and so on. By the same token, every concrete and organized collectivity, whether a church, a household, or a friendship *a deux* has by virtue of organization some collective goal to pursue, needs some means for that, has to face potential conflict inside, and has to agree on basic meaning patterns if for no other reason than the need to communicate. Thus every concrete organization regardless of type has political, economic, integrative, and pattern maintenance "aspects." Hence every concrete collectivity as a social system is multifunctional, and, however rudimentarily developed, also multistructural. Yet the criterion of overlapping memberships seems hardly sufficient to justify the tortuous English required to keep the distinction clear. There must be better reasons than these of common sense to justify it.

One other reason for these abstract formulations was the need to deny common sociological sense to the economist's usual practice of treating goods and services jointly as outputs of economic action. A set of empirical differences here seemed to counsel separation. In contrast to physical factors the human factor has to be motivated; next, "labor" is "produced" in households or formal education systems, not in the economy; also, because of multiple role incumbencies the labor market is subject to far more stringent imperfections than a goods market, and the relation of "service" to product is quite asymmetrical when compared to the relation between physical factors and production in that service cannot be divorced entirely from the personality performing it.[18] The result was that output destinations were classified differently. Goods, i.e., property rights in physical objects of possession as consumables, ultimately go to households. "Services," as commitment of human role performance to occupational structures, ultimately constitute a contribution to the effective organization of the societal collectivity. As such they constitute an output to the polity.[19] But again, even sociological common sense seems insufficient to justify such departures. There must be better reasons yet to ground such a departure from common sense.

Turning to these, the four-function paradigm of action demands a somewhat unusual view of action, one that is geared in the manner of a Weberian ideal type to illuminate the sources for the increasing rationality in action. Though most clearly articulated in a later work of Smelser and Parsons,[20] this was already in their *Economy and Society* a conception of action in general as the result of a value-added process. Accordingly, an action was a product of a combinatorial process. Somewhat analogous to the familiar categories of economic theory wherein land, organization, labor, and capital are combined to yield a good with more exchange value than the combined "factors" of production, any kind of action could be conceived of as a result of the combination of (1) value-commitment, (2) normative specification, (3) properly organized and socialized motive force, and (4) facilities. Though essentials did not differ from an earlier definition of action with its emphasis on (1) goal-orientation, (2) situational selectivity (the actor could have oriented differently than he did in the observed case at hand), (3) normative regulation, and (4) effort expenditure,[21] the combinatorial view not only sounded more dynamic but also blatantly invited an attempt at generalizing the basic questions asked by economics to action theory.

"Suggested" by the array of the principle components of action—values, norms, organization, and facilities—action was seen as the product of the operation of successive constraints on the queries (1) *what shall be done,* (2) *in what situation,* (3) *by whom and for whom* as participants-recipients, and (4) *with what means?* As a program for action analysis this is not just reminiscent of Samuelson-type economics. It is very close indeed. Therefore, it is important to elucidate the effort to generalize beyond

economics but retain its principle perspective as a science concerned with problems of rational choice.

Actually this use of the economic perspective took the form of a subtle two-step search for useful analogies. First, surely the critical role of the concept of "price" in the form of "the capacity to impute value in exchange into an incredible variety of objects (physical and social) with quite varying values in use" was only a rather special case of the more general concept of "meaning" in the Weber-Durkheim-Mead tradition of sociological theory. Second, if so, value of exchange was just as surely only one kind of special meaning differentiated for one type of functionally specialized subsystem, the economic, and there must be others of a cognate standing that aid the organization of the other three function-specific subsystems, the political, the integrative, and the pattern-maintaining. In fact Parsons has not done much work in generalizing the category of price. Instead he has confined himself to applying the basic idea of equilibrium between inputs and outputs to all relations between subsystems. However, the role of price is so central in the operation of media as mechanisms of choice that one may confidently expect work attempting to trace the analogues of price in the other media in the near future. To encourage such work a few more remarks concerning price may be in order.

The price concept in economic theory suggested that in the case of general action that to which value is added is meaning. A rational combinatorial process here would demand that the value of meaning that can be experienced actually in the final implementive act is more than that carried and expended in combining the components. However, although it was a common element in sociological theorizing, the concept "ability to impute a common property of meaningfulness into an incredible variety of concrete shared meaning experiences" had not advanced sociological theory in any way comparable to the role of price in economic theory. Sociologists had treated it merely as a necessary though not sufficient prerequisite for any kind of order at all to be maintained. Empirically it did not signal much more than postulating some minimally shared common language-competency.

Analytically, however, the story was not quite that dismal. Marx, for example, had a very dynamic conception of interest going far beyond this or that concrete object or experience. Using such notions as "the whole of history is a preparation for . . . the development of human needs (the needs of man as such)," "It will be seen from this how in the place of the *wealth* and *poverty* of political economy, we have . . . the plenitude of human need," "The sway of . . . the sensuous eruption of my life activity, is the passion which here becomes the *activity* of my being,"[22] one can see that Marx had a historical-evolutionary conception of interest culminating in "man's capacity to experience want as such." This is not want for specifics like the stilling of hunger, the ease of pain. This is "interest as the generalized capacity to experience a gap between what is and could be," encompassing everything from salvation to satisfaction of a bodily need. One of the unfortunate consequences of this important insight among later writers was indiscriminate interest reductions, despite and perhaps even because of Marx' equally important recognition of a medium that aids man in articulating unlimited wants. Quoting Shakespeare to the effect that gold "speak'st with every tongue, to every purpose!" Marx concludes "that which exists for me through the *medium* of money, that which I can pay for, . . . that I am." "As an individual I am *lame*, but money provides me with twenty-four legs."[23] A shared language such as money was utterly important for wants as such to be experienced as in principle realizable. Yet given only one such medium, the subsequent fate of Marx' important insight proved less productive of advancing our understanding of increasing rationalization than one could expect. It unleashed an ideological academic tempest in the teapot concerning conflicting views about the allegedly real and more real. It also encouraged unenlightening interest reductions, as prevalent among utilitarian exchange theorists.

For illustration on both points the eminently clear position of a famous "self-conscious psychological reductionist" might be the best. In Homans' view[24] the theoretical resources for the study of action are in principle invariant between non-social and social behavior and between size of units, small group to total society, This does not deny that explanations become more complex as phenomena become more complex, but it does deny assigning to larger aggregated phenomena partly independently and variable "reality." Hence Homans is a bit of an anti-wholistic ideologue, seeing some greater "reality" in individuals and what they say than, for instance, in party-systems of different countries who "directly" say nothing. The counter-position is simple. It asserts that assuming that more complex phenomena have "reality" in their own right, and hence need additional conceptual representation in explanatory models, is useful for theory construction.

Without being an ideological wholist in turn, I should like to endorse the latter view. Such a position need not be based on a priori considerations. It can be based rather on a need for logical complementarity of the category of collective interest, more precisely aggregate phenomenon, that in turn arises from, to me, very convincing results of empirical research.

Ever since Gehlke and Biehl's[25] apparently original discovery of the "Robinson problem" well-known to sociologists,[26] facts demonstrating the ecological fallacy have accumulated. Now, for all who take these facts seriously, Scheuch's[27] discovery of the logical complement to this "group effect" of the ecological fallacy is important. This is known as the "individualist fallacy." In the ecological fallacy an opportunity for error in inference-making exists when the units of observation are larger than the units of inference. Anyone impressed by the wide discrepancy between the sizes of correlations based on grouped as opposed to individual observations can hardly doubt the significance of the possibility of *error in reverse*. Such an opportunity to commit the individualist fallacy exists when the unit of observation is smaller than the unit of inference, as for instance making connective statements between the opinions of voters or even other individuals not enfranchised and the characteristics of regimes. Now, one need not realize more than the fact that Homans' position amounts to no less than making the possibility of committing the individualist fallacy the very basis of his research program to be a little wary of such a position.[28]

These observations permit four conclusions. One, the inference problems associated with fallacies such as these *do not* reflect just difficulties with "size of units," data manipulations, or numbers. They reflect problems of the relation between theory and observation. Strictly put, a logical error of inference can exist if the units of observation and inference belong to conflicting theoretical universes. Two, from an action-theoretical perspective, the problematical relation between individual and group in these fallacies is classifiable as a "level" or subsystem problem. It involves the articulation of personalities and social systems. Therefore, it is but a special case of the problem encountered in relating observations from different subsystems of action to each other. Minimally therefore, taking a principled anti-wholistic stance deprives one of using system theory, a rather widespread theoretical resource in several sciences. Such a deprivation seems quite unnecessary. Three, it is axiomatic in action theory that cross-level explanations (best with evidence on each level, of course) are superior to single-level data and explanations. Minimally this should provide a powerful leverage against unenlightening uniform interest reductionisms in explaining. Furthermore, as the principle of system-environment relations applies to the relations between any type of subsystem at any level, notably of course the societal, one way to avoid uniform interest reductions is the search for function-specific "interests" to serve in action theory what the concept "price" does in economic theory. And four, caution against slipping into the individualist fallacy when engaging in empirical references to media and those who use them should be constantly before one's eye.

The requisite of some shared language competency was also instrumental in forging the linkage between values and norms as *institutionalized* in social relations and as *internalized* in personalities. As epitomized in Dahrendorf's[29] emphatic cry, "Out of Utopia," for many this important insight did not fare much better than Marx's discovery of generalized interest. While one was misread as material interest reductionism, the other was seen as ideationalist reduction. The cost of such ideological academic warfare is not negligible. Important insights get lost in the shuffle. Thus to give one last illustration, Scheuch's[30] critique of Almond and Verba's Civic Culture study as an exercise in the individualist fallacy cannot be accepted *prima facie* as a logical error in inference unless one can prove that the data gathered on internalized values and norms are not those whose institutionalization is a requisite for stable democracy. One can still criticize the study on its narrow scope. Values and norms are after all only one set of variables involved in regime stability. But that is another issue. The point here is that useful methodological consequences which are the concomitants of genuine theoretical advances remain underutilized at least relative to their full potential as long as ideological debates revolve in futility about different preferences to impute some greater "reality" to this or that unit or phenomenon of observation. Let us now consider some conceptual prerequisites that Parsons and Smelser used in their efforts to generalize economics beyond the utilitarian realm.

If we envisage a societal system composed of four functionally differentiated subsystems, each specializing for the production of one of the four basic components of action as it were, it is also feasible to see all four in mutual contingency on each other. Each one needs "inputs" from the other three and similarly needs to dispose of its share of product to the other three. Such an interchange model precludes another piece of common sense. Strictly speaking, because each subsystem is contingent for its functioning on the other three any one is quite incapable of producing anything. Real things are the product of relations between them. Real wealth, for example "results from" a process of interrelating economic roles and norms with political, societal-communal, and household roles and norms. Clarifying this even somewhat better, however, demands brief recapitulation of the concepts of system, structure, function, and process.

A system is, simply conceived, a structure of interdependent phenomena that shows some premanence of patterning over time and retains its distinctiveness vis-à-vis its environs. For a society the immediately contiguous environments are personality on the "lower" and culture on the "higher" side, meaning that "culture" controls societal structure and the latter does the controlling over personality structure whereas the provisioning of necessary conditions runs in the opposite direction.[31] The essential idea of positing a control and a conditions hierarchy involves the notion of selectivity on the one hand and provisioning of conditions which permit certain kinds of choices to be made in the first place on the other. These run in reverse order: "Control" is exercised in the form of culture over social system; social system over personality; personality over behavioral organism. But the behavioral organism provides conditions for personality; personality does so for social system; and social system "conditions" culture.[32] The lower system provides a supply of necessary conditions on the basis of which the higher can control through selection.

Let us give two simple illustrations. Taking interest on loans is one way to finance in an economically rational fashion. So long as taking money for helping someone out with money was seen as in principle usurious and hence illegitimate, interest on loans could not be securely institutionalized. It took a change in the religious significance of economic relations to break this barrier. But culture could not have done this "controlling" had there not been sufficient mobility of possessions in society. The phenomenon of indebtedness had to exist before it could be redefined. Society had to provide the necessary condition—indebtedness—for culture to act as a selector — away from usury or in some other direction. Similarly, it is a commonplace that the social system "family" shapes the personality through socialization. But "plasticity of the infant" is a necessary condition for such socialization-shaping to be possible. The principle idea of a cybernetic control hierarchy is that systems are posited as programmed to behave in an ascertainable way within limits of variation in their environments. In conjunction with conditions providing levels of energy this allows for feedback about the consequences of past behavior and about changing contingencies relative to environments.[33] A system perspective focuses attention on three conceptual objects: system, environment(s), and system-environment relations. Relative to one or more environments a system is defined as having lower complexity and higher stability. Hence, in order to preserve these which constitute its distinctive pattern, the system must be "protected" against great vicissitudes in the environments on which it depends for resources. The system-environment relation as a boundary maintaining process aims at preserving this differential incomplexity and stability. Media are posited as mechanisms operating to maintain this internal-external difference. The rationale applies to systems and subsystems that treat each other as environments.

Structure, too, is not ontological. Structure is those elements of order in a system of interdependencies which for purposes of a given analysis are deemed stable relative to changes in the system's environments. The principle heuristic value of this concept is also simple. There must be some basis to generalize Schumpeter's "circular flow model of a stable economy"[34] to a societal circular flow model in societal equilibrium in order that one can distinguish change in some of the internal arrangements from change of the whole system as such.[35] As for any system of action, the most important structural elements in society are the symbolic codes of the function-specific societal languages, to be discussed in more detail below.

Again abstractly, function is mediation between two sets of contingencies a system is subject to. These are contingencies on environments and, through time, the mediation of processes which (1) "preserve and protect the system's potential for actualization of its pattern (instrumental functioning) and (2) 'mortgage the future' in some kind of consummatory interest" in the present.[36] Thus function is mediation of processes across a set of double boundaries: external-internal and instrumental-consummatory. A boundary means simply that a theoretically and empirically significant difference in structure and process between system or subsystem and environments exists and tends to be maintained.[37]

Finally, process refers to those aspects of a system which undergo change of state within the time period of significance to some investigative purpose. Process is in principle communication: the transmission of meaning from one unit to another, a transmission that rests on symbolic codes shared to some minimal extent by both participants in communication. Whereas structure is code, message-flow is process. In the prototypical case message-flow is two-way. Here too there is mutual contigency between pairs of sender-receivers. Inputs to one unit in terms of messages received influence that unit's output. But in keeping with the voluntarist position of action, there is no strict determination whereby some given input "triggers" an automatically programmed response without any internal selectivity in the receiving unit. That is why a second important characteristic of process is *decision*, wherein antecedent inputs of communication are related to subsequent message output through selectivity operating on stored information.[38] Plural inputs are related to plural outputs with the unit having some choice in relating them.

Thus the primitive conceptual tools—system, structure, function, and process—are all defined in terms of each other. A system is a meaning complex that differs in specifiable respects from others, and process and meaning-flow "closes" the circle of definitions again. The concept of differentiated function can now be introduced to finalize our preparation for an answer to the query "Why media?" Differentiated function is specialized mediation for one of the four functional problems that results from the cross-classification of external-internal and instrumental-consummatory exigencies of any living system. Specialization is used here in the general division of labor sense. Thus *adaptive* function (external and instrumental) is mediation of resources for all functions, itself and the other three. *Goal-attainment* function (external and consummatory) is mediation of the other three functions in the service of actualizing the patterned meaning of the system. *Integrative* function (internal and consummatory) is mediation of the other three functions towards a harmonious balance among all of them. *Pattern-maintenance and tension management* function (internal and instrumental) is mediation of meaning elements in the service of maintaining and adjusting their patterned institutionalization and internalization.[39] Thus A-functioning is mediation in the service of providing disposable facilities independently of any particular goal; G-functioning is mediation aiming at the reduction of the inevitable discrepancy between inner need and external dependency; I-functioning is mediation aiming at regulation of unit contributions to over-all functioning of the system; and L-functioning is mediation in the service of maintaining the integrity of the meaning pattern itself. The meaning of these terms for the societal system case will be supplied below. All we now need is an image of a system functionally differentiated into four subsystems specializing for these functions. Given that this perspective takes function as the master concept in terms of which both structure and process are analyzed, i.e., this being *not* a structural-functional paradigm but rather a *junctional paradigm for* structure and process,[40] let us see what is meant by a state description of functional differentiation.

Illustration being easier with greater specification, the societal labels of these functions will be used, though definitions have to be delayed a little. At the societal level one speaks of economic (A), political (G), normatively-integrative or societal-communal (I), and social-order legitimating (L) functions. *When differentiated* the goal of the economic is the provisioning of economic resources to society; that of the political, the mobilization of collective effort for the attainment of collective goals; the normatively-integrative specializes for the production of belongingness; and the legitimacy subsystem does that for a sense of integrity in social relations as such. This renders the basic clue about a state of differentiation at a given level. Simply put, a set of structures and processes is functionally differentiated to the extent that their operation can specialize for the function-specific goals at hand in the sense of *being liberated* from the need to concern themselves with matters not *directly* relevant for their specific function. This is known as the principle of exoneration or freeing from impediments in the service of function-specialization. Exaggerating a bit, it means that any structure and process is differentiated to the extent that one can afford to disregard function-specific irrelevancies on *prima facie* grounds. An economic structure is differentiated to the extent that its operations can proceed as if political, normatively-integrative, and legitimacy contingencies were taken care of by their appropriate function-primary structures. Strictly speaking, there are of course no genuine irrelevancies. What is of merely indirect relevance for one structure is the major business of the other. But any differentiated structure is exonerated from responsibility about functional problems outside its purview of specialization.

The basic idea is simple. Specialized performance of a function is cheaper because it can be more efficient performance. But in the aggregate it is not that simple. If functional specialization is to eventuate in savings of effort there must be a genuine institutionalization of a network of reciprocal exonerations. And this depends rather directly on a proper balancing of inputs and outputs. Such four-way function specialization therefore presumes at whatever level of differentiation a requisite amount of *adaptive upgrading* such that facilities become alienable from source and available to specialized structures. The same applies to shares of output. These two must be sufficiently alienable to flow to their destination points. At the societal level, media are the regulators of these flows. If they are to do their job, furthermore, there must be *normative upgrading* such that appeals can be made on the grounds of *inclusion* in wider and wider solidarity systems. Finally, if these differentiated structures and processes are to be institutionalized there must be *value-generalization* to supply the requisite value standards on which function-specific legitimations can flow.[41] Put differently, with a rising level of societal complexity in organization, values themselves have to be couched at higher levels of generality to insure some degree of stability.

Finally, when each subsystem becomes a resource and share-of-product recipient-supplier for all the other three, there must be regulated interchange across three boundaries looked at from the point of view of one subsystem. Taking the economic case as paradigmatic here presented a bit of an anomaly. There are after all four factors—labor, land, capital, and organization—and four shares of income— wages, rent, interest, and profit. But there are only three exchange flows. Aiming at numerical balance here led Parsons and Smelser to take out the land category, arguing that for a given "political economy" land is a given at the aggregate level of resources. They also redefined the land category "as the unconditional commitment of economically significant resources to the function of economic production, thereby withdrawing them from other potential uses"[42] and thereby also withdrawing them from interchange. What this means is that at a given level of differentiation of any function the respective resource is treated as a meaningful function in an unproblematical sense. The same is true for the other three subsystems, the political, the normative-integrative, and the legitimative. All L-boxes are placed at the extreme periphery of the interchange paradigm, hence do not "participate" in interchange.[43] This is a severe limitation which cannot be justified on grounds of simple numerical balancing of the model of interchange. The reason is simple: treatment of the differentiated resource and share categories in its meaning-aspect of function — i.e., being able to agree what economic, political, integrative, or pattern-maintaining resources *are* at whatever level of differentiation as simply given, hence unproblematical and therefore excluded from interchange—might be quite sufficient with equilibrium analysis (a Schumpeterian societal circular flow at whatever level of differentiation), but it also prevents one from articulating this model with the dynamic growth model of differentiation as a theory of structural change. This seems already sufficient reason to change the matter; there are other reasons as well. In a reconsideration of the interchange paradigm Gould addresses this issue directly. His reformulations should prove very helpful in two respects: a better logical structure of the interchange paradigm and a more powerful conception of its relation to models of change.

What still needs review is the requisite of double-interchange. That there must be regular input-output interchange is clear. After all, each subsystem depends for its functioning on adequate provisions from the other three *because* meaningful action needs the addition of all four basic components: facilities, organization, norms, and legitimation. But why double-interchange? Again Parsons and Smelser[44] generalized from the economic case of an economy already fairly differentiated. There are several reasons: First, a household cannot draw its total income of goods from the one employing organization of the breadwinner if one is at a stage of any reasonable level of specialization. This is a bit of a weak reason depending on the definition of "employing organization." One need not consider even the "socialist state" as employer; some superduper conglomerate could be conceived as able to satisfy most consumer wants. The point rather is that at a stage beyond simple bartering many sellers and many buyers must be articulated as suppliers-recipients of many resources and shares in product. This requires of course some monetary mechanism to regulate the flows. Thus households have to supply generalized labor capacity (a form of commitment) to the economic subsystem that returns wages to the household (a form of money). This is a factor interchange signaling the principle instrumental significance of *both* categories in *both* subsystems. Labor commitment as capacity to take the occupational role as such for granted is clearly labor as factor of production for an employing agency. But breadwinner is equally clearly of instrumental significance in disposing of one's family role obligation. The same holds for wages. In the firm they are a differential instrument of reward for economic performance; in the household an instrument of sustaining the family.[45] Thus factors have to be exchanged, and the requisite of balance demands two flows. From the point of one subsystem any output is balanced by an appropriate category input. This then should hold for shares as well.

But second, for the latter there is a more profound reason. The goals of the sub-system connected through interchange are different. Households want to live according to some style of life, firms want to "produce" generalized facilities, polities aim to generate effective goal-attainment, societal communities strive for a sense of belongingness, and the functionally differentiated *primary* legitimation structures "aim" at the provisioning of supplies of a sense of integrity in belonging to different structures. Shares of product then have to be "shared." Each subsystem requires that it receive-dispose some requisite share of the proceeds of the other three. Thus the aggregate of households provide to the economy effective demand for consumer goods as a share in their product, consuming a style of life. The economy receives this share in the form of money. It in return disposes of its share to households in the form of a commitment to produce goods covering a minimally requisite range of consumption styles on "satisfactory" market terms. In the general case any one subsystem needs shares of proceeds of the other three, hence it also has to dispose of shares of its proceeds to them. Now, all of these flows are regulated

by media. Furthermore, as a consequence of multi-functionality in the concrete case, there must be a supply of all four media to a given structure of whatever differentiated functional primacy.

Finally, third, double-interchange between systems is the theoretical analogue to double-contingency in social interaction, wherein A's situation is composed in part by B's action and vice versa. Double-contingency between two actors signals that they are both conditions and means to each other virtually *ad infinitum* unless shared meanings and a commitment between both parties to these put a stop to this feedback regress. However, the theoretical correspondence between systems and double-contingency between two individuals-in-roles is anything but obvious and unproblematical. Furthermore, this connection has not been much explored by Parsons. Luhmann's contribution here fills this relative void. He explores generalized media as one type of mechanism "solving" the double-contingency problem in the format social organization of individually dispersed human selectivity from indefinite possibilities of meaning and action.

Again abstractly, a functional subsystem can enjoy exoneration of responsibility for irrelevancies to its function-specialization only if its state of differentiation is ensured through the fact that its inputs and outputs flow in differentiated markets. Otherwise the inevitable contamination of function-specific factors and shares of product would amout to actual de-differentiation pressure. Generalizing from the economic case, a market could be defined as a social system specialized for mediating interests in which there are institutionalized expectations of willingness to exchange disposable resources for a medium and vice versa under a set of rules for settling terms and for the rights and obligations assumed and relinquished in the process.[46] In the model at hand we have four types of interest. These are economic, political, normatively-integrative, and legitimative interests. We also have four media to be described shortly. These are money, power, influence, and value-commitments. Taking Parsons'[47] interchange paradigm as given for present purposes, there are three flows that articulate a given subsystem with each of the other three. But each of the other three are similarly articulated. In short, there are six markets, and they can be considered differentiated from each other to the extent that each articulates only two interests with the aid of two media, *provided* each of the media are the ones functionally specialized for the subsystems in interchange. Thus, first, we have a consumption-goods and effective consumer-goods demand market (A-L) in which economic and legitimacy interests are articulated with the media of money and value-commitments. Second, there is a credit (for production) and employment market (A-G) in which economic and political interests are articulated with the media of money and power. (The categories of interchange so far worked out make the placement of consumer credit difficult.) Third, there is a political support and "policy-priority-setting-for-collective-goal-attainment" market (G-I) in which political and normatively-integrative interests are articulated with power and influence. We have a fourth market in which differential loyalties to sub-groups and societal loyalty are mediated (L-I). Here normatively-integrative and legitimacy interests are mediated with the media of influence and value-commitments.

There is a special status about the last two markets, those mediating interchanges across the diagonals in the usual presentation of the four-function paradigm. This requires brief pause and comment. It may be recalled that the "Economy and Society" format of this functional interchange paradigm[48] on which this account is based specifically excluded the capacity to take a differentiated function-interest for granted from market regulation. I interpret this in two ways. First, as to cause, Parsons and Smelser deemed it necessary to posit a source of value consensus at the societal level on the basis of which function-specific interests could be subjected to combinatorial marketing. Second, they chose at whatever level of differentiation "the capacity to take function-specific interest as such for granted." If one applies the four-function division to the societal subsystems themselves, i.e., to the economy, the polity, and so on, such that they too have their own adaptive, goal-attaining, integrative, and pattern-maintaining sub-systems, then this decision is schematically shown by flipping the societal subsystems in such a manner that their own L-subsystems are all placed at the peripheral extremes of the interchange paradigm. This does four things: (1) it excludes the L-sub-systems from participation in interchange (they do not supply a functional boundary across which shares and resources flow); (2) it designates "horizontal" flows (mediating A-G and L-I) as specialized for adaptive functioning *because* the respective interests here are flowing only across the instrumental-consummatory boundary (compare earlier discussion); (3) the arrangement designates "vertical" flows (mediating A-L and G-I) as specialized for goal-attainment functioning *because* the respective interests there are flowing only across the external-internal functional boundary; and (4) it designates the "diagonal" flows (mediating A-I and G-L) as specialized for integrative functioning *because* the respective "interests" here are flowing across *both* instrumental-consummatory and external-internal functional

boundaries *at the same time* (see Gould, Figure 20-1). Now it is important to recognize that Gould changed matters concerning point (1) but not the rest. This excludes but one value-element from participation in marketed interchange at the societal level, viz. those commitments (L_L) most directly articulated with cultural commitments, particularly of the religious kind. But societal function-specific commitments such as "commitment to economic rationality" and the analogous commitments to political and integrative-solidary rationalities are *included* in interchange (see Gould, Figure 20-2). But this does not affect the special standing of *diagonal interchanges*. A double boundary is always crossed here, and this is an exclusive characteristic, not occurring elsewhere in the paradigm. What can be said about it?

First there is the "settlement and justification of differential claims" market (A-I) in which economic and normatively-integrative interests are mediated with money and influence. Apart from emphasis on its integrative functional significance and the role of "organization" in economic theory we learn precious little about the special status of this market. Media are exchanged here for factors and shares as in the "horizontal" and "vertical" markets. This lacuna becomes particularly obvious because the other function-specific integration "market" is given explicit special status. This last legality-legitimacy "market" articulates political and legitimacy interests, not with media but only with direct codes. For "the assumption of operative responsibility, which is treated as a 'factor of integrity' *is* responsibility for sovereignty (original: success) in the implementation of the value-*principles*, not *only* of collective effectiveness, but of integrity of the paramount societal value-pattern."[49] And legalizing powers of office, as for example through the franchise, *"is an application of the standard of pattern-consistency."* Thus the two last interchange markets remained unbalanced. There is a special status in one but not in the other, despite the fact that both mediate interests across the functional double boundary. One contributor specifically addresses himself to this problem, suggesting one direction in which further closing of this lacuna might be fruitfully pursued (see Baum: "Communication and Media").

This part raises one query demanding an answer, though it must be excessively brief. In this image of four function-specific subsystems, each of which needs supplies from the other three, hence also media inputs from the other three which it in turn can spend, what is it that "enables" a function-specific medium to "govern" intrasubsystem process? The answer is to be found in a rule not detailed here lest this preparation becomes truly interminable. The rule is this: From the perspective of any *one* functional subsystem, such as the economy or the polity, the inputs of shares of product received from the neighboring subsystems always come in the form of that medium functionally specialized for internal process of the *recipient* subsystem. The obverse holds for factor inputs. They always come in the form of the media functionally specialized for internal processes of the respective *emitting* subsystems.[50] For example, money can "govern" economic affairs because relative to commitments, influence, and power inputs there is a greater money input. For each "set" of factor inputs with one "unit of each of the nonmonetary media" there is a triple set of product inputs all coming in the monetary medium. Hence inputs come in forms of media favoring the function-specific medium of the recipient subsystem in a ratio of 3 to 1. I am almost ashamed to give such schematic numerical-magical "reason." It hints at only one part of an explanation. But it will have to do.

There is one more preparatory observation. This involves Smelser's model of structural change and a hint of how media relate to it. Only the briefest explication can be rendered here. First, in contrast to a state-description of a given level of functional differentiation in a system, Smelser's is a model of a certain kind of change of structure—the functionally differentiating—through a change in process. Smelser[51] defines structural differentiation as *"a process* whereby *one* social role or organization . . . differentiates [perhaps better "separates," lest the term to be defined is part of the definition] into *two or more* roles or organizations which function more effectively in the new historical circumstances." The terms "more effectively" and "new historical circumstances" alert one that more than separation in the form of increased specialization in the division of labor must happen in order for effectiveness to increase in fact. And there is more. Based on empirical research, far greater specification than can be found in nineteenth-century notions of evolution was supplied. These specifications concern four interrelated processes.[52] Incidentally illustrating a reflexive use of the four-function paradigm, involving it not only with observations to be explained but also with the mode of explaining, these were: (1) differentiation (G-function); (2) adaptive upgrading (A-function); (3) normative inclusion (I-function); and (4) value-generalization (L-function). They are all treated as processes here, not as states of differentiated structure, but as process leading to structural differentiation and its maintenance once achieved. It deserves emphasis that this model is deemed evolutionary because the result (of this rather than other kinds of

change) is an increase in the rationality of problem solving in society. All four processes are constituted as a set of dependent variables in the form of a net-rationalization-of-action responses to some forces, constituted as independent variables. What about the impetus; whence the source for this particularly crucial type of change?

Though unfortunately blurred with a more detailed stage or phase description of the process of differentiation itself, the major sources for the process to get started seem to be four: (1) perceived strain with performance and resource allocation (facility level); (2) shared value standards that legitimate expression of dissatisfaction and demands that something be done to alleviate strains; (3) a structure of opportunities and available facilities to effect some change; and (4) a demonstrated inability to alleviate strain by marginal adjustments within the extent structural arrangements.[53] One frequently hears the charge that Parsonians tend to presume what they wish to explain in the sense of blurring the lines between the explanans and the explanata. Hopefully the preceding short exposition shows that the theory of differentiation as one kind of change does not suffer from a blur of independent and dependent variables.

For our purposes, however, the question of moment is whether the element of rationality does not appear on both sides of the fence? The difficulty here turns on two essential assumptions underlying the postulated sources for change. One is that personalities will respond with "disturbance" to inadequate role performance and insufficient resource allocations; the other that extant values legitimate sufficiently that something be done about such strain.[54] Mindful of Max Weber's China, the absence of a value system with sufficient stress on the performance dimension may prevent a response in the form of differentiating change because of a symbolic deficit to do something about strains as such and/or because personalities respond neither with distress nor anxiety but, for example, with fatalism instead. This raises the question whether the nature of values (item two among four preconditions for differentiating change) does not already include an action and rational-response tendency to strain which should appear as a consequent variable most notably in the form of step 3 (covert social control of tension in a direction of "socialized motivation"), step 4 (experimentation), and step 5 (specification of solutions found)?[55] It should be emphasized that steps 3, 4, and 5 are postulated as specifications of the differentiation process. Of course different levels of generality are invoked to avoid the possible impasse. Nevertheless, the idea that a change of a kind that enhances rational problem-solving in society is to be explained, even if only to the tune of one fourth of the precipitating conditions, by the role of values already stressing action-solutions in society in a rational manner leaves one dissatisfied.

Also, doubts concerning the utility of the model appear in a different sense as well. This time the universality is questioned. Grounding the differentiation model *empirically* in the Western case of the emergence (differentiation) of the modern family household and the modern employing organization (occupational structure) from the fused family-economy of the peasant, the cottage textile case, or the family firm, and *theoretically* in the application of economic theory of the West to more general sociological theory raises the possibility that understanding of the boundary relations between subsystems apply only to the kind of society "which stress the economic aspect of their structure and functioning."[56] However, that this could actually mean restriction of the model to societies with value systems characterized by adaptive primacy is hastily denied and explicitly so. Yet again in the very same paragraph it is also conceded that the correspondence between analytical and concrete categories and the applicability of categories of economic theory to differentiated structures and their relations "apply more directly . . . as adaptive or economic values approach greater primacy over others."[57] One might conclude that the pre-media stage of attempts to provide greater specificity to Weber's problem of rationalization remained ambiguous in part both on grounds of logic and universality of applying the model. Media were a next step in a continuing enterprise with an unchanging aim.

But for systematic inclusion into Smelser's model they were either not yet available in fact or not available for use.[58] To my knowledge their systematic inclusion is still to come. Yet they have an obvious place. If step 2 (disturbance) is to have the requisite effect, there must be commitments that can legitimate the demand for change. If step 4 (experimentation) is to take place at all, sufficient influence must guarantee a requisite level of trust given to those who are supposed to look for new solutions. Once found, there must be power to back up "suggestions" about new solutions for specifying them down the line in the organization of action, if for no other reason than the obvious: Structural change always hurts interests, vested or other, in the short run. One could go on, but this may suffice to establish the crucial role of media in Smelser's model of evolutionary change. But there are instances of course where power is lacking to back up "suggestions." Perhaps the utility of a model is most impressively demonstrated when its use can shed light on phenomena nearly opposite in nature to those for which it was overtly developed. If so, this model of evolutionary change can shed light on cases with lots of change but little evolution. Here such fruitful application to "negative" cases is provided by Bourricaud's analysis of power deficit in France and two Latin American countries. His specifications of some of the conditions underlying persistent political anomie in the face of considerable economic evolution contribute significantly to our as yet meagre grasp of societal praetorianism and, more generally, of the problem of differential rates of institutional development in different sectors of society.

SOCIETAL MEDIA: PRINCIPAL COMPONENTS

We are finally in a position to give a brief technical exposé of media proper. This account will outline (1) function-specific interests; (2) function-specific *Zweckrationalitäten* as selective standards for rational choice, and (3) function-specific media to articulate both in action. The account will be limited entirely to a societal system functionally differentiated to a fairly high extent. The four cases will be taken up in the order of the AGIL sequence, starting with the economic medium and ending with the integrity medium.

The starting point is always the conception of differentiated function. "*Economic* function is exercised only when important available resources are means to alternative ends, and at some stage are not committed to a specific use."[59] When differentiated, such function presumes (1) an orientation to means as scarce, (2) the alienability of resources from their source (notably important in the case of human services), and (3) the characterization of resources as generalized facilities disposable for their own production as well as entirely different functions, i.e., their disposability for political, integrative, and pattern-maintenance functions. As funny as it may sound at first glance, a function-specific resource, the "economic" one, is defined in terms of function nonspecific disposability. That is the meaning of an *adaptively* instrumental resource in general. But the ability to impute a common significance of meaning, in the restricted sense of something being a generalized facility into an indefinite range of objects, rests on the internalization and institutionalization of a function-specific *value-principle* differentiated out from meaning. This is *utility*. Having such a principle of valuation as utility makes possible in turn "having an economic interest" in objects, physical, social, and cultural, in the sense of assigning to them generalized facilitative significance *for all manner and types of social interaction.* Hence solitary action whether it involves contemplating nature, God, or consuming a painting by oneself is specifically excluded from the realm where economic interest can operate. Hanging a painting in one's home *in order to* impress others with some ascertainable effect on either party can of course be governed by economic interest. In the advanced economies here at issue the value-principle "utility" is typically combined with *solvency* as a *coordinating standard* into a rational choice mechanism for making decisions about utilities. This is known as "economic rationality."[60] Acting in accord with economic rationality means to decide about possible means-end relations, involving both selectivity about means and ends in the social realm, in such a fashion as to maximize general utilities. A Soviet manager attempts to do this just as much in trying to reach assigned plan objectives as does his capitalist counterpart.[61] That solvency requisites as social control mechanisms act more directly through overtly political agencies in the Soviet Union than in North America is for present purposes a matter of quite secondary import. What is more important is that given four types of function-specific rationalities, space commands that their description has to be left at the intuitive level, rather than giving them definitions.

Last, no amount of economic interests could ever control action in any satisfactory manner by sheer "emanation." A special language in the form of a function-specific medium is necessary to articulate means and ends in the decision process. For the economic function this is *money.* Given the present perspective with its interest in a stage beyond barter, it is necessary to emphasize the symbolic aspect. Despite commonsense usage in financial circles engaged in financing money with money where different kinds are commonly considered as a commodity, this notion has to be denied here. Thus "money is not a commodity."[62] It is not a factor of production either. As a *medium* of exchange and a "measure of utility-value" it is symbolic "in that, though measuring and thus 'standing for' economic value or utility, it does not itself possess utility in the primary consumption sense. . . ."[63] As medium of exchange and measure of utility-value, money is a mechanism of rational choice connecting "value in exchange" with "value in use" for *different social functions.* Standing for potential control over objects having utility, it is also a *store of value* and as such a mechanism for control in the future held in the present. To spend money, then, is to mobilize resources for social interaction through the activation of economic interests.

It always involves sacrificing some utilitarian options that could have been taken instead. Spending is action in the present to mortgage the future by placing restrictions on options left. Broadly put, money *"is a very specialized language through which intentions and conditional consequences of action are communicated."*[64] The same definition covers the other three function-specific media. What varies are the nature of the intentions and that of the conditional consequences.

Taking a cue from general language, like English wherein grammar and syntax supply this pattern-maintaining function, any language has a code. The code is a set of rules delimiting the range of normatively legitimate use and assemblage of symbols into messages. In all four specialized societal media, the symbols that comprise messages consist of two kinds, words and sentences of the general language in the context of the requisite function-specific symbols. In the case of money the latter are monetary signs such as dollars and cents. Forms of money are of course quite varied. There are cash, promissory notes, debentures, mortgage certificates, drawing rights on accounts, and so on. Important for their flexible use which also makes the medium subject to inflationary and deflationary volatility is that they all refer to identical units as a measure of utility-value and value in exchange.

Money is special in this last respect, as it has units of account that are uniform between different forms. They are also subject to the most rational measurement device, ratio-scaling, at least in principle, as fractionalization of cents can be carried as far as desired. The units of account in the other media remain to be explored. But even in the absence of greater knowledge about these one can conceive of inflationary and deflationary pressure operating among the other media as well. Let influence serve as one illustration. Inflation connotes a change in the amount of symbols expended for a given amount of unit control over "real things" in the direction of increasing the symbols necessary to exercise this control. The change can be thought of as taking place between two points in time. Whereas at point t_1 one needed only x amount of symbols, at t_2 one needs $x + n$ symbols to control the same amount of intrinsic satisfiers. In the case of influence whereas at t_1 it took but 10 sentences with x words to successfully suggest a strategy of therapy to a patient at t_2, it takes 20 sentences with $x + n$ words to get compliance. Deflation is simply the reverse: Fewer symbols control what took more symbols before. This is an oversimplified and literal analogy to the monetary case where changes in price involve changes in the quantitative relation between symbolic and "real" units. Changes in the context that makes symbols functionally authoritative yield a better conception of inflation and deflation. Although definitionally not much of a problem, media dynamics in general constitute a fairly complex phenomenon deriving from intermedia contingency. This issue is explored by Baum (see "On Societal Media Dynamics").

Concerning the code of money, the three aspects of value-principle utility, coordinating standard solvency, and economic rationality have already been mentioned. To complete this part let us add the fourth code element, the *operative code*. For money this is the *law of property* specifying (1) the range of objects (e.g., to permit slavery or not), (2) the range of aspects of objects (e.g., delimiting labor power), and (3) the situations in which (4) exclusive rights in possession in the sense of control over use and disposal can be granted to units in society.

Finally, just as a community of language users in the modern world with its educational institutions usually deploys various kinds of dictionaries with specifications of permissable connotative variety of words in use during delimited time periods, so some such "security base" seems also necessary for function-specific languages. Parsons suggested gold as filling this role for the medium money. Other bases can probably be found in ethnographic records. In the contemporary world it is often claimed that confidence in the American economy and hence the American dollar "determines" the price of gold, rather than the other way around. These are not very important matters concerning the role of a security base. Special Drawing Rights with the IMF under discussion for many years will likely replace the traditional role of gold. What is important is that there be a security base standard with units acceptable to an incredibly diversified user community of money who, furthermore, use a large variety of forms of money. Without it the smooth functioning of an intrinsically worthless symbolic medium would be endangered. The "intrinsic satisfiers" or the "real things" symbolically represented by money are consumable utility-resources for different functions. They can range from bread eaten by individuals to electricity consumed in a factory.

Turning to political function let us recall that this involves mediation of a system with some external environment in such a manner that a state of contingency defined as desirable is either maintained or attained. This is the general-action sense of the goal-attainment function. At the societal level, political function proper is "essentially the facilitation of attaining collective goals" in the sense of (1) making decisions about such goals and (2) mobilizing societal resources for their attainment.[65] When differentiated, such function presumes (1) an orientation to

political means as scarce, (2) the alienability of political resources from their source, as for example the mobilization of generalized support rather than votes for policy-specifics, and (3) the capacity to characterize resources as having specific-function relevance for cooperation only.

This ability to impute a common significance of meaning in the restricted sense of political resource into an indefinite range of objects, physical and social, rests on the internalization and on the institutionalization of a function-specific *value-principle*. Cognate to utility in the economic case, this is *effectiveness* in the political. Having such a principle of valuing effectiveness in cooperation on its own makes possible in turn "having political interests" in all manner of objects, physical, social, and cultural. Taking a political interest amounts to assigning generalized effectiveness significance to objects which in principle have many other competing "values-in-use" quite apart from human cooperation. In the advanced polities here at issue (and it should be emphasized the collectivity reference covers all associations from the small group to society at large), the value-principle effectiveness is typically combined with *sovereignty* as a *coordinating standard* to yield a rational-choice mechanism known as "political rationality." Acting in accord with political rationality means to select from possible means-end relations those that promise to maximize effectiveness over a range of potential collective goals. In part, therefore, political rationality guides priority setting in collective goals.

Again, just plain having political interests could not conceivably control action in a reliable manner. A special language in the form of a function-specific medium is necessary. Here it is *power*. As a medium, power is neither a factor in effectiveness nor some goal attained. Power has no effectiveness in itself in the primary implementation sense. It is a language as intrinsically worthless as money, and again like money oriented to something scarce. But in contrast, power as a control mechanism is not deemed as indiscriminately and unproblematically desirable as money. The reason for this first difference is simple. Having power and spending it "burdens" the spender with far more stringent responsibilities than the money spender has in his role as free agent in an exchange economy. There is a far more direct element of bindingness and of hierarchy in power relations which, though factually present in the economic case frequently as well (rich and poor have differential marginal utility for a given amount of money), is mitigated in the economic case by norms emphasizing principled equality.

In the present sense, as language, the elements legitimacy, bindingness, and generalization characterize power as a medium. It is defined as the "generalized capacity to secure the performance of binding obligations by units in a system of collective organization when the obligations are legitimized with reference to their bearing on collective goals and where in the case of recalcitrance (non-compliance) there is a presumption of enforcement by negative situation sanctions" (punishment of some kind.)[66] Given legitimacy and mobilizing binding commitments to a collectivity, the power spender cannot just forget it if he encounters non-compliance; he is supposed to enforce his decision by virtue of bearing primary responsibility for the consequences of failure. This contrasts with money in the ideal-typical free market exchange relation. In the latter case there is the principled presumption of equality and voluntarism in the relation. In line with this is that mobilizing economic interest pure and simple always involves offering differential advantage (not punishment). In economic relations, if A's offer is spurned by B, A can simply try to find more satisfactory terms of settlement with C. Not so in power relations: here A has to force B. This indicates inequality as the principled presumption in power relations. It is only one of three important differences from economic relations in ideal-typical form. This is of course well known in the formulation" "A has power over B."

There are two differences remaining. First, there must be a priority system of commitments among the units in a collectivity such that power holders can reliably draw on it relative to competing claims on obligations of these units from non-political sources of interest. Second, if the hierarchy principle is to work at all smoothly, there must be a fairly clearcut rank ordering of differential powers among those units entitled to make binding decisions. The most important rank ordering here concerns scope or domain wherein decisions are to be binding.

Two further differences deserve mention even in such brief account as this. One concerns the unit of measure. Money is measured on, minimally, an interval scale, if not a ratio scale. Power amounts, however, do not lend themselves to precisely comparable quantifications at different levels because of more and more inclusive scopes which involve objects of different functional significance for society as a whole. Power therefore might be measurable on an ordinal scale, but it seems doubtful that significantly more precise quantifications would make theoretical sense. The other difference bears on a near-reversal in the operation of the voluntary principle. Le us keep in mind that power as conceived here applies to collectivities of any size. This provides an illuminating contrast in the cases of both a genuinely "monetized" economy and a genuinely "powerized"

polity. In the former, as we all know, there is practically no option as to the acceptance of money as legally binding tender for economic transactions. The tender is not optional. But what a unit likes to do with money is highly optional in terms of spending it. In a polity sufficiently "developed" to be highly contingent on institutionalized mechanisms of support, whatever the form of this institutionalization, the question of just where a power relation shall exist is quite optional; but once it is entered for whatever specified domain, both parties have few options left.[67]

Finally, one must add merely one other general restriction applicable to the operation of all societal media. Participants have no option to accept a medium but then not to use it themselves nor to make it available for use by others. This, in the form of storing money under one's pillow rather than depositing it in a bank that renders credit, is Keynes's famous liquidity trap. However differently legally regulated as yet — voting is a duty subject to a fine for non-compliance in some democracies only — such "liquidity traps" could not be permitted to any substantial degree if mediated interchange is to be protected against the possibility of excessive inflationary and deflationary pressures.

These differences apart, power as a medium of exchange and a measure of effectiveness value is a mechanism of rational choice connecting the allocation of resources of a given "value in effectiveness" with "value in use" for different social functions. Standing for potential control over objects having effectiveness significance, it is also a store of value because one may or may not mobilize resources for given goals at given times. Clearly, however, in the case of public office the expected level of activity restricts the incumbent concerning saving and spending far more than is the case with the proverbial private man and his money. The utility of this analogy may well turn out better for the case of overtly non-governmental collectivities. Whatever the variations on the empirical level, analytically power too is a mechanism of control over the future with respect to potential mobilization of collective effort held in the present. To spend power is to sacrifice alternative decisions, those that could have been or could be made.[68]

Messages of power appear in the form of commands of the general language *in the context of* such symbols of office as uniforms or seals of office — in short, a variety of "power signs." Forms of power vary as well covering votes, policy statements, legal decisions, and the like. As to codes, the three aspects of value-principle effectiveness, coordinating standard of sovereignty, and "political rationality" have already been mentioned. The fourth element, the operative code, in the case of power is authority in the sense of the *jurisdiction of office* specifying the domain and scope of power.[69] Domain is a function of membership in the collectivity; scope specifies the range of obligations and conditions under which they can be mobilized. Finally, as in any language, there must be some security base. In the case of power this is force. The "real thing" or intrinsic satisfier of power, on the other hand, is goal realization of the collectivity.

Integrative function is mediation of units and subsystems in the service of their mutual adjustment and harmony, which forms one basis of their capacity to contribute to the over-all functioning of the system. In order to spell this out for the societal level let us once more run through the four necessary conditions underlying the operation of any symbolic medium. These are: (1) a category of *value*, (2) a category of *interest*, (3) *giving meaning to a situation* such that it becomes "exploitable," and (4) a set of rules discriminating between legitimate and illegitimate modes of exploiting. Be it emphasized that only with institutionalization in all four conditional respects "can the risks inherently involved in accepting the 'symbolic' in lieu of the 'real' be expected to be widely assumed by whole categories of acting units."[70]

At the societal level integrative function is mediation of collectivities and individuals-in-roles in the service of gaining a harmonious balance among a multiplicity of potentially conflicting sets of rights and obligations. When differentiated such function presumes (1) an orientation to the "level of balance" in rights and obligations mutually expected as a scarce attribute of relations, (2) the alienability of a sense of belonging from their source, and (3) the characterization of belonging-experiences as generalizable and disposable across a variety of situations. These conditions demand an ability to impute one common meaning significance, this time a sense of normative fit, into an indefinite range of social relations. The differentiated function-specific category of value that must exist with some sufficiency in internalization and institutionalization is *solidarity*. Sharing the *value-principle solidarity* in turn makes possible "having an integrative interest" in objects, physical — as for example the body in medical practice — social, and cultural. Taking an integrative interest in objects is assigning to them generalized "bondedness-potential" for social relations and being desirous of gaining control over them in that respect. In advanced societal communities at issue here the value-principle solidarity is typically combined with the *coordination standard* of *consensus* to yield a rational choice mechanism known as "integrative rationality." Acting in accord with the latter means to decide about means-end relations in the social realm in a fashion designed to minimize the level of conflict — particularly its unregulated varieties.

Again, no amount of integrative interests, simply desires for harmony in relations, could ever reliably control action by sheer "emanation." The function-specific medium that regulates these interests is *influence*. Here messages appear in the form of the symbols of general language — words and sentences — accompanied by such function-specific symbols as titles and degrees that represent a superior capacity to contribute to solidarity imputed to the holder. Influence too is intrinsically worthless. It is not experienced belongingness; neither is it a factor deployed in the construction of belongingness as, for example, justifying one's allocation of loyalties. As *medium* of exchange and measure of solidarity-value it is symbolic in that, though measuring and thus "standing for" belongingness, it does not itself possess belongingness-value in the primary consumption sense of experiencing being bound to others. As medium, influence is a rational mechanism of choice connecting "value in solidarity" of relations with their values-in-use for different social functions. Standing for potential control over objects having solidarity-value, influence is also a store of value, a mechanism of control over the future held in the present. To spend influence is to mobilize resources for social integration through the activation of integrative interests.

The relation between influencer and influencee, somewhat parallel to power, rests on presumptive inequality. The language of influence takes the general form of persuasion. A influences B if he suggests to B what is good for him concerning his role-set bundles of obligation-rights on the presumption that A knows better. The whole process rests on a presumed consensus on ends and an equally presumed superiority concerning means ascribed to the influencer. Taking the professional-client relation as prototypical, influence is the making of credible assertions which *in principle* could be verified according to prevailing standards of validity but are *in practice* never verified. The point is that he who possesses influence need not give detail justification for the suggestions he makes in order to elicit compliance. His competence is trusted. With presumptive inequality and hierarchy, influence, like power, demands careful scope and domain hierarchization of influence users. Hence also, ordinal scaling might be the theoretically tolerable limit. What differs from power is that the sanctions involved are positive. This follows from the presumption of perfect agreement on ends. The typical doctor-patient relation demands that both parties take for granted and unproblematical the notion that health is preferable to illness at least as a general principle.

Finally, we need to add to the three code aspects for influence already mentioned the fourth element, the operative code. What authority of office is to power, *prestige* is to influence. Neither "circulate," as both are characteristics imputed to positions in a collectivity. Prestige here is defined as "the criteria by which units in a (collectivity) are given *generalized* status-rank, one which transcends specificity of function or situation."[71] As to the "security-base" of influence Parsons originally suggested *Gemeinschaft* and then changed it to "certain types of knowledge, treated as forms of information."[72] The latter is too vague to be serviceable. It also treats information in too commonsensical a fashion. A third reason for rejecting ·this formulation is that it gives "information" a special status in only one medium, while media as such of course involve transfer of information. Nevertheless, as the "experience of belongingness" aspect of *Gemeinschaft* constitutes the intrinsic satisfier, one cannot simply retain it either. One possible way out might be to define ascriptive aspects of social ties as the security base of influences. As a generalized mechanism of information-saving ascription points to base-line commonalities typically taken for granted.

Several of these technical aspects are covered in very illuminating ways by Johnson, whose primary interest focuses on the sources that underlie the institutionalization of public news media as a mechanism of influence in society. This essay should be of particular interest to those impressed with recent attempts in North American society to "force" advertisers to use influence rather than continue making statements which most of the time turn out to be *in principle* non-verifiable. This involves a subtle interplay of the expenditure of influence to generate power in the form of legislation designed to turn reluctant advertisers into genuine influentials. To my knowledge nothing like it has happened as yet in Western Europe. Johnson's sensitive pen traces some of the most important developmental trends in the United States that help one understand its relative uniqueness in this respect.

Last, we turn to the legitimation function. At the societal level legitimation involves societal values defined as "conceptions of the desirable type of society held by the members of the society of reference and applied to the particular society of which they are members." It also involves a commitment on the part of such members to implement this value pattern.[73] Legitimation function is mediation of units and subsystems in the service of their capacity to contribute to implementing societal values. When differentiated such function presumes (1) an orientation to legitimacy in social action as scarce and variably manageable, (2) the alienability of legitimacy as loyalty to a pattern from its source of construction, and (3) the characterization of legitimacy as generalizable and disposable across functions and situations. A value-relevant "integrous aspect" here is the common meaning significance imputed to an indefinite range of objects. The differentiated function-specific *category of value* is *integrity*. Sharing this value-principle to some sufficient degree of internalization and institutionalization again makes possible having "integrity interests." Taking such an interest in objects signals assigning to them legitimation potential for social relations and being desirous of obtaining control over them in that respect. In advanced societies at issue here, the value-principle of integrity is typically combined with a similarly function-specific *coordination standard of pattern consistency* implying both cognitive and cathectic symbolic stability in patterning. The combination yields an evaluational rational choice mechanism labeled "moral rationality" by Loubser.[74] Acting in accordance with the latter means to decide about means-end relations in the social realm with the aim of implementing commitments to the good society that ought to be.

For the last time, no amount of integrity interests could steer action in any reliable fashion by *ex machina* emergence. Just calling for "value relevance" in social relations is insufficient. A language is necessary for this function as well. The specific-function medium *value-commitments* or *sociomoral rhetoric* has a message structure composed again of general language components, this time appearing in the context of what one might call "rhetorical symbols." They cover a wide variety, ranging from slogans of "motherhood," "fatherland," and "socialism" over more composite forms such as national anthems to "concretizations" such as monuments signifying crucial collective moral tests. As a medium, sociomoral rhetoric is also intrinsically worthless. An appeal as such cannot be consumed. It is not experienced integrity in social relations; neither is it a factor of integrity. Sociomoral rhetoric is but a selection mechanism guiding shares and factors for integrity constructions. As a medium, sociomoral rhetoric is a rational mechanism of choice connecting "value in integrity" of relations with their values-in-use for other functions. Standing for potential control over objects with integrity significance, sociomoral rhetoric can also be "saved," acting as a store of integrity value, because of some flexibility in options where and when to spend. This medium is a mechanism to mobilize integrity interests. One spends sociomoral rhetoric through "activation of obligations, which are presumptively morally binding by virtue of values which ego and alter share."[75] This connotes a presumption of principled equality in the relation between an "appellant" and he who is appealed to. A presumes that B has been socialized into the same moral community as himself, such that B can be expected to respond or else experience guilt. The sanction is therefore negative but its efficacy operates through the personality system making sufficient internationalization particularly crucial in this medium.

In contrast to power, however, responsibility for failure to effect action in the desired direction does not directly sit with the appellant but rather with the recipient of an appeal to his "moral obligations." Despite the egalitarian aspect involved, empirically this does not preclude some moral stratification which for obvious reasons is a generational phenomenon in all societies. But beyond that, in highly differentiated societies there are positions whose incumbency demands differential capacity for moral leadership. Some of these are political, as the office of President in the United States; others have cultural primacy, as the office-charisma of the papacy. In these cases one imputes a differential capacity to contribute to the implementation of societal commitments into the position and hence some appropriate expectation to do so as a role requirement. This illustrates well the need for careful husbanding of the use of this medium lest the office becomes delegitimized simply through proof of demonstrated incapacity to effect anything. If a pope decries some specific condition, such as a war, too often without visibly effecting the principal agents involved, the willingness to deposit one's fiduciary trust into the office of papacy declines. Hence again, with spending options somewhat flexible, sociomoral rhetoric is also a store of integrity value, a mechanism of control over the future held in the present.

With value-principle, coordination standard, and "moral rationality" already mentioned, there remains the question of the appropriate operative code for sociomoral rhetoric. This has not been adequately defined. Parsons merely mentions *"moral authority in its societal reference."*[76] At best this suggests that some particular skill in articulating "practical reason" and aesthetic judgment. It might be exercised blatantly by charismatic types, sometimes "latently" floated by intellectuals or church leaders with access to political, economic, and legal elites. Moral authority can also be genuinely institutionalized in society. Office-charisma is a prototypical case. However, keeping in mind that societal legitimation function is mediation in the service of maintaining the effective cybernetic control of the societal value pattern itself, one experiences also some conceptual noise in learning that the security base takes "primarily" the form of a personality medium, the operation of guilt. This does, however, emphasize that sociomoral rhetoric demands a high development of individuation before it can be institutionalized as medium. It also demonstrates impressively the continuity in Parsons' Durkheim perspective over several decades.[77]

But such continuity also causes problems not quite resolved as yet. The medium of sociomoral rhetoric is the only one of the four discussed wherein the security base rests "primarily" in a subsystem of action different from the societal one, the personality. Where else it rests remains fuzzy. Neither gold nor force nor ascriptive communality share this feature. All of these are contained within the societal subsystem of action. Deciding on a difference in the case of the medium of value-commitments or sociomoral rhetoric therefore signals the crucial role of this medium as the Archimedian point of articulation between the revived perspective of Pareto and the permanently valid precipitate of Durkheim. Gould's revised interchange paradigm should be consumed with attention to this point.

To provide a convenient overview, the following table summarizes the characteristics of the societal media just discussed.

To live on liquidity rather than possessing real things for a good portion of the time is of course a life shot through with risk. It is also one demanding unusual amounts of trust. But such life makes available temporarily stored and inactive controls over "real things" to others who may deploy such resources for innovations. Hence one might close this introductory review with a brief remark on the "zero-sum" problem. The question of import is whether the institutionalization of such media permits the operation of credit mechanisms. Are there four types of function-specific entrepreneurship? Indeed for an attempt to extend and provide greater specification to Weber's problem of the increasing rationality in the organization of society an answer to this question is the moment of moment. Parsons' answer to this question is an emphatic yes. Leaving aside the familiar monetary case wherein additions to money are made through deposits in the banking system whether these be interpreted as genuinely new creations or increased rates in circulation, all three media papers are liberally sprinkled with analogous phenomena in power, influence, and commitments. One finds illustrations wherein some roles act as bankers and others as entrepreneurs. These cover moral-fiduciary, integrative, and political entrepreneurship. Holders of charisma, genuine or routinized, illustrate the

Major Code Aspects

Medium	Differentiated function specialization	Value-principle	Coordination standard	Operative code	Communications mode	"Security Base"	"Intrinsic satisfier"
MONEY	Economy (A)	Utility	Solvency	Law of Property	Inducement	Gold (SDR's)*	Consummable utilities
POWER	Polity (G)	Effectiveness	Sovereignty	"Authority" (Jurisdiction of office)	Commandment	Force	Goal realization
INFLUENCE	Societal community (I)	Solidarity	Consensus	"Prestige" (Criteria of generalized status-rank)	Persuasion	Ascriptive social bonds	Belongingness
VALUE COMMITMENTS	Fiduciary legitimation subsystem (L)	Integrity	Pattern consistency	Moral authority	Moral appellation	Guilt	Experience of relational integrity

An outline of the principle components of the societal media.
*SDR's = Special Drawing Rights on the IMF.

first; representatives of professional associations who can speak in the name of the aggregate expertise of their members without asking for their detail endorsement exemplify the second; electoral politics wherein political influence expenditure generates generalized support for the polity, thus enabling leaders to undertake new ventures not expected nor foreseen by voters, elucidates the last. But illustrative instances for additions to a medium are one thing, conceptual "fixation" of the quantitative aspects of medium expansion another. Further advance in this area clearly hinges on giving the forms of all the media far greater specification than they have received so far. Particularly relevant in this respect is supplying them with appropriate units of account. This is especially crucial of course in the case of the forms in which legitimation flows. Just above one analytical reason for the special importance of this medium has been mentioned. In the present context one merely needs to remind oneself that the societal media are interdependent to suggest that this greater specification of forms should start out with commitments.

There remains of course the question whether such reasons as just given suffice to justify a commitment to the pursuit of further media theorizing. One man's epiphany may be another's boredom; and where one sees promising utility another's skepticism may remain unshaken. On this point Cartwright and Warner present a lengthy dissent from the views prevailing in this introduction and the other essays in this section. They argue in effect that a concept of media as symbolic entities fashioned on an analogy to money (or language!) is *neither necessary* in the

analysis of complexly organized systems *nor representative* of Parsons' own practice when his work on power is closely scrutinized.

Finally, although this is a question of commitment to cognitive rationality, thus remaining in the utterly familiar, the very fact that Parsons tried to portray a thoroughly rationalized use-conception of value-commitments invites a closing comment. As all of us know, there comes a point where the rational manipulation of even "merely" social legitimations must stop lest legality and legitimacy of social action diverge so far as to make a mockery of either one or the other. Just where this point is reached in any generalized empirical sense, I do not know. Nevertheless, having some analytical handle on it should prove helpful to those with a tendency for alienation yet still responsive to cognitively relevant information. For members of developed societies, and particularly for those with some commitment to a civic religion of whatever variety, the articulation of a sense of inner integrity with authentic implementation on the societal level has become one central problem. As America's "instant philosopher" of the CBS-news network in the United States recently reminded his listeners: "Politics demands above all the operation of heads that can sustain the sheer facticity of a tremendous complexity in leadership responsibility. But democracies on the support level rely on the great simplification." The same *pari passu* seems true of any differentiated polity, however it manages its contingency on the societal community. Soviet-man or American, both face the same dilemma. "And there comes a point when the head must yield to the heart, a point reached just before the heart breaks"; thus, in essence, Eric Sevareid. There is in common sense an urgency to which concerned men cannot but respond. In a differentiated society, doing that responsibly demands above all attempting to use the special tools that society provides to different occupations, however humble the result. The contributors have tried; the reader be the judge.

NOTES

1. See T. Parsons, "On the Concept of Influence," *Public Opinion Quarterly* 27, 1 (Spring, 1963), pp. 37-62; T. Parsons, "On the Concept of Power," Proceedings of the *American Philosophical Society* 107, 3 (June, 1963), pp. 232-262; T. Parsons, "On the Concept of Value-Commitments," *Sociological Inquiry* 38, 2 (Spring, 1968), pp. 135-160.

2. T. Parsons, "Some Problems of General Theory in Sociology," pp. 27-68 in John C. McKinney, and Edward A. Tiryakian (eds.), *Theoretical Sociology: Perspectives and Development* (New York: Appleton-Century-Crofts, 1969).

3. T. Parsons, *Politics and Social Structure* (New York: The Free Press, 1969), p. 433.

4. Parsons, "Some Problems . . . ," *op. cit.*, p. 68.

5. T. Parsons, "The Political Aspect of Social Structure and Process," pp. 71-112 in David Easton (ed.), *Varieties of Political Theory* (Englewood Cliffs: Prentice-Hall, 1966), especially p. 99.

6. Parsons, *Politics and Social Structure*, p. 403. Personal communication from Victor Lidz, whose help is greatly appreciated.

7. T. Parsons, "Some Considerations on the Theory of Social Change," *Rural Sociology* 26, 3 (September, 1961); T. Parsons, "An Outline of the Social System," pp. 30-79, in T. Parsons, *et al.* (eds.), *Theories of Society,* Vol. 1 (New York: The Free Press, 1961); T. Parsons, "Evolutionary Universals in Society," *American Sociological Review* 29, 3 (June, 1964), pp. 339-357; T. Parsons, *Societies: Evolutionary and Comparative Perspectives* (Englewood Cliffs: Prentice-Hall, 1966); T. Parsons, *The System of Modern Societies* (Englewood Cliffs: Prentice-Hall, 1971).

8. Parsons, "Some Problems . . . ," *op. cit.*, pp. 28-30.

9. Parsons, *Politics and Social Structure*, p. 313.

10. Parsons, "Some Problems . . . ," *op. cit.*

11. T. Parsons, and N. J. Smelser, *Economy and Society* (Glencoe, Ill.: The Free Press, 1956), p. 292.

12. N. J. Smelser, *Social Change in the Industrial Revolution* (Chicago: University of Chicago Press, 1959).

13. Parsons, *Societies.*

14. Parsons and Smelser, *op. cit.*, pp. 39-100.

15. T. Parsons, *The Structure of Social Action* (New York: The Free Press, 1949), p. 710.

16. T. Parsons, *The Social System* (Glencoe, Ill.: The Free Press, 1951), pp. 161-163.

17. Parsons and Smelser, *op. cit.*, p. 14.

18. *Ibid.*, pp. 131-137, 141; Parsons, "An Outline . . . ," *op. . cit.*, pp. 50-51.

19. Parsons, "On the Concept of Power," *op. cit.*, p. 235.

20. N. J. Smelser, *The Theory of Collective Behavior* (New York: The Free Press, 1963), pp. 23-45; Parsons, "On the Concept of Power," *op. cit.*, p. 233.

21. Parsons, *The Structure of Social Action*, p. 48; T. Parsons, *et al., Toward a General Theory of Action* (Cambridge: Harvard University Press, 1951), p. 53.

22. T. B. Bottomore (tr. and ed.), *Karl Marx, Early Writings* (New York: McGraw-Hill Book Co., 1963), especially pp. 145-219; 164-165.

23. *Ibid.*, p. 191 (emphasis on the medium added).

24. George C. Homans, *Social Behavior: Its Elementary Forms* (New York: Harcourt, Brace and World, 1961); George C. Homans, "Fundamental Social Processes," pp. 30-78, in N. J. Smelser (ed.), *Sociology: An Introduction* (New York: John Wiley and Sons, 1967), especially pp. 32, 41-77.

25. C. E. Gehlke, and K. Biehl, "Certain Effects of Grouping upon the Size of the Correlation Coefficient in Census Tract Material," *Journal of the American Statistical Association* 29 (1934), pp. 169-170. Acknowledgement and appreciation is duly registered as due to my colleague Gilbert Shapiro, who alerted me to this early formulation of the ecological fallacy.

26. W. S. Robinson, "Ecological Correlations and the Behavior of Individuals," *American Sociological Review* 15, 3 (June, 1950), pp. 351-357.

27. Erwin K. Scheuch, "Cross-National Comparisons Using Aggregate Data," pp. 131-167, in R. Merrit and S. Rokkan (eds.), *Comparing Nations* (New Haven, Conn.: Yale University Press, 1966); Erwin K. Scheuch, "Social Context and individual Behavior," pp. 133-155, in M. Dogan and S. Rokkan (eds.), *Quantitative Ecological Analysis* (Cambridge: MIT Press, 1969).

28. The Homans' indictment comes from Scheuch, "Cross-National Comparisons," *op. cit.*, pp. 159-162. Yet his critique remained incomplete and not incisive enough, as there was too much attention to the size of units. That a logical error exists only if *different and conflicting* theoretical schemes are involved is a sharp insight I owe to Cristina Molina.

29. R. Dahrendorf, "Out of Utopia," *American Journal of Sociology* 63 (1958), pp. 115-127.

30. Scheuch, "Cross-National Comparisons . . . ," *op. cit.*, p. 165.

31. Parsons, "An Outline . . . ," *op. cit.*, pp. 37-38.

32. *Ibid.*, p. 38; Parsons, *Societies*, p. 28.

33. Parsons, "Some Problems . . . ," *op. cit.*, pp. 33-34.

34. J. A. Schumpeter, *The Theory of Economic Development* (Cambridge: Harvard University Press, 1934).

35. Parsons, "An Outline . . . ," *op. cit.*, pp. 36-37; Parsons, "Some Problems . . . ," *op. cit.*, pp. 35-36.

36. Parsons, "An Outline . . . ," *op. cit.*, p. 36; Parsons, "Some Problems . . . ," *op. cit.*, pp. 31-32.

37. Parsons, "An Outline . . . ," *op. cit.*, p. 36.

38. Parsons, "Some Problems . . . ," *op. cit.*, p. 36.

39. Parsons, "An Outline . . . ," *op. cit.*, pp. 38-40.

40. Parsons, "Some Problems . . . ," *op. cit.*, p. 36.

41. Parsons, *The System of Modern Societies*, pp. 26-28.

42. Parsons, "Some Problems . . . ," *op. cit.*, p. 38.

43. Parsons, and Smelser, *op. cit.*, p. 68.

44. *Ibid.*, pp. 70-71.

45. Parsons, "On the Concept of Power," *op. cit.*, p. 260.

46. Parsons, "An Outline . . . ," *op. cit.*, p. 52.

47. Parsons, "On the Concept of Power," *op. cit.*, pp. 259-260.

48. Parsons and Smelser, *op. cit.*, p. 68.

49. Parsons, "On the Concept of Power," *op. cit.*, p. 262 (emphasis added).

50. Parsons, *Politics and Social Structure*, p. 487.

51. N. J. Smelser, "Mechanisms of Change and Adjustment to Change," pp. 32-54 in Bert F. Hoselitz, and Wilber E. Moore (eds.), *Industrialization and Society* (Paris: UNESCO-Mouton, 1968), p. 35.

52. Smelser, *Social Change*; Parsons, "Some Considerations. . . ." *op. cit.*

53. Smelser, *Social Change*, pp. 32-40; Smelser, *The Theory of Collective Behavior*, pp. 42-66.

54. N. J. Smelser, *Essays in Sociological Explanation* (Englewood Cliffs: Prentice-Hall, 1968), p. 81.

55. Smelser, *Social Change*, pp. 39-40.

56. Parsons and Smelser, *op. cit.,* p. 79.

57. *Ibid.,* p. 83.

58. Smelser, *Social Change*; Smelser, *The Theory of Collective Behavior*, Smelser, "Mechanisms . . .," *op. cit.*

59. Parsons, "An Outline . . .," *op. cit.,* p. 31.

60. Parsons, "On the Concept of Power," *op. cit.,* pp. 261-262.

61. In general no comparable levels of rationality and nonrationality between centrally planned and free market economic models are implied here. The complexity of this issue prohibits its consideration in this paper. Further, unless they are deemed especially crucial this account will henceforth dispense with detailed source indications. The interpretive and in fact mostly recapitulative effort here is based on Parsons' societal media papers — those on influence, on power, and on value-commitments in that order — as cited previously.

62. Parsons, "An Outline . . .," *op. cit.,* p. 52.

63. Parsons, "On the Concept of Power," *op. cit.,* p. 236.

64. Parsons, "Some Problems . . .," *op. cit.,* p. 40.

65. Parsons, "An Outline . . .," *op. cit.,* pp. 51-52.

66. Parsons, "On the Concept of Power," *op. cit.,* p. 237; Parsons, "An Outline . . .," *op. cit.,* p. 53.

67. Parsons, "On the Concept of Power," *op. cit.,* pp. 241-242.

68. *Ibid.,* p. 246.

69. *Ibid.,* p. 244.

70. Parsons, *Politics and Social Structure*, p. 409.

71. *Ibid.,* p. 435.

72. *Ibid.,* pp. 432-433.

73. Parsons, "On the Concept of Value-Commitments," *op. cit.,* pp. 136-137; Parsons, "An Outline . . .," *op. cit.,* p. 47.

74. Jan J. Loubser, "The Contribution of Schools to Moral Development; A Working Paper in the Theory of Action," *Interchange* 1 (April, 1970), pp. 99-116.

75. Parsons, "On the Concept of Value-Commitments," *op. cit.,* p. 143.

76. *Ibid.,* p. 148.

77. Parsons, *The Structure of Social Action*, pp. 324-338.

20

SYSTEMS ANALYSIS, MACROSOCIOLOGY, AND THE GENERALIZED MEDIA OF SOCIAL ACTION

Mark Gould

This essay is an attempt to enunciate a basic and highly selective outline of a media theory, applicable—with modifications—to money, power, influence, and value-commitments. I have included two interconnected discussions. The first criticizes and reorganizes the Parsonsian system paradigm, providing a foundation for the following analysis. The second explicates certain basics of monetary and macroeconomic theory within the context of this paradigm and then indicates how the monetary model might be generalized. My discussions are schematic and simplified in this presentation. I decided, after much consideration, that a broad overview of certain work in progress, even if presented as a working paper, was a more appropriate contribution to this symposium than a more narrow discussion of one aspect of my current work.[1]

A REVISED PARADIGM

At one level of analysis Parsons deals with the classification of processes within the contexts of a

---

This essay does not presuppose an expertise in Parsonsian sociology, but such an expertise will make it easier to follow my arguments and to develop them. The reader with no background in Parsons' work will at times find the going difficult, and some of my arguments will seem to him incomplete. I have not explicated in any detail the positions which I criticize, and I often assume or modify components of Parsons' work without explicit note.

The essay represents a partial product of four years of discussion and argument with Professor Parsons. My debt to his writing is clear, my debt to his person is, perhaps, even more important. During those same four years these ideas have been tried out on successive groups of students, many of whom have commented and criticized with a candor and intelligence which has forced numerous revisions and developments. It is comforting that my debts fall to the man this book honors and to the students for whom it is written.

functional paradigm. Collectivities, as such, are not classified except insofar as they are structures definitive of the categorized processes.[2] Thus at one level I will be concerned with aggregate measures, summations of processes categorized in accord with their functional consequences for the system as a whole. In order to deal effectively with the import of summary variables, however, it is often necessary to deal with the structural organization of the system under discussion.[3] In empirical studies the two types of analysis should always overlap, as they must for a complete theoretical picture to emerge.[4]

The Economy and Society Format

Figure 20-1 illustrates the paradigm within which Parsons and his associates, especially Neil Smelser, have conceptualized all systems interchanges. (I will call this version of the paradigm the Economy and Society format (E & S).) Each set of exchanges entails a double boundary interchange. Each involves a factor and a product exchange where the point of origin and culmination within each subsystem are theoretically determinate.[5] For example, consider the exchanges between the latency and the economic societal subsystems:[6] The factor exchange concerns the provision of the real commitment of labor capacity in exchange for wage income. Labor is then transformed within the economy, along with other factor inputs, and in part emerges as the consumer goods to be exchanged for that segment of wage income utilized to purchase goods produced. Such income serves as a support input for the receiving organizations within the economy. In Parsons' work these exchanges are between the goal-attainment subsectors of the economy and latency subsystems (A_G and L_G).[7]

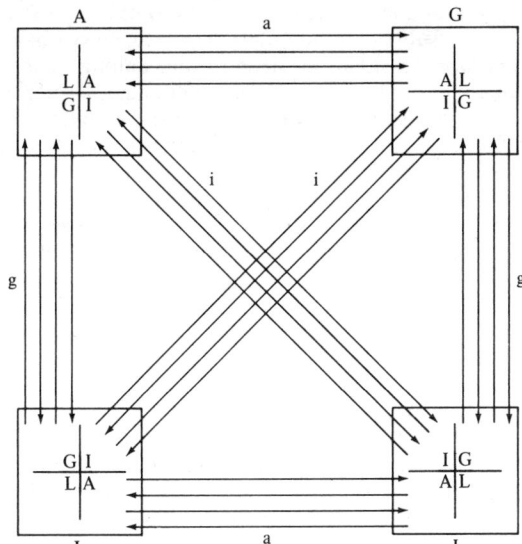

Figure 20-1. The Economy and Society paradigm. Adapted from Parsons and Smelser, *op. cit.,* p. 68.

Parsons further specifies, within the exchange paradigm, at which boundaries the four functional requisites for the action system are met. Taking a social system as our unit of analysis, the integrative function is met at the diagonal ($I_I \longleftrightarrow A_I$ and $L_I \longleftrightarrow G_I$), the adaptive function on the horizontal ($G_A \longleftrightarrow A_A$ and $L_A \longleftrightarrow I_A$), and the goal-attainment function on the vertical ($L_G \longleftrightarrow A_G$ and $I_G \longleftrightarrow G_G$). The latency function is, presumably, met for the system as a unit within A_L, G_L, I_L, and L_L. For Parsons the last exemplifies the special status of the pattern-maintenance subsystem. Maintenance involves a cultural, not a social boundary[8]; as such, L subsystems are not articulated in an interactive exchange, in part owing to the relative stability of cultural patterns.

It is necessary, I think, to take issue with Parsons' presentation at a number of points and for a number of reasons. In the first instance, the notion of system functions being fulfilled across specified boundary interchanges (*supra*) indicates a confusion of system levels. The four-function schema is based on the assumption that each subsystem is concerned with the fulfillment of one functional problem for the system of reference, taken as the unit of analysis; thus processes are categorized in terms of functional consequence for the total system of reference. For example, the economy is concerned with the production and the allocation of scarce resources within the society as a social system. In Parsons' presentation, however, this function for the system is met in exchanges between the adaptive *subsectors*, so that not only is A_A concerned with this

problem, but also G_A and, somewhat incongruously, L_A and I_A.[9]

Thus the adaptive function for the system as unit is met (within the E & S format) without reference to the adaptive subsystem (excepting the tangential utilization of A_A). If this be the case, speaking of the function of adaptation loses all meaning, for the economic processes necessary for the functioning of the system need not be located in the economy but can be located in the adaptive subsectors of other subsystems. In the E & S format the adaptive subsector of the societal community is erroneously seen as fulfilling the adaptive function for the society and not for the societal community as a subsystem. Taking a different example, the functional consequences of a business firm's activities, those which have political primacy in the economy, are political insofar as they relate to the economic subsystem, but economic insofar as they relate to the society (not goal-attaining as the E & S format would have it).

This difficulty can be most vividly portrayed in an examination of the pattern-maintenance function. Here the latency functions for both the system of reference and the subsystem of reference appear to merge. For a society the L function is not met within the latency subsystem, but rather within the latency subsectors of the economy, polity, societal community, and pattern-maintenance subsystems. Although it is possible to argue that there is no confusion, because the L function of the subsystems might be fulfilled not by their respective L subsectors but by subsystems one level further developed, surely this argument is not acceptable. For the systems paradigm to remain coherent its conceptualization must be cogent and must include an assignment of functions without confusing levels of analysis.

The focal point of the outputs that serve the pattern-maintenance needs of the total system must be within the latency subsystem, not within the maintenance subsectors of the four subsystems. If there is some problem in the provision of maintenance resources within the latency subsector of the economy, the first *subsystem* to feel the consequences should be the economy. Thus the first consequences for the total system should be adaptive, not pattern-maintenance, Likewise, if the latency subsystem, for whatever reason, possesses insufficient adaptive resources to fulfill its tasks, the first consequences should appear in L, not in A.[10]

Further problems are generated within this format of the systems paradigm; it was articulated prior to the systematic development of the generalized media, and it is my opinion that the notion of a circulating medium is incompatible with it.[11] Unlike many economists and political scientists, Parsons does not define all transactions involving money and power as belonging within the economy and the polity (respectively) as societal subsystems. Rather he views money and power (influence and value commitments) as circulating media, moving across the boundaries of the subsystems wherein they are centered and articulated within subsystems other than those with which they are identified. Power is, for example, an active medium within the economy, within the economy's political subsector.

This conceptual necessity of including offices utilizing power within nonpolitical subsystems[12] cannot be dealt with in E&S format. Within that schema power is an input from the polity to the I_G subsector, but not to the A_G subsector (nor to the L_G subsector). Rather, because the $G \longleftrightarrow A$ interchange is conceptualized as an "adaptive interchange," the power input to the economy goes to its adaptive subsector (A_A). Consequently, there is conceptual contradiction in the attempt to handle power within the economy: it belongs both in A_G and in A_A. Thus, in using the E&S format, offices concerned with power must sometimes be miscategorized within the adaptive (and integrative) *subsectors* of the economic (and latency) *subsystems.* Similar problems arise within two thirds of the receiving subsystems; in the other third, the "proper" subsector receives the input, e.g., the I_G subsector receives the power input from the polity and thus no contradiction arises.

The Economy and Society paradigm also puts Parsons in the position of arguing that, for example, the primary goal of the economy is the provision of consumer goods to the latency subsystem.[13] This is so because he specifically defines the $L \longleftrightarrow A$ boundary as the economy's goal attainment boundary. Yet this definition contradicts the view that the goal of the economy is defined internally, although not ignoring specifications of higher-order goals and values, and concerns the implementation of adaptive functions within substantive situational contexts.[14] More concretely, within Parsons' paradigm the goal of the economy is fixed across situation; in fact he has isolated one aspect of the functional task of the economy (one of its product outputs) and defined it (without, of course, specifying the substantive context) as the economy's goal. Provision of this product output is not always the paramount "goal" of the economy, for example in national emergencies wherein consumer production is sacrificed in the provision of services for the polity (e.g., soldiers) and wherein government control over the system of economic production is enforced.[15] In this situation (and goals are situationally defined, as distinct from values)[16] the major goal of the economy is not the provision of consumer goods.

More analytically, Parsons' error lies in identifying the goal of the subsystem with the output across a specified subsystem boundary. Once again we have come upon a situation of confusion among system levels. The goal of the pattern-maintenance system is not the provision of labor but rather the mobilization of "maintenance resources" to the other subsystems, in order to fulfill the latency function for the system as a whole. And, as will be seen, "the goal of the polity . . . is the *mobilization* of the necessary prerequisites for the *attainment* of given system goals of the society."[17] The goals of other subsystems are also defined in terms of the necessity of mobilizing resources to implement their functions within a concrete situation (in part delimited by the goal attainment subsystem of the total system).

Another major problem with the E&S format must be mentioned. Parsons has consistently argued that the latency function merits special consideration within the interchange schema, a consideration derived from the relative stability of its contents and from its functional role as the "gene" within an action system.[18] In the case of the "land" factors relevant to the economy, A_L, their defining characteristic "lies in the segregation of these commitments from the operation of ordinary price mechanisms, i.e., the insulation of supply from the fluctuations of demand."[19] Thus "land" and, more generally, all latency factors are insulated from the exchange system.

Without taking exception to Parsons' general orientation to the latency quadrant and its functions, I must still take issue with his theoretical treatment of this aspect of the functional schema. Relative isolation is not complete isolation; even the available quantity of physical earth varies with the price paid and with certain other noneconomic considerations. Parsons' treatment, on the other hand, contains an aspect of an idealistic notion of immanence which must be removed from the system. The difficulties involved are most easily seen at the general action level.

In *Economy and Society* Parsons and Smelser assume the input to A_L, G_L, I_L, L_L (at the social system level) comes from the cultural system (or at least this is my understanding of their discussion). This tacit assumption provides for a possible derivation of the content within A_L, but it collapses for the other "land factors". I say "possible" for the economy because the cultural input to the social system (in the E&S format) does go to the economy, although it is not specified to which subsector of the economy. But within the E&S paradigm there is no way to get inputs to the "land" component of the noneconomic sectors. This is so even if one recognizes the legitimacy, as I do, of treating any societal subsystem, for example, the polity, as the social system directly receiving the cultural input. In such a case the adaptive subsector of the polity would be the receiving subsector, not the latency subsector (see Figure 20-1). Thus even if we ignore what seems to me to be an awkward situation, the fact that all cultural inputs to a social system are mediated through the adaptive rather than the latency subsystem, within the current format of the paradigm there is no way to remove the immanent quality of G_L, I_L and L_L.[20]

As will be seen, I rectify this problem by demanding that the maintenance function be fulfilled at the societal level (more generally, at every system level). Thus the latency function as well as the latency subsystem (an subsectors) must be represented in the interchange paradigm. Parsons and Smelser deliberately do not allow for a latency interchange; my system demands three such interchanges, i.e., interchanges where maintenance resources are provided, thus reinstating the L function to its proper *social* role. I endeavor to do this while retaining the valuable insights Parsons has generated about the function of pattern-maintenance.

The Systems Paradigm: A Revised Format

What follows is a schematic presentation of components of a revised paradigm. As should be obvious, the major distinctions between this and the older version lie in the following: The location of the sending and receiving subsectors is altered, and the labelling of functional effect across the boundary interchanges eliminated. The reader should note that Figure 20-2 is arranged so that the subsectors within each subsystem are facing the subsystem of cognate function. This reordering possesses both theoretical and empirical consequences of major import. I will discuss some of the former in the paragraphs which follow.

In this version processes categorized within subsystems are viewed as specializing in the provision of resources defined in accord with subsystem tasks. These resources are utilized to enable the entire system to meet the relevant functional exigencies, e.g., economic resources enable a society to meet adaptive exigencies and, further, are allocated to the cognate subsector of the other subsystem, better enabling them to meet the functional exigency under discussion and thus to complete their own tasks, e.g., economic resources provided to the G_A subsector help political structures meet their adaptive exigencies and thus fulfill the goal-attainment function for the society.

To take another example, the societal community provides integrative resources relevant to the adequate functioning of the society. It does this by

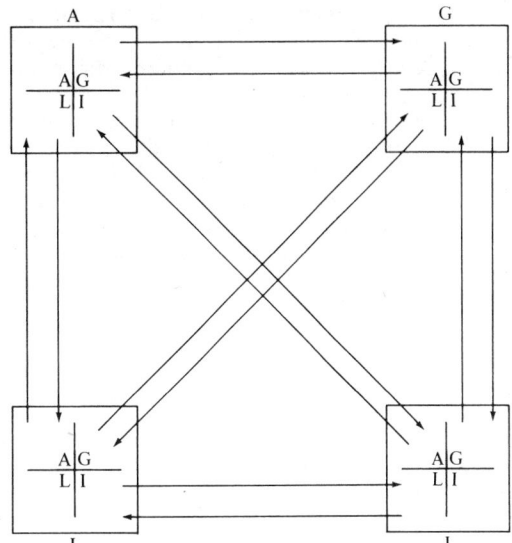

Figure 20-2. Simplified version of the revised interchange format.

allocating these resources to the integrative subsector of the other subsystems, thus providing those subsectors with the integrative resources necessary for the subsystem to function and therein contributing to the functioning of the society. If one wanted to label boundary exchanges in terms of functional import, all six outputs from the societal community are concerned with the integrative coordination of the system as a whole. The same logic holds for all subsystems, at all levels of discussion. I fulfills the integrative function for the system, X_I for the X subsystem.

This modification also enables us to systematically deal with the generalized media. Each medium is viewed as centrally located within one of the societal subsystems and, when circulated beyond the boundaries of that subsystem, as remaining within the cognate subsectors of the neighboring subsystem. The focus of power is, for example, within the polity; when utilized in the factor inputs to the economy and in the product outputs from the economy, it is always based in a goal-attainment subsector of the economy. This placement occurs because the polity always exchanges with the political subsector of the economy, societal community, and maintenance subsystems.

The necessity for this revision may become clearer with one further example. Within the latency subsector, consumption, utilizing money, is "located"—in the revised version—within the adaptive subsector of the latency subsystem (L_A). The original framework locates this role (of consumer) in L_G and thus, if consistency is to be maintained, should have him utilize either commitments or power. The revised version never falls into this dilemma: The medium is always properly classified within either the appropriate subsystem or subsector.

The revised format is also helpful in eliminating the problem of specifying system goals. No longer is the goal of any system conceptualized as limited to a specific output across any one boundary; rather, the goal-attainment subsystem (or subsector) is viewed as the focal point of collective mobilization of system resources for the attainment of situationally specifiable goals. The goal-attainment subsector of the economic, integrative, and maintenance subsystems articulates with the polity and thus accepts inputs of political resources generated for over-all system goal-attainment. Similarly, each of the goal-attainment subsectors provides the polity with resources relevant to both functions. For example, mobilized services may be put under the control of governmental collectivities (in G), or political support may be mobilized for the incumbent political system. These assets are directly concerned with the utilization of power within and between subsystems.[21]

Different problems are raised in Parsons' treatment of the latency function. First, it should be noted that I do not disagree with Parsons' contention that "land" factors, as closely related to, and sometimes interpenetrating with, cultural factors, possess a special place in the interchange system. It is in the revised format, not in the *Economy and Society* paradigm, that the latency subsystem (of the social system) and latency subsectors articulate most closely with the cultural system. The cultural input to the social system is to the adaptive subsystem in the old format (and to the adaptive subsector when the subsystem is taken as the receiving subsystem), while it is to the latency subsystem in the new format (and to the latency subsector when the subsystem is taken as the receiving system).[22]

I believe that the special features of the "land" categories can be adequately treated within the confines of the revised paradigm I have devised if we develop a few scattered references found in Parsons' own works. The exposition will be more readily followed if I begin with a brief consideration of the L$\longleftrightarrow$A boundary interchange: "There is a pattern-maintenance subsystem *below* the adaptive subsystem in the hierarchy of control of any system of action and another *above* the integrative subsystem in the series."[23] Parsons goes on to tell us that the interchange that he and Smelser considered in *Economy and Society* (A$\longleftrightarrow$L) dealt with the lower level L, LIG*AL*.[24] It is my contention that this view is correct, that the reference is to the real commitment of labor capacity when the L is below A, A$\longleftrightarrow$L,

LIG*AL* but further that when the reference is to the L above A, *LIGAL*, the discussion should concern "land," as a component of value commitment.

In the labor interchange, A$\longleftrightarrow$L, as Parsons has commented in the technical notes to the media papers, money is the controlling medium in the interchange. In the case of "land," value commitment becomes the cybernetically higher medium. Labor capacity concerns the provision of real commitments to a task orientation, although

> at the time of commitment to employment, the content of these specifications need not be known or agreed to by either party.
>
> Per se, the act of employment excludes units other than the employing one from encroaching on the rights of the employing unit; it also defines both the obligations assumed by the employee within the organization, and the obligations assumed by the employing organization for remuneration, type of work expected, times, etc.
>
> The allocation of real commitments in this sense is controlled by the monetary mechanism, while these commitments constitute mechanisms governing the processes of further specification of the utilization of resources.[25]

In the case of "land," L$\longleftrightarrow$A, value commitment becomes the governing medium. Here we are concerned with a higher ordered commitment to work, of the type Weber treated in *The Protestant Ethic,* and with the value principles in terms of which the work is evaluated. The specification of interpenetrating cultural traits into the social system, owing to their locale on the cybernetic scale, involves the relative "isolation" of these commitments from the exchange system. This is not to say that the commitment to work can not be influenced by monetary incentives in the selection of a specific job (this is a concern of the A$\longleftrightarrow$L, LIG*AL*, exchange), but only that under normal circumstances the value commitment to work, or to leisure, will dominate one's over-all attitude towards membership in the work force; in this exchange commitments are higher on the cybernetic scale than money. Thus in Parsons' own terms, in the LIG*AL* interchange "land" factors are insulated from immediate dependency upon market price.[26]

More generally, a parallel argument is tenable for the polity and the societal community, as well as for the action system considered as a whole. This framework provides a context within which it is possible to conceptualize Parsons' insights about the "land" factors, whatever the functional context, owing to the fact that in the revised paradigm L subsectors always exchanging with L subsystems; yet at the same time it provides systematic channels along which one can trace the influences of "land" factors on the rest of the system, and reciprocally, the influence of the system upon the "land" factors. Stability does not imply theoretical transcendence.[27] Stability is, after all, only relative; the development of the Protestant Ethic must itself be explained. The possibility of such treatment is dependent upon the inclusion of the latency *subsectors* within the exchange system, the inclusion of the latency *function* (subsystem) within the exchange system (in terms of the six maintenance outputs), and finally, the articulation between the L subsectors of the economy, the polity, and the societal community with the latency subsystem. All of these imply the revision of the E&S format.

One additional criterion for judging the adequacy of the interchange paradigm was pointed out to me by Professor Parsons. He believes, correctly I think, that the paradigm must be arranged so as to display cybernetic hierarchy among the various subsystems and subsectors. Thus if one accepts the LIGA hierarchy, the various subsystems and subsectors must be arranged in a fashion wherein this ordering is maintained.

Referring to Figure 20-1, the *Economy and Society* paradigm, it is apparent that this condition of theoretical adequacy is not met. Here, if we treat the lower left corner as the point of cybernetic control, we find the subsystems are properly ordered: L above I, G, and A (reading counterclockwise). But the subsectors are not so ordered. L_L is above L_A, which is above I_A, which is above I_L. The last is not correct. Such discrepancies occur on the horizontal, the vertical and the diagonal.

Refer to the new paradigm, Figure 20-2. Here the subsystems are correctly ordered (counterclockwise as the table is printed), and so are the subsectors: L_L above L_I above I_L above I_I. This hierarchy is always in evidence, no matter where in the paradigm one begins. Another example: A_A is below A_G below G_A below G_G. Only with the revised schema can this cybernetic ordering be theoretically exemplified.

The External-Internal Axis of the System

The four-fold schema can be generated by conceptualizing it along two axes:[28]

	Instrumental	*Consummatory*
External	A	G
Internal	L	I

The modified format does not alter the status of the instrumental-consummatory division, but it does alter the status of the external-internal axis; and therefore, although the former may be ignored, I must briefly state my understanding of the import of this alteration for the latter.

The external-internal axis indicates that for Parsons only at adaptive and goal-attainment boundaries is a system open to exchanges beyond its boundaries. Thus the latency and integrative subsystems should not take part in boundary exchanges. As a matter of fact, within the E&S paradigm this rule is not applied to subsystems but to subsectors. The latency and integrative subsystems take part in boundary exchanges of the same type as the goal-attainment and adaptive subsystems.

The axis does come into consideration, however, in a discussion of subsectors. The exchanges between subsystems are never over the latency boundary, and those across the integrative boundary Parsons attempts to differentiate from those crossing the goal-attainment and adaptive boundaries. He tells us that at the diagonal boundaries (between I subsectors) each medium is operative not as a message but in its code component. This presumably is sufficient to explain the apparent deviation from the theory. Nowhere, to my recollection, are we told whether the "assumption of operative responsibility" (the factor output, power output, from G to L) is a utilization of power as a message or as a code, nor is explicit reference made to the factor output from A to I, the "assertion of claims to resources."[29] His discussion is tortured at best: He means the term code to specify the "grammar" within which the media flow and forgets that such a "grammar" must be institutionalized in all positions wherein the media are "intelligible," utilizable. His argument might be defensible if influence were the only medium flowing across the diagonal boundaries and if he chose to define influence as noncirculating, thus viewing the central axis as a focus of normative interpenetration, not exchange. But as the interchange schema is constructed this is not possible: Although the content across these boundaries is, perhaps, different from those at the horizontal and vertical boundaries, these are still exchanges involving all of the media.[30]

It is my contention that Parsons has misplaced the import of the external-internal axis and that to understand its theoretical relevance one must focus not upon the interaction between subsectors within an integrated system, but rather upon the process of integration between two systems at the same system level.[31] The external-internal division is seen as essential to the understanding of system development.[32] I can do no more than illustrate this without presenting a completed version of a highly tentative developmental model, a task well beyond the boundaries of this exposition.

The model hypothesizes that system development occurs in the following sequence: A, A——G, G——L, G——I, I——A, I——L, L——G, L——A (where the subsystems are connected with lines, not arrows, the ordering within the interchange does not follow the cybernetic hierarchy).[33] Only with stage three, G——L, do we have the beginning of the internal axis of the system.

The import of this model for the questions under discussion is two-fold: First, it forces us to add an explicit developmental perspective to our work. We cannot analyze any system without forcing ourselves to assess the developmental potential of its current position. If this schema proves useful it will immediately orient us to the next stage of the system and, at a more sophisticated level, to the processes inherent in any system which might lead to this development.[34]

Second, the schema emphasizes that, prior to the development of intrasystem exchanges, interrelationships between units are across the adaptive and goal-attainment "subsystems" (stages one and two). This fact remains constant from interaction between infants to interaction between nation states. Only with the G——L interchange does the internal organization of the system appear. The external boundaries between two systems at the same level of generality are across the A and G boundaries of the separate systems (whatever their level of internal differentiation). This does not imply that there are no G and A boundaries when the two separate systems merge into one. It does imply, however, that the internal exchanges involving the polity and the economy are mediated through their respective integrative and maintenance subsectors, and that the externally oriented exchanges concerning the latency and integrative subsystems are mediated through their goal-attainment and adaptive subsectors. Further, all externally directed exchanges beyond the boundaries of the extant system are mediated through the A and G subsystems; the integrative and maintenance subsystems (and subsectors) figure in boundary relationships only within a system. (See Figure 20-2.)

In other words, the merging of two segmented systems into one system involves the functional elaboration of a set of internal boundaries. In unifying, two independent (yet perhaps interdependent) systems that exchanged across their A and G boundaries they articulate a set of internal exchanges, although they may continue exchanges across their A and G boundaries because of the possible specialization of the systems with functional subsystems. In the prototypical case, the integration of two structurally monadic systems into one differentiated system involves the elaboration of I and L subsectors within

the then extant A and G subsystems and the consequent development of subsystems specializing in integrative and maintenance functions (these subsystems imply the generation of processes, not necessarily of differentiated structures). In no case are the I and L subsystems involved in "external" exchanges.[35]

Thus I see the analytical utility of the external-internal dichotomy relating to the developmental process leading the integration of two segmented systems into one differentiated system. Not only is it not erroneous to conceptualize the integrative and latency subsystems as being involved in intrasystem boundary exchanges, it is absolutely necessary that such conceptualizations be included (as they are in the E&S paradigm). But further, it is imperative that I and L subsectors be involved in boundary exchanges; these exchanges are also internal to the analyzed system. They involve the intrasystem maintenance of patterns and the integration of subsystems within the context of a differentiated system. The A and G subsectors of the I and L subsystems are involved only in externally directed exchanges *within* an integrated system; only the A and G subsystems are involved in externally directed exchanges beyond the borders of an integrated system.

The Systems Paradigm: A Suggested Complication

In concluding this section of the paper I do little more than articulate a refined version of the interchange paradigm. I do not pretend to enunciate theoretically conclusive arguments for this version of the model, but have found it useful in empirical work and want it available to others who might care to consider, utilize, evaluate and modify it.

The major change in the model outlined above is simple: here all factor inputs are between the core subsectors within each subsystem (e.g., $G_{G_a} \longleftrightarrow A_{AG}$ or $L_{L_i} \longleftrightarrow I_{I_l}$), while the product outputs are as enunciated in the text (e.g., $G_A \longleftrightarrow A_G$ or $L_I \longleftrightarrow I_L$). The schema appears in Figure 20-3. Note that in the figure the core subsectors of each subsystem (A_A, G_G, I_I, L_L) are drawn out of context, for easier understanding.

The inner exchanges are product inputs, the rewards effectively evaluating past and prospective subsystem performance. These are defined in terms of the medium of the receptive subsystem and are equivalent to the intrinsic satisfiers controlled by the medium focused within the sending system.

The outer exchanges indicate the factor inputs, defined in terms of the media of the sending subsystem. These are the "factors of production," definitive of constituent intent, opportunity, and

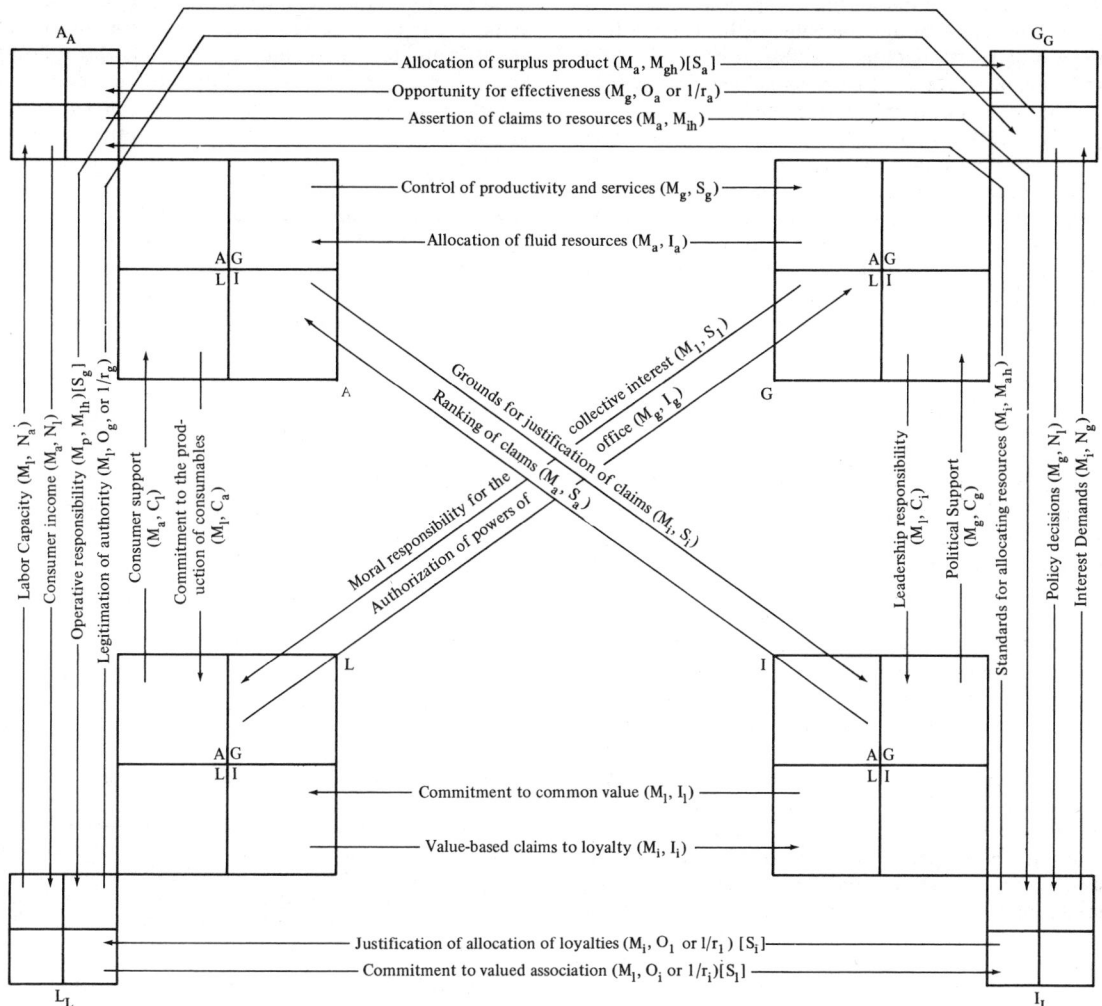

Figure 20-3. Revised interchange paradigm.

KEY:

All symbols are explicated in the appendix to this chapter.

Inner exchanges are product exchanges; outer exchanges are factor exchanges.

The *first symbol in each parenthesis* refers to the medium in control of the output. The *second symbol* refers to the discussions within part two of this chapter. For example: "Value based claims to loyalty (M_i, I_i)" refers to (Influence, Investment input to integrative subsystem). The reader will note some overlap in terminology, e.g., "I," for integrative subsystem and investment. These overlaps were unavoidable unless standard conventions were thrown to the winds. Meanings should be clear within contexts.

available media resources for production with the system.[36]

Factor inputs flow to and from core subsectors for these subsectors are viewed as the immediate foci of the subsystem media. Thus the procurement of factor resources is the task of the medium focused within each core subsector, each procurement being a provision for some other subsystem.[37]

Within a developmental context the core subsector of each subsystem is the first affected by conditional and/or cybernetically controlling developments. It is the analytical focus of the emergence of each subsector within the context of developing interchange relationships. It occupies a special position within the framework in that it is involved in each interchange affecting its cognate subsystem and, at levels of structural differentiation, is the center of intra-subsystem relationships relevant to the value-added processing of the factors of subsystem production. At levels of structural fusion its subsectors and the cognate subsystems are indistinguishable.[38]

This model thus indicates the patterns involved in the differentiation of function and the possible differentiation of structure. It isolates the framework within which the double boundary interchanges between subsystems are manifest and, further, forces the analyst to elaborate the intrasubsystem interchanges which are presumed in the double boundary notion and which are not extant in the E&S model nor in the simple model previously discussed. Thus the elaborated model enables us to assess the emerging complexity and differentiation within a system and to isolate the intrasystem exchanges which make this development possible; for example, the double boundary exchange between A and G involves the adaptive subsectors A_{A_g} and A_G and, implicitly, the interchange between them, $(A_{G_g} \longleftrightarrow A_{G_a} \longleftrightarrow A_{A_g})$. In those instances where the categorized structures are equivalent, no interchanges occur; in those where they are functionally differentiated (not simply segmented), the interchanges must be portrayed.

Of the many examples I could provide illustrating the utility of the elaborated model I will briefly describe only one. I have devoted much time to studying the importance of the charismatic expansion and contraction of the media in the study of social disorder. It appears that charismatic effects occur in the first instance in the expansion or contraction of value commitments and perhaps, via the flow of value commitments, then affect the other media and their subsystems. These possible effects on the other media concern the definition of the opportunity structure (O_i and O_g) affecting media utilization, and thus medium investment (I_i and I_g), located at the exchange with the immediately higher cybernetic system than the one affected, which wields a negative sanction).[39]

But this does not explain the charismatic expansion or contraction of value commitments, a phenomenon clearly related to the cultural input to the social system. If the cultural input is to A or L no leverage is provided explicating the expansion of value commitments, via the investment input (I_l), as effected by the input from the cultural system. In the elaborated model, however, the "definition of the situation" input, the factor input from the cultural to the social system, is to the I_L subsystem of the societal community, the locus of the investment input to L. This is clearly the focus of the cultural effect upon the charismatic expansion or contraction of value commitments.

Thus, although the societal community does not have the cybernetic leverage to control the investment input to the latency subsystem, the cultural system is higher cybernetically and does possess a negatively sanctioned medium, "definition of the situation."[40] Therefore, the charismatic expansion of value commitments is placed within an intelligible context in the revised paradigm. In Weber's terms, "Prophets systematized religion with a view to unifying the relationship of man to the world, by reference to an ultimate and *integrated* value position."[41] The charismatic prophet, the individual who claims a personal relationship with the divine, with the source of meaning for society, the individual who provides an apparently unified and meaningful view of the world and who defines moral obligations as the duty of his followers—the personality in this role often merges the I_L and L_I subsystems in redefining the scope of value commitments for his following. He draws upon the cultural heritage of those whom he affects in redefining the content and breadth of their moral beliefs.

INTERCHANGE ANALYSIS

The object of our analysis is, not to provide a machine, or a method of blind manipulation, which will furnish an infallible answer, but to provide ourselves with an organized and orderly method of thinking our particular problems; and, after we have reached a provisional conclusion by isolating the complicating factors one by one, we then have to go back on ourselves and allow, as well as we can, for the probable interactions of the factors amongst themselves. This is the nature of economic thinking. Any other way of applying our formal principles of thought (without which, however, we shall be lost in the wood) will lead us into error.[42]

The remainder of this chapter uses the interchange paradigm as a framework within which to isolate and outline a series of propositions relating to the conditions regulating subsystem output. Working at a macrosociological level I put forward a set of analytical propositions concerning the interrelationships between factor and product inputs to any subsystem. In this presentation my focus is upon the economy and the polity. While the model will undoubtedly prove in need of modification, its utility is, I feel, apparent even in this introductory presentation.

More specifically, I will develop this system within the context of a societal analysis; societies are "a type of social system, in any universe of social systems, which attains the highest level of self-sufficiency as a system in relation to other systems."[43] In this exposition I will not be concerned with interchanges between societies and will be only peripherally concerned with the interchanges between a society, as a social system, and the cultural, personality, and behavioral organism systems which make up a major portion of its non-social environment; nor will I treat questions of development. Thus while I view the social system as open — "spatially and temporally" — I have here limited my perspective to the internal exchanges within any one societal system, within the context of a given stage of development, and generally, from a short term comparative static perspective.

The presentation which follows is incomplete in numerous ways: I have not provided operational definitions for the concepts, and further, many of the concepts are better termed search devices, less precisely stated, with regard to inclusion and exclusion criteria, than even I am capable of at the moment. This has been done to avoid a premature closure and, frankly, to enable my reader to cheat. Cheating I would define as allowing that the presumed falsification of a proposition might be avoided by changing the categorization of the empirical materials examined. To take a crude example: if examining a specific revolutionary movement leads to the conclusion that the hypothesized determining variables for a revolutionary coup d'etat are present, yet the actual revolution falls outside the boundaries of this concept, it is permissible to redefine the concept to include the historical case. The checks on this seemingly arbitrary procedure occur in examining the next coup d'etat similarly defined (and this definition must be rigorously drawn), and in determining if one's propositions lead to correct explanations and avoid incorrect ones. Such procedures are commonplace in survey research work, where I fear they too often are not recognized, as I would have it, as aspects of theory construction, but are treated as aspects of verification. We must be wary of throwing out good propositions simply because we do not completely understand to what our conceptualizations refer before we dig into the empirical, historically specific, materials.[44] We should also recognize that papers like this one, stated at very high levels of generality, remain of limited value until utilized within many historical contexts.

Second, the model identifies only the major determinants of the subsystem outputs discussed and ignores auxiliary determinants, as expressed, for example, within the other interchanges involving the subsystem under discussion. Any predictions from the model will, therefore, be crude and assume the *ceteris paribus* condition. To alleviate this "problem" would entail the specification of numerous middle-range theories, clearly a task which must be left undone in this context.

Related to this, I have often only indicated the direction of interrelationships, not the exact nature of those relationships. Such a specification involves processes of disaggregation, structural analysis, and historical particularization. I hope, nonetheless, to have been both sufficiently precise and suggestive to solicit error and commentary.

Subsystem Inputs: Product

It is my ruling assumption that it is possible to specify a series of interrelationships between inputs to a given social system and the product output of that system. Such a model can be stated at various levels of complexity and with various degrees of completeness. Here I will attempt to be brief and will, therefore, be very schematic. In intoducing the model my discussion is very abstract, focusing on the three product inputs to *any societal subsystem*. Initially I seek to outline certain general implications which can be drawn from well-known and basic economic theory.[45] Later in the paper I specify this discussion to the economy itself and then to the polity.

The level of media input ("expenditure") provided for each subsystem is dependent upon the balance between the amount of media withheld from current consumer support (C) S, and the amount invested (I), the amount of media utilized to add value to future productive potential. (Appendix A is a guide to the symbols utilized.) My central concern will be to explicate the relationships between subsystem production (output, Y) and various breakdowns in the spending of subsystem derived income (Y).

There are two perspectives which we might adopt regarding the support the consumer provides the producing subsystem. In the aggregate, his consumption input (what I call consumer support) provides the resources, the income, enabling subsystem units to regenerate their product. With regard to individual units, the consumer provides support to individual productive enterprises — which can be analyzed at many levels of specificity, e.g., within the economy by industry, or by firm within the context of an industry, or between industries providing interchangeable products. Products consumed (the product output from the subsystem of reference to the consuming subsystem) are utilized within the context of the time period under analysis (although, even with this period delimited, it is often difficult to draw an exact line between consumer and investment "goods").

Savings refers to the total income, derived from a subsystem, withheld from current consumption and thus defines the total of subsystem resources that might be made available for purposes of investment.

Savings is thus a measure of income not utilized in current support of the subsystem, while investment refers to nonconsumption utilization of income. Thus investment involves the allocation of media resources (a form of "support") towards the addition (over a specifiable period) to the value of produced "capital," produce reserved for further production.[46] Investment is therefore equivalent to the total value of subsystem production minus product consumed. Likewise, since the value of subsystem output is equivalent to subsystem income, actual investment will be equivalent to actual saving. Both saving and investment are equivalent to total product minus consumed product; savings plus consumption is equivalent to subsystem-derived income ($C + I \equiv Y$; $C + S \equiv Y$; $I \equiv S$).

Subsystem Product Inputs: Specified to the Economy

Thus far, while utilizing terminology drawn from the discipline of economics I have endeavored to couch my discussion at a level of generality encompassing product inputs to any societal subsystem. In order to make what follows a bit more concrete I will specify these terms to the economy and identify their location within the interchange paradigm Parsons has developed. Later, in complicating the model, I will return to the more general formulations.[47]

Economic consumption (C_a) concerns the product input of monetarily defined resources to the economy at the $L \longleftrightarrow A$ interchange. Economic investment (I_a) refers to the monetary product input from the polity to the economy ($G \rightarrow A$), what Parsons has termed "allocation of fluid resources, financial." Economic savings (S_a) is a two-pronged concept, in the first instance referring to the "ranking of claims" between money allocated towards consumption and money withheld from current consumption and thus available for purposes of investment. Second, it concerns those resources actually made available within the context of an investment market, those resources not hoarded. Functionally the first occurs across the $I \longleftrightarrow A$ boundary as the product input to A, a definition of the rate of surplus value, the second across the $G \longleftrightarrow A$ boundary, as the factor input to G, what I will call the allocation of surplus value, surplus product.

The preceding is in need of clarification. First, for the reader familiar with Parsons: at the $G \longleftrightarrow A$ boundary, the product input from G to A concerns the allocation of liquid capital; the specification of funds in particular uses, including hoarded cash, occurs within the economy, $A_G \longleftrightarrow A_A$.[48] Savings

is viewed as dependent upon the allocation of income within the economy — as Keynes would have it — and thus is not specifically concerned with intralatency decisions. It involves, therefore, questions of business saving as well as saving by wage-earners; it further involves the much-debated "forced savings," and "saving" enforced by the government. The question is one of solvency, the coordination standard of money in A, not pattern-consistency, the coordination standard of commitments in L. Insofar as the former is relevant to latency decisions it is concerned with the allocation of funds within the boundaries of a consumer's budget; thus dissaving can occur within the context of the $A \longleftrightarrow L$ boundary. I assume, therefore, that hoarded cash remains within the economy, not within the latency subsystem.

For the reader familiar with Marx, I view the factor output from A to L as involving the monetary payment for necessary labor power (while recognizing the ambiguity of this social and cultural definition within the Marxian framework). Marx's variable capital is here treated, for simplicity's sake, as a segment of the money income allocated to L and returned in consumer expenditure. But not all consumption stems from what Parsons calls "wage income" — although all wage income is consumed. Some derives from an allocation of surplus, e.g., transfer payments drawn from government taxes, conspicuous consumption drawn from, for example, profits or rents;[49] both of these examples involve an allocation of funds via $G - (product) \rightarrow A - (factor) \rightarrow L$, although various levels of dedifferentiation may be manifest.[50] I have, therefore, labeled the $A \rightarrow L$ factor output, "consumer income," a category including, but extending beyond, the monetary payment for necessary labor power.

The boundary interchange at $I \longleftrightarrow A$ is obscure in the economic literature. The factor output from A to I clearly refers, in part, to economically necessary costs of sales and distribution; in part, however, it includes the costs of advertising and publicity that do no more than waste income; thus some part of these are cost of production and some are waste.[51] In any case, it does not involve the actual export of income across this boundary; the total economic product is a Summation of the real (nonmonetary) products at $A \rightarrow L$ and $A \rightarrow G$ (not all of which actually cross the boundaries), and the total income, the factor (monetary) outputs across the same boundaries. The factor output from A to I concerns rational, nonrational, and irrational assertions of claims for funds, but not the actual provision of income (which involves the hiring of labor capacity and the actual export of surplus product). The product output from the economy to I concerns the justification of the allocation of claims within the societal community, between individualistic demands and more general loyalties. It does not concern the aggregate scope of economic produce, only its possible uses.[52]

Thus at the I $\longleftrightarrow$ A boundary questions of the scope of economic output are not at issue — although the scope can be and usually is influenced by what occurs at this boundary. Rather issues concerning the allocation of available resources to "make good" the symbolic definition of scope are of paramount importance. (See the later discussion of inflation and deflation.) Something comparable occurs at each subsystem. The product input to the subsystem which delineates the level of the sending subsystem's saving (e.g., I $-$ [product] $\rightarrow$ A and A $-$ [product] $\rightarrow$ G) is always allocational regarding recipient functions, although not necessarily with regard to the sending product. The product output to the subsystem which defines savings for the outputting subsystem (e.g., A $-$ [product] $\rightarrow$ I and G $-$ [product] $\rightarrow$ A) is always allocational (although not necessarily as a savings input). It always concerns the distribution of the sending subsystem's product among receiving units. This is so even when these allocational priorities become relevant to the determination of the aggregate total product for the sender in the next period. And it is also true when this output (to the subsystem which defines total saving) involves the "purchase" of real product from the sending subsystem. For example, the G product output to A concerns the allocation of fluid resources (I_a) in return for the control of productivity and services (S_g). Here the economy receives from the polity an allocational product, relevant to the distribution of the total political product, not, in this time period, to the scope of political output (see later discussion); the return product from the economy is allocational with regard to the mobilization of political resources. It concerns the availability of "real economic product" in the implementation of the powers inherent in the political subsystem. Thus while this boundary involves the scope of economic output, the I $\longleftrightarrow$ A boundary deals with the distribution of both economic and integrative product. Only in the following period can this interchange be determinative of the aggregate level of such output.

Economic output is equivalent in value to total income which is equivalent to consumption plus investment, and/or consumption plus saving. Thus within the context of the model income is either defined, across the I $\longleftrightarrow$ A boundary, as available for consumption which occurs across the A $\longleftrightarrow$ L boundary, (A $-$ [Factor] $\rightarrow$ L $-$ [Product] $\rightarrow$ A), or saving on the G $\longleftrightarrow$ A boundary (A $-$ [Factor] $\rightarrow$ G $+$ hoard). In the simplest case all the surplus will

be allocated to investment purposes; thus surplus value would be equal to value saved equal to value invested. In the more complicated reality, the "government" allocates certain of it to its own labor force, as "wage income" (here there is a de-differentiation between the economy and the polity). Certain of it is transfered to others for the purpose of consumption, and certain is consumed by political groups (here there is a de-differentiation between the polity and the latency subsystem).[53] But still, income is allocated for either consumption or investment, or differently, for consumption and saving. The equivalence between savings and investment appears over the A $\longleftrightarrow$ G boundary in money allocated to the polity and not utilized for purposes of consumption (either by transfer or by de-differentiation), thus in Keynesian terms only the surplus of tax is properly called "savings," or more generally, the surplus not redistributed as consumer income.

It is now possible to explicate a simple model of income determination. At this point let us view investment as constant, with regard to income, and view savings as positively related to income. In this case 20-4 can be constructed. The intersection of the savings and investment curves, and the intersection of the aggregate support curve ($C_a + I_a$) with the 45° line ($C_a + S_a$), is the equilibrium point determining the level of economic output. The actual slope of the curves produced will be determined by the structural characteristics of the system under examination, as will the disaggregated character of the terms utilized.[54] But in any case, the point of equality between saving and investment should be determinative of the level of output and income.

We can make verbal sense out of this if we first imagine a case where output exceeds the point marked by the equilibrium; here intended aggregate

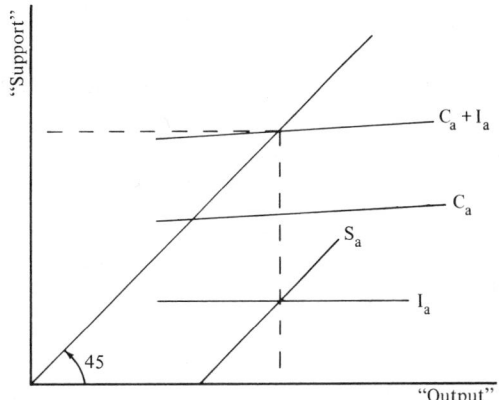

Figure 20-4. The determination of aggregate equilibrium output.

savings will exceed intended aggregate investment, thus some firms will find themselves incapable of selling the goods produced and inventories will begin to accumulate. These firms will thus be forced to curtail production, thus curtailing aggregate output and intended saving.

If output should fall below the presumed equilibrium point, intended investment would exceed intended saving. Here there will occur, for some firms, an involuntary disinvestment — for example, the selling of inventories. Aggregate intended support (consumption plus investment) will exceed output, thus generating pressures for an increase in output (and an actual increase, assuming the availability of the necessary factors of production). As only at the equilibrium point does aggregate support equal aggregate output, only here is a stable level of output specified.[55]

In the last paragraph mention was made of aggregate support. This approach to income distribution adds intended aggregate consumer support to intended aggregate investment to form the $C_a + I_a$ schedule in Figure 20-4. The reader will note that the intersection of the $C_a + I_a$ curve with the 45° line is equivalent to the equilibrium point where desired savings equals desired investment. Here total output equals total spending (aggregate demand equals aggregate supply), and aggregate saving equals aggregate investment.

In concluding this segment of the paper I will introduce only one further economic concept, the multiplier. This term is used to denote the numerical coefficient which shows the ultimate change in output and income which results from a change in spending, e.g., a shift upwards in the investment curve. The general formula for this relationship is as follows:

$$\text{Change in output} = \frac{1}{\text{MPS}_a} \times \text{change in investment}$$

$$= \frac{1}{1 - \text{MPC}_a} \times \text{change in investment}$$

where MPS_a (Keynes' marginal propensity to save) indicates what percentage of the increased income will be allocated to savings instead of consumption and the MPC_a (marginal propensities to consume) indicates what percentage of the increase in aggregate income will be allocated to consumption. ($\text{MPC}_a + \text{MPS}_a \equiv I$.) Unlike some economists, I define these terms solely in terms of aggregate measures and make no psychological assumptions concerning them. Again, the actual arithmetic value of the curves is determined by the structural conditions within any given economy.[56]

A simple example shows that if the MPS_a is one fifth,

a $10 billion shift in the investment cruve, at any given level of output, would increase output by $5 \times \$10$ billion, or $50 billion. Likewise, a shift upwards in the savings curve of $10 billion will decrease output by $50 billion; this is equivalent to saying that a shift downward of $10 billion in consumer support at any given level of income has occurred, with the consequent fall in output.[57]

The shift upward in the saving schedule is often referred to as the paradox of thrift, for thrift ultimately yields both a decrease in output and, if we drop the assumption of a horizontal investment schedule — introducing a more realistic schedule showing a positive relationship between output and investment (Figure 20-5) — a decrease in aggregate saving. Conversely, an increase in the consumption schedule — a decrease in the savings schedule — yields an increase in output and an increase in saving. This paradox will reappear in my discussion of the polity and is very important to bear in mind.

Subsystem Inputs: Factor

If we now execute a mental shift and go back to the level of generality referring to any subsystem, it will be possible to elaborate upon our model. Here the terminology I have adopted is not drawn from economics, and therefore it will, perhaps, be a bit more difficult to follow than earlier discussions. The following concerns the factor inputs to any given subsystem and the interrelationships among the six inputs to that subsystem, as they affect output. Later in this section I will examine questions dealing with the relationships between symbolic output, measured in terms of the medium of reference, and real output — problems of inflation and deflation.

One of these factor inputs involves a specification of intent, one a definition of resources, and the last a definition of opportunity. Three varieties of the first,

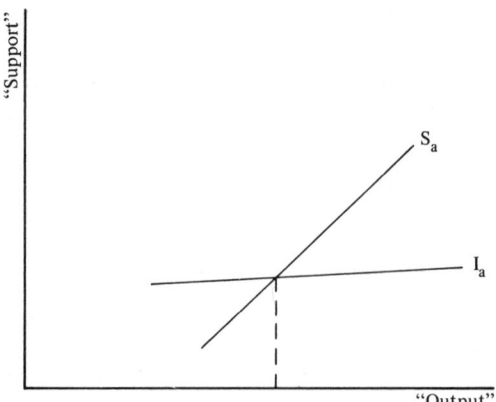

Figure 20-5. Equilibrium of saving and investment showing both as positive functions of output (income).

constituent intent, are labor, interest demands, and policy decisions. Marshall defines "*labour* as any exertion of mind or body undergone partly or wholly with a view to some good other than the pleasure derived directly from the work. And if we had to make a fresh start it would be best to regard all labour as productive except that which failed to promote the aim towards which it was directed, and so produced no utility."[58] Easton tells us that "a demand may be defined as an expression of opinion that an authoritative allocation with regard to a particular subject matter should or should not be made by those responsible for doing so."[59] Parsons defines policy decisions as "the process of altering priorities in such a way that the new pattern comes to be binding on the collectivity."[60] All of these resources involve the specification of constituent intentionality.[61] All, however, are objectified in exchange; all may be generalized, and within the system we call "democratic capitalism," all are alienated.

I will call this factor of production, for lack of a better term, "constituent intent" (N). It involves a factor input to the subsystem of reference defined in "real terms," that is, defined in terms of a medium other than that centered in the subsystem of reference. This input is the "real" measure of value produced and embodied within the subsystem's intrinsic satisfiers, the product outputs purchased with media input, with the product outputs of other subsystems.

It is important to recognize that in a capitalist society—and here I paraphrase Marcuse in quoting a Hegelian discussion of labor—the intention of the individual [any unit under examination] fails to guarantee that his wants will be attended to. A force alien to the individual and over which he remains powerless determines whether or not his needs will be fulfilled. The value of the product of such intentions is independent of the individual and is subject to constant change.[62]

Continuing the paraphrase: The particular intention becomes a universal one in the process of exchange; it becomes a commodity. The universality also transforms the subject, the constituent, and his individual activity. He is forced to set aside his particular faculties and desires. Nothing counts but the distribution of the product of intention; nothing counts but abstract and universal intention.[63]

It should be apparant that constituent intention is not a homogeneous quality; neither, however, are any of its specifications: labor, interest demands, and policy decisions. Just as certain forms of labor command more income—in certain social situations—so with interest demands and policy decisions. An important task, one which lies beyond the boundaries of this paper, is the development of a theory of distribution applicable to these inputs, disaggregated by unit (individuals, occupational groupings, racially or ethnically defined collectivities, classes, etc.). Here we will concern ourselves only with aggregate inputs of intent.[64]

The second factor input concerns the definition of allocatable media resources available for actual utilization within the subsystem (M_h). It defines one component of the "demand for the media," the amount to be held in the context of various levels of acceptable opportunity within the system. A relatively high level of opportunity (defined by the third factor input) implies a relatively low inducement to part with the medium in question; the second factor input is thus concerned with the hoarding of media resources, that subsystem asset with the greatest liquidity.

The second factor input thus specifies the allocational priorities of the demand for the media of reference. One aspect of this concerns the structure of the response (in the monetary case, the slope of the "speculative demand cure") to available opportunities (defined in monetary theory by "the interest rate"). Another component of "liquidity preference" is defined by the transactions demand for the medium (M_t) and is dependent upon the level of output and income generated by the subsystem within which the medium is centrally located. An excess of produced output will be equivalent in value to the excess of the relevant medium demanded.

The last factor input concerns the availability of acceptable opportunities. The varieties of opportunity, and the indexes thereof, differ according to the subsystem of reference. All concern, however, a definition of the directionality of attitudes towards production within the subsystem. All define the return expected for the provision of media to the subsystem encompassing "banking" functions for the subsystem under discussion and serve to equilibrate the amount of any medium held with the amount of the medium supplied.

Subsystem Factor Inputs: Specified to the Economy

It is possible to specify each of these variables as factor inputs to the economy. The first, "constituent intent," becomes, as has already been noted, the input of labor capacity ($L \rightarrow A$, N_a). The second, the definition of available resources, concerns what Parsons has labelled "standards for the allocation of resources" ($I \rightarrow A$), more precisely within the context of economic theory, it partially defines the structure of the demand for money, the slope of the "speculative demand for money," that aspect of liquidity preference which is correlated with acceptable opportunities for the utilization of money (M_{ah}).[65]

The last factor input to the economy ($G \rightarrow A$)

Parsons has labelled "opportunity for effectiveness." In specifying this within conceptualizations available in academic economic theory we enter into an area of controversy and confusion. I am here concerned with the determinants of investment and the demand for money. Here I will only summarize: I am convinced that one index of opportunity is contained in the notion of the interest rate,[66] and it seems reasonable, at this level of schematism, to outline a model assuming one interest rate within the economy.[67]

Second, opportunity must involve some measure of the possibility of profitable investment. This factor may itself involve a number of components, varying from wealth effects to the levels of security and return manifest within banks and obtainable in various types of investments, Third, the level of opportunity can encompass questions related to political incentives to investment. e.g., the availability of subsidies. More generally, such factors concern the political reallocation of income. Last, at least from our restricted point of view, types of political policy, might vary from one or another form of governmental regulation to a policy of overt (or covert) imperialism—for example, involving direct or indirect opportunities for investment and/or for the control of markets and materials. All of these define the relative position of units within the system.

For our purposes, in the following discussion, I will deal only with one variable across this boundary: the interest rate, treated as an index of opportunity. An increase in the interest rate (r_a) measures a decrease in opportunity for productive, profitable investment (O_a). I assume, with tongue in cheek, that the other components of the process will appear in the measure of income, which is a way of saying that implicitly they do appear in the slopes of the curves I will draw.[68]

For our purposes it will be possible to discuss the relationships among the six inputs to the economy in the two market contexts: a production market and a money market. I will only make an abbreviated reference to the market for labor capacity. My comments are brief and nonrigorous, suited more to the inexact nature of the discussions which follow than the (apparently) rigorous discussions economists engage in.[69]

Figures 20-6 and 20-7 represent the relations between investment (I_a) and the rate of interest (r_a), and saving (S_a) and income (Y_a).

I assume, unless I indicate otherwise, the parameters M_a, the money supply, and P_a, the price level, as given. As such I often obscure distinctions between real measures and monetary measures.

Investment is taken as a decreasing function of the interest rate, an increasing function of opportunity,

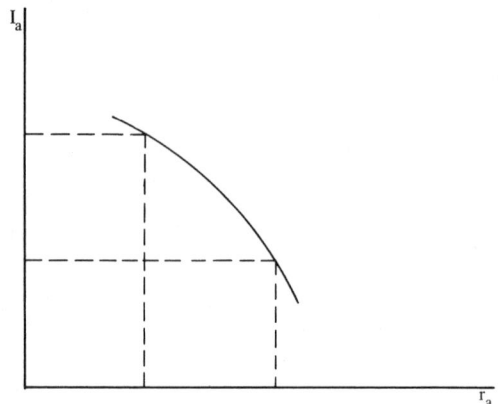

Figure 20-6. Investment and interest rate.

and saving as an increasing function of income. Figure 20-8 shows the Hicks *IS* curve. It represents the combination of income and interest rates that equilibrate the real sector of the economy, those points where saving equals investment, where consumption plus investment equals income. It is downward sloping; as the rate of interest falls investment rises, income rises and therefore saving rises.

Figures 20-9 and 20-10 represent the relations between the demand for money and income and the rate of interest. The transaction demand (M_{at}) is an increasing function of income, the demand for money to hold (M_{ah})[70]—comparable to Keynes' speculative demand—is a decreasing function of the interest rate. In other words, as opportunity increases it is reasonable to "trade off" influence for money (at I⟷A money becomes relatively more attractive); in addition, since the reward for relinquishing money (r_a) decreases, hoarding becomes more attractive. The LM curve, Figure 20-11, represents those combinations of income and interest rate which

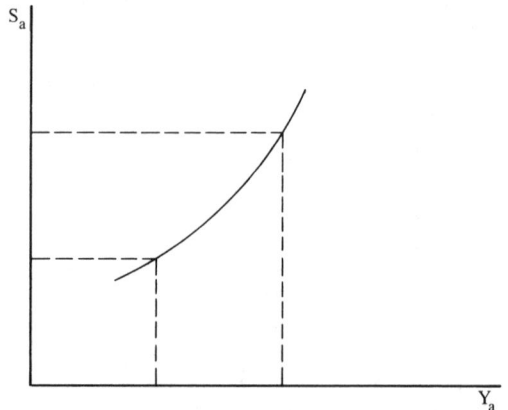

Figure 20-7. Saving and income.

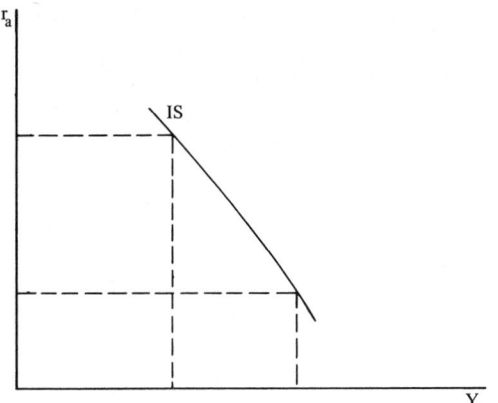

Figure 20-8. Combinations of Y_a and r_a which yield an equality of I_a and S_a (given the I_a and S_aY functions).

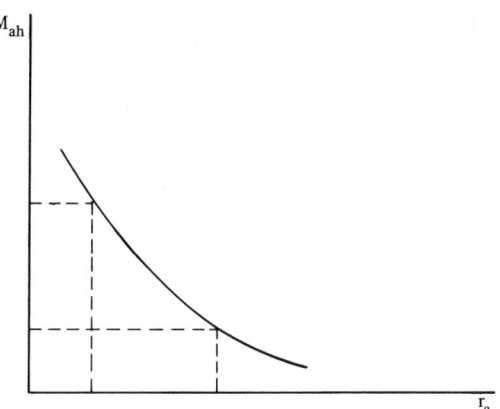

Figure 20-10. Demand for holding, "speculative demand."

result in an equilibrium of the money market, wherein the money supplied equals the money demands $(M_{as} = M_{ad})$, when the parameters remain: the stock of money is fixed and the price level given. The LM curve is upward sloping; at high levels of income more money will be required for transactions, leaving less for holding, and necessitating a rise in the interest rates to induce those holding money to part with it.

Figure 20-12 shows the IS and the LM curves on the Y_a, r_a plane. The intersection of the two curves displays the income and interest rate which balances both the money and the real sectors. It thus identifies the level of subsystem outputs which equilibrates the factor and product markets for the economic subsystem, the level at which utilized real factors, secured with money, balance the input of money, secured in exchange for real products, "intrinsic satisfiers." The utility of the model is that it identifies, using only a few equations, key positions in the interrelationship of these inputs, and

specifies the importance of the variable of opportunity in linking the two market contexts.

To display the model fully, especially the effects of monetary considerations upon the thus-far excluded factor input, labor capacity, would require a detailed elaboration of the IS-LM model. For our purposes it will be sufficient if we treat the demand for labor capacity as an increasing function of output. Thus if we draw this relationship, in Figure 20-13, below the LM-IS curves, the specification of output determines the amount of labor demanded. A major thrust of Keynes' work was, of course, that at the equilibrium level not all labor available need necessarily be utilized.[71]

Variations in the parameters of the model can be indicated within the context of this analysis and predictions generated as to the resultant effects upon other variables. It should be remembered that the variables within the model are mutually determined and that all the variables are interdependent. With this in mind let us take the example of an increase in

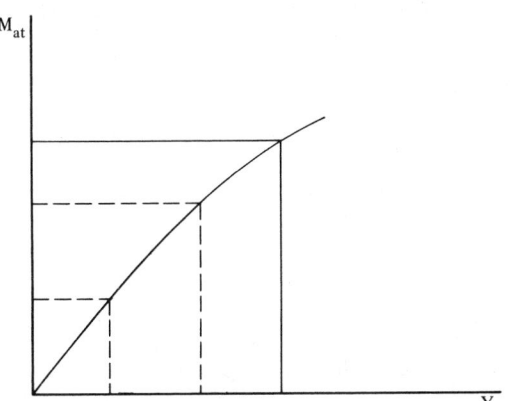

Figure 20-9. Transactions demand for money.

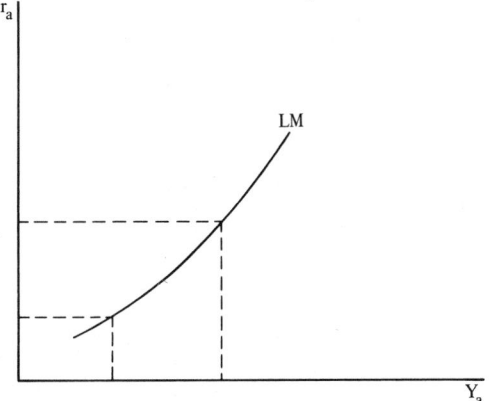

Figure 20-11. The combinations of r_a and Y_a which yield an equality of M_{as} and M_{ad}, for a given stock of money and a given price level.

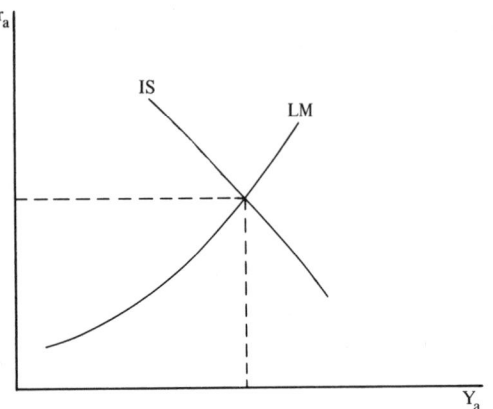

Figure 20-12. The equilibrium of money and production markets.

the propensity to invest, or a decrease in the propensity to save; the latter is, of course, equivalent to an increase in the propensity to consume, $1 - MPS$. In the former case the I_a curve, Figure 20-6, shifts upward and to the right, in the latter, the S_a curve, Figure 20-7, downward and to the right. In Figures 20-8 and 20-12 these changes result in an upward and to the right shift of the IS curve, and an increase in r_a and/or Y_a—depending upon the slope of the curves. Here, unlike the simple multiplier model outlined previously, part of the expansion is absorbed in higher interest rates and thus only part in an increase of income.[72]

It is also possible to vary the supply of money within the simple IS-LM analysis.[73] Very simply, an increase in the supply of money (or a downward shift in the M_{ah} schedule) will pull the LM curve out and to the right; such an increase yields an increase in Y_a and a decrease in r_a, as well as yielding

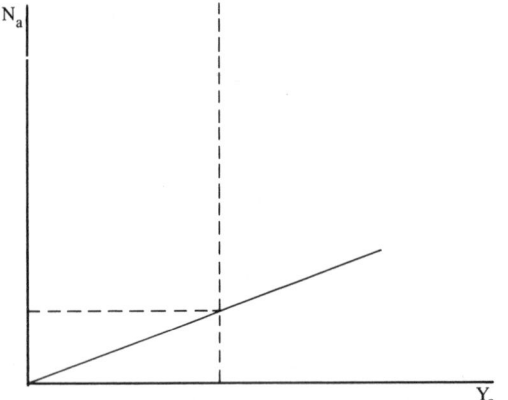

Figure 20-13. Labor and income.

and increase in investment, consumption and saving.

Subsystem Product Inputs: The Polity

I have now outlined a general framework within which it is possible to discuss subsystem output as it relates to the interrelationships among factor and product inputs to the subsystem. To do this I generalized the basic national income model utilized in contemporary macroeconomics, making it abstract enough to encompass all four societal subsystems. Then I placed the economic case within the social system interchange paradigm outlined in the first part of this chapter. I will now specify the generalities of this model to the polity, showing how it is possible to generate propositions of some interest concerning the inputs to that subsystem. The discussion will be easier to follow if we begin by looking at the three product inputs to the polity: political support ($I \rightarrow G$; G_g), control of productivity and services ($A \rightarrow G$; S_g), and authorization of powers of office ($L \rightarrow G$; I_g).

In the aggregate political support (consumer support, G_g) concerns the product input (defined in terms of power) to the polity at the $I \longleftrightarrow G$ boundary. It provides the resources, the income, enabling political units to regenerate their consumed product. With regard to individual units, the consumer provides support to individual collectivities, e.g., to one or another party in an election. This is the provision of diffuse, yet contingent, support for units assuming leadership responsibility. The source of support derives from the factor output from G to I, policy decisions.[74] Thus the scope of support in any given time period is delimited by the income of power from the polity to the societal community. Subsequently this support can be expanded, but the primary leverage for expansion is within the political "banking system," located in L, not in either G or I.[75]

Political investment (I_g) refers to the power (product) input from the latency subsystem to the polity. This input has been labelled by Parsons "the legality of powers of office." I change this term to "authorization of powers of office," for I am concerned not so much with delimiting the code of the political authority system but rather with the actual specification of the permission to utilize authority within classifiable types of situations. While the definition of the particulars of usage is an intrapolity decision, the investment input to the polity delimits the scope of discretion within which authorized units may act.[76]

Both political consumption and investment (authorization) involve the allocation of subsystem derived income in support of units classified within the polity. Consumption refers to the satisfaction of "immediate wants" (within the time period of reference), and investment involves the allocation of power in the generation of legitimate political institutions to be utilized in the production of future outputs.[77]

Political saving is dependent upon the allocation of income within the polity, not within the societal community. It refers to the total of political income withheld from the societal community and thus not available for current consumer support. Like economic saving, S_g is a two-pronged concept, first referring to the definition of the total of subsystem resources which might be made available for investment and second delimiting those resources actually made available for political authorization (I_g), those resources not hoarded. The first occurs across the $G \longleftrightarrow A$ boundary as the product input to the polity. It specifies the economic resources (services and productivity) over which the polity can exercise political control. The second occurs across the $L \longleftrightarrow G$ boundary, as the factor input to L, the assumption of operative responsibility.

Control over services and productivity indicates the allocation of position, relative to the political control over economic processes, exchanged for inputs of monetary resources. "This has often been put as presenting to political organization the 'problem' of *mobilization* of adequate manpower [and economic productivity] to meet its obligations in the society or to attain its collective goals."[78] Such resources are utilized in the assumption of operative responsibility within the system, unless the input is hoarded ("when qualified members of the labor force simply refuse to accept 'opportunities for effectiveness' [within the polity] and remain passive so far as contributions to collective goal-attainment are concerned"[79]), where available economic productivity is not allocated in the attainment of collective goals.

The reader conversant with the Parsonsian interchange paradigm will have noted modifications across the $G \longleftrightarrow A$ boundary. In this presentation the control of both productivity and services is relinquished across the product interchange. The control of productivity indicates "not managerial control of particular plants . . . but control of a share of general productivity of the economy through market mechanisms, without the specification of particulars."[80] I do not mean to refer to a factor of effectiveness, but to the "political control"[81] (via mechanisms of banking and credit, among others) over productive capacity and over the inreased potential for generating economic output.[82] I conceptualized this product output as including control

over those components of services which economists have come to label "human capital," but I do not view all services as passing into the control of the polity.[83] Rather a service is, in the first instance, an economic, occupational category.[84] In the second place services should be categorized in terms of their consequences, function, implying in many instances a de-differentiation in the noneconomic case;[85] only such services as pass into the control of the polity are considered at this boundary.

The control of productivity and services is granted in exchange for the monetary investment input—at the product boundaries—while the provision of opportunities is exchanged for the allocation of monetarily defined economic surplus.[86] One would predict, therefore, that opportunity would not be defined in terms of the quality of units, across the $G \longleftrightarrow A$ boundary, unless those units are "monetarily equal."[87] The input of surplus is a factor component of effectiveness, providing monetary resources to the polity.

Actual authorization (I_g) is equivalent to actual operative responsibility (S_g). The extent of *ex post* investment is by the actual scope of the political control of economic resources (S_g). It should thus be apparent that political income is equivalent in value to political investment plus political consumption and/or political investment plus political saving. Political income is allocated either for consumption ($G - [factor] \rightarrow I - [product] \rightarrow G$) or as saving ($G - [factor] \rightarrow L$), for investment ($L - [product] \rightarrow G$), or hoarded in G, as "saving" and as "investment."[88]

It is now possible to present a simple model of the determinants of political output and income. Paralleling the presentation of the economic model let us begin by treating investment, authorization, as constant with regard to income, and savings, control over productivity and services in operative responsibility, as related to income. Figure 20-14 represents these relationships.[89] Within the context of any single stage of political development an increase in income will yield a greater proportional increase in saving, i.e., the MPS_g (marginal propensity to save) will be greater than the APS_g (average propensity to save). The reason for this is that an increase in the scope of political output will necessitate the greater proportional allocation of power resources into *police* functions, paralleled by a greater input of authorization of powers of office. The intersection of the authorization and savings "curves,"[90] and the intersection of the aggregate support (authorization plus political support) "curve" with the 45° line ($C_g + S_g$), is the equilibrium condition determining the level of political output.

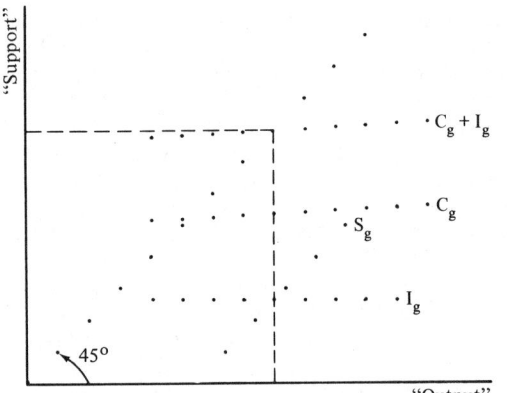

Figure 20-14. The determination of aggregate equilibrium political output.

Political output in a specifiable period is the sum of the real (nonpower) products, leadership responsibility and moral responsibility for the collective interest, political income is the sum of operative responsibility and policy decisions, measured in terms of power. The two products are the intrinsic satisfiers exchanged for incomes of support (consumption, political support and investment, authorization). The specification of the opportunities for effectiveness (G — [factor]→ A) is an indication of position within the political system, an output of information relative to power position, not an allocation of an income of power. The allocation of fluid resources (G — [product]→ A) involves the distribution of political output among economically classified units. Although evincing a reallocation and perhaps an expansion of economic resources within a credit structure organized by the polity, it is not relevant to the immediate scope of political output.

In short, at the G ⟷ A boundary questions of the scope of power are not at issue, rather questions of the allocation of the resources available to make good the symbolic definition of that scope (see the following discussion of inflation and deflation).

Once it is formulated in this fashion, it is easy to make verbal sense out of my hypothesis. Assume for a moment that output exceeds the place marked by the equilibrium condition. In this case intended aggregate saving will exceed intended aggregate investment, i.e., the provision and utilization of economic resources in the assumption of operative responsibility (and not transferred to the societal community) will be greater than the authorized powers of office. In this case the assumed level of leadership responsibility will not meet with the requisite level of support. Thus, in a situation analogous to the economic, some political production will be curtailed, decreasing the level of aggregate

output and intended saving. That is, a decrease in the input of politically controlled economic resources and in the assumption of operative responsibility will occur.[91]

If output and income fall below the hypothesized equilibrium condition, intended investment, authorization, would be in excess of intended saving, i.e., aggregate intended support (consumption plus investment, political support plus the authorization of power of office) will exceed output, thus generating pressures for an increase in output. Only at the equilibrium condition will aggregate intended output be equal to aggregate intended support, thus only at this "point" will an equilibrium be generated.

This model, like the macroeconomic model, is constructed so that intended aggregate political support plus intended aggregate authorization form the $C_g + I_g$ "schedule" in Figure 20-14. The 45° line, measuring aggregate income, support plus saving, intersects the aggregate support line at the "point" where desired saving equals desired investment; here total output equals total support, and aggregate saving equals aggregate investment.

Without the generation of ratio scales measuring power, a strict numerical analysis of the multiplier becomes impossible. If I nonetheless outline the form it would take, it is because the approximation would be theoretically interesting, even if difficult to carry out in practice. (Once the graphs are drawn, lines approximating the actual data can, of course, be fitted to the distributions.) Here the multiplier can be viewed as the numerical coefficient approximating the ultimate change in output and income which results from a change in support, for example, a shift upwards in the investment "curve." The general formula for this relationship is identical to the economic multiplier:

$$\text{Change in output} = \frac{1}{\text{MPS}_g} \times \text{change in investment}$$

$$= \frac{1}{1 - \text{MPC}_g} \times \text{change in investment}$$

where MPS_g indicates what percentage of the increased income will be allocated to savings (operative responsibility) instead of consumption and the MPC_g indicates what percentage of the increase in aggregate income will be allocated to consumption ($\text{MPC}_g + \text{MPS}_g = 1$). As in the economic case, I define these terms in aggregate measures, making no psychological assumptions. The actual arithmetic value of the curves—as approximated—will be determined by the structural properties of the polity under examination.

The important point for us to note is that an increase in the scope of authorized power generates an increase in the scope of political output far greater than might appear at first glance. The reverberations of this increase are magnified in inverse proportion to the new power income allocated for operative responsibility, MPS_g. The less allocated towards contingent, consumer support, the less the magnification of the increase in the scope of defined powers.

As in the economic case, there is a "political paradox of thrift." A shift upwards in the saving "schedule" will decrease output a commensurate amount. In other words, a simple increase in the political control of economic resources for *police* functions will decrease, not increase, output. Such a shift will also yield—where investment varies positively with output—a decrease in aggregate saving. Conversely, an increase in the consumption "schedule" $(I \rightarrow G)$, a decrease in the saving schedule $(G \rightarrow L)$, generates an increase in output and an increase in aggregate saving.

It is worth pausing for a moment to draw one, among the many, conclusions from the "political paradox of thrift." We are in a position to begin evaluating one of the most important problems of classical normative theory in light of the results of a systematic body of theory and in the process to help explain a wide variety of empirical findings. Although the simple utilization of resources, often repressive, in maintaining order in obedience will, in the short run, yield greater "acceptance" of authority, in the longer run it will yield a deterioration of the political system, a deflation in the scope of its output and a diminution of the very "powers" those in authority sought to maximize.

There is no way within this aggregate model to identify the effect of an increase in political savings, relative to other utilizations of power, upon specific units within the system. It is, however, possible to say that for the entire political system the morality which preaches "law and order" is, in the long run, inimical to order through law. The "conservative" who emphasizes "law and order" will, under certain conditions, get it, although he will narrow the scope of what is politically enforceable; in other conditions he will create a severe enough deflation of power to generate political disorder.[92] Wisdom lies with those who attempt to alleviate the disorder through the generation of political support, in meeting the interest demands of the constituencies involved.

Subsystem Factor Inputs: The Polity

It is now possible to introduce the factor inputs to the polity. The first concerns the "specification of intent," interest demands, the factor input from the societal community (N_g). Interest demand

is conceived to be the primary basis on which leadership elements of the polity are put in a position, through the use of their influence, to appeal for political support.... Thus we conclude that knowing constituents' wants, as well as partly "shaping" them through leadership initiative ... is a crucial factor in political effectiveness. As such, however, it must be combined, with some approach to "optimization," with other factors. From this analysis it is perfectly clear that it is neither desirable nor realistically possible for political leadership. in governmental collectivities, to attempt to "satisfy" all demands or wishes of its constituents.[93]

Thus interest demands are a factor input of influence definitive of the value of the polity's product. As in the case of labor capacity, the individual unit's intent does not guarantee the satisfaction of his desires. The structure of the control over output differs markedly in various types of polities and thus differs the degree to the alienation of intent.

The second factor input concerns the allocation of economic, monetary resources (M_{gh}), to the polity. The input of monetary resources defines the response of holders of power to fluctuations in the legitimacy of the political system. An increase in the input of money to the polity generates an increase in the power held, power available for, but not utilized in, transactions. It concerns, therefore, the hoarding of power. Greater legitimacy generates more authorization, but less "payment" for the relinquishment of power.

This second factor input thus specifies the monetary resources available to finance political output. It defines the structure—on the charts, the "slope"—of one aspect of the allocational structure of power, as a medium of exchange, that aspect which is respondent to fluctuations in opportunity, legitimacy. If the rate of alienation is low, little benefit is accured from relinquishing control of power held.[94] In addition there is a "transactions demand for power" (M_{gt}), dependent upon the level of output generated by the polity. As in the case of the economy, an excess of political product will be equivalent in value to the excess of power held.

The final factor input delimits the evaluational status of the political system and thus serves as an index of attitude towards the legitimacy of the system (O_g). There are many possible indices of legitimacy; perhaps the major one is the rate of perceived alienation from the values implemented within the political system (r_g).[95] An increase in political alienation marks a decrease in legitimacy for the political structures.[96]

As in the case of the economy I will discuss the interrelationships between the discussed political variables in two market contexts: a production and a power market. I shall only make a passing reference to the market for "constituent intent," interest demands.[97]

Figure 20-15 represents the relations between authorization (I_g) and legitimacy (O_g); in order to avoid confusion and to maintain parallels, O_g will be represented in the figures by an index of political alienation, r_g, which varies inversely with legitimacy. Figure 20-16 displays the relationships between the assumption of operative responsibility (S_g) and income (Y_g). Unless indicated otherwise the parameters M_g, the amount of power in circulation, and P_g, the ratio of power to the capacity to secure binding obligations, and therefore, political intrinsic satisfiers, are given.[98] Authorization decreases with an increase in alienation, increases with an increase in granted legitimacy; the scope of assumed operative responsibility increases with political income.

Figure 20-17 is a modified version of the IS "curve," as specified to the polity. It represents the variations of income and legitimacy levels which equilibrate the real sector of the polity. The "curve" shown is downward "sloping," with increases in opportunity (increases in legitimacy, decreases in the rate of political alienation), investment rises (the scope of authorization is enlarged), the scope of output and income broadens and therefore saving rises (the scope of assumed operative responsibility grows). Figure 20-17 does not identify any single level of equilibrium, rather it demarcates a series of positions where political saving balances political investment, a series of possible political outputs. To find a "single" equilibrium position requires a discussion of the "market for power."

Figure 20-18 displays the relation between the definition of available resources and the level of opportunity. The input of monetary resources (M_{gh}) varies positively with the level of legitimacy, nega-

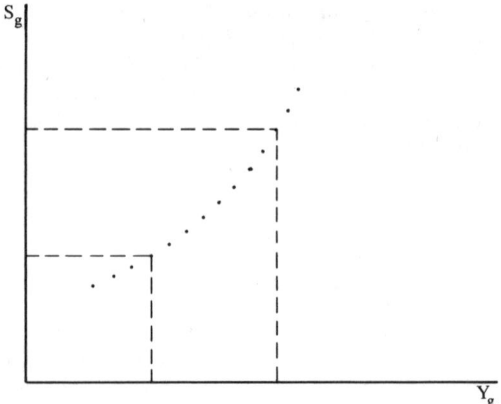

Figure 20-16. Political saving and political income.

tively with the rate of political alienation (r_g). As political opportunity increases it becomes more attractive for units to "trade off" monetary resources for the access to power: power becomes a more secure resource to hold, increases in relative value. Thus as the level of legitimacy rises, the level of power hoarded grows.

As legitimacy, opportunity, grows, less positive sanction is needed to induce units to make power available for transactions. The autonomous level of investment varies positively with the level of legitimacy; as legitimacy increases, investment increases. Also, power becomes more valuable relative to money as its legitimacy grows, and the "trading" of money for power increases. This power is held, not made available for transactions or made available within the investment market. It becomes apparent that legitimacy symbols set a balance between production and money markets, as we will see in Figure 20-21.

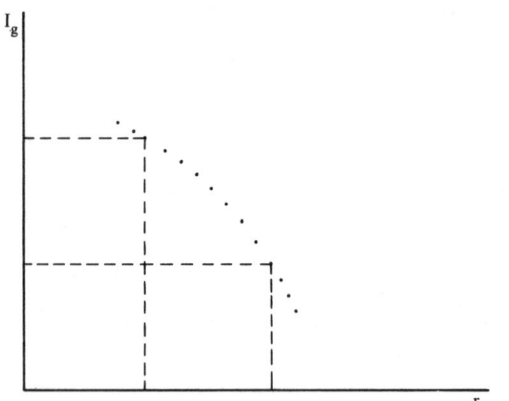

Figure 20-15. Political investment (authorization) and the rate of alienation.

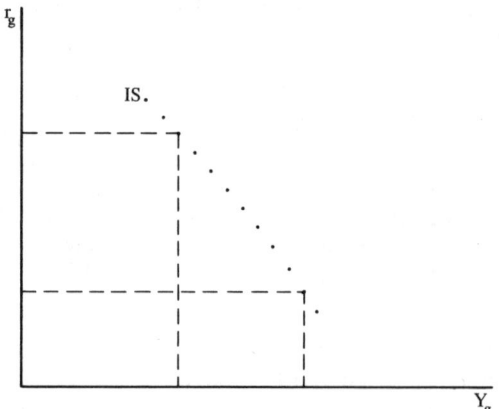

Figure 20-17. Combinations of Y_g and r_g which yield an equality of I_g and S_g (given the I_g and S_g functions).

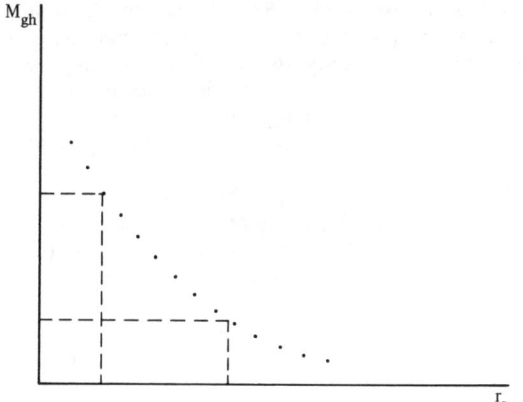

Figure 20-18. Allocation of surplus economic resources.

If the reader refers back to the discussion of the economy he will find a strikingly parallel set of circumstances. Only in the economic case it is influence which is "traded" for money. An increase in the "flow of influence" generates an increase in the demand for money to hold. In that instance, as in this, I categorize hoarded media in the system of immediate reference, thus the quotes around "traded."

Figure 20-19 represents the transactions demand for power (M_{gt}) as increasing with income. An increase in income from the polity will generate an increase in the number of political transactions and thus an increase in the demand for power, to be utilized in those transactions. The LM curve in Figure 20-20 displays those combinations of income and legitimacy which result in an equilibrium of the power market, where the total amount of power equals the power demanded ($M_{gs} = M_{gd}$), and where our parameters are a fixed amount of power and a fixed ratio between the amount of power controlled and the capacity of secure the intrinsic satisfiers available. The LM curve slopes upward.

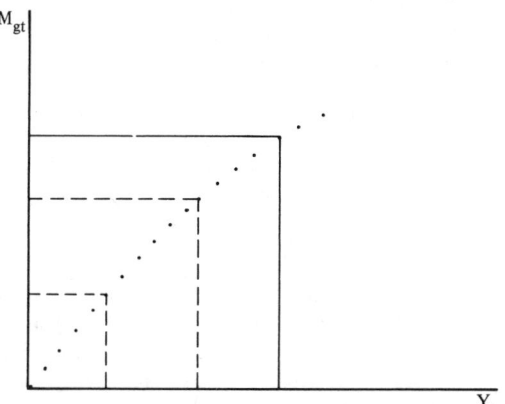

Figure 20-19. "Transactions demand" for power.

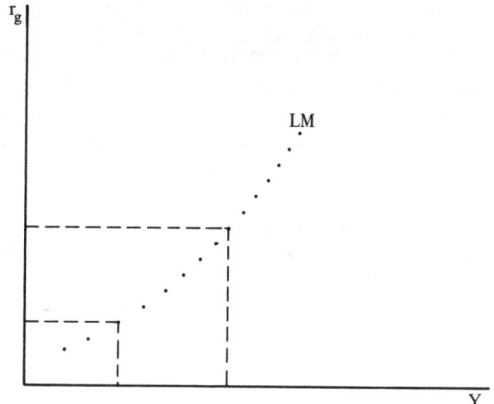

Figure 20-20. For a given stock of power and a fixed ratio between the amount of power controlled and the capacity to secure available intrinsic satisfiers, the combinations of r_g and Y_g which yield an equality of M_{gs} and M_{gd}.

At high levels of income more power is required for transactions, leaving less for holding, yielding a decrease in opportunity (the legitimacy of the available fringe opportunities will be less secure than those closer to the center of the power system) and an increase in return for parting with money. In other words, an increase in the rate of political alienation implies that a greater reward will have to be offered to individuals in order to induce them to make held power available within the investment market.

Figure 20-21 represents the political LM-IS curves. On this graph the intersection of the two curves identifies the level of political output and political legitimacy which balance the two market systems. Figure 20-21 also identifies the aggregate measure of interest demands which will be fulfilled; the output specified by the LM-IS curves determines the scope of interest demands met, but not, as I have mentioned before, the important question of which interest demands are to be fulfilled.[99] Figure 20-21 thus specifies the level of subsystem output which exemplifies a balance between the factor and product inputs to the polity.

It is possible, of course, to vary the parameters in the model and to generate predictions of effect upon the other variables. As in the economic case, all of the variables are mutually determined and interdependent.

An increase in the "inducement to invest," the aggregate level of authorization at any level of opportunity, or a decrease in the "propensity to save," a smaller assumption of operative responsibility at any level of output and consequently the provision and utilization of a relatively greater proportion of income for consumption, political support, involves the following reactions: in the former case the I_g curve in Figure 20-16 shifts upward and to the right; in the latter case the S_g "curve" in Figure 20-17 shifts downward and to the right. In Figures 20-17 and 20-21, either of these changes would result in an upward and to the right shift in the IS curve, yielding an increase in r_g and/or Y_g, a decrease in political legitimacy and/or an increase in output (depending upon the "slope of the curve"). Unlike the simpler multiplier model proposed previously, part of the expansion of output and income will be swallowed by a growth in the sense of political alienation, a decrease in legitimacy.

In the short run the decrease in legitimacy can be countered with an increase in the amount of power within the system. This might involve, for example, a redefinition of the assets which might come under political control or an inclusion of

previously excluded persons within the jurisdiction of control. In any case it involves an increase in the generalized capacity to command binding obligations, and if the power is not inflated, to secure the performance of those obligations.

An increase in the amount of power within the system or a decrease in the M_{gh} "schedule" shifts the LM curve (in Figures 20-20 and 20-22) out and to the right, yielding an increase in Y_g and a decrease in r_g, and in addition, an increase in the authorized powers of office, in the level of political support, and in the assumed control of productivity and services in the assumption of *police* powers. These effects retain their meaning only if an inflation of the medium can be avoided, and it is to this issue that I turn in a few paragraphs.

As should be apparent, the historical analysis of any society might place it anywhere along the curve I have drawn or might effect the shape of those curves. Let me note two examples whose economic analogies have received much attention. The first is the so-called classical case, wherein there are relatively high levels of investment and saving and the relationship between a decrease in legitimacy and the demand for power is low. In this situation an increased inducement to invest or consume will result in little change in income and a relatively large change (downward) in the legitimacy of authority (an increase in the rate of political alienation). On the other hand, an increase in the amount of power will yield a large effect in the scope of political income and output, as shown by the movement of the LM curve outward and to the right. This situation is typified graphically when the equilibrium "point" lies along a nearly vertical segment of the LM curve, i.e., where the IS curve intersects with the LM curve along a nearly vertical segment of the latter.

The converse case is represented for the economy in the Keynesian discussion of the "liquidity trap": Here levels of investment and saving are low, unmet interest demands generally high. The equilibrium point is found on the nearly horizontal section of the LM curve, or the entire curve may be horizontal, and thus a movement upwards in the authorization "schedule" (a movement of the curve, not along it) will result in little increase in alienation and a great increase in income. This would involve an upward and to the right shift of the IS curve. An increase in the supply of power (a shift to the right in the LM curve) would involve only a slight increase in income, and a slight reduction in the level of political alienation.[100] Thus the impact of an expansion of power might well differ markedly according to the historical context.

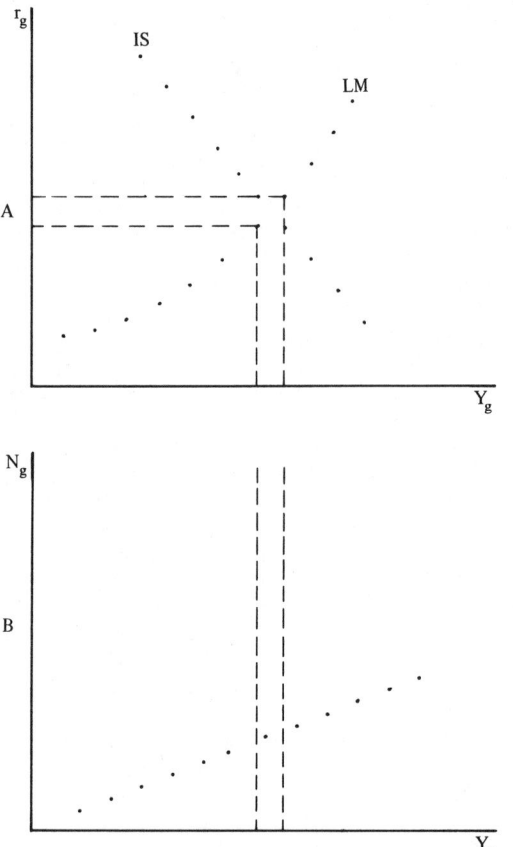

Figure 20-21. (A) The equilibrium of power and production markets; (B) Scope of implemented interest demands.

Inflation and Deflation

In discussing inbalances in the media I am again entering an area of much controversy within contemporary economic theory. I will, therefore, once again limit my arguments to basic points generally accepted within the context of short-term analysis. Rather than taking the space to elaborate upon the specifics of the economic case, I will focus upon a discussion of the polity, interspersing comments applicable to all the generalized media.[101]

A medium may be said to be inflated when its symbolic scope exceeds, or is growing more rapidly than, its capacity to command real resources. Such a situation will be manifest where the accepted credit standing of the units commanding the medium exceed their capacity to control the income of the medium withheld from current consumption, where investment exceeds savings, or where the total of aggregate support exceeds total real output. "True inflation" is the situation where an increase in support produces no increase in output, but simply raises the cost per unit output in full proportion to the increase in the scope of support.[102] At this point an expansion of the amount of the symbolic medium will produce no increase in real output and will be inflationary.[103]

Power inflation is the situation wherein the scope of the powers of office exceeds the capacity to implement binding decisions; this is a situation where the polity would provide relatively less in intrinsic satisfiers for the same amount of power. Power inflation will be manifest if granted authorization of the powers of office exceeds control over economic resources by the polity and if in a situation of rising support the potential to assume operative responsibility is held constant, decreases, or rises more slowly.

Support inflation can be portrayed within the context of the LM-IS diagram, although the portrayal is awkward. Therefore I begin with a simple example utilizing the Figure 20-14 model. In Figure 20-22 we see political consumption, investment, and savings plotted on an axis of income and expenditure. Point F marks the equilibrium level of output and also the level of interest demands fulfilled.

Let us assume that there occurs an increase in the political investment "schedule," owing, for example to a constitutional expansion of the powers of selected offices.[104] This is shown by the upward movement of the aggregate support "curve," $(C_g + I_g)_2$, and the investment "curve," I_{g2}. Output will increase to F_2 and accepted interest demands to F_2. It is possible that both these points, F and F_2, mark situations comparable to "full employment equilibria," where the difference between the interest demands, $F_2 - F$ is equivalent to demands induced by the polity, a

situation of "low full demand" and "high full demand." (In the economy this is a situation in which persons are induced into the labor market.) It is also possible, however, owing to circumstances explicable only in an examination of the societal community, that F marked the total level of interest demands capable of extraction from the public. Stated differently, F_2 would mark a situation where certain outputs from the polity were not adequately justified by inputs of demand.[105] In this instance we confront an inflationary gap, A—B, a situation where the excess of support will generate an inflationary spiral until curtailed by an increase of political alienation. The spiral can also be halted, on Figure 20-22 (but not shown), by a decrease in the support "schedule," an increase in the saving "schedule," the political control of economic resources in the assumption of operative responsibility. In the latter case the new point of intersection would be to the left of F_2: the inflationary gap would close when the level of output once again reached point F.

An expansion of power will generate similar inflationary pressures. If, on Figure 20-22, a shift in the LM curve out and to the right increases political output beyond the level adequately justified by the input of interest demands, an inflationary push will be generated. Assuming a situation of "true inflation," with no real increase in output, the fall in the value of power would be halted when the decrease in symbolic value approximated the increase in the amount of power.[106]

If both an expansion of power and a shift upward in the inducement to invest curve occur simultaneously, the pressures are compounded. And this latter case is not unlikely: An increase in the political authoriza-

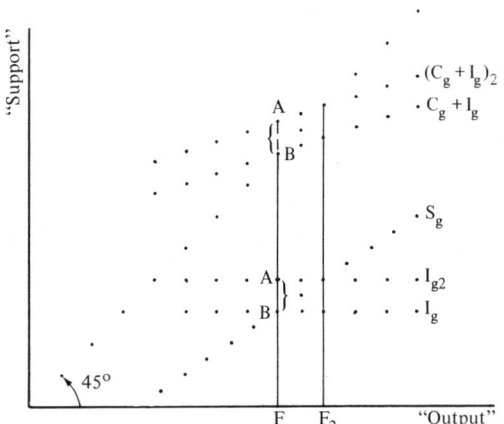

Figure 20-22. A shift upward in the political investment "schedule" and the inflationary gap.

tion "schedule" will generate an increase in output (even assuming no inflation) only by leading to an increase in political alienation. A remedy for the latter might be found in the increase of the amount of power within the system, perhaps through an extention of the franchise. Clearly a more complete model would specify the conditions under which any medium would undergo expansion, and just as clearly, such an explanation would broaden our focus beyond a single subsystem.

The interchange model provides us with a framework within which to trace certain effects of a media inflation. The effects of an inflaction of power are manifest in the power outputs from the polity. Policy decisions are called into question; if the medium is inflated their bindingness is dubious; and further, if the medium is inflated the capacity of politically categorized collectivities to wield effective force, the security base of power[107] is also called into question across the G $\rightarrow$ L boundary, in the implementation of operative responsibility. Thus the ability of the government to enforce its decrees is doubtful when power is inflated.

A simple example will also display the value of the interchange paradigm in this regard. An inflation of money will involve an alteration in the A factor input to G. *Ceteris paribus,* as money inflates it becomes less valuable relative to power, thus it will be more likely to be "traded off" for power. Thus the M_{gh} "curve" will shift upward, moving the LM "curve" in and to the left. This will generate a decrease in Y_g and an increase in r_g, the rate of political alienation, and more generally, a contraction of the entire political subsystem. In the same way knowledge of the conditions in one subsystem often enables us to generate predictions concerning other subsystems.

A major qualification to the points in the last paragraphs must be added. Generally, in speaking of money inflation an economist expects to find an upward change in the general price level, not an increase in prices in one sector (perhaps coupled with a smaller decrease in others). Admittedly, however, sectorial inflation occurs, where prices remain stable, sometimes because prices remain stable, in other sectors.[108] Sectorial inflation is even more common in the polity. Power is often inflated for certain collectivities, for certain uses and not others. Let me elucidate by way of example.

The successful utilization of power depends upon the combinatorial addition of inputs to the polity. Within a value-added model we can view a balance of I, A, and L resource inputs as the necessary and sufficient condition for the actual implementation of political output without engendering disequilib-

rium. It is possible, within any given set of conditions, to identify a maximum "real output" from the polity in terms of the limits of the resources available to the polity. Within this framework the limit upon the scope of the control of economic productivity and services available in the assumption of operative responsibility is a primary conditioning (in the cybernetic sense) variable.

An elected communist government in a nation with economic capitalism would be in a situation of holding inflated power. Such a government would be incapable of implementing policy decisions essential to the generation of a communist system, even if there was support for such a program. Unless it were to drastically alter the capitalist character of the economy, eliminating profit as the criterion of economic success and requisitioning control over economic resources in an attempt to restructure the economy, it would be unable to secure the necessary control of economic resources to assume the operative responsibility for the implementation of essential programs. In other words, it would be unable to secure the required economic inputs to "make good" its promises within the context of leadership responsibility, as the extent of its capacity to assume operative responsibility (real, not inflated) is defined by its control of productivity and services. A government unwilling to abide by the conditions of action delimited by the economic system extant in capitalist countries would be in a position of cybernetic control with an energy system refusing to respond to inputs of information. This is one aspect of what Marx meant by the dictatorship of the bourgeoisie,[109] that class in control of the economy in a "capitalist country."[110]

In this hypothetical situation[111] those who support the government in its anticapitalist policies do so with inflated power, i.e., the government is incapable of generating the resources to make its decisions binding and, relatively, their support is thus for a lesser scope of leadership responsibility.[112] Those who oppose the government in these policies may well be able to utilize their power with greater effect elsewhere, and their power is not necessarily inflated. (Not being able to purchase a specific painting because it has already been sold, or increased in price, does not mean that money is "inflated" for the actor; likewise, not being in control of some decision does not mean that power is "inflated" for the actor when he turns to some other issue. If, however, the power [or money] the actor controls is only utilized in one sector of the polity [or economy], and that sector is where the inflation has occurred, perhaps as a consequence of his support, then the medium, as he utilizes it, is "inflated.") Thus in certain situations power may be inflated with regard to only some sectors of the polity. The same sectorial breakdown in the effects of inflation is also present in circumstances of deflation.

"In the field of power it [deflation] is toward progressively increasing reliance on strict authority and coercive sanctions, culminating in the threat and use of physical force."[113] A deflationary situation for part of the polity occurs where the assumption of operative responsibility exceeds the authorized powers of office, or where political output exceeds the input of support. Diagramatically, in the aggregate, if the saving "schedule" shifts upward, moving the aggregate support "curve," $(C_g + I_g)$, downward, in Figure 20-23; we have a situation of a deflationary gap, A—B, and would predict decreasing output and greater demands for binding decisions, "to which the demander has some kind of right, but which . . . [are] out of line with the normal expectations of the operation of the system."[114]

Deflation is a situation wherein the economic resources are present to increase in the scope of political output, but aggregate intended support falls short of the intended output at which all justifiable interest demands would be met. It becomes a situation in which individuals demand power to hold, but this power is in danger of losing its symbolic nature, and as a result, the appeal to force becomes a method of coercion. The capacity to command force in the implementation of operative responsibility is present for the scope of output extant prior to the deflationary downswing in output. In deflation, power is "more valuable," but within a limited scope of discretion; its distinction from "real," intrinsic satisfiers can become blurred, and political barter may well develop.[115]

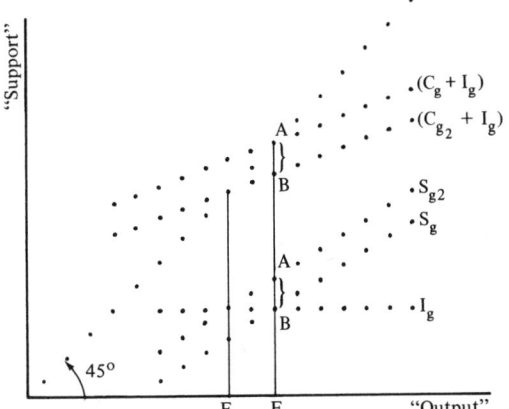

Figure 20-23. A shift upward in the political saving "schedule" and the deflationary gap.

In cases of acute deflation, the situation becomes too complex to be adequately dealt with in an aggregate model. Paradoxically, depending upon the location of the deflation, it can result in an inflationary spiral. If the government in power attempts to enforce a scope of output for which it is unable to generate sufficient support; if, for example, it enunciates policy decisions which are in violation of the interest demands of some segment of the public and which those persons believe to be in violation of authorized powers, then the equilibrium of the system will be impaired. In such a situation those individuals in deflated sectors of the polity—those who, for example, view the excess political output as unauthorized — will withdraw their affirmations of legitimacy from the system and will adopt a calculating attitude towards presumptively binding decisions,[116] obeying when it is in their interest to do so, disobeying when it is in their interest to disobey.[117]

If these segments of the society are either numerous enough or, under conditions of normalcy, are in key positions, e.g., if they make up the governmental bureaucrary — including the army and police — and/or are in crucial positions in control of the economy, then a situation of inflation may occur, wherein previously acceptable and authorized powers of office are incapable of implementation because of a lack of resources in the assumption of operative responsibility. Thus a situation of political alienation in one sector of the society might generate "excessive support" in the aggregate. A situation of inflation will exist alongside a situation of deflation. (This is the situation of a communist government trying to rule in a country possessing a capitalist economy.) The deflation in one sector of the polity curtails saving to a level below the authorized powers of incumbent officials. If the situation becomes one of coercion, the incumbents might not be capable of enforcing their decrees.[118]

CONCLUSION

I have outlined the rudiments of a macrosociology; expansions upon what I have done, involving more detailed and satisfactory treatments of the issues raised and in the expansion of the scope of issues to include, for example, a theory of subsystem cycles and a growth theory, are clearly called for and clearly possible. As important will be advances enabling us to better integrate structural and aggregative perspectives, so that we will be able to predict the "slopes of curves" in specifiable developmental situations.[119]

The relationships I have enunciated are hypothetical. I have chosen to present them in an abstract form and to avoid presenting examples illustrating them. Too often the example is taken as evidence of truth, not as an aid to exposition. I am aware of the difficulties which will be confronted in systematically operationalizing the terms identified in the discussed propositions, and of the difficulties in doing systematic research to verify their truth or to demonstrate their falsity. I can only hope that this discussion has been sufficiently cogent and sufficiently illuminating to entice others to join me in the theoretical and empirical tasks which lie ahead. The recent awarding of the Nobel Prize to Professor Kuznets is a reminder of the intellectual difficulties of the empirical side of this endeavor. If this working paper stimulates criticism, corrections, and developments upon what I have done so that in its revision my task will be lightened, I will be content with its reception.

APPENDIX

A   adaptive subsystem, economy
C   consumer support
C_a economic consumer support $(L-[product] \rightarrow A)$
C_g political support $(I-[product] \rightarrow G)$
G   goal-attainment subsystem, polity
I   integrative subsystem, societal community *and* investment
I_a economic investment, allocation of fluid resources $(G-[product] \rightarrow A)$
I_g authorization of powers of office $(L-[product] \rightarrow G)$
L   pattern maintenance subsystem, latency subsystem
M_a money
M_{ad} money demanded
M_{ah} demand for money to hold, standards for allocation resources $(I-[factor] \rightarrow A)$
M_{as} money supplied
M_{at} transactions demand for money
M_d medium demanded
M_g power
M_{gd} power demanded
M_{gh} allocation of surplus product $(A-[factor] \rightarrow G)$
M_{gs} power supplied
M_{gt} transactions demand for power
M_h definition of allocatable medium resources, demand for medium to hold
M_i influence
M_l value-commitments or real commitments
M_s medium supplied
M_t transactions demand for medium

N   constituent intent
N_a labor capacity $(L-[factor] \rightarrow A)$
N_g interest demands $(I-[factor] \rightarrow G)$
O   definition of opportunity
O_a opportunity for effectiveness $(G-[factor] \rightarrow A)$
O_g legitimation of authority $(L-[factor] \rightarrow G)$
r   rate of opportunity
r_a rate of economic opportunity, interest rate
r_g rate of legitimation, rate of alienation
S   saving
S_a economic saving $(A-[factor] \rightarrow G)$, extent delimited by ranking of claims $(I-[product] \rightarrow A)$
S_g operative responsibility $(G-[factor] \rightarrow L)$, extent delimited by control of productivity and services $(A-[product] \rightarrow G)$
Y   subsystem output, income
Y_a economic output $(A-[product] \rightarrow L, A-[product] \rightarrow G)$, income $(A-[factor] \rightarrow L, A-[factor] \rightarrow G)$
Y_g political output $(G-[product] \rightarrow I, G-[product] \rightarrow L)$ income $(G-[factor] \rightarrow I, G-[factor] \rightarrow L)$

NOTES

1. This paper might best be viewed as a first statement leading to a theory of internal disorder and, from a longer perspective, to a theory of social development. My major substantive interest is the United States, now and in the future, and thus I am concerned with formulating a framework within which to analyze total societies and their development.

2. Very simply, a social structure is a set of patterned and presumptively sanctioned interactions which are taken as stable for the period of analysis.

3. Institutional structures are legitimized normative patterns defining regularized expectations for actors in situations in which the requisite facilities for performance are provided and in which conforming performance is, in the idealized case, rewarded and "disorder" (motivated behaviors in violation of the normative component of any institutional structure) negatively sanctioned. Collectivities are groups of actors distinguishable by specifiable higher levels of interaction, or potentiality for interaction; and organizational structures indicate the links between norm and collectivity, the stable patterns of expectations for collectivities, and in the limiting case, roles, as units of analysis.

4. A good introductory discussion of the problem of aggregation is found in G. Ackley, *Macro-economic Theory* (New York: Macmillan, 1961), Chap. XX. See also T. Parsons, "Some Problems of General Theory in Sociology," in J. McKinney and E. Tiryakian (eds.), *Theoretical Sociology* (New York: Appleton-Century-Crofts, 1970). Later in this paper I briefly outline a developmental scheme which attempts to insert a dynamic perspective into the core of our conceptual framework. There are hopeful indications that the notion of developmental stages (including discussions of mechanisms of change) will serve as the focal point for the systematic interrelating of aggregate and structural propositions (see note 54).

5. See T. Parsons, "An Outline of the Social System," in T. Parsons, *et al.* (eds.), *Theories of Society* (2 vols.) (New York: The Free Press, 1961); "On Building Social Systems Theory:

A Personal History," *Daedalus* (1970); T. Parsons and N. Smelser, *Economy and Society* (New York: The Free Press, 1956); and N. Smelser; *Social Change in the Industrial Revolution* (Chicago: Chicago University Press, 1959). Throughout this paper I will adopt the following terminological convention: The word *system* will refer to the action system under discussion, generally to a social system, and most regularly to a society. The word *subsystem* will refer to the four functionally defined subsystems of reference, e.g., when the system is a society, to the "economy," "polity," "societal community," and "latency" subsystems. The word *subsector* will refer to the four functionally defined subsectors of the subsystem of reference.

Symbolically I will adhere to the usage of Parsons and Smelser: A will refer to the adaptive subsystem of the system of reference and A$_A$ to the adaptive subsector of the adaptive subsystem.

6. In this brief discussion of the A$\longleftrightarrow$L boundary I will be speaking of the lower level L, the L cybernetically below A, LIG*AL*. The import of distinguishing this as a second set of A$\longleftrightarrow$L exchanges is discussed further along.

7. It is sometimes difficult when discussing boundary interchanges to avoid using misleading conceptualizations. It should be remembered that we are always discussing social relationships between men in roles, even if the historical system under discussion obfuscates this truth. See, to illustrate this point, K. Marx, *Capital* Vol. 1, F. Engles (ed.), translated from the third German edition by S. Moore and E. Aveling (New York: International Publishers, 1967), pp. 71-84; G. Lukacs, "The Dialectic of Labor: Beyond Causality and Teleology," A. GuCinski (tr.), *Telos* (Fall, 1970); G. Lukacs, *History and Class Consciousness,* R. Livingstone (tr.) (Cambridge: M.I.T. Press, 1971, first published in 1923); and M. Merleau-Ponty, "Western Marxism," translated from *Les Aventures de la Dialectique* (Paris: 1955), Chap. 2, pp. 43-80, in *Telso,* (Fall, 1970). Merleau-Ponty quotes Marx: "Capital . . . is 'not a thing, but a social relation among men mediated by things.'" (p. 142; from Marx, *op. cit.,* p. 766).

8. See Parsons and Smelser, *op. cit.,* p. 69.

9. The preceding discussion is elliptical, referring to functional subsystems as actors. As I do not mean to reify these subsystems, in each instance I should refer to structures and processes classified within these systems (even this is elliptic); to do so, however, would be tedious and pedantic.

10. Victor Lidz has argued, in a personal communication to the author, that Parsons "has not conceived the interchanges as being 'functional' directly at the societal level . . . but rather through the co-ordination of sectors of the subsystems. Thus the functionality of the interchanges is classified not at the societal level but at the subsystem level. For example, the 'adaptive' interchanges provide linkages between adaptive sectors of subsystems, etc. I take it that the principal formal problem is whether there is adequate rationale for hypothesizing that the linkages should be located as Parsons has claimed."

I take no issue with Lidz's interpretation if it is treated as an "ought," rather than as an "is." In that regard he is making points I have previously enunciated here. My only reservation is as follows: Granted this favorable interpretation, why then the redundant marking of the boundary exchanges, as well as the already extant notation of the subsystem boundary, i.e., the identification of the relevant subsectors at the social system (societal) level? Why has Parsons persisted in such statements as the following? ". . . the distinctions between the three interchange sets—namely, in the figures, horizontal, vertical and diagonal respectively—had functional significance. Specifically, the horizontal interchanges had mainly adaptive significance [for what?], the vertical ones, goal-attaining, and the diagonals, integrative significance." [Parsons, "Equality and Inequality in Modern Society, or Social Stratification Revisited," *Sociological Inquiry,* 40 (Spring, 1970), p. 62.] Although this statement

is ambiguous, throughout his discussion in the quoted paper Parsons treats the diagonals as of integrative significance for the societal system. The only sense I can make of the labels attached to the boundary exchanges is when it is assumed that they indicate the location of system function for the total system under examination. If one does not assume this, but accepts Lidz's view of Parsons' intentions, then my criticisms remain valid in their conclusions but are somewhat misplaced, thus far in the paper, in their forms of attack.

11. It should be noted that Parsons has recently reaffirmed, in print as well as personally to the author, his belief in the utility of the E&S format (see Parsons, *op. cit.,* pp. 62-3), and he is skeptical of the need for the revisions which I make on the following pages.

12. See, for example, T. Parsons, *Politics and Social Structure* (New York: The Free Press, 1969), p. 488.

13. See Parsons and Smelser, *op. cit.,* pp. 42, 52, and others.

14. *Ibid.,* p. 47.

15. To avoid misunderstanding it is best to note explicitly that I am not speaking of "governmental consumption," where certain activities of an organizational structure (the government), largely classified in G, are properly classified in L. Rather I am referring to the A outputs to G: the allocation of surplus product and the control of productivity and services. See Parsons and Smelser, *op. cit.,* pp. 59-60.

16. Parsons has commented that "values are, for sociological purposes, deliberately defined at a level of generality higher than that of goals—they [values] are directions of action rather than specific objectives, the latter depending on the particular character of the situation in which the system is placed as well as on its values and structure as a system." Parsons, *Structure and Process in Modern Society* (New York: The Free Press, 1960), p. 172.

17. Parsons and Smelser, *op. cit.,* p. 48. Parsons is, in this quotation, utilizing the word "goal" in a double sense—first within the context of the generalized function of the polity, second with reference to the implementation of that functional task in the context of a specified goal. The latter may well involve the assumption of political leadership responsibility—just as the goal of the economy might well be the production of consumer goods—but the former can not be relegated to the output across a specified boundary.

It is also worth noting that in *Economy and Society* the goal of the economy was said to be the provision of goods *and* services; later a revision was made in the schema whereby services were conceptualized as an output to the polity, across the economy's adaptive boundary. The revision was made in T. Parsons, "On the Concept of Political Power," *Proceedings of the American Philosophical Society,* Vol. 107 (June, 1963), reprinted in T. Parsons, *Sociological Theory and Modern Society* (New York: The Free Press, 1967). See also T. Parsons, *Politics and Social Structure,* Chapters 13 and 17. Presumably this means that Parsons no longer considers the provision of services as part of the economy's goal-orientation. If so, this theoretical determination considered in light of the United States' service-oriented economy should give pause to those who utilize the old format.

18. See T. Parsons, "On Building Social Systems Theory" *op. cit.,* and "Some Problems in General Theory in Sociology," *op. cit.*

19. Parsons and Smelser, *op. cit.,* p. 41.

20. It is necessary, perhaps, to refer briefly to the difficulties involved in treating the *L* subsystems within the cultural system. Within the current interchange format the L_L subsector (of culture) must literally derive from "the beyond," and while conceptualizing this subsector as concerned with ultimate orientations to meaning is quite acceptable, deriving its contents from a nonempirical source is not satisfactory. It must be integrated into the action system.

21. I will return to the problem of system goal-attainment when I briefly examine the rationale Parsons has provided for the four-fold framework.

22. Parsons has on numerous occasions indicated that the cultural subsystem interchanges with and interpenetrates the latency (and integrative) subsystems of the social system. For example, he says, "in social system terms, higher education is located mainly in the pattern-maintenance subsystem, the primary zone of interpenetration with the cultural system." T. Parsons, "On the Concept of Value-Commitments," *Sociological Inquiry* 38 (1968), reprinted in T. Parsons, *Politics and Social Structure*, p. 454; and ". . . the interpenetration between social and cultural systems concerns, most saliently, the place of religion in relation to social structure." T. Parsons, "Systems Analysis: Social System" in D. Sills (ed.), *International Encyclopedia of the Social Sciences* (New York: Macmillan and The Free Press, 1968), p. 472. Finally, he states, "Pattern-maintenance structures in this connection have cultural primacy only in that their societal functions concern interchange with the cultural system and in that they interpenetrate with the latter." *Ibid.*, 468. Yet this interchange is not conceptualizable within the old format. In fact, Parsons often implicitly utilize the new format in his more concrete discussions (of this and other issues), thus generating similar problems of conceptualization.

I will discuss some "special" characteristics of L within the social system; one must also, however, emphasize the "special" characteristics of A due to its direct relationship with the behaviroal organism, and of G, due to its direct relationship with personality systems. It should be obvious that there are non-social constraints that occur in A and G (as against cybernetic controls in L), constraints which must be systematically articulated (see *ibid.*, p. 472).

23. Parsons. T., "Pattern Variables Revisited," *American Sociological Review,* 25 (1960). Reprinted in T. Parsons, *Sociological Theory and Modern Society,* p. 199 note 4. See also T. Parsons, "Some Problems of General Theory in Sociology" *op. cit.,* p. 63.

24. I have adopted a simple terminological convention in an attempt to keep this discussion unambiguous. In a symbolic reference to a boundary interchange, the subsystem *higher* on the cybernetic hierarchy is listed *first*. Second, when symbolic reference is made to a boundary interchange involving the pattern-maintenance subsystem below A the former will be italicized: thus A$\longleftrightarrow$*L* refers to an interchange between LIG*AL* and *L*$\longleftrightarrow$I to an interchange between LIG*A*L.

25. Parsons, T., "An Outline of the Social System," in Parsons, *et al.* (eds.), *op. cit.,* p. 67. I have reversed the order of the quotations. The discussion from which the quotations are taken was completed prior to the systematic discussions of the media. It does not include a consideration of influence, but rather of "integrative communication." The latter is considered as the highest mechanism of control; thus what was later referred to as "value-commitments," of which "real commitments" may be specifications, was not included.

I should note that in Parsons' view exchanges involving L occur outside the interchange paradigm and are concerned with the process of specification (oral communication). See also Parsons and Smelser, *op. cit.,* p. 69, and T. Parsons, R.F. Bales, and E.A. Shils, *Working Papers in the Theory of Action* (New York: The Free Press, 1953), pp. 185ff. In my own view, processes of specification must be conceptualized as one type of input *within* the interchange paradigm. Thus in terms which will be utilized later in this discussion, the process of legitimation of authority involves a subsumption of political values within the confines of more general social values—this is a process of specification of values according to functional context. See Parsons: "Legitimation, therefore, is a mechanism of *allocation* of authority to different subcollectivities and statuses within them, by virtue of which they are 'put in position' to acquire and use power. It is a case of the specficiation

of value-commitments" (Parsons, *Politics and Social Structure,* p. 488). Clearly this instance of specification belongs within the interchange system. Another type of specification concerns the level of generality, within one functional context, at which the value of defined (LIG*AL*). One example of this concerns the definition of general and particular callings within Puritan theology. See D. Little, *Religion, Order and Law* (New York: Harper Torchbooks 1969), pp. 118ff.: M. Walzer, *The Revolution of the Saints* (New York: Atheneum, 1965), pp. 212-219; and C. George and K. George, *The Protestant Mind of the English Reformation* 1570-1640 (Princeton: Princeton University Press, 1961), pp. 126ff. The former is clearly relevant to the definition, within L, of the "land" component of A, and the latter to the definition of the labor component. A final form concerns the specification of value according to the differentiation of function (re: norms) and according to situation (re: goals). This is similar to the first mentioned, but generally viewed within the context of one subsystem. On this paragraph, see Parsons *et al.* (eds.), *op. cit.,* pp. 45, 55, 977; T. Parsons, "Some Considerations on the Theory of Social Change," *Rural Sociology,* 26 (1961), pp. 219-39, at p. 238; and T. Parsons, *Politics and Social Structure,* p. 477.

26. The validity of the preceding discussion is dependent upon the acceptability of the revised paradigm. If the L input to the economy is A$_G$, rather than A$_L$, the argument has no merit.

27. See Parsons *et al.* (eds.), *op. cit.,* p. 968.

28. See for example, T. Parsons, "Some Problems of General Theory in Sociology," *op. cit.*

29. The only reference to these is by exclusion; they are not included as messages on the charts contained in the technical appendices of the media papers (for example, T. Parsons, *Sociological Theory and Modern Society,* p. 353). Neither are they listed as code components, although this may be an aspect of Parsons' confusion between the code and what are called codes in these charts, the value principles and coordination standards. On the latter see the somewhat obscure discussion of "operative responsibility" in Parsons, *Politics and Social Structure,* pp. 514-15; here Parsons seems to treat "operative responsibility" as defined by value commitments, not power.

30. My view is that the code component of a medium is defined within the integrative subsystems (and subsectors) wherein the medium flows. Value-commitment inputs, from L to X, are concerned with the definition of value principles, and influence inputs, from L to X, with the definition of coordination standards. Both possess a "special" place within the system (as regards to the legitimation and justification of codes), both extend across the diagonal, vertical and horizontal, and both are interactional in nature.

Parsons' discussion of code components is jumbled and confused. This is not the place to enter into the contradictions among his various positions; some selected references follow: "General Theory in Sociology," in R. Merton, L. Broom, and L. S. Cottrell, Jr. (eds.), *Sociology Today* (New York: Basic Books, 1959), p. 17; *Theories of Society,* pp. 53, 974; *Sociological Theory and Modern Society,* pp. 351, 357 (note 3), 364, 374; *Politics and Social Structure,* pp. 435, 447 (note 11), 456, 482, 486, 488; "Systems Analysis: Social Systems" *op. cit.,* pp. 465-6; and "Some Problems of General Theory in Sociology" *op. cit.,* pp. 44, 66-8.

31. The idea that the external-internal boundary was especially concerned with interchanges between and the integration of segmented systems was first suggested to me by Ms. Sandrah Whipple.

32. It is my contention that theory in the social sciences must utilize concepts that incorporate three interrelated foci: the concepts must help us to understand the place of the unit under discussion with reference to the total system—sometimes referred to as "functional" (e.g., the place of the proletariat

within a capitalist system)—with reference to other units in the system—sometimes referred to as "structural" (other actors at the same level of analysis—the proletariat with reference to the bourgeoisie)—and within a developmental perspective (how may the proletariat develop?). As hinted in the parentheses, the Marxian conception of class possesses these three dimensions; most Parsonian concepts do not, and I believe that one of the basic weaknesses within action theory is this lack of a built-in developmental dimension in the concepts utilized.

Parsons' recent work on evolution does not strike me as being well integrated with the systems basis of the theory. To remedy this deficiency one must recognize that the sociologist's task is not completed with a systematic model at one time but that the model must be developmental (dialectical, critical) and concern itself with processes and potentialities through time. A "fourth dimension" must be incorporated into the conceptual center of the framework.

33. Such a listing indicates a hypothesized sequence of stages in the development of an action system and ignores the mechanisms (internal and/or external) generating the transcendence of one stage by another, especially the many types of disorder which occur in social systems. Nor does the listing consider the multiple forms of stagnation, regression, and debilitating breakdown which must be incorporated into the model. It also gives the impression that the model is linear in time, which is not correct; rather, the model is subsumed under the rubric of the value-added.

It is possible to interpret much Marxian sociology (especially discussions of movement between stages of development) as articulated within a modified value-added perspective. On the value-added process see N. Smelser, *Theory of Collective Behavior* (New York: The Free Press, 1962). The modification is, however, essential. For Marx a set of economic and noneconomic variables are seen as the necessary and sufficient conditions for some occurrence. Like the value-added model, these variables are ordered in effect, i.e., for the "second" variable(s) (the noneconomic) to have an effect in generating the result, the first (the economic) must be present. Unlike the value-added model, for Marx the presence of the economic variables leads to the generation of the noneconomic conditions, resulting in the predicted event. Thus (autonomous) developments within the economy will necessarily be followed by parallel developments in other social subsystems.

Marx does indicate that ideological structures, for example, may precede, in time, the material structures; in this case, however, they are ineffective in generating change. Thus he accepts, at least with regard to the conditions generating a transition between stages, the ordering of the variables as posited by the value-added model, and he rejects, along with the model, notions of a specified sequence. (Marx's explanations of how the ideological conditions arise are not, to my mind, satisfactory.) The disagreement concerns the independence of the variables.

Weber, on the other hand, felt that each of these social realms, while interdependent, was independent. For him, as for Marx, the first ordered variables in the explanatory schema was the economic; its presence was necessary in order for the other variables to add value, but its presence was neither necessary nor sufficient for the development of the other variables (together leading, for example, to the rise of modern rationalistic capitalism). This simple difference, even ignoring other reasons, forced him to generate an elaborate set of theoretical constructs within which he sought to analyze the development of political, legal, and religious orders. It also forced him to seek independent explanations for the autonomous, even if interrelated with the economic, changes within the noneconomic systems of a society.

34. One consequence of the developmental addition is simply stated: When analyzing any structure or process

within a system one is concerned to categorize it not simply "spatially" but also developmentally (and concretely, historically), that is, our perspective is diachronic. Thus some process might be categorized within the adaptive subsystem of a society at stage four of its development. Such a perspective forces us to look backwards as well as "sideways."

Another possible consequence is the adoption—at least in part—of a Hegelian method of defining terms, wherein the definition refers to the whole and to a moment within the whole—the latter is unintelligible without reference to the development in time (and, for us, in space) of the former. Thus one would not speak of a collectivity acting, as sociologists tend to state it, but rather of a collectivity being definitive of a set of actions.

35. One further aspect of the model relevant to questions of development involves an elaboration of the interchange paradigm itself. Here the concern is to explicate the parallel processes in the different subsystems as they relate to the mutuality of "growth" and level of differentiation. For example, and speaking very crudely, an economic system at stage three (G—L) will condition the development of all other social subsystems as well as affect those action systems involved in its development (e.g., it will exert a cybernetic control over personalities working with a feudal system). These effects must be traceable within the paradigm, which appears to be possible within the context of a complex helical model involving four (perhaps differentiated) threads (AGIL by AGIL, GALI, IGAL, LIGA). In such a model the complexities of organizations would be pictured horizontally, the complexities of development vertically, and the complex interrelationships between changing subsystems by the entanglement of the threads, interchanges between the threads, on the cylinder.

36. Parsons has never satisfactorily elaborated upon the explicit relationship between these factor inputs, which differ from those elaborated in *Economy and Society* (and which incorporate my own minor revisions of Parsons' latest version), and the "factors of economic production." See the "technical note" to T. Parsons "On the Concept of Political Power" in *Sociological Theory and Modern Society*, pp. 347-354. Here it is necessary to remark only that factor inputs define the scope of available resources (generalized or not) for the productive performance "judged" in terms of the product inputs, in terms of the medium for which these products are intrinsic satisfiers. This is a simplification, but within this context it will suffice.

37. On the last two paragraphs see Parsons, *Politics and Social Structure*, pp. 486-7.

38. The following chart is descriptive of the subsystem interchanges within the context of system development. It should be noted that within this model the instrumental subsystems follow the "performance sequence" of development Parsons described in *The Working Papers*, progressing up the cybernetic order, and the consummatory subsystems follow the "learning sequence," progressing down the cybernetic order (Parsons, Bales, and Shils, *op. cit.*, Ch. 5). There is one exception in each case. L follows the described sequence when the L—G interchange is included, and the G—L interchange excluded, and G follows the sequence in the reverse instance, with stage three included and stage seven excluded. I do not know why these apparent discrepancies occur, but I suspect that it concerns the placement of the lower level L (LIGA*L*) within the context of this model. Eventually the helical, or some other, formulation must provide a framework indicative of (1) the interface between core subsystems and (2) how the generation of "lower-level" subsystems is involved within system development.

Another complication of great importance concerns the autonomous development of each subsystem, a development which follows the order of the original developmental model. This involves the issues concerning the historical progression

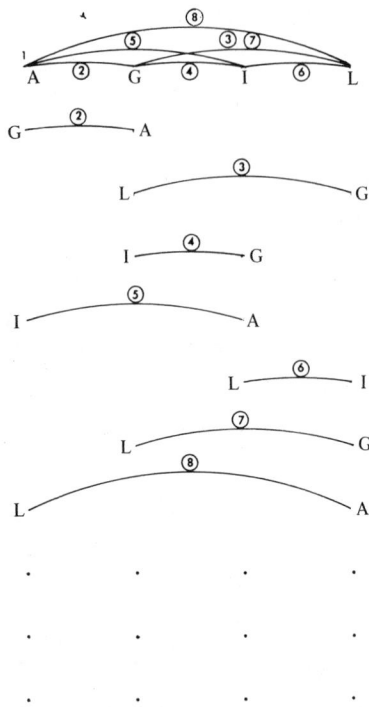

A straight line version of a four-strand version of the developmental model.

(in time) of specific phases and the sociological generation of the conditions of structural consolidation.

39. The model used in this paragraph and the next is outlined in the second part of this paper. For both power and influence the investment input occurs in exchange with the latency subsystem; for money, at the G⟷A boundary, and thus the economy presents different results in an analysis of the effects of charisma upon non-pattern-maintenance phenomena. This finding helps explain Weber's conclusion that although "charisma" is fundamental in the generation of a new economic system, its routinization at high levels of moral control is not as important in an already developed economy as in the political or the societal community. In the economy, at least within the "formally free labor market" or a capitalist economy, a "real commitment" in work is easier to obtain without extensive, and intensive, moral support than, for example, the real commitment of obedience without extensive and intensive moral legitimacy.

40. See Parsons, "On Building Social Systems Theory," *op. cit.*, and "Some Problems of General Theory in Sociology," *op. cit.*

41. Max Weber, *Economy and Society* (Kansas: Bedminister Press, 1968 first published in German in 1922), p. 460, my italics.

42. J.M. Keynes, *The General Theory of Employment, Interest and Money* (New York: Harcourt, Brace and World, 1965, First published in 1935), p. 297.

43. T. Parsons, *Societies: Comparative and Evolutionary Perspectives* (Englewood Cliffs: Prentice-Hall, 1966), p. 9 and ff. Although this brief definition is not, for many purposes, adequate, here it will suffice.

44. See B. De Jouvenal, *On Power*, J.F. Huntington (tr.) (Boston: Beacon Press, 1962, first published in 1945), p. 114.

45. Although a background in macroeconomic theory is not essential to follow the discussion, familiarity with a middle-level text, such as Ackley, *op. cit.*, would be helpful. In economic terms my discussion does not go beyond the degree of sophistication found in such a text. A few basic sources are listed: Keynes, *op. cit*; D. Patinkin, *Money, Interest and Prices*, second edition (New York: Harper and Row, 1964); A. Leijonhufvud, *On Keynesian Economics and the Economics of Keynes* (New York: Oxford University Press, 1968); P. Samuelson, *Foundations of Economic Analysis* (New York: Atheneum, 1965, first published in 1947); M. Friedman, "A Theoretical Framework for Monetary Analysis," *Journal of Political Economy* (March/April 1970); H. Johnson, *Money, Trade and Economic Growth* (Cambridge: Harvard University Press, 1967) and *Essays in Monetary Economics* (Cambridge: Harvard University Press, 1969), for summary articles and a bibliography. Some middle-level texts: Ackley, *op. cit.*; R.G.D. Allen, *Macro-economic Theory: A Mathematical Treatment* (New York: St. Martins, 1968). Some good readers: R. Thorne (ed.), *Monetary Theory and Policy* (New York: Random House, 1966); W. Smith and R. Teigen (eds.), *Readings in Money, National Income and Stabilization Policy* (Homewood, Ill,: Irwin, 1965); M.G. Mueller (ed.), *op. cit.*, and H. Williams and J.D. Huffnagle (eds.), *Macroeconomic Theory: Selected Readings* (New York: Appleton-Century-Crofts, 1969).

46. Both consumption and investment involve the allocation of subsystem-derived income in support of units within the subsystem of reference. The point is that consumed output is utilized in satisfying "immediate" wants (within the time period or reference), while investment involves the provision of media resources for the production of "goods" to be utilized in the production of future "goods" (beyond the time period of reference). I have chosen the term consumer support, as against consumer demand, because although there is inevitably a type of demand involved in every variety of consumption, the actual allocation of the media resources is a form of support for the producing collectivity. This distinction will be elaborated upon in the following discussion of the polity.

47. Terminological difficulties have haunted the writer in composing this paper. The economic terms utilized in certain discussions applicable to all social subsystems were chosen because of their familiarity and because the only alternatives which came to mind were either complicated in phrasing or abysmal neologisms. The drawbacks in proceeding as I have are two-fold. First, it is difficult to distinguish the general level of reference from the economic. Second and, for the discussions in this paper, more importantly, the economic terms have connotations not always appropriate to their political, integrative, and maintenance references. When the latter is the case, I attempt to clarify the points at issue.

48. See Parsons and Smelser, *op. cit.*, pp. 123 ff. and 210 ff.

49. See P. Baran and P. Sweezy, *Monopoly Capital* (New York: Monthly Review Press, 1966), appendix, for an attempt at calculating the economic surplus in the United States.

50. One can question whether there is a necessary labor power component manifest in all work, thus inevitably arguing about the total "real production" within an economic system. Although such discussions are important, they will not concern us here. See *ibid.*; P. Baran, *The Political Economy of Growth*, second edition (New York: Monthly Review Press, 1968), and the criticism by E. Mandel, "The Labor Theory of Value and 'Monopoly Capital,'" *International Socialist Review* (July-August, 1967).

51. On these points, which require more space than I have here, see E. Chamberlain, *The Theory of Monopolistic Competition* (Cambridge: Harvard University Press, 1962, first edition 1933, and Baran and Sweezy, *op. cit.*

52. The reader will note the similarity between this discussion and Parsons' arguments that at this boundary money appears not as a circulating medium but rather as a measure of value. See *Sociological Theory and Modern Society,*

pp. 373-5. In fact Parsons is effectively quite correct, especially in noting that "the economist's ideal of free competition is here the limiting case in which influence as an independent factor disappears" (*Ibid.*, 375). His errors are three-fold. One, in his assertions, elsewhere, that this boundary is the major focal point of the code components of the media, money, and influence. Two, in his sharp division between money as a circulating medium and as a measure of value: As the former it is both; as the latter, actual money is characterized by levels of liquidity and has the potentiality of circulating; as a simple measure of relative value "money" would not be money but any scale of equivalence and relative difference, e.g. Marx's labor unit. Three, at this boundary the "measure of value" aspect of money, insofar as it relates to the value principle of utility, is not relevant. Rather our concern is with the co-ordination standard of money, "solvency," as identified in the factor output from I to A, "standards for the allocation of resources." Nor does "measure of value" directly refer, in the context of the I$\longleftrightarrow$A boundary, to the value of labor power as expended in economic production, at A$\longleftrightarrow$L. However, the I$\rightarrow$A product input does concern the ranking of claims made by labor regarding actual wages received in payment for labor power. Within the Marxian system there is an ambiguity between the two, as the value of labor power is not adequately specified (as Marx tells us) by physical necessities and thus cannot be unambiguously specified. Thus an increase in wages might involve an increase in the value of labor power socially and culturally determined) or a capture of surplus product by workers. In the latter case, even assuming no increase in productivity, no inflation should occur; in the former, unless there is a proportional increase in productivity, a price rise should follow, as the rate of surplus-value would remain exactly what it was prior to the increase in the money value of labor power (see Marx, *op. cit.*, vi, Chs. 17 and 18). The I$\longleftrightarrow$A interchange is relevant to the specification of the actual rate of surplus-value.

53. Let me remind the reader that the term polity is functional in reference and includes processes which are not necessarily governmental, for example, certain banking functions. Likewise, not all governmental processes are political in function.

54. To many readers, and certainly to the author, this caveat should be an indication of the necessity of coupling simple functional, aggregative analysis with structural, historically specific analyses. Let me provide a simple example: Weber argued that in traditional social systems workers might work less, beyond a specifiable point, if wages were raised. The aggregative relationship between wages and labor capacity is thus not determined on simple a priori grounds; rather, it must be determined within the context of a specific class of social situations. Given the historical, social-structural determination of the "slope" of certain relationships, general propositions, of the type I go on to discuss, are presumably valid. A more sophisticated theory would be able to correlate types of historical structure with stages in the development of social systems, thus identifying in general terms for a more narrowly delimited range of systems — those categorized within a developmental stage — the specifics of the relationship.

55. In such an analysis the economist hypothesizes that where planned savings equals planned investment an equilibrium situation occurs. *Ex ante* saving and investment need not be equivalent, even though by definition *ex post* saving is identical with *ex post* investment. This is roughly comparable to the situation where desired demand is greater than desired supply, whereas the actual amount of goods sold and purchased must be equivalent. Only where the desired supply equals desired demand is equilibrium arrived at.

For the economist an equilibrium situation is where all the wants of all individuals are satisfied, as Schumpeter puts it (I quote slightly out of context): economic equilibrium

"corresponds to a position . . . whose constituent parts cannot be altered (if all the data remain the same) without any . . . individual's having the experience that he is worse off than before." Schumpeter, J., *Theory of Economic Development*, R. Opie (tr.) (New York: Oxford University Press, 1949) first published in English in 1934), p. 40. See also Samuelson, *op. cit.*; R.E. Kuenne, *The Theory of General Economic Equilibrium* (Princeton: Princeton University Press, 1963); and N. Smelser, *Essays in Sociological Explanation* (Englewood Cliffs: Prentice-Hall, 1968). In this condition we are assuming the possibility of a meaningful aggregation of consumer proclivities in a stable curve related to productive output, total income. A change in the slope of the curve, as against a move on the given curve, for any of the variables, would change the level of equilibrium output.

Much of the elegance and power of macroeconomics is based on the possibility of making such assumptions. The existence of singular equilibrium points is based upon (1) the ability to measure in ratio scale terms levels of income and (2) the existence of monotonic functional relationships between the processes measured. Although the first is reasonable in economics, the second is based upon the rather simplistic assumption of the sameness of the units aggregated, thus eliminating qualitative jumps across income levels. See R.M. Clower, *Monetary Theory* (Baltimore: Penguin Books, 1969), Part III.

Once we leave the realm of utilitarian, psychologistic economics the world of the economy gains in complexity and becomes more difficult to treat "rationally." Here I allow the simple assumptions of the economist and further "sin" (later in this paper) by making even simpler assumptions about the polity. It should be noted, in both instances, that empirically the equilibrium points identified are at best approximations allowable within the context of short-terms analysis.

56. If the MPC >1, the model provides no equilibrium condition. This involves dynamic assumptions assuming a single lag, consumption behind income. See Ackley, *op. cit.*, pp. 326-30 and 347ff. This fact has multiple consequences for internal disorder, especially in nonindustrialized nations, and most especially in the cognate political case.

57. For more detailed discussions of these phenomena see Samuelson, *op. cit.*

58. A. Marshall, *Principles of Economics,* eighth edition (London: Macmillan, 1920, first edition 1890), p. 65.

59. D. Easton, *A Systems Analysis of Political Life* (New York: J. Wiley & Sons, 1965), p. 38. Let me immediately clear up a misconception which might confuse the reader. Interest demands are a factor of political effectiveness, an input of influence to the polity. As such they parallel the factor input of labor to the economy (as will be elaborated upon), not the product input of consumer support (not "consumer demand" in part for this reason, rather, in certain contexts, intended support). See M. Bronfenbrenner and S. Holzman, "A Summary of Inflation Theory," in *Surveys in Economic Theory* (New York: St. Martins, 1965), p. 53 and footnote, who use the term "aggregate expenditure." With regard to the societal community the power, product, input to the polity is political support — "The product inputs of power to the polity from its neighboring subsystems thus constitute a mechanism for evaluating past and prospective political performance of collective agencies" (Parsons, *Politics and Social Structure,* p. 486) — the accurate theoretical parallel to consumer support. The reader should note the importance of the concepts of "good will," "brand names," and "party loyalty" within this context.

Labor and interest demands are factor inputs processed within the economy and polity; the respective economic and political products — intrinsic satisfiers — are exchanged for product inputs, in the broad sense, inputs of "support," investment and consumption. Parsons' views on these matters have been inconsistent; see, for example, " 'Voting' and the

Equilibrium of the American Political System" (1959), reprinted in *Sociological Theory and Modern Society*, "Some Reflections on the Place of Force in Social Processes" (1964), reprinted in *ibid.*; "On the Concept of Political Power," in *ibid.*, especially page 302; and *Politics and Social Structure*, especially pp. 489 ff. With regard to the last reference, it is especially important to note that interest demands are *not* a component of the so-called "effective demand" of the polity; rather, this term should be "effective support" and encompasses what I will later call $C_g I_g$, political support plus authorization of powers of office.

60. Parsons, *Sociological Theory and Modern Society*, p. 321.

61. My usage of "intentionality" differs from Parsons in "On the Concept of Influence" and the "postscript" to it in *Politics and Social Structure*.

62. H. Marcuse, *Reason and Revolution*, second edition (Boston: Beacon Press, 1960), p. 58.

63. *Ibid.*, pp. 77-78. See the discussion of K. Marx, *Economic and Philosophic Manuscripts of 1844*, early writings translated by T.B. Bottomore (New York: McGraw-Hill, 1964), and *Capital*; G. Lukacs, *op. cit.*; and E. Durkheim, *The Division of Labor in Society*, G. Simpson (tr.) (New York: The Free Press, 1933). The literature on the processing of interest demands and on the sabotage of policy decisions is voluminous.

64. Pragmatically this is, of course, much easier with labor than interest demands or policy decisions. One assumes each individual can occupy one job and sums the number of individuals. Realistically, however, one must remember that the structural location of the intention is often of great import in determining its productive effect and the return granted. This is as true for labor capacity as it is for interest demands and policy decisions.

65. It does not seem reasonable at this point to engage in an analysis of the controversies monetary theorists have engendered over the notion of the demand for money. Here I assume that this demand is a function of income and opportunity. As will be seen, this latter term is broader than the usual conceptualization of the interest rate. Although the interested reader will find much food for thought if he refers to the sources cited in footnote 45, he may emerge with indigestion.

Some confusion might arise if I don't explicitly note that an increase in the speculative demand for money — more generally, the demand for money to hold — implies an increase in the amount of money retained in A, and therefore a decrease in the amount of money going across the A $\to$ G and/or the A $\to$ L factor boundaries. (See Leijonhufvud, *op. cit.*, pp. 29-30, and footnote 35.)

66. See Parsons and Smelser, *op. cit.*, pp. 63-64 and 75-76.

67. For a summary of the economic literature see G.L.S. Shakle, "Recent Theories Concerning the Rate of Interest," reprinted in Thorne (ed.), *op. cit.*

68. For clarity's sake much of the preceding discussion utilizes terminology appropriate to a capitalist system. Cognate terms descriptive of the same processes can be found for any economy, although the level of differentiation manifest in a capitalist system might not be present.

At this level of generality our concepts are necessarily broad. This once again emphasizes the necessity of concrete historical analyses of specific situations. But this problem is not resolved by simply assembling "objective data" without understanding the functional import of specific structures and processes within the context of the society under analysis. In Weber's terms, structures have meaning, and meaning varies within the context of social and cultural situations. To presume to use "objective indices" without an analysis of their meaning, in context, is to obscure relationships and to generate a false surety in the objectivity of one's data. See Lukacs: "Thus the objective forms of all social phenomena change

constantly in the course of their ceaseless dialectical interactions with each other. The intelligibility of objects develops in proportion as we grasp their function in the totality to which they belong" (*History and Class Consciousness*, p. 13).

69. Brief discussions of the model I am utilizing are found in J.R. Hicks, "Mr. Keynes and the 'Classics': A Suggested Interpretation," reprinted in Thorne (ed.), *op. cit.*; H. Johnson, "Monetary Theory and Keynesian Economics," reprinted in Johnson, *Money, Trade and Economic Growth*; Ackley, *op. cit.*; Allen, *op. cit.*, and Smith and Tergin, *op. cit.* The best source, as Leijonhufvud has recently emphasized, is Keynes himself. Complicating factors are introduced into the model by both Leijonhufvud, *op. cit.*, and G. Horwick, *Money, Capital and Prices* (Homewood, Ill.: Irwin, 1964), among numerous others, while Allen provides a very brief discussion of two sector models (consumption and investment output), *op. cit.*, pp. 150-54. Models including a separate governmental sector can also be constructed. Before continuing, the reader might want to reread the quotation from Keynes on page 478.

70. Modigliani's term. F. Modigliani, "Liquidity Reference and the Theory of Interest and Money," reprinted in Williams and Huffnagle, *op. cit.*, p. 266.

71. This is very simplistic, ignoring wages, both real and monetary, as they reflect demand; technology, and supply, assuming its existence. For discussions of these factors, see Keynes, *op. cit.*; Leijonhufvud, *op. cit.*; Patinkin, *op. cit.*, J. Tobin, "Money Wage Rates and Employment," reprinted in Mueller (ed.), *op. cit.*: and, more briefly, Ackley, *op. cit.*, and Allen, *op. cit.*

The following equations define the system I have been discussing:

$$I_a = I_a(r_a)$$
$$S_a = S_a(Y_a)$$
$$M_a = M_{at}(Y_a) + M_{ah}(r_a)$$
$$S_a = I_a$$
$$Y_a = Y_a(N_a)$$

For the restrictions upon the first four equations yielding an equilibrium value of Y_a and r_a see Allen, *op. cit.*, Ch. 7. Treating investment as a function of Y_a and r_a and saving as a function of r_a and Y_a does not markedly alter the results of our discussion.

72. For a similar analysis using a more complicated graphic model see Ackley, *op. cit.*, pp. 373ff. For cogent, brief numerical examples see Smith and Teigen, *op. cit.*, Ch. 1.

73. Here I do not have the space to discuss the complex theory of the supply of money. Within the system paradigm outlined the supply is treated as specified within the polity. For a brief description of the complications involved, see R. Teigen, "The Demand for and Supply of Money," in Smith and Teigen, *op. cit.* I treat an increase in supply as an increase in the "amount of money," yielding in the analysis which follows, except in situations of "true inflation" (see p. 493), an increase in its scope (Y_a). See H. Lasswell and A. Kaplan, *Power and Society* (New Haven: Yale University Press, 1950); Parsons, *Politics and Social Structure*, Chap. 15, "postscript."

74. Policy decision is "a process of power output from the polity to its constituencies through the support system, . . . an output of power to the societal community. . . . The crucial feature of . . . policy decision is the bindingness of policy decisions on all elements obligated to the collectivity as either associational or bureaucratic members. Policies, however, impinge differentially, not equally, on members. They generally favor certain interests over others and impose varying obligations so that they somewhat reallocate resources" (Parsons, *Politics and Social Structure*, p. 334. See also Parsons, *Sociological Theory and Modern Society*, p. 321). I interpret policy decision in the fashion just used, not in the narrower sense of

Barnard (see Parsons, *Structure and Process in Modern Society*, pp. 28ff and *Politics and Social Structure*, p. 334). My meaning is close to Easton's "authoritative statements," as a political output. Likewise, my usage of operative responsibility is close to, but not so substantive as, his "authoritative performances," as output. His "associated outputs" seems to encompass both influence and commitment outputs from the polity (see D. Easton, *op. cit.*, Chapter 22).

75. See Parsons, *Sociological Theory and Modern Society*, pp. 338-45.

76. See *Ibid.*, Chapter 5. The scope of power in any office is related to the concept of discretion, i.e., the range within which the incumbent's decision (1) need not be referred to higher authority, (2) need not be referred to a constituency, and (3) need not be referred to adjudication (or in retrospect where adjudication will support the decision as justifiable within the authority structure). (See Parsons, *Politics and Social Structure*, the "postscript" to Chapter 15, pp. 482-5.) An increase in the range of discretion for an office, e.g., a constitutional increase, would involve an increase in the amount of power and the scope of power within the office, except in the case of "true inflation," where only the amount of power would be increased (see p. 493).

77. See Ş.P. Huntingdon, *Political Order in Changing Societies* (New Haven: Yale University Press, 1968), vii, and passim; and S.N. Eisenstadt, *The Political Systems of Empires* (New York: The Free Press, 1963), p. 380: "Institutionalization of powers; i.e., extent of clearcut definition of powers." Note that this usage of "institutionalization" is narrower than the one indicated in note 3.

78. Parsons, *Politics and Social Structure*, p. 479. The bracketed words are my insertion.

79. *Ibid.*, p. 430.

80. Parsons, *Sociological Theory and Modern Society*, p. 349.

81. *Ibid.*, p. 304.

82. See Parsons and Smelser, *op. cit.*, p. 72, and Parsons, *Politics and Social Structure*, pp. 487-88, for Parsons' views.

83. For an estimate of the importance of investment in persons and things in economic growth, see E. Denison, *The Sources of Economic Growth in the United States* (New York: The Committee for Economic Development, 1962), and *Why Growth Rates Differ* (Washington: The Brookings Institution, 1967). Parsons' arguments in favor of all services passing into the polity confuse the structural term "collectivity" with the functional term "polity." See Parsons, *Sociological Theory and Modern Society*, pp. 279 and 303, and *Politics and Social Structure*, pp. 324 and 479.

84. Services are allocated "human role-performances to an 'employer,' or contracting agent" (Parsons, *Sociological Theory and Modern Society*, p. 303). In quoting out of context I have altered the meaning of Parsons' usage. See K. Marx, *Theories of Surplus Value* (Moscow: Progress Publishers, 1968), addenda, 12: "Productivity of Capital, Productive and Unproductive Labor."

85. Not necessarily, it is possible to imagine a system wherein certain individuals would have a guaranteed income and provide services outside of an occupational category, as in much charity work. Such cases may not involve de-differentiation within the economy, nor categorization within the polity.

86. See Parsons, *Sociological Theory and Modern Society*, p. 304. For simplicity's sake I have not analyzed the dependence of economic saving and the surplus on granted opportunity. As noted, such an analysis does not markedly affect the propositions generated, but it does greatly complicate their graphical presentation.

87. See *ibid.*, pp. 329-30, and *Politics and Social Structure*, p. 324. This inequality is certainly the case both with regard

to the generation of human capital through educational opportunity and in the "opportunity" to fill higher appointive office within the polity.

88. The term operative responsibility often causes confusion: "Operative responsibility . . . which is treated as a factor of integrity, is responsibility for sovereign implementation of the value-principles, and involves not only collective effectiveness, but also integrity to the paramount societal value pattern." Parsons, "The Political Aspect of Social Structure and Process," in D. Easton (ed.), *Verieties of Political Theory* (Englewood Cliffs: Prentice-Hall, 1966), p. 112. See also, Parsons, *Sociological Theory and Modern Society*, p. 354. I am thus not directly concerned with bureaucratic responsibility, but with police powers: "Police, the French word here [in Montesquieu] referred to the function or branch of government involving the keeping of public order and Morality." Montesquieu, *The Greatness of the Romans and their Decline*, D. Lowenthal (tr.) (Ithaca, Cornell University Press, 1965), note by the editor, p. 58. Thus I am referring to the assumption of operative responsibility for the implementation of legitimized constitutional powers. $LIGAL$. The extent of the polity's capacity to implement operative responsibility, in any set of circumstances, is delimited by its control over productivity and services.

89. The figure is drawn to indicate that the direction of the relationships is known, but not to indicate ratio scales. As such, all equilibriums will be approximations. The only assumption that the graphical presentations make is that it will be possible to operationalize notions like the scope of power in terms of interval scales. Later, when I speak of the "multiplier," I assume the sensibility of the process of multiplication and thus ratio scales. In the latter case, I think it theoretically unlikely that power will ever be operationalized in "stronger than" interval scale terms, and thus some distortion will be introduced in the process of multiplication. In the former, approximations of much utility can be made with indices of only ordinal strength. See S.S. Stevens, "Measurement, Statistics and the Schemapiric View," *Science*, 161 (August 1968).

90. Let me remind the reader that L refers to a functional subsystem. Not all power allocated as "operative responsibility" need necessarily be utilized in investment. Rather, units within L may redistribute some of it to the societal community (L— [product]→ G— [factor]→I or through de-differentiation) where it might be utilized as a component of political support. This seems to occur, for example, in situations where administrative workers are expected to campaign and vote for the party in power (see p. 480).

91. The preceding paragraph deals with movements along the drawn "curves," not movements in the "curves" themselves, in which case the equilibrium conditions themselves are subject to modification. The study of the movement of the "curves" is comparable to the economic study of the middle range theories of consumption and investment.

92. Later in this paper I will discuss the conditions of inflation and deflation of the generalized media of social action. Deflation of a medium plays an important role in the generation of disorder and inflation in its prolongation and in its success if the "disorderly movement" is one which attempts to restructure some component of social action. An increase in political saving might well be the wisest course of action in a situation of power inflation. I will discuss the generating conditions of internal disorder in another publication.

93. Parsons, *Politics and Social Structure*, pp. 490-1.

94. The rate of alienation is indicative of the value of the stock of political capital, powers of office, within the polity. Greater alienation, relevant to any office, implies that the true domain of power (the number of persons who view pronouncements as binding) is lessened. This implies an increase

in the number of units adopting a calculating attitude towards the political order, and thus an increase in the rate of alienation indicates that the political productivity must increase in order to justify the current level of political authorization. Conversely, as the rate of alienation falls less payment is required to induce authorization of powers, but because power becomes more valuable, more of it will be hoarded. The rate of alienation is, therefore, as we will see below, the link balancing the market for power and the market for political product. The rate of alienation is separate from the "alienation of constituent intent."

95. Political alienation involves a strain at the level of values where units are ambivalent towards or consciously reject what they believe are the dominant institutionalized values of their political system.

96. As in the case of the L⟷A interchange, there are in the L⟷G interchange two levels of reference (see p. 474). At the lower level, LI$\underline{G}$AL, the factor input to G, is a real commitment to compliance with specified political obligations—here power is the governing medium. The upper level case, L$\underline{I}$GAL, involves the input of value commitment to the generalized legitimacy of the polity.

97. The observant reader will have noted in the earlier discussion of the economy that the variables considered in the production market were monetarily defined, except for the variable of opportunity, the interest rate, and that the variables considered in the money market—given a specified supply of money—were defined in terms of real (nonmonetary) inputs. The same apparent paradox holds for the polity; the variables in the production market, again excluding the factor of opportunity, the legitimacy of authority, are defined in terms of power, and the variables in the power market are defined in terms of real inputs. All this means is that the output of a subsystem is determined by the spending of income for intrinsic satisfiers, while the liquidity preference—each medium is the most liquid resource for obtaining the real products of the subsystem of reference—manifest for the medium is determined by information conveyed by inputs of real assets, perhaps defined in terms of some other generalized medium, but never in terms of the medium under examination (see *ibid.,* "postscript" to Ch. 15).

98. Working within these parameters allows me to blur distinctions between real and medium measures of the variables. I will, in part, remedy this ambiguity in the concluding segment of this section when I discuss questions of inflation and deflation of the media.

99. Here the necessity of disaggregation is of paramount import. To say that an increase in output implies that more interest demands are met is as obvious as it is trivial. It is not, of course, trivial to know what proportion of interest demands go unsatisfied, but it is also necessary to explicate the notion of the "wages of demand," the return of power for the influence provided. It is essential to know how policy decisions are distributed within the society.

100. See Allen, *op. cit.,* p. 123, and Smith and Teigin, *op. cit.,* pp. 15-18, for introductory discussions of the economic analogies.

101. Bronfenbrenner and Holzman, *op. cit.,* provide a review of the economic literature and a list of references. R.J. Ball, and P. Doyle, *Inflation* (Baltimore: Penguin Books, 1970), also includes a list of references.

102. See Keynes, *op. cit.,* p. 303.

103. For a brief discussion of monetary definitions of inflation see Bronfonbrenner and Holzman, *op. cit.,* pp. 47-52.

104. This might, but need not, imply a situation comparable to deficit spending by governmental collectivities. It would imply deficit spending, for example, if a constitutional court exceeded the level of provided operative responsibility in its authorization of the powers of elective office. It seems to me

that such phenomena have occurred on multiple occasions in the history of the United States and are especially likely to occur in the founding of new states. They may, but surely need not, involve an inflation of power.

105. See Parsons, *Politics and Social Structure,* p. 490.

106. Inflation cannot be adequately portrayed on the LM-IS diagram unless we make the inputs to the polity a function of real, nonpower, variables, e.g., the level of political saving a function of real output, not measured in terms of power. Then a shift to the left of the LM curve indicates a decrease in the value of power, where a position with a given level of authorization is, for example, less able to secure and to see implemented binding decisions; the "price level" is no longer a given. See Allen, *op. cit.,* pp. 147-9, for the economic case.

.107. See Parsons, *Sociological Theory and Modern Society,* Chapter 9.

108. See C. Schultze, *Recent Inflation in the United States,* study paper #1, U.S. Congress Joint Economic Committee. Study of Employment, Growth and Price Levels, 1959) and Schultze, *National Income Analysis,* second edition (Englewood Cliffs: Prentice-Hall, 1967), pp. 108-9.

109. The old dictatorship of the bourgeoisie refers to those in whose interest the government must function, not necessarily to who rules. The point is as follows: even if "Lenin and Mao" were elected President and Vice-President in the U.S.A., the conditions imposed upon political action by a capitalist economy would thwart any electoral transition to socialism and communism. The question is not "Who Governs?" but rather, "What are the conditions of successful governance?" and, therefore, "What must the governor do, what are the constraints upon his capabilities in acting?" This is the same question one should ask about economic leaders. Queries concerning their satanic or saintly values are not irrelevant, the conditions of action do not define the content of action, but we should be especially concerned with the structural constraints upon their actions and the limits thereby imposed. Successful governance within a "capitalist society" requires the furtherance of the interest of the bourgeoisie; success in managerial positions within a capitalist economy requires adherence to the rules of capitalist success, solvency and profit. See M. Gould, "Review of Michael Harrington, Toward a Democratic Left," *Sociological Inquiry,* 40 (Winter 1970).

110. A governmental alteration of the basic structure of the economy would involve a situation of disorder by doing "violence" to the property rights institutionalized within the economy. (See Hannah Arendt, *On Revolution* (New York: Viking Press, 1965), p. 10: "Cain slew Abel, and Romulus slew Remus; violence was the beginning and, by the same token, no beginning could be made without using violence, without violating." See also H. Blumer, "Collective Behavior," in A.M. Lee (ed.), *Principles of Sociology* (New York: Barnes and Noble, 1955), pp. 168ff.) The necessity of utilizing force in such a transformation would be largely dependent upon the response of those expropriated; surely coercion would be essential.

It would be an interesting exercise to trace within the interchange system the multiple political effects (directly from the economy and secondarily from I and L) of instituting a policy fundamentally detrimental to controlling economic interests, yet without fundamentally redefining the institutional structure of the economy. A good case study might be the economic imperialism of post-World War Two America. One would find, I think, that it would be very difficult for a popularly elected government to both implement a policy eliminating U.S. imperialism and to maintain its political support. Other cases which might be examined within this framework are the policies of the so-called democratic socialists. It is not coincidental that no victory of any socialist democratic party has brought about fundamental realignments within the stratification system of its country, let alone developing a socialist society.

111. But we may watch Chile if she attempts to implement a communist program. See P. Sweezy and H. Magdorf, "Review of the Month: Peaceful Transition to Socialism?" *Monthly Review* (January 1971).

112. See Parsons, *Sociological Theory and Modern Society*, p. 342.

113. *Ibid.*, p. 382.

114. *Ibid.*, p. 291.

115. Another aspect of Marx's dictatorship of the bourgeoisie can be made intelligible within the context of power deflation. "Ideally," known violations of the system's authority code are met with coercive reactions, not excepting the case of parliamentary democracy. It was Marx's point that in a "capitalist system" the rules exist to protect the interests of the bourgeoisie as a class (an empirical question in any society) and that classes which, in a position of deflated power, act in violation of the authority code will be forced to conform. This gains in import if one accepts the argument, previously made, that communist programs can not be implemented in a "capitalist system" without generating power inflation. Thus the communist is forcibly attacked when he acts as a minority within the polity in seeking to attain his interest demands; and when he wields sufficient political support to act "democratically," his power inflates. His only alternative is to wrest control of the economy and the polity from bourgeois interests and thus begin the development of a new type of societal order.

Marx recognized the validity of those arguments within the context of a "socialist economy"; economic conditions necessitate the protection of those in whose interest the economy operates. The dictatorship of the proletariat means that the authority code specifies that policies on behalf of the proletariat are acceptable, while those on behalf of the bourgeoisie are not acceptable. It defines the "rules of the game," which for Marx necessarily benefit one class, in socialism the proletariat, and harm another, in socialism the bourgeoisie. (Marx often seems to imagine a zero-sum system, but even in an expanding system he emphasizes the relative benefits between the two classes and the structure of control over those benefits. The strength of the proletariat within the capitalist economy lies in the fact that his labor power is the condition LIGAL of economic production). Theoretically, however, the dictatorship of the proletariat need no more lead to totalitarianism than must democratic capitalism, "the dictatorship of the bourgeoisie," lead to fascism.

116. Here the assumption of a single "rate of alienation," of an aggregate measure of alienation across collectivities, clearly becomes misleading.

117. I have not discussed the effects of an increase in the amount of power here for two reasons: To determine the credibility of such an expansion demands a study of the mechanisms of power creation, within the latency subsystem, and my thoughts about this are still in the process of formulation. Suffice it to say that more power cannot be created by fiat, thus lowering the rate of alienation. Here it would be as accurate to say that lowering the rate of alienation leads to the creation of more power. Second, insofar as more symbolic power can be created by fiat (actual, not "counterfeit power"), by the constitutional functionaries in L and G, this will lower the "rate of alienation," through the manipulation of legitimacy symbols, but not necessarily the "real rate of alienation." Thus it will not necessarily markedly affect political support and, if the "real rate of alienation" rises, will yield a decrease in "real authorization."

118. De Jouvenal, *op. cit.*, correctly emphasizes the importance of the increasing ability of the political system to control

conscription and taxation. It is not fortuitous that the "new type" of revolution that Arendt, *op. cit.*, analyzes begins with the onset of the increase of such control and thus with the onset of the growing importance of acute power deflation.

119. I regret not having the space to treat the societal community and latency subsystems in this paper. My thinking about these subsystems is less developed than about the polity, but it might help others if I simply indicate symbolically a few parallels, as I tentatively see them:

C_i Leadership responsibility (G − [product]→I)
S_i Justification for allocations of loyalties (I − [factor]→L), extent delimited by grounds for justification of claims (A − [product]→I)
I_i Value-based claims to loyalties (L − [product]→I)
N_i Policy decisions (G − [factor]→I)
M_{it} Transactions demand for influence
M_{ih} Assertions of claims for resources (A − [factor]→I)
O_i Commitment to valued association (L→[factor]→I)
r_i Rate of alienation from commitment to valued association
C_l Commitment to the production of goods (A − [product]→L)
S_l Commitment to valued association (L − [factor] →I), extent delimited by moral responsibility for the collective interest (G − [product]→L)
I_l Commitments to common value (I − [product]→L)
N_l Consumer income (A − [factor]→L)
M_{lt} Transactions demand for commitments
M_{lh} Operative responsibility (G − [factor]→L)
O_l Justifications for allocation of loyalties (I − [factor]→L)
r_l Rate of distrust

I have generally retained Parsons' terminology, which might cause some confusion, especially in the case of commitments.

A number of comments need to be made. First, some outputs occupy a double role: $M_{ih} = S_a$, $M_{lh} = S_g$, $O_i = S_l$ and $O_l = S_i$ (see Figure 20-3). These nodes are, I believe, the keys to integrating the partial theories developed about the subsystems into a total theory of societal scope.

Second, the rationales I have provided for the classification of the various subsystem inputs has been neither elaborate nor complete. I have generalized economic usages to the social subsystem and then specified the content of these concepts for the polity. I have not explicitly discussed the functional import of the consumption, investment, and similar inputs because my focus has not been upon the total social system. These inputs, for example economic and political investment, do not necessarily involve the same functional consequences for each receiving subsystem; and they cannot be identified as if they did.

The theoretical parallels we must draw concern cognate systems: any two social systems may be compared if they are treated as the total system of reference; subsystems must be compared with their cognate subsystems. Thus the fact that all subsystems require an input of "consumer support" does not mean that they all receive that input from the same source, nor that the consequences involved in its receipt are the same for each subsystem; rather, the consequences are necessarily the same only for congate subsystems, i.e., for two different adaptive subsystems, not for the adaptive and goal-attainment subsystems of the same social system.

An example might clarify this point. The investment input to any subsystem must come from a subsystem higher on the cybernetic hierarchy to be able to exert the leverage that will enable an expansion in the scope of subsystem output (both real and symbolic). This leverage must also be backed by a binding obligation or commitment, by a negative sanction, in order to "enforce" the required actions. Thus the subsystems involved in the generation of investment outputs are the polity and latency subsystems (the exception to this rule is discussed on pages

476-78); the investment input comes from the next highest sub-system wielding a medium utilizing a negative sanction. It is within these subsystems that the "banking process" occurs for the subsystems of reference. Thus, although I_a has immediate consequences for the goal-attainment subsector of the economy, I_g has immediate consequences for the latency subsector of the polity.

It is a tempting "simplification" to utilize the *Economy and Society* interchange format and to categorize G inputs as consumer support and constituent intent, A inputs as invest-ment and opportunity, and I inputs as saving and the demand for medium to hold. Such a categorization would once again involve a confusion of system levels. Processes like political consumption must be identified functionally within the context of the total system under examination; and within the context of the polity, in both instances integrative i.e., the consumption input to the polity is from the I subsystem to the I subsector of the polity (G_i). (Although product inputs always emphasize the same function for the total system and the receiving subsystem, the case of factor inputs is complicated in that they are always directed to the central subsector for each subsystem, for example, in the polity to G_g.) Consumption, as a set of four processes, can only be spoken of functionally in terms of the specific locale of each variety of consumer support.

21

GENERALIZED MEDIA AND THE PROBLEM OF CONTINGENCY

Niklas Luhmann

Sociology needs a general theory which reflects enduring structures of social experience and action. Actors, however, have the possibility of choice and may choose in unpredictable ways. If they hear of a theory, they may feel stimulated to refute it by action. The old European tradition of thinking about society, law, and politics recognized this problem and tried to solve it. It was a humanistic tradition and an ethical one insofar as it reflected the possibility of choice. Its theory of social systems (*koinoniai, societates*) was a normative theory of right and prudent choices. The breakdown of this tradition was an unavoidable consequence of the scientific movement. This, however, does not do away with the problem of structure and choice, which therefore has to be solved in other ways.

Thomas Hobbes redefined this problem as the natural preference for unethical choice, i.e., war, and hence as the necessity of government to establish and guarantee order in social relations. The instrument which transforms nature into order was for him a legal one, a covenant, and the science which conceptually reconstructs the establishment of order was for Hobbes a natural science of law and politics. With this conception Hobbes remains in the tradition of legal and political philosophy in at least two ways: (1) defining the principal problem in ethical terms, albeit by negation,[1] and (2) looking to law and politics as the realm of problem solving. These limitations can, in Parsons' terms, be interpreted as recognition of the functional primacy of the political subsystem of society.

This primacy can no longer be taken for granted. Since Hobbes the theory of political society (*societas civilis*) has been replaced by a theory of economic society (*bürgerliche Gesellschaft*, in the sense of Hegel and Marx). Today we are inclined to differentiate between the system of society and its subsystems. This means that the concept of society no longer

contains a decision for an essential primacy of specific subsystems. The theory of society has to be, therefore, elaborated on a higher level of generalization. On this conceptual level of the social system the question of structure and choice has to be confronted once again.

A serious effort to cope with this problem and all its implications has been made by Talcott Parsons,[2] who elaborates on it in terms of system and action and tries to solve it by the statement "action is a system".[3] This leads, with remarkable consistency, into his well-known theory of the action system, which emphasizes differentiation, evolution of differentiation, generalization, and processes of interchange between differentiated subsystems. The concept of generalized media refers, then, to interchange processes between subsystems of the social system of society. Generalized media are conceived as specialized languages regulating interchange processes between sub-systems. Consequently, the differentiation of media follows the differentiation of systems and not vice versa. There is no direct relation between the theory of generalized media and the subjective experience of choice.

Critical commentators have made the point that the early Parsons began with a voluntaristic concept of action, i.e., a concept which is defined by the contingency of subjective orientation and choice, and slowly changed over to a neobehavioristic theory of structurally defined systems.[4] Other critics hold that he conceives actors in interaction only as individuals structuring their action in terms of ends and means and adaptively maximizing their satisfaction and not as subjects with a self-conscious potential for critique, innovation, and emancipation.[5] These criticisms may be overdrawn. The subjectivity of human orientation and choice remains the fundamental human condition on which Parsons founds his argument that choice has to be guided by structural limitations and that actions are, by necessity, units of normatively integrated systems. In this way Parsons redefines the Hobbesian problem of order on a higher level of abstraction. However, we can and should refuse to believe that the problem of subjective contingency has already been solved by an existing social system. We have to advance slowly.

If we accept the fundamental thesis that meaningful systems are necessary to cope with the subjective contingency of choice, we are, as Parsons certainly would agree, not yet logically committed to any concrete social or cultural system. We cannot treat that problem as solved by systems while it constantly remains a problem for interaction.[6] It is quite possible to think of contingency as a problem which continues in and pervades all systems. The concept of contingency serves, then, not only as argument for the necessity of systems as systems, but furthermore as a guideline for the functional analysis of structures and processes. That makes it possible to link the analysis of structures and processes in a more direct way to the function of system-building as such.

Overstating the opposition to Parsons we could speak of functional-structural analysis in contrast to structural-functional analysis. This formulates the intention to relate functional analysis not only to the structure of systems but also to the function of the structure of systems, i.e., the function of reducing the complexity of contingent possibilities.[7] It would be interesting to see how far Parsons' concepts could be reformulated in this perspective. This would require a functional theory of differentiation (e.g., in the sense of Ashby) to replace a deductive theory of functional differentiation. We would need a functional conception of norms that explains the "oughtness" of norms and not only the meaning of particular norms.[8] Furthermore, we should try to link the concept of generalized media more directly to the central problem of the subjective contingency of orientation and choice. This is the attempt of the present study.

DOUBLE CONTINGENCY: ACTION AND EXPERIENCE

The index of *Toward a General Theory of Action*[9] contains no entry on "contingency." The concept has, nevertheless, central significance in Parsons' work, without finding adequate attention and elaboration. The main chain of arguments is reduced to this conception: Social systems need normatively institutionalized structures to secure complementarity of expectations. This complementarity is problematical because of the "double contingency" inherent in interaction. The gratification of ego is contingent on the action alter chooses. Alter's selection among his

available alternatives is, in turn, contingent on ego's selection. There is, then, an infinity problem, as in all relations which can change on both sides. This infinity problem was taken by Parsons to be solved by shared meanings in relatively stable symbolic systems.

In transferring this conception from the microsociological theory of interaction to the macrosociological theory of system differentiation, Parsons substitutes "double interchange" for "double contingency." This is intelligible only if we realize that Parsons, from the very beginning, has seen action in terms of ends and means[10] and interaction as interconnection of ends and means, which is problematical only insofar as ends and means are differentially evaluated. Under these presuppositions it makes sense to reconstruct double contingency as double interchange,[11] which can be organized in a way that each participant may pursue his individual preferences. Generalized media, then, are symbolic rules of interchange which integrate actors of systems with different ends into a high level of reciprocal satisfaction.

This line of thought renders the meaning of "contingency" inadequately and runs the risk of missing it completely. Parsons' choice of the concept of contingency was not a matter of contingent choice. In a very superficial sense, we could reconstruct Parsons' argument by substituting "dependency" for "contingency" and interpreting "dependency" as dependence of the realization of ends upon means. But the original connotation of contingency would thus be lost. If I understand correctly the English term contingency in its present use, it has its core meaning in dependency and draws the attention primarily to the fact that the cause on which something depends performs itself a selction from other possibilities so that the contingent fact comes about in a somewhat chancy, accidental way. If we look into the theological and philosophical tradition of the term, our findings confirm this interpretation.[12] In scholastic philosophy, the term *contingens* belonged to the theory of modal forms. Used to translate the Aristotelian ενδεχορνον (=possible) and mixed up with the classical Latin sense of *accidens* or *eveniens*, it was narrowed down to signify a special type of possibility, i.e., "possibility not to be."[13] This "possibility not to be" was attributed to a world created by the unlimited will of God. Only a contingent world, as the nominalistic scholastics found out, could be conceived as created by God. *Contingens* was used in a double sense as a general category of modal logic and as a term which includes causal selection as the factor which decides between being and not-being.[14] Contingency of the world came to be a corollary of the absoluteness of God. Contingency, therefore, also meant dependency on His creation or the visibility of His free will in His creation. This led the pious to look to God for the elimination of infinite other possibilities and for a guarantee that the selected world was the best of all possible worlds.

This tradition was, of course, known in its results to Descartes and to Hobbes. Finding the transcendent God liberated from any essential commitment to a preexisting "cosmic" order of nature or ideas, they drew the consequences for the individual and for the social order. They secularized the problem of selectivity. Descartes transformed it into a theory of individual and cognitive processes and Hobbes into one of social-political and normative processes. Not yet sociologists, they did not reflect on the interdependence of individual and social processes; nor could they pay sufficient attention to the fact that the problem of contingent selection became urgently relevant in connection with evolutionary changes in the social system of society.[15] Nevertheless, this background of conceptual history helps to see why, and in what sense, contingency is inherent in interaction.

Summarizing what we have discussed so far, contingency means that being depends on selection which, in turn, implies the possibility of not being and the being of other possibilities.[16] A fact is contingent when seen as selection from other possibilities which remain in some sense possibilities despite a selection. Implying a potential for negation and the visibility of other possibilities, the concept can be applied only to the meaning of subjective experience and action. This does not limit the range of application and does not, of course, mean that contingency is accessible only by "introspection." Every fact may be seen as contingent: the objective world,[17] the concrete self with its biography, conscious life,[18] decisions and expectations and other persons with their experiences and choices. Contingency is a universal, but it nevertheless presupposes a subjective point of view. It can be applied to all facts but not independently of a subjective potential to negate and conceive other possibilities.

We are now prepared to analyze the special problem of *double contingency* in interaction. Contingency does not double by erasing the twofold dependence;[19] nor does double contingency signify two contingencies in the sense of a simple addition; nor does it simply mean interdependence in the sense that ego depends on alter and vice versa, the subjective point of view coming in later and only as an interpretation of this interdependence.[20] The doubling comprehends the whole structure: the generalized potential to conceive of facts as selections implying negations, to negate these negations and to reconstruct other possibilities. Double contingency is "double négation virtuelle"[21] meaning that possibilities of negation can be retained and

stabilized as reciprocally not actualized but implied possibilities. The doubling of contingencies is possible because this potential is located in subjects, and subjects can experience other subjects. The doubling does not double the world and does not construct two separated realms of contingency. The potential is universal for each subject and is an aspect of the meaningful constitutions of his encompassing world so that ego has to identify alter as being another subject in his world, and vice versa. Double contingency rests on the fact that contingency is subjective and universal at once.

All this may sound unnecessarily complicated, particularly to readers for whom the contact with and the continuation of themes, problems, and motives of European thought have no significance. There are, however, for this renewal specific sociological reasons and payoffs. The point is that we have to conceive of meaningfully organized selectivity as the specific human condition and that we need the outlined conceptual framework to understand evolutionary gains as higher forms of problematization and organization of selective processes. Double contingency is not simply a problematical fact inherent in the nature of interaction. It has the double aspect of high achievement and high risks. It makes the *selctivity* of other subjects *selectively available*[22] at increasing risks. The selection chain may be broken and expectations disappointed — a risk which, then, can become a specific (secondary) problem and be solved by specialized mechanisms.

The main ethical as well as sociological tradition has tried to solve this problem by reference to the existence of norms and values in all human societies, explaining the "oughtness" of norms and values either by nature or by consensus or by some tautological circumscription.[23] If we relate the function of oughtness to the problem of surprise and disappointment inherent in double contingency we can work out a functional definition. There are two (and only two) possible ways to react to disappointments: by learning and adapting expectations and by maintaining expectations contrary to fact. The decision as to the way to settle the issue may be made in advance and then colors the expectation. If it is to be adjusted to contrary behavior the expectation has *cognitive* character and refers to future facts. If it is to be maintained in case of deviant behavior the decision has *normative* character and is symbolized by "ought."[24] To learn or not to learn, that is the question.

The decision as to this characterization of expectations and ensuing disappointment reaction implies the risk of fixing future behavior in advance. It may be made in advance or postponed, leaving the choice between normative and cognitive character open for situational adjustment. If made in advance it requires institutional support, i.e., an institutionalization of the differentiation of cognitive and normative expectations. It must be possible to expect that others expect normative characterization of expectations in certain cases and cognitive characterization in others, otherwise normative expectations would be simply private projections. Institutionalization helps also to impute to others the same choice of characterization.

On one level I may expect deviant behavior from a known criminal. Even then I can retain normative expectations of correct behavior and remain sure about them because I can expect that the criminal expects my expectations to be normative. The "oughtness" of norms symbolizes this counterfactual maintenance of expectations on the level of expectations concerning expectations over time.

We cannot develop this conception of the oughtness of norms into further details.[25] Our refined conception of norms shows, however, that the problem of double contingency cannot be "solved" simply by reference to norms because norms have a very special relation to double contingency. Aside from the problem of *nonfulfillment of expectations* which becomes redefined by the differentiation of normative and cognitive expectations, there are other problematical aspects of doubly contingent selectivity. We shall use the concept of *transmission of selections* to define the function of media. To prepare the elaboration of this idea we have to conceptualize another problem outside the scope of (but not independent of) the theory of norms, namely the problem of *attribution of selections*, which has likewise far-reaching consequences for sociological theory.[26] If we define interaction by double contingency and understand ego and alter as subjects with their own potentials of meaningful selection, we shall have to question the idea that sociology can be founded on one basic concept of action. There are two modes of meaningful selection, action and experience.[27] We conceive a process as *action* if its selectivity is attributed to a system[28] and as *experience* if its selectivity is attributed to the situation or the environment of the system.

These definitions imply

1. that the concepts of system and environment are used to define action (and not vice versa); and that systems theory, therefore, is more basic than action theory;[29]
2. that the classification of selection as action or experience depends on the choice of a system reference: an action of a system can be the experience of another system;
3. that action and experience can be seen as functionally equivalent ways of selection and, to some extent, be substituted for one another;

4. that we have to look for rules of attribution which may differ in different societies; that we have to explore the reasons for these differences, the reasons that make one or the other rule advantageous and allows for their institutionalization;
5. that there are chains of selective processes in different constellations: we experience actions, we act out (express) experiences and experiences of experiences or experiences of actions; we prepare actions by experiences and experiences by actions; we experience actions of alter as expressing his experience of our own action. The pragmatic view that all experience is instrumental to action is a dogmatic preference for one of these forms.[30]

Action and experience work together by a kind of division of labor. If two subjects meet, they constitute the world as a vast horizon of possibilities which cannot be reduced by action and reaction alone. They also have to use the other mode of selection, experience; and so they constitute "social systems to which they attribute selective action of its own."[31] In other words, they have to use the difference of actor and situation and, simultaneously, the difference of the social system and its environment to distribute and organize selection.

Every personal and social system identifies itself by its own selectivity, i.e., as an action system. Nevertheless, the conceptual framework of sociology cannot be derived from the concept of action or interaction alone. Systems are systems-in-an-environment, and their own selectivity is organized in relation to a selected and selecting environment. Environmental selections are, for the system, experiences. Sociological theory has to put both interaction and interexperience as intersubjective selections on an equal footing; then it can incorporate the conceptual tradition which stresses the social reflexivity of consciousness (ego is conscious that alter is conscious of ego's consciousness) which is, to Americans, mainly known under the name of "looking-glass self" (Cooley) and "role-taking" (Mead). And it will be possible to integrate both traditions which compete for the position of a general sociological theory: sociology of action systems and sociology of knowledge.

DOUBLE CONTINGENCY AND MEDIATION

The problem of double contingency finds an institutional solution by normative integration of the expectations of actors. This statement of Parsons remains true. There is, however, a dangerous inclination to bypass the theoretical significance of the problem. The fact that all social systems have institutionally patterned solutions and cannot exist otherwise does not mean that the sociologist, by some kind of theoretical uncertainty absorption,[32] may treat the problem as solved and forget about it. Having reconstructed the concept of contingency in terms of selection processes, we are in a position to see its pervasive importance and to link the theory of the generalized media more directly to the problem of contingency. Parsons treats the problem of double contingency as solved by the institutionalization of social systems and of symbolic language codes which then, following the lines of system differentiation, are differentiated as media of interchange between subsystems. I shall propose to explore generalized media as one type of solution of the problem of double contingency, i.e., as social organization of individually dispersed human selectivity.

Individual subjects have a very narrow span of consciousness and, consequently, a very limited potential for conscious choice. Nevertheless, they live consciously in an infinite world of other possibilities of experience and action constituted by communication with other subjects. They experience themselves and other subjects as systems which select their own experiences and actions, but neither ego nor alter can choose all possibilities which are open to him for choice. This human condition makes a complete dissociation of selective systems impossible—even logically impossible, if MacKay is right.[33] One consequence is the emergence of social systems which restrict and distribute the real possibilities of selection and can be treated as separate systems for analytical purposes as well as in situations of daily life. Put in a dynamic perspective and seen as a process, this means that transmission of selections is unavoidable. It is performed by communication. Thus, there are two interdependent modes of coping with high contingency which have to be treated on an equal level of conceptual abstraction: restriction of the possibilities of choice by *social systems* and transmission of performed choices by *communication.*

Communication presupposes language. It is organized by double selectivity—by a differentiation of a generalized symbolic code from concrete speaking behavior. But linguistically it is perfectly possible to lie and deceive, to negate, to refute acceptance, to be silent. As a generalized symbolic code, language does limit possibilities but does not commit motives.[34] This combination of limitation with openness provides for high structural complexity but does not, by itself, provide for transmission of selections. Communication, in other words, is not necessarily effective. This is another way to express double contingency. Language alone does not suffice for solving the problem of double contingency. It requires the additional function of generalized media to make sure that the selection of experience of action by ego will be accepted by alter as premise of his own selections. Therefore, we cannot describe generalized media as a linguistic code or a specialized language alone. This would not account for the transmission of selections. Like social systems, media are mechanisms for narrowing choices which linguistically remain open.

To explain transmission of reduced complexity, we have to look for motivational mechanisms which operate in spite of other possibilities. These mechanisms have two roots; the limited capacity for conscious information processing and the pattern of selection. The limitation of consciousness makes it impossible to follow up all visible possibilities of experience and action, nor is it possible to choose without accepting choices—a point of very general importance for money, power, truth, and love. To some extent everyone has to accept what others have chosen simply because others have chosen. Consciousness always organizes its own selectivity in relation to the selection of other subjects. It predisposes actors to accept selections as condition of their own freedom of choice on specific issues. This limited capacity can, in sociological theory, be treated as constant, but the organization of its selectivity is variable. Its organization is open for evolutionary change and for learning on the level of social systems and personality systems.

To account for these changes we have to focus on the second root of the motivational mechanism: the pattern of selection. Selection has the general form of "one out of more than one." These "one out of more than one" have to be combined by patterns that ensure that one selection continues and reinforces others. Described as process such patterns have the general form of "one out of more than one out of more than one out of . . . ." But with its narrow span of attention, consciousness cannot grasp concretely elaborated patterns of this type (or it would limit itself to the use of very simple selection chains). It uses generalized symbols to represent such patterns on a higher level of abstraction. These generalized symbols have to be phenomenally simple (to be representable) and functionally complex (to function adequately as substitutes for concrete chain descriptions). Functionally, they have to be "form" as a reliable promise of "content" and to be a cue for quick evocation of attention.

Generalized symbolic patterns that fulfill these requirements can be concepts that organize individual selection chains. They can embrace different systems and organize the selectivity of one system in relation to the way in which others use their power of selection. This type of pattern we call generalized media of communication. Media, then, solve the problem of double contingency through transmission of reduced complexity. They employ their selection pattern as a motive to accept the reduction, so that people join with others in a narrow world of common understandings, complementary expectations, and determinable issues. Media are not only words, symbols, or codes; they are meaningful constellations of combined selectivity which can be signified by words, symbolized, and codified legally, methodologically or otherwise. Prominent examples are money and power, and we would like to add truth, love, and perhaps art.

Media transmit contingent selections which are perceived as *past* performances. Trust, on the other hand, refers to *future* contingencies.[35] The two horizons of time provide the base for a clear analytical distinction. Man, however, is always conscious of both horizons. He conceives of himself as enduring and remembers events as more or less reliable indicators of future events. Media, therefore, involve trust insofar as the reliability of past selections becomes a problem.[36] Accepting alter's selections may narrow or even bind ego's possibilities of future choice. It therefore requires institutional securities, e.g., law and special strategies of risk control, the result of which is trust. Trust, then, is not a special type of general media. It conditions the futurity of all mediated selections. The need for trust increases and changes into higher generalized and more specialized forms inasmuch as the time horizon expands into an open future, and the differentiation of media involves a corresponding differentiation of trust.

THE MEDIA OF LOVE, TRUTH, AND POWER IN EVOLUTIONARY PERSPECTIVE

The differentiation of language, media, and systems has important consequences for social evolution. Evolution requires three different types of mechanisms: mechanisms of *variation* that realize plain possibilities; mechanisms of *selection* that select the useful realizations and eliminate the not useful; and mechanisms of *stabilization* that incorporate selected innovation into the structure of existing systems.[37] The rate of evolution depends on the extent to which these mechanisms can be differentiated so that they generate viable possibilities which are not identical with the existing systems, i.e., reduced to zero.

Evolutionary change in social relations also presupposes a differentiation of such mechanisms so that they can, although interdependent, operate under different conditions of effectiveness. *Language* performs a permanent overproduction of

possibilities, stimulates the current realization of some of these possibilities, and serves in this way as the primary mechanism of *variation*. *Media* channel the socially acceptable and transmittable selections, i.e., choices that can have social success. They use the effectiveness of the communication process as a criterion and function in this way as mechanisms of *selection*. *Systems* provide for discontinuities (boundaries) and *stabilize* themselves by successful selection of structures. Discontinuities means differential contingencies. The possibilities (next moves, choices) of the environment are not the same as the possibilities of the systems. The possibilities of the system are conditioned by the fact that they need not to continue in its environment. This constitution of its own possibilities implies chances and risks at the same time. The chances, therefore, cannot be realized randomly; they have to be used to counterbalance risks—in other words, to solve system problems. Stabilization by system building is the way in which this balance of specific chances and specific risks is maintained and its problem solutions become continuously available. Stability is the capacity to reproduce problem solutions under simplified conditions of limited contingency.[38] It reproduces the solution of problems which are generated and made solvable by system boundaries, i.e., by differentiation and limitation of possibilities. This performance can be multiplied by system differention, i.e., by repetition of system building within the boundaries of a system.

In a logical and operational sense, stabilization seems to depend on the selection of problem solutions and selection on variation in the sense of generation of other possibilities. The real mechanisms, however, presuppose one another in the reverse order. The maintainance of boundaries comes first in the sense that it generates contingency by differentiation of possibilities. What is possible depends on what is stabilized. Furthermore, the stabilizing function of system building and system differentiation has primacy insofar as it founds the interdependence of the evolutionary mechanisms. Variation and selection refer to possible states of systems; and the structure that is stabilized determines how far specialized mechanisms for variation, selection, and stabilization (in the case of society: language, media, and system differentiation) can be separated.

Very simple societies can afford only a low degree of differentiation between these mechanisms.[39] These systems are structured by relatively concrete expectations: by an "ethos" in the archaic, preclassic sense. This does not provide for possibilities of legitimate structural change. Their language is, to them, the meaning of the world; words are the essence of things. A new, unusual way of speaking comes close to erring or lying. Language does not serve to open the access to other possibilities. Even in more highly developed societies, words limit the possibilities. The development of Roman law was possible, considering its high regard for words as institutions, only by some kind of "practical nominalism." It had its social roots in a professional group of legal specialists able to judge the differing consequences of differing legal constructions, i.e., in functional differentiation of roles.

Under these conditions the function of transmission of selections cannot and need not be institutionalized separately. Men live oriented to a communal "reality construction"[40] that gives to shared meanings the character of obvious facts. Contingency and selectivity are problems of very limited impact, manageable in terms of moral and technical categories of everyday life. Everyone can easily grasp the meaning of experiences and actions which others wish to elicit. There are a few visible alternatives and acceptance is usually (exept for a very few contested issues that are solved by violence or threat of violence) not a question of conscious choice. These societies stabilize their social systems primarily by lack of alternatives. There is little need for specialized media, not even for power,[41] because the functions of language and media are fused.[42] Words and patterns for truth, love, friendship, power, reciprocal help, and so on either symbolize the order of society as a whole or point to marginal institutions.[43]

The Greek tradition of thinking about law and society testifies to a significant and conscious break with archaic societies. It reflects a new level of social organization and a conscious interpretation of its problems, its institutional forms, and its proper risks. A new range of institutional selectivity and individual choice becomes visible and requires a generalized understanding and legal political formations compatible with higher degrees of freedom. In the leading conceptualizations (i.e., the distinction of *physis* and *nomos,* the ethical conception of human action, and the political, i.e., institutional, constitution of common affairs) we can recognize the underlying problem: the quest for natural limitations of human selectivity.[44]

In this context of institutional and conceptual development we find the origin of symptomatic innovations which indicate new needs for generalized mechanisms to transmit selectivity. One of them is connected with the new, artificially coined word *philia*,[45] later translated as *amicitia, amour,* friendship, love but originally indicating social relations of mutual acceptance in a very large sense. The concept clearly meant a motivational mechanism with strong moral implications. From these roots grew a very important conceptual development that can be characterized as a slow process of elimination of functionally diffuse connotations. The first classical Greek discussion centered around the value of only useful (i.e., purely economic) "love" against which Plato put his eros speculations. Aristotle and his followers saw love in its essence and its highest form as public virtue, as political love, and thereby, as an essential element of society itself. After the collapse of the polis and the spread of Christian religious thought, the political connotation lost its importance and the societal function of love was expressed by religious symbols. Love became, in its essence, love of God himself and of God in His creation. This idea was accepted and elaborated during the Middle Ages. It finally was torn asunder on the rocks of modern reflective subjectivism, which could offer no convincing solution to the crucial problem of self-interest in love (as the famous contest about *amour pur* between Fénélon and Bossuet showed to a large European public). A few decades later the more or less literary idea of passionate (or romantic) love became generally accepted as essential expression of true love. "True love" now meant a serious and deep individual feeling committing to one (and only one) other individual, and "passion" symbolized relinquishment of normative social control of love matches. These, it was hoped, led to marriage. Love is now institutionalized as specialized symbolic medium. It regulates the mutual selections of individuals for common family life in terms of compatible personalities and compatible personal worlds. It thereby provides, as we shall see, for special motives to accept reduced complexity.

Another line of development has its focus in the problem of truth. It is far from obvious that truth in itself can be a problem, and for archaic societies this was simply inconceivable. They questioned, of course, the existence of facts and the trustworthiness of reports, but not truth in an abstract sense. It required the social conditions of more highly developed, politically constituted, economically differentiated societies to visualize truth as such, (i.e., to conceive of *aletheia* as manifestation and accessibility of being in its phenomenal evidence). This idea had its roots in unquestioned communal reality constructions thought of as "being" or "nature"; but it could already specialize goal-oriented, truth-seeking human striving and it could organize social interaction, (i.e. dialogue), around this idea. The parallel with *philia* is remarkable and goes so far that *aletheia,* too, was conceived as possible only in politically constituted societies. i.e., societies that are based on a differentation of family systems (*oikos*) and political system (*polis*).

Classical Greek thinking saw truth no longer as manifestation of being but as correspondence of thinking and reality. This concept allowed for combinations of freedom and limitations (freedom of thinking and limitations by the objective world) which could be institutionalized and which remained stable under varying social conditions. Limitations on thinking became conscious as acceptance of reality as it is and not primarily as moral constraints of thinking or as social, organizational, or methodological limits of science as a social system. The main stages of further development were marked by an increasing differentiation of language from reality as objects of knowledge. This was stimulated by the nominalistic school of medieval scholastics and closely connected with the problem of contingency. Language became emancipated for instrumental use, abstracted from any innate truth value, by the conceptual differentiation of thinking and being. The increasing differentiation of language, media, and systems required conscious control. This intellectual tradition founded the need and offered the possibility to elaborate a new conception of scientific truth based on the idea of methodically controlled certainty of intersubjective transmission. Knowledge is scientific, "when he that pretendeth the science of any thing, can teach the same; that is to say, demonstrate the truth thereof perspicuously to another."[46] The "other," in this context, is the reasonable subject and not a concrete person oriented by his own status, roles, interests, or biographic history. The source of knowledge, again, is the reasonable subject and not a social authority of high status which relies upon functionally diffuse resources for attention and credit.[47] The new idea of "the subject," the subjectivity not of substance but of consciousness, symbolizes a higher degree of role differentiation, namely the relative independence of scientific, truth-seeking communication from social status, political, economic, or family interests and from historic commitments. The details of this development are, of course, very intricate. We are able to grasp its essential aspects as (1) increasing differentiation of language, medium, and system as varying, selecting, and stabilizing mechanisms; (2) an increasing generalization and specialization of truth as medium for scientific communication; (3) an increasing differentation of truth from other media, e.g., love or power; and (4) corresponding role differentiations.

Our last example concerns power. Here, too, we can outline a very significant trend of conceptual development within the older European tradition that accompanies and interprets increasing system differentiation of society. Since the separation of family systems from political systems lies at the roots of all higher forms of functionally differentiated societies, political power is a fact for all early thinkers. It has the legitimate authority to issue collectively binding decisions. Already ancient thought relates power to a system, at least to an office, and not, as in the case of love or truth, to an idea or a public virtue which only much later will become principles of subsystems.[48] Nevertheless, political power remained institutionalized on the level of the society, like love and truth, and was not treated as a specialized political (and only political) medium. This was expressed, on the one hand, by the fact that society itself was conceived of as the political system (*societas civilis*) with political roles as its leading parts and, on the other hand, by the idea that power was founded on moral and legal grounds. The transmittibility of binding decisions was seen as a moral phenomenon, called *potestas*, until a new concept of power as causal force gained prominence. For a time, both concepts were used side by side;[49] then, the concept of *potestas* passed away without an adequate substitute, leaving behind a purely causal conception of power in the sense of "A's behavior intentionally causes B's behavior." We can note however, growing doubts in this prevailing view.[50] Parsons' idea to conceive of power in analogy to money as a generalized symbolic medium[51] seems to indicate the solution, i.e., an adequate interpretation of power as a highly specialized regulatory mechanism used in the political subsystem of functionally differentiated social systems.

MEDIATION OF ACTION AND EXPERIENCE

The resuscitated ideas and conceptualizations of the older European tradition do, of course, offer no valid proofs. We do not revive them as scientific arguments on the same level with sociological theory. Even the modern concept of scientific truth is, in itself, not a scientific concept of truth. We have, on the other hand, to concede that it is not simply a matter of chance what thinkers think. We were able to point at notable parallels between different lines of conceptual development and between these conceptual developments and societal evolution. These parallels suggest that conceptual developments lead or follow the evolution of society. They reflect the changing needs of symbolization emerging in the flow of increasing system differentiation and social complexity—increasingly conscious contingency and selectivity of action and experience. We, therefore, have to expect that symbolic work focusses to some extent on the problems of contingency, selectivity, and transmission of choices, which means that it elaborates generalized media of communication and prepares their institutionalization.[52]

By now it has become obvious that we have to deviate from the scheme of media that Parsons has outlined. Parsons prefers a more deductive and analytical approach. He tries to deduce his well-known AGIL scheme of system problems from a general theory of action and gives priority to system differentiation according to these four functions. He relates, then, the concept of generalized media to the interchange processes growing out of this differentiation.[53] Media are, for him, functionally related to subsystem problems and not to the general problem of contingency. He conceives consequently of four and only four media: money, power, influence, and commitments. There is, on the level of the social system at least, no place to account for truth although science is a social system in much the same sense as the economy or the polity. In its present unfinished state, the theory is difficult to review, but there seems to be a danger of arbitrariness in a purely analytical linking of problems, systems, subsystems, interchange processes, and media that cannot be controlled sufficiently by a simple repetition of the AGIL scheme. Without daring to give a final opinion about the approach of Parsons it may be worthwhile to explore other possibilities.

We shall take the idea of the evolutionary emergence of generalized media and transfer it into an enlarged and flexible conceptual frame of reference.[54] The salient difference, can be summarized under three points: First, we have related the concept of medium functionally to the problem of double contingency, and not primarily to the consequences of system differentiation (therefore we prefer to speak of media of communication and not of media of interchange). The possibilities and problems of system differentiation come in later when we have to consider which media in the context of societal evolution can be articulated with functional system problems and stabilized by differentiation of functional subsystems. This implies, second, that we cannot use a scheme of system differentiation as a guideline of deductive reasoning; we cannot be sure to know axiomatically the kind and number of possible media in advance. We have rather to use an inductive and heuristic approach, sensitized, but not logically determined, by the problem of contingency. We are, then, not fixed as to kind and number of media. We shall investigate the cases of "power," "money," "truth," and "love" and leave open other, functionally equivalent possibilities, strongly suggesting that "art" could be included. Third, we might thus advance the theory of evolution. We may conceive concrete, functionally differentiated social systems as organized around culturally developed generalized media or as concretizations of different ways to solve the problem of double contingency (while Parsons, on the other hand, would have to maintain that functionally differentiated systems have to exist, at least analytically, before a need for organizing their interchanges can evolve).

Starting with contingency as our "sensitizing concept" (Blumer), we can recapitulate that contingency becomes conscious as selectivity in the twofold form of action and experience. There are selective actions if the selection is attributed to meaningfully acting systems; and there are selective experiences if selectivity is seen as "the state of the world." This difference in attribution becomes itself experience (i.e., ego knows whether the selections of alter are alter's experiences or alter's actions). The problem of acceptance of reduced complexity branches out in these two directions: the acceptance of alter's experiences and the acceptance of alter's actions. Both cases may be relevant for ego's experiences or for ego's actions. This general scheme provides for four possible constellations and suggests different types of problems in each of them: (1) The experience of alter may be accepted as vicarious experience of ego $(A_e \rightarrow E)$. (2) The experience of alter may be accepted by ego in the form of a corresponding action $(A_e \rightarrow E_a)$. (3) The action of alter may select an experience of ego and be accepted as such $(A_a \rightarrow E_e)$. (4) The action of alter may be accepted as action of ego $(A_a \rightarrow E_a)$. We assume that each constellation differs from the others and will generate very different problems in the way reduced complexity can be transmitted. It will, therefore, be advantageous for the society to specialize generalized media in relation to these different problem areas. We have, indeed, found in our survey of the European tradition some indications that the societal differentiation of media and social systems has developed in the direction of increasing separation and functional specialization. We now want to argue that this functional differentiation of media and systems follows the outlined four-fold problem differentiation. That is to say: that truth, love, money, and power transmit reduced complexity in different types of situations which combine selectivity by experience or by action of alter and ego.[55] If this is true, the development of media out of primitive reality constructions can be understood as a way of coping with double contingency on the level of the social system of society.

The *first* case, in which alter's experiences are adopted (and, of course, adapted) as ego's experiences, is symbolized by *truth*. Truth expresses, in other words, the equivalence of experiences of alter and ego. In the course of social interaction truth emerges as a symbol in reference to which critical cases of transmission can be interpreted, normalized, and justified. As only experiences are involved and not actions selected by actors on their own account, truth at first and most easily is symbolized as reality itself. The problematical cases typically are those connected with "vicarious learning", i.e., with establishing and changing expectations on the ground of the experiences of others.[56] Vicarious learning is not simply imitation. It involves higher risks and higher responsibilities. Ego does not imitate actions which have led and may lead again to good results, avoiding the bad ones. Learning from others, he accepts on notice experiences as results of selection processes without taking the pain, or the time, or even without being able to repeat these processes. He may substitute communication control for experience and, finally, medium control for communication control. In any case, ego uses "context" as a guide for his own selection. Yet the relevant "context" may shift from personal familiarity with concrete alters to a very vague notion about the reliability of science.

This use of alter's experiences means paying for alleviation by higher risks, and these risks require symbolic elaboration and control. The institutionalization of truth as an increasingly generalized and specialized medium of communication satisfies this need of symbolic control of vicarious learning. Vicarious learning, then, seems to be the intervening variable between social and cultural evolution. This evolution requires more and quicker vicarious learning processes and the increasing functional refinement and elaboration of truth as symbolic medium. The mediating function of truth makes it possible to rely to an ever-increasing degree upon the experience of others, even without ever knowing them.[57]

The modern idea of truth, the development of which we have previously traced, has its most significant trait in a high degree of commitment to a cognitive, i.e., learning, style of expectation and disappointment reaction. This is, although obvious today, by no means an unproblematical matter, of course. Our differentiation of problems of selection transmission and problems of disappointment in the face of counterexpected selections, as introduced before, allows us to see the problem. The transmission of the selectivity of alter's experience to ego's experience ($A \rightarrow E$) is not necessarily controlled only by cognitive expectations and readiness to learn.[58] To treat transmission of experiences as a matter of cognition is too risky a choice to be universally valid. We can suppose, therefore, that for the same constellation ($A_e \rightarrow E_e$) a complementary medium has been developed on a normative basis.[59] Responding to this need Parsons has conceptualized a special medium as value commitments.[60] The concept of value is appropriate because it refers more to experience than to action, leaving the choice of action open to a large extent.[61] It remains to be explored precisely how reference to values works in the process of transmission of selected experiences covering normative restrictions on possible choices of topics, contents, and reasons.

Love is the medium in the *second* constellation ($A_e \rightarrow E_a$) where ego commits himself by action to the experiences and possible experiences of alter. Love is not only mutually gratifying action, common experience, and mutual "understanding" but also reciprocal selection. It requires that ego selects his action, and thereby identifies himself as a system, in relation to the world (including ego himself) as alter sees it; and that alter, as the other ego, acts in the same way. The transmission of reduced complexity crosses from experience to action. If love becomes reality, the selectivity of experience is reinforced by action.

Thus, the cultural history of love is not simply a history of varying conditions of sexual gratification. It depends on the evolution of society which changes the horizon of possibilities and the conditions of selectivity in respect to both experience and action. The enlargement of the public world makes it possible to conceive of love in the ancient way as public virtue. The contingency and selectivity not only of actions but also of experiences become visible. and love becomes functionally specialized to relate privately selected "worlds" of opinions, living style, taste, judgment, and preferences to privately selected action which no longer pertain to truth or universally shared meaning.[62] Love even claims not to be comprehendible by others.

As it is the case with truth, love also becomes specialized under modern conditions. Conceived as passionate affection it becomes unable to mediate all cases in which alter's experience selects ego's action ($A_e \rightarrow E_a$). Alongside of truth develops, although in a highly precarious and problematical way, a generalized medium of value commitments. Alongside of private, passionate love we can, following Parsons, identify *influence* as a complement for public situations.[63] In the case of influence, alter refers to his experiences, his reasons, and his "potentiality or reasoned elaboration,"[64] which indicate a certain course of action to ego, who is expected to direct his intentions accordingly.[65] Influence is appropriate for public use because it refers to the common world of accessible experiences and not to the private condition of reciprocal affection. As medium of communication it seems to be much less consolidated than love. It lacks a specialized supporting system and a symbiotic base and lives to a large extent on overdrawing truth.

Love and influence, then, are not truth and are not an exchange. It is shameful, as Hegel remarks,[66] to think of marriage as a contract. The idea of contractual exchange develops in another direction and comes close to our third type of constellation, $A_a \rightarrow E_e$, which can be ruled by *money*. In these cases the problem is that highly selective specification of interests by action of alter becomes experience for ego and has to be accepted at least as experience. The institutionalization of high selectivity of action would not be possible if the results were not accepted as experience (albeit disappointing experience) but were confronted with moral requirements and normative standards of right selection. It is, on the other hand, not possible to abandon moral criteria of choice wihout functional substitutes. Their function can be recovered on a higher level of abstraction in the form of money. The monetary mechanism formalizes the conditions of acceptance of action as experience (i.e., the conditions of laissez faire) in a way that does not restrict the contingency of choice except in a purely quantitative sense. It convinces people that they can deal with others who pursue actively their own selected interests, simply as an experience. The acceptance of selected action as experience is motivated by the artificially established fact that alter loses freedom insofar as he uses it; he "pays" for selection by transmitting the possibility of selection to others. Thus, money transmits selections under the condition that the freedom of selection is transmitted too. The complexity of possible choices is reduced for the actor, not for the system in which it fluctuates. Other media tend to blur this distinction of acting reduction (or processual reduction) and system reduction (or structural reduction). Acceptance of truth, or values, or love, or power in interaction binds in a way *both* sides. It narrows the possibilities of choice down to accepted reality or custom. To retain high contingency, i.e., other possibilities of experience or action, in the system needs a counter-current of motivation to change and innovate, an enduring struggle against habit. Money, on the other hand, has its unique feature in the fact that it continually regenerates contingency by the conditions of selection; it allows for specification of wants under the condition that indeterminateness is restored in others who accept money in exchange. A society which gives institutional primacy to the monetary mechanism (i.e., on the system level, to its economy) will, therefore, orient itself to an "open" future and will conceive of itself as moving ahead.

The well-known Marxist criticism of "political economy" relates precisely to the fact that the societal system could not differentiate, on the part of ego, experience and action. In other words the action of alter would define action, not only experience, of ego. As long as ego has no alternatives of action, the constellations $A_a \to E_e$ and $A_a \to E_a$ tend to merge. As long as the society cannot constitute very high complexity and contingency, money serves as a way to exercise power.

Our *fourth* problematic constellation, $A_a \to E_a$, clearly points to *power*. Power relates not only action to action, but the selectivity of action to the selectivity of another action.[67] It presupposes double contingency and furthermore a certain constellation of alternatives in the positions of both alter and ego. These alternatives are structured by social systems.

A system generates power if it constitutes alternatives of action for alter and of experience for ego which are negatively evaluated and consequently avoided by both, but more so by ego than by alter. Given these conditions a short cut on the level of expectations becomes possible. Alter can realize that ego realizes the possibility that alter chooses the unwanted alternative, and furthermore ego realizes this awareness of alter and alter this awareness of ego. Alter, then, can use that shortcut on the level of action by choosing one among his alternatives which defines, more or less, the action of ego. The "source" of his power remains invisible. It consists of unchosen alternatives and, finally, in system structures which provide these alternatives *and* the possibility to use them as unchosen alternatives. Although continually treated as negative, the sources of power are symbolized as *positive* values by reference to religious foundations of order, hierarchy, legitimate authority, democracy, or whatever. And legitimated by symbolization they offer differential communication advantages for those who are in a position of power.[68]

It is important to illuminate this complicated conditional context which generates power as a generalized medium of communication. If we recognize that the relation between system structure, power and selected actions is mediated by avoided alternatives, the relation between contingency and power becomes visible, and we can trace links between power and other system variables. Power may be founded on access to physical force, knowledge of shameful facts, the possibility to retire and live independently, the possibility to increase the burden of uncertainty or complexity for others, the possibility of timing or of refusing important contributions. Therefore, availability of power depends on very different structural conditions which generate avoidable alternatives. It depends on the degree to which actors rely on complementary expectations regarding the avoidance of available alternatives and on the differentiation of situations in which different sources of power are used.

There are, of course, other cases in which the selection of alter's action is transmitted as selection of ego's action. We may think of imitation or of naturally corresponding activities like question and answer, pointing and looking, giving and taking things.[69] But these are more or less unproblematical

Generalized Media in Action

cases (i.e., situations without conscious or available or attractive alternatives). Specialized media are, as we already know from the other types, differentiated and developed to cover problematical cases where the selections of alter would not be accepted as obvious. Media, and particularly power, make the transmission of reduced complexity from one selective event to another independent of what we could call the natural suitability of situations. This independence of processes from conditions that come about by themselves (from *physis,* in the Greek sense) seems to be required in all large and complex societal systems. In this sense, media seem to "mobilize resources."[70] This formulation of Parsons, however, needs careful interpretation. It does not mean access to a given stock of resources nor exploitation of usable realities. In the case of power, it does not mean that men can be brought to work hard on collective goals. It refers to possibilities, not to realities, and means that we can choose from more possibilities if we can institutionalize improbable choices and choice connections. In other words, we can say that media replace older forms of communal reality construction and reorganize the human possibilities of choice in a way which is compatible with high contingency.

MEDIATION AND THE DIFFERENTIATION OF ACTION AND EXPERIENCE

The differentiation of media, in my view, depends on the possibility to differentiate experience and action. It requires that alter knows and can treat ego either as experiencing or as acting and vice versa. Both ego and alter are supposed to be able to know in advance which way to attribute selections (experience or action) is appropriate in what situation, and both are supposed to be able to expect the complementary attitude of the other. This is, of course, a highly artificial condition. Fundamentally, all experience implies action in the sense of incessant bodily movement and ever-changing choice of topics.[71] Action, on the other hand, presupposes previous and accompanying experience to limit the range of responsible choice. On the level of the psychic system there is a permanent alternation of experience leading to action and action leading to experience. This fluctuation of primacy of function adjusts the psychic system to its environment. The differentiation of experience and action refers, therefore, not to psychic functions but to different ways to account for reduction of complexity. It has to be seen as a (psychologically improbable) achievement of social systems.

The need to differentiate experience and action

emerges with the increasing complexity and contingencies of social life.[72] This requires a more effective organization of specialized selective processes— more effective not simply in the sense of better perception or active goal attainment but in the sense of more effective combinations of selective performances which cope with highly complex and contingent possibilities. Differentiation of experience and action provides for a specialization of trust. The confidence in the experience of others can be ruled by other constraints than the confidence in the decision of others.[73] There may be, furthermore, institutionalized control relations between fields of experience and fields of action. Experience can, if differentiated, be organized to prepare and control conditions of action without taking the responsibility for decision. The advantages, however, of such a "division of labor" between experience and action can be realized only if sufficiently specialized media are available which differentiate the motives for accepting selections by experience or by action. It is in relation to this need, and not primarily in relation to a preestablished system differentiation, that media develop as successful solutions of interaction problems, and that they begin to organize reliable complementary expectations, so that they can be symbolically represented, institutionalized, and integrated in the cultural tradition. On this cultural level we can reconstruct their conceptual history and recognize distinct types.

These media, however, remain at the level of the social system "institutionalized improbabilities." They are improbable because they presuppose a differentiation of experience and action which lacks a sufficient base in the psychic systems. Media are, furthermore, supposed to bring about improbable connections of choices; they also are generalized, specialized, and function as routine solution of problem cases. They presuppose very complicated institutional arrangements for information selection, organization of role support, neutralization of dysfunctions, and so on. Only in social systems can improbable selection chains become expectable and reliable performances. Their stabilization depends on the maintenance of systems as areas of reduced complexity, of structured patterns, and of boundaries which, by their selective function, guarantee the higher order of an "internal environment" to every part of the action process.

Generalized media evolve, then, in close interdependence with social systems. Although stimulated, as we have seen, by recurrent problems in interaction, the differentiation of media into distinct institutional mechanisms depends on the social evolution at the level of society. It would not suffice to explain the development of generalized media as a consequence of system differentiation. On the contrary, system differentiation seems rather to follow the lines of possible media. There are, besides, other important interdependencies which have their roots in the changing complexity of the social system of the society. The main points are that higher complexity of the societal system means, on the whole, higher contingency of every item, higher risks of selection, higher improbability of selection transmission, increasing needs for media and, again, higher risks at the level on which media are institutionalized.

Older societies begin to differentiate media at the level of elementary interaction, relying sometimes more on power, sometimes more on truth or on personal attachment. We know examples of institutional differentiation of specific media even in primitive societies.[74] These institutions are related to dysfunctions of the main structure of the societal system; they are not this structure itself. In the course of further evolution, particularly in societies of higher culture, we observe increasing specialization which may find its center in the palace or the courthouse, in the market or in the academy. These centers remain institutions of city life with almost no impact on village life. Until the newer times no society could build its system structure on the principle of functional differentiation and specialization of generalized media. In its main structures e.g., the household and the institutions of political rule, the older societies tended, on the contrary, to attain acceptance of communications by a *combination* of different media. The powerful ruler should be at the same time the source of true communication, the beloved, and one of the rich who distributes favors. Such functionally diffused, combinations show remarkable advantages. They stabilize selection transmission by an amalgamation of different motivational patterns and provide for a limited elasticity of institutions. The ruler can rely on truth *and* love *and* power *and* money, and he can shift emphasis in different interactional contexts and use truth *or* love *or* power *or* money as circumstances suggest. It seems natural and unavoidable for him not only to long for power but to accumulate wealth, to claim truth, and also to expect the love of his people. He finds himself, therefore, under severe tactical limitations. Using his power he should not exhaust his financial resources, endanger his possibility to think of himself as beloved, or lose the connection of action with accepted truth. He may exploit institutional elasticities. He may interpret truth, or bribe the interpreters, and dream up the heroic history of his clan.[75] He may augment his riches by means of power and vice versa. He may, with the aid of his entourage, continue to think or himself as beloved

though contrary to fact. He will, nevertheless, be immobilized by considerations for other media and, consequently, will not be able to attain the abstract freedom of choice inherent in specialization. The ruler could not afford to concentrate on power and to be indifferent against truth, love, and money except insofar as they have an impact on power.[76] In this respect Machiavelli's *Prince* opens a new epoch.

Modern society has one of its distinguishing features in the fact that media differentiation has become the principle of subsystem-building at the level of the societal system. Society itself is no longer the politically constituted social system (*societas civilis*) but the encompassing system which constitutes a political system for the special function of the generation and administration of power. The economy, too, changes from household with occasional external market relations into a societal subsystem which uses money to mediate communications between firms, markets, and households. In the case of love we have accepted and institutionalized the highly improbable principle that marriage has to be based on and maintained by love and not by economic reason or by power relations. Finally, scientific research has become a social system in which scientists are supposed to produce true sentences and control their communications by standards of intersubjective transmissibility.

Functional-structural differentiations of this kind are, of course, highly artificial. They split up the reciprocal institutional supports between media and have to substitute, therefore, specialized systems. This differentiation and specialization increases the social visibility of selective processes and spreads the consciousness of contingency. These changes uproot the hitherto unquestioned institutional framework of the society. The quest for other possibilities, and thereby the quest for certainty, becomes universal; the world itself appears as contingent. All this changes the level at which uncertainties have to be absorbed and implies new kinds of risks and performances. The societal system seems to attain a new evolutionary level of system complexity, structural generalization, and selection control which differs in significant ways from any older type.

DOUBLE CONTINGENCY, MEDIATION, AND SYSTEM EVOLUTION

A theoretical explanation of this evolutionary development has to accept the fact that there is no one-way causal relation between the development of differentiated and specialized media on the one hand and the development of system differentiation. Evolution depends on possibilities of selection which presuppose interdependence as well as independence between the evolutionary mechanism.[77] This means, in our case, that on the general level of culture a broader range of media becomes available for the different constellations of selection transmission. There are, for example, many cultural possibilities to symbolize "influence" which could fit into the constellation of alter's experience and ego's action. The evolutionary success and the societal prominence of some of these media depends on their systematization. Some of them are more capable than others to solve system problems which arise in the course of societal evolution. The case of art, particularly modern "aesthetic" art, shows that media can survive as abstract cultural possibilities without adequate systematization as subsystems of society.[78] Other media like power, money, love, and truth had a more successful career.

The conceptual articulation of generalized media, therefore, is not sufficient to predict or explain evolutionary success and stabilization in functionally specialized subsystems of the society. Although all media relate to the general problem of double contingency they differ in respect to additional functions and constraints they might have in particular subsystems. This question remains to a large extent open, because a theory of society which could answer it is not available. We can only offer some suggestions to close the gap.

If we are right in our assumption that system-building increases the range of possibilities (and thereby contingency) by differentiation and limitation,[79] one main societal problem consists in the increasing complexity of possibilities. This accounts for the fact that the society prefers and develops media which can cope with high complexity. Coping with high complexity means, in the case of media, the capacity to regulate the transmission of selections for many different and variable topics. Media have to be, to a large extent, generalized, i.e., indifferent as to content. This generalization is required on two levels, the symbolic level and the symbiotic level; and its success depends on their integration. At the symbolic level it refers to the symbolization of meaning as a code for the communication process, that has to be compatible with many possibilities of interpretation and application. Generalization generates problems of "respecification."[80] Media differ in respect to the possibilities of respecification, i.e., in their "ease of use." It is easier to refer to money in the communication process—you have simply to add the intended amount—than to refer to beauty; it is easier to talk power than to communicate in terms of influence. The gain of time, the advantage of speed, is an invaluable asset in the processing of complex systems and gives some media priority over others.

The term "symbiotic level" refers to the necessity

for ego and alter to share the same organic and physical world.[81] They have to live together—not simply to experience the same impressions or to act complementarily. Some processes of the organic system, e.g., sensual perception or sexuality, have a high plasticity and social sensitivity and carry organic and social selectivity at the same time.

The capacity of symbiotic processes to motivate the acceptance of meaning is not simply a function of organic complexity. It depends essentially on the dimension of time which enlarges the realm of relevant facts. Men can, as Hobbes argues, expect want and bodily suffrances, and this expected continuity of organic problems gives reason a chance to generalize power, to establish the Leviathan. That sexual interests are more or less chronic is a condition of love. That past perceptions can be remembered, reported, and their recurrence anticipated is a condition of truth. In this regard, the evolutionary success of some media seems to depend on the meaningful interpretation, control, and utilization of sufficiently plastic organic capacities.[82] Their symbiotic base is generalized in the sense that it broadens the range of compatibility between organic and social processes. This makes it possible to differentiate organic and social systems further in the direction of relative independence of variation.

By generalization on both the symbolic and the symbiotic level, the code function as well as the motivational function of certain media open possibilities of application and combination under varying conditions. One can combine clearly superior physical force with a very broad range of meaningful commands;[83] the sources of influence, on the other hand, e.g., scientific reputation or professional standing, impose many more restrictions on effective communication. More highly generalized media are superior in combinatorial and adaptive capacity. They can regulate more topics, they can be used under highly varying circumstances and yet remain identical, in very different situations. They can operate, therefore, in the context of different system problems. Truth may be useful for technological and educational purposes, power may be useful in enforcing justice and in deterring enemies, love has its recreational and its procreational uses. Thus, media are specialized in respect to the cultural interpretation of interactional constellations, particularly in respect to experience and action of ego and alter; they are not necessarily tied to specific system problems, i.e., not functionally specialized in the system sense.[84]

These considerations suggest that there is no one-way relationship between the evolutionary development of media and system differentiation, but a relation of complex interdependence not only in the empirical but also in the analytical sense.

Analytically, we can distinguish at least three relationships:

1. The generalization of media is related to system differentiation in so far as *both are related to the problem of contingency*. System building and system differentiation differentiate possibilities and increase contingencies. This requires the solution of problems of selection by mechanisms, e.g., media, which have to be incorporated into the system structure. Given an elementary (archaic) system of society which constitutes its possibilities primarily by language, further system differentiation can develop only if sufficiently generalized mechanisms are available to handle contingency. The generalization of media, then, becomes a strategic prerequisite of further differentiation of society in a two-fold sense: To adjust itself to an ever-changing internal environment of the societal system each subsystem needs, on the one hand, higher adaptive capacities, particularly capacities to "socialize" selective experiences and actions, e.g., media. On the other hand, each subsystem has to rely on corresponding mechanisms in other subsystems. Power, for example, has to be available for collectively binding decisions on whatever decision problems arise in the family (this is the turning point from archaic to high culture societies) and in the economy (this is the turning point from high culture to modern societies). The use of political power, on the other hand, can be autonomous and flexible only if it can assume that family life adjusts to political decisions, that even strains of democratic participation in politics does not destroy love, that the economy adjusts to (not only: is obligated by) political decisions, because the respective media are sufficiently generalized.[85]

2. In another sense, the interdependence of the generalization of media and the differentiation of systems consists in the fact that *specialized media become the primary focus* of system *differentiation*. It seems that the integration of subsystems goes according to the rule of one system, one medium. At least the primary subsystems of the society, the political system, the economic system, the families, and the social system of science are organized around the specialized media of power, money, love, and truth respectively. As a result, media are selected, symbolized, and institutionalized not only in response to the interaction constellations of experience and action, but also in response to the requirements and consequences of system differentiation. The primary division of possible media according to experience or action of ego and alter remains fundamental because their primary function of selection transmission differentiates along these lines. This gives each societal subsystems its distinctive style of selection. Additional requirements grow out of the problems of system differentiation. The evolutionary differentiation of politics and household did require constitution and cultural interpretation, i.e., legitimation of power; the differentiation of the economy and family-households did require a new interpretation of love as purely private, intimate affection and it gave money a new meaning involving not only the exchange of goods but the interpretation of actions as work and of goods as commodities.[86]

The critical position of specialized media implies that other structural decisions of subsystems, particularly their internal differentiation, refer to media. The differentiation of the political system is conceived as division of power; the differentiation of the small modern family is qualified by love. The central relevance of media becomes also apparent in the fact that it explains the particular combination of societal problems which are delegated to one particular subsystem: Education and research are combined by the common use of truth; production, exchange, and consumption by the common use of money. Recreation and procreation belong to the family because and insofar as they use love. The main societal functions of politics, peace and justice, both involve the medium of power. From a purely analytical point of view all these functions could be separated as referring to different system problems. Therefore, their combination in the process of societal differentiation cannot be explained by reference to societal problems, prerequisites, or functions alone; it depends upon the identity of specialized media.

3. A third relationship between media and societal differentiation depends on the fact that language and cultural development produce a surplus of possible media from which social systems can select those which can best be connected with systems problems. The symbolization of reasons for confidence, influence, and cooperation which are possible and actually in use exceeds the possibilities of system differentiation. Only some of the possible ways to code and motivate selection transmission are chosen as focus for subsystems of the society and, thereby, gain prominence and stability on the system level of the society.

We have discussed one of the reasons for this revolutionary career: capacity for generalization. Besides this important aspect, societal differentiation generates problems of interchange between subsystems. At this point, our theory of media links closely with the problems on which Parsons has elaborated. Differentiation does not inhibit the flow of communications between subsystems; on the contrary, it increases it. This problem of communication overload produced by high-contingency system differentiation provides the point of reference for a reformulation of the theory of interchange processes. The object of interchange cannot be defined in terms of specific media such as commodities, or decisions, or affection because such a definition would be only partially correct. It has to be conceived of in general terms as reduced complexity. The need for interchange is the need to accept the selection performances of other systems without duplicating their choice processes. Systems contribute, on the other hand, the interchange process selections organized in terms of a specialized medium. Therefore, the interchange process is ruled by the media of the transmitting system: The communication from the economy to the polity has to be stated and accepted in terms of money, the communication from the polity to the economy in terms of power. The interchange process depends, then, on translation, on decoding and recoding of inputs. The scientific system contributes true knowledge that can, nevertheless be reevaluated by standards of money, or power, or love in the other systems. Science itself receives money to be used in research under criteria of truth. The current crises of the universities show that it also needs power inputs from the political system to establish peaceful longterm cooperation. In both cases it is essential that money remain money and power remain power and that both, nevertheless, can be reevaluated in terms of research and can structure the scientific communication from this point of view. To sum up, the processes of societal interchange depend on translatable media that are institutionalized in other subsystems. This requirement is, in addition to generalization, a further condition which media have to satisfy in the context of system differentiation.

A final point concerns the increasing risks which accompany the process of differentiation, generalization, and specialization of media as well as of systems. We shall elaborate on this point later. At the moment it may suffice to state that further conditions of evolutionary success are to be sought in the availability of risk-absorbing mechanisms. The institutionalization of interdependencies between power and law is the best example;[87] interdependencies of money and competition and of love and habit may be others. These examples show again some of the symbolic as well as institutional difficulties which had to be solved in the course of the evolutionary career of specific media.

LEVELS OF MEDIATION

When symbolic media loosen their anchorage to concrete and multifunctional institutions, and when they function without support and constraint by other media, they change their meaning. They lose their reference to a "cosmic" image of the world and become more process-oriented. This process orientation has two aspects: complexity and performance.

If media are functionally specialized and related to special problems of double contingency, their domain of possible processes enlarges and more selections can be transmitted. This effect has been called, by Parsons, "mobilization of resources." It comes about by an interesting relation between restriction and expansion of possibilities. Very strict modern conditions of truth exclude the whole area of goals, norms, and values and, nevertheless, increase the number of true sentences that can be formulated. Romantic love is praised as a 'rare, unique, almost unbearable passion and, at the same time, links more couples than ever before in intimate relations which are supposed to be ruled by love. The exercise of power is, under the condition of political peace, severely restricted by the state monopoly to decide on physical coercion[88]; it expands by the same fact, enormously since the legal rules governing property, contract, and organizational authority provide a basis for nonviolent power relations. Money, finally, is characterized by chronic scarcity, without regard to felt needs, and regulates, through scarcity, an economy which satisfies more needs than ever before.

These remarkable parallels cannot be explained by the particular meaning of the different media, by the essence of truth, love, or the like. This supports our main thesis that generalized media are related to the problem of contingency. We had defined contingency as visibility of other possibilities in selective events, and this visibility seems to change with increasing differentiation and specialization of media. Some layers of possible experiences and actions become accessible only by effective exclusion of others. The specialization of media, then, performs a strategic reduction which opens access to other possibilities. These other possibilities of experience and action depend on the type of reduction that constitutes them. The contingencies of truth are not the contingencies of love, and the risks of power not identical with the risks of money. This divergence has important consequences for system problems and system boundaries, which will be discussed later. It puts, furthermore, media themselves and the mediated communication processes under performance stress. They have to perform selection transmission in very complex systems and are judged by results.[89]

Under such conditions of independence, high contingency, and specific performance stress, media develop some common traits whose similarity is again remarkable. Three special features are of particular interest to us: (1) the higher generalization with increasing strains in the relation between the symbolic level and its symbiotic base, (2) the suppression of what we may call self-satisfying activities which elude the motivational mechanisms, and (3) the need for reflexive processes that can be applied to themselves.

1. Every generalized medium is based on symbiotic processes which connect it with the organic systems but overdraws their selective potential. By generalization the social selectivity of these processes becomes, to some extent, independent from their organic selectivity, especially in the sense that temporal synchronization is not necessary. Perception, sexual gratification, subjection to physical violence, fulfillment or nonfulfillment of organic needs can be anticipated or remembered and used as motive without immediate connection with problem solutions in the organic system.[90]

This being so, we have to expect that admission of more contingent possibilities of experience or action in the domain of a medium does increase the distance between the symbolic and the symbiotic level. Higher generalized capacities on the symbolic level lead to increasing strain in its relation to the symbiotic base. We know, for example, that the modern abstraction of "scientific" truth in the sense of certainty of intersubjective transmission has changed the relation between theory and empirical reference of knowledge. The problem of this relation has become the main issue of the theory of knowledge and its methodological refinements and remains, without institutional solution, an enduring burden of scientific progress. In the case of *love*, the parallel problem lies in its reference to sexual relations. Older cultural traditions knew, of course, passionate sexual love as a fact of human life but distinguished clearly between love as public virtue and sexual interests. In modern times love became redefined and institutionalized as passionate individual feeling without regard to status, wealth, family interest or even personal biography and, therefore, culminates in sexual relations as proof and fulfillment. *Money* has its symbiotic base in consumption. Higher contingency of consumptive choices is attainable only by generalization of the monetary mechanism. This generalization makes it unavoidable to accept that the value of money does not exist in its own possible consumption or its inherent value, nor in legal rights to certain goods, but that it depends on the functioning of the economic system under changing conditions. High economic contingency demands the use of *changing* prices as an adaptive mechanism, which requires giving up the institutionalization of confidence on more concrete levels (for example, the moral-legal idea of "just prices").[91] Political *power* was always connected, on the symbiotic level, with the real assets of physical force. But here, too, we observe corresponding changes in the relations between the symbolic and the symbiotic level. A higher generalization of power was attainable only by legitimation and legalization in the sense that the use of power was bound to the form and procedures of jurisdiction and legislation. This formalization of power requires not only concentration but effective monopolization of access to physical force in the political system. Political power is not only backed by physical force but, in a new way, responsible for physical force, for the reasonable use of its organizational potential and for all interests which need a protection by force.

2. The management of increasing strains in the relations between symbolic and symbiotic levels is a necessary, but not sufficient, condition of further evolution. Moreover, the motivational force of generalized media depends on the institutionalization of barriers against certain self-sufficient practices. There are possible shortcuts on the symbiotic level which offer functionally equivalent problem solutions without interaction. The use of these shortcuts has to be discouraged, if not suppressed. An equivalent for truth may be attained by the private means of intuition, by subjective experience of evidence. In newer times such private ways to truth became increasingly suspected and disapproved.[92] Sexual self-sufficiency has a long history of moral incrimination which could be extended to all sexual practices for shunning the social commitment of love, including prostitution and homosexuality. The monetary mechanism, too, is highly vulnerable to shortcuts. The punishment of forgery becomes necessary as soon as the symbolic value differentiates from the material value. But the dangers grow with increasing complexity and increasing distances between the symbolic and the symbiotic levels. The incrimination of certain credit practices and controls of the banking system have to be added, and finally the danger of self-sufficiency has to be banned on the critical level of political decisions which steer the monetary mechanism or simply make money for political purposes. The political independence of central banks can be judged in this context. In the case of power, self-sufficiency means violent self-help. Its control is connected with the spread of peace, from house peace to territorial peace. The prohibition of immediate violence makes power accumulation dependent on the social conditions of interaction and to expectational control. The increase of power can become independent of further increases in physical force and can organize higher contingencies of action. On higher levels of power organization, then, new possible shortcuts emerge, e.g., corruption in office, and these have to be excluded.

3. Here, we recognize, besides generalization, another requirement of high contingency, namely, strategic negation of motivational shortcuts on different structural levels. These different levels cannot be constituted simply by different degrees of symbolic abstraction. They emerge by an arrangement of processes which could be called "reflexive." Processes are reflexive if they can be applied to themselves or to processes of the same kind before reaching their objectives.[93] One can teach teaching before teaching the children, think about thinking, decide about decisions, expect expectations, and so on. Reflexive arrangements intend to increase the selective capacity by building and connecting different levels of selective activities, by choosing possible choices. They emerge with increasing complexity and contingency of social systems.

This very general phenomenon can also be observed in the realm of generalized media. Transmission of reduced complexity can become reflexive if the special constellations of transmission by truth, love, money, or power are applied to processes which select special constellations of the same type which makes effective transmission, possible. In a short, inadequate way, we can speak of true conditions of the search for truth (or theory of knowledge, or research about research), of loving love, of financing money, of overpowering power. These formulations already suggest the question of the evolutionary conditions which can support reflexivity of this kind.

We know of roots in old high-culture societies, but only in the modern age does the societal system attain a degree of complexity which requires and supports the institutionalization of reflexive media. The eighteenth century, in particular, brings the breakthrough of conscious elaboration which establishes this new level of evolutionary universals.[94] It brings, with Kant, a new way to ask for true (a priori) conditions of true knowledge on a different, "transcendental," metascientific level. It brings the romantic idea of loving for love[95] (and not for rank, or riches, or beauty, or any other particular qualities or relations). It sees the first conscious attempts to create money above the level of the credit system.[96] The concept of power begins to lose its hierarchic connotations, first by the theory of the separation of power and then by providing for democratic government in the sense that even the highest power is subjected to power and that superior power yields, under specified circumstances, to lesser powers.[97]

The essential point seems to be that reflexive mechanisms demand identity of process, at least of process type, and are, therefore, compatible with functional differentiation and specialization of systems. They do not combine different media into one arrangement of reciprocal support characteristic (as we have seen) of older societies. They do not provide power by truth or love or money. On the contrary, the strengthening of the selective function for a highly contingent environment requires that code and process remain the same, that power preselects and structures the conditions for the exercise of power—and not for research or lovemaking; or that alter's love preselects and structures the conditions for ego's love—and not for his intellectual, truth-seeking curiosity or his power drive. This, of course, does not preclude the interpenetration or interdependence of processes.

The loss of reciprocal support implies, as we know, higher risks. It may, in part, be compensated by reflexive differentiation of processes. Disturbing events may upset the reflexive mechanism on one level, but not on all levels at the same time. Occasional doubts in one's own love may be overcome by the continuing love of the other. Scientific revolutions may hit theoretical conceptions but not "facts," or methods, nor end the metascientific controversies. Insolvency of firms, even of banks, may cause somebody to lose his money without deranging the monetary mechanism; and crises on the level of monetary policy may, on the other hand, not mean bad business for all firms. Reflexive differentiation explains a feature which characterizes modern society, it combines high disturbability with high recuperative capacity.

Reflexiveness seems, furthermore, to be a correlate of "double interchange." Parsons has shown that subsystems of a highly differentiated society communicate on different levels at the same time.[98] They cannot rely exclusively on exchange relations which satisfy both sides immediately. The flexibility of interchanges and the range of choice open to the participants is enhanced if they are able to accept input in generalized form, e.g., money, or generalized political support, or patterned readiness for loving love. This requires internal mechanisms that specify and apply generalized potentialities. Parsons has tried to identify "integrative standards" which rule this process of respecification. In addition, the coining of generalized input into small usable money seems to require either translatability of media into other types—we have already used the example of the scientific system transforming the input of money and power into potentialities of research—or reflexiveness in the sense that the medium controls its own application. The general readiness for loving love, which can be learned, becomes attached to specific persons; money is spent; power is used to program binding decisions. In all these cases, the generalized resource constitutes freedom of choice in its use and restrains, at the same time, the possibilities of its use by code identity.

MEDIATION, RISKS, AND THE EMERGENCE OF A WORLD SOCIETY

Very complex societies produce high contingency of experience and action and reorganize their communication processes by symbolic media in the direction of differentiation, specialization, generalization, strategic negation, and reflexiveness. This combination of patterns seem to be selected as structure of a very complex societal system. In the evolutionary perspective it has to be understood as a structural choice which makes social systems compatible with high contingency and strengthens their selective capacity.

Under these conditions, social systems are all the more forced to focus their structure on the problem of selectivity transmission. Generalized media, their institutional prerequisites, and the dysfunctions of their specialization move into a position of central concern. They gain prominence in the value structure of the society, displacing religious values in their function to symbolize the collective unity of the system; and they regulate the boundary definition and boundary maintenance. Finally, we shall track some of these consequences to illustrate, once again, our main thesis, that double contingency, selection transmission, and generalized media are interdependent evolutionary achievements.

If truth seeking and communication of knowledge for its own sake become the main goals of a specific social system, this structural decision generates secondary problems. Problems of *information overload* and problems of *motivation* to continue without immediate, tangible rewards come up and have to be solved within the social system of scientific research. The system has to incorporate in its value structure two kinds of contradictions: The first is a stress on thoroughness of research and publications over against the impossibility of comprehensiveness and complete access to all relevant knowledge; the second is the goal of universal intersubjective transmissibility of knowledge and the abstraction from any personal source of knowledge over against the importance of priorities in discovery and of personal reputation.[99] The social system of science has, in these specific respects, to provide for sufficiently ambivalent institutions and for the possibility to act according to contradictory values.

There are analogous, but highly different, secondary problems in systems which focus on love. To found marriage and family on passionate love and nothing else than love is, as any unifunctional prescription,[100] a highly unrealistic structural choice and needs correctives. Love, in other words, is not a complete description of structural requirements of family life. The problem of disappointment and family

disorganization by romantic love is a well-known topic in fiction and science[101] and may not be solved simply by comprehensive premarital sexual "learning". The smallness of the system as well as love itself inhibits a structural solution, by strict role differentiation.[102] The contradictory requirements are embodied in the myth of romantic love,[103] and the ensuing problems have to be solved partly by the accumulation of a history of common life which serves as a substitute for structure and partly by a continuing process of strategic behavior and adaptive response on both sides.[104]

In the case of the economy, the monetary mechanism stimulates high differentiation of the economic system (division of labor) and, in consequence, has a high innovating potential. It sets free internal dynamics, which then have to be equilibrated. This means that strategies of stabilization and strategies of growth begin to diverge and that economic measures at all system levels have highly differentiated consequences in different subsystems and different time horizons. The ensuing problems have to be solved either by the market or by political decision making, but neither of the two guarantees optimal or even secure solutions.

The dysfunctions of political power have been the most obvious of all, and their discussion has had an important impact on the organization of the political system. The famous device of "division of powers" and its various institutional realizations were thought to sift out all use of power which could not appear as law. This solution, however, neglected the problem of power generation. Mainly for this reason, the governmental system which separated legislative, executive, and judicial competencies was infiltrated by the tendency to build subsystems for politics and for administration.[105] Politics, then, serves as the subsystem for power generation and the administration serves as the subsystem for programmed power spending. The question remains open as to how far it is possible to realize and maintain the functional separation of politics and administration not only as separation of situations[106] or differentiation of roles but as differentiation of specialized interactional subsystems which work under different criteria of success and rationality. This structural differentiation of politics and administration has to be maintained in the interest of high and diversified political power against tendencies which inhere in the power mechanism itself, namely, tendencies to narrow the possibilities of choice by a more or less concrete fusion of political and administrative considerations.

We could go farther into these researchable fields and specify the subsystem problems, contradictory requirements, dysfunctions, and burdens of concrete behavior that follow from an institutional and organizational differentiation of media. It is more important, however, to change the system reference and to consider. in conclusion, the consequences on the level of the society. The society is the encompassing social system and the only system which is complex enough to institutionalize the functional differentiation of generalized media. This differentiation requires structural changes on the level of the societal system itself. Usually, these changes have been described as corresponding generalizations of the integrative mechanisms.[107] Another, perhaps even more important, set of consequences concerns the boundaries of the societal system.

In general we know that increasing system differentiation means increasing diversification of system boundaries.[108] .In segmentary societies we find several layers of narrower and larger societal boundaries which can be activated according to circumstances, e.g., for purposes of conflict resolution.[109] With increasing functional differentiation the subsystems begin to stabilize their own intrasocietal boundaries and, at the same time, their own demand for societal boundaries.[110] For a long time the integration of societies by common territorial boundaries remained possible. This possibility seems to correlate with low effectiveness of communication. The external boundaries could symbolize internal unity in spite of differentiation of interests because they did transcend the possibilities of effective communication in everyday life and, therefore, did not motivate internal conflicts.

This situation has changed drastically. Subsystems which focus on different generalized media of communication can no longer agree on common external frontiers. Territorial frontiers are reduced to political ones. They are boundaries of political power insofar as power accepts the form of jurisdiction. The political territory does not define boundaries of the society that are meaningful for possible love matches, for common search of truth, or for profitable economic exchanges. In the abstract perspectives of specialized media and on the basis of improved communication techniques and mobility, any subuniversal formulas for the boundaries of society become obsolete.[111] It is not compatible with modern scientific truth to refuse its acceptance from partners who live outside the reach of political power. It makes no sense, economically, to refuse to compare the advantages of exchanges with persons whom one does not love. The functional specialization of selection transmission produces permanent spillover effects which destroy the meaning of territorial frontiers and, thereby, the idea of regional societies. In fact, there exists today only one society on earth: the world society.[112]

The environment of this one global society cannot consist of other human societies, and it can no longer be marked by territorial frontiers. It consists of other possibilities of experience and action which are not selected by social systems but are contingently available to human beings. It contains the possibilities which cannot be treated as rightfully selected and cannot be transmitted as reduced complexity by one medium or the other, but which exist, nevertheless, as language and the human capacity for negation constitute more possibilities than can be accepted.

It is remarkable, moreover, that the evolution of one single world society came to be reflected in the concept of the world itself. This concept has changed in a significant way, namely, in its relation to the problem of contingency.

The scholastics could think of the contingency of the world only as the infinite possibility of other worlds, as a plurality of possible worlds.[113] Only in modern times has it become possible to conceive the world itself as an infinity of other possibilities of human experience and action. In his famous phenomenological analysis of human consciousness, Edmund Husserl described the world as the last "horizon" of conscious human acts.[114] Conceived as the last horizon which accompanies every act that tries to transcend previously given horizons, the world is an immanent infinity of other possibilities, an "and so on and so forth" of experience and action.

If we accept this view of a single and infinite world, the definition of possibilities (and, consequently, the possibility of possibilities) becomes a problem.[115] It is at this point that the transcendental phenomenology became unreliable, falling back into intuitive essentialism. And it is at this point that the theory of interaction systems comes in. Social systems (including all levels from global society to a cocktail party) are selective performances which constitute limited and viable realms of action and experience.[116] The world is the contingency of systems.

Put into this context of integrated thinking about "world," "possibilities," "systems," and "interaction," the classical theory of society as the comprehensive social system can be reformulated. The society is a social system whose selective structure constitutes the meaningful world as its environment and guarantees, at the same time, narrower, domesticated environments for other social systems. We know successful evolutionary solutions of this problem on the basis of limited territories, plural societies, religiously closed world definitions, incomplete functional differentiation of subsystems and media, and functional primacy of the political subsystem. But the conditions for this type of solution have changed in all respects. The main disruptive, innovating, enlarging force has been a reorganization of the mechanism which transmit selections: a reorganization in the direction of higher differentiation, specialization, and symbolic generalization of media and with the effect of higher social complexity and contingency. This has changed the conditions under which a social system can operate effectively as society. If we continue to think in terms of the old European tradition, the place of society seems almost void today. Even the most formalized abstraction from this tradition (the principle of self-sufficiency of the society, the definition of systems in terms of wholes and parts, the postulate of the hierarchic priority of normative over cognitively conditioned mechanisms, and communal solidarity, which Parsons carries on) have become questionable. If we are unbiased in our observation, the emergence of a new global system of world society appears as an undeniable fact. This requires corresponding changes in the concept of society. And if we are right in our assumption that the reorganization of media has propelled society up to this new level of evolution, the further exploration of these generalized media may contribute, on the conceptual as well as the empirical level, to an adequate understanding of this new phenomenon.

NOTES

1. For comments on the specific form of negation and its contrast to the Aristotelian tradition see Manfred Riedel, "Zum Verhältnis von Ontologie und politischer Theorie bei Hobbes" in Reinhart Koselleck and Roman Schnur (eds.), *Hobbes-Forschungen* (Berlin: Dunker & Humblot, 1969), pp. 103-118.

2. For an explicit statement see the formulations in: Talcott Parsons and Edward A. Shils (eds.), *Toward a General Theory of Action* (Cambridge: Harvard University Press, 1951), pp. 63ff.

3. See "The Position of Identity in the General Theory of Action," in Chad Gordon and Kenneth J. Gergen (eds.), *The Self in Social Interaction*, Vol. 1 (New York: J. Wiley, 1968), pp. 11-23 (14).

4. See John Finley Scott, "The Changing Foundations of the Parsonian Action Scheme," *American Sociological Review*, 28 (1963), pp. 716-735.

5. See Jürgen Ritsert, "Substratbegriffe in der Theorie des sozialen Handelns: Über das Interaktionsschema bei Parsons und in der Parsonskritik," *Soziale Welt*, 19 (1968), pp. 119-137.

6. As is the case with fundamental problems, there is an almost irresistible temptation to solve it by "sub-stantivation" by putting substantives like system, institution, community, leadership at the place of the problem of contingency. This is, of course, the way the problem finds its solution in the language of daily life, but sociology needs a more careful and sophisticated way to retrace and reconstruct the problem solutions of daily life—if only to preserve the possibility of other solutions, i.e., the contingency of solution.

7. For a short general exposition of this point of view see Niklas Luhmann, "Soziologie als Theorie sozialer Systeme,"

Kölner Zeitschrift für Soziologie und Sozial psychologie, 19 (1967), pp. 615-644, reprinted in Niklas Luhmann, *Soziologische Aufklärung: Aufsätze zur Theorie sozialer Systeme* (Köln-Opladen, Westdeutscher Verlag, 1970), pp. 113-136.

8. See Niklas Luhmann, "Normen in soziologischer Perspektive," *Soziale Welt*, 20 (1969), pp. 28-48.

9. Talcott Parsons and Edward A. Shils (eds.), *op. cit.* See, however, the index of *The Social System* (Glencoe, Ill.: The Free Press, 1951) on "double contingency."

10. The critical point is, of course, not only that action is conceived of as evaluated causality, but that this conception is, following Max Weber, who himself draws in this respect on Heinrich Rickert, maintained on the analytical as well as on the concrete level for scientific conceptualization as well as for the description of the intended meaning of actors themselves; and that the scheme of ends and means is supposed to integrate both levels. The historic roots of this pragmatic theory of knowledge are exposed by a very careful study of Horst Baier, "Von der Erkenntnistheorie zur Wirklichkeitswissenschaft: Eine Studie über die Begründung der Soziologie bei Max Weber," Ms. Münster 1969.

11. See Wsevolod W. Isajiw, *Causation and Functionalism in Sociology* (London: Schocken Books, 1968), pp. 83ff.

12. See Hans Blumenberg, "Kontingenz," in *Die Religion in Geschichte und Gegenwart*, Vol. III (Tübingen: 1959), pp. 1793-4, with further indications. For newer research see Heinrich Schepers, "Möglichkeit und Kontingenz: Zur Geschichte der philosophischen Terminologie vor Leibniz," *Studi e Ricerche di Storia della Filosofia* No. 55, (Torino: 1963); Heinrich Schepers, "Zum Problem der Kontingenz bei Leibniz: Die beste der möglichen Welten," in *Collegium Philosophicum: Studien J. Ritter zum 60 Geburtstag* (Basel-Stuttgart 1965), pp. 326-350.

English-speaking readers may consult Philotheus Boehner, "The Tractatus de praesdestinatione et de praescientia Dei et de futuris contingentibus of William Ockham *St. Bonaventura N. 4* (1945), pp. 41ff.; B. Wright, "Necessary and Contingent Being in St. Thomas," *The New Scholasticism*, 25 (1951), pp. 439-466; Edmund F. Byrne, *Probability and Opinion* (Den Haag: M. Nijhoff, 1968), pp. 188ff.

13. The negation refers, as Leibniz did make clear, not to the possibility itself—this would mean impossibility—but to the being whose possibility is stated. *Contingens* is a positive statement about the possibility of negative being.

14. See Gerard Smith, "Avicenna and the Possibles," *The New Scholasticism*, 17 (1943), pp. 340-357; Celestino Solaguren, "Contingencia y creación en la filosofía de Duns Escoto," *Verdad y Vida*, 24 (1966), pp. 55-100.

Particularly clear on the double sense of the term is the statement of an anonymous author of the fifteenth century, reprinted by Léon Baudry (ed.), *La querelle des futurs contingents* (Louvain 1465-1475) (Paris: J. Vrin, 1950), pp. 126-133 (127): "contingens igitur in prima sui divisione est duplex. Unum quod ex significato idem est quod possibile; et si accipitur contingens absolute, non considerando contingens per habitudinem et respectum ad causam suam. *Aliud est contingens* quod est et potest non esse, et non est et potest esse, quod distinguitur a possibili quia includit habitudinem et respectum ad causam que in producendo (procedendo?) potest inhibiri."

15. We shall pick up this problem again. Here, we should note at least the astonishing fact that the conceptual preparation for modern society preceded its institutionalization: High, contingent, selectivity was a problem of thinking, before any real needs came up to organize mechanisms for contingent selection on a large scale. Parsons could see here a corroboration of his hypothesis, that large-scale evolutionary change is controlled on the highest cybernetic level, i.e., by the cultural subsystem of the action system. Cf. *Societies: Evolutionary and Comparative Perspectives* (Englewood Cliffs: Prentice-Hall, 1966), pp. 113ff.

16. The scientific and empirical status of these "other possibilities" is, bluntly stated, unknown. Its clarification will be one of the most important theoretical and methodological tasks of social sciences in the future. Max Black in his important essay on "possibility" leads us into doubts about the "ghostly view" of other possibilities as pure illusions, shatters *en passant* the traditional construction of possibilities in terms of a theory of modalities — and leaves the scared reader on the edge of this precipice with the advise "to undertake a detailed survey of how we do in fact use the words possible, possibility, and their cognates." See (*Models and Metaphors: Studies in Language and Philosophy* (Ithaca, N.Y.: Cornell University Press, 1962), pp. 140-152.

17. The contingency of "the" world implies, however, a metaworld as the horizon of all possibilities from which the actual world is selected by creation or by evolution.

18. The Cartesian tradition of subjective metaphysics would deny this statement and exempt consciousness from contingency. But the immediacy of experience of one's own consciousness is no sufficient reason to exclude its contingency.

19. See, however, James Olds, *The Growth and Structure of Motives: Psychological Studies in the Theory of Action* (Glencoe, Ill.: The Free Press, 1956), pp. 198ff.: "Within a presented object system, contingency is single in the sense that if *I perform a particular set of behaviors* I will achieve a particular outcome for my labors. Within a non-presented object system, there is a double contingency: If *I perform the behaviors that will take me to that object* successfully, then, if I perform a certain set of behaviors (manipulating the object) I will achieve a particular outcome for my labors." Social contingency (double contingency in the sense of Parsons), then, is only a special case of this two-step dependence. But this argument confounds contingency and dependence. Consequently, social contingency, i.e., the interaction of subjects knowing each other as subjects, is constructed as a special case of a much too simple case.

20. Parsons in some formulations comes close to this view. See Talcott Parsons, Robert F. Bales and Edward A. Shils, *Working Papers in the Theory of Action* (Glencoe, Ill.: The Free Press, 1953), p. 35.

21. We owe this splendid formulation to Paul Valéry, *Animalités, Oeuvres,* (Paris: ed. La Pléiade, 1957), p. 402.

22. James Olds *op. cit.* touches upon this point at p. 205 describing the gain in terms of economy of time and movement. See also Donald M. MacKay, "Communication and Meaning — A Functional Approach" F.S.C. Northrop and Helen H. Livingston (eds.), *Cross-Cultural Understanding: Epistemology in Anthropology,* (New York: Harper & Row, 1964), pp. 162-179 (163).

23. "A norm is a rule, more or less overt, which expresses 'ought' aspects of relationships between human beings" [Paul Bohannan, "The Differing Realms of the Law," reprinted in Paul Bohannan (ed.), *Law and Warfare: Studies in the Anthropology of Conflict* (Garden City, N.Y.: The Natural History Press, 1967), pp. 43-56, 45] is a typical way to bypass the problem.

24. This distinction has been first made by John Galtung, "Expectations and Interaction Processes," *Inquiry,* 2 (1959), pp. 213-234. Its analytical power is clearly superior to previous distinctions which usually refered to psychic or even metaphysical factors like reason, emotion, or will.

25. See also Niklas Luhmann, "Normen in soziologischer Perspektive," *Soziale Welt,* 20 (1969), pp. 28-48. A further elaboration shall be published in my *Rechtssoziologie* (Reinbeck: Rowohalt, 1972).

26. We shall not be able in this essay to trace all the possible connections between these different problem areas: e.g., to pursue the question under what special conditions problems of attribution and transmission of selections are, in regard to possible disappointments, to be treated as either normative or cognitive or ambiguous expectations; or to explore if the differentiation of normative and cognitive expectations presup-

poses certain ways to solve the problem of attribution and transmission of selections, i.e., a differentiation of experience and action and a differentiation of specialized media, e.g., power and truth.

27. I use the term experience in the large and freighted sense of the German *"Erleben."*

28. There exists some research concerning the personality system. See Fritz Heider, "Social Perception and Phenomenal Causality," *Psychological Review,* 51 (1944), pp. 358-374; Edward E. Jones and Keith E. Davis, "From Acts to Dispositions: The Attribution Process in Person Perception," in Leonard Berkowitz (ed.), *Advances in Experimental Social Psychology* (New York: Academic Press, 1965), pp. 212-266.

29. There are several reasons to propose this reversal within the general theoretical framework. It offers changes to integrate the theory of action systems into the general systems theory. It lays, thereby, the ground for comparative and evolutionary analyses which may compare physical and organic systems with systems of meaningful action. It may elucidate the adaptive advantages of action systems over organic systems and physical systems and may find these advantages in the higher complexity of meaning as a special way to relate a system with other possibilities to an environment with other possibilities in regard to these other possibilities. There are, furthermore, immanent reasons in the concept of action which point to the primacy of the system concept. The identity of one action in the continuing flow of behavior is definable only by reference to a system which limits the possibilities of meaningful action, i.e., in terms of what could be changed in a system. (Parsons uses a comparable argument for the relation of unit and system.) And the components of the structure of action (Parsons identifies actor, situation, ends, means, conditions, norms, values, and states explicitly that they are not conceivable at the level of the isolated unit act) presuppose limitations of possibility, change, and compatibility, which can not be identified without accepting a discontinuity between system and environment. It is not sufficient to clarify the relations *between* these components, because these relations change with the changing complexity of the relations between system and environment. For the concepts of ends and means I have elaborated on this point in Niklas Luhmann, *Zweckbegriff und Systemrationalität* (Tübingen: Mohr, 1968).

30. Talcott Parsons, "Interaction: Social Interaction," in D. Sills (ed.), *International Encyclopedia of the Social Sciences,* Vol. 7 (New York: The Free Press, 1968), pp. 429-441 (436), formulates the same idea "that each actor is *both* acting agent and object of orientation both to himself and to the others."

31. For this concept see Ronald D. Laing, *The Politics of Experience* (New York: Pantheon Books, 1967). See also Ronald D. Laing, Harbert Phillipson and A. Russell Lee, *Interpersonal Perception: A Theory and a Method of Research* (New York: Springer Publ. Co., 1966).

32. In the sense of James G. March and Herbert A Simon, *Organizations* (New York: J. Wiley, 1958), pp. 164ff.

33. Donald MacKey, *op. cit.,* 1964, p. 163.

34. Parsons, too, recognizes this limitation of language. He tries, however, to overcome it by specialization of language itself, namely by one specialized symbolic medium "commitment". See Talcott Parsons, "On the Concept of Value-Commitments," *Sociological Inquiry,* 38 (1968) pp. 135-159. In my view, all media involve commitments to reduced complexity (not only to values!), and this function distinguishes media as a special kind of mechanism from language.

35. See Niklas Luhmann, *Vertrauen: Ein Mechanismus der Reduktion sozialer Komplexität* (Stuttgart: F. Enke, 1968).

36. Parsons treats the symbolic structure of generalized media as a basis for trust in special human intentions in "On the Concept of Influence," *Public Opinion Quarterly,* 27 (1963), pp. 37-62 (47ff.). Furthermore, media presuppose a more generalized trust in the continuity and operational efficiency of systems which use them. This trust has the "reflexive" form of

trust in the fact that others will trust the systems and their media. "The rational ground for confidence in money is that others have confidence in money" (Talcott Parsons, "Some Reflections on the Place of Force in Social Process," in Harry Eckstein (ed.), *Internal War: Problems and Approaches* (New York: The Free Press, 1964), pp. 33-70 (45). See also Luhmann, *Vertrauen,* pp. 44ff., 63ff.

37.   This very general conceptual scheme can be applied on different levels to different types of systems. See Donald T. Campbell, "Variations and Selective Retention in Socio-Cultural Evolution," *General Systems,* 14 (1969), pp. 69-85. The best-known application exists on the level of organisms (mutations, natural selection, reproductive isolation). For the Development of cognitive personality systems (learning) see Donald T. Campbell, "Methodological Suggestions from a Comparative Psychology of Knowledge Processes," *Inquiry,* 2 (1959), pp. 152-182 (163). A related view on the change of social systems is published by Alvin Boskoff, "Functional Analyses as a Source of a Theoretical Repertory and Research Tasks in the Study of Social Change," in Walter Hirsch and G. K. Zollschan (eds.), *Explorations in Social Change* (Boston: Houghton Mifflin, 1964), pp. 213-243 (224ff.). The case of legal evolution is treated with the same conceptual scheme by Niklas Luhmann, "Evolution des Rechts," *Rechtstheorie,* 1 (1970), pp. 3-22.

38.   The philosophical theory complains about "alienation," "objectivation," "reification" which imply the oblivion of "the world" and the "transcendental subjectivity." See Edmund Husserl, "Die Krisis der europäischen Wissenschaften und die transzendentale Phänomenologie," *Husserliana* Vol. VI, (Den Haag: M. Nijhoff, 1954); Lothar Eley, *Metakritik der Formalen Logik,* (Den Haag: M. Nijhoff, 1969). This can be reinterpreted as complaint about limitations of freedom for structural change. The cybernetic theory, on the other hand, points to the important advantage of time-saving by reproduction.

39.   The question of differentiation of evolutionary mechanisms has to be distinguished, analytically, from the question of system differentiation, i.e., segmentary or functional differentiation. There are, of course, interdependencies in the sense that societies, which are differentiated primarily into segments do not have the possibility to go very far in the differentiation of evolutionary mechanisms. And that means that they evolve slowly.

40.   In the sense of Peter L. Berger and Thomas Luckmann, *The Social Construction of Reality: A Treatise in The Sociology of Knowledge* (Garden City, N.Y.: Doubleday, 1966).

41.   See Siegried F. Nadel, "Social Control and Self-Regulation," *Social Forces,* 31 (1953), pp. 265-273.

42.   Another view, therefore, would be appropriate for authors who use the language concept of media and look mainly for a differentiation of codes and messages as condition of social influence. See Terence S. Turner, "Parsons' Concept of 'Generalized Media of Social Interaction' and Its Relevance for Social Anthropology," *Sociological Inquiry,* 38 (1968), pp. 121-134.

43.   See Shmuel N. Eisenstadt, "Ritualized Personal Relations," *Man,* 96 (1956), pp. 90-95, for the latter case. See also note 74.

44.   This interpretation of Greek thought follows Joachim Ritter, *Metaphysik und Politik: Studien zu Aristoteles und Hegel* (Frankfurt: Suhrkamp, 1969). At the same time, it gives classical evidence for Parsons' thesis that differentiation involves universalization, generalization, and the need for respecification of the generalized norms. See Charles Ackerman and Talcott Parsons, "The Concept of 'Social System' as a Theoretical Device," in Gordon J. DiRenzo (ed.), *Concepts, Theory and Explanation in the Behavioral Sciences* (New York: Random House, 1966), pp. 19-40 (36ff.).

45.   The archaic Greek language knew only *philos,* meaning attached to, close to, belonging to, and therefore estimated by.

It had no concept expressing friendship or love in an abstract sense. See Franz Dirlmeier, *PHILOS und PHILIA im vorhellenischen Griechentum,* Thesis (München: 1931).

46.   See Thomas Hobbes, *Leviathan* (London—New York: Everyman's Library, 1953), p. 22.

47.   For comments on the exceptional and artificial character of this "Western" conception of truth see Ithiel de Sola Pool, "The Mass Media and Politics in the Modernization Processes," in Lucian W. Pye (ed.), *Communications and Political Development* (Princeton: Princeton University Press, 1963), pp. 234-253 (242ff.). For the same idea in a philosophical and minor key see Edmund Husserl, "Die Krisis der europäischen Wissenschaften und die transzendentale Phänomenologie," *Husserliana* Vol. VI (Den Haag: M. Nijhoff, 1954).

48.   We shall account for this difference by the distinction of two types of media: Media that regulate the transmission of selectivity of *action,* e.g., power, are more easily to differentiate and to institutionalize in specialized patterns than media that regulate the transmission of selectivity of experience, e.g., love and truth. The reason for this difference is found in the fact that the selectivity of action from other possibilities is more easily visible than the selectivity of experience. This partly explains the fact that some societal subsystems are differentiated earlier than others and that only fully developed, highly complex societies can afford to specialize subsystems around the media love and truth.

49.   See Christian Wolff, *Vernünftige Gedanken von dem gesellschafftlichen Leben der Menschen und insonderheit dem gemeinen Wesen,* 5th ed. (Frankfurt—Leipzig: 1740), p. 456.

50.   See James G. March, "The Power of Power," in David Easton (ed.), *Varieties of Political Theory* (Englewood Cliffs, N.J.: Prentice-Hall, 1966), pp. 39-70; Niklas Luhmann, "Klassische Theorie der Macht: Kritik ihrer Prämissen," *Zeitschrift für Politik,* 16 (1969), pp. 149-170. For the legal point of view become important Jürgen Rödig, *Die Denkform der Alternative in der Jurisprudenz,* (Berlin—Heidelberg—New York: Springer, 1969).

51.   See Talcott Parsons, "On the Concept of Political Power," *Proceedings of the American Philosophical Society,* 107 (1963), pp. 232-262.

52.   There are, of course, other topics of symbolic work, e.g., the normative order of law and the system concept, articulated in terms of wholes and parts, goals and means, and hierarchical order.

53.   "The need for generalized media of interchange is a function of the differentiatedness of social structures." Talcott Parsons, "Systems Analysis: Social Systems," D. Sills (ed.), *op. cit.,* Vol. 15, pp. 458-473, 471.

54.   For a general outline see Luhmann, *Vertrauen.* It is, of course, questionable whether the concept of medium can be defined abstractly enough to survive this transfer from one context into another. We think that the important theoretical insights regarding money and power, the elaboration of analogies between different media, the idea of generalization and symbolic regulation of processes, and, most important, the connection of these aspects can be preserved.

55.   We may use the technique of cross-tabulation to present our view:

	Ego's experience	Ego's action
Alter's experience	$A_e \rightarrow E_e$ (truth; value commitments)	$A_e \rightarrow E_a$ (love; influence)
Alter's action	$A_a \rightarrow E_e$ (money; art)	$A_a \rightarrow E_a$ (power)

but we should add, then, several warnings. The boxes should be read as definition of problem areas, not of problem solutions (not even in an analytical sense), i.e., not as definitions of the corresponding media. The deduction of a differentiation of problems simply means that a development of different media along these lines will bring about the advantages of functional specialization. It does not allow us to conclude that such media, in fact, exist nor that such problem areas will be served each by one and only one medium; nor that problems and problem solutions will be congruent in the sense that existing media will solve without further specialization all problems in their particular area. Compared with the level of theory to which Parsons aspires, we feel again the need for a logical discounting.

56. See Albert Bandura, "Vicarious Processes: No Trial Learning," in Leonard Berkowitz (ed.), *Advances in Experimental Social Psychology* (New York: Academic Press, 1965), pp. 1-56; Alfred R. Lindesmith and Anselm R. Strauss, *Social Psychology,* 3rd ed. (New York: Holt, Rinehart, and Winston, 1968), pp. 283ff.

57. See Robert E. Lane, "The Decline of Politics and Ideology in a Knowledgeable Society," *American Sociological Review,* 31 (1966), pp. 649-662, with interesting implications as to the interdependence of truth and power in this respect.

58. And precisely because a cognitive pattern of truth is by no means unproblematical, commitment to *cognitive* expectations and learning in science is itself normatively expected and ruled by very strict conditions. The cognitive character of truth is institutionalized on one level of expectation by normative expectations on another level.

59. The philosophical reflection of this need can be found in German Idealism, confronting the realm of nature and the realm of freedom in the sense of freedom to value commitment. The sociologist scanning this literature may learn that it has not been possible to establish the realm of freedom outside of truth and natural causation. The "necessity" of commitment, symbolizing the transmissibility of value orientation, remained a postulate, a failure which indicates some of the problems of a special medium for normative orientations.

60. See Talcott Parsons, "On the Concept of Value-Commitments," *op. cit.*

61. I even venture to say that reference to value *never* justifies the selection of a particular action, because every action depends on a decision as to preference between conflicting values which are not transitively ordered on the level of the general code of the medium.

62. See Peter L. Berger and Hansfried Kellner, "Le Mariage et la construction de la réalité," *Diogène* 46 (1964), pp. 3-32, German transl., *"Die Ehe* und die Konstruktion der Wirklichkeit: Eine Abhandlung Zur Mikrosoziologie des Wissens," *Soziale Welt,* 16 (1965), pp. 220-235.

63. See Talcott Parsons, "On the Concept of Influence," *op. cit.*

64. See Friedrich's definition of authority in "Authority, Reason, and Discretion," in Friedrich, Carl J. (ed.), *Authority* (Nomos I) (Cambridge; Harvard University Press 1958), pp. 28-48 (35).

65. Parsons defines his concept of influence as persuasion, forming the intentions of the other by positive sanctions. The difference seems to be a minor one because the channeling through intentions and reference to positive sanctions will be particularly appropriate if selective experiences and not decisions are communicated.

66. See Hegel, *Grundlinien der Philosophie des Rechts,* § 75.

67. This requires a reinterpretation of the conception of power as causal relation, which is the source of the most problematical aspects in the classical theory of power. See Niklas Luhmann, "Klassische Theorie der Macht: Kritik ihrer Prämissen," *op. cit.,* pp. 149-170. Causality, too, has to be understood not simply as necessary chain of facts, but as a chain of selective events connected by their selectivity. Seen in this

way causality presupposes a structural limitation of possibilities, i.e., systems.

68. We meet here Kenneth Burke. *A Grammar of Motives* (New York: Prentice-Hall, 1945), and *A Rhetoric of Motives* (Berkeley: University of California Press, 1969), and Hugh Dalziel Duncan, *Communication and Social Order* (New York: Bedminister Press, 1962), and *Symbols in Society* (New York: Oxford University Press, 1968), who propose to study these symbolic expressions as well as those of truth, money, and love. We have, however, to go beyond a purely hermeneutic or a dramatic exposition and recognize that these positively evaluated values are symbols insofar as they stand for and point to *negated* possibilities. Symbols have dramatic relevance because they save the trouble to articulate negated possibilities in the communication process. They have structural relevance insofar as they refer to these possibilities and depend upon their maintenance.

69. These acts, too, are of course symbolic acts, culturally defined and forcing insofar as it is difficult to refuse the complementary act.

70. Cf. Talcott Parsons, "Durkheim's Contribution to the Theory of Integration of Social Systems," in Kurt H. Wolff (ed.), *Emile Durkheim* 1858-1917 (Columbus, Ohio: Ohio State University Press, 1960), pp. 118-153.

71. For a theory of motivation built on this fundamental condition see Edward L. Walker, "Psychological Complexity as a Basis for a Theory of Motivation and Choice," *Nebraska Symposium on Motivation* (1964), pp. 47-95.

72. It is important, however, to note the serious restraints on the differentiation of experience and action in the religious system.

73. It is even possible to gain confidence in the experience of others where the selection is, actually, a matter of decision if the selection is socially prescribed as experience, e.g., confidence in the professional advice of doctors and lawyers.

74. A good example offers Kenelm O. L. Burridge, "Friendship in Tangu," *Oceania* 27 (1957), pp. 177-189. Another type is the institutionalized possibility of special power concentration in case of war, far spread in Germanic tribes.

75. These are reasons to suppose that differentiation and political specialization of rulership roles in archaic societies correlate with a deeper and more articulate historic consciousness which provides sources of legitimation. Cf. Rüdiger Schott, "Das Geschichtsbewuβtsein schriftloser Völker," *Archiv für Begriffsgeschichte,* 12 (1968), pp. 166-205.

76. We reconstruct, in other concepts, the main argument of S. N. Eisenstadt, *The Political Systems of Empires* (New York: The Free Press, 1963), that relatively autonomous political rule in the historical bureaucratic empires was a premature differentiation, permanently endangered by the fact that it had no control over the sources of its legitimation.

77. Our model of mechanisms of variation, selection, and stabilization therefore cannot be interpreted as a phase model in the sense that one mechanism must operate before the other can begin to develop. (This is the interpretation of Boskoff, *op. cit.*) It is a model of concommitment requirements which can be applied to itself. That is to say: The differentiation of mechanisms of variation, selection, and stabilization is itself a function of possibilities of variation, selection, and stabilization so that a surplus of possible selective mechanisms has to be created for selective use in the process of stabilization.

78. Norman W. Storer, *The Social System of Science* (New York: Holt, Rinehart and Winston, 1966), pp. 94, 96ff., compares art and scientific truth in this respect.

79. See our previous discussion.

80. See Charles Ackerman and Talcott Parsons, *op. cit.,* p. 37.

81. See the paragraph, "Symbiotic Patterns versus Social Organization" in Daniel Katz and Robert L. Kahn, *The Social Psychology of Organizations* (New York: J. Wiley, 1966),

pp. 34ff. Parsons, using the language of economics, speaks of "real assets," "On the Concept of Political Power," *op. cit.* Explicit comparisons of media on the level of their symbiotic processes are rare.

82. Some of the consequences and possible dysfunctions of this performance are discussed later in this chapter.

83. There are, of course, limits to the types of commands that can be backed by physical force. See Roscoe Pound, "The Limits of Effective Legal Action," *International Journal of Ethics,* 27 (1917), pp. 150-167. And there are further limitations imposed by the conditions of legitimation.

84. We have already stated the intention to modify the formulations of Parsons in this respect.

85. The German experience with family life during, and economic recovery after, political catastrophes show that this holds even under the condition of very high political risks.

86. We take up this topic later in regard to some problematical consequences.

87. The famous Chinese politicians called "legalists" failed at this point, not being able to link absolute power with law as interdependent. A good presentation of their thinking and fate is Léon Vandermeersch, *La formation du légisme* (Paris: L'École Française d'Extrême-Oriente, 1965). The counterexample is the European conception of the rule of law and of "Rechtsstaat" and its classical philosophic reflection, Hegel's *Philosophie des Rechts.*

88. Talcott Parsons, "Some Reflections on the Place of Force in Social Process," *op. cit.,* compares the state monopoly of coercive power with the banking system of the economy—both seen as generalization of media.

89. Performance, here, means simply that behavior is judged as a selective event intentionally related to other selective events in a process. It does not necessarily imply inherently valuable goals, nor a distinguishible causal effect on system maintenance. Performance pressure in modern society can be understood as a result of an aimless evolution in the direction of high differentiation and system complexity, which then seeks its goals; it is not sufficiently explained as a result of cultural change in the evaluation of system states. This is, of course, not the sense in which Parsons has introduced the concept of performance in Talcott Parsons, Robert F. Bales, and Edward A. Shils, *op. cit.,* pp. 163ff.

90. See Olds, *op. cit.*; Robert L. Marcus, "The Nature of Instinct and the Physical Bases of Libido," *General Systems,* 7 (1962), pp. 133-156.

91. For corresponding changes in the law of contract see Emmanuel Gounot, *Le principe de l'autonomie de la volonté en droit privé: Contribution à l'etude critique de l'individualism juridique* (Paris: 1912), pp. 43ff.

92. The Enlightenment had a special polemic concept against such shortcuts to truth: fanaticism. This concept became fashionable in the theological debates of the seventeenth century, incriminating at first private zealotic opinion against accepted orthodoxy, and was, then, secularized into a verdict against occult idiosyncratic sources of knowledge which are not open to control according to general rules of reason. With further accumulation of scientific successes the moral verdict against fanatics could be softened down, and today it suffices to doubt the scientific character of statements. For the conceptual history of fanaticism, see Robert Spaemann, *Reflexion und Spontaneität: Studien über Fénelon* (Stuttgart: Kohlhammer, 1963), pp. 163ff.

93. See Niklas Luhmann, "Reflexive Mechanismen," *Soziale Welt* 17 (1966), pp. 1-23, reprinted in Luhmann, *Soziologische Aufklärung,* pp. 92-112.

94. In the sense of Talcott Parsons, "Evolutionary Universals in Society, *American Sociological Review,* 29 (1964), pp. 339-357.

95. Jean Paul's formula is "Liebe um Liebe"; See Jean Paul's *Sämtliche Werke,* Vol. 23 (Berlin: 1842), p. 47.

96. Money itself is already reflexive on a first level because it symbolizes that the possibility of exchanges is taken into exchange. On a second level, money itself can be bought in the credit system when the obligation to pay interest becomes legalized. Finally it becomes possible to finance even the credit system, e.g., by changing strategic interest rates.

97. That the people is called sovereign and the government democratic is, of course, not an adequate description of the real power distribution in the system but indicates the difficulty to think and express reflexiveness of power in traditional (hierarchic) terms.

98. See Talcott Parsons and Neil J. Smelser, *Economy and Society* (Glencoe, Ill.: The Free Press, 1956), pp. 70ff.

99. See Robert K. Merton, "Singletons and Multiples in Scientific Discovery: A Chapter in the Sociology of Science," *Proceedings of the American Philosophical Society,* 105 (1961), pp. 470-486; Warren O. Hägstrom, *The Scientific Community* (New York: Basic Books 1965); Norman W. Storer, *op. cit.*; Niklas Luhmann. "Selbststeuerung der Wissenschaft," *Jahrbunch für Sozialwissenschaft,* 19 (1968), pp. 147-170, reprinted in *Soziologische Aufklärung.*

100. See Talcott Parsons, "An Outline of the Social System" in Talcott Parsons, Edward Shils, Kaspar D. Naegele, and Jesse R. Pitts (eds.), *Theories of Society* (Glencoe, Ill.: The Free Press, 1961), pp. 30-79 (53ff.).

101. See Willard Waller and Reuben Hill, *The Family: A Dynamic Interpretation,* 2nd ed. (New York: Dryden Press, 1951), pp. 120ff.; Hugo G. Beigel, "Romantic Love," *American Sociological Review,* 16 (1951), pp. 326-334.

102. See Robert K. Leik, "Instrumentality and Emotionality in Family Interaction," *Sociometry,* 26 (1963), pp. 131-145.

103. A good statement of this point is "A Note on Love" in Vilhelm Aubert, *The Hidden Society* (Totowa, N.J.: Bedminster Press, 1965), pp. 201-235.

104. See John P. Spiegel, "The Resolution of Role Conflict Within the Family," *Psychiatry,* 20 (1957), pp. 1-16.

105. The early American discussion is particularly clear on this point. See Frank J. Goodnow, *Politics and Administration: A Study in Government* (New York: Macmillan Co., 1900), and for later developments Herbert Kaufman, "Emerging Conflicts in the Doctrine of Public Administration," *The American Political Science Review,* 50 (1956), pp. 1057-1073. Compare also Albert Schäffle, Über den wissenschaftlichen Begriff der Politik," *Zeitschrift für die gesamte Staatswissenschaft,* 53 (1897), pp. 579-600.

106. Such a separation of situations can be traced back into archaic societies. See Michael G. Smith, "On segmentary Lineage Systems," *The Journal of the Royal Anthropological Institute of Great Britain and Ireland,* 86 (1956), pp. 39-80, and *Government in Zazzau* 1800-1950 (London: Oxford University Press, 1960).

107. These remarks refer, of course, to the Spencer-Durkheim-Parsons tradition. See Talcott Parsons, "Durkheim's Contribution to the Theory of Integration of Social Systems," *op. cit.*

108. See Georg Simmel, *Über sociale Differenzierung* (Leipzig: Duncker & Humblot, 1890); Guillaume de Greef, *La Structure Générale des Sociétés,* 3 vol. (Bruxelles-Paris: 1908), vol. II, pp. 245ff., 299ff.

109. For this fluctuation of boundaries see Lloyd Fallers, "Political Sociology and the Anthropological Study of African Politics," *Europäisches Archiv für Soziologie* 4 (1963), pp. 311-329.

110. S. N. Eisenstadt, "Religious Organizations and Political Process in Centralized Empires," *The Journal of Asian Studies,* 21 (1962), pp. 271-294, has shown that in the ancient empires the group referent of the religious and the political community begin to diverge. This was on the one hand a consequence of increasing territorial size. On the other hand, the ensuing conflicts could be solved by the enlargement of territorial

boundaries beyond the possibilities of effective interaction.

111. Not, as Leon H. Mayhew, "Society," in D. Sills (ed.),
op. cit., Vol 14, pp. 577-586 (583), concludes, the concept of
a society with exclusive boundaries.

112. Curiously enough, the existence of this global system
is acknowledged, but the concept of society is not applied to
it. Usually, societies are seen as subsystems of the global system,
as "national" societies. See Herbert J. Spiro, *World Politics:
The Global System* (Homewood, Ill.: Dorsey Press, 1966);
Wilbert E. Moore, "Global Sociology: The World as a Singular
System," *The American Journal of Sociology*, 71 (1966), pp.
475-482. This can be explained only as conceptual survival of
the old "civil society" tradition which postulated the societal
system as constituted by one (and only one) political system.

113. The main reason for this conceptual choice was the
fact that infinity was seen as an essential attribute of God which
could not be reproduced in the world. The contingency of all
essentials could, therefore, be admitted only as actual infinity
of possible creations by God, who could, however, produce
only finite worlds. See Hans Blumenberg, *Die Legitimität der
Neuzeit* (Frankfurt: Suhrkamp, 1966), pp. 122ff. *et passim*; Celestino Solaguren, "Contingencia y creaction en la filosofia de
Duns Escoto," *Verdad y Vida*, 24 (1966).

114. See Helmut Kuhn, "The Phenomenological Concept of
"Horizon," in Marvin Farber, *Philosophical Essays in Memory
of Edmund Husserl* (Cambridge: Harvard University Press,
1940), pp. 106-123; Ludwig Landgrebe, "The World as a Phenomenological Problem," *Philosophy and Phenomenological
Research*, 1 (1940), pp. 38-58. Husserl himself did elaborate
his concept of the world in the framework of the *contingentia*
tradition; see "Erste Philosophie II" (1923/24), *Husserliana*
Vol. VIII (Den Haag: M. Nyhoff, 1959), and also see Hans
Blumenberg, *Lebenswelt und Technisierung unter den Aspek-
ten der Phänomenologie* (Torino: Edizioni di Filosofia, 1963).

115. This problem, too, has its noteworthy tradition. It
became obvious in the nominalistic revolution: Whereas Aristotle saw the difficulty in explaining the possible in a necessary
world, Duns Scotus inverted for theological reasons the priorities in modal theory and his problem was then to explain
the necessary in a contingent world. This moved the modern
quest for natural laws, the Cartesian discovery of the *cogito ergo
sum*, and the Hobbesian problem of political order. It motivated
Leibniz to postulate limitations of "compossibility" in every
possible world. It made the problem of a priori conditions of
knowledge relevant. It gives to the interaction theory "from
the standpoint of a social behaviorist" its importance. And it
may stimulate systems theory to set out for a new solution.

116. See Niklas Luhmann, "Soziologie als Theorie sozialer
Systeme," *Kölner Zeitschrift für Soziologie und Sozial psychologie,* 19 (1967), pp. 615-644, reprinted in: *Soziologische Aufklärung.*

22

COMMUNICATION AND MEDIA

Rainer C. Baum

The conception of the generalized symbolic medium marks an important new departure in the theory of action. Its addition to the conceptual array of the theory aims in two directions. One is substantive, the other technical-theoretical. Generalized symbolic media are to give flesh—primarily of a processual nature—to the earlier skeletal-structural problem formulation of the question: How can there be unity and order in diversity.[1] By the early 1960's it had become quite clear that the emphasis on values and norms, no matter how differentially specified and subjected to a ramified complex system of normative mechanisms, was insufficient. It was not a question that the emphasis on values, norms, collectivities, and roles in the functional LIGA order was somehow mistaken. It was rather found that the freight that normative specification was to carry proved too heavy. Some more general mechanisms of control had to be found. These are the generalized symbolic media.[2] Apart from any substantive problem concern, however, the importance of the media has also another aspect. They signaled a shift in action theory from a structural-functional focus to a theory that takes the concepts system and function as primary and gives the concepts structure and process derived status.[3] With the emphasis on process and mechanisms that control them, media, this perspective lays a foundation for a far more dynamic theory, one with heightened potential to deal with the analysis of change.

Clearly one starting point here was the desire to make economic theory continuous with sociological concerns.[4] Knowledge about the role of money as a medium, controlling factors and shares in the economy, served as a model to develop media in other than economic relations.[5] Although money was designated as a type of language, its special feature of uniform units of account measurable on a ratio scale underplayed a little the more general language aspect. There is a simple reason why emphasizing a systems and language perspective may be more pertinent at this stage of theoretical development, regardless of the actual history of ideas in Parsons' work. Seeing in media theorizing "merely" extensions of economic theory, as some have apparently done, may be quite misleading in that it encourages premature and therefore misplaced concreteness. Instead of focusing on the language analogy in general, attention is directed to the special language of money and quite concretely to cash, of all things. At that level, in those terms, similarities are found more wanting than present. As often, the outcome is quite varied. Either some commitment to intriguing possibilities is maintained,[6] disillusion sets in,[7] or even abandonment of the whole direction of theoretical effort is counseled.[8] Whichever, premature concreteness diverts attention from the basic problem. This is to develop a conception of media of interchange adequate for a complex social science paradigm. I do not regard the available materials on media as satisfactory; I intend to say why and to suggest in what direction greater adequacy might be found.

If the particular, in this case money, causes some confusion, the normal strategy is to go to the more general, in this case communication as such. If, further, the particular case—here the economy—is also associated for some at least with this misdirection, one response is to go to the more general, hence the emphasis should shift to system as such. But confusion and despair among some readers is hardly sufficient legitimation to start on a travel demanding considerable effort expenditure before the destination is reached. Parsons' own work on media to date is characterized by disbalance. Granted that the whole effort of media theorizing aims at upgrading action theory in a more dynamic direction, the sources of this disbalance seem to be three. First, media at the societal level have been far better developed than general action media.[9] This applies particularly for such components as code-aspects, "security bases," and intrinsic satisfiers (see introduction to this part). Thus by not starting "at the top" of the action-theoretical paradigm Parsons himself fell prey to premature specification. He found it necessary, for example, to change one code aspect of a societal medium. The coordination standard of power, first designated as "success," was later shifted to serve as the cognate standard of the general action medium performance capacity, and "sovereignty" took its place at the societal level.[10]

Second, the extant formulations of the interchange paradigm at the societal level show internal disbalance. It must be remembered that in the usual format of presentation, the diagonal interchanges in the four-function paradigm provide for integration of the system. Compared with the vertical (G-function) and horizontal (A-function) interchanges, the diagonal have a special "integrative status" because controlling flows of input and output here have to cross the double cleavage of both the instrumental-consummatory and the external-internal boundaries. Yet this special status is recognized for only one interchange market, the legitimation-legality (L-G) interchange, and not the other, the societal-communal and the occupational market (I-A). We only learn that across L-G it is not media but code aspects that do the controlling. We learn nothing like that in the case of controlling flows between economy and societal community (A-I).[11] There is something missing here, and it needs fixing.

Third, there seems to be some lingering confusion about information and its role in media theorizing. Parsons assigned a very special role to information in the operation of one particular societal medium, influence. Because the professional-client relation serves as the paradigmatic case for formulating what influence in a technical sense is all about, one is not surprised to find such a special link between information and influence. The major problem in the professional-client relation turns on the management and proper exploitation of the competence gap. A client is supposed to live with ignorance in impunity because he can trust the professional. This highlights the information-saving function in the operation of media. However, that is a characteristic of all media, not just influence. Furthermore, if mediation implies communication, information plays a role in all. This is not to deny that information may play a special role in influence not duplicated among the other media, but just what this might be can hardly become clear before the general role of information has been worked out. Hence Parsons' disbalanced linkage

between information and influence[12] needs rebalancing.

Having identified three sources of conceptual noise, the aim of this paper can be specified. Contrary to what the reader might reasonably expect, I do not plan to provide a conceptual repair job at the level of societal media themselves. My reason is cognitive incapacity. The answer to the equally reasonable query "Then why bother to write about these disbalances?" should be found in the identification of the first disbalance. It depends how one interprets Parsons' incompleteness in developing the general action media. I allocate the absence of operative codes, the paucity concerning security bases, and intrinsic satisfiers to an underdeveloped conception of communication. As the general action media are to operate at the most general level conceivable in action theory, a four-function conception of communication may be a requisite to gain greater clarity about the mentioned lacunae. *Pari passu*, the same applies to the disbalance across the diagonals, and the problematical role of information. Perhaps the last case illustrates my position best. When things do not work out, one suspects commonsense usage of terms such as information for highly technical purposes as the source of fault. My response in such a situation—and I do not think it unique but rather the universal scientific response—is to try to abandon commonsense, for a while at least. Hence I shall try to make communication and information problematical, attempt to decompose these terms, and give the newly gained concepts more precise specification. Therefore my central objective in this paper is to provide a better foundation for doing the conceptual repair job for the media already posed at two levels of action theory, the general action level and the societal. If I succeed at all plausibly, however, I trust I will also have supplied a useful base from which to attempt development of cultural, personality, and behavioral organism media. That is a bit of a tall order. I therefore beg the reader's indulgence for remaining at the illustrative suggestive level when it comes to articulating some of the results of this effort with the societal media as we know them.

The issues to be addressed here can be presented conveniently in four parts. First, one very general answer to the question of why one should bother with media may be attempted. Here I shall emphasize a historical and loosely evolutionary perspective as a good reason to analyze action in the contemporary world as mediated action. Principally, such need increases with the relative modernity of conditions one is interested in. I shall couch this rationalization in the form of a historical sketch of a burgeoning problem of meaning. It should be emphasized here that this sketch does not pretend to the status of historical analysis. Drawing on what I believe to be widely shared images of historical change, the sketch has only one message: *This invitation to concern oneself with media as a conceptual tool in the social sciences is one that can reasonably be extended to any analyst, whatever his theoretical preferences.* Anyone who has not lost all enchantment with Max Weber's central preoccupation of the "rationalization" of instrumental and expressive, of "this" and "other-wordly" concerns, can, I believe, "trust" the potential utility of media theorizing. Hence he can also trust the potential utility of considering communication as problematical. In short, both communication and media have importance far beyond the peculiar technical requirements of action theory.

Following up on this, a second section is devoted to emphasizing that any system's perspective in the analysis of action demands attention to media. The aim here is to provide a broader base than could be gleaned from economics for a conception of an increase in the rationality of organization of society. Building on this in turn, I shall outline a general and functional communications model in a third section. Its aim is to aid us in thinking constructively about the use of any kind of language. Finally, in a fourth part, there follow a few ilustrations of a more concrete empirical nature. These concern the functioning of societal media. They aim at sustaining our trust in media theorizing as potentially useful for empirical research.

LEVELS OF MEDIATED ACTION IN HISTORICAL PERSPECTIVE

Media are mechanisms which provide a double function. On the one hand, media serve to *reduce* complexity (by saving decisions); on the other hand, they serve to *produce* complexity (by generalizing meaning and widening ranges of choice). This is of course a contradiction, but only a logical fetishist might prefer to give up already.[13] As will be seen later, that they can do both hinges on the division of labor between debtor and creditor and differential uses of time. At this point, however, the decision-saving function will be stressed. This is also most consistent with Parsons' conception of mediation. The message is to concrete historical change and reads: As societies differentiate, the need for decision-saving mechanisms increases.

Some mechanism of decision-saving very likely constitutes a universal attribute of human action. Turner[14] recently argued for the applicability of a frame of reference that takes "mediated action" as its problem focus for societies at rather low levels of

development. ". . . it is far more practicable and efficient to channel communal sanctions . . . through a standardized system of symbolic tokens . . . than to try to bring collective norms and values directly to bear on every instance of social interaction of a particular type. . . ."[15] Efficiency is probably the wrong reason. One might substitute language and religion, the demarcation line between the nonhuman and the human. Because the latter term implies the capacity for reflection, one might attribute mediated action to some degree of differentiation between experience and the world which is indeed constitutive of the human realm. In short, even primitive man can dream of alternatives. This facilitates representing what is and what might be symbolically. It also makes it possible to act on symbols rather than on detail-negotiated agreement, which amounts to a saving of decisions concerning meaningful interaction. The question of motivations seems far too complex to be solved by recourse to a few simple notions such as efficiency, particularly for men who live by custom. Nevertheless, the insight that men always face some choice between the risks attendant on the relatively effortless implementation of mediated action and the security inherent in the labor of negotiating certainty about expectations is important. It points to the fact that at higher levels of development the latter option becomes both less necessary and more costly, being implementable primarily at the price of dedifferentiation. Furthermore, focusing on the problem of choice—to decide or not—also defines the maintenance and management of trust as the central integrative problem in modern life, particularly at the societal level. This suggests that societal media can be understood best as function-specialized yet generalized languages of trust. Let us illustrate by describing schematically the unfolding of complexity in religious development.

It must be emphasized that the following account is very compressed and looks very simple—but not so simplistic, I hope, as to delegitimize the purpose. In a nutshell, the central message is as follows: as structural sources of uncertainty become differentiated and specialized media develop that serve to reduce complexity, the load of complexity management develops in opposite directions for the individual and society. Individuals face more and more uncertainty, hence experience greater and greater potential for social and personal alienation; societies become more and more immune against individual disturbance.

In Bellah's felicitous terms the primitive symbol system is myth par excellence, and with it action is ritual par excellence. Church and society are one, so are society and man; life is a given, and essentially a "one possibility thing."[16] If one adds the absence of a conception of a man-made order, one sees that such a fused sociocultural realm of familiarity constituted reduced world complexity. People lived in a *given* world. The general action media probably suffice for analyzing the relatively small amount of mediated action in such a case. Certainly, where neither society nor culture have become differentiated, neither cultural nor societal media proper have applicability. Another reason why a benign neglect of specialized media seems justified here is the presumed inability to orient to specific structural sources of genuinely institutionalized continuous change. Living in a given order, one is not constantly anticipating that problems of change in that order have to be dealt with. This does not imply of course an image of an institutional order without change, but it does imply a generalized lack of preparedness for change. For those to whom action had prescribed meanings most of the time change always came as a surprise. Most action was enacted meaning experience. Specific structural sources of uncertainty were not perceived. Therefore special languages of trust to manage uncertainty were underdeveloped. Subsequent developments, however, did give rise to specific structural sources of uncertainty; and they did so in increasing number.

For the individual, uncertainty grew, first with the birth of the gods, of worship and sacrifice. Now a sense of the tragic could emerge; error was not just a joke. If there are higher beings who must be propitiated, there is the possibility that they may not respond. The expected results of action here became contingent on forces beyond the immediacy of the action situation. Culture and society differentiated. This implies that at this stage *experience and action became differentiated.* Ever after their relationship was problematical. It could no longer be taken for granted. Following Luhmann,[17] we can say that experience denotes the allocation of meaning to a given order that lies beyond what men can touch. Action, on the other hand, sees meaning as a product of men's relations. Here the alter-ego system of action reduces complexity. The difference then rests on where one "localizes" the formation of meaning. It should not be confused with subjectivity in the sense of individual uniqueness. That would be to slip back into the utilitarian dilemma.

Experience is the acceptance of reduced complexity or meaning from sources beyond the social-interaction scene. *Action* is acceptance of reduced complexity from and treated as an achievement of the system of interaction itself. The former deals with manipulables and entities beyond manipulation, the latter with manipulables only. With the differentiation between the two, action became a source of uncertainty because self-constituted meaning could be subject to error.

In the remaining stages of Bellah's schema, either uncertainties deepened or new sources of uncertainty were added as a product of the differentiation process. The emergence of transcendence increased the culture-society gap. The problem of salvation was posed. Now tendencies both to reject the world profoundly or to escape from it became serious options. In addition to the action source, perceived uncertainty now came to include the need to understand an ordered set of realities because one was to be saved through partaking of them. Cosmos and chaos became radical alternatives at the level of symbols. Hence, action became more complicated as it had to ensure inclusion into cosmos. The Reformation's insistence on faith accompanied by the denial of any valid withdrawal from the world brought the final differentiation of self and society, adding to the uncertainty of action another source, the need of the individual to work for self-created congruence between his spiritual and worldly aspects of being.

Action now further differentiated into two realms of validity. One of these was the public realm, wherein action came to focus on the legitimacy of the larger insitutional structures—from the family to the economy—characterized by their functionally specialized normative orders. The other was the private sphere, wherein individuals in small nonassociational groups achieved complexity reduction. Sociologists of religion refer to the latter as the privatization thesis, emphasizing that the meaning constructions produced in nonassociational settings lack any clear-cut intersubjective bindingness in the public realm. That is the major source of the growing relative immunity of function-specialized structures in differentiated society against strains experienced by individuals, provided function-specialized media do their job of information-saving.

But the relations between the public and the private realm became problematical.[18] In part this development was the social-organizational consequence of contradictory theological symbols that insisted on "works" in the face of a concomitant commitments' stress on "sola fide." Nevertheless, here there was still a plan, an ultimate given which in principle at least could be known. But this next-to-last "bit" of genuine experience as *given* meaning too fell away with the emergence of the conception of man as his own creator of all realities, or what Bellah's ingenious formulation denoted as the "conception of life as an infinite possibility thing." Here experience differentiated.

If I understand Bellah correctly, the underlying

dynamics of this differentiation involve a sharper contrast between the inescapability of the meaning problem as such and the freedom of the modes of solving it. On the one hand, there is almost infinite choice, certainly indefinite ranges of choice concerning the question of how to solve the problem of meaning; on the other, there is no choice at all, whether to solve it. Precisely because of the increase in contrast, the meaning problem poses itself more radically than it ever could before with respect to both inescapability and ultimacy. The situation is somewhat analogous here to an economic market where there is tremendously wide choice in how to use money, but practically no choice at all whether to use it or not.

The rationale for the absence of choice in confronting the meaning problem in this context has minimally two roots. One root is a part of our image of personality, part assumption, part fact resting on findings of clinical psychology. This is that one component of personality is a "continuous self," an identity that both poses and serves as reference for an integration problem as man moves through his life-cycle shot through with increasing variety in social involvements.[19] The other root is a technical theoretical constraint imposed by the theory of action. This is the cardinal tenet that action when analyzed as a system must have a reference base to articulate with which remains beyond interchange, a theoretical function served by posing a pattern maintenance subsystem. There may well be alternative interpretations of Bellah's conception of life as an infinite possibility thing that claim that it breaks with this tenet of the theory of action. Mine is an attempt to keep it within the framework. The solution, little more than suggestive, is the differentiation of experience in Luhmann's sense as described previously.

To bridge the gap between indefinite modes of solving the meaning problem and the inescapable need to do it, experience differentiates into two kinds. On the one hand men come increasingly to rely on secondhand experience. For a given individual this occurs through his involvement in simulated interaction.[20] The solitary TV viewer is one example; partaking of the meaning achievement of interacting fictional characters in a book is another. The distinctive criterion of "secondhand experience" is the relatively unreflected acceptance of reduced complexity from a distant social source mediated in such a way that the individual cannot supply his own feedback. Hence the source of experience is action, but one that lies beyond reach. This must involve some reflexive mechanism that transforms vicarious interaction into experience. The other type of experience is genuinely individualized self-generated "subjective experience." In distinction to secondhand experience, reduced complexity by others here is merely a stimulus supply for the individual to work up his very own meaning. Again, the relation between subjective and secondhand experience poses a problem of integration. Mismatch at this juncture also constitutes a source of uncertainty.

This sketch of historical evolution of the meaning problem suggests that structural sources of perceived and anticipated uncertainty have multiplied. Older sources were retained, though in altered form, and newer ones were added as one moves from stage to stage. Unless the sketch is quite wrong, the intensity of facing the problem of meaning in uncertainty and the attendant sense of risk have increased at each step as well. Certainly, life in a relatively fused order was not ever objectively more secure. On the contrary, meaning was probably intrinsically more threatened. Any extraordinary event in nature such as climatic disaster or in personality such as insanity threatened directly the cosmologically interpreted institutional order. Perhaps it is not even exaggerated to say that the more intrinsically fused the meaning system the greater the chance for a disturbance on one part to reverberate throughout the whole. This would be an image of the primitive given order as virtually flooded with threats to its stability from unrecognized environments. But the latter is the point here: there were no recognized structural sources of uncertainty which one could *fear* (and hence attempt to mitigate by special mechanisms of reduction), there was only generalized diffuse uncertainty one could be generally *anxious* about. But with specific structural sources of uncertainty being symbolically recognized as multiplying, the demands for reduction through mediation and neutralization increased as well. Hence the need for mediating mechanisms should be a function of the level of development. Such mechanisms must be operative simultaneously and mutually contingently in culture, society, and personality; and they must cover both types of action and types of experience. Certainly one of their main functions must be to reduce complexity.

However, the proceding is but one aspect of the story of development. Its complement, the mechanisms of complexity production, needs emphasis as well. Certainly a long and continuing intellectual tradition that sees in development a movement from the simple to the complex invites a search for mechanisms of complexity production. The idea that it is also media that perform this function has been the major *result* of the fascination with the role of money in economics. Money has the fundamental property of facilitating credit, which permits innovation in and expansion of economic activities. Schumpeter's[21] insight locating the source of creative economic activities in the relation between banker and entrepreneur that "risked other people's money" was one stimulus. The recognition that money could be viewed usefully as a special case of speech was another, and the more important. Language, minimally consisting of a code—a rule-set defining the basic elements of meaning—and permissible symbol combinations constituting messages to serve as information for meaning of a more generalized nature, then served as the basic model of a mechanism of mediation that both produces and reduces complexity. The need for such double function can be rendered best by emphasizing the system-theoretical element of the theory of action.

SYSTEMICS AND NEED FOR MEDIA

Laying out the relevant backbround material for the two issues of the unbalanced diagonal interchanges and the uncertain status of the concept information demands, above all, attention to the concept system and system-environment relations. These form the bedrock for the concepts of function, structure, and process.

The concepts function and system constitute the baseline in the theory of action, "Indeed, it (function) is simply the corollary of the concept living system, delineating certain features in the first instance of the system-environment relation, and in the second, of the internal differentiation of the system itself".[22] Actually this biological perspective has three foci. Attention is placed on the characteristics of the system, those of the environment, and those of the relation between the two. Relative to an environment a system is characterized by lower complexity (and greater order or organization in it) and greater stability. Second, therefore, there is a difference with greater variety and lower stability "located" on the outside. And third, the most fundamental functional problem of a system turns on maintaining this difference through interchanges with the environment. This is to emphasize that contingency on the environment rather than autarchy is constitutive of the concept system. The principal mode of adapting to greater variety and lower stability outside occurs through partial replication inside. Internal differentiation increases both the system's internal complexity and its ability to change relations between the parts *without* endangering its basic pattern. A system has autonomy (capability of self-steering) to the extent that it can select "what it wants to be dependent upon" in the environment and use that selectivity to

guide its own internal differentiation process. This of course implies a conception of will. When combined with the idea of plural environments posing contingencies partly independently variable relative to each other, this yields the basic rationale for the familiar four-function differentiation that enables a system to specialize its functioning for external and internal problems of exchange and for instrumental and consummatory interests.[23]

For present purposes the nature of these basic axiomatics of the theory of action have two important implications. The first is that all subsystems in action systems are constituted as meaning systems, not as "physical thing" systems. The second import involves the recognition that evolution in meaning systems takes the form of reproducing complexity. Both of course assert that the analysis of symbolic mediation is what action analysis amounts to and that it goes beyond "sociological analysis".[24] Though always emphasizing this central aspect of meaning— as for example in the conception of role as shared expectations about rights and obligations in the case of social system—there have been formulations such as "a patterned conception of membership which distinguishes between those individuals who do and do not belong,"[25] which obscured the matter by making it possible for the reader to misplace his attention to concrete individuals rather than the patterned conception. That at least has been one of my errors for a fairly long time.

The same holds for the concept self-sufficiency as a criterion for the societal boundary. Even relatively recent formulations here remained somewhat ambiguous. Self-sufficiency in: (1) cultural components to meet societal exigencies, (2) role opportunities to meet personal exigencies for all stages of the life cycle, (3) self-recruitment by birth and socialization, and (4) adequate self-control over the economic-technological complex could be read to imply such nonsense as cultural and economic autarchy.[26] To my reading only one of the most recent formulations has definitely precluded such misinterpretation. "Self-sufficiency in relation to environments [the three nonsocial subsystems of the action system and the two nonaction environments], then, means stability of interchange relations and *capacity to control interchanges* in the interest of societal functioning."[27] This specifies autonomy in the sense of self-determined selectivity about contingencies as self-sufficiency.

If all four subsystems of action are meaning systems, then their difference rests with functional primacies. Some systems specialize for the production, modification, and maintenance of symbols and meanings themselves (culture), others for the cognate problems involved in meaningful interaction (social systems), yet others for the cognate problems of experience (personality), and still others for those of the behavioral response base underlying both action and experience. But all are meaning systems, and symbolic mediation constitutes their "action." As subsystems, all "act" in the sense of being involved in the production and reduction of complexity. What varies is the aim of such activities. In this light the best boundary criteria are undoubtedly conceptualized as language jurisdictions.[28] Different and functionally specialized codes are used to manipulate meanings from different sources for different "aims."

Viewing action systems as meaning systems has at least two distinct advantages. First, it exposes two glaring lacunae in the theory of action. Second, it suggests the direction in which an answer to these may be found. Let us elaborate.

One of the open questions in the theory of action is how far one can carry the utility of an evolutionary model of change. Evolutionary change of a system is a change in its reproduction of external complexity inside when and if the resulting increase in and stabilization of internal variety amounts to an institutionalized capacity to deal more effectively with variety and instability in its environments. Clearly the crucial point here is the integrative internal load. If the system becomes so busy with managing its own internal variety that its ability to deal with external conditions stays constant or even declines, no evolutionary change has taken place. Some other kind of change has resulted involving internal dissociation rather than differentiation. The idea of functional differentiation as a mode of reproducing external complexity inside contains, after all, two aspects. One is the liberation of a differentiated subsystem from problems irrelevant to its specialized tasks. The other is that such liberation is possible only to the extent that these problems are taken care of by other differentiated subsystems specializing for them. Hence functional differentiation by subsystem formation can only proceed in mutual contingency. If an economy, for example, is really to be free to specialize for the continuous production of generalized utilities, not only does it need inputs of factors of effectiveness in cooperation, factors of solideratiy underlying organization, and factors of integrity in the form of unreflected commitments to goods production, but it can count on some adequate level of supply in these only to the extent that they are produced by primarily noneconomic institutions which for their specialization in turn draw on utilities. Such mutual contingency in variety is endemic to the theory of action, which conceives of the production of meaniful action as a value-added process.[29] Hence it makes sense to speak of the evolutionary development of

one language jurisdiction only if one can demonstrate appropriate changes in neighboring language jurisdictions.

Where some growth of meaning systems is the issue, then, the use of such indicators as GNP growth or more broadly the standard of living become problematical. First of all, they may "reflect" but analytically they are not what evolves.[30] Second, a perspective of meaningful action as a value-added process links the concept evolution with a generalization of "economizing." To economize, as may be recalled, involves a process of change whereby the utility-value of inputs declines relative to the unit value of output. Money as a measure of value of utilities enables one to determine this, at least in principle. The formulation of power, influence, and commitments as media is premised on the desirability to view "bureaucratizing" (in the positive sense of increasing rational organization of collaborative effort), "solidarizing," and "legitimizing" as processes strictly parallel to economizing but involving values-in-effectiveness, solidarity, and integrity instead. Hence "bureaucratizing" involves a decline of effectiveness cost on the input side per unit of effectiveness output, the exact opposite of the commonsense notion of bureaucratic red tape.[31] The same holds for the remaining two processes where their function-specific values are at stake. Furthermore, what is combined stays constant: Factors of meaningful action always cover utilities, effectiveness, solidarity, and legitimacy. What varies is the form of their combinations and the "aims" pursued in their productive combination. This is a useful view even in the absence of the respective "measures of value" involved in practical application. It allows us to distinguish evolutionary change from nonevolutionary change. Economic change as a true resultant of "economizing" would still not amount to evolutionary change if it proceeds at demonstrable cost to political, solidary, and authentic exigencies. The reason is charmingly simple. Economic development regardless of cost in other institutional spheres does not incorporate variety from personality and culture into society but rather represses the need for their expression. It is a form of overselection over one societal boundary and minimally raises the interesting research problem of how long it might last.

Next, this view raises another problem, of how far one might usefully attempt to take a model of evolutionary change when analyzing subsystem differentiation. Should one look upon subsystem differentiation within an already fairly well differentiated economy as another potential candidate for evolutionary change? The system-environment conceptualization might provide a tentative answer. Accordingly, a system itself is seen as constituted of organized selections from its environments. Luhmann[32] used this perspective to give an abstract definition of modernity as consisting in the institutionalization of evolutionary change. This type of change can occur through the differentiation of three evolutionary mechanisms. These are: (1) variation in the form of mechanisms that permit internal structures to generate novelty by copying external variety; (2) selection in the form of mechanisms that select from novelties what is functional for the system under observation, and (3) stabilization in the form of a mechanism that stores selections that have proven their worth as types of problem solutions. Thus variation produces complexity, selection reduces it, and stabilization retains the higher level of internal variety achieved through subsystem formation.

As will be shown, the mechanisms of complexity production and reduction are media. Furthermore, in Parsons'[33] interchange paradigm, media control the production of functionally specialized action. Hence media are prior to function-specific subsystem formation and sustain it once formed. Therefore, we have at least two sources suggesting a methodological rule of thumb where the utility of asserting evolutionary stages might conveniently stop. Whether in their role as differentiated mechanisms of evolution or as regulators of the flow between differentiated subsystems, the number of media conceptualizable at a given stage determine whether one can speak of evolution or not. In the present state of action theory, this means that the primary differentiation of the action system into culture, society, personality, and behavioral organism is an evolutionary state description because four general action media have been proposed. At a secondary level of differentiation applicable to any one of these four primary subsystems, society too seems analyzable in terms of evolutionary change into its own subststems of economy, polity, societal community, and legitimacy subsystem because four societal media have been proposed.

And here is where the story ends. A theory of action study of the evolution of culture as a symbol system, for example, is not likely to be impressively successful until we have developed its four subsystem media. "Cognitive truth" in terms of a combination of the methodological requisites of both validity and reliability as a medium in science, a likely candidate for the status of the adaptive subsystem of culture, might be an appropriate example. But until some such conception as "cognitive truth" (for the A-subsystem) together with such possible candidates as "aesthetic judgment" (for the G-subsystem), "consistency" (for the I-subsystem), and perhaps some religiously musical "axiomatics" (for the L-subsystem of constitutive symbolism) have been elaborated as media, i.e., as symbolic mechanisms

effecting symbolic combinations, a study of cultural evolution in the action frame remains fraught with problems.[34] The methodological rule of thumb is that with no four-member family of media at the requisite level, no evolutionary advance can be demonstrated at that level. This does not deny the utility of looking at an economy or polity as themselves further internally organized around their own four functions in general; but it does deny viewing such internal differentiation as a further instance of evolution. No language differentiation, no subsystem formation in an evolutionary sense. But such an assertion needs better grounding. Therefore we turn to the problem of communication.

COMMUNICATION: MEANING, SIGNIFICANCE, RELEVANCE, AND INFORMATION

Parsons[35] maintains that, with economics, linguistics is the theoretically best developed discipline in the action field. I cannot claim expertise in it. Neither do I possess an adequate command over sociolinguistics and psycholinguistics, the other "natural sources" for decomposing communication. Hence it is with an especially appropriate sense of trepidation that I offer some suggestions of how to think about communication from a four-function perspective. That such an effort could conceivably be justified despite massive ignorance of the relevant disciplines hinges quite closely on the narrow aim pursued. I merely want to show one way in which a medium could perform contrary functions. If I can show a plausible basis for this in the structure of any kind of communication, it should aid in developing the proper qualifications to make the principle of double function applicable to media, which are after all forms of communication. The starting point here is the consideration that information is always involved in communication, and so is meaning. But these are not the only aspects involved, and they must be assigned a "role."

If role assignment to components is the issue, it may be useful to conceive of communication itself as an action system facing the familiar four-function dilemma. The starting point here is the consideration that when A supplies information to B, the latter gains something without the former incurring a loss *in the same currency,* that is, information. Hence, one can share something like scarce information without altering its status as information. One can also repeat statements without affecting their significance linguistically. But other aspects may be affected. These may include the value of information or its relevance in a set of situations.[36] Shared meaning in terms of language competency, furthermore, is presupposed in communicating; it is not transported. This suggests the need to distinguish information and meaning as Luhmann[37] emphasizes. But it seems also useful to conceptualize both as aspects of meaning and add two more. The four-function paradigm "inspires" one to pursue the problem in this direction.

The problem of this kind of cogitation is that it poses the classical philosophical dilemma: cogitating about meaning as if this did not already presuppose meaning. It might be useful to recall that Parsons in his earlier work avoided this dilemma in defining his most "premitive" concept. The definition of action in terms of: (1) conditions (environmental aspects beyond manipulation), (2) means (manipulable environmental aspects), (3) ends, and (4) guiding norms[38] with its intrinsic teleology presupposes some agency capable of realizing meaning. Meaning itself is taken for granted, rather than treated as problematical. Normally there is no doubt that this is the wisest choice for nonphilosophers. But it cannot be endorsed when the effort is to get at the components of communication, which is a meaning construction process as is the case here. Furthermore, when using the system-environment relation as his starting point for articulating the concept function, Parsons[39] comes close to taking meaning itself as problematical. But to my taste this is not done explicitly enough. Making it blatant might contribute further clarity, though this is not very easy. Hence, with a real sense of trepidation I shall try to use yet more primitive terms from which the four-function paradigm itself could be derived. By its very nature such a formulation must sound quite artificial and near-meaningless.

The two terms to be connected are system and function. It was stated above that system connotes a difference in complexity and stability between two phenomena. This "means" that, relative to some X, system is more organized, i.e., a configuration with lower complexity and higher stability. The only necessary postulate here is that a system aims at maintaining this differential. Boundary maintenance is the ultimate survival goal, as it were. At this most general level there are two possible threats to maintaining the boundary. Either the complexity differential is dangerously low, or the stability differential is dangerously low. Combining both sources of threat yields four types of entropic danger conditions. Given the notion of greater organization in complexity as constitutive of the concept system, there are only two necessary system responses to these dangers of entropy: increase internal complexity, or decrease it. Next, function is mediation of complexity differentials. Mediation is going from one to many, or the reverse, from many to one. It should be noted that stability is a special case of complexity.

Complexity is time-invariant; stability is not, as it involves change through time. But such change operates on complexity in the organization of components. Hence, complexity is the more general, stability the less general. This is important because function as mediation over the boundary operates on the more general regardless of the potentially different centrality of time.

Function, then, is mediation of the differential between system and environment. It involves adjustments in complexity differentials regardless of the source of the pressure, whether the threat to boundary maintenance comes immediately from too low a stability differential or too low a complexity differential. This has a direct implication for viewing evolutionary change in societies. Such change always involves upgrading internal complexity in the organization of society, not just any kind of change, as for example urbanization, growth in GNP, and the like. Though I cannot develop this theme fully here, evolutionary change involves primarily complexity change in patterns, never just social change as ordinarily described.

Already we may pause a moment for the sake of illustration. In an enterprise such as this, trying to make sense out of sense, illustration because it presumes meaning involves committing the illegitimate, taking for granted what we wish to derive. Supposing that meaning were known, the notion of complexification, one to many, or the reverse, simplification through generalization, many to one, underlies a great deal of scientific analysis. The notion "one to many" underlies analysis in the strict sense. This involves breaking down or disaggregating one proposition, concept, or phenomenon observed into several. Familiar procedure in science also illustrates the reverse: from many to one. This is what we do in ideal-type, in proposition, and in law constructions. Here several parts are combined into a meaningful configuration.

Next to a conception of system as outlined, we only need one other assumption. This involves a special characteristic of living as contrasted with nonliving systems. The assumption is that life is intrinsically a constant struggle against entropy.[40] In our case of the system-environment relation there are two principal sources for entropy, and hence death: Either the complexity differential between system and environment reaches dangerously low limits, or the same happens involving its special case, the stability differential between the inside and the outside. Function is mediation of complexities in response to such threats and in the service of ameliorating them. Principally this can happen in two ways: internal complexity is either increased or decreased. But system response to boundary breakdown potential always involves operations on the general, complexity, rather than the particular, stability. Yet on the side of the outside environment these two entropic threats operate partly independently of each other. That is why a system involves mediation over a double boundary.

Let us dichotomize the principal environmental variables for a system and speak of high or low complexity differential and high or low stability differential. In both cases low designates an entropic threat, high a state of security. Combining the two variables with their two values yields four combinations of different types of threat to system survival.

Obviously, the most severe threat is a combination of low differentials on both dimensions: low stability and complexity differentials at the same time. What can be done? If life is an effort aimed against entropy, the response here must be to work up complexity. The system response must be operation on the more general to defeat the double threat from the general and the particular. Parts inside are not only insufficiently differentially complex from the outside, but low stability differential signals that they also lack organization. Hence the only lifesaving strategy is to increase complexity inside to subject disorganized parts to greater control. Now, as the level of fit among parts inside is the primary aim, one might denote this complexity-productive response as integrative functioning. Somewhat contrary to commonsense expectation, integrative functioning operates through complexity production.

The next possibility to be taken up involves a threat from too low complexity differentials but no threat from stability differentials. This, given the interdependence between complexity and stability, is only a short-run contingency. What response on the part of the system seems reasonable here? With no immediate threat from stability differentials, the path of least resistance and least effort suggests itself. This is the reduction of complexity inside in order to increase the differential on this dimension. Such reduction of course involves a modification in the patterned organization of parts. Therefore, this complexity reduction response yields a broader conception of the pattern-maintenance function; instead of just pattern-maintenance function it should read pattern-maintenance and modification function. This is not a new idea but merely a more economical formulation than that of Parsons.[41]

The third combination might be simply the reverse of the one just considered: a threat from a low stability differential, but no threat from the complexity differential. This then, involves the particular, not the general. Nevertheless, the path of least effort suggests itself once more. Low stability differential in the face of adequate complexity differentials is directly a short run problem. The most adequate response would be reduction of complexity inside in order to gain greater stability inside relative to the outside. In addition to repairing the threatened stability boundary, the use of internal complexity reduction inside yields an extra kind of bonus, viz., an increase in the complexity differential where none on its own ground was called for. Complexity differentials are increased at no extra cost through reduction inside. Not only is a desired state attained (increase in stability differential), the over-all distinctiveness of the system is also improved. Given this "catching of two birds with one stone," this complexity reduction response has a distinctly consummatory flavor. More importantly, though, regaining a lost security state vis-à-vis the outside being the issue, mediating this combination is the goal-attainment function.

Before leaving these two cases and turning to the last, a brief comment is in order. They share a feature: the system response is complexity reduction. But they also contrast in two ways. First, the same response is due to different kinds of boundary threats, too low a complexity differential in the pattern maintenance function and too low a stability differential in the goal-attainment function. Second, the significance of the same response, complexity reduction inside, is different for the system. In the pattern case, it is of instrumental significance; in the goal-attainment case, it is consummatory. Clearly this must involve the time factor in different ways. When there is no direct threat in the short run, due to sufficient stability differential but a pattern distinctiveness threat, as there is in the pattern case, reducing complexity does not mortgage the future because repairing the complexity boundary (1) does not occur in response to time pressures and (2) constitutes a kind of future insurance because of the absence of need to attend to the immediacy of external threat. (Obviously the role of time is crucial here. Obviously too this theme is insufficiently developed as it stands. But at least it should point to the direction whence better grounding could be found.) Reducing complexity in response to low stability differentials, however, is quite the opposite. Low stability differentials signal rates of change inside and out too similar for boundary maintenance. There are changes in complexity, but they run through time, involving such similar units that distinctiveness is threatened. The response itself is time-triggered and time-oriented, and to the here and now. Reduction of complexity in this case therefore involves mortgaging the future.

Finally, the last possible combination involves high differentials on both dimensions of complexity and stability. No entropic threat to system maintenance exists at all. System and environment are in equilibrium. Hence, there is no "response" one could expect on the part of the system in ways analogous to the previous combinations. But drawing on life as an intrinsically anti-entropic process suggests adaptive functioning through complexity production. When there is no threat at all, further internal complexity is worked up to prepare for future contingencies up to the point where one of the boundaries is threatened.

For a convenient overview, Figure 22-1 summarizes the discussion graphically.

Having derived some, though necessarily very general, notion of the "meanings" of four functions, one can now proceed to take these four functions for granted in constructing a functional model of communication as a meaning production process. As meaning is always selection from multiple possibilities, production here also works through combining complexity production and reduction functions.

Combining the idea of "sources of meaning" fairly current in linguistics with the four-function paradigm just outlined as a derivative of the system-environment relation, communication as a four-function process productive of meaning can now be considered in outline form. Though not following it in detail, the central idea underlying this functional paradigm is borrowed from Beneviste's insistence that "language is a system in which nothing is significant in and of itself, but in which everything is significant as an element of the pattern; structure confers upon the parts their 'meaning' or their function."[42] Accordingly, two general sources of meaning productions can be suggested. One of these, semantics, is "more" linguistic intrinsically than the other, contextual. These are the marginal variables for the function table. Each needs dichotomization.[43]

Turning to the first, one might dichotomize semantics into lexicals on the one hand and syntax and grammar on the other. As used here lexicals refers to symbolic elements characterized by: (1) cognitive-denotative primacy, and (2) marginality of meaning. Thus lexicals belong to a category of symbols which in contrast to all others are least invested linguistically with meaning. They are the raw-material base on which meaning constructions rely, but they themselves have hardly any meaning. This formulation is to be compatible with an early action-theoretical recognition that sheer object denotations are the least "creative" symbols conceivable.[44] In the present perspective lexicals have primarily external reference outside communication, selecting from environs what communication as a functional process requires. Syntax plus grammar, on the other hand, with primarily internal reference constitute the code aspects used to make selections from lexicals to form types of languages. It should be emphasized that "language" as used here refers to all manner of communicating, covering music, dance, ordinary language such as the English tongue, and so on.

As to the second marginal variable, context, this is to fill another requisite of any four-function paradigm, that of mediation over the instrumental-consummatory functional cleavage through time. Dichotomizing again, let "situation" refer to the instrumental side and "behavior" to the consummatory. The former denotes situation in the traditional action-theoretical sense. It covers conditions which are beyond the ability of communicators to manipulate and to which, as a consequence, communication has to adapt, as well as means for communication. This is quite parallel to situation in Parsons' sanctions paradigm. However, on the consummatory

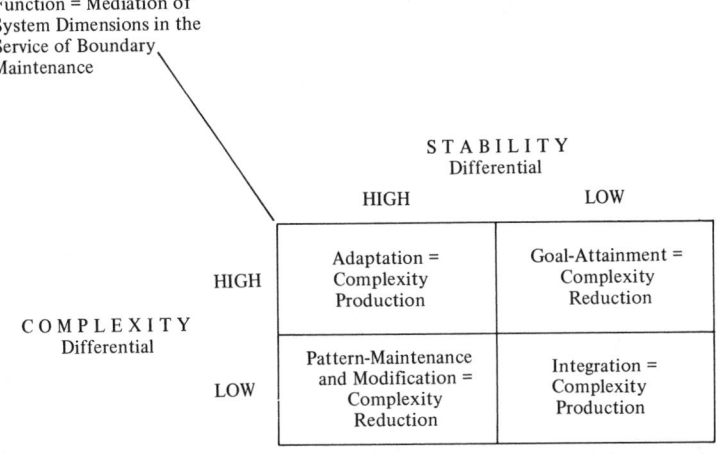

Figure 22-1.

side of the paradigm, behavior instead of intention is used. Behavior as used here refers to a context aspect, not to intentions of others' as in interaction. The reason is simple. Intention would restrict communication to social interaction, hence preclude meaning productions associated with reading a book, for example. Sticking to a minimalist definition, behavior as used here refers to the teleological aspect of the definition of action: the end pursued. Here in the broadest sense this means "striving for some understanding." Parallel to semantics, context is a selector mechanism. It denotes what is to constitute means, what conditions (situational side), and what are the class of understanding to be pursued. For example, for the solitary prayer in an otherwise empty church, context is constituted in the devotional paraphernalia constituting means, some elements of orthodoxy constituting the conditional realm. On the behavioral side, experience here would be selected as the goal of communication.

With these conceptual elements at hand, the next step is to combine the dichotomized values of the marginals in order to define functionally the content of the four cells. Situation and lexicals function to provide information in the sense of a symbolic raw-materials stock made available for communication to draw on. Behavior and lexicals function to provide a selective guidance component. This is relevance. Conceived as a goal-attainment component, relevance selects from information aspects adequate for whatever particular "striving for understanding" is at issue. Situation and syntax with grammar function to provide significance. As a pattern-maintenance and modification function significance selects criteria for gauging consistency in the flow of statements. Finally, syntax with grammar and behavior functions to yield implication. Conceived as integrative function for the elements of communication, implication provides that level of richness in symbolic

variety sufficient for realizing whatever the particular understandings aimed at require. For a convenient overview, Figure 22-2 presents a summary of communication as a four-function problem. This retains the location of the complexity production (P) and complexity reduction (R) functions derived before.

As Figure 22-2 shows some resemblance with Parsons'[45] sanctions paradigm, a comment is in order. They are not the same. The major difference rests in the fact that Parsons' sanctions paradigm is not a functional one in the technical sense. Using positive and negative sanctions in the commonsense terminology, this is immediately visible in the placement of function-specialized media in a format at variance with the usual presentation of the four-function paradigm. Making it a functional paradigm should of course be possible. According to the perspective of this paper, one possible way would be to substitute action and experience for positive and negative sanctions and then let the combinatories of this new marginal variable with the channel variable "dictate" the use of positive and negative sanctions. Such a strategy of revision would look as in Figure 22-3.

Returning to communication, before putting some flesh on the skeleton provided by Fig. 22-2, a few cautionary notes. First, the term semantic, as used here, refers to the generic, as a structural aspect of any kind of language, verbal, musical, mime, or whatever. Thus cowhorse is a designation with an irreducible lexical component, and so is the note designated as middle C with reference to a set of musical lexicals. Second, the distinction between the contextual and the semantic is relative, not absolute. If contextual symbols are to symbolize anything, they too must be parts of some semantics. Third, this base model of communication is designed to cover any conceivable type, verbal, nonverbal, with cognitive, cathectic, evaluational, or constitutive symbol primacy, one-way, two-way, or combinations of all

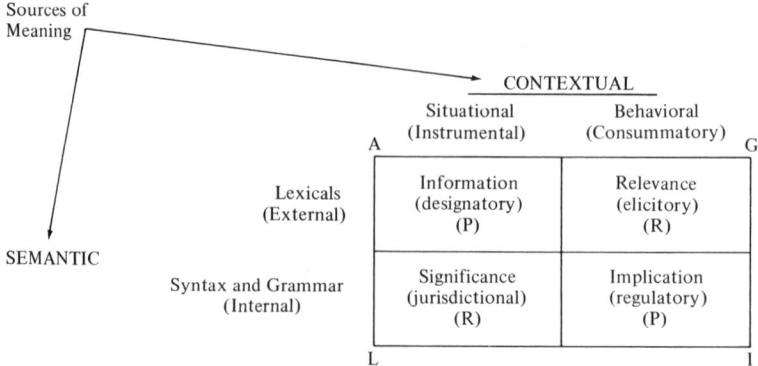

Figure 22-2. The structure of communication in functional perspective.

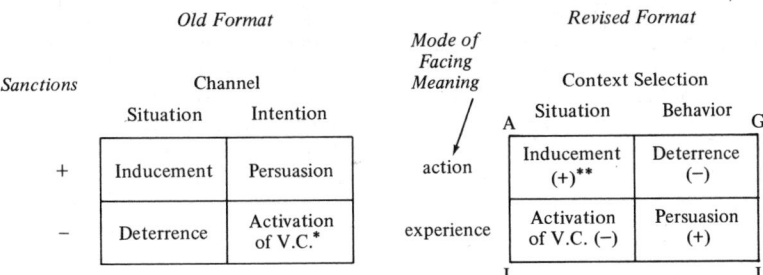

Figure 22-3. Sanctions paradigm.
*V.C. = Value Commitments.
** = sanction type as a result of meaning source and context combinations.

of these. Last, the purpose is narrow indeed: showing just one way in which communicating meaning produces and reduces complexity. Put differently, communication as a flow of intrinsically worthless statements achieves its "aim," which is a sense of comprehension, by varying sources of meaning and scope of meaning.

Communication is a process of extending invitations to partake of understandings. Always extended by an actor to an object(s), social or nonsocial, the primary case here used for illustration will be the social one. Invitations appearing in the form of statements have no intrinsic worth. They have "value in exchange," not in use. Parsons' "intrinsic satisfier" here is the realization of some understanding. Next, as a value-added process "aiming at understanding," communication relies on the combination of four basic components. These, indicated inside the boxes in Figure 22-2, are modes of effecting meaning by tapping different sources of it: syntactic-grammarial, lexical, situational, and behavioral. The basic view here is that only when all four sources have been activated and only after each has made its functional contribution have the necessary prerequisites for the chance of an understanding been fulfilled. The proposed "family" of functional components of: (1) significance, (2) implication, (3) relevance, and (4) information constitute analytical aspects of any concrete medium of communicating such as speech, music, dance, mime, and combinations of these. They are not to be confused with such concrete forms as making statements. It follows that communication cannot be defined in terms of any class of concretely observable statements. A functional definition may be possible, however.

The same statement can be of informational value to some, of relevance to others, full or devoid of implications for yet others, and so on. The announcement "heavy snow blanketed the East throughout the night" may mean "no school today" for children, the expectation of cancelled appointments for the commuting father, reminiscences of *temps perdu* for grandmother. In a seminar discussion on "feudal aspects of modern Japan" announcing that Japan had a faster growth of GNP throughout the post-World War II period than the established industrial nations of the West may be supporting evidence "relevant" for a functional theoretician of modernization insisting on the need to distinguish political and economic development; it may be "full of implications" demanding a comparative assessment for him who views development as a push-pull process between different functional sectors of society; for one convinced that modernization is all of one package it might be a threateningly "significant" statement; and for another participant, never seriously interested in the potential utility of the modern-traditional contrast in the first place, it may be "mere information" for unspecified future use. This illustration suggests that the functional status of a statement in a communication depends on its purposes and the participants' role in pursuing them. This is always a result of the combination of all four components.

Let us specify more details. Significance is a selector mechanism that allocates a concrete medium to a given context of communication, and with that, defines the major sources of meaning to be legitimately used for it. In the two-way communication context of a seminar, for example, the concrete medium appropriate is talk and the legitimate sources of meaning to be exploited are primarily of the action variety, either in the public or private sense described in the first section of this essay or combinations of the two. The amount of the ratio between public and private action sources surely depends minimally on restricting seminar participation by disciplinary specialization, i.e., to those who share a special vocabulary of discourse. Relatively open seminars rely more on commonsense language competence, more specialized ones on the esoteric language shared by smaller circles of specialists.

On the other hand, where music is selected as a medium in a context of the performing arts, the sources of meaning to be legitimately utilized are typically a mixture of action types and experience types. The audience has to assume bona fide performance by the musicians according to prevailing standards. Given this, the audience is expected to accept complexity reduction from performers in order to produce-reduce their own experience. What seems to distinguish the "live" from the "canned" context of the acceptance of complexity reduction from others primarily is the element of surprise intrinsically given in the former but absent in the latter, at least after repeated exposure. The fact that no repeated performance is ever exactly identical when done by man affords the listener a greater chance to vary his own experiences. Secondhand experience as music from the "can" demands more of the listener concerning his experience construction. Here he has to manage to surprise himself without the aid of others.

In setting a language jurisdiction, significance selects the latitude permitted between alter's action as a constituent of ego's experience. In a typical seminar the two are set equal. Unarticulable "subjective experience" or similarly unarticulated secondhand insight, as simply quoting expert opinion, are not legitimate contributions. In a typical concert the two are set as unequal. Whatever the performer(s) may experience, his/their action constitute but invitations for the listener's own construction of a musical experience. Finally, although such traditional mixed media shows as a Wagner opera makes one appropriately hesitant about saying so, significance by selecting a concrete medium seems also to select at least some rough ranking of the differential importance to be attached to different symbols. Thus despite the fact that a Wagner opera "operates" on several planes in being simultaneously a symphony, chamber music, dramatic theatre, and, given its notorious length, perhaps even a novel, hence involving music, speech, and mime, significance here nevertheless for most seems to select music as the major medium. With that it also selects expressive symbols as primary over cognitive symbolization. In a seminar, presumably, the situation is reversed: cognitive rationality "rules" and expressiveness is supposed to be mute. Clearly, however, the seminar with its talk and talk-simulative aids such as graphing designates expressive symbolism as instrumental at best while giving consummatory significance to cognitions. The significance inherent in musical communication reverses this relation. Clearly, humans can be "turned on" by the Beatles whether they understand cognitively what the Beatles are doing or not. A traditional Roman Catholic mass, on the other hand, with its phasing of music-song and sermon-talk aims at some complex blend of maximizing expressiveness and evaluational symbolism. These illustrations should indicate that significance in the present conception does the defining of the definition of the situation. As multiple selections are involved covering context, concrete medium, and legitimate sources of meaning, significance functions primarily to reduce complexity.

Implication mediates bits of communication by regulating their flow. It owes its integrative primacy in the present schema to the relative indeterminateness observable by common sense in "natural" every-day verbal speech. Neither given words, nor sentences carry precise meanings. The same is true of a note or even a theme in music, provided "precise meaning" is that ready for consumption, be that through types of action or experience. Such relative lack of selectivity is that which gives implication its integrative role. Hence implication can be defined as a communications element that functions to focus attention on some selections of sense while retaining alternative connotations.[46] Retention of additional variety is the central function here. Hence, although implication selects, as do all components, relative to significance and relevance, implication produces complexity. Such selection points to a given sense of the statement(s) without abandoning in principle other alternatives. Put differently, implication selects very incompletely. Only "implausible alternatives" to explicit sense are excluded. Whole ranges of "neighbouring plausible alternatives" to explicit sense are implicitly retained in the ongoing speaker-listener exchange. Circumlocutions like "I think you must imply x in your statement y," so characteristic in the use of speech for joint cognitive reflection, testify to this regulatory role. A similar function can be observed in music, at least in the West since its "break-out" of the medieval cantus firmus. The presentation of a theme carries an implication. The "announcement" of a theme constitutes at the same time an invitation to expect a variation in the future, which may be in the form of a change of key, a mirror image, a reversal of notes, or combinations. Such invitation reduces surprise when the expectation is fulfilled, increases attention to unfulfilled plausibilities when not.

Viewed in this manner, implication can be said to facilitate speaker-listener sensitivity about the gap between speech intent and speech realization and the constraints exercised on communication by time. As implication sensitizes speaker-listeners to what might, should, or will be said, it plays a primarily consummatory role in communication as an invitation for partaking of understandings. The meaning source involved, however, is syntactical-grammarial and behavioral in the main, in that it is the connotative variety inherent in the medium that allows implication to become an input into communication. Thus by operating through the retention of plausible alternatives to explicits, implication functions as a mechanism of complexity production. It is admittedly a bit of a curious idea that an integrative mechanism should function by complexity production. Yet the matter is not quite so absurd as might appear at first glance when communication is viewed as process creative of meaning by virtue of imperfections inherent in one element used in it.

Relevance functions as a guidance mechanism for the communication process. By calling for relevance we exhort another (through question and comment) to stick to the topic. Again, what is true for verbal speech communication holds for music too. It is said of Glenn Gould, contemporary pianist and Bach interpreter of some repute, that he knows but fans and foes. For some he makes Bach relevant in ways they never expected; for others he romanticizes Bach to the point of irrelevance. For the latter group, whatever else he may be doing, he is not interpreting Bach, perhaps not even playing him, but rather displaying himself. Whether in speech, music, mime, or dance, letting the implications run wild or succumbing to information wealth constitute the principle threats to relevance. The achievement of meaning is always the product of selection from possibilities into a configuration of sense. Meaning is symbolic *Gestalt*, and relevance a steering mechanism by which speaker-listeners discard that which lacks sufficient configuration. Thus, in contrast to implication, relevance is a mechanism that represses alternatives of sense. Given the orientation to other and the underlying fear of getting lost rather than moving towards a partaking of an understanding, the meaning sources activated are primarily behavioral and lexical. With selectivity primary, relevance functions to reduce complexity.

Finally, with two of the mediating mechanisms identified as complexity reducers and one as producing complexity, the last one, information, should again be viewed as a source of complexity production to balance the model. But apart from balancing the model the adaptive dimension has a special place in communication as a process aiming at the achievement of meaning. All "meanings," except the adaptive, are superimposed on the intrinsic properties of objects. As a condition of viability, sufficient external complexity must be admitted for internal processing in minimally distorted form, lest external complexity and instability overwhelm the system. Information, therefore, can be defined as a mechanism that admits

sufficient variety from situational and lexical sources of meaning for implication to play its regulatory role and relevance to "pick and choose" that external contingency most promising for the achievement of configurational sense. For example, whether a seminar discourse remains one depends among other things on whether sufficient variety from the situation of some academic context is admitted. If not, a seminar may change into another kind of communication process where cathectic rather than cognitive symbols "rule." A kind of status competition characterized by "flight and fight" may be one outcome, the feeding of affiliational needs at the expense of cognitive ones another. Similarly, whether a musical communication retains the primacy of cathectic symbols rather than degenerating into a sheer display of technical brilliance depends at least also on admittance of sufficient situational variety. The accomplished artist asked to play a simple piece may get bored, the less proficient accepting a complex obligation may just struggle to maintain cognitive control over his performance. In both cases neither implication nor relevance can do their work because of insufficient selection or overselection from situational supplies outside the given communication episode.

This perspective permits one to view communication as a value-added process which aims at the construction of meaning through alternating phases of complexity production and reduction. The precise sequences of such phasing cannot be described here. They are probably quite variable. What can be identified are the relations between the function-specific components that specialize for one or the other and for the utilization of different sources of meaning. This is indicated in Figure 22-4 which summarizes the preceding discussion.

No doubt one could supply a set of suggestive labels for the input-output flow of functionally different productions and reductions of complexity. However, this would not materially advance the analysis. For that, one needs more than labels which in turn requires considerably more work. It might suffice, therefore, to state that this model is quite parallel to Parsons' media interchange paradigm in all respects save one. Beginning with the common elements, the principle functional significance of the horizontal and vertical interchanges have been kept unaltered as they were first presented.[47] Horizontal interchanges facilitate adaptive needs in that they articulate the instrumental with the consummatory aspects of system functioning. Vertical interchanges facilitate goal-attainment needs in that they articulate external with internal contingencies "enabling" a system to select from environments what it wants to be contingent on and hence facilitating the principal survival goal of maintaining the

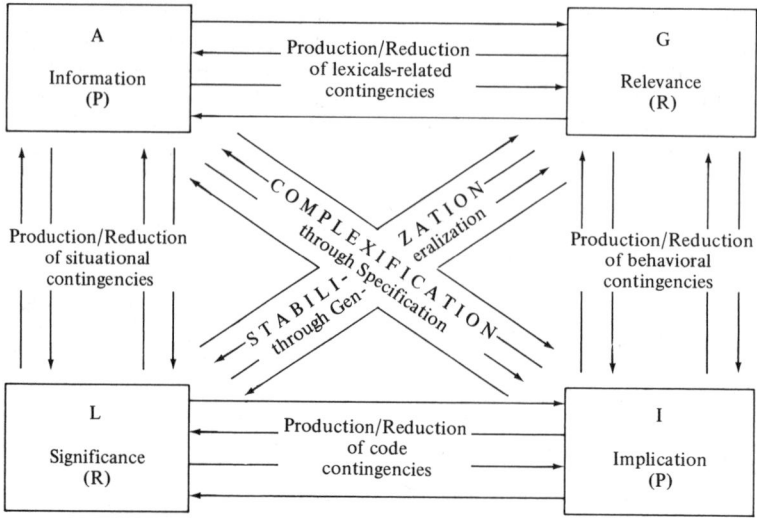

Where: Complexification = Production of External and Internal variety.
Stabilization = Reduction of External and Internal variety.
P = Component productive of complexity.
R = Component reductive of complexity.

Figure 22-4. The process of communication in functional perspective.

threshold of differential complexity and stability between the inside and the outside.

On the diagonal interchanges, however, there is a departure from Parsons. Here I accept the principal message of Gould's revised interchange format (in this volume). Rather than set the diagonals as integrative on the presumption that meaning problems have been met, which is of course impossible for a model that treats the construction of meaning as problematical, the present schema allocates the production of complexity to the A-I interchange where information "feeds" implications and implication "generates" more information by producing more and more specifications of meanings. Specialization for reduction, and reduction only, is allocated to the L-G interchange where significance restricts relevance and vice versa. If one accepts the notion of complexification through specification as a process of replicating more and more environmental complexity inside the system and stabilization through generalization as the appropriate balancing process of preserving this gain in internal complexity, then the always-noted special status of the diagonal interchanges is preserved. But it also seems improved. That there must be something special is recognized by Parsons in claiming that the L-G interchange involves code elements directly, while the others do not. The schema presented here intends to preserve this insight but complement it more adequately by giving a similar special status to the A-I interchange. This is done by allocating to both antonym

functions. Interchanges in both cases "cross" the double cleavage of the four-function paradigm, the external-internal *and* the instrumental-consummatory, *at the same time.* But effects and functions performed for the system are precisely opposite, viz. complexification in A-I and stabilization in L-G.

Two further implications of this view of communication deserve mention. One is a kind of finding. Components productive of complexity are cognate with societal media employing positive sanctions; components reductive of complexity, with those involving negative sanctions. The other is a kind of coincidence in viewing the integration problem writ large. There is a tie here between stabilization and Parsons'[48] analysis of Durkheim's mechanical solidarity on the one hand, and between complexification and organic solidarity on the other.[49]

As can be gleaned from Figure 22-4, the components productive of complexity parallel the case of the media of money and influence at the societal level, both of which involve positive sanctions. This suggests that these media operate to provide greater complexity in the organization of society primarily. In the case of money this does not come as that much of a surprise. Money is defined functionally as of primarily adaptive significance. Also, the tremendous possibilities open under the freedom to contract suggest a basic role in providing social arrangement with increasing variety. Influence, however, with its function-specialization for internal and consummatory interests does not seem to fit the picture as well at first glance. Yet Schumpeter's economic entrepreneur does point to influence as a necessary complement to money if the latter is to play its most important role. This is clearly making it available through credit. That influence as such produces variety analogously to money, though with a different aim, has been implicitly recognized by Parsons. He presented four types of influence,[50] of which one, "fiduciary" influence, has primarily resource allocation significance. As, then, in a highly monetized society money becomes one of the major allocation mechanisms, with respect not only to commodities but also to human services, and as influence importantly guides banking of monetary funds in the credit-extension sense, the production of complexity function underlying this medium can also be seen without too much a strain on credibility.

That two of the communications functions here associated with putting an end to speculation about meaning possibilities should find their parallel among the societal media with power and value-commitments, both deploying negative sanctions, seems quite reasonable as well. They are the parallels. To go into a g-phase collectively is the exercise of collective will; it connotes a temporary stop to learning, paying attention to differential implications and other contingency vicissitudes. A command constitutes action; it is reduced complexity that must be accepted from others. One need not put a narrow military or authoritarian interpretation on this, with very narrow detail specifications coupled with total unreflectiveness "where orders are orders," which could cost one seeing power as circulating medium. But if it were not a question of action as acceptance of reduced complexity from others, the whole idea of bindingness would be lost. The case of activating societal value-commitments through sociomoral rhetoric seems similarly simple. This process relies on experience as a security base. Appealing to another on moral considerations presumes he has been socialized to be committed to the same ideals. He is supposed to feel guilty in the case of recalcitrance. Excluding the possibility that he has an acceptable excuse, which could only be a higher moral obligation than the one invoked, he is expected upon stimulation from another to accept reduced moral complexity stored in his super-ego from the past. In fact then he is expected to accept reduced complexity from a source over which he never had and never could gain a degree of control comparable at all to that he exercises over other spheres in his life. Psychoanalysts like to characterize this state of affairs as the ineluctible fate of the infancy scene.

As these connections between complexity production-reduction and the sanction types imply, this whole issue also implies Durkheim's contrasting conceptions of mechanical and organic solidarity. These two interchanges—A-I involving complexification through specification and L-G involving stabilization through generalization—share a characteristic in that they are the diagonal interchanges in the four-function paradigm; but they also contrast in that they connect different functional problems. The most important common element is one of nonrationality. This is most evident in the operation of influences and value commitments. As a condition of its efficacy, influence rests on the complete taken-for-grantedness of ends. There must be unproblematical consensus on ends and adequately institutionalized trust in recognized expertise; otherwise, suggestions as to means will not evoke compliance but rather demands for detail justifications. But when assertions of intent are actually subjected to verification, influence has stopped. In the doctor-patient relation the unproblematical consensus on ends concerns the preference of health over illness and life over death. Such unreflectiveness must be the result of powerful social control forces of the past and the present, as the forces pressuring men towards escape from performance in society and indeed from life itself cannot be presumed to be weak.

There is a similarly nonrational base to the operation of commitments. No one chooses his parents and his infant socialization scene; hence at the requisite level of common societal values no one chooses his commitments, and most are slaves to them. Minimally, in a highly differentiated society this involves the inescapability of willingly taking individual responsibility for one's action. Out of this "Protestant" bind hardly anyone is permitted to opt out. This kind of willing acceptance of responsibility constitutes a necessary precondition for the freedom to contract, which is indeed wide. What one contracts and how one settles terms can be subjected to wider and wider ranges of variety, primarily to the extent that the element of unit responsibility can be taken for granted. But as long as requisite relevance can be presumed on responsibility, normative variety which constitutes the essence of organic solidarity[51] can grow. For the function of the latter (I-A) is above all to connect institutionalized norms with the incredible growth in the complexity of the role structure. Mechanical solidarity, on the other hand, concerns the relation between societal values and society's primary agency of implementing them, governmental function. "Mechanical solidarity is the integration of the common values of the society with the commitments of units within it to contribute to the attainment of collective goals either negatively by refraining from interference or positively by taking responsibility for it.[52] Hence this involves directly the citizenship complex through the processing of legitimation and legalization of power agents (L-G). The central connecting link to complexity reduction here remains Durkheim's discovery of the interpenetration of personality and society. In this famous analysis of suicide under conditions of expanding economic fortunes, where the utilitarisns would have had to predict rising "happiness," one cause of suicide was clearly not a lack of means to attain goals but rather an inability to integrate new goal possibilities meaningfully with old institutionalized expectations. Clearly too this signaled the possibility of a malintegration between the meaningfulness of situations and alternatives to action. As, finally, internalized commitments are in important respects beyond the control of "reason," they play a conditions role in the situation. Hence, unless pressures for complexification are counteracted by complexity reduction, mental ill-health and anomie would be the inevitable result.[53]

Finding such links with previous work in the theory of action can be taken as some sign that the present effort to dig deeper into the assumptions-soil of the four-function paradigm and the status of information cannot be wholly mistaken. If so, it should be possible to draw some empirical implications from the above. Hence, in closing, one may attempt some illustrations of the functioning of societal media from this vantage point.

SOCIETAL MEDIA AS MECHANISMS OF DECISION-SAVING AND DECISION-MAKING

Two "findings" of the preceding analysis are important in teasing out some implications for understanding the functioning of societal media. These are: (1) that when analyzed as a communications system the same medium-in-use, speech for example, can be conceived as simultaneously productive and reductive of meaning complexity *because* using it actually involves activating four communications functions and (2) that adaptive integrative interchanges always complexify the world, while pattern maintenance and goal-attainment exigencies stabilize it. In addition, trust has been repeatedly emphasized as central to an understanding of media. It is therefore time to define it.

"Whosoever renders trust puts the future into the present." "Acting in trust is to reduce the complexity of future possibilities." "Trust, however, exists only if a trusting expectation (concerning the future) decisively effects decision-making in the present." "Trust depends therefore on a critical alternative where the noxious effects consequent upon a breach

of trust could exceed the advantage gained in rendering it."[54] There are three important elements in Luhmann's conception of trust: time, uncertainty, and risk-taking. One might summarize this conception to read: trust is a generalized mechanism to risk the *exclusion* of specific future undesirable contingencies from current decision-making, whether consciously or not, and where disappointment forces one to regret the decision taken. For most men, for example, to take a plane amounts to excluding the crash possibility. This contrasts with hope, defined as a generalized mechanism to base current decision-making on the *inclusion* of generalized future desirable contingencies expected. He who acts on hope does not even consider critical alternatives. The difference between the two has less to do with the admixture of knowledge and ignorance, more with a normative standard of rationality concerning odds. The extension of trust that resulted in disappointment can be justified. Disappointed hope, however, is met with the criticism of naïveté. In being composed of expectations about expectations and characterized by risktaking that finds social acceptance, the language of trust seems to be the most general mechanism of complexity production-reduction operant as a medium. All other media, like the societal, are merely special forms with specialized functions.

The communication model outlined previously asserted that to communicate is to combine significance with implication, relevance, and information. Transporting this Smelserian view to society suggests that one cannot implement any commitment to an image of the desirable type of society save through combining with that commitment normative specification (what such a value should mean in a given context), organization (how and who should do what), and facilities. In the action-theoretical perspective one useful way to conceive of the division of labor in the broad sense is to posit four functional subsystems of society, each specializing for the production of one of the four components of meaningful action. And as recounted in the second section of this chapter, this implies mutual contingency and the need for media as mechanisms that regulate flow of components.[55]

There are of course more reasons, both technical-theoretical and empirical, one could adduce for the heuristic value of such a perspective. Two more may suffice here. As indicated earlier, the model depicts a relatively developed society as a system. This system is composed of four subsystems: a fiduciary subsystem (with integrity-function), a societal community, a polity, and an economy. These four exist in mutual contingency. This implies two more technical reasons for the indispensable need for media. One is that any change in such a system has two consequences: A subsystem is changed and three environments are changed.[56] If it were not for generalized media of societal interchange any change would threaten the boundaries between the subsystems. The other is that this model defines society as that language jurisdiction constituted of "talk" in four tongues and four tongues only, societal commitments, influence, power, and money. Smaller social systems within this society, as for example, friendship groups, may not be small-scale societies, as, given face-to-face grounded familiarity of the members *inside*, there may be no need to talk in specialized tongues such as these societal media. From an empirical point of view, in a small and stable group members know much about each other. They may know social position, interests, personal idiosyncrasies. These enable them to "effect" each other's behavior instantaneously through diffuse modes of talk that need no formalization.

Nevertheless in a complex society life *inside* the small group is one thing, dependency on an *outside* another. This is particularly important in view of function-specialization of small groups, as for example families for early childhood socialization. Here they must not only transmit-produce commitments, they also need supplies from anonymous others to perform that function. Hence their principle "leader" members must be able to speak in tongues of money, influence, and power, as well as sociomoral rhetoric. Thus when one comes to depend on performances of anonymous others about whom little is known, one needs formalized tongues. Then choosing a context-appropriate medium defines the relation sufficiently to be understood in one's attempt to effect behavior. One can communicate with minimal knowledge about alter. This points to one important function of societal media. They save information: using a societal medium allows one to underutilize others whose significances can be taken for granted and to do so with impunity. Any complex arrangement demands mechanisms that permit interacting units to live and interact reliably and predictably in the face of ignorance. But that is only one aspect. By allowing for ignorance, societal media certainly reduce potentially significant, relevant, and implicatory possibilities. When used as regulatory mechanisms between functionally specialized subsystems, however, they also enable others to produce complexity.

Again to repeat, functional specialization through subsystem organization means exemption from responsibility for all problems of societal functioning save the one that the subsystem specializes for. Such freedom from having to care about subfunction-irrelevant though in other contexts very relevant

problems enables specialists to innovate solutions to problems within their special domain. Economists as economists always produce more economically sound solutions to economic problems than can be implemented. Some of these solutions cannot be implemented because they are politically intolerable, others because they would upset strata relations in the societal community, yet others because they would threaten one's ability to maintain commitment to societal values. What can be said of economists, *pari passu* can also be said of the respective specialists in the other functional subsystems. Political leaders produce always more "politically rational" solutions to political problems than can be implemented because some lack feasibility on economic grounds, others on solidarity grounds, yet others on integrity grounds. This recognition led Luhmann[57] to propose an interesting reversal of the old saw about "the whole being more than the sum of the parts." Society as a language jurisdiction is in terms of problem solutions implemented always less than its variety of problem solutions produced. Put differently, the societally feasible always constitutes a selection from four sets of perfectly rational subfunction feasibilities. But our analysis of antonym functions across the diagonals in the usual format also permit the proposition: the growth of rationality is a direct function of the degree of equilibrated growth in complexification and stabilization.

How can one conceive of such processes in more concrete terms? Presumably by doing the hazardous in the theory of action, by descending to the level of empirical hypothesizing. Hazardous or not, this is indispensable for preparing the way for empirical research.

My subsequent remarks will deal with three topics. First, one way to concretize societal media as mechanisms simultaneously productive and reductive of complexity is to view them as means that enable some to make decisions and face complexity because others refrain from doing both. Second, living on liquidity rather than achieved meaning—which is what saving decisions is all about—constitutes institutionalized forms of future insurance. Thus there is a differential use of time. Decision-savers who live on liquidity expand the present into the future. Decision-makers who spend liquidity do the reverse, constraining the future by acting in the present. Third, contrary to Luhmann,[58] who argues for motiveless acceptance of political decisions and claims that power needs no legitimation in complex societies, a box he gets himself into on the grounds of claiming unlimited substitutability of the system-environment relation between all societal subsystems, I shall argue that orderly complex mediation in society requires that influence grow in tandem with economic expansion and that societal commitments always constrain power.

The crucial focus for an understanding of evolutionary expansion of societally regulatory symbols is always the pressure of money on influence. The level of monetization serves as a rough indicator of the complexity in the division of labor achieved (A-L). As mediated through money this complexity triggers demands for more influence (A-I implications increase). Influence expansion in turn facilitates power expansion (G-I). The latter, however, threatens to turn humans into nothing but service opportunists (A-G) through a potential growth in anomic confusion concerning the sorting out of differential loyalties (L-I), unless stabilization of the legitimacy-legality contingency (L-G) controls the net increase in symbolic supplies. Cumbersome as this statement is, and as summary of a complex set of relations must be, the main idea should be clear. The diagonals are crucial. This does not mean that cybernetic features of adaptive and goal-attainment interchanges can be ignored. It only means that mismatch of supplies across the diagonals cannot be substituted for by the others, except in the shortest of short runs.

In an earlier formulation Luhmann[59] thought of media as mechanisms of information-saving. Information was there still treated in some commonsense sense. The argument, in brief, was that perceived complexity had tremendously increased in modern society. And if men, increasingly conscious of themselves as the creators of their own realities, were to act at all, they had to have mechanisms of complexity reduction. There are simply too many sources of perceived uncertainty to live without insurance mechanisms. If men make society, society can be different tomorrow or, minimally, at a time when one's children face adult responsibilities. This of course makes a kind of institutionalized mockery of socialization as a preparation for life. For how are parents to raise children for future contingencies if they know that they cannot know what these might be? When the future becomes a source of uncertainty, there must be mechanisms to reduce its impact on current action. But, in addition, another located at a different spot in the division of labor than myself can see what is differently. When I meet him, he can subject me to radical uncertainty as to what is. Therefore, the division of labor constitutes a source of uncertainty in the present. Since, third, men can reinterpret the significance of their past, and even have specialized roles like historians to do that for them, the past becomes a source of uncertainty. Hence the past becomes less and less a constraint on the present and the future. With multiple sources of perceived uncertainty, mechanisms to reduce it had to be posited.

This perspective led him to conceive of the societal media as forms of societal liquidity, and "liquidity saves information."[60]

Once one abandons the unspecified commonsense sense of information, however, the matter becomes quite difficult. Hence it might be advantageous to view societal media as mechanisms of decision-saving and decision-facing. Of course a conception of voluntaristic action is one of action that always involves some deciding. But considering the limiting case may be useful. I can decide not to decide. This comes close to avoiding complexity. Positive action, in the sense of deciding, then would be exposure to complexity. Now, in a mutually contingent set of subsystems, when some do not decide, others can because nondeciding is to leave real entities available for deciders, provided only that the symbolic representations are kept institutionally accessible as money is through banking.

Nondeciding about a resource and keeping it liquid and accessible amounts to refraining from investment by some and the possibility of investment by others. When voters remain content with keeping their liquid franchise liquid during the inter-electoral period rather than abandoning it through forms of extraparliamentary political action, leaders are enabled to make policies unanticipated during the election. When most keep their membership badges as a valid token of what voluntary association stands for rather than insisting on detail negotiations of just what the collective judgment is in every instance of communicating an organized interest, influentials are enabled to exercise persuasion beyond the expectation of any one of their constituents. When men are content with moral liquidity in the form of some conventional moral wisdom most of the time, they give integrity specialists — be they existential psychiatrists, priests, intellectuals, counter-culture devotees or whoever — a chance to innovate morals.

Symbols can be viewed as mechanisms that connect the unknown with the known.[61] In the case of societal media the unknown is the future, the known only an apparently known in the form of constructed familiarity about anonymous alters. This can be elucidated by a brief answer to three questions. They are: (1) Just what is one giving up when accepting the intrinsically worthless liquidity of societal media? (2) How does one manage to maintain trust in convertibility of media? and (3) What is the wider abstract system whose working one assumes?

In the case of money he who is content with keeping deposits relinquishes direct control over consumables. He has lost certainty, but at the tremendous gain of being emancipated from economic self-sufficiency. He places his trust in impersonal others in the commodity and labor markets. As long as he finds opportunities to buy at prices within his expectation range, each purchase made shores up trust in keeping liquidity. Beyond that, however, he also assumes the working of an abstract system called "the economy."[62] In view of the usually dire reports in the news about this system in the form of threats to it through strikes, monetary crises, balance of payments, and the like, this is rather remarkable. One possibility here is that most entertain some beliefs that maintain their trust in an essentially nonunderstood abstract system. In the economy such beliefs may involve such potentially naïve but useful notions as "no matter what, 1929 can't happen again." Implied here is of course that relevant experts have not only learned effective control techniques but that they can also implement them. With beliefs of this kind specific future contingencies such as runaway inflation are screened off from current spending and investment decisions.

In the case of power, holding its liquid form, such as the franchise, amounts to the temporary abandonment of two real entities. In view of the monopolization of the means of destruction, the first real thing forsaken is coercive self-sufficiency. Instead of "packing one's own gun," citizens generally rely on the working of the institutions charged with the maintenance of law and order. But the wider and increasing number of services provided through governmental channels also suggests that he who holds the vote in effect renounced the need for self-sufficiency in creating his own opportunities for participation in society. The obvious examples here are education, health, and transport. The slogan "equal opportunity" suggests the first objects of trust. These are service provisions, i.e., receiving fair opportunities. But again beyond these, trust in the general working of the political system and reasonable protection is also involved. For Western societies one of the more concrete beliefs that generates and maintains this kind of trust may be the assumption that "coups may be the Latin American thing, but they can't really happen here." Hence one trusts "equality of rights."[63]

Concerning influence, he who "respects" the symbols of superiority gives up a need to know the facts himself. Holding an empty symbol in this area is a way of being able to afford ignorance without suffering from it. That one will get fair advice and help when and where one needs it constitutes the expectation-base of trust. Again, in addition, a more general trust in a society's reputational system is also involved. One of the more concrete beliefs that maintains this kind of trust may be the assumption that "by and large certified superiority in our society is a source of responsible statements made in good faith." Here the first part asserts that certification does

represent qualification, the second that professional standards do prevail, i.e., exploitation of the unaware is the exception.

Last, with respect to commitments, he who goes by the proven road of conventional moral wisdom forsakes the need to know in any concrete way just how conventional moral formulas are philosophically and/or religiously grounded. Being a conventional moralist saves man the effort — and likely the failure — of attempting to be his own Immanuel Kant. The first objects of trust in this case are simply one's fellow men. Following conventional moral wisdom and occasionally translating the symbols into one's own moral position means trusting that: (1) one will receive respect for one's decision and behavior from peers, and (2) through that one can enjoy a clear conscience. A more diffuse object of trust here, however, involves assumptions about the general working of the system of civic morals. The most important general belief in this area may well be that "there certainly is no longer any obvious and self-evident connection between moral principle and moral action." Other relevant beliefs in this area very likely embrace the twin concepts of tolerance and relativity. One such assumption incorporating tolerance might be the conviction: "the fact that another comes to a different decision than myself does not mean that he is a villain nor that I am morally corrupt." Decisions on birth control might serve as a contemporary example. Another maxim might be: "what is moral today," self-realization through disciplined work, for example, "might well become morally irrelevant tomorrow." However, if one is to enjoy the freedom to make occasional investments, to decide a moral question according to one's own light without fear of interference from one's immediate milieu, one has lost that milieu as a source of certainty. Men who are expected to stand on their own feet morally must have the strength to do so. Living off moral liquidity most of the time means to face loneliness at investment time. It also means giving legitimacy entrepreneurs a chance to surprise one with their innovations.

One may observe that the indicated kinds of illustrative beliefs maintaining trust in the working of abstract systems probably involve generalized negations. They refer to things that will not happen. Whether it is a past event deemed unlikely to recur, such as 1929 in economics, contemporary political events precluded from one's own polity such as Latin American coups, certification deemed to preclude charlatanism, or the possibility of meeting rejection from one's peers for concrete moral decisions taken on one's own responsibility, trust excludes specific future contingencies. It is this feature that gives decision-makers who constrain the future in their present the capacity to be innovative in their problem solutions.

The point about living off liquidity is that men can face complexity in decision-making piecemeal, as it were. When confronting a moral problem, for example, they can presume that economics, effectiveness, and belongingness is taken care of. The same holds when confronting an economic investment problem. Then, if there is a functioning media market and specialized subsystems that operate, they can presume that morality, cooperative effectiveness, and solidarity are taken care of. Clearly this presupposes sufficient variety in deciding. The ways in which particular cases are decided must leave the rest of decisions unaffected. Pluralization of investments and expectations about investments is a necessary condition for stability in any medium. Luhmann has called this aspect "system indifference." Clearly, if all were to invest their savings in tourism, the demand could not be filled, or if filled somehow, vacations would have to be something drastically different from what they are understood to be. Again, if all votes were invested into the same party, the party system would collapse. Similarly, if all membership tokens were to be cashed in for the identical kind of solidarity experience the complex of voluntary associations would collapse. Mass effects resulting from a desire for the same kinds of intrinsic satisfiers have one immediate consequence: dedifferentiation in society. Accordingly, system indifference is a prerequisite for the same medium to be used for contrary ends: *reducing complexity by decision-savers, and producing complexity by decision-makers.*

Yet, while avoiding mass effects is a necessary requirements for diversity through symbolic organization, sufficient variety in decision-making is not a sufficient requirement for the operation of a complex society. Acting as if the future had limited liabilities demands extraordinary amounts of trust. The medium most directly involved influence, which is following unverified but in principle verifiable statements. Influence must expand in response to complexity if stability is to be maintained. Most immediately two reasons suggest themselves. First, as the banker-creditor relation risks the money of third parties, influence expansion seems to be the crucial variable in wealth expansion. Second, it has been a commonplace in sociology that changes in the level of wealth or economic development have an immediate impact on strata relations. An increase in the level of property to be distributed has an impact on the code of influence, the set of rules justifying societal inequalities of any kind. Hence, where influence fails to grow in real terms with money, conflicts about inequalities tend to become destructured. On the other hand, if these two media do

expand, acting as motors of complexity production in societal relations, there must be more countervailing force than is provided by simple variety in investments. The latter could not by itself suffice to sustain trust, i.e., preclude specific future noxious contingencies. In addition, if stability in expansion is to be maintained, value-commitments must always constrain power lest legitimacy and legality diverge to the point of confusion in anomie.[64] Unless commitments to societal integrity do in fact constrain law-making, no one could preclude anything from the future. Legitimation by sheer procedure and that alone—as implied in Max Weber's category of rational-legal authority and identified as the characteristically modern form by Luhmann[65]—constitutes a limiting case of legitimation, at least for authority and power at the national level. How such commitments control the scope of authority of office (the code of power) may vary widely. The U.S. supreme court's recourse to presumed intentions of the founding fathers is one such mechanism, the diffuse anchorage of Britain's unwritten constitution another. But that a condition of minimal stability demands the operation of assured complexity reduction via commitments and power is amply attested to by recent German history where societal modernity turned to a system of anarchical systemlessness.

According to Parsons,[66] ". . . it is imperative to treat the media as a 'family,' and hence to attempt *systematically* to work out their similarities and differences, and their relations to each other." This essay has tried to stress one analytically common element, communication as a four-function process. If not wholly mistaken, this constitutes an invitation to regard all media as mechanisms simultaneously productive and reductive of meaning complexity. In addition, one relational characteristic has been singled out as of central importance for their functioning. This is a primary division of labor concerning these two functions among media. Without it their single-function specialization cannot be adequately understood.

NOTES

1. Talcott Parsons, "Durkheim's Contribution to the Theory of Integration of Social Systems," in Talcott Parsons, *Sociological Theory and Modern Society* (New York: The Free Press, 1967), pp. 3-34.

2. See the media papers of Talcott Parsons, "On the Concept of Influence," *Public Opinion Quarterly* 27 (Spring, 1963): 37-62; "On the Concept of Power," *Proceedings of the American Philosophical Society* 107 (June, 1963), pp. 232-262; "On the Concept of Value-Commitments," *Sociological Inquiry* 38 (Spring, 1968), pp. 135-160; and the general action media as developed in "Some Problems of General Theory in Sociology," in John C. McKinney and Edward Tiryakian (eds.), *Theoretical Sociology: Perspectives and Development* (New York: Appleton-Century-Crofts, 1969), pp. 27-68.

3. Parsons, "Some Problems . . .," *op. cit.,* pp. 28-36.

4. T. Parsons and N. J. Smelser, *Economy and Society* (Glencoe, Ill.: The Free Press, 1956).

5. Talcott Parsons, *Politics and Social Structure* (New York: The Free Press, 1969), p. 313.

6. J. S. Coleman, "Comment on 'The Concept of Influence,'" *Public Opinion Quarterly* 27 (Spring, 1963): 63-82; J. S. Coleman, "Political Money," *American Political Science Review* LXIV (December, 1970), pp. 1074-1087.

7. D. A. Baldwin, "Money and Power," *Journal of Politics* 33 (August, 1971), pp. 578-614.

8. R. R. Blaine, "An Alternative to Parsons' Four-Function Paradigm as a Basis for Developing General Sociological Theory," *American Sociological Review* 36 (August, 1971), pp. 678-692.

9. Compare and contrast Parsons' treatment of societal media—power, influence, and value commitments—with the general action media (intelligence, performance capacity, affect, and definition of the situation). Sources for these are listed in note 2.

10. See Parsons, "On the Concept of Power," *op. cit.,* p. 262; T. Parsons, "The Political Aspects of Social Structure and Process," in David Easton (ed.), *Varieties of Political Theory* (Englewood Cliffs: Prentice-Hall, 1966), pp. 71-112; Parsons, "Some Problems . . .," *op. cit.,* p. 67.

11. Parsons, "On the Concept of Power," *op. cit.,* pp. 259-262.

12. Parsons, *Politics and Social Structure,* pp. 432-433.

13. The approach taken here, including this bold assertion, is based directly on Luhmann's work. See particularly J. Habermas and N. Luhmann, *Theorie der Gesellschaft oder Sozialtechnologie* (Frankfurt: Suhrkamp Verlag, 1971), p. 309.

14. T. S. Turner, "Parsons' Concept of Generalized Media of Social Interaction and Its Relevance for Social Anthropology," *Sociological Inquiry* 38 (Spring, 1968), pp. 121-134.

15. *Ibid.,* p. 132.

16. R. N. Bellah, "Religious Evolution," *American Sociological Review* 29 (June, 1964), pp. 358-374. This is also as good a place as any to acknowledge deep indebtedness to colleagues who helped. First among these were my fellow editors Victor Lidz and Jan Loubser, who encouraged me to drop issues as yet beyond my capacity of complexity management and aided considerably in clarifying many others. Of course neither bears responsibility for what has remained wrong or obscure. This may apply particularly to my possibly simplistic notions of primitive society appearing later. Against their urging to drop the notion about the differentiation of experience and action I decided to retain it because it seems to me indispensable for coming to grips with communication. Wolfgang Schluchter's willingness to discuss just this problem sustained my faith in its potential fruitfulness. To him I owe the idea of partaking of "secondhand experience" mentioned later. Further yet, where I draw in a very tentative and brief fashion on linguistics, it was Helen Douglass whose aid proved very helpful.

17. Habermas and Luhmann, *op. cit.,* p. 77.

18. In contrast to differentiation, recognition of a public-private dichotomy and *segregation* between the two could of course occur earlier. An example involving the suppression of the private realm has been described for Bali where a system of naming, giving primacy to public titles, a permutational calendar defining time as episodes, a highly stylized form of interpersonal etiquette, and a personality medium "stagefright" conjoined to depersonalize, detemporalize, and ceremonialize social life. See C. Geertz, *Person, Time, and Conduct in Bali* (New Haven: Yale University, South East Asian Studies, 1966).

19. T. Parsons, "The Position of Identity in the General Theory of Action," in Chad Gordon and K. Gergen (eds.), *The Self in Social Interaction* (New York: John Wiley and Sons, 1968), pp. 11-23.

20. This formulation was suggested by Wofgang Schluchter, whose help is gratefully acknowledged.

21. J. A. Schumpeter, *The Theory of Economic Development* (Cambridge: Harvard University Press, 1934).

22. Parsons, "Some Problems . . .," *op. cit.,* p. 29.

23. *Ibid.,* pp. 30-32.

24. Parsons, *Politics and Social Structure* p. 316.

25. Talcott Parsons, *Societies: Evolutionary and Comparative Perspectives* (Englewood Cliffs.: Prentice-Hall, 1966), p. 10.

26. *Ibid.,* pp. 16-17.

27. Talcott Parsons, *The System of Modern Societies* (Englewood Cliffs.: Prentice-Hall, 1971), p. 8 (emphasis added).

28. Parsons, "Some Problems . . .," *op. cit.,* p. 36.

29. N. J. Smelser, *The Theory of Collective Behavior* (New York: The Free Press, 1963), Table 5, p. 44.

30. For details see Luhmann, in Habermas and Luhmann, *op. cit.,* p. 362.

31. A rationally constructed bureaucracy, for example, can result in an organization of the division of labor where self-generated internal adaptation problems absorb more of the members' energies than the pursuit of the organization's goals. For a pertinent and brilliant case analysis see Michael Crozier, *The Bureaucratic Phenomenon* (Chicago: University of Chicago Press, 1964). Such outcomes diametrically opposite to intentions are always a possibility. But here the interest centers on relating costs of means combinations to unit value of goals attained *in the same currencies.*

32. Habermas and Luhmann, *op. cit.,* p. 364.

33. Parsons, *Politics and Social Structure,* pp. 398-399.

34. In this connection I regard Bellah's religious evolution as symptomatic. Its success in terms of the differentiation of culture, society, and personality was paralleled by relative paucity in supporting the claim of an increasing level of complexity in theological symbols. Because of greater abstraction, monotheism is symbolically more simple than polytheism. Again, it may not be an accident that an earlier truly heroic effort to pursue the same end in the format of a 256-boxes schema was never taken up again by its author. See R. N. Bellah, *Beyond Belief* (New York: Harper & Row, 1970), pp. 260-287.

35. Parsons, "Some Problems . . .," *op. cit.,* p. 39.

36. Habermas and Luhmann, *op. cit.,* p. 41.

37. *Ibid.,* pp. 34-56, 304-309.

38. Talcott Parsons, *The Structure of Social Action* (New York: The Free Press, 1949), p. 44.

39. Parsons, "Some Problems . . .," *op. cit.,* pp. 28-33.

40. See L. V. Bertalanffy, *General Systems Theory* (New York: George Braziller, 1968), pp. 42, 144.

41. Talcott Parsons, "An Outline of the Social System," in T. Parsons, *et al.* (eds.), *Theories of Society.* Volume I (New York: The Free Press, 1961), pp. 30-79, p, 57.

42. E. Beneviste, *Problems in General Linguistics* (Coral Gables, Florida: University of Miami Press, 1971), p. 21.

43. The assistance of Helen Douglass for these selections is gratefully acknowledged.

44. T. Parsons, R. F. Bales, and E. Shils, *Working Papers in the Theory of Action* (Glencoe, Ill.: The Free Press, 1953), p. 231.

45. Parsons, *Politics and Social Structure.* pp. 412-413.

46. Habermas and Luhmann, *op. cit.,* p. 34.

47. Parsons and Smelser. *op. cit.,* p. 68.

48. See Parsons, "Durkheim's Contribution. . . ." *op. cit.*

49. I owe recognizing the first linkage to Jan Loubser, the second to Victor Lidz. I am deeply indebted to both for sustaining courage in attempting the level of abstraction which underlies this whole effort. Without learning about these "findings" I am not sure at all whether "abstracting even beyond Parsons" would be a useful undertaking.

50. Parsons, *Politics and Social Structure,* pp. 419-426.

51. See Parsons, "Durkheim's Contribution . . . ." *op. cit.,* p. 13.

52. *Ibid.,* pp. 12-13.

53. *Ibid.*, pp. 24-28.

54. Niklas Luhmann *Vertrauen* (Stuttgart: F. Enke Verlag, 1968), pp. 7, 22, 18.

55. Parsons, "On the Concept of Value-Commitments," *op. cit.*, p. 147.

56. Habermas and Luhmann, *op. cit.*, p. 363.

57. Niklas Luhmann, *Zweckbegriff und Systemrationalität* (Tübingen: J.C.B. Mohr, 1968), pp. 121ff.

58. Niklas Luhmann, *Soziologische Aufklärung* (Köln-Opladen: Westdeutscher Verlag, 1970), pp. 154-177; and Habermas and Luhmann, *op. cit.*, p. 386.

59. Luhmann, *Vertrauen.*

60. *Ibid.*, pp. 46-47.

61. V. Turner, *The Forest of Symbols* (Ithaca, N.Y.: Cornell University Press, 1967), p. 48.

62. Luhmann, *Vertrauen,* p. 46.

63. Parsons, *Politics and Social Structure*, p. 503.

64. See J. Winckelmann, *Legitimität und Legalität in Max Weber's Herrschaftssoziologie* (Tübingen: J.C.B. Mohr, 1952).

65. Niklas Luhmann, *Legitimation durch Verfahren* (Neuwied am Rhein: Luchterhand Verlag, 1969).

66. Parsons, *Politics and Social Structure*, p. 520.

23

PENURY AND DEFICIT OR THE PROBLEMS OF POLITICAL UNDERUTILIZATION

François Bourricaud

The present paper is an attempt to analyze two studies conducted by the author in the two very dissimilar societies of France and Peru. The analysis is largely based on the political theory of Talcott Parsons. Difficulties encountered in this analysis have led to a tentative but perhaps useful extension of the theory of action framework.

In his political writings Parsons regards power as an essentially *social* phenomenon, i.e., as a society's ability to implement certain common goals. On the face of it this concept appears different from the concept of power used by conflict theorists like C. Wright Mills, for whom power is always used by one group against another. In their view, even when power is used "in the name of the majority" it is, in fact, being used for the benefit of the "rich and powerful at the expense of the poor and the oppressed."

If we adopt the theory of action perspective as developed by Parsons, however, and then seek to identify the conditions enabling a society to formulate certain goals and to enlist its members in the pursuit of these goals, the debate over power as a "zero-sum game" loses much of its meaning and the concept of power becomes much more encompassing. The significant factor becomes the set of conditions allowing maximum utilization of the collectivity's various resources or at least a degree of utilization sufficient to allow the attainment of collective goals. Although it includes the meaning of a discrepancy between the intrinsic value of resources and the value they acquire according to the use the society makes of them, "full employment" of resources must not be interpreted in a restricted Keynesian sense.

The discrepancy in question may take the form of an asset as well as a liability. Conflict theorists have stressed the liability aspect. Saint-Simon, for example,

argues that societies possess capacities that are held and checked by the privileged classes. Moreover, he believed that because of the support these classes got from the State they not only retained an overly large proportion of collective products but they actively sought to prevent, or at the very least to slow down, growth and development. The Marxian thesis differs from this position in that it emphasizes exploitation and repression for the profit of "capitalists," whereas Saint-Simon speaks of "feudal landowners." But both these positions belong to the same tradition. They concur in denouncing the evil of the discrepancy between man's capacity for unlimited innovation and growth and the restrictions placed upon this capacity by the tactics of monopolizing capitalists or, more generally speaking, of the establishment.

At this point it will be useful to look at the syncretic notion of "malthusianism,"[1] which has enjoyed much popularity in France in the post-World War II period. The appeal of this loose concept is most probably explained by the fact that it allows the ills of society to be imputed to society's "corruption" or to the "greed" of the "powerful." *Malthusianism*, as Sauvy broadly applies the term to the demographic sphere ("concern for limiting the number of children") and to the economic sphere (caution vis-a-vis increasing wealth) has two meanings: First, it refers to a "fear of scarcity" related to a possible increase in the number of mouths to feed. In this sense it applies to "traditional societies" which undergo little or no technological progress. But this fear of scarcity is also related to the fear that abundance, (of harvest, for example), might result in a decrease in the market value of goods.[2] This second meaning of Malthusian "cautiousness," therefore, not only means preventing an increase in population so as to protect the level of the individual's share of *real income*; it also means avoiding an increase in total production to maintain *the relative*

Translated from the French by Dr. J. B. Haché.

positions of the various beneficiaries. This last meaning is especially emphasized in reference to industrialized societies where the "haves," supposedly in order to maintain their monopoly over the "means of production" and to safeguard their "privilege," are accused of standing in the way of growth and progress or, at least, of modifying its course and outcomes.

According to this interpretation, social organization is tainted with a double injustice: Not only do the powerful take a disproportionate share of the collective *good*, but they also stand in the way of growth in order to ensure the perpetuation of their own privilege, particularly to safeguard "the monopoly" they have acquired over the means of production.[3]

There is a more optimistic tradition which sees society as a surplus-producing machine and stands in contrast to the pessimism of conflict theory. Neil Smelser[4] has indicated that the notion of "value added," which is borrowed from economics, is a helpful one in understanding the development of social movements as well as the creativity of certain individuals. Smelser places particular emphasis on the notion that the increase in value which enriches a producer (his activity engenders an increase in the activity of the collectivity) results from the fact that his activity is being used in combination with the activities of others according to a given rule for combining activities. The "surplus" occurs as the result of a division of labor. As such it can be taken as a measure of the effects of the division of labor.

This thesis tells an overly optimistic story when it is oversimplified to mean that the division of labor adds — automatically as it were — efficiency to the individual producer, especially if we attribute to a reputedly benevolent authority, or to an infallible mechanism as the market, the capacity to allot the working force according to an optimum formula. Conflict critics, however, insist on the feality of unearned incomes and privileges with arguments of corruption of governments and selfishness of the rich.

As long as they hold to these arguments, the conflict theorists are able to condemn social systems on the basis of the discrepancy which they claim exists between the society's effective capacities and the infinite "potentialities" they attribute to human nature, or even to technology. According to them these potentialities will surely be developed when we rid ourselves of the chains that hold them back.

This position is strongly upheld by many writers who discuss underdevelopment. Although it was customary in the past to blame underdevelopment on a rigorous climate or infertile soil, today's authors stress the importance of mobilizing the "unused resources" — e.g., the unemployed portion of the labor force, abandoned land, and idle capital — for the collective good.

Unfortunately the ambiguity surrounding the notion of "full employment" in economy becomes even greater when we try to define it in a political context, even according to simple criteria.[5] But what are these "infinite potentialities" of society which conflict critics accuse the establishment of not developing and not actualizing? Seemingly they are invoked simply to highlight insufficiencies and deficiencies — as if the Law of Progress, by some version of the position of Comte, had meaning only when invoked to disqualify the Law of Order. The conflict school views these potentialities so broadly that their essential characteristics may be said to be that they can never be completely actualized. Conflict theorists arrive at this position via the push-pull effect, the "push" being constituted by the requirements of "irrepressible" basic needs, and the "pull" by aspiration drives that incessantly "create" greater needs.

This in essence is the interpretation which Darras offers in his account of growing discontent, in spite (or because) of rising standards of living:

> Demands increase as the general standard of living improves and as the homogeneity of aspirations—resulting from urbanization and the direct, or immediate awareness of various life-styles—increases.... Is it not true that even the most disenfranchised class will resent all the more strongly the economic and social obstacles to better education and greater social mobility, for example, when they acquire the ability to recognize the obstacles that these economic and social hindrances hide from their view?[6]

Malthusianism artificially produces poverty for some members of society by condemning a society to use only a fraction of its "infinite" resources and capabilities. This occurs as the result of a more or less deliberate failure on the part of rulers to acknowledge the demands of the poorest classes.

The discrepancy between the reality of what societies make available to their members and the members' expectations had previously been noted by Durkheim. His interpretation of the phenomenon was, however, radically different from the one just discussed. He spoke of "appetites" and "desires" rather than of "needs":

> Having no limits, appetites do not recognize boundaries beyond which they must cease to seek more. They are in a natural state of arousal and cause general vitality to be intense. Because prosperity has increased more desires have been satisfied . . . The state of immoderation, or anomie, is further reinforced by the fact that passions are less disciplined at the very time when they are in greater need of discipline.[7]

It is not at all certain that this text of Durkheim must be interpreted as a plea for asceticism and abstinence in spite of the fact that, in his time, "cautiousness" — or even distrust — in the face of increasing wealth, to use the language of Alfred Sauvy, was a part of French moral rhetoric. Alain's prescription, for example, was for "lead coinage and a simple life."[8] Durkheim's concern was with "moderation." On the other hand, he clearly suggests that a society characterized by functional interdependence can provide its members with the opportunity for full development of their potentials. Therefore, societies of this type can be characterized by an institutionalized functional interdependence between individual personal development and the achievement of societal goals. This congruence between individual motivation and societal discipline is achieved by the proper socialization of the individual to a "collective conscience." At any rate, only an extremely superficial understanding of Durkheim's conception of socialization would lead one to believe that anomie might be remedied by external repressive forces. Durkheim's concept of socialization, as Parsons has clearly shown, rests not only with externally imposed sanctions but mainly on sanctions that are legitimized in identifications with models for behaviour and in internalizations of common values.[9]

CENTER AND PERIPHERY: THEIR REAL AND SYMBOLIC RESOURCES

The increase of collective power appears to be the common concern of those whose main referent concepts are full employment of resources, surplus, added value or, more traditionally, division of labor. Parsons' concept of power is obviously formulated along these lines. But it has one decisive advantage in that it allows to bypass the debate between those who contend that the surplus created as a result of social organization is reserved and misused by monopolists and those who believe that full use of collective resources — or at least the progressive growth of these resources — comes about as the result of some natural harmony, resulting from the application of the principle of the division of labor. Parsons has formulated certain guidelines concerning the conditions that regulate the growth, the use, and the preservation of collective power. These guidelines allow us to avoid the futility of that dispute.

The main proposition one finds in Parsons' theory, in my view, is that the mobilization of collective resources, principally when it is for the purpose of reaching attainable goals — goals that may not, however, necessarily be obtained — is not an entirely automatic or spontaneous process. It is one, on the contrary, that requires guidance.[10]

This guidance, which is too often interpreted on a trial and error approach, is only possible in a society that has at least a minimally effective system of communication within itself and between itself and other systems and that is also at least minimally self-regulating. Obviously a political society does not function with the predictability of a thermostat. Nevertheless, information flow and self-regulation are characteristics of both cybernetic and social systems. To give precision to our concept of guidance, or steering, it is necessary to enquire as to the extent of a system's autonomy, of the constraints within which it is free to operate. These constraints are of two kinds: external to the system and internal to the system. In reference to the first we will say only that a hostile environment (temperature, terrain) can break the physical unity of a system. It can also more or less seriously disrupt it by scrambling the messages it can emit, receive, or transmit by feeding it signals that are not part of its code or by ceasing to supply it with signals it can decode. The autonomy of a system, however, is not exclusively dependent on these boundary exchanges. It also depends on the system's capacity to link together and control its own component subsystems. The risk of low internal cohesion increases with the multiplication and diversification of the system's component parts. The disequilibrium producing centrifugal tendencies of the peripheral areas can be neutralized by the mobilization — under a central control — of forces that can be used when required to counter peripheral disruptive forces.

The power of a group, or its capacity to achieve certain collective goals, depends both on its relations with the environment and on the relationship of its center to its periphery. This latter distinction, which is not found in the Parsonian framework, is consistent with it if we define "center" as the unit, which, in the end, makes decisions for the execution of which it is considered accountable.[11] It now becomes possible to determine what the necessary resources of a center are and to evaluate its capacity to attain common goals — or more exactly, to attain common goals in concert with the periphery. The capacity of a group to attain its own goals, i.e., its power, is dependent on different resources. Naked force is the strongest sanction that holders of power can bring to bear in order to ensure obedience. Parsons, however, recognized that, although force is the ultimate sanction, it is by no means the only one. In fact, force works only in extreme and therefore exceptional circumstances. A society that assigned a policeman to each citizen would perhaps ensure that unlawful behaviour did not occur; however, it is less certain that it would be successful in eliciting prescribed behavior. As popular wisdom has it, you can lead a horse to water, but you cannot make it drink. It is also a disputable hypothesis that societies succeed always in "manipulating" their members from the inside by inculcating in them certain common values. Given that individuals can internalize only relatively indeterminate patterns, there is still the matter of giving them content, of making them specific in terms of experience. Just as power is not reducible to force, it is not exact to conceive of it as the external manifestation of a collective conscience or as an automatic realization of common values.

Power as generally conceived in its broadest sense, that is, as the capacity to mobilize societal resources to pursue collective goals, depends upon many conditions. Let us now ask how the center A, charged with the responsibility of achieving certain goals, goes about bringing the periphery B to cooperate with it? Parsons has distinguished between the resources available to A in its relation to B and has classified them as positive and negative. They may be considered as rewards and punishments respectively. These sanctions (both the positive and the negative) can also be classified into two categories according to how they affect B's objective state: They can deprive B of resources or increase its supply of them, or they can affect either positively or negatively the degree of satisfaction B derives from its own activity. In combination these two dimensions yield four modalities of power:

1. *Inducement*, whereby A induces B to do what is asked by making B realize the material advantages of doing so.
2. *Coercion*, whereby A makes B realize the disadvantages and negative consequences of failure to concur.
3. *Persuasion*, whereby A persuades B to concur on the basis of internal rewards or inner satisfaction to be gained by cooperating with other units.
4. *Activation of commitments*, whereby A brings B into line by pointing out some of the common values of the group of which they are both members.

A must operate with these four basic resources. We may now attempt to arrange them on a continuum, going from left to right, that will allow an appraisal of the nature of A's control over B. If A, having threatened reprisal, has not been able to prevent B from acting in a negative direction nor to apply sanctions to B for doing so, A can be said to have no effective means for acting on B. Otherwise stated, A is powerless in its relations with B. In this connection, minimum power can then be defined as the *threshold* below which an attempt at coercion fails. Let us now consider the case which, on the face of it at least, appears to be the opposite. Suppose that A obtains the cooperation of B simply by indicating how much better it would be to do what A suggests. There is no need for A to resort to threats and hence there is no

risk that the threats might not be taken seriously. Moreover A is not put in a position where it must make, let alone keep, promises.[12]

Can it be said that power based on the threat of reprisal is less power than power based on the fact that those subject to it would find themselves guilty if they indulge in disobedience? The answer is not an easy one, and the nature and the extent of the area in which power relations are exercised are first to be known. Suppose that A always obtains concurrence from B without threats or promises of material rewards: This might be due to A's acting in ways congruent with B's interests. In this case this does not mean that A is omnipotent, as its power is still conditional on being exercised in a prescribed manner, in nonconflicting areas, and according to well-accepted formulae.

As the basis of power consists of a range of diversified resources, the question arises whether these resources constitute an integrated and hierarchical system of control. A society whose center could never have recourse to force in order to bring a rebellious periphery into line could not be properly called a political society. On the other hand, a society that could make executive decisions solely on the basis of force may be said to have weak and questionable principles of legitimacy. In such cases intense hostility would be found to exist between the leaders and the remainder of the population; indeed, it would be safe to predict that leaders would experience difficulty in appropriating from the population the resources required for public services. The political capacity of a society therefore depends on the manner in which it maintains the solidarity of its membership, in providing a minimal legitimating basis for the goals it proposes to persue, and in the effectiveness with which it mobilizes its resources and retains a portion of them for its own operations.

In dealing with problem of the hierarchy of these functions, we are led to distinguish between the real and the symbolic aspects of power relationships. The existence of a threshold below which power holders can be challenged has already been recognized. Another is that which exists when the center can no longer provide the periphery with convincing arguments for the legitimacy of its decision making. We therefore define as real those elements in the power system that have the intrinsic capacity for producing obedience. Naked force in sufficient quantity or certain collective presentations through which the center can assure itself of the cooperation of the periphery are examples of real elements of power. It is clear, however, that power also rests on elements that do not immediately possess that capacity. Such elements may be referred to as symbolic.

Remember now that the conflict school emphasizes

the importance of force and violence in power relations, in a word, the *real* elements of power. They do so to such an extent that certain writers[13] no longer distinguish between "naked force" and the "force of law," but rather go to the extreme of suggesting that law, culture, and the like are always their force under the guise of social norms, which they term "symbolic violence." Parsons avoids these equivocations by pointing out that power is the capacity to formulate "binding obligations." These obligations are binding on both the party that orders and the one that obeys. Naturally, the content of the obligation is different for each party; but the essential point is that there is equal commitment on the part of both. Were this reciprocity to break down, the legitimacy of the obligation would disappear and social power would be reduced to force. It must be emphasized that the relationship between force and power is much more complex than those who identify the second term with the first would have us believe. Were there only force, Parsons, who always has taken Hobbes' challenge very seriously, would simply say that there is no social system. On the other hand, there can be no society without force because, in the absence of effectively binding collective obligations, individuals could exercise a kind of *liberum veto* at any time against any other individual. Although they must eventually be enforceable, the basis of social obligations must be of a substance other than force.

Here the analogy with money becomes very useful.[14] Everyone knows that money is a symbol. Its value is in unspecified goods and services. Money, however, is not only a substitute; not only does it render possible the standardization and efficiency of trade, but also it acquires its own value such that, by anticipating the rate of substitution between money and goods the economic agent can be led to spend more or save more. Money is not only a symbol of real or actual goods, but it is also the indicator of a promise of future goods, though of unknown quantity and cost. For this reason money is sought after for its own sake. Power has in common with money not only the feature that it is real to the extent to which it can guarantee the periphery's obedience to the center (just as the value of money rests finally on its capacity to be exchanged for goods), but, like all symbols (and like money in particular), power acquires an intrinsic value and hence comes to be sought for its own sake. This is especially so as its concentration or possession in sufficient amounts constitutes one of the conditions for mobilizing collective resources. The reasons for this is the same as for money: Power produces for third parties effects which depend on the preferences of those who hold it. Control over money and power is of such importance that the acquisition and disposition of both constitute two

of the main stakes of social competition. This is the reason why, like money, power is subject to cycles of inflation and depression. It is through these cycles that projects are launched into action, adjusting more or less successfully to the effective capacities of the social system to have them performed.

It is by analyzing the relationship between the real and the symbolic aspects of power systems that we can best come to an understanding of why they so often seem to function in a state of structural deficiency. The study of two very different countries, Peru and France, yields a complex picture of this phenomenon, a picture that allows us to gain meaningful insight into the conditions affecting the center's ability (or inability) to mobilize the resources of the periphery and to guide society in the direction of the achievement of given common goals. Our puspose in this paper, in the more detailed analysis that follows, is to go beyond the classical view of social power which explains symbolic discrepancies by referring to actual poverty or to the malice of those who govern.

"DECENTRALIZED VIOLENCE," INTELLECTUAL "VOLUNTARISM," AND MILITARY ENFORCEMENT: THE CASE OF PERU

Most observers are agreed that the violent disruption of the political system in a society like Peru is inevitable.[15] When I began my observations of Peruvian society some fifteen years ago I did not question the inevitability of the predicted catastrophe. However, as the years passed and the conflict between the privileged and the destitute did not reach its predicted climax, I began to reflect upon the catastrophe thesis and its underlying assumptions. The thesis rested on certain implicit assumptions: that the misery of the masses resulted from the policies of the ruling class and that, therefore, the solution was simply to overthrow the ruling class: *sublata causa tollitur effectus*. By combining these assumptions the substance of the apocalyptic message becomes clear: political struggles have only one goal— the seizure of power. From this conclusion there arise a number of problems relative to the equivalence between center and power and to the opposition between center and periphery.

Two sets of reflections have helped me to see through these problems. I first looked at the center-periphery tension, which I conceptualize as the totality of linkages between social groups and the established hierarchies among these groups. The nature of these relations and of their hierarchies varies with the type of society in which they are found. In a segmented society such as defined by Durkheim,[16] the center-periphery relationship is very different from that characteristic of modern societies. In such societies this relationship is characterized by two essential traits. A segmented society is made up of juxtaposed units which are distinct but identical. One cannot really speak of a center possessing a differentiated organ—effectively in control of the whole society. In fact, a segmented society does not exist as a whole that is conscious of itself as such. Each constituent unit, being identical to all others, operates in isolation and severely limits the field of activity and the liberty of its individual members. According to Durkheim,[17] differentiation—resulting mainly from technological progress—and consequent competition leads to the specialization of social groups, to a greater interdependence among them, and especially to a greater dependence on an authority of higher rank which alone can manage and regulate their interrelations. Relationships develop between the center and the periphery, which is made up of an increasingly large number of differentiated groups that are simultaneously cooperating and competing, of which coexistence is more or less viable. It is these relationships that allow us to gauge the degree of integration in the society.

In the case of a country like contemporary Peru, the relationship between center and periphery seems quite removed from any functional principle of integration. From all evidence, Peru does not belong to the category of segmented societies because, like all other posttraditional societies, its center has an importance never found in really traditional societies. On the other hand, Peru is not, either, characterized by strong functional integration because its peripheral units operate in relative isolation from one another and from the center. Indeed, the rural masses have long continued to live in isolated groups, communities, or haciendas on the fringes of society. This marginality is also characteristic of the organized urban masses crowded into the *barriadas*. As for the Peruvian ruling classes, particularly the old oligarchy, their origins, activities, interests, and attitudes give them a more external than internal orientation. Their profits are realized on foreign markets; the products they consume are imported from other countries, and the life style toward which they are drawn originates in London, Paris or New York. In brief, the periphery is composed mainly of isolated units and, in relation to it, the center appears to be both heterogeneous and indifferent. One consequence of these structural features cannot fail to strike the observer: it is the inequality between the various social strata. For most peripheral units this inequality is represented in extreme hardship and poverty, a poverty which has been borne by the marginals for a long time and

to a certain extent, still is today. Surprisingly, however, there is no sign that these peripheral units ever possessed the desire or the means to put an end to their intolerable situation. This is the paradox with which the naïve observer is confronted.

Albert Hirschman suggests that there is a simple explanation for this paradox. If a situation so apparently untenable does persist it must be that it possesses certain change potentialities generally disregarded by conflict theorists who fear that their prophesies may be dismissed. These limited changes —which go unnoticed by those who cause them— are not the consequence of any plan or strategy; rather, they result from what Hirschman calls nicely "decentralized violence." In Colombia, he writes,[18] violence has been scattered, local and decentralized. Over the past hundred years the peasants have occupied and continued to occupy lands which are not theirs. At times they have had recourse to force, and force has been used against them by those who declare themselves to be the proprietors. In some instances the forceful appropriation of large parcels of land has, in the end, been sanctioned by the government either through specific intervention or through the process of "general measures."

Two ideas that also apply *mutatis mutandi* to Peru emerge from this account. Violence, the use of force to achieve illegal ends, is endemic. It manifests itself in a series of intense but local and short-term confrontations and has two principal consequences. At the local level, the use of violence allows landless peasants to limit the power of rich landowners to acquire additional lands. At the societal level—as in Colombia—violence acts as a safety valve to release built up tensions and also as a warning signal for political authorities. The insufficiency of this optimistic interpretation becomes apparent, however, when we reflect upon the fact that the easing of a situation occurs only *after* the marginal groups have exerted pressure upon the authorities and, even then, only under certain conditions: that these authorities are able to "decode" the message and that the "marginals" are either disposed or forced to moderate their pressure. This is indeed what Hirschman went on to suggest: "Thus the peasantry's propensity for occupying unused land . . . has hastened legislative reform." He poses the problem, at least implicitly, of the communication network through which "decentralized violence" becomes an element that "facilitates" social and political change.

The following is the model suggested by Hirschman:

> the land is occupied by the peasants and, in general, there is no immediate resistance to their doing so. It is true, however, that local tribunals can sometimes be taken over and made to rule that the occupants of these lands be evicted either by the police or even by the

armed forces. It is equally probable that for long periods of time nothing of the sort will happen. When political authorities decide that it is necessary to end such states of uncertainty without using force against the peasants, they are themselves disposed to buy the land and try to resell it to the peasants. For their part the peasants are prepared to pay something to acquire a land deed which among other things gives them the advantage of being able to obtain credit.[19]

The question that we must now ask is whether this model, which is based on an analysis of the Colombian situation as it existed in the 1930's and under the presidency of Alfonso Lopez applies in the case of Peru? It did not in the years prior to 1956, but it was becoming applicable during the Bellaunde administration. We must note that it is not the validity of Hirschman's interpretation nor even its relevance to the Peruvian case that is pertinent here. What is important is the content of his hypothesis. First, Hirschman assumes the existence of a constitutional government, that of Alfonso Lopez, for example, requiring, in order to function, a parliamentary majority of which a significant proportion must be progressive reformers. Secondly, Hirschman assumes that the chief executive has a sincere desire to bring about a certain number of more or less radical reforms, such as in the area of land ownership. Third, he assumes that the executive is more liberal — more "to the left" — than the parliamentary majority that must be sold a certain number of policies with which it is not in sympathy. He also assumes that, at the local level, the executive can rely on some degree of loyalty of the police and of the armed forces and on the impartiality of the courts that would resist the claims of the owners of occupied lands for "chains and reprisal" for the peasants. Fourth, Hirschman assumes that, at the parliamentary level, the executive is able to neutralize the opposition of the "hardliners" who, for ideological reasons, refuse to entertain any consideration of altering the *status quo* and to offer compensation through appropriate concessions to material interests threatened by reform, to which the conservative "ideologists" offer a more or less effective support. Hirschman himself summarizes his model in the following words: "The reforms which have taken place in Latin America are an example of extraordinary skill in the art of manipulation whereby certain initially hostile power groups are won over to the need for reform, others neutralized and outplayed and the remaining 'hardliners' checkmated by a coalition of extremely heterogeneous forces."[20]

"Decentralized violence" is an effective lever in bringing about change — and perhaps the only lever in countries like Colombia and Peru. Its effectiveness, however, depends on the political power being in the hands of well-meaning but also skillful "reformers" (reform-mongers as Hirschman calls them).

This condition can be viewed in an entirely negative perspective. Indeed, if the government is dominated by the "hardliners," all agitation will be repressed and the society will be caught in a vicious circle of repression. Hirschman's thesis, however, can also be seen in a positive manner: The "release" of the society will be facilitated if the more or less coordinated activities of the "center reformers" at the government level are consistent with the claims and agitations of the "marginals." Although I did point out the extraordinary difficulties which the reformers encountered, I have nonetheless attempted to apply this framework to the analysis of the Peruvian case.[21] I did so in spite of the fact that many obscure points remain with respect to the identity of the "reformers," to the content of reform programs, and to certain conditions related to the effectiveness of these programs.

The political effectiveness of the "reformers" is not only dependent on their modernization project or on the methods they select to put it into action. It also depends on the *initial* power of the reform group, on the position which its members occupy in the society, and on the resources and advantages these positions give them. All of these contribute in assuring them a more or less favourable starting point. Finally, in order to estimate the "reform" group's chances for success, we must take into account its ability to negotiate and to form coalitions with other groups. In discussing the various attempts at reform which have taken place in Peru recently, three main trends stand out that also correspond to distinct phases of the mobilization process. I shall distinguish among populist, technocratic, and military reform styles. Responsibility for the "historic mission" to "modernize" or to "Peruvianize" Peru has been successively and concurrently claimed by politicians, by technocrats, and by the military.

At this point, I cannot enter into a detailed analysis of the conditions surrounding the organization of each of these reform groups. What must be pointed out, however, is that the populist group appeared first. It emerged in the early 1930's as a distinct force in the context of the *Aprista* movement. It was Haya de la Torre in his Acho speech of August 1931 who proposed radical changes in the political orientations of Peru. He challenged the traditional Peruvian dualism and denounced the separation between the externally-oriented "center" and the "peripheral" marginal groups which it exploited. "Lessen the differences," that is, the distance between the "dominants" of the "center" and the "dominated" of the "periphery," was a slogan pointing not only to a radical change or reversal of the relationships between the "masses" and the Peruvian "elites" (between the "oligarchy" and the nation — *la oligarquia y las mayorias nacionales,* to use the populist terminology) but also to international relations, in particular to relationships between underdeveloped countries—"new" or nonindustrialized countries in 1930—and "imperialist" countries. "Dependence" and "exploitation" must cease and be replaced by solidaristic if not egalitarian cooperative relations.

The objectives set out by Haya de la Torre in 1931 have been the frame of reference for all subsequent attempts at "reform" and "modernization." Although the populist ideal has been maintained alive through successive generations of Peruvian politicians who have inherited their orientation and inspiration from Haya de la Torre (naturally without acknowledging their debt), the populist model has nonetheless progressively receded. To illustrate the features of the populist action model we must begin by underlining the very particular kind of legitimacy which its protagonists claimed for it. Haya de la Torre insisted on the urgency of the task and on the absolute commitment required. This urgent task of life or death, not only for the committed but for the entire country, was one that could be carried out successfully only by those who had taken themselves the responsibility for doing so. This charismatic character or radical populism is expressed in the notion of *compromiso generacional.* Only "the young," whether students or workers, having become conscious of their situation and their mission, can become completely committed to a task that will oppose them to an older generation that "has not understood," that cannot "understand," because it lacks the intellectual tool of "political science" and because it is irreparably entangled in the "politicking" of a neocolonial society and its folklore. Radical departure from the status quo and youthful mobilization are intimately associated in the populist movement: "Los viejos a la tumba, los jovenes a la obra."

But charisma—even that of "youth"—is not everything. *Aprist* populism would be a coalition attempting to bring together all forces that are "young," "modern," and "dynamic." The *APRA* and its leader must therefore attract and hold to its ranks the different "forces" that make up "las mayorias nacionales." Pertinent questions here have to do with whether the populist coalition is capable of attracting adherents; whether, once organized, its leader will be able to arbitrate differences among the various constituent groups. But it is not clear whether *APRA* has succeeded in passing from its "take-off" stage into a stage of "self-sustained growth", whether the youth reform movement has succeeded in making itself into an authentic Front of "active forces" (Fuerzas vivas) and national energies. Certainly it has succeeded in becoming known and imposing itself as a partner with which conservative interests have finally had to deal and which has obliged its

enemies to "coexist" (convivir) with it. This survival condition of having to coexist with rivals goes both ways: it means that the conservative interests could not get rid of the *APRA* reformers, but it also means that the APRA had to somehow "appease" and placate the conservatives. This is, in fact, what explains the lack of success the *Aprist* reformers have had in their attempt to impose the most radical parts of their program.

I see two basic reasons for this failure (or only partial success). First, the social forces which the *APRA* proposed to form into a coalition in 1931 were essentially weak. This was particularly the case of the middle classes and of the "national bourgeoisie." The problem was not only one of numerical weakness, however, for the bulk of the Peruvian population at that time consisted of Indian peasants. A serious part of the problem was that these Indian peasants are marginal citizens at best. Regardless of their numerical importance, therefore, they played very little part in the political life of Peru between 1930 and 1960. But the fundamental weakness of the *mayorias nationales,* whose cause Victor Raul had taken on, was their lack of organization. Moreover, the "decentralized" character of their protest did not produce the effects that Hirschman's optimistic hypothesis predicted: Violence, even decentralized, can only be effective if its vibrations reach the center. On the other hand, to be politically effective the protest of the marginals must be sufficiently decentralized so as not to touch off repression. But, it must not be so weak as to remain unheard at the summit, as seems to have been the case for a long time in Peru. This circumstance has made the *Aprist* reformers' task of political mobilization ("agitation" or "education," whatever we wish to call it) extremely difficult.

The *Aprist* of the 1930's were would-be reformers caught in the snare of a society that had very little feeling for Reform. I will not pretend to be able to explain each of the various aspects of this situation, which is common to many other Latin American countries besides Peru. I shall be content to outline here the disparity between the reform plans and the actual evolution of the society. Whether in response to their own regulations or to external provocations, societies change. It would be absurd to believe that the Peru of 1960 remained identical with the Peru of 1930. The trend towards urbanization of the coastal region has continued; agriculture, which was in the main an export agriculture, has been constantly modernized. Changes have occurred, but they have been precisely of the kind and in the direction that the early "reformers" condemned. Restricted by the limitations of their own projects, the "reformers" went out of touch with a rapidly changing society:

They were condemned to each other's company within a clandestine party not only because of the strength and efficiency of the repressive forces but also because they had failed to find allies in outside (and especially nonpoliticized) groups undergoing modernization. Although it is true that a relatively effective union movement had begun to organize, its influence was restricted to the plantations of the coastal region and to the mining camps. The mass of peasants and the bulk of the very limited working class remained unorganized.

The second wave of Peruvian reformers rose in the late 1950's. By this time the great *Aprist* plan had undergone the test of the first "convivencia"; between 1945 and 1948 the *APRA* party had been associated with the civil government of Bustamante Rivero. The conditions of this association had been exceptionally difficult and confused. The arrangement went from bad to worse and was climaxed, at the end of October 1948, by the coup d'état led by General Odria. A second "convivencia" began eight years later when, for better or for worse, Odria handed over his regime to a civilian, Manuel Prado. The *Aprist* reformers, emerging once more in 1956 from their clandestine life, were by this time moving towards a quite clearly "reformist" position although they themselves did not like to admit it. The emphasis shifted from the content of the Reform to the process whereby it would be accomplished. The goals of 1931 remained holy writ and Haya de la Torre continued to refer to them, but it became increasingly apparent that the realization of these goals depended on two conditions which severely limited the *APRA*'s freedom of movement: survival and the freedom of the party, a priority of priorities which put off to *mañana* what could not be obviously achieved in the short term. The *Apristas* counted, above all—rather like Hirschman—on obtaining positions in centers of power (particularly in the administration) and on the success of a certain number of structural reforms that had been legally introduced (land reform,[22] educational reform, and the like) to overcome *à la larga* conservative interests. But at the very moment when the second "convivencia" gave a second change to *APRA*, a second wave of Peruvian reformers rose, around 1956, which was bitterly antiprista.

Several basic differences between the reformers of the 1955-60 period and those of the first wave are worth noting: the new-brand reformers were passionate in their rejection of *reformism*. The *Apristas*, on the other hand, had never considered the reformism-revolution antithesis as an alternative. Very early Haya had made a distinction between a maximum and a minimum program. He gave priority to "leading"—a regulating activity dominated by an intellectual and moral type of leadership—over "ruling—defined as arbitrary injunction and brutal exploitation of the weak by the strong. The constant movement back and forth between these two approaches lost to the Revolution much of its dynamic impact and substituted for it political action characterized by a series of forward and backward initiatives that required skill, patience, and dedication. This gradualist approach was strongly denounced by *los Revolucionarias* of 1955-1960. They considered it a betrayal, a "social-democratic capitulation to the national oligarchy and to world imperialism." Any real reform program must be "integral" or nothing. As opposed to the *Aprist* approach, which they accused of being gradual, they called for "immediate action." The *Aprists* of 1930 had invoked the example of the Mexican Revolution. The generation of the early 1960's found its hero in Fidel Castro, as did the majority of Latin American radicals. Their program was not very original in content. Its originality was in the more or less implicit position taken with regard to development. On the one hand, they placed much confidence in the techniques of planning (integral, of course), while displaying, on the other hand, an increasingly strong distrust toward the "oligarchy" and also toward the "national bourgeoisie." Contrary to the position taken by *Aprist* reformers, the new wave surrendered to the dream of an "autonomous" and "accelerated" development and accepted, with little concern, the risk of a rupture with foreign sources of capital.

This direction may be called voluntarist if we take this term to mean the absolute priority that the new wave gave to the objectives which they themselves selected and, more important still, the contempt for resistance groups, which they did not intend merely to drive back, but to destroy. The justification for this "voluntarist" attitude is found in their technocratic pretensions. Both waves of Reformers that we have examined were composed of "intellectuals." This common label, however, conceals profound differences. Although they opposed their own "scientific" politics to those of politicians (*à la criolla*)— their conservative adversaries— the *Aprist* intellectuals were "generalists." Haya de la Torre was more familiar, for instance, with the works of Romain Rolland, Ghandi, and Toynbee than with those of Keynes or Irving Fisher. The new wave of reformers, on the other hand, were educated at a time when concepts like linear programming and gross national product were current and when Leontieff input-output analysis was often referred to. These intellectuals learned the language, if not the techniques, at the *CEPAL* of Santiago and in North American or European universities. More often than not, their knowledge was superficial, but it served to provide a common language between and to unite otherwise incongruous groups. Architects, anthropologists, sociologists, economists, doctors, hygenists, or urbanists had different training backgrounds, but they shared a common concern: by applying their knowledge to social problems they would contribute to the development of their country. These new wave reformers can, in the main, be said to be (or think of themselves as) specialists in terms of developmental problems. They find the symbol of their identity and of their mission in a few grand themes of planning.

Naturally enough, these ideas alienated the "new-wave" Reformers from—and brought them into conflict with — both the politicians and the bureaucrats and the traditional interest groups. They accused the politicians of being impotent and the bureaucrats of being inefficient and both of cooperating with the oligarchy, with the "reactionaries," the "imperialists," and so on. Possibilities for change (integral, of course) are seen by the new Reformers as linked with their own capacity to organize the masses and the marginal groups and, following this, to impose centralized planning with a view to accelerate development. Two images are associated with this conception: the "spontaneous" and "populistic" orientation (the peasants, the indigenous communities still faithful to the old Incaic socialism, will take control of their destiny) and the voluntarist (technicians determine and implement the most effective use of collective resources). The new Reformers have the conviction that they reconcile these two orientations within their own persons. On the one hand, they are as if by divine right in contact with the people of whose needs and aspirations they are aware and, on the other hand, they master modern knowledge and techniques of development.

Another feature must be added. It is the political indetermination or the absence of clear party identification of the New Reformers. A number of them had belonged to the *Aprist* Party; others were active in the party of Fernando Belaunde where they were a fairly active "left wing." Most of them, however, were found in splinter groups without electorates, like the *Movimento Social Progresista* or even the Christian Democratic Party. Others, still, held membership in no party and belonged to no movement. At certain times a few of them were tempted by the Castro adventure. At first sight at least we may say that the new Reformers are best suited for "groupuscule" agitation or factionalism, whereas the *Aprista* were set on organizing a "mass party" of their own capable of surviving persecution. This political indetermination is such that the new Reformers, unlike the *Aprista,* can easily be co-opted — and used — by successive governments. In the case of the *Aprista,* loyalty to a mass organization would

make it difficult for any of them to individually support a government that persecuted the "fellows" (*compañeros*) given the personal costs in case of rupture with the party. The splinter group setup of far left-wing Reformers is much more accommodating. This is exemplified by the case of a certain number of them who, having worked for the Belaunde government, are now advisors to the military Junta.

The fact is that the technocratic voluntarism of the new Reformers has a certain authoritarian streak that makes it relatively easy for them to collaborate with the "military progressives." This authoritarianism has two sources. First, it is related to the pessimism of the new Reformers: They surrender themselves to an idealization of the "masses" when they insist on the capacity of the peasants to organize and when they evoke the vitality of Indian communities. Yet, at the same time, many of them complain of the narrow-minded empiricism of the peasants, whose submission to ancient ways causes them to meet with distrust and indifference the innovations which agricultural and health technicians bring them and causes them to be incurably docile vis-à-vis the landed class towards which they remain submitted and deferential. Furthermore, the new Reformers often experience a strong feeling of their own powerlessness. Having no well-defined ties with the society which they would transform and isolated in their different and higher-status positions, they are particularly vulnerable to two complementary temptations. For those who are most deeply committed, the Castro-type revolution constitutes a last magical solution. However, the failure of Peruvian Castroism—after the escapade of Luis de la Puente and Lobaton in 1965 — brings the most realist among them to dream of a progressive military power which they would radicalize.

Whatever the nature of the relationships between the military progressives and the new Reformers, albeit only temporary, the latter's authoritarian tendency tends to crystallize and find expression in a "state-socialist" concept of development — "*el estado solidario*" — to which General Velasco refers in his speeches. The rapid decline of the model that entrusted the responsibility for development to the "national bourgeoisie" led to the gradual admission in the early 1960's that a more authoritarian approach was necessary in order to get out of the vicious circle of underdevelopment. The post-World War II variant of the *desarrollismo* would have been compatible enough with the views of the populist reformers of the *APRA* variety. The "substitution of imports" policy was consistent with their own watchword: a state able to resist imperialist interests and firm in its decision to mobilize the popular masses against the abuses of foreign capitalists in order to impose on them more equitable conditions. But neither populism nor *desarrollismo* in its first variant required that the state, though a guiding force, take the responsibility for planning the economy as a whole and even less for its detailed administration. In fact, *desarrollismo* was never pushed very far in Peru because of the resistance and distrust with which the populist reformers, met and the difficulty they encountered, if not in gaining credibility, at least in making themselves tolerable to the vested interests. When the second wave of reformers came out in the late 1950's they began by denouncing the cautiousness of the first wave and immediately advocated policies going very much beyond the policy of substitution of imports. The function assigned to the State would not be any longer one of mere animation, regulation, and gradual correction through the well-intended Machiavellian techniques to which Hirschman refers. Rather, in the precisely defined framework of the new reformers, where there was no longer a place for the national bourgeoisie or for foreign capital which served only to bring about dependence, the State must now conceive, plan, execute and control. The paradox is that such a state, at least in Peru, was nonexistent: It must therefore be created from top to bottom. And who would be better suited to this task than the military, when they are made aware of their historic mission?

The present Peruvian situation seems to be one where, paradoxically, the reformers, while in danger of becoming impotent, find themselves in a power position. The growth of the reform group cannot be explained simply in terms of the increasing and intensifying awareness of the need for a reform of structures. An understanding of the phenonemon must include the fact that Reform is no longer envisaged as a series of piecemeal initiatives, that it can no longer look for leadership to a small group of men of good will using their position to exert pressure on those holding wealth. The reform movement is, in fact, so comprehensive that it can be directed only by the centre itself, or, at the very least, eye to eye with it. Obviously, the "marginals" cannot be fully relied upon to take responsibility for their own affairs. While it is true that the motto *cooperacion popular*, so advantageously used by Belaunde, has still a strong appeal, neither the land nor the education reform program, nor even the large investments of infrastructures has been — and can be — left in the charge of the "masses." And given the weakness of the "national bourgeoisie" and the sharply reduced autonomy of the middle class, it is difficult to see who, apart from the most committed among the intellectuals, can assume responsibility for the Reform. In short, the intellectuals have branded the Reform

movement with their own style of action (which they like to call Revolution). As most of the intellectuals, they have a tendency to make judgements on the basis of general principles and are not very good at the game of bargaining, compromise, and coalition-building, except perhaps for those who have had executive responsibilities in large administrative organizations or in mass parties. Whereas they are experts and engineers in their own fields, in political matters they are amateurs, the most committed of whom have at one time or another been part of the schizoid life of splinter radical groups.

The urgency of the Reform combined with the weak organizational capabilities of the periphery have led the new Reformers — the closest to the center — to the conclusion that the first thing to do is to capture and control the center. The question is whether the technologist (or pseudo-technologists) of development possess the resources to realize their ambition. Do they see their power in relation to the power of other social groups in a realistic perspective? Are they aware of the extent of their ability to control spontaneous evolution that might not necessarily follow their prescribed directions? I am inclined to interpret the authoritarian orientation of the new Reformers as a reaction formation to their own sense of powerlessness. The inability of a group to come to a realistic evaluation of its position in society or to a realistic estimate of its power in the existing power structure, is most likely to result in its own "alienation," which can take two main forms. The first is passivity, which corresponds to a withdrawing attitude. It combines a narcissistic tendency to give supreme value to the activities and objectives of the group with the admission that actual achievement is extremely difficult, if not wholly impossible. The well-known "ivory-tower" symbol is often invoked in Latin America to describe — and usually to condemn — the escapist and high-minded attitudes of these intellectuals disillusioned by their society. (It may be noted that the hippie variety of escapism has so far met with very little success. It is as soundly condemned as the ivory-tower variety.) Second, alienation can also take a form which is active and, eventually, compulsive. This active form has three main components to which Peruvian new Reformers are particularly susceptible: voluntarism, technocraticism, and authoritarianism.

The relationship between the alienation of the intellectuals and their passive or active attitude is dependent upon the ideal which the intellectuals as a group set for themselves — their "mission" — and upon the congruence between this mission and expectations other groups have of them. The causes of an eventual dissonance may be seen at the level of the individual member of the group — student or young professional, for example—at the point of articulation of their intellectual, personal (especially within the framework of the family, both of orientation and of procreation), and professional roles.[23]

Whatever the hypotheses to which this research may lead, I shall limit my task to a few summary observations allowing some insight into the fundamental weaknesses of the new Reform movement. The movement seems to be deficient at both the symbolic and material levels. As well, it appears incapable of persuading, constraining, or negotiating. These capacities, it must be noted, are those which serve as the criteria whereby the power of any group can best be evaluated. As for the lack of material resources, it is not enough to simply say that Peru is a "poor country" and to dismiss the new Reformers dream of a program of accelerated development as an illusion. One must also consider that the new Reformers do not control the crucial resources: the administration of the armed forces and the production of wealth. To make some fairly arbitrary comparisons, it could be said that the "enlightened despots" of the 18th century who had the sovereign state at their disposal as an instrument for their modernization programs were better equipped than the new Reformers in Peru; so also were the British or French bourgeoisie who, although barred by the traditional aristocracy from positions of political power, were conscious, to use Saint-Simon's term, of being the authentic and genuine group of "producers."

The new Reformers are *intellectuals* first of all: other than *aspiring* to organize the sector of production they play no part in it; and as for the real "producers," the reformers at best can only attempt to *influence* them, for they hold no power of constraint over them, save perhaps through the sword of the soldier (if it can be put into motion) or through the manipulation of existing organizations like unions (if these can be won over). In sum, the new Reformers have more influence than power. If we agree with Parsons that influence is the reactivation of a latent consensus between "influencers" and "influencees" we must then ask what the consensual basis for the new Reformers influence might be. The consensus approach allowed a watered-down land reform bill to be passed in 1964. And while it is also true that the military *Junta* of 1968 acted, at least at the beginning, on the basis of a broad consensus, it has the advantage that the closing of Parliament served to silence the vested invested interests: who for instance, could, on the day following the coup d'état, oppose the nationalization of the oil fields of the International Petroleum Company? Or who, in June 1969, could come to the defence of the "oligarchy" when its sugar plantations were expropriated? On the other

hand, there is less certainty as to the success of the voluntarist policy of August 1970 that tried imposing an administrative program for industry, including workers' participation in management, while at the same time trying to curtail the influence of the unions.

It seems obvious that the two categories of reformers to which we have referred have had very little power. The first group had to operate on the basis of a survival strategy because of the fierce opposition they encountered. They were forced to be content with limited compromises that made little inroad into the traditional structure. In contrast to their gradualist or incrementalist powerlessness, there is the powerlessness of the voluntarist approach that leads to the alienation and progressive isolation of the new Reformers from the society they seek to change. Both these forms of powerlessness—one ending in the dissolution of the reform program, the other in the isolation of the reformers in unrealistic programs—have as common origins the conditions in which power is achieved, retained, and distributed in a society like Peru.

Hirschman suggested a comprehensive framework in which reform and change are explicitly related not only to the ability of "reformers" to manipulate conservative forces but also — and this is less explicit but no less important — to the existence of a consensus or a quasi-consensus among "reform-mongers." But Hirschman's main point — and it is only implicit in his theory — is that reform and change are dependent upon some degree of congruence between the *conscious* orientations of the reformist consensus and some of the *spontaneous* trends in the over-all society. The emergence of the new Reformers suggests that the first two conditions have not yet been met. And it remains to be seen whether the voluntarist orientation can overcome the forces of resistance or whether it can work with them while still maintaining control over them.

It is reasonable to ask whether Peru, as we have described it, is in fact "governable" or "guidable." To clarify this somewhat vague question, it is necessary to pose two others of a more precise nature: Is Peruvian society capable of defining collective goals that are feasible, and has it capabilities to mobilize the resources required to attain these goals? As to the nature of the goals, none of the development policies seems till now to have really concerned the collectivity. To the extent that the old ruling classes had a development policy, it has been challenged more or less forcefully by the various reform groups, all of which, for a variety of reasons, refused to grant to the schemes of the oligarchy any legitimacy. For their part the reform groups claim to speak for the "masses," confident in their innate knowledge of good and evil and in their right to speak for the

Common Good. Their dogmatism, however, fails to guarantee not only the rationality of their reform programs but also their very acceptability to the masses.

Considering the resources that the society could bring to bear in order to attain the reform goals, the extreme weakness of the center relative to the periphery is striking. So far the center under oligarchic rule has just been able to contain or suppress, and in certain instances prevent, "wild" violence. Even when it is directed, as it is today, by "progressive" military forces that are supported by radical intellectuals, the chief weakness of the center remains that it cannot be legitimized on a common value base although such a base is necessary to obtain the lasting cooperation of the various social groups. Undoubtedly, governments like to talk of development. However, on the one hand, there is increasingly bitter conflict between the old oligarchy and the urban and professional upper-middle classes from which the reformers come; on the other hand, the demands of the masses are likely to move farther and farther away from the goals set up by the reformers. Thus any alliances became difficult and increasingly improbable. "National independence" and "autonomous development" are abstract goals that provide enthusiasm only in exceptional circumstances such as under direct enemy threat. In this respect slogans of the *justicialista* type, which long assured Peronism (Juan Peron) the support of the *descamisados,* are much more effective as long as some slices of the cake remain to be divided. Finally, we must not exclude the possibility that the requirements of development and of autonomy may be perceived as contradictory. Indeed, they may even be perceived as contradictory in terms of personal ambitions. This is true not only of the well-to-do but also of individuals belonging to less favored but socially ascended groups like the *cholos,* whose value system is probably very different from that of the reformers who like to think that they speak for them.

The absence of common orientations that makes collective mobilization difficult also hampers bilateral negotiations between the center and the peripheral groups. It is true that the reformers experience no difficulty in coming to mutual understandings with professionals — at least as long as the professional interests are not threatened by the reformers. However, it would appear that, for the present at least, the center has nothing much to offer to the peripheral groups.

The confrontation between the "real" and the "symbolic" resources of the Peruvian power structure invites another look at what Parsons has called "inflation and deflation" of social systems, particularly in political systems. The comparison between the economic phenomenon of credit and the social phenomenon of confidence is a good starting point for our analysis.[24] Credit may be defined as the advance, for the benefit of an economic actor, of resources which the actor has not earned himself and of which he has only provisional use — on the understanding that at a given date he will return the funds loaned to him. In terms of the person who extends the credit, therefore, credit is based on the anticipation that the terms of the transaction (the lender parts with his liquid assets on the understanding that the borrower will pay him interest during the term of the loan) be met in due time; by the end of the loan period the borrower must demonstrate his solvency by being able to pay back the loan. Extending credit involves taking calculated risks because there is no real guarantee that, at the end of the term, the borrower will be solvent. Both banker and client can be mistaken. By being either overly optimistic or pessimistic they can fail to make a correct prediction of the state of the market at the time of reimbursement.

According to Parsons, inflation in the economic system is the result of an overextension of credit that leads economic actors to faulty anticipations of prices, costs, and revenues, resulting in a generalized crisis of insolvency. The causes of inflation are found to be an excessive offer of credit on the part of creditors, a buoyant demand on the part of economic agents, or a combination of both these factors.

Two points must be stressed which will facilitate our analysis. First, "crisis" is defined as the moment of truth, *le moment de Vérité,* when the system must demonstrate its solvency. The analogy between this and the political situation is striking, particularly in the case of confrontation between power holders and groups who defy them to use that power. This analogy rests on a characteristic common to all symbol systems. Symbols are adequate substitutes of a given reality only if they have the capacity, when necessary, to provide us with the essential characteristics of that reality. Second, the process of inflation, which Parsons presents as a kind of symbolic disequilibrium, stimulates anticipations in different classes of actors that eventually become both conflicting and mutually reinforcing. Whereas the phenomenon of credit has commanded much attention, little has been given to an equally important and analogous situation found in the political system, the simultaneity of inflationary and deflationary trends.

To return to Peru, it is easy to see that there exists a "general crisis" of confidence. Therefore it is difficult however to determine whether this

Peruvian crisis should be qualified as categorically "deflationary" or "inflationary." At first sight, it seems that for various reasons and to various degrees, the capacity of Peruvian society to reach collective goals or even to satisfy the most essential requirements of its situation — its solvency, to use economic terms — is highly questionable. Contrary to what the economic analogy suggests, the crisis *à la Peruvienne* cannot be treated as a merely cyclical episode which would follow a "credit" boom: It is not a momentary return to earth for actors who have been carried away in excessive involvements whose success depended upon the magic of endless expansion. The crisis *à la Peruvienne* is a *structural* crisis and has a character of permanence. It does not arise solely from the conflict between the reality principle and inflated expectations but also from the structural discrepancy between the various expectations that characterize each group.

The position of the various reform groups may be said to be inflationary in relation to the center though deflationary in relation to be traditional ruling classes. In other words, there is a tendency for the reform group to exaggerate the capacity of the center as such, to underestimate the effectiveness of the "real" elites, and to believe themselves to be somehow all-powerful. It is likely that according to the reference they choose (themselves as powerful, the others as powerless) they tend to experience shifts of moods that extend in cyclical fashion from extreme pessimism to the most unrealistic optimism and that vary with their proximity to centers of political decision-making. The masses, on the other hand, like the traditional elites but for different reasons, are characterized by an attitude of withdrawal and noninvolvement.

The degree of confidence social groups possess toward the over-all society is related to the congruence or incongruence of their attitudes toward one another. In Peru, it would seem, the reform group plays a major role in determining this degree of confidence; it decides what the collective goals shall be or, more exactly, the goals it specifies in a usually abstract and arbitrary manner have good chances to be acknowledged as valid for the society as a whole. The explanation for this privilege is easily discovered. In relation to the masses, the reform group has an overwhelming superiority in symbolic manipulation; and in similar fashion, it can dismiss the power of the traditional ruling class as devoid of legitimacy on account of its egotistic self-interest.

The reformers tend to presume that they alone know the common good. Apart from the resistance of the old ruling classes and the apathy of the masses which hamper their attainment, the most important tensions affecting the reformers are not those between themselves and other groups. They are those found within their own ranks. So long as they can point to the self-centeredness of the oligarchy or to the apathy of the masses in order to explain their failures or their slow pace in implementing their policies, their arguments are not very different from those of the conflict school: the development of society's "limitless potential" is hampered by archaic and oppressive institutions. On the other hand, once underutilization of resources ceases to appear as the exclusive effect of material poverty or of exploitation by the rich and powerful it has to be admitted that society, even when rid of its "parasites," does not respond immediately to the inducements of the center and that more or less pronounced "leads" and "lags" between the center and the periphery are an expression of the tenuous and fragile relations between the "real" and the "symbolic" aspects of the power system.

CENTER ALOOFNESS, BUREAUCRATIC ACTIVISM, AND PERIPHERAL RESTLESSNESS: THE CASE OF FRANCE

The case of France will help us to understand the nature of the symbolic discrepancy characteristic of center-periphery relationships. Observers from Marx to Tocqueville have agreed that, as a look at the following two basic and related questions will show, in France the center is more powerful than the periphery. The questions are the following: Is it the State which constitutes the "center", or is it the bureaucracy, or are State and bureaucracy one single thing? The hypothesis can be entertained that bureaucrats are primarily interested in *administration* through hierarchical control exerted on sectors which are more or less distant, but nonetheless special and distinct, while the power of the State is more explicitly geared to defining and reaching a certain number of goals of common concern to all sectors of society. It is more in the nature of the bureaucratic structure to deal with the management of day-to-day affairs than to deal with policy-making matters. In France, a symbiotic relationship has come to exist between the two. The bureaucracy has always had more than simply a *fonction d'execution*. The State, on the other hand (and this is especially true of periods when it works through a parliamentary arrangement, as in the period from 1870 to 1958), has often been incapable of exercising its arbitration or decision-making powers.

Whatever the relationships between the bureaucracy and the State, the importance of the center has always been great and, more often than not, decisive.

This was already the case under the Old Monarchy, as Tocqueville pointed out. The Revolution consolidated and, perhaps, even increased this importance (although perhaps less than traditionalists like Taine or Maurras would have us believe)[25] by substituting the sovereignty of the people for that of the Monarch. It remains to be seen what the explicit or latent goals of the center are and how it would impose its own goals on, or negotiate them with, the periphery.

The orientation of the center to affirm its own primacy finds expression in the ideology of either sovereignty or the common good. Its most powerful expression is found in democratic rationalism, which acts both as a centralizing and levelling force. The French refer to it as Jacobinism. This orientation is still found today, although to a lesser degree, in the ideology which top-ranking civil servants refer to as "service to the State." Second, the center sees its responsibility in the area of maintaining order and as such feels obliged to use, if necessary, repressive measures. It tends to perceive its functions in terms of policing, rather than in terms of overseeing. Last, the center is eager to take on the responsibilities for development. This is a point which Tocqueville underscored in his study of the expansion of the monarchic administration at the end of the old regime. The intendant was not content with levying taxes and with commanding the militia: he built roads, beautified towns, concerned himself with what is now referred to as urbanism or regional development. "The central government did not confine its activity to helping peasants with their miseries, but concerned itself with helping them learn how to prosper — helping them and even forcing them on occasion."[26] The center assumed for itself a role of initiator and guide in matters of economic development. It is unlikely however that it desired to subjugate completely the periphery. The often-used expression "colbertism" obscures the question by focusing exclusively on one of the many intervention techniques: direct state control of production. In fact the intendants under Louis XV and Louis XVI — as was also the case of high officials under de Gaulle — preferred a pattern of goal-setting and regulatory intervention.

The Leninist thesis[27] holds that the State is the "instrument of the ruling class." This thesis must be understood in the light of the fact that it was a response to the traditional thesis that equates the State with the embodiment of the common good. The French case gives us a clear example of such a claim from the center attempting to set itself up as an autonomous, benevolent, and transcendent body. The way the center attempts to make this claim good allows us to gain insight into the characteristics of

the strategies, behaviors, hard stances, and sudden failures of the State in contemporary French history.

The periodic crisis of French political history since the Revolution lend themselves to two kinds of interpretations that stand in contrast to each other but that nonetheless are not mutually exclusive. The first, and by far the most popular, consists in looking for the causes of political revolutions in social conflicts or in economic crises. The conflict between the rising bourgeoise and the nobility at the end of the eighteenth century and later on the confrontation between the emerging social forces and the established political structures would explain the downfall of the old Monarchy and the almost permanent turmoil of French life in the nineteenth century.[28]

Although this interpretation has the merit of linking disruptions at the center with movements occurring in the most remote areas of the periphery, three basic reservations must be made as to its adequacy. In the first place, it does not allow the establishment of meaningful relationship between political movements and economic phenomena. Basically, it does not determine in any clear way the threshold beyond which an economic fluctuation becomes a tidal wave shaking the entire political fabric. After all, the crisis of the years 1846-1847 was not much more severe than many others which the Louis Philippe regime had to face previously. Basically, the "economistic" explanation fails in that it neglects to consider the center's capacity to confront movements which originate outside of itself but over which it can keep a more or less effective control. In brief, it neglects to consider the center's capacity to constitute and maintain itself as an *autonomous* force. A second difficulty encountered in this explanation is that it described crises in terms that did mean very little for most of the protagonists. In relation to the events of 1848, for example, Marxist historians underscore the building up of economic tensions. On the other hand, Tocqueville, in his *Souvenirs*, describes the events in the following words: "The Revolution was *unforeseen* by all and perhaps least of all expected by the King. No sign had prepared him for it, since for years, his spirit had withdrawn in that kind of proud solitude to which the intellects of undisturbed princes almost always find their way. Mistaking power for genius they no longer wish to listen since they have nothing more to learn from anyone."[29]

Tocqueville's comments on the old King withdrawn in his "proud solitude" were applicable, without modification, to the entire political class, including the enemies of the King and Crown, or at least to those among them who, as visible chiefs of His Majesty's opposition, belonged to the world of the officials. Here is what Tocqueville had to say of the political world on the eve of the February Revolution of 1848. One of the leaders of the opposition, then raising many questions about the "Banquet" campaign, told him: "Be confident that the outcome of all this will be favourable; at any rate there must be some risk . . . . Besides, the government is less worried than the opposition." It is true that the "radical leaders" were better informed than anyone; but they were unwilling to fight it out, so convinced were they that, in the event of trouble, things would turn out to the favour of the government. "On the eve of these events Madame de Lamartine, who had come to pay Madame de Tocqueville a visit, was so openly anxious, that the many sinister ideas she expressed excited and troubled her hostess to the point that she (Madame de Tocqueville) became upset and that very evening told me of her fears." The observer concludes: "That the events which formented this singular revolution were brought on and almost desired by those who were to be abruptly deposed from power and foreseen and feared only by those who would conquer by the revolution was not the least among the bizarre characteristics of the revolution."[30]

What is worth noting in Tocqueville's description is that it offers an explanation contrary to the commonly accepted view: For him the main cause of the Revolution was not in the class conflict. Tocqueville looks at things from the angle of the center and attempts to explain why the center lost over the periphery. What strikes him is the extent to which the political class was uninformed about events occuring outside its immediate boundaries. The King's "proud solitude" made him "incapable of learning anything from anyone." It led him, along with his Prime Minister to commit errors in judging the behavior of the parliamentary opposition; it rendered the political class almost totally unaware of public opinion and of the attitude of the mass of the population. Second, the lack of adequate communication between the various parts of the center led to a wavering that caused unenlightened and other inconsistent decisions to be taken, for the most part, abruptly and too late. Finally, Tocqueville strongly emphasized the center's selfishness: "Toward the end, the existing government had come to look like an industrial company in which all operations are geared to the benefit of shareholders."[31] This overriding concern for personal and family enrichment had two effects: the internal corruption of the political class and the subsequent contempt of the public for the ruling group.

The crisis of 1848 was related to a loss of confidence, but one which was not obviously so severe as in the Peruvian case, where the society's capacity to attain any set of collective goals — goals acceptable to the various component groups — is so deeply undermined. The crisis that Tocqueville analyzed resulted from the loss of confidence of the general public in the political leadership and profound mistrust of the official leaders in each other, rather than from an over-all loss of confidence in the society itself. It is more a case of a regime's "wearing out" rather than a fight to the finish between two irreconcilable classes. Of course, the boundary between the two is difficult to determine, the more so since the cumulative aspects of the phenomenon must be taken into account, as they progressively revealed the very nature of the developing crisis, which was far from being clear at the onset.

Tocqueville emphasized the miscalculation that brought the leaders of the parliamentary opposition — Thiers and Odilon Barrot — to bring about the downfall of a regime (to which they remained committed to the end) when all that they had in mind was forcing Louis Philippe to dismiss Guizot and to summon them to his Council. In order to grasp the nature of the cumulative process that explains the rapid elimination of the Moderates in the crisis of 1848 as well as in the early phases of the 1789 Revolution, we must begin by looking at the chance elements of the historical starting point. Were an observer to limit himself to the events of February 1848, he would not have readily seen a "crisis of civilization" or a "class conflict" in the strictly political episode that brought about the downfall of Louis Philippe. But he could possibly have changed his mind after the terrible bloodbath of June. Once the political center had become virtually powerless as the result of divisions and inconsistencies in the provisional government, led by Lamartine, the very bases of social control — particularly the principles of private ownership and even monogamy — were overtly questioned by the most radical of the "utopian socialists."[32] Here Parsons' "hierarchy of controls" enables us to understand the paradox of apparently unshakeable conservative positions which crumbled at one stroke as soon as their front lines were overcome with the downfall of the King. And similarly, though in a reverse sequence, we see the apparently irresistible strength of the radical tide receding massively because *its very success* had forced into opposition those who had initially been supportive but now realized that "things had gone too far."[33]

The crisis of the 1848 variety appears to be a loss of control on the part of the center. The extent of this loss of control depends on the effectiveness of the regulatory mechanisms, which were either simultaneously or successively loosened but could be put into motion again in the subsequent phases of the process. In order to predict the seriousness of a crisis of this type at its very onset, it would be necessary to know whether the center can still count on some degree of control over certain essential peripheral units or whether it has become so completely isolated that it is definitely out of the picture and has no chance to play a significant role in the further phase of the crisis.

Let us begin by noting that, in France, the relations between center and periphery are comparable to those between the top layers of the hierarchical structure and the lower-rank clerks in a traditional bureaucracy. This comparison, however, if pushed too far, becomes arbitrary. France is not, and never has been, a really bureaucratic society — if such a thing has ever existed anywhere. The existence of a market and a private sector made up of small and medium-sized enterprises which even if subsidized retained a large degree of managerial autonomy, and the continued existence in rural areas of traditional peasantry surviving on the subsistence economy which their small land plots provided had reduced the power of the State over French society as a whole during all of the nineteenth century and perhaps even up until the Second World War. With all these restrictions and qualifications, we can nevertheless, following Michel Crozier, adopt the bureaucratic model as the most appropriate model for analyzing some notorious dysfunctions in French society.

Although those in the top positions have to grant their subordinates many guarantees in the areas of recruitment, promotion, and discipline, the principal characteristic of bureaucracy *à la française* is the reluctance of its center to negotiate its power with the periphery. In this respect one of the latent bureaucratic functions, as the history of French public administration well demonstrates, is the protection of acquired rights — not to say privileges — of lower-ranking officials to the extent that the bureaucracy, which in theory is all-powerful, finds itself progressively bound and paralyzed, like Gulliver by Lilliput. If, however, instead of considering the relations between the hierarchy and its administrators, we look at the manner in which the bureaucracy defines its major orientations, we note that its mode of operations puts it out of touch with society, in relation to whose demands or needs it always either "leads" or "lags" behind. To the extent that the bureaucracy is capable of foresight, it tends to select goals that are not of immediate interest to the public at large. To use Karl Deutsch's words,[34] its decisions are based mainly on the discrepancy between the actual state of affairs (which, supposedly at least, it knows in a more extensive and synthetic manner than the public at large) and the anticipated (bureaucracy credits itself with a broad capacity to foresee, even at the expense of considerable error margins) set of

goals that it holds (often alone) as "socially desirable." In this regard, discussions at the French "planning commission" are characteristic.

On the other hand, the bureaucracy is most subject to "lags" in relation to public opinion, especially in cases of slight variations in the public mood; it is slow to recognize those ambiguous and sometimes misleading signs to which the clinician has to be constantly alert. It is fashionable to attribute this "lag" of the bureaucratic machine to the complexity of its communication networks. It must be remembered that bureaucratic systems are highly selective. They can transmit and receive only a limited range of messages. Consequently, they are able to attend to certain kinds of demands only by disregarding information that may be lost unless other circuits routed to the center are established.

Far from being mutually exclusive, the two risks — the systematic "lead" and "lag" — are cumulative. In terms of the selection of its overall objectives, the bureaucratic system pretends to lead the society; in terms of realizing these objectives it tends to lag behind. Persuing Deutsch's line of reasoning, we can state that the system reacts through two seemingly different behaviors: voluntarism and opportunism. The bureaucratic system is voluntaristic inasmuch as it tends to substitute the goals of the top dogs for those of the people and to impose them without regard to societal need or want. It is opportunistic inasmuch as, at the bottom, it proceeds by compromises aimed at getting the consent of administrators, even at the risk of completely altering the objectives defined at the top.

It is therefore both exact and inexact to say that the French-style bureaucratic system is incapable of negotiation. The proposition is exact if it refers to the over-all objectives of an organization or of the society as a whole, but at the level of particularistic exchanges of favors and privileges, the system retains a high degree of flexibility. As a result, its ability to function and its survival are assured, in part at least, by its ability to accommodate the universalistic principles it proclaims. Above all, this procedure results in the fragmentation of the public into a number of clienteles with which the center laboriously barters, trying to avoid the danger that the particular demands of any of them might become a serious concern to the others.

The method of negotiations imposed by the State and its bureaucracy on French society is not without resemblance to the "decentralized violence" of which Hirschman speaks. In order to "force the Power to draw back," the interests that are not fairly treated have no recourse but to make their nuisance value felt. The small French businessman or farmer is not unlike the Peruvian or Colombian peasant who occupies lands which are not his in order to give himself some breathing space and to force the State to care for his needs. Michel Crozier is correct in seeing that in the French-style process of negotiation, blackmail — the meeting of two antagonists seeking to feel out each other's propensity to force or yield — holds a decisive place.[35] Blackmailing is attempted before bargaining in order to overcome the resistance of vested interests which stick to their guns. And very often, it also concludes the whole affair. In both instances power is perceived more as a particularistic and bilateral relationship than as a *binding obligation* involving the entire society.

Many observers, for different reasons, believe that the alienation of the center in French political life has reached the point of no return.[36] Not taking into account the hyperbolic and metaphysical form that the thesis has in the eyes of some of the most radical of its adherents, its defenders generally appeal to two arguments: The first is that the center's increasing rigidity intensifies its growing inability to assume responsibility for the whole nation;[37] the second is that the center is captive and a perfectly subjugated instrument of the interests of the ruling class.[38]

The French policy can be characterized by a combination of rigid enforcement on the one hand and low capacity inducement on the other hand. The inducement mechanisms seem to belong mainly to two categories. First, within the framework of an apparently rigid bureaucracy, a highly sophisticated exchange of tiny particularistic favors (material and symbolic) has always been going back and forth between the representatives of the central government — the *préfet* — and the lower ladders of the political class, mainly small town mayors, *conseillers généraux,* and so on. The local *notables* could use another channel in order to get connected to the center: through personal relationships they carefully cultivate with congressmen and senators, they may have an access to the Parisian *bureaux.* But in both cases, it has dealt mainly with very particular problems, which by common agreement are referred to not as really "political" but merely "administrative" matters. These ingratiation techniques please the bureaucracy while, at the expense of a few favors, it keeps its control over the really important matters and are tolerable to the "notables," who may insist when they report to the voters on their total independance from the "Power."[39]

But these mechanisms, if they provide a link between the "notables" and the center, do not seem to constitute the most adequate tool to deal with the issues that interest the larger sections of the population. Moreover, the exchange of particularistic favors no longer seems to work satisfactorily since the congressmen themselves have lost much power and influence at the national level, and the bureaucracy at the local level is consequently less responsive to the notables. Any way the basic question remains whether the over-all nature of the influence process has not changed in the last years. When it deals with the opening of a new job at some rural school, the pressure a notable may exert through the *député* upon the *Inspection Académique* is reasonably efficient and adequate to the nature of the case. But when it deals with complex problems like regional development, the poor articulation of the local interests, or the arrogance of the technocrats, the insensitivity of the administration leads into an impossible situation wherein any decision finally has to be taken by the government and it resented as arbitrary, clumsy, and obnoxious.

The weak inducement capacity of the center in relation to the periphery can also be looked at from the angle of the over-all participation by groups which dedicate themselves to problems of (more or less common) interest. The mistrust does not point only at the government. Party affiliation, union membership for instance, even in relation to countries like Italy which are not by any standard more industrialized than France, seems constantly low.[40] More generally, the concern for the common good does not seem quite lively. The "science of association" of which Tocqueville spoke so eloquently is certainly not a strong point in French political culture.

It may be argued that the sort of exchange of particularistic favors we have been referring to tends to be superseded by the emergence and consolidation of "mass parties" such as the Communist Party and the Gaullist U. D. R., but let us notice that the Gaullist party still remains relatively weak at the grass-root level and that the communist party still insists on its being a "revolutionary party," "the vanguard of the proletariat." Moreover, the special links between the U. D. R. apparatus and the group of leaders who have run French national politics since 1958 constrain its capacity of taking initiatives, because of a somehow crippling fear "to embarrass the government." Anyway, the center (government and bureaucracy) remains aloof and lonely, the only exchange it has with the periphery dealing with specific grievances and very special and narrow demands. The more general goals of the polity are kept at the discretion of the center, whose style in proposing change has been aptly described by Michel Crozier: As a succession of ambitious bold moves engineered and decided at the top level performed by reluctant *fonctionnaires,* which finally stumble at the obstinate resistance of the threatened interests. That clinical descriptions of so many failures at "Reform-mongering" does not apply only to bureaucratic engineered change. When the innovation is carried by a group of private citizens, though the picture is different, the outcome is basically the same. Of course, whereas the bureaucratic Reformer is secretive, the member of the private association tend to be vociferous and strident. The first tries to take advantage of his position at the center: the second is not loath to raise the mob against "Le Pouvoir." Everyone sticks to his guns; and if some change occurs, it has to be imposed by the center or wrested from it after a severe confrontation.[41]

The merit of these analyses is that they remind us of the oligarchic tendencies of all societies and of French society in particular. They rejoin the conflict theme which was the starting point of this paper: the inability of societies to ensure full use of their capabilities. This tendency of withdrawing and withholding benefits for themselves from other sectors of society, which is particularly noticeable in the political behaviour of the ruling classes, is also expressed on the cultural level by the mandarin tendency towards ritualism and esoterism. At the political level, it is expressed in the setting up of an "apparatus" which, in order to preserve its autonomy and to extend its grip, seeks to exert strict control over the society in which it operates. I acknowledge the existence and generality of this tendency. Nevertheless, comparisons must be made between the different forms of the said tendency if we are to undertake a study of its causes and attain as far as possible a level of understanding going beyond the trivial explanations of "human nature" and "laws of capitalism."

CONCLUSION

If we define power as a society's capacity to attain a set of common goals, the first step we must take in giving substance to this highly abstract concept is to examine the relationship between center and periphery. It is not possible to localize the center of different societies in the same manner. However, in all societies the center does fill a number of relatively comparable functions. Specifically, it contributes in an important and often decisive manner to defining a plan for the use of collective resources, whatever their extent, which, of course, varies from one society to another. It also serves as a kind of last resort in the enforcement of sanctions that can be applied to a reluctant sector of the periphery. It has to do this regardless of the type of intervention it must adopt under different circumstances.

The capability of the center is dependent upon a certain number of real resources, the intrinsic effectiveness of which it is important to assess. However, in the same way that power is not reducible to

physical constraint, exchange is not to be confused with the barter. Hence the effectiveness of the center's resources is affected by the increasing multilateral nature of the exchange network in which these resources are involved, and by the extension, through the mechanism of credit and confidence, of the span of time during which they can be used. It is through this double temporal and special extension that the symbolic dimension of power may be understood.

Like all symbolic relationships, power involves two kinds of phenomena. On the one hand, it reduces the effort of resorting to physical operations. The political authority which calls upon its power "so as not to be required to use it" is in the same position, comparatively speaking, as an individual who uses the words of a language correctly. On the other hand, the operations evoked by power as threats or persuasions must, when necessary, be translatable into practice. Moving to the symbolic realm involves substitution of *possible* relationships for real ones. But symbolic resources cannot completely be substituted for real ones: the symbolic must be submitted to reality testing from time to time.

This process of testing can be institutionalized on a regular basis as in the case of democratic regimes, through the mechanism of elections. It can also take the form of an insolvency crisis or of a prolonged period of economic stagnation, during which more or less important "real" resources remain unused. Parallel situations can be found in the political realm. Here we find short-run crises, on the one hand, from which recovery is rapid despite their intensity; on the other hand, there are structural crises of longer duration which involve long-term underutilization of a large proportion of the collective resources. This underutilization — to which conflict ideologists justly attach so much importance — results from a disturbance of the symbolic function, which in turn causes the system to fall back on the effectiveness of its real resources, or, so that it may "pull out of it," to engage in a process of wild threats and unrealistic promises.

Unfortunately, it is difficult to arrive at a classification scheme for political crises on the basis of these considerations. Moreover, inflationary and deflationary tendencies are often found to exist side by side in the same system and, what is worth noting, originate in the same groups. Peruvian reformers, for example, helped to destroy confidence in the traditional ruling classes while also creating excessive expectations in the achieving capacities of State. Similarly, in France, the weight of the bureaucratic structure engenders two series of consequences. First, it limits *current* demands in that, because of bureaucratic rigidities, groups are discouraged from attempting to bring their grievances to the center.

Second, inasmuch as the bureaucracy attempts to impose too ambitious collective goals, it raises public expectations and hence public claims on the center which it will find difficult to meet.

The benefit of studying the responsiveness of a political system to inflation or deflation, especially when these occur simultaneously, is that it provides a basis from which to evaluate the capacity of a political center. In this respect the cumulative process phenomenon is particularly enlightening. In the last section of his *Ancien régime et la révolution,* Tocqueville gives a characteristically precise and detached analysis of the phenomenon. His analysis rests on the hypothesis that an erratic situation developed in the last years of the Monarchy as the result of the combination of commitments made by reform ministers and the Crown's reluctance to move in the direction it had itself prescribed.[42] The "drift" (in the sense in which Karl Deutsch uses it) that resulted was characterized by a sort of structural indecision that gave the last years of the Old Regime the staggered pace of a series of bold ventures followed by hasty retreats. The center's incapacity was the result of a paralysis of decision-making units combined with an overloaded communication system and contradictory projects of reform ministers. The result was the complete disruption of the system.[43]

The difference between this and the contemporary Peruvian situation (though both are obviously "structural" and long-term crises) is easily seen, as is the difference between it and the present state of the French society.[44] The Peruvian type of situation is characterized by the isolation of the political center in relation to the remainder of society and by the corresponding tendency either to settle itself in a cynical attitude of exploitation and manipulation or to claim for itself the exclusive responsibility to define societal goals. The oligarchic tendency found in the old ruling classes is also found in the authoritarian reformers who replaced them. It remains to be seen whether the reformers will succeed in activating the latent capacities of groups that the traditional system of domination neglected.

A society whose center is aloof is exposed to disruptions that lead not only to a violent but also to a lasting deflation of power. In this respect the French case appears to be very different from the pure oligarchic case in that as the periphery is more diversified and integrated, it is difficult if not impossible for the center to set itself up in lasting cynical or defiant attitudes of exploitation in the manner of the traditional Peruvian ruling classes. This complete alienation is, indeed, as unlikely as would be the implementation by the revolutionaries of the daydreams of the new Reformers, were they to gain power. Both these risks, which are cumulative, are not absent

from the French case; generally speaking, they can be found in the case of any society politically structured on the model of a centralized hierarchy. In the French case, however, a certain counteracting and stabilizing effect is found in the partial congruence between the common values of the society and some of the goals proposed by the center.

Ideological cleavages within the French political class are very apparent. Nonetheless all the available data suggest that not only does there exist a fairly widespread *consensus* at a public level but that this consensus is supported by a degree of in-depth understanding between the various groups. In the areas of civil liberties and adherence to basic forms of personal existence (family, inheritance) there is a certain apparent agreement that serves to guide the "center" in certain relatively fixed directions and to dissuade politicians from deviating very much from them.[45] It is true that the agreement on these values is not always explicit and that the consensus, far from being self-evident, must be built up by the political leadership. Precisely on this point rests the principal failure and greatest weakness of French society. This lack of an explicit consensus is related to the absence of any real network of influence between the center and the periphery, with the result that most communications must be routed through bureaucratic channels — official and unofficial.[46]

It must be clear that it was not my purpose to suggest some comparisons between two societies so obviously different as France and Peru. But I wanted to suggest the fruitfulness of an approach that would systematically elaborate on the relations between center and periphery and would analyze the various resources the center can count on, in the process of controlling or mobilizing the periphery. Two things seem now reasonably clear. First, the effective mobilization of *all* the social forces is extremely hard to achieve; and it is not surprising if some, or many, resources remain idle — even if, taken as a whole, the society is quite able to produce added value. Second, the setting and implementation of collective goals can by no means be reduced to their coercion through force or immediate fulfillment through charisma. One of the remarkable convergences — which obviously needs further elucidation — in this analysis I have presented is the importance of influence networks, which seem so notoriously ineffective, though for different reasons, in both France and Peru.

I do not maintain that the questions raised at the beginning of this paper have been answered. But the attempt to employ a theory of action framework to study the problem of the underutilization of political capacities has, I believe, accomplished three things: It has permitted the identification of a number of political consequences of the nature and extent of the control the center exerts over the periphery. Second, it has permitted the description of the processes influencing the ralationship between center and periphery. Last, it has facilitated a certain clarification of the relationships between the "real" and "symbolic" aspects of political power as they affect the center-periphery relationship.

NOTES

1. See Alfred Sauvy, *Théorie générale de la population*, Tome II (Paris: Editions Presses Universitaires de France, 1966), Ch. 9.

2. A famous "law" stated by King establishes a relation between the net revenue of farmers, the volume of the harvests, and the price level of foodstuffs. Taking into account the slight variation of food demand, even in traditional societies, the maximum net revenue (for the maximum physical volume of the harvest) is not necessarily attained.

3. The Marxist doctrine, with its distinction between "relative" and "absolute" impoverishment, undoubtedly supplies the best picture of these two aspects of exploitation (appropriation of the product and underemployment of the producer).

4. See Neil J. Smelser, *Theory of Collective Behavior* (New York: The Free Press, 1962).

5. When Keynes wrote that it was preferable to employ workers to place bank notes into bottles and bury these bottles so that they could then dig them up and break them to recover the bank notes in order to place them in other bottles and so on indefinitely, rather than let workers go unemployed, the notion of employment, although intuitive and normative, was relatively clear. Intuitively, employment is the opposite of unemployment and, from a normative stance, it is any measure which reduces the number of the unemployed whatever its cost. But outside of extreme situations, such as "the great depression," this view is obviously not very illuminating.

6. Darras, *Le Partage des bénéfices* (Paris: Les Editions de Minuit, 1966), pp. 17-19.

7. See Emile Durkheim, *Le Suicide* (Paris: Editions Presses Universitaires de France, 1967), p. 281.

8. Alain, *Propos* (Edition de la Pléiade) (Paris: Editions Gallimard, 1956), p. 1205.

9. Talcott Parsons, *The Structure of Social Action* (New York: The Free Press, 1949), pp. 378-90.

10. This guidance function defines political activity in both specific and general terms: in specific terms because it allows the distinction between political and economic activity and in general terms because this definition includes government action but goes beyond it. See my distinction between political activity *lato sensu* and *stricto sensu* in François Bourricaud, *Esquisse d'une théorie de l'autorité* (Paris: Librarie Plon, 1961).

11. I prefer the opposition "center—periphery" to "base—summit" for reasons that will' become obvious further on; briefly stated, however, the principal reason is that the first, as opposed to the second, does not over-emphasize a hierarchical relationship (top-bottom) but stresses functional exchanges that are not all vertical.

12. The power to influence is relatively less costly than the power to coerce: A loses less when its attempts to influence B are not successful than it loses when its attempts to coerce are rejected. The same applies to B: it risks less in not allowing itself to be persuaded than it does in acting in a prohibited direction. The sanctions are different. They are material in the first instance, symbolic in the second.

13. See Pierre Bourdieu and Jean-Claude Passeron, *La Réproduction* (Paris: Les Editions de Minuit, 1970).

14. See Talcott Parsons, "On the Concept of Political Power," *Proceedings of American Philosophical Society,* 107 (June 1963), pp. 232-262.

15. See Carlos A. Astiz, *Pressure Groups and Power Elites in Peruvian Politics* (New York: Oxford University Press, 1969); Julio Cotler, "The Mechanics of Internal Domination and Social Change in Peru." Pp. 407-444 in Irving L. Horowitz (ed.), *Masses in Latin America* (New York: Oxford University Press, 1970); and Alonso Quijano "Contemporary Peasant Movements." Pp. 301-340 in Seymour M. Lipset and A. Solari (eds.), *Elites in Latin America* (New York: Oxford University Press, 1967).

16. See Emile Durkheim, *De la Division du travail Social* (Paris: Editions Presses Universitaires de France, 1967).

17. *Ibid.*

18. See Albert O. Hirschman, *Journeys Toward Progress* (New York: Greenwood Press, 1968), p. 257.

19. *Ibid.,* p. 258.

20. *Ibid.,* p. 272.

21. See the conclusion of François Bourricaud, *Pouvoir et société dans le Pérou contemporain* (Paris: Librairie Armand Colin, 1967), which I have titled "E puor se muove."

22. On the conditions surrounding the land reform of 1964, see *ibid.,* Part III, Ch. 3. These conditions are very similar to those suggested in the Hirschman model.

23. I have referred to this very difficult problem in a yet unpublished paper dealing with the university crisis in Latin American countries.

24. See Parsons, "On the Concept of Political Power," *op. cit.*

25. In assessing, quite correctly I think, the strength of the State in nineteenth century France, the traditionalists forget that industrialization during that period, even if conducted within a protectionist framework, implied, in the economic order (in so far as the industrialists claimed a certain autonomy in the conduct of their business), that the center could exert less pressure on the periphery than it could under Louis XV or Louis XVI (through their intendants) or under General de Gaulle.

26. See Alexis de Tocqueville, *L'Ancien régime et la révolution* (Paris: Editions Gallimard, 1964), Book 2, Ch. 2: "There are royal orders, prohibiting the cultivation of certain produce on lands that the King's council judges unfit. There are others whereby the council orders the uprooting of vineyards judged to be in bad soil. Such was the extent of the government's move beyond the role of sovereign to that of tutor." p. 114.

27. Marx himself takes a much more realistic position in Karl Marx, *Le dix-huit brumaire de Louis Bonaparte* (Paris: Les Editions Sociales, 1950).

28. The conflict between "emerging bourgeoisie and decaying nobility has traditionally been quoted as the main cause of the French Revolution. For a brilliantly devastating criticism of this thesis, see François Furet, "Le catéchisme de la Revolution francaise," *Annales,* 26 (Juillet 1970), pp. 255-289.

29. Alexis de Tocqueville, *Souvenirs* (Paris: Editions Gallimard, 1942), p. 73. Tocqueville's italics.

30. *Ibid.,* pp. 38-39.

31. *Ibid.,* p. 27.

32. A vivid description of that fascinating "Cultural Revolution" may be found in Gustave Flaubert, *L'Education sentimentale.*

33. For an analysis of the events of May 1968, which reflect similar tendencies, see François Bourricaud, "Une reprise en main difficile," *Preuves*, 218 (Mai-Juin 1969), pp. 38-48.

34. Karl W. Deutsch, *The Nerves of Government* (New York: The Free Press, 1963). pp. 197-198. From another perspective I have attempted to measure the impact of expanding "public goods," the production of which rests with the major state agencies, in the functioning of modern society. See Francois Bourricaud, "Le modèle polyarchique et les conditions de sa

survie," in *Revue française de science politique*, 20 (Oct, 1970), pp. 893-923.

35. Michel Crozier, *La Société bloquée* (Paris: Editions de Seuil, 1970), pp. 33-34.

36. According to a declaration of "leftist" leaders, the Third World and underdevelopment begins at the suburb, at the "door of our cities." They arrive at the conclusion that "urban guerilla warfare" is, in France as in Latin America, the only argument that a corrupt ruling class understands: "Power grows out of the end of a gun" (Mao Tse-Tung).

37. This is Michel Crozier's thesis in *La Société bloquée*.

38. This theme has been elaborated by a famous publicist, J. J. Servan-Schreiber.

39. See Jean-Pierre Worms, "Le préfet et ses notables," *Sociologie du travail*, 8 (Juillet-Sept. 1966), pp. 249-271.

40. I shall make that comparison in a forthcoming publication.

41. This sketchy description will be expanded and discussed in a forthcoming publication.

42. See in particular Chapters IV and V of Book III of de Tocqueville, *L'Ancien régime*.

43. Tocqueville's description of the crisis of the years immediately preceding the 1789 Revolution is therefore different from that of the short crisis of 1848 as described in his *Souvenirs*.

44. On this point see my "note" on M. Crozier, *La Société bloquée* in *Critique*, 285 (November 1970), pp. 960-978.

45. I plan to elaborate this important point in a later publication.

46. Tocqueville was quite perceptive of the contrasting ways interest groups make themselves heard in France and the United States when he referred to the beginnings of the prohibitionist movement: ". . . had the 100,000 (American) men who publicly pledged not to consume strong liquor been Frenchmen, each individually would have requested that the government supervise all bars in the Kingdom". *De la Démocratie en Amerique*. Tome II (Paris: Pagnère, 1850), Ch. 5, p. 124.

24

ON SOCIETAL MEDIA DYNAMICS

Rainer C. Baum

Media theorizing is still in its infancy. It has been relatively recently that Parsons has rounded out his scheme of "generalized societal media of interchange" by adding the concept of value-commitments *as medium* to his earlier writing on influence and power. With the money analogue prominent in all, conceptualizations of four societal languages functionally specialized for four universal problems now exist. Work on the general conditions relating to inflationary and deflationary pressures among these four has not gone far, however; neither have we formalized definitions of such phenomena. As yet, we have suggestive descriptions and illustrations.[1] The purpose of this paper is to take a modest step beyond the illustrative. The aim is to present a set of hypotheses concerning the inflation and deflation potential of such media in different societies. Organizing the task into three parts, the first tries to suggest how media theorizing ought to be anchored in action theory. Second, recognizing that analytically the values medium controls the other media cybernetically, the introduction of empirical variation in substantive societal values should help in approaching the prediction of the inflation-deflation potential in media in general. For this purpose a simple functional typology of substantive values is developed. Variation in substantive commitments can then be treated as a variable intervening between variable liquidity preferences of the values medium on the one hand and the influence and power media on the other. I shall argue that the empirical consequences of inflationary-deflationary pressures on the values medium for the other two media depends primarily on substantive societal values. Finally, in the third part, we return to the illustrative, attempting to demonstrate the potential utility of the scheme by a

very speculative interpretation of past and prominent commitment deflation events in American and German society.

My approach differs from Parsons'[2] earlier view of the role of values in two ways. First, rather than treat cultural boundary interchanges as presumptively met when analyzing interchange at the societal level, I treat values as more directly involved in institutional interaction. Second, rather than regarding values as primarily relevant for the maintenance of appropriate motivations, the emphasis here is shifted towards their role in defining the situation in novel ways. If continual structural change is a defining characteristic of modernity, then there must be mechanisms for novel and therefore potentially immoral definitions. Commitments as a medium of interchange can inflate, and it is this feature which provides the intellectual or similar "moral expert" with the necessary tool to act as a Schumpeterian innovator with respect to changing definitions of the situation in society.

MEDIA AND THE PROBLEM OF "CONFLATION"

In placing the problem of "conflation" (either in or deflation) into the complex analytical edifice that is action theory I use Smelser's "production" metaphor of social action.[3] Social action is conceived of as a product. The "production process" involves the combination of four basic elements. These "factors of production" are; (1) values (patterned conception of the desirable), (2) norms (regulatory rules specifying how values are to be implemented through interaction), (3) roles (organized effort), and (4) facilities (means). Social action exists only after all four elements have been combined. But once combined, such products can be variably symbolically represented as the experience of action. Symbolically represented products constituting experiences can in turn

The receipt of constructive criticism from the co-editors is greatly appreciated. This applies to Victor Lidz in particular. I am especially grateful to Helen Douglass whose wide-ranging interests and considerable commitment to theory helped to reduce many complexities.

be used to guide new combinations or new productions of action.

These elements of action have two properties of central importance for our purpose. They stand in a relation of decreasing generality or increasing specificity of meaning to each other, and such meaning can be symbolically represented. The direction of decreasing generality in meaning runs from values to norms, to roles, and to facilities, with the last being the least general or the most specific. Therefore the production process of social action is said to involve the progressive additions of placing restrictions on meaning. The end result of the combinatorial process is a specific act that is experienced as intrinsically meaningful. Using the logic of a *value-added* process presupposes the capacity to impute a common attribute into diverse elements. For social action in general this is increasing specificity in meaning.

Turning to the symbolic representation of action, let us denote the elements of action just described as real entities and those entities that do the representing as symbols. A medium then consists of symbols that can be combined into messages about real entities and a code, or set of rules, specifying the set of permissible combinations and delimiting the real entities referred to. The use of media is probably a general characteristic of humanity regardless of the level of development. Discussing media in primitive society, Turner recently pointed out the basic reason: "From the standpoint of society as a whole, it is far more practicable and efficient to channel communal sanctions and support through a standardized system of symbolic tokens and institutions than to try to bring collective norms and values directly to bear on every instance of social interaction of a particular type, without the aid of a mediating symbolic system."[4] This suggests the principal function of media. Using them saves information.[5] Instead of negotiating to consensus *ad idem* on all four elements of action, i.e., setting the elements in a perfect one-to-one relation of specification each time they are combined into an interact and thus assuring themselves of an ironclad and total guarantee for the experience of shared meaning in each particular act, men rely on symbols "promising" the experience of meaning as a statistical probability over many acts. They are freed from the efforts to negotiate basics all the time. But their action also becomes more risky. The more men act on media, the greater the risks they assume but also the larger the amount of information they save, and hence the less the effort required in coming to terms with each other.

Taking a cue from Luhmann and Bellah,[6] this perspective implies that some differentiation between experience and action is constitutive of the human condition. Men can use symbolic media only because they can act and reflectively represent their experience to themselves. But only when this differentiation has gone so far as to permit functionally specialized media do generalized societal media emerge; and only once these have emerged to some degree of shared recognition can their functionally analogous social subsystems be organized. Put otherwise, a differentiated economy, polity, societal community, and formal socialization system presupposes to some degree the operation of societal media. The reason for this priority arrangement rests directly on the operational requisites of functionally specialized subsystems. If, in any one of these, meaningful action is to be possible at all, then they need inputs from the other subsystems. No economic action specialized for the production of "utilities as such" is possible without commitments, influence, and power and the real entities these represent. The same is true for those specialized institutions engaged in the production of societal effectiveness, integration, and authenticity. Hence one needs to emphasize that it is never the economy, in some literal sense of the sum of all firms, or the polity, in some literal sense of the sum of all overtly political organizations, and so on that produce the societal attributes of growing wealth, growth in goal-attainment effectiveness, and the like but rather that the latter are a result of interchanges between the subsystems that produce them. Without bits of values, norms, roles, and means, *already treated as* factors of authenticity, solidarity, effectiveness, and utility, there is no institutionalized production of continuously expanding wealth, collective effectiveness, solidarity, and societal authenticity. But also, without the same kinds of bits occurring as well in preprocessed form as products of utilitarian, effective, solidary and authentic interaction *already constituting four kinds of experiences*, no such institutionalized and functionally specialized productions are possible either. Both are necessary factors or raw materials of action to be manipulated into functionally specialized outputs and experiences, i.e., already-produced action to guide their combination. This is why any one functional subsystem needs both factor and product inputs from all of the other three.

This conception of a functionally differentiated society permits two conclusions. First, it is the differentiation of experience and action to the point of the symbolic representations of the four components of interaction that makes "conflation" possible. Second, media can guide interchange processes only because they possess the attribute of reflexivity. They can represent themselves and each other with respect to their real entities but only concerning products, not factors. Both of these points need elucidation; let us start with the second.

Self-reflectivity[7] is illustrated by our ability to "finance money" when one issues stocks, "over-power" when votes lead to a change in policies, "influence influence bankers" when a student suggests to a professor that concrete illustrations might enhance teaching of abstract principles, and "out-commit commitments" when propaganda invites counterpropaganda. Substitutability, however, occurs when one medium represents a real entity "primarily" associated with another. Commodity demand, for example, appears in the form of money; but it represents the authentic experience of units — households or other spenders — concerning a commitment to spend and a propensity to save in the pursuit of primarily other than strictly utilitarian ends, as for example socialization of the young or production of intimacy between lovers. Value-based claims to differential loyalties (a product output from L to I) appear in the form of influence but represent the experience of authenticity in multiple role incumbency. Budgeting or ranking of claims appears in the form of money but represents the experience of integrative efficacy of limited combinations. Allocating fluid resources again appears in the form of money but represents the experience of a decisional outcome bearing on the effectiveness of commiting resources.

Substitutability among different societal media to represent real entities does not, however, apply to the factors in the production of action. Though for different reasons than are implicit here, Parsons' "law of the forms of interchange"[8] recognizes the difference as follows: at the societal level product inputs into any one subsystem always come in the form of the medium anchored in the receptor system, but factor inputs always come in the forms of the media anchored in the emit subsystems. Let us make explicit our reason. Any social system, so it seems, can store only experiences, i.e., already constitutive action, in more than one medium. Regardless of function specialization, action always involves combinations of the four basic elements. Once combined, however, the experience can be stored subsequently in one medium rather than another. This takes but a slight shift in emphasis from one basic element of action to another in the interaction process that activates memory. If that were not so, men could not give variant meaning significance to past events. Whether associated in the pursuit of economic, political, solidary, or directly moral-meaningful objectives, subsequent to the event men can reorder the primary significance of their past at least four ways. But given the absence of combinations when

it comes to the sheer raw materials of social action in its original production, no such substitution among media is possible in their symbolic representation. Hence, factors can only be represented by their base media.

The fact that "the buck of symbolic substitutability stops at the level of factors" leads to two more conclusions, one quite commonplace, the other rather disturbingly at variance with Parsons' interchange paradigm. In genuinely differentiated economic action, combining the four elements is a process immediately governed by money. Whether we look upon it in terms of combining land, labor, capital, and entrepreneurship or organization — or in terms of combining labor capacity (a commitment factor), standards for allocating resources (an influence factor), and opportunity for effectiveness (a power factor) — *insofar as the action is economic* the monetary consideration constitutes the paramount guidance standard. Analogously, the same applies to differentiated political, solidary, and meaning-oriented action, which is what we mean when we speak of each of the four societal media as "anchored" in one functionally specialized subsystem of society. But what enables a given medium to exercise that control over factors which often appear in the form of a higher medium remains for me a problem for which — in the absence of a clear development of four types of each of money, power, and commitments analogous to Parsons' four types of influence, themselves cybernetically arranged — I have but a feeble "solution." It is this: The product inputs supply a given subfunction medium with such extraordinary controlling capacity. When a businessman chooses among different strategies for his enterprise according to monetary criteria, he selects only from those alternatives under which the conditions affecting commitments, solidarity, and effectiveness of the firm as collectivity are presumptively met. When an economy readjusts itself according to market criteria then here too the alternatives open are already constrained by what is ethically meaningful, tolerable by the prevailing structure of the societal community, and politically tolerable. In the normal case this is so because in the normal case it is experience that guides action rather than the other way around. Hence it also follows that at the equilibrium point in societal interchange, when things follow institutionalized patterns, it is ultimately always products that control factors. The reverse typically happens when behavior becomes de-institutionalized. This conclusion is, however, quite at variance with Parsons.[9] But it has the advantage of providing compass for examining conflation phenomena.

My attempt to approach this problem from the vantage point of Smelser's resource table rests on the conviction that collective behavior by no means exhausts the category of responses to a felt de-institutionalization of action. I do not think that such was Smelser's intention, but he remained relatively silent about alternatives. I suggest there are far less blatant forms of bringing about and responding to de-institutionalization. These are also forms not subsumable under deviance. They can take rather subtle features where a simple lack of prudence starts a self-feeding mechanism that may or may not finally bring down the whole edifice of complexity achieved through the use of symbols in functionally differentiated institutions. Simply put, conflation refers to a process by which the use of symbolic media of interchange alters their mutual contingency such that reliance on any one or all either increases or decreases the risks of uncertainty beyond the advantages gained from complex differentiation. This definition rests on the claim that the societal media are the most prominent representations of the four components of action at the social system level.[10] If it were not for these, action indeed would be no more than a successive spelling out as the value-adding process moves from higher-order to lower-order components, resulting in a narrowly determined unit act. Life would be certain, but also "overdetermined" and "primitive."

A Smelserian View of Conflation

Conflation involves processes analogous to Smelser's "short-circuiting beliefs." Though restricted to a careless use of symbols that disregards their mutual contingency, the analogy retains a complexity that refuses simple description. A brief reference to one condition underlying the equilibrium point in mutual contingency may be in order to emphasize that it is the conditions permitting departure from equilibrium which constitute the focus of interest here. Elsewhere I described one condition that keeps the use of media balanced in terms of a hierarchical operation of trust.[11] The efficacy of any medium was seen there to rest on the *exclusion* of specific operations in another, next higher in the usual cybernetic order. For example, at any given time reliance on money by citizens rests on their excluding the possibility of a *future arbitrary* change in the money supply, i.e., a specific power deployment on the part of government, from their *current* decision making. Similarly, for the voter the efficacy of the voting act rests on the exclusion of specific future influence operations on the part of extranational foreign actors that would alter the power of national office beyond all reasonable expectation. Such a future possibility

must be excluded from his current voting decision. Last, influence efficacy—for example in the doctor-patient collectivity—rests again on the exclusion of such commitment contingencies as the valuing of sickness over health or of death over life from current decisions in going along with suggestions ostensibly made for the "patient's own best interest." This application of Luhmann's perspective on trust[12] can be broadened, however to provide a handle in grasping the essentials of the conflation phenomenon in media operations as such.

For the sake of convenience, unraveling this complexity might be presented in three steps, which vary in level of abstraction from a higher to the near-phenomenal. The first task is to specify the meaning of inflation and deflation in terms of the "production of meaningful action as such." Second, one level down in abstraction, the principle of conflation as such can be subjected to additional constraints deriving from a functional perspective. Third, on the near-phenomenal level, conflation will be shown to involve always alterations in minimally four reference standards.

To begin with, on the most general level conflation refers to either a "tightening up" or a "loosening off" of articulating the principle components of action in the process of its production. Crude as it is, a graphic representation of this "tightening up" and "loosening off" might be helpful. Accordingly, Figure 24-1 suggests that inflation involves some process whereby the "setting into a relation to each other" of the components of action loses in specification. Deflation then involves the obverse process, whereby the production of action proceeds with a degree of specification in excess of that necessary relative to the level of institutional differentiation reached in society *and* its media development guaranteeing that level. Once again crudely put, the metaphor may be likened to the behavior of some gas. Inflation would be a process that so extends the volatility that the gas loses its structure and with that its essence and effect. Deflation, on the other hand, would be a process compressing the gas to the point of solidity or liquidity where its essential characteristic as a gas, its volatility, drops to zero. Concerning mediated action this point would be reached when action and experience "fuse" in the unmediated value-implementive act. Beyond the spatiophysical metaphor, and as a first approximation, one might say that inflation involves acting with the mediation between the components so loosely structured that the experience of meaning becomes impaired. On the social level inflation manifests itself, for example, in the form of a disorientation because of increasing role conflict. Correspondingly, an example of a

Principle Components of Action				Mode of Conflation
Values	Norms	Mobilization for action	Facilities	
←→	←→	←→		Inflation
→←	→←	→←		Deflation

Figure 24-1. Conflation in symbolically mediated action.

personal-level manifestation would be a self-alienation due to inner integrative failure, or the inability to experience a "sense of a continuous self" in the multilayered action implementations of the personality's need-dispositions.[13] Deflation, on the other hand, involves acting with the mediations between the components so tightly structured that acts become "overdetermined with meaning" to the point where adaptiveness becomes impaired. For the sake of illustration, on the social level one form of deflation might manifest itself in the experience of "unnecessary regimentation." On the personal level one form might be compulsion neurosis.

Two conclusions may be derived from this crude view of the matter. First, as suggested in the figure, both inflation and deflation can proceed in two directions, "up" and "down" the hierarchy of control. Second, next to the familiar view of conflation involving an alteration in the quantitative relation between symbols and the "real entities" they represent, as for example between the volume of money and the goods and services it can command which can change between two points in time, conflation phenomena also have code aspects. When one medium gets out of line in the real entities it commands relative to those of another then the codes tend to encroach upon one another. To be sure this involves codes primarily in their role as objects of social significance and orientation and not in their legal aspects where applicable. Nevertheless, as will be shown, this is a matter of some import in understanding intermedia dynamics.

Going somewhat beyond crude analogizing, the .analysis of conflation phenomena may start with two observations. First, it is a product of evolutionary development, that is a considerable amount of well-institutionalized differentiation between experience and action which gives rise to both the fact of symbolically mediated action and the capacity to use media in inflationary and deflationary ways. Second, conflation phenomena involve functionally confused usages of social space and social time, both increasingly regarded as resources and therefore seen as scarce.

Language, the most general of the media, might illustrate the fact that some degree of differentiation between experience and action is intrinsic to the human condition. It is language communication with its inherent possibility for error that stimulates self-reflectivity and yields an irreducible amount of individuality to man. When men interact through language they "trust" that they will understand each other as a statistical probability over a series of communication messages through time. By trust, and following Luhmann, I mean they exclude the possibility of total misunderstanding from their current decision to enter into communication, Misunderstanding remains a contingency even in the face of repeated trials in good faith. But such possible unintended future consequence of present action is "neutralized," i.e., screened off from attention in each moment of present. However, the contingency of error is not just "forgotten." That would be "reckless" language use. It would constitute "primitive hope." Here understanding would be expected in the future rather than excluding the opposite, complete misunderstanding. Trust, in contrast, calls for memory to use past experience and a past-future trend extrapolation to monitor restricted attentiveness regarding all possibilities in present action. Speaking trustingly clearly requires a prudent use of language involving corrective feedback in small steps throughout the communication flow. Therefore trust is not primitive hope, the expectation that "our minds will meet all right" regardless of the details of the communication at each step. Using a medium with trust, then, rests on the awareness of uncertainty as well as the "understanding," however dim, that the medium serves to reduce complexity and enables one to act in an uncertain world. Hope lacks these dimensions. He who hopes still orients to a simple world with inherently limited possibilities, a characteristic of tradition, though that world may in fact have passed.

In short, language is not and never has been an all-or-nothing game. Its connotative meaning variety, or built-in ambiguity, is too large for such a game. Moreover, in contrast to some specialized languages, such as mathematics which aim at reducing ambiguity to a minimum, the ambiguity of "natural language" facilitates human voluntaristic action.

With George Herbert Mead one might say that

language use produces an irreducible amount of individuation. For it is this medium primarily that makes it possible to compare the "I" reality-construction of personality with its preceived "Me" reality-constructions of others. Goffman's actor[14] presents merely a vastly more self-conscious orientation to the contingency of personality and society. He can "present" an inflated "I"—for example, in terms of pretended performance capacity—and then spend the rest of his life straining himself to the utmost in a futile attempt to catch up with a "Me" that does not actually suit his need-dispositions. The reverse is equally possible. Having once presented a deflated "I" he may have to escape the social circle where he presented it if he is to increase the action opportunities made available to his "Me."

Conflation and the Four-Function Division of Labor

What is only marginally visible in the case of language, however, becomes blatant in the case of "functionally specialized" yet general societal media of interchange. An acceptance of "liquidity"—for example, intrinsically useless paper money in lieu of actual utilities for some good or service rendered—amounts to a drastic saving of information for the receiver. Trusting only that prices will not change in an unexpected direction to an unexpected amount in the range of future considered for spending it again, money saves the receiver the need to know anything in detail about the complex nature of his potential consumption experiences. Trusting the operation of a market he does not have to know about his needs. He can also save the time necessary to generate relevant information for experiencing the bliss that is consumption. He can delay producing the experience into the future and therefore attend more fully to maximizing general profitability chances in the present. It is this distance between action and selected experiences which enables one to act instrumentally.

There are of course parallels in the other media. Let us take the example of morality. Feeling entitled normally to go along with the symbols of "conventional wisdom" amounts to making choices with the aid of moral liquidity instead of the "real thing," a sense of inner integrity. Such liquidity saves one information and time. One spares oneself the effort as well as the likely failure of trying to become one's own Immanuel Kant. At least one does this most of the time. In this respect the distance between action and experience enables men to concentrate on the external problems of a system of action, leaving internal problems of integrity and solidarity at bay

temporarily. When media work, accepting them amounts to the capacity to live in a world of "multiply" reduced complexity, to save oneself an extraordinary amount of information and time about many aspects of action while generating and spending lots of information and expending lots of time wherever the situation demands that some piecemeal complexity be faced. The division of labor grants one the opportunity to face some complexity really thoroughly *because,* trusting the operation of media, one can rely on function-specific services to be performed elsewhere in continuous fashion while one attends to the malfunction of one relatively immunized part in a differentiated system of action.

In the preceding paragraphs inferences about the use of media concerning the saving of information and time have been generated from the perspective of the individual placed in a market situation. Matters change unfortunately when considered from the perspective of sets of interactions. From the point of view of any two or more mutually contingent and collaborating towards such common ends as the production of utilities or solidarity, the special-function appropriate orientations call for more complex patterns of time and information use. Given our treatment of this problem at the social level, and unless otherwise specified, the term information always refers to social information about alter's other role obligations. It seems that the logic of the four-function paradigm at the social level involves two dichotomous orientations. One of these refers to social space, the social embeddedness of alter, the other to social time. I wish to contrast both with physical space-time. Social space, it seems, relates primarily to the external-internal division of labor in a system of social action, social time more to the instrumental-consummatory division. Let us take each in turn.

One way—perhaps the principal way—that enables the Goffman actor to present a calculated "self" is to select from his inescapable embeddedness in complex social space (the sum of his dependencies on others) one dimension, distance to alter. Whether the actor be a collective or an individual, relative to the sheer quantity of social contingency which remains for most ascribed, distance to others is the one element in the situation that permits manipulation in a differentiated social system. Regulating one's closeness or intimacy to other is, however, a way of regulating amount and type of information revealed about the self. What ego does, alter does; and the two manipulated distances may not coincide. Amount and selectivity of information revealed may vary somewhat from both sides. For more stable relations requiring collaboration this produces tensions.

There remain margins of uncertainty, of curiosity, and also of danger. Given this inherent double-perspective in ego-alter contingency and the primacy of orientation to distance, let us call this "reduced" orientation to social embeddedness diascopy. Though there is so far only intimacy as a variable and with that information the two dimensions suggested in "dia-scopy" have another reason. If ego is to have some control in a role through presenting himself, this calls for management of another "proper" distance. Ego as role-incumbent, anticipated and actual, has to keep a distance to his total "I" involved in other roles and that individuality which remains forever beyond the hold of society if he is to make proper selections from personality for presentation in society and achieve proper distribution in his multifaceted involvement there.

Minimally, social relations involve two additional spaces. One is hierarchy, i.e., some vertical dimension. Wherever men collaborate, action has to flow across a dependency and frequently a competency gap. Interdependence means to give and to receive. Often when collaboration eventuates in a stable group formation there is an authority gap, a special aspect of dependency. Always, however, there is the third social space, an ingroup-outgroup dimension. Here interdependence has to flow across a belongingness gap. Just where a man stands on vertical dimensions and with respect to groups in society is for him manipulable to some degree primarily through the regulation of intimacy. It is a function of what he has to offer and what he wishes to offer and what others have and are willing to grant. But being in society is hardly a matter of choice, Once a role-set has been set, most have to live with the consequences for a considerable time. Most general role incumbencies are an inescapable given for man. Furthermore, within the developed world, changing one's society of residence does not help much. Role-sets remain rather similar. Everyone has to grow up. One may marry or not and can therefore choose a particular marital status, but one cannot escape having one, be it single, married, or divorced. Similarly, there is some choice as to what or even whether concerning work. But no one can avoid a work status. Unemployment too constitutes a role. Most again have to assimilate to some work organization and be a citizen. Hermitage becoming less possible with the shrinkage of "white polityless spots on the maps," there is of course some choice about being in society while avoiding being of it in sickness and in crime. But neither permits one avoiding authority. In short, social contingency is inescapable. Further, given one's helplessness during the crucial years of early socialization, a great deal remains an inescapably

ascribed "primordial stereoscopy" where each has a place in a three-dimensional space bounded by intimacy, hierarchy, and belongingness. In sum, there are probably at least two primary orientations to social space. One of these, diascopy, leads one to view it as a resource and therefore subject to the principle of scarcity. Another, stereoscopy, leads one to accept what is inescapable anyway; since the inescapable is beyond manipulation, neither the notion of resource nor that of scarcity plays any commensurate role.

When seen in terms of information control relevant for role performance, social space apparently relates primarily to the external-internal boundary and its division of labor. For it is on this axis that the problem of autonomy or self-steering capacity in the face of the system's contingency on several environments finds its major focus. For a differentiated and relatively autonomous society these environments involves culture, personality, "nature," and other societies. But autonomy does not mean independence. The notion of independence denies the principle of contingency or interdependence. Rather, autonomy refers to a system's capacity to select from its environments *what it wants* to be dependent upon. Such action of selecting occurs first of all over the external boundary. It involves the twin functions of adaptation and goal-attainment. To adapt is to maintain one's distinctiveness in the face of dependence on changing environments. To maintain some acceptable gratificatory-deprivational balance in the sense of selecting goals on one's own terms is highly dependent on successful adaptation. Maladaptation impairs autonomous goal pursuits. This is the perspective emphasized by Deutsch,[15] who maintains that boundary maintenance deals primarily with maintaining self-selectivity of contingencies. A creative level of boundary maintenance—or learning in his terminology—then constitutes a strategy of selecting in the present that which increases the range of future selectivity; a viable level is one that maintains the level of selectivity achieved over time, a pathological level one that decreases the range of future selectivity.

This view suggests that the functional subsystems specializing in external problems orient to social space primarily as a diascopy. Selecting from other systems over a boundary largely involves prudent control over proper distance. Goffman's actor as a calculating *homo sociologicus* attempts to control intimacy to his personality and his role partner. If he loses distance to himself he may reveal too much and load onto the role what it cannot or should not bear. The murky matters of the repressed come to muddy the pond of social reality constructions. If he keeps too much distance to himself, and reveals not enough, he may underinvest himself in society. This leads to underutilization of human potential for both society and self. Current pollution consciousness invites one to illustrate the same point on the macro level involving the society-nature boundary. Here again two distances have to be monitored. The guidance center has to keep a proper distance to society's "natural trends" in technology, economics, and urbanization in order to be in any position to keep a distance vis-à-vis the natural environment in the sense of being able to select there what it wants to be dependent on. When societies lose distance vis-à-vis themselves and as a consequence "penetrate" too much into nature, they may deprive themselves of any future choice.

Now, the great advantage of the division of labor across the external-internal cleavage rests precisely in the fact that social subsystems dealing with the problem of contingency on environments can afford to save themselves information about a considerable range of societal problems *provided* subsystems specializing for internality do their job. As selecting from an environment demands considerable information about it, the subsystem involved in this task requires relief from the need to know a lot about the complex requisites of the total system of which it is a part. In order to make adequate selections about contingency on "nature," agencies involved can afford to concentrate on survival limits of an industrial order. They need not be concerned with human happiness or fulfillment, leaving these problems to other agents.

Institutional specialization for internal problems, however, faces the joint contingency of pattern authenticity or identity in the context of the inevitable ambivalent vicissitudes of present interests. It is here that one locates the old problems of sociology; "continuity in change" and "unity in diversity," If so, adequate functioning in these subsystems calls for a far more complex orientation to social space than simple diascopy. Here constant comparisons between levels of intimacy, height and distribution along the dimension of hierarchy, and complex composites of ingroup-outgroup relations must be made simultaneously. For questions about authenticity and solidarity social information is at premium. One cannot afford to save it in attempts to maximize internal problems of identity and cohesion; one needs to save other information about environments. Instead of saving information about society, performance of these functions demands spending it.

Turning to social time, this dimension appears to relate more directly to the instrumental-consummatory cleavage in differentiated society. Here again

one might usefully distinguish two principal orientations. On the one hand, one can orient to time as a diachrony. This means that one experiences time as flowing through a continuum connecting the three "points" of past, present, and future. The present continuously slips into the past, and the future continuously encroaches onto the present. It is in this sense of time as something that "slips by" that one orients to it in terms of a scarce resource to be saved wherever possible. Attempting to save time seems appropriate too in all action intended to lead to some end rather than being an end in itself. For the consummatory state, or action that affords the blissful experience of genuine consumption, however, one has to be willing to spend time. To attain and experience any genuine consumption man requires —so it would seem—suspension into a three-dimensional temporal order. Being a historical creature but accepting his finitude primarily on the cognitive level, he must achieve some trancendence over physical time if he is to experience consummation. This is facilitated through orienting to and using time as a synchrony. A synchronous use of time involves minimally a simultaneous experience of the actor-object relation with respect to three points in time: an actual as compared to a fictionalized past, an actual versus a potential present, and a probable as compared with a desirable future.[16] Therefore, for man in his inevitable historicity the experience of consummation demands time; and he who is unwilling to spend it deprives himself of consummatory experience. For an easy overview Figure 24-2 presents the suggested relation between social time and space and the four-function paradigm at the social level.

As can be seen, combining the dichotomous orientations to social time and space yields different combinations for functionally specialized social action depending on whether time and social space are used as resource or as inescapable givens beyond manipulation. In the absence of confusion, well-differentiated instrumental adaptive social action (A-function) calls for the saving of both time and information about the other. Social organization specialized for the production of generalized utilities can save social information to that minimum relevant for the task-performance at hand. This provides the organization with increased capacity to generate information about the environments to be manipulated into generalized resources. As consummatory experience is not its business either, time can be used as a simple diachrony as well. In social action differentiated for goal attainment (G-function), matters are different. In the case of romantic love, for example, a willingness to spend time is crucial.

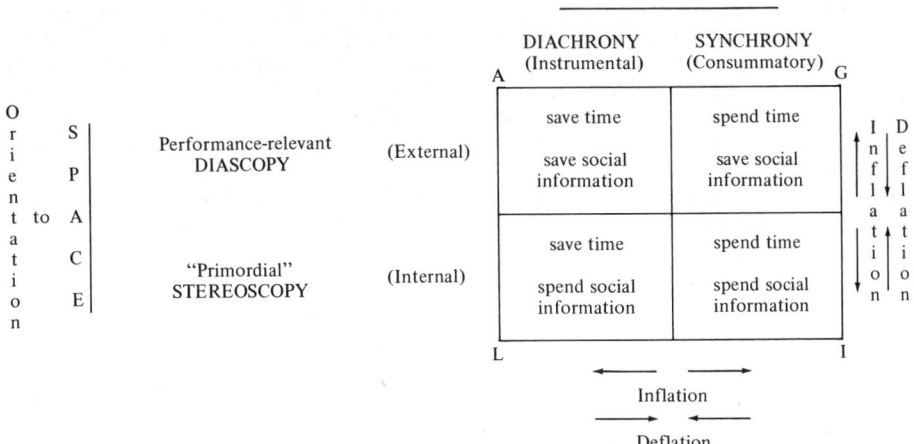

Figure 24-2. Social time/space and functionally specialized social action.

Ritualized, step-by-step give and take must be observed; tension must be maintained. Both demand the spending of time. Here it is also important to save information about other. Total familiarity means near-perfect predictability, and there is nothing more suited to diminish tension and cool romance. In contrast, social action specialized for the consummatory experience of solidarity in multiple-role incumbency (I-function) rather than in any one given special tie demands both time and information spending. For collective solidarity rituals to be effective, George Herbert Mead's perspective suggests, multiple "Me's" have to be matched with many "I's." One has to know a great deal about the multiple role demands on alter in order to "let him be," i.e., permit him to "present" what "selected composite I" he wants, if one is to experience a sense of kinship with such autonomous selections. And autonomous self-selectivity in presentations has to be maximized if affiliation rituals for generalized solidarity are to minimize the chance of alienation. Intimacy and hierarchy have to enter in all their distributional variety of all members if a sense of belongingness is to be experienced by each. Lastly, in the case of social action specialized for the maintenance and modification of over-all societal identity (L-function), the provisioning of adequate societal sociocentric patterns is the issue. One cannot save information about society here. Social variety is a requisite of life for any complex society. But as the issue is not the production of experiences but rather the production of patterns that guide experiences, considering time a scarce resource is function-adequate.

These observations about Figure 24-2 permit four conclusions. First, the principle of autonomy in contingency mentioned above applies to the relations between subsystems as well. Therefore, inflationary behavior refers to action patterns that tend to neglect intersubsystem contingency. Mediated action of course makes this possible. One can let the money standard in economic action rule to the point where no other considerations exist at all. Deflationary behavior, on the other hand, would derive from a reaction against a distance between action and experience that is felt to be too much. Deflationary behavior refers to action patterns that tend to neglect intersubsystem autonomy. One introduces media controls into a subsystem that—given the level of differentiation achieved—simply do not "belong" there anymore.

Second, in addition to the earlier observation that inflationary and deflationary pressures can occur in both directions, both "up" and "down" the control hierarchy, this figure identifies two principle fissures where conflation may arise. The first, running across the instrumental-consummatory cleavage in differentiated social action, suggests the possibility of "instrumentalizing" consumption and "consumptionalizing" instrumental action. The second, running across the external-internal cleavage, provides the potential to "externalize" internal problem solutions sought and vice versa. This involves a misapplication of internal standards and procedures for the solution of external problems or the reverse.

Third, the figure also suggests that conflation phenomena involve function-inadequate orientation to and use of social space and time. Action within one functionally differentiated subsystem may come to be guided by orientations appropriate to another. This potential for confusion arises from the principle of substitutability among media to represent the products of more than one subsystem. As achieved effectiveness in cooperation lends itself to monetary measurement—for example, income tax—the possibility exists to apply more and more economic considerations to the solution of political problems. Attempts are made to "diachronize" a synchrony. This might take the form of trying out different political schemas in rapid succession without giving any one sufficient time to work out. In general then, functionally inadequate behavior ultimately rests on oversaving or underspending time and social information. A few examples might be helpful.

On the A-G interchange a whole series of increasing complaints about "the quality of life" in the rich countries has become prominent. According to Linder, there is at the base of this curiosum a kind of production orientation misapplied to consumption behavior. The harried leisure class is here portrayed as pathetic income oligarchs who fail to take sufficient time to consume.[17] Given the fact that services in general are less efficiently produced than goods,[18] men attempt to consume "goods-intensively." They pile more and more goods into shorter and shorter consumption moments. For example, they listen to the radio, read a magazine, talk to each other, eat, drink, and do all that while "travelling" in a jet, that is regarded the better the faster it gets them the longest distance, curiously, therefore, the more it shortens the travel experience. Because they oversave time relative to probably minimal levels required to have any consummatory experience, they "use" things and each other rather than "consume" them, and therefore their restless chase after more and more consumption opportunities. Scheuch believes that such piling up of goods into consumption moments serves to relieve men from the need to pay intensive attention to anything. Paying partial attention to many things and real to none may be some pleasure in leisure,[19] but this pleasure may be more an escape from pressure than the experience of happiness. Our paradigm suggests that these harried rich practice as a matter of course that kind of institutionalized confusion which in earlier times was a more temporary aberration. Goethe's sigh of fleeting romance in Faust—"Oh, moment of bliss, why could thou not last longer"—might serve as the basic paradigm of this "functional sin": to diachronize what by function is a synchrony. Recently when Italian Fiat workers went on strike not for higher wages or fringe benefits of any utilitarian nature but rather to enforce "the rehumanization of work," they not only attempted to synchronize what should be a diachrony under conditions of differentiation,

they also demanded spending more social information than is requisite for the production of utilities. Hence their behavior constituted deflationary pressure on both variables, time and information. This would be an example of a double deflationary pressure across both fissures in a differentiated social action system, here from I to A, for which Marx's early humanism with its principled antipathy against social differentiation provides the classic example in social science literature. Finally, across the internal-external cleavage xenophobia as an input into national identity formation may serve as an example involving the relative "externalization" of an internal problem. This occurs primarily through function-inadequate oversaving of social information.

Fourth, Figure 24-2 also indicates that the net conflation potential in a society is in part a function of the rank order of importance imposed on the four functions. This is of course an aspect of the society's value system. If one regards the second-order function as supplying a reserve of commitments that become most immediately mobilized when primary commitments "get out of hand," our paradigm suggests greatest stability for the diagonal case. When functions placed diagonally constitute the most and secondmost important functions, a conflationary pressure on any one is relatively offset by the mobilization of precisely the opposite "directives" for the use of time and information in the other. Hence one requisite for the understanding of macro-sociological conflation phenomena is the development and empirical measurement of a functional typology of societal value systems. Some evidence on both will be presented in later sections of this chapter.

Illustrations of Code Confusions

It might be useful to present a few more concrete observations concerning the preceding fairly abstract analysis. Endeavoring to underscore the practical import of media analysis, these will emphasize changes in the social significance of the codes that accompany conflation. Hence it may be advisable to stress that nothing in subsequent remarks is intended to change the now familiar view that inflation and deflation are processes of change in the quantitative relation between the net supply of symbols and the real entities they represent. In inflation this change involves an increase in symbols relative to the real thing, as when the growth of money outstrips that of real wealth; in deflation it is the reverse, as when the claims of "institutionalized social wisdom" outstrip growth in credibility, an example of influence deflation. There is, however, a code aspect in such changes, and that is the one of interest here.[20]

Men inflate media when they use them by acting

on primitive hope rather than trust which, as previously stressed, involves the inclusion of anticipated specific benefices in current decision making rather than the exclusion of anticipated specific noxious consequences. He who acts with hope in modern society acts indiscriminately, in the manner of a child believing that "somehow everything will work out all right." A child of course is enabled to hope by reliance on powerful parental figures who can take care within the diffuse family setting where diffuseness guarantees control. The prominence of institutionalized expertise in modern society, however, carries some built-in temptation for adults to regress in their decisional behavior. Frequently our response to a rising cost of living is simply to clamor for higher wages, and "let the money doctors take care." But in contrast to parents in the family setting, money authorities command a functionally specialized subsystem, not diffuse generalized superiority in society at large. Hence by imposing parental roles on them one subjects them to unrealistic expectations.

The essential reason for this is charmingly simple. A society so far differentiated as to need special languages of trust like the four media can no longer cope with hope. Intuitively we all know this by appreciating how difficult it is to control an inflationary money psychology. In part this difficulty results from the effect of inflation on the code. If it is believed that tomorrow's goods in general will be dearer than today's, the wage-price spiral governs consumer demand and its commitments' response. Then factors come to control products in interchange, which changes the social significance of property. In inflationary times the debtor after all enjoys the advantage. It pays not to own. In fact to owe becomes a form of economic wisdom. The creditor suffers because his right to use and control becomes vacuous. It appears more reasonable to live on credit than on achievement. The significance of ownership declines because its role becomes doubtful.

Once a medium has lost credibility because of hope, however, the central reason for the difficulty of repair by substitution with another medium also becomes apparent. Already used to the advantages accruing to functionally specialized languages, and acting in the euphoria of eating one's cake and having it, higher-order media cannot be easily substituted because their codes are set the way they are on the presumption of adequate functioning of the codes of lower-order media. This does not mean that control is impossible, only that it is difficult. In a so-called free enterprise system the use of power to defeat an inflationary mentality remains so precarious because the scope of authority of political office itself is sufficiently restricted as to characterize a whole host of potential political control remedies as

constitutionally uncertain. There is simply too much doubt about the jurisdictional authority of office to pay much heed to the politicians' dire warning and promises to solve the problem. Little may happen unless a change in the power code is pending. Inflation of a medium then involves the generalization of the use of symbols beyond the institutional capacity of the system for their normally expected translation into real entities *because* the code has lost its constraining control. Concerning the impact on codes, then, and formally put, inflation in any given medium involves an unspecified enlargement of its code relative to the operant scope of the codes in other media. Deflation involves the opposite, the constriction of a code of a given medium relative to the breadth of claims made under the operant codes of other media. In both cases claims advanced with a given symbolic token encroach upon the jurisdictional territory of another specialized language. This produces confusion.

According to the view stressed here, monetary inflation should lead to an encroachment of specifically economic rationality into the power realm. When the usual expectations about creditors and debtors erode the social significance of ownership and nonownership, there may well be attempts to substitute for the dissolution of this particular authority gap by other authority gaps, yet using largely the same language. As a result, such attempts at substitution often do not work. Also, there is a considerable practical implication. Our perspective sheds some light on Kuznets'[21] finding of greater productivity in the primary and secondary than the tertiary sectors of the economy. As the tertiary sector tends to expand relatively in modernization, this points to a "double trouble" in modernity. First, services do not add directly and primarily to a society's stock of utilities but rather to other stocks, such as effectiveness, solidarity, and through education to authenticity. Hence monetary measurement of value added to these stocks is at least partially misleading because it involves a use of money for purposes for which it was not designed. Second, such misuse of money is likely to continue until we develop and actually use the other media as stores of value and units of account. Misuse here primarily operates through an oversaving of social information. Very likely this results from carrying with money also its characteristic narrow utilitarian outlook quite inappropriately to activities aiming at the production of solidarity or "authenticity in the quality of life" where social information is at premium. The utilitarian outlook is of course quite appropriate within its own domain of the production of utilities, where under differentiated conditions a great deal of social information constitutes irrelevancies.

Taking one more example, influence inflation involves the substitution of "considered opinion" that could be verified on demand with cheap "mere opinion" that could not. Such oversaving of information might operate with false claims concerning the advice rendered, through concealing dissensus about goals between influencer and influencee, or both. Here too the code is enlarged. Mere opinion alters the presumed competence gap between the parties: mere opinion "creates" one where there is none. This affects other competence gaps. Therefore, it constitutes an encroachment onto the power realm. Concealed dissensus on ends alters their presumed identity, on which solidarity between the parties rests. Spending influence on nonexistent identities, however, is likely to affect other identities, notably the qualitative ones, "normally" steered with moral appeals. Thus, when influence lacks efficacy because of hope, its claims cannot be backed up easily by value commitments because their code is too narrow and the distinction becomes eroded. Neither can they be implemented easily, because the power code is too narrow and the voluntary and obligatory aspects of influence on the one hand and power on the other have become confused. Again, such backing from "above" and implementing "lower down" do not become impossible, but they are more difficult than in the absence of conflation. After all, when "orders" become "suggestions," obedience becomes less certain. Not only does the influence message lack selectivity, but under influence inflation this loss of selectivity may spill over "downwards" into the power realm and "upwards" into the values realm. Nevertheless no overt intent need be involved. Men can think they will find backing; they can falsely assess their implementation capacities; and they can do both honestly. Men can genuinely fool themselves and others in using a multiplicity of messages that actually lack adequate selectivity about the conditions that limit their freedom because of the inherent ambiguity in differentiation that tempts one to confuse autonomy with independence.

In contrast, deflation results from a wariness of the risks accompanying symbolic organization. Here men attempt to return to a simpler age wherein experience and action were more closely tied up with each other. They try to collapse the two. Instead of producing meaningful action in multiple diverse forms, each functionally specialized, and the whole set complex and mutually contingent but not ever easily grasped and fully understood at any one moment, men attempt to realize meaning simply and directly. However, when they reorient to already extant media in this fashion the process is far less obvious than any simple reference to value absolutism would suggest.

After all, value absolutism with its associated propensity to collective behavior ordinarily refers to conditions where preparedness to produce action through symbolic mediation has already been largely abandoned or, minimally, considerably reduced. Strictly speaking, media here have almost completely "deflated out" of circulation. In this merely extreme case the risks involved in acting on intrinsically worthless symbols have been largely defeated because medium symbolicity itself has been abandoned. A deflated use of media, however, presupposes their existence and operation: no media, no media deflation. Hence using media in a deflated way only involves imposing greater selectivity on messages than is warranted in the light of the degree of symbolically mediated institutional differentiation already achieved in society. Scared of the uncertainties inevitable in symbolic control, but not despairing enough to abandon its considerable advantages, men deflate media when they send messages restricted in meaning below the latitude of interpretation in implementation previously enjoyed by the receiver. This involves reduction in the code relative to the breadth of the codes of neighboring media. For illustration, influence may serve once more.

Having "functionalized" trust mechanisms four ways in terms of function-adequate time and information use leads me to retain solidarity as the security base of influence despite Parsons'[22] later misgivings about this early formulation. To deflate influence then means to restrict confidence in accepting essentially nonunderstood advice to those of one's own kind, where shared commitments in the form of total *consensus ad idem on ends* can be taken for granted. Naturally this excludes private and socially illegitimate desirable ends such as the wish to die and presumes that for influence to work solidary ties must be strong enough to suppress these. In the modern case ultimately this solidary group is the family. When influence deflates, its efficacy is displaced from formal and essentially voluntary bonds towards increasingly inescapable social bonds, i.e., artificially created "kinship certainty." It is not the competence gap as such that is in doubt but the presumed identity on ends across this gap instead. Once superior knowledge has proven its capability one does not subsequently doubt its superiority as specialized knowledge, rather one suspects its specialization. Doubt centers on the necessarily increased complexity of its deployment and the greater wisdom this demands.

For many Americans today going along with the advice of their "national security doctors" has become increasingly difficult because they no longer trust the industrial-military complex. In part they suspect that interests of institutional advancement rather than real national welfare have come to structure the advice. It is this contingency which can no longer be excluded in decisions to go along with expertise. But it is not just a simple imputation of egotistical self-interest that has robbed these experts of their Durkheimian professional status as monopoly bearers of responsibility for a functionally specialized problem of society. It is rather a creeping doubt about the possibility of genuine professionalism in an increasingly specialized world. The adage of the expert as knowing more and more about less and less has posed the contingency of overselectivity. The expert, so his doubting client senses, somehow prestructures the real world differently. The specially informed reality-construction, it is felt, might indeed work in the long run. But patience with the long run has run out and saving time becomes the order of the day. Perhaps one needs to wage more war for peace, who can really know? Most Americans, I suspect, still grant their relevant institutional experts authenticity in their professed commitment to peace. But differential time preferences and suspect complexity in reality constructions have tended to erode the capacity for proper distinctions in the means-end schema on which all media efficacy necessarily depends. Some explain to themselves their lack of trust in messages of euphemistic language by conspiracy theories. Others deduce the appearance of a seemingly perverted language from increasing complexity. The result is the same: where means and ends lose distinction, both are in doubt. Hence when the code of influence, the rules of justification for societal inequalities, has shrunk, there is pressure "downward" narrowing the scope of legitimate political authority. There is also pressure "upwards" because the language of persuasion becomes mixed up with that of moral appeals. For that which enables men to withdraw trust from formally institutionalized expertise in the first place is a reduction in the number of solutions they are capable of identifying as authentic experience because they can no longer wait so long as before. When they save time with a language that demands its spending, they confound at least the neighboring media.

A message "if you want to end the war, follow me to widen it temporarily," already implies that negation of the suggested means signifies negation of the declared end. Hence immorality is implied. A presidential stance of "I must do what IS RIGHT regardless of my popularity" connotes a not too subtle shift from presidential democracy to absolutist monarchy where authority was far less contingent on influence and therefore narrower in scope. It is a *subsequent* loss of the capacity to make distinctions which has

been gained *before* that justifies the neologism of conflation. It emphasizes that inflation and deflation are mutually contingent; that each implies the other; and that when codes lose their boundaries, the messages start encroaching on each other. In short, conflation is to media — these specialized mechanisms of complexity reduction — what confusion is to ordinary language discourse. But because of their specialization, conflation often takes far longer to show its dismal results than is the case when two talk to each other but fail to communicate effectively. The former is far more difficult to correct than the latter.

A Summary Perspective on the Conflation Problem

Conflation becomes possible only with the development of functionally specialized action and only when such action is organized into differentiated subsystems in society, each governed by its functionally specialized medium. It seems essential to recognize that functionally specialized action involves different orientations to and different uses of time and social information. Although media constitute special kinds of liquidity which one accepts in lieu of the "real thing," thus saving oneself information for a while about their translation potential into experiences, the penalties for over or undersaving information about social partners are quite different. For a social system these tend to be more severe for solving internal than external problems. A roughly similar generalization seems to hold for time. Oversaving of time causes more immediate and more severe problems for consummatory action, undersaving for instrumental action. Hence the question of how the saving and spending of time and social information relates to conflation in the different media may well be far more complex than one might expect at first.

Nevertheless conflation probably always involves a change in the relation between a medium and four other reference systems. An alteration in the time and information horizons constitutes the first of these. A second is the now familiar view. This concerns a changing relation between the quantity of symbols and the real entities they command.

A third referent concerns the level of organization in society, i.e., the degree to which functionally differentiated subsystems have emerged and the clarity of their boundaries. Clearly the general case of conflation makes sense only with reference to level of differentiation. Inflation involves attempts to effect action that goes beyond the capacity of a subsystem *because* of its contingencies on others. Deflation is felt as "unduly constricting" by opponents because their immediate past experience teaches them that differentiated social action is organizationally institutionalized well enough to risk greater delays between experience and action. On the other side of the fence, deflation is such an urgent business *because* of their anxiety that "differentiation has gone too far." For them intersubsystem contingency is experienced as autonomy due to simple independence. That generates anomie. A fourth referent concerns the effect on codes. When a given medium inflates or deflates its messages encroach on the "language territory" of the neighboring media. The general result is confusion. Such confusion derives from a double source. On the one hand, the means-end schema which is crucial in the rational organization of differentiated action itself loses distinctiveness. As has been pointed out, money-conscious men can confuse production and consumption. Harried nation builders in societies without any indigenous territorial consolidation can confuse external and internal problems. On the other hand, confusion results also from multilingualism. Under conflation a given message loses distinctiveness concerning the security base. When orders appear to be suggestions or vice versa, disobedience may be a response to the former and cynicism to the latter.

All this is not much of an advance in theory. Mostly it has only been suggested how media theorizing ought to be anchored in action theory. Once the central concern of Luhmann's work with its focus on intersystem contingency and complexity reduction was brought to bear on Smelser's "production of social action" as a value-added process, the suggestions proposed here flowed more or less directly by articulating the two with time and information use. What needs emphasis perhaps is that in part media constitute double symbolicity. They are symbols of some entities already themselves symbolic, though they also represent real things. This has been pointed out with the distinction between "factors" and "products" of action, in which only the latter permit substitutive symbolic representation by several media. It is this feature which makes for built-in ambiguity in differentiated society. Finally, it is only in societies with fairly high levels of institutional differentiation that regulation by double symbolicity becomes a necessity. For it is here that man has to act often in contexts completely beyond his intellectual and emotional grasp, accept some liquidity, and delay its translation into a personally comprehensible experience for considerable periods of time. Such delays make modern life uncomfortable most of the time for some and some of the time for most. Yet, when they work, media grant us the opportunity to live with ignorance and impunity as individuals and

with a tremendously increased capacity to solve functional problems as a collectivity. They also afford us far more variety in the experience of meaning than was available before. But this is clearly contingent on prudent use to avoid chronic conflation. As Henry Kissinger allegedly said: Where ambiguity becomes the guiding principle, disaster is courted.

To court disaster is an intrinsic temptation in modern society. However, recognizing on purely analytical grounds that there is some pressure for spillover into other media when any one either inflates or deflates is one thing. The empirical world is another. Therefore Parsons' claim[23] about America's first McCarthyism as involving deflated influence which necessarily "propagated to deflated power" needs far more empirical evidence than he could give it in the political power paper. Off-set mechanisms are always a possibility in the real world. Parsons and Lidz[24] recognized this when hypothesizing that elaborate funeral rites might constitute inflated influence in the private realm in response to deflated status communication ability in the public realm. The reverse possibility, public status inflation and a deflationary discounting in the private sphere, was also pointed out. Providing room in theory for such empirical contingencies is therefore an urgent task. A first step in this direction is taken in the remainder of this paper.

VALUE SYSTEMS AND INTERMEDIA DYNAMICS

Perhaps the best way to start bringing some analytical variety into media dynamics is the development of a typology of societal value systems. Keeping this within manageable boundaries, values can be thought of as varying according to which functional aspect and its differentiated institutional expression is deemed the most important and hence ranked highest among the four functional problems and their institutions. As the media are linked in this model with functionally differentiated institutions, a particularly high emphasis on one institutional sector would signify a tendency to overvalue the efficacy of its medium. A G-primacy case, for example, suggests that men have a tendency to entertain unreasonable expectations about power solutions to all kinds of social problems. Very simply put, they think first and foremost of organization when responding to problems, deeming that nearly all that counts is will-power. Given such an intrinsically inflated *orientation* to power, we would expect a net propensity for *actual* power to deflate. If there is a tendency to issue commands going beyond the jurisdiction of office, disobedience should be chronic, and resort to force where possible the necessary outcome. Whether this comes about through an inflationary pressure on influence, however, or through relative influence scarcity would in turn depend primarily on the location of the integrative sector in the functional rank order that values define as authentic. When the I-function is placed next to G in importance we might expect an inflationary spillover into the influence medium; if ranked lower down, scarcity might be the outcome. To take another example, in the A-primacy case we would expect a tendency to view the "profit motive" as the primary and near universal means to solve problems. This need have nothing to do with the particular way the economy is organized or legitimated. It means merely that economic solutions are attempted in preference to other alternatives such as the mobilization of collective obligations, the institutionalized regulation of conflicts, or the upgrading of consensual commitments. A net preference to regard the creation of more and more wealth as a first necessary requisite to the solution of "everything" then ought to be associated with inflationary expectations about the "power of money." What this does to the actual operation of money should depend on the kinds of problems at issue and their location in functional significance on the extant value-hierarchy, as well as whether or not something approaching "units of account" and "stores of value" have been developed concerning the intrinsic satisfier that causes the problem.

As always, matters are complex. Let us take a simple illustrative example. Suppose the problem at issue is a political one. Suppose further that the power medium lacks clearly institutionalized forms to be used effectively as a "store of value" and a "unit of account," as seems to be still empirically the case in most industrially advanced societies. Suppose, third, that the G problem ranks next to A in order of importance as defined by values. Then, in a society characterized by "economic fetishism," there ought to be (1) an inflationary spillover of expectations into the power realm, (2) a substitution of the missing power resources by money or corruption, and therefore (3) a spooning off of money from utility to collective effectiveness which remains unmeasurable. The same result could be sustained through different combinations, depending on other rank-preference locations of G and whatever would take its place next to A. And yet, empirically "economic fetishism" may have very little to do with A-primacy. As indicated later, it may be a temptation intrinsic to contemporary society.

These introductory remarks should serve to make three modest points. First, it has been clearly recognized that social problems must necessarily grow in quantity and intensity through modernization and into modernity. This is a direct result of increased interdependence.[25] Second, particularly in the economically advanced world where genuine utility needs are declining in significance, the blatantly apparent intractability of many social problems evident in the now familiar series of crises—urban, transport, regional cleavages, farmers' revolt, youth, all these seeming "tertiary mobilizations"—are so intractable primarily because the rationalization inherent in Western culture demands now more than ever that we "account." But most of these disturbances do not reflect problems of utility of genuine demands for more wealth but rather demands for more authenticity, more solidarity, and more collective effectiveness. The media governing these latter problems, though already in use, have empirically remained so far relatively underdeveloped, not rendering themselves adequately as "stores of values" and "units of accounts."[26] Our commitment to rationality has outpaced the available means. As "everything" demands rational justification and "accounting" of performance in the only terms still "convincing," in numbers, grows rampant, this seemingly leads to an increasing misuse of money to control action for which it is not functionally specialized at all. It is not the idea of "cost-effectiveness" that is misused, but the use of money to measure change in "intrinsic social satisfiers" other than wealth. Again, one need not be a conspiracy theorist to see some validity in the charge of "consumption fetishism" somehow alienating men. The same mechanism may simply operate on the subunit level of family or individual. Because men lack the relevant measures but prefer accountable to nonaccountable performances, they try to solve L, I, and G problems by consumption of utilities which for the more affluent certainly have very little bearing on their actual needs. To some extent affluent societies no longer add to their "stocks" of utilities, they just add to a utilities' "flow." Hence the sheer practical implications of our problem are enormous. One might wax poetic, declare that the discovery of media will be to society what the X-ray was to radiology, and hence demand a Nobel prize for the discoverer. This is the second point. The third is, that given the tremendous complexity of the problem of media dynamics, expecting more than an outline of one source of principle variation amounts to inflated expectations.

A Four-Function Typology of Commitments

Societal values as conceptions of the desirable type of society[27] refers to an image of society "one ought to be committed to." Given the normative bindingness, such an image provides men with an evaluation standard. They can use it to assess actual conditions they find in their society. In this sense societal values probably constitute a feature of relatively developed societies. If society rather than "everything" or life as such is to be the object of evaluation, some degree of differentiation seems presumed. Citizens, not people, are to assume responsibility for societal events. Furthermore, such an image of society as a guidance standard to making judgments implies the presence of two beliefs. The first is the recognition and acceptance of the idea that men create their society; the second, the notion that they can change extant societal arrangements into a multitude of possible alternatives without changing everything in a preperceived "overdetermined" fashion, as for example themselves, their personalities, or their religious beliefs. The image of society prevalent constitutes reduced societal complexity, not reduced world complexity in which everything hangs closely together.[28] In having such a differentiated guidance standard men can confront "bits" of life-complexity, i.e., aspects of their existence, and contemplate rearranging them in light of what they deem desirable without being frozen into anxiety about change that stems from a perception that sees in any change a change of the whole world of the familiar. In primitive society men's relation to the supernatural, the natural, and themselves presumably constituted one single package; and the ascriptive regulation of social life was rigid precisely because the image involved reduced world complexity. Ongoing institutionalized change presumably could not be entertained because a voluntary confrontation with any given change did amount to the unbearable, the confrontation of world-uncertainty. So much for locating societal values as guidance standards in developed societies.

This image of the good society can be thought of as a kind of master blueprint constitutive in turn of legitimacy beliefs about association as such. Such beliefs are probably variably general, with some being more abstract than others, the set as a whole applying to any kind of human association. For in modern conditions men do not ordinarily live "in society." As captured in the concept of multiple role-incumbency, concretely they live in families, work associations, recreational clubs, and so on. Generalized legitimacy beliefs about association as such are used to develop and "float," more specialized legitimacy beliefs appropriate to organizations in a division of social labor. The present interest is confined to such generalized beliefs.

First a cautionary comment: when Parsons introduced the concept of value commitments as a medium he no more intended to deny the earlier emphasis on values as the most stable aspect of social structure[29] than Einstein's introduction of relativity intended to negate the law of gravity. Therefore there is an aspect of values which cannot be considered a medium in the present context. If a society is conceived as subject to a four-function dilemma, then the priority ranking of the four functions can be considered the structural aspect.[30] I shall treat the possibilities of valuing goal-attainment over integration, adaptation over goal-attainment, and so on, as a given. Dealing with modern societies of course means dealing with active ones, i.e., those involving the continual mobilization of resources on a national level, in order to narrow the ideal-real gap. But even within this range one can distinguish those societies that put a primary emphasis on the perfection of distributive justice (integrative primacy), where "just" distribution of resources and access to opportunities are the predominant concern, from those wherein the development of generalized resources takes priority (adaptive primacy). Similarly one can distinguish those types wherein the transformation of the social order in the service of an abstract ideal or the construction of social authenticity looms as the most pressing problem (pattern primacy) from others wherein the validating of the presumed superior effectiveness of a given type of social organization constitutes the primary business of men's efforts (goal-attainment primacy). In the perspective adopted here, beliefs concerning this rank-ordering of all four functions constitutes the structural aspect of societal values. The image of the good society on the other hand constitutes already a set of more specific beliefs that spell out the desirable in terms of such variable priority ordering of the four functions. The notion of a need for some priority ordering derives of course from the postulate that no two functions can be maximized at the same time. With four functions to be ranked, twenty-four types of rank orders are possible. Hence there should be twenty-four types of images of the good society reflecting somewhat reduced societal complexity in accordance with such functional preference sets. In order to avoid unmanageable complexity we shall have to confine the construction of such images to four basic types reflecting primacy of one function each.

As a belief system, an image of the good society itself is subject to the four-function constraint. As legitimacy beliefs about human association as such are the issue, the commitments specifying the purpose of association constitute the goal output. Commitments to images of man, time, nature, and supranature would constitute the way in which a societal image is grounded in more encompassing meanings.

Commitments to rationales concerning social rights and obligations would serve to integrate the varied components of a societal image. Finally, a set of legitimacy beliefs about association needs to be adapted to other sets of commitments, as for example personality ideals or religious imperatives. On the side of societal images the management of competing pressures between sets of different commitments is probably handled through commitments to rationales involved in changing associational arrangements. Thus any adequate delineation of a given societal image would have to include at least four different sets of beliefs and the relations among them. Just how simplistic our outline remains can therefore be effectively communicated. In each of the four sets we shall present but one belief and outline the structure of a given image by the relations pertaining among them.

Given the much simplified single-function primacy case as a purely heuristic device, our first task is to establish a link between assigning priority to a given functional problem, the structural aspect of societal values, and a given image of the good society, the medium aspect. The link is the now familiar paradigm of the differentiation of four function-specific actions, governed by standards of utility for the adaptive, effectiveness for the goal-attainment, solidarity for the integrative, and authenticity for the pattern spheres.

Second, let us indicate some systematic sources whence the components of images of society attain some content even though such content must be fairly general. A few universal features shared by all developed societies provide such sources. Given the notion of a man-created rather than a taken-for-granted social world, there is a universal problem of legitimating association in accordance with some perceived purpose. Specifications of a general purpose of association in the image serves as our link to the structural aspect of values. Also, as individuals have been sufficiently emancipated from the web of primary ties in developed societies, another general problem asking for continual solution concerns the question as to how the rights of individuals are to be balanced off relative to the demands of organization. Touching on the image of man, this individual-group dilemma constitutes one of the beliefs in the pattern sphere of images as belief systems. Further, although all developed societies have inequalities, in none is the unequal distribution of rewards and facilities self-legitimating. Hence there is the problem of legitimating inequalities. Involving rationales for evaluating unit contributions, this set of beliefs has integrative significance for the image. Finally, all modern societies are characterized by forces making for change and others resisting it as an institutionalized pattern. Thus the legitimation of change and stability and the rationales underlying them are the last component of a societal image considered here. As indicated, these are seen as serving adaptive functions relative to commitments other than societal. These preliminaries done, four ideal-type images are outlined below.

Four Images of the Good Society

When the principle of utility reigns in the structural realm, denoting the choice of adaptation as the most pressing problem to solve, men tend to view association in intrinsically instrumental fashion. Organization exists, as it were, to achieve something for man. One joins an organization, so goes the prevalent notion on the medium level, in order to satisfy needs which have been set before. This is one source which gives this image its individualistic slant. Another is the emphasis on learning that adaptive primacy dictates. No collectivity, however constituted, can pry loose resources from allocated uses to recombine them for new uses, which is learning, with as much agility as the individual mind.[31] Furthermore, with human bonds being the instrumental clay of history, the goals pursued in organization are not only extrinsic to organization itself,[32] they are also of an empirical pragmatic nature and relative success or failure in their attainment has no direct bearing on the ultimate meaning of human bonds as such. The underlying model for organization is the voluntary association for mutual advantage. Where such a model is generalized to society at large, an atomist version of *Organic Association*[33] constitutes the image of the good society. An atomist aspect in the image as a derivative of individualism and voluntarism is stressed deliberately. When components of this image inflate, i.e., are carried to excess, the problem directly affected becomes integration. The crucial balancing act in an A-primary societal value system concerns the tension between "development" of resources and its inevitable impact of change on the societal community.

Given the individualist strain, in principle the rights of the individual always outrank those of the needs of effective organization. The burden of proof in conflicts tends to go to him who demands buckling-under. He has to show why adjusting to organizational demands is necessary. The implication is always to adjust in the service of the members' strategies that led them to join in the first place. Thus in this case the individual-group dilemma is "solved" by assigning consummatory significance to the individual and instrumental meaning to the organization.

Given an overriding concern with usefulness, prestige tends to be allocated on the clearest measure of utility available, monetary income. The important criterion is "wealth period," not command over specific kinds of resources such as land rather than "crude sacks of cash," reflecting qualitatively different ways of generating resources. The rich are the recognized top dogs because their wealth is presumed to attest to their superior utility. The poor are identified as "low achievers" deserving special attention primarily because of the possibility that low achievement derives from structural sources of opportunity constraints rather than from free will. If the former, something is wrong in the system because there are constraints on full resource utilization. That is bad and needs repair. If the latter, however, helping the poor is problematical because legitimation of such action needs to draw on other than primary societal values.

Finally, where organization is an instrument designed to produce generalized usefulness, the search for improvements is constant and built into the design as an ideal. As a result, social change, usually thought of as finding new ways of doing things better, is an end valued in itself. It means progress. Hence in this image the status quo is on the defensive; those who oppose changing arrangements must show why change should not occur.[34]

On the other hand, where goal-attainment ranks supreme on the structural level, the presumed purpose of association in general tends to be to prove the effectiveness of organization itself. Men are seen as "joined" for the sake of demonstrating that the specifically human resides in the capacity of effective collaboration. The concrete ends pursued are again extrinsic to organization. But here they are of instrumental significance to organization, not the ends of organization. Concrete goals tend to be selected to demonstrate organizational efficacy. Improvement in the power position of the organization vis-a-vis others tends to be the measure of success. He who emphasizes organizational effectiveness must also emphasize power and discipline. Consequently, leadership and follower status, authority and obedience stand at the center of men's relations. When the organizational purpose of this kind is generalized to the society at large, a militaristic, hierarchical model prevails. This template of the good society denotes a plurality of corporate structures arranged into a tight system of superordination and subordination extant "to prevail in the world despite all its vicissitudes." Society exists in order to continuously enhance its standing in the international stratification system. Let us call this image *Corporate Gesellschaft*. Instead of "just plain growth in everything useful," as the preceding case, improvement

in world power status constitutes the overriding goal in this case.

Given organizational effectiveness as the overriding sense of being human, a pervasive collectivism characterizes this image. The individual-group dilemma is "solved" by an emphasis on "freedom for" rather than "freedom from." The individual is expected to let the requisites of organizational effectiveness become his own needs. Men are not seen as joining society. They are seen as born to it in order to serve. Consequently, instrumental significance tends to be assigned to the individual and consummatory significance goes to the group.

The allocation of prestige tends to emphasize contribution to collective societal welfare. Standing in, and association with particularly powerful corporate structures whose functioning has the widest societal repercussions tends to be the basis of prestige assignment. Service in the public realm here usually outranks that in the private, and association with large corporate structures outranks that with small. "Strategic position," i.e., having the greatest impact on all, tends to control highest prestige.

Given the ideal of collective development, the status quo is again on the defensive. But contrary to the preceding case, change here is intrinsically problematic. First, G-primacy connotes emphasis on will. But to will is to have decided, to strain towards an objective itself no longer in doubt. Will implies one no longer wants to learn about alternative ends, for to have these before one's eye is to hesitate and weigh. Hence concerning ends, G-primacy involves some intrinsic aversion to learning. It therefore poses an enormous adaptation problem. The purer the case of G-primacy, the more maladaptive it tends to be. Therein lies the brilliance of Deutsch's observation that wherever will-power looms as an overriding concern, symbols of death abound in evocative messages.[35] Second, large-scale change in society always involves redistributing scarce resources from one use to another. In a society where all corporate structures operate under an explicit service ethos, all are expected to compete for resources as "proof" of their commitment to collective welfare. Hence any demands for more by one must be immediately opposed by others as an inevitable infringement on their potential to prove their effectiveness. Thus corporate rivalry tends to be the motor of change, a vigorous defense of vested interests the major brake, and both are being legitimated by appeal to presumed national interest. Finally, as change calls for learning, will opposes it, but success in a developing world requires it, the basic orientation to change as such is deeply fraught with intense ambivalence. One must learn to prevail, but in learning can one prevail? Neither change nor the status quo are clearly on the defensive. The onus of proof for and against change rests on both sides.

Third, where the integrative function looms as the most pressing problem at the structural level, social harmony tends to be the guidance conception in association. Human association is to serve human affiliational needs. Where the notion of the specifically human as being together rather than as doing something together prevails, the ideal type of society is one where "everything fits" for the multitudes of human needs. Activism not withstanding, this is a kind of organismic image where proper balance among the parts counts as the criterion of success. Let us call this image of the good society *Corporate Gemeinschaft.*

With the idea of "enjoying harmony in balance" as the major purpose in association, the whole issue of the individual-group dilemma tends to be rejected as a false alternative. The image of man as primarily a social being by nature prevents a principled priority ordering concerning the rights of individuals as compared to the demands of social organization. Consummatory significance tends to be assigned to both the individual and the group.

Given the organismic template with its emphasis on proper fit, prestige tends to be assigned to interstitial roles specializing in social integration. The professions in their role as "influentials" constitute the higher-ups of institutionalized wisdom. The grounds for distributing resources unequally tend to reside in perceived role-capacity to make contributions to the perfection of distributive justice in the social order.

In this organismic image, the goals pursued in association are intrinsic to organization and man, seen as inseparable. If for no other reason than the fact that structural change in society always proves upsetting to many groups and their relations, change in principle here is on the defensive despite the fact that perfecting justice constitutes the major legitimating ground for dynamics in this case. In view of the over-all disturbing effect of structural change, it is the advocates for change who have to supply proof of its necessity. They can do so best by arguing that inequities have to be removed. With equity being the principal consideration, those opposed to change argue vested rights rather than vested interests. The typical sequences involved in efforts at change are quite different from the preceding case. One argues for intended change on the grounds of a need to respond to unintended changes presumptively assumed to have already taken place, and in a manner that "unbalanced" equity. Anticipated change is then legitimated on the presumed need to "rebalance" distributive justice.

Finally where pattern consistency and authentic experience of commitments through social action rank highest among the functional problems, the predominant purpose of association at the image level tends to be an interest in realizing ultimate ideals. Organization exists, as it were to transform society and man (personality) in accordance with some ultimate cultural idea of an authentic way of life. Where the realization of some authenticity as the central rationale for association is projected onto the wider society, a bifurcated image of true believers and reprobates tends to prevail. Let us label this image *Mechanical Bund.* Regardless of the content of ethical concerns, absolute idealists tend to denigrate everything but direct moral involvement as corrupt. They always live in a wicked world, i.e., an imperfect extant present is seen as corrupt, usually in some intrinsic way. Such a commitment to total transformation in the service of some humane ideal involves a bifurcated social reality construction focused on the quality of human existence. Usually some inverted mirror-image of what is constitutes the model of what should be.[36] As the corrupt is to give way to the pure, extant relations and men constitute the clay of history. Consequently, instrumental significance tends to be attached to extant organization and extant corrupt man, while consummatory significance is shifted into the future of the saved.

Here superiority in standing tends to be assigned to those best suited to symbolize whichever nature of ultimate concerns is in vogue. Superior man may be the bearded revolutionary of a distant land, a mythical personage of a distant time, a flower child of meek sensitivity, or a phalanx of the shirt-uniformed toughs marching towards the glory of a future era out of the misery of contemporary hopelessness. Because prestige goes to the truly committed and converts are sought, access tends to be inherently open, giving a preferential advantage to those adept in the presentation of credible sincerity.

As to change, men who see themselves as the instruments of compelling ideals derogate defenders of the status quo as criminals. For the believers the need for change is self-evident. For the reprobates the advocated change is an alternative equally to be feared and opposed. Change is always legitimated on grounds of "nothing but" ideological commitments, and the only source of stability rests on the routinization of charisma, without which defenders of the status quo have to rely on illegitimate means. This case then is a marginal one in a double sense. On the one hand, more is involved in change than just rearranging social relations. Minimally personality too is involved. Put differently, when a modern society puts pattern consistency as a primary concern, its modernity tends to be impaired. However, this is not so for a modernizing transitional society which has still little to lose in modernity and everything to gain. Second, the legitimation beliefs all tend to be diffusely and abstractly "meshed" with higher cultural ideals.

For a convenient overview Figure 24-3 presents four legitimacy beliefs as illustrations of types we take to be constitutive of any image of the good society. The components are arranged by function for the image of the good society as an evaluational symbol system. Briefly summarizing, as can be seen, the Organic Association involves: (1) the development of generalized resources as the primary reason for association; (2) defining the individual as an end and the organization as means; (3) allocation of prestige on the basis of utility or "productiveness"; and (4) placing the burden of proof on the forces of preservation. In the Corporate *Gesellschaft* legitimacy beliefs (1) stress a search for superior effectiveness in organization as the major reason in association, (2) assign instrumental significance to the individual, (3) allocate prestige on the basis of presumed power in society, and (4) attribute intrinsic ambivalence to orientations to change with the result that change comes to depend primarily on corporate rivalry and stability on vested interests. In the Corporate *Gemeinschaft* case the corresponding normative beliefs involve: (1) realizing social harmony, (2) the assignment of consummatory significance to both individual and group, (3) the allocation of prestige on integrative capacity, and (4) justifying change in the name of a claimed inequity needing adjustment while defending stability in the name of vested rights.

Finally in the *Mechanical Bund* variety the image components stress: (1) the search for moral fulfillment as the predominant reason in association, (2) the assignment of instrumental significance to both individual and group, (3) allocating prestige on the basis of capacity to represent a cultural ideal, and (4) the justification of change in the name of ideology and that of stability in terms of routinized charisma, if at all.

The I column lists the primary grounds on which differential standing is recognized which involves the societal media. This is to indicate a feature of intrinsic inflationary pressure, inherent in the conception of single-function primacy. But only in the *Mechanical Bund* type does this inflationary pressure involve societal values themselves. Where men take the *Bund* as a standard, they tend to expect too much from sheer commitments. It signifies an inherent propensity towards relative neglect of the potential efficacy of the other media. How much any one of these tends to be "undervalued," however, is again a function of values in their structural aspect, hierarchical order imposed on the remaining three functional problems of society. In the *Gemeinschaft* case, influence is under some inflationary pressure. The emphasis on "equity above all" in societal values tempts men to overestimate "the power of influence." In the *Gesellschaft* case the central concern with organization and effectiveness leads men to overestimate "the power of power," while the *Organic Association* model tempts them to overestimate "the power of money" because of the identification of the social as of utilitarian-instrumental significance to

Legitimacy Beliefs in Terms of Functions for the Image as a Belief-System

Structural Aspect: Function of Priority	Type of "Good Society"	L		I	G	A	
		Consummatory-Instrumental Significance Attached to		Basis of Prestige Allocation	Perceived Main Purpose of Association	Principle Modes of Legitimating	
		Individual	Group			Change	Stability
L	Mechanical *Bund*	Instrumental	Instrumental	symbolizing Cultural Ideal: "commitments"	search for moral fulfillment	ideology	routinized charisma
I	Corporate *Gemeinschaft*	Consummatory	Consummatory	contributions to harmony "influence"	search for distributive justice	disturbed equity	vested rights
G	Corporate *Gesellschaft*	Instrumental	Consummatory	service *for* society: "power"	search for national effectiveness	corporate rivalry	vested interests
A	Organic Association	Consummatory	Instrumental	utility *in* society: "money"	search for useful opportunities	progress	stalemate among interests

Figure 24-3. Components beliefs in four types of societal images.

the individual. Positing this link between societal values and the other media in terms of some intrinsic inflationary propensity proves useful to some hypothesizing on intermedia dynamics, as will be discussed later. For the moment, however, let us consider the nature of a values code and how in very general terms values as such inflate or deflate. The question here is, what does value conflation mean when considered outside the context of intermedia comparisons?

The Nature of the Code and the Nature of Value Inflation and Deflation

As already indicated, a code is a set of rules ordering the number of ways in which symbols can be combined into meaningful messages. In music the *Kontrapunkt* is one example. In societal values the code is the rationale that connects the four basic belief components about human association into a meaningful set. Given the Smelser perspective deployed here, such "rationalization" always starts with the column at the left and works itself progressively to the right. For example, compressed into a minimally meaningful rationale, the basic codes of two of these primary types might be formulated as follows. The code of the *Mechanical Bund*: (1) Given that man is above all a religious creature, a being striving for self-realization foremost through self-reflection (L), he must evaluate his action (2) primarily in terms of their potential for experiencing meaning (I). Therefore he who best manages to represent his commitment to some cultural ideal through interaction, the most blatantly virtuous, deserves the most prestige. But if one ranks contributions to interaction on experiencing meaning, then (3) the major purpose of association surely must be the search for moral fulfillment (G). But given (3) the problem of whether and how the forms of association must be changed has to be evaluated above all in light of what ideology dictates (A). A similarly primitive mutually reinforcing reasoning set in the case of *Corporate Gemeinschaft* could read as follows: Given that by nature man is social, so that the individual-group dilemma is a false one (L), (2) action has to be evaluated primarily in terms of a mediating-potential that overcomes the false dilemma (I). But if one ranks contributions to interactions on the principle of harmony primarily, then surely (3) the major reason in the false dilemma that constitutes association is the achievement of distributive justice (G). But given (3), the only really good reason to change or not to change the forms of association has to be the presence or absence of disturbed equity (A). These two might suffice as illustrations. The effectiveness of codes to restrict the

variety of ways in which commitments can be mobilized should then be a function of two properties: the degree of tautological tightness in mutual contingency and the generality of terms connecting the elements in the rationale.

As to conflation phenomena, if we use Figure 24-3 in a way similar to Smelser's resource table, there are principally two ways in which a code can restrict or expand. Both across the rows and through the columns, deflationary restriction occurs in the AGIL direction and inflationary expansion in the LIGA direction. Because these types of images reflect a different evaluation of the four components of action, they themselves are ordered on a scale of varying tolerance for the distance between experience and action, with A, G, I, and L ranging from high to low. It follows, therefore, that when a specific legitimation for a concrete association is floated which, relative to the prevailing primary case of commitments to "the good society," happens to fall "stepwise" one row lower and one column to the right, the floating of such a belief signals inflationary pressure or expansion of the code. When the reverse takes place, i.e., some concrete legitimation is floated that fits better a category "up" and "to the left," deflationary pressure is exerted. Where under a prevailing *Bund* image some legitimation for some concrete association such as in factory, university, or party is broadcast, which takes a form actually better fitting the logic of *Gemeinschaft*, *Gesellschaft*, or Organic Association models, inflation is at hand. Deflationary pressure takes the reverse order. This general principle is particularly easy to appreciate also at the exterme boundaries of the societal realm. Strictly speaking, Organic Association beliefs cannot inflate any more at the societal level. Inflation here means transition into the realm of personality media. As McClelland[37] recognized, rampant individualism means anarchy, the denial of social constraints as a matter of principle. At the other end, strictly speaking, Schmalenbach's *Bund* beliefs cannot deflate at the societal level. Their deflation involves a tip-over into the purely cultural realm. A cultural revolution is an attempt to deny the conditionality of the social realm on meaning attainment for man. When experience and action have been fairly highly differentiated, inflation involves the neglect of a control element in action, deflation the disregard of a conditions' element. Both are characteristically modern sins. Both involve primitive hope instead of prudent trust. But the former amounts to an attempt to desocialize man under the mistaken notion that man can be completely emancipated from his existence as a lengthened shadow of his childhood dependency, and the latter amounts to an attempt to "decondition" experience from social history under the mistaken notion that society is an "all-possibility thing."

As already indicated in connection with function-adequate use of time and social information, the functional perspective on societal values deployed here permits positing a stability theorem. Any value system that assigns primary and secondary import to functions diagonally placed to each other in the usual manner of presenting the four-function paradigm will make for greater stability in intermedia dynamics than any other combination. Hence, among the twenty-four possible types of value systems, there are four which are special in this sense. If we denote by the appropriate letter that function stressed the most, and the function given secondary emphasis in the value formula by a second appropriate letter, while leaving the order among the remaining two unspecified, these four special types are the A-I value system and its reversed type I-A and the G-L value system and its reversed type L-G. Any one of these permits a greater chance for long-term historical identity in the production of societal authenticity under varying economic and scientific-technological conditions than any other type. The reason for this greater stability resides in an intrinsic capacity for mutually contingent correction of inflationary or deflationary excess in terms of the societal values involved and their function-analogue media.

Such societies can oscillate across the diagonal, as it were. They can correct excess in one function because, given the ready availability in secondary place of the relevant components, they have a means for correction in that functional area most immediately threatened. In the A-I case for example, inflation under a prevailing image of Organic Association most directly threatens integration in society. But as legitimacy beliefs of the Corporate *Gemeinschaft* variety are in secondary reserve, the relevant counter-foils are available. The same holds for the reverse value formula of I-A. Here an excess on the harmony theme most immediately threatens adaptiveness. Vested rights keep the system from adjusting to external change; but when this occurs the very fact that Organic Association beliefs do constitute the secondary stress in the value formula poses a high probability of their mobilization and with that of the restabilization of the system. There is of course a similar connection in the G-L case and its reversed type. When a society goes "all out" in goal attainment the strains on the individual become particularly acute in terms of the meaning of it all. Why is the constant demand for sacrifices necessary? When a primary commitment to the over-all importance of organization threatens to get out of hand here, however, the classic reversal of means and

ends tends to be forestalled before it can go very far, because the function-relevant opposite, the authenticity problem, does rank second in the formula, thus leading to relatively early mobilization of precisely those commitments needed to restabilize this situation. The same holds in its reverse case. When the principle of hope comes to pervert a primary commitment to authenticity in society, above all through first inflating claims of values and then rapid deflation "out" to the cultural realm, then here, because of the second rank given to the kinds of commitments representing exactly that component of action most directly threatened, organization, it is again likely that these rather than others will be mobilized secondarily, thus helping to rebalance the situation. Because conflation does involve confusion in media, there is of course no guarantee of rebalancing even in these cases. Compared to the others there is merely a far greater probability of it. Relatively, these types have an important self-corrective capacity built into them.

This feature of special long-term stability through oscillation is further adumbrated by the role of the other media involved. Let us return to the A-I case. When the principle of utility gets out of hand and the profit imperative or monetary standards begin to run wild, here, because of the secondary placement of I, influence too tends to outrank in expected efficacy and, therefore, in net preference of use the two remaining media. Thus precisely that medium best suited to stop an inflationary psychology, influence, should be in relatively ample supply, available for ready deployment. In the reverse case, it would be the profit imperative that would be readily available. This is of course the most directly relevant standard to overcome the immobility deriving from vested rights. In the G-L case, the inflationary trend in the power medium is more easily corrected because the most immediate problem created by power inflation is legitimacy. Hence having *Bund* commitments ready at hand to draw on also implies restabilization, either through redefining the power code or by "throwing the rascals out." In the reverse case, when commitments run wild, it is order in a differentiated society which is most immediately strained. Hence having power as "the most favored medium" over influence and money shores up the efficacy of political authority in recreating order.

In the remaining twenty types of value-systems, no such offset mechanisms are built in. They lack both the easy availability of counterfoiling commitments and the requisite supplies of the most directly appropriate media which, given a crisis situation, *must* be mobilizable in extraordinary amounts if restabilization is to occur without change in the production of societal authenticity under changing economic and scientific-technological conditions and, therefore, without a change in the basic identity of society itself. Unless mechanisms such as these or functionally equivalent ones do operate, modern society with built-in structural change would have to suffer from a permanent crisis in meaning.

Turning to application, the next and final section of this chapter suggests the potential utility of the preceding model by a rather speculative interpretation of recent conflation phenomena in American and German society.

APPLYING THE MODEL: A SPECULATIVE INTERPRETATION OF AMERICAN AND GERMAN MEDIA CONFLATION

Recently, when developed societies engaged in total war, their nationalism or other mission appeared as propaganda. This always involves the activation of moral commitments in a somewhat deflated way. On was to feel secure and accepted as a citizen in good standing only on condition of "doing everything for the war effort." The profit imperative became "profiteering." A good deal of political action, in particular disputes over national objectives, became "politicking." A whole host of social conflicts were redefined as close to a treasonous lack of loyalty. The whole idea of differential association was seen as inherently problematical and perhaps basically incompatible with the need for national comitment. On the job one was to wage the "production battle," in bed *a deux* the "fertility battle," in church the "spiritual battle," and on the social class line the "solidarity battle." In fact of course, social relations were not altered that drastically. Profits continued to be made, love was enjoyed for its own sake, spiritual experiences were attained, and strikes continued if not *de jure* then *de facto*. The quickening itensity of life that the war emergency brought probably advanced further the differentiation of experiences, of action, and of experience and action. All this happened despite and partly because of the massive efforts to activate commitments in a deflated way. For most followed the propaganda line in spirit and not in a literal sense but needed the latter to mobilize their energies. Expected or not, this outcome was the only one compatible with the imperative of success. To many it was quite apparent that modern war needs effective managers with their profit imperative more than heroes of the medieval variety, reliable factory operatives with their notions of "an honest day's work for an honest buck" more than fiery idealists, therapeutically effective religiosity or art more than their political perversion, and moments of escape from a more demanding society

more than "nothing but warriors" in whatever form. For to deprive society of the capacity to operate at the level of actual differentiation of its institutions reached was in fact to deprive it of the chance to win.

But Germany had a propaganda ministry, America had not. There can also be little doubt that the messages about the New Order were more innovative, hence potentially more immoral, than America's "crusade for democracy." In Germany the departure from her past seemed more radical than in America, where one actually carried one's own civil war past onto the international scene. Furthermore, as Hannah Arendt[38] correctly emphasized, the Nazis' "nationalism" was intrinsically antinationalist. This points to early inflation probably followed later by rapid and severe deflation in Germany, whereas the American case involved slight unidirectional deflation. There are further differences. In 1942 Germany returned to the production of peacetime consumption goods disproportionately to America and England. Furthermore it has also been shown that Nazism and the war accelerated the modernizing differentiation trends in German society in ways directly opposite to the image of the good society officially propagated.[39] Acceleration of differentiation was probably also a feature of American society during that time, but, and this is the decisive point here, this was not a development diametrically opposed to official propaganda, though it was at variance with deflated commitments. Different types of societal values and different effects of their deflation on power and influence can shed some light on this contrast. Let us take both in turn.

As to America, it might be recalled that prior to the start, the war was opposed by an "America-First" movement. Its defeat lent itself subsequently to interpretations relevant for a view of the past civil war experience. To let England and European democracy in the lurch would have amounted to "the same thing" as having permitted slavery in the South earlier. This points to the kind of blatantly social moral fundamentalism that carries integrative primacy. America's other prominent deflationary commitments episode occurred with the McCarthyite movement under the pressure of the Korean war. This, as might be recalled, involved a search and destroy tactics of un-Americanism. Parsons related this phenomenon to experienced status threat, and general integrative strains in American society.[40] Both the terminology of redefinitions of Americanism and the differential susceptibility to McCarthy on the part of socially marginal groups again point to the link between American commitments deflation and a strained societal community. In response to large-scale status disequilibria Americans, so it seems, react with moral outrage.

That American values involve A-primacy seems hardly in dispute. Far more difficult is the clearcut delineation of a secondary stress on the other three functions. Of the fourteen major value themes outlined by Williams,[41] eight clearly reflect A-primacy, four a stress on integration, and two on blatant morality. I interpret a primary orientation to egalitarianism in terms of a concern with equity for opportunity, a conception of freedom as guaranteed better through operation of diffuse cultural controls than explicit social organization, a stress on conformity through a notion of "group individualism," and a definition of patriotism in terms of a concern with "un-Americanisms" as reflecting a concern with solidarity in diversity. The often noted "moral overstrain" and the widespread presence of humanitarian mores in the form of the charity complex, however, seems to signal some form of deflated solidarity concerns. Hence, deflated societal values in America tend to take the form of deflated components of the Corporate *Gemeinschaft* image of the good society. In short, America's societal value-system involves an A-I type where a primary stress is placed on *Organic Association* and a secondary one on some intrinsically deflated belief components of the Corporate *Gemeinschaft* model. According to our hypothesis, this means that America belongs to those few types that are inherently better balanced internally. For when the atomist version of Organic Association commitments "get out of hand," the very fact that a secondary stress in the value formula is placed on integrative ties means that deflated commitments sooner than later become counterbalanced by the effective mobilization of influence, which can put a stop to further deflation in the values medium.

The case of Nazi Germany may provide an interesting contrast in this respect. More recent research has developed the highly suggestive hypothesis that Germany was a totalitarian state in name only, to the extent that the term denotes perfect control from the political center. In the practice of every-day reality, her polity was a caricature of total control, a system of anarchical systemlessness."[42] It seems now fairly well established that after the seizure of power the barrage of blood-and-soil propaganda never succeeded in covering up the meaninglessness, in the sense of goallessness, of the tremendous efforts demanded. This was a meaninglessness primarily experienced by the very units who generated the demands, i.e., the leadership cadres in army, party, economy, and so on. The perspective of this chapter would suggest a new hypothesis for the interpretation of Nazism as a "system of systemlessness." All the propaganda notwithstanding, available evidence points to the fact that societal value commitments

in the sense of an over-all conception of the good society were hardly involved at all in Nazi Germany, at least after 1939. Instead, a terrific escalation of corporate rivalries was combined with a deflated power medium and an exceedingly inflated influence medium, particularly in the area of purely technical expertise.

This perspective may help account for some of the more prominent mysteries in this case that continue to baffle even the empathic analyst. It touches upon Hannah Arendt's "banality of evil phenomenon" at the elite level, i.e., the involvement of apparently normal and well-educated men in the spectacularly unscrupulous use of power. The case of the writing desk murderers is one of these mysteries; the apparent extreme helplessness on the part of intelligent men to avoid clearly impending disaster is another.

Germany's value system seems to have been one in which a primary stress went to Corporate *Gesellschaft* and a secondary one to Corporate *Gemeinschaft*. The former was very characteristic of Prussia, the latter far more prominent in the South.[43] But the Bismark solution to nation-building from the top down had put its Prussian stamp on the nation, at least in the political use of value commitments at the national level. We might therefore identify Germany's societal values as having been a G-I system. This means that it belonged to those types of value-systems inherently more mobile, less capable of correction for conflation than the American type. If so, the apparent failure of a breakthrough to mechanical ties in the form of an emergence for a clear specification of the "meaning of it all" in the public realm and with intersubjective bindingness in that realm might be due to two conditions. The first is the relatively low placement of *Bund* type commitments in a value-formula with G-primacy. Those commitments precisely necessary to counterbalance the early inflation of nationalist commitments remained relatively inaccessible. When later, therefore, Corporate *Gesellschaft* commitments deflated, this could happen to the point of the actual disappearance of societal values from circulation in the public realm because the secondary commitments that became mobilized were of a type emphasizing solidarity, getting along with others, rather than those more directly having bearing on the problem of societal authenticity. Hence the stress was displaced from a function which is objectively of paramount importance to one which is relatively less relevant. Because deflationary pressures "got stuck" in concerns with insuring tighter solidarity, this system with G-primacy lacked corrective capability. At this secondary level, however, *Gemeinschaft* messages do not get deflated, hence they leave the operation of influence relatively unaffected. This, with deflated value media, however, means automatic relative inflation of the influence medium.

Put in less abstract language, the banality of evil phenomenon and the apparent helpless drift towards total defeat at the elite level probably had little if anything to do with some "fixation on *Götterdämmerung*." Instead, two far less esoteric factors suggest themselves. The particularism of *Gemeinschaft* symbols made it impossible for meaning symbols to be effectively mediated in the public channels available in a Corporate *Gesellschaft*. Asking "where are we all headed" simply was not the thing to do in the normatively differentiated context of one's *Gesellschaft*-role. Second, excessive trust in technical experts, i.e., inflated influence, in some form of institutionalized naiveté placed in functionally specialized institutions and their functionaries seems to have been involved. After all, these Germans might have reasoned, these specialists possess the requisite qualifications, therefore naturally one can expect them to know and perform responsibly.[44]

In other words, most Germans in elite positions did not place any spectacular trust in their "charismatic Führer." Their behavior amounted to sheer formal support, that could be rendered without any self-conscious scrutiny. They could do this because and so long as they placed their "trust" in the kinds of institutions they were familiar with, the traditional bureaucracies in the public and private sectors which were not eliminated by the Nazis. Given the altered conditions in the political regime, this of course was a replacement of trust with hope. They mutually presumed normal operations and functioning of each other's institutions without realizing that they were engaged in mutual deceit. The question therefore is: Why did they fail to find out? But to find out requires getting together. And although the lack of elite cohesion across functional sectors has been emphasized,[45] this constitutes a description of the phenomenon in need of explanation. Our perspective suggests that when the question as to the general meaning of societal association arises in a society with a G-I type of value system, then this problem tends to be "handled" at a level where it cannot be solved, with little but renewed commitments to solidarity "regardless why." And so, when "bothered" or "worried" about the dynamic direction of society, everyone focused on its cohesion. Where *Gemeinschaft* commitments operate, one tends to do this renewal with one's own kind. The "bothered" army officer raised doubts with his comrade in the casino; his naval counterpart in his mess; and business executives in their clubs. Thus the question of societal authenticity was not only circumvented by redefinition into a problem of solidarity, it was

also raised in this falsified form in mutually isolated milieux where nothing essential had really changed. Hence personality was reassured, at the wrong place, on erroneous ground, but reassured nevertheless. Thus relieved of creeping doubt, a personality could resume his role duties as member of a Corporate *Gesellschaft*. Finding the familiar at one's own place, one hoped that the familiar also existed still at other relevant places. Thus with an inflated influence medium, doubters tended to be identified as lacking loyalty deserving treatment with deflated power. And "hence to camp with him, who constituted a threat to solidarity."

Now it can be observed that in both the American and the recent German value formulas, the secondary value theme involved a societal image higher in the control hierarchy, i.e., one where experience and action were symbolized as more tightly integrated than in the image given first priority. Therefore a generalization covering these two and similarly constituted cases may be suggested. It is this: "under stress, current primary symbols of societal association are being exchanged in relevant areas of concern with the respective cybernetically higherplaced patterns." Secondary value themes always function to provide a kind of security backup for primary themes. Just as "disturbed" Americans may attempt to find security by reverting to the "mechanicalized" *Gemeinshaft* solidarity of their Pilgrim forefathers, the German elites "went back" into the deceptive security of their unperverted *Gemeinschaft* patterns. The crucial difference is that the Pilgrims had universalist commitments which can be floated in the public realm. But the Germans had to rely on a reserve of genuine, not "mechanicalized" *Gemeinschaft* commitments, which cannot be floated in the public realm of a modern society.

Two further aspects of deflation in societal commitments deserve emphasis, however. First, this is not just a phenomenon operating at the individual level. When such symbols deflate, legitimacy beliefs relevant for the extant level of differentiation in society lose in consensus on shared meaning content. In Germany as the war progressed, nobody was a Nazi anymore in any identifiable way because there was too little agreement left as to what Nazi status might entail. Thus the security service became a police, the SS an army, and the party an administrative bureaucracy. "Security" legitimacy beliefs concerning societal association were "remobilized" because only these retained a semblance of shared meaning after the radical symbols of the New Order had become no more than "word-salad" through propagandistic over-use. Second, it might be observed that such "sliding back" into the relevant gold base of primary societal values involves forms predominantly, not necessarily content. In the American case, given the universalism inherent in intrinsically deflated *Gemeinschaft* symbols, the actual content of deflated messages might cover the whole range from "revolutionary New Leftist" conceptions to a "nationalist Rightist" response to strain.

The essential difference in political consequences between these two cases seems to be this: Apparently America can afford her proverbial "pendulum-swing" political history with somewhat more than a mere chance expectation of finding herself ending up somewhere near the center. Germany cannot. The reason seems to be that for this kind of problem — the meaning of societal solidarity as constituted — a return to some "mechanicalized" *Gemeinschaft* security base *from* an experience of adaptive commitments having "gone out of hand" would appear to be potentially far more adaptive than a return into solid *Gemeinschaft* security in response to strain in Corporate *Gesellschaft* commitments. There are two features in the former case presenting an inherent chance to solve the problem. First, remobilizing "security commitments" here involves the "antonym function" most directly under stress through "overstrain" in Organic Association. Second, because of the mechanical elements in the secondary *Gemeinschaft* symbols, the chance for solution is heightened because these permit the relevant questions to be raised in the adequate arena, the public sphere. Because the dispute can circulate there, sooner or later precisely that medium most necessary to push a right or left drift back towards the center, influence, becomes mobilized. And influence here can be corrective because the glare of public transparency prevents it from inflating to serve mutual conceit. However, the absorption of attempts to handle a meaning problem of societal association into the relative isolation of subunits does not permit this to begin with. In this latter case a built-in self-correcting device against media conflation is missing. In Germany, it would appear as though the "handling" of this problem at the subunit level merely had further maladaptive consequences for society, although it may have been effective in the maintenance of personality stability. This, however, made available to a society bent on a maladaptive course only further personality-resources, in the form of relevant "maladaptive" role-playing capacities. In society this contributed to further inflation of the influence medium as well as further deflation of power. Trapped in this vicious circle of deflationary and inflationary trends among two media with the apparently relatively complete withdrawal from public circulation of the relevant third, societal value commitments, the society could not but go on to its bitter end.

Conclusion: A Tentative Analytical Approach to Media Conflation

Modernity implies the institutionalization of continuous structural change in society.[46] But profound change in values as structural aspects of society has to be excluded in the formulation of this widespread conception of modernity. If not, modernity would imply that societal death becomes the norm rather than the exception in just those cases usually identified as successful in survival. It is, after all, values at that general level of a rank-preference order imposed on the four functional problems which give societies their distinct identity, more commonly known as "a cherished way of life" or "the quality of life," i.e., a set of priorities that legitimate the social order. Furthermore, if change simply included everything in society, the adaptation problem would dissolve largely. If the old adage of *tempora mutantur, et nos mutamur in illis* were literally valid, there would be nothing left to pose a problem of adaptation to a changing environment. The usual critique of modernity, whether appearing in the form of an alleged reversal in the master-servant relation between technology and man or in the threat of "Americanization," clearly reflects concern with the preservation of a style of interaction, a societal identity, and indeed a call for its better implementation with the help of modern means.

Yet the rapidly expanding means base and its deployment through media brings forth two principal types of "modern social sin." One, and the more general, is to replace trust with hope. This amounts to the temptation to prefer "business in action" and delay indefinitely the hard day of judgment that is experience. Media facilitate this. They can be used in a generally inflationary way, as if men could live on credit for ever. Also, all four media are already fairly institutionalized in advanced industrial societies, but, excepting money, none have yet been developed to the point of rendering clear "measures of account" and "stores of value." Their partial institutionalization further encourages their reckless use where the rhetoric-reality gap widens. Furthermore, this inherent temptation toward inflation is partially due to "apparent reasonableness." This involves the second characteristically modern sin, the misuse of money. The tremendous trend towards increasing rationalization in the Western world so brilliantly exposed by Max Weber amounts to a net preference to use the most rational yardsticks available in legitimating social action. Relative to the other media and in measurement efficacy this is money. Men, therefore, may prefer to use money as a yardstick even in efforts which do not have the aim of making additions to a society's stock of utility. Even where the aim is to add to solidarity, collective effectiveness, or societal authenticity, men, once committed to rationalization, deploy a variety of cost-benefit analyses to measure their performance. As neither power, influence nor value commitments as media have as yet proved usable as measures of account, they use money instead. But money, designed, so to speak, to measure utility, cannot reflect adequately what it is supposed to reflect, — additions to the other realities of societal functioning. A whole host of classically modern social problems from urban renewal to delinquency prevention projects remain a mess, in part because of the use of money for ends that money alone cannot serve, particularly not when used as a measure of performance. It would appear that these two sins apply to all advanced industrial societies regardless of their values in the sense of societal identity. Nevertheless, the amount of temptation to fall prey to these sins seems to be a function of (1) values as a structural aspect of society and (2) the type of commitments medium. For it seems to be the former that "determines" the potential of conflation in the latter, and with that the conflation impact on the other three media. Let us attempt a general formulation of systematic variation in society's media conflation potential.

First, first-order function primacy in the structural aspect of values implies the existence of a normative image of the good society at the medium level that carries its particular vice. In the A-primacy case, for example, the legitimacy components of Organic Association with their stress on individualism, use of money in assigning generalized prestige, constant search for pragmatic opportunities in association, and nearly total openness to change carry the inherent vice of "rampant individualism." When carried to the extreme these commitments spell an anarchy of "reckless interest pursuits" that threatens normative integration. And it is this tendency to push implementation of value commitments as far as possible that overstrains the function-relevant medium, in this case money. One tries to do too much with it. Hence it seems that function-primacy in values as structure is associated with some inherent inflationary pressure on the function-relevant medium through an inflationary pressure on societal values as medium implicit in the demand to implement a set of value-commitments as far as possible. One other example might suffice. In the G-primacy case the legitimacy components of Corporate *Gesellschaft* with their stress on collectivism, use of power as a determinant of generalized standing, constant search for expanding national effectiveness, and intense ambivalence

toward the problem of change carry the inherent vice of driving the commitment to will to the point of a flirt with death. The constant buckling under, the incessant pressure to assert the superiority of organization here implies inflationary pressure on power. But second, how far such inflationary pressure inherent in functional value primacy and its associated societal values can go would seem to depend on the secondary value theme, the function that it stresses, and the associated societal values it holds as a "back-up reserve" for the primary commitments.

Three broad types can be distinguished here. These range from a relatively low potential in conflation through inherent self-correcting mechanisms to a high potential where such rebalancing mechanisms are absent.

The first broad type involves the kinds of value systems wherein the functions given first-order and second-order priority are "antonym functions," i.e., those arranged across the diagonal in the usual format of A-I and G-L. The self-correction potential against a general escalation of inflationary pressure upwards, or deflation down, here derives from the fact that the order in the functional areas stressed cross-cuts the double cleavage of any functionally differentiated social system, the external-internal axis and at the same time the instrumental-consummatory axis of differentiation. When the instrumentalism and externality inherent in the maximization of adaptive interests with the emphasis on saving time and social information run wild, then, here in this example, the secondary value theme mobilizes the internal consummation interests that can counterfoil the inflationary pressure among the former because of the ready availability of relevant societal belief commitments with an opposite stress on time and information use. In short, where the value structure makes available for ready disposal commitments as medium that involve the opposite functional aspects of differentiated action, mutual self-correcting balance is built in. In this broad category two sub-types can be distinguished, involving again a differential in conflation potential. This potential should be maximum in the two cases cited, the A-I and G-L combinations, because here the secondary backup theme involves societal value commitments of a cybernetically higher order than the primary theme. The legitimacy beliefs of Corporate *Gemeinschaft* involve a tighter connection between social action and experience than those of Organic Association. The same holds true for those of the Mechanical *Bund* relative to Corporate *Gesellschaft*. In the reverse cases, I-A and L-G, the fact of cross-cutting the double cleavage notwithstanding, it is the cybernetically lower media that provide the backup for the primary commitments. Therefore, despite the fact that the primary and secondary patterns again involve exactly opposite directives for time and information use, the capacity to control conflationary pressure should be somewhat lower relative to the former case. However, it should be much larger still than in the succeeding cases.

The next two broad types share one property. Here the primary and secondary value themes cross-cut only one of the two cleavages inherent in functional differentiation, either the instrumental-consummatory axis or the external-internal axis. The second broad type then involves a primary and secondary stress on "horizontally adjacent" functions in the usual format, on either the external side or the internal side involving A and G or I and L. The only cleavage cross-cut is the instrumental-consummatory axis. In the primary and secondary patterns there are only opposite instructions for the use of time. But this cleavage is still more inherently parallel to the general one involved in the differentiation of action and experience than the external-internal cleavage. Hence cross-cutting it constitutes a somewhat greater potential for conflation control than the last broad type to be considered. Parallel to our subtypology in the first case, the A-G and I-L combinations should prove superior in controlling conflation than the reverse combinations of G-A and L-I because the former two pairs utilize a cybernetically higher medium as a backup security on first-order commitments, while the latter two reverse that order. This should hold of course for all media. It is easier for power to control money than the reverse and again easier for societal value-commitments, particularly those quite closely related to a sense of authenticity, to control influence than the reverse.

Finally the last broad type involves a differential primary and secondary stress on functions "vertically adjacent" in the usual format, A-L, L-A, and G-I, I-G. Here primary and secondary value themes cross-cut only one functional cleavage, the external-internal. In the primary and secondary patterns there are only opposite instructions for the use of information. Both most stressed commitment patterns are also on the same side of the consummatory-instrumental axis. Hence there is no correction capability on the time variable. This should be the most conflation-prone arrangement within the range of variation here considered.[47] When instrumental interests start running wild, i.e., when action is emphasized and experience indefinitely delayed and no one takes time, there is little of potency here in ready reserve that involves the opposite, and vice versa. The control potential hinges entirely on perceived incompatabilities between the pursuit of internal and external

imperatives, i.e., opposite commands for information use. These tend to be ignored with merely apparent impunity in the short run far easier than incompatabilities between instrumental and consummatory aspects of action. The classic political example is of course the use of the "foreign relations imperative" for domestic political control problems and vice versa. Subtyping can of course be suggested here again on the same lines. Where the secondary societal value theme as a reserve backing takes cybernetically lower forms than the primary theme of commitments (the L-A and I-G combinations), the situation should be worse yet than in the reverse cases. Given the great structural latitude on conflation in this last broad type, however, the empirical consequences likely to flow from this distinction of subtypes are likely to be minimal. The fact that modern Germany as a nation belonged into this last broad category suggests two things. First, it sheds considerable light on the double attempt and the double failure to go all out in trying to establish a *Mitteleuropa*. But going beyond this single case, the typology itself suggests that some types of societies demand far greater skills in political guidance if they are to survive in modernity than others, because they face inherently greater conflation problems as a derivative of the very structure of their societal identity.

NOTES

1. See for example the identification of commitments deflation as restricting freedom of implementation at any level — cultural, social, and personal — and the statement that such deflationary pressure automatically propagates to influence, power and money. Further, commitments inflation is described as "making so many commitments as cannot be reasonably expected to be implemented, or as involving a discrepancy between the claims of implementation and control over operative resources." T. Parsons, "On the Concept of Value-Commitments," *Sociological Inquiry*, 38 (Spring, 1968), especially pp. 153, 154, and 157. Influence deflation was first identified as "questioning of broader loyalties to multiple groups and insisting on in-groupism," later as a "reduction of accepted information to solidly, verified information." Influence inflation has been defined as "extension of authoritative claims to situations that cannot be validated by information," and also as "declarations of intentions that will not be backed by commitments." T. Parsons, "On the Concept of Influence," *Public Opinion Quarterly*, 27 (Spring, 1963), especially p. 62; and the "Postscript" to the influence paper in *Politics and Social Structure* (New York: The Free Press, 1969), p. 434.
2. T. Parsons and N. J. Smelser, *Economy and Society* (Glencoe, Ill.: The Free Press, 1956), p. 68.
3. N. J. Smelser, *Theory of Collective Behavior* (New York: The Free Press of Glencoe, 1963), Chapter II, especially pp. 24-34.
4. T. S. Turner, "Parsons' Concept of Generalized Media of Social Interaction and its Relevance for Social Anthropology," *Sociological Inquiry*, 38 (Spring, 1968), p. 132.
5. This whole analysis is deeply indebted to the work of

Niklas Luhmann. Use has been made throughout of Niklas Luhmann, *Vertrauen* (Stuttgart: F. Enke, 1968); *Soziologische Aufklärung* (Köln and Opladen: Westdeutscher Verlag, 1970); and *Zweckbegriff und Systemrationalität* (Tübingen: J. C. B. Mohr, 1968).

6. N. Luhmann, "Die Praxis der Theorie," pp. 253-267, in Luhmann, *Sociologische Aufklärung*; R. N. Bellah, "Religious Evolution," *American Sociological Review*, 29 (June, 1964), pp. 358-374.

7. N. Luhmann, "Reflexive Mechanismen," pp. 92-112, in Luhmann, *Soziologische Aufklärung*.

8. Parsons, *Politics and Social Structure*, p. 487.

9. Parsons, "On the Concept of Value-Commitments," *op. cit.*, p. 138. It should be noted that experience can take a variety of forms. It can be formalized, generalized, gained in one situation, applied to another, and represented by all four societal media. The meaning of the term used here is not restricted to Schumpeter's usage in his ideal-typical circular flow, but it includes that meaning. I have to leave it at that, foregoing a formal definition of experience at this point.

10. Such horrid language suggests the familiar difficulty experienced by the beginner in Parsonian analysis. It is a problem of restriction in the scope of one's effort. Societal media are of course not the only ones of import. Culture and personality too clearly operate with media. As to the former there are media in science and art, and concerning the latter dreams operate as media. Furthermore, general action media have also been developed. See T. Parsons, "Some Problems of General Theory in Sociology," pp. 27-68, in John C. McKinney and Edward A. Tiryakian (eds.), *Theoretical Sociology: Perspectives and Development* (New York: Appleton-Century-Crofts, 1969). Scope seems an inescapable and often an intractable problem in action theory.

11. R. C. Baum, "Zpusoby redukovani komplexnosti v moderni spolecnosti," *Sociologicky Casopis*, 6 (1969), pp. 600-607.

12. Luhmann, *Vertrauen*, pp. 46-47. Though excluding *future* contingencies from current decision modes is the principal time-direction involved in using media with trust, it is not the only one. A *past* restriction on options can undermine the efficacy of voting for example as well. The Wilson budget of 1968 in the United Kingdom might serve as an illustration. This budget was altered and approved by officials of the IMF *before* it was submitted to parliament, a procedure that raised profoundly disquieting questions concerning the principle of "no taxation without representation."

13. Irene Taviss, "Changes in the Form of Alienation: The 1900's vs. the 1950's," *American Sociological Review*, 34 (February, 1969), pp. 46-57.

14. Erving Goffman, *The Presentation of Self in Everyday Life* (New York: Doubleday and Company, 1959).

15. Karl W. Deutsch, *Nationalism and Social Communication* (Cambridge, Mass.: The M.I.T. Press, 1966).

16. This formulation has been adapted from Claude Levi-Strauss, *The Raw and the Cooked: Introduction to a Science of Mythology*, Vol. I (New York: Harper and Row Torchbooks, 1969), pp. 15-16ff.

17. Staffan B. Linder, *The Harried Leisure Class* (New York: Columbia University Press, 1970), pp. 64-76.

18. Simon Kuznets, *Modern Economic Growth* (New Haven: Yale University Press, 1966).

19. Erwin K. Scheuch, *Massenmedien und Religion in der Freizeitgesellschaft* (Essen: Verlag Fredebeul and Koenen, 1971).

20. The source of this code aspect in conflation rests on the hierarchical contingency among codes. The code of money, the institution of property embodying the principle of the exclusive right to use and dispose over objects of utility, is of course a special case of the power code, the jurisdictional scope of office. The idea of "property as an office" prevalent among European conservatives was an explicit recognition of this fact. The power code, the scope of authority of office, is of course a special case of the influence code, the rules of justification of societal inequalities, because authority is only one form of inequality. As Parsons' earlier work on stratification emphasized (cf. T. Parsons, "A Revised Analytical Approach to the Theory of Stratification," pp. 92-128, in R. Bendix and S. M. Lipset (eds.), *Class, Status, and Power* (Glencoe, Ill.: The Free Press, 1953), the nature of the influence code in terms of its content is a result of that aspect of the societal value system manifest in a differential rank ordering of the four functional problems.

21. Kuznets, *op. cit.*

22. Parsons, "Postscript" to the influence paper, *op. cit.*

23. T. Parsons, "On the Concept of Political Power," *Proceedings of the American Philosophical Society*, Vol. 107 (1963), p. 257.

24. T. Parsons and V. Lidz, "Death in American Society," pp. 131-170, in Edwin S. Shneidman (ed.), *Essays in Self-Destruction* (New York: Science House Inc., 1967).

25. I. Weinberg, "Social Problems that Are No More," University of Toronto, Department of Sociology, mimeographed.

26. For an examination of this point related to money and power cf. James S. Coleman, "Political Money," *American Political Science Review*, LXIV (December, 1970), pp. 1074-1087. Yet such money analogies cannot be pushed too far. Victor Lidz remined me that some sound analytical reasons argue against the possibility of ever developing the measures of nonmonetary media to the ratio-scale level. Strictly in measurement terms they may be intrinsically "inferior." This does not deny that they could be improved as stores of value and units of accont. Nevertheless there may be a continuing temptation to use the most efficient measure, money, regardless of its functional limitations.

27. Parsons, "On the Concept of Value Commitments," *op. cit.*

28. Luhmann, *Vertrauen*, Chapter 3, pp. 15ff.

29. T. Parsons, E. A. Shils, and J. Olds, "Values, Motives, and Systems of Action," especially pp. 159-189, in T. Parsons and E. A. Shils (eds.), *Toward a General Theory of Action* (Cambridge. Mass.: Harvard University Press, 1959).

30. Curiously Parsons constructed such a typology most explicitly only for personality systems. T. Parsons, "An Approach to Psychological Theory in Terms of the Theory of Action," pp. 612-711 in S. Koch (ed.), *Psychology: A Science*, Vol. III (New York: McGraw-Hill Book Company, 1959). A societal typology based on the pattern variables can be found in T. Parsons, *The Social System* (Glencoe, Ill.: The Free Press, 1951), pp. 182-200.

31. Deutsch, *op. cit.*, pp. 170-172.

32. P. Blau, *Exchange and Power in Social Life* (New York: Wiley and Sons, 1967), p. 312.

33. In order to avoid coining new terms, familiar concepts from the work of Durkheim, Toennies, and Schmalenbach will be used here. See E. Durkheim, *The Division of Labor* (Glencoe, Ill.: The Free Press, 1949); F. Toennies, *Community and Society* (East Lansing, Mich.: Michigan State University Press, 1957); H. Schmalenbach, "The Sociological Category of Communion," pp. 331-347, in T. Parsons *et al.* (eds.), *Theories of Society*, Vol. I (New York: The Free Press of Glencoe, 1961). It should be kept in mind, however, that as used in the present context they stand for simple images of the good society, not for actual structural characteristics.

34. This approach to the nature of legitimacy beliefs in terms of allocating the onus of proof derives from M. J. Levy, "A Revision of the *Gemeinschaft-Gesellschaft* Categories and Some Aspects of the Interdependencies of Minority and Host

Systems," pp. 233-266 in H. Eskstein (ed.), *Internal War* (New York: Macmillan-Free Press, 1964).

35. Deutsch, *op. cit.*, pp. 181-186.

36. E. Scheuch, "Das Gesellschaftsbild der Neuen Linken," pp. 103-123 in E. Scheuch (ed.), *Die Wiedertäufer der Wohlstandsgesellschaft* (Köln: Markus Verlag, 1968).

37. D. C. McClelland, *The Roots of Consciousness* (Princeton, N. J.: D. van Nostrand Co. Inc., 1964), pp. 62-92. Concerning the unidirectionality in deflation and inflation mentioned before, it should be pointed out that this is probably a special feature of the subtypes of any functionally specialized societal medium. It should hold for Parsons' four types of influence as well. At that lower level there seems to be tighter contingency between symbolic tokens which results from the single function served. Hence this contrasts sharply with intermedia dynamics involving separate functions where conflation runs both ways, "up and down" the control hierarchy.

38. H. Arendt, *The Origins of Totalitarianism* (New York: Meridian Books, 1958).

39. R. Dahrendorf, *Gesellschaft und Demokratie in Deutschland* (München: Piper, 1965).

40. Parsons, "On the Concept of Political Power," *op. cit.*, pp. 256-257.

41. R. M. Williams, *American Society* (New York: A. Knopf, 1961), pp. 415-470.

42. H. Höhne, *The Order of the Death's Heads* (London: Secker and Warburg, 1970).

43. R. C. Baum, "Values and Democracy in Imperial Germany." *Sociological Inquiry*, 38 (Spring, 1968). pp. 179-196.

44. McClelland, *op. cit.*, p. 86.

45. W. Zapf, *Wandlungen der Deutschen Elite* (München: Piper, 1966).

46. S. N. Eisenstadt, "Social Change and Development," pp. 1-33, in S. N. Eisenstadt (ed.), *Readings in Social Evolution and Development* (New York: Pergamon Press, 1970).

47. It might be noted parenthetically that this total of 12 types considered here exhausts the range of variation in a classification based on primary and secondary functional ordering only. The complement of 12 cases to the total number of ways one can order four functions all involve variations in third and fourth rank-order of preference.

25

THE MASS MEDIA, IDEOLOGY, AND COMMUNITY STANDARDS

Harry M. Johnson

The so-called mass media, by fairly general agreement, include newspapers, radio, and television, as well as some magazines, books, and films. They all involve elaborate production technology and specialized social organizations, and they are addressed to large, heterogeneous audiences, the members of which have little direct interaction with one another or with the authors of the "mass" communications. These criteria for the mass media, however, are matters of degree. The organizations most directly involved are newspaper publishing companies, radio and TV stations and networks, book and magazine publishers, and film-producing companies. Extremely important ancillary organizations include the press associations (wire services), press syndicates (for "features"), rating services, and advertising agencies. There are also many distributing and storing organizations such as bookstores, libraries, theaters, and museums. Important in another way are schools and university departments of journalism, cinema, radio, and television. The mass media have also developed several trade and professional associations. Finally, many business firms, government agencies, universities, churches, and voluntary associations maintain public relations departments, publicity agents, or advertising departments.

As the term "community standards" suggests, we assume in this chapter that the mass media are rooted mainly in the integrative subsystem of society (the societal community). As Parsons has made clear, the symbolic medium anchored in the integrative subsystem of the social system is influence. In the first part of the present chapter, therefore, we consider the sense in which the mass media involve influence. In the second section, we consider the functions of the mass media in more detail, having in mind in particular the United States and other "free" societies. Here we also consider briefly the

possible malfunctioning of the mass media in the form of spreading ideological distortion instead of valid information. As the mass media have somewhat different functions in a totalitarian society, we compare very briefly a "free" press and a press with high government control. This selective comparison will consider the functioning of the press only in the "political support system" (the interchanges between the polity and the societal community). The functions being somewhat different, the "community standards" for the press are of course also different. In both types of system, however, community standards for the press include values and various kinds of specification (norms). In the next two sections of the chapter, therefore, we consider the social controls, in a broad sense, that operate in and over the mass media in a "free" society. At various points we consider ideology in the mass media, but in the final section we take up, briefly, ideological distortions about the mass media.[1]

INFLUENCE AND THE MASS MEDIA

In Parsons' technical sense, "influence" is one of the four generalized symbolic media that control the processes of interchange in the social system. All four media are special languages, involving "codes" and "messages." (This point highlights the fact that communication and decision making are the most general social processes). Influence is the medium anchored in the integrative subsystem of the social system. In exercising influence (i.e., attempting to persuade), "ego" (any collective unit or individual-in-role) offers a suggestion to "alter" (another such unit or individual), a suggestion to the effect that alter should do such and such, both for his own good and for the good of some collectivity or community to which both ego and alter belong or could belong. Ego does not offer an inducement to alter for compliance or threaten any negative sanction in case of noncompliance; he simply suggests that alter's situation is such that a certain course of action would be beneficial to alter and to some collectivity of which alter is a member. At least implicitly and often explicitly, ego is also suggesting that the recommended course of action is better for alter than one or more alternatives would be.

Another possible form in which influence may be exercised—a variation of the one just described—is ego's offering an *opinion* describing alter's situation in such a way that alter himself can decide which of certain specific alternative courses of action would be the best for him. For example, this is what a medical doctor does when he describes for a patient the possible and probable outcomes of two lines of treatment, say surgery and something less drastic. (Once the patient decides to engage the doctor for a certain course of treatment, then the doctor can give "orders" in a stricter sense; having exercised "influence" successfully, he now exercises "power," backed up by the contingent negative sanction of breaking the relationship if the patient disobeys him too much, i.e., refuses to cooperate.)

Influence is symbolic in at least a double sense. The suggestions or opinions of which it consists are not intrinsic "persuaders" but *stand for* a combination of presumed competence of judgment and presumed trustworthiness (i.e., loyalty to some solidary collectivity or community to which ego and alter already belong or which they might form by agreement). The corresponding *intrinsic* "persuader" would be some kind of detailed demonstration or elaborate argument showing why alter should do what is suggested. The presentation of such a detailed rationale would not be an example of the exercise of influence in the technical sense. The "influential" aspect of a doctor's suggestion or opinion rests not on the reasons the doctor may give (reasons that as stated to the patient will be quite incomplete from a "logico-experimental" point of view, to use Pareto's expression), but on the patient's belief that the doctor is competent in such matters and his trust that the doctor is giving advice in the patient's interest. As Parsons frequently puts it, influence bridges the "competence gap" between expert and layman.

Thus influence symbolizes solidarity (the value of the integrative system). It both *rests on* solidarity and *contributes to* solidarity. As Parsons points out, however, "influence" depends upon two types of commitment (or potential commitment), one more general, one more specific. The doctor's influence, for example, depends first upon his general commitment to life and health and second upon his readiness to make a commitment to contribute to this specific patient's health (a form of particularistic loyalty as distinguished from universalistic value commitment).

How does this type of analysis apply to the mass media, particularly in view of the fact that one of the chief purposes of the mass media is to provide "relevant" information? The problem arises from the fact that information, as just argued, might be supposed to have intrinsic as opposed to symbolic value. I shall argue that the organs of the mass media receive influence in the technical sense and that, in addition to transmitting the influence of other units in the social system, they create influence and exercise or "spend" it according to their own judgment (while also adhering more or less faithfully, however, to a normative *code* for the exercise of influence, a code analogous to authority for the exercise of power). This analysis, of course, is only a modest extension of Parsons' work on influence in general and on the mass media in particular.

Insofar as the mass media editorialize (that is, attempt to persuade), they are obviously exercising influence. The editorials of a newspaper, for example, may present reasons for such and such an opinion, but these reasons hardly even pretend to be adequate from a logico-experimental point of view. What does the "influential" aspect of the editorial rest on? It seems to rest on at least two bases. First, the author or authors, representing the newspaper as an organization, may be presumed to have command of at least some of the facts that are relevant to an intelligent opinion about the issue with which the editorial is concerned. After all, the chief business of the newspaper is gathering and presenting information about events of public interest. The second basis of the editorial's influence is the presumption that the editors have some loyalty to some sort of community of which the main readers are members. That is to say, the influence of the editorial rests on the presumption of competence and judgment and the presumption of solidarity. The newspaper's presumed loyal concern for the welfare of some solidary public (of course, solidary to some degree) is an aspect of the newspaper's reputation or prestige. ("Prestige" is a term for the generalized status or rank of a particular social unit or category of social units in a community of units. Prestige, according to Parsons, may be regarded as an indicator of the quantitative aspect of a unit's influence.) The prestige of a particular newspaper (or other mass communication channel) will be enhanced or reduced by its actual performances in gathering and reporting the "news" accurately and "completely," by its courage in exposing dangers to the solidary public, by its proven judgment on issues whose outcome has become known to some extent, and by other factors to be considered. Obviously, then, the worth or effectiveness of the newspaper's *loyalty* to the public depends upon the more general commitment of its staff to the value of cognitive rationality (its effort to live up to the criteria of objective truth and fairness).

But it seems to me that the "influence" of the mass media is not confined to their editorial content or even to editorial content and the interpretation of the news, which also is meaningful only within a context of presumed loyalties and interests. There is an inescapable element of influence even in the reporting of "straight news." I am not now referring to the allegedly irreducible element of bias that is perhaps present in all reporting and that may be due to all sorts of conscious and unconscious extraneous factors. What I am referring to, rather, is the inescapable fact that it is impossible to gather and present all the news. Selection is absolutely inevitable. Part of the influence of the mass media, it seems to me, is based on the presumption (more or less well founded in particular cases) that the newspaper or other organ is attempting to select on the basis of what will be "of interest" to its particular audience. Thus, an item that might or might not find a little spot in *The New York Times,* according to the exigencies of the actually limited though apparently ample space available in that paper, might "have" to be published, as it were, in some much smaller and purely local paper such as the Champaign-Urbana *Gazette* or *Courier.* This would be true of, let us say, a teachers' strike in Champaign. Thus, the completeness of coverage of a particular mass communication channel will depend upon the extent and character of its main audience (the public or publics it serves). The community or public that an organ of the mass media serve may be local, regional, national or worldwide; and it may be narrow or broad in its common interests.

What to include and exclude depends on integrity, loyalty, knowledge, and judgment: integrity in the sense of commitment to truth and fair play, loyalty to this particular public, knowledge of the interests and needs of this public and knowledge of its average capacity to understand, and judgment with regard to the relative importance of all the items competing as it were for inclusion. It is impossible for the newspaper or other channel of mass communication to present in detail to its audience all the reasons for its particular selection in each issue or broadcast. The very attempt to present those reasons would defeat the purpose of the selection in the first place. The "competence gap" discussed by Parsons (which is also involved in the relation between the mass media and their publics) is a specific aspect of the general pressure to economize on time and effort—in short, to preserve the benefits of the division of labor. The patient may be as bright as the doctor and might be able eventually to understand a comprehensive explanation, but there would be no competent doctors or lawyers or bakers or candlestick makers if we all insisted on such comprehensive explanations. Moreover, in some cases, of course, the patient is not so bright as the doctor and would never be able to understand. Similar remarks apply to journalism (in a broad sense). Thus trust must be involved. In the case of journalism it is a large element, as the reader or listener has little or no immediate indication of the relative success of the journalist's report (as he does for example with respect to a wristwatch, which at least roughly "goes" or not, whether or not he can understand why). Thus when we take seriously even the news or reporting aspect of the mass media, let alone the editorial aspect, we are submitting to "influence."

It is because of the enormous part that influence plays in the mass media that the identity of news and opinion *sources* is generally important. In the United States at least, the name of the publisher and certain other facts about the "channel" as source of news and opinion must be made public. More important, probably, than a newspaper's own editorial opinions, are the opinions it reports as part of the news. *Whose* opinion is being reported is important, because if this source is not known the reader cannot properly judge how much weight (or influence) he should allow the opinion to have. He will be more inclined to be guided in his own opinions and action by the opinions and news emanating from a known and trusted source, and he will probably be more inclined to distrust as "propaganda" the opinions and even the "facts" emanating from an unknown or a distrusted source (one with which he feels little or no solidarity).[2] Hence one constantly finds in the mass media references to the sources of opinion and to the sources of news. "According to official spokesmen at the 3rd Army headquarters," "reliable sources in the White House," "our own correspondent on the scene," "Senator So-and-So said. . .," "a usually reliable source indicated. . ."—such phrases are quite common.

Moreover, newspapers ordinarily refuse to sell space for political advertisements or for the expression of controversial opinion unless the source can be printed. We are all somewhat indignant upon finding out that information or opinion apparently coming from one source actually came from another for which the first was only a "front." We are even fussier: there was a scandal when it was revealed that the CIA had been secretly and indirectly supporting certain "cultural" publications with funds. It made no difference that the publications were generally acknowledged to be of high quality.[3]

The mass media customarily not only give the

source of news and opinion but also mention the audience to which an opinion was addressed and the occasion upon which it was uttered. These facts are also important for enabling the reader or listener to judge how much influence he should allow the opinion to have. The reason is that we want to know to whose solidarity the speaker was presumably committed and how much consideration the speaker had presumably given to his utterance. These circumstances, we assume, to some extent guided the selection of facts and interpretations. The mass media exert influence by transmitting more or less legitimately selected news, and an important category of news is the expressions of opinion (attempts to persuade or to use influence) of known sources other than the mass media themselves, sources that are presumed to have various kinds and degrees of competence, various kinds of specialized value commitments, and various loyalties to specific publics ("solidary" collectivities, status groups, or social categories). One of the most important aspects of the media's commitment to truth, therefore, is their accuracy in reporting the opinions of others. It goes without saying that this accuracy is a matter of degree, varying from one organ to another. The pressure of time under which the mass media labor often contributes to inaccuracy. To some extent, the more responsible organs make up for lapses by publishing corrections.

It was said above that the mass media receive an "income" of influence and then "spend" it. Some aspects of this process can be brought out by considering the interchanges, not between functional subsystems of the social system, but between specific organizations in the publics of the mass media, on the one hand, and specific mass-media organizations, on the other. In this discussion we have in mind for the moment the mass-media system of the United States. It will be convenient to consider first the interchanges between organs of mass communication, on the one hand, and business firms and other organizations in their capacity as advertisers in the mass media, on the other. Then we may consider the interchanges between the mass-communication organs and all the other collectivities that compose their publics or audiences. Concretely, of course, these collectivities include some organizations that advertise in the mass media. We might say that virtually all collectivities in society are part of the clientele of the mass media in general, insofar as they "consume" the information and opinion "produced" by the mass media, but that some collectivities are part of the clientele in another sense, in that they use the mass media as channels for advertising and thus help in producing some of the information that "consumers" in general are looking for.

Newspapers and most magazines depend upon advertising for funds. They can afford to sell copies at a low price, and thus reach a larger audience, only because advertisers pay for "space." Radio and TV stations can provide programs "free" to the public only because advertisers pay for "time." "Space" and "time" here mean essentially the opportunity to present an advertising message to an audience of a size and with social characteristics more or less well known in each case.

The interchange between mass-communication organs and the "consuming" units has two principal aspects. In the more obvious aspect of the interchange, the subscriber, newsstand buyer, or wireless listener or watcher spends time and often money in return for information, opinion, and entertainment. He pays directly for his subscription to newspaper or magazine, of course, but he also helps to pay for it indirectly by buying the products it advertises. (In some cases, advertisements in newspapers and magazines that must be answered by mailing a coupon contain a code indication of the organ and the specific issue, so that advertisers can tell which ads in which media and organs were the most effective.)

In a perhaps less obvious but equally important aspect of the interchange, the members of the public are able to receive information and opinion only if they in general are willing to *give* information and opinion. As we have seen, the mass media collect and transmit or broadcast. In one sense the willingness to give information and opinion is part of the price the public has to pay for the benefits of the mass media. But in another sense the organs of mass communication are of course providing the collectivities (and individuals) in their publics with the opportunity to extend or amplify their influence. The organs of mass communication must of course seek news from various sources, but many organizations, eager to provide information about themselves, maintain public relations departments. There are well over 100,000 voluntary organizations in the United States, and many of them write letters to editors of newspapers and magazines (especially newsmagazines).[4] These are formal representations, but of course any individual may send a letter to an editor, a letter that will by some readers be taken to represent informally some segment of public opinion. The prestige (hence influence) of a mass-communication organ depends, in part, upon the prestige of the writers of these letters, who are frequently identified not only by name but by their occupation or even their specific position. Some people are as much interested in the letters printed in *The New York Times* as they are in any other news items or features.

More generally, however, the prestige of an organ of mass communication (hence its influence) depends to some extent upon the average prestige of its audience. Not all readers write letters to the editor. The enormous prestige of *The New York Times* rests partly on the fact that its readers are known to include a large proportion of the most important and influential individuals in the United States and indeed the world. The *size* of an organ's audience is also a factor in its prestige, but hardly more important than this factor of average "quality" (in terms of social prestige).

A channel of mass communication may be "independent" or it may be the special organ of some collectivity such as a political party or a church. Being affiliated as against being independent has an advantage and a disadvantage. The advantage is that for a special audience it is likely to have more influence. The disadvantage is that it may be less able to mediate between the various groups of which a pluralist society is composed. Influence, as Parsons says, is a circulating medium, but for any particular source of influence the size of the "market," so to speak, varies.

Thus the influence of a channel of mass communication derives from at least five interdependent factors: (1) its reputation for competence and integrity (commitments to values of cognitive rationality and fair play and to the welfare of one or more publics), (2) the quality of the contributions made to it by members of its audience, (3) the size of its audience, (4) the average prestige of its audience, and (5) the number and diversity of the publics it reaches.

These factors are also important for its ability to sell advertising space or time. Advertisers watch closely the Nielsen ratings of television programs. Newspapers and magazines must submit to an impartial audit of their circulation figures by the Audit Bureau of Circulations, and the Bureau wants to know how many subscriptions are fully paid and how many are low-cost subscriptions. The assumption is that subscribers who pay the full amount are more likely to be really interested in the publication and to read it. The channels of communication, when advertising themselves to prospective buyers of advertising space, emphasize the size of their circulation (if it is large) and the average education and income of subscribers (if the facts are impressive). At the same time, the conferral of prestige may be two-way: the advertiser buys some of the influence of the communication channel, but the latter may also profit to some extent from the prestige of its advertisers. A relatively small or rising channel of communication will no doubt feel that its prestige has been enhanced if an important company pays for space or time. This is not only a matter of financial income.

Not every attempt to persuade succeeds. The measure or indicator of success is not the same for all types of influence. A doctor's influence in general is measured by the number and prestige of his clients and by the number and prestige of the other doctors who consult him or his publications. A doctor can often know which particular persons he has influenced; for example, a person who becomes his patient has obviously accepted his influence (although in many cases it is really the influence of the profession or a hospital rather than of a particular doctor). The success of a newspaper or other organ of mass communication cannot be measured precisely. Even the success of the influence of a candidate for political office has at least a fairly precise aggregate measure in the relative number of votes he wins. The voters are persuaded in part by sources of influence other than the candidate himself, but these other sources are in part transmitting the influence of the candidate, which "circulates" among those who are exposed to it. A newspaper, however, can seldom be sure how many readers, in how many choices, were influenced how much by reading it, for all the readers were presumably exposed to its influence on many choices and to many other sources of influence on each one. The best over-all indicators of a newspaper's influence are probably the size of its circulation and the social composition of its readership, followed by the total monetary value of its sale of advertising space. These are only rough indicators, however.

In the foregoing discussion we have, following Parsons, deliberately used the term interchanges rather than exchanges. The term interchange is appropriate where one or more of the four generalized symbolic media are involved and the exchanges are indirect. A member of the public does not send a letter to the editor in return for a specific and measurable effect on the rest of the public, either of the letter itself or of the channel's transmission of it. When he gives information to an inquiring reporter, his *immediate* payoff may actually be outweighed by the nuisance of having to give his time; and if he derives benefit from information he receives from the press, it will probably be information supplied by some other reporter, perhaps in a different publication. But, above all, when he buys a newspaper, he does not insist on being shown absolutely all the evidence that would be necessary to convince a fanatical skeptic to accept the information as genuine. Moreover, the element of trust is especially remarkable (that is, requires analysis) because he extends this trust to people who are strangers to him personally. He knows (if he thinks about it) that sometimes he will be wrong to accept a particular item, but he goes on assuming that on the whole he is better informed than he would be if he (and everybody else) did not have the mass media. He also knows (if he thinks about it) that the system of the mass media, like the monetary system, could certainly be improved.

Although an organ of mass communication certainly creates influence by inviting an income of influence and then using its own aggregate prestige, this creation of influence should probably be distinguished from its function of merely transmitting the influence of specific other sources. By reporting the opinions of others, the mass media certainly extend or amplify the influence of these opinions. But it is important to understand that this amplification is not quite the same thing as creating influence out of whole cloth. For example, the mass media certainly amplified the influence of Senator Joseph McCarthy when they reported the Senator's irresponsible utterances regarding alleged Communists in the State Department and in other sensitive posts in American society; but the public utterances of Senators are rightly regarded as important news, as Senators, by virtue of the position they already have, have a great deal of prestige, hence influence. The same statements, if they had been made by some obscure inmate of a mental hospital, would have been rightly ignored by the mass media. To ignore McCarthy's statements, however, would have been a gross breach of trust. In the McCarthy case, the public was already predisposed to seek scapegoats and to distrust certain public officials.[5]

Nevertheless (or perhaps all the more), the mass media (or some organs) were certainly at fault in failing to counteract adequately the known falsehood of McCarthy's utterances by reporting corrective results of independent investigations. It was at first possible, of course, that McCarthy had information not available to the press, but as time went on it became reasonably clear, at least, that McCarthy would have produced hard information if he had had any. Herbert J. Gans has recently remarked that the mass media sometimes err by injudiciously drawing the line between reporting the news and commenting upon it.[6] It is probably true that journalists today more often accept the responsibility of correcting distortions in the news and opinions they transmit. Even in the McCarthy case, it was the televised Army-McCarthy hearings that finally made the public at large aware of McCarthy's untrustworthiness.

The distinction between reporting (giving information) and either interpreting or editorializing is of course an important one, and professional journalists rightly try to let the audience know which is being conveyed at any particular point, a report of news, the organ's interpretation of it, or an expression of the organ's opinion about it. Strictly speaking, as Parsons says, influence involves an attempt to persuade; therefore, the reporting of straight news is not use of influence on the part of a channel of information, although it may involve amplification of some other unit's influence. As Parsons remarks, *all* the functions of the action system require communication of information. Only some of this information should be regarded as being involved in influence. There remains, however, the irreducible element of selection of news, to which we referred above.

To some extent, it may be true that journalists are becoming more aware of their duty to expose distortions in the news reported. This is a very complex matter, however. The complexity may be brought out with reference to another case. When a professor of psychology at a leading university published a technical article in a leading technical journal, in which he argued that there may indeed be real differences in intelligence between races, despite preponderant expert opinion to the contrary, the appearance of the article was rightly regarded as "news," for two reasons. First, as we have just mentioned, the preponderance of expert opinion (which in a sense is no longer news and is often simply taken for granted) is (briefly) that average differences in I.Q. between "Negroes" and "whites," for example, are *not* due to biological factors. Second, the "new" opinion came from a reputable source (a professor at the University of California at Berkeley) and was published in a reputable journal (*The Harvard Educational Review*).

In this situation, I think that professors of journalism would probably agree that the mass media should have reported the maverick opinion but also, at the same time and in the same place, should have alerted all readers to the fact that most experts do not agree with it and should have given prominent space to the views of this large majority of experts. Moreover, the mass media should have made clear that even if the opinion should ultimately turn out to be true it would in no way justify making *a priori* judgments about particular individuals of any race nor would it justify social practices such as "racial" segregation in schools. The justification for this procedure is that the mass media amplify influence and have the responsibility of seeking truth and serving the interests of "the community." The potential damage and injustice to Negroes, for example, in reporting the professor's news-worthy but highly controversial views demanded extremely careful handling of that news item. Some organs of mass communication showed better judgment than others.[7]

A question that continually arises in connection with the mass media is the extent to which they create events. Rivers and Schramm provide us with several examples in their book *Responsibility in Mass Communication*.[8] They believe that the mass media contributed to the development of the various conspiracy theories after the assassination of President John F. Kennedy in Dallas, Texas, in 1963. These theories were more than academically significant because they tended to undermine confidence in the integrity and good faith of high officials. According to Rivers and Schramm, the mass media provided ammunition for the conspiracy theoreticians simply by reporting "all" of the "facts" without always checking beforehand the accuracy of the reports they received on the spot. How many shots were fired? What kind and make of gun was used? In the initial confusion of the tragedy, reports made in good faith often differed. Two of the persons most directly involved, Governor John Connally of Texas and his wife, gave reporters differing statements about the exact location of the moving car at the time of the shooting—and both statements turned out to be inaccurate. This case brings out the extreme difficulty the responsible journalist faces in his attempt to carry out the commitments underlying influence. Ideally the journalist is trained to be skeptical about even eyewitness reports, considering the fallibility of even quite honest observers and reporters. Ideally, also, the journalist would be aware of the possible consequences for public morale of confused reports, however well-intentioned and honest.

Another case was the reporting of the Watts (Los Angeles) "race" riot while the riot was going on. The gist of the criticism of the mass media, here, is that some "news" reports (of unverified rumors, for example) may have helped to inflame passions and shops, and that even accurate reporting of ongoing events may, under specified circumstances, have inadvertently helped roving participants in the riots, who were carrying hand radios, by letting them know just where they could operate with maximum destructiveness and impunity. Thus the magnitude of the riot and to some extent its specific course were affected by the operations of the mass media—the spreading of rumors, which became self-fulfilling prophecies, and the spreading of accurate information about the location of the police. These criticisms of the performance of some organs of mass communication, like the criticisms of their handling of the Kennedy assassination, have led not only to greater sensitivity to the pitfalls of reporting but also to the formulation of more specific guidelines for the future.[9]

But these are fairly special types of case, however important. The unwitting provision of material for weaving ingenious speculations, as in the conspiracy theories, which of course were partly inspired also by ideological preconceptions, is not the main activity of the mass media. Nor do the mass media *typically* guide the course of events as in the riot case—thus

in a sense putting into the hat the rabbits they then solemnly pull out and exhibit. However, the more typical role of the mass media in reporting events and opinions and in transmitting and so amplifying influence does indeed help to shape events.

The discussion about whether or not the mass media create events can easily become confused. To create events may mean either to report actual events inaccurately or to bring about the occurrence of actual events. It might be helpful to say a few words about each of these possibilities.

No one would deny that the mass media sometimes report events inaccurately. In the United States this is probably due more often to ignorance and error than to deliberate policy. Perhaps a good example, referred to by Daniel Boorstin,[10] was the TV coverage of the parade for General Douglas MacArthur in Chicago in 1951, after MacArthur had been relieved of his command in Korea for his failure to keep his military action within limits that had been set by President Harry S. Truman. Apparently the TV coverage exaggerated the degree and extent of enthusiasm for MacArthur that the crowd in Chicago showed. Some observers complained that if you were in the crowd you might have had a dreary time trying to keep awake or trying to see something. We must be careful, however, not to equate the "real" event with what any one observer on the spot might have been able to see. One of the great advantages of the mass media, from which we all presumably benefit much of the time, is that they can bring large teams of observers to bear on the presentation of events from many different vantage points. The TV viewer may have the visual and auditory benefit of several vantage points while the event is taking place, plus the benefit of a running commentary from someone more knowledgeable than he is. Nevertheless, it is certainly possible, even probable, that the TV producers, perhaps anxious to make a dull event more entertaining, perhaps eager to pay tribute to a general who had given notable service to his country in times past and who might now be chagrined at the end of his military career, did make the parade appear more exciting and the crowd more enthusiastic than they were in reality.

Some years later in the same city the TV producers gave their audience a view of the Democratic Convention that was to contribute a great deal toward changing American political life thereafter. One could not reasonably say, however, that the reporters produced a pseudo-event, for what they showed and described were indeed aspects of what went on in Chicago in November, 1968. In my opinion, Boorstin goes much too far in his exposé of the alleged deterioration of the mass media, an exposé heralded in the title of the first chapter of his book *The Image*, to wit, "From News Gathering to News Making: A Flood of Pseudo-Events." In this chapter Boorstin seems to be deploring not only image-building and ghost-writing but all publicity releases, all planned interviews, arranged debates, news leaks, trial balloons, and even background stories. Boorstin's interpretation is that God does not make enough events for newsmen, so the latter must create pseudo-events. Another possible interpretation, however, is that the multitudinous events that occur regardless of the participation of newsmen are too many and too complex to be understood without analysis, interviews ("spontaneous" or arranged), and even press handouts.

As we shall see, the journalists who are seeking to be socially responsible try to maintain a critical attitude toward all sources of news, including the sources they seek out themselves. It is now obvious to professional journalists that the "facts" do not speak for themselves, however many of them one might gather. If the mass media could be criticized for the handling of the 1968 Democratic Convention, they might be criticized for not having provided *enough* background and for not helping the public to see the event in enough perspectives. Another perspective on so-called pseudo-events might be given by considering the functions of the mass media.

FUNCTIONS OF THE MASS MEDIA IN A "FREE" SOCIETY

Communication, in its widest sense, is of course much broader than the mass media; it is involved in all the interchanges of the action system as a whole. The term mass media refers to the differentiated complex of collectivities, with their physical plants, that specialize in mass communication. The functions of the mass media in this sense are still very broad. We might begin by saying a few words about functions in the general action system, then turn to the social system in somewhat greater detail.

Readers of Parsons will remember that in the general action system the social system is only one of four primary subsystems.[11] Each of these subsystems, in turn, has four subsystems of its own. Moreover, each subsystem of the general action system has its characteristic symbolic medium, which is involved in the interchanges between that subsystem and the other three subsystems of the general action system; and, in turn, each subsystem of the *social* system also has its characteristic symbolic medium, which of course is involved in the interchanges between that subsystem and the three other subsystems of the social system. All these interchanges — those within the general action system and

then those within the social system — have functions for both members of each interchanging pair of subsystems. All the symbolic media are subject to more or less strict normative regulation. (Thus the basic concepts of the theory of action — action system and subsystem, function, process [interchange], structure [regulation], and symbolic medium are of course closely interrelated. The units that take part in the functional interchanges vary, of course, according to the particular type of system or subsystem being considered. The units of *social* systems are more-or-less specialized collectivities or roles.)

The question, then, is: What are the functional contributions of mass media organs within the general action system and within the social system? I cannot answer this question in detail. I can only give some suggestive examples, in largely nontechnical terms. We have located the mass media primarily in the integrative subsystem of the social system, in which influence is anchored. In general, however, *organizations* or collectivities such as organs of the mass media are seldom if ever involved in one functional subsystem only. In fact, mass media organs are involved not only in the social system but also in the cultural.

Unfortunately, the relations between the symbolic media of the general action system and those of the social system have not been worked out in detail. There is a certain analogy between *influence* (the medium in the I position in the social system) and *affect* (the medium in the I position in the general action system). Each is integrative: *affect* in the general action system, *influence* in the social system. Both can be characterized in terms of the same combination of values of the pattern variables, namely, affectivity and quality.

Although Charles Horton Cooley did not think explicitly in terms of special circulating symbolic media, to some extent he anticipated Parsons's view that affect is the circulating medium of the social system. Noting that whatever one may mean by human nature, it will be something possessed by all human beings regardless of time and cultural variation, and something that will distinguish human beings from animals, Cooley finds this something in the capacity of human beings to have sympathy and empathy, and he says that this capacity underlies all specific affects such as love, admiration, or envy. The capacity for sympathy and empathy is not innate, says Cooley, although it does depend upon genetically grounded innate capacities such as intelligence. According to Cooley, human nature or the capacity for (meaningful) affect, comes from participation in primary groups, of which the family and neighborhood playgroups are universal examples. In one of Cooley's phrases, the primary group is "the cradle of human nature." This "human nature," moreover, is social in a double sense. It arises in social interaction in primary groups, and it underlies or makes possible all the more elaborate aspects of human societies as more or less integrated systems. In Cooley's words, human nature is "the primitive phase of society."[12]

Most sociologists would agree with Cooley that the capacity for affect, which of course underlies affect itself as the basic circulating medium anchored in the social system, derives largely from experience in primary groups. Cooley also emphasizes, however, that the capacity for sympathy (his "human nature") is not equally strong in all adults. It has to be renewed and cultivated. Presumably it is for this reason that among the prototypical primary groups (that are the cradle of human nature) Cooley includes, along with the family and the playgroup, the neighborhood group of elders. It might be added that one of the basic functions of art in its symbolic aspects is to extend and refine the imagination — in other words, the capacity to take the role of the other, the capacity for affect (socially meaningful feelings, as distinguished from genetically determined physiological energy, to which affects give form and direction). It is obvious that whatever the artistic merits of mass media entertainment may be, it makes a highly general contribution of the sort Cooley had in mind in his treatment of primary groups. The production of works of art, even of so-called horse operas or soap operas, is cultural, and in analyzing their social effects one is discussing the relations between the cultural system and the social system.

One of the most common forms of ideological distortion within a society and between societies is more or less gross misunderstanding and misrepresentation of the motives of one unit by another. Some whites, for example, perceive black nationalists, especially if the latter use violent rhetoric, as little better than thugs, while the black nationalists perceive themselves as righteously indignant and rationally disenchanted with whites' hypocritical value commitments. It is obvious that mass media entertainment and art could do much more to reduce this kind of ideological distortion; but many film makers, for example, do accept this responsibility and discharge it according to their lights. Many film critics, moreover, are obviously conscious of this aspect of films. On the other hand, there is no doubt that the popular art purveyed in the mass media also diffuses and confirms ideological distortions. It is difficult to tell what the net effects are, for the mass media as a whole or for any particular work, say a film. Simple content-analysis would not be enough: one would have to study the actual responses of audiences. There is no reason to believe, moreover, that different segments of the audience react in the same way.

We may take as an example the film *Little Big Man*, directed by Arthur Penn. (The name Little Big Man is given to the white non-hero by his friend, a Cheyenne chief). By showing the arrogance and ruthlessness of white Americans when they took the land away from the Indians, the film perhaps helps to gain political support for efforts to do something good for Indians now. On the other hand, the murderousness of whites in the film is not very well motivated: Is it possible that the message evokes defensiveness in some members of the audience? Ambiguity more or less pervades the film. The makers have a hilarious time satirizing many aspects of frontier life, leaving it ambiguous whether we should extend the satire to present American society. Thus, religion is presented as repulsive hypocrisy and prudishness. Family life is shown only in revolting examples (the minister and his wife, Little Big Man's sister's attempt to create a "home" for him). Free enterprise is presented as a matter of deceit and greed (the panacea huckster, who later takes part in destroying the Plains in his mad greed for buffalo skins). In highly entertaining scenes the cult of masculinity and guns is exposed and ridiculed. Alcoholism (another aspect of fake masculinity?) is presented as a white man's disease, which he spread to the Indians. Before that the Indians only smoked the peaceful pipe together (like smoking pot?). A nymphomaniac prostitute would make a *good* senator's wife, the hero thinks.

All this is great fun, if you don't take it too seriously; the question is: How do various segments of the public actually take it? There are some indications that the makers of this film sympathize with hippie culture or perhaps are trying to win the approval of hippies. The "simple" Indians are idealized to some extent. By contrast with the hypocritical whites, they enjoy sex frankly and are tolerant toward homosexuality. Indian family life is pictured as humane and peaceful (the one shrew is a white woman, ironically captured in an ambush). The Cheyenne chief has the ability to see into the future in his dreams. To be sure, the Indians have minor faults: The old chief is harmlessly prejudiced in that he thinks whites are ugly-looking; he is also undogmatically, even lovably superstitious and gullible (he is easily convinced that he has become invisible, and he believes that "Snake" women have intercourse with horses). An Indian brave, humiliated as a young man, nourishes his vengefulness for years and finally lets out a bloodcurdling cry of rejoicing when he becomes free to kill the man who (unwittingly) has humiliated him; the old chief smiles, puffing his pipe, and remarks sympathetically that the brave is going out to dance his joy.

Again, how the fictional Indians will on balance strike various segments of the audience is a question. Deep in the film, obsured by the fashionable propaganda, so deeply buried that they may not even have been intended, are some "lessons" of universal value. One of these lessons is that hatred and cruelty tend to breed hatred and cruelty, in a vicious circle or a self-fulfilling prophecy: The film shows in conscientious gory detail the "genocide" committed by whites, but it does touch (much more lightly, to be sure) upon the cruelty of the Indians also; they gleefully trap Custer's men and wipe them out in revenge. The Cheyenne (like many other primitive peoples) call themselves the human beings, but when the wise old chief remarks that the human beings are few, perhaps we are supposed to apply his remark not only to the Cheyenne. Indeed, the very name of the film, after the decent but terribly fallible hero, perhaps applies not only to him but to human beings in general, who in all societies tend to be "little big men." *If* such points as these "get across," this film might make a contribution to the "human nature" of the audience. Only careful, controlled investigation could answer our questions.

Another example: In *Little Big Man*, the old Cheyenne chief reacts to a reference to the Negroes: "The Negroes!" he says (I am recollecting roughly), "Oh, yes, the *black* white men! They're not so ugly as the whites, maybe, but otherwise they're about the same." This remark to the white "hero" about blacks may be supposed to carry some weight symbolically, in that the old Indian chief (as a fictional character, of course) speaks from a point of view relatively neutral as far as black-white relations are concerned. The remark is a small joke, of course, in that the red man on the one hand confirms the fairly common belief in the solidarity of the "colored" races vis-à-vis the whites, with his judgment that whites are "ugly" (merely ugly-looking or just plain ugly?), but on the other hand, with unconscious irony disconfirms it by treating whites and blacks as essentially alike from the Indian's point of view. The chief's remark has a message both for those whites who exaggerate the differences between themselves and blacks and for those blacks who imagine that "white" culture is alien to them and that culturally they are "really" African, or at least should be.

It should be obvious that this informal functional analysis of one example involves treating the mass-media organizations ("channels" or "organs") as both cultural and social in the technical senses of the theory of action. Insofar as the mass media aid in socialization, they contribute to the social system

and to the personality. They do contribute to socialization directly in TV programs for children, for example, and indirectly by offering advice to parents. Most sociologists would agree, I think, that other communications are more important in socialization. The effect of TV programs on children has, however, been a major focus of concern. The mass media also affect personality, of course, in other ways than by socialization in a narrow sense.

In an early paper, Parsons treats the mass media as the integrative subsystem of the community, where the latter is defined as those aspects of the social system that have to do with the behavioral organism (and, through the behavioral organism, with the physical environment).[13] This early paper was an attempt to tie together the four-function scheme with the traditional concept of community as a *local* group of some kind. Thus, the residential aspect of family life connects physical location with pattern maintenance; the territorial aspect of the political organization of societies connects physical location with the goal-attainment system; and, finally, the place of work connects physical location with the adaptive system. It is my impression, however, that Parsons in later works has adopted a somewhat different conception of community. Now he uses the term community with emphasis on *Gemeinschaft* (solidarity and integration). Thus the societal community is the integrative subsystem of the society. *All* social life must be located some how in space. All interaction involves communication, and all communication involves some physical vehicle, hence some of the effectors and receptors of the behavioral organism. The mass media, as communicating systems, are of course tied to the behavioral organism, but no more than other media of communication.[14]

Both news stories and editorial comment frequently add to or detract from the reputation and prestige of individuals and collective units. There is also, of course, a social-control aspect in publicity; there can be no doubt that fear of unfavorable publicity and desire for favorable, help to keep social units within the normative order. Thus by helping to contribute "standards for allocation of affect" and "priorities for allocation of loyalties" the mass media help to shape the stratification system of society and, more broadly, all social ranking.

Somewhat similar in one aspect of its functioning is mass media advertising. It helps indirectly in the interchanges that reward entrepreneurs with profit and allocate rewards to individual and collective units for their unequally valued contributions to the social system. The products advertised in the media symbolize social prestige in many different contexts in which individual and collective units are invidiously compared. The themes stressed in advertising, and its very format and style, help to define the symbolic meaning of the products themselves. This aspect of advertising is frequently attacked, but not always realistically. What is sometimes contemptuously called "snob appeal" depends upon the fact that consumers' goods not only satisfy household needs but also have the inevitable aspect that they reveal taste and financial means. To be sure, it is well known that financial means are a very rough and imperfect indicator of the relative value of their possessors' functional contributions to society. It is also known that evidence of "good" taste can be bought by ignoramuses. Perhaps we could express this uncertain aspect of consumers' goods (which is partly an effect of mass media advertising) by saying that possession of particular consumers' goods may not *signalize* precisely what it symbolizes: That is to say, like words themselves goods not only have a somewhat unstable symbolic meaning but they may or may not indicate the actual presence or existence of the things symbolized—in this case, good taste and highly valued contributions to society. In one sense of the term, a "snob" is a person who attempts to take "unfair" advantage of this ambiguity and uncertainty. But snobbishness in this sense is a derivative, not a primary phenomenon.

The allocation of rewards of course involves some grievances and envy, but the stratification system, of which the symbolization of relative prestige is an aspect, is nevertheless primarily integrative in function. As Parsons among others has pointed out, in no social system is it likely that all the differentiated units, individual and collective, will make equally valued functional contributions. Consequently it would be regarded as unjust if they were rewarded equally. Needless to say, however, the actual allocation of rewards frequently causes a sense of grievance, produces strain in the social system, and thus leads to the reexamination of the allocation itself. This fact does not disconfirm the idea that allocation of rewards is integrative; it shows only that this integrative function is not performed once and for all but requires a continuous process.

In the legitimation system of the social system (L-G: the interchanges between pattern-maintenance and goal attainment), the major role is performed by court decisions and, perhaps, the activation of moral commitments by religious and other moral leaders; but the mass media at least report all such activities and hence amplify their effect. Radio and TV also broadcast sermons. Religious groups sometimes even buy radio time for "spot" activation of moral commitments.

In the resource mobilization system, also (G-A: the interchanges between the polity and economy), the mass media play a secondary role. Newspapers are used to some extent to advertise employment and investment opportunities, but the actual interchanges are consummated in contracts. Probably newspapers are more important than other vehicles for advertising employment opportunities, and less important for advertising investment opportunities. Similarly, in the labor-consumption market system (L-A: the interchanges between pattern-maintenance and the economy), the mass media play an important part in advertising consumers' goods. The postal system is also involved.[15]

As compared with their other functions, those performed by the mass media in the political support system (I-G: the interchanges between the integrative system and the goal-attainment system) are perhaps the most important, in the sense that the mechanisms involving the mass media are probably more important than most other mechanisms with regard to these interchanges, whereas in the other interchanges mechanisms that do not involve the mass media are relatively more important.

In the terms Parsons has made familiar, the mass media spend their influence in part by making interest demands, technically a form of influence going from the integrative system to the goal-attainment system, as a factor of effectiveness. Interest demands, it should be remembered, are not to be regarded merely as a burden or a "thorn" to the polity. Political officials may gladly accept demands as well as support. Indeed, officials frequently seek expression of interest demands and work to generate them. The news media also transmit and amplify the interest demands of other units in the societal community (or lesser integrative subsystem). By interpreting these other interest demands and putting them in the context of one another and the "news" organs' own demands, the news media also modify them to some extent. This is another way of saying that the news media play a kind of entrepreneurial role in the complex process of producing some degree of consensus among the various publics that compose the integrative subsystem of the social system.[16]

The product that the polity contributes to the integrative system, in return for interest demands, is also a form of influence, namely, leadership responsibility. This takes the form of programs and proposals for which the political leaders, whether in office or competing for office, are seeking public support in one form or another. The news media report these offers of leadership, interpret them, and by commenting upon them help to generate public response that will eventually take the shape of areas of consensus. A special type of offer of leadership, called the trial balloon, is tentative. This is a valuable mechanism because it permits political leaders to generate a public debate without jeopardizing their influence too much. The leaders can confirm their offer or abandon it, depending upon their assessment of public reaction to it. The mass media frequently help both the political leaders and their constituencies by noting the tentative nature of the trial balloon, examining its merits, and mobilizing and reporting public reaction.

The factor of solidarity that the polity contributes to the integrative system is of course a form of power—namely, binding decisions about collective goals. Here again the mass media report the binding decisions to the public (or publics), interpret them, comment upon their probable effects, evaluate them, and report the range and extent of reaction to them. The product of power that the integrative system returns to the polity is political support (in a democratic system, in the form of votes, the aggregate of which is binding upon the system as a whole). The mass media, again, play an important role by reporting the results of elections and referenda and by attempting to assess their political meaning. This is an important task since the mandate conferred by electoral victory is often less precise than the community support given in the form of interest demands (exercises of *influence* by units in the public vis-à-vis the occupants or potential occupants of positions of power defined by the institution of authority).

The chief functions of theory (such as that of Parsons) are to help to codify existing knowledge and to expose, or disclose, for further investigation problems that might not otherwise have been recognized. In closing this brief illustrative discussion of the functions of the mass media in the general action system and in the social system, we should emphasize that only elaborate empirical research could ascertain the relative importance of the mass media in the several interchange systems. The assessment in this paper is tentative and impressionistic.

Other mechanisms of communication are interdependent with the mass media. For instance, religious leaders, delivering sermons to their congregations and influencing various publics through specialized religious publications, are influenced and activated in part by their reception of mass media communications. This point will be elaborated somewhat in our discussion of social controls in and over the mass media. Before considering them, however, we should take account, however briefly, of the fact that there is considerable variation between one system of mass media and another.

DILEMMAS AND COMPROMISES

In their book *Four Theories of the Press,* Siebert, Peterson, and Schramm describe four different mass media systems.[17] The "authoritarian" system, which arose in England in the sixteenth and seventeenth centuries, forbids "criticism of political machinery and officials in power," whereas the "Soviet totalitarian" system forbids "criticism of [Communist] party objectives as distinguished from tactics"; and whereas the "authoritarian" type of system is an "instrument for effecting government policy," the chief purpose of the Soviet system is "to contribute to the success and continuance of the Soviet socialist system, and especially to the dictatorship of the party." In both types of system, the government controls the mass media very closely; but in the "authoritarian" type, ownership is public or private, whereas in the Soviet system ownership is public only. For our purpose, we can lump both systems together and refer to them as "high control" systems (i.e., systems having a high degree of government control).

The other two types of system distinguished by Siebert, Peterson, and Schramm may be called "low control" systems. The first of these, the "libertarian" type, was "adopted by England after 1688, and in [the] U.S." and has been "influential elsewhere." The second, characterized by a doctrine of "social responsibility," arose in the United States in the twentieth century. This type is still very imperfectly developed, but its main characteristics are already fairly clear. Even as it has developed thus far, it is more different from the "libertarian" type than the Soviet type is different from the "authoritarian." The "libertarian" press and, by extension, all the other mass media were open chiefly to the owners themselves, i.e., "anyone with economic means" to publish, and perhaps their chief social responsibility was to check on government. By contrast, the evolving mass-media system of "social responsibility" is in principle open to "everyone who has something to say," and the channels of communication, though still largely private organizations, must assume much wider social responsibilities. What these are will be specified hereafter, because in our discussion of the low-control type of system we shall have the present system in the United States chiefly in mind.[18]

For the purpose of simplification we can compare a system of relatively complete government control of the mass media with a system of relatively little control. To some extent we can speak of advantages and disadvantages to the government *versus* advantages and disadvantages to the public, but this is an only partly tenable distinction, as in all societies government and public are interdependent, and in the long run what is functional for the public is also functional for the government. This derives from the interdependence of the functional subsystems of society and from the fact that they compose a hierarchy of control and conditioning. The term government, however, is ambiguous. A mass-media system that is functional for the "government" in the sense that it enables the government to perform its functions better, may not be functional for the "government" in the sense of enabling a particular group of men to continue in power.

It cannot be said that one or the other of the two "ideal types" of system (great direct government control versus little) is functionally preferable under all circumstances. In particular, in a society in which one societal value system is only precariously dominant, we must expect that government will tend to be more repressive and depend more on coercion as against legitimacy and broad consensus.

All modern societies have certain things in common, among which we might mention, for present purposes, the following. First, they are all highly differentiated, and in particular even if the mass media are owned outright by the government there will still be differential responsibility for what goes into them (or through them). Second, any mass-media system is subject to normative controls of several levels of generality (or specificity). Third, in any system the government will certainly exercise *some* control, and therefore some degree of coercion will be involved in the mass media.

Nevertheless, there are of course great differences in the amount and kinds of government control. Beyond that, at least equally important is the basis of government control itself—in particular whether the government is a self-perpetuating elite of some kind or is democratically elected. This in turn will affect both the content of law and the extent to which the law may be regarded as a mechanism of control independent of the government.

There are many forms of government control of the mass media.[19] There can be control at the "consumer" end of the producer-consumer relationship, in the form of jamming broadcasts; interference with buying books, issues, or receivers; or punishment for possession of materials or equipment. But most of the controls are exercised at the "publication" end. These controls may take effect before publication or after publication. Discrimination may be exercised before publication in the form of licences to publish, subsidies, bribes, discriminatory access to important news sources, injunctions against publishing, and allocation of newsprint. All the mass media may be subject to censorship, surety bonds against libel, special taxes, and compulsory disclosure of ownership and management. As for controls exercised after publication (but of course operative as threats before publication), probably the most important are compulsory cessation of publication, seizure of published material, and prosecution for "offenses."

We may now turn to the functional advantages and disadvantages of the two "ideal types" of mass-media systems.[20]

In presenting the advantages and disadvantages of each type of system, we shall make use of Parsons' well-known LIGA scheme. L stands for "latent pattern maintenance," which has to do with continuity, stability, and change in the societal value system, the "highest" level of social structure in the hierarchy of control. In the present context, however, an L advantage to government, for instance, is an advantage to it in its relations with the pattern-maintenance system of society. The power of government depends in part on the (more or less) institutionalized pattern of authority, and the legitimation of authority depends on its consonance (or lack of it) with the dominant societal value system. Many difficult research problems are involved in this formulation, but there is no doubt of its theoretical importance. An I advantage then, will be an advantage to government in its relations with the integrative system; a G advantage, one to its own effectiveness in goal attainment and to the effectiveness of nongovernmental collectivities (upon which government may partly depend); and an A advantage, one to its relations with the adaptive system (the economy) upon which the government, like all other collectivities of the society, depends for resources.

We shall present the advantages and disadvantages of a High-Government-Control System, first to the government, then to the public. It must be borne in mind that "the government" means, here, not a certain group of men but a specialized type of collectivity. The advantages and disadvantages of the Low-Government-Control System will be evident from the discussion of the High-Government-Control System.

HIGH GOVERNMENT CONTROL OF MASS MEDIA
ADVANTAGES AND DISADVANTAGES TO GOVERNMENT AND PUBLIC

L Advantages

To government: Through use of the mass media for socialization and education, the government can promote the purity of its value system or ideology and do much to suppress "undesirable" doctrines. "Desirable" cultural standards can be maintained in entertainment.

To public: The public may indeed be protected to some extent from crackpot, frivolous, or pernicious value systems or ideologies.

I Advantages

To government: The government can mobilize public support for its policies, suppress opposition views, and prevent special-interest groups from having too much influence (from the point of view of the government).[21]

To public: There may be less confusion in the discussion of public questions.

G Advantages

To government: The government can publicize and interpret its decisions and achievements favorably, and to a considerable extent can protect the secrecy of its operations, a secrecy upon which effectiveness may partly depend. The government can also, to some extent, protect itself against "unfair" or embarrassing criticism.

To public: There may well be a certain kind of stability in government.

A Advantages

To government: If it wishes, the government can concentrate the influence of the mass media on the goal of productivity.

To public: The government's possible concern for productivity may be effective to some extent, insofar as it can mobilize support and coordinate services for this policy as for others.

L Disadvantages

To government: The value commitments of part of the population may be spurious or superficial.

To public: The government's value system or ideology may not be very popular, and people who do not agree with it may either have to risk a great deal to oppose it or have to suffer a bad conscience for their cowardice.

I Disadvantages

To government: To some extent the government may have to rely on indirect, unpleasant, and perhaps unreliable means to find out what the public is thinking (i.e., to get feedback); there may be troublesome underground movements.[22]

To public: The public may have difficulty getting more than one point of view. They may have

inadequate protection against injustice and the abuse of authority. It may be difficult to get a fair trial, also.

G Disadvantages

To government: Although ruling circles (including the government) may have considerable diversity of views, still the government will not be able to profit from the information, analysis, and advice that a more open press would make available. Moreover, being relatively unchecked by the press, government officials may yield more readily to their own worst impulses.

To public: The public may suffer from the fact that the government deprives itself of potential help and may not have, within itself, all the wisdom it needs in making binding decisions for collective goal-attainment. The public also suffers, of course, from the worst impulses referred to previously.

A Disadvantages

To government: Relatively speaking, the government will lack the benefit that can be derived from many categories of scientists and other intellectuals, who need freedom to search for truth, free communication with the world, and the sense of personal dignity that might impel them to cooperate with the government freely and enthusiastically.

To public: The public will of course also suffer from the trammeling of the professionals.

Looking at this catalog, one will be differently impressed, no doubt, according to whether or not one accepts as absolute a religious or quasireligious elitist ideology in the sense of accepting some kind of self-appointed, self-perpetuating governmental elite. The High-Government-Control System tends to be less impressive to members of the public who do not happen to approve of the existing government. Moreover, the disadvantages of the High-Government-Control System tend to be very serious for both government and public. Provided a Low-Government-Control System is possible at all, its advantages to both the public and the governmental *system* are impressive. The chief disadvantage of the Low-Government-Control System, by contrast, is that it tends to put greater demands for performance and judgment on both government and public. This is perhaps obvious as far as government is concerned. Being obliged to contend with open criticism in the mass media, government officials are kept on their toes. But the responsibility of the public is also greater. It needs more widespread and more flexible commitment to societal values (L), a greater and more widespread sense of responsibility for mobilizing support for specific collective goals (an aspect of consensus) (I), more alertness to the problems and performance of government (G), and more effort to meet high standards of cognitive rationality (rather than ideological orthodoxy) (A).

It is interesting that the historical movement from an "authoritarian" press to a "libertarian" press to a free press devoted to "social responsibility" corresponds to the development of democracy itself. Democracy provides a broader base for the support of government, and the free mass media provide a broader base for meaningful participation in the processes of consensus formation.[23] If there is a kind of evolutionary pressure toward democracy,[24] there must also be evolutionary pressure toward a "free" system of mass media. We may expect, therefore, that these will develop eventually in the Soviet Union.[25] This does not mean, of course, that anyone can predict just when this will occur; too many things in the Soviet Union itself, in the satellite countries, in the rest of the Communist world, and in the world as a whole are concretely involved.[26] But there are signs that the advantages of democracy, including a "free" mass-media system, are already beginning to be appreciated in the Soviet Union. An example is the letter addressed by two distinguished Soviet scientists and a distinguished Soviet historian to "Deeply Esteemed Leonid Ilyich [Brezhnev], Aleksei Nikolayevich [Kosygin], and Nikolai Viktorovich [Podgorny]."[27] This letter provides as cogent a statement as one can find of the I, G, and A advantages of democracy, including an open system of mass media. The value system of Communism, as opposed to the present institutional arrangements in the Soviet Union, could legitimate democracy in the sense of competing parties, free elections, a parliament with actual legislative authority, and a free system of mass media. The distinguished letter-writers stress this point repeatedly (and courageously). They ask for "a statement from the highest party and government authorities on the necessity of further democratization, on its rate and methods." They speak of the rigidity and hypocrisy caused by fear of ideological impurity and the suppression of intellectual dissent.

With regard to integrative problems, they say, "Restrictions in the exchange of information make difficult any kind of control over the leadership and frustrate the people's initiative. . . ." They propose amnesty for political prisoners and separation of the courts and the government. They propose "establishment of an institute for the study of public opinion with initially restricted but eventually complete publication of material showing the attitude of the population to the most important problems of internal and external policy." A proposal with both I and G significance is "extension of the rights

and responsibilities of the [Parliament]." Referring to goal attainment, they point out that, as a result of restriction of the exchange of information, "the top administrators receive incomplete, falsified information and thus cannot exercise their power completely. . . ."

The authors of this remarkable letter are especially concerned about the extreme backwardness of the Soviet Union in the economic realm (A), which they treat in some detail. A modern economy, they point out, demands "the creative participation of millions of people on all levels . . . ." They stress the necessity of freedom for professionals in particular: "Freedom of information and creative labor are necessary for the intelligentsia due to the nature of its activities, due to the nature of its social function. The desire of the intelligentsia to have greater freedom is legal and natural. The state, however, suppresses this desire by introducing various restrictions, administrative pressure, dismissals and even the holding of trials. This brings about a gap, mutual distrust and a complete mutual lack of understanding, which makes it difficult for the state and the most active strata of the intelligentsia to cooperate fruitfully. In the conditions of the present-day industrial society, where the role of the intelligentsia is growing, this gap cannot but be termed suicidal." Recognizing that the community of intellectuals is international, they call for "an end to the jamming of foreign broadcasts. Free sale of foreign books and periodicals. Admission of our country to the international copyright system. Gradual expansion of international tourism. Unrestricted international correspondence and other measures for the expansion of international contacts."

The functional advantages of a free mass-media system do not mean, of course, that there are no longer any problems to be solved. The struggle to break through the secretive tendency of government goes on. Government can still spend enormous amounts extolling its own achievements.[28] The perhaps excessive power and influence of advertisers could probably be brought under better control. It is still a question whether the proper balance has been attained between the rights of publishers and the needs of the general public. A relatively free system must and does have social controls, however, and to these we now turn.

EXTERNAL CONTROLS IN A FREE MASS-MEDIA SYSTEM

Although the mass-media system in the United States is relatively free, there are many pressures upon it that work to control the operation of the system, in the sense of maintaining some degree of conformity to community standards. As we have suggested several times above, these standards are themselves being sharpened as the system develops. They are summed up, however vaguely, in the phrase "system of social responsibility." Some of the controls exist as the result of conscious planning. Others are more or less inherent in the nature of American society apart from the mass media. Of whichever kind, all the controls are subject to criticism, revision, and supplementation in the light of increased understanding of how the system works out in practice. In discussing these controls, it will be convenient to distinguish at least roughly between those that in some sense operate upon the mass-media "industry" from the "outside" and those that are part of the "industry" itself. Needless to say, all the controls together do not prevent the mass media from being "bad" according to one or another point of view; they only prevent the mass media from being worse than they are as measured by the values indicated in the phrase "social responsibility."[29]

The main United States *government agency* directly concerned with the mass media is the FCC (Federal Communications Commission), which was established by the Radio Act of 1927 as a five-man commission but which in 1934 became a seven-man commission. Among its concerns are keeping down the tendency toward monopoly in radio and TV, preventing or correcting conflicts of interest, and seeking to ensure broadly fair or balanced program content in editorializing and entertainment.[30] The FCC grants and reviews licenses to radio and TV stations and assigns wavelengths ("channels"). In 1941 it published *A Report on Chain Broadcasting* and forced the Radio Corporation of America to give up some of its stations. In 1970 it announced that henceforth it will not grant a license for a radio or TV station to anyone who already has a license in the same area. It is holding hearings on a more drastic proposal: to bring about a state of affairs in which no one would own more than one station in the same urban area and no one who owns a newspaper in the area could also own a radio or TV station. Existing combinations would have to be broken up within five years.[31] The FCC has frequently been criticized for conservatism, but its activities are by no means negligible.

There are also *special commissions* of inquiry such as the Commission on the Freedom of the Press, in the United States, which published *A Free and Responsible Press* in 1947, and the British Royal Commission on the Press, which published a long report in 1947-1948.

A more remote control that helps to make government agencies responsible is a *democratic electoral*

system. It is widely believed that the widespread popular revulsion that led to President Lyndon B. Johnson's decision not to run for a second term was due in part to his lack of candor with the press. We might note, in passing, that the "credibility gap," as it was called, was revealed directly by the fact that the press faithfully reported the Administration's words about Vietnam but also reported and commented on its own. In general, the executive branches of governments usually try to conceal some of their operations from the public, but in the end democratically elected legislatures can withhold funds and in other ways exert their control. It may take a long time, of course, before popular pressure can be translated into legislation. It took from 1819 to 1855 for the British to get rid of the discriminatory taxes against the so-called penny press.[32]

General law, especially in a democratic system, is also an important control over the mass media. The relative separation of the courts from the political system, the separation of church and state, and even the system of private enterprise (the relative separation of government from other specialized collectivities)—all these partly support a free mass-media system. The law of contract and property underlies mass-media channels as well as more specifically economic enterprises. Especially relevant, however, are the laws protecting intellectual property.

The FCC is not alone in fighting against a degree of monopoly that might interfere with impartial communication of information and opinion; for example, it was mainly the activity of the Department of Justice and the Supreme Court, from 1938 to 1952, that finally brought about separation of film-producing from film-exhibiting companies.

Special law, in the sense of law applying particularly to the mass media, is a large and important topic, worthy of far more attention than I have been able to give it. We might touch upon seven especially important types of regulation in a system whose merits we are perhaps more likely to overlook or take for granted than its defects. We take for granted, for instance, the simple right of the press to criticize the government; but "seditious libel" originally designated the crime of criticizing public authority—not criticizing it unfairly, but criticizing it at all. In the United States, it was, of course, the famous case of John Peter Zenger in 1735 that changed all this, or at least that marked an important turning point. Today, if anything, the protection of public authority from even outrageous criticism depends more upon the discretion of the press than upon the courts, which are inclined to lean over backwards protecting the freedom of the press to criticize. Another important right of the press is the right of access to public records and to many legislative and public-committee proceedings. This right is sometimes hard to enforce, but it is not negligible.[33]

While the government may not withhold certain information from the press, it now appears that the courts may not require journalists to disclose information that would interfere with their getting the news and reporting it to the public. In a 1970 case, Earl Caldwell, a reporter for *The New York Times*, was subpoenaed "to produce tape recordings and notes of interviews he conducted with [Black] Panther leaders David Hilliard and Raymond (Masai) Hewitt. Caldwell refused to comply," and the attorney for him and the *Times*, Anthony G. Amsterdam, a Stanford law professor, "contended that his client's professional standing would be 'utterly destroyed' if his sources could not trust him to protect their confidence." Federal District Judge Alfonso J. Zirpoli

said he was prepared to issue a court order, if necessary, to restrict the questioning of Caldwell. In a clear attempt to define the permissible limits of government pressure on the media, the judge declared: "When the exercise of grand jury power . . . may impinge upon or repress First Amendment rights of freedom of speech, press and association, which centuries of experience have found to be indispensable to the survival of a free society, such power shall not be exercised in a manner likely to do so until there has been a clear showing of compelling and overriding national interest that cannot be served by alternative means."[34]

The special law we have mentioned so far, having to do with the right to criticize, the right of access, and the right to confidentiality, protects the functions of the mass media by imposing controls over government or the courts. Other special law protects mass-media functions by restricting the mass media themselves. An example is the vague restriction against revealing information that might endanger national security. The press is not overawed by this restriction. Another rather unpopular restriction, perhaps more with the old-fashioned libertarian type of reporter, is the newly developing right of privacy. Four types of cases are coming to be internationally recognized:[35]

1. Intrusion upon the plaintiff's seclusion or solitude, or into his private affairs.
2. Public disclosure of embarrassing private facts about the plaintiff.
3. Publicity which places the plaintiff in a false light in the public eye.
4. Appropriation, for the defendant's advantage, of the plaintiff's name or likeness.

The mass media are also restricted, of course, by the laws against libel. Finally, special laws such as the Radio Act of 1927 and the Communications Act of 1934 restrict the development of monopoly and provide the legal basis for the FCC.

As in the case of Caldwell and the Black Panthers, the efficacy of the law (general and special) is enhanced by the activity of *watchdog and legal-aid groups*, of which probably the most important in the United States is the American Civil Liberties Union.

Turning to a very different kind of control over the mass media, we should say something about *personal experience and personal contacts*. The consumers of mass communication still have all the means of communication available to people in the allegedly golden age before alleged manipulation by the mass media. We can travel, have face-to-face conversations, write letters, talk with others by telephone. Moreover, the same governments that permit a free press are less likely to restrict travel unduly, "bug" homes and offices, censor the mail, and "tap" telephone conversations, except within strict limits of law. According to the well-established "2-step flow" theory of mass communication, the influence of the mass media is to a considerable extent filtered through opinion leaders in each community.[36] There are two types of opinion leaders, "cosmopolitans" and "locals."[37] The cosmopolitans are either involved in a national or international "community" of people who are interested in some special field such as medicine, or they are concerned about world affairs in a broad sense. The first type of cosmopolitan reads in a narrow field; the second keeps up with a broader range of the communications of the mass media about a broader range of problems. As opinion leaders, both types can help people to be critical of any one mass-communications source or item. The "locals" are people who make it their business to know personally a great many others in the local community and to be familiar with their personal problems. Insofar as the mass media deal with local problems directly or touch upon matters that effect local interests, the "local" type of opinion leader helps to amplify, interpret, and perhaps modify the "information" from more distant and impersonal sources.

Somewhat similar in effect to local opinion leaders are *filter groups*, such as trade unions, churches, and many types of voluntary associations, which often produce periodicals for their specialized audiences. These publications help to provide a check on the mass media, although, as we noted, McQuail points out that the mass media also affect the reception of communications from the specialized press.

Among the personal contacts that must be taken into account are those that take place during the viewing of television and, to a lesser extent, listening to radio. It has been pointed out that many exposures to the mass media are not lonely confrontations in which the individual is helplessly brainwashed but social situations in which a good deal of discussion goes on.

At a different level of control from the ones we have been considering are at least three other external controls of great though not easily measurable importance. One is the process of early *socialization*, which of course takes place largely in the family. It might be objected that in these days socialization itself is very much affected by the mass media, from TV to women's magazines. No doubt this is true, but socialization is also affected by social and cultural forces that have a continuous history going back well before the present importance of the mass media and extending into the present time. Some of the social controls we have touched upon in connection with the mass media themselves also affect socialization.

Another control over the mass media is the *educational system*. It is not alone the prohibitive cost of mass-media "excellence" or the perversity of journalists that prevents us from having more newspapers at the level of *Le Monde*, *Die Zeit*, or *The New York Times*. The major obstacle, perhaps, is that the channels of mass communication are intended for the people as they are, people who switch the radio or TV set on or off and subscribe or do not subscribe to the papers and magazines, people whose level of taste and comprehension can hardly be better than the education they have. There can be no doubt that more people are educated today in the free societies than ever before in history, but of course much remains to be done. In the meantime, there must be channels of communication for the uneducated and the poorly educated as well as the well educated (however these terms are defined). Education, moreover, not only implies limits to what the mass media can do, it also provides a control in the more positive sense that it helps to make people critical.

Finally, standing behind all the controls we have mentioned is the *cultural system* itself. In terms of Parsons' theory of the action system, culture is the highest subsystem in the hierarchy of control. It is a living action system insofar as men and women are directing their efforts, in universities for instance, to maintaining and extending symbolic systems such as science and religion and to solving the intellectual, artistic, and moral problems raised by such symbolic systems. The cultural action system, in this technical sense, depends upon the systems below it in the hierarchy of control — the social system, the personality, and the behavioral organism; but changes in the cultural system eventually redirect these lower systems in ways that could not be fully foreseen or manipulated even if there were any groups with

the sinister power sometimes attributed to Madison Avenue. Thus universities are of central importance in modern societies. We should also mention professional congresses and all the professional journals that are circulated internationally, as well as the great and small museums and libraries that help to store, arrange, and distribute specialized books, models, exhibits, magazines, firms, photographs, drawings, maps, tapes, and disks, as well as the works of the mass media. The importance of these cultural products cannot be gauged simply by comparing, for instance, the number of people who read Keynes with the number who read comic strips. It must be remembered that the influential people who write for the mass media, for instance, use libraries much more than ordinary people.[38]

Among cultural influences on the mass media the development of technology is only the most striking. But one aspect of technology that deserves special mention is the pressure it exerts toward ultimate democratization and a free mass-media system. The very fact that communication with the help of man-made earth satellites is now available means, among other things, that it will be more difficult for totalitarian regimes to resist the demand for worldwide contacts.

INTERNAL CONTROLS IN A FREE SYSTEM

Competition, which may be international as well as national and local, is one of the most important social controls within the mass-media "industry" itself, although, as we have seen, this "market" control, so to speak, depends on external controls also. There is considerable competition within each medium, competition between different media, and competition of all the mass media with other sources of information, opinion, and entertainment. The consumers' expenditure of money and time determines the sale of advertising time and space, and the sale of advertising time and space largely determines whether a particular channel of communication will be solvent and profitable. Producers of television programs dread the drift of listeners from their program to another at the same time. The Associated Press is in competition with the United Press International, and, less directly, with the rest of the 155 press agencies in 80 countries (1964). The AP and the UPI, moreover, keep watch to see whose story gets printed in those newspapers that subscribe to both services.[39]

An important aspect of the competition between organs, media, and the wire services is that the public benefits doubly: first, each organ of mass communication is kept busy trying to be more effective and second, the competing organs supplement one another by copying items, in effect exchanging the benefits of their separate facilities and staffs.

The competition *between* advertisers is perhaps just as important as the competition of channels for advertising funds. Advertisers sometimes attempt to exert undue pressure on organs of the press, by threatening to withdraw their ads. This form of undesirable pressure probably cannot be eliminated entirely, but it is certainly often exaggerated; and one thing that keeps it down is the fact that advertisers are competing with one another, they need the mass media, and they are especially dependent upon the larger channels. The latter can afford to resist pressure.

As we have noted, the Audit Bureau of Circulation and the Nielsen rating service help to provide relatively objective checks on the accuracy of claims that the public is reading, watching, or listening.

Competition is meaningful only when one knows what the competition is about. What are the standards of success? Sales, one might say. Yes, but what determines sales? The answer is complex, of course, as people read, watch, and listen for different reasons. But insofar as information and opinion are concerned, people are certainly interested in the qualities commonly referred to as objectivity, relevance, coverage, and good faith: the qualities we discussed earlier as part of the basis of journalistic influence. We must regard *professionalization*, therefore, as one of the most important internal controls of the mass media. Rivers and Schramm[40] have too narrow a conception of professionalism, which to them implies self-employment, but their concept of journalistic "responsibility" comes close to what we mean here.

Full-fledged professionalism implies, first, that the occupation in question requires competence in and special responsibility for some well-developed intellectual cultural tradition. Second, professionalism implies a well-developed ethical code governing the relations between professionals and their clients. Third, this code must be to a considerable extent institutionalized. Fourth, although professionals may or may not be self-employed, their judgment is regarded in the community as at least relatively "authoritative" in the area of the well-developed intellectual discipline in which they are competent or expert. Finally, a profession is marked by a sense of a common status, which may seek expression in professional associations. These associations have some success in setting standards, maintaining them through some control over professional performance, disseminating technical information, and protecting the common interests of members of the profession. We should bear in mind

that common "interests" include interests in maintaining or raising "community standards." For example, the defense lawyer in the Caldwell case, which established the principle of professional confidentiality in journalism, was supported by five *amicus curiae* briefs. The five briefs were submitted by the Reporters Committee on Freedom of the Press, the Columbia Broadcasting System, the Associated Press, *Newsweek*, and the American Civil Liberties Union.

Can journalism be regarded as a profession by these criteria? It is obvious, I think, that journalism could not be regarded as an outstanding example of a profession. But the criteria are important for indicating possible trends or approximations as well as defining full-fledged cases. Much of journalism is too little specialized and involves too little competence in a highly developed (complex and relatively generalized or abstract) intellectual field. Nevertheless, at least the beginnings of professionalism are present in journalism and constitute an enormously important internal control.

One such beginning is the trend toward increasing specialization within journalism. (Compare specialization within law or the academic profession.) Where a high degree of specialized competence is demanded, one can surely speak of a trend toward professionalism. *The New York Times* does not assign just any reporter to cover the fields of law or science or finance. Rivers and Schramm comment on the tremendous improvement in the average competence of the corps of Washington correspondents between Rosten's study in the thirties and that of Rivers in the sixties.[41]

The basic ethical code of journalism has been well stated, in part, by Rivers and Schramm, as follows: "Taught from the beginning to seek out and report fact, the young journalist takes it as an article of faith that he is not to slant news toward private, personal, or group interest. This ethic pervades the news operation, touching those who are in its orbit— including owners—as well as those who have been schooled in its tradition."[42] The growth of this ethic has made it increasingly unacceptable for journalists to have other employment that might conflict with their duty to try to be objective. According to Emery, Ault, and McGee,[43] the impartial gathering and reporting of news had become a recognized standard by the early 1900's.

Moreover, this ethic is to some extent institutionalized. This means not only that it is internalized by working journalists in the course of their training but that, as Rivers and Schramm recognize, its "sacred" character as a value is widely accepted by others, including owners and advertisers. I think it is clearly in store that the principle of separation of ownership and control will become more widely taken for granted in the mass media. It has been slower to take hold there than in ordinary business because many organs of the mass media are still owned by individuals. Separation of ownership and control in large industrial corporations was of course facilitated by the fact that these corporations came to be owned by a very large number of shareholders, no one of whom (or which) owned enough shares to control the identity or activity of management. But the principle of separation of ownership and control is of course at least as relevant to the press as it is to soap production.[44]

Another sign of the institutionalization of the professional quasi-professional status of journalism is the incipient recognition of the journalist's right of confidentiality in his relation with news sources.

There are also many schools and departments of journalism, which are developing common standards through such organizations as the American Association of Teachers of Journalism, the American Association of Schools and Departments of Journalism, the National Council on Professional Education for Journalism, the American Society of Journalism School Administrators. We have already mentioned the increasing degree of subject-matter specialization in journalism, a trend encouraged by the Nieman Fellowships at Harvard and by the grants for refresher courses made by the Ford Foundation. But there is also something like a common background of ethics, skill, and more or less technical lore that schools of journalism impart to student journalists regardless of their eventual specialties. Difficult ethical questions in journalism can be studied by means of the case method. Writing conventions and skills can be taught. Even for relatively specialized reporting such as science news there are at least precepts that are relevant to science reporters for the mass media, as opposed to science teachers or researchers. A very important function of professional schools of journalism is research, extending the basis for teaching and also for more effective social controls. Within every profession there tends to be some specialization with regard to research, teaching, and practice.

Finally, there are professional associations. In addition to those already named, we might mention the American Society of Newspaper Editors; the National Conference of Editorial Writers; the Radio-Television News Directors Association; the National Association of Broadcasters; and Sigma Chi Delta, the professional journalists' fraternity. The American Society of Newspaper Editors publishes an annual, *Problems of Journalism*. It also

commissioned the Cross report called *The People's Right to Know* (cited in note 33).

In some countries, England for example, there are professional boards of review, which take up cases of alleged malpractice and help to correct and prevent them. There is some opinion in favor of creating in the United States a government or, rather, "public" commission, free from "political" interference in the narrow sense, that would investigate complaints. For example, it might be alleged in some cases that advertisers had sought to put undue pressure on a channel of communication or that an owner had sought to put undue pressure on his professional staff. Some newspapermen would understandably favor professional boards of review conducted by the mass media themselves and possessed of no disciplinary power other than painful publicity. The American Association of University Professors provides an excellent model; its operations to protect the value of academic freedom are widely acknowledged to be quite effective.

One source of resistance to the idea that journalism is to some extent a profession is no doubt the fact that organs of mass communication are engaged in a competitive business or industry. This, however, is not a valid objection. Professionalization, after all, is not incompatible with other businesses; for example, lawyers, accountants, and economists are expected to adhere to professional standards even when they are employed by corporations. In the mass media, "separation of ownership and control" essentially means that business owners are not free to dictate standards to professional journalists within the sphere of their professional competence. Professionalization in this sense also makes possible the integrity of broadcasting in government-owned TV systems in "free" societies such as Great Britain or West Germany or government-owned systems such as the Canadian Broadcasting Corporation. Without this professionalization, the integrity of journalism would surely be no less threatened by government than by private business. Another example of professional integrity maintained despite the otherwise inherent dangers of nonprofessional interference is the existence of academic integrity in state-owned universities in "free" societies.

Professional doctors and lawyers do not compete with their colleagues through advertising. Neither do professional journalists. The organs that employ them do compete through advertising (as do many colleges and universities). The units engaged in such competition, however, are restrained and limited by the institutionalization of *cultural* standards of cognitive validity and truthfulness; and the professionalization of journalism, as of teaching and research in the university, is an aspect of this institutionalization.

Turning now to a different type of social control, there are *international agencies*, which deal with the complex technical, legal, and economic problems of international communication. We have already mentioned the European Broadcasting Union and its *Review*. The International Telecommunication Union, a United Nations agency, has 135 member countries (1969). These agencies are partly external controls, but of course the most active people in them are professionals in the mass media, notably television and radio (as well as telephone and telegraph).

Among the intangible internal controls in the mass media is the desire of specific organs of mass communication to maintain or improve their reputation, both with the public at large and within the industry or profession. Newsmen like to compile lists of "the top ten" newspapers. There is even an international elite, the members of which must be somewhat concerned not to act in such a way as to jeopardize their high prestige.[45] Louis Lyons, the first curator of the Nieman Fellowhips, stressed the desire to maintain family reputation,[46] and this no doubt has helped either to encourage separation of ownership and control or to make it less necessary; but the staff of a famous newspaper is no doubt conscious of the reputation it has to live up to, whether the paper is still associated with a family name or not.

The last type of internal control I should like to comment upon briefly is the *conventions* with regard to the content and the layout of newspapers in particular, although some of them apply also to radio and television. Of these, perhaps the most important is the distinction between news and opinion.[47] Some effort is made to let the reader know which he is giving his attention to at any given moment. Regardless of the grave difficulties there may be in maintaining the distinction perfectly in practice, it is important in principle. Reporters give the "news," in principle, without any conscious intention of swaying the reader this way or that, whereas editorial writers and often columnists are of course intent on persuading.

The convention of grouping news items according to subject is also important, for it helps to counteract whatever biases may be present in the relative emphasis given to particular items by the size and location of headlines. It is well established that a reader's interests mainly guide what he pays attention to,[48] and the convention of dividing a newspaper into sections helps him both to save time and to avoid missing items that he would like to see. The sports fan has no trouble finding sports items even though they may be in the inside pages. Indexes are an aid in the same way.

Another important convention is the adversary principle. According to Rivers and Schramm (page 3), most newspapers now have the policy of presenting more than one point of view even in the editorial pages. Letters to the editor often correct or counteract the biases of the editorial staff (although sometimes one has the impression, especially in the newsweeklies, that one object of the editorial selection of letters is to prove to the reader that the original news item or commentary was fairly well balanced, since some readers thought it was biased one way while others thought it was biased in just the opposite way). Good newspapers feature columnists of both "liberal" and "conservative" tendencies. Sometimes newspapers even give more than one review of the same book, film, or TV show.

Another feature that reveals to the public that more than one view is possible is the publication of the results of opinion polls. These are also of special interest for the evidence they contain of the amount of knowledge or awareness the public has about a given question, and the amount of support a public policy or politician has or would probably have.

Good newspapers and radio and TV stations also help the public to be aware of a spectrum of opinion by arranging for interviews with political leaders, professional experts, and artists of various kinds. Skill in interviewing can be taught to some extent and should not be taken for granted. A good interviewer knows something about the subject matter of the field involved and about the probable capacities of his audience, and he guides the interview in order to give the interviewee a chance to present and explain his main views and to bring out objections to these views and to give the interviewee a chance to answer them. Apart from interviews that are sought or arranged by the news organ itself, it routinely prints as news the opinions of leaders and experts that were presented in public places or even in technical publications. Many organs of the mass media print reviews of books, films, and radio and TV shows, as well as announcements of publications and programs. To a large extent, indeed, the mass media are mutually complementary as well as competitive. Interviews with experts; reports of research findings; reviews of books, especially nonfiction; and informative or thoughtful letters to the editor are among the well-established means the mass media have for tapping cultural systems to some extent and at least helping to make the so-called mass audience aware of them.

In very special cases, such as the best periodical reports or assessments of products for consumers, particular magazines may not accept any advertising at all, thus precluding the most obvious possibility of advertiser influence or power in the evaluations (in other cases, products that are reviewed or assessed may also be advertised, but the assessments will emphasize the results of objective tests, and the organs will rely on their own great importance to the advertiser to permit them to be unintimidated by the possible withdrawal of advertising).

Finally, one of the most important forms of internal control in and over the mass media is publicity. Readers of *Newsweek*, *Time*, and *The Saturday Review*, for example, are kept informed about events and decisions that may affect or reflect the level of performance of the mass media themselves; I mention these publications because they are among those that have specific sections devoted to the mass media. Publicity is also used by the mass media to protect themselves from undue external influence, to punish incursions on the liberty of the press, and to reward and encourage a high level of performance by the mass media. Advertisers who withdraw advertising in protest can be given publicity that might harm them, and advertisers who threaten to withdraw, as a means of pressure, can be treated as a reporter that Rivers and Schramm (p. 108) tell about, treated one such advertiser: "'I told him,' the reporter said, 'what an interesting story the threat would make for the next day's paper. The advertising stayed.'" It is difficult to believe that the people in San Diego who were persecuting the editors of the "underground" paper there will continue to be so brazen, or to go unpunished, after receiving such publicity as we cited from *Time*, The Weekly Newsmagazine (note 22). The press sometimes gives publicity to its own shortcomings, and corrections at least are fairly common. But in the long run it is perhaps just as important to reward and encourage individuals, broadcasting stations and networks, and newspapers for their good performance. Use of by-lines, awarding prizes such as the Pulitzer prizes, write-ups on individual journalists at retirement, death, or change of assignment — all help to encourage others to win recognition and to make the public conscious of high standards and high performance. There are even annual international prizes, such as the Italia Prizes for radio and television programs; the Prix Futura, given by Germany, but not necessarily to a German, for a TV program illuminating the future; the Golden Harp Festival prizes given by Ireland for TV programs conveying the cultural heritages of the competing countries; and the radio and TV prizes awarded by Japan for educational programs. In the 1969 competition in Japan, there were 177 entries from five continents and fifty-six countries.[49]

IDEOLOGY AND THE MASS MEDIA

The term ideology is rather widely used in two interrelated but distinguishable senses. In one sense, it refers to widely held ideas about the functioning of social system and its significance in a wider field of social systems. In this sense, an ideology is an amalgam of social values and ideas about their realization and importance. Part of such an ideology may consist of ideas about and evaluations of other social systems with which the system of reference is in interaction. In this sense, ideology is to a social system something like a self-image or sense of identity to an individual personality. Being an aspect of the orientation of a social system, however, an ideology is cultural.

In the second sense, ideology consists of selective or distorted ideas and evaluations, with reference to one's own social system or others or both. Such distorted ideas are also to some extent cultural. For present purposes we may speak of an ideology in the first sense and use the term ideological distortion for the second.

In considering ideology in relation to the mass media, therefore, we might ask whether or to what extent the mass media foster ideologies and ideological distortions and, second, whether any ideological distortions are current about the mass media.

It is to be expected that the mass media of any society will in some sense reflect the ideology of the society. It is no accident (as the Marxists say) that the mass media of the Soviet Union are of the Soviet totalitarian type or that the mass media of the United States are moving away from the "libertarian" type toward the "social responsibility" type. The relation between the broadly accepted ideology of the United States and the mass media, however, is understandably not clearcut. Many views appear in the press that not only question more or less conventional ideas about the place and mission of the United States in the world but go so far as to treat the American value system and its related ideas as a fairly thin veil of hypocrisy covering vicious greed, imperialism, and in general the pursuit of self-interest by just about everybody except the observers themselves and a few other people of like mind.

At the very least, the American mass media transmit ideologies in fulfilling their role of reporting the news. As we have already indicated, however, there seems to be a growing feeling that the press ought to be critical and skeptical as well as impartial. This means that, increasingly, professional journalists regard it as part of their duty to be aware of ideological distortions and to expose them. It seems probable that the episode of Senator Joseph McCarthy's use of the press to spread a wildly distorted conception of the United States was traumatic and helped to bring about something like a crisis of conscience in the industry. The result has probably been a step forward for the social responsibility doctrine. How successful the mass media are in exposing ideological distortions cannot be answered, of course, without many detailed investigations of the question.

What about ideological distortions about the mass media? To some extent this question can be considered in the light of the article by Parsons and White about the mass media.[50] They suggest that the mass media (in a free society) have in effect added four "degrees of freedom" in the communications field comparable to those created by money in the economic system, but that in principle every one of the new degrees of freedom could be "canceled out." First, the mass media have given us new sources of information and opinion. Second, they have added to the variety of information and opinion available. Third, they have reduced the cost of obtaining at least certain kinds of information and opinion. Fourth, they make it possible for anyone to choose his own time, to a greater extent, for informing himself about public events and opinions. Possible ideological distortion comes in with regard to the extent to which these degrees of freedom have been canceled out. This is a controversial question, but it seems at least that the extreme negative position involves considerable ideological distortion.

The extreme negative position, in effect, is not only that all four degrees of freedom have been canceled out but, apparently, that we are worse off than we were before we had the mass media; moreover, if we are not now as badly off as possible, things at least are steadily getting worse. The indictment is familiar: Monopoly of ownership is growing; anyway, business advertisers call the tune directly or indirectly, for they also supply the bulk of campaign funds, and these are spent entertaining a gullible public instead of informing and arousing it; paid professional minions slip over fake images, make the public actually like its manipulated conformism, and thus keep the shiny putrescent system alive.

There is, of course, no doubt that some concentration of control of mass-media organs has taken place; the facts are well known.[51] But a great deal of competition remains, and the social controls protecting competition are perhaps becoming stronger. Moreover, it is a mistake to think that all the concentration that has occurred is necessarily bad. Weaker channels with poor facilities have been eliminated or combined; some quite uneconomical duplication of effort in very small towns has been eliminated, at the same time that these towns have access to various channels from nearby big cities; and the larger organs of communication, financially stronger, have much more ability to resist undue pressure from "busybody" groups and from advertisers. The AP and the UPI, which compete vigorously with each other, are forced to try to be politically neutral precisely because they both serve some newspapers and broadcasting stations that editorially support one of the political parties, some that support the other, and some that are independent.

The idea that the mass media support the system (or the status quo) is another aspect of the mass-society thesis. The "system" is of course bad; therefore, anything that allegedly supports it must also be bad. Whatever may be meant specifically by this criticism, several comments are perhaps appropriate. First, it is quite unrealistic to suppose that the main social forces in any society can be in a permanent state of revolution, if revolution is taken to mean change in the basic societal value system and political regime. Second, whatever the more subtle effects of the mass media may be, it is hard to see how any one can seriously believe that the day-to-day news presented by radio, TV, and newspapers could make people complacent about society. Government policies are criticized freely, and we hear or read discussions calling into question practices of the police and the courts. If we know about Ralph Nader's attacks on the rich and powerful General Motors Company or the federal Food and Drug Administration, it is because we read the newsweeklies. It is quite possible that the mass media are playing a fundamental role in helping to make people in the United States aware of injustice to Negroes and other minorities and aware also of the strong forces both pressing for change and opposing it.

One reason ideologists sometimes accept rather uncritically the idea that the mass media merely support the status quo is that they often exaggerate the part of advertisers and rich owners in determining the content of the press. The dogma of advertiser control has been mindlessly repeated by Communists ever since the days of Marx and Lenin (when there was probably more truth in it), but of course one does not have to be a Communist to give it credence.[52] Yet, Richard D. Altick writes: ". . .down to the time of Pitt the newspaper's appeal and influence were limited chiefly to the upper and the urban commercial classes. As organs of opinion the daily papers were simply the hired mouthpieces of one party or the other. Not until the nineteenth century was decades old would the increasing value of newspapers as advertising mediums allow them gradually to shake off government or party control and to become independent voices of public sentiment."[53] "Undue influence" does still exist to some extent, but it arises mostly where small papers and stations are involved; and the mass media in general are not without defenses against it. In 1962, Donald I. Rogers, business and financial editor of the "conservative" New York *Herald Tribune*, complained rather bitterly that "conservative" business gave more advertising money to the liberal papers in Washington and New York than to the conservative papers; and Rivers and Schramm, pointing up the significance of his statement, note that by 1967 the liberal *Post* had increased its lead in Washington, and the two conservative papers in New York were dead.[54]

As for the idea that we are all being manipulated into a depraved conformity, so subtle and sinister that we succumb to it happily, again, this kind of thing is difficult to appraise, but several comments seem to be in order. We should be careful to distinguish between having the same focus of attention and having the same reactions. For example, it is true that millions of people all over the world were watching the Apollo II landing on the moon, but it is not true that they all had the same reactions to this event. Second, the mass media present much more highly differentiated material to "the" public than this thesis of homogenation would suggest. For example, the great increase in the time spent on television (now the mass medium par excellence) has made it possible for the radio (and probably newspapers) to become more specialized. The radio, in order to survive, had to take advantage of the facts that one can be otherwise occupied while listening to it and that a small radio set can be carried about almost anywhere. Hence there is a trend all over the world toward an emphasis on light background music and light chitchat. But there are also special programs for people listening to their car radios during peak traffic hours, special programs for housewives who have just finished the breakfast dishes, for teenagers who have just come out of school, and so on. Moreover, the radio takes advantage of the fact that it can broadcast the news more quickly than newspapers and can leave to the latter reports in greater detail and also, to some extent, in greater depth.[55] In all the mass media, there are offerings at several different levels. A particular newspaper tends perhaps to have a certain level of presentation, but it may well have sections that are of interest to rather different publics.

If the alleged pressure toward uniformity or even toward conformity were as great as some people think, we should have very little social controversy or conflict in the so-called mass societies, but there is actually controversy and conflict enough for riots, "confrontations," and threats of revolution. Jean Cazeneuve, Director of Research at the French Press Institute and Professor at the Sorbonne, has the following to say about the allegedly helpless but happy docility of the mass-media audience: "Indeed, it was believed for a long time that the effect of television was to 'depoliticize' the citizens by getting them interested in unimportant things, by putting them to sleep, by conditioning them to accept the existing order. This opinion moreover has proved extremely tenacious, for it has been able to resist a good deal of contrary evidence and we still find it cropping up in thinkers who, like Marcuse, are otherwise not ordinarily inclined to accept all received ideas.[56]

A specific aspect of the mass-society thesis is the alleged manipulation of the public by Madison Avenue counselors, who ghost-write speeches, advise candidates how to make themselves up for TV appearances, and in general are said to create an "image" of the candidates that may have little to do with reality. The element of distortion here lies not in the assertion that such attempts are made but rather in the idea that they are completely successful or that they are the main factor in successful political campaigns. This is at least doubtful. In considering it, we should bear several things in mind. Candidates since ancient times have studied rhetoric and practiced deceit to some extent. Today the press is rather toughminded and unsympathetic toward obvious efforts to sell fake images and tends to expose them. A skillful interviewer, for example, can help to force candidates either to say something definite or to reveal themselves as uninformed or evasive. Moreover, during political campaigns for important offices each candidate tends to criticize the actual record of his rivals. After reviewing carefully the research on televised political debates in the United States, England, and France, Cazeneuve felt inclined to reach a conclusion very different from that of the mass-society theorists. He thinks that on the whole television, in reasonably long presentations of the candidates to the public, is "merciless toward pretense" (*impitoyable aux travestissements*: literally, merciless toward disguises).[57] This judgment may lean too far the other way, but it is obviously the carefully considered opinion of someone who has actually studied the question empirically.

It remains true, however, that thoughtful people are very much dissatisfied with the performance of the mass media in covering public questions. Even educational TV is poor in its coverage at the height of a political campaign, to say nothing of ordinary times.[58] There is perhaps more agreement about the gaps in mass-media performance than about the harm it allegedly does. The idea that we are all brainwashed by advertisers and are living in "an air-conditioned nightmare" without knowing it, reflects the assumption many people make, against the facts, that the mass media have limitless power to shape our thinking. This idea ignores all the other influences on our lives. Moreover, as social psychologists have well established, the audience for most controversial messages is largely self-selected; that is, it consists of people who already believe. People have a tendency to distort what they hear or read, finding in it what confirms their existing beliefs, even to the point of missing what the intention of the message was. Advertising copywriters are said to daydream wistfully sometimes about the riches they would have as "hidden persuaders" if their methods had the potency sometimes attributed to them.

To be sure, Mendelsohn and Crespi point out that the professional manipulators do their best to keep up with the social psychologists' findings and to circumvent obstacles. If the people listen only to what they already agree with, the manipulators will catch them unawares and feed them "spots" of "exposure." If the people like to be entertained, the manipulators will gladly oblige by making their pitch as bland as possible, building up favorable images of their candidates by much repetition of palatable snippets. The question is, how successful are these tactics? It is becoming increasingly clear that their success is not great, and therefore we may expect changes. Perhaps the most important solvent of this light film of obfuscation is ridicule by professional journalists (as opposed to professional admen and image-makers). During the 1970 midterm election campaign in the United States, the term "rhetoric" (as applied for example to the phrases concocted, we were frequently reminded, by Vice-President Spiro Agnew's speechwriters) was obviously understood as a polite term for "claptrap." When the campaign was over, journalists made it known that the president and his agent were not very happy with the results of their tactics.

There will certainly be continuing and continuous need for sophisticated and vigilant professional journalists, for much of the image-building and campaigning are being done between the regular campaign seasons.

In general, Mendelsohn and Crespi point out that the public is becoming more sophisticated (less gullible). There is greater openness to reform. Serious proposals have been made to reduce the importance of money in political campaigns and to strengthen the responsibility of TV. One proposal is to require all stations by law to reserve a certain amount of prime time equally for both major political parties. This time could be free or could be paid for at reduced rates by the parties themselves or by the government. (Time could be given to third parties in proportion to the number of votes they won in the previous election, provided they present candidates in a certain proportion of the states.)

If the mass media do not have the magical potency sometimes attributed to them, they are by no means without influence. They not only confirm people's beliefs through the well-known mechanisms of self-selection and selective perception, but under some circumstances they change them. The information and opinion carried in the mass media have a better chance of making a difference in time of crisis; with people under cross-pressures; with people who are unfamiliar with the topic discussed; and with people who have weak social attachments. As for people who do not have abnormally weak social attachments, we must keep in mind the "2-step flow." Thus mass-media communications have first a direct influence, then an indirect influence, which may be greater because the local leaders can tailor their arguments to the individual and reward him immediately by giving him approval when he accepts them. The mass media are exerting influence, not necessarily for harm, every day, and one cannot gauge the extent of it simply by studying their immediate effect in a political campaign.[59]

If the worst charges were true, it would be possible to say that monopoly and inflation have wiped out the degrees of freedom that might have been conferred by the appearance of the mass media. "Inflation," here, could be interpreted as a decline in the value of "units" of influence, similar to a decline in the purchasing power of money. As far as the mass media are concerned, inflation, I take it, would mean that the performance of the mass media has been declining in average quality, so that the reader or listener or viewer is getting less and less for his time and money. Most serious students of the mass media, however, seem to agree that over time a great improvement has taken place. As Emery, Ault, and McGee remark (page 70), the earlier mass press was terribly sensational and tended to give views first, then news as a poor second. I think we can speak of ideological distortion where the emphasis is overwhelmingly on alleged manipulation and "class"-based selectivity, where it is assumed that the system makes improvement impossible, or where actual improvement is simply pooh-poohed.[60]

As I understand Parsons, he means by "deflation" a decline in public confidence with regard to one or more of the circulating generalized symbolic media, hence a tightening up of the circular flow, a reluctance to accept the symbolic money instead of solid gold. As far as the mass media are concerned, we should remember that in one aspect they are vehicles for transmitting the influence of others but in another aspect are recipients and spenders of influence on their own. Decline in public trust of government announcements about Vietnam, for example, is not necessarily the same thing as decline in public confidence in the mass media. It is true, however, that the growth of general alienation from all authority or from the so-called establishment can spread to the mass media, especially if the alienation is somewhat blurred in focus. Thus, lack of confidence in the regular press presumably lies behind the emergence in the United States of the so-called underground press. As for the most part it is not in danger of being suppressed, it has a kind of theatrical make-believe quality, as if people were enjoying playing at being revolutionaries. Nevertheless, this is a serious phenomenon, reflecting at least some degree of alienation, bewilderment, and frustration.

It should be clear, however, that this kind of deflation may or may not be based on a sound analysis. Senator Joseph McCarthy managed to bring about a fairly drastic deflation in influence by casting doubt on the loyalty of high government officials; but after a time it became clear that this deflation was due largely to ideological distortion.

Detection and analysis of ideological distortions should be among the major tasks of social scientists.[61] The elaborate development of all the symbolic media has involved a process of increasing social differentiation. One aspect of this is the progressive emancipation from ascriptive ties. The elaboration of the special symbolic media has been functional for society in that it has introduced new degrees of freedom, of which the prototypes are the well-known degrees of freedom made possible by the use of money. However, as against these functional advantages (which permit us to speak of social evolution), societal dependence upon the special symbolic media has involved the risks of greater social interdependence for the interdependent units; the need for the extension of trust to "strangers"; the necessity of adjusting to more complex forms of social integration; and Marx's alienation of the individual, in the sense of loss of the apparent "wholeness" and "naturalness" of earlier social life which, with its relative fusion of functions (lack of structural differentiation), its relatively unproblematic ascriptive ties, and its relatively small communities, seemed, at least in romanticizing retrospect, to have been more satisfying and secure by comparison. This alienation should be distinguished from alienation in the sense of a negative attitude toward norms, persons, or collectivities to which or to whom one was once committed. Marx's alienation is much closer to Durkheim's anomie (although Marx understood it less completely than Durkheim). This alienation (or anomie) has led both to the development of

constructive normative and collective mechanisms and to various "regressive" manifestations, such as some of the romantic and utopian ideologies of both the Right and the Left.[62]

The mass media, of course, are changing all the time, and they have only begun to realize their great potentialities. Technical developments will make it possible to expand greatly the number of channels available for radio and television, to have stereo television, to have a central store of programs from which an individual can select a program to be played to him personally at any time.[63] Communication satellites will soon make it possible to send the complete text of *The New York Times* from one coast to the other in seconds.[64] We can expect further specialization.[65] There will be a few competing newspapers dealing with national and international events and issues, and local newspapers will be freed to cover local areas more fully. All channels of mass communication will be able to raise their standards as the average level of education is raised. Robert Lindsay and Raymond B. Nixon, writing in the United Nations magazine *The Courier* (July-August 1966), point out that 40 percent of the adults in the world in 1965 could not read and that half the children of school age were not going to school. The possibilities of television for education, not only in the developing but in the more advanced countries, are beginning to be appreciated and exploited. There has been much enthusiasm recently in the United States over the program *Sesame Street*, which seems to be reaching ghetto children not easy to reach in the past. National Educational Television has recently opened a relatively new field by doing a four-part series of niney-minute films on the court trial of a Black Panther who was accused of resisting arrest for speeding and of causing a disturbance. (He was acquitted.) The judge in the case thought that the possible good that could come from televising court trials outweighs the possible harm. At the present time only two states (Texas and Colorado) permit television cameras in the courtroom, with the important proviso that both sides in the case agree to their presence.[66]

As far as ideological distortion about the mass media is concerned, my main purpose has been to emphasize the relevance of theory, upon which Parsons has insisted all his life. Among basic theoretical concepts developed in part by Parsons himself may be included the conception of levels of social structure, the distinction of the four functional subsystems with their symbolic media, and the conception of institutionalized and *de facto* social controls. Theory alone, of course, is not enough to detect and analyze ideological distortion or anything else about social systems. It is also necessary to have "all" the relevant facts, gathered with the aid of theory, assembled in comparative perspective, and certified by sound methodology. The present chapter is of course only a sketch. Many of the statements made in it are tentative or merely presumptive, and a good deal of research is desirable on all the topics touched upon.

NOTES

1. The author is grateful to the editors of the present volume for some helpful suggestions. For help in finding pertinent books and articles I am indebted to Jacqueline Riat-Cousin and Danielle Cousin Johnson. The chief works of Talcott Parsons that are important as background for the present paper are all included in his *Politics and Social Structure* (New York: The Free Press, 1969); see especially Chapters 10, 14, 15, 16, and 17.

2. The trust that mass-media influence (and all other influence) depends upon is not based solely on the competence and integrity of the influence source. There must be a *cultural bond* between communicator and audience; and there must be some *social solidarity* to be symbolized, or at least social alienation must not have gone too far. These points were illustrated recently in a striking case. The Knight newspaper group interviewed 1,721 persons in the United States and found that many, "particularly among the old, the poor and the black" (especially if they were not well educated?) doubted that Neil Armstrong had actually walked on the moon, even if they had watched him on TV. In a black ghetto in Washington, D.C., more than half of those interviewed suspected that the whole thing may have been a trick. "'It's all a deliberate effort to mask problems at home,' explained a Negro preacher. 'The people are unhappy—and this takes their minds off their problems.'" (*Newsweek*, July 20, 1970, page 51). Many factors besides alienation and ignorance may have been involved in this lack of trust. For instance, the blacks interviewed would probably have reacted quite differently if Armstrong had been black—partly because they could have trusted him more, partly because it would have been more gratifying to identify with his achievement.

3. Perhaps we could say that inauthentic communications are analogous to counterfeit money. "Authentic" means "coming from the source implied or stated. " It hardly needs stressing that the government is running the risk of "deflating" the influence of the mass media if it supports certain channels secretly and if this fact becomes known; the public could be pardoned for wondering how many other channels are being supported and at what cost to integrity.

4. Arnold M. Rose, *The Power Structure: Political Processes in American Society* (New York: Oxford University Press, 1967), pp. 110-111, 218.

5. See Parsons, "Social Strains in America," Ch. 7 in Parsons, *op. cit.*

6. See Herbert J. Gans in *The New York Times Magazine* of January 11, 1970.

7. The way the mass media handled this news item is itself somewhat controversial. See the acrimonious set of exchanges between Elizabeth Alfert and Arthur R. Jensen (the professor challenging orthodoxy) in the *Journal of Social Issues*, XXV (Autumn 1969).

8. William L. Rivers and Wilbur Schramm, *Responsibility in Mass Communication*, revised edition (New York: Harper & Row, 1969).

9. See the formulation of rules for reporting riots, in Rivers and Schramm, *op. cit.*, pp. 186-187.

10. Daniel J. Boorstin, *The Image, or What Happened to the American Dream* (New York: Atheneum, 1962), pp. 26-28.

11. See Talcott Parsons, "Some Problems of General Theory in Sociology," in John C. McKinney and Edward A. Tiryakian (eds.), *Theoretical Sociology: Perspectives and Developments* (New York: Appleton-Century-Crofts, 1970), pp. 27-68.

12. Cooley's analysis is somewhat similar to that of George Herbert Mead; at least, Cooley and Mead are compatible. "Taking the role of the other," in Mead's sense, is a fundamental social process that involves communication—in its more developed forms, communication in terms of "significant symbols" (cultural symbolic media). "Taking the role of the other" also involves the capacity for sympathy and empathy.

13. "The principal Structures of Community: A Sociological View," in C. J. Friedrich, ed., *Community* (New York: The Liberal Arts Press, 1959), reprinted as Chapter 8 in Talcott Parsons, *Structure and Process in Modern Societies* (Glencoe, Illinois: The Free Press, 1960).

14. See reference in note 11.

15. A few comments may help to distinguish between the L-A interchanges in the general action system and the L-A interchanges in the social system. As Parsons says, these interchanges, defining "codes" rather than conveying "messages," are integrative in their respective systems, and they have to do with allocation. But (1) the A subsystem in the general action system is the behavioral organism, whereas the A subsystem of the social system is the economy (no more nor less an abstraction but an abstraction of a different kind, involving aspects of the activity of many collective units, not to speak of many individuals). (2) The L subsystem of the general action system is "culture," whereas the L subsystem of the social system is a "specified" type of pattern-maintenance system. (3) The symbolic media involved in the general action system are "definition of the situation" and "intelligence," whereas in the social system the symbolic media involved are "commitments" and money. (4) In the general action system it is rewards that are allocated, whereas in the social system it is resources. (5) All these distinctions are analytical: A given concrete communication may involve two or more types of interchange simultaneously.

16. To say that the mass media are mainly integrative is not to ignore or deny the fact that mass-media communications may also contribute to controversy and conflict. The integrative function (expressed in one way) is to forestall, check, reduce, resolve, or settle conflict and potential conflict between units of a system. This function is performed with only partial success. To be successful at all, however, the function requires that potential conflict be to some extent anticipated and that conflict that cannot be forestalled be brought into the open. Conflicts of opinions or of interests cannot be resolved, or settled somehow short of perfect resolution, unless the issues are aired and joined. It might be less misleading to say that the main function of the mass media, viewed objectively, is to deal with integrative problems.

17. Fred S. Siebert, Theodore Peterson, and Wilbur Schramm (Urbana: Univeristy of Illinois Press, 1956); paperback edition. For a detailed treatment of the Soviet systems, see Alex Inkeles, *Public Opinion in Soviet Russia: A Study in Mass Persuasion* (Cambridge: Harvard University Press, 1950).

18. For the phrases characterizing the four types, see Siebert, Peterson, and Schramm, *op. cit.*, the chart on page 7. All four systems are well described, but see especially Peterson's chapter on the "social responsibility" type. On the same type, see also Rivers and Schramm, *op. cit.*

19. See Wilbur Schramm, "Communication, Mass: Controls and Public Policy," in D. Sills (ed.), *International Encyclopedia of the Social Sciences*, III (New York: Macmillan-Free Press, 1968), pp. 55-63.

20. For comparison with the present discussion, see Charles R. Wright, *Mass Communications: A Sociological Perspective*

(New York: Random House, 1959), and Rivers and Schramm, *op. cit.,* Ch. 2.

21. In the early nineteenth century, "right-thinking" people in England were afraid that radicals might win over the giddy public if there were no restrictions on the press. Accordingly, in 1819 the government put a high tax on newspapers selling at less than 6d, so that the price of cheap papers had to go up. See Richard D. Altick, *The English Common Reader: A Social History of the Mass Reading Public* 1800-1900 (Chicago: University of Chicago Press, 1957), pp. 327-328. In the Soviet Union today the government suppresses "objectivism" and "escapism." "Objectivism" is the presentation of news without regard to its meaning in Marxist-Leninist perspective. "Escapism," though perhaps superficially entertaining, is dangerous or frivolous distraction from the matters regarded by the government as important. Rivers and Schramm, *op. cit.,* pp. 43-44.

22. In the Soviet Union there is the phenomenon known as *samizdat* ("self-publishing"). For example, in 1968-1969 the underground "press" published a "Chronicle of Human Rights Year in the Soviet Union"; according to Anatole Shub, who was the Moscow and Eastern Europe correspondent for the highly respected *Washington Post* from 1967 to 1969, when he was expelled by the Soviet government, "The 'publishers' and 'reporters' of its six fat issues managed to assemble data and texts on arrests, searches, Party sanctions, trials, protests, and demonstrations in Moscow, Leningrad, Gorki, Pskov, Kiev, Kharkov, Lvov, Riga, Talinn, Dubno, Obninsk, Novosibirsk, and the Potma concentration camp." *Samizdat* may be smuggled out to the West and broadcast by radio back to Russia. *Samizdat* (plus people's knowledge that the regular press is closely controlled) leads to suspicion and distrust of the regular press and of government activities. Anatole Shub, *The New Russian Tragedy,* (New York: W. W. Norton, 1969), Ch. 5, "Russia's New Free Press," pp. 62-63). Many stories about this new "Free Press" are appearing in the West now. In a dispatch of July 28, 1970, the AP reports that William Cole, CBS correspondent expelled from the Soviet Union, smuggled out with him taped recordings made by Soviet intellectuals who are in Soviet concentration camps or prisons. Four well-known intellectuals, whose voices can be recognized on the tapes, are named in the dispatch. They tell about the system of killing and torturing dissenters in Soviet prisons and "insane asylums," and they "all sent messages that 'no matter what the consequences' they wanted the film and the spoken tapes broadcast in America."

There is also a flourishing so-called underground press in the United States, most of whose publications are sold quite openly. Some, however, are harassed by vigilante types and even by the police. An extreme example is the *Street Journal & San Diego Free Press,* which got into trouble for a story it printed about a San Diego financier. But the editors are still at large, the paper is still being published, and even in San Diego it has defenders among public officials. (This is not to take lightly the harassment, which is not funny.) Two other points are also interesting. The "offensive" story in the so-called underground weekly was "essentially a rehash of a *Wall Street Journal* story," and I read about the harassment in *Time,* The Weekly Newsmagazine (March 23, 1970), in its section on The Press, under the heading "Not so *Free Press.*"

23. Denis McQuail, referring to Louis Wirth's "proposition that mass societies are 'aggregations of people who participate to a much greater degree in the common life,'" notes that the mass media supplement, perhaps correct, and possibly modify other means of communication, with the result that greater consensus is achieved. "Examples would include members of trade unions, where industrial action is reported, the police where police actions are publicly discussed, or religious groups where church teachings attract public attention. Members of these . . . will become aware of the wider public's attitude to them, they may acquire information suppressed or changed

by their own specialized communication sources. The resolution of any resulting cross-pressures and conflicts will have a bearing on the level of consensus in society. . . ." In the next paragraph: ". . . the rise of television has affected democratic politics in numerous ways, without necessarily altering the balance between contending forces. It promotes centralization, the substitution of national for local issues and increased consensus across party lines, at least in open public debate. There is a probable softening of the tone of argument; a greater public accountability of individual politicians. . . . The task of the sociologist is to devise concepts and research strategies for handling the analysis of such effects." Denis McQuail, *Towards a Sociology of Mass Communications:* (London: Collier-Macmillan, 1969), pp. 92-93.

24. See Talcott Parsons, "Evolutionary Universals in Society," *American Sociological Review,* 29 (June 1964), pp. 339-357 and *Societies: Evolutionary and Comparative Perspectives* (Englewood Cliffs: Prentice-Hall, 1966).

25. See Talcott Parsons, "Communism and the West: The Sociology of the Conflict," in Eva and Amitai Etzioni (eds.), *Social Change* (New York: Basic Books, 1964), pp. 390-399.

26. Paul Hollander, who as editor of *American and Soviet Society* (Englewood Cliffs: Prentice-Hall, 1969) reprinted the article by Parsons referred to in the previous footnote, thinks that Parsons is excessively idealistic and optimistic; perhaps so, but I interpret Parsons' article in the spirit of my text above.

27. The three Soviet scholars are A. D. Sakharov, V. F. Turchin, and R. A. Medvedev. An abridged but verbatim translation of their letter was published in *Newsweek.* See the text and accompanying story in the issue of April 13, 1970.

28. For an estimate of "federal expenditures on telling and showing the taxpayers" of the U.S., see Rivers and Schramm, *op. cit.,* p. 97. I hesitate to quote their (very high) estimate because I do not know what part of this expenditure can be regarded as "illegitimate" (although legal) horn-blowing. For an alarmist view, see Herbert I. Schiller, *Mass Communications and American Empire* (Urbana: University of Illinois Press, 1969).

29. For an analysis somewhat similar to the one in this and the following section, but in a quite different field, see Talcott Parsons, "Research with Human Subjects and the 'Professional Complex,'" *Daedalus,* 98 (Spring 1969), pp. 325-360.

30. Rivers and Schramm, *op. cit.,* pp. 63-64, give the standards of the FCC under twenty-five headings.

31. *Newsweek,* April 6, 1970, pp. 66-67.

32. Altick, *op. cit.,* Chapters 14 and 15. See note 21.

33. See Harold L. Cross, *The People's Right to Know: Legal Access to Public Records and Proceedings* (New York: Columbia University Press, 1953).

34. *Newsweek,* April 13, 1970, pp. 40-41. The decision was later upheld in a higher court. The principle of professional confidentiality is now established.

35. Fachtna O. Hannrachain, "Privacy and Broadcasting," *BBU Review: Radio and Television News General and Legal* (January 1970), pp. 50-55. In the same issue, see "Notes on United States Privacy Law," by three attorneys for TV networks, pp. 55-59. The *Review* is published every two months, in French and English editions, by the European Broadcasting Union (which also has associate members outside Europe).

36. See P. F. Lazarsfeld, B. Berelson, and H. Gaudet, *The People's Choice: How the Voter Makes Up His Mind in a Presidential Campaign* (New York: Duell, Sloan & Pearce, 1944); I. N. Stycos, "Patterns of Communication in a Small Greek Village," *Public Opinion Quarterly,* 16 (1952), pp. 59-72; E. Katz and P. F. Lazarsfeld, *Personal Influence: The Part Played by People in the Flow of Mass Communications* (Glencoe, Illinois: The Free Press, 1955); and E. Katz, "The Two-Step Flow of Communication," *Public Opinion Quarterly,* 21 (1957), pp. 61-68. McQuail, *op. cit.,* gives a good secondary treatment of these works.

37. See Robert K. Merton, "Patterns of Influence: Local and Cosmopolitan Influentials," in *Social Theory and Social Structure* (Glencoe, Illinois: The Free Press, 1957), pp. 387-420.

38. See Fritz Machlup, *The Production and Distribution of Knowledge in the United States* (Princeton.: Princeton University Press, 1962); and Bernard Berelson, with the assistance of Lester Asheim. *The Library's Public: A Report of the Public Library Inquiry* (New York: Columbia University Press, 1949).

39. Edwin Emery, Phillip H. Ault, and Waren K. McGee, *Introduction to Mass Communications* (New York: Dodd, Mead, 1960), p. 297.

40. Rivers and Schramm, *op. cit.*, pp. 240-241.

41. *Ibid.*, p, 102; Leo C. Rosten, *The Washington Correspondents* (New York: Harcourt Brace, 1937); William L. Rivers, *The Opinion Makers* (Boston: Beacon Press, 1965). See also the striking remarks by Benjamin Bradlee in his Foreword to Anatole Shub, *op. cit.* It should be emphasized that professionalism is only getting started and has a long way to go. Even *The New York Times* has been severely criticized, and quite fairly, for amateurishness and bias. See, for example, Irving Kristol, "The Underdeveloped Profession," *The Public Interest* (Winter 1967); pp. 36-52, and the exchange between Kristol and Clifton Daniel (managing editor of the *Times*) in the Spring 1967 issue, pp. 119-123. See also Herman H. Dinsmore, *All The News That Fits* (New Rochelle: Arlington House, 1969). As far as bias is concerned, in view of a common charge from the Left that "capitalist" papers are essentially organs of "capitalist" owners and advertisers, it is interesting that the *Times* is most frequently accused of being too "anti-Establishment." It should be remembered that the *Times* is by far the most influential paper in the U.S., its columns widely syndicated and even more widely copied. Fifty copies of the *Times* are delivered to the White House every day.

42. Rivers and Schramm, *op. cit.*, p. 49. See also the official Canons of Journalism, published as Appendix A in their book. This book, to which I have referred several times, is itself an important clarifying contribution to the tradition the professional. authors refer to in the passage quoted. The National Association of Broadcasters has an operational guide, "Broadcasting the News." The official Television Code, however, and the Radio Code, and the Code of Self-Regulation—Motion Picture Association of America, (Rivers and Schramm, Appendices B-D), are somewhat different; they have a good deal of practical effect, but they are concerned to a large extent with the entertainment aspects of the mass media, and they were formulated largely to stave off more government control of radio, TV, and films. The Public Relations Code (Appendix E) no doubt excites a few smiles here and there, but its effect is probably not negligible either. We tend to take a fairly high level of adherence to the Canons of Journalism for granted.

43. Emery, Ault, and Agee, *op. cit.*, p. 79.

44. A recent interesting sign of what is coming was the revolt by the staff of *Time* after the death of the founder, Henry Luce. This was the result of the dissatisfaction of professionals with nonprofessional control of the *professional aspect* of news-gathering and -reporting, a dissatisfaction emboldened by the increasingly successful competition of *Newsweek*. See R. Pollack, "Time: After Luce," *Harper*, 239 (July 1969), pp. 42-52.

45. John C. Merrill, *The Elite Press: Great Newspapers of the World* (New York: Pitman, 1968). A paper such as *Pravda* is included because it speaks for the rulers of a great country.

46. Louis Lyons in *The Reporter* of December 8, 1960; reprinted in part in A. Fontenilles and J. Marty, *The Mass Media in the United States*: *Communications et Relations Sociales* (Paris: Dunod, 1967), pp. 30-31.

47. The difference if not the distinction between news and opinion is in effect denied by Violette Morin in *l'Ecriture de presse* (The Hague: Mouton & Co., 1969). This book is a systematic and quantitative study of the treatment of the same event in sixteen Paris newspapers: seven dailies and nine weeklies. The event was the state visit to France of Premier Nikita Krushchev, at the invitation of General Charles de Gaulle, from March 21 to April 4, 1960. All the papers gave their readers the "main" facts: that the Premier came to France with his wife and a large entourage, that he had talks with General de Gaulle, that he toured France, amiably sampling the gastronomic specialities of several regions, etc. But each paper, over time, managed to convey or suggest its own view and evaluation of these people and events, not so much by blatant partiality as by subtle selection and omission and above all by repetition of certain facts.

Actually, of the 8,532 "units of information" (including repetitions) that the analysis found in all the papers, 6,467 were judged to be "neutral," 1,215 "positive," and 850 "negative." An example of a "negative" item was the report that some students demonstrated at the Rond-Point against Krushchev on account of Hungary. In this study, some interpretations seem to me ingenious but rather strained, if not far-fetched. Where the papers tend to agree in seeing political obstacles to any far-reaching agreement between the two countries—a "negative" residue—the author makes no attempt to assess whether this agreement was objectively sound or not. The analysis of the residue presumably left in the reader's mind by the total coverage in each of the papers is subtle and plausible in each case, but speculative.

The whole work is most vitiated, however, by the practice of treating together all items, whether news reports, background stories, editorials, cartoons, or photographs; and by the refusal to take seriously, as guides to relative importance, the relative size of headlines or the placement of an item in the paper. After all, few people will be surprised to learn that *l'Aurore* is not pro-Communist while *l'Humanité* is. The book does show, however, the extreme difficulty if not impossibility of being "objective" in news reporting. It would be interesting to study the same event and the same papers but (1) to analyze separately the news and background material and the editorial material, and (2) to study both against some sort of grid representing relevant questions that *might have been asked* about the event and its significance. Incidentally, it might be a contribution to "objectivity" if on "important" stories a newspaper published some such grid in addition to its attempts to answer the questions.

48. See, for example, the summary of social-psychological findings with regard to the mass media in Bernard Berelson and Gary A. Steiner, *Human Behavior: An Inventory of Scientific Findings* (New York: Harcourt Brace & World, 1964), pp. 527-555.

49. The programs that were given awards for 1969 in the Italian, German, Irish, and Japanese contests are announced in the *EBU Review*, (January 1970), pp. 37-39.

50. Talcott Parsons and Winston White, "The Mass Media and the Structure of American Society," *Journal of Social Issues*, 16 (1960), pp. 67-77; reprinted as Chapter 10 in Parsons, *Politics and Social Structure*.

51. See, for example, the pages from Theodore Peterson, J. W. Jensen, and W. L. Rivers, *The Mass Media and Modern Society* (New York: Holt, Rinehart & Winston, 1965) reprinted in Fontenilles and Marty, *op. cit.*; see also *Newsweek*, April 6, 1970, pp. 66-67.

52. It seems to me that V. O. Key, Jr., who of course was a serious scholar, tended to ignore the operation of social controls in his treatment of the press, and hence to exaggerate the tyranny of owners and advertisers. See his *Public Opinion and American Democracy* (New York: Alfred A. Knopf, 1961). Characteristic of the "hardheaded," "realistic" approach is the following: "Over the long run, the innate conservatism

of the proprietors of the communication industry is reinforced by scattered acts of discipline of individual deviates, which episodes have a wider exemplary impact" (p. 381). No doubt; but this is far from being the whole story.

53. Altick, *op. cit.*, p. 322. See also Steven Shaw, "Colonial Newspaper Advertising: A Step Toward Freedom of the Press," *The Business History Review*, 33 (1959). It is theoretically possible, of course, to have a system in which the mass media would be privately controlled and directly supported by the public, while advertisers would have to develop their own mass media. Such a system would tend to benefit the rich since the price of newspapers and other "broadcasts" would have to be high, and the relatively poor would still have to pay for advertising in the prices of consumers' products. To some extent, we already recognize that organs of the press are not simply economic enterprises in the analytical sense and, therefore, need not be solvent as a business firm would be. Some magazines, for instance, are partly subsidized by financial contributions. Indirect government subsidy is also possible and might be regarded as desirable if it is kept free from control by the administration in power.

54. Rivers and Schramm, *op. cit.*, pp. 104-106.

55. See Robert Wangermee, "The evolution of sound broadcasting: An EBU Radio Programme Committee enquiry," *EBU Review* (January 1969), pp. 10-17.

56. Jean Cazeneuve, *Les pouvoirs de la television* (Paris: Gallimard, 1970), p. 334 (my translation). For other criticisms of the "theory of mass society," see E. A. Shils, "Daydreams and Nightmares: Reflections on the Criticism of Mass Culture," *The Sewanee Review*, 65 (1957), pp. 586-608; R. A. Bauer and Alice Bauer, "America, Mass Society and Mass Media," *Journal of Social Issues*, 16 (1960), pp. 3-66; Parsons and White, "The Mass Media and the Structure of American Society," *op. cit.*; Arnold M. Rose, *The Power Structure: Political Processes in American Society* (New York: Oxford University Press, 1967); and McQuail, *op. cit.*, Chapter II, especially pp. 32-35.

57. Cazeneuve, *op. cit.*, p. 312.

58. See Harold Mendelsohn and Irving Crespi, *Polls, Television, and the New Politics* (Scranton, Penn.: Chandler Publishing Company, 1970), especially Chapter 5, "Indirect Political Effects of Mass Media." See also the quotation from Denis McQuail in note 8.

59. On the influence of the mass media in psychological terms, see Berelson and Steiner, *op. cit.*, Morris Janowitz, "Communication, Mass: The Study of Mass Communication,"
in Sills (ed.), *op. cit.*, III, pp. 41-53; and Cazeneuve, *op. cit.*, Chapter 7.

60. The following statement by Rivers and Schramm seems just: "What can be claimed, clearly, is that the level of Mass Culture has risen perceptibility even as the mass media have become more powerful. Dwight Macdonald admits this, saying that Stephen Vincent Benet has replaced Edgar Guest (whose best-known line is probably 'It takes a heap o' livin' in a house t' make it home'), Walter Lippmann has replaced Arthur Brisbane [an old Hearst man], and 'There are no widely influential critics so completely terrible as, say, the late William Lyon Phelps.' Typically, Macdonald holds that the seeming improvement is simply a corruption of High Culture: 'There is nothing more vulgar than sophisticated 'kitsch.' But it must be obvious that one who does not approve the advance from Guest to Benet or from Brisbane to Lippmann is simply dedicated to negativism" (pp. 195-196; footnote reference omitted).

61. See Talcott Parsons, "An Approach to the Sociology of Knowledge," in Parsons, *Sociological Theory and Modern Society* (New York: The Free Press, 1967), pp. 139-165. For a few additional comments, see Harry M. Johnson, "Ideology and the Social System," in Sills (ed.), *op. cit.*, IV, pp. 76-78.

62. See Talcott Parsons, "Some Comments on the Sociology of Karl Marx," in Parsons, *Sociological Theory and Modern Society*, Chapter 4; "Durkheim's Contribution to the Theory of Integration of Social Systems," *ibid.*, Chapter 1; and "The Distribution of Power in American Society," in Parsons, *Politics and Social Structure*. See also Robert V. Daniels, "Marxian Theories of Historical Dynamics," in Werner J. Cahnman and Alvin Boskoff (eds.), *Sociology and History: Theory and Research* (New York: Collier-Macmillan, 1964), pp. 62-85; Robert N. Bellah, "Durkheim and History," *American Sociological Review*, 24 (August 1959) (reprinted in abridged form in *ibid.*, pp. 85-103); and Winston White, *Beyond Conformity* (New York: The Free Press, 1961). Also relevant are two of Parsons's earlier articles (both reprinted in *Politics and Social Structure*): "Democracy and Social Structure in Pre-Nazi Germany" and "Some Sociological Aspects of the Fascist Movements."

63. See Franz Josef In der Smitten, "Possible Developments in Radio and Television Techniques in the Next Few Decades," *EBU Review* (January 1969), pp. 28-32.

64. UPI story, December 31, 1969.

65. See "The End of the Mass Magazine?" *The Public Interest* (Summer 1970), pp. 119-121.

66. *Newsweek,* March 30, 1970, page 49.

26

THE MEDIUM IS NOT THE MESSAGE

Bliss C. Cartwright and R. Stephen Warner

During the past two decades, Parsons' theoretical attention has turned increasingly to the explanation of dynamic processes in advanced systems. Having formulated four functional problems of all systems (adaptation, goal-attainment, integration, and pattern maintenance), he and his co-workers postulated that system evolution entails increasing structural differentiation into these four cells. With Durkheim, he recognized that such structural differentiation raises problems of social integration. To explicate the processes of integration and communication in advanced systems, Parsons by the early 1960's had articulated a concept of "generalized media of social interchange." The media concept was seen to be an answer to questions concerning the variable adaptive capacities of systems. Four media were conceptualized as grounded in the social system: money, power, influence, and value commitments.

The purpose of this essay is to assess the usefulness of Parsons's conceptualization by examining closely his arguments concerning power as a medium and his parallel between media and language. The essay has five parts:

1. We begin with an exposition of Parsons' media concept, particularly his argument that power ought to be understood as a medium analogous to money, and a statement of what he takes to be the contributions of the concept.

2. Then we proceed through a critical analysis of the derivations concerning the political system that Parsons claims to follow from the power-money analogy. Parsons' theoretical program asserts that

> certain structural arrangements generate and support a *medium* of power which has certain consequences for the political system.

However, in practice, we find that most of his derivations rely on two-variable models, that is, that certain *structural* arrangements have certain *consequences*, which, from the point of view of parsimony, do not require media as intervening mechanisms.

3. In order better to understand why Parsons postulates a concept he does not use, we attempt a historical reconstruction of the theoretical steps that led him up to the media concept. We suggest that the media concept can best be viewed as a convenient name or rubric for certain *dependent* variables that Parsons believes ought to be explained, rather than as an explanatory variable in its own right.

4. Looking closely at Parsons' parallel between money and language, we find that Parsons' justification for the media concept relies on philosophical (rather than empirical) arguments and that numerous empirical difficulties are created by attempting to view resource-processing issues within the framework of symbolic *objects* which are either present or absent.

5. We conclude with suggestions for directing research toward questions posed in *adverbial* terms, e.g., under what circumstances are efforts at communication and control accomplished with minimal expenditure of resources? The major primary texts for our analysis will be Parsons' essays, "On the Concept of Political Power" and "On the Concept of Influence" which treatments, especially the former, Parsons has recently claimed to be paradigmatic.[1]

We are indebted for advice, suggestions, comments, and encouragement given by Rainer Baum, Ludlow Brown, Yoon Choe, Randall Collins, Liewellyn Gross, Robert Kagan, Jan Loubser, Jonathan Ratner, Ronnie Steinberg Ratner, Katharine Snyder, Neil Smelser, Ross Starr, Ronald Weinstock, and Stanton Wheeler.

The order of authors' names was determined by a random assignment, as this paper is in every sense a joint enterprise. It began several years ago as an informal debate between two incurable conflict-functionalist colleagues and ended as a scholarly collaboration between friends.

A BRIEF EXPOSITION

Parsons begins by recognizing some controversial problems in the literature on power: the conceptual diffuseness of the term, the issue of whether coercion of consensus is "really" basic to power, and the zero-sum problem.[2] By conceiving of power as a *specified type* of mechanism, by articulating the centrality of *confidence* to both power and money, and by conceiving of power as playing a role in political *"investment,"* Parsons claims to have resolved these problems. The crux of the argument is that "power is here conceived as a circulating medium, analogous to money, within what is here called the political system, but notably over its boundaries into all three of the other neighboring functional subsystems of a society . . . , the economic, integrative, and pattern-maintenance systems."[3] What does Parsons mean?

Generalized Media

Power and money, along with influence and value commitments—with which we shall not deal directly here—are alike conceived to be "generalized media of exchange," "circulating media," "symbolic media," or "mechanisms of interaction" (Parsons seems to use these various locutions interchangeably). They share the following properties:

1. Such media are forms of language; they are "symbolic," in the sense that they are intrinsically worthless. Power and money are sought after not for what they "are," but for what they can be "exchanged" for. They are modes of communication in the sense that they are used to make offers. As modes of communication, they are effective only within defined social boundaries. Just as the *guaranteed acceptibility* of the dollar is limited to the United States, so the dictates of the government are binding only within the territorial boundaries of the United States. Just as any language, they operate on the basis of an institutionalized "code," a lexicon within which meanings are understood. But money and power are a special kind of language whose "message" is in the "imperative" mood; they are ways of getting things done. Their usefulness stems from their symbolic nature: One need rely neither on gold nor on force for economic and political transactions. Just as an economy using only monetary metal is an undeveloped one, so also the regular recourse to overt force is not an index of power but of political weakness. This symbolic aspect of power seems to be part of Parsons' answer to the question of why there is not a cop on every street corner.

2. They are "generalized" media in the sense that their use is not confined to any particular relationship. Just as money is an advance over a barter system in providing a number of degrees of freedom in what one can buy and when and in what context one can exchange something of intrinsic worth for it, so also power is conceived by Parsons as not being confined to the context of any particular sanctioning. It is *generalized* capacity to secure the performance of binding obligations . . . .[4] Whereas traditional economies and polities operate on the basis of ascribed relationships and barter exchanges, social evolution and differentiation require more flexible mechanisms of exchange and allocation. Just as money and monetary institutions (e.g., banks) appear only with social development, so also "power" in the strict technical sense is not an attribute of traditional (e.g., patriarchal) politics.[5]

3. As a consequence of their symbolic nature and their generality, such media as power and money require a large measure of confidence for their effective operation (i.e., their acceptability). For Parsons, the question of why one should accept "worthless" money in exchange, say, for one's week's labor is parallel to the question of why one should perform a citizen's obligation—say, registering for the draft—with only a rather vague and general guarantee of rights corresponding to obligations in return. He insists that the easy answers—money is backed by gold and Uncle Sam's dictate is backed by his penitentiary—are inadequate, even if containing a grain of truth. In fact, a backing for money equal to or better than gold is an economic system which regularly produces economic utilities. So also, in the political sphere, the imperative command is backed by an "effective" political system, one that manifestly performs up to expectation. Thus, just as *both* gold and the GNP back our "confidence" in money, so also *both* force and effectiveness back the "legitimacy" of power.

4. Finally, money and power are "circulating" media. Each is, in economists' terms, a medium of exchange and a store of value. They may be "hoarded" and they may be spent.[6] "The spending of power is to be thought of, just as the spending of money, as essentially consisting in the sacrifice of alternative decisions, which are precluded by the commitments undertaken under a policy".[7] Yet, being spent, such media are not dissipated; rather, they circulate.[8] From the point of view of the unit, in terms of Parsons' familiar interaction paradigm, the money ego uses to induce alter to relinquish something of value can in turn be used by alter. Although it is exceedingly unclear in his treatment,[9] Parsons appears to have in mind that alter's exercise of power over ego creates expectations on the part of ego (1) that other similarly

situated units will be subject to similar exercises ("If I have to register for the draft; so do they") and (2) that alter will be *generally* obligated to perform his duties to ego ("If I pay my taxes, I'd better receive adequate governmental services"), this *general* expectation being backed by ego's own power (e.g., the right to vote[10]). From the point to view of the system, circulating media are mechanisms moving back and forth to facilitate exchanges and communications. "Spending" media does not consume them.[11] Such, then, are the common properties of money and power and the other generalized media — they are symbolic, generalized, based in large part on confidence, and circulating.

Power as a Medium

Having discussed some common properties of media, we now turn to a consideration of the special properties of the medium Parsons calls "power." The provision of a definition is always an involved matter for Parsons. He will not have recourse to merely commonsensical notions, nor will he rely simply on the "literature." Indeed, he is aware that his concept of power and the political system violates many widely accepted usages. These problems of definition are due to Parsons' emphatic and self-conscious use of analytical-functional (rather than concrete-structural) reference points.[12] Thus, Parsons refuses to begin the definition of "power" by reference to "government" or "police forces." But because he also rightly wants to cut through the conceptual diffuseness that has surrounded the term, he avoids defining power as simply "the ability to get things done." Rather, he converges on a definition from two perspectives, by creating a typology of sanctions and by invoking the logic of his AGIL scheme.

Power is certainly, at the most general level, a way of getting things done. Parsons outlines four types of sanctions at "ego's" disposal on the basis of two dimensions, (1) whether the sanction is negative or positive, and (2) whether the sanction operates through the channel of the situation of alter or through alter's intentions. "Negative-situational" sanctions or "coercion" will turn out to have an intimate relationship to power, though the two terms are not identical.[13] ("Power," for one thing, is generalized and symbolic; "coercion" is intrinsically effective.) Power, it will be seen, involves a particular kind of symbolization of coercion.

To specify what kind of coercion is at issue, Parsons brings to bear his four-function paradigm of adaptation, goal-attainment, integration, and (latent) pattern maintenance. Just as in the economy (or A subsystem of a society) transactions are mediated by money, so also in the "polity" (or G subsystem) transactions are mediated by power; so Parsons asserts. Thus, power has a locus. But as the polity is the analytic subsystem specializing in collective goal attainment, this means that power becomes a medium for the attainment of collective goals. Thus to speak of "political" power is a redundancy.

Thus we see that Parsons has converged on the idea that power is somehow to be defined by the bearing of *force* or coercion on *collective goals*. Without being very explicit, he has thus joined two of the classical definitions of the category of the "political," the one Weberian, emphasizing monopoly over the legitimate use of force,[14] the other stemming from the literature on public finance and concerning the provision of public goods.[15] Note also that the intersection of these two criteria — force and collective goals — turns out to resemble intimately the definition of the concrete institution of the "state," notwithstanding Parsons' analytical emphasis.[16]

With these considerations in mind, Parsons proffers a formal definition of "power." "Power, then, is generalized capacity to secure the performance of binding obligations by units in a system of collective organization when the obligations are legitimized with reference to their bearing on collective goals and where in case of recalcitrance there is a presumption of enforcement by negative situational sanctions — whatever the actual agency of that enforcement."[17] Four aspects of this definition deserve highlighting.

1. Power is a *generalized* capacity; it is not confined to situationally specific acts of coercion.
2. The obligations mobilized by power are by definition binding (e.g., legally prescribed) and legitimized by collectivity-orientation. Power is thus inherently institutionalized.[18]
3. It *may* be necessary to enforce the bindingness of obligations through the use of coercion, but such enforcement is not required by definition.
4. The agency of enforcement is not (in the formal definition) specified; it may be government, a citizen, or another agent. Power, that is to say, circulates.

Having stated that power is a generalized medium "directly parallel in logical structure" to money, Parsons goes on to note one important but often overemphasized disanalogy. That is that power is hierarchical in a way that money is not. A has *more money than* B; but A may have *power over* B. Presumably it is this invidious, hierarchical aspect of power that stimulated the zero-sum school of thought. Yet Parsons maintains that hierarchy is a *functional* aspect of power and that its potentially cumulative, indivious nature is *mitigated* by its circulation.

Hierarchy is *functional* because in matters as "serious" as force and collective goals "there must be priorities in the matter of which decisions take precedence over others, and back of that, of which decision-making agencies have the right to make decisions at what levels."[19] (The institutionalized code specifying the proper uses and users of power Parsons calls, reasonably enough, "authority." Authority is thus comparable to rights in property, on which the legitimate use of money is based.)

The hierarchical aspect of power is *mitigated*, in modern, differentiated, pluralistic societies, by equalization of the franchise — a vote may be very little "power" but it is power, just as a dollar is money[20] — and by "equality of opportunity" for collective service, whereby government becomes no longer the special preserve of a highly privileged stratum. Hierarchy, therefore, is neither necessarily ascribed nor cumulative.[21] These features of modern society, apparently, are aspects of the "circulation" of power. Moreover, Parsons points out, even the supply of money has to be centrally controlled (e.g., by the Federal Reserve system) in the interest of system functioning. Thus the hierarchical aspect of power is not, when fully considered, a serious qualification on the analogy of money and power.[22]

Some Theoretical Consequences

Having stated this conception of power, Parsons maintains that it enables him to resolve the controversies cited at the outset of this essay, as well as to make independent theoretical contributions:

1. Neither money nor power are zero-sum media. Additions to the supply[23] of both media may be made by a "banking" process. A multiple of dollars deposited in a bank may be loaned out. In this way the banker is enabled to create a greater quantity of money and thus to contribute to investment and increases in total economic utility. Dollars on deposit do a "double duty." Similarly, votes as a form of generalized support enable the "political banker" or official to *increase* the total of power and through it the total of political effectiveness in the system. Parsons insists that this is a major theoretical breakthrough, and we acknowledge that his emphasis that neither economic nor political processes are necessarily zero-sum is a salutary one.

2. However, precisely because of the symbolic character of the media and the risks involved in the combinatorial process, both banks and governments in advanced societies are necessarily "insolvent" at any given time. Neither the media nor the values that they represent are infinitely and immediately expandable; there are opportunity costs connected with their allocation. Thus widespread demands for immediate payoff (comparable to panic withdrawals) are an inherent risk of advanced systems. Deflationary spirals eventuating in a devolution to barter-like conditions are an ever-present possibility. The McCarthyism of the fifties, a movement demanding the "hard currency" of "loyalty" and "patriotism," represented a withdrawal of a form of generalized support.[24] Here again Parsons has performed a valuable service to sociologists, who are perhaps overly inclined to envy the "hard realities" of the economist.[25] By emphasing the symbolic aspect of money, Parsons suggests a potentially fruitful area of a sociology of money.

3. Finally, though Parsons does not emphasize it, we should like to note that he has presented a conception of power that transcends the sterile behavioral-reputational debate.[26] For Parsons, power is a *capacity*, not to be measured by reference to an overt sanction. Power is often most effective precisely where it is least noticed.

CRITIQUE: THE MEDIUM IS NOT THE MESSAGE

We have seen that Parsons maintains that he has largely resolved a number of outstanding issues in political sociology by means of his postulation of "power" as one among a family of generalized media of interaction. Now a number of commentators have pointed out that Parsons has succeeded in this endeavor only insofar as he has so narrowly circumscribed the understanding of power as to exclude many of its most problematic aspects (e.g., illegitimate power) and that he has presented a quite conventional and uncritical) analysis of those phenomena he has determined to study.[27] Other critics have analyzed disanalogies in the media concepts.[28] Although by no means necessarily disagreeing with these critiques, we intend to proceed in the present section of our paper to meet Parsons on his own ground, to examine, that is, the structure of his argument itself. The major conclusion of this examination is that the postulation of a "medium" of power is unnecessary to the derivations regarding advanced political systems (especially that of the United States) that Parsons provides. In this sense, a medium of "power" turns out not to be an operative intervening variable in the conclusions Parsons draws.[29]

Our argument will proceed through the following four issues: (1) zero-sum; (2) confidence, including legitimation, trust, and deflation and inflation; (3) circulation; and (4) generalization of the mandate. With respect to each issue, it will develop that a generalized medium of power is irrelevant to the message about the polity Parsons wishes to convey.

Zero-sum

By means of the media conception, Parsons claims to have answered those other theorists who maintain a zero-sum conception of power.[30] Now in considering this issue, it is crucial to make, as Parsons does, the distinction between the properties of *media* (money and power) which are, we remember, intrinsically worthless and the *outputs* of the *system* (utility and effectiveness) which are the actual "value principles" on the basis of which the performance of systems is evaluated. Without *expandable* generalized media, Parsons insists, the economic and political systems would be trapped in a mere "circular flow" of sanctions, which would be characterized by a "zero-sum." Contrary to Parsons, however, the variable-sum attribute of the outputs of the economic and political *system* is not inherently dependent on a non-zero-sum *medium*. Robinson Crusoe is called upon by writers of textbooks in economics to illustrate the way in which investment and savings (and hence growth) occur in a primitive (one-person, non-monetary) economy. Obviously, it is not only advanced, differentiated systems that are capable of economic growth. Even in a differentiated system, it is at least highly controversial among monetary theorists whether money is necessarily required for growth to take place.[31] More generally, what is important ultimately both for the actors in Parsons' system and for the system as a whole is not whether the supply of money or power is a constant or a variable. As Parsons well knows, merely to increase the supply of money, *ceteris paribus*, is to create inflation. Thus what is important is whether the total "pie" of economic utility is increased and whether, analogously, the total of political "effectiveness" is increased. Parsons recognized this, evidently, in his original refutation of Mills's zero-sum conception.[32] There Parsons presented an analogy of (intrinsically valuable) *wealth* to power. By the time of his media analysis, however, the concentration was on *money* and power had become a *symbolic* phenomenon, as well as one oriented, by definition, to collective goals.[33] In this fashion, the "zero-sum" question, stressing the invidious distribution of something of importance to social actors, was not so much refuted as rendered meaningless. If, however, we wish to investigate the conditions under which "real" utility and effectiveness can be increased, we should want to inquire into, among other factors, the level of mobilization within the system (e.g., unemployed resources) as well as the attributes of the specific

political and economic investments being contemplated (e.g., their cumulative character). Thus the *structural* attribute of levels of mobilization is in this respect more important than a "medium" in explaining a variable sum *system*. (Now manipulation of the money supply is surely a part of the economist's strategy of growth in a monetized economy. Yet what Parsons wants to do is to explain the advantages of the phenomenon [and concept] of media in the first place; it cannot be part of such an explanation to assume their existence as a first premise. Such reasoning is circular.)

To take a political example, Robert Dahl, whom Parsons regularly cites as a member of the zero-sum-of-power school, found it possible nonetheless to analyze what he regarded as creative politics (in Parsons' terms, a system of enhanced political "effectiveness") in his study of New Haven, *Who Governs?*[34] Whatever the empirical or ideological merits of that study, Dahl clearly regarded Mayor Lee as a successful political entrepreneur who contributed to political welfare and consensus but who operated within a zero-sum world of power (in the sense that insofar as he had power, other actors did not). Other zero-sum theorists more in the tradition of C. Wright Mills might be inclined to dismiss the possibility of a non-zero-sum *system*; yet holding a zero-sum conception of power did not prevent Dahl from analyzing political entrepreneurship. What such entrepreneurship involves has been stated in general terms by Stinchcombe:

> . . . a tentative proposal draws a preliminary nucleus of support, generally from among those to whom the proposal has the highest utility. The nucleus is often not yet a feasible coalition. Then the project is modified toward what will be acceptable to, and feasible to, a coalition which "appears on the horizon." For coalitions involving a large number or a variety of powers, a broker, or a holding company, or a politicians' politician is needed. In order to carry such a coalition to fruition, the trust of a large number of people and knowledge of their resources have to be concentrated in a man or a committee. Thus this kind of entrepreneurship is preeminently a political phenomenon—a fiduciary-brokerage function in a network of influence. But it is also a creative phenomenon, creating and modifying proposals so that they can be the basis of a coalition.[35]

The structure of powers, the distribution of their utility functions relative to each other,[36] a broker (who aggregates specific proposals and preferences, not media)—these are the elements that go into the understanding of creative politics. Parsons' attempt to arrive deductively at the necessity of a concept of a variable-sum political *medium* on the premise of his intuitive observation of the variable-sum property of the political system thus fails and proves unnecessary.[37]

We conclude, then, that: (1) a question of at least as great importance as that of a constant or variable supply of the (symbolic) *medium* is that of a constant or variable sum of those matters of "real" value, what Parsons calls utility and effectiveness; (2) to achieve enhanced utility and effectiveness, it is not necessary to postulate a variable-sum medium.

Confidence

Parsons has clearly highlighted a pivotal problematic for political and economic systems (indeed for all advanced systems) in their dependence on high levels of confidence. Yet it is questionable whether Parsons' contribution to the understanding of these phenomena through the media conception is as compelling as it may first appear. We will look at three of the ostensible derivations of the media analogy.

Legitimation

Parsons claims to answer the paradox of the acceptability of intrinsically worthless media by adducing an analogy between the *confidence* we have in money and the *legitimacy* we accord to power. Whatever the merits of Parsons' own view of social processes, it is clear that societies operate on a large measure of trust. His analogy, however, is a questionable one. Confidence in money is accorded to the medium itself; legitimacy, however, insofar as it is granted, is granted to the *user* and *uses* of "power" in Parsons' definition, rather than to the medium. Let us look again at Parsons' definition: "Power, then, is generalized capacity to secure the performance of binding obligations . . . when the *obligations* are legitimized with reference to their bearing on collective goals . . . ."[38] The "obligations," rather than the "capacity," are legitimized. This is no mere linguistic oversight, but is central to the message Parsons wants to convey. Whereas the uses to which money is put are in principle irrelevant to its acceptability in the payment of debts—money can be illegally or legally appropriated and illegally or legally spent, and all the while retains its character as a medium—for Parsons it is crucial that power, properly speaking, is socially regarded as being employed for collective purposes.

We conclude: legitimation, which may or may not be an appropriate qualification on the definition of power in the reader's view, for Parsons is less an attribute of a *medium* of power than of the *mode of its employment.*

Trust

Parsons' argument on the necessity of trust involves a difficulty similar to that regarding legitimacy.

Indeed Parsons systematically confuses trust in the medium with trust in agents and institutions.[39] Parsons notes that ego expresses his trust when he *accepts* from alter a "worthless' piece of *money* for an item of value he is selling. Parsons claims that this is a trust similar to that expressed by ego's *voting* for an alter over whom he has no day-to-day control but whom he expects to provide responsible leadership.[40] Both examples are indeed remarkable phenomena of trust, and Parsons is right to render them problematic. Yet the lack of parallelism is instructive. The phenomena are not quite precisely inverse of each other. Note that in the first case ego surrenders an object of value for a quantity of the medium of exchange; in the second, ego surrenders a quantity of the medium (his vote) not for an object of value, but for a mere expectation. The "trust" in the second case is in the *candidates* and their presumed responsibility;[41] in the first case it is in the acceptability of the *currency*. Granted, the two types of trust are closely parallel in Parsons' favored analogy of the special case of the banking and electoral systems, where ego "deposits" dollars and votes to the trust of bankers and political leaders. But it is questionable to erect a general analogy between power and money on the basis of this restricted example.[42] The "trust" phenomena that seem most to interest Parsons are those in which social actors manifest a kind of "patience," foregoing immediate demands for "payoffs" in the expectation that greater rewards will be forthcoming. But for the analysis of such phenomena, the money-power analogy serves primarily as a suggestive metaphor; it does not provide the actual analysis. Monetary and political *institutions* do depend on trust; but, for Parsons' analysis itself, the media concept does not serve as the variable linking the two.

More generally, Parsons' discussions of legitimation and trust illustrate the extent to which Parsons has collapsed the long-standing distinction between power and authority. Power for Parsons, must be specified as to the legitimacy of its user and its uses. Between the overriding concerns for these "end" points, the promised analysis of the *medium* is hard to find.

Deflation and Inflation

Parsons' argument that the inherent day-to-day "insolvency" of both banks and the polity creates the risk of deflation exhibits a similar confusion.[43] Parsons notes that trust in banks and in political institutions may be withdrawn. If the differentiated but vulnerable structures of the economy and the polity fail because of a "vicious circle" of such withdrawals, exchanges in society revert to a "barter" level, where the medium no longer enjoys public confidence. (More on Parsons' category of "barter" will follow.) Parsons tends to conflate the phenomena of deflation and declining confidence in the media, but what he is primarily interested in is decline in confidence in monetary and political institutions and leadership (e.g., banking panics and McCarthyism).

Yet, consider what happens in an economic deflation. (Granted that it has been many years since the United States has experienced economic deflation; our recessions have tended to be, in current parlance, "stagflationary.") A deflation involves a decline in prices and hence, temporarily at least, a *rise* in the exchange value of money. If it is severe, the rise in the value of money, combined with the lower level of economic activity usually coinciding with deflation, will cause a default on bank assets, which in turn can cause banks to fail. If this process is severe and prolonged enough, the entire monetary structure can collapse and a reversion to barter occur. However, note that, by definition, a deflation involves a *rise* in the value of money and a decline in its quantity; whereas it is *inflation* that involves a decline of confidence in the medium and a rush into commodities of intrinsic value. As of this writing (in the summer of 1973) the American economic system is experiencing a rather severe spate of inflation. Consumers are hoarding goods, particularly foodstuffs, in the expectation of higher prices. Savings institutions are experiencing worrisome withdrawals of funds by depositors who, in view of the shrinking value of their dollars, are seeking the extremely high rates of interest offered for short-term securities. These are precisely the sort of nontrusting behaviors that distress Parsons and that he labels "deflationary." But they are the result of monetary *inflation*. Thus, for short-run phenomena, Parsons has inverted the relationship between confidence in the medium (money) and inflation-deflation. (In the long run, as Parsons recognizes,[44] hyperinflation and depression can both bring about barterlike conditions in the rush to "real" assets and commodities. Germany in the early 1920's and America in the 1930's are examples, respectively, of such occurrences.)

Nor does this inversion seem to be a mere mistake on Parsons' part. "Deflation," as a decline in the confidence in *institutions* (banks, government), does concern him greatly. It restricts the adaptive potential of leadership; it inhibits a flexible approach to unforeseen contingencies. It tends to lock leadership into positions that Parsons would like to see transcended. DeGaulle's reliance on gold, a *force de frappe,* and ethnicity and the McCarthyites' insistence on *bona fide* patriotism and "security" are recidivisms from Parsons' point of view, involving as they did a withdrawal of trust from social institutions.[45]

He labels them "deflationary." But as we have seen, economic deflation, *per se,* is not a decline of confidence in the *medium.*[46]

Circulation

Parsons' attribution of the quality of "circulating" to his medium of power is most troublesome. It is, of course, intuitively obvious that money circulates and that its advent immensely facilitates economic exchange. Parsons and Smelser were able to derive the functionality of money in a differentiated society from a paradigm of exchanges between household and firm; money functioned to mediate the labor-to-commodity exchange.[47] One could readily picture commodities and services moving back and forth, and the medium of money moving 'round and round.' Parsons gives few clues as to what an analogous circulation of power would look like, except to assert that power legitimates expectations of effective political process and that the "spending" of power by an actor does not dissipate its quantity in the system. It is difficult to follow Parsons on this score. In the type of creative political entrepreneurship analyzed by Dahl and Stinchcombe (and evidently indicated in general by Parsons) power may not be "spent" at all if the distribution of preferences is such as to make all or nearly all participating actors "better off" by the consequences of the new policy. Moreover, it is not at all clear that "power" can be "saved" or "hoarded." Surely, under our current political institutions a vote cannot be saved.[48] Power, indeed, may not share that nonperishable property of money that allows money to serve as a "store of value." In that Parsons' "power" is by definition limited to collectivity-oriented and authorized uses, it is difficult to see how a nice analogy with the circulation of money could be constructed. Increasingly, then, Parsons' concern for circulation devolves to a macroscopic, analytical level, wherein power is conceptualized as "moving back and forth over the boundaries of the polity."[49] Thus, in the I-G interchange (between the "societal community" and the "polity"), "policy decisions" and "political support" (both forms of power) are interchanged; and in the A-G (economy-polity) interchange, "opportunity for effectiveness" and "commitment of services to the collectivity" are interchanged.[50] Insofar as these interchanges have empirical content, they seem to refer, respectively to reciprocity between voting and governmental actions, on the one hand, and hiring of personnel by government and acceptance of employment on the other. Yet, other than developing a set of obscure labels, Parsons seems to have done little here to present a concept of circulating *media.*[51]

Once again, the postulation of "power" as "circulating" is not a mere aberration for Parsons. He insists that to see power as circulating is a corrective to the view that power is hierarchical in a pejorative sense. The undoubted hierarchical aspect of "power" (or authority) is mitigated by "equality of opportunity" (to enter government service) and universal franchise, Parsons insists. Yet so far as these tendencies do counteract the hierarchical aspect of power, they are *structural* features of society, not properties of a medium. Increasingly, it appears[52] that Parsons' emphasis on circulation is little other than a reiteration of the functionalist's faith in integration and reciprocity between institutions and groups.[53] The concern for a *circulating medium* of power in other than a hortatory fashion is lost. Nor could it be otherwise, given Parsons' definition of power.[54]

Generalization of the Mandate

Perhaps the most crucial attribute of media for Parsons is that they are, as he terms it, "generalized." He claims that the degrees of freedom for consumers facilitated by the advent of money is parallel to the degrees of freedom granted political leadership by generalized power. Flexibility in foreign policy, domestic initiatives, and support of productive programs lacking powerful constituencies (such as scientific research) all are facilitated, he claims, by power-generalization.[55] Direct exchange of political support for particular policies (such as the AFL-CIO's attitude toward Congressmen and section 14b of the Taft-Hartley Act) is to Parsons a form of barter which, if widely practiced, would severely inhibit the adaptive capacity of society. His earlier commentary on *Voting* made the point that the American electoral process generalizes political support and so facilitates flexibility and leadership discretion.[56] The more recent work on power as a medium ostensibly builds on that earlier base.

Here, however, the most damaging confusions enter Parsons' arguments, and we shall require some space to straighten them out. As Parsons recognizes, it is the *structural* conditions of the American political system that render the electoral mandate a highly "general" one. As political sociologists have long known, it is the simultaneous pluralist social structure and dual party, single member, majoritarian electoral system of the United States that facilitates the discretion (Parsons' "generalized power") of our elected leaders.[57] Parsons acknowledges the role of such variables as electoral rules and social pluralism,[58] but he fails to take the next step of *analyzing* the operation of such variables. In Fourth Republic France, for example, the attributes of Parsons' generalized

medium of power were present (including nearly-universal franchise and equality of opportunity to enter government service), but political leadership was nonetheless constrained by an electoral and party system that particularized rather than generalized the political *mandate*. Innovations were difficult, and action was taken only under the pressure of *force majeure*.[59] What is crucial in the contrast of this system and that of the United States are the *structures* of interest articulation and aggregation.[60] Of course such structures must be supported by an institutionalization of the "rules of the game,"[61] but that is true of "nonmediated" processes as well.

This point will become clearer if we investigate what Parsons means by the category of "political barter." The term barter, presented diffusely by Parsons as an opposite of media-exchanges, sometimes implies reliance on intrinsic effectors, more frequently implies *quid pro quo* arrangements. Political barter apparently subsumes such phenomena as vote-trading and voting for a candidate in order to enforce a *particular* policy alternative.[62] Here are two quasi-definitional statements: "the *quid pro quo* of political barter" is exemplified by the exchange, "'you vote for my measure, and I'll vote for yours.'"[63] "In some cases election is tied to barterlike conditions of expectation of carrying out certain specific measures favored by the strategically crucial voters and only these."[64] Presumably, generalization of power in advanced, differentiated systems tends to overcome such barterlike arrangements, and their persistence (at whatever minimal level) is a form of atavism.

Now in what sense are giving political support contingent on specific policy actions and vote-trading as political phenomena analogous to the economic category of barter? Barter is a *direct* exchange of commodities of *intrinsic* value, unmediated by money. It requires a "double coincidence of wants." Voting for a candidate only if he will promise to use his position to enact specific measures is to trade a bit of a *medium* (the vote) for a promissory note on future action. Its economic analogue is not barter but, for example, buying wheat futures (with money) on a commodity market (except that the purely economic case has the advantage to the buyer of being legally enforceable). Such an exchange *is* transacted through the use of a symbolic medium of exchange; thus it cannot be barter.

Vote-trading is similarly remote from barter. It often looks like this: Senator Jones wants measure *a* passed. He approaches Senator X (who may be *any* Senator) and proposes a deal. "You vote yes on *a*, and I'll vote yes on *b*, or *c*, or *d*." What strikes many citizens as shady about this transaction is *precisely* the irrelevance to senator Jones of the *particularities* of the other party and the other measure. Jones is using his vote as a highly *general* medium, apparently to be used for any and all transactions (in the extreme case), in just the way money can be used. (In a sense, our civic culture expects legislation to proceed on more of a barter basis than a generalized basis. We expect legislators to form coalitions that are less ad hoc in character; we expect coalitions to be based on a multiple coincidence of wants. Presumably, political parties involve at least a measure of such coincidence.)

Now why should Parsons refer to such mediated transactions as barterlike? Perhaps because they involve an exchange of sanction for sanction. But at least one of the sanctions is a *symbolic* one, just as is true when a commodity is exchanged for money. Just as Parsons' discussion of trust was more about a patient public attitude toward the exigencies of leadership and financial institutions than about a medium, so also his discussion of generalization says little about a medium and much about institutions. He seems to be interested in structured situations where actors must "go out on a limb," for example, manufacturing thousands of automobiles that no one has contracted to buy in the expectation that they will be purchased or voting for a candidate who is an unknown quantity in the hope that he will prove to be a responsible leader, or signing a legislative bill that will hopefully benefit some public need but that might backfire. These phenomena are truly market-like, but the nonmarket phenomena of contractual and custom-order transactions, which Parsons finds it possible to characterized as ascriptive or barter-like,[65] are equally transacted with the use of the generalized *medium,* money.

What seems likely is that Parsons regards *quid pro quo* voting as barter because it *circumscribes the discretion of political leadership.*[66] We remember that Parsons pointed out that the advent of money facilitates degrees of freedom for the consumer. So also Parsons' "power" facilitates degrees of freedom, but this freedom is enjoyed by leadership precisely in that it is restricted for the voter.[67] Those systems in which structural conditions (especially the electoral rules and social pluralism that facilitate a two-party system) are such as to discourage *quid pro quo* voting are those that encourage a large scope of discretion for elected leaders. Perhaps a "generalized medium of power" could be defined as "those structural conditions conducive to leadership discretion," but that would be to reduce Parsons' argument to a tautology.

Once again, Parsons has not simply made a mistake. Collectivity-orientation is for him an aspect of power by definition; and Parsons increasingly views flexible, responsible leadership as necessary to the well-being of the collectivity.[68] If the polity were simply that subsystem in which socially-organized force and symbolizations thereof were used to enforce the provision of public goods, some analogies with money might be selectively made. James Coleman has shown how a "political money" might be instituted to facilitate both the provision of public goods *and* the enforceable choice of the individual elector. He writes:

> When the consequences of an activity are indivisible among the members, and yet each has a claim to some control over the activity, this claim must be exercised by a *fraction* of control over the indivisible activity, rather than total control over the divisible activity.[69]

Coleman's hypothetical innovation, which might involve divisible quantifiable units of political support to be given by the voter to legislators whose policies he supports, would for Parsons fall under the pejorative label of "barter." For Parsons, "policy decisions" are "a factor in the integration of the system, not . . . a consumable output of the political process."[70] The "populistic" practice of tying leadership to popularly supported policies is counterproductive in Parsons' view.[71]

Parsons' characterization of "power" as "generalized," then, seems to conflate at least three dimensions: (1) elitism vs. populism ("power" facilitates leadership discretion), (2) collectivity-orientation vs. unit-orientation, and (3) symbolization vs. intrinsic effectiveness.[72] Parsons' "power" is elitist, collectivity-oriented, and symbolic. Money is symbolic but is neutral regarding the first two dimensions. Force is intrinsically effective but highly general with respect to its potential users and uses. (It is thereby also neutral with respect to the first two dimensions.)

It would seem that under the rubric of "generalization," an attribute of money as a medium, Parsons has included a number of attributes of "power" in his special sense. These attributions have the effect of providing a theoretical rationale for the formal operation of the American political system, but they increasingly make it difficult to sustain Parsons' claim that power is "a generalized medium in a sense *directly parrallel in logical structure,* though very different substantively, to money as the generalized medium of the economic process."[73] The parallels are generated in part at the expense of consistency and clarity in the use of such terms as generalization.

We conclude as follows: The important observations regarding the political process that Parsons makes—its variable-sum character; its dependence on confidence and trust and consequent vulnerability to crises of confidence; its egalitarianism and responsiveness; and its facilitation of leadership discretion—are derived in his argument from institutional and social structural variables and not from the concept of a medium of power analogous to money. The money analogy serves primarily as a suggestive metaphor under which to subsume a large variety of phenomena, which in turn are explained without recourse to the media concept.

SUBSTANTIVE INGREDIENTS OF THE MEDIA ANALYSIS: SKETCH OF AN INTELLECTUAL HISTORY

Parsons' Emphasis on the Media Concept

Having demonstrated that, contrary to Parsons' explicit programmatic position, the medium of power does not function as an intervening variable in his theoretical derivations, we now turn to a reconstruction of the analyses of modern political systems that led Parsons up to the postulation of the media concept. It will be seen that several of what later appear ostensibly as derivations from the concept were earlier derived from more particular substantive premises, all of them, nonetheless, involving economic-political analogies. First, however, we must be clear that Parsons' programmatic position is an emphatic one.

Notwithstanding the claim advanced here and elsewhere[74] that the logic of Parsons' media concept is lacking in rigor, it ought not be supposed that the object of our theoretical attention is a poor relation in the family of Parsons' ideas. While the very enterprise of comparing political and economic processes in Parsons' fashion at first startles the reader and encounters obvious and serious disanalogies, we grant that Parsons is aware of the revolutionary nature of the theoretical step he is taking. It must be supposed that he has a self-conscious theoretical agenda.

No doubt one must be wary of assigning undue weight to Parsons' protestations of the crucial nature of each of his conceptions. Yet he seems to have emphasized the importance of the media concept—and particularly the monetary analogy aspect of it—to an extraordinary degree. He recently took to task one of his critics for failing to appreciate the extent to which his analysis of equilibrium has been extended in his theoretical work on power. He notes that a "very substantial proportion of [his] theoretical work for over a dozen years" has been devoted to the media.[75] In a collection of his writings including the

essays on power, influence, and value commitments, a collection appearing over five years after the publication of the power essay with its money-power analogy, he reiterates his conviction of the strategic significance of his concept of power and goes on to address a theoretical admonition to political scientists:

It may sound strange for a noneconomist, and a sociologist at that, to be "lecturing" political scientists about the theoretical virtues of monetary theory, but this is indeed the main key to the significance of this idea[i.e., power].[76]

In an even more sweeping statement addressed to an even broader audience, Parsons concluded his article on "Social System" in the *International Encyclopedia of the Social Sciences* with the statement that the media "constitute the master scheme for the systematic analysis of social system processes."[77] Clearly the critic of Parsons' media work is not concerning himself with merely an aberrant phase in Parsons' theoretical development.[78]

Parsons' media analysis, especially the essay on power (which was the first and is still the most highly developed of the several treatments) is in fact a theoretical *tour de force* in which Parsons brings together a very great range of the theoretical and political commitments that have informed the whole body of his work for decades. The publication of the media concept in 1963 represented the culmination of years of theoretical development and was a step Parsons took with some deliberation. Unlike most of the essays he has published in the past two decades, the essay on power was a spontaneous effort,[79] delivered as an inaugural address to the American Philosophical Society and conceived independently of editors' and publishers' priorities. It contains, ostensibly, an elaboration and theoretical undergirding of his commentaries on Mills' *Power Elite* and Berelson, Lazarsfeld, and McPhee's *Voting*. It continues for the polity Parsons and Smelser's analytic efforts in *Economy and Society*. It reinforces his attempt to answer those critics who claim that his theory is unresponsive to phenomena of force and societal vulnerability. It anticipates his explicit return to evolutionary theory in the mid-1960's. It draws together these and other threads in a remarkably small space.

A Case Approach to Reconstruction

Parsons is inclined to characterize such examples of continuity in his work as evidence of logical derivation, but in a rather more accurate and revealing passage he has drawn an analogy between the development of his own theory and that of the common-law system.[80] To recognize that common law has grown by means of the justification of decisions on a case-by-case basis is not to say that common-law has no continuity or coherence. It does mean, however, that the *understanding* of its continuity is best approached through a historical, rather than axiomatic, reconstruction. And so it is for Parsons' theory. He admonishes those critics who would understand his theory that they must understand its development.[81] Just as a judicial decision in a common law system involves recourse to intellectually compelling reasoning and subsumption under general principles, so each of the steps in Parsons' theoretical development mobilizes his brilliance at providing justifications and at drawing upon a wide variety of general principles. Often enough, these justifications-under-a-principle involve analogical reasoning.

A few words, then, on the events, the "cases," so to speak, with which Parsons has grappled intellectually. (As we proceed through this sympathetic reconstruction, we ask the reader to bear in mind that we will be chronicling not a logically coherent development but a number of variations on the theme of economic-political analogies, with different aspects of what Parsons later attempted to work into the media concept being elaborated in particular contexts.) We will be seeking to answer the question of how Parsons arrives at a concept that proves unnecessary to his treatment of the polity.

Parsons makes no secret of the fact that he has long had an interest in political affairs, and that, as an "incurable theorist," he has attempted to subsume his understanding of political matters under an over-arching theoretical scheme. Two broad classes of events seem particularly to have demanded attention from him. One is the large-scale changes in the United States, particularly in the relationship between state and society, occasioned first by the depression and second by the decisive arrival of the United States as the pre-eminent world power after World War II. For Parsons, these trends have brought about higher levels of differentiation and integration in our society than had been manifest before. They were, thus, spurs to a further move in the direction of social evolution. The second broad class of events is that of fascist and quasi-fascist movements and regimes, Naziism and (Joe) McCarthyism particularly. Parsons regarded these movements as regressive (rather than as being the fruit of advanced capitalism) and thus as being, in part, reactions against precisely the broad evolutionary trends that also concerned him. Although his analyses of Naziism and McCarthyism concentrated on the *special* features of, respectively, German and American social structure that gave rise to them,[82] he increasingly found it possible to discuss progress and regress in similar terms and to show how it is precisely advanced systems

that are vulnerable to the damage that can be wrought by fascist movements. The media concept, especially its postulation of inflationary and deflationary phenomena, seemed to allow him to subsume these theoretical considerations under a single rubric.

Institutionalized Trust and McCarthyism

Although Parsons's own analysis of McCarthyism focused on the sources of support for the movement, showing that it was not likely to become a predominant political force in the United States, he took a lead from Edward Shils' *The Torment of Secrecy* for an understanding of the systemic *effects* of the movement.[83] Shils, not only an eminent sociologist but also a confidante of a number of scientists involved in the development of the atomic bomb and then in efforts at civilian control of atomic energy, had maintained that the paradoxical passion for publicity and secrecy characteristic of American populism was actually counterproductive to the enhancement of American power. In those societies, such as Britain, where political elites are freer of day-to-day public surveillance, Shils held, policies can be made on a more rational basis than in those where the *bona fide* credentials of leadership are called continually into question.[84] By the time of his reconsideration of the American right wing in 1962, Parsons had come to interpret the demands for absolute security put forth by the McCarthyites as an instance of "deflation" of public confidence in leadership. But as such a deflation, it was more analogous to a financial panic than to a full-scale depression, and thus once the downward spiral was stopped — the bubble pricked — by McCarthy's censure, an equilibrium based on confidence could be restored. From considerations of this sort, among others, Parsons drew the conclusion emphasizing the importance of confidence and the willingness of constituents to forego demands for continual demonstration of a solid basis for their confidence in their leaders. Note, however, that although this is the germ of the idea of symbolization in the media concept, so far Parsons is speaking of confidence in leadership and concrete institutions — bankers, and politicians such as Acheson — not confidence in the medium.

Zero-sum: The Debate with Mills

Perhaps the decisive step toward the variable-sum aspect of the media concept came with Parsons' confrontation with Mills' *Power Elite*. Unlike many of Mills' critics, Parsons did not take him to task for sloppy methodology,[85] nor, for the most part, did he take issue with Mills' over-all findings regarding an increasing centralization of power in the United States. He does claim that Mills' picture of a "military ascendancy" overinterprets short-run trends, and he reasserts the Berle-Means thesis regarding the differentiation of property and power in the face of Mills' attempt to refute it. His main argument with Mills, however, is a theoretical and ideological one. As might be expected, he is put off by the sarcastic and moralistic tone of Mills' analysis, but the theoretical issues are more serious than that. Generally speaking, Parsons accepts the view that American society is more subject to the decisions made by elites than our Jeffersonian heritage would find comfortable. He wants to show, contrary to Mills, first, that such a development is to be "expected"[86] and, second, that it must be interpreted in a light other than that cast by the individualistic assumptions inherent in much of American political thought, assumptions that, according to Parsons, Mills uncritically accepts.[87]

Mills' error, in Parsons' view, was to conceive of power solely in its distributive and particularistically oriented aspect. Concentration of power in the hands of an elite seems for Mills to be *ipso facto* a bad thing; but this conclusion can be drawn, Parsons points out, only if we fail to consider the extent to which power is a facility for the performance of system functions. What Mills does, says Parsons, "is to elevate a secondary and derived aspect of a total phenomenon into the central place."[88] Here Parsons introduces an economic-political analogy, pointing out that, although *wealth* can be invidiously distributed, it is nonetheless a resource for society and a good thing. So also for power: "it has collective as well as distributive functions,"[89] and just as it is better for a society to have more wealth than less of it, so also it is better to have more power, *ceteris paribus,* than less.[90] The argument is certainly persuasive on its face and, in modified form, it became one of the leading ideas of Parsons' sustained analysis of power, an idea for which he has been justly praised.[91] Note, however, that the refutation of Mills' zero-sum concept was made here on the basis of an analogy of wealth (not money) and power and that the collectivity-oriented aspect of the concept is not held to exhaust its meaning. The 1963 argument for power as a *medium* analogizes to *money* and defines power as (solely) a capacity for *collective* goal attainment.

We thus see the manner in which two threads of Parsons' media analysis were informed by his interest in political affairs; he clearly intended to make a contribution to a more rational public discussion of the political effect of social changes in America. For Parsons, Mills and the McCarthyites were reacting against social developments they did not comprehend. Neither side had the conceptual tools for the proper understanding of the role of responsible elites in society, whose freedom of action was necessary for the successful performance of system functions. The McCarthyites demanded a "hard currency" of absolute loyalty; Mills demanded a decentralization of power. Neither conceived of the political order as legitimately a differentiated subsystem of society, organized around the attainment of collective goals and requiring, for that function, high levels of public trust and social integration. Such a theoretical step was necessary for Parsons to provide a "defense" of pluralist democracy,[92] "asserting and justifying the increased importance of government."[93] He intended to contribute both to scientific and political discourse. As he concluded his essay on Mills:

> It is necessary not only to criticize existing conditions from the order philosophical or ideological points of view, but to take serious stock of the ideological assumptions underlying the bulk of American political discussion of such problems as power.[94]

Generalization: The Analysis of Voting

Parsons' invitation by Burdick and Brodbeck to take stock of the theoretical significance of the large body of data being accumulated on voting behavior provided him with an opportunity to articulate, in a sustained fashion, a theory of pluralist democracy that would transcend individualist assumptions. The result was his commentary on *Voting.*[95] The voting-behavior literature is multifaceted, but Parsons chose to concentrate on the systemic effects of voting. From one point of view, the voting data cast unflattering light on the electoral process: the outcome of an election is apparently decided by those who care least about it. But this apparent paradox provided Parsons (as it had also Berelson and his colleagues) with an opportunity to demonstrate the emergence of *system-level* functionality, providing for stability and change. The problem he faces is thus formally parallel to that addressed by Mandeville and Smith: private vices become public virtues. Voting on the basis of dominantly ascriptive solidarity provides an element of stability, whereas social mobility between social groupings, among other factors, contributes to flexibility.

For our purposes the most relevant part of Parsons' answer to the problem of orderly flexibility and change in his *Voting* essay is the theoretical framework with which it begins. Here Parsons builds a model of the two-party system. The party system is said to be the focus of the mechanisms by which the American political process works. A two-party system, assuming a pluralistic social structure and a sufficient degree of social integration, is a mechanism for generating *generalized* political support from constituents. The candidate, particularly in the Presidential elections that are the focus of Parsons' attention, must appeal to diverse interests; he must compromise and synthesize between varied points of view. Whatever the actual motivation of the voter, his vote is counted only for the one or the other major candidate.[96] Thus, from the point of view of the successful candidate, the "general meaning of the aggregate of the support he receives cannot be more than the endorsement of a broad *direction* of action for the polity."[97] From structural premises, therefore, Parsons has been able to show how the American political system generalizes support so as to facilitate effective political leadership.

Yet the process clearly cannot be one-way; Parsons expects that there is an output corresponding to this input of support. In order to grasp what it might be, he introduces another economic analogy, this time using a parallel between the situation of the wage worker and that of the voter. The wage worker relinquishes control over the product of his labor and in return accepts money income on the basis of the faith that it may at some time in the (immediate or distant) future be used to secure for him something of consumable value. Similarly, the voter relinquishes control of his expression of political support in the expectation that political leadership will provide the general *kind* of policies he favors.[98] Parsons has thus not yet hit upon the technical money-power analogy where voting is analogous to depositing money in a bank. In 1959, voting is said to be analogous to the provision of labor service, and confidence is reposited not in a medium but in leadership. Generalized support "takes the form of broadly based confidence in those assuming responsibility for leadership in governmental affairs which is necessary to enable them to act with real power . . . ."[99] Yet Parsons has clearly focused on the mechanisms making for the generalization of political power.

Wrapping It Up: Convergence on the Media Concept

There are a number of other threads that Parsons seizes upon in weaving his media argument. It brings him back to his original (1937) concern with the bearing of economic theory on sociology, but using structural economic analogies that allow him to transcend the "elementary" (and, Parsons would say, "barter-level") quasi-economic modeling of Homans.[100] It allows him to pose another "voluntaristic" solution to the Hobbesian problem of order, as he can emphasize that power, just as money, is

not intrinsically effective. It allows him to present a serious answer to the crescendo of critics who chided him for ignoring questions of power and change.[101] Yet these opportunities, combined with the "case-events" of political interest we have chronicled, do not yet provide an answer to the question how they could all be wrapped up in Parsons' particular concept of generalized symbolic media of social interaction.

We shall, then, consider four additional of Parsons' theoretical commitments that might have served as inputs to the media concept.

General Theory

In the foregoing pages, we have devoted attention to several essays of the genre Parsons used to call "applied" theory. Each of them concerns explicitly American social phenomena, as is reflected in each of the titles.[102] Yet they are not merely applications of a previously elaborated theory, as Parsons[103] acknowledges and emphasizes; they are rather new extensions and developments of the theory (or, perhaps, each is a new theory). Nonetheless, it is and has long been Parsons' aspiration to develop the most general kind of theory, one applicable across cultural, historical, and system-level boundaries. And as Parsons' unit of analysis is the *system,* it is not enough for him merely to be able to apply some of the same analytic concepts across these boundaries—as could be done with his marvelously flexible "pattern-variables." He clearly wants to be able to generalize entire structural patterns. The answer to this problem seems to have been to conceive of these American patterns, particularly pluralism and a two-party system, as aspects of an all-round evolutionary superiority of American society.[104] The particularities of the American political system and of the "medium" of power embedded in it could thus be attributed to a uniquely high level of societal "differentiation," a characterization of American society Parsons rather uncritically accepts.[105] The structural derivation (1959) of generalization of support could thus be down-played and the argument made that generalization was a concomitant of a medium of power which appears only in advanced systems.

The Primacy of Culture

We have seen in the preceding "case-studies" that the independent variables (e.g., party-systems, pluralism) and dependent variables (e.g., elites) tend to be structural factors. To be sure, they are surrounded and supported by normative commitments—"the operation of such a system is dependent on the firm institutionalization of the 'rules of the game.'"[106] But the concept of generalized media is at one remove higher. With it, the very control mechanisms and inputs and outputs are *symbolic* and are, in their very essence, constituted by consensus. It is in the analysis of cybernetic mechanisms that Parsons has acknowledged being a "cultural determinist".[107] Presumably this is one reason for Parsons' abandonment of the wealth-power analogy[109] and his elaboration of a money-power analogy. Wealth is "real"; money is symbolic.[109] Insofar as cultural patterns are on a higher level of generality than social-structural ones and, indeed, tend to integrate the contemporary world of modern societies into one system,[110] the media as symbolic entities are a further step toward a more general theory.

Pareto Optimality

Clearly, as we have seen above, part of the input to Parsons' media analysis is a political polemic. To alleviate public apprehensions regarding the appearance, during the past four decades, of a hugely powerful federal government, the conception of power as a medium serves quite well. After all, it is not intrinsically valuable, so no one ought to be motivated to secure it *per se*. But, like money and language, "power" is a mechanism the invention of which redounds to the benefit of nearly everyone, while making no one[111] worse off. Language, money, and "power" are good things. Because "power" is, by definition, oriented to collective goals, the question of its *distribution* is not raised (as, of course, it is raised by economists for money). As we have seen above, too, the vague conception of power as "circulating" is directed against an overemphasis on the necessarily hierarchical nature of power. Power and its mechanisms are in the interest of society.

Cognitive Style

Two well-recognized and self-acknowledged[112] aspects of Parsons' cognitive style may well have forced the final step toward the media concept. They are (1) his evidently deep-seated conviction that convergence is a form of proof and (2) his attraction to, and facility with, analogies.[113] In the several case studies discussed above, one or another aspect of the generalized medium of money was said to hold true of the political system: symbolization, generalization, variable sum, degrees of freedom, vulnerability to panic, and so on. To Parsons, these converged on a *complete* picture of "power" as analogous to money, with only the problem of "circulation" to be solved. As Parsons later reconstructed his thinking at this time, the question was:

> If there is a parallel between economy and polity, why not between money, which has come to be so very central to economic theory, and a corresponding medium centered in the polity?[114]

Parsons states his answer in particularly forceful terms; the urge to analogize and extrapolate was overwhelming:

> The most important sequel to his development [the understanding of money as a language] has been the emergence of a "sociology" of money as a generalized *symbolic* medium of societal interchange, along with a growing conviction that money *could not* be an isolated phenomenon, but must be a member of a family of media. An obvious place to look for one of its siblings was the political sphere. The search eventuated in a conception of political power as another such generalized symbolic medium . . . .[115]

But as we have seen, Parsons makes little other than hortatory use of this final conceptual step. The important derivations had already been made in the earlier treatments. What the "power" essay does is to bring them all together under one umbrella. It is a remarkable tour de force. But the umbrella is unnecessary.

Summary

This section of our essay has been devoted to an understanding of how it was that Parsons developed a concept that, to put it bluntly, his theory does not really use. We have seen that the process of reasoning must be understood in context rather than in fine isolation. The characteristic mode of Parsons' recent major publications — the collection of essays — is mute testimony to this necessity. Like the common law, Parsons' theory grows more by accretion on a bookshelf than by revision, codification, and supersession. The *Parsons-Forscher* can make the reasonable complaint that Parsons rarely, if ever,[116] lets it be easily known when he has subtly, but crucially, changed his position. That generalization of support is derived from particularly American structural variables; that the variable-sum argument was most compellingly made comparing wealth, not money, to power; that confidence is reposed in political leadership, not power; that deflation was originally conceived to be a decline of confidence in institutions, not media — these and other changes are obscured in Parsons' power essay. Perhaps we cannot expect him to provide revised editions of his works in order to render them consistent.[117] We might expect him to cite passages that he no longer accepts.

FROM NOUNS TO ADVERBS: A TENTATIVE RECONSTRUCTION

Having discussed Parsons treatment of power and the chronological development of his theory, we would like to conclude by examining the media concept itself.

The basic questions will be:

What does it mean to postulate the existence of a generalized medium?
What theoretical function does this perform?
What are the alternatives to media explanations?

Although we believe that Parsons has performed a major service in emphasizing

1. the theoretical importance of explaining variations in the operating *capacity* of social systems,
2. the significance of resource-processing mechanisms (particularly technological innovations which reduce transaction and information costs) as critical components in this process, and
3. the relative trade-offs between systemic flexibility and vulnerability in transactions requiring a high degree of trust and confidence,

we would like to raise some doubts about the wisdom of formulating those issues in terms of relationships between symbolic media and intrinsic satisfiers.

As a means of unpacking these themes, let us begin with Parsons' interaction paradigm.[118] The core feature of this paradigm is the interaction sequence,

Alter: Do X.
Ego: Why should I?
Alter: You ought to do X because . . .

For example,

Alter: Pay $1,000 in taxes.
Ego: Why should I?
Alter: Because you earned $10,000 last year and the tax on $10,000 is $1,000.
Ego: Why should I obey that rule?
Alter: Because you are a citizen and the rule applies to you.
Ego: Why should citizens have to pay taxes?
Alter: Because governments need money to provide services.
Ego: Why should people support their government?
Alter: Because they will be thrown in prison if they do not.
Ego: What's the likelihood of that happening to me? What is so bad about prison?

On the basis of this sequence, one can say,

1. when confronted by imperatives of the form "Do X because . . .," people can demand varying degrees of supporting evidence before deciding to act;
2. assessing arguments critically or uncritically

affects the resource-processing costs of a system (particularly when alter feels compelled to mobilize overt sanctions);

and begin asking:

Under what conditions will these resource-processing costs be high or low and with what consequences?

Parsons, however, takes a slightly different tack. He assumes that

1. every system has certain intrinsic sanctions (such as physical force and consumable commodities);
2. it is possible to construct symbolic substitutes for those sanctions which offer systemic benefits such as high flexibility and low transaction costs (but no inherent worth);
3. the systemic benefits of these symbols occur only if they are used and accepted by large numbers of people;

and then asks:

Since modern societies exhibit high levels of systemic benefits, what symbolic substitutes exist in these societies?

The first approach focuses on the amount of energy, effort, and evidence required to convince ego. It selects problems of the form:

Under what conditions will ego pay his taxes at varying costs to alter?

and examines alter's cost-benefits for all available sanctions. The second approach, however, gives a privileged status to certain kinds of sanctions (intrinsic sanctions). By invoking the tacit principle:

Low-cost compliance *without* intrinsic sanctions implies widely-accepted symbolic substitutes,

Parsons transforms a search for causal relations (linking alter's cost-benefits to differing sanctions) into an ontological problem (linking the presence or absence of intrinsic sanctions to the existence of certain symbolic objects). For example, in terms of the ego-alter interchange. Parsons would presumably say, ego obeys alter's command. "Pay $1,000," because he accepts alter's legitimacy arguments (about the legality and desirability of paying taxes) as a symbolic *substitute* for the sanctions alter could mobilize if ego resisted.

Given that both approaches are concerned about resource-processing costs, why does Parsons emphasize the importance of the symbol-sanction distinction? The answer lies in his analogy between language and money. Parsons argues that:

1. Social communication represents a process of

conveying thoughts, intentions, and experiences from one person to another.

2. Language forms a set of arbitrary signs and symbols which can be used to express these thoughts and feelings (i.e., the "meaning" of a word is derived from a non-inferential knowledge of physical and cognitive states).

3. The relationship between money and consumable commodities parallels the relationship between linguistic signs and their referents. "Just as the word 'dog' can neither bark nor bite, yet 'signifies' the animal that can, so a dollar has no intrinsic utility, yet signifies commodities that do, in the special sense that it can in certain circumstances be substituted for them and can evoke control of relations with them in the special kind of process of social interaction we call economic exchange."[119]

4. Therefore, as the adequacy of linguistic symbols depends on the clarity and specificity with which they are defined, it follows that people will accept monetary symbols only when the risks "involved in accepting the symbolic in lieu of the real"[120] are designed and delineated by well-defined normative standards.

Now, as a model of language, Parsons' analysis has severe shortcomings:[121]

1. By portraying language as a technological invention which increases communication efficiency, Parsons implies that it is logically possible to conceive of social action and communication in the absence of language (a claim which underestimates the close conceptual ties between communicating intelligibly and using a language correctly).

2. By stressing a person's immediate recognition of intrinsic sanctions, Parsons implies that it is possible to distinguish between primitive givens which are known directly and derivative constructs which are uncertain and error-prone (a claim which underestimates the epistemological differences between having an X sensation and knowing that something is X).

3. By viewing language as a relation between unidimensional symbols and their referents (without differentiating among nouns, verbs, adjectives, adverbs, propositions, arguments, and theories), Parsons reduces all issues to a single criterion, definitional clarity and specificity, without analyzing the weighting of *multiple* criteria implicit in the construction of cultural and institutional systems (a claim which underestimates the methodological differences in evaluating the truth of a proposition, the rigor of an argument, the generality of a theory, and so on).

For present purposes, the main point is to recognize

that Parsons' justification of the symbol-sanction distinction rests on a particular *philosophical* theory of meaning (frequently called a relational theory of meaning) which is simply one point of view, highly controversial and by no means widely accepted.

Even if one subscribes to Parsons' views on language (and we do not), the critical justification for the symbol-sanction distinction must be its empirical credentials, but the problems here are equally severe. As symbolic media are necessary conditions for systemic benefits, the following is a valid logical inference:

1. Systemic benefits occur only if media are accepted;
2. media are not accepted;
3. therefore, systemic benefits will not occur.

But it is difficult, if not impossible, to separate step (2) from step (3), because *ipso facto*,

> not accepting imperative commands at their symbolic value means either (a) lack of compliance, or (b) compliance based on intrinsic sanctions, and by definition, both states automatically increase a system's cost-benefit ratio.

Parsons claims that systemic benefits and symbolic media are independent theoretical constructs, but without clear measurement criteria for distinguishing among,

1. ego's acceptance of a command as a symbolic medium,
2. ego's acceptance of a command with minimal cost to alter, and
3. ego's acceptance of a command because of intrinsic sanctions,

the media concept tends to spawn borderline tautologies that reiterate the resource-processing characteristics of a system without providing explanatory mechanisms for increasing and decreasing *rates* of systemic capacity.

In addition, the symbol-sanction distinction tends to create the impression that society is faced with only bipolar choices: Either a society accepts the services of an intrinsically worthless medium (almost as an act of blind faith and devotion) or it suffers the consequence of reverting to barter or worse. Having constructed a dichotomous media concept, Parsons tends to see any deviation from the status quo as a forerunner of doom rather than as an occasion for investigating and adopting structural alternatives. For example, in the economic sphere:

1. The real alternative to a particular currency is usually a cost-benefit assessment of competing currencies rather than an automatic reversion to barter.

2. Strains and inefficiencies in market allocations frequently set the stage for examining the feasibility of various nonmarket allocation mechanisms (such as the provision of public goods through budget procedures).[122]

Likewise, in the political sphere, dissatisfaction with one governmental agency usually leads to a reallocation of jurisdiction and mandates to other agencies (witness the cyclical progression of problems from the legislature to the courts to the executive branch and back again during the life cycle of regulatory agencies).

Finally, the symbol-sanction distinction tends to overestimate the consensual character of institutional evaluations. By invoking the logical equivalence:[123]

1. Systemic benefits occur only if media are accepted,
2. if systemic benefits occur, then media are accepted,

Parsons frequently allows himself to slide from the general principle that the monopolization of almost any kind of social activity reduces the costs of resources-processing to the dubious conclusion that, therefore, one must accept and utilize the services of any given monopoly, without fully exploring countervailing values which might want to limit the options and discretion of authoritative leadership (particularly in political contexts). For example, in analyzing social influence (exemplified by a relationship between professional advice and scientific facts), it may be true that

1. There would be high information costs if each patient had to process all the medical "facts" himself.
2. A division of labor between doctors and patients cuts these costs, but the system could not work if everyone was "testy" (demanded frequent and lengthy justifications).
3. Increased professional discretion allows a greater range and depth of services to be performed (e.g., doctors can work on long-term causes rather than short-term symptoms). However, none of this implies that there cannot be serious and legitimate theoretical disagreements about what constitutes a medical "fact," how it should be interpreted, or what is an appropriate therapy. The basic problem here is that by establishing a definitional substitution between "intrinsic persuaders" and the total set of alter's legitimacy arguments, the symbol-sanction distinction implies that ego accepts all of alter's arguments in place of the sanction which automatically eliminates the possibility of wide-ranging, legitimate objections to the status quo.

What is the alternative? On the one hand, Parsons' theory of symbolic media raises numerous philosophical and empirical difficulties. On the other hand, his substantive arguments often raise important insights and problems. How can these points be reconciled? The critical move is to recognize that resource-processing problems involve the modification of ongoing activities or events rather than the presence or absence of certain objects. That is, instead of trying to force resource-processing problems into the *noun* form: Under what conditions do certain objects increase or decrease the resource-processing costs of a system? it is more natural to use the *adverbial* form: Under what conditions does a system operate efficiently and effectively? and focus on a marginal cost-benefit analysis.

For example, in the case of legal institutions, one might ask: In what situations will the generation of legal norms by a central authority be able to combine high levels of social integration (based on unified policy objectives) with decentralized mechanisms of dispute-resolution so that by invoking the appropriate norm, parties can resolve their disputes with minimal dependence on the sanctioning and interpretive facilities of the state?[124]

In analyzing a problem of this kind, it will be important to examine such variables as (1) the flow and dissemination of legal information ("the circulation of messages"), (2) distribution of disputant activities and transactions (e.g., variations in the frequency, intensity, and duration of conflicts), and (3) the perceived evaluation of authoritative performances (e.g., popular impressions of legal legitimacy, procedural fairness, and sanctioning effectiveness). But the core problem will not be the presence or absence of a "symbolic medium" (as if "the medium" were a hidden, ether-like substance accompanying every legal command). Rather the basic issue will be the structural conditions under which maximal conflict-resolving effectiveness can be achieved with minimal investments in the judicial machinery of the state (where the operative metaphor is the adverbial activity-modifier, "communicating effectively and efficiently").

We are now in a position to see precisely why the media concept raises so many problems for Parsons. By talking the language of "symbolic objects," Parsons implies that he is postulating the media as a new kind of explanatory variable (which naturally leads to questions of the form, "where is it and how is it causally related to other variables?"); whereas, in fact, the media are essentially names and shorthand descriptions for a complex *dependent* variable (variations in the operative efficiency of communicated information) which ultimately must be explained in structural terms. To adopt the media framework means that one is constantly searching for conjoint conjunctions between two objects, messages and media:

1. When resource-processing costs are low, alter issues a message and the message *is* accompanied (or conveyed) by a medium;
2. When resource-processing costs are high, alter issues a message and the message *is not* accompanied by a medium;

whereas parsimony, and Parsons' own substantive practice, indicates that little is lost (and much is gained) by using the adverbial form:

3. Ego can either obey alter's commands readily or unreadily,

to formulate the basic empirical variations which need to be explained.

CONCLUSION

In this essay, we have surveyed many different aspects of Parsons' media discussions, placing a primary emphasis on his treatment of money, power, and language. Although the media analogy subsumes many suggestive and fruitful observations, it also raises many questions and puzzles — not the least of which is the fact that when examined carefully, most of Parsons' substantive arguments rely on structural conditions, rather than media properties, for their basic explanatory variables. As an over-all impression, one gets the feeling that Parsons has somehow overloaded a valuable, heuristic model with theoretical burdens it was never meant to carry.

Does this mean that one should reject the concept of a generalized medium of exchange? The skeptical tone of this paper might imply we are inevitably bound to answer "yes," but that would be to misunderstand our purpose. What is required in this situation is not a major amputation but a selective pruning and trimming. For we strongly believe that the core of Parsons' analysis raises a very important and basic theoretical problem, namely,

1. given that the operating capacity of a social system is inversely related to the marginal costs of mobilizing, processing, and allocating basic social resources (such as motivational energy and organizational capacity);
2. given that information-processing systems generally combine maximal energy-control with a minimal consumption of productive resources;
3. given that information-processing (particularly the transmission of generalized promises and expectations) require high levels of trust and confidence;

the critical question becomes,

4. under what conditions will social systems be able to increase their operating capacity by developing high levels of trust in the *messages* transmitted across multiple spheres of specialization and authority?

By mapping the relations between social integration and mechanisms of communication, Parsons has fundamentally altered and expanded our understanding of the systemic consequences of social processes based on varying degrees of public trust and confidence. What remains as the next stage of research is to explore the causal determinants of confidence variations, particularly in terms of dynamic processes over time. As examples of potential questions for future research, we would suggest the following issues deserve serious consideration:

1. What are the structural conditions that encourage steady cumulations and erosions of confidence (as opposed to rapid accelerations and decelerations)?
2. Under what conditions will procedural considerations (as opposed to substantive outcomes) become the primary components in public evaluations of authoritative performance?
3. Under what conditions does the technical elaboration ("rationalization") of normative rules and specifications increase or decrease confidence in institutional operations?
4. What are the relative costs and benefits of attempts to achieve national integration through the institutionalization of multiple official languages?
5. Under what conditions does knowledge about the confidence levels of other persons affect evaluations of institutional performance?

NOTES

1. See T. Parsons, *Politics and Social Structure* (New York: The Free Press, 1969), pp. 352-404, for "On the Concept of Political Power," and pp. 405-429 for "On the Concept of Influence." For Parsons' recent claims, see T. Parsons, "Some Problems of General Theory in Sociology," pp. 27-68 in John C. McKinney and Edward A. Tiryakian (eds.), *Theoretical Sociology: Perspectives and Developments* (New York: Appleton-Century-Crofts, Inc., 1970); and T. Parsons, (with Gerald Platt), *The American University* (Cambridge: Harvard University Press, 1973).

2. That is the claim that A's gain in power must necessarily be B's loss and that, in reference to hierarchical systems what A (superordinate) has, he has precisely at the expense of B (subordinate). See R. Dahrendorf, *Class and Class Conflict in Industrial Society* (Stanford: Stanford University Press, 1959), p. 169. The term "zero-sum", when applied to the economic arena and money, is misleading. It might better be called the "constant-sum" theory, as here also A's gain is B's loss. To avoid confusion, however, we shall follow Parsons' usage. Parsons' view we shall call a "variable-sum" theory.

3. Parsons, *Politics and Social Structure,* p. 360.

4. *Ibid.,* p. 361, emphasis added.

5. Parsons, "Social Systems," pp. 458-473, in David Sills (ed.), *International Encyclopedia of the Social Sciences,* Vol. XV (New York: MacMillan, 1968), p. 471.

6. Parsons, *Politics and Social Structure,* p. 478.

7. *Ibid.,* p. 375. Rhetoric expressing caution regarding the spending of scarce political capital issued regularly from Washington during the Kennedy years, during which period Parsons' power paper was written.

8. *Ibid.,* p. 325.

9. *Ibid.,* pp. 330 and 362.

10. The use, however, of a large bloc of votes to enforce a particular policy preference (e.g., the AFL-CIO organizing its members to vote for Congressmen solely on their past or promised vote on section 14b of the Taft-Hartley act) approximates what Parsons calls "political barter" and is thus not an exercise of "power," properly speaking. We shall return to this problem below.

11. Parsons, "An Outline of the Social System," pp. 30-79, in T. Parsons, E.A. Shils, K.D. Naegele, and J.R. Pitts (eds.), *Theories of Society* (New York: The Free Press, 1961), p. 66.

12. For a sophisticated attempt to grapple with a Parsonsian definition of "economic" activity, see N.J. Smelser, "The Methodology of Comparative Analysis of Economic Activity", pp. 62-75, in Smelser, *Essays in Sociological Explanation* (Englewood Cliffs: Prentice-Hall, 1968), pp. 64-69.

13. The other types are positive-situational ("inducement"), positive-intentional ("persuasion"), and negative-intentional ("activation of commitments").

14. M. Weber, *From Max Weber: Essays in Sociology,* H.H. Gerth and C.W. Mills (trs. and eds.), (New York: Oxford University Press, 1946), Ch. IV.

15. See for example, J. Buchanan and Gordon Tullock, *The Calculus of Consent* (Ann Arbor: University of Michigan Press, 1962).

16. Parsons, *Politics and Social Structure,* pp. 368, 374.

17. *Ibid.,* p. 361.

18. *Ibid.,* pp. 486, 518.

19. *Ibid.,* p. 370.

20. *Ibid.,* p. 488.

21. *Ibid.,* p. 192.

22. Another apparent disanalogy was the fact that there is "obviously no generalized unit of power comparable to a currency unit." Yet, for Parsons, "linear measurability in terms of money . . . seems to be a special empirical advantage of the monetary system which derives from factors other that its status as a generalized medium" (*ibid.,* p. 486). Economists, who speak of one of the functions of money as its status as a "unit of account," might be inclined to disagree. At any rate, Parsons' strategy seems to be to render the analogy a homology by paring off from money the aspects in which it is dissimilar to power (see also note 42).

23. Perhaps velocity, rather than supply, increases; Parsons claims that the effect, and therefore the concept for sociological purposes, is the same (*ibid.,* p. 384n.).

24. Strictly speaking, for Parsons, McCarthyism was an example of deflation in the "influence" sphere. But since "influence" is higher on Parsons' cybernetic hierarchy than "power," its vicissitudes necessarily involve the latter (*ibid.,* p. 393). This aspect of Parsons' technical system theory need not concern us here.

25. He does, however, (*ibid.,* pp. 517-522), append to his media analyses an intimidating reference to the virtues of studying sophisticated monetary theory. The economics on which Parsons' treatment is based is quite elementary, however (derived for the most part from nineteenth century arguments against mercantilism). For example, nowhere does Parsons discuss the serious and difficult problems of trying

to incorporate monetary phenomena into classical equilibrium theory. By assuming perfect information, instantaneous exchanges, and equilibrium prices, the classical competitive model relied entirely on barter mechanisms in a money-free economy (a prime counterexample to Parsons' emphasis on the theoretical indispensability of money), and even in the most sophisticated "transaction-costs" models, the issue of how to weaken the classical assumptions to admit money is by no means resolved. See R.W. Clower (ed.), *Monetary Theory* (Harmondsworth: Penguin Books, 1969); and H.G. Johnson, *Macroeconomics and Monetary Theory* (Chicago: Aldine, 1972).

26. See N. Polsby, *Community Power and Political Theory* (New Haven: Yale University Press, 1963), p. 60.

27. See for example, L.A. Coser, "The Structure of Power: What Have We Learned? The Theoretical Aspects," Paper delivered at the 68th Annual Meetings of the American Sociological Association, 1973, and A. Giddens, "Power in the Recent Writings of Talcott Parsons," *Sociology,* 2 (September 1968), pp. 257-272; and A.W. Gouldner, *The Coming Crisis of Western Sociology* (New York: Basic Books, 1970).

28. See J.S. Coleman, "Comment on 'On the Concept of Influence,'" *Public Opinion Quarterly,* 27 (Spring 1963), pp. 63-82.

29. The title, "the medium is not the message," is a double entendre as well as a pun. We wish to suggest that structural variables (not media properties) constitute the main explanatory contributions of Parsons' analysis. We also suggest that the transmission of imperative "messages" (statements, commands, orders) efficiently and effectively constitute Parsons' main dependent variable.

30. See for example R.A. Dahl, "The Concept of Power," *Behavioral Science,* 2 (July 1957), pp. 201-215; and C.W. Mills, *The Power Elite* (New York: Oxford University Press, 1956).

31. H.G. Johnson, *op. cit.,* pp. 171-173.

32. See Parsons, "The Distribution of Power in American Society," in *Politics and Social Structure,* pp. 185-203, first published in 1957.

33. *Ibid.,* in "On the Concept of Political Power," first published in 1963.

34. R.A. Dahl, *Who Governs?* (New Haven: Yale University Press, 1961).

35. A.L. Stinchcombe, *Constructing Social Theories* (New York: Harcourt, Brace, and World, 1968), p. 194.

36. As Parsons acknowledges in *Politics and Social Structure* p. 219, power generation is possible only under conditions of social integration. This is to say little other than that the structuring of politically significant interests must be such as to make coalitions feasible. In a way, it is analogous to saying that (short-term) economic expansion is not possible when the requisite factors of production (especially idle plant, workers, and, increasingly, natural resources) are not at hand. It is to say nothing, *per se,* about a medium.

37. Parsons, "Higher Education as a Theoretical Focus," pp. 233-252, in H. Turk and R.L. Simpson (eds.), *Institutions and Social Exchange: The Sociologies of Talcott Parsons and George C. Homans* (Indianapolis: Bobbs-Merrill, 1971), pp. 249-250.

38. Parsons, *Politics and Social Structure,* p. 361, emphasis added.

39. See also Coleman, *op. cit.,* p. 76.

40. Parsons, "Some Reflections on the Place of Force in Social Process," pp. 264-296, in T. Parsons, *Sociological Theory and Modern Society* (New York: The Free Press, 1967), p. 276.

41. In "'Voting' and the Equilibrium of the American Political System," pp. 204-240, in T. Parsons, *Politics and Social Structure,* p. 208 (first published in 1959).

42. The banking-electoral analogy is itself open to serious

question in a number of ways, but consider only the following: as Parsons' "power" is "binding," what matters about an election is who wins The *size* of the winner's plurality and the total *number of votes* are, in a two-party system, irrelevant to the "power" input. *Mutatis mutandis,* such matters, of course, are decisively relevant for the banker. (Parsons' logic would require him to subsume President Nixon's erstwhile interpretation of the "mandate" signified by his landslide victory of 1972 as an instance of "influence".)

And what are we to make of those who vote, but for the losing candidate? Are they less bound by the results of the election? Of course not. But then what has happened to "circulation"? And for those who vote not at all?

In other kinds of electoral systems, such as those having several parties and proportional representation, the number or proportion of votes does matter. But it matters because of the interaction of the factors of (1) a particular structure of the rules of the game and (2) competing parties. What remains true is that from the point of view of the whole political system, the number of units of input (votes) is irrelevant, strictly speaking, to the "power" input.

Such questions may have diminishing intellectual marginal utility. They come up only because of Parsons' insistence on the thoroughness of the analogy.

43. *Ibid.,* pp. 392-94, and *Sociological Theory and Modern Society,* p. 288.

44. *Ibid.,* p. 292.

45. Parsons, *Politics and Social Structure,* pp. 179-180.

46. It might be more appropriate to pose an analogy between McCarthyism and Gresham's law. A poor currency (jingoistic demagoguery) circulates—no one wants to hold it, only to use it—and a good currency(statesmanship) is hoarded—liberal ideas are expressed only in private; liberals retreat to their own circles. Parsons and White (*ibid;* pp. 245-247) considered, but rejected, a Gresham's law imagery, as suggested for the analysis of the poor quality of mass culture, by Dwight Macdonald. Evidently, Parsons and White did this because they perceived that the mass media were not inevitably pernicious. Yet, more than that, to consider a Gresham's law analogy seriously would have required Parsons to treat *competing media,* whereas his whole analysis assumes only an either/or image of media: a society either has media or it does not. He thus is not attuned to the analysis of different kinds of media within any given subsystem.

47. T. Parsons and N.J. Smelser, *Economy and Society* (New York: The Free Press, 1956), pp. 70-71.

48. But see J.S. Coleman, "Political Money," *American Political Science Review,* 64 (December 1970), pp. 1074-1087.

49. Parsons, *Politics and Social Structure,* p. 375.

50. *Ibid.,* p. 399.

51. Indeed, in that Parsons' double interchanges between functional subsystems (see *ibid.,* p. 399) involve inputs and outputs *solely* of "media" and not intrinsically valuable goods, services, and the like, it is difficult to take them seriously. Surely societies operate on large measures of trust, promises, commitments, and expectations; yet hard realities are exchanged as well.

52. *Ibid.,* pp. 488, 520.

53. See A.W. Gouldner, "The Norm of Reciprocity: A Preliminary Statement," *American Sociological Review,* 25 (April 1960), pp. 161-178.

54. For some further critical remarks on the concept of power as circulating, see M. Weber, *Economy and Society,* Vol. III, Guenther Roth and Claus Wittich (eds.) (New York: Bedminister Press, 1968), p. 942.

55. Parsons, *Political and Social Structure,* pp. 391-2.

56. *Ibid.*

57. See M. Duverger, *Political Parties* (New York: Wiley Science Editions, 1963); and S.M. Lipset, "Party Systems and the Representation of Social Groups," pp. 276-294, in Reinhard

Bendix *et al.* (eds.), *State and Society* (Boston: Little, Brown, 1968).

For a social psychological derivation see W. Lippmann, *Public Opinion* (New York: Harcourt, Brace, 1922), Part V.

58. Parsons, *Politics and Social Structure,* pp. 378, 389, 483.

59. See N. Leites, *On the Game of Politics in France* (Stanford: Stanford University Press, 1959).

60. See G. Almond and G.B. Powell, Jr., *Comparative Politics: A Developmental Approach* (Boston: Little, Brown, 1966).

61. Parsons, *Politics and Social Structure,* p. 214.

62. *Ibid.,* pp. 247, 333, 340, 343-346, 389-392, 408, 421, 455, 483-85, See also N. J. Smelser, "Stability, Instability and the Analysis of Political Corruption," pp. 7-29, in Bernard Barber and Alex Inkeles (eds.), *Stability and Social Change* (Boston: Little, Brown, 1971), p. 14.

63. Parsons, *Politics and Social Structure,* p. 333.

64. *Ibid.,* p. 389.

65. *Ibid.,* pp. 245-247.

66. *Ibid.,* p. 343, pp. 483-485.

67. But see his earlier statement, *ibid.,* p. 248.

68. For some observations see A. W. Gouldner, *The Coming Crisis of Western Sociology,* pp. 341-351.

69. Coleman, "Political Money," *op. cit.,* at p. 1086.

70. Parsons, *Politics and Social Structure,* p. 359.

71. *Ibid.,* p. 391n.

72. *Ibid.,* p. 382.

73. *Ibid.,* p. 355, emphasis added.

74. See the reviews of *Sociological Theory and Modern Society* by J. Berger and M. Zelditch, Jr. in *American Sociological Review,* 33 (June 1968), pp. 446-450, and by A.J. Gregor, pp. 450-453.

75. Parsons, "Commentary," pp. 380-399, in Turk and Simpson (eds.), *op. cit.,* p. 384.

76. Parsons, *Politics and Social Structure,* p. 517.

77. Parsons, "Social Systems," *op. cit.,* p. 472.

78. Other analysts who find Parsons' media concept attractive, at least in some respects, are S. N. Eisenstadt (ed.), *Political Sociology: A Reader* (New York: Basic Books, 1971); W. A. Gamson, Review of *Politics and Social Structure, American Sociological Review,* 36 (June 1971), pp. 523-4; W. C. Mitchell, *Sociological Analysis and Politics: The Theories of Talcott Parsons* (Englewood Cliffs: Prentice-Hall, 1967), pp. 87-97; N. J. Smelser, "Stability, Instability and the Analysis of Political Corruption," *op. cit.,* and T. S. Turner, "Parsons' Concept of Generalized Media of Social Interaction and its Relevance for Social Anthropology," *Sociological Inquiry,* 38 (Spring 1968), pp. 121-134.

79. Parsons, *Politics and Social Structure,* p. 314.

80. Parsons, "On Building Social System Theory: A Personal History," *Daedalus,* 99 (Fall 1970), pp. 826-881, at pp. 866-868.

81. Parsons, "Commentary" in Turk and Simpson (eds.), *op. cit.,* p. 384.

82. This is a characteristic aspect of evolutionary thinking: one explains progressive change by reference to *general* factors, stagnation or regress by *special* factors; see K. E. Bock, "Evolution, Function, and Change," *American Sociological Review,* 28 (April 1963), pp. 229-237.

83. E. A. Shils, *The Torment of Secrecy* (New York: The Free Press, 1956).

84. It is not irrelevant to note, as Parsons does, that his own Harvard was a target of the McCarthyites' attacks (*Politics and Social Structure,* pp. 157-8). For a serious attempt to refute Parsons' and Shils' (and Lipset's, Bell's, Hofstadter's, etc.) analysis of McCarthyism, see M. P. Rogin, *The Intellectuals and McCarthy: The Radical Specter* (Cambridge: M.I.T. Press, 1967).

85. Parsons, *Politics and Social Structure,* p. 185.

86. *Ibid.*, p. 193.

87. *Ibid.*, pp. 202-203.

88. *Ibid.*, p. 199. Parsons has been accused of disregarding the distributive aspect of power by, among others, Coser (*op. cit.*). Indeed, Parsons does so by definition.

89. *Ibid.*, p. 200.

90. Power enhancement, in this sense, is more problematic, and Parsons is taking a greater theoretical risk than might first be supposed on considering this idea. He is *not* primarily referring to increases of power of a system *over* its environing systems (e.g., the U.S.A. vis-à-vis the U.S.S.R), but rather to the enhancement of power *internal* to the system (e.g., the capacity of Washington to respond effectively to the "energy crisis").

91. Eisenstadt (ed.), *op. cit.*, p. 15.

92. Parsons, *Politics and Social Structure*, p. 159.

93. *Ibid.*, p. 202.

94. *Ibid.*, p. 203.

95. *Ibid.*, pp. 204-240.

96. The objection, "What about third-party candidates?" cannot be sustained. The electoral rules under which the American system operates provide a disincentive for third-party voting and, thereby, for third-party candidates.

97. *Ibid.*, p. 212.

98. *Ibid.*, p. 213.

99. *Ibid.*, p. 208. It is not our purpose here to evaluate the appropriateness of this analogy; rather it is to analyze the vicissitudes of Parsons' economic analogies. For this purpose, a note on Parsons' technical usages may be in order.

In 1959, he presented the polity-societal community interchange in the following terms (*Ibid.*, p. 209):

where "generalized support" and "effective leadership" are *general* inputs and outputs and "advocacy of policies" and "binding decisions" are more *specific*. Presumably the more general interchange at top provides the requisite flexibility such that specific measures can be taken responsibly.

By 1963, however, the interchange looks like this (*ibid.*, p. 399):

where P is power, I is influence; 1, 2 is order of hierarchical control as between media, and a, b is order of hierarchical control within interchange systems. "Decisions" and "support" are both binding and therefore forms of "power," and lower on Parsons' cybernetic hierarchy of control than the "influence" arrows of "interest-demands" and "leadership responsibility."

In 1959, then, before the full-blown media concept had been developed, "generalization" was seen to be an attribute of one *binding* input (support or votes) and of one *nonbinding* input (leadership). Here, "generalization" refers to an attribute of the message, i.e., that an element of latitude or discretion is allowed. By 1963, however, *all* of the interchange elements are "generalized media" (power and influence); and, therefore, "generalization" is no longer a variable *between* these interchanges.

This substantial change in interpretation is, it seems, obscured rather than illuminated by a brief footnote to the 1963

"Technical Note," which reads, in part (*ibid.*, p. 397n); "Early and partial versions of the application to political subject-matter [of the system paradigm in *Economy and Society*] are found in my contributions to Roland Young, ed., *Approaches to the Study of Politics*, and Burdick and Brodbeck, eds., *American Voting Behavior*" [the last is Parsons, "Voting, . . .," *ibid.*, pp. 204-240].

100. Parsons, "Levels of Organization and the Mediation of Social Interaction," pp. 23-35, in Turk and Simpson (eds.), *op. cit.*, pp. 26-28.

101. For example, R. Dahrendorf, *op. cit.*

102. "The Distribution of Power in American Society," "'Voting' and the Equilibrium of the American Political system," and "Social Strains in America: A Postscript," all in *Politics and Social Structure*.

103. See Parsons, "On Building Social System Theory: A Personal History," *op. cit.;* "Some Problems of General Theory in Sociology" *op. cit.*, and "Commentary" in Turk and Simpson (eds.), *op. cit.*

104. See T. Parsons, "Evolutionary Universals in Society," *American Sociological Review,* 29 (June 1964), pp. 339-357; and especially, T. Parsons, *The System of Modern Societies* (Englewood Cliffs: Prentice-Hall, 1971), Chapter 6.

105. For a contrary view, see S. P. Huntington, "Political Modernization: America vs. Europe," pp. 170-200, in Reinhard, Bendix, *et al.* (eds.), *op. cit.*

106. Parsons, *Politics and Social Structure*, p. 214.

107. T. Parsons, *Societies: Evolutionary and Comparative Prespectives* (Englewood Cliffs: Prentice-Hall, 1966), p. 113.

108. See Parsons and Smelser, *op. cit.*, pp. 48-49; Parsons, *Politics and Social Structure,* p. 200; and N. J. Smelser, "Stability, Instability, and the Analysis of Political Corruption," in B. Barber and A. Inkeles (eds.), *op. cit.*, p. 9.

109. Parsons, Shils, Naegele, and Pitts (eds.), *op. cit.*, pp. 66-67.

110. See T. Parsons, *The System of Modern Societies.*

111. Perhaps users of sign language are disadvantaged by others' use of a spoken language, gold miners by the advance of paper currency, handgun manufacturers by state-building, village elders by codified law, and fundamentalist preachers by mass literacy (although these are controversial assertions). Nonetheless, they would appear to be minor qualifications (if such be allowed!) on the Pareto welfare criterion.

112. Parsons, "On Building Social System Theory: A Personal History," *op. cit.*, p. 870.

113. See for example, the social control-psychotherapy analogy in Parsons, *The Social System*, p. 301; the personality system-family system analogy in *Family, Socialization and Interaction Process* (with R. F. Bales) (New York: The Free Press, 1953), Chapter II; the ambitious, but brief, sketch on biological analogies (*ibid.*, pp. 395-399); and the throughgoing system-to-subsystem analogy in *Economy and Society* (with N.J. Smelser) pp. 196-218, among many other instances.

114. Parsons, *Politics and Social Structure*, p. 313.

115. Parsons, "Higher Education as a Theoretical Focus," pp. 233-252, in Turk and Simpson (eds.), *op. cit.*, p. 241.

116. An exception is his explicit recantation (*Politics and Social Structure,* p. 395n) of his earlier (*The Social System,* pp. 161-163) conception of the political system as concretely, rather than analytically, defined.

117. To our knowledge, the last time Parsons promised such a revision was in the preface to *The Social System* p. x. The revision was not forthcoming.

118. Parsons, *Politics and Social Structure*, pp. 410-415.

119. *Ibid.*, p. 407.

120. *Ibid.*, p. 409.

121. For example, W. Sellars, *Science, Perception and Reality* (London: Routledge and Kegan Paul, 1963), pp. 127-242, 321-358, among others, has criticized this model on various grounds.

122. An important logical point here is to recognize that to identify something as an intrinsic satisfier says nothing about the social organization of its use. In particular, the inference, that, as (1) money is a symbolic representation of intrinsically valuable commodities, (2) therefore, in the absence of money, goods will be allocated through barter is simply *invalid* without a large number of structural assumptions about the infeasibility of autarchy, the commitment to market mechanisms, and so on. Conversely, one should note that in economies where "tastes, technology, anticipations, population, and types of products are either invariant or change in a known fully anticipated way at a steady rate," the marginal cost of acquiring information approaches zero and there may be no incentives for switching from a barter to a money economy; see K. Brunner and A. Meltzer, "The Uses of Money: Money in the Theory of an Exchange Economy," *American Economic Review,* 61 (December 1971), pp. 784-805, p. 800.

123. Now one could attribute the form of these hypotheses to Parsons' functionalism, but the real villain lies elsewhere. The crux of the matter is the inference, —money is not a consumable commodity; therefore, it can only be a meaningless, "symbolic" substitute for things that are. Parsons assumes what is essentially a request for a *definition:* Put crudely, he assumes that when confronted with money, people want to know, "If you can't consume it, what is this stuff? What can you do with it?" and in response, society develops elaborate normative institutions (i.e., specialized languages) outlining what things can and cannot be bought, how to calculate the units of account, and the like. Once media are defined in this way, people will be able to understand what they are getting and what they can do with it, but ultimately all they can do is accept or reject what is offered since "only mutual acceptability can make money a functioning medium" (*Politics and Social Structure,* p. 409).

But notice that this is only part of the story. For someone who already knows what money is and what it does (who recognizes that even though you cannot eat it, the essential services of money lie elsewhere) the critical question is not a definitional request ("what are you giving me?"), but a request for supporting *evidence* designed to show that this is, in fact, money and that the institutions backing it really work. That is, one does not accept money simply on the grounds that it is a substitute for something else—one accepts it because it fits into a family of other potentially checkable facts and hypotheses (e.g., "If cash, is it green? Whose picture is on it? Will my banker take it? What's the exchange rate today?"). The fact that one might want to get more guidance before accepting a car from Honest John, the used car salesman, than taking money from a bank is not a difference in principle, but a matter of *degree*—how much evidence one demands will depend on the circumstances, and it is precisely such circumstances which can be used to *explain* varying degrees of confidence in all matter of things which people say, offer for sale, promise, command, or exhort.

124. See B. C. Cartwright and R. D. Schwartz, "The Invocation of Legal Norms: An Empirical Investigation of Durkheim and Weber," *American Sociological Review,* 38 (June 1973), pp. 340-354.

V

SOCIAL CHANGE
AND DEVELOPMENT

INTRODUCTION

Andrew Effrat

To attempt to pull together or even to map the various strands that constitute the theory of change in the theory of action is truly a Herculean task. As for which task — many critics would no doubt suggest that it is comparable to the cleaning of the Augean stables; I prefer the comparison of the securing of the golden apples of the Hesperides. To cover properly the theory would involve pulling together a very extensive, rich, and rather disjointed body of literature. In the corpus of Parsons' own work and the work of those who have relied heavily on the theory of action, not only are there a number of overlapping but incomplete essays and books dealing primarily with the theory of change[1] and many specific empirical works concerned mainly with historical material,[2] but there are many specific points or issues directly relevant to the theory of change scattered throughout. Further, given that much of the theory is concerned with the sources of equilibrium and homeostasis or the problematics of maintaining "systemicness," essentially all the rest of their work can be seen as at least indirectly relevant because, in a sense, it attempts to analyze the conditions that may prevent or inhibit change in general or of a particular sort.

I shall try to focus on a somewhat more manageable task. My overriding aim is to provide a blueprint or roadmap of the main features of the theory of change and how they fit together in some relatively obvious ways. This introduction is not intended to stand on its own, but rests on a reading and understanding of the other editorial introductions in this book for relevant background information. My discussion will be organized in terms of some of the major questions that any general theory of change should attempt to handle: What is change, and how might it be conceptualized? What are the principle sources of

change and factors in change? And what are some of the main sequences, patterns, stages, and consequences of change? Along the way, I shall touch briefly on some of the basic orienting notions, concepts, and propositions of the theory, allude to some of the major empirical work that is relevant to the theory, and weave in some of the highlights of the essays in this section. I also want to deal with some criticisms that have been made of the analysis of change in the theory of action, and I will do so after my overview of its substance.

I shall not attempt to spell out the theory in definitional and substantive detail, nor will I attempt to deal in depth with change at all of the system and subsystem levels of action. Rather I will focus on the social system level, primarily the societal system. Further, I will not deal systematically with the roots of the change theory (which of course run deep through Durkheim/Weber country) or even its evolution in Parsons' own work. My focus will be on mapping the theory essentially as it now seems to stand.

Before turning to the three focal questions let me offer a brief over-all characterization of the action theory of change that may help the reader make more sense of the specifics that are to follow. To oversimplify greatly, I think the theory can be seen as a distinctive blend of four basic positions — evolutionary theory, an equilibrium model, cybernetic theory, and a voluntaristic perspective. Each of these positions would of course bring with it a particular set of conceptual baggage.

Contemporary evolutionary theory[3] would draw our attention to questions concerning the over-all directions of change, the principle stages that crystallize, and the qualitatively different modes of organization that emerge, the processes of struggle or competition and survival of the "best-adapted" patterns, the various mechanisms of adaptation, the processes of differentiation, and the like. Equilibrium models would concern us with system tendencies towards consistency and mechanisms blocking

I wish to express my gratitude for their critical comments and valuable suggestion to Robert Baker, Rainer Baum, Ronnie Leah (and for her typing this — truly a work of alienated labour). Victor Lidz, Jan Loubser, Paul Paschke, Gail Regan, and Jonathan Turner.

662

that or making it unnecessary for system stability, sources of strain and mechanisms of adaptation to such, as well as factors inhibiting system change or adaptation and the problems in overcoming them. Cybernetic theory would involve a distinctive conception of causality and change (to be discussed later) and emphasize the importance of various control mechanisms and the role of generalized informational components in guiding and regulating energy and lower-level information components, as well as systemic learning capacity, and a distinctive set of processes characteristic of informational components (such as generalization and specification).[4] Finally, the voluntaristic position would emphasize the goal-directedness of action, the general importance of actors' orientations and motives, the adaptive or problem-oriented and problem-solving nature of action and systems, and the like.[5]

Of course, these points do not completely characterize either these four positions or the theory of action but I offer them as sensitizing orientations to help us through the maze we are about to enter.

WHAT IS "CHANGE" IN GENERAL, AND HOW IS IT TO BE CONCEPTUALIZED?

Structural change is the principal set of change processes on which Parsons and most action theorists have focussed. By "structural change" they generally mean change at the social structural or social system level — usually, but not necessarily, societal. Change is also analyzed at other levels, such as personality and cultural levels and within the social system, but not nearly to the same extent.

Structural change may be defined as an alteration in the normative culture governing the relationship among social units.[6] This follows from Parsons' general conceptualization of social systems as consisting in "patterns of institutionalized normative culture."[7] A more general and encompassing definition that would apply to all levels would equate change essentially with an alteration in the basic components of the system in question and/or their relationships. For example, important here be the emphasis that the theory has placed on a change such as structural differentiation which represents a distinct qualitative structural reorganization (as opposed to "adjustment") of the components of the system.[8]

The question would naturally arise as to whether the theory would also deal with changes in processes. It does discuss these (e.g., in considering the development of rationalization, inflation, and so on) but the focus is generally on structure, as structural components are treated as, by definition, the basic stable reference points of the system. Changes in structure

are most likely to reflect changes in the basic nature of the system as well as its processes. Further, most of the major patterns of change (such as differentiation or integration) refer primarily to structural rearrangements.

The importance of not confusing the levels of analysis and system reference relates to some crucial distinctions that Parsons virtually constantly[9] emphasizes in his general discussions of the conceptualization of change. Perhaps the first basic distinction to be made is that between process and change. This distinction is more accurately represented as that between processes that operate to maintain the systems essentially as they are (call them "boundary-maintaining processes") and processes that operate to change systems.

A related distinction is that between "change in" or within systems and "change of" systems.[10] The former concerns changes in specified states of units or subsystems (e.g., roles or families within societal systems), while "change of" concerns alteration in a specified state of the system itself. Of course, these can vary independently. For example, change can occur at a lower level of the system (say, in the polity from a two-party to a multi-party system) without changing any defining and essential features at the higher system reference (say, in whether the society remains a "modern" system or not). Indeed, change at the lower level may be necessary for stability or equilibrium at the higher level. Parsons had emphasized this in observing that "structural change in systems is an inevitable part of equilibrating process in larger systems."[11]

To ground these distinctions and to explicate further the conceptualization of change, it is perhaps useful to remind the reader of the theory of action's general conception of action systems as basically homeostatic (within limits) or characterized largely by equilibrating processes. Thus, a great many structures and processes can be seen as serving to continue action systems in their existing state (either maintaining them in that state or returning them to it should they digress from it). None of this is to suggest (as some critics seem to believe) that change is impossible or does not occur as, for example, when homeostatic mechanisms break down. Rather, the model emphasizes institutional obstacles to change and the difficulties of overcoming vested interests and resistances to change.[12] Parsons has also suggested a "watershed" image of the relationship between boundary-maintaining processes and change processes such that, once the boundary or resistances are overcome, there is a tendency for social control mechanisms to break down further and for a cumulative process of change to build.

These emphases would also make sense of the rather striking statement that "all processes change something"[13] Related to the equilibrium model is the notion of action systems as "open systems" that are constantly threatened by entropic tendencies. That is, the system is constantly consuming energies (for example, motivational resources of actors). Action systems must therefore constantly draw resources from their various environments to maintain themselves. (In a sense, they must keep running merely to stay in the same place.) An apt analogy is the relationship of an organism to its situation. In a sense, it is constantly consuming its energies and moving into, say, a state of hunger and weakness. *If it is to remain stable,* it must therefore constantly engage in re-equilibrating or counter-entropic processes that shift it or change it back to nonhungry states. In this sense, then, even boundary maintaining processes are changing certain states (albeit often rather low-level ones) of the system.

Finally, this should help to clarify the sense in which Parsons argued that it is essential to have an understanding of the basic processes and structures of action systems before we could develop a *general* theory of change. This was not to claim that we could not develop many specific propositions and limited theories about change, but that a full-scale *general* theory of such must *logically* rest on a fuller understanding of structure and process. See, for example, Parsons' statement that

> It is, of course, entirely possible and appropriate to theorize about many *particular* processes of change within social systems, without attempting to build up a theory of the processes of change *of* social systems as systems. It is this latter task which logically presupposes a theory of social structure and a theory of motivational process within the system.[14]

WHAT ARE THE PRINCIPAL SOURCES OF CHANGE?

One major distinction that Parsons emphasizes in conceptualizing the sources of change is between sources exogenous to the action system in question and those endogenous. In part, this emphasis seems to rest on Parsons' relatively self-conscious borrowing of the "principle of inertia"[15] — which in effect holds that systems will continue in the same state unless interfered with by internal or external factors. Reliance on this principle might seem inconsistent with the emphasis on action systems as open systems — systems whose existence is constantly threatened by entropic tendencies. However, I think the apparent inconsistency would be reconciled by emphasizing that action theory takes as given the homeostatic or boundary-maintaining properties of action systems. The inertia principle then is that they will continue

to maintain their boundaries unless internal or external factors overcome the tendencies (often institutionalized) for maintenance of the status quo.[16]

One crucial point to be made in regard to the exogenous factors is that action systems and subsystems are treated as exogenous to each other and are generally the most immediate and important environments for each other. For example, at the general action level, from the viewpoint of the social system, the other principle environments at the same level of generality are cultural, personality, and organismic systems. Thus for example, the mobilization and channeling of cathexes or personality system energies are major environmental concerns of and constraints on the social system.

Another implication is that for the social system the physical environment is largely mediated through these other systems. But in an analogous fashion within social systems, the economy, polity, and pattern maintenance institutions (such as the family and the church) would be the immediate environments at the same level of generality for the societal community. One set of implications is that the immediate environment and the generally established channels of interchange would vary for each subsystem, depending on its place in the hierarchy of control or conditions. Some would be "closer to" or "contiguous with" the pattern maintenance level, some with the goal attainment level, and so on. Also, each subsystem would have different immediately juxtaposed environments. For example, in the hierarchy of control, I would have G and L as its immediate "neighbors," while G would have A and I, and so on. I am not aware of any work that has systematically developed the implications of this point for the analysis of system change.

I shall focus my discussion of the sources of change on endogenous factors, as most action theorists have also done. Suffice it to note that a number of the points that follow might equally well apply to exogenous factors (for example, that strain in relationships between system and environment is a major source of change). Of course, from the viewpoint of the system, it is probably easier, *ceteris paribus,* to deal with and control internal sources rather than external.

Parsons has treated *strain* as one of the principal catalysts to change in and of systems. The nature and content of normative orientations is another major factor emphasized in the theory. It will be dealt with at greater length later. "Strain" may be characterized, at the unit level, as "disturbance of the expectation system of actors."[17] Another satisfactory definition that would more readily apply to all action systems would be "disequilibrium in the input-output balance between two or more units of the system."[18] Some of the principle general manifestations and/or sources of strain would be inadequate functioning of a unit or structure, frustration of a system's or subsystem's capacities to attain its goals or fulfill its expectations, conflict among competing structures or groups, ambiguity in allocating facilities, incomplete institutionalization or specification of values, and contradiction or inconsistency among patterns. [19]

One example of inadequate functioning or "deficit of input at the goal attainment boundary of the social system" that action theorists seem particularly fond of is the inadequacies in the productive capacities of the family farm and cottage industries in England in the late eighteenth and early nineteenth centuries which laid the groundwork for the subsequent differentiation of occupational units from kinship units. [20]

Tominaga's essay in this collection also provides a number of quite concrete examples of inadequate functioning, dysfunctions of incompatible structures, and the like, and their role in the economic and political development of nineteenth and twentieth century Japan. A particularly fruitful avenue for further development is his attempt to conceptualize strains and functional inadequacies in terms of imbalances among interchanges. [21]

It is particularly important to emphasize that strain (or any of its various manifestations) *per se* does not "lead to" change and is not seen as the principle "cause" of change in itself. A number of possible outcomes may occur in response to the processes set in motion by strain — resolution and arrestation or isolation, stagnation and decline, revolution, and continuous or discontinuous development being among the prominent alternatives. [22] The main point is that various aspects of the system in question shape its response and influence the outcome. Smelser's discussion of the determinants of collective behavior [23] provides a good example of the set of other factors that can shape the response to strain. Those factors include structural conduciveness, a generalized belief, precipitating factors such as a dramatic event, mobilization of participants, and the operation of social control mechanisms, particularly the actions and effectiveness of relevant political authorities.

In effect, then, change must be conceptualized as the outcome of the *interaction of a multiplicity of factors.* One "striking" way of putting this is to state that the emphasis on monocausal or single-factor theories of change would be regarded by an action theorist as being as naïve as a theory attributing the start of a fire to a match *per se.* Obviously one must consider the match's interaction with the combustibility of the material, the availability of oxygen, and so on. Similarly, system vulnerabilities, value patterns, organizational arrangements, actors

skills, and social control mechanisms would all interact with the strains or dissatisfactions to shape the system's response.

One of Parsons' strongest statements on this is the following:

> . . . the conception of a system of interdependent variables, on the one hand, and of units or parts, on the other, by its nature implies that there is no necessary order of teleological significance in the sources of change. This applies particularly to such old controversies as economic or interest explanations *versus* explanations in terms of ideas or values. This problem is logically parallel to the problem of the relations between heredity and environment. Of a set of "factors," *any or all may be sources of change,* whose nature will depend on the ways an initial impetus is propagated through the system by types of dynamic process. . . . [24]

This is a particularly crucial statement in light of the many criticisms of Parsons' theory as having a simple "idealist" or value emanationist bias.

Although the theory of action model rests on this sort of multifactorial logic, it is not a "formless eclecticism." Factors in change are analyzed systematically in at least three respects: substantively, in terms of the AGIL four-functions scheme, cybernetically, in terms of the hierarchies of control and conditions, and sequentially in terms of a "value-added" model. Let us briefly take up each of these.

1. First, the principle substantive factors that an analysis of change would identify would, in some way, be a manifestation of the AGIL scheme. The structures specialized in performing these functions would be conceptualized at the appropriate level of system reference, their interchanges and contributions to each other and system development would be mapped, balances and imbalances would be identified, and their various ramifications would be traced over time. Regardless of the adequacy of its specific content, I think the Tominaga paper in this part of the book provides one of the clearest examples of the form of this kind of systematic analysis. He points not only to the ways in which factors (conceptualized in AGIL terms) may contribute to aspects of system growth and development, but also to how incompatibilities and imbalances can derail development or help to channel it in particular directions that seek to deal with the strains (such as totalitarianism). [25] Robertson's article can be seen as pointing to the way that some factors, primarily political, could serve as obstacles to or promoters of broader-scale system integration.

In some respects, this material can be viewed as providing answers to one of the most crucial questions in evolutionary theory, i.e., what factors account for evolutionary success or failure of given patterns, or the survival and growth or the decline and death of given systems? Among these answers, then, would be the nature, extent, and level of generality of resources available, the level of political integration and centralization, the extent and foundation of community solidarity, and the content of value orientations.

2. Factors are also treated systematically in that they are conceptualized in terms of the cybernetic model. As just indicated (and as in Loubser's essay) this model emphasizes that, generally, components high in information guide and regulate, through processes of specification and generalization, components that are low in information and/or high in energy. The classic examples are a thermostat regulating the performance of a furnace or a governor regulating a steam engine.

In discussing cybernetic governance, it should be noted that we speak of *factors* that *channel* energies, *components* that *shape* outcomes, and the like—and not in terms of *a* simple cause, *the* determining factor. I think this cybernetic conception of causality is rather different from the more mechanistic conception which seems prevalent in this culture.

Analogies or models of information control are perhaps clearest in the realms of language and logic, where I think we can more readily appreciate the sense in which higher-level components, such as the grammatical rules or the major premises, can be seen as guiding and shaping through processes of specification the more specific outcomes in speech or deduction. These analogies would also bring out the sense in which more proximate factors (the immediate preceding sentences in language or the immediately preceding but low-level link in a syllogistic chain) can appear to be more determinative of specific outcomes.

Even while propounding the cybernetic model Parsons is careful to dissociate himself from a simple antimaterialist or pro-idealist position:

> In the sense, and *only* that sense, of emphasizing the importance of the cybernetically highest elements in patterning action systems, I am a cultural determinist, rather than a social determinist. Similarly, I believe that, within the social system, the normative elements are more important for social change than the "material interests" of constituted units. The longer the time perspective, and the broader the system involved, the greater is the *relative* importance of higher rather than lower factors in the control hierarchy, regardless of whether it is pattern maintenance or pattern change that requires explanation.[26]

It should be stressed that the theory recognizes that each level has its own distinctive exigencies, control mechanisms, and autonomous or independent variability. Eisenstadt's paper in this collection can be seen as one illustration of this point in the way that codes may continue autonomous of other system changes and may influence structural patterns independently of other changes.

Further, obviously none of this is to claim that energy components or lower-level information components do not influence structures and processes in action systems or effect more general information components any more than to emphasize that the strength of boundary-maintaining mechanisms implies that they cannot be overcome. One analogy that Parsons is fond of in this regard is the relationship between a horse and its rider drawn from Freud's discussion of the relationship between id and ego.[27] Although the rider (and ego) may generally guide and regulate the behavior of the horse (or id) there are unquestionably circumstances in which the system higher in energy but lower in information can and does overthrow the higher information system. Smelser's discussion of the ways that conditional strains may generalize up the hierarchy of control and precipitate reorganization in the higher-level components is one particularly apt example of these processes.[28] Similarly, it should be observed that although the cybernetic model emphasizes the stability of value orientations relative to other components, it does not treat these orientations as rigidly fixed and unchanging. Discussions and processes of value extension and normative upgrading[29] and the generalization of strain up the hierarchy of control are clear instances of value change that theorists of action have dealt with.

More socioculturally, an example would be the way that more general normative components structure and regulate more specific levels of social action. One of the best developed sets of examples is in Smelser's *Theory of Collective Behavior.* Table V-1[30] summarizes the levels of specificity of societal values.

Note that the hierarchy of specificity runs not only vertically from 1 to 7 but also horizontally from left to right or from column (2) to column (4). Further, note that the levels correspond essentially to an L-I-G-A-I-G-A pattern.[31] Table V-2[32] summarizes all four components of action at the social system level.

Let me turn to a number of general considerations concerning these tables and cybernetic conceptions of change. First, theorists of action generally regard components closer to the "peak" of generality (that is higher and to the left in these tables) as being relatively the most stable components. For example, the higher-level components would be generally the best insulated from everyday exigencies and the least likely to change readily. Further, the higher com-

Table V-1. LEVELS OF SPECIFICITY OF VALUES

(1) Level	(2) General character of specification	(3) Specification of economic values	(4) Example from "free enterprise"
1	Societal values	Societal values	Commitment to "freedom"
2	Legitimization of values for institutional sectors	Economic definition of societal value	Commitment to "free enterprise"
3	Legitimization of rewards	Definition of rewards for economic activity	Commitment to "profit-making"
4	Legitimization of individual commitment	Definition of values for individual actor in economic world	Commitment to "personal success"
5	Legitimization of competing values	Definition of values which compete with economic values	Commitment to "ethics of business"
6	Legitimization of values for realizing organizational goals	Definition of values for running business firm	Commitment to "efficiency"
7	Legitimization of values for expenditure of effort	Definition of values of "work" and "the job"	Commitment to "personal responsibility"

Less specific (↑) — *More specific* (↓)

Source: N. J. Smelser, *Theory of Collective Behavior* (New York: The Free Press, 1962).

ponents are regarded as most influential in channeling energies, shaping outcomes, and guiding action in general; and a change in them is likely to have the most serious repercussions throughout the system. This does not imply that the components will appear to have the greatest predictive power or be the most determinative of quite specific lower-level changes. For most purposes, the components immediately superior in the hierarchy of control or immediately inferior (that is, the most relevant conditions) would probably *appear* as most influential. Thus, in general, the higher the component in the hierarchy of control the greater the probability of its effects on system functioning, or ". . . the probability of producing structural change is greater in proportion to the position in the order of control at which the impact of its principle disturbing influence occurs."[33]

Another way of putting this would be to say that change processes and resistance to change are likely to be guided or patterned by the highest-level components. However, this is not to go so far as to say that *any* change in a component necessitates or automatically implies change in a component below it or to the right of it in this scheme. To maintain that position would be to ignore the analytical possibilities and empirical probabilities of degrees of autonomy and freedom among levels and components. It would also border on an idealist emanationism and

neglect of mechanisms that establish or institutionalize linkages among components.

Mayhew has crystallized a number of other assumptions involved in this model as follows:

1) Changes in patterns of structure occur relatively rapidly at lower levels in the hierarchy of control and slowly at higher levels.

2) Disturbances at any given level are solved at the next highest level or, if they cannot be stabilized at that level, cause disturbances at higher levels until they reach a level where a solution can be found.

3) Whenever a solution occurs, it is shaped by the constraints deriving from a preexisting stable structure which lies above it in the hierarchy, e.g., new political coalitions that form in response to changing patterns of interest will still compete within the framework of an established set of political institutions, and these institutions help to determine which groupings will be politically viable and effective. Consider the difficulty of establishing a third party in the United States.

4) Progressively higher levels of structure unite larger and larger groups of people.

5) History is the progressive institutionalization of values; as actors face problems they draw upon the high levels of structure that unite large numbers of people, and, in consequence, institutional arrangements come to be more accurate reflections of value traditions. This, in the United States the fundamental legal norms of the society have come more and more to reflect the American value of equal opportunity.[34]

Table V-2. LEVELS OF SPECIFICITY OF THE COMPONENTS OF SOCIAL ACTION

Level	Values	Norms	Mobilization of motivation for organized action	Situational facilities
1	Societal values	General conformity	Socialized motivation	Proconceptions concerning causality
2	Legitimization of values for institutionalized sectors	Specification of norms according to institutional sectors	Generalized performance capacity	Codification of knowledge
3	Legitimization of rewards	Specification of norms according to types of roles and organizations	Trained capacity	Technology, or specification of knowledge in situational terms
4	Legitimization of individual commitment	Specification of requirements for individual observation of norms	Transition to adult-role assumption	Procurement of wealth, power, or prestige to activate Level 3
5	Legitimization of competing values	Specification of norms of competing institutional sectors	Allocation to sector of society	Allocation of effective technology to sector of society
6	Legitimization of values for realizing organizational roles	Specification of rules of cooperation and coordination within organization	Allocation to specific roles or organizations	Allocation of effective technology to roles or organization
7	Legitimization of values for expenditure of effort	Specification of schedules and programs to regulate activity	Allocation to roles and tasks within organization	Allocation of facilities within organization to attain concrete goals

More specific (vertical axis)

More specific →

Source: N. J. Smelser, *Theory of Collective Behavior* (New York: The Free Press, 1962).

Mayhew's second statement may seem to point to some contradiction in the theory. Smelser seems to locate the typical strain at the lower levels of the system (5 to 7), while Parsons emphasizes that long-term evolutionary change occurs at the higher levels. But these are compatible positions. Smelser in effect is suggesting that strains may be first evident at the lower, operative levels and that if they cannot be handled there they would keep generalizing up the hierarchy, in a sense "searching" for solutions, until they are adequately handled. Thus, most serious strains would reach higher levels and most major changes would emanate from there.

At this point, let us consider somewhat more substantively some of these higher-level value or orientational components. As previously indicated, the theory of action treats values or, more generally, orientations as one of the principal sets of factors in promoting change. One way of bringing this home would be to point out that "norms may *demand* flexibility and change."[35] For example, one of the principal orientational complexes is what Parsons has referred to as instrumental activism. This implies an orientation toward active mastery of the environment which could be seen as having affinities with and roots in the West, in the Protestant Ethic. In the theory of action, it is generally regarded as one of the major value orientations that has guided and influenced development in North American society for the past several hundred years. For example, Fox in this collection notes the role of instrumental activism in shaping the development of modern science, conceptions of illness, health practices, and so on. More generally, perhaps this orientation could be seen as operating in a way parallel to the Oedipus complex at the personality-system level. Both seem to bind affectivity, energy, and the like into investing in instrumental action such that "work" can be done and aspects of "development" can occur.[36]

3. The *sequence* of activation and combination of factors is a third respect in which the theory tends to be systematic in assessing the relationships among factors. I shall deal with several examples of this sequencing in the next section. Smelser, who has perhaps been most rigorous in efforts to deal with relatively microlevel and intermediate-level sequential issues, has characterized this aspect of the approach as a "value-added model." The nature of this approach can be illustrated by referring to Smelser's example of the conversion of iron ore into finished automobiles. Smelser observes:

> Each stage "adds its value" to the final cost of the finished product. The key element in this example is that the earlier stages must combine *according to a certain pattern* before the next stage can contribute its particular value to the finished product. It is impossible to paint iron ore and hope that the painting will thereby contribute to the final product, an automobile. Painting, in order to be effective as a "determinant" in shaping the product, has to "wait" for the completion of the earlier processes. Every stage in the value-added process, therefore, is a necessary condition for the appropriate and effective addition of value in the next stage. The sufficient condition for final production, moreover, is the combination of *every* necessary condition, according to a definite pattern.[37]

Another important distinction in this approach is between the occurrence of an event such as the "preparation" of a factor and the actual activation of this event as a determinant. For example, obviously the paint may be prepared and processed prior to its use, but it can be activated as a determinant and enter into the "causal chain" only at the appropriate time in the sequence.

Even the quite macrolevel discussion of evolutionary stages in the next section can be seen as a value-added series, with one tentative product to date being "modern" societies. Of course, the present conceptualization of stages is not a particularly detailed mapping of the sequential relationships.

WHAT ARE THE PRINCIPAL PATTERNS, OUTCOMES, SEQUENCES, AND STAGES OF CHANGE?

This section is principally concerned with the way that outcomes or consequences of change have been conceptualized in action theory. There are perhaps two principal ways that can be identified—the stage schemes and major developmental patterns. The

stage schemes may be seen as levels of crystallization or ideal types of a number of relatively congruent patterns that can be treated as having coalesced. I shall first deal with some of the principal patterns or dimensions that seem to characterize change and then turn to a discussion of the several major stage and sequencing schemes.

I have deliberately selected as general and vague a term as "patterns." Depending on the questions under consideration, the starting points, the time perspective, and the givens of the analysis, the same pattern (such as structural differentiation or adaptive upgrading) can be consequences or outcomes of change processes, sources of or facilitating and inhibiting factors in change, and over-all directions or trends in which action systems seem to be moving in the long run. Of course, this would also be part of the logic of the value-added model. I do not think this is a weakness in the theoretical system but rather an important complexity in the analysis to which the theory sensitizes us. I shall try to keep these various different analytical statuses relatively clear in my discussion.

An Evolutionary Direction: Enhanced Adaptive Capacity

Perhaps the focal question under the heading of outcomes that an evolutionary theory must deal with is what the basic over-all trend or direction of change is. What, in effect, is the criterion of evolutionary advancement or development? For action theory, the over-all evolutionary direction and the chief criterion are clearly the growth in the system's *generalized adaptive capacity*.[38] "Adaptive capacity" can be characterized in several ways—as the ability of a system to cope, survive, and prosper in the long run, as its ability to "learn" and solve problems, reduce contingencies, or control environmental exigencies that may exist or arise,[39] and as the ability to continue to evolve or further enhance adaptive capacity. As Parsons has emphasized,

> This capacity includes an active concern with mastery, or the ability to change the environment to meet the needs of the system, as well as an ability to survive in the face of its unalterable features. Hence the capacity to cope with broad *ranges* of environmental factors, through adjustment or active control, or both, is crucial. Finally, a very critical point is the capacity to cope with unstable relations between system and environment, and hence with *uncertainty*.[40]

In a sense, enhanced adaptive capacity can be seen as part of the trend in which systems differentiate out of their environments and come to be autonomous of and have control over the vagaries of the environments. In this regard, systems can also be said to be characterized by an increasing "internality" in that their distinctive patterns are able to develop, maintain themselves, and guide their action.

Much of the theory of action's analysis of change can be seen as concerned with identifying and analyzing ways in which various mechanisms promote (or fail to promote) adaptive capacity. In one of Parsons' first explicitly evolutionary articles,[41] he identifies six "evolutionary universals"—social stratification, cultural legitimation, bureaucratic organization, money and markets, a universalistic legal system, and the democratic association in governmental and private forms. These are complexes of structures and associated processes which systems must develop if they are to be able to attain still higher levels of generalized adaptive capacity. There are many other general and specific mechanisms which presumably promote adaptive capacity that are analyzed in the theory of action.[42] I shall take up two of these— structural differentiation and development of generalized integrative mechanisms.

Let me first make several general observations about the implications of the notion of adaptive capacity. One way Parsons has emphasized that certain structural arrangements can bestow generalized adaptive capacity is with the observation "Trees can't move." Critics may be tempted to respond that "Trees don't need to move."

I think that the obvious evolutionary rejoinder would be that, should some conditional catastrophe threaten— such as flood, fire, or forester— trees would not be able to move and would be severely limited in their "choice" of mechanisms to cope with threats to their individual or species existence (although various mechanisms of adaptation have of course evolved).

In a cybernetic sense, their lack of certain generalized adaptive mechanisms that might help them anticipate, analyze, prescribe, or mobilize resources severely limits their capacity to control and be autonomous from (or, in a sense, differentiated out of) aspects of their immediate environment and ways it might change.

Let us explore another line of criticism of the theory which brings out some other possible problems and implications of the evolutionary approach. One might have responded that not only don't trees need to move, but if they could and did, they would then have all sorts of other problems. In social system terms, for example, the larger and more differentiated a structure becomes, the more its integrative problems are likely to increase and the greater the need for more complex communications channels. Along these lines, Robertson in this collection observes that modern societies are not as flexible as they

are thought to be, given their problems of coordination and centralization.

One rejoinder would of course be that these counterexamples are pointing to systems that have not adequately evolved and dealt with, among other things, their integrative problems effectively. The second rejoinder would be that, at the risk of continuing the pastoral analogy, evolutionary theory never promised us a rose garden. The theory does not imply that problems (including problems brought on by complex solutions) necessarily become fewer and simpler. (Indeed, it might imply that they become more complex.[43]) What it does imply is that systems gain in their capacity to perform higher-level functions more effectively— functions that are more complex and difficult, that provide greater generalized learning and problem-solving abilities, that provide units with a greater number and higher-level range of choices,[44] and that involve cybernetically higher components.

But further it should be acknowledged that as systems evolve and gain in the capacity to perform higher-order functions, they pay certain costs or in a sense suffer certain losses. For example, in one sense, certain choices or freedoms must be foregone as resources and structures are committed to and processed into certain outcomes. To return to the value-added model example, as the iron ore becomes "committed" to an automobile, the system (sometimes only temporarily) must forego other uses and products of the raw material, while at the same time gaining the freedoms of this mode of transportation. A related set of losses concerns the ways in which evolution involves creating more complex and intricate dependencies (the notion of organic solidarity goes far to capture this). Actors and subsystems would increasingly cease to be self-sufficient in regard to many lower-level functions (e.g., with urbanization most of us are dependent on a long chain of food growers, processors, shippers, sales and distribution organizations). Thus, for example, actors and systems become more vulnerable to a considerably larger array of possible malfunctions or demands.[45]

Structural Differentiation

Perhaps the evolutionary pattern that has received the most attention from Parsons and most theorists of action is structural differentiation.[46] As Parsons now presents this pattern, it is one of four major patterns — the other three being adaptive upgrading, inclusion, and value generalization.

Structural differentiation generally refers to the change within a system from a state in which certain functions or activities are performed by a given unit to a situation in which two or more relatively distinct units or substructures varying in their characteristics perform these separated functions and do so in a fashion such that the joint output of these separate units is more efficient and effective. Examples of structural differentiation at the societal level would concern the progressive separation in the last few hundred years in Western society of occupational roles and activities from family and domestic life, leading to the emergence of the modern family and the modern employing organization. Another example would be the disestablishment of legal norms and governmental structures from religious institutions. Also, Fox's discussion in this collection of the development of modern medicine traces the differentiation of the treatment of illness out of the previous broader religious and kinship nexus. Other prominent examples in modern society of specialized collectivities that have crystallized around activities once performed in more diffuse groupings would be hospitals and universities. An instance of role differentiation within an organization would be the separation and specialization of activities such as the development of the role of the trained, full-time psychological counsellor in a school.

Differentiation should be distinguished from another important concept, segmentation. Segmentation refers to a process of generating two or more essentially similar structures performing essentially similar functions. Examples would include the proliferation of additional nuclear families or business organizations or the splitting off of one group from a tribe to form a separate tribe. Occasionally, as in the last example, segmentation can serve as an important safety valve in societies — a way of avoiding or minimizing contact and strain.[47] Alternatively it can be a major base of primordial attachments and consequent conflicts (comparable to a geological fault, to use Rueschemeyer's imagery). Segmentation does not seem to involve the same qualitative structural reorganization that differentiation does and is not extensively treated in the theory of action.

All action systems — not just social systems — would of course be analyzed as structurally differentiating over time. What the differentiating units are would depend on the system level of analysis. They could for example, be roles or collectivities at the social system level, general beliefs or symbols at the cultural level,[48] and motives or schema at the personality level.[49] Differentiation is seen as occurring even at the general action level itself — of organism, personality, social system, and cultural system from each other and from the nonaction environment.

I should perhaps hasten to add that, although the theory of action emphasizes structural differentiation as one of the major trends or patterns characterizing change and development in all action systems, differentiation is not regarded as inevitable or unilinear (any more than any of the other patterns). De-differentiation[50] is recognized as occurring and as being one type of possible response to strain or systems' attempts to adapt. Nevertheless, differentiation is treated as one of the principal over-all trends that, despite setbacks and difficulties, continues to develop or to be "selected out" as one of the more effective responses or adaptations to system strain and malfunctioning.

One of action theory's major observations concerning differentiation is that, over time, systems tend to differentiation along the lines of the major functional problems. That is, structures tend to arise or differentiate out which are specialized in the performance of adaptation, goal attainment, integration, and pattern maintenance. This of course is congruent with the general view of evolution as, in a sense, the efforts of a system over time to engage in problem solving, with the AGIL scheme characterizing the major problems to be solved.

Differentiation is seen as enhancing adaptive capacity in a variety of ways. For one, in the case of institutionalization at the social system level, differentiation would enable, sanction, or require actors to specialize in the performance of a given set of activities. This can involve offering and demanding more intensive specialized and advanced training and skill development, the concentration in a given collectivity of necessary and appropriate resources, and the provision of opportunities for making a more effective match of skills and tasks. Specialization can also make possible the development of more sophisticated technical information, which in turn can require more specialization, and so on.[51]

Second, differentiation usually involves sorting out or compartmentalizing to a high degree expectations and principles of organization that may conflict. For example, families tend to operate primarily in terms of affectivity, particularism, ascription, and diffuseness. While more "modern" business organizations and other occupational settings involve some elements of these pattern variables, they seem to rely primarily on the opposite pattern variable choices — affective neutrality, universalism, achievement, and specificity. It presumably minimizes role conflicts, personal strains, and normative ambiguities to differentiate to a significant extent functions and activities that would seem to necessarily rest on these alternative principles.

Further, differentiation often involves liberation of actors and resources from being bound to a variety of ascriptive commitments that would limit the flexibility of their "choice" or allocation, mobilization, and combination. Perhaps the classic example would be the increased flexibility of the labor market as this factor of production has become liberated from such ascriptive ties as particular geographic locations, particular employers (or employees) who are related by kinship or common ethnicity. The development of generalized media of exchange such as money can also be seen as introducing degrees of freedom, relative, say, to a barter economy in regard to the time at which items may be exchanged, the sources with which one deals, and so on. Of course, this phenomenon would not be limited to the social system level. One important example from the personality system would be the liberation of cathectic energies from early primordial attachments to enable a person to engage in ever broader solidarity groupings and to leave the family of orientation for a family of procreation.[52]

As I have already noted, differentiation is not without its problems. "Excessive" or too-rapid differentiation, for example, can be a major source of alienation or of a romanticist backlash.[53] Parsons has discussed some of the conditions or reorganizations necessary for successful differentiation: the provision of opportunity through the emancipation of facilities from ascriptive ties, inclusion of differentiated units in higher-level collectivity structures, upgrading of norms to higher levels of generality, and extension or generalization of values to legitimize new functional units.

A crude summary formulation of the point here would be that as differentiation in an action system grows, so grow the integrative problems.[54] Obviously, then, if the system is to be relatively stable and to be able to continue to develop, mechanisms of integration must be further developed. A number of phenomena can be seen as dealing with integrative problems, such as the development of a more inclusive ideology, a universalistic legal system, voluntary associations, the extension of community membership rights and privileges, and increases in the level of generality of the media of exchange.[55]

Indeed, even written language can be seen as the development of a more powerful and generalized medium of exchange, liberated as it would be from many constraints on the exchange of information. This suggests that the crucial evolutionary breakthroughs that characterize watersheds between the major evolutionary stages (symbols, written language, universalistic law — to be discussed later) can be seen as responses to and solutions of major integrative problems. These "solutions" enable significantly more differentiated and expanded systems to be viable and, in a sense, facilitate the birth

of new, more complex emergent levels of organization. This point is congruent with Mayhew's presentation of the evolutionary theory in which he emphasizes seeing the evolutionary stages as *"new levels of consolidation of the relationships between aggregates"* and the discussion of the nature of the societies at each stage as focussing on the relative integrative and incorporative capacities of various societies and cultures.[56]

I shall pass over a number of other patterns, such as modernization, industrialization, societal growth, rationalization, and professionalization. These will be woven into the discussion of evolutionary stages that follows.

Sequences and Stages

Let us turn now to some of the principal sequence and stage schemes that have been employed in action theory. The patterns previously discussed are crucial dimensions or directional trends in some of these schemes, but others are also involved.

Essentially three kinds of schemes have been employed — a seven-stage model of sequences in structural differentiation, a four-stage model of phase movements, and a stage model of societal evolution that has been divided into three stages by Parsons and, in its usage in connection with religious evolution, into five stages by Bellah.

Differentiation Schemes

Perhaps the most developed version of the model of structural differentiation has been presented by Smelser, who divides the sequence into seven steps.

(1) Dissatisfaction with the goal-achievements of the social system or subsystem in question and a sense of opportunity for change in terms of the potential availability of facilities.

(2) Symptoms of disturbance in the form of "unjustified" negative emotional reactions and "unrealistic" aspirations on the part of various elements in the social system.

(3) A covert handling of these tensions and a mobilization of motivational resources for new attempts to realize the implications of the existing value-system.

(4) Encouragement of the resulting proliferation of "new ideas" without imposing specific responsibility for their implementation or for "taking the consequences."

(5) Positive attempts to reach specification of the new ideas and institutional patterns which will become the objects of commitments.

(6) "Responsible" implementation of innovations carried out by persons or collectivities which are either rewarded or punished, depending on their acceptability or reprehensibility in terms of the existing value-system.

(7) If the implementations of Step 6 are received favorably, they are gradually routinized into the usual patterns of performance and sanction; their extraordinary character thereby diminishes.[57]

Of course this is intended as a model of a complete sequence. Depending on a variety of relevant factors, the change sequence may stop, fixate, regress from, on spend more actual time at any of the points in this sequence.

The scheme could readily generalize to any social system level change sequence concerning, say, value generalization or inclusion. There is nothing in the content that seems to limit it to structural differentiation. Further, if the steps were conceptualized more generally, the scheme would seem applicable to any action level. One would of course need to drop out the social system content. For example, step 1 might be reformulated as "inadequate functioning or deficit in the goal attainment sector of the system of subsystem in question and the availability of facilities providing an opportunity for change." The second step might be simply "symptoms of disturbance," with the content being appropriate to the system level under analysis.

Phase Movement Schemes

A second major model employs the four functional categories, AGIL. It has been used mainly to describe the phase movements in small groups and the process of learning or socialization.[58] Phases are characterized in terms of the overt acts and associated attitudes oriented to the solution of particular system problems. Thus,

phases are *technically* described by the specification of the direction and amount of movement taking place within the time interval on *each* of the four dimensions, but for purposes of convenience, are named in terms of the dimension of major movement.[59]

Before discussing the principal sequences of phase movements which Parsons and Bales suggested, let us introduce several of their cautionary notes. They emphasize that they are not contending that only one sequence is possible. Not only do they suggest several sequences (depending on the type of group), but they even go so far as to assert that ". . . regular phase movements are in a way a limiting case, depending upon unusual stability of inputs, a relatively closed system, and a number of other factors."[60] They also suggest it is dependent on the time span, number of units, ease of communication, and so on.

A second important cautionary note is that there is not necessarily a one-to-one relationship between system and unit phases. They introduce the concept

of "orbit" to underline the relatively autonomous movement of units vis-à-vis the system of which they are members.

The systematic application of the phase movement scheme and logic to more macrolevel systems remains to be done (although there are the hints of a beginning, as for example in Parsons' suggestion that integrative problems have become primary in the U.S.[61]). An extension of the use of this scheme to characterize the development of personality and other action systems (perhaps most obviously in articulating it with Erikson's eight phases of personality development) also holds much promise for refining the theory.

Essentially two basic patterns or sequences of stages are suggested. One is a clockwise sequence or task performance set of phases running A-G-I-L, thought to characterize groups that are mainly instrumentally oriented to the performance of a group task. The principal instance of such groups which is dealt with are the experimental five-person decision-making groups, but this pattern would presumably also be thought to apply to work groups, say in a factory setting, and conceivably to such groups as families insofar as they are focussing on some instrumental task. The second is a counterclockwise sequence of "learning-social control phases" running L-I-G-A, thought to characterize such systems as therapy groups or families engaged in long-term socialization.

One factor offered to account for phase movement is that there are similarities between cells such that there is a "pull" to the adjacent cell. For example, the G and I sectors have in common an emphasis on the affectivity and particularism pattern variables which would supposedly pull activity from, say, I to G or G to I. Of course, this would not be enough in itself to account for the direction of movement (I to G or I to L), as L also has two pattern variables in common with I.

A second factor noted is rather inconsistent with the first. This is one of *compensatory alternation*. It is maintained that, given its limited resources, an action system cannot concentrate adequately on both instrumental and consummatory activity simultaneously. Concentration on one type then leads to deficits in the other, which necessitates and promotes a shift to the diagonal of a given sector (G to L or I to A, for example) in order to reestablish the system's equilibrium. Of course, this in itself would be directly contradictory to an LIGA or AGIL pattern, unless, of course, one accepted some of the revisions proposed by Loubser in his essay, "Action and Experience," in this collection.

Perhaps the main point to be observed here is that

acceptance of this sort of argument and development of its implications would go very far to establish an inherent dialectic in the theory of action.

A third set of considerations offered is that

> . . . a system of action is considered to involve a *one-way process* . . . . "Energy" is continually "fed into" the system and "expended." There is no spontaneous reversal of this process from sources within the system itself. Energy is converted into goal-attainment and consequences . . . ."[62]

Thus it would seem that action systems are conceived of as inherently counterentropic. This would seem to imply that higher-level informational components are constantly structuring lower-level energy (or energy controlling) components — which would be, in effect, an LIGA sequence presumably. Of course, an important qualification in the quote should be emphasized — that "there is no spontaneous reversal of this process from sources within the system." Obviously, then, external factors could "overwhelm" the system and promote entropy on balance.

Evolutionary Schemes

Finally, we come to the schemes characterizing evolutionary stages. Parsons' version of such a scheme is couched essentially at the societal level (although it does seem to include in rather unsystematic fashion aspects of other levels[63]). There is no comparable sustained effort that I know of for other system levels, although Bellah's scheme of religious evolution[64] would presumably be readily generalizeable to the cultural system level. Clearly this is a major need not only for the extension of the theory but for the refinement of social system level analysis to which it is likely to lead.

Parsons has offered a three-fold scheme with two subdivisions in the first two stages that makes this scheme roughly equivalent to Bellah's five-fold scheme of religious evolution. Bellah's treatment of religious evolution concerns four principal aspects — religious symbol systems, religious action, religious organization, and social implications. In regard to each of these, he maps what is essentially a pattern of increasing differentiation, generalization or symbolization, rationalization, and autonomy relative to the environment.

I shall deal with Parsons' scheme in somewhat greater detail. He distinguishes three stages: primitive (subdivided into primitive and advanced primitive); intermediate (with archaic and advanced intermediate being distinguished); and modern (with some suggestions of what an advanced modern stage might be). Without going into the full complexity of the nature of each stage in Parsons' scheme, let us briefly note some of the principle distinguishing features that are suggested.

Action theorists (in part through their adaptation of biological evolutionary theory) emphasize the continuity of human evolution with biological evolution and so-called subhuman species. The first major watershed — or evolutionary help — that Parsons touches on is that from subhuman to primitive human society. Human beings, it is suggested, are the only cultural animals,[65] and, as Parsons puts it, "in the realm of action, the gene has been replaced by the symbol as the basic structural element."[66] This breakthrough to symbolization in turn implies very significantly different attributes about the social system, personality, and organismic levels.

Primitive systems are characterized by a high degree of fusion or undifferentiatedness among components at the action level or among action subsystems. Primitive social organizations are particularly characterized by the high degree of importance of religious orientations and kinship relationships in all spheres of action. Further, a high degree of normative prescriptiveness and low level of generality of information components present the actor with a minimum degree of choice and has led to the characterization of life in this system as a "one-possibility thing." In a sense, only a few degrees of freedom beyond the constraints imposed by the operation of instinct, genes, heredity, and the like seem to be in control at the subhuman levels. Other features are of course also distinctive of primitive human systems, such as the simplicity of economic and political organization. I shall pass over the details of the advanced primitive type, save to note its distinctive development of stratification and some kind of central political organization.

The transition from primitive to intermediate is marked by the emergence (and institutionalization in some sectors) of written language. This development significantly increases the differentiation between the social and cultural systems as well as the range and the power of the cultural system. The first substage termed "archaic," is distinguished by craft literacy and cosmological religion. The second or "advanced intermediate" stage involves the institutionalization of full male upper-class literacy and an "historic" religion — a religion which has broken through to philosophical levels of generalization and systematization.

The watershed to "modern" societies is conceived by Parsons as the development and institutionalization of a legal system that is highly generalized according to universalistic principles and formal rationality. This development significantly enhances the autonomy of societal normative components from the exigencies of political and economic interests and other lower-level factors operating on them (although still integrating them). Thus, this represents another major step in the increased differentiation out of and cybernetic control by higher-level components over conditional exigencies. Further, for the individual a great range of choices and opportunities has opened up. Life has become an "infinite possibility" thing.

Parsons has discussed many other features that seem to be characteristic of modern society,[67] such as the rationalization and professionalization[68] of many forms of activity (note particularly developments in business and the various natural and social sciences, both pure and applied), the institutionalization of far broader ranges of freedom for larger masses of people than ever before, the development of more decentralized and associational forms of power and authority (with an emphasis on the trend not towards increased bureaucracy but towards associationism).

Let me make several general qualifications or cautionary notes in regard to the stage schemes. First, it is important to emphasize that Parsons by no means regards contemporary examples of modern society as having fully evolved as yet. He stresses that the type would still seem to have a long way to go in regard to problems of inequality and social injustice, the development of broader and perhaps more profound forms of freedom, and the extension of various forms of democratic association. More generally, it should be obvious that no specific historical instance would necessarily be a full and complete "realization" of the ideal type of the stage in which it is classified.

Further, Parsons traces a number of ways in which modern societies constitute a single system whose loose differentiation has enhanced the long-run adaptive capacity and evolution of this system. The point here is of course that there is still a long way to go in the evolutionary development of this stage before a more emergent and adequately integrated system will have been reached.

A third cautionary note that I would like to make concerns the pattern variables. The evolutionary stage scheme does not hypothesize or imply a simple emergence of the more *gesellschaft* pattern variables (affective neutrality, universalism, achievement, and specificity) and the disappearance of the more *gemeinschaft* type (affectivity, particularism, ascription, and diffuseness). It does map an increase of the former, while, far from positing the complete withering away of the elements or institutions with *gemeinschaft* primacy, the theory sees these patterns as tending to become focussed in institutions and collectivities that increasingly specialize in operation on these principles or meet needs apparently related to these principles — such as the family and perhaps even more specialized units that seem to be emerging (communes, psychotherapeutic relationships,

and other forms of premarital and nonmarital dyads) that could represent even further differentiation out of the kinship nexus of sex, procreation, and socialization activities.

A related problem for the scheme concerns societies that appear to be stable and durable mixtures of the components of more than one stage. Rueschemeyer's second essay in this collection deals at length and quite effectively with this and related issues. Although I am not completely convinced that most instances of "partial modernization" or, more generally, "durable inconsistencies" are not indeed transitional and/or unstable systems, Rueschemeyer does usefully call attention to the phenomenon and indicates some of its sources[69] and mechanisms for maintaining what might ordinarily be conflicting and change-inducing patterns. None of these points are incompatible with the theory of action, which would also recognize that action systems vary in their degree of integration, strain to consistency, and the like, depending on a variety of factors such as the content of the value system, the nature of structural arrangements, the development of organic solidarity, and mediating roles and mechanisms.[70] Rueschemeyer's analysis is also relevant to the position that certain structural arrangements (for example, a high degree of segmentation) can inhibit further system evolution, and he points to some additional factors necessary for continued modernization.

What the next major breakthroughs are to "advanced modern" and "beyond modern" stages — analytically and/or empirically — have received disappointingly little attention. Various suggestions have been or might be made in regard to such developments as the institutionalization of universal literacy in the entire adult population,[71] the development and integration of a genuinely transnational system (extrapolating from Robertson in this collection), the development of more fully social or collectivistic conceptions of human action and ways of dealing with social and individual problems (extrapolating from Fox's essay in this collection), and other developments related to some probable future occurrences (such as the establishment of relationships with extraterrestrial action systems, minimization of age and sex chauvinism, or the establishment of greatly increased human longevity if not virtual immortality). Whether any of these developments represent sufficient qualitative "leaps" and restructurings as opposed to merely further development of the modern stage remains quite problematic.

It may be observed[72] that there is an important contradiction (or at least tension) in the theory between the evolutionary universals and apparent trends stratification, on the one hand, and, on the other, the trend towards greater equality and (possibly) democratic association. Without entering into this rather complex controversy, two main possibilities seem likely. One is that these principles or evolutionary patterns will continue in some sort of dialectical and creative tension (as are other evolutionary universals and pattern variables). In a sense, both might continue to grow, with society developing still new forms of synthesizing or integrating these patterns. A second possibility is that one of these patterns emerges as predominant, with the other tending to wither, having made its evolutionary contribution. The probable development of ever more socialistic societies would represent one version of this path. Indeed, solution to the fundamental dilemmas of integrating stratification and egalitarianism, commitment to technical standards and democratic association, and the like may well represent the crucial breakthroughs to an advanced modern or post-modern stage.

It certainly "boggles the scheme" to try to contemplate the extent of social and cultural evolution that could occur over the coming centuries, given what appears to have occurred in, say, a mere ten to twenty thousand years, and given the apparently exponential increase in the rate of evolution that breakthroughs seem to bring. However, these considerations do not point merely to interesting or amusing empirical concerns but, in a sense, to an important analytical problem and deficiency in the evolutionary theory to date. That is, although it is systematic in its conceptualization of processes of differentiation, generalization, and liberation of factors, the stage theory does not seem to be formulated in terms of a systematic series such that we could readily generate a set of future stages and provide a clear theoretical rationale for past and present ones. An effort at a more systematic conceptualization might try to identify a stage sequence somewhat along the lines of the work on small groups in regard to phase movements, for example. Thus, assuming the theoretical utility of characterizing the major watersheds as marked by the emergence of culture, written language, universalistic law, it might ask whether these form a series of differentiations, generalizations, or liberations of factors— first at the total action L level, then at some subsystem of L, then at some subsystem of the societal system (law or I_i). Obviously this scheme is not particularly "neat" and might call for some reconceptualization of the whole stage scheme that might look for patterns of differentiation first at the total action level, with subsystems then emerging within each system, and so on.

Alternatively, the dialectical logic of alternation

among instrumental and consummatory foci noted in regard to phase movement might suggest a different pattern. Obviously considerably more work remains to be done.

CONCLUDING REMARKS AND RESPONSE TO SOME CRITICISMS

I shall not discuss each essay included in this part of the collection in specific detail, as I have woven into my text comments and criticisms concerning their main points. The final portion of this essay will instead be devoted to discussing some of the principle general criticisms of the theory of action.[73] I shall focus on three, the claims that the theory is essentially static, conservative, and conflictless.

It is often suggested that action theory lacks a theory of change and/or is essentially static. I think this criticism may rest on a variety of assumptions. In part it seems to involve ignorance of large parts of Parsons' work—particularly his recent work on evolution—and the work of other theorists of action such as Smelser and Bellah.

This line of criticism also seems to rely on sources that have wrenched from context Parsons' statements about not being able to have a general theory of change until we have a theory of structure and process. More importantly it may be based on regarding equilibrium models as incapable of dealing with change. Such models supposedly treat homeostatic mechanisms as inexorably returning systems to equilibrium, regard societies as stable and well-integrated with every element as functional. I trust I have indicated sufficiently here that the theory of action does not have this rigid a conception of systems. The theory quite explicitly sees homeostatic mechanisms as capable of being "overcome" by specifiable factors. It has certainly emphasized that systems can and do change, often quite radically, and are far from being perfectly integrated. Further, the theory would rely in part on a notion like "moving equilibrium" in which aspects of the system's control processes may remain viable and stable while guiding lower-level change processes.[74]

Another important criticism often raised in this context is that the theory treats values as the determinants of change but has no way of explaining change in values. This, too, seems based on a very limited grasp of the theory. As indicated before, a great many components other than values are treated as factors in change. Further, values are treated as quite susceptible to change under the influence of higher-level cultural components and strains or pressures from other conditional factors.

Further, many aspects of change that analysts would wish to attribute to value change may in fact be due to stability at the level of values and change at lower levels to which they are specified and institutionalized, such as roles and collectivities. Relevant here would be Eisenstadt's treatment in this collection of the importance of codes in system continuity as well as Parsons' concept of "instrumental activism" as an important value in American society that accounts for development and change in specific subsystems such as the economy.

Let me turn to the second set of criticisms—that the theory has neglected conflict in action systems, sees conflict (and even change) as "bad," and postulates no inherent sources of strain in these systems. I would agree that the theory has failed to develop as explicit and systematic a treatment of conflict as would be useful and desirable (e.g., for all the typologizing, I do not know of even one typology of conflict in action theory). However, I do not see that this treatment of conflict is a limitation inherent in the theory. For example, many of the specific empirical analyses discuss conflicts among competing groups and interests (social class, religious, political) for various scarce resources. Perhaps the principle form of the analysis of conflict has been in regard to contradictions among alternative normative patterns. For example, Parsons' classic essay on fascism in Germany discusses the way that differential institutionalization of rational and traditional patterns in different societal sectors was conducive to the rise of Nazism.[75] Further, the thrust of many of the analyses of industrial societies points to incompatabilities among alternative patterns and structures (often conceptualized in pattern variable terms).[76] The problems that these incompatabilities do or might create and ways in which they are resolved are usually dealt with. There is no necessary assumption that perfect consistency or integration is necessary for system functioning or is likely to arise. Rueschemeyer's analyses of stable inconsistencies and ways that they can be maintained is instructive in this regard.

Further, competition, as one major form of conflict, is recognized as a crucial evolutionary mechanism. Examples of more systematic and analytical treatments of conflict might concern the pattern variables, which represent—not only dilemmas of choice for individual actors but principles of organizing collective social conduct that often seem to conflict and present fundamental tensions. Extending this use of the pattern variables could go a long way towards incorporating a notion of strains and contradictions in action systems that are fundamental and inherent as well as dialectical in nature.

Further, along these lines, recognition of inherent tensions that act as constant stimuli to change would relate to the basically "open-system" conceptualization of action systems. As Parsons emphasizes, action systems are faced with a constant need to mobilize resources from their environments,[77] which are themselves generally changing. The tension then is not only how to deal with these ever present problems, but how to allocate fundamentally scarce resources among competing functional sectors. In this sense, one can see the AGIL scheme as a way of conceptualizing and typologizing basic tensions.[78]

The third set of criticisms with which I will deal concerns the claim that the theory of action is conservative (or liberal in the pejorative sense). I think it is probably true that most theorists of action are liberals (and I see important differences among even today's conservatives and liberals). But I think it is important to distinguish between what most theorists of action may themselves believe and have done to date in developing the theory, on the one hand, and, on the other, what ideological and analytical potentials are inherent in the theory.

Further, while theorists of action have praised American society in particular and modern societies in general in a number of ways, they are at least praising it in terms of values and criteria that are often generally shared by more radical critics of contemporary society.

Finally, they have also criticized many aspects of modern societies and American society in terms of their lack of institutionalization of justice, equality, genuine pluralism, and so on.[79]

A related line of criticism concerns action theory's use of equilibrium models. While action theory may have focussed on equilibrium models and even highly integrated systems, these are, for the most part, treated as analytical ideal types and arguing points. They do not imply or necessitate a preference for equilibrium and integration any more than using largely nonexistent abstractions for analytical purposes such as "the vacuum" implies a preference for or belief in the prevalence of vacuums.

But even if the theory is not inherently conservative or liberal, one might ask if it has any radical or critical potential. For example, what in the theory might lead one to at least an analytical concern with justice, equality, and freedom. First, it might be observed that in many respects these value terms in Western society have come to be associated with the treatment of individuals in terms of "achievement" standards (as opposed to "ascriptive") and "universalistic" norms (as opposed to "particularistic"). Further, as I trust I have indicated, the theory places a high evolutionary value on the liberation of actors and other components from conditional and ascriptive constraints—and surely that is, in many senses, what most of the struggles and revolutions of the oppressed have been for.[80]

Of course, none of this is to imply that there is not still much work to be done. I am sure that most theorists of action would agree that the theory of action has far to go in its own evolution before it will have begun to realize its full generalized adaptive capacity.

NOTES

1. Probably most important would be the following works by Talcott Parsons: "Some Considerations on the Theory of Social Change," *Rural Sociology,* 26 (September 1961). pp. 219-239; "An Outline of the Social System," pp. 70-79, in Talcott Parsons *et al.* (eds.), *Theories of Society* (New York: The Free Press, 1961); *Societies: Evolutionary and Comparative Perspectives* (Englewood Cliffs: Prentice Hall, 1966); *The System of Modern Societies* (Englewood Cliffs: Prentice-Hall, 1971).
Also see Neil J. Smelser, *Social Change in the Industrial Revolution* (Chicago: University of Chicago Press, 1959).

2. See, for example, the following works by Talcott Parsons: "Democracy and the Social Structure in Pre-Nazi Germany," and "Some Sociological Aspects of the Fascist Movements," in *Essays in Sociological Theory,* revised edition, Glencoe, Ill.: The Free Press, 1954); Chapter 7, pp. 226-247, in *Structure and Process in Modern Societies* (Glencoe, Ill.: The Free Press, 1960); "Christianity and Modern Industrial Society," pp. 33-70, in Edward A. Tiryakian (ed.), *Sociological Theory, Values and Sociocultural Change* (New York: The Free Press, 1963); "Full Citizenship for the Negro American?" pp. 422-65, in *Sociological Theory and Modern Society* (New York: The Free Press, 1967).
See also Robert N. Bellah, *Tokugawa Religion* (Glencoe, Ill. The Free Press, 1957); and Winston White, *Beyond Conformity* (New York: The Free Press, 1961).

3. I think it is fair to say that contemporary evolutionary theory, at least as developed by Parsons, is no longer vulnerable to the criticisms of postulating a unilineal, inevitable, or irreversible pattern and of ignoring mechanisms accounting for change and adaptation.

4. For other discussions of the nature of the cybernetic model in general, see particularly Robert N. Bellah, "The Sociology of Religion," in David L. Sills (ed.), *International Encyclopedia of the Social Sciences,* Vol. 13 (New York: Macmillan and Free Press, 1968), p. 410; Karl W. Deutsch, *The Nerves of Government* (New York: The Free Press, 1963); and Parsons, *Societies,* Chapter 2.

5. Whether there is any fit between the AGIL scheme and these four characteristics or "orientations" of the theory remains to be explored.

6. See, for example, Parsons, "An Outline of the Social System," *op. cit.,* p. 72. Smelser's definition, *op. cit.,* p. 14, varies in emphasizing change in social system roles and social structural change at the social system level. This seems to be a less useful formulation than Parsons'.

7. See Parsons, "An Outline . . . ," *op. cit.,* p. 30. Of course this is consistent with his general cybernetic conception of action systems as, to an important extent, though not wholly, a series of successive specifications of general

cultural components to ever more concrete levels from cultural to social system to personality system to organism.

8. Whether any particular alteration is a "sufficiently significant" reorganization to be classified as a "change" is (1) in part a matter of definition or conceptualization of what the state of the system is, (2) in part a matter of choice of the indices for measurement of the nature of the system, and (3) in part a matter of theoretical judgement or explanatory power.

9. See Talcott Parsons, *The Social System* (Glencoe, Ill.: The Free Press, 1951), p. 481; and *Societies,* pp. 20-21.

10. See particularly Parsons, *The Social System,* pp. 481-90, and Parsons, "Outline. . . ," *op. cit.,* pp. 70-79.

11. *Ibid.,* p. 70.

12. See Parsons, *The Social System,* pp. 491ff and Parsons, "Outline. . . ," pp. 70-79.

13. See Parsons, *Societies,* p. 21.

14. See Parsons, *The Social System,* p. 480. Also consider his statement on p. 486 that

. . . it should be clear, that so far as our knowledge goes beyond description and sheer empirical generalization it is always to some degree knowledge of processes of change. It is not possible to segregate *theoretical* knowledge of the laws of the processes within systems, and of their processes of change. They are both different contexts of *application* of our knowledge of the relations between variations of conditions and the outcomes of processes going forward under the conditions in question. When, therefore, we combine our knowledge of structural imperatives in the above sense, our paradigmatic knowledge of motivational process, and our fragmentary knowledge of laws, we do in fact have considerable knowledge of many processes of change, and the progress of research will steadily increase it.

15. See Talcott Parsons, Robert F. Bales, and Edward A. Shils, *Working Papers in the Theory of Action* (New York: The Free Press, 1953), Chapter 3, pp. 63-109.

16. Again, it should probably be emphasized that this is not to imply that systems will remain stable, but that their change or stability is contingent on the relative strength of internal and external forces which promote stability or change.

17. Parsons, *The Social System,* p. 491.

18. Parsons, "Outline. . . ," *op. cit.,* p. 71. There is some ambiguity about the meaning of strain. For example, "strain here refers to a condition in the *relation* between two or more structured units . . . that constitutes a tendency or pressure toward changing that relation to one incompatible with the relevant part of the system . . . a strain is a tendency to disequilibrium in the input-output balance between two or more units of the system" (p. 72). One ambiguity is whether the "tendency or pressure toward changing" is part of the definition of strain or merely one of its principle consequences and potentially correlated outcomes. I think the more theoretically useful conceptualization would be not to treat this as part of the definition of strain. Also, in an earlier treatment (*The Social System* p. 491), Parsons quite explicitly includes the initiation of re-equilibrating processes as part of the definition of strain. I think this is also a theoretically unnecessary strategy.

19. For a particularly systematic effort at conceptualizing types of strain in social systems, see Neil J. Smelser, *Theory of Collective Behavior* (New York: The Free Press, 1963), Chapter 3.

20. See particularly Smelser, *Social Change in the Industrial Revolution* and Parsons, "Some Considerations on the Theory of Change," *op. cit.*

21. However, some theorists of action would take issue with the overly strong position that "a structure can continue to exist only so long as the density and the volume of

activity generated by the structure satisfies the functional imperatives of the system" (Tominaga, p. 692). This would seem to be a conception of action systems as being more tightly integrated and adaptively attuned than they are in actuality such that in fact many dysfunctional patterns and structures may persist. Further, it is difficult to agree with Tominaga's position that "an endogenous variable model is likely to result in a conclusion that change is cyclical or that it is short-run" (p. 690). Concepts in action theory such as value generalization, inclusion, differentiation, and adaptive upgrading would probably overcome these supposed limitations as they conceptualize significant internal structural alterations which can also promote further internal changes.

22. See Neil J. Smelser, *Essays in Sociological Explanation* (Englewood Cliffs: Prentice-Hall, 1968), p. 277; and Parsons, "Outline. . . ," *op. cit.*, p. 72.

23. Smelser, *Theory of Collective Behavior*, pp. 15-18, *et passim*.

24. Parsons, "Outline. . . ," *op. cit.*, p. 72.

25. Tominaga, like most other theorists of action, does not expend much analytic effort analyzing ways in which workers and others may have been exploited and oppressed, However, these considerations could well be built into an interchange model and might help more adequately account for the development of unions, socialist movements, and the like.

26. Parsons, *Societies*, p. 113.

27. Sigmund Freud, *The Ego and the Id*, Joan Riviere (tr.) (London: Hogarth Press, 1950), p. 30.

28. See Smelser, *Theory of Collective Behavior*.

29. Parsons, "Some Considerations. . . ," *op. cit.*

30. From Smelser, *Theory of Collective Behavior*, p. 38.

31. The first four levels would be, respectively, societal, institutional, collectivity, and role. Levels 5, 6, and 7 would parallel 2, 3, and 4 and would be the day-to-day operative specification levels of the system.

32. From Smelser, *Theory of Collective Behavior*, p. 29.

33. Parsons, "Outline. . . ," *op. cit.*, p. 74.

34. Leon Mayhew, *Society: Institutions and Activity* (Glenview, Ill.: Scott, Foresman, 1971), pp. 41-42.

35. Mayhew, *op. cit.*, p. 38.

36. Many other examples could be cited, of important values or orientational complexes that are regarded as relevant to promoting or inhibiting change. See for particularly salient instances Eisenstadt's discussion of various "codes" in his contribution to this collection and Bellah, *Tokugawa Religion*.

37. Smelser, *Theory of Collective Behavior*, pp. 13-14.

38. It should be clear that "adaptive" is being used in a much broader sense in this context. The narrow definition would be the sense in which adaptation is one of four particular functional problems, representing an intersection of the external and instrumental dimensions for characterizing action systems. The broad definition in this context would in effect be equivalent to generalized "successful" relationships to environmental exigencies. In one sense this broader definition could be seen as some sort of summary of effectiveness in dealing with all four functional problems in any given system level.

39. Bellah's definition of "progress" in Robert N. Bellah (ed.), *Religion and Progress in Modern Asia* (New York: The Free Press, 1965), p. 170, as the increased capacity "to receive and process information from within and without the system and to respond appropriately to it" could be seen as another way of characterizing enhanced adaptive capacity. Another useful general discussion of adaptive capacity as well as structural differentiation can be found in White, *op. cit.*, Chapter 6.

40. Talcott Parsons, "Evolutionary Universals in Society," *American Sociological Review*, 29 (June, 1964), p. 340.

41. Parsons, "Evolutionary Universals," *op. cit.*, pp. 339-57.

42. For an extension of the concept of adaptive capacity to the personality system level and a discussion of some of its sources, see Michael Fullan and Jan J. Loubser, "Education and Adaptive Capacity," *Sociology of Education*, 45 (Summer, 1972), pp. 271-87.

43. Characterizing evolution as the movement from simple to complex societies or structures is somewhat simplistic. As Parsons has observed, the increased "organizedness" (or counter-entropic patterns) that emerges in evolution introduces degrees of simplification or "complexity reduction" that are not readily captured in this single dimension.

44. See White, *op. cit.*, pp. 87-100.

45. These losses often have been the focus of "romantic" backlash against various evolutionary developments.

46. See particularly Parsons, "Outline. . . ;" *op. cit*; Parsons, "Some Considerations. . . ;" *op. cit*; Smelser, *Social Change in the Industrial Revolution*; T. Parsons, R. F. Bales *et al.*, *Family, Socialization and Interaction Process* (Glencoe, Ill.: The Free Press, 1955), Chapter 2, pp. 35-131. One of Parsons' strongest statements in this regard is that

> The great processes of elaboration of social structures — such as those involved in the development of modern industrial societies, took place mainly by a process of differentiation within the same social systems from simpler antecedents. "External influence" has played a part, but surely the big thing is the process of internal system-differentiation (*ibid.*, p. 55).

47. See Rueschemeyer's essay in this collection on partial modernization.

48. Bellah's very brief summary of religious evolution would be relevant here:

> The central focus of religious evolution is the religious symbol system itself. Here the main line of development is from compact to differentiated symbolism, that is, from a situation in which world, self, and society are seen to involve the immediate expression of occult powers to one in which the exercise of religious influence is seen to be more indirect and "rational." This is the process of the "disenchantment of the world" that was described by Weber. Part of this process is the gradual differentiation of art, science, and other cultural systems as separate from religious symbolism.

Bellah, "The Sociology of Religion," in Sills (ed.) *op. cit.*, p. 413. For a fuller explication see R. Bellah "Religious Evolution," *American Sociological Review*, 29 (June, 1964), pp. 358-374.

49. Parsons has even suggested that differentiation at the personality level can be seen as following a pattern of binary fission. This suggestion occurs in a relatively early work (*Family, Socialization and Interaction Process* Chapter 2). It has not to my knowledge been explicitly developed, although the binary fission pattern can be seen to underlie Parsons' and Bellah's mapping of the evolutionary stages.

50. De-differentiation would obviously be a reversing of the process of differentiation in which the functions performed in separate, relatively specialized and distinctive roles are in some way fused back together or with other roles. It is important to distinguish this phenomenon from the process of integration in which the differentiated component would remain clearly differentiated but linked by some over-arching structure. For further discussion see Talcott Parsons, "On the Concept of Value-Commitments," *Sociological Inquiry*, 38 (Spring, 1968), pp. 157ff. Also see

Jean Lipman-Blumen, "Role De-differentiation as a System Response to Crisis: Occupational and Political Roles of Women," *Sociological Inquiry,* 43 (1973), pp. 105-129. The general phenomenon of de-differentiation is rather important but relatively unexplored in the theory of action.

51. See, for example, Winston White's discussion (*op. cit.,* p. 76) of the advantages of differentiating family and firm that enable specialized, technical, and independent "managerial control" of family and firm decisions, financial matters, and personnel recruitment or dismissal.

52. See particularly Parsons, Bales *et al., op. cit.* and Philip Slater, "On Social Regression," *American Sociological Review* 38 (June, 1963), pp. 339-64.

53. See particularly Smelser, *Social Change in the Industrial Revolution* and Rueschemeyer's essay on ideology in this collection.

54. See Smelser, *Social Change in the Industrial Revolution,* Chapter 9.

55. See, for example, other papers in this collection by Fox, Baum, and Rueschemeyer on ideology, as well as Parsons, *The System of Modern Societies;* Parsons, "Full Citizenship for the Negro American," *op. cit.,* and Smelser's *Essays,* p. 138.

56. Mayhew, *op. cit.,* p. 237 *et passim.*

57. Smelser, *Social Change in the Industrial Revolution,* pp. 15-16. Versions also appear in Talcott Parsons and Neil J. Smelser, *Economy and Society* (New York: The Free Press, 1956).

58. See Parsons, Bales and Shils, *op. cit.,* Parsons, Bales *et al., op. cit.,* and also Cottle's contribution in Part III of this collection.

59. Parsons, Bales and Shils, *op. cit.,* p. 181. This suggests some interesting possibilities concerning subtypes of phases. That is, in addition to characterizing a phase in terms of the dimension which is being given maximal attention relative to the other three dimensions (such as the adaptive phase), one might be concerned with the differences there are between an adaptive phase in which integrative problems are secondary in importance and attention or one in which pattern-maintenance problems take precedence in being second-most important. A second sort of possibility is developing the intensity aspect — that is, differentiating among phases with the same primacy, say integrative, in terms of the extent to which that problem is primary.

60. *Ibid.,* p. 188.

61. See T. Parsons, "Some Problems of General Theory in Sociology," in John C. McKinney and Edward A. Tiryakian (eds.), *Theoretical Sociology: Perspectives and Developments* (New York: Appleton Century Crofts, 1970), pp. 27-68.

62. Parsons, Bales and Shils, *op. cit.,* p. 97.

63. See especially Parsons, *The System of Modern Societies* and *Societies.*

64. See Bellah, "Religious Evolution," *op. cit.*

65. Porpoises are at least one species on which considerably more information is needed before my scepticism is satisfied on this point.

66. Parsons, *Societies,* p. 30. In a sense, this represents a breakthrough in the differentiation of culture out of the conditional environment.

67. See particularly Parsons, *The System of Modern Societies,* pp. 114-60, and Rueschemeyer's essay on ideology in this collection.

68. See, for example, Fox's discussion in this collection of the development and nature of the "professional complex" and the rationalization of medical treatment.

69. Eisenstadt's "codes" would also be relevant here as potential sources of inconsistencies, promoting the continuation of previously institutionalized patterns. Of course, one would have to be methodologically cautious here not to get involved in a circular argument by abstracting the codes from particular structural arrangements and then using those abstractions *per se* to explain the structural arrangements.

70. See Parsons, *The System of Modern Societies,* pp. 139ff.

71. See Parsons, *Societies,* p. 27.

72. As suggested in part by a personal communication from Rainer Baum.

73. See, for example, Albert Szymanski, "Toward a Radical Sociology," *Sociological Inquiry* 40 (Winter, 1970), pp. 3-13; Wolf Heydbrand, "Review Symposium," *Contemporary Sociology* 1 (September 1972), pp. 387-95; and Ralf Dahrendorf, *Class and Class Conflict in Industrial Society,* (Stanford: Stanford University Press, 1959).

74. A number of aspects of Tominaga's discussion in this collection are particularly good on how equilibrium models can deal with change.

75. See the two essays on fascism and Nazism in Germany cited in footnote 2.

76. See, for example, Parsons, *The System of Modern Societies,* pp. 140-42.

77. Recalling that environments can be other action systems.

78. As for example, between A-G, A-I, and so on. This would produce a simple six-fold scheme. Of course one might conceive of various combinations as particularly likely to be in conflict, such as the instrumental as opposed to the consummatory pair.

79. See, for example, Parsons, *System of Modern Societies* and Parsons, "Full Citizenship for the Negro American" *op. cit.* Also note the following from Robert N. Bellah, *Beyond Belief* (New York: Harper and Row, 1970), p. xvii:

> Behind them [certain essays in the book] lies my dismay at the failure of our society to move quickly and efficiently to correct racial injustice, distress at the growing turbulence, much of it meaningless and self-destructive, in the academic community and above all horror at the profoundly immoral and unjustified war in Vietnam. These experiences have led me increasingly in the last few years to feel that the problems of American society, not of the developing societies, are the really most serious ones today.

80. To take this one step further here, one might consider this set: exploitation, oppression, particularization (a form of "dividing and conquering" on segmental lines, as in racism), and the inculcation of "false consciousness" as an application of the AGIL scheme.

27

GROWTH, DEVELOPMENT, AND STRUCTURAL CHANGE OF THE SOCIAL SYSTEM

Ken'ichi Tominaga

SOCIAL SYSTEM ANALYSIS AND SOCIAL CHANGE

Problem

The essay will present the results of both theoretical and empirical research on the macrosocial change accompanying Japan's industrialization. An old Japanese proverb says "those who chase two rabbits at the same time will catch neither one." It may be that it is difficult to achieve success in pursuing two objectives in one essay. However, it is necessary to test theoretical propositions with empirical data in order to evaluate their usefulness. A macrosocial change theory is an aspect of the theory of history; its validity depends upon the adequacy with which it explains historical facts. Hence the empirical data presented here will consist of historical facts and events.

The theoretical objective of this essay is to construct an analytical model of social change at the societal level. This model will focus on the growth and development of total societies that is stimulated by industrialization. Theories of social change are not limited to industrialization theories. Other examples of social change theories at the societal level would be cycle theories and theories of acculturation; in addition there are microtheories of change which deal with partial systems such as organizations and small groups. In this sense, there are definite limits to the generalizability of the model presented here.

Since the time of Saint-Simon, Comte, Spencer, Marx, and Durkheim, macrosociology has concentrated on the problem of societal change or development. It is necessary for contemporary sociology to go beyond mere interest in the problem to the formulation in analytical terms of the processes of social change and development — even if these formulations are only middle range, that is, limited in their generality.

One of the most prominent of contemporary efforts to analyze social change at the societal level is that of Talcott Parsons and his collaborators. In preparing the model of social change and development presented here, I have borrowed the conceptual apparatus of Parsons, especially the AGIL scheme and the underlying methodology of social system analysis. What I plan to do is to construct a generalized explanatory model for industrialization using the conceptual apparatus and methodology of the theory of action.

In 1951 Parsons wrote that *"a general theory of the processes of change of social systems is not possible in the present state of knowledge."*[1] What Parsons meant by this statement was that the construction of a general theory of social change is extremely difficult because it must be based upon comprehensive scientific knowledge over both time and space, and knowledge of this scope has not been assembled; he did not mean that his theory and methodology were inapplicable for explaining change. In fact, increasingly Parsons himself has taken up the problem of explaining change. However, there has been an obstinate tendency among the critics of Parsons (both in Japan and in the West) to blindly reject his efforts, claiming his theory has a static bias. This tendency arises from a fundamental misunderstanding on the part of the critics of the nature of equilibrium

The writer owes Mr. William K. Cummings thanks for great help in improving his English expression as well as discussing the substantive content of this chapter.

theory. In view of this, the first part of this essay will be devoted to showing that social system analysis and the equilibrium assumption are suitable for explaining social change. Following this, I will present a social system model of the processes of social change stimulated by industrialization.

Then I will apply the model of industrialization to the analysis of social change in Japan since the Meiji restoration. The doctrines which have been influential in the study of social and economic change in Japan have been historicism and Marxism. Historicism has rejected the relevance of a generalized theory. In contrast, Marxism has emphasized the importance of generalized theory, and therefore the only influential theories we have in Japan of historical change are Marxist. Marxism, by its nature, explains development, but as the theory narrowly focuses on a particular process of transformation — the series of contradictions that occur in capitalism and the consequent class revolution — there is a tendency in Marxist thought to focus only on the "distorted" elements in Japan's modernization.

The defeat of Japan in 1945 and the setbacks of capitalism are congenial to explanation by Marxist theory. For example, Marxists tend to view the defeat of Japan in 1945 and the accompanying difficulties of Japan's capitalist economy as a stage in the catastrophes leading to capitalism's decline; however, the fact is that the period from 1930 to 1945 was only a short-run interruption of a long-term trend of growth in various indices of modernization such as gross national product, urbanization, and increase in numbers and upgrading in job content of the non-agricultural labor force. It is necessary for a theory of change to explain how it has been possible for Japan to have experienced this long-term growth over both the prewar and the postwar periods. However, at the same time, a theory of change must explain why the success in industrialization was followed by short-run deterioration. I think that by using an industrialization model one can explain both of these phenomena.

In the empirical parts of this essay, I will first analyze the conditions favoring change at the end of the Tokugawa and Meiji restoration periods. Then I will proceed to the analysis of the internal social processes of rapid development in the Meiji era and the short-run deterioration in the early Showa period.

Equilibrium Analysis and Social System Analysis

When Parsons calls an orderly mutual interaction of actors a "social system," the concept "system" has an intrinsic analytical logic; this logic emphasizes the necessity of "the treatment of body of *interdependent* phenomena simultaneously."[2] Variables comprising social system simultaneously depend on one another and, therefore, the actions within the system feed back on each other. In such a condition, if the value of one variable changes for some reason, it affects other variables and the changes of other variables again affect the original variable. Furthermore, at the next stage, a second cycle occurs in the same manner, resulting in new pressure on the original variable. In this way, the value of a variable continues indefinitely to affect other variables. When change gradually diminishes, the social system moves toward a new equilibrium. Conversely, when the nature of the effects of the initial change is nondampening, the system cannot restore its stability. Only systems of differential equations common in analytical mechanics can satisfactorily handle changes of variables related in a state of mutual dependence. The general theory of equilibrium in economics had adopted systems of differential equations for the analysis of price determination in the market.

"Analytical logic" has to be the same, be it in physics, economics, or sociology. It is thus very natural that Parsons thinks that, so long as he uses the concept of "social system," he should, ideally, employ the logic common to these disciplines. But the unmodified application of the mathematical method of systems of differential equations is possible only when variables are measured at least on an ordinal scale; it is not possible to use differential equation analysis without modification in sociology because most of the sociological variables are expressed in terms of sets of discrete categories. Seeking a simplified formula as a substitute for differential equation analysis, Parsons invented "structural-functional" analysis. As the term indicates, the central concepts of this mode of analysis are structure and function.

Structure is the relatively constant connection of various parts of the system. In the ideal type of equilibrium analysis the concept of structure "dissolves into interdependent process."[3] The concept of structure is not in principle introduced in analytical dynamics or the general equilibrium theory of economics. In the case of social systems, too, it is fundamentally true that everything is undergoing continuous changes in processes. But, because there is no analytical instrument to express the law of movement in the social system in its totality, we are obliged to designate structural concepts, hypothesizing that certain parts of the system are tentatively stabilized.

Function is the contribution of these structural

elements to the functioning of the system as a whole. In order to explain how one structural arrangement is such and such and not otherwise, it is necessary to test the functional relevance[4] of its various structural elements. If it is apparent that the structure is functional to the maintenance and development of the system, one can judge that the system can be stable. And, if it is clear that the structure is dysfunctional to the system as a whole, one predicts that the system will change from the present structural condition to another. One might say that the test of functional relevance in sociology is equivalent to the "stability condition" in the equilibrium analysis of economics.[5]

I have presented an outline of "structural-functional" analysis, which Parsons has developed into social system analysis. It is necessary to stress that this mode of analysis was presented as a substitute for original equilibrium analysis. The original equilibrium analysis does not involve structural concepts; its objective is to formulate the mutual interdependence among variables, that is, the endless feedback movements of action and reaction. Thus the equilibrium analysis is of a dynamic nature in the sense that it always analyzes processes. "Structural-functional" analysis was introduced as a substitute for the original equilibrium analysis, and unlike equilibrium analysis it involves structural concepts. But, in that it clearly inherits the original logic of the equilibrium analysis, it deals with the process of the moving aspect as well as the maintenance aspect of the system. In spite of such a nature of the structural-functional analysis, why has Parsons' system of sociological analysis been criticized as having a "static bias" or being inappropriate for the analysis of social change?

On this question I have to point out that not infrequently the critics naively misunderstand the analytical logic of equilibrium theory, which serves as the basis for "structural-functional" analysis. Let me for a while refer to the economic analysis for illustration. The Walrasian general equilibrium theory was certainly a static analytical tool when it was used for determining the equilibrium solution using simultaneous equations. However, the development of theoretical economics has advanced since then towards dynamic treatment of equilibrium theory. Let us examine the most simplified case. We hypothesize that a system consists of a certain number of mutually dependent endogenous variables and one parameter (exogenous variable). These endogenous variables are in an equilibrium state with regard to the given value of the parameter. If we change the value of the parameter in this situation, the change affects the endogenous variables in a

system one after another. And, if the system satisfies the stability condition of the first kind in the Samuelsonian sense,[6] all these effects converge towards a new equilibrium value. However, this new equilibrium point generally is different from the original equilibrium point. Thus, *the condition of the system was changed by the change in its parameter.* In this case, we can say that the logic of equilibrium analysis explains the change of the condition of the system by change in the parameter.

The Problem of "Structure" in the Social System

Parsons' analytical method was not the original equilibrium analysis but a modified form, namely, "structural-functional" analysis. I have previously stated that the distinct difference between equilibrium analysis and "structural-functional" analysis is that in the latter the concept of structure is added as one of the central components. Structure is certainly a static concept in itself. Thus, if the model which is built in structural-functional terms does not involve any possibility for forces to emerge which may change the existing structure, certainly it has a static bias. Now, I will examine what happens when the concept of structure is introduced to conceptualize systems, as Parsons has done.

In the first place, in the pure system concept, the various constituting elements of the system can vary individually, whereas once the concept of structure is introduced into the system concept, at least some of the variables that constitute the structure become stabilized or constant. Thus, the degree of freedom diminishes. Basically, an equilibrium is a limiting state achieved as a result of infinite interaction of variables. Therefore, when the concept of structure is introduced, the equilibrium concept should be redefined to match the context of "structural functional" analysis. Here the concept of function is indispensable. For the system, the crucial issue is whether or not the present structure meets the functions of the system. When the present structure completely satisfies the necessary functions of the system, we can say that the system is in a state of an equilibrium in that structure.[7] On the other hand, when the present structure does not completely satisfy the functional needs of the system, there will be forces within the system which act to change the existing structure.

In the second place, as the social system is a system consisting of mutual interaction of actors, whether or not the structure of the system is maintained depends on the behavior mode of its constituent members. Because of the definition of the concept, the analysis should take into account the motivational factors of action. The problem that a "structural-functional" analysis poses is whether the motivation for action is of such a character as to maintain the system or to alter it. It is true that motivation is developed within the framework of the existing structure, and so a large proportion of the people acting with reference to this structure will acquire motivations consistent with it. However, we cannot assume a priori that this motivation will maintain the existing structure.[8] We cannot derive a definite conclusion about the system-maintaining effects of motivational processes without first determining whether the existing structure satisfies the functional needs of the system.

Equilibrium analysis of the social system aims at formulating the conditions for the system to arrive at an equilibrium state; equilibrium analysis does not assume that the system is always in an equilibrium state. Equilibrium theory posits that in the limiting case of perfect equilibrium, the processes of complementary interaction will be fully developed and that the functional needs of the system will be maximally satisfied. In this limiting case, there will be no instances of deviant behavior. However, the achievement of this state of perfect equilibrium depends on the fulfillment of a strict condition: the structure must perfectly satisfy the functional needs of the system. Structures, by definition, are relatively unchanging, whereas their environments (exogenous conditions) are incessantly changing. Therefore, while a certain structure may at one moment fulfill the strict condition of perfectly satisfying its system's functional needs, the same structure in the next moment may fail to fulfill this condition. The possibility that a system's structure will perfectly fulfill the equilibrium condition is low.

Let us be concrete. For example, in industrial societies, it is unlikely that the institutionalized value system will be transmitted without modification from generation to generation. Ongoing changes in the industrial, occupational, and educational structure bring about modifications in institutionalized value standards, and as a result there are strains between those who learn the modified value standards and those who hold to old standards. We are familiar with the strains created in the family and school because of different value standards held by different generations. In these cases, the complementary character of parent-child or teacher-student role sets cannot be fully realized. Equilibrium analysis, in investigating the nature and conditions for equilibrium, brings out the fact that disequilibrium of greater or lesser degree is the common state of social systems. Positing a tendency to equilibrium in an existing structure never implies that structure is in equilibrium.

"Equilibrium Model" or "Conflict Model"?

Some writers assert that the theory of action only attempts to explain equilibration, integration, and stabilization of social structure and that therefore it cannot explain the change of social structure. Thus these writers tend to characterize Parsons' theory that emphasizes, according to their argument, the forces for equilibration, integration, and stabilization as an "equilibrium model" or "integration model"; they contrast it with a "tension model" or "conflict model" which, they argue, recognizes the forces for opposition, tension, conflict and so forth. Typical of such an argument is that of Ralf Dahrendorf.[9] He once severely attacked the equilibrium model as presented in the theory of action, saying that it is blind to the origin of current social problems. He said Parsons' theory overly emphasizes social harmony and has escaped into an "utopian image" of society. But, when Dahrendorf finally systemized his own "conflict theory" or "coercion theory," he began to assert that these two models abstracted and theorized two different aspects of society. In other words, Dahrendorf gave up the idea of integrating the two contrasting dimensions of social process such as association versus dissociation, accommodation versus antagonism, and cooperation versus conflict into a unified theory. Instead, he proposed the coexistence of two kinds of theory, each representing different aspects.

Shall we accept Dahrendorf's proposal to distinguish the "equilibrium model" from the "conflict model" and to regard them as partial theories of mutually irreconcilable parts? In my opinion, Dahrendorf's view is wrong because of his misunderstanding of the nature of equilibrium theory. It seems evident that Dahrendorf's assertion is based on a misunderstanding of the basic nature of equilibrium theory in that he assumed that equilibrating mechanisms were necessarily mechanisms to maintain the status quo. When a parameter changes under the stability condition just stated, the variables in the system generally can no longer assume their previous values, because the change affects them one after another and they move towards a new equilibrium point. Equilibration denotes the process through which a system moves from one state to another. In terms of equilibrium theory, strain and conflict are the temporary disequilibrating states that appear in the process towards a new equilibrium. In the actual social process it is highly probable that such a disequilibrium state may continue as more than a mere temporary state because of certain structural rigidities of the system such as the presence of vested interests. Thus, it is very common in the real world for such disequilibrium conditions to continue to exist. Although the structural-functional model assumes a more or less smooth process of resolving such a condition, conflicts and tensions are not outside the scope of equilibrium theory. The equilibrium assumption leads to the thesis that if structural rigidity such as vested interests is naturally preventing change toward an equilibrium point from occurring, the tension within the system will increase. Another proposition of structural-functional theory will predict that if such tension steadily accumulates within the system, such an accumulation will inevitably end up in a radical explosion in that system, like a "revolution."

When one examines Parsons' own discussion, it is not difficult to prove that Dahrendorf's distinction between the "equilibrium model" and the "tension model" is irrelevant. For instance, Parsons states that "the process of structural change may be considered the obverse of an equilibrating process"[10] and "structural change in subsystems is an inevitable part of the equilibrating process in larger systems."[11] These statements indicate that Parsons interprets the equilibrating process as a dynamic process. As long as equilibration is a dynamic process, concepts such as tension and conflict which Dahrendorf thinks are separated from the concept of equilibrium are in fact included in the very process of equilibration. In fact, whenever Parsons discusses social change, he always refers to the problem of tension.[12] Furthermore, he very frequently quotes concrete examples of conflict or tension such as Nazism in Germany, McCarthyism in America, and the Cold War as illustrations. It does not seem necessary to point out the many other past examples.

Association versus dissociation, accommodation versus antagonism, cooperation versus conflict, organization versus disorganization, conformity versus deviance—these dichotomous social conditions do not exist separately in actual social life but alternate in the actions of the same human groups and coexist in the same space. Thus, generally speaking, it is more desirable to construct a theory to explain them together rather than separately. Therefore, Dahrendorf's proposal to establish two separate bodies of theory are acceptable only when no better alternatives are available. Structural-functional analysis, however, can handle equilibrating processes and change processes as two sides of the same coin, if it is applied properly. Thus, I conclude that contrasts such as "equilibrium model" versus "conflict model" or "integration model" versus "tension model"

are unnecessary. I believe that a well-formulated social system analysis can include both types of model. This will be shown in my later argument, wherein the social system model is applied to the analysis of industrialization in Japan.

INDUSTRIALIZATION AND THE CHANGE OF THE SOCIAL SYSTEM

Problem

The theory of social change that I am going to discuss now is not a general theory in the sense that it can handle any kind of social change. It is an analytical framework to explain social structural change resulting from or as a concomitant of industrialization.

We define "industrialization," in the narrow sense, as the process of technological progress in mechanized production and, in a broad sense, as the whole process of cumulative economic and social development resulting from and concomitant with technological progress.[13] The general characteristics of the culture and society after the emergence of mechanized factory production systems is referred to as "industrialism." As it is a clear empirical fact that technological progress was made cumulatively after the "take-off" in each nation, social change occurring as a result of industrialization is a change directed toward a definite trend. By concentrating on the analysis of industrialization I exclude cyclical fluctuation and irregular change. Change towards a definite direction, that is, irreversible and cumulative change, is generally called "development" or "growth." Therefore, I will use the term "social development" or "societal growth" to distinguish the kind of social change I am going to deal with from social change in general.[14] Compared to the concepts of economic development and economic growth in economic theory, which are firmly established as technical terms, the concepts of social development and societal growth in sociology are not established as technical terms with clear definitions. I would like to postpone my own definition of these concepts until I have introduced the technical arguments.

I can anticipate a number of criticisms of my approach of limiting my study of social change to the process of industrialization. First, one might argue that other important problems will be omitted from my definition of the problem. It is true that I am excluding problems within the pre-industrial society,[15] on the one hand, and the problem of cyclical change, on the other. I can, however, defend my position against this criticism.

In the first place, as the theories of the nineteenth-century social theorists such as Saint-Simon, Comte, Spencer, Marx, and Durkheim indicate, it was after people became impressed by the remarkable consequences of the industrial revolution or became worried about unfortunate phenomena brought by it 'that social change emerged as our problem. The daily mode of social life did not rapidly change in pre-industrial society, where most people were engaged in agriculture. A radical change of the mode of social life in a short span of time is characteristic of industrialized societies. In this sense, an acute concern with the problem of social change is nothing but a product of industrialism.

In the second place, it is certainly true that a part of the theory of change has been concerned with cyclical change, as we see in Pareto's "circulation of elites," Sorokin's thesis of cyclical alternation of "Ideational Culture," "Sensate Culture," and "Idealistic Culture," and Toynbee's thesis of the succession of civilizations, including his theory of the repeated succession of "Growth, Decline, and Disintegration."[16] Furthermore, the rhythm of social life which progresses by days, weeks, months, and years is cyclical. Temporal units such as days, weeks, months, and years are regulated by the rotation of the earth or the revolution of the solar system. However, superlongitudinal observations such as the history of the rise and decline of civilization go beyond the temporal scope that contemporary social science can deal with. For this reason, concepts and arguments in such superlongitudinal observations tend to be roughly defined, and the discussions are mainly philosophical speculations or literary motifs.

The second anticipated criticism of my approach to view social change only from the perspective of industrialization is that it remains within the traditional framework of the theory of social change in that it is not different from the unilineal developmental theories of history of the nineteenth century. Certainly, my definition of the problem is basically identical with the classical theories of social change since Spencer. I am concerned, too, with distinct differences between pre-industrial and industrialized societies, as were Durkheim and Tönnies. This does not mean, however, that my attempt is merely a repeat of the nineteenth-century theories of social change that tended to characterize developmental stages in dichotomous terms such as "*Gemeinschaft* versus *Gesellschaft*," "mechanical solidarity versus organic solidarity," and so forth. One of the most serious shortcomings of these dichotomies is that they ignore the diverse patterns of development. For instance, some pre-industrial societies were feudalistic, as were the Western nations and Japan, while India had

a caste society and China had a prebendal bureaucracy; some contemporary industrialized societies are capitalistic while others are socialistic or of an intermediate nature. Studies of social change in this century have begun to pay attention to the wide vareity observed in both the pre-industrial and the industrial societies. On the other hand, the dichotomous conceptualizations omit the aspect of continuous growth and development in the industrialization process. To any society, industrialization brings rapid upward changes such as depicted in logistic curves or exponential curves, when we take such indices as population growth, national income growth, increasing rates of urban population, increasing rates of nonagricultural population, and so on. The dichotomous approach is not adequate to deal with this aspect of the social change.

The third anticipated criticism against limiting my analysis only to changes toward growth development is that my approach may handle only the aspects of "progress," ignoring dysfunctional aspects of industrialization; that is, one might say that it excludes the social disintegration resulting from industrialization. Theories of social change during the dark period between the First and Second World Wars stressed the crisis of industrial civilization instead of its development.[17] The emphasis on the imbalance between material and nonmaterial civilizations is one such example. It is true that in contrast to the theory of social change in this period. theories of industrialization after World War II tend to paint a brighter prediction of the future; many theories predict that industrialization will smoothly progress without serious conflict such as opposition between management and labor or between ethnic groups.[18] However, the reality is that, although industrialization has overcome a number of difficulties, it has not developed smoothly. For instance, population problems, unemployment problems, problems of poverty, class struggles, and so forth were serious factors challenging industrialism. They might have led industrialism into destruction. But industrialism has dealt with each of them more effectively than had been anticipated. In Toynbee's words, industrialism had a strength to "respond" actively towards "challenges"; because of this strength, it has successfully developed. Therefore, in discussing the development of society, it is necessary to regard development as embracing the dynamic relationship between "challenge" and "response." Malthus' and Ricardo's dismal predictions in the early industrialization period were not fully realized, but new problems and pessimism continue to challenge industrialism. The pollution problem is one example. It should be emphasized that the forces toward the development of industrialism and toward its disintegration are not separate but interwoven.

Structure and Function

I stated earlier that social system analysis as introduced by Parsons is the biggest contribution to and fundamentally an appropriate method for the analysis of dynamic processes and that I would utilize it in this paper. Structure and function are the two basic categories in our sociological analysis. The important point here is that social system analysis assumes that the functional imperatives do not guarantee the preservation of a given structure. Whether the existing structure can be preserved or not is the essential problem of the "test of functional relevance."

When we say that social systems have a structure, it means that there are certain norms of behavior which are accepted by its members and backed up by sanctions. In other words, there are institutionalized and legitimized normative standards. The institutionalized norms (1) distribute their members to various roles in the system and (2) distribute physical and relational goods as facilities and rewards for role behavior. Thus, social structure is defined as a relatively stable arrangement of the distribution of actors and possessions according to institutionalized norms.

Social change is a change of social structure, a self-evident definition considering that structure denotes constant elements of social system and change implies that these constant elements are no longer constant. The definition of social change can be easily drawn from the definition of social structure: social change is a process through which the distribution of actors and possessions change as the institutionalized norms change.

Function is the activity of any segment of the system which satisfies the needs of the system. The segment engaged in these activities has a certain structure, and because of this structure it can satisfy the needs of the system. In this sense it is for the time being correct to say that structure precedes function. On the other hand, if the various segments of the system are always in flux, the system does not have a fixed structure; in this respect, it is acceptable to say that structure is a static concept expressing a more or less stabilized set of various elements. However, the satisfaction of functional imperatives is indispensable for the system to survive, and thus, if the activities of the various segments of the system do not satisfactorily meet the functional imperatives under the existing structure, the functional imperatives will act to change the existing structure. Functional imperatives do not work for the maintenance of the existing structure, but for *the maintenance of the system.* Thus, it is impossible that the system maintain a structure which is not sufficiently effective for the continuation of the system. When the structure is ineffective, the system will reorganize the structure so that it becomes sufficiently effective for the continuation of the system. In this sense I would argue that *function precedes structure.* The process of reorganizing structure corresponds to the equilibrating process in the equilibrium analysis. When one structure is not sufficiently effective for the maintenance of the system, there will be tensions and difficulties within the system. These tensions and difficulties will be solved only when a modified structure is organized, that is, when a new equilibrium is achieved. If the process of equilibration is prevented by some sort of structural rigidity such as the presence of vested interests, tensions and difficulties within the system will be further intensified. As such an intensification will be changed by nothing but the change of the structure, if structural change continues to be prevented, accumulated tensions and difficulties blow up to a point where the structure can no longer take their pressure. Thus the structure will be destroyed in this process.

The kind of activities to meet the functional imperatives of the system must be quite diverse. To distinguish and categorize them is to a certain extent a matter of convenience. Parsons and his collaborators classified the functional requisites of social action systems into four categories and named them adaptation (A), goal-attainment (G), integration (I), and pattern-maintenance (L). There is no a priori reason why it is best to classify them into four categories or that the categories must be these four. Other scholars have employed different lists of functional requisites. However, in this paper I will employ Parsons' categorization of AGIL without modification.

AGIL, being the terms for "functions," are highly abstract. When one attempts to determine the correspondence between these categories and actual activities and their agents, one faces some problems, because the former are "analytical" categories while the latter are "substantive" empirical realities. In order to apply the AGIL framework to the empirical study of actual society, however, at least an approximate correspondence should be established between the two. Parsons is not always consistent in his efforts to match empirical referents and the analytical categories. He uses different expressions for empirical referents of the analytical categories in different contexts. I will select the terms for empirical referents most appropriate to the objectives of my theory building. Also I would add that the theory presented here deals with change within the social system and does not consider change within the other systems of action, that is, the cultural system, the personality system, and the behavioral organism system.

The goal of the adaptive subsystem (A) is economic production. The output produced by this subsystem is economically valuable goods and services. The units which primarily perform this activity are firms. The goal of the goal-attainment subsystem (G) is policy decisions. The output of this subsystem is power for mobilizing the facilities necessary for the attainment of system goals. The units which perform this function as their primary task are the various governmental organizations. The goal of the integrative subsystem (I) is maintenance of the working of the system. The output produced by this subsystem is national solidarity. The units which perform this function as their primary tasks are communities and voluntary associations. The goal of the pattern-maintenance subsystem (L) is maintenance of the individual members' lives. The output of this subsystem is reproduction of the motivation for daily activities. The units which perform this function primarily are families and schools. Table 27-1 shows these relationships.

Each subsystem trades its output in exchange for the output of other subsystems to utilize it for its own activity. Thus, a subsystem regards the output of other subsystems as "raw material" for its own output. Maintaining balance between inputs and outputs results in smooth functioning of the system. In equilibrium states, inputs and outputs are supposed to circulate without deficit in any interchange.

The empirical referents for the six sets of interchanges linking each respective subsystem with the remaining three are presented in Figure 27-1. Among these six sets of interchanges, three directly involve

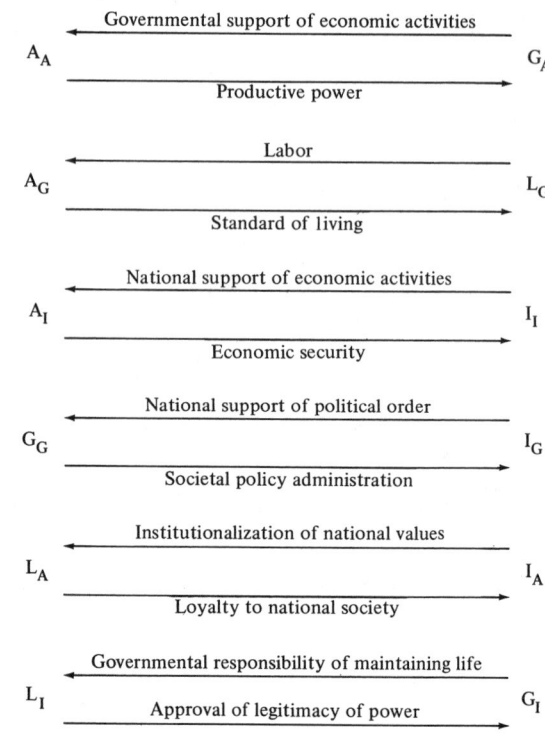

Figure 27-1. Empirical referents of the six interchanges.

the A subsystems; they are listed first in Figure 27-1. Change according to the industrialization model starts with economic growth stimulated by technological change; thus these three sets of interchanges are of direct concern here. The other three sets of interchanges will enter into our discussion only indirectly.

The inputs received by the economic subsystem

Table 27-1. **EMPIRICAL REFERENTS OF THE FOUR SUBSYSTEMS.**

NAME OF FUNCTION	GOAL OF SUBSYSTEM	OUTPUT	TYPICAL PERFORMING UNIT
A: Adaptation	Economic production	Economically valuable goods and services	Firm
G: Goal attainment	Policy decisions	Power: ability to mobilize facilities necessary for the attainment of system goals	Government
I: Integration	Maintenance of the working of the system	National Solidarity: institutionalization of **value-orientations**	Community and voluntary association
L: Pattern maintenance	Maintenance of the individual members' lives	Reproduction of the motivation for daily activities: internalization of norms	Family and school

are: (1) governmental support from the G subsystem (the result of policy decisions), (2) labor from the L subsystem (the result of motivational reproduction), and (3) national support of economic activities from the I subsystem (the result of maintenance of the working of the system). It must be noted that the input (1), governmental support of economic activities, is the basis for the accumulation and distribution of capital by actors in the A subsystem.

The economy, as the A subsystem, provides the following outputs in exchange for its inputs: (1) the economy provides productive power to the G subsystem which governments can mobilize for collective goals; (2) the economy provides consumption goods and services to the L subsystem, and with these the family households are able to maintain a certain living standard and provide the resources to support educational institutions; (3) the economy provides economic security to the I subsystem which enables communities and voluntary associations to maintain themselves.

The role of the remaining three sets of subsystem interchanges (in Figure 27-1) in the process of economic development is not direct. But from the point of view of the over-all equilibrium of the system these also become important conditions for economic development.

The Source of Change

When the inputs and outputs respectively of the four subsystems are in equilibrium, there exists no source of change endogenous to the system. Parsons has said that in the equilibrium situation the "law of inertia" prevails. Schumpeter termed this a "stationary cycle," contrasting it with "development." Pre-industrial societies prior to developing the preconditions for take-off can be viewed as in a state close to the stationary cycle. That is, the inputs and outputs between the subsystems are low in volume and close to being equally balanced. Of course, the stationary cycle is an analytical picture—even the pre-industrial societies are distinguished from it by modest rates of change and development.

How can we explain the way change occurs in a system which approaches the state of inertia? Different methodologies of model-building result in different explanations. The methods of constructing a model for explaining change can for heuristic purposes be divided into the following two types.

The first type assumes the source of change comes from outside the system. A variable which is located outside the system and not affected by the actions of the system but which itself affects the system is called an exogenous variable. A change in the exogenous variable will cause a shock to the system

resulting in processes of change within the system until it reaches a new state of equilibrium under the stability condition. However, when the exogenous variable changes repeatedly in some clear direction (for whatever reason) the exogenous variable will continually shock the system. The system will continually change in a consistent direction, though without obtaining equilibrium. This logic is used to explain change and development within the system. No effort is made in the exogenous variable model to explain the movement of the exogenous variable (see Figure 27-2(1)).

The second type assumes that all of the impetus for change comes from within the system. In this case, the concept of "source of change" becomes meaningless. The change is an outcome of the nature of the system itself rather than the outcome of any particular identifiable factor. That is, a system changes because of the special character of interdependence between the units of the system which in some manner favors change. In the endogenous model, system change can be one of three possibilities as illustrated in Figure 27-2 (2): (a) a gradual acceleration of change leading to increasing dispersion of the system, (b) a gradual diminution of change to a steady state, and (c) a

(1) Exogenous model

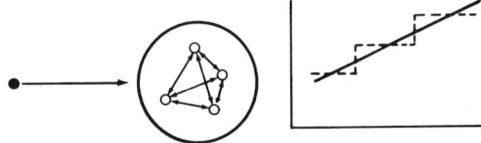

(2) Endogenous model

(a)

(b)

(c)

(3) Strategic variable model

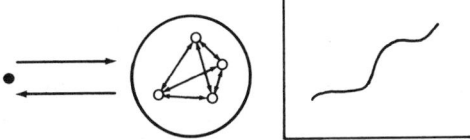

Figure 27-2. Types of change models.

regular cycle of change resulting neither in dispersion nor in a steady state.

One classical example of the exogenous model might be Karl Marx's theory of historical materialism.[19] For Marx the development of productive power is self-actualizing, not the outcome of interaction with the system. Actually historical materialism might best be viewed as a special case of the exogenous model, as Marx did not view the various units of society as mutually interdependent in the strict sense of this concept (the superstructure was dependent on the substructure), and he portrayed change as occurring in stages rather than as linear.

Another example of the exogenous model might be the theory of Yasuma Takada[20] who, influenced by Durkheim, developed a "third view of history" locating population growth as the exogenous variable. In this case also the exogenous variable (population growth) is regarded as a self-actualizing variable and its influence is regarded as one-way.

Thus the theories of Marx and Takada can be viewed as the prototypes of the exogenous variable model. This model would be convincing for explaining "development." The major difficulty with this model, however, is that the mode of explanation tends to be deterministic, because the exogenous variable is supposed to be a self-actualizing agent regardless of what occurs within the system.

A classical example of the endogenous variable model is Samuelson's theory of business cycles, employing differential equations.[21] There are many examples of this kind of model in economics though it is rarely found in sociology. The sociological theory which comes closest to the endogenous variable theory might be Pareto's theory of the circulation of elites; however, Pareto's theory is restricted to predicting a cyclical pattern of change and does not view development as a possibility.

The endogenous variable model is attractive in that it satisfies the conditions of equilibrium analysis. However, the application of this model for explaining a process of *social* development is extremely difficult. This is because in sociological theory our thinking is still couched in a structural-functional framework. The combination of a structural-functional framework with an endogenous variable model is likely to result in a conclusion that change is cyclical or that it is short-run. Continuous development is not a likely conclusion.

Because the endogenous variable model is weak in explaining social development, we will not use it. Rather what we will endeavor to do here is to improve on the exogenous variable model by emancipating it from its usual deterministic character.

The improvement of the exogenous variable model is to include within the model reactions of the system on the exogenous variable. Thus the exogenous variable is no longer viewed as strictly self-actualizing. Figure 27-2 (3) illustrates the improved model. In this improved model, a certain designated variable plays a strategic role in the change process. Hence, it will be called the strategic variable model. The important modification is that the strategic variable receives feedback from the system.

By limiting the problem here to the social change stimulated by industrialization, we can regard technological progress as such a strategic variable. Technological progress would not be designated a priori the strategic variable for the explanation of all processes of social change. The reason we chose technological progress as the strategic variable is that we have limited our investigation to the process of industrialization. If we were to attempt to explain another process of social change, we might choose a different strategic variable.

It does not seem that the social sciences have given a definite answer to the question of why technology advances. Many scholars have held that human nature is desire for change; for instance, Sombart's "Faust-like" nature, Veblen's "instinct of curiosity," and Rostow's "propensity to accept innovation" or "propensity to wish for material improvement." But these desires or natures do not explain why technology progresses. This is the very reason why I have thought it is convenient to treat technological progress as an exogenous variable. My model does not require the answer to the primordial question of why technology progresses. I can tentatively assume the cumulative progress of technology as an empirical generalization. It is, however, misleading to conceive that technology progresses by means of its innate force alone, totally independent of other causal factors. Technological progress first appeared in the now advanced nations and then was introduced to underdeveloped countries. In order to answer the question of why some late-coming nations could easily adopt technological progress and catch up with advanced nations, while others failed to do so, it is indispensable to take into account the feedback effect from the system towards technological progress.

For the late-coming countries modern technology exists as something already given rather than something they have to develop by themselves. Moreover, unlike religion or ideology, technology has a universalistic nature. Therefore, it is much easier to borrow technology than religion or ideology. Nevertheless, some countries adopt it with relative ease, while others do not. Why such a difference exists may be explained by the difference of social structure in each country's pre-industrial state. By this, I mean that the social system does give feedback to technological progress.

Societal Growth and Social Development

Through what courses does technology as an exogenous variable enter the social system? It is easily understood that its primary route is through the economic subsystem A, as technology in this study is defined as production technology. What is the effect of technology on this subsystem A? It can be summed up in the following: (1) technological progress enables the production of new kinds of products and makes it possible to supply them through mass production; (2) technological progress enables changes in the production function, that is, the coefficients of human labor factors among all the other factors of production can be diminished; and (3) technological progress lowers the cost of the product. These three changes will be summarized in one sentence: Technological progress increases the volume and the density of economic activities.

The increase of volume and density of activities in the A subsystem causes a matching increase of demand for "factors of production." The factors of production here have a broader meaning than in usual economic theory: They mean the inputs from each of three subsystems to A subsystem.

1. Capital, one of the factors of production, is in itself provided through the internal boundary exchange within the A subsystem, $A_{Ag} - A_{Gg}$. However, capital provision is closely related with political power in the widened sense of the term; power means here the governmental decision to support enterprises. Thus the first input into the economy in our model can be better called governmental support than capital. Actually it means power over capital; thus it will be permissible in the following argument to regard capital provision as included in it. This input is supplied by the G subsystem through the $G_A - A_A$ boundary interchange.[22]

2. Labor, another factor of production, is more broadly defined here than in economics and is understood as an aspect of the output of the L subsystem, motivation. It is emphasized in this context that labor acquires a definite quality in the L subsystem, that is, "labor commitment" equipped with the will to work is achieved through family life and education. The L subsystem supplies this input to the economy through the $L_G - A_G$ boundary exchange.

3. Organization, the third factor of production, is also given a broader sociological meaning and is understood as an aspect of the output of the I subsystem, solidarity. We can call this input national support of economic activities. Some concrete

examples are formation of national consensus supporting the goal of industrialization, acceptance of the power and prestige of the industrialists, coordination of the economic interests, leadership at the national economy level, and so forth. Economy receives this output from the I subsystem through the $I_I - A_I$ boundary exchange.

4. Land, as the remaining factor of production, is omitted from our model because it is simply a natural resource.

It goes without saying that the A subsystem supplies its output to the G, I, and L subsystems in exchange for these inputs. Technological progress plus the increase of these inputs provides the condition for economic development to occur, which further supplies more outputs to the three noneconomic subsystems than before. The concept of the output of the economy (A subsystem) here is broader than the usual conceptualization in GNP terms in economics, so we may call it economic development rather than economic growth.[23]

The boundary exchange which was in equilibrium on a low level loses its balance by the increase of amount of density of activities in the A subsystem. Then the system moves towards a new equilibrium point through the mechanism of mutual dependence between supply and demand. Its effects spread indefinitely and finally end by establishing a new equilibrium. By this process, the volume and density of actions at the G, I, and L subsystems increase in proportion to the increase in the A subsystem. In reality, however, it is very likely that this equilibrating process experiences various bottlenecks and time lags. The presence of a bottleneck hinders technological progress from penetrating into the economic subsystem. When all the bottlenecks are overcome, a new equilibrium is realized on a higher level by the increase of the volume and the density of activities in all of the AGIL subsystems, and these have an accelerating feedback effect on technological process; I say that in such a situation the society grows. "Societal growth" means that in all the subsystems the volume and density of activities increase, and consequently the volume of their output and flow at the boundary exchanges increase. On the other hand, by "social development" I mean that such a quantitative growth of the social system causes structural change in certain directions. In the next section, I will discuss the issue of structural change.

General Trends in Structural Change

The process from economic development to societal growth that is started by technological impact is a "quantitative" change. This "quantitative" change has to proceed to a "qualitative" change, namely, a structural change; this is the issue discussed in this section. We have to pay attention to the fact that this proposition is established on the basis of the assumption that the *function precedes the structure*. The hypothesis that the impact of technological progress causes economic development which in turn causes societal growth is drawn from my concern with the function in terms of the AGIL scheme. It is appropriate that I use the concept of "activity" to explain this process. Societal growth is caused by the functional imperatives of the social system.

Structural-functional analysis emphasizes that the social system has a structure and that structure cannot exist apart from function. A structure can continue to exist only as long as the density and the volume of activities generated by the structure satisfy the functional imperatives of the system. Continuously progressive technology functionally demands incessant societal growth. Its functional imperative is powerful and irreversible. In this lies the reason why the institutional structures of the various sectors are always under pressure for change in the present highly industrialized society.

Under such pressure, the institutional structures of society are, in fact, changing. Unavoidably, however, tension rises within the system when the structural change cannot satisfactorily meet the functional imperatives of the system or when some subsystems lag behind in their ability to respond to the functional imperatives. It is only a slight exaggeration to state that the social structures within the various subsystems in highly industrialized societies are under constant pressure for structural change because of the powerful functional imperatives. Thus they are always facing the possibility of tensions. There are a number of known empirical generalizations concerning the general direction of structural change resulting from industrialization. Obviously empirical generalizations come from the empirical observations and cannot be deduced from theory. Theory, however, can give integration to the intepretation and explanation of empirical generalizations. Now I will formulate some empirical generalizations according to my definition of social change.

Let me repeat my definition of social change: social change is a process in which the mode of distribution of actors and/or possessions change as the institutionalized norms change. Because this definition has two pillars, that is, "distribution of actors" and "distribution of possessions," I can divide it into two parts. "Possessions" in this context means a wide range of things. It includes four kinds of items, that is, material facilities (e.g. means of production), nonmaterial facilities (e.g., power), material rewards

(e.g., income), and nonmaterial rewards (e.g., prestige). Next "the change of institutionalized norms" is a necessary condition for social change in this definition in the sense that it is the change in the mode of distribution, and the mode of distribution is defined by the institutionalized norms. But this part of the definition embraces a question, because changes without change of institutionalized norms such as change of mere distribution of actors or possessions are existing.[24] I tentatively call this "semichange" (distributional change) contrasting it with "change" (change in the mode of distribution), and include it in our inquiry. Then, I will get four boxes by combining those two pairs of axis, that is, (1) semichange versus change and (2) distribution of actors versus distribution of possessions. I will then introduce four subsystem concepts in AGIL terms in each of the four boxes, and thus will order major empirical generalizations in these four-times-four boxes.

1. Semichange
  1.1 Semichange in the distribution of actors
    A Economic subsystem
       Industrialization tends to transform the relative distribution of actors in the industries such that increasing proportions are in secondary relative to primary industry and in tertiary industry relative to secondary industry.
    G Political subsystem
       Industrialization tends to increase the opportunities for upward mobility towards those positions which have power.
    I Integrative subsystem
       Industrialization tends to heighten the mobility of people between occupation and prestige groups.
    L Pattern-maintenance subsystem
       Industrialization tends to increase the numbers of those who develop the ability to manipulate complex symbols, that is, the average educational attainment advances and more people have access to "culture."
  1.2 Semichange in the distribution of possessions
    A Economic subsystem
       Industrialization tends to result in an increasing proportion of people working with means of production that they do not own (decline of self-employed workers).
    G Political subsystem
       Industrialization tends to be accompanied by the diffusion of hierarchical structures of power within workplaces as these are

effective for attaining the goals of industrial production. The result is that an increasing proportion of the labor force have little power to control their work life.

    I Integrative subsystem

       Industrialization tends to result in the distribution of high prestige to those occupations which contribute most to the functioning of the industrial system.

    L Pattern-maintenance subsystem

       Industrialization tends to result in the levelling of the distribution of income.

2. Change

  2.1 Change in the mode of distribution of actors

    A Economic subsystem

       Industrialization tends to increase the number of occupations where activity is evaluated on the basis of achievement.

    G Political subsystem

       Industrialization tends to be accompained by an increasing proportion of people working in positions that are organized along bureaucratic principles.

    I Integrative subsystem

       Industrialization tends to produce an ever-increasing specialization of occupational roles.

    L Pattern-maintenance subsystem

       Industrialization tends to increase the degree to which manpower distribution is based on formal educational attainments.

  2.2 Change in the mode of distribution of possessions

    A Economic subsystem

       Industrialization tends to increase the extent to which access to possessions is mediated by market mechanisms.

    G Political subsystem

       Industrialization tends to increase the opportunity for mass participation in the political system through voting.

    I Integrative subsystem

       Industrialization tends to be accompanied by the emergence of various types of organizations with countervailing power.

    L Pattern-maintenance subsystem

       Industrialization tends to result increasingly in the distribution of possessions being determined by personal achievement.

I have classified according to the AGIL framework major empirical generalizations about structural semichange and change occurring with industrialization. In collecting these empirical generalizations, I have not differentiated the developmental stages of industrialization. Therefore, my list does not distinguish the phenomena in the early stage of industrialization from those in the advanced stage. This list includes controversial generalizations, but in this paper I do not go into the details of the individual problematic issues. I regard these generalizations as examples indicating the major trend of structural change.

An important theoretical point is that these structural changes are interpreted as consequences of the functional imperatives demanded by the societal growth. In order to increase the output of individual subsystems in the social system, all the structures are reorganized to increase the "social density" of activities. I tentatively call an increase of the social density of activities "functional rationalization." Hence these empirical generalizations are examples of structural changes in the direction of increasing functional rationalization. However, functional rationalization as used here cannot be measured by a single index such as maximization of production. Intrinsic to the AGIL framework is the assumption that systems must simultaneously satisfy the four functional problems; hence, functional rationalization must be evaluated in terms of complementary changes in the structures oriented to each of these four functional problems.

Time Lag and Imbalance of Development

Then, in view of these accumulated empirical generalizations, is it possible to reduce all the structural change caused by industrialization to a unilineal process of rationalization? Our model assumes the causal nexus of technological progress to economic growth, economic growth to societal growth, societal growth to social structural change. Therefore, it might appear that the model is unilineal. But, it is necessary to add at least two further conditional qualifications about it. The two conditional qualifications are the problems of time lag and imbalance between subsystems.

The problem of time lag occurs because it takes time for the institutionalized structures within the various subsystems to respond to the functional imperatives of the system.[25] Let us list three classical examples to illustrate this issue.

1. In *The Condition of Working Class in Britain*, Friedrich Engels clearly described the devastating life of the laborers' families in a British industrial city during the early stage of industrialization. The wretched living conditions of the working class are

reported as evidence that the early phase of industrialization, despite the rise of productivity, does not improve the working-class people's living standard. Rather, if living standard is measured by indices such as infant mortality rate, the early stages of industrialization seem to cause a decline in the living standard of the working class. This indicates that the mechanism by which the increase of the output of the A subsystem is introduced to the L subsystem does not work properly, and hence the output of the L subsystem is dampened.

2. In his *Division of Labor*, Emile Durkheim pointed out that the abnormal division of labor in France brings about anomie, as the outcome of excessive competition in industry and the antagonistic relations between labor and management. Such a situation indicates that the boundary exchange between the outputs of the A subsystem and the I subsystem does not work smoothly, and hence the output of the I subsystem deteriorates.

3. J. M. Keynes argued in his *General Theory of Employment, Interest, and Money* that a large amount of "involuntary unemployment" during the great depression was due to insufficient effective demand rather than to excessively high wages for workers. This situation represents the case in which the output of the A subsystem to be exchanged for the output of the G subsystem is not sufficient.

These classical examples tell that many social problems can be explained as the lags of social development vis-a-vis economic growth. The same principles of explanation can be applied to contemporary social issues, such as the pollution problems of factories, traffic jams in large cities, housing problems, disorganization of community life, juvenile delinquency, and so forth. The causes for the lags vary by case and are quite diverse. But, it is possible to classify them into three classes: (1) lag in discovering problems, (2) lag in discovering the remedies, and (3) lag in realizing the remedy. The main sources of these lags would be insufficient communication between victims and administrators, the lack of enthusiasm on the part of administrators for solving the problem, and the assertion of vested interests by some people.

The problem of imbalance between subsystems originates in the fact that the abilities of subsystems in successfully responding to the functional imperatives of the systems are not necessarily the same. As I cannot systematically investigate this issue here, I merely list a few fragmentary examples. First, in some cases subsystems at different developmental stages coexist. Because the empirical processes summarized in the preceding section do not occur simultaneously, inevitably some of the sectors of the social system are more efficient than others when they are measured at a given point in time. Second, the various social activities are different in nature. For instance, of all human activities economic activities most easily respond to the demand for higher efficiency, while it is most difficult to raise the productivity of education. Third, each subsystem has organizations such as enterpreneurs' associations, community groups, and professional groups, and these insist on their own interest and independence. Quite a few of such interest groups resist change, trying to maintain the old structure.

The problem of time lag and imbalance among subsystems are not separate. The former conceives the problem on the temporal dimension, the latter on the spatial dimension. But the substantive effects are identical. That is, social structural change functionally demanded by economic development does not necessarily in fact progress as the functional imperatives order. Therefore, the dynamics of actual change of the social system stimulated by industrialization follow not a unilineal course but a very complex one, with forces directed toward different directions. Between functional imperatives and such a complex movement of forces in reality, the system experiences many tensions. The accumulation of tensions serves as the momentum to cause explosive change, on the one hand, and it can cause feedback which prevents economic development and technological progress, on the other. Present sociological research is not prepared to provide a comprehensive explanation for this complex process. What is needed today is to set apart individual causal factors of this complex process through empirical research and to examine them in theoretical perspectives.

INDUSTRIALIZATION AND SOCIAL CHANGE IN JAPAN (1): THE BEGINNING OF CHANGE

Problem

The so-called Meiji Restoration was a political revolution which through civil war brought about the overthrow and dissolution of the Tokugawa feudal system. In its first few years (1868-1873) the new Meiji Government energetically pursued a program of institutional reform. Changes were effected such as the abolition of feudal *han* and the establishment of prefectures, the reform of the land-tax system and the establishment of the legal right for commoners to possess land, the abolition of the feudal system of hereditary claims to land and the revenue thereof, and the issue of bonds to compensate those samurais deprived of income and possessions through these changes.

These institutional changes were introduced in rapid succession and marked a dramatic break with the past. In contrast, change related to industrialization has been gradual and cumulative. Historians have tended to favor the phrase "industrial revolution" to describe industrial change. However, the use of the term revolution insofar as it implies a sudden transformation (as in the political case) is misleading when applied to industrialization. Change of the industrial system does not occur overnight, but rather over a long period. Using indices for industrialization such as the number of factories or number of factory workers, we find that there was a steady increase in industrialization from the late 1880's. Many accounts of Japan's early industrial history in Meiji have tended to emphasize the role of governmental enterprises; the importance of government enterprises cannot be denied, but it must be emphasized that numerically they constituted only a small proportion of the industrial sector even in the 1880's.

It is inconceivable that rapid industrialization could have occurred in Japan without the political revolution brought about by the new Meiji government. There have been many controversies over the extent of development of rural industries prior to the Meiji restoration. Many scholars have asked if these rural industries of the late Tokugawa period might not appropriately be viewed as predecessors of the modern "factory." Most scholars, though with notable exceptions, have come to conclude as follows: The major form of production in the rural industries of the Tokugawa period was the putting-out system. While there were a few examples of prototypes of factories (houses where workers, mainly female, worked together in a common place separate from their households), there is no apparent link between these and the later introduction of mechanization after the Meiji restoration.[26]

The following propositions will be the focus of discussion in this chapter. Although light industries (especially spinning and weaving) developed somewhat during the late Tokugawa period, free development of them was hindered by the Tokugawa institutional setting. Some of the intellectual leaders of the late Tokugawa period, recognizing the problems of financial deterioration of the bakufu and han governments (in spite of the heavy taxes they collected from peasants) as well as the imperative of national defense, advocated economic development. These men gradually came to understand that the Tokugawa system did not have the potential for realizing economic development. This recognition as it spread to lower samurais and the peripheral areas, especially Satsuma and Choshu, was the driving force for the Meiji restoration.

In that there was an intellectual force behind the armed conflict of the Satsuma-Choshu coalition and the bakufu, the Meiji restoration was different from the coups d'etat frequently seen today in underdeveloped countries. In the case of the Meiji restoration economic development was recognized as an imperative for survival as an autonomous nation, and the Meiji government when it established itself confronted this imperative as its central objective. Because of both the accumulation in the Tokugawa period of many prerequisites of growth and the effective leadership of the Meiji government, success in the development effort gradually began to be manifest from the 1890's. Our model using the AGIL framework and analysing the interchanges of the economic subsystem with the other subsystems will attempt to explain why Japan was successful in its development effort.

In Japan, up to today Marxism has been the general theoretical system most frequently used in interpreting Japanese history and economic development. The Meiji restoration is congenial to Marxist explanation in that an armed conflict occurred between those who wished to maintain the status quo and those wishing to overthrow it. However, in that the central agent for the revolution was the samurai class, not the merchant class, the Marxist class conflict theory cannot adequately explain Japan's revolution. An explanation using structural-functional analysis can be parallel to the Marxist approach in that it also uses as its starting point tensions and disturbances within the system. However, the tensions and disturbances on which structural-functional analysis focuses are those that are indications of the inability of the structures to solve the functional problems; these tensions and disturbances may be, but are not necessarily, the expressions of class conflict which Marxism views as the source of revolution.

We already have Robert N. Bellah's excellent study[27] applying the structural-functional framework to an analysis of Japan's modernizing process. Bellah's study and the analysis here are methodologically similar; however, the focuses are different. Bellah focused on the role that religion in the broad sense, or the value system, played in stimulating political rationalization. The approach here focuses on the inputs to the economy from the other subsystems during industrialization. These two studies relate to each other in the same way that Max Weber's sociology of religion and his economic sociology supplement each other.

Imperative of Structural Change

We suppose that structures change when internal tensions and disturbances appear within the system.

In the late Tokugawa period, the major focus of discontent was insufficient economic productivity relative to system demand with the consequence that the economic situation of the samurais was declining and national defense was inadequate. In that the governments increased taxes in an effort to maintain the standard of living of the samurai class, the economic situation of the peasants declined, and, in fact, there were peasant disturbances.

The data on economic conditions in the early Meiji period are very fragmentary (those for the Tokugawa period are even less satisfactory). An estimation of national income extending back to 1878 using the 1928-1932 wholesale price level as an index of commodity value was made by Yuzo Yamada and Kazushi Ohkawa[28] (Table 27-2). International comparisons of national income over time are not very reliable; however, using Yamada and Ohkawa's data and assuming that one dollar in 1928-1932 was equal to two yen of the same period, a rough conclusion is that the per capita income of the Japanese people in early Meiji was even lower than the per capita income of various Southeast Asian societies today.

The percentage of the population in primary industry in early Meiji is estimated to have been 75%-80%, roughly equal to the percentage in contemporary Southeast Asian societies. Agricultural productivity was apparently not much higher than in contemporary Southeast Asia. For example, rice productivity in Japan in 1880 was 1.9 tons per hectare. The average productivity of rice between 1950-1960 was 1.2 tons per hectare in the Philippines, 1.4 tons per hectare in Thailand, and 1.7 tons per hectare in Indonesia. In sum, in so far as conclusions can be drawn from the fragmentary data, the economic level of early Meiji Japan was not far in many ways from that of contemporary Southeast Asian societies.

The consciousness of crisis in the late Tokugawa period was based on a recognition of Japan's poor economic situation relative to the demand. The first indication was the deterioration in the financial situation of the bakufu and han governments. Among the samurai class, roughly 10% of the population, expenses exceeded income due to the rising standards of expected consumption. The only way to redress the balance was to increase taxes. Shonan Yokoi (1809-1869), a lower samurai of the Kumamoto han and one of the top intellectuals of his day, on the request of the daimyo of the Fukui han provided in 1860 the following analysis of the economic system:

> In the closed feudal regime daimyos are isolated from one another; they think only of their own interests and always trying to improve their personal situation. Thus they impose heavy taxes on the peasants to obtain revenue to finance their private activities. But still the revenue is insufficient. To relieve their financial difficulties diamyos are known to forcibly borrow portions of the stipends they are supposed to pay to their retainers and to exploit not only merchants and wealthy farmers but even lowly paupers. For this reason the peasants and merchants are becoming impoverished and exhausted. They want to avoid impoverishment so they tend to raise the prices for their commodities. A vicious circle develops. From all parties there are deviations from the traditional status system with its prescribed privileges and obligations. The people are losing respect for the daimyo and there are frequent popular riots demanding relief. If such a situation continues, Japan will soon be in the throes of desperate turmoil.[29]

The second indication was the urgent problem of national defense. England's subjugation of China after the Opium War caused deep fear among Japanese intellectuals that Japan might also suffer foreign defeat and occupation. They came to realize that the Tokugawa government did not have the resources to provide adequate defense for Japan. The urgent need to develop economic strength was one of the biggest issues among intellectuals at that time. Zozan Sakuma (1811-1864), a political adviser

Table 27-2.   NATIONAL INCOME IN REAL TERMS, 1878-1938.

Year	National Income Produced (Million Yen)	Population (Thousands)	National Income Per Capita (Yen)
1878	1,106	36,166	30.6
1883	1,454	37,569	38.8
1888	2,049	39,029	52.5
1893	2,555	40,860	62.5
1898	3,694	42,886	86.1
1903	3,915	45,546	86.0
1908	4,482	47,965	93.5
1913	5,706	51,305	111.2
1918	6,397	54,739	116.8
1923	8,042	58,120	138.3
1928	10,450	62,600	167.0
1933	13,375	67,430	198.3
1938	16,657	71,010	234.5

The data source of the estimate of national income produced is: Kazushi Ohkawa (ed.), *Nihon Keizai no Seichoritsu* (The Growth Rate of the Japanese Economy) (Tokyo: Iwanami-shoten, 1956), p. 161.

of Matsushiro han and widely known as an expert on Western military technology, wrote of this problem in about 1854:

> It is said that Japan has abundant rice and gold. But this country has little land and many people. Actually after the needs for everyday living are met, there is little surplus left. The pressure to develop naval defense is upon us and in a short time we will need to build large numbers of naval fortifications, guns and batteries, and warships. The expenditures for these defense facilities will be tremendous; and as defense facilities do not last forever we will have to begin replacing them in ten or twenty years. Looking at our relations with outside countries we will need money to entertain the foreigners who come to Japan. Looking at the domestic situation we must provide the expenses for soldiers to man naval forts. How is it possible to obtain the necessary money? If a poor family squanders money in excessive entertainment, it will become bankrupt and be forced to give up its land. The contemporary Japanese situation is not far from that of a poor family. What skills are required to help us manage our affairs? Those who study the nation's government and economy must somehow develop the solutions to our problems.[30]

The policies which the scholars at that time advocated were diverse and conflicting. For example Yokai asserted that foreign trade would make it possible for Japan to enlarge national revenues and lower taxes. On the other hand, Seishisai Aizawa (1782-1863),[31] a central figure of the Mito school, asserted that the real cause of financial deterioration could be found in the behavior of merchants; he charged that the merchants manipulated their prices, obtaining great profits. Aizawa advocated the exclusion of foreigners, whereas Sakuma as well as Yokoi emphasized the advantages of foreign trade. However, Sakuma felt that the existing decentralized feudal society was viable and that the bakufu was a satisfactory agency for regulating foreign trade, whereas Yokoi felt that the existing society lacked sufficient integration; Yokoi implied that changes in the society would be necessary before Japan would be able to reap advantages from foreign trade. Despite these big differences, one thing was common to all of these writers: Japan's difficulties were seen as lack of economic strength and inadequate national defense, and the identification of these difficulties implied — even if an explicit statement was not made in all cases — a criticism of the bakufu government.

We can recast this analysis in AGIL terms as follows (Figure 27-3):

1. The bakufu and han governments had inadequate economic policies for national enrichment and thus brought about an insufficient capacity for national defense. That is, the output from G_A to A_A resulted in an insufficient output from A_A to G_A.

2. Because of the exploitation of the farmers and other groups the bakufu and han governments gradually lost popular support. That is, insufficient output from G_I to L_I resulted in insufficient output from L_I to G_I.

3. The bakufu wished to weaken the strength of the han, the various han were antagonistic to each other, and the integration of the nation (national

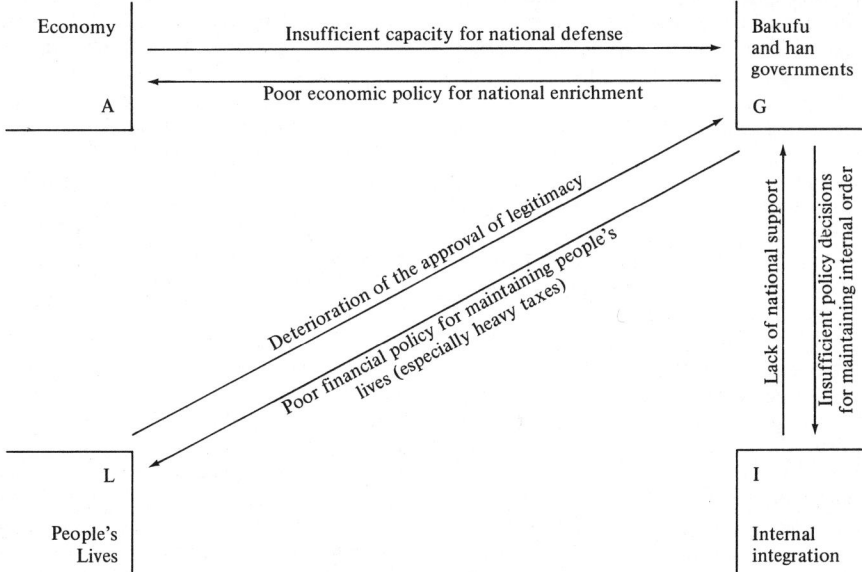

Figure 27-3. State of inputs and outputs as the end of the Tokugawa period.

unity) declined. Some of the hans began to qualify their support for the bakufu. That is, insufficient output from G_G to I_G resulted in insufficient output from I_G to G_G. In this way, these insufficient interchanges resulted in the system becoming unable to meet the functional imperatives. This situation produced the crisis of the bakufu. The gap between structural interchanges and functional imperatives indicated the need for a change in the system.

Commercialization and Industrialization

Tokugawa society was a feudal society, but monetary exchange was widespread. The economic system was based on rice, which the bakufu and han governments received as a tax in kind. However, considering that it was a feudal society, the extent of urbanization was exceptionally high. The growth of the urban sector stimulated the development of monetary exchange. Looking at the hans, most samurais of the han governments were separated from the land and received rice as a salary in kind rather than being granted the rights to a fief. They lived in the central castle towns of the numerous hans. In Edo, the capital of the bakufu, the *hatamoto* (retainers of the Tokugawa family) were obliged to live. Also the daimyos of every han were required to maintain a household in Edo where their wives and several official representatives must permanently reside; the daimyos were required to live in their Edo residences at least one year out of every two (the *sankin-kotai* system). Thus the daimyos, samurais, and their families living in the castle towns and Edo constituted a large mass of urban consumers. The large number of urban consumers provided the opportunity for the development of a merchant class.

I would like to examine the organization of the social units of the merchant class that developed under these circumstances as a background for asking what role, if any, this class might have played in Japan's industrialization. According to Takashi Nakano,[32] who studied through official registration documents the structure of merchant households in Kyoto, 30% to 40% of the merchant population were "employees" living in a master's household. The average merchant household had four family members and two or three "employees" who lived with the family. The employees were divided into apprentice servants (*detchi* and *tedai*) and other servants. The age of the apprentices living in the master's household usually ranged from 10 to 25 years. After a *detchi* (junior apprentice) reached a certain age, he became a *tedai* (senior apprentice). Often senior apprentices when about 25 years old were allowed to establish a branch household and continue

serving the master either by commuting to and working in the main shop or managing a branch shop. In large merchant households (with over ten members), there was a tendency to differentiate the household as a unit of consumption from the shop as a unit of management, a sort of bureaucratization. Mitsui, one of the largest merchant households of the late Tokugawa period with more than 1000 employees, essentially came even to differentiate management from ownership.

It is without doubt that commercialization reached a high degree of development in the Tokugawa period, but this commercialization did not result in industrialization. The controversial issue is how to interpret the relationship between commercialization prior to the Meiji period and industrialization after that. To simplify, there are two contrasting points of view.

The first is that the development of commercialization would have led inevitably to industrialization. According to this view, the rapid industrialization during and after Meiji is said to have been possible because Tokugawa commercialization established the necessary foundations. There is even an assertion that the activities of the merchants in the Tokugawa age were essentially capitalistic in the sense that the activities were rational and profit-seeking.[33]

The second view is that, as commercialization and industrialization are distinctive phenomena, the development of commercialization does not automatically lead to industrialization. There are many pre-industrial examples of the development of commercialization and a monetary economy that were not followed by industrialization.[34] Even today the accumulation of capital by the Chinese merchants in Southeast Asia is not being accompanied by the emergence of industrial entrepreneurship. If we take this second view, commercialization in the Tokugawa period was not necessarily the driving force for industrialization that began after the restoration.

The first view is challenged by noting that many of the large merchant families which had survived from the early Tokugawa period collapsed after the Meiji restoration. Kizaemon Ariga and Takashi Nakano,[35] emphasizing the fact that among the *zaibatsu* (the large industrial combines of the pre-war period) there were two, Sumitomo and Mitsui, which had their origins in merchant households of the Tokugawa period, asserted that industrialization from the Meiji period is best understood as a transformation of the functions performed by several of the large Tokugawa merchant familial groups. Certainly it is an important fact that Mitsui and Sumitomo, which had survived since the sixteenth century, could transform and engage in modern industrial entrepreneurship. However, when we view the large

Tokugawa merchant families as a whole, Mitsui and Sumitomo are exceptional cases. When the merchant guild system supported by the bakufu was disorganized after the Meiji restoration, many of the traditional merchant families proved to be unable to adapt to a free competition economy and collapsed. The Ono and Shimada families who collapsed in early Meiji are typical examples. Indeed there are quite a few among the big industrial capitalists who trace their kinship lineage back to Tokugawa large merchant families. In the case of Mitsui and Sumitomo, the transformation to industrial production was led not by family members themselves but by modern-style entrepreneurs who came from outside. That is, the separation of ownership and management facilitated the transformation.[36]

On the other hand, the second view tends to ignore the fact that the development of commercialization promoted a system of specialization in domestic production and achieved increased productivity over the Tokugawa period. For example, socio-economic historians[37] report that as early as 1707 61.7% of the agricultural land of Hirano village of Settsu was specialized in growing cotton. Such a high degree of specialization in a cash crop presupposes a wide range of merchant activities. Another example is that according to a 1836 document from the peripheral han of Akita, most of the farmers there sold rice and bought clothing and many of their other necessities at the market; among the total amount export to other han, 90.7% was rice, and of import from other han 45.3% was clothing. If commercialization was well developed in the peripheral han of Akita, we may infer that commercialization was well developed throughout much of Tokugawa Japan and that a nationwide division of labor in production of commodities had developed.

Casting the commercial activities of the Tokugawa period in terms of the AGIL scheme, we can say the following (Figure 27-4):

1. Commercial activities in the Tokugawa period were stimulated by the consumption demands of the urbanized population ($A_G \rightleftharpoons L_G$).

2. The interests of the merchant class in the cities were deeply connected with the bakufu and han governments; for example, the bakufu received payment for its support of merchant guilds. Because of this interdependence, few merchants played a supporting role in the Meiji restoration. What is more, many merchant households collapsed after the dissolution of the bakufu ($A_A \rightleftharpoons G_A$).

3. However, the development of commerce in the Tokugawa period facilitated specialization in domestic production and thus contributed to increased productivity. In this sense, we can see that commercialization was one of the preconditions for industrialization after the Meiji restoration ($A_I \rightleftharpoons I_I$).

Import of Western Technology

There existed almost no technology in the late Tokugawa period appropriate for modern mechanized production. As expressed in Zozan Sakuma's well-known slogan "Eastern Morality versus Western Technology," Eastern learning had developed principally in letters, political and administrative sciences, and ethics; but technology was a virtually neglected field and had to be imported. Before the Meiji period Japanese technology was restricted to techniques for producing handicrafts. Most of the exports of raw

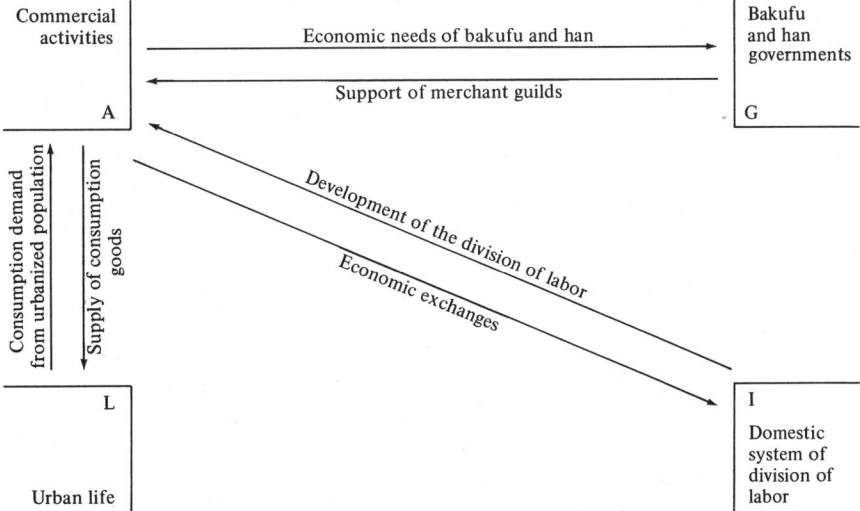

Figure 27-4. Input and output analysis of commercial activities in the Tokugawa period.

silk in the early days after Japan's ports were opened in 1859 were produced as side-work by peasants in their homes using the *zaguri* method (a simple hand-operated machine for spinning raw silk thread). As the volume of raw silk exports increased, the export merchants developed a putting-out system, buying the raw cocoons and paying peasants on a piece-rate basis to spin the silk. Historical documents of the Misawa area[38] report a few workhouses there; this suggests the workhouse was not an unknown institution. But this was the limit to the indigenous development of mechanized technology. Additional technology had to be imported from the West. When the Maebashi spinning factory was built in 1870 under the auspices of the Maebashi han government, foreign engineers were invited to manage it. Similarly the Tomioka spinning mill built by the Meiji government in 1872 invited engineers from France. These early Western-style spinning mills were not always successful, but they played a prominent role in the nation-wide diffusion of Western technology.

In almost all industrial sectors such as shipbuilding, mining, railroads, telegraphs, spinning, weaving, and machine production, Western engineers were employed. The Yokosuka shipyard built by the bakufu in 1865 invited 43 Frenchmen to work in positions from head manager right down to skilled worker.[39] The number of foreigners employed to work in Japanese industry peaked in the 1870's. According to a document of 1872, the central government employed 214 foreigners and local governments employed 164.[40] The number of foreigners employed by government increased over the next few years, but declined by the late seventies. Mitsutomo Yuasa reports that the number of engineers working with the Kobusho (Department of Engineering) reached 270 at its peak in 1874. The same study tells us that the number of engineers employed in private enterprises reached a peak of 237 in 1878.[41] The salary of these foreigners was extremely high when compared with the salary of Japanese. For example, the foreign head of the Yokosuka shipyard was paid a sum amounting to $10,000 in currency of that day[42] — far more than the income of the heads of government departments. But the foreigners were hired for only a short period, the longest a foreigner stayed being about ten years. The Yokosuka shipyards ceased to employ foreigners after 1877.

The importation of spinning and weaving technology ceased at a relatively early date, and Japan developed its own mechanized technology from the late 1890's. It was in 1898 that the famous Toyota power loom was invented. This power loom was so cheap compared to imported looms that it diffused rapidly, displacing hand looms. In contrast as heavy industry was still in the nascent stages at the turn of the century, in the heavy industrial sector foreigners continued to be hired. For example, the Yahata steel mill built by the government in 1896 hired several foreign engineers, paying them ten times the going salary for engineers of Japanese nationality.[43]

It seems that one of the important reasons for Japan's success in rapid industrialization was that Japan as a late developer was able to import the most advanced technology of the West, technology which Western nations had spent many decades developing. Japan through importing and mastering the latest technology was able relatively quickly to close the gap between her own technological level and that of the Western nations. To cite one example, the Tokyo Dento Company provided power for lighting Ginza in 1882, only three years after Edison invented the lightbulb. But as all late developers had the same opportunity to take advantage of "borrowed technology," we cannot explain Japan's success in rapid development simply in terms of this availability of advanced technology. What was impressive was the ability of the Japanese engineers to master the technology it imported. Although Japan entirely lacked experience with mechanized technology, the long experience of many Japanese with handicrafts surely played a role in enabling them to learn quickly. For example, the handicraft skill of zaguri spinning was a useful background for mastering the techniques of mechanized spinning. It would have been extremely difficult to quickly master the imported technology if there had been a large gap between indigenous skills and the imported technology. It is likely in Japan's case that the gap between indigenous skills and the skills required by the imported technology was not so large.[44]

In our change model, technology is located as the strategic variable explaining industrialization. According to the logic of the model, technological progress, once "embodied" within the economic subsystem, can become the driving force for change. That technological progress came to be embodied in the economic subsystem indicates that the social system was able to provide the capital and labor which the technology itself required. In the next chapter we shall turn to the analysis of the internal processes of input-output relations brought about by the embodiment of technological progress.

INDUSTRIALIZATION AND SOCIAL CHANGE IN JAPAN (2): THE INTERNAL PROCESSES OF CHANGE

Problem

According to our model using the AGIL framework, the social conditions for realizing economic development are increases in the supply of inputs to the economy from the other three subsystems in proportion to the economy's demand. If these conditions can be realized, increases in the outputs of the economic subsystem are possible; the balance of exchanges will be maintained if the economy provides increasing outputs to the other three subsystems corresponding to the inputs it has received.

When the above-mentioned exchanges proceed without major disturbance, we say the social system experiences a balanced growth. In the present state of knowledge it is not possible to measure with a satisfactory degree of precision the exchanges between the subsystems, and thus it is extremely difficult to say definitely when there is or is not balanced growth. However, inferences are possible using indirect evidence. Looking at Japan's case, it seems, relatively speaking, that balanced growth was achieved through the Meiji period. In contrast, the first two decades of the Showa period were a time when imbalanced growth was prominent. Various abnormal events, especially the rise to dominance of the military fascist regime, can be interpreted as brought about by imbalanced growth. The objective of this section is to discuss balanced and imbalanced growth in these two periods of Japanese history.

The objective is not to present historical description, but rather to analyze historical events in terms of my change model; hence I chose these two periods, the early stage of industrialization in the former half of Meiji and the mature stage of industrialization in the first two decades of Showa, which allow me to illustrate the nature of balanced and imbalanced growth. In the analysis of the early stages of industrialization I will emphasize how economic development was launched, and in the latter period I will emphasize why in spite of economic development there was imbalanced growth.

We will look primarily in this section at the exchanges between the economic subsystem and the other three subsystems. The other three sets of exchanges do not have a direct effect on economic development, as they do not include the economic subsystem. But of course these exchanges play a role in the growth and development of the social system as a whole. Here, in view of the important role of the polity in Japan's development, I will take up the sets of exchanges this subsystem has with all of the other subsystems. Thus the only exchange not treated will be that between the I and L subsystems.

Internal Processes in the Early Stage of Industrialization

Interchange between the Economy and the Polity ($A_A \rightleftharpoons G_A$)

It was stated earlier that one of the functional imperatives of the increase of economic output in the late Tokugawa came from the recognition of the national defense problem. Was this imperative successfully solved? Unlike many of the other Asian countries at the time, Meiji Japan did not become a colony of a Western nation nor was it ever subordinated to a Western nation; what is more, Japan triumphed over China in 1894-1895 and Russia in 1904-1905. Thus we can claim that Japan was able to solve her problem of national defense. In AGIL terms the input to the G subsystem from the A subsystem was supplied in adequate volume for the functional imperative of national defense to be met. What then was the nature of the complementary exchange from the G subsystem to the A subsystem?

It is commonly recognized that the government played an important role in the early stage of Japan's industrialization. But it was only in a few national enterprises that the Meiji government actually supplied the capital; in the other cases of entrepreneurship the government's role was limited to promotion and encouragement of capital provision through its economic policy. Though there was monetary accumulation among the people they did not necessarily have to provide this as capital; investment only occurs when there is the will to take a risk with money. Much of the activity of the Meiji government was to persuade those with money to invest it.

The first policy of the Meiji government related to encouraging investment was the establishment of a national bank system from 1872. These national banks, numbered one to 153 in order of their establishment, were Japan's first nationwide financial institutions. They were national in the sense that they were authorized by governmental decree; but actually the government did not supply capital to aid in establishing these banks. The banks operated purely as commercial banks owned by investors; although the type of people investing in these banks varied, major proportions of the banks' funds came from wealthy merchants and former upper-samurais who deposited the bonds they had received as government compensation. It is significant that these 153 banks were established in rapid succession from 1872 to 1879. That the banks could be established so rapidly was an indication of the substantial amounts of money in private hands. Especially noteworthy is that the accumulation dating back to the Tokugawa period of merchants was effectively mobilized through the establishment of these banks.

The role of government in establishing these banks can be summed up as follows: First, the government issued the legal decree and by doing so introduced the principle and legal basis for banks at a time when few people knew of this type of institution. Second, the national and local governments provided the banks with important business by depositing their annual revenues from tax and other sources and then withdrawing as needed for governmental expenditure. According to Tsutomu Ouchi and Toshihiko Kato's study group,[45] Nearly 80% of the deposits to the First National Bank (Tokyo) in its early days and 80% to 100% in the case of the Fourth National Banks (Niigata) was from governments. Third, government persuaded those who had money to invest it. One significant illustration is that Eiichi Shibusawa, a higher official of the Treasury Department, persuaded the Mitsui and Ono families to establish the First National Bank and he himself became the president of this bank in 1875.

The second policy of the Meiji government was the issue of currency not backed by gold as well as the issue of government securities to meet the expense of the large number of governmental activities. These activities included the establishment of governmental enterprises such as shipyards, mines, arsenals, and so forth, as well as railway construction and national communications services. The important point is that the government purchased quite a large amount of goods through these activities and thus created a large volume of effective demand. Quite a few entrepreneurs succeeded in rapidly expanding their businesses by providing the government with goods and services. We can say that government encouraged business activities through its creation of effective demand. There are many other sorts of governmental activities which encouraged the growth of business; above all two deserving mention are the promotion of foreign trade, especially the export of silk and tea and the transfer of governmental enterprises to private entrepreneurs.

However, it would be wrong to place too much emphasis on the direct role of government in promoting industrialization and economic development. Certainly the government engaged in many economic activities, but government alone cannot create business activities in the private sector. These business activities depend on the emergence of people willing and able to engage in them. Government activity alone will not automatically result in the emergence of entrepreneurial activities. In the past, historians have tended to emphasize the importance of the transfer of government enterprises to private owners. Apart from the fact that the number of these transfers as a proportion of all enterprises established was quite small, what needs to be emphasized is that these enterprises in most cases operated in the red while under government management although after the transfer there were able entrepreneurs who could turn these enterprises into successful private businesses. Within the framework of AGIL we cannot form conclusions about the predominant importance of one particular factor but must take account of the

mutual interrelations between all the major factors involved. Now we will turn to some of the other factors.

Interchange between the Economy and the Pattern-Maintenance Subsystem ($A_G \rightleftharpoons L_G$)

It is difficult to say to what extent the national standard of living was elevated over the early Meiji period by virtue of the output of the A subsystem to the L subsystem.

In the early Meiji it is estimated that the national standard of living did not necessarily improve. In the land tax reform of 1872 the property value of land was determined and a tax rate of 3% on property value was instituted, but it is generally argued that the reform did not result in any reduction in the tax burden of the peasants.[46] Moreover, as is shown in Table 27-3, agricultural productivity over the early Meiji only slowly increased. Therefore it is unlikely that the peasants enjoyed improvement in their living standard.

The wage level of workers in the newly established factories was set by reference to the peasants' living standard; Table 27-4 shows that in 1885 the average daily wage of a male skilled worker was around 22 sen while that of a female worker in silk spinning was 11 sen.[47] In 1872 one *koku* (5.3 bushels) of rice was officially evaluated as equivalent to three yen; from this we can estimate that the amount of rice eaten daily by a typical adult cost three sen. Of course the adult diet consisted of more than rice, as there were expenses for clothing, housing, and other items; moreover, an adult male had to support his family. Thus we can conclude that the wage paid to factory workers was close to the subsistence level.

However, the situation improved as the governmental policy helped to stimulate economic growth and in turn the economy was able to provide an increasing level of outputs to the L subsystem. As is shown in Table 27-4 the wages of factory workers began to improve relatively rapidly from the 1890's; from that period agricultural productivity also began to increase as is seen in Table 27-3.

One illustration of the rising living standards was that the common people increasingly availed themselves of the opportunity to enjoy culture. For example, the government promoted a national school system from 1872 and obliged all cities, towns, and villages to establish primary schools. By 1873 there were 11,558 primary schools, and by 1880 28,410. R.P. Dore estimates that the proportion of the appropriate age brackets across the nation attending primary schools in 1875 was 54% for boys and 19% for girls.[48] Another example is the development of mass communications. The first of the modern newspapers was the Yokohama Mainichi Shimbun printed

Table 27-3. RICE PRODUCTION, 1880-1965

YEAR	AREA UNDER CULTIVATION OF RICE (1,000 HECTARES)	AMOUNT OF RICE PRODUCTION (1,000 TONS)	RICE PRODUCTION IN TONS PER HECTARE
1880	2,549	4,715	1.850
1885	2,590	5,106	1.972
1890	2,729	6,463	2.368
1895	2,762	5,994	2.170
1900	2,805	6,220	2.217
1905	2,858	5,726	2.004
1910	2,925	6,995	2.391
1915	3,031	8,389	2.767
1920	3,101	9,481	2.058
1925	3,128	8,956	2.863
1930	3,213	10,031	3.123
1935	3,178	8,619	2.712
1940	3,152	9,131	2.897
1945	3,869	5,872	2.470
1950	3,011	9,651	3.205
1955	3,222	12,385	3.844
1960	3,308	12,858	3.887
1965	3,255	12,409	3.812

Data source: The Section of Statistical Research, The Ministry of Agriculture.

from 1870; this was followed by the Yubinhochi Shinbun and the Tokyo Nichinichi Shinbun in 1872. National postal, telegraph, and telephone systems and railroads are examples of other facilities that became available to the public.

Let us examine the labor inputs from the L subsystem to the economy. When the government established the Tomioka spinning factory it requested several prefectures to provide a quota of workers; the number of applicants was so small that the prefectures had to resort to making special requests of the daughters of samurai in order to fill their quota. However, as is illustrated in Table 27-5 the number of factory workers began to increase rapidly towards the latter half of the 1880's. The following four sources were the major sources of demand and supply.

1. Rural industries: As the scale of rural industries was small and production accomplished by the putting-out system or handicraft workhouse, most of the labor could be supplied from daughters of agricultural families and seasonal labor.

2. Mechanized factories of silk and cotton spinning: The early factories had a policy of employing the landless lower samurais, but as the number of factories increased and the supply of lower samurais became exhausted the practice developed of employing unmarried girls from the families of lower peasants. Mechanized silk spinning from around 1890 was introduced especially in Nagano prefecture; girls were at first collected from nearby rural areas but as the demand increased they were brought from more distant areas and were provided residence in factory dormitories. In contrast, cotton spinning developed in the large cities from the late 1880's; necessarily the girls employed were from distant places, and the dormitory system was instituted from

Table 27-4. SOME EXAMPLES OF THE AVERAGE NOMINAL WAGE LEVEL OF WORKERS IN THE EARLY STAGE OF INDUSTRIALIZATION (UNIT : SEN)

YEAR	FEMALE WORKER OF SILK SPINNING	MALE WORKER OF FOUNDRY	MALE METAL WORKER	MALE JOINERY WORKER	DAY LABORER
1885	11.3	—	20.5	22.3	15.7
1892	13.3	—	25.2	25.1	18.4
1895	13.4	30.2	28.5	29.8	22.1
1897	18.2	39.3	39.2	38.8	28.6
1900	20.0	46.8	47.5	50.0	36.5
1905	21.5	53.3	55.0	54.8	42.5
1910	30.5	68.5	69.0	76.3	53.3

Data Source: Tokyo Statistical Association (ed.), *Nihon Teikoku Tokei Zensho* (Statistical Book of Imperial Japan).

Table 27-5.   THE NUMBER OF FACTORY
WORKERS, 1886-1900

1886	112,779	1894	381,390
1887	100,728	1895	418,140
1888	123,327	1896	436,616
1889	220,138	1897	439,549
1890	346,979	1898	412,205
1891	321,624	1899	408,029
1892	294,425	1900	403,474

Data Source: 1886-1892 Statistical Bureau, Prime
Minister's Office (ed.), *Teikoku Tokei Nenkan* (Statistical
Year Book of the Empire).
1894-1900 Tokyo Statistical Association (ed.), *Nihon
Teikoku Tokei Zensho* (Statistical Book of Imperial
Japan).

the beginning.[49] As the demand increased for girls,
recruitment became more and more difficult and
factories competed fiercely. Girls frequently moved
between factories when they found better opportunities. As the girls typically worked in the factories
for only a few short years of their lives we would
not say that they constituted a fixed working-class
strata.

3. Mechanized factories of heavy industry: In the
early days of Meiji, heavy industry factories were
limited to a few for shipbuilding, arsenals, and
machine manufacturing. Male skilled workers were
trained in these factories. There were two categories
of these skilled workers. One worked at those tasks
requiring indigenous handicraft skills, as wood-
workers and blacksmiths; these workers were recruited from among the traditional craftsmen who
could not make an independent living by their skills.
The other category worked at newly created tasks, as
lathesmen, sheet-metal workers, boilermakers; for
this latter category of skilled workers, a training
system in the factory was necessary.[50] As these skilled
workers were extremely rare, factories competed with
each other to obtain them and there was high mobility.

4. Unskilled workers: Day workers in the factory,
contruction workers, mining workers, and other unskilled laborers were recruited from among the
urban poor. In big cities such as Tokyo and Osaka
those without a steady job lived in slums. The factories
did not hire these unskilled workers directly but
through subcontractors.[51]

The important point is that the L subsystem was,
generally speaking, able to effectively meet the
rapidly growing demand for labor and thus did not
hinder rapid industrialization. Earlier we noted that
indigenously trained engineers were able to master
Western technology, but what is equally important
is that the male skilled workers had the ability to
master quickly the skills required by Western technology. Dore rightly points out that the diffusion
of education among the common people in the

Tokuwaga period was an essential factor in their
ability to master these new skills. Dore, estimating
that in the late Tokugawa period more than 40%
of all Japanese boys and 10% of all girls were getting
some kind of education, argues:

"Widespread literacy . . . at the very least . . . constitutes
a training in being trained. . . . Japan had already got over
the first hurdle in a process of purposeful development,
the diffusion of a simple notion of the possibility of
'improvement.'"[52]

The accumulation of handicraft skills among
craftsmen as well as the tradition of rural industries
also were advantageous. Mikio Sumiya[53] claims that
in the case of shipyards traditional skills made it
easier to master Western skills. In addition, the development of rural industries in the Tokugawa period
staffed by girls prepared the way for females to be
recruited as labor in the new factories. That women
could be recruited is very important; there was a
limitation on the number of male workers free to
respond to the demand for factory labor; as there
were no prominent laborsaving innovations in agricultural technology. As Japan's early industrialization was primarily in silk and cotton manufacturing,
it was possible for there to be a fit between the type
of labor demanded and the workers, principally
female, that the rural villages could provide.

Let me add one more observation. There is a commonly held notion that there has always been a
surplus of labor in Japan, but this is not correct. As
mechanized industry began to develop rapidly after
1900, both the male skilled workers and female laborers were in short supply. There was also labor
shortage from the early 1930's. However, even under
such circumstances, the number of people who
engaged in agriculture remained unchanged; so
the industrial workers had to be supplied from the
rapid increase in the total population. It was only
after 1955 that the absolute number of people
engaged in agriculture began to decline.

Interchange between the Economy and the
Integrative Subsystem ($A_I \rightleftharpoons I_I$)

Saint-Simon stated, 150 years ago, that industrial
society is a society wherein secular power is in the
hands of the industrialists, and the activities of
industrialists receive high evaluation. For industrialists to gain this prominence there must be a
change in institutionalized norms. Bendix has pointed
out[54] that is common in the early stages of industrialization for the industrialists to find that they are
not highly evaluated and hence they need to work
for social recognition. Especially in Japan the concept
of hierarchical social ranking based on *shi-no-ko-sho*
(samurai-farmers-artisans-merchants) persisted, and

the industrial entrepreneurs were given a low evaluation. Yukichi Fukuzawa wrote in 1872 on this point as follows:

> Those who are highly educated wish for a governmental position and look down upon jobs in private companies. They know only how to work within government and have no idea of what work in private companies is like. Youthful students after reading a handful of books can think only of entering government employment; ambitious merchants with an abundance of capital want to do business in the name of government; schools are licensed by government, teaching is licensed by government, grazing is permitted by government, silkworm culture is permitted by government. Seven or eight of every ten "private" businesses have some connection with government. . . . In sum, we can go so far as to say in Japan there is only government, no people.[55]

Considering that one of the driving forces for the Meiji restoration was the crisis of national defense and that industrialization as the state's purpose was stressed thereafter, it is easy to understand why the people of Meiji Japan always were conscious of the state and the state's purpose. It seems that such a situation is more or less common to the late-developing societies. Such a situation is disadvantageous to those entrepreneurs who want to be highly rational in their business practices, an approach essential for successful capitalism.

Japanese entrepreneurs adapted to this disadvantageous situation by saying that their private business activities served the interests of the state. This is not to say that businessmen attempted to rationalize their activities in this way; they tended naturally to think this way given the aforementioned general climate in Japan. It is quite natural that the crisis of national defense gave birth to nationalism; as economic growth was viewed as essential for solving the national defense problem and maintaining national integration, successful entrepreneurship was welcomed as contributing to the nation and entrepreneurs took pride that they could help in the national effort. Entrepreneurial activities came to be viewed as something more than the mere pursuit of private interest; in AGIL terms entrepreneurship was felt to offer "economic security" for maintaining solidarity. National support for the economic activities of entrepreneurs was given as the input to the economy from the integrative subsystem in exchange for this economic security.

The traditional merchants of the Tokugawa period had no consciousness of serving the state purpose; they thought only of preserving their family treasures. It seems that it was only from Meiji that the emphasis on state purpose became a part of the motivation for economic activity. Japanese, generally speaking, did not have a religious orientation analogous to the ascetic Calvinism which Max Weber regarded as the spiritual basis for capitalism. There were some Christian entrepreneurs such as Sanji Muto, founder of the Kanebo spinning company, and Ichizaemon Morimura, who started the Morimura commercial empire, but they were a small minority. It is hard to demonstrate that Buddhism motivated modern entrepreneurship in the Meiji period. It seems that the consciousness of serving the state's purpose played for Japanese entrepreneurs a role analogous to ascetic Calvinism in the West. Confucianism, not as religious belief in the usual sense but rather as philosophical conviction of the need to serve the state, was the typical rationale for entrepreneurship. This can be best illustrated in the case of Eiichi Shibusawa; he systematically collected from the Analects of Confucius the advice bearing on economic activity and used these in his writings to present the philosophy that activity to enrich people is a basic obligation of national policy.[56]

Interchanges between the Polity and the Integrative and Pattern-Maintenance Subsystems ($G_G \rightleftarrows I_G$, $G_I \rightleftarrows L_I$)

Japan's successful industrialization in the Meiji period seems to have been highly dependent on the ability of the government to maintain stability and gain national support. Having already considered the interchange of the polity with the economy, let us turn briefly to the interchanges of the polity with the two other subsystems.

It is possible to argue that the Meiji government, at least in its early stages, had relatively weak foundations. For example the frequency of peasant uprisings was greater in early Meiji than in late Tokugawa; the peak of these uprisings was in 1873. Peasant dissatisfaction was directed against the assessment of land value, the government's acquisition of the common-use land of villages or the incorporation of common-use land in private estates, and the institution of a military conscription system. Also the dissatisfaction of those ex-samurais who did not obtain positions in the new government was a potential danger; the somewhat violent Jiyu Minken Undo (Movement for Freedom and People's Rights) which began in 1874 and reached its height in 1881 gained part of its support from these ex-samurais.

Why didn't these uprisings seriously threaten the authority of the Meiji government? We may answer this question, in the first place, by noting the stability the Meiji government acquired from the nationalism developed in the integrative subsystem and the Tenno (Emperor) ideology developed in the pattern-maintenance system. I mentioned already the effect of nationalism on the economy, but nationalism also had effects on the polity. The nationalism that developed in the late Tokugawa period had two faces: one, which we might call "internal nationalism," focused on the imperative of disorganizing the feudal structure and developing true national unity under the emperor; a second nationalism which we might call "xenophobic nationalism," focused on the need to defend the nation from the threat of foreign invasion. One of the brilliant successes of the Meiji government was the transformation of those energies directed to xenophobic nationalism towards application in the projects it conceived to realize the ideals of internal nationalism.[57] Thus the government was able purposely to make use of the broad sentiment of nationalism to reinforce its actions.

In the second place, the Meiji government was able to make use of the widespread sentiment that the people had for the charismatic institution of the emperor. In Max Weber's sense, the traditional authority of the Japanese emperor was based on "hereditary charisma."[58] The Meiji government redefined the meaning of the imperial institution, giving it a systematic formulation, and claimed legitimacy for its government on the basis of this new formulation.

The legal formulation of the redefined imperial institution was elaborated in the Constitution issued in 1889; the related moral code was formalized in the Imperial Rescript on Education of 1890 which all primary school students were expected to learn. Without doubt the indoctrination of students with the Tenno ideology led to growing cooperation with the state among the new generations. In this way the Meiji government succeeded in mobilizing the traditional sentiment toward the emperor to support its exercise of power. However, this indoctrination set the stage for demands of superpatriotism in the Showa period, focused on the old theme of xenophobic nationalism. We will turn now to this period of imbalanced growth.

Internal Processes in the Maturity Stage of Industrialization

Bellah, in the concluding chapter of his excellent study of Tokugawa religion, argues to the effect that late-coming nations can enjoy successful industrialization only if they have a powerful government and an emphasis on the polity in their value system. He further states, after noting the examples of China, the U.S.S.R. and Japan, that the situation in these three nations is "perilously close to totalitarianism."[59] Bellah does not discuss the Tenno ideology leading to totalitarian fascism in the early Showa period, but his statement is suggestive when one places Japan from 1930 to 1945 in the framework of his analysis.

But I believe that if Bellah had attempted even a cursory analysis of "Tenno fascism," he would have immediately recognized that it is quite irrelevant to discuss Japan, China, and the Soviet Russia as if they belonged to one category. Soviet Russia and China have been achieving industrialization *in the framework* of a politically centralized system. On the other hand, a form of totalitarianism in Japan appeared *in the course* of industrialization in response to tensions and disturbances resulting from imbalanced growth due to excessively rapid industrialization. In this respect, it would be Germany and Italy, not China and Soviet Russia, that should be placed in the same category with Japan.

Internally, Japan experienced during the early Showa years the age of totalitarianism generally called Tenno fascism; the normal development towards democracy during the Taisho period was reversed in this totalitarian period. Externally, Japan expanded herself during this time into Manchuria and China, resulting in the Pacific War and its defeat. When we contrast the period between 1930 and 1945 with the years before and after that, it appears to be an abnormal period. I interpret this totalitarian phenomena not as something suddenly thrust upon the system from the outside, but as a phenomenon which emerged because the system had a functional need for it. To be more concrete, I view it as a consequence of the system's imbalance in the process of development due to the rapid industrialization since the Meiji period. It is a phenomena which could have been avoided if the system took certain precautions; I by no means imply that rapid industrialization inevitably leads to such a consequence. I would say that, other things being equal, excessively rapid industrialization is more likely to bring about serious tensions and disturbances than moderately rapid industrialization. According to our model of social change it is assumed that imbalance as well as time lags will potentially accompany the process of development; the only assumption to be added here is that the more rapid the development, the more likely that imbalance as well as time lags will result in serious tensions and disturbances. The Tenno fascism ideology began from around 1920, and it reached its maturity after the Manchuria Incident of 1931, when Japan's heavy industries progressed in accordance with military needs.[60]

In order fully to test this hypothesis it would be necessary to develop a detailed analysis of the external and internal factors of the system and the subsystems of Japan during this period. The analysis I can do now is limited to presenting a sketch which shows the imbalances in the boundary exchanges. In the preceding sections I explained the successful industrialization in Meiji Japan as the realization of relatively balanced growth. Now I would like to argue that in terms of the long-term trend in Japanese development the period of the former half of Showa can best be viewed as abnormal and due to imbalanced growth which brought about serious tensions and disturbances.

Interchange between the Economy and the Polity $(A_A \rightleftharpoons G_A)$

The A subsystem supplies the G subsystem with productive power in exchange for input from the latter. The task of the A subsystem ends when it achieves production. How the G subsystem "consumes" the increased inputs supplied by the economy depends on the decisions within the polity. Thus we come to realize that when a country reaches a highly industrialized stage, the government faces a serious problem of decision-making. The government can use the increased productivity in attempting a big war, elevating national welfare, raising the level of mass consumption, or anything else it wishes. Which of these alternatives is chosen depends on the

always introduces a risk concerning what the productive power will be used for.

The index of manufacturing production, as is shown in Table 27-6 when 1909 is taken as the base year, is 293 in 1920, 558 in 1930, and 1,247 in 1940.[61] This statistic shows a remarkably rapid growth of productivity available to the polity subsystem. Then, what was the nature of Japan's political power? During the Taisho period, democracy gradually developed, achieving a major formal advance when the Diet passed the universal male suffrage law in 1925. But in the very same year, the Diet passed the Law for Maintenance of the Public Peace which restricted freedom of speech, thought, and association. The issuing of this law indicates that democracy was not in substance established at all. Under this law, the government suppressed labor movements by depriving labor union activities of their legitimacy. This raised the level of domestic tension, for in these actions the government blocked with power the general direction of structural change due to industrialization. On the other hand, by depriving intellectuals of the freedom of speech, the government

Table 27-6. THE DEVELOPMENT OF THE MANUFACTURING INDUSTRY, 1909-1940

YEAR	NUMBER OF FACTORIES		NUMBER OF FACTORY WORKERS		AMOUNT OF MANUFACTURING PRODUCTION		INDEX OF WAGES		RETAIL PRICE INDEX IN TOKYO
	Number (1)	*Index* (2)	*Number* (3)	*Index* (4)	*Nominal Amount* (5)	*Real Index* (6)	*Nominal Index* (7)	*Real Index* (8)	(9)
1909	32,032	100	780	100	796	100	100	100	—
1914	31,458	98	942	121	1,372	163	115	115	100
1920	45,576	142	1,548	198	5,912	293	363	139	261
1925	48,850	153	1,802	231	6,925	403	399	183	218
1930	61,768	193	1,676	215	5,937	558	374	241	155
1935	84,625	264	2,361	303	10,816	836	389	256	152
1940	137,142	429	3,830	491	27,093	1,247	609	234	260

Original data source: The Ministry of International Trade and Industry, *Kogyo Tokei* (Statistics of Industries).
(6), (7), (8), and (9) are taken from Showa Dojinkai (ed.), *Wagakuni Chinginkozo no Shiteki Kenkyu* (Historical Study of Wage Structure in Japan) (Tokyo: Shiseido, 1960), pp. 463-464.
Unit: (3) 1,000 persons.
     (5) 1,000,000 Yen.
Computation: (6) See footnote 61.
     (8) = (7) / (9).

character of the government and the international condition at this crucial time. When the international environment does not place too great a strain on the system and when internal democracy is institutionalized to a sufficient degree, the increased productivity will probably be used for the realization of national welfare, the elevation of mass consumption, or for the mobilization of more investment for future development. However, when these conditions are not met, attaining the stage of high industrialization

eliminated the mechanism that might have checked the rise of totalitarianism. In addition to such a domestic situation, the emergence of Nazism in Germany and of fascism in Italy generated severe tension in Europe in the 1930's. This international situation also influenced Japan. In Asia, the very increase of Japan's national power caused serious tension in Manchuria and China. All of these circumstances led Japan to decide to invest the increased productivity in warfare.

Thus the increasing productivity was used neither for realization of national welfare, the elevation of mass consumption, or the mobilization of more investment for future development; rather it was used for the unproductive consumption of military facilities and activities. The G subsystem received a large amount of productivity from the A subsystem; however, because of the excessive demand for military use, the G subsystem could not afford to supply adequate inputs to the other subsystems to meet the functional imperatives for the growth and development of the social system.

Interchange between the Economy and the Pattern-Maintenance Subsystem ($A_G \rightleftharpoons L_G$)

Other things being equal, the increase of productivity in the A subsystem makes it possible to increase the input from the economy to the household. If this is the case then the household can enjoy a higher living standard. How much did Japan's rapid industrialization after the Meiji period raise the standard of living?

Let us look once more at some statistics. When 1909 is taken as the base year, the index of real wages was 139 in 1920, 241 in 1930, 234 in 1940 (Table 27-6).[62] Even though the rate of increase of real wages is slow, when compared to the explosive rate of the industrial production index, real wages continued to increase until 1930. The decade between 1930 and 1940, however, saw no increase in real wages. It is widely known that farmers were more severely affected by the impact of the great Depression of the 1930's. There are no available data which shows the long-term trend of the income of farmers during this period. But various documents indicate that there was a turn for the worse: at that time the top-level officials of the army worried that the depression situation in the villages might negatively affect the most important source of soldiers; a group agrarian ideologists blamed industrialists for the depressed situation of the villages. Thus, during the decade of the thirties both industrial workers and farmers experienced a decline in their living standards. Furthermore, according to a historical study by Miyohei Shinohara of trends in propensity to consume, there was an actual decrease in the consumption rates of all income strata between 1930 and 1940; this was an abnormal pattern not observed at other times.[63]

These data clearly indicate that there was an imbalance in the boundary exchanges between A_G and L_G during the decade. In these days the increase of productivity was invested exclusively for military expansion at the sacrifice of civilian life. As the rapid increase of productivity indices indicates, people worked hard; but they were rewarded with negligible improvement in their living standard compared to the rise of their productivity.

Interchange between the Economy and the Integrative Subsystem ($A_I \rightleftharpoons I_I$)

The A subsystem guarantees the I subsystem economic security in exchange for the input from the latter, national support. Economic security designates the functional contribution of the economy in strengthening national solidarity, when the rise in productivity provides social and psychological stability for the people. When the boundary exchanges between the A and I subsystems are growing in balance, economic development appears to the people to bring national safety and sociopsychological stability. But, once this balance is disturbed and the I subsystem experiences a kind of deficit situation, they become hostile and indignant towards economic development. Then, they start labelling economic development as "exploitation by monopolistic capitalism," "corruption of the business world," "pursuit only of self-interest," "the evil virtue of commercialism," and so forth.

Such was the situation in the 1930's. The nationalistic ideology of the Tenno system advocated the supremacy of Japan's "traditional spiritual culture" vis-a-vis the "materialism of corrupted waste." An anti-urban and anti-industry ideology called "agrarianism" further reinforced such a trend.[64] This gave logical justification to the assertion that Japan had to achieve a spiritual revolution by destroying the existing Japanese society, which had been spoiled by materialism. Such an ideology captured the minds of the young people who were brought up in the traditional conservatism of the impoverished villages. Nationalistic rightists attacked capitalism and socialism without making any distinction between them because for them they were equally materialistic ideologies. The Labor movement and the Communist movement also evoked the nationalistic rightist's antagonism. On the other hand, it should not be overlooked that the leftists' warning against "monopolistic capitalism" in certain respects invited the rightists' attack on materialism. Thus, Tenno fascism, being based on the structural tension generated by the imbalance in the boundary exchanges between the A and I subsystem, rapidly gained supporters.

Interchanges between the Polity and the Integrative and Pattern-Maintenance Subsystems ($G_G \rightleftharpoons I_G, G_I \rightleftharpoons L_I$)

Similar imbalances also existed between the polity and the other two subsystems. The upsurge of Tenno ideology had the consequence of fostering xenophobic nationalism analogous to that found in the "expel the foreigner" movement of the late Tokugawa period. Intensive conduct by the polity of a practice such as war results in the polity demanding far greater inputs from the other subsystems than it can repay to them. Thus when the China War which began in 1937 reached a stalemate, the polity lost its ability to maintain the national standard of living (output of G to L); by inspiring and through social pressure forcing a high level of patriotism the state was able to obtain a substantial input of loyalty (input to G from L). At the same time the polity lost its ability to maintain national integration (output of G to I); by emphasizing the threat from foreign countries it endeavored to maintain a strong input of internal solidarity (input to G from I). Inspiring patriotism and emphasizing the threat posed by foreign countries led to a continued strengthening of xenophobic nationalism. Thus the vicious circle was intensified. Possibilities within the system of preventing the government from extending its military campaign disappeared. The result was that in 1941 the government began the Pacific War against the Allies.

SUMMARY AND CONCLUSION

The social system analysis developed by Parsons is by its nature an appropriate method for analysing dynamic processes of change in social systems. It takes for granted that such phenomena as tensions and disturbances are incorporated in the very processes leading to equilibration. Thus it is useful to borrow the basic framework of social system analysis to build a model for explaining societal growth and social development stimulated by industrialization. In this model it is supposed that the functional imperatives do not necessarily encourage the maintenance of existing social structure; when a structure is inadequate for meeting the functional imperatives, pressure for change develops. Technological progress is placed as a strategic variable, considering the effect of this variable on the system and, at the same time, the feedback effect of the system on this variable. By viewing function as a leading concept, this model is able to explain the route through which technological progress affects structural change. The structural changes accompanying industrialization can be viewed as integrated movements toward functional rationalization; sixteen empirical generalizations were presented as illustrations. However, these changes do not necessarily proceed linearly; thus the model was modified by introducing the concepts of time lag and imbalanced growth.

By applying this model to the modern history of Japan I have endeavored to answer two questions: (1)

how Japan was able to achieve rapid industrialization from the Meiji period, and (2) what the sources were of the tensions and disturbances accompanied by industrialization that appeared in the Showa period and their consequences. In the analysis of the late Tokugawa period the imperatives for change were found to be the financial impoverishment of the bakufu and han treasuries and the need for national defense. To meet the functional imperatives the import of Western technology was essential; the embodiment of the new technology was eased by the background of handicraft skills and traditional knowledge of production. A major impediment to the embodiment of new technology was the economic policy of the traditional decentralized governmental structure, and thus the establishment of centralized government with the Meiji restoration was critical. The analysis of internal processes using the AGIL framework indicates that in the early stage of industrialization relatively balanced growth was maintained. However, the success in rapid industrialization opened new possibilities for imbalanced growth. In particular, the A and G subsystems exploited the other subsystems, returning a lower volume of output than they received. Thus xenophobic nationalism backed up by the Tenno ideology became rapidly diffused as new tensions and disturbances emerged in the Showa period.

For sociological theorists, the empirical analysis of Japan's industrialization may be useful as an illustration; for historians and social analysts of Japan it may be useful for reorganizing materials. From the theoretical point of view, it is satisfying to find that the structural-functional analysis and the AGIL framework help us to understand the nature of Japan's process of social change. I have no doubt that Parsons' theory has wide applicability that extends far beyond the type of analysis presented here.

From the point of view of the empirical analysis of social change, the model presents an analytical tool for analyzing historical materials and, we may add, of attempting international comparisons. Macrosocial change is a topic of great currency. As we look around the world today, we find many societies systematically attempting to bring about changes in their social structure which resemble the changes effected by Japan over the process of her industrialization and development. In this context, it is inevitable that one who studies social change in Japan will be tempted to draw implications from Japan's experience for the societies of the Third World. Frequently in this essay I did so, though not systematically, as the habit of comparison has become an intrinsic part of my thinking. It would be desirable for someone to use a model of this kind for systematic international comparisons. However, it must be emphasized that this essay is not directed to answering the question of why Japan was able to do it and other nations were not. It is rather directed to the presentation of a theoretical model and an illustration and verification of this model, using Japan as a case study.

NOTES

1. Talcott Parsons, *The Social System* (Glencoe, Ill.: The Free Press, 1951), p. 486.

2. Talcott Parsons, *Essays in Sociological Theory* (rev. ed.,) (Glencoe, Ill.: The Free Press, 1954), p. 215.

3. *Ibid.*, p. 217.

4. *The Social System,* p. 21.

5. On this point it is essential to note that functional analysis is a special kind of equilibrium analysis. The simplest definition of the nature of functional analysis from the point of view of equilibrium analysis is that the former is the latter plus the teleological assumption for the system. Naoki Komuro, "Kozokino Bunseki to Kinko Bunseki* (Structural-functional Analysis and Equilibrium Analysis)," *Japanese Sociological Review* 16 (1966), pp. 77-103, demonstrated this point in clear terms. (A title followed by an* is written in Japanese.)

6. Paul A. Samuelson, *Foundations of Economic Analysis* (Cambridge: Harvard University Press, 1947), pp. 260-263.

7. Both equilibrium analysis and functional analysis use the common concept of equilibrium. But the equilibrium concept must be redefined in the case of structural-functional analysis, because for the latter the idea of the functional imperative for the system is indispensable. For the sake of realizing such an equilibrium state, structure and function demand each other so as to fit together. The structure being given, the "functional imperative" arises. The function being given, the "structural imperative" arises. See *The Social System,* p. 484.

8. See *The Social System,* pp. 202-203.

9. Ralf Dahrendorf, "Out of Utopia," *American Journal of Sociology* 64 (1958), pp. 115-127; *Class and Class Conflict in Industrial Society* (Stanford: Stanford University Press, 1959), esp. pp. 157-173.

10. Talcott Parsons, "An Outline of the Social System," in T. Parsons *et al.* (eds.), *Theories of Society* (Glencoe, Ill.: The Free Press, 1961), p. 70.

11. *Ibid.*, p. 71.

12. For example, *The Social System*, pp. 485, 491f., 510f. and *passim.*; *Theories of Society*, p. 72; Talcott Parsons and Neil J. Smelser, *Economy and Society* (London: Kegan Paul, 1956), pp. 263f. However, there are at the same time misleading paragraphs in Parsons' own writing. Here is one typical bad example:

> The "equilibrium" conception is that such relatively small changes tend to be "counteracted" by the effects of their repercussions on the parts of the system, in such a way that the original state tends to be restored (*Economy and Society,* p. 247).

Obviously this is too narrow a definition of the equilibrium, which is a strictly special case of the equilibrating process in the wider sense stated in my text.

13. Industrialization as broadly defined here could also be called "modernization" by other writers. But I would prefer industrialization to modernization, because the former concept has an external criterion of technological progress in mechanized production while the latter concept has no such external criterion. See K. Tominaga, *Shakaihendo no Riron** (The Theory of Social Change) (Tokyo: Iwanami-Shoten, 1965), pp. 171-199. Because of the lack of external criterion, the concept of modernization always has an ambiguity, "What is

'modern'?" Cf. Alex Inkeles. "The Modernization of Man," in M. Weiner (ed.), *Modernization* (New York: Basic Books, 1966), pp. 138-150.

14. Economists tend to define economic growth in purely quantitative terms as increments to GNP, while they tend to define economic development in wider terms, including structural and institutional change. We can distinguish between social development and societal growth in the same manner. I will discuss this issue later.

15. The preindustrial society is an extremely important research subject for the study of industrialization, as industrial society is prepared within the preindustrial societal framework. In the analysis of the industrialization process in Japan, I will analyze the nature of the preindustrial state of Tokugawa Japan in AGIL terms, focusing on the preconditions indispensable for successful industrialization.

16. V. Pareto, *The Mind and Society,* 4 vols. (New York: Harcourt, 1935), Ch. XIII; P. A. Sorokin, *Social and Cultural Dynamics,* 4 vols. (New York: American Book, 1937-41), Ch. II; A. J. Toynbee, *A Study of History* (abr. ed. by Somerville), 2 vols. (London: Oxford Univ. Press, 1946-57).

17. The works of Alfred Weber and Oswald Spengler are typical examples. In more moderate form, the works of Karl Mannheim and William Ogburn would be other examples.

18. Examples are W. W. Rostow, *Stages of Economic Growth* (London: Cambridge Univ. Press, 1960); C. Kerr., F. H. Harbison, J. T. Dunlop, and C. A. Myers, *Industrialism and Industrial Man* (Cambridge: Harvard University Press, 1960).

19. Karl Marx, *Zur Kritik der politischen Ekonomie* (A Contribution to the Critique of Political Economy) (Berlin: Duncker, 1859), Foreword.

20. Yasuma Takada, *Kaikyu oyobi Daisan-shikan** (Social Class and the Third View of History) (Tokyo: Kaizosha, 1925, rev. ed., Tokyo: Seki-shoin, 1948); *Kaitei Shakaigaku Gairon** (Principles of Sociology, rev. ed.) (Tokyo: Iwanami-shoten, 1950), esp. pp. 321-332. Takada (1883-) is the greatest sociological theorist Japan has ever had. In the magnitude of his theoretical scope, originality in theory building, and the systematically deductive character, his whole body of work is equal to that of Parsons. He published a large number of important theoretical works intensively during 1918-1926 in the field of sociology; then he switched his major concern to theoretical especially mathematical economics, but up to 1952 he still continued to publish sociological works. The title of "the third view of history" means that, contrasting the "first view" or idealistic interpretation of history of Comte and Hegel with the "second view" or materialistic interpretation of Marx, he designated his own position as "third view" or sociological interpretation. It is interesting that his conflict theory reminds us of Simmel, and his methodological individualism of Max Weber, while his "third view" is reminiscent of Durkheim. If his voluminous work *Principles of Sociology* had been translated into English, it might have been one of the world's classics in sociology. For a fuller discussion see my article in *Sociological Inquiry,* 45 (1975).

21. Samuelson, Paul A., "Interaction between the Multiplier Analysis and the Principle of Acceleration," *Review of Economic Statistics* (1939), pp. 75-78.

22. Being influenced by Schumpeter, Parsons and Smelser emphasized that the supply of capital depends in its most important respect upon the activity of credit creation by banks, and this can be interpreted as a kind of "political power." Thus they asserted that capital is supplied by the G subsystem (*Economy and Society,* pp. 72-75). In my view, capital accumulation in itself must be an internal process of the A subsystem, that is, the process of internal boundary exchange within the economy. Political input intervenes in so far as the governmental activity encourages or discourages capital accumulation. I would like to stress that this view was adopted because the latter interpretation is more adequate for the analysis of what the Meiji Government did in the early Meiji era in Japan than Parsons and Smelser's.

23. Parsons and Smelser treat each boundary exchange as a "double interchange" (*ibid.*, pp. 70-85). Unavoidably this treatment makes it hard to correspond to empirical referents. For the sake of simplicity I do not introduce the double interchange idea.

24. In actual situations the distinction between "change" and "semichange" is only a matter of degree. Some of the institutionalized norms of distribution change as a result of accumulations of "mere" distributional change. To that extent the distinction becomes fluid.

25. It was Ogburn who formulated and illustrated this fact for the first time, although his term "cultural lag" is ambiguous, reflecting too wide a usage of the term "culture" in cultural sociology at that time. It is necessary to reformulate it as the process within the social system in structural-functional terms.

26. It was Shiso Hattori who asserted for the first time that there was a "fairly high level" of the development of capitalist production among the rural industries in the late Tokugawa period; there have been controversies over Hattori's claim. See Shiso Hattori, *Meijiishin-shi Kenkyu** (Studies in the History of Meiji Restoration) (Tokyo: Kureha-shoten, 1948), esp. pp. 10-13.

27. Robert N. Bellah, *Tokugawa Religion: The Values of Pre-industrial Japan* (Glencoe, Ill.: The Free Press, 1957). As the subtitle of this book suggests, Bellah's definition of religion is so broad that it covers the entire field of the value system, which he places in the L subsystem. In contrast, my analysis is focused on the A subsystem.

28. Kazushi Ohkawa (ed.), *The Growth Rate of the Japanese Economy Since 1878* (Tokyo: Institute of Economic Research, Hitotsubashi University, 1957). Ohkawa improves on those parts of Yamada's estimate which were concerned with the national income produced.

29. Shonan Yokoi, *Kokuze Sanron** (Three Essays on National Policy), written in 1860 as manuscript and first published in: *Yokoi Shonan Iko** (Collected Essays in one volume of Shonan Yokoi), Masatsugu Yamazaki (ed.) (Tokyo: Nisshin-Shoin, 1942), p. 31.

30. Zozan Sakuma, *Seikenroku** (Reflection), written in 1854 as manuscript and first published in: *Zozan Zenshu** (Complete Works of Zozan) Vol. 1 (Nagano: Shinano Mainichi Shimbun-sha, 1934), p. 11.

31. Seishisai Aizawa, *Shinron** (New Essay), completed in 1825 as manuscript and published in *Aizawa Seishisai-shu* (Collected Works of Seishisai Aizawa), Yoshijiro Takasu (ed.) (Mitogaku Zenshu, Vol. 2) (Tokyo: Ida-Shoten, 1941), pp. 108-110.

32. Takashi Nakano, *Shokadozokudan no Kenkyu** (Studies of Merchants' Dozokudan) (Tokyo: Mirai-sha, 1964), pp. 194-208.

33. One typical formulation is: Takao Tsuchiya, *Nihon Keieirinen-shi** (History of Management Ideology in Japan) (Tokyo: Nihon Keizai Shimbun-sha, 1964), pp. 94-95, 99-117.

34. Among the authors of this view, the most influential works are Hisao Ohtsuka's, though his formulation is derived from the study of economic history in England, not in Japan. Hisao Ohtsuka, "Kindai Shihonshugi Hattatsu-shi niokeru Shogyo no Chii"* (The Role of Merchants in the Development of Modern Capitalism), in *Ohtsuka Hisao Chosaku-shu* (Selected Works of Hisao Ohtsuka), Vol. 3 (Tokyo: Iwanami-shoten, 1969), pp. 119-185.

35. Kizaemon Ariga, *Nihon Kazokuseido to Kosakuseido** (Family System and Tenancy System in Japan) (Tokyo: Kawade-shobo, 1943), reprinted in: Ariga Kizaemon Chosaku-shu (Selected Works of Kizaemon Ariga), Vol. 2 (Tokyo: Mirai-sha, 1968), p. 712; Nakano, *op. cit.*, p.45.

36. See Shigeaki Yasuoka, *Zaibatsu Keisei-shi no Kenkyu** (Studies in the History of Zaibatsu Formation) (Tokyo; Minerva-shobo, 1970).

37. Eiichi Horie, *Meijiishin no Shakaikozo** (Social Structure at the Time of the Meiji Restoration) (Tokyo: Yuhikaku, 1954), pp. 106-108, 113-114.

38. Hajime Tamaki, *Gendai Nihon Sangyohattatsu-shi Soron** (General Considerations on the Development of Industry in Modern Japan) (Tokyo: Kojun-sha, 1967), p. 82.

39. *Yokosuka Kaigun Sensho-shi** (History of the Yokosuka Naval Shipyard) (Yokosuka: Yokosuka Kaigun Kosho, Vol. 1, 1915), pp. 75-77.

40. Takao Tsuchiya, "Obeijin no Nihon Shihonshugi Seiritsu ni Hatashita Yakuwari"* (The Role played by the Westerners in the Formation of Capitalism in Japan), in: *Keizaishutaisei Koza* (Lectures on Agents in Economic Development), Vol. 6 (Tokyo: Chuokoron-sha, 1960), pp. 266-306.

41. Mitsutomo Yuasa, "Scientific Revolution in Nineteenth Century in Japan," *Japanese Studies in the History of Science,* No. 2 (Tokyo: The History of Science Society of Japan, 1963), p. 126.

42. *Yokosuka Kaigun Sensho-shi*, p. 75.

43. Yoshiro Hoshino, "Kogyo Gijutsu no Hatten"* (The Development of Industrial Technology), in: *Keizaishutaisei Koza* pp. 80-119.

44. Cf. Akira Ono, "Gijutsu Shinpo to 'Borrowed Technology' no Ruikei"* (Technological Progress and the Types of 'Borrowed Technology') in: J. Tsukui and Y. Murakami (eds.). *Keizai Seicho Riron no Tenbo* (Perspectives on the Theory of Economic Growth) (Tokyo: Iwanami-shoten, 1968), pp. 199-214.

45. Tsutomu Ouchi and Toshihiko Kato, *Kokuritsuginko no Kenkyu** (Studies of the National Banks) (Tokyo: Keiso-shobo, 1963). pp. 35-36, 115-117.

46. For example, see: M. Kajinishi, T. Kato, K. Oshima, and T. Ouchi, *Nihon Shihonshugi no Seiritsu** (Formation of Capitalism in Japan), Vol. II (Tokyo: Todai Shuppankai, 1965), p. 297.

47. Data source is shown in the bottom of Table 27-3. Statistical data of wages are fragmentary until Kogyo Tokei (Statistics of Industry) began in 1909.

48. Ronald P. Dore, *Education in Tokugawa Japan* (Berkeley and Los Angeles: University of California Press, 1965), p. 317.

49. Wakizo Yokoi wrote in 1925, "A dormitory of female workers—in a word it is a 'pigpen.'" Yokoi, *Joko Aishi** (Miserable History of Female Workers) (Tokyo: Kaizo-sha, 1925, Iwanami-shoten, 1954), p. 164.

50. Mikio Sumiya, *Nihon Chinrodo-shi Ron** (History of Wage Workers in Japan) (Tokyo: Todai Shuppankai, 1955), pp. 208-238.

51. Gennosuke Yokoyama, *Nihon no Kasoshakai** (Lower Class of Japan) (Tokyo: Kyobunkan, 1898, Iwanami-shoten, 1949), pp. 28-29.

52. Dore, *op. cit.*, p. 292.

53. Sumiya, *op. cit.*, pp. 216-217.

54. Reinhard Bendix, *Work and Authority in Industry* (New York: Wiley, 1956), p. 7.

55. Yukichi Fukuzawa, *Gakumon no Susume** (An Encouragement of Learning), first published in 1972-1976, now in: *Fukuzawa Yukichi Zenshu* (Complete Works of Yukichi Fukuzawa), Vol. 3 (Tokyo: Iwanami-shoten, 1958-1964), p. 52.

56. See Takao Tsuchiya, *Zoku Nihon Keieirinen-shi** (History of Management Ideology in Japan, continued) (Tokyo: Nihon Keizai Shimbun-sha, 1967), pp. 56-71.

57. An illustration is that Masao Maruyama calls the nationalistic aspect of the radical anti-bakufu thought represented by Shoin Yoshida "Prenationalism," where the prefix "pre-" means that it developed within the framework of the feudal society but established a basis for later national integration. Masao Maruyama, *Nihon Seijishiso-shi Kenkyu** (Studies in the History of Political Thought in Japan) (Tokyo: Todai Shuppankai), pp. 339-363.

58. Max Weber, *The Theory of Social and Economic Organization*, Henderson and Parsons (trs.) (New York: Oxford University Press, 1947), p. 366.

59. Bellah, *op. cit.*, p. 193.

60. The term "maturity" of Tenno facism was borrowed from: Masao Maruyama, *Gendai Seiji no Shiso to Kodo** (Thought and Behavior in Modern Politics), Vol. 1 (Tokyo: Mirai-sha, 1956), pp. 28-35.

61. The original source of the amount of manufacturing production is Kogyo Tokei (Statistics of Industries). Indices are derived by the following formula:

[Amount of production (yen)/Price index/Amount of base year (yen)] x 100

62. Data source and index calculation are parallel to those in footnote 61.

63. Miyohei Shinohara, *Shohi Kansu* (Consumption Function) (Tokyo: Keisoshobo, 1958), pp. 256-258.

64. Maruyama, *op. cit.*, Vol. 1, pp. 39-42.

28

SOCIETAL ATTRIBUTES AND INTERNATIONAL RELATIONS

Roland Robertson

The study of international relations has suffered particularly from a failure of theoretical crystallization, although many attempts have been made to improve this situation during the past few years. Undoubtedly this has something to do, *inter alia*, with the social and cultural conditions under which knowledge about international affairs has been produced and disseminated, the sociocultural characteristics of specialists in the field, and the history of the discipline. But purely in terms of the nature of international affairs we can readily observe some crucial elements of intractability.[1] From a sociological angle the backdrop to this intractability is to be seen in the ambiguous status of the conventionally regarded basic unit of international system, namely, the national society. The society is in sociological terms a macroscopic analytical entity, and it has long been regarded by sociologists as the highest-order sociological entity: many — probably most — sociologists take the society to be their inclusive frame of reference, while most of recent comparative sociology has employed the society as the basic unit of analysis.[2] Many sociologists have, then, worked on the assumption that it is at the level of the society that their analyses stop; and the recent revival of interest in macrosociology has in itself done little to offset this.[3]

When, however, we consider the analytic emphasis

upon the society in the context of a global sociocultural complex, serious problems arise. Strictly speaking, sociology has not emphasized the national society as the pivotal macroscopic unit of analysis. When Parsons speaks of the society as "the typecase" of his theoretical system, he has not tended to see it as a national entity operating in an environment of other societies. Indeed, in the case of action theory, the environment has been dealt with basically in analytic as opposed to phenomenal terms. That is, the analytic systems, cultural, social-psychological, and biological, comprising a total action system have been taken as the relevant span of systems needing sociological attention. Thus, at least until very recently, we have found in Parsons' work an emphasis upon treating the social system as the focal system of analysis with the other three analytic systems constituting the environment of that system. It is precisely this "intra" as opposed to "inter" emphasis which puts critical difficulties in the way of adequate sociological treatments of international relations.[4] These difficulties may be summed up in the observation that whereas the society is frequently regarded as the major macro-unit of analysis, when seen in the context of an international system it is a *micro-unit*.

If, however, this is all there is to say about the problem, we ought to be satisfied with merely applying our microsociological propositions to national societies when our major empirical interest is in international relations. In fact, this has been attempted from time to time, and a few sociologists have applied the general principles of relationships between micro-units and macro-units, between statements about the behavior of units within a system and the over-all attributes of the system itself, to the international field.[5] In principle, then, there appear to be no problems in treating international

I am indebted to the editors for their incisive criticisms of earlier drafts of this essay. In particular I wish to acknowledge the constructive suggestions of Rainer Baum — although I have been unable to capitalize upon these as much as I would have ideally wished. The essay was completed before the occurrence of some major recent political events: most notably the enlargement of the European Economic Community to include Britain, the Republic of Ireland, and Denmark; and "Watergate." Neither of these circumstances have changed my views as expressed in what follows.

systems as analogous or homologous to the society (or indeed any sociocultural system). Some analysts have claimed more. Thus Modelski has written:

> Sociological generalizations about social systems are, *mutatis mutandis*, applicable also to the study of international systems. Like other systems, international systems consist of a set of objects, plus the relationships between these objects and between their attributes. Since international systems are systems of action and interaction between collectivities and between individuals acting on their behalf, and hence social systems, the objects of which the international systems are composed may be defined, on the analogy of Talcott Parsons' fundamental unit of social system, as international status-roles (examples of these are the roles of a great power, of a United Nations member, or of a neutral).[6]

This is not the appropriate context for delving into the problems posed by Parsons' insistence that the status-role is the basic unit of sociological analysis proper, the elemental analytic constituent of a social system. Suffice it to say here that whatever the merits or demerits of Parsons' arguments, the idea that at the international level we can safely eschew analysis of the concrete units of the system, i.e., national societies — as is suggested by Modelski's argument — seems, to put it mildly, to be misplaced. To argue *sociologically* that we can ignore the internal attributes of national societies in the same way that we ignore or make primitive assumptions about the internal attributes of the psychological individual implies the existence of a normatively integrated system or at least assumes the heuristic worthwhileness of such a predicate.

The basic problem in the present context revolves around the *interstitial* analytic status of the national society; interstitial, that is, between the study of international relations, on the one hand, and comparative sociology, on the other. And it seems that the only way to approach international relations from a sociological standpoint is through a synthesis of the approaches of comparative sociology and the discipline of international relations. This would involve treating societies as distinct structural entities in interaction on a comparative basis. This argument conforms to Singer's persuasive statement that

> political science, sociology, and to a lesser extent, anthropology, have shown a growing tendency to theorize around the concepts of relationship and of role. One consequence of this emphasis has been a gradually diminishing concern with the social entities which share these relationships and fill these roles; one almost gets the feeling that the entity which experiences these relationships and occupies these roles is of no consequence, and that its immanent properties have *no* effect on the way in which the role or relationship is handled.[7]

What we have just said implies a three-level conception of the study of international relations: at the lowest level, there is the study on a comparative basis of concrete national societies; at the second level there is the microanalysis of international relations; and at the third level there is the macroanalysis of international relations. The delineation is clearly an oversimplification of the issues at stake, mainly because when we use the term "international" we usually include social processes which, strictly speaking, do not fall into the domain of relations between nations (or national societies) *per se*. The debates which have been concerned with the appropriateness of treating the nation as an actor (themes hinging upon the behavior of nations as actors falling into the category of international microanalysis in terms of our delineation) have usually been concerned with the philosophical problems of "personalizing" a large-scale collectivity; but there are more profound substantive issues involved. These mainly have to do with the degree of integralness and boundedness of the national society. The analogy with the personality system does not work out, simply because many interactions across the boundaries of the national unit do not represent the unit as such in interaction, nor are they interactions for which the unit has responsibility. The closest analogy to the individual actor which we find in the international system is the "successful" authoritarian-totalitarian society, that is, the national society which successfully exercises comprehensive controls over the interaction of its parts and its members with other entities in the global complex. In this sense, it is intuitively more meaningful and realistic to say "Russia acts" than it is to say "Belgium acts." Similarly it makes more sense to say "Portugal acts" than it does to say "Norway acts," and so on.

However, the "actorness" of national societies is not merely a matter of the degree to which the system is an authoritarian-totalitarian one. It is a multifaceted notion, and much of this essay can be read as an attempt to distill a more adequate and comprehensive conception of what is involved in this problem area, with particular reference to the modes of legitimation of governmental action and decision and to the relationship between state and society within the national societies which constitute collectively the global international system or subsystems of the latter.

International systems will be regarded as consisting in sets of relationships between what have been classically known as states, more frequently labelled political subsystem or polities in modern social science, although we will have occasion to consider the more complex themes of transnational and supernational systems. Any analysis which seeks, like this one, to tap the relationship between societal processes and extranational systems must of necessity inquire into the variety of, and the changes taking place in, the area of polity-society relations. Thus we are committed here to "coming at" international relations primarily the terms of the attributes of national societies which relate most directly to developments in the global international system. We will be particularly interested in impediments to the development of a relatively autonomous system of relations between national societies. Our analysis will thus say relatively little about the structure of the global international system itself, as we are more interested here in the societal boundaries of that system.[8]

SOCIETAL STRAINS IN THEIR INTERNATIONAL CONTEXTS

The relationship between intranational events and processes, on the one hand, and international events and processes, on the other hand, is a complex one, about which it is almost impossible to generalize with parsimony and analytic closure.[9] What, however, will lie at the heart of our analysis is the simple and by now widely-accepted proposition that polities in the contemporary world are encountering ever-expanding "problem loads" — an expansion which is bringing about increasing strains between polity and "society."[10] In terms of Parsons' theory of action, the term society will be taken to refer to all of the remaining subsystems of the over-all social system: the economy (A); the societal community (I); and the pattern-maintenance subsystem (L). But in our analysis the economy will be considered not so much as a source of pressure upon the polity but rather as a societal sector requiring political "treatment." The L and I subsystems constitute the social matrix which is in a major sense prior to the operation of political processes. The fact that adaptive-economic problems are highly conspicuous and seemingly intractable in a number of societies is, of course, a matter of considerable importance, although there does seem to have been a shift away from the position of regarding the problems of modern societies as primarily (and "merely") economic in nature.[11] In the present context adaptive-economic problems clearly cannot be ignored, if only because of their significance as links between national societies. And at a later stage we will have occasion to consider briefly the significance of developments in the economic sphere — such as the increase in salience of so-called multinational corporations and attendant labor union responses — as they affect the survival of nation-state systems of international relations; for such developments involve in some cases the direct interpenetration of the A subsystems of modern societies.

In sum, much of our analysis rests on the assumption that economic factors, including associated technological change, are — insofar as they can be separated empirically from other social and cultural developments — "undermining" the nation-state system. But a, perhaps the, major thesis adumbrated here is that social factors of a kind more internal to societal systems, categorizable as pattern-maintenance and integrative factors, are working, if not directly at odds with adaptive-economic factors, in complex respects which make the operation of the political subsystems of modern societies particularly important foci for sociological analysis. Thus we are above all concerned with the ways in which governments and governmental agencies seek to cope with what we describe as problem loads. We will, in other words, attend to what Parsons has called the "'inner circle' of political problems" — a circle which comprises, as he puts it, a "typology of 'political problems'" and which consists in the relationships between the polity and each of the other three subsystems of any social system — in our case, the national society.[12]

Parsons has recently argued that American society — in particular — is in a phase of change

> in which integrative problems have for the time being assumed primacy. . . . It is particularly striking that the malaise of our time does not seem to have its internal focus in the structure of the industrial economy as such. . . but in the generation structure with its close relation to the system of higher education, and in the status of those population groups who are, relative to the societal community, the most marginal.[13]

It seems, however, that even though this is where the recent problems of a number of modern societies have begun — in the American case in the civil rights movement and in an international manner in the mid-1960's student-protest quasi-movement — these essentially integrative problems have escalated to the level of societal values and, indeed, as we shall have occasion to note, to the *cultural* level of societal consciousness.[14]

We may briefly indicate some of the contents of the categories of political problems derivable from the LIGA schema. In the category of *adaptation* we locate such factors as increasing role differentiation, notably differentiation of occupational roles and collectivities and the complexity of managing and controlling such processes. As we have already suggested, this economic-adaptive cluster of problems encountered by polities relates beyond the strictly social level of analysis to technological change and strains attendant upon the technification of modern societies. It is this over-all set of social and "material" factors centering upon the economies of contemporary societies which conventionally receive most attention in discussions of nation-state dissolution — in terms of technostructures and economic collectivity complexes crosscutting national boundaries, nonnationally directed monetary management programs, and so on.

In the case of the second category, the societal community (I), we refer at the most general level to problems faced by polities in respect of citizenship definitions and political mobilization. More specifically we are thinking of demands for inclusion within the societal community with respect to political relevance in that community on the part of a large range of quasi-groups and collectivities in modern societies. The most conspicuous of these have been in recent years ethnic groups and the young; but we also include here certain aspects of "sexual" citizenship, most notably of course the demands for political and community upgrading advanced by women's movements. Less dramatic, but in the long run not of much less significance, consumer groups and special-purpose collectivities and associations, including "the poor," have relevance here.

The third category of problem load bearing upon the activities of contemporary governments concerns the pattern-maintenance subsystem. Some elemental aspects of developments mentioned under the heading of the societal community are important in this connection. Thus the citizenship and community inclusion aspects of both the role of women in modern societies and the position of deprived ethnic groups, notably blacks, have more profound counterparts in a pattern-maintenance respect. In the latter sense the concern is more diffusely with questions of identity and meaning — that is, what femininity means, what being black "really involves," and so on. In the broadest sense, then, personal identity and changing definitions of the societal situation as a whole have come increasingly to the fore in a number of modern societies.

It is clear that in view of these brief characterizations of the political problems of modern societies questions concerning the relationship among the A, I, and L systems are of considerable theoretical importance. In particular the L/I relationship (what Parsons calls the loyalty, solidarity, commitment system) is implicitly at analytic stake in the present discussion. Focussing as we are on political problems, we will define the L subsystem as having to do with the questions of protopolitical identity and I problems as relating to issues concerning conceptions of citizenship.

Our immediate requirement at this stage is to obtain an image of the ways in which governments may seek to cope with problem loads. This we attempt in terms of a typology of pure strategies. These pure strategies consist in general diagnoses of how the problems are to be dealt with. In explicating these types of strategy it should be emphasized that even though we have spoken mainly in terms of pressures on polities from within the national societies of which they are subsystems, this does not mean that governments will necessarily perceive these pressures to be internal in any clearcut manner. In any case, it is obvious that many problems perceived as being of an internal kind have, in fact, crucially important external origins. Economic crises frequently have international or transnational origins, many of the recent strains in American society stem from the war in Indochina, and so on.

The two basic axes upon which the typology is found are: first, whether there is a positive or a negative orientation to the load problem (whether the problems are "appreciated" or not); second, whether the problem is to be solved or dissolved on a primarily internal or on a primarily external basis.

Four possible strategies will be considered. The first, engagement, involves a disposition on the part of the relevant political elites to deal with the problems of internal load by devoting a great deal of attention to the meeting of the demands and problems of internally-generated resources, in other words, to treat the problems as internally soluble and manageable.

	Mode of dealing with problems	
	Primarily internal	Primarily external
Orientation to problems		
Positive	Engage	Allocate
Negative	Dispose	Deflect

Allocation involves looking for positive solutions in terms of perceiving the problem as having a significant international, transnational, or supernational aspect; as warranting recourse to external agencies.

Disposal involves an inclination to "put problems down" — to regard problems as having to be coped with by manipulatively neglecting them or, if they "won't go away," to dampen them. The political notion of benign neglect is a form of disposal.

Deflection involves translating the internal problems into external ones; for example, by claiming that what has gone wrong internally is a consequence of an external or alien factor or agency. The notion of blame is crucial here.

The economy of exposition facilitated by the use of a "box typology" has to be contrasted with the empirically more satisfying depiction of strategies in terms of a more "fluid" property space:

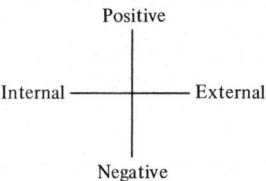

In the ensuing discussion, we will employ dichotomized variables, but this continuum form of presentation should be borne carefully in mind as being empirically more appropriate — as it permits the *relative* locations of actual societies with greater precision than the box procedure. At a later stage we will attempt to tie these strategic alternatives to a typology of relations between polity and society — to suggest which types are most congruent situationally with particular strategic mixes. However, a point requiring more immediate attention is the kind of *societal conditions* which impose constraints on the probable adoption and continuation of a particular strategic stance. Whereas specific types of society (characterized in terms of the polity-society relationship) are, as we shall see, more likely to manifest particular strategies in relation to their internal problem loads, the precise nature of the loads themselves and their internal settings, as well as the prevalent international context, limit (as a matter of degree) the range of viable strategic choices:

STRATEGY	MINIMUM CONDITIONS	
	National	*International*
Engagement	Compatible inputs	Absence of threat; nonlikelihood of interference
Allocation	Divisibility of inputs	Availability of "partners"
Disposal	Relatively weak opposition	Nonintervention
Deflection	Mobilizability of populace	Availability of enemies and scapegoats

A more satisfactory elaboration of this attempt to pinpoint the critical variables directing adoption of a particular strategy, or a particular strategic mix, would involve distinguishing, within each category of conditions, between general structural conditions obtaining in the given society and "existential" conditions, i.e., the ideographic characteristics of the society at a particular point in time. As it is, the conditions which we have listed tend to cut across and amalgamate these two aspects of minimum conditions. We will merely offer an indication of the relevance of the schema to one society, namely Britain, at this juncture.

A government faced with numerous demands for social reform cannot hope to sustain a pure strategy of engagement unless the demands are consistent in relation to each other or can be treated on a perceived priority basis. And even if these conditions are fulfilled, the government in question cannot hope to succeed unless it can bank on noninterference from outside. The situation in Northern Ireland has "excellently" illustrated this point. Catholic and Protestant demands are not separable or congruent, while Eire has been committed to some degree of involvement in the affairs of Northern Ireland. The British Labor Government until 1970 apparently attempted a policy of engagement, with little success; while the Northern Ireland Government, having relied largely in the past on a strategy of deflection (Protestant mobilization, Eire as the "enemy") split in the late 1960's into groups demanding respectively each type of strategy.[15]

In the case of the strategy of engagement it is clear that the condition "compatibility of inputs" covers both the specific nature of the inputs themselves and the pregovernmental institutional mechanisms for dealing with the inputs. A society which has institutionalized procedures for articulating and aggregating inputs to the polity or one with effective "gatekeeping" institutions clearly has an advantage with respect to making inputs relatively compatible through the process of establishing priorities and what might be called "input queues."[16] Some societies, such as Britain, have greater, noncoercive capacities for establishing queues of demand inputs to the polity than do other societies (an attribute which, as Lipset suggests, is undoubtedly based on the salient elitism of British society[17] — that is, there is a phenomenal link between respect for social hierarchy and the cultural disposition to "queue" in the political input sphere).

Nevertheless, it is worth noting that the last few years have seemingly witnessed a decreasing capacity for British society to maintain this queueing political attribute. British politicians and political commentators have evidently become more and more aware of the overload of demands on the polity, notably with respect to the various social services which simply in terms of money available cannot be adequately met. Thus British society, like others, has witnessed over the last few years numerous attempts to meet the overload situation with strategies other than that of engagement. A hard core of politicians of all major parties have sought a solution in the allocation strategy, particularly with respect to economic problems, in relation to the European Economic Community; others, on the right wing of the Conservative party and "beyond," have followed the strategy of deflection. The latter have sought to find an "enemy" upon which to displace the blame for the increasing load of political demands.[18] Although mainly internally alien—in an objective sense—in its focus, the Powellite strategy bears strong international overtones, as did fascism in Germany and McCarthyism in America before it, insofar as the "black menace" is clearly related to an international or transnational category of individuals.

As we have indicated, none of the foregoing should be construed as arguments against the idea that domestic problems originate in many important cases from foreign sources. Many of the movements which confront the governments of contemporary societies, both relatively developed and relatively undeveloped, clearly receive many of their assets and inspirations, indeed guidance, from external sources. Foreign policy considerations have been and are frequently major bases for the centralization of economies in societies which are, in fact, culturally and politically pledged to the principles of private, competitive industrial enterprise (not to speak of societies which are more naturally disposed to economic centralization). For example, American society has experienced major centralizing shifts as consequences of war mobilization, economic depression, and increasing internal complexity; as well as major changes in its occupational and stratification systems attendant upon the same process.[19] Thus, to repeat, the issue of increasing international and transnational interdependence is not in the present context a problematic one. The global system *is* becoming increasingly interdependent. But a fundamental query is whether increasing interdependence between societies is being "overmatched" by the increasing internal interdependence (not to be confused analytically with integration or internal coordination) of national societies. Another equally important problem is the degree to which national governments seek to or actually do regulate the various facets of increasing interdependence.

It is a commonplace of much sociological theory that so-called advanced or modern societies are more adaptable than less advanced ones, primarily because their greater structural differentiation allows for more flexibility.[20] The involuted nature of pre-industrial societies — the contingency of their activities, the lack of differentiation between institutional sectors—allegedly makes for a tighter social structure which is more liable to holistic disturbance than modern societies. Persuasive as such views often are, the increasingly centralized nature of government in many industrial societies tends to offset the flexibility advantages granted by the high degree of differentiation of institutional sectors and of their respective media of control and interchange. And so the "real" problem for modern industrial societies in this respect is, we would argue, one of their gaining an efficient mode of control, in the cybernetic

sense, over their modes of operation. This is the basic attribute of what Etzioni calls the active society.[21]

The pressures to attain this kind of cybernetic control are sufficient to make the national society the primary point of reference. Or, to state the point in another way, the pressures towards the attainment of societal control capacity appear greater than those having to do with international control; although in order to obtain societal control a governmental elite may have to seek adjustments in its international environment, which process falls into our category of an allocative governmental strategy. Loose or tentative forms of political unification, such as EFTA or the Nordic Community, are relevant to this point.[22] Within these two groups, Sweden is a particularly interesting case, in which the balance between efforts to gain societal control and the necessity to seek consonant external arrangements has been delicately managed.[23] Speaking in reference to the policies of national governments in the face of increasing transnational interactions, Kaiser observes that the former.

> theoretically have the option between on the one hand national self-encapsulation (what is here called *engagement:* RR) to stop inter-societal interaction or to bring it under complete national control and, on the other, regularized consultation, and even co-ordination of policies, with the governments of other national systems involved, in order to cope with the problems created on the level of societies.

The EFTA and Nordic cases would appear to fall between these two strategies.

One of the major unintended consequences of the contemporary upsurge of interest in social planning is indeed probably that of consolidating the national-societal structure; although it may be that in some cases national-societal planning is in part motivated by the goal of holding the line against penetration by, or on the part of an agency within, another national society. It is to the level of the society that planning primarily refers. This results mainly from the (clearly accurate) perception on the part of most planners and planning theorists that the central-governmental level of the society is the highest level to which they can reach in terms of gaining effective control leverage. Of course there are many international and supranational planners and planning agencies, and these continue to multiply in all parts of the world. But supranational agencies such as EEC and Comecon have to cope with the considerable resilience of national societies as the units of their planning endeavors. The example of Russian coercion of Czechoslovakia (1968), or more accurately the latter's resistance to the former, shows just how formidable is the task of coordinated planning at the extranational level, as does the relatively successful resistance of Rumania to the dictates of Russian-controlled Comecon. Worldwide planning agencies such as the United Nations development system (which has been described as "probably the most complex organization in the world"[25]) are even less successful at the moment. In this connection it is significant to note that the Jackson Report (see note 25) on the UN development system warned that the latter was in danger of being in effect taken over by the (Western-controlled) World Bank system, which, of course, operates very much on the assumption, and in terms of the persistence, of a nation-state form of international system.

In the general context of these remarks about the resilience of the nation-state as a political referent, it is worth noting that one of the most famous advocates of international planning and coordination, Gunnar Myrdal, pointed some time ago to the international-disintegrative consequences of the rapidly expanding scope of intrasocietal activities undertaken by modern governments.[26] However, the situation is more complex than this. Myrdal's argument fails to distinguish among sources of problems generating governmental activity. It is from the societal community that problems requiring expansion of governmental activity most explicitly originate—while problems of an economic-adaptive kind are frequently external in their significance, problems suggesting the need for international collaboration or problems deriving from the penetration of one national society by business enterprises from another society.

Such considerations do not, however, cast much doubt on the main thrust of Myrdal's thesis. For example, Angell has recently concluded that the general effect of business activity in "host" societies is to sustain or arouse negative attitudes towards the society of which the relevant business personnel are members.[27] Angell's data come mainly from business and industrial activity in developed societies. In the case of such activity on the part of industrial corporations in the less-developed societies, the negative attitudes are much more intense, on all available evidence, a circumstance which is in large part contingent upon the fact that investment in less-developed countries involves bringing in a wider variety and greater proportionate numbers of personnel, including even semiskilled labor.[28] It might be argued that in some cases where societies are threatened by a powerful economic "intruder"— such as those of Western Europe in relation to American business enterprise — they are likely to escalate international-integrative moves *in response* to the threat.[29] But the degree to which they are able in fact to do this depends in large part precisely on the variables delineated in the present discussion.

SOCIETIES, STATES, AND POLITIES

We turn again, and in more detail, to the relationships between political subsystems and their societal contexts, maintaining at the same time a sensitivity to the implications which these have for interactions between national societies. Although the present essay is not directed in any specific or concentrated sense toward Parsons' (highly problematic, but very important) discussion of media of interchange, it is clear that in view of the recent prominence of those media in action theory we will have to remain conscious of their relevance. In particular we have to keep an eye on the relationships between power (the medium centered on the polity) and value commitments (centered on the L subsystem) and between power and influence (centered on the I subsystem). In principle, clarification of processes of inflation and deflation of these media in relation to each other ought to be developed through discussion of the emphases which specific societies place upon interchanges between particular subsystems (see Appendix).

Galtung argues that the basic structural condition for change in the international system (and the global sociocultural system as a whole) should be seen as "the consequences of the incompatibilities between state and society, between the nation-state and the social orders that it contains or is contained by it."[30] The elemental ideas entailed in this proposition are: first, that modern industrial societies are growing out of the nation-state "shell": second, that developing or modernizing societies are growing into that "shell."

The "logic of the socio-economic forces currently in operation (in industrialized societies) is such as to lead to the breakup of national boundaries, and this logic . . . will prevail over ideological distinctions."[31] Galtung envisages that, given contemporary trends, the flow of personnel, goods, and information across national boundaries "will contribute tremendously to the erosion of the nation-state. . . . Nations will look more like Armenians and Jews before Israel. This may also sometime in the 1970s facilitate the solution of the German problem in Central Europe."[32] In contrast the immediate problems of less-developed societies consist in evolving a nation-state structure. Galtung predicts that as such trends unfold the world will come to consist in a highly developed complex of interlocked "nations" embracing "the Kennedy Grand Design vision of an Atlantic Community, the de Gaulle vision of a Europe expressed in the 1957 Treaty of Rome. . . ."[33] faced by a group of less-developed nations which will in the early 1970s organize themselves in a "heavily ideological, rather than organic co-operative" manner against the developed nations.[34] These are challenging propositions, which merit close attention in their own right, although we use them here mainly as a discussive springboard. It should also be noted that Angell has produced data-backed arguments in favor of the idea that transnational participation is slowly but inexorably yielding more accommodative relations between most national societies.[35]

The socioeconomic forces whose "logic" Galtung dwells upon are primarily those connected with the rapid growth of the tertiary sector of modern occupational systems. He foresees a situation in which the vast majority of the populations of the more developed industrial societies will be employed in tertiary, professional-technological occupations. It is, he contends, precisely this kind of occupation that yields political identifications and loyalties which deny the relevance of the nation state. Typically, he sees loyalties as therefore going beyond the national level in the direction of crossnational commitments (identification with two or more societies) transnational commitments (identifications which transcend national boundaries as such), or supranational commitments (identification with supranational agencies or organizations such as UNO). Of these three possibilities, the transnational form of identification is the most threatening to the survival of the nation-state international system. It is also the one to which Galtung devotes particular attention. His arguments in this respect hinge particularly on the rapid growth in the number of International Non-Governmental Organizations (INGOs). At present there are about 1600. Loyalties to INGOs constitute in fact both a subnational identification (to the collectivity or quasi-group within the national society)and a transnational identification (to the collectivity formed across national boundaries by constituent collectivities). The growth in INGOs is connected by Galtung with such developments as the internationalization of political ideologies, of age-sets, and of peace specialists and development engineers.

Meanwhile, Galtung predicts that, apart from new professions being created, old professions will become increasingly "denationalized." We could add that in the late 1960s and up to the time of writing nonprofessional forms of work have seen a significant degree of denationalization—at least at the top-leadership level—in the sense that Galtung uses the term. We think here in particular of the attempts early in 1971 on the part of labor union leaders in the Ford section of the automobile industry to coordinate union actions across national boundaries in protection of Ford workers generally. This was a consequence of threats by the Ford company to reduce its investments and scale of production in Britain, threats based—at least ostensibly—upon the demands of Ford workers in the latter country

for substantial pay increases. Whether this and other less publicized developments of a similar kind constitute genuine denationalization is a question which will be subsumed under more general considerations in subsequent sections of this essay.

It is not possible to deny either the facts or the importance of Galtung's focus on the expansion of tertiary occupations and the rapid growth rate of INGOs; but his interpretation is open to serious question. Here we will present three sets of objections to his arguments.

The first objection is a purely methodological one. Galtung's thesis is based on the assumption that we can and should hold constant the presumed values of occupational quasi-groups. If we discern that tertiary occupations are expanding, then we should concomitantly assume that the values now held by those in tertiary occupations will also expand. In such terms, a society consisting only in tertiary occupations would be a society which aggregatively exhibited tertiary occupational values, where our conception of tertiary occupational values depended solely upon what such values are at the present time. The reasoning is inadequate, principally because it takes no account of general structural changes which may occur between times t_1 and t_2. It is also suspect because of the predicate that major values necessarily have an occupational basis. As we shall have cause to mention again, if major changes in values are occurring in the modern period, it is extremely doubtful whether this is a direct outcome of occupational change, although it may well be partly *in response to* occupational restructuring.

Furthermore, and this connects with the point about structural change, Galtung's argument is neglectful of the *stratification* aspects of his extra-polations. He tends to assume that, whereas we can now make distinctions between primary, secondary, and tertiary occupations—distinctions which undoubtedly relate closely to systems of stratification—a society consisting completely of tertiary occupations would not itself manifest significant stratification differentials. One has to hold to the functional theory of stratification only in a very minimal respect to argue that in a society consisting solely in tertiary occupational categories there would be stratification within that range of categories; or, to put the matter differently, the notions of center and periphery so central to Galtung's arguments ought to be conceived of as relative attributes, not absolute ones: in a society where all or nearly all people are employed in tertiary occupations there will be central and peripheral *tertiary* activities.[36]

A second, more substantive criticism concerns the nature of the tertiary occupations which Galtung dwells upon. What he fails to note is the extent to which the employment rates of governments have increased in recent years—the extent to which, in other words, tertiary employment is directed into central governmental channels. It may well be in order to anticipate changes in the operative policies of governmental agencies as a consequence of this; but we seem to have enough evidence to suggest that the selective entry of professional social scientists into the governmental arena does not automatically lead to radicalization of policies or to greater internationalism in the ideological sense.[37] The technification of political problems which Galtung predicts—as have many social scientists before him (notably end-of-ideology theorists)—does not in itself guarantee an attenuation of identification with the national society as the primary and most salient political allegiance. Thus, Galtung's basing of his argument on selected aspects of the changing occupational structure leads him into a dubious sociology-of-knowledge stance, which at root consists in a commitment to the occupational determinism of social values.

Third, Galtung's theses, at least as they apply to the relatively developed sector of the international system, assume all too readily that the polity, or as he puts it, the state, yields before the pressure of the social order. This aspect of his argument is, of course, most relevant to the central concerns of this essay. It can be faulted on two principal grounds: first, it fails to take into reckoning the possibility of considerable variation in the structure of the relationships between polity and society in the highly industrialized societies of the world; second, it omits sustained attention to the reactions of central governmental personnel and collectivities to changes in political loyalties away from the national society as such. Governmental reactions to the political defection of radicals or "protorevolution" in France and, most conspicuously of all, the U.S.A. show just how vital a consideration this should be.

Clearly, this is where our previously adumbrated typology of pure strategies of governmental response to internal problem loads becomes particularly relevant. Systematic analysis of particular societies in terms of this typology and elaborations of it presented in this essay would, we suggest, considerably illuminate the work of those who have examined themes such as the structural interlocking of industrial societies, transnational attenuations of the nation state, and so on.

De Jouvenel has warned us well about the dangers of being led into "thinking that events in the political order fit the needs of the social economy. . . ."[38] He argues that "since these needs can be grasped by rational analysis, we end up assuming that politics is the rational adjuvant of social change—an assumption which unfortunately is without foundation."[39] Thus, what we should not do is to deduce political

changes from forecasts, predictions, or extrapolations based on social structural, technological, or economic changes. As De Jouvenel says, "this is not to say that such changes do not affect politics, but that our knowledge or forecasts of such changes do not entail necessary political forecasts."[40] In order to get at political changes, in the context of social structural, economic, and technological change, we have to move to another level of forecasting, which involves, again to invoke De Jouvenel, a form of prediction oriented to the behavior of those in positions of societal power and authority—one which is clearly tenuous and difficult, involving "guesses concerning the choice and timing of unique moves by a few individuals. . . ."[41] Increasing transnational interactions and communications alter the environment in which central governments operate, but clearly governments do not leave such developments to themselves.

Recently there has been a tendency for those working within the broad domain of political science and political sociology to question the sociological tendency to see politics as a projection of social structure or as a translation of conflicts and processes of change within the wider society. One of the most telling of such critiques is that of Sartori, whose general position is captured well by the following: "As long as we take for granted that cleavages are *reflected in*, not *produced by*, the political system itself, we necessarily neglect to ask to what extent conflicts and cleavages may either be channelled, deflected, and repressed or, *vice versa*, activated and reinforced, precisely by the operations and operators of the political system."[42] In terms of the present discussion, the significance of Sartori's argument lies in his pointing to the need for the "simultaneous exploration" of how the political system is affected by the society and how, reciprocally, the society is affected by the polity.

The main thrust of our criticisms of what we would describe as neo-utopian views of the future shape of international and transnational relations is that they fail to take into account political variables which relate closely to the maintenance of national boundaries and of nationhood itself—that is, the polity-society relationship in its international context. Galtung includes attention to such variables only in their dependency function and does not consider seriously the possibility of their being independent or even intervening variables. At least this is true of his focus on the more highly developed nations—for Third World societies he sees, as we have indicated, as growing into the nation-state situation. Lest our criticisms of neo-utopian views seem to be too prominent, it should be said that it is only through comprehension of the "harsh realities" of the international scene that we can gain anything approaching control over it. In any case "international" models are not necessarily any more liberal than so-called national ones. The debate about the "brain drain" has shown that the international approach may be, to take but one aspect, much less egalitarian than the national approach.[43]

It is a matter of simple intuitive observation that some societies are more prone to transnational penetration or emanation than are others.[44] It is equally clear that membership of INGOs emanating from some societies is more definitely sponsored and overseered, indeed censored, than others. Some Communist societies seem to allow only "reliable" individuals to join in the activities of INGOs, while many non-Communist societies are, so to speak, "careful" about transnational penetrations of their societies, and others are "careless." Some societies of the "careful" type, such as contemporary Britain, show few signs of liberalizing their relatively tight surveillance of immigration patterns. Britain in particular has become increasingly rigid in this respect during the past decade, as exemplified by its policy on Asians in East Africa; its financial discrimination against overseas students; and its 1971 legislation on immigration. Operationally, the delineation of transnational and international communications is exceedingly difficult. Any individual INGO may have have a relatively free, voluntaristic, and uncontrolled set of memberships from one cluster of countries but a governmentally-sifted set of memberships from another cluster. The former might safely be labelled conceptually as transnational communication, but there are good grounds for calling the latter international. Even in the area of capitalistic industrial enterprise and investment the matter is by no means analytically simple, as industrial firms very frequently work in conjunction with and under terms and facilities specified by governmental agencies (see our later comments on the "multinational" corporation). It is clear also that the significance of membership and participation in INGOs varies among the different kinds of society. To belong to an INGO on the basis of prior attachment to the relevant collectivity in a relatively more-developed society is less likely to lead, it would seem, to attenuation of national-cultural commitment than is the case with participation on the basis of prior attachment to a collectivity in a less-developed society. It would be expected that greater prestige accrues to the participant in his home society in the latter case. Confirmation of such a hypothesis would at the very least complicate Galtung's ideas about less-developed societies growing into the nation state "shell."

The strong version of the thesis that the more-developed societies are undergoing processes of mutual structural interlocking is thus suspect primarily because it assumes at least a neutral attitude on the part of governments to such tendencies and also because it assumes too readily that national loyalties are easily eschewed. It probably is the case that there is occurring a diminution of the prestige of central-governmental politicians, at least among some sections of a number of modern societies. Many arguments of this kind seem to rest on the claim that while the populations of industrial societies become more restless or more apathetic in relation to central-governmental politics the latter remain unchanged and their societal significance thereby becomes seriously attenuated—to the point that central-governmental politicians no longer have legitimacy and the nation-state situation collapses in favor of either structurally interlocked international complexes or subnational developments. But why assume that strains centering on conceptions of citizenship and social values will not yield relatively internal changes in political organization and participation—a circumstance that would be facilitated by the governmental strategy which we have conceptualized as one of engagement? Strategies of deflection or disposal would both inhibit the consequences of internal occupational change and increasing transnational participation foreseen by Galtung. It should be said that the phenomenon of increasing transnational participation has been examined explicitly by Angell in terms of its impact upon political elites, which is really the only adequate way of tackling the problem. In our judgement, however, the evidence and reasoning produced by Angell to support his view about the positive, accommodative effects on elites of increasing transnational participation is not conclusive.[45]

In the existing body of social-scientific work, two sets of foci stand out as being especially relevant to estimating the degree to which national societies are undergoing processes of boundary breakdown and loss of integralness: first, the analysis of changing patterns of political involvement, and second, the analysis of the relationship between interaction and communication across national boundaries and the intensity of interaction and communication within national boundaries. In this latter area of inquiry the work of Deutsch has been particularly vital. We will deal with each of these in turn and, subsequently, try to bring them together with some analytic and interpretive consistency.

A major thrust of work in recent political sociology has been the examination of the long-term processes by and through which previously excluded groups and quasi-groups become incorporated into the societal community in such a way as to attenuate the salience of sociocultural cleavages, which in turn ramify into the operation of the political system.[46] There has been, undoubtedly, a marked tendency for mainstream social scientists to argue that, at least in the liberal democracies, processes of citizenship inclusion have in the modern period come to some kind of stable head. Exceptions have been recognized, particularly in view of various political developments in the late 1960s. A good example of the latter recognition, expressed in the context of the general tendency to view citizenship inclusion as a kind of unfolding, evolutionary process is Parsons' discussion of the status of the black American.[47] Recognizing the trauma and explosive potential of the current relationships between black and white in American society, Parsons does nevertheless project the view that black Americans generally will be included politically within the societal community on roughly the same terms as other relatively deprived ethnic quasi-groups have in the past. He does stress that the inclusion of this particular ethnic group will, because of the circumstances of color and race, occur on a more pluralistic basis than many previous cases of ethnic inclusion. Conventional conceptions of processes of citizenship inclusion, in broad outline at least, converge upon the idea of "total" citizenship as involving the attainment of legal, political and social rights (and obligations)—respectively equality before the law; franchise access and equality; and some form of social welfare protection.[48]

However, the last decade or so has clearly witnessed pressures for an extension of citizenship beyond this point to a more definitely political *power* level —a form of power which connects with diffuse considerations of control over life-chances, a more adequate synchronization in effect of basic value-commitments and political power. In many liberal-democratic societies there have arisen a variety of demands for further control over both differentiated sectors of modern societies and more diffuse aspects of the life-opportunities of individuals and groups. In this latter connection we may mention the resurgence of nationalism among a large number of ethnic and territorial groups in the Western world—Welsh, Scots, and Irish in the U.K.; Bretons in France; the French in Canada; Indians, Negroes, and Chicanos in the U.S., and so on. In the former, more specialized and differentiated category we need note only the generalized phenomenon of the rapid proliferation of organizations and movements from many sectors of modern societies demanding control over such aspects of life as education, air and food quality, noise abatement, and so on—almost *ad infinitum.*

Clearly it would be a major research task to make sociological sense of such developments.[49] Major analytic clues to the evident recent dissatisfaction with conventional political procedures in Western democracies may be found in, for example, Parsons' conception of evolutionary universals, which sequentially generate new societal problems to be solved.[50] The most modern of Parsons' universals is that of the development of structures of "democratic association." Although Parsons himself sees these structures as having in fact already in large part been developed in a number of Western societies, notably the U.S., it seems clear now that such processes of democratization have not yet reached their peak. We suggest that political democratization of the liberal type in itself engenders further demands for wider participation, for processes of "fundamental democratization," to adopt and extend Mannheim's phrase.[51]

In examining the structure of political oppositions in Western democracies, Dahl has asked whether there are "possible sources of (political) alienation . . . that might foster new structural oppositions?" Tentatively, he suggests that there are three likely sources: conflicts over distribution, international politics, and "the new democratic Leviathan itself."[52] Writing before many of the more salient political crises of the last few years—in America, France, Italy, Northern Ireland, and so on—Dahl wondered whether the traditionally rightist opposition to the "new Democratic Leviathan" might well not be equalled or surpassed by a leftist opposition, a circumstance which has been significantly realized. In respect of the third source Dahl underlines the development of ideas concerning the remoteness, distance, and impersonality of democracies which are welfare-oriented, bureaucratic, centralized, and controlled by competition and bargaining among highly organized elites.

Undoubtedly, social-structural factors are of great importance in our coming to terms sociologically with the recent presentation of new political demands in Western societies—the strains between institutions of higher education and the structure of modern occupational systems, the proliferation of increasingly comprehensive professional organizations, the intensification of generational conflict on some critical sites in most societies, the economic and political exigencies that have led to pressures for greater functionalization of political structures, and so on. But no complete understanding of these could be obtained without a thorough analysis of the cultural factors which have constrained and guided the situational interpretation of them. It is these cultural factors which ultimately, we feel, in line with Parsons' similar insistence in respect of societal evolution generally, will be of greater long-run significance.[53] Although it is outside the scope of our present discussion to explore these, since they would lead us into an analysis of action systems in their entirety, it is worth noting that what appears to have come to a head in the modern period is an essentially secular utopianism, the leading attributes of which are: a concern with wide *control* over life chances, a commitment to *anticipating* and *planning* for the future, and a preoccupation with *well-being* at both the individual and collectivity levels. Such developments have remarkably significant implications for the exercise of political control and governmental activities generally, in a way which may well have a cultural and societal importance equalling the reconstruction of value systems involved in the Protestant Reformation. We are, it should be emphasized, not arguing that such cultural changes of Western cultural systems are autonomous and emanative. Clearly, the structural strains which we have pinpointed are critical; but, to repeat, it is the cultural changes that, once crystallized, function as the long-term variables of greater independent significance.

The cultural changes of which we have spoken constitute basic redefinitions of "the societal situation." (In the total action system this has to do with the medium operative in the L-subsystem.) No exact empirical evidence of which we are aware taps this problem; increasing theoretical interest in the relationship between structural change and patterns of symbolic meaning holds great promise. The work of Douglas on this theme bears directly upon demands for control over life-chances and participation in modern societies. Douglas has shown how structural differentiation is yielding fundamental problems of individual identity in the modern period, developments which she has linked to various forms of radical deviance in Western societies.[54] Douglas also explores the respects in which differentiation within action systems and differentiation of the action system from its physical and natural environments yield *symbolic* crises, although her work is not expounded in the terms of action theory. Clearly, this style of work is highly compatible with Parsons' approach to the inflation and deflation of value commitments.[55]

We turn now to a consideration of the relationship between interaction and communication across national boundaries and interaction and communication within such boundaries. As has been noted, this sphere of discussion and analysis is one in which conceptual clarity has been singularly lacking and in which we again lack the appropriate data. More precisely, we lack empirical evidence which is adequate in determining the extent to which interaction across national boundaries is having any significant effect on the structure of international relations or upon allegiance to the national society—Angell's work being nearest to adequacy in this respect.[56] There is a danger, indeed a strong likelihood, that social scientists generalize in part from their own

dispositions and circumstances when they speak strongly of rejections of the national political loyalty.

The empirical evidence bearing on this problem which we do possess is extremely difficult to interpret.[57] It definitely points to an increase in transactions and communications across national boundaries and an increase in membership of International Non-Governmental Organizations. On the other hand, as Deutsch in particular has shown, the increase in communications across national boundaries has been, on many indicators, relatively smaller than the increase of communication across national boundaries; but the ratio of internal to external communications has in many instances also increased. This pattern of communication flows—an absolute increase but a relative decline—is almost certainly paralleled in the area of membership of organizations. Although it should be emphasized that we possess no empirical proof of this, our firm speculation is that whereas membership of INGOs and number of INGOs has increased substantially, as has membership of supranational organizations, the increase in membership of and growth in number of organizations within societies has been relatively greater.[58] Thus we are proposing that what Deutsch has found for certain types of transaction flow is paralleled by organizational involvement—an overmatching of transnational communication by intrasocietal communication.

A further illustration of this argument is that for all the developments in the direction of nonnationally prescribed communication and participation, it is probably the case that these are overmatched by such important phenomena as increasing governmental attempts to localize planning and government in a number of societies. For example, we may cite the development in Britain of regional planning agencies and in America the proliferation of community-controlled welfare and economic agencies of various kinds. It might be argued that some developments of this kind may actually undercut the loyalty salience of the national political center, leading eventually to the development of what Kaiser calls transnational societies or subsystems.[59] But there are no grounds for assuming that many of the developments mentioned here do more than lead to increasing interdependence within the international system, which as we have already suggested does not necessarily impair the boundary-maintaining capacities of the national society as such.

The proliferation of intrasocietal collectivities is, we suggest, part of the more general tendency for the members of modern societies to become increasingly concerned to "put their own houses in order." Many of these collectivities are antigovernmental, "extraparliamentary," or oriented to grassroots political issues. But the major point is that they are primarily concerned with internal problems; a lot of them have international consequences only through governmental translation of the problems into extranational terms (*allocation* or *deflection*).

Of course, many intrasocietal collectivities are not ostensibly antigovernmental, although some are militantly progovernmental ("silent majorities" can become "vocal majorities"). But ultimately the most serious sociological point to be made about intrasocietal collectivity proliferation is that the "density" of intrasocietal affairs is increasing, we suggest, disproportionally in relation to the "density" of transnational and international affairs. Unless this feature of modern societies is precipitated into the international arena by governments, we see no short-term likelihood of this having an extranational significance. Thus, national boundaries could remain resilient by default, as it were. It should quickly be added at this juncture that what we have just argued in no way implies that the affairs and attributes of other societies are of no consequence for the members of a given society. But the emergence of an international system in which modernization consists in the process of societies selectively adopting other societies as reference points, positive or negative (a phenomenon with which we have dealt elsewhere[60]) is in no way incompatible with a situation in which social energy is focused primarily upon the internal problems of national societies.

These tendencies, in the direction of further processes of citizenship inclusion and increasing organizational involvement within societies, point to the necessity of our seriously considering the view that the internal integration of societies may well have much further to go than is claimed by many of those social scientists who have explored issues such as the development of transnational systems, supranational systems, and processes of political unification. As we will propose more fully towards the end of this essay, the arguments that we have produced in favor of this idea do not entail the conclusion that international relations will thereby persist in modes similar to those prevailing at the present time. But many of the likely changes will be, we contend, largely contingent upon the increasing concern with modernization, the latter term having to do with the acquisition of "societal quality."

TYPES OF RELATIONSHIP BETWEEN POLITY AND SOCIETY

Nettl drew a distinction between elitist and constitutional political cultures, which he saw as a special adaptation of Parsons' diffuseness-specificity pattern

variable. In an elitist society, of which the Soviet Union and Britain are claimed as examples, political relationships are "viewed as informal and distinct." There is an emphasis upon "consensus and its corollary, obscurity, as against definition and proclamation. . . . Differentiation tends to be confined to the relatively 'low' hierarchical level of roles rather than collectivities. In extreme cases even political roles fail to crystallize clearly and differentiatedly: *role consensus is low because roles are not to be seen as sharply defined.*"[61] Consensus functions to sustain the existing state of affairs or to adapt given institutions to new exigencies. In contrast, in constitutional societies, such as the U.S., the political subsystem is "strongly differentiated," with "an autonomously recruited and specific authority structure within it, and above all one that is based on formal institutions. These are stable objects of reverence and utility."[62]

It is clear that this aspect of Nettl's approach to the analysis of political systems involves some confusion of cultural and social-structural levels of analysis. This slippage produces the idea of there being a simple straightforward connection between the elitist-constitutional culture distinction and the degree of (social) differentiation of and within the polity. There is, however, evidence that societies manifesting a constitutional political culture do not necessarily possess congruently differentiated political subsystems, as has been convincingly demonstrated by Huntingdon in his comparison of European and American processes of modernization.[63] On the other side of the coin, it would be highly misleading to conceive of elitist cultures as having little or no differentiation of their political subsystems. What is frequently found in such cases, particularly in totalitarian societies, is a compressed form of differentiation. Compressed differentiation is closely related to what Fischer has called "dual leadership patterns" (i.e., political and economic) in reference to Soviet society and what Almond and Powell refer to as a lack of subsystemic autonomy under conditions of role and task differentiation.[64]

In spite of this and associated difficulties in deploying Nettl's concepts, we believe that the elitist-constitutional distinction is viable. It should be made as clear as possible, however, that the designation "elitist" does not imply that there are no constitutional apparati in the relevant society nor, conversely, that constitutional societies possess no elites. The distinction has to do, in the broadest sense, with processes, mechanisms, and rationales underlying claims to political legitimacy. In the constitutionalistic U.S., political elites tend to be fashioned in, and in a sense *by,* a complex web of formal institutions.[65] In contrast, in another relatively constitutionalistic society, France, there has been a greater tendency, notably in the Gaullist era, for the elites themselves to fashion the formal institutions. This statement cannot be applied to the administrative bureaucracy, given the salience of the Ecole National d'Administration and the extensive in-service training norms traditional to the bureaucracy. In this latter, administrative, respect there are some strong elitist elements in the French societal context.[66] Over-all, however, France has clearly been, since the French Revolution, a constitution-oriented society.

Legitimacy claims, including of course in some cases claims to use force extensively, are referred directly in elitist societies to categories of personnel, traditions, and political doctrines. Clearly there is variation in this domain, as there is in the constitutional category. In the Soviet Union the self-conscious visibility of a political elite maintaining continuous supremacy in reference to a frequently manipulated self-serving political doctrine contrasts strongly with the more implicit, less continuous and relatively non-doctrinaire form of elitism in British society. What these two societies do have in common at a higher level of abstraction is their subordination of explicated and differentiated rules and procedures to groups, group cohesiveness, and, in the broadest sense, political philosophy. As we will shortly see, the variation on deployment of political philosophy can be highlighted by the introduction of another variable.

It is evident that societies vary a great deal in respect of the congruity between their internal sociocultural attributes and the requirements of participation in international systems, and indeed that they also vary in respect of the degree to which they manifest state-like qualities. Nettl suggested (mainly in a context other than that in which the elitist/constitutionalistic distinction was developed) that we should regard the notion of the state as a conceptual variable; his basic contention was that stateness is externally invariant insofar as societies interact as national-political entities but that it varies in internal-societal terms.[67] That is, societies differ in the degree to which they manifest stateness in their internal operation. Clearly, most African and Asian societies are disjunctive in respect of the internal-external distinction. Their ambassadors, diplomats, delegates to the U.N., and so on have been rapidly inducted into the norms of international interaction on a basically Western model, whereas their internal cultural and social systems are characterized by very different principles.[68] Such disjunctiveness is especially evident in the case of those less-developed societies which traditionally have had a definite cultural consciousness, and some structural characteristics, of stateness—societies such as Ceylon, Burma, and Indonesia—but which have had to find a new form of stateness in the (formally defined) post-colonial period.[69] (There is also the added complication that some languages—such as Arabic and other Middle Eastern languages — have had major difficulties in dealing with many abstract political terms, like that of "the state.")[70]

However, stateness as a variable also applies to the more-developed societies, which is our more immediate concern. France and Russia have, in continuous historical respects, manifested greater degrees of stateness than have, for example, Britain or the U.S. In the modern world we have to acknowledge, then, that, as Rokkan puts it, "the national centre can be organized around collectivities and coalitions varying markedly in power resources and styles of legitimation: the national centre need not constitute a 'state' except in the elementary sense that it is the locus of external representation."[71]

Rokkan's important synthesis of the work of leading theorists of political processes has to be further refined. We have defined the elitism/constitutionalism distinction as having to do with modes of legitimation. As we see it, the stateness variable has to do with phenomenal imagery concerning the center of the societal-political process, that is, whether there is an orientational emphasis upon an agency "out there" in which resides the basis for societally organized effectiveness or whether the effectiveness of the society is considered (phenomenally speaking) to reside more diffusely in the society qua society. It is worth noting in passing that this analytic distinction seems to echo disagreements within the social contract debates of the seventeenth and eighteenth centuries. It is thus a good example of the transition from political philosophizing to empirical-analytic explication. It may also be added that our characterization of the stateness variable injects an important "ethno" consideration into the center/periphery distinction. In our terms this distinction cannot be imposed upon a society in an objectivist manner; it is a matter of subjective, symbolic significance.[72]

We can now cross-tabulate our elitism/constitutionalism and stateness/nonstateness distinctions:

Mode of political legitimation

		Elitism	Constitutionalism
Image of societally organized effectiveness	Stateness	1	3
	Nonstateness	2	4

This typology of polity/society relationships has to be related to the LIGA schema, bearing in mind what was said earlier concerning the nature of the problem loads of modern societies. It will be recalled that we argued in terms of there being both L/G and I/G problems in a number of societies, most notably the U.S. Our characterizations of the elitism/constitutionalism and stateness/nonstateness variables connect with these (sociopolitically) problematic relationships in the following ways.

Priority of Input/Output Emphasis	Variable Type
Into G:	
L→G	Constitutionalism
I→G	Elitism
Out from G:	
G→L	Stateness
G→I	Nonstateness

The arrows denoting the relationships between functional subsystems show the direction of *impact* of one subsystem upon another subsystem. Our presentation thus departs from the normal use of Parsons' subsystem interchange model. It glosses over, particularly, the emphasis upon the double-interchange nature of that model. We do not believe, however, that it actually violates any basic principle of action theory. It must be recognized in particular that we are addressing here rather specialized relationships between subsystems, with G as the pivot in each case. Thus, in the case of constitutionalism there is an emphasis upon the formation of pre-political identities, involving particularly rituals and symbols of political significance. Societal values are explicitly and directly at stake in the L→G input. A stress upon constitutionality is in effect an explicit attempt to articulate politically the values of a society. The polity, even though it may have a differentiated form of autonomy is, so to speak, "there" as a concrete mode of value expression and implementation. As Rokkan has put it, the L→G relationship involves acceptance (or nonacceptance) of and support (or nonsupport) for what he calls "territorial agencies."[73] In contrast, the I→G relationship has to do in Rokkan's terms with questions concerning acceptance of and support for the distribution of "control powers." This clearly is in line with the tendency in action theory to regard the I subsystem as encompassing the stratificational aspects of a social system. What the polity receives is in the I→G case a relatively implicit set of inputs, concerning not explicated values and commitments and a corresponding emphasis upon socializative translation of those values into the political arena but rather norms

and influence capacities associated with a relatively "tight" system of stratification, in which values get raised only in times of societal strain.[74] Conversely, in the constitutional case it is norms and stratificational aspects of inclusion which get raised in periods of strain. Thus, the "master notion" which distinguishes constitutionalism from elitism is the explicit nature of the legitimation process of the former and the implicit process involved in the latter.

Turning to our second variable, stateness/nonstateness, we see that stateness (an emphasis upon the G→L relationship) involves according the polity what — rephrasing Rokkan — we can call penetrative capacities.[75] The polity is traditionally regarded in societies manifesting stateness as being the center of that society. To put the matter in a different way, the polity is regarded as being something more distant, more separate, from the rest of society than in the nonstate cases. The latter involve the polity in treating individuals and collectivities as already part of a societal community and less in need of direct "political treatment." In line with the LIGA hierarchy the closer proximity of the societal community, cybernetically speaking, to the polity as compared with the pattern-maintenance subsystems relationship, highlights this point. Nonstate societies thus do not have a center/periphery problem, relatively speaking. The paramountcy of the G→I relationship makes the impact of the polity on "society" more concerned with allocation than with penetration.

There is an intimate connection between this typological elaboration of the political attributes of a society and the manner in which governmental agencies and personnel cope with internal problem loads. The way in which this connection will be explicated is by linking stateness, nonstateness, elitism, and constitutionalism to a "correspondent" in the category of governmental strategies.

It is proposed that stateness tends to facilitate *disposing* strategies. The distance between "society" and polity lends to the latter a capacity to "get rid" of problems and demands on a primarily internal basis. In contrast, nonstateness facilitates the strategy of engagement — a willingness to come to terms with problems and to meet many internally-generated demands. This contrast may be further highlighted by observing that a state society is likely to have brittle loyalties but a relatively great capacity for exercising political leverage over its members. The reverse is the case with a society manifesting a condition of nonstateness. In the latter case, loyalty is relatively unproblematic, as it is diffusely embedded in and across the society; on the other hand, governmental leverage capacity is relatively brittle.[76]

Elitism, we suggest, is particularly facilitative of deflective strategies. Governmental elites in societies manifesting this attribute are able, in the face of large problem loads, to "get away" from internal problems through the deference they command and their ability to diagnose problems as being due to an agency other than themselves. Constitutionalism is more facilitative of allocative strategies, as it manifests in structural terms a tendency to establish special-purpose agencies and roles for dealing with particular problems. A society manifesting the attribute of constitutionalism is more likely than others to have a range of institutional devices to match the range of internal (and for that matter, external) problems. Let it quickly be said, however, that this does not mean that a society with constitutional attributes will thereby be more successful in coping with its problems. All that we are saying here is that such a society is more facilitative than others with respect to "sharing" its problems with other societies. Actually sharing may well involve imposing problems on other societies, which is precisely why earlier we put the word "partners" in quotation marks when speaking of the external (international) conditions required for the adoption of an allocative strategy.

Because we have already cross-tabulated the variables of stateness/nonstateness and elitism/constitutionalism, we are logically required to indicate that specific types of society tend to work within certain corresponding ranges of pure strategies:

Type 1 (Elitism/Stateness): Deflect/Dispose
Type 2 (Elitism/Nonstateness): Deflect/Engage
Type 3 (Constitutionalism/Stateness): Allocate/ Dispose
Type 4 (Constitutionalism/Nonstateness): Allocate/Engage

It must be emphasized that this set of relationships has to do only with tendencies based upon the polity/society relationship of the national society in question. It is not intended that one should be able to predict the strategies (or rather, the range of strategies) in the righthand column solely on the basis of the categorization of a given society in the appropriate lefthand column. As we have suggested, we also need to know about the internal circumstances and the international context in which the society operates in order to do this. All we are saying here is that the characteristics of the lefthand column tend to predispose the relevant society to work within the range of categories indicated in the corresponding row in the righthand column. Its ability to do this successfully depends upon its conditions of legitimation and effectiveness, as previously diagrammed. Thus, any given society possesses a specific "structural set" (defined here in terms of the elitism/constitutionalism and stateness/nonstateness di-

chotomies, or, in more elaborate forms, continua). This set yields a "normal" range of pure strategies, strategies which are, so to speak, *natural* to the society in question. On the other hand, as we have seen, these strategies may not work, because either the internal or external circumstances (or even both of these) are resistant to such treatment. Indeed, sustained intractibility of adaptive problems and escalation of demands from other subsystem sources will, in terms of our model, lead to changes in the structural set and its corresponding range of governmental strategies. We may indicate, as examples of each of our types, Russia as approximating type 1; Britain, type 2; France, type 3; the U.S., type 4. This does not mean, however, that there is fixity with respect to the appropriate characteristics. In any case, it must be very heavily emphasized that it is best to think in terms of societies as distributable across a property space defined by the two continua of elitism/constitutionalism and stateness/nonstateness. In such a more elaborate depiction, France would be placed less definitely at the state/elitist extreme than the respective locations of our three other examples.

We propose that societies with statelike attributes tend to be relatively unlikely to become involved in transnational systems. Stateness provides a clear focal point for internal political activity; and statist societies are more inclined towards and have "good" facilities for putting down their internal problems. State societies are more prone to revolutionary situations because there is one single visible reference point for the expression of political grievance, although it is also the case that societies may become more statelike in response to heavy problem loads directed at the governmental apparatus and personnel, as has almost certainly occurred in recent American history. Thus societies such as France and Russia are on this score relatively resistant to transnational "emanations," quite apart from the question of whether they allow transnational "intrusions" into their societal "selves."[77] In contrast, societies with nonstate attributes are more facilitative of transnational emanations and intrusions; and, therefore, if structural interlocking and the bypassing of national political centers is to take place on any significant scale it will, in our terms, necessarily involve most typically societies with nonstate characteristics in the special sense in which we have defined nonstateness.

Supernational developments are probably best facilitated by societies possessing constitutional attributes, attributes which facilitate their developing institutional complexes with sufficient flexibility to cope simultaneously both internally and externally. If the constitutionalism is combined with statism the society can shed some of its problems externally — as France has done in respect of its economic problems — while holding its more resiliently internal problems at bay. If constitutionalism is combined with nonstatism, then a more "schizoid" situation may arise if internal problem loads become very heavy. American governments have become increasingly subject to dilemmas arising from the relationship between external and internal issues. Type 4 societies are prone to strains arising from coordinating and integrating differentiated governmental structures. In the present context, the most significant of such strains are those centering upon the relationship between internally oriented and externally oriented problems. Elitism tends to consolidate the "internality" of state forms and to mitigate the transnational flexibilities provided by nonstateness. Elitist, nonstate societies — notably Britain — tend to be "organically holistic." They may manifest a high degree of politicocultural sensitivity to international and transnational affairs, but their internal unity inhibits structural interlocking vis-à-vis other societies.

It would be beyond the scope and space limitations of this paper to explore in detail the full empirical implications of the schemata which have been presented here. We have in effect argued that the development of a more integrated international system and/or the emergence of relatively permanent transnational systems crosscutting relations between national societies qua nations are contingent upon the spread of governmental strategies of the engaging and allocating types. In turn the existences of these types of strategy are conditioned by the relationship between what we have called structural sets and internal societal problems, as well as by the external conditions, confronting any given society. Such stipulations would suggest, admittedly at this stage in a highly intuitive respect, that social-science optimism about the attenuation of national boundaries and the emergence of more peaceful international affairs is to be looked at very sceptically indeed.

The general trend of our argument has been that societies in the developed parts of the world are becoming more introverted because of the increasing difficulty in managing such societies. In these societies internal pressures from "below" are, we have argued, in the direction of more inclusive and wider-ranging forms of citizenship and participation. Governmental elites are having their attentional apparati brought increasingly to bear on these problems.

Although it has deliberately not been a major concern of the present essay, it is necessary to say a few words at this juncture about the less-developed,

Third World sector of the international scene. It is fairly conventional to lump these societies together (except for variations in the inclusion or exclusion of Latin American societies), as is done by Galtung when he makes the previously invoked generalization about the less-developed societies being a situation of growing into the nation-state "shell." However, given the vast number of internal-war situations in these societies, it is difficult to see precisely in what way one can say those societies are becoming more integrated politically.[78]

A more accurate generalization would seem to be that these societies are in large part experiencing processes of primary mobilization. We conceptualize primary mobilization as detachment from primordial loyalties (although these are frequently reasserted in internal-war circumstances). Relatively few of these societies have undergone thorough processes of secondary mobilization, which involves mobilization toward new, non-ascriptive political objects of attachment.

In order to get a more accurate comparative picture we might add a tertiary phase to the distinction between primary and secondary mobilization.[79] This would cover the processes of "post-representational" democratization, which we discussed earlier in reference to the more developed, especially Western, societies. Tertiary mobilization, then, is a process predicated situationally on the motivation to obtain power for the individuals and/or quasi-groups within the context of an already-constituted national society. This difference between more and less developed societies — involving problems attendant upon secondary mobilization in the less developed societies and problems of tertiary mobilization in the developed societies — is, we believe, a major contrast in attributes, a contrast which makes for, at least in the short run, increasing exaggeration of the sociocultural gap between these two international groups.[80] The less-developed societies are more prone to transnational emanations and penetrations in relation to the more developed societies — this being truer of those less-developed societies which have a very low degree of stateness. It is this which makes for a marked fluidity of relations among Third World societies and between those same societies individually and societies in the more developed section.[81]

A general tendency of our discussion has been the avoidance of the view that Western, highly industrialized societies manifest some kind of relatively end-state pattern of political structures. The idea of sequential generation of new political problems is central to our arguments. The concept of tertiary mobilization is illustrative of this standpoint. Technically, we would express primary mobilization as the differentiation of G processes from the ascriptive matrix of an L/I base; secondary mobilization as the differentiation of I processes from an L matrix in relation to G; and tertiary mobilization as a "triangulated" process of bringing G, L, and I into a more stable alignment. Tertiary mobilization is not regarded here as any kind of end-state. Problems centering on the A subsystem may well generate another phase of mobilization.

CONCLUSION

We have attempted to sketch in some of the major considerations necessary to the analysis of relations between societies as national entities. That we have adopted this tack does not entail a commitment to the view that national societies are the only significant actors on the international scene. We have tended to adhere to the so-called conservative view of the resilience of the nation-state, or, as Etzioni puts it, "tribal" system — but not, it should be emphasized, through any philosophical or political commitment to its attractiveness.[82] Moreover, in arguing in this way we have not intended to support views which see relations between nations as solely and necessarily understood in terms of power considerations. On the contrary, one thread of the discussion underlines the growing concern in the contemporary world with *the internal quality* of societies. Clearly there are important areas of the international system where such a concern is not specially conspicuous at the present time. But "welfarism" in the broadest sense does seem to be increasing in importance. In spite of the tendency we do adhere to the distinction between "high" and "welfare" politics, the former being one of major conservers of the national-societal structure.[83]

There has deliberately been no attempt here to discern an emergent pattern of international global relations as such.[84] We have been more concerned with the society→international-system theme than the international-system→society theme. This is mainly because of our assessment of the importance of the societal constraints operating in the modern period. On the other hand, the implications of what has been said for changes in the structure of relations between nations should be briefly noted. In the more developed sector of the worldwide international system, the introversional preoccupations of national societies (which as such should not be identified with isolationism) makes for a much greater potential flexibility and fluidity in relations between nations — with a high prominence accorded to the selective diffusion of cultural ideals and technical procedures which are considered relevant to any given society's internal problems. However, the discussion has also indicated certain potentials for more violent forms of international relations, notably those having to do with the governmental strategy which we have called deflection. Clearly the strategies we have labelled allocative carry potentially violent consequences, although this does not mean that such strategies automatically entail violent intentions. Additionally, and perhaps of even more threatening significance, the incongruity between the more-developed and the less-developed societies carries a violent potential, which is, of course, a frequent focus of attention among social scientists. Generally, the view of patterns of international relations implied here is one marked by what Young calls political discontinuities — a world of partially overlapping subordinate international systems — where the national society remains the basic acting unit.[85]

The international-system conception projected here is perhaps best captured by Hanson's comments upon social-science optimism about West European integration:

> Three factors led to an overestimation of the expansiveness of functional integration in Europe of the Six. They were first, a failure to relate the process of regional integration closely enough to relevant international system factors; second, a tendency to deny rather than to investigate the discontinuity between high and welfare politics proclaimed by traditionalists; and third, a failure to recognize that sizeable (and equitably distributed) economic gains would result from a common market *coordinated* by sovereign states rather than managed by ceaselessly expanding supranational authorities.[86]

Of course, these comments cannot be regarded as pinpointing the definitive character of the contemporary international scene. We have attempted here to establish some of the more salient attributes of national societies which affect the nature of international and transnational relations. Many predictions and prophecies about the changing structure of such relations have been falsified in the modern period, and in the case of Hanson's conclusions we cannot claim strongly that the pattern he projects will prevail. The European Economic Community has undoubtedly developed so far along the lines which he suggests; but it could be that the growth of so-called multinational corporations will produce sufficient pressures to lead to an "enforced" development of extranational institutions to deal with them.[87]

Of all the transnational developments which we have touched upon, it is almost certainly the industrial corporation which is the most significant. But, given what we have said about the significance of governmental control variables, it would be extremely unwise to assume that the "logic" of multinational industrial enterprise will prevail over the nation-state system. It is very tempting to assume that linkages between societies such as those exhibited in workers putting pressures on employers in one society in order to assist the cause of employees of the same corporation in another society are of far-reaching significance with respect to the viability of nation-state entities. But, as we have said, increasing interdependence should not be confused with integration, either at the nation-state level or at a subnational level. Kindleberger, in the process of delineating the differences between national firms with foreign operations, multinational corporations, and international corporations (all of which frequently are lumped indiscriminately into the same category), has emphasized that their impact depends largely on *national* policies.[88]

The main point of this essay has been to point up the major societal features of the nation-state system and to examine what it is about modern societies that sustains or modifies that system. We have in the main focused upon interplays between societal problems and governmental-control variables. This interplay is a crucial factor in exploring modern trends in international affairs, the major boundary condition of international systems. There are of course important facets of this boundary condition which we have not explored—for example, the kinds of international relationship obtaining between different types of society. Our intention here, however, has been to underline the salience of the societal boundaries of international systems and to initiate analytic tacks with which to handle this problem area. We are well aware that our analysis neither encompasses all relevant variables nor focusses simply on a small number of variables which would facilitate parsimonious manipulation. We take it that the theory of action has been particularly conspicuous for its adoption of precisely this kind of analytic stance, that is, for its steering a path between the Scylla of naturalistic empiricism and the Charybdis of over-facile analytic closure.

APPENDIX

During the course of our discussion we have referred to the symbolic media of interchange which have become so central to Parsons' recent theorizing. Because much of the discussion rested upon ideas drawn from the functional subsystem (LIGA) model, it is obvious that our typology of polity/society relationships is bound up with the connections between those media. Two particular problems of Parsons' development of the media interchange schema have to be borne in mind in this respect. First, Parsons has emphasized that exchanges take place involving two or more of the media—for example, power can be exchanged for influence—and yet the precise nature of such exchanges and their circumstances remains relatively unelaborated. A second, closely associated problem revolves around the hierarchical nature of the media. In this respect Parsons has emphatically stated that the control principles of the LIGA model are equally applicable to the four media: value commitments, influence, power, and money. That is to say that inflationary or deflationary processes—as the case may be—operate on a "downward" basis. Deflation at the level of value commitments, for example, will have deflationary implications at the level of influence, and so on. The degree to which this precludes the autonomous generation of deflationary or inflationary processes at levels below the top one and the possibility of upward escalation of deflation or inflation are not clearly spelled out. The upward-flow process is definitely implied by the thrust of Smelser's analysis of collective behavior; although it is worth noting that the kind of upward-flow process elaborated by Smelser seems to involve what for Parsons are deflationary processes only.[89] This probably emerges most clearly in the case where escalation occurs all the way from what Smelser calls facilities to values, resulting in value-oriented movements. The latter bear a striking resemblance to the situation of fundamentalism and de-differentiation which Parsons uses to characterize the process of deflation of value commitments.[90]

Theoretical progress in this problem area would seem to hinge upon a more complete and elaborate comprehension of the direction of flows and interchanges. In view of this requisite we offer very tentatively a set of suggestions concerning such processes in reference to their bearing upon political power. The basic idea is that deflation and inflation of power are conditioned by the form in which power is gained by a government and the aspect (functionally speaking) of the society upon which the government acts. In other words, we are attempting to isolate of what, in terms of specific subsystems, the government is the pivot. Our four basic patterns are:

Suggested Implications for Power

Type 1:	$I \rightarrow G \rightarrow L$	inflationary
Type 2:	$I \rightarrow G \rightarrow I$	inflationary-deflationary vacillations (small range)
Type 3:	$L \rightarrow G \rightarrow L$	deflationary-inflationary vacillations (small range)
Type 4:	$L \rightarrow G \rightarrow I$	deflationary

We suggest that Type 1 is inflationary in a dispositional sense, as power is generated within the polity on the basis of its elitist relationship to the societal community and is used in a penetrative manner vis a vis the value commitments of the relevant society. Structurally, the location of G is such as to make it the pivot of a set of political interchanges which "end" at the most fundamental (cybernetically) aspects of the social system as a whole. In most direct contrast, Type 4 societies are more prone to deflationary processes. In this case the interchange flow is in the opposite direction. Type 4 societies are much more open, therefore, to the threat of withdrawal of support for the polity. Type 3 societies are, on the one hand, susceptible to withdrawal of fundamental commitments but, on the other hand, the polity tends to act more directly on those commitments. This circumstance would seem productive of both deflationary and inflationary processes, each of a relatively wide-ranging nature. Type 2 societies differ in the relatively constricted nature of their interchanges of a political kind. But, like Type 2 societies, their interchange flows are reciprocal in structure (in contrast to the spiral form manifested in the other two types). Thus, they are also susceptible to both inflation and deflation of power—but, we suggest, the ranges of inflation and deflation are not so large.

NOTES

1. One of the most cogent and comprehensive demonstrations of such intractability is Raymond Aron, *Peace and War*, Richard Howard and Annette Baker Fox (trs.) (New York and London: Wiedenfieds, 1966). See, *inter alia*, Klaus Knorr and Sidney Verba (eds.), *The International System* (Princeton: Princeton University Press, 1961); Ernst B. Haas, *Beyond the Nation State* (Stanford: Stanford University Press, 1964); Stanley Hoffman (ed.), *Contemporary Theory in International Relations* (Englewood Cliffs: Prentice-Hall, 1960), esp. pp. 174-84; Hedley Bull, "International Theory: The Case for a Classical Approach," *World Politics* 18 (April 1966), pp. 361-77; Morton A. Kaplan, "The New Great Debate: Traditionalism vs. Science in International Relations," *World Politics* 19 (October 1966); Hayward R. Alker Jr., "The Long Road to International Relations Theory: Problems of Statistical Nonadditivity," *World Politics* 18 (July 1966) pp. 623-55; See also J. David Singer (ed.), *Quantitative International Politics* (Englewood Cliffs: Prentice-Hall, 1968). For a comparison of the major distinctively sociological approaches, see J. P. Nettl and Roland Robertson, *International Systems and the Modernization of Societies* (London and New York: Basic Books, 1968), Part 3.

2. See Robert A. Nisbet, *Social Change and History* (New York: Oxford University Press, 1969), Chs. 6-8. More technically see Erwin K. Scheuch, "The Cross-Cultural Use of Sample Surveys: Problems of Comparability," in Stein Rokkan (ed.), *Comparative Research Across Cultures and Nations* (Paris, The Hague: Humanities, 1968), Ch. 12, esp. pp. 197-203; and Terence K. Hopkins and Immanuel Wallerstein, "The Comparative Study of National Societies," in Amitai Etzioni

and Frederic L. Dubow (eds.), *Comparative Perspectives* (Boston: Little, Brown, 1970), pp. 183-204.

3. One of the very notable exceptions to this is the macrosociology of Amitai Etzioni, *The Active Society* (New York: The Free Press, 1968).

4. See Talcott Parsons, *Politics and Social Structure* (New York: The Free Press, 1969), Chs. 1 and 2. Parsons' major essays on international systems are contained in *ibid.* (Ch. 12) and in *Sociological Theory and Modern Society* (New York: The Free Press, 1967), Ch. 14. (The author was unable to consult Parsons' *The System of Modern Societies* (Englewood Cliffs: Prentice-Hall, pending). See Roland Robertson, "The Analysis of Social and Political Systems," *British Journal of Sociology* 16 (September 1965), pp. 252-9.

5. See discussion in Nettl and Robertson, *op. cit.*, Part III.

6. George Modelski, "Agraria and Industria: Two Models of International Relations," in Knorr and Verba (eds.), *op. cit.*, pp. 121-122.

7. J. David Singer, "The Global System and its Subsystems: A Developmental View", in James N. Rosenau (ed.), *Linkage Politics* (New York: The Free Press 1969), p. 35. The present argument is in close agreement with other presentations of Singer, notably: "The Level of Analysis Problem in International Relations," in Knorr and Verba (eds.), *op. cit.*, pp. 77-92; and "The Political Science of Human Conflict", in Elton McNeil (ed.), *The Nature of Human Conflict* (Englewood Cliffs: Prentice-Hall, 1965), pp. 139-154.

8. See. Amitai Etzioni. *Political Unification* (New York: Holt, Rinehart and Winston, 1965).

9. See Karl W. Deutsch and Richard L. Merritt, "Effects of Events on National and International Images," in Herbert C. Kelman (ed.), *International Behavior* (New York: Holt, Rinehart and Winston, 1965), pp. 132-87.

10. A useful, sensitizing and "prophetic" essay on this point is Karl W. Deutsch, "The Future of World Politics," *Political Quarterly* 37 (1966), pp. 9-32. See also the contributions of Deutsch to Philip Jacob and James V. Toscana (eds.), *The Integration of Political Communities* (Philadelphia: Lippincott, 1964). The theme now gets attention in many essays on the nature of government in modern societies. We mention only two at this particular point, as between them they encompass most of the relevant intrasocietal issues: John K. Galbraith, *The New Industrial State* (New York: Houghton Mifflin, 1967); and S. M. Miller and Pamela Roby, *The Future of Inequality* (New York: Basic Books, 1970). Governmental surveys can be regarded as indicators of the rising load problem—for example the HEW inquiry, *Towards a Social Report* (Washington, D.C.: G.P.O., 1969).

11. See Nettl and Robertson, *op. cit.*, Part 1; and Talcott Parsons, "Some Problems of General Theory in Sociology," in John C. McKinney and Edward A. Tiryakian (eds.), *Theoretical Sociology* (New York: Appleton, 1970), p. 59. But compare Susan Strange, "The Politics of International Currencies," *World Politics*, 23 (January, 1971), pp. 215-31.

12. Parsons, *Politics and Social Structure,* p. 477.

13. Parsons, "Some Problems of General Theory," *op. cit.*

14. See Parsons' emphasis upon the total system of action in *ibid.*

15. The Northern Ireland case is particularly interesting (and complex), owing to the fact that Ulster is a kind of sub-nation within British society. For a brilliantly succinct political appraisal of the Irish situation as of early 1971, see Conor Cruise O'Brien, "The Irish Troubles: Boys in the Backroom," *New York Review of Books* 16 (April 8, 1971), pp. 35-39.

16. See David Easton, *A Systems Analysis of Political Life* (New York: Wiley, 1965).

17. See especially Seymour Martin Lipset, *The First New Nation* (New York: Basic Books, 1964). (In conformity with the earlier depiction of Russia and Britain as elitist societies

we may note the intuitive conspicuousness of both of these societies as nations of queuers; although one might distinguish between deferential British-type queueing and regimental Russian-type queueing.)

18. The international aspects of blaming have been explored fruitfully by Helge Hveem, "'Blame' as International Behavior: A Contribution to Inter-State Interaction Theory," *Journal of Peace Research* 7 (1970), pp. 49-66. Hveem presents some scales of intensity of international blaming and hypothesizes relationships between disposition to blame and two other variables: rank distance in the international system and political-ideological distance.

19. For a very useful discussion of the empirical issues, see Arthur L. Stinchcombe, "American Society and the International System," in David Street and Robert W. Hodge (eds.), *Social Change in America* (Chicago: University of Chicago Press, 1971). Stinchcombe emphasizes the extent to which such changes are in a major sense planned changes in the stratification and occupational systems. For detailed analysis of the American occupational system, see Peter M. Blau and Otis Dudley Duncan, *The American Occupational Structure* (New York: Wiley, 1967), especially in the present context, Ch. 6. See Johan Galtung, "On the Future of the International System, "*Journal of Peace Research* 4 (1967), pp. 305-333, and the discussion later in this chapter.

20. This is a highly prominent theme in Parsons' work, especially since Talcott Parsons and Neil J. Smelser, *Economy and Society*, (Glencoe: The Free Press, 1956). See Gabriel A. Almond and C. Bingham Powell, *Comparative Politics: A Developmental Approach* (Boston: Little, Brown, 1966). For critiques see, *inter alia*, Nettl and Robertson, *op. cit.*, pp. 42-50; Etzioni, *The Active Society*; Roland Robertson and Andrew Tudor, *The Sociology of Talcott Parsons: A Critical Exposition* (London 1971).

21. Etzioni, *The Active Society, passim*. See Karl W. Deutsch, *The Nerves of Government* (Glencoe: The Free Press, 1963); and, in a more political context, Jeremy Bray, *Decision in Government* (London: International Publications Service, 1970). Etzioni's conception of cybernetic control differs considerably from that of Parsons. The former puts great emphasis upon the interdependency of power and information; the latter emphasizes cultural and normative factors in his "hierarchy of normative control." although at the same time acknowledging "conditional" factors. See especially Talcott Parsons, *Societies: Evolutionary and Comparative Perspectives* (Englewood Cliffs: Prentice-Hall, 1966).

22. See Etzioni, *Political Unification*.

23. *Ibid.*, Ch. 6. More generally, see Richard Tomasson, *Sweden: Prototype of Modern Society* (New York: Random House, 1970).

24. Karl Kaiser, "The Interaction of Regional Subsystems," *World Politics* 21 (October 1968), pp. 84-107. Kaiser argues that the first course is not feasible, given the stake which many societies have in trade, investment, and so on.

25. *The Times*, London, December 10, 1969, p. 10. (*A Study of the Capacity of The United Nations Development System* Geneva, 1969).

26. Gunnar Myrdal, *Beyond the Welfare State* (New Haven: Yale University Press, 1958). See also Kaiser, *op. cit.,* p. 91.

27. Robert C. Angell, *Peace on the March: Transnational Participation* (New York: Van Nostrand, 1969), Ch. 7.

28. See Charles P. Kindleberger, *American Business Abroad* (New Haven: Yale University Press, 1969), esp. pp. 145-78.

29. See Jean-Jacques Servan-Schreiber, *The American Challenge* (London: Hamilton, 1968). In June 1970, a "secret" internal paper was prepared for the executive commission of the EEC, censuring American corporate activity in Europe. See *The Times* (London, June 25, 1970). The converse, American-based idea of the "European Challenge" also exists.

30. Galtung, *op. cit.* See also Kaiser, *op. cit.*

31. Galtung, *op. cit.*, p. 317.

32. *Ibid.* (The major steps taken towards an East-West German *modus vivendi* in 1970 have occurred since Galtung's analysis was published. It would be difficult at this stage to estimate the degree to which these developments help to corroborate Galtung's thesis.)

33. *Ibid.*

34. *Ibid.*, p. 325.

35. Angell, *op. cit., passim.*

36. See, *inter alia*, Johan Galtung, "Social Position, Party Identification and Foreign Policy Orientation," in James N. Rosenau (ed.), *Domestic Sources of Foreign Policy* (New York: The Free Press, 1967), pp. 161-193.

37. Although creating a very misleading impression on the intrinsic nature of social science, Noam Chomsky's writing are on this theme highly relevant. See his *American Power and the New Mandarins* (New York: Pantheon, 1968). See Lee Rainwater and William L. Yancey, *The Moynihan Report and the Politics of Controversy* (Cambridge: MIT Press, 1967); Paul F. Lazarsfeld *et al.* (eds.), *The Uses of Sociology* (New York: Basic Books, 1967); Irving Louis Horowitz (ed.), *The Rise and Fall of Project Camelot* (Cambridge, Mass.: MIT Press, 1967). See also Robert E. Lane, "The Decline of Politics and Ideology In a Knowledgeable Society," *American Sociological Review* 31 (October 1966), pp. 649-62.

38. Bertrand de Jouvenel, *The Art of Conjecture* (New York: Basic Books, 1967), p. 239.

39. *Ibid.*

40. *Ibid.*

41. *Ibid.*, p. 240.

42. Giovanni Sartori, "From the Sociology of Politics to Political Sociology," in Seymour Martin Lipset (ed.), *Politics and the Social Sciences* (New York: Oxford University Press, 1969), p. 89. See also Roland Robertson, review essay on Raymond Aron, *Main Currents in Sociological Thought*, Vol. I, in *History and Theory*, 5 (1966), pp. 191-98; and Nettl and Robertson, *op. cit.*, Part I. This problem is a major theme in Etzioni, *The Active Society*; and in Reinhard Bendix, *Nation-Building and Citizenship* (New York: Wiley, 1964), esp. p. 73.

43. See in particular the respective positions of Harry G. Johnson and Don Patinkin in Walter Adams (ed.), *The Brain Drain* (New York: Macmillan, 1968), Chs. 5 and 6.

44. For empirical discussion, see Louis Kriesberg, "U.S. and U.S.S.R. Participation in International Non-Governmental Organizations," in Kriesberg (ed.), *Social Process in International Relations* (New York: Wiley, 1968), pp. 466-485. See also Robert C. Angell, "The Growth of Transnational Participation," *Journal of Social Issues* 23 (January 1967), pp. 108-129; Angell, *Peace on the March*; and Steven J. Brams, "Transaction Flows in the International System," *American Political Science Review* 60 (December 1966), pp. 880-88. (See the cogent critique of the latter in Kaiser, *op. cit.*, p. 97.) More generally, see Rosenau (ed.), *op. cit.*

45. See Angell, *Peace on the March*, esp. Ch. 2.

46. See in particular S. M. Lipset and S. Rokkan (eds.), *Party Systems and Voter Alignments* (New York: The Free Press, 1967); and S. Rokkan *et al.*, *Citizens, Elections, Parties* (Oslo: McKay, 1970).

47. Parsons, *Sociological Theory and Modern Society*, Ch. 13.

48. The classic in the field is T. H. Marshall, *Class, Citizenship and Social Development* (Garden City, N. Y.: Doubleday, 1965). See also Bendix, *op. cit.*; Rokkan *et al.*, *op. cit.*; Miller and Roby, *op. cit.*; Sidney Verba, "Democratic Participation," *Annals of the American Academy of Political and Social Science* 373 (September 1967), pp. 53-78. Parsons has recently added *cultural* and *personality* considerations to Marshall's dimensions of citizenship — which bears closely on this phase of

our discussion: Parsons, "Some Problems of General Theory," *op. cit.* See also, Talcott Parsons, "Equality and Inequality in Modern Society, or Social Stratification Revisited," *Sociological Inquiry* 40 (Spring 1970), pp. 13-72.

49. The author is currently exploring these issues with special reference to the function of changes in cultural patterns. See Roland Robertson, *Culture and Cultural Change* (Oxford: Oxford University Press, 1972). See also, Roland Robertson and Laurie Taylor, "Problems of Comparative Analysis of Deviancy: A Survey and a Proposal" (Paper given to British Sociological Association Annual Conference, London, April 1971), Department of Sociology, University of York (mimeo).

50. Talcott Parsons, "Evolutionary Universals in Society," in Parsons, *Sociological Theory in Modern Society,* Ch. 15. This differs somewhat from the way in which Parsons himself has presented the evolutionary universals schema. See also Robertson and Tudor, *op. cit.* For sequential structural change, see Wilbert E. Moore, "Toward a System of Sequences," in McKinney and Tiryakian (eds.), *op. cit.,* pp. 156-66.

51. See Deutsch's reference to these processes in the context of international relations: Karl W. Deutsch, "The Propensity to International Transactions," *Political Studies* 8 (1960), pp. 147-55.

52. Robert A. Dahl (ed.), *Political Oppositions in Western Democracies,* paperback edition (New Haven: Yale University Press, 1968), p. 399.

53. See especially Parsons, *Societies: Evolutionary and Comparative Perspectives,* esp. Ch. 7. See Roland Robertson, "The Sociocultural Implications of Sociology: A Reconnaissance," in T. Nossiter and S. Rokkan (eds.), *Imagination and Precision in Political Science* (London: Faber, 1972).

54. See especially Mary Douglas, *Natural Symbols* (London: Pantheon, 1970).

55. Parsons, *Politics and Social Structure,* pp. 463ff.

56. Angell, *Peace on the March.*

57. See, *inter alia,* Karl W. Deutsch, "Toward an Inventory of Basic Trends and Patterns in Comparative and International Politics," *American Political Science Review* 54 (March 1960), pp. 34-57; "Shifts in the Balance of Communication Flows," *Public Opinion Quarterly* 20 (Spring 1966), pp. 143-160; Karl W. Deutsch and Walter Isard, "A Note on the Generalized Concept of Effective Distance," *Behavioral Science* 6 (October 1961), pp. 308-11; Karl W. Deutsch and Alexander Eckstein, "National Industrialization and the Declining Share of the International Economic Sector," *World Politics* 13 (January 1961), pp. 267-299; Haas, *op. cit.*; Brams, *op. cit.* See Singer, "The Global System and its Sub-Systems," *op. cit.,* p. 23, n. 1, for a statement on just how confusing the evidence is.

58. In this domain there is a lack of evidence; for in spite of the vast body of literature on organizational participation, notably in the U.S.A., this author is not acquainted with contributions which synthesize empirical findings to the national level. For fairly old overview appraisals of general tendencies, see Kenneth Boulding, *The Organizational Revolution* (New York: Harper, 1953); Robert Presthus, *The Organizational Society* (New York: Random House, 1962). Clearly this theme relates closely to the question of growth in organizational attachments and social integration — see James Thompson, "Organizational Interdependence and Social Integration," (paper delivered at University of Pittsburgh, February 1970). See Angell, *Peace on the March.*

59. See the helpful conceptual discussion in Kaiser, *op. cit.*

60. Nettl and Robertson, *op. cit.*

61. J. P. Nettl, *Political Mobilization* (London: Faber, 1967), p. 88, emphasis added.

62. *Ibid.,* p. 81.

63. Samuel P. Huntington, *Political Order in Changing Societies* (New Haven: Yale University Press, 1968), pp. 93-139.

64. For elaboration see Nettl and Robertson, *op. cit.,* pp. 42-57; G. Fischer, *The Soviet System and Modern Society* (New York: Aldine, 1969); P. D. Stewart, "Soviet Interest Groups and the Policy Process," *World Politics* 22 (October 1969), pp. 29-51; and Almond and Powell, *op. cit.,* pp. 307-308.

65. See Z. Brzezinski and S. Huntington, *Political Power: U.S.A./U.S.S.R.* (London: Viking, 1964). This institutional basis of elite formation in American society is a glaring lacuna in the theses of C. Wright Mills. See, in particular, *The Power Elite* (New York: Oxford University Press, 1956). The relationship between elites and "masses" explicated here differ significantly from another well-known attempt to analyze similar problems, Willian Kornhauser, *The Politics of Mass Society* (New York: The Free Press, 1960).

66. See J. Hackett and A. Hackett, *Economic Planning in France* (Cambridge: Harvard University Press, 1963); and F. Ridley and J. Blondel, *Public Administration in France* (London: Routledge and Kegan Paul, 1964), esp. Ch. 2.

67. J. P. Nettl, "The State as a Conceptual Variable," *World Politics* 20 (January 1968), pp. 559-592.

68. See Nettl and Robertson, *op. cit.,* pp. 152ff; see also Adda B. Bozeman, *Politics and Culture in International History* (Princeton: Princeton University Press, 1960); J. D. B. Miller, *The Politics of the Third World* (London: Oxford University Press, 1966).

69. See Charles H. Alexandrowicz, "New and Original States' The Issue of Reversion to Sovereignity," *International Affairs* 45 (July 1969), pp. 465-480.

70. For a useful discussion, involving a comparison of Turkish, Modern Arabic, Israeli Hebrew, Persian, Bahasa Indonesia, and Japanese, see Charles, F. Gallagher, "Language Rationalization and Scientific Progress," in Kalman H. Silvert (ed.). *The Social Reality of Scientific Myth* (New York: American Universities Field Staff, 1969), Ch. 3, especially pp. 58-65. See Parsons' emphasis upon language as the major link between culture and social system: Talcott Parsons, "Introduction" (to "Culture and the Social System"), in Parsons *et al., Theories of Society* (New York: The Free Press, 1961), pp. 963-993.

71. Rokkan, *Citizens, Elections, Parties,* p. 54. See also Rokkan's attempt (pp. 54-60) to formalize the findings of Barrington Moore, Jr., *Social Origins of Dictatorship and Democracy* (Boston: Beacon Press, 1966).

72. The phenomenal perception of the location of the governmental core of societies receives detailed comparative-historical attention in Guy E. Swanson, *Religion and Regime: A Sociological Account of the Reformation* (Ann Arbor: University of Michigan Press, 1967). See Robert T. Holt and John E. Turner, *The Political Basis of Economic Development* (Princeton: Princeton University Press, 1966).

73. Rokkan, *Citizens, Elections, Parties,* pp. 61ff.

74. See Andrew Tudor, "The Dynamics of Stratification Systems," *International Journal of Comparative Sociology* 10 (September and December 1969), pp. 211-233.

75. Rokkan, *Citizens, Elections, Parties.* Our presentation differs in some salient respects from that of Rokkan, notably in its application to so-called developed societies — in contrast to Rokkan's explicit developmental interests.

76. I am indebted to Rainer Baum for this observation.

77. For the latter see, *inter alia,* Rosenau (ed.) *op. cit.*; A. M. Scott, *The Revolution in Statecraft* (New York:Random House, 1965). See also the influential contribution of John Herz, "The Rise and Demise of the Territorial State," *World Politics* 9 (July 1957), pp. 473-493.

78. Adapting data compiled by Kathleen Gough, Worsley has calculated that in the late 1960's armed revolutionary movements existed in at least twenty countries of the Third World (including Latin America), while several others had unarmed movements or parties with wide support; Peter Worsley, *The Third World,* 2nd edition (Chicago: University of Chicago

Press, 1967), p. 308. For further data, see Huntington, *op. cit.,* pp. 1-11. See also various chapters in Hugh Davis Graham and Ted Robert Gurr (eds.), *The History of Violence in America* (New York: Praeger, 1969), especially Part IV.

79. See G. Germani, "Fascism and Class", in S.J. Woolf (ed.), *The Nature of Fascism* (New York: Random House, 1969), pp. 65-96, esp. 83ff. The present distinction differs from that of Germani in that secondary mobilization consists for him solely in displacement in a radical direction. See Deutsch and Merritt, *op. cit.,* pp. 174ff; Nettl, *Political Mobilization,* Kornhauser, *op. cit.*

80. Worsley's emphasis in *op. cit.* on Third World populism should be compared with these views. See also Karl W. Deutsch, *Nationalism and Social Communication* (Cambridge, Mass.: MIT Press, 1953).

81. See Worsely, *op. cit.,* especially Ch. 7; Galtung, *op. cit.*; Roland Robertson and Andrew Tudor, "The Third World and International Stratification," *Sociology* 2 (January 1968), pp. 47-64.

82. Etzioni, *The Active Society,* Part 5. See Stanley Hoffman, "Obstinate or Obsolete? The Fate of the Nation-State and the Case of Western Europe," in S. Hoffman (ed.), *Conditions of World Order* (Boston: Little Brown, 1968), pp. 110-163. More generally, see Stanley Hoffman, *Gulliver's Troubles, Or the Setting of American Foreign Policy* (New York: McGraw-Hill, 1968).

83. See the evaluation of this distinction contained in Roger D. Hansen, "Regional Integration: Reflections on a Decade of Theoretical Efforts," *World Politics* 21 (January 1969), pp. 242-271.

84. This has been attempted elsewhere, in, Nettl and Robertson, *op. cit.,* Roland Robertson, "Strategic Relations between National Societies," *Journal of Conflict Resolution* 12 (March 1968), pp. 16-33; and Robertson and Tudor, "The Third World and International Stratification." See also Robertson and Tudor, "Patterns of Change in International Stratification" (pending).

85. See Oran R. Young, "Political Discontinuities in the International System," *World Politics* 20 (April 1968), pp. 369-392.

86. Hansen, *op. cit.,* p. 256; see also Hansen's comments on less-developed societies.

87. See Charles P. Kindleberger (ed.), *The International Corporation* (Cambridge: MIT Press, 1970).

88. Kindleberger, *American Business Abroad,* pp. 179ff.

89. Neil J. Smelser, *Theory of Collective Behavior* (New York: The Free Press, 1962).

90. Parsons, *Politics and Social Structure,* Ch. 16, especially pp. 463ff.

29

IDEOLOGY AND MODERNIZATION

Dietrich Rueschemeyer

If ideologies are not specifically modern phenomena, they do have, at least in certain forms, a peculiarly close relation to modernization—to the early modernization of Western Europe and to the contemporary scene both in relatively advanced countries and in the "developing areas." I wish to present some theoretical reflections on the conditions of ideological developments, beginning with some basic conceptual considerations and decisions, proceeding to discuss certain general theoretical orientations about ideologies in complex social systems, and finally considering ideological developments in the process of modernization.

THE CONCEPTUALIZATION OF IDEOLOGY AND MODERNIZATION

Both ideology and modernization designate areas of sociological inquiry where problems of definition loom large. As in the case of other topics—power or law may serve as examples—much of the total effort is spent on concept formation; a multitude of different concepts are used side by side and are labeled with the same terms; and a good deal of the propositions advanced turn out, upon closer scrutiny, to be tautological formulations of implicit or explicit components of the definitions chosen.

In this situation it seems wise to reverse the emphasis and to work, at least initially, with relatively simple and crude concepts. Furthermore, it may be useful to choose rather wide definitions so that the

This essay was written in connection with empirical work on value conflicts in German modernization. I wish to thank the Ford Foundation and the Deutsche Forschungsgemeinschaft for support of both theoretical and empirical research during the academic year of 1968-1969; of course, neither the Ford Foundation nor the DFG are responsible for the content of this essay. Colin K. Loftin of Brown University and the editors of this symposium made comments on a first draft from which I profited gratefully.

wealth of alternative conceptual formulations can be understood as dealing with special cases, the diverse characteristics of which can provide hunches as to empirical interrelations between specific patterns. The assumption underlying this procedure is that much of the previous conceptual discussion is not merely concerned with creating language tools for analysis but involves important, if loose and unsystematic, references to empirical regularities.

Ideologies are defined here as belief systems, shared by a plurality of actors, which combine cognitive and evaluative elements in relatively undifferentiated fashion and which concern major cognitive and evaluative orientations of the individuals and groups involved. The cognitive components have primarily empirical reference, although nonempirical beliefs play a more or less important role in any concrete instance. This formulation does not "decide by definition" whether ideologies distort reality or not, whether they are held "sincerely" or are espoused with the intent of manipulation of others, whether they are formulated in highly systematic and explicit fashion or left largely implicit and loosely structured, whether they constitute comprehensive world views or leave major areas of potential concern untouched, whether they are associated with specific ideological collectivities such as parties and "schools" or not, whether they are upholding the status quo or seek to establish a new order, whether they contain prominently a program for action or are largely content with interpretation, whether they are espoused by dominant or by relatively powerless groups, and whether they are associated with collective and individual states of "mobilization" and affective agitation or not. All these and a number of related dimensions may be used to characterize special properties of ideologies. The clustering of several such characterizations suggested by various more narrow definitions can be restated as hypotheses about specific types of ideology.

The proposed definition is deliberately formulated in such a way that it articulates easily with more general theoretical frameworks which link systemic patterns of culture to social and personality systems as well as, more specifically, values and cognitive beliefs to other elements of cultural, social, and personality structures. It is, in other words, more consonant with the conceptual framework of the theory of action than with the tradition of the sociology of knowledge.[1]

The problems of defining modernization are perhaps even more complex. It does not seem necessary to enter into a full discussion here. Max Weber's concept of rationalization of social and cultural life is the basis of recent definitions that appear most useful. These put modernization into the context of societal evolution and combine the conception of increasing "adaptive capacity"—a reformulation of Weber's rationalization in system terms—which the consideration of specific characteristics that set off the highest level of adaptive capacity from previously evolved levels.[2]

Increased ability for adaptation does not leave the adapting system unaffected but requires far-reaching changes even in its inner core. In Weber's terms, sociocultural rationalization not only involves an examination, evaluation, and selection of means for given goals but also entails a critical examination of goals and values—of their consequences, interrelations, and compatibilities. Values become in the course of modernization increasingly the objects of choice and selection based on such examination, although any choice involves always some underived value orientations. These considerations give a first indication of intrinsic relations between modernization and ideologies—belief systems that combine empirical analysis with evaluation: Modern ideologies incorporate this critical examination of goals and values and provide a basis for their selection where the unquestioned provisions of tradition have been eroded.[3] This does not mean, however, that ideologies as presently defined are found only in modern societies or in periods of transition. In different forms, ideological orientations are a universal aspect of human social life. The differentiation of these forms and their differential interrelations with the process of modernization will be one of our concerns in this chapter.

IDEOLOGY AND OTHER COMPONENTS OF ACTION

Ideologies are patterns of culture that play a crucial part in structuring both social and personality systems. They spell out central values and basic assumptions about reality and link them to each other. They give answers to such questions at the borderline of evaluation and cognition as "Who am I?" and "Who are we?"—suggesting bases for identity and solidarity. They give an interpretation and evaluation of the past of the actors in question, they present an analysis of their present situation and offer a perspective—again in both cognitive and evaluative terms—on the future.

Joining formulations of the desirable with interpretations of reality, ideologies provide a more or less inclusive orientation for individual or collective actors in terms of which discrete experiences and actions can be organized and given meaning. They provide a common symbolic framework that facilitates communication and consensus among their adherents. They define the baselines from which morally legitimate and intellectually sensible demands can be made—demands by the concerned actors on themselves and on others as well as demands by others on these actors. Because values, "conceptions of the desirable," are never fully implemented, ideologies deal with the tension between actual and ideal states of affairs. Whether this results in an activist or passive, conservative or innovative stance, however, depends on the conceptions about reality espoused as well as on the strains and opportunities the adherents are facing.

As patterns of culture, ideologies not only stand in systemic relationships with personality and society or societal subsystems—structuring these systems of action and being subject to various influences and pressures generated in these systems—but also have to be viewed in relation to other components of the cultural system. This point, an argument for analytic differentiation in order to grasp the peculiar regularities in the structuring and restructuring of complex symbolizations, has been stressed recently by Talcott Parsons and Clifford Geertz.[4] The stability and change of ideologies cannot, according to this reasoning, fully be explained in terms of their interdependence with socially patterned personality dispositions, aggregations of interest of collectivities, and strains in the social system. Their internal symbolic structure as well as their interdependence with other components of the cultural system have to be taken into account, too.

The significance of this insistence on a double analytic perspective is made clearer by two considerations. First, the cultural heritage always contains elements that are rather weakly and only partially institutionalized in a given society. Yet, the components of the cultural system — values, empirical knowledge, expressive symbolization of what constitutes rewards and fulfillment of desires, and religious or quasi-religious conceptions of ultimate reality and meaning—even if only precariously anchored in social institutions may limit and give direction to changes in ideological orientations by virtue of their symbolic interrelationships.

The second consideration derives from Parsons' conception of a "cybernetic hierarchy" in the relations between the systems and subsystems of action. The analogue referred to here is, of course, the governor programmed for specific goal states and touching off mechanisms designed to change a physical system in the direction of these goal states. A common example is the thermostat set for a given temperature which switches furnace action on and off. The conception of a cybernetic hierarchy sees "lower-level" patterns of action as programmed by a series of higher-level ones. Strains and disturbances at lower levels are dealt with not simply on their own terms but within the framework of more generalized higher-level programs still intact. Stability of an overall pattern in a changing environment would lead to the inference that there are mechanisms protecting the functioning of higher-level subsystems. For example, values inform the restructuring of norms and, judging from many instances of stability within change, tend to be better protected against rapid change than the more specific normative patterns they legitimate. In turn, if values are affected by processes of change, the reverberations of change throughout the social system are in the long run more far-reaching than if the initial changes concerned specific norms only. What is not implied by this conception, though often read into it, is a value determinism for social change or a cultural determinism for change in the total system of action. Cultural patterns do not by themselves effect social or personality change, but they do constitute more or less systematically interrelated programs "informing" processes in the social and personality systems by setting out limits and directions, plausibilities and implausibilities.[5]

A DIVISION OF LABOR IN IDEOLOGICAL CONCERNS

These very broad theoretical orientations regarding the interrelations of ideologies with other components of social action may give rise to certain skeptical questions. Invoking common sense as well as the observation of "common people" one may ask, do "basic cognitive-evaluative belief systems," do ideologies really matter? The question may be put in somewhat more circumspect fashion: Although for some people in some situations ideologies may indeed be meaningful and consequential orientations, is not the life of most people more "down to earth,"

more concerned with making a living, with getting along with their kin, friends, partners, and opponents and with pursuing short-run interests in changing situations?

The assertion of the latter rhetorical question is indeed valid, but the seemingly obvious conclusion stated in the first, that therefore ideologies do not "really" matter, is definitely not. Explaining this judgment requires discussion of certain aspects of ideologies crucial to a fuller understanding of the phenomenon. Furthermore, this discussion will suggest conceptual differentiations that seem important for the analysis of ideological developments in the context of modernization.

Ideological orientations are taken for granted by most people in the daily routines of life. Being taken for granted and being of low salience, they are typically held in highly inarticulate fashion. Thus, attempts to elicit ideological convictions in standardized interviews often produce meaningless results—ad hoc responses more shaped by the wording of questions than by coherent opinions and orientations of the respondents. More carefully probing interviews typically reveal ideas of diffuse contours, related to each other by loose association and often mutually contradictory.[6] Except under special conditions, ideas concerning basic matters of cognitive and evaluative orientation are in a state of "latency." These special conditions are, however, by no means only, or even typically, quasi-pathological circumstances.

There is a variety of situations in which "ordinary" people become more sensitive to such matters—when they occupy roles in which they are confronted with contradictory value and reality premises, when they have to make consequential choices between different major roles and social affiliations, when they encounter crises that upset or threaten major life interests and systems of reference groups. The socialization of children is an undertaking in which some of these experiences are, in modern society, commonplace—thus the greater concern for ideological questions in the educational sphere and in certain sections of youth culture.

In response to such situations people become receptive to ideological interpretations offered by others. Accepting others as a source for ideological "information" or for confirmation of one's own tentative responses requires trust. In the simplest and "safest" case, this trust may be grounded in the shared membership in diffuse solidary groups. Often the resources of such groups may be perfectly sufficient to provide adequate answers to ideological problems. The disturbing and sensitizing experiences may be extraordinary only for subgroups or individuals while they are routine problems from the point of view of the collectivity, routine problems for which standardized solutions are held ready. In addition, many transitory problems of limited scope can be handled on an ad hoc basis with the consent of such primary groups "guaranteeing" the validity of the solution. What is used and accumulated here are relatively simple "philosophies of life" which may involve little articulation with the more elaborate cultural heritage of the wider society. They are often so unreflected that it might be useful to set them aside terminologically and to speak of "mentalities" shaped by the recurrent problems and their workable interpretations in a given milieu of a society.

However, there are many conditions under which social relations of this type are incapable of stilling the quest for meaningful interpretation of disturbing and sensitizing experiences. The intellectual sophistication of ideological responses by people whose primary concerns are the preoccupations of routine social life is necessarily limited. In very simply structured societies with a great deal of stability over time it may be rare that an ideological problem cannot be handled by the collective wisdom of such undifferentiated solidary groups. The likelihood of such inability increases with greater social complexity and with sociocultural change that introduces sharp discontinuities between the experience of different generations. Furthermore, the more interdependent the parts of a society become—and this is one of the correlates of increasing differentiation—the more will the affirmative power of such solidary groups become questionable: the interpenetration of previously isolated milieux is likely to lead to clashes between divergent interpretations which will give rise to more far-reaching ideological problems.

In all moderately complex societies we find therefore a *division of labor* regarding ideological concern and authority that goes beyond the confines of small primary groups, although it does not replace the latter in their ideological functions. Some such specialization in cultural matters is actually found in all but the least complex societies known or imaginable.[7] It is of increasing importance with each higher level of societal evolution, and its development — its reorganization and expansion — is one major problem in modernization.

It is clear that such a division of labor reinforces the tendency to take basic ideological orientations for granted in routine social life. To put the point with some exaggeration, just as the ordinary car driver has little knowledge of or interest in the production of his vehicle, taken care of by the automobile industry, so ordinary people in the daily round of life take for granted that their actions and expressed attitudes and orientations fit together and make sense in terms of what they ultimately hold sacred, while the ways in which these might be shown to make sense and in which their congruence might be examined are largely left to cultural specialists.

The conception of a division of labor in ideological matters gives rise to two sets of questions: First, what are the bases of more sustained and more explicit ideological concern, how do such ideological "centers" relate to other aspects of social structure, and how are they related to each other? Second, in which ways are developments in such centers articulated with the more intermittent ideological questioning at the "periphery" discussed previously, and what are the bases of trust that permit ideological solutions developed in various centers to be accepted at the periphery?

It would lead far beyond the confines of this essay to discuss adequately the bases of trust that are required for the transmission of ideological orientations across the boundaries of diffuse solidary groups. Therefore, a few suggestions about different forms of what may be called "mediated trust" have to suffice. Some of these forms are merely variations of the primary case and are in a broad evolutionary perspective only moderately more flexible than this pattern of trust. The ideological specialist may be part of a collectivity which, although somewhat differentiated, retains much of the character of diffuse primary relations; or primary ties may be symbolically extended to a source of ideological "information" which for all other purposes is outside the collectivity in question.

A more significant departure from the primary case is found where an extension of trust outside of primary relations is backed up by the consensus of a primary group. Such an indirect rooting of trust in primary relations through the confirmation of trustworthiness is of great theoretical importance. However, conditions beyond the confines of these primary relations seem to determine in good measure whether and to whom such endorsements are given. Shared membership in collectivities which are more differentiated and impersonal but still command loyalty and public commitments to common basic values seem important among these determinants, as do shared antagonisms towards the same evils and outgroups. High status, which may be based on one's membership and position in such collectivities, on a particular closeness to shared values, and/or on the possession of knowledge relevant, but not accessible to all, makes it more likely that trust is extended and trustworthiness confirmed. Interwoven with such generalized positional prestige or honor is the specific reputation of a person or group for reliable knowledge, moral integrity, and good judgment. The positional prestige is in modern societies generally less protected and stabilized by ascriptive mechanisms than in traditional agrarian societies. Furthermore, the institutionalization of freedom of association, freedom of speech, and freedom of the press provides in Western liberal societies open arenas in which extensions of trust can be established, tested, and revised.[8]

It was noted before that extensions of trust beyond diffuse solidary relations do not replace the latter in their ideological functions. This does not mean only that primary relations of various kinds respond to the intermittent and limited ideological questioning at the periphery of complex sociocultural systems. Diffuse solidary groups are also of crucial importance for the development of what I will call below "radical" ideologies — the forms of ideology most flexible relative to ascriptive traditions. Close-knit groups with an intense solidarity typically develop and give early support to such ideologies. However, personal relations of trust tend, in this case, not to be a given condition but to develop with and even to be contingent on a sharing of ideological commitments. Finding in each other a similar awareness of problems and common ideological inclinations creates a basis for solidarity which in turn lends "social reality" to the developing ideological orientation.[9] Often, the need for ideological reorientation goes along with being cut off from other, more ordinary supportive social contexts. This constellation in particular seems to be conducive to the development of a charismatic fervor which frequently has been thought of as characteristic of all ideological commitments.

CENTERS OF SUSTAINED IDEOLOGICAL CONCERN

A discussion of some loci of more sustained ideological concern may give more specific meaning to the conception of a division of labor pertaining to ideological awareness, competence, and authority. Wherever the conditions for ideological sensitivity just indicated have a higher and more continuous incidence, a concentration of ideological questioning should be expected. Certain occupational roles and organizations deal routinely with matters that involve major societal values, require the use of wide-ranging and relatively systematic knowledge, and demand consequential choices between alternative decisions. Major examples, drawn from modern society but also found in somewhat different form in less differentiated societies, are the institutions of education and scholarship, the learned professions, positions and institutions in which far-reaching decisions affecting the rest of society are made— positions and institutions of political authority as well as those of visible economic and other power

and religious institutions. Associated with all these we find more or less coherent belief systems dealing with the place of the profession or institution in society and with its particular moral problems and possibly branching out to include subject matter of much wider scope.

All of these "ideological centers" also exhibit, though to a varying degree, major conditions of that trust which helps make their beliefs acceptable to audiences outside. They specialize in the implementation of major values, they in a sense represent these values in wider society, and they derive prestige and moral authority from this fact to the extent that such values are shared throughout the society and that the competence and commitment of the groups involved are not put into question.

The various centers differ from each other in a number of ways which affect the nature and the direction of ideological developments characteristic of each. Thus, they may be preoccupied primarily with the orientations of outside groups rather than with their own orientations and beliefs. The ideologies espoused may then acquire a more or less "manipulative" character. This is particularly likely where consent or support from the outside is crucial to carrying out the center's primary function and/or to the maintenance of an advantageous status quo and where a spread of mistrust and a challenge to authority and privilege are serious possibilities.

Further, the specialized concern of these occupations and institutions may have a wider or narrower scope, which will affect the range of ideological problems and ideas. The problems of education in a changing society create pressures toward more far-flung ideological concerns than we find in the professional ideology of medicine, but they are likely to stay within more narrow limits than the ideological interpretations of social and personal experience derived from a specialized concern with religion. Similarly, the nature of the specialized concern varies in the extent to which the symbolic interpretation of reality and "ideal interests" are central, which also will determine in part the content as well as the intellectual sophistication of the respective ideologies.

Parsons' conceptions about four categories of system problems may be helpful for ordering and interrelating a great variety of such hypotheses and for generating new propositions about these problems, as they specify analytically the major characteristics of four functional subsystems of a society. The location of the specialized concern of a profession or institution in the economy (primacy of adaptive problems), the polity (primacy of goal-attainment problems), the societal "community" (primacy of integration problems) or the "latency" subsystem (primacy of problems of pattern maintenance) should have important implications for most of the questions indicated—for the characteristic problems and strains encountered, for the degree and sophistication of symbolization, for the pertinence which the problems and solutions developed in one sphere have for other subsystems, or for the remoteness of the respective ideological problems from the experience of routine social life.

For instance, the ideological problems encountered in the political sphere are likely to center around the mobilization and maintenance of support as well as the legitimation of the structure of authority, of prevalent types of encumbency, and of the goals envisaged, while in religion and in the more basic phases of education ideological sensitivity will focus on problems of personal and collective identity, generalized responsibility, the integrity of values, and ultimate meaning and motivation. Compared to ideological orientations of this latter origin, beliefs sponsored by political elites are likely to be more "manipulative," less symbolically differentiated and less concerned with "ideal interests," more confined in their relevance for other spheres of life, but also less remote from the routine concerns characteristic of the periphery.

The different centers of ideological concern and authority are in various ways interrelated with each other and with the periphery, and these interrelations, too, will shape the respective ideological problems and solutions. First, they may share in varying degrees the same personnel, be it through actual multiple participation or through sequences of involvement in the course of typical careers. Such personnel linkages are a simple but significant mechanism of integration. It may be exemplified by the importance which education at centers of learning has for the orientations of the modern professions. Ideological developments in the different centers are similarly affected by the mentalities and ideological inclinations characteristic of the various milieux in which members spent their childhood and received their early formation.

A second pattern of interrelations is found in shared or overlapping audiences. Of special significance for the analysis of modernization is the rise of audiences with fairly generalized ideological interests. This requires, of course, a high level of literacy and the development of relatively autonomous and responsible positions for educated people. What is of interest here is that such audiences constitute a general "marketplace of ideas" in which ideological formulations of different origin are discussed.[10]

Third, the very idea of a division of labor in these matters suggests that the centers stand in a relation of complementary specialization and interdependence to each other. While in each case the connection between primary specialized concern and ideological beliefs is a loose one and awareness of ideas in other centers may be limited, there should indeed be a tendency of varying strength to take ideas developed in other centers into account, to respect special competence and moral authority, to delegate intellectual responsibility for certain matters to others, and to make value and reality premises developed by others the foundation of one's own problem formulations and solutions. As to the direction such a delegation of ideological authority takes, Parsons' conception of a cybernetic hierarchy among the functional subsystems of a society is suggestive.

Intentional social control of ideological developments is an important fourth aspect of these interrelationships. Attempts at such control may be made by various quarters and they will be based on a variety of mechanisms. Direct attempts at influence may range from ideological persuasion to threats of violence. More indirect mechanisms include control over access to centers of ideological concern, over their resources, over the further career patterns of the participants, and over the means of dissemination of ideas. A very indirect but quite important type of influence, finally, is control over structural conditions that give rise to ideological preoccupations.[11]

Modernization, as will become more clear below, has far-reaching consequences for these patterns of interrelation. There will typically arise pressures for broader contact with the periphery and for less ascriptive access to various centers. Increasing specialization and the erosion of traditional definitions of grounds for respect and authority will upset the old patterns of influence and information; and the over-all premises of the system are likely to come under questioning.

These are not changes which accompany smoothly and predictably a process known as "modernization." It is more useful to think of them as characteristic problems, the solutions for which are by no means obvious. While the structures of a division of labor in ideological matters are inevitably upset in the course of modernization, their past shape is always one of the factors that determine the search for such solutions and generally the future course of ideological development.

SOURCES OF "RADICAL" IDEOLOGIES

For a discussion of the specific interrelations between ideological developments and modernization it is useful to distinguish a specific type of ideology.

In the preceding discussion, sustained ideological concern resulting in complex and coherent belief systems was contrasted with the much more widespread intermittent forms of ideological questioning which find typically simpler and less consistent answers. In either case, most of the ideological orientations discussed tend to be limited in scope. They are likely to leave major areas of potential concern in a state of latency and to take the more basic evaluative and cognitive premises for granted. Finally, what is formulated in these ideologies is typically understood as a mere explication of generally accepted value and reality premises.

By contrast, we may conceive of ideologies that attempt to develop a total analysis and design of the major aspects of a society and civilization, that do not take for granted but critically examine usually latent value and reality premises. These can be called "radical" ideologies in the original, rather than the narrower political meaning of that term.

Before we consider the conditions that give rise to radical ideologies and the determinants that shape their content, the problem of the latency of basic assumptions deserves some comment. We have noted above that in routine social life ideological questions in general tend to be latent. These tendencies toward latency are not simply due to inattention. It appears to be impossible, even in radical ideological questioning, to overcome them ever completely. The more general evaluative and cognitive frameworks even of radical ideologies remain to a large extent latent. This is one aspect of what Mannheim grasped in his "total conception" of ideology. We cannot attempt an explanation of this phenomenon here. Aside from intrinsic intellectual difficulties, due to the complexity of human systems of action and to the problems of "reflecting while doing," there seem to exist a variety of psychological and social mechanisms which make such reduction of latency beyond certain limits a difficult, unrewarding, and even fearful undertaking.[12] The fact that radical ideologies do reduce latency is one major reason that, as was noted, the people most involved in such ideologies seek close association in solidary groups where they find emotional support as well as intellectual validation.

What gives rise to such more inclusive ideological orientations minimizing latency? Basically, the same kinds of conditions seem to be relevant here that we considered in connection with intermittent ideological questioning and the more sustained but relatively limited ideological concerns. Strain between components of a system of action is the broadest common characterization of these conditions. In the case of the most incipient and transient ideological questioning these strains—contradictions in the structure

of roles and group affiliations, crises, and indeterminancies of choice—are isolated from one another, they can be absorbed largely within routine social life and do not give rise to more far-reaching questions. Centers of more sustained ideological concern are located at points in the division of labor where such strains have a higher and more continuous incidence; but here, too, the questioning is often confined, focusing on the particular problems of a given specialized pursuit. It is strains that are more pervasive, relevant to a wide variety of specific conditions, which give rise to critical questions about the more generalized cultural codes.

Interpretation of experience plays, of course, an important role in these matters. A new definition of the situation may turn isolated troubles and uncertainties into manifestations of pervasive social and cultural disorders. Effective ideological communication among established ideological centers and between them and the periphery tends to militate against an "escalation" of ideological interpretation. Conversely, tensions and breakdowns in the structure of a division of labor in ideological matters may be crucial elements in the development of radical ideologies.

Pervasive strains may take different forms. A very broad distinction is the following. Pervasive strains may arise primarily out of developing inconsistencies in the cultural system, for instance out of new knowledge that casts doubt on the appropriateness of inherited reality assumptions and values or out of reinterpretations of religious themes that make certain values more salient than before and render others problematic. Socially, such cultural developments are likely to be related to quite narrow circles set free in the societal division of labor to devote themselves to cultural matters. Their spread may be limited for very long periods by barriers of communication and by differences in scope and type of ideological concern between these and other subsystems of the society.[13]

Pervasive strain may arise also in the interrelations between cultural codes and the patterns of social life they are supposed to govern—between widespread aspirations and opportunity structures on the one hand and cultural legitimations on the other, between enforced norms or policies and widely held values, between different structurally available answers to relatively limited needs for ideological orientation. Such strains create a readiness for more inclusive ideological interpretation. Whether acceptable formulations come forth depends in part on the intellectual resources of the various groups affected. Available formulations, even if well articulated with the sociocultural strains in question, may be kept from gaining wide acceptance because of problems of communication between subcultures with different levels of ideological awareness and intellectual sophistication and because of intergroup relations that may render crosscutting appeals of ideological leadership ineffectual.

A secondary source of inclusive ideological formulations, which can also be understood as a special case of strain, is the development of innovative ideological systems challenging the tacit assumptions of the dominant order. Karl Mannheim has analyzed the transformation of largely latent traditional tenets into an explicit conservative ideology in response to the challenge of liberalism in nineteenth-century Germany.[14]

The content of relatively full-fledged ideological belief systems seeking to reorder the cultural codes and horizons of a society will be shaped by a number of factors suggested by the previous analysis. It is likely to reflect, first, the sociocultural strains to which the ideology constitutes a response; second, the material and ideal interests, the mentality and limited ideological orientations of the groups involved in the more explicit formulation as well as of the various categories of people to whom the ideological innovators appeal; third, the influence and challenge of other ideologies; and finally, fourth, the features of the cultural tradition, or traditions, which remain as stable reference points.

The first point is fairly obvious in principle. A later section which seeks to identify the ideological issues predominant in developing areas will be concerned primarily with the effects of these strains. It is worth pointing out one implication here, namely that ideologies tend to "conserve" themes arising out of a historical constellation of sociocultural strain well beyond this period of origin. Historical tensions may thus, if the ideology in question gains some measure of institutionalization, imprint their stamp on the cultural codes of a society for very long periods of time.

The second point generalizes Mannheim's thesis that conservatism has its roots in, is in an important sense an explication of, less reflected and systematized traditionalist orientations. This constitutes, of course, a reformulation of Marx's assertion that consciousness is determined by socio-economic position as well as of Durkheim's view of *représentations collectives* as "emanations" of underlying social structures. However, such determination of ideological content should be viewed as partial only, limited and specified by the influence of stable cultural orientations and of competing alternative ideological positions. Furthermore, it should be analyzed in differentiated fashion, taking into account the social position as well as the corresponding mentalities and ideological inclinations of both divers

originating groups and different audiences of their ideological appeals.

Reformulating certain ideas of Mannheim in the light of social-psychological insights about social validation, one can see that the perceived orientations of audiences are of influence beyond the fact that their adherence is sought. As noted previously, comprehensive ideological reorientations generate considerable insecurity, especially if the social integration of originating groups is uncertain and ambiguous. This insecurity may be compensated by leaning towards the "sound sense" of certain strata considered "healthy," embodying the "future," or symbolizing in other ways central ideals of the new orientations.

Rival ideologies, the third major influence, not only force problem formulations on each other which may be answered in opposite directions; they also may provide answers of so general persuasiveness that they are taken over by an ideology of different over-all orientation. Two possible outcomes of this latter type of process are of special importance. One is the more or less complete absorption of one ideological position by another or, in the more balanced case, the merger of two positions. Such concentration may go hand in hand with, and be furthered by, increasing polarization from an opposing cluster of ideological positions. Polarization may, however, be counteracted by the other outcome of interest here, a generalization of certain views across all major lines of ideological orientation. Which of these outcomes is the more likely depends on the other factors influencing ideological content just indicated. Of particular relevance, aside from cultural premises shared across different subdivisions, is whether or not different ideologies seek to win over the same audiences and how the inclinations of these audiences relate to the contentions of the competing ideologies. This in turn is contingent on the patterns of interest conflict and of cleavages in mentalities and limited ideological inclinations. If major cleavages and conflict alignments divide the same groupings and strata on a variety of central issues, polarization is more likely than generalization, while a "criss-cross" pattern of alignments and cleavages would be more favorable to generalization.[15]

Among the consequences of conflict and competition between ideologies, then, is a certain decrease in latency: What is problematic to one ideological position tends to become problematic for others as well. Furthermore, such competition paradoxically tends to contribute, under a variety of conditions, to consensus about central ideological issues if not necessarily about the appropriate answers.

The fourth point, finally, concerns issues that are among those most heatedly debated in contemporary sociological theory. What is argued here in the first place is a minimum of continuity in the cultural premises of social structures even in radical social change. I would hesitate to go further and posit simply a greater resistance to change the higher a cultural or social pattern ranks in the hierarchy of cybernetic control. Although an assumption of such differential protection against change is plausible, and fruitful as a perspective generating hypothesis, it is not the only reasonable assumption pertinent here. For instance, certain elements of empirical knowledge, especially those related to survival, would rank low in the hierarchy of cybernetic controls but are likely to exhibit similar if not greater stability than basic values and religious ideas, except for change in the direction of greater adequacy and completeness. Still, the insistence that the most remotely controlling cultural codes, higher level values and ultimate orientations of a religious nature, are also likely to be rather stable seems to be more correct than an orientation that treats these elements of culture as a mere, and highly variable, reflection of underlying—more "real"—social conditions.

Continuity in certain components of cultural orientation, which then shape and give direction to ideological innovations, is not identical with societal consensus about them. The continuity may be specific to certain subsystems, and in different subsystems of a society different aspects of previous cultural traditions may persist as stable reference points. Continuity and consensus are not unrelated to each other, however. Continuities are the more likely to entail consensus the greater the homogeneity of previous orientations, the stronger the interdependence and contact between subsystems, and the more similar and simultaneous the tensions that induce ideological reorientations. Conversely, consensus increases the chances of continuity through multiple social anchorage for the same cultural tenets. On the basis of these considerations, we should expect in many developing countries far fewer cultural continuities and less consensus transcending ideological orientations and conflicts than in relatively modernized societies. A likely response to the disruptive possibilities this entails are attempts to constrict and curtail ideological developments by political means.

MODERNIZATION AND THE IDEOLOGICAL QUEST

Radical ideologies seeking to reorder the cultural codes of social action are particularly likely to arise in the course of modernization. The "great transformation" of society, personality and culture which we term modernization has only few parallels in human history. What is upset in its course are cultural traditions accumulated over centuries and consonant with patterns of social and personal life which, in spite of significant variations and developments, have remained basically similar through several millenia.

While a full analysis of even the major conditions engendering a readiness for the ideological quest in the course of modernization is obviously beyond the limits of this essay, a few points may be highlighted. These will be useful for an identification of recurrent ideological issues raised by processes of modernization. Modernization tends to dissolve the isolation and the traditional stability of the parochial units characteristic of large-scale agrarian societies. In these, most people come into contact primarily with members of their own "primordial" groups. Such a limited range of social experience results in a mutual reinforcement of the major reference groups, both positive and negative. Social relations as well as cognitive and moral outlooks can be and are in such circumscribed social contexts predominantly ascriptive, particularistic, and diffuse in orientation.[16]

The self-sufficiency of these units breaks down with increasing, even if limited, functional differentiation and interdependence. Related technological changes, especially in transportation and communication, add to the same effect independently. It is crucial that widened horizons and broadened social contacts as well as the promise of a better life in incipient modern structures may undermine the traditional patterns of life and orientation without leading to an institutionalization of modern alternatives in their stead, alternatives which would be characterized by a variety of types of affiliation, multiple and potentially dissonant reference groups, and predominantly specific, universalistic, and performance-related orientations. In the poignant phrase of Marion Levy, modern patterns of behavior and outlook act as a "universal social solvent" on premodern social structures.[17]

These processes, which do not, then, coincide with successful modernization on a large scale but are set off in some measure from the very beginning by efforts at modernization, raise ideological problems by taking away the "natural," inevitable character of the traditional forms of social organization and culture, by confronting people with crucial choices of roles and affiliations, by rendering the future less certain and by stimulating dissonant preliminary solutions offered to ideological questions. The ideological questioning thus engendered may be stilled temporarily by limited answers developed from the traditional cultural background or from some ad hoc compromises between old and modern orientations. However, uncertainty and dissatisfaction with the old cultural codes and their implementation are, in view of the radical divergence between traditional and modern orientations and of the peculiar vulnerability of traditional patterns in these situations, likely not only to persist but to escalate in scope and depth, creating a fairly widespread readiness for inclusive ideological reorientations. Both this readiness and the difficulties of gaining a firm institutional grounding for new orientations will be increased when for longer periods of time old patterns of social life and cultural orientation have been uprooted without new ones being firmly established, when, that is, life has acquired a persistent anomic quality.

In all societies where modernization has met with some success there are parts of the population that in their work roles and related group affiliations experience little difficulty in judging and being judged by performance, using universalistic standards and applying them in highly specific contexts and that have these and similar roles and affiliations fairly well integrated with others of different quality. Here the pressures for ideological questioning may be less immediate and less drastic than in transitory and anomic social contexts. However, the very acceptance of such a complex of modern orientations increases intellectual sensitivity and versatility to a certain extent; and even if at the levels of role performance and collectivity membership things are relatively smoothly aligned, there remain—in an inconsistent and ever-changing societal context—unresolved problems of intergroup relations, of wider collective identities, of societal values, and of even more remote cultural orientation.

One aspect of modernization, implicit in some of the foregoing considerations, is particularly important in fostering a readiness for radical ideological reorientations. The processes discussed undermine the inherited division of labor in ideological matters, which thus loses its capacity to contain the ideological quest and limit its "radicalization."

The old centers of ideological interpretation find their influence declining as its bases in the traditional structures of group affiliation, authority, prestige, and communication are eroded. Aside from the adequacy of their orientations, new forms of "mediated trust" would be required but are not easily developed. Whatever integration and mutual articulation existed previously between different centers is likely to be upset and turned into contradiction and competition, as new groups claim the right and the competence to develop their own ideological answers, as specialization changes spheres of competence, and as the impact of modernization is felt unevenly in different centers. These conditions make it more likely that ideological developments in any one center will go beyond its particular specialized concern and approach the scope of radical ideologies.

Old as well as new elites are likely to find themselves with a more volatile and insecure support than in traditional times. This is of particular importance for political elites, but relevant for others, too. They will therefore increasingly tend to resort to ideological appeals to their constituencies in order to maintain and widen their base.

Ideological controversy at the top may engender considerable strains and open further horizons for ideological questioning at the base. Much of these controversies will, of course, be relatively remote from the broad public. They may also be kept intentionally out of the open. Furthermore, coalition formation may limit the acting out of conflicts, and attempts may be made by political elites to end controversy and strife and to substitute authoritarian decree for ideological diversity and debate. However, even if these reactions succeed in confining certain issues to relatively narrow social realms, they do not solve them. The issues remain as problems for inclusive ideological reorientation.

One peculiar aspect of the elite structure in contemporary developing societies deserves special mention. In all contemporary cases of modernization diffusion of knowledge, technical equipment, forms of organization, and patterns of orientation from more advanced countries is of paramount importance. This entails that the groups particularly associated with such intersocietal transfer of cultural items will rise in functional importance and gain in power, prestige, and self-evaluation. Reinhard Bendix goes so far as to compare the strategic importance of educated minorities in "follower societies" to the role assigned to social classes like workers and capitalists in earlier analyses of modernization in Europe.[18] The fact that these groups are mediating between cultures increases their awareness of ideological problems beyond the level characteristic of equivalent occupational groups in relatively modernized societies. Obstacles encountered in the pursuit of their modernizing goals, imbalances between the development and the utilization of educated manpower, and conflict with more established cultural elites threatened by the rise of these groups tend to sharpen their problem consciousness and give a distinctive character to their emergent ideological orientations.

In the search for solutions these groups are able and likely to draw on ideological developments in more advanced countries. Yet they are in varying degree anchored in the indigenous culture and exposed to indigenous ideological responses. Under special circumstances of relative insulation from their own society and culture their orientations may come close to being a replica of foreign ideologies. A more likely outcome is a variety of syncretist patterns of thought, borrowing and reinterpreting foreign elements and relating them to indigenous problems and ideological inclinations. In either case and whether their ideological orientations are formulated as full-fledged ideological systems or not, the new cultural elites are likely to be extremely influential in shaping the development of ideologies.

MODERNIZATION AND RECURRENT IDEOLOGICAL THEMES

What are the major ideological issues and themes that arise repeatedly, or perhaps universally, in the course of modernization? It may seem that no generalizations are possible because of the diversity of foreign influences and pressures, internal cultural traditions, levels and types of economic organization and performance, stratification patterns, cleavages and alignments of primordial affiliations, and forms of political process, characterizing in an endless variety of combinations the situation in the different developing countries. Yet, if direct empirical generalizations describing patterns common to all developing nations are impossible, the previous considerations provide some basis for propositions holding true under certain conditions.

Some of these conditions must remain implicit in the following discussion for reasons of space, others will be indicated specifically. Generally the following considerations confine themselves to "late-comers" of modernization, countries which can take others as models, as "reference societies," and which attempt to modernize in a context of foreign influence, help, pressure, and, possibly, threat.[19] A specific type of such foreign influence are, of course, the varieties of colonial domination leaving in their wake "new states" shaped by the experience of emancipation as well as by the past and the continuing exigencies of the international environment. For most arguments, furthermore, a model of large-scale agrarian societies will serve as a baseline, of societies to some extent held together by governmental institutions, dominant religion, and a few other specialized activities such as limited market exchange but otherwise characterized by a high level of parochial segmentation and a strong development of primordial ingroup-outgroup relations. Patterns of primordial solidarity and alienation, based on ethnicity, religion, language, community, region, and status categories, are in their origin closely related to segmentation but tend, at least in the early

phases of development, to overlay functional differentiation also. Thus, various functionally specialized elites, merchant groups, and religious and other experts may be identical in personnel with certain primordial groups or may be defined and articulated with the rest of the societal structure in a fashion analogous to primordial relations. Finally, the assumption will be made, valid in most contemporary cases, that any serious attempt at development will give government agencies a more significant role than in the earlier European processes of modernization and than under either colonial or premodern indigenous rule. In virtually all contemporary developing countries, government action is, for a variety of reasons not to be discussed here, crucial for initiating and implementing developmental policies and for maintaining order in the face of tensions engendered directly and indirectly by such policies.

Perhaps the most obvious recurrent problem for modernizing societies is the redefinition of collective identities. Established solidary units, their boundaries, their interrelations with each other, and their relative importance to those affiliated are made problematic by growing interdependence between previously segregated parts of the society as well as by contact and exchange with other countries. At the same time, but by no means synchronized in successful implementation, there are functional exigencies of development requiring new social identifications and redefinitions of the interrelations between collective objects of loyalty. It is sufficient to mention here a few such imperatives only. Identifications with groups and social categories have to be compatible with the allocation of people to differentiated work roles relatively independent of various ascriptive origins. Cooperation on the job as well as in voluntary associations focusing on specific goals would be hampered by narrow and inflexible ascriptive solidarities with their attendant mistrust of and hostility towards outgroups. New broader identifications coextensive in scope with the framework of government have to be built up as an underpinning of efforts to reach collective goals. The same identifications are also crucial in developing a comprehensive solidarity within which differences of origin, value orientation, and interest can be seen as not ultimately divisive — which allow, in other words, conflict and cooperation on a society-wide basis.

These social identifications, loyalties, and hostilities in the aggregate constitute one of the fundamental bases of social existence. They define who "we" and "they" are and provide the social context for personal identity as well. This suggests that these beliefs and commitments are not likely to be changed easily and that actual changes as well as problems and threats in this respect engender profound anxieties and set loose tremendous energies.

Nationalism, in all its varieties, can be broadly understood as an ideological response to the facts that old social identities become problematic and crumble and that new ones and new alignments of groupings and social identifications are required by modernization. Nationalism, to be sure, has one important source in conflict with other nations: in the struggle for independence, in competition with other countries, and in quarrels over the geographic and, more generally, the social boundaries between national social systems. This can be understood, though, as a special case of the more general problem. Whether it is or not, however, it seems likely that the internal problems of nation-building are of greater importance. The modernizing elites in virtually all developing countries face the need to build up broad support for collective efforts; and a comprehensive framework of solidarity is required if the strains generated are not to threaten any internal order. That conflict with national outgroups is not unrelated to such efforts and may serve unifying functions is one of the oldest insights of statecraft and sociology.

A nationalist ideology can engage furthermore the quest for identification of those uprooted from their previous social locations. This is not to say that it can provide a real equivalent for more immediate and more stably meaningful affiliations, but it can capture some of the dislocated commitments and give ideological meaning to some of the most affected groups and individuals. It thus taps a tremendous source of support for collective national endeavours.

That nationalism can easily be defined broad enough to embrace a variety of substantively different orientations is another source of its utility for societal integration. However, if nationalist orientations can be made highly salient — and for several reasons indicated that should be the case in many instances — they are unlikely to be without influence on the content of ideologies incorporating them. Dominant elites may thus manipulate competing ideologies by "playing up" nationalist issues and by linking other ideological commitments to national issues.

Any given nationalist ideology is likely to encounter opposition, too, as well as qualified and ambivalent reactions. In most developing countries there are likely to be minorities excluded from full membership in the national community, whether the primary criterion for definition chosen is language, ethnicity, religion, participation in a common history, or a combination of such bases. These groups may attempt to promote a different conception of what really constitutes the nation, develop a separatist nationalism of their own, or adopt a more universalistic posture and seek to moderate nationalist feeling. However, if their exclusion is contingent on orientations attributed to them rather than on ascriptive qualities and if the appeals of nationalism are strong, such groups may develop a secondary and often particularly intense nationalism always ready to prove that they, too, are good members of the community.

Other sources of opposition, qualification, and ambivalence are vested interests in local and regional patterns of loyalty, adherence to ideologies different from the particular content of a given nationalist ideology, and close association with modernizing cultural transfers from other countries, particularly when the latter are seen by the majority as hostile or are used as a foil against which national self-definition takes place. People involved in cultural diffusion from more advanced countries may of course be ardent nationalists, but their mediating role is then likely to qualify their nationalist orientations and will under certain circumstances induce intense ambivalences. One frequent outcome is a compensatory emphasis on the indigenous virtues inherited from a real or imagined past, side by side with an embrace of the foreign technical civilization. Of this, the dichotomies between German "culture" and Western "civilization" or between Eastern "depth" and Western "efficiency" are examples.

The near-universal emergence of nationalism in developing countries points to the centrality of problems of social integration in the process of modernization. This centrality is the greater the more we can take for granted — and to some extent I think we can — that old forms of social integration are particularly vulnerable when confronted with modern social patterns and that some modernization and differentiation on the levels of roles and operative organizations may be difficult to establish but can proceed with little elaborate ideological justification, although discipline and performance orientation are likely to receive strong emphasis in most modernizing ideological indoctrination.

However, nationalism by no means offers answers to all or even most integrative social problems raised in the course of modernization, at least if the lowest common denominator of the diversity of nationalist ideologies is examined. In addition, there are recurrent ideological issues pertaining to other functional problem areas than that of integration.

Two related sources of ideological concern that pertain to the problem area of integration are reactions to a system of stratification in transition and the demands of newly mobilized strata to be included in spheres of political and cultural life previously open only to a privileged few. Several factors combine to make stratification patterns an object of ideological redefinition and contention: (1) the decomposition of old legitimations for differential privilege, (2) the emergence of new criteria for judging a man's or a group's worth, (3) the persistence of stark contrasts in wealth and other privilege characteristic of traditional agrarian societies, (4) the accumulation of wealth and power due to allocating mechanisms unrelated to either old or new bases of legitimation, and (5) the development of the contrast between workers and employers outside the context of traditional relations.

One response to situations of this type is, of course, radical socialism. However, its mass base is likely to be limited, especially in the very early phases of development, by the limited size of the urban working class, by the disorganization of large parts of the lower classes that are relatively emancipated from tradition, and by residues of primordial cleavages dividing the potential following. A crucial and rather unpredictable source of support are members of various intellectual elites. They are more open to sweeping ideological reformulations, and they are receptive to ideological belief systems developed in more advanced countries, a factor more important in this context than in regard to problems of national unification. The critical and very complicated question is in what ways they are tied to privileged strata and groups interested in the status quo and, conversely, to what extent they define their inevitable frustrations and partial alienation in terms of social class.

The inclinations toward radical socialism are modified and generally moderated by the fact that a variety of groups and strata with greater stakes in differential privilege are led by different paths also to adopt socialist or quasi-socialist ideological orientations. Nationalism as such has little to offer in response to the divisive issues arising from changes in the system of stratification. However, where both ideological elites and relatively broad strata define themselves as neutral in the conflicts between old and new, top and bottom, while embracing nationalist ideals, they are likely to insist on mediation in the name of internal peace, "objectivity," and national strength. Such mediation, especially when combined with assigning a strong role to government intervention, typically entails ideological orientations that have a close similarity to socialist ideology. Intertwined with such responses or developing independently are typical orientations of traditional elites. It has long been noticed that the conservative criticisms of capitalism in Europe bore a certain similarity to the socialist critique. These inclinations, it appears,

were not unique to specific European constellations but are characteristic of the value orientations of traditional elites in most large-scale agrarian societies and of their predominant concern with political and religious matters.[20]

These arguments would be misunderstood if the conclusion were drawn that different versions of socialism are as likely to constitute a formula for broad ideological consensus as the varieties of nationalism do. This may be the outcome, and such instances indicate that socialism often is little but another expression for ideological gropings toward societal integration. However, ideological division is much more likely in these matters pertaining to stratification than in regard to the imperatives of national unity conceived more narrowly.

The probability of divergent ideological responses to problems of stratification is increased by the second and closely related integration issue mentioned. The mobilization of people previously tied to narrow social units through interaction and orientation patterns characterized by ascription, particularism, and diffuseness implies that new groups demand participation in as yet relatively closed cultural and political centers.[21] Social mobilization, however, proceeds quite unevenly and applies to the clienteles and audiences of various ideological elites in different degrees. Thus, it is likely that these elites will respond to demands for increased participation with different images of actual and ideal elite-mass relations.

While issues of this kind arise in many fields, for instance with regard to "mass education" and the intrusion of plebeian and mere utilitarian ideas into the inner sanctum of learned culture, the most obvious area is the political one. The issues here may be conventionally labeled as problems of "democratization." However, all the different interpretations of democratic rule that historical and philosophical scholarship has identified in European ideological developments are found, in a different and varying quantitative mix, in contemporary developing countries, too. They tend to be associated with different ideological positions according to differential chances of political success as well as in terms of ideological consistency. Perhaps the weakest is a conception of democratic rule anchored in the decisions of individuals freely associating with each other to pursue common political goals. This would be in line with the relatively low levels of mobilization and the even less-developed reintegration of people into more flexible organizational frameworks. Competing with this classic liberal conception, which may receive a measure of support through ideological imports from the West, are various — explicitly or implicitly — more elitist notions. Traditional ideas of representation of the populace through its established superiors stand in conflict and/or interpenetrate with charismatic, plebiscitarian demands for assent, claims to expression of the *volonté générale* based on intricate ideological arguments about the nature of society and history, and a disenchantment with popular rule turning to the enlightened rule of the few as the true representation of the real needs of the populace.

Total rejection of the masses is unlikely except for exclusive and esoteric intellectual elites that do not aim at a popular following and disdain political success. Even here, a certain idealization of broad segments of the population is not rare because of the need to seek social validation, if only fictionally, discussed earlier. On the other hand, the images of the masses in other ideologies tend to be selective, and the debunking and glorification of different parts of the populace varies with ideological orientation and political strategy. Whether the common man, the free peasant, the serf, the solidier, the worker, the *petit bourgeois*, or the *Lumpenproletarier* is praised or seen as debased, supposed to be yet unspoiled or to provide the key to the future, is not only indicative of ideological dispositions, but also shapes in turn the ideological responses to the demands for democratization in the wide sense of the word.

Of the recurrent ideological issues concerning other types of problems, those pertaining to collective goal attainment are the most prominent in the foreground of ideological concern. Aside from justifying or questioning the role of government institutions in the efforts to achieve development — a set of issues which on balance contributes to the prevalence of nationalist and quasi-socialist orientations — it is the various measures and paths toward development that are argued here: which areas of the economy and of technological development should be given priority, the relative importance of mass education, the timing of savings and investments favoring present or future generations, or the use of coercive measures in government action. Although these questions are the most immediately pressing political problems, the answers seem to be either relatively pragmatic and variable or to follow from ideological orientations formulated with regard to integrative problems higher in the "cybernetic hierarchy" of sociocultural systems. While specifying ideological controversies and engaging more specific collective interests of different groups and strata, these problems do not constitute typically the primary focus of comprehensive ideology formation.

Extending this argument schematically, one could reach the conclusion that problems of societal integration are also not the most important focus of ideology formation as, in terms of Parsons' hypothetical hierarchy of cybernetic controls, they are in turn subject to control and information from higher-level sociocultural codes: ultimate values defining the identity of a society, the patterning of values in the cultural system, and religious orientations especially. I am inclined, though, to argue that the central ideological problem focus is indeed in the area of integration — not that higher-level orientations do not become problematic and in the extreme cases shattered, although in contemporary developing countries disturbances may very well be greatest in the patterns of social integration. I would rather argue that the latency character of these higher-level sociocultural patterns persists even if their internal order and the interrelations with other components of social structure are fundamentally disturbed. Such disturbances are not without consequences. They may engender, in limited groups, unease and *malaise* and in the long run would seem to be crucial for the resolution of persistent ideological problems. However, for shorter time periods — and these may extend as long as several generations — I would advance the hypothesis that most ideologies, especially those which seek a broad following, treat such problems vaguely and develop their answers as an outgrowth of ideological orientations pertaining to societal integration.[22]

Among the latency problems that are treated in such fashion are clashes between ultimate societal values which are of consequence for the legitimation of the governmental structure and of the integrative order; furthermore the ideals concerning the future shape of the society, visions of a long-run path from early origins through recent history to the distant future, and conceptions of the ultimate place, possibly the mission, of one's own society in the community of nations, the family of man or, depending on the conception adopted, a jungle world of evil and inferior outgroups.

Instead of a tentative examination of how these themes can be related to different conditions shaping ideological orientations, two other and more subtle phenomena pertaining to latency problems should at least be mentioned. The first concerns the place of religion or of functional equivalents of religion in the sociocultural order of modernizing societies, the second certain responses of particularly sensitized intellectuals to unresolved problems of ultimate meaning.

Robert Bellah and Talcott Parsons have argued that one condition for a sustained sociocultural accommodation of modernity and continuing change is a differentiation between religion and the more specific institutional order of a society. Such differentiation allows ultimate beliefs and values to inform lower-level structures and processes without introducing the rigidities of a less-differentiated and more directly prescriptive pattern.[23] It appears that such a balance between irrelevance and too close involvement is extremely difficult to achieve and to maintain. One type of problem arises when religious communities cling to traditional prescriptive control of behavior. This tends to engender sharp ideological conflicts which center, however, more often on resulting integration problems such as church-state relations or the conditions of full membership in a developing national community than on the underlying more general problem.

Related phenomena are found in tendencies of ideologies, particularly of those that have achieved a high level of inclusive and systematic formulation, to reach into the realms of ultimate meaning and of religious orientations to extend towards persistent "involvement" in ideological and other more pragmatic concerns. These extensions of belief systems may be more flexible than the traditional concatenation of religious meaning and routine patterns of social life. Furthermore, they are often concerned only with matters of general consensus dramatized for different audiences by being rendered in religious or secular language, respectively. However, when understood as dedifferentiations, the parallel between these tendencies and the traditional case becomes clear. This would suggest that such developments can under certain circumstances engender ideological conflicts which are difficult to contain within the institutions of conflict regulation and in which compromise becomes virtually impossible.

On the other hand, religious orientations may, rather than becoming closely involved with the institutional order and its problems, lose their relevance for social and personal life altogether. They may be seen as a residue of the past incapable of giving an ultimate basis of meaning to complex personal, social, and cultural problems. Such a disjunction between inherited and currently offered beliefs about ultimate meanings and other central orientations towards the sociocultural order will be experienced as deeply disturbing only by a small number of people sufficiently preoccupied with complex problems remote from daily routines.

Immersion into activities one has a stake and a chance of success in, be they familial, professional, or administrative-political, may serve to evade these questions, and this is probably the most frequent response. It may be associated with a critical disdain for the prevailing "shallow optimism," for the fierce ideological and political contention over lesser issues and for what is seen as an age of superficiality and cultural decay. Where the immediate ties to routine tasks and careers are weaker and where the intellectuals involved see little chance to influence ideological and cultural developments, the tendencies toward withdrawal and "alienation" from modernity and tradition are likely to become dominant. Small esoteric ideological groupings often spring up under these conditions. Their orientations tend to be elitist and often exhibit a romantic vagueness and intellectual poverty due to the fact that they are cut off from both pragmatic problems and the more differentiated cultural resources of the community. They may gain a broad following if widespread and persistent dissatisfaction with integrative problems and a lack of national success make wider strata receptive to ideas about a radical reordering of social and cultural orientations advanced by such groups.[24]

Concluding this—necessarily incomplete—review of ideological issues and responses likely to arise in the course of "secondary" modernization, I wish to draw attention to a few formal aspects of the problem. It seems that it is far easier to identify, predict, and explain with some confidence ideological problems and issues than the responses to them. Aside from a certain degree of creativity, responses are shaped by indigenous cultural traditions and a continuing proliferation of foreign influences and models which introduce a greater amount of variability than is found with respect to the basic structural changes that give rise to a number of fairly general ideological problems. In addition to such basic similarities, there are, of course, many variations between societies on the issue side, too.

One reason why this asymmetry between the determination of ideological problems and that of ideological responses does not typically make for a greater variety of distinct full-fledged ideological formulations is found in the fact that the people sufficiently mobilized and exposed to cultural matters to engage in ideological discourse constitute often a very thin stratum only. The small size of this stratum is frequently combined with a fairly homogeneous education as well as other mutual social ties. Furthermore, shared collective ambitions may cut across incipient lines of ideological cleavage. Finally, the limited degree of more general social mobilization and the very fact of rapid, if limited, change impede the crystallization of stable audiences and followings. Thus, what is characteristic of the ideological scene in many developing countries is a great fluidity of ideological positions allowing for coalitions and mergers based on broad common denominators such as nationalism and "socialism."

The paramount role of government and of political

elites in contemporary developing countries contributes similarly to this aggregation and amalgamation of ideological inclinations. However, it introduces in many cases an important further element: purposive ideological indoctrination and manipulation. The focus of the preceding discussion was predominantly on structural determinants of relatively spontaneous and autonomous ideological inclinations. It paid only passing and indirect attention to calculated mass persuasion informed by policy goals of the dominant elites. Such mass persuasion cannot be successful without being responsive to widely felt ideological problems and inclinations, but it can shape ideological responses and prevent, in combination with coercive control, extremes of ideological diversity and strife.

CONCLUSION

The major arguments of this essay can be stated in seven theses.

1. If the study of ideology is concerned with certain mechanisms of change in the cultural contexts of elementary social behavior and of more complex social structures and processes, it seems useful to remove cognitive distortion as well as other pejorative qualifications from the definition of ideology; furthermore, the concept of ideology should then be integrated with a more inclusive theoretical framework such as that of the theory of action. Within this framework the proposed definition focuses on the relatively undifferentiated combination of basic cognitive and evaluative orientations without denying the utility of keeping evaluation and cognition analytically distinct.

2. There is no radical discontinuity in the processes of ideological developments in relatively stable societal structures and in societies undergoing fundamental change. General considerations about the incidence and salience of ideological beliefs suggest (1) that there exist strong strains toward latency of basic cognitive-evaluative orientations; (2) that normative contradictions, situations of choice with long-term consequences and changes in the structural "scene" of routine activities engender increased ideological concern; (3) that certain occasions of increased ideological concern are routine events for collectivities while they are extraordinary for subgroups and individuals and that for these there are often standardized ideological interpretations offered; (4) that in every complex society there exist "centers" of more sustained ideological concern corresponding to a continuous incidence of conditions that generally give rise to ideological questioning; and (5) that these centers of sustained ideological

concern are interrelated in complex and varying ways with each other, with the more peripheral intermittent ideological questioning, and with other aspects of the social structure such as the distribution of power; two especially important aspects of these interrelations are the extent to which there is a division of labor, a pattern of functional differentiation rather than segmentation, and the degree of direct and indirect control the different centers are subject to.

3. In addition to the distinction between intermittent and sustained ideological concerns, ideologies which limit themselves to one institutional sphere of society leave many cognitive-evaluative premises of social life latent and understand themselves largely as explications of a perceived consensus may be distinguished from those that tend to be inclusive in their concerns, minimize latency, and aim for a further consensus rather than spelling out an existing one. Although it is realized that concrete ideologies are likely to fall in between these polar types and in the three dimensions indicated there may be variations which are to some extent independent of each other, attention in the context of modernization is focused on the conditions leading to radical ideologies that approximate the inclusive, nonconsensual type minimizing latency.

4. Strain between the components of a sociocultural system is the broadest characterization of these conditions. Aside from certain specifications of the nature of such strains, it seems important to distinguish strains within the cultural system from strains in the relations between institutionalized aspects of the cultural tradition and other components of the social structure. While in the first case obstacles to a widespread diffusion of radical ideological questioning are greater than in the second, they deserve careful consideration in each case. An examination of central features of the processes of modernization shows that they make strains of both types virtually inevitable. One important aspect of these changes is that they upset the inherited division of labor in ideological matters. Furthermore, such strains are likely to occur even if modern institutions do not—or not yet—become operative on a wide scale. In contemporary cases of modernization, diffusion of technology, patterns of social organization, and ideological interpretations give the educated classes a particularly important role and modify both the conditions of ideological concerns and the direction ideological responses take.

5. The content of radical ideological belief systems is determined by four types of factors: (1) the nature of strains to which an ideology responds, (2) the less inclusive and more routinized ideological inclinations and orientations of the originating groups as

well as of their audiences and reference groups, (3) the content of competing ideologies, and (4) the cultural traditions that remain as unquestioned value and reality premises.

6. Among the most prominent ideological orientations in developing countries are varieties of nationalist, socialist, and democratic ideals. These are interpreted as responses to pervasive integrative problems of the societies in question: the crumbling of old and the need for new patterns of collective solidarity and identification, the problems of stratification systems in transition, and the demands of newly mobilized strata to be included in previously exclusive spheres of political and cultural life. Opposing responses are often partially co-opted, a tendency which, in conjunction with certain typical characteristics and problems of the cultural and political elites, results in the variety and the characteristic fluidity and dilution of these belief systems.

7. A final hypothesis presented is that integrative problems rather than the economic and political ones of adaptation and goal attainment tend to constitute the primary focus of ideological developments in the course of modernization and that integrative problems also are likely to predominate over questions of ultimate meaning in shaping the content and the direction of ideological formulations. The first assertion differs from models espoused by vulgar Marxisms which take economic interests as the decisive determinants of ideology. This assumption is at odds with the fact that ideological formations often unify collectivities with quite divergent economic interests, and it makes it difficult to explain why ideological formations tend to persist long after constellations of economic interest remotely plausible as explanations have vanished. The second assertion differs from a schematic application of Parsons' hypothetical hierarchy of cybernetic controls. My argument here is not that religious problems do not arise in the course of modernization, in which case there would be no serious theoretical issue, nor that their solution is irrelevant to sustained support for modernization, in which case any version of the cybernetic hierarchy conception would be rejected, but rather that these matters tend to remain latent even if past conceptions become highly problematic and that integrative problems are typically so much at the center of ideological concern that religious responses tend to merge with and become translated into ideas pertaining to integration.

In conclusion, it should be noted that one major complex of questions about the interrelations between ideological developments and modernization has virtually been excluded from consideration here. A good deal of sociological theory has been concerned with the functional problems of which ideological developments aid or impede, are required for or prevent, breakthroughs towards modernization, which are positively or negatively functional for the maintenance of thrusts towards modernity, and which specific mechanisms are involved in the effects of these ideological developments on various aspects of modernization.[25] These problems have been neglected here except for certain constellations where functional exigencies were assumed to be perceived by ideological elites and to have feedback effects on ideological orientations.

NOTES

1. In fact, the definition is quite similar to the one developed by Talcott Parsons in *The Social System* (Glencoe, Ill.: The Free Press, 1951), p. 349, except that I interpret Parsons' formulation to stipulate that ideologies have by definition certain functions for collectivities. In the sociology of knowledge tradition, cognitive inadequacy is typically made a defining characteristic and the focus of the analysis. Parsons adopts in "An Approach to the Sociology of Knowledge," *Sociological Theory and Modern Society* (New York: The Free Press, 1967), pp. 139-165, a similar concept in which "deviations from scientific objectivity are essential criteria of an ideology" (p. 153). While the study of cognitive selectivity and distortion is a perfectly legitimate pursuit, it appears not helpful to make intellectual inferiority a part of the definition of a concept central to the understanding of symbolic orientations of people and their reorganization; see on this point the polemic arguments of Clifford Geertz in "Ideology as a Cultural System," D. A. Apter (ed.), *Ideology and Discontent* (New York: The Free Press, 1964), pp. 47-76.

2. See, for instance, Robert N. Bellah, "Epilogue," R. N. Bellah (ed.), *Religion and Progress in Modern Asia* (New York: The Free Press, 1965), pp. 169-171, who in turn relies on the theoretical work of Parsons and Karl W. Deutsch. Structural differentiation is, in the long run, one of the major conditions of increased adaptive capacity—a necessary though not sufficient condition, incidentally. Important advances in its theoretical analysis have laid the foundations for the conception of modernization referred to. Attempts to formulate specific characteristics of modern patterns of social and cultural life have long centered around Parsons' pattern variables; see for instance Marion J. Levy, Jr., *Modernization and the Structure of Societies* (Princeton: Princeton University Press, 1966). Work that goes significantly beyond this level of analysis is represented by Talcott Parsons, "Evolutionary Universals in Society," *American Sociological Review,* 29 (June 1964), pp. 339-357; Robert N. Bellah, "Religious Evolution," *American Sociological Review,* 29 (June 1964), pp. 358-374; and S. N. Eisenstadt, *Modernization: Protest and Change* (Englewood Cliffs: Prentice-Hall, 1966). See also my "Partial Modernization," in this volume.

3. Niklas Luhmann, "Positives Recht und Ideologie," *Archives for Philosophy of Law and Social Philosophy,* 53 (1967), pp. 531-571, makes the "evaluation of values" achieved by ideologies the crucial link between modernization and the emergence of ideologies of the specifically modern type. Positive law, the "norming of norms" without recourse to a stable higher or natural law, is seen as an analogous mechanism of coping with extreme sociocultural complexity. A highly suggestive discussion, this paper underrates in my opinion the

extent to which even modern ideologies typically rely on unquestioned value premises. These value premises may consist predominantly of values which are considered absolute, or they may be more flexible and highly generalized value orientations which govern a wide range of specific value choices in accordance with varying circumstance. Max Weber analyzed these matters in his discussion of *Gesinnungsethik* and *Verantwortungsethik*, respectively. Complex mixtures of the features of these pure types are likely. See also note 25.

4. Parsons, "Approach to the Sociology of Knowledge," *op. cit.*, and Geertz, "Ideology as a Cultural System," *op. cit.*

5. An early formulation of Parsons, pointing back to Weber, contains this conception in embryonic form:

> It was not Weber's view that religious ideas constitute the principal driving force in the determination of the relevant kinds of action. This role was rather played by what he called religious interests. A typical example is the interest in salvation. . . . But the mere interest in salvation is not enough. The question arises as to what kinds of specific action it will motivate. This, Weber's comparative analysis shows, will be very different according to the structure of the existential religious ideas according to which the individual achieves cognitive orientation to the principal nonempirical problems he faces in his situation ["The Role of Ideas in Social Action," T. Parsons, *Essays in Sociological Theory*, rev. ed. (Glencoe, Ill.: The Free Press, 1954) p. 28].

A fuller development of the conception is found in "An Outline of the Social System," Talcott Parsons *et al.*, (eds.), *Theories of Society* (New York: The Free Press, 1961), pp. 30-79, and in Talcott Parsons, *Societies: Evolutionary and Comparative Perspectives* (Englewood Cliffs: Prentice-Hall, 1966), Ch. 2.

6. See, for instance, M. Brewster Smith, Jerome S. Bruner, and Robert W. White, *Opinions and Personality* (New York: Wiley, 1955), and the cogent argument of Philip E. Converse, "The Nature of Belief Systems in Mass Publics," in David E. Apter (ed.), *Ideology and Discontent* (New York: The Free Press, 1964), pp. 206-261.

For the following I learned a great deal from recent discussions by Edward Shils and S. N. Eisenstadt of dispersed and attenuated forms of "charisma"—a phenomenon related to, but distinct from, what is called here "ideology." As I understand these extensions of Max Weber's concept, they include values, cognitive orientations as well as religious and quasi-religious orientations, focusing on the latter as grounds of order and meaning. See Edward Shils, "Charisma, Order and Status," *American Sociological Review*, 30 (April 1965), pp. 199-213; "Charisma," in David L. Sills (ed.), *International Encyclopedia of the Social Sciences* (New York: Macmillan and the Free Press, 1968); and especially S. N. Eisenstadt, (ed.), *Max Weber on Charisma and Institution Building* (Chicago: University of Chicago Press, 1968), pp. ix-lvi.

7. Thus, "specialized cultural legitimation" constitutes together with stratification the first pair of Parsons' evolutionary universals that goes beyond the earliest and simplest level of human social life; see Parsons, "Evolutionary Universals in Society," *op. cit.*

8. The two preceding paragraphs relate to a number of problems discussed in recent theoretical publications. Instead of expanding the sketch further, it may be useful to point to some of these ramifications. There is first and perhaps most obviously reference group theory. Although some suggestive ideas about the choice of normative reference groups have been developed in this tradition, the dearth of substantive generalizations and theoretical formulations is perhaps more noteworthy in this instance of "middle-range theory" launched to bring theory and research more closely together; for a recent review see Herbert H. Hyman and Eleanor Singer, (eds.), *Readings in Reference Group Theory and Research* (New York: The Free Press, 1968).

The problem discussed can further be seen as an instance of exchanges that utilize generalized media of exchange, which have been a central concern of the recent work of Talcott Parsons. Parsons treats money, power, influence, and value commitments as such generalized media. The exchanges discussed in the text involve, in the terminology of Parsons, influence and value commitments. What is said relates in particular to Parsons' preliminary treatment of influence as a medium of exchange; see Talcott Parsons, "On the Concept of Influence," *Sociological Theory and Modern Society*, Ch. 11, esp. pp. 368ff.; see also his "On the Concept of Political Power," *ibid*, Ch. 10, and "On the Concept of Value-Commitments," *Sociological Inquiry*, 38 (Spring 1968), pp. 135-169. Niklas Luhmann, *Vertrauen. Ein Mechanismus der Reduktion sozialer Komplexität* (Stuttgart: Enke, 1968), combines Parsons' conception of generalized media of exchange with phenomenological considerations of trust and notions taken from cybernetic system theory.

Finally, the recent work of S. N. Eisenstadt on processes of strata formation which focuses on a conceptual and empirical reconsideration of the phenomenon of prestige is pertinent here. Eisenstadt also uses the conception of generalized media of exchange, of which he sees prestige as one instance; but he emphasizes the structural limitations of its exchangeability which are crucial for the character of the stratification system of a society. See "Prestige, Participation and Strata Formation," J. A. Jackson, (ed.), *Social Stratification* (Cambridge: Cambridge University Press, 1968), pp. 62-103.

9. In a chapter of his *Delinquent Boys* (Glencoe: The Free Press, 1955), entitled "A General Theory of Subcultures," Albert K. Cohen gives a brilliant analysis of "the emergence of new cultural forms" which is directly pertinent to our concretely quite different problem; see esp. pp. 59-69. Edward A. Shils has, following Herman Schmalenbach, differentiated Toennies' concept of *Gemeinschaft* and has emphasized the role of the "ideological primary group." See his "Primordial, Personal, Sacred and Civil Ties," *British Journal of Sociology*, 8 (1957), pp. 130-145, and "Ideology," *International Encyclopedia of the Social Sciences*, 7 (1968), pp. 66-85, esp. p. 70. Shils' analysis of different modes of human affiliation and attachments as well as his work on charisma (see note 6) and on the concepts of "center" and "periphery" [see his "Centre and Periphery," *The Logic of Personal Knowledge. Essays Presented to Michael Polanyi* (London: Routledge and Kegan Paul, 1961), pp. 117-131] should be added to the set of recent theoretical discussions listed in the previous note which, in conjunction, promise significant advances in the understanding of ideological developments.

Problems of the extension of trust analogous to those discussed previously arise when a radical ideology faces the necessities of differentiation and growth beyond this close ideological community, problems of the delegation and specialization of responsibility which come with increasing success in seeking a following and with attempts to implement the new orientations. For some further discussion related to these problems see note 25.

10. This can, of course, also be understood as the development of another "center" which may have rather open and unclear boundaries but which is by no means lacking in structure. Aside from the composition of these audiences, questions about the authors who produce directly for such a market of ideas are pertinent to a structural analysis—questions concerning their typical education and career, their association with each other and their affiliation with other groups and collectivities, as well as the economic and organizational circumstances of the creation and marketing of their products.

11. A famous example of this last type of influence is the labor and welfare legislation in Imperial Germany which was initiated in part as a measure against the appeals of socialism.

12. On Mannheim's "total conception" of ideology see Karl Mannheim, *Ideology and Utopia* (London: Routledge and

Kegan Paul, 1936), Ch. 2. There are some interesting parallels between the conception of latency and Marx's concept of "reification" which would be worth exploring. For a differentiated discussion of the interrelations between division of labor, alienation, reification, religion, and ideology in the thought of Marx see Hans Barth, "Ideologie und ideologisches Bewusstsein in der Philosophie von Karl Marx," H. Barth, *Wahrheit und Ideologie* (Zürich: Manesse, 1945).

13. An example that does not pertain directly to ideologies but illustrates well what is meant here is the development of liberal theology in nineteenth century Germany which dominated the professional education of most ministers but found expression at the parish level only in exceptional cases.

14. See Karl Mannheim, "Das konservative Denken," *Archiv für Sozialwissenschaft und Sozialpolitik,* 57, pp. 68-142 and 470-495; transl. in K. Mannheim, *Essays on Sociology and Social Psychology* (London: Routledge and Kegan Paul, 1953).

15. Mannheim discussed some aspects of polarization and generalization in "Die Bedeutung der Konkurrenz im Geistigen," *Verhandlungen des sechsten deutschen Soziologentages* (Tübingen, 1929), pp. 35-83, transl. in K. Mannheim, *Essays on the Sociology of Knowledge* (London: Routledge and Kegan Paul, 1952). On coinciding versus crisscross patterns of conflict, E. A. Ross, *The Principles of Sociology* (New York: Century, 1920), and Georg Simmel, *Soziologie* (Berlin: Duncker & Humblot, 1923 and 1958), partly translated in *Conflict and the Web of Group Affiliations* (New York: The Free Press 1964), are the now-classic early discussions.

16. On primordial groupings see Clifford Geertz, "The Integrative Revolution: Primordial Sentiments and Civil Politics in the New States," C. Geertz (ed.), *Old Societies and New States* (New York: The Free Press, 1963), pp. 105-151, who takes off from Shils' essay referred to in note 9.

The pattern-variable scheme is a powerful tool for analyzing the relations between a mode of social organization based on parochial solidary units that are segmented from each other and held together primarily by limited market exchange and a few political and religious centers and agrarian means of production on the one hand, and a traditionalized cultural system on the other. See, for instance, S. N. Eisenstadt, *The Political System of Empires* (New York: The Free Press, 1963), and Levy, *op. cit.*

17. Levy, *op. cit.,* pp. 741-764.

18. Reinhard Bendix, "Tradition and Modernity Reconsidered," *Comparative Studies in Society and History,* 9 (April 1967), p. 334.

19. See Talcott Parsons, "Some Reflections on the Institutional Framework of Economic Development," in T. Parsons, *Structure and Process in Modern Societies* (New York: The Free Press, 1960), pp. 98-131, and Bendix, *op. cit.,* for two broad analyses emphasizing the differences between the first emergence of modern patterns and the interaction between diffusion and indigenous innovation in all other cases.

20. See, for instance, Parsons, "Some Reflections on . . . Economic Development," *op. cit.,* p. 123f. The affinity of the resulting policy orientation to socialism was recognized by Lenin who, when faced with the success of a Marxist revolution in an underdeveloped land, urged a policy of following the lead of Germany's "state capitalism," a model which had developed along the lines indicated in the text.

21. On the concept of social mobilization see Karl W. Deutsch, "Social Mobilization and Political Development," *American Political Science Review,* 55 (September 1961), pp. 493-514, who refers to Mannheim's conception of "fundamental democratization" accompanying modernization; see Karl Mannheim, *Man and Society in an Age of Reconstruction* (London: Paul, Trench and Trubner, 1940).

22. Primacy of integration problems seems to be built into the definition of ideology used by Parsons in *The Social System,* p. 349. In the later "Approach to the Sociology of Knowledge,"

op. cit., such primacy is not decreed by definition; it rather is strongly suggested as the result of the argument: "Perhaps it is not too much to say, in summary, that ideology is a special manifestation of the strains associated with the increasing division of labor, and that in turn it is an integrative mechanism which operates to mitigate those strains" (p. 164). However, in part this conclusion seems to be due to conceptual decisions, too, as Parsons treats ideologies here as deviations from the superordinate "value-science integrate," defined by consistency at the cultural level, and focuses on belief systems espoused in different subsystems by such groups as businessmen and intellectuals—the more generalized versions of our limited ideologies embedded in a system of division of labor (pp. 151-154). The case where a "revolutionary ideology" does not protect the institutionalized values of society as a whole is excluded from consideration as "a different order of theoretical problem" (p. 162).

I wish to include this case, but would still argue that it is the values and reality premises pertaining to adaptation, goal-attainment, and integration which will be at the center of the ideological concerns, with the last typically, though not always, having primacy. Values and reality beliefs, which concern directly ultimate pattern maintenance at the societal level, as well as higher-level cultural and especially religious orientations are, of course, not absolutely inaccessible to critical examination. However, the broader the participation in the development of an ideology and the wider the audiences appealed to, the less likely that these matters will be the center of concern.

In a limited sense, this issue is affected and prejudged by the definition chosen here, too, because primacy of empirical beliefs was stipulated, which would exclude central religious ideas by definition (see my first section). However, I would argue that modernization—the implementation of high levels of rationality—makes the boundary between empirical and nonempirical beliefs more important and tips the balance of—culturally defined—saliency and reliability in favor of empirical beliefs.

One final point. Primacy of concern with one sphere rather than another is not identical with "cybernetic control" of one set of ideas and commitments over another. I do not wish to exclude the possibility that an inherited system of higher-level sociocultural codes remains intact and, although largely latent, guides radical transformations of reality assumptions and value orientations at lower levels. What is more likely, however, is that these beliefs lose much of their perceived relevance and/or are themselves fundamentally disturbed. In either case they become less effective, though not altogether insignificant, in steering lower-level developments.

23. In addition to their pertinent works cited previously, see Robert N. Bellah, "Religious Aspects of Modernization in Turkey and Japan," *American Journal of Sociology,* 64 (July 1958), pp. 1-5, and Talcott Parsons, "The Pattern of Religious Organization in the United States," in T. Parsons, *Structure and Process in Modern Societies,* pp. 65-85.

24. For a case analysis focusing on the intellectual biographies of three originators of such ideological orientations see Fritz Stern, *The Politics of Cultural Despair. A Study in the Rise of the Germanic Ideology* (Berkeley: University of California Press, 1961). It is ironic, though in line with what was suggested here that, especially when these ideological orientations gained wider acceptance, their focus turned from latency to integration problems.

25. Much of the recent work of Parsons, Bellah, and Eisenstadt is concerned with this set of problems. See, in addition to previous references, S. N. Eisenstadt (ed.), *The Protestant Ethic and Modernization* (New York: Basic Books, 1968), with an introduction by Eisenstadt which constitutes a theoretical review of the prolonged discussion that is relevant for the analysis of ideologies, too.

These analyses face all the difficulties of dealing with not only complex but also very long-term developments. There are good reasons, in part connected with Parsons' conception of a hierarchy of cybernetic controls, why in the short run a great diversity of ideological developments may have consequences contributing to modernization or at least compatible with certain modernizing processes, while more restrictive requirements enter the picture as far as the long-term maintenance of thrusts toward modernity is concerned.

One specific problem which deserves theoretical exploration links up with matters discussed briefly in the first section of this chapter and in notes 3, 8, and 9—the consequences ideological developments have for the use of generalized media of exchange. The extension of the scope of this use and the related expansion of the "amounts" of money, power, influence, and value commitments in "circulation" can be seen as crucial aspects of increased adaptive capacity of a societal system. High levels of such symbolic generalization increase freedom of choice and the range of options in combining various elements of the societal system.

In analogy to monetary metal in the case of money, Parsons treats force, a *Gemeinschaft* kind of solidary relation (later certain kinds of incontrovertible information) and absolute commitments to specific values as the "security base" of the other three media—of power, influence, and generalized value commitments, respectively. It is to these that the participants in the exchange systems revert if they lose trust in the symbolic extensions; at the same time, however, such moves deprive the social system of the flexibility the use of the symbolic media

yields and on which the functioning of highly complex societal systems is contingent.

In the last parts of his essay "On the Concept of Value-Commitments," *op. cit.,* Parsons develops some ideas that are pertinent to the analysis of the consequences "radical" ideologies have on these systems of generalized media of exchange. On the one hand, such ideologies very often insist on absolute commitment to selected values. They thus tend to undermine —not only to change in content—the existing system of extensions of generalized value commitments. In other respects, too, ideological movements can be seen as phenomena of de-differentiation; thus they tend to make their adherents responsible for the whole transformation of society and to pry them loose from more differentiated obligations.

However, de-differentiations of certain kinds may be required for breakthroughs that open up the possibility of significant advances in differentiation and adaptive capacity. Specifically, it seems that radical ideologies are necessary for reaching those sociocultural redefinitions which allow extensions of the use of generalized value commitments.

In this perspective, a number of further questions acquire special significance. What are the characteristics of social and cultural systems that make them more or less capable of absorbing the tensions, and in particular the abridgments of trust, associated with ideological innovation? What are different patterns of articulation between existing sociocultural orientations and ideological innovations? What are the special problems radical ideologies encounter in turning towards implementation and the attendant processes of differentiation?

30

PARTIAL MODERNIZATION

Dietrich Rueschemeyer

THE PROBLEM IN THEORETICAL PERSPECTIVE

During the last twenty-five years, research on economic development and other forms of modernization has made abundantly clear that few if any contemporary societies exhibit patterns of culture and social organization consistent enough to warrant straightforward characterizations as "modern" or "traditional." Yet, the theoretical orientations of social research on modernization have largely been molded by a dichotomy that contrasts "relatively modernized" and "relatively nonmodernized" societies, both with strong "strains toward consistency."[1] This dichotomy dates back to the beginnings of modern sociology and has continued, in spite of strong and well-founded critiques, to inform theory formation in sociology, especially on those higher levels of abstraction which are not often explicitly discussed.[2]

To insist that in rapidly modernizing courtries old and new patterns often coexist is in one sense trivial. The different parts and features of a society can never be transformed simultaneously. Large-scale social change always involves leads and lags. What is at stake here is something different. Most if not all societies which have experienced economic and other forms of development for decades and even generations retain in varying degrees important elements of an older social and cultural order, elements that theoretically seem inconsistent with full modernization. The coexistence and cooperation of traditional small shops with highly advanced industrial firms in Japan and the traditional features of labor relations reported of even the most modern Japanese enterprises are examples of such persistent partial modernity in one country that can easily be matched by similar patterns in other societies.[3]

It is this widespread phenomenon of a *stable coexistence* of modern and nonmodern elements that concerns us here. Several types of problems are raised for social research and theory by these conditions. With respect to any instance one can ask, first, whether closer inspection does not reveal conditions more in line with theoretical reasoning: Are labor relations in Japan indeed so particularistic and ascriptive in character as reported, and are they indeed combined with high productivity and other specifically modern features of production? Second, one may question the adequacy of hypotheses about the character of modern societies contradicted by the conditions reported: Is productivity actually limited by the Japanese patterns of labor relations referred to? Are these in fact incompatible with other rational production arrangements? And conversely: Are the hypothesized modern labour relations realized in any society, and are they realizable at all?

The fact that durable inconsistencies of social and cultural structure appear to exist in many, if not all modern societies may lead one, third, to question the "theoretical orientations" underlying a whole bundle of specific hypotheses. Thus, Ralf Dahrendorf and Herbert Blumer have argued, I assume with hyperbole born of exasperation: "Contrary to the beliefs of many, the industrial revolution

The central ideas of this chapter were first presented in a paper at a conference on Partial Modernization in March 1966, at the University of Toronto. The essay is part of a research project on ideological tensions engendered by modernization in nineteenth century Germany, for which the Canada Council and later the Ford Foundation have provided partial support. Of course, neither of these institutions is to be identified with the ideas formulated. I had the opportunity to discuss these ideas with many colleagues; in particular, I wish to thank Harry K. Nishio (University of Toronto), Richard P. Taub (University of Chicago), C. Parker Wolf and Peter Evans (Brown University), Fritz Sack (Universität Regensburg), Heiner Treinen (Universität Köln), and the editors of this symposium for their critical comments. Parts of an earlier version of this essay were published in W. Zapf (ed.), *Theorien des sozialen Wandels* (Cologne: Kiepenheuer and Witsch, 1969).

is not the prime mover of the modern world at all;" and: "Sociologists and other students will do well to reexamine their naive assumption that the industrializing process has definite results."[4]

Finally, the theoretical concern may move one more step away from specific hypotheses and even further into the realm of metatheoretical considerations about the strategy of theory formation. If so many modern societies are characterized by fundamental inconsistencies, it may seem reasonable to abandon — or at least to relegate from center stage — the conception of societies as systems with "strains toward consistency." After applying in a number of case studies a perspective that emphasizes "the various amalgams of tradition and modernity which make all development 'partial,'" Reinhard Bendix concludes: "To future historians it may appear as a touching if minor irony that an organic conception of society based on the idea of equilibrium is one of the major perspectives of our time."[5]

This last set of problems deserves additional comment. Bendix and a number of younger colleagues, most notably Randall Collins, have moved from occasional critiques of societal system models to the development of an alternative theoretical framework for social analysis, a framework that is primarily grounded in Max Weber's sociology. While the Bendix group shares this root in Weber's work with Talcott Parsons' action theory, it not only emphasizes the role of conflict between groups and organizations, but specifically denies the utility of viewing societies as systems of interdependent parts: "The interpretation of Weber presented . . . [is intended] as an alternative to all social-system models, be they functionalist, Marxist, or a combination of the two."[6]

Although the framework of analysis developed by Bendix and his collaborators is attractive in many respects, I consider it an ill-advised strategy of theory development to discard the system conception of societies at this point. There are several reasons. First, I would contend that this perspective has advanced our understanding of societies to a great extent even when it was formulated in glaringly unrealistic terms. Second, unless any utility of a given theoretical formulation is denied, continuity with past theorizing, guess-work, and speculation has obvious advantages for a cumulative development of social theory. Third, it is well to remember that we are dealing here with metatheoretical frameworks consisting of sociological orientations, not testable hypotheses. The relevant criteria for accepting or rejecting are those of utility in generating and integrating specific hypotheses rather than those of empirical confirmation or falsification. This also implies that there is no inescapable necessity to choose — once

and forever, and for all purposes — between alternative frameworks.

Finally, there are reasons for retaining the system perspective that bear specifically on the problem at hand. Phenomena of persistent partial modernity become problematic precisely because they are at odds with reasoned consistency assumptions. The system perspective raises with particular acuity questions about causal constellations, conditions of persistence, and consequences of partial modernization. Whether such an analysis of inconsistent societal patterns leads only to qualifications and differentiations of the system perspective or whether its results in the end will suggest the discarding of this perspective for the analysis of societies can be left open at this point. The crucial consideration here and at present is which orientation raises the sharpest questions about the problem under discussion. In this sense, the system conception of societies appears to be a better heuristic device than a perspective that emphasizes the wide range of factual compatibility of different institutional arrangements.

This essay will explore some of the theoretical implications of partial modernization. While retaining the conception of societies as systems with equilibrium tendencies, it not only recognizes but insists that developmental inconsistencies of societal structures are not necessarily mere transition phenomena. I will discuss some of the recurrent causal conditions that give rise to relatively stable patterns of partial modernity. This discussion will be followed by an analysis of social mechanisms and arrangements that accommodate divergent social patterns and thus can account for the stability of such inconsistent constellations in spite of hypothesized strains toward consistency. A final section will consider some consequences of inconsistencies of culture and social structure. In order to put these discussions on firm conceptual ground it is necessary, in a first step, to clarify certain definitions.

PROBLEMS OF CONCEPTUALIZATION

Partial modernization is defined as *the institutionalization of relatively modern patterns side by side with significantly less modern patterns in the same society.* Where the resultant state of society rather than the process that leads to it is referred to we speak of partial modernity.

Because changes in large social systems are never simultaneous, it is necessary to establish a cutting point beyond which we shall speak of relatively stable partial modernity in contrast to the short-run phenomenon of uneven change. To define this difference meaningfully by length of time period is at present virtually impossible. A qualitative threshold separating stable from transitory patterns is, however, indicated by the concept of institutionalization — the development of effective social controls, including internal controls based on socialization, which support a given normative structure.[7]

The term modern is, of course, central to the proposed definition. It raises complex conceptual problems. Perhaps the most useful starting point for a definition that suits present purposes is Max Weber's concept of rationalization of social and cultural life. Rationalization means an increased emphasis on rationality. Rationality, based on an active search for information relevant to action, has in this Weberian use a double meaning: rationality in the choice of means for a given goal, comparing the characteristics of different factor combinations; and rationality with respect to goals, considering the consequences of different goals and choosing in terms of higher-order preferences. In the extreme case virtually all goals are subjected to such scrutiny — nothing is unthinkable — although the choice always implies a reference to ultimate standards.

Rationalization in the latter sense is of tremendous consequence for culture and society; however, it allows for a large number of different sociocultural patterns because the ultimate standards used remain unspecified.[8] Variants of this definition therefore tend to emphasize rationalization in the choice of means. Robert N. Bellah defines progress as an increase in the capacity of a sociocultural system to gain information about its internal and external conditions and to act on it in accordance with basic orientations that are relatively stable but in the long run also subject to change. Talcott Parsons' analysis of the direction of societal evolution as increased adaptive capacity goes in a similar direction. These conceptualizations are grounded in an evolutionary perspective without, however, agreeing with the assumptions of an older evolutionary theory that the process be irreversible, unilinear, or inevitable.[9]

With such a "controlling definition" of the core of modernity in mind we can ask empirical questions — whether particular sociocultural arrangements are conducive to higher or lower levels of rationalization of social activities, what the immediate consequences of different levels of such rationalization are, and which institutional forms are most, which least compatible with those more immediately associated with a given level of rationalization. Answers to these questions — often rather crude and always hypothetical answers, to be sure — result in ideal types of societies differing in over-all level of rationalization. The construct that incorporates the most advanced forms of rationalization known would be the ideal type of modern society.[10]

Although it is required for the determination whether a particular sociocultural arrangement is more or less — or not at all — modern, it is plainly impossible here to spell out in any detail such a theoretical model of "modern society." I suggest that most sociologists accept one version of such a model as valid and that most versions are in substantial agreement with each other. Major lines of thought since the inception of modern sociology have been concerned with these issues, and although a good deal of later empirical research has confined itself to more limited and primarily descriptive problems, a number of hypotheses have found substantial empirical support, the credibility of others rests on theoretical reasoning and an absence of contrary evidence, and some are at present subject to a debate that involves both theoretical and empirical arguments.[11] A few analytic indications about the model of modern society may be useful. They illustrate the kinds of theoretical statements involved and set the stage for a number of observations important for the present context.

One distinctive feature that sets modern societies apart from societies with lower levels of rationalization is the institutionalization of scientific research and its systematic application in the economy as well as in other spheres of social life. Closely related is an increased emphasis on achievement in a variety of roles, especially occupational ones, although there are good reasons to assume that achievement orientation never can be extended to all of an individual's roles and that there are limits to its implementation even in instrumental roles, where it appears most appropriate. Differentiating roles with relatively specific tasks from more diffuse role complexes and adopting universalistic rather than particularistic standards are preconditions for rational judgments of performance. Achievement orientation, universalism, and differentiation of instrumental pursuits from more holistic concerns have to be accorded high rank in the dominant value orientations in order to give these role patterns legitimacy.

The counterpart to instrumental role patterns at the organizational level are bureaucracies — formal organizations with relatively specific goals in terms of which the organization can be viewed as an instrument to be constructed rationally. Judgment and action according to universalistic standards, specificity and explicitness of task definitions, and a high degree of affective neutrality are among the features of such organizations that aid rational administration. As in the case of roles, social theory and research suggest cogently that this organizational form is not suitable for all collectivities and that even in the most suitable organizations the rational features are tempered in ways that seem inevitable under most circumstances. However, in relation to the parallel "imperfections" at the role level, an interesting hypothesis argues that bureaucracies make efficient use of the less able and thus compensate for the "protection of the inept."[12]

Instrumental roles and organizations require a far-reaching differentiation of social structure. Aside from the specialization of these roles and organizations themselves, their differentiation from the kinship system and other institutional complexes serving primarily noninstrumental functions is crucial for rationalization. Such differentiation insures flexibility in the allocation of resources unhampered by ascriptive traditional fixations. Functional differentiation results in greater interdependence of the differentiated parts, thus giving modern society a more systemic character than traditional agrarian societies in which segmentation plays such an important role.

Differentiation of social structure raises problems of societal integration fundamentally different from those of societies that give less room to instrumental orientations and activities. Among the institutional patterns required for the solution of these integration problems are a system of universalistic legal norms, impersonal market exchange, associations of varied purpose, and ultimate values generalized enough to inform and legitimate values, norms, and goals in a great variety of subsystems.[13]

The modern polity is perhaps more than any other part of the model a subject of disagreement and debate. It appears that considerable variation is possible with respect to features that are highly valued in Western political culture, such as civil liberties and democratic representation. Among the characteristics about which there is less doubt are a systematic alignment and centralization of public authority, bureaucratic administration, increased popular participation in politics, and more fluid support for political institutions, leaders, and policies. It is possible to state over-all problems the polity has to cope with — such as maintaining the capacity for effective collective action in the face of continuous change within the system — but the requirements for meeting these problems and their correlates are only partially understood.

Sketchy as this outline necessarily is, it gives rise to a number of observations on the nature of the theoretical model of modern society. First, it is clear that many areas of social life can vary considerably in different societies even as far as the "ideal" construct is concerned. There are several reasons for this. The criterion of rationality itself is, as we have seen, not fully determinate as far as rationalization in the choice of ends is concerned. Further, some spheres of social life are indifferent to conditions and consequences of the modern level of rationalization. In others, several alternative social arrangements may be equally compatible with a certain form of institutionalized rationality. Different forms of rationalization may come into conflict, the outcome of which is not necessarily predictable from the criterion of rationalization and from acceptable hypotheses about systemic interdependencies. Finally, and by no means of least importance, new social arrangements, may be invented or "hit upon" that make new systemic combinations of sociocultural patterns possible. There is no reason to assume that modern social forms are the end of history and social evolution.

The second observation has a more direct bearing on the use of the model in identifying social patterns with different degrees of modernity. It might be tempting to look for a straightforward definition of modernity in terms of the pattern variables which Parsons developed out of the older concept of *Gesellschaft* in contrast to *Gemeinschaft,* that is, to suggest that all major institutions of modern societies are characterized by universalism, performance orientation, affective neutrality, and specificity.

The preceding sketch made clear, however, that this would run counter to some rather definitive results of research and theory. No social form can combine a modicum of stability, effectiveness, and satisfaction for the people involved, if it is structured purely in terms of one side of the pattern variables. Nor is it possible to extend one combination of such features to all major institutions of a society. Although we may postulate a generalized "strain towards homogeneity" — supported by certain psychological theorems and findings — that would suggest that all differences between social patterns in which the same people are involved, are sources of strain and stress, it seems that the gratifications derived from diversity can outweight the rewards of similarity and that no social system can persist without some differentiation because of the inherently diverse problems with which all social systems have to cope.[14] Moreover, modern sociocultural patterns are characterized by a particularly high degree of differentiation which sets *Gesellschaft*-like patterns, such as bureaucratic work roles, in sharp contrast next to *Gemeinschaft*-like ones, such as the family. Such differentiation is one necessary condition for the institutionalization of high levels of rationality. There is, of course, in modern society, too, a minimum of Durkheim's "likeness of conscience," and it is in these ultimate intellectual and moral orientations that one would expect a dominant rank accorded to performance orientation and universalism as well as an elevated place for specifity and affective neutrality.

We can now bring these conceptual considerations to a conclusion. Whether a given component of social structure and culture can be considered more or less — or not at all — modern is determined by the available propositions about the conditions and consequences of sociocultural rationalization. Patterns of partial modernity combine characteristically modern features with others that squarely deviate from theoretical statements about the immediate requisites and consequences of a high level of rationality and about social and cultural arrangements which are most compatible with these conditions and results. Although this formula may leave the identification of partial modernity in some cases open to dispute, there is sufficient agreement about such theoretical statements to allow for unambiguous identification in many cases. We are now in a position to turn to the substantive discussion of partial modernization. First, some major causal constellations will be considered that lead to developmental inconsistencies. In some cases the long-run character of such patterns results from the initial constellation, and in others their stabilization is due to special mediating and accommodating conditions, the subject of the next section following the discussion of recurrent causes of partial modernization.

RECURRENT CAUSES OF PARTIAL MODERNIZATION

In exploring the conditions that generate lasting developmental inconsistencies it appears fruitful to focus on central features of a society — on basic religious, intellectual, and moral orientations and on patterns of political power — which are of special significance for the ways of dealing with sociocultural change. Other reference points for this analysis which seem pertinent to virtually all modernizing societies are the differences in character between the major functional subsystems of society and between segmental divisions of a country, certain pervasive aspects of social structure in large-scale agrarian societies, and the process of intercultural and international diffusion.

In an evolutionary perspective one of the basic causes of partial modernization is the diffusion of modern sociocultural complexes to societies at lower levels of development.[15] A corollary of this proposition is that societies which experience few outside disturbances, especially from more advanced societies, exhibit a greater degree of consistency than less isolated societies. Because of their general scope, these are crude propositions, but some indications of how they can be specified are possible at this point.

It seems that there are great variations in the effectiveness of cultural diffusion, which is partially determined by the social and cultural character of the receiving country as well as by the kinds of things transmitted. Although some relatively isolated techniques of obvious and universal utility, such as techniques of death prevention, have been successfully transmitted to societies of the most divergent types, it appears that even limited rationalization of economic and political structures approximating the level of modern societies requires a fairly high degree of previous differentiation of societal structure. On the other hand, cases like Japan or India make it clear that diffusion of the more complex elements of modern social organization is not confined to societies that are on the verge of developing these patterns indigenously.

Such diffusion would not lead to stable structural inconsistencies if there were a tendency toward pervasive transformation of the receiving society in response to the initial process of diffusion. That this tendency is limited by a variety of factors is the theme of the following paragraphs. In addition, the special circumstances of the diffusion process itself may account, in part at least, for rather limited repercussions throughout the host society.

Modern techniques and institutions imported by a colonial power may be, and often are or were, purposely confined to the colonial administration and a few areas of indigenous social life. Inevitably, there are some further consequences of colonial rule that penetrate the fabric of society and culture more deeply, but these are typically quite limited. Exchange and authority relations engendering "strains toward consistency" link these modern bridgeheads more closely with the centers of the colonial home country than with the hinterland of the colony. Patterns of partial modernization growing out of the colonial penetration of the non-Western world were actually the first to be noticed and analyzed by social scientists.[16]

Although the demise of colonialism after World War II made these particular forms of partial modernity obsolete, some of their features can be generalized and used to interpret analogous patterns of considerable present importance. In virtually all contemporary developing countries, there are relatively modernized organizations or even whole institutional sectors that form part of an international system of interdependencies. Relations with their counterparts in other societies are of at least as great significance as relations with other institutions in their own society. Examples are international organizations with agencies operating in developing countries, scientific institutes in these countries that share educational bases and channels of communication with their counterparts in more advanced societies, and business firms that are parts of an international network of financial and commercial relations. What is important in the present context is not the dominant position occupied by the most advanced nations in such an international system of interrelations — its "neocolonial" aspect — but rather the discontinuities which such interdependencies and the related power differentials introduce into the less-developed societies.

Historical evidence as well as theoretical considerations suggest that religious orientations and the ultimate value system of a society tend to be rather resistant to change, even in the long run. A modernization of technical facilities and of specific social roles, organizations, and norms can under certain conditions proceed far without effecting a change in the religious and value orientations.[17] A major exception to this generalization would be the societies with so low a level of differentiation that virtually every significant activity is imbued with religious meaning and that, in turn, religion is bound up in daily rituals and avoidances. In this case, the premodern system is likely to resist institutionalization of crucial modern patterns or to break down as a whole.[18]

An extension of the proposition of the relative stability of religion and central value patterns is the thesis that successful modernization has always been associated with a *gradual* transformation of the core of the indigenous culture, emphasizing in a complex process those elements of the heritage that are most compatible with increasing rationalization and differentiation, rather than with a radically new development starting from a *tabula rasa*. If this thesis is fundamentally correct, one would expect long periods of inconsistency between new patterns of behavior and organization, on the one hand, and the haltingly changing forms of ultimate orientation and those norms, organizations, and roles more immediately associated with it, on the other hand. This expectation would be particularly strong for those societies that exhibit few internal conditions conducive to modernization and receive the major impetus towards change from contact with the West, although some partialities should result, or have resulted, on this basis in all cases, including the European "pioneers."

Premodern value orientations may receive strong reinforcements from the very process of modernization. Three interrelated patterns are especially relevant: the development of explicit conservative ideologies in response to modern challenges, widespread emergence of images of a golden past in response to strain, and nationalist emphases on the uniqueness of the society in transition and the glories of its past.

The changes which make established orientations problematic, subject them to strains, and threaten to undermine them are likely to provoke efforts to re-state and revalidate the tradition. Karl Mannheim has analyzed "conservatism" as a transformation of traditional orientations into a set of positions which exhibit a greater degree of reflected consciousness, intellectual organization, and political determination.[19] However, although in their form these ideologies are thus more systematically rationalized, more "modern," in substance and intent they are designed to preserve older patterns, and they are by no means doomed to fail in all cases.

The process of modernization broadens the ranks of people capable of dealing with complex intellectual problems and responsive to ideological appeals. The later modernization occurs, the more important is the diffusion of technology and patterns of social organization from more advanced countries. This gives a strategic role to the educated classes in developing societies.[20] Although most of the educated will be concerned with specialized technical problems, the process is also conducive to the emergence of an *intelligentsia* concerned with the moral and cultural significance of modernization for their societies.

The dual orientation of these intellectuals to their own society and culture as well as to more advanced foreign countries is the basis for a differentiation of positions along the dimensions of cosmopolitanism-nationalism and modernization-traditionalism. Conservative orientations will draw strength from traditional religious, political, and economic interests that need ideological support. The differentiation of contrasting ideological positions may turn into a polarization of sharply opposed camps. Such a development in which ideological positions harden and coalesce firmly with different group solidarities and interests is likely to contribute to the survival of conservative orientations beyond the constellation of their origin.[21] Finally, conservatism frequently is strengthened because it is intertwined with the two other correlates of late and accelerated modernization previously mentioned: nationalism and popular regressive reactions to frustration and anomie.

Nationalism can be interpreted along the lines of Max Weber's analysis of the role of Calvinist Protestantism in the modernization of Europe. In addition to its capacity of mobilizing great energies, nationalism can provide a basis for large-scale political integration and for the strong political authority required to contain the strains and tensions engendered by modernization. What I wish to emphasize here is another side of its multifaceted character. A positive orientation to the nation's past cannot easily be separated from the nationalist emphasis on the country's greatness and unique value. The ideological models of nationalism in Europe as well as the socio-cultural conditions of new nations make such traditionalist components in contemporary nationalist ideologies even more likely. Among the latter conditions are hostile attitudes toward the more advanced countries caused by the ex-colonial status of new nations and the utility of nationalist appeals in establishing a base for alliances between traditional and modern elites.

Any societal change brings serious deprivations to some segments of the population. One particularly important source of such frustrations in the case of modernization processes is the fact that frequently the old order and its controls are undermined before new patterns of orientation, integration, and control are operating efficiently. The result is anomie in the literal meaning of the term. Among the consequences of frustration, irrational action, aggression, and apathy are the more familiar ones; the first two of these frequently are associated with, distorted or reinforced by, simplified images of good and evil, salvation and degradation. This popular imagery, often intensely emotional in character, assumes particular importance when the origin of frustration is not easily understood. Under these conditions we obtain the familiar pattern in which certain cultural features and social groups associated with the new ways are turned into scapegoats. The positive contrast is often provided by the supposedly good old days, and even if radically progressive designs represent the ideal state of affairs they frequently bear the earmarks of nostalgic references to the past. Thus, while widespread strains generated by deprivation and anomie encourage radical mobilization politics, they also often provide a receptive ground for retrospective ideologies.

The role of the state in modernization and industrialization is by far greater in most contemporary developing societies than it was in the "primary" development of modern patterns. Development, economic and otherwise, has become an explicit goal toward which collective energies can be politically directed. Furthermore, the tour de force of accelerated development envisaged by most latecomers requires particularly strong controls and integrative mechanisms that in most cases are only imaginable on the basis of a strong political authority. This constellation has crucial consequences for the consistency of developing patterns. A consideration of certain aspects of modernization in Prussia/Germany and Japan, "early latecomers" which had strong political authority traditions, can provide instructive insights into this problem.

In both Prussia and Japan a fairly rational and manipulative political elite had a largely traditional support in wide segments of the population. One would expect such an elite to be extremely wary of uncontrolled modernization and industrialization because such processes would tend to undermine its authority positions. In both cases, this elite vigorously sponsored the modernization process when it became clear that external threats could be met only by moving in this direction. Economic development and other forms of modernization were thus adopted as means for the protection and enhancement of national power. At the same time, a series of measures was taken to preserve the traditional bases of political power. Of course, not all persons and groups who participated in these efforts to keep the old order intact conceived of their labor as means for the maintenance of a given pattern of domination; rather, these measures tied in with institutionalized religious patterns, with the concerns of conservative secular intellectuals, and with the vested material interests of many groups other than those participating in national power. Even within the political elite and among its various retainers, intrinsic attachments merged with political manipulation.

"Dynastic modernization" of this particular kind may be obsolete, but political sponsorship of modernization has become the standard case, and with the exception of truly revolutionary elites, the elites of mobilization systems in David Apter's terminology,[22] all of these ruling groups have *some* interest in stabilizing support through tradition. What is characteristically lacking in contemporary new nations, when compared with Prussia and Japan, is the extraordinary power differential and the great stability of the power patterns in these two countries. However, extreme cases are often instructive.

A few examples from Germany and Japan may illustrate the ways in which power interests lead to the maintenance and creation of relatively nonmodern patterns side by side with modern developments. In both cases traditional patterns of power in rural sectors were more or less consciously protected by tariff, tax, and credit policies. These policies were supported by populist ideologies that centered in Germany around the noncommercial *Bauer* and his contribution to social "health" and stability.

Such modern institutions as public schools and armies, based on general conscription and run along fairly bureaucratic lines, were simultaneously used for imparting modern skills, discipline suited for either type of pattern and traditional political loyalty grounded, for the lower classes at least, in religion.

A final example concerns developments within the modern industrial sectors. Paralleling elements of partial modernization in the relations between government and industry, especially large-scale industry,[23] the internal patterns in the developing industries were influenced by governmental, military, and neofeudal models. Thus, employer-worker relations frequently combined quasi-military discipline with a strongly particularistic paternalism.

These illustrations from two societies have interesting implications beyond the fact that modernizing elites may find it useful to husband their traditional power resources. They point to the general possibility of using modern means for the implementation of traditional goals as well as the reverse pattern, the utility of certain elements of traditional life for modern goals. The use of traditional forms of authority for containing the strains and tensions engendered by modernization would be an instance of the latter, indoctrination of traditional religious and political orientations in modern schools or armies an instance of the former. For intensely sought goals, people take as means whatever is at hand as long as the *immediate* problems involved in these means are not too great.

Examples abound in the literature. Bellah mentions cases of effective missionizing with modern facilities that allowed the dominant traditional religion for the first time to penetrate successfully various non-elite groups.[24] In a discussion of unexpected changes in birth rate in Mexico, Zarate suggests, following other observers, that industrialization may have made resources available that allowed greater conformity with traditional standards.[25]

The reverse combination of traditional means for modern goals may be illustrated by the utility of solid extended-family connections for raising entrepreneurial capital funds.[26] Other patterns are more subtle and complex and do not involve consciously intended "use" of traditional patterns. Modernization creates wider horizons and new activities for which frameworks of orientation are relatively undeveloped. Frequently traditional conceptions and social identifications provide frames of reference for orientation in these uncharted fields of social life. An example would be the considerable importance of tribal, ethnic, and caste affiliations in voting and other forms of modern political behavior, although undoubtedly other factors are involved here too.[27] Another example is indicated in an observation by Tumin about developments in Puerto Rico: "Typically we find that among Puerto Rican peasants who have entered upon the new ways of life there is virtually no sense of danger to their conceptions of themselves as worthy individuals. This confidence is based on part on the shared concept of *dignidad*. . . ."[28]

So far, I have primarily dealt with two functional subsystems of society, with religion and the system of societal value orientation and with the polity. For both it was argued that potentially stable combinations of old and new are generated by the intrinsic character of the functional subsystem and by its responses to developments in other subsystems, provided some moves toward modernization have occurred in the society.

Religion and basic value orientations seem under most circumstances to possess considerable stability over time, which may furthermore be required for sustained modernization of a society. Yet these old forms will stand in contrast to new formulations seeking to sustain meaning and motivation and to map out new features of the "good life." This contrast remains even if various more or less stable amalgamations are formed. Furthermore, there will be inconsistencies between the heritage of ultimate orientations and new behavior patterns, new organizational forms and new normative developments. In the case of the polity, partial modernization is related closely to what may be called the "opportunistic" character of politics — the inclination of all but the most radical and the most traditional elites to forge available support from however heterogeneous constituencies into as stable a power base as possible. Where large sectors of the society are as yet little touched by modern forces undermining traditional patterns, this inclination will introduce strong traditional elements into policy making and ideological justification, and it will evoke in many cases policies specifically designed to protect traditional sectors supporting a powerful elite. At the same time, the goal of modernization—conceived in whatever form and scope—is nearly universal among contemporary political elites, as are attempts to develop bureaucratic organizations as instruments of political rule.

This line of analysis may usefully be extended to include the other two major functional subsystems of society — the economy and the different interrelated modes of societal integration. Such an extension could show in greater detail that it is not only the inherently different dynamics of different functional subsystems that are conducive to partial modernization but also their interrelations with each other. Here it must be sufficient to state more explicitly the basic underlying assumption. Due to the nature of the problems they are primarily concerned with, the various functional subsystems of a society differ considerably in their receptivity to modern innovations. Although the different subsystems are interdependent, and become increasingly so with each move toward greater functional differentiation, these differences may well be retained over farily extended periods of time precisely because they correspond to basic incompatibilities in the functional requirements of a societal system.

The same reasoning can be applied to functional

differentiation within a societal subsystem. Thus, not only the differences in function between the economy and, say, the law as a part of the integrative subsystem of the society, but also the differences between banking and production, between agriculture and commerce, are likely to give rise to developmental inconsistencies which may or may not be stabilized.

If functional differentiation is conducive to certain developmental inconsistencies, its other face is the interdependence between the differentiated structural units which should set off strong forces encouraging greater consistency. The situation is reversed in the case of segmentation. Segmented units "perform essentially similar functions"[29] and are therefore more self-contained than functionally differentiated units which perform different but complementary functions. Examples of segmentation are different households or different firms producing the same goods. There is no reason inherent in the functional contribution of segmented units to expect divergent developments. However, differences not directly related to function, differences in the situation or differences in the association with certain cultural traditions, may well exist between several aggregates of segmented units, which may engender contrasts in receptivity to modern innovations. For instance, commercial farming may develop in response to opportunities confined to, say, coastal areas, and it may be hampered or encouraged by the religious traditions of peasants in different parts of a country. As segmented parts of the social structure are, in relation to other segments, relatively self-contained, there are likely to be fewer pressures toward consistency than in the case of functional differentiation.

Patterns of partial development are, in the over-all picture of social evolution, not confined to modernizing societies. The coexistence of not easily compatible elements that is frequent in agrarian societies before modernization becomes a significant tendency may later provide the basis for patterns of partial modernization. The classic case of differential advance in premodern societies is the coexistence of urban and rural patterns of life. Tied in with this division is the partial development of literacy and literate culture, which tend to be confined to the upper urban strata. Other divisions, more segmental in character, are the often deep cultural divergencies between regional, ethnic, and religious groups.

Large-scale agrarian societies are much more loosely bound together by interdependencies than either modern or simpler tribal societies. They are the prototype of what Wolfram Eberhard calls layer societies. Different layers of people form "truly self-contained societies" which "can exist side by side without functional social relations and without acculturation or assimilation."[30] Because it is in agrarian societies, nearly without exception, that modernization develops and has a chance to mature into sustained growth, divisions of this kind may give rise to developmental inconsistencies. They are likely to be accentuated by modernization processes, as the various sectors of agrarian society offer differential opportunities to modernizing measures and the traditional modes of coexistence tend to contain such developments within a given sector.

In conclusion, causal constellations that are likely to lead to potentially stable inconsistencies in modernization are quite common and variegated in character. They are related to the nature of central cultural traditions and political institutions and their response to pervasive change. More generally, they seem inherent in the different dynamics of functional subsystems of a society. Functional differentiation as well as segmentation may become the basis for patterns of partial modernization. Partial modernization may have its roots in the typical structure of agrarian societies; and, finally, it may develop out of the relations between societies — out of processes of diffusion from more-advanced societies to less-developed ones or out of international networks of institutions that often are more responsive to each other than to the particular society in which they find themselves.

It should be possible and theoretically fruitful to develop a typology of patterns of partial modernization that would distinguish inconsistencies both in terms of broad forms of causation and in terms of likely outcome. A conceptual base for such a typology might be found in recently developed paradigms of the theory of action which concern functional and structural subsystems of society and the types and media of exchange between them. To approach this task of a systematic taxonomy of patterns of partial modernization appears premature, however. It seems more fruitful first to analyze some of the conditions that affect the stabilization of the coexistence of incongruent patterns and to explore some of the consequences of partial modernization. At this point, I therefore wish to make only two sets of preliminary distinctions between different kinds of developmental inconsistencies which were implied in the preceding and are useful for the following discussion.

The inconsistencies that develop may exist between different structural subsystems of a society, but they may also be found within the same institutional complexes or within the same organization, and incompatible normative and cognitive orientations may be held by actors in closely complementary roles or even by the same actors. Conditions of stabilization and consequences of developmental inconsistencies are likely to vary according to how "close" incongruent elements are brought together. The following discussions focus on contrasts between rather discrete parts of social structure, but do not neglect the more intimate amalgamations of contradictory patterns.

The second kind of distinction I wish to emphasize here is related to what Parsons has called the hierarchy of cybernetic controls. Thus we may distinguish between four principal components of social structure that stand in a relation of cybernetic control to each other, with the first-named informing and steering developments at each subsequent level: values, institutions or normative complexes, collectivities and organizations, and roles that structure individual behavior and motivation.[31] It appears to make a difference whether the contrasts studied obtain between different levels or are found between divergent elements at the same level, whether it is, for instance, traditional values of humane treatment of others that stand in tension with bureaucratic forms of authority — which according to other value orientations need not be inhumane at all — or whether values of such a traditional cast are contradicted by the ideals of more modern value orientations.

CONDITIONS FOR CONTAINING THE EFFECTS OF PARTIAL DEVELOPMENTS

According to assumptions made initially, one should expect that developmental incongruities engender tendencies toward consistency which in the long run eliminate inconsistent sociocultural patterns. Such tendencies may take different forms. Modern social forces may undermine incompatible traditional patterns — or vice versa — by raising the costs of maintaining the latter, by curtailing the bases of power of elites protecting them, by changing value orientations that make labor and sacrifice in their support meaningful, and in other similar ways. This need not entail open social conflict or exceptional strains, though it often does.

Conflict may be a direct consequence of partial modernization. This is especially likely whenever contrasting normative patterns and value orientations set different groups apart from and against each other and give simultaneous legitimation to opposed interests. Depending on its outcome, open conflict may contribute to greater sociocultural consistency. If ending in stalemate or less than decisive victory of

one side it may, on the other hand, result in complex compromises and amalgamations of heterogeneous patterns or in a hardening and consolidation of contrasting positions.

Strains are also a likely consequence of partial modernization, which in turn may feed both into social conflict and tendencies of modern or nonmodern patterns to spread at the expense of the other. Strain has been defined as a "disturbance of the expectation system" of actors.[32] Such disturbances occur when contradictory normative demands are addressed to the same actors and collectivities or when values, norms and regulations, motivated desires, opportunities for action, and rewards are out of step with each other. Discrepancies of this kind are of course commonplace, but they are especially likely to occur if inconsistent sociocultural elements are brought so closely together that many people have to live with contradictory expectations.

The experience of strain involves frustrations of varying intensity. A rational response could be social action and commitments supporting one or the other side of the contradictory pattern, thus lending strength to the postulated tendencies toward consistency. Such rational action is by no means to be ruled out. However, several conditions which would make rational action unlikely rather favor the translation of such strains into a hostility which is deflected from the source of frustration and fairly indeterminate in its choice of objects. Among these conditions are difficulties of understanding the situation, obstacles to effective action once the problems are understood, and the fact that the contradiction and confusion may affect the very commitment to ultimate ends in terms of which rational action makes sense. Conflicts resulting from, or substantially feeding on, such deflected hostility are not easily resolved and are not particularly likely to contribute to greater consistency of culture and social structure.

Simple social system models that stress integration tendencies to the point of organicism would suggest the following sequence: uneven change; reverberations of the initial change, including strains and conflicts which engender further change; equilibrium with consistent patterns. I have argued that strains and conflicts may contribute, but not necessarily to greater consistency. These problems will be pursued further. Another qualification of the sequence model, which is central to the thesis that developmental inconsistencies can be stabilized for long periods of time, maintains that partial developments of modern patterns can be contained in such a way that the propagation of their effects throughout the society is prevented. It is possible to identify a number of social arrangements which inhibit the spreading of partial developments of rationalization and reassertions of the traditional order and which may avoid strains and conflicts.

The most fundamental pattern containing the effects of partial development is a phenomenon widespread in all large-scale agrarian societies which was already discussed among the conditions conducive to partial modernization: a high degree of segmentation of economic and social activities reinforced frequently by religious, ethnic, and regional subcultural divisions. Segmentation requires fewer integrative links between different social units than functional differentiation; it thus reduces contact and exchange except within narrowly confined localities. Of course, certain political, religious, and economic functions are in varying degree differentiated from the more diffuse kinship and communal groups in most agrarian societies, and these specialized forms of organization have a society-wide impact; but in comparison to modern societies the prevalence of segmentation results typically in high degrees of parochical and regional self-sufficiency. The low levels of contact and exchange across many group boundaries inhibit reverberations of partial developments. Societies of this kind can cope with disturbing changes in ways analogous to the capacity of a ship with watertight compartments to stay afloat in spite of leaks.

Subcultural divisions along ethnic, religious, linguistic, regional, and status lines, while in origin closely associated with segmentation, are in many agrarian societies elaborated in a stable enough way to minimize contact and exchange even between functionally differentiated and interdependent subsystems, though they then require more complicated integrative arrangements. The intrusion of modern political and economic processes into such patterns and the increase of communication they bring beyond parochial boundaries tend, paradoxically, to activate these primordial ties rather than weaken them. Local accomodations between the different groups are upset, "consciousness of kind," independent of particular local definitions becomes more salient, and complex tensions are touched off by these developments.[33]

Consciousness of primordial identities and divisions, and even moderate tension and conflict along these lines engendered by modernization, reinforce or simulate the containing effects of segmentation. Acceptance and spread of new patterns are under these conditions hindered because they are perceived as associated with an outgroup. Geertz speaks of a " 'contextual relativism' which sees certain values as appropriate to context"; it both facilitates the co-existence of divergent old forms of life and limits the

diffusion of new ones.[34] Such contextual relativism has to be distinguished analytically from the moral grounding of functionally differentiated patterns in modern societies. In the latter case legitimation rests on common ultimate orientations, while its equivalent in the former is the consciousness of deep cleavages.

Wherever contact between relatively modern and relatively nonmodern social structures occurs, mediating roles are frequently found that deal with both sides on their terms, or at least on terms which are less inconsistent than unmediated interaction would be. Merchants, certain kinds of foremen and labor subcontractors, local administrators, chieftains, political bosses, attorneys, teachers, and missionaries are among those who frequently fill such intermediary roles.

To make these roles viable they have to be partially exempted from the full impact of either one or both of the normative patterns associated with the disparate structures. Such exemption, particularly problematic on the relatively nonmodern side, where role obligations tend to be diffuse, is frequently based on different ethnic status, which generally narrows obligations and rights, and on positions of authority, which allow for some denial of reciprocity. Further support for partial deviance from contradictory role expectations is gained by offering services and goods that otherwise are not easily available. Great cleavages between disparate social structures are often bridged by a series of linked mediating roles, each of which then has to cope only with more limited disparities.

Premodern agrarian societies, too, typically exhibit a broad range of roles which both link and shield different subsystems to and from each other. The most important examples are the local and regional representatives of more centralized political and religious institutions and merchants involved in trading beyond communal boundaries. These can form the base and model from which new roles and new uses of old roles are developed that link and segregate modern and relatively nonmodern sectors. Furthermore, complicated relations of tension and accommodation may grow up between intermediary roles of the old and the new type concerned with identical or overlapping clienteles.

Roles of this kind are made viable by being partially exempted from the normative context into which their partners are integrated, but such exemption has other consequences, too. Cheating, fraud, and exploitation are likely to be endemic in these situations. Where the limitations of reciprocity are not grounded in power and authority, the intermediate roles themselves are ill protected against their role partners. Where intermediary roles are based on power and where their relations with the less developed community cover a broad range of spheres, they may coalesce into fairly tight collectivities which effectively control certain sectors of society and seal them off against outside influence. An example of this is the clientele system that exists between peasants and the regional bourgeoisie in Southern Italy. The terms of the labor market make the peasants extremely dependent on landlords and other elements of the middle class, and this dependency is highly diffuse, covering many spheres of life. Organizational disadvantages to the peasants arising out of this situation prevent their interests from being expressed in effective movements for protest and social change. On the other hand, it is fairly clear that the central government, though aiming for modernization in the area, does not care to upset the pattern radically because of the explosive political potential of the situation.[35]

In analyzing these mediating role complexes, I have found helpful the concepts and propositions developed for the analysis of role strain and "role sets" in modern societies,[36] although allowance has to be made for greater disparities in role expectations and for a narrower common ground of cognitive and value orientations among the various role partners. Such theoretically well-understood mechanisms as the segregation of activities and role partners in time and space, their symbolic insulation through rituals and manners of interaction, and the establishment of priorities between conflicting obligations explain many specific aspects of such intermediary roles.

The capability of various individuals and groups for evading or minimizing strain is related to their position in the stratification system. More privileged strata have a greater range of options regarding an individual's exposure to traditional and modern patterns, and the various accommodating arrangements that moderate the impact of inconsistencies are more available to them. It is the peasants and artisans bent on escaping traditional misery who can be most ruthlessly subjected to the routines and disciplines of factory work, while the spread of specificity, universalism, and performance norms into the higher ranks of administrative structures is likely to encounter greater obstacles. It is the guild organization of occupations like lawyers that is preserved and, through complicated compromises, adapted to new situations in contrast to the fate of the traditional associations of many lower occupations.

This negative correlation between exposure to strain and command over resources has important implications for the sequence model of equilibration referred to above. Strain there is assumed to stimulate awareness of inconsistencies and to generate motivation for changes in the direction of greater consistency. If strains and tensions have a much greater incidence in one group than in another, intergroup conflict tends to arise which might accelerate change toward reduction of strains. This outcome is unlikely, however, if strains are concentrated in the weakest strata of a society. Here it is well to remember that the organizational disadvantages of the lower strata are particularly great in agrarian societies with their parochialism and their limited forms of communication and cooperation.

I have discussed a few of the mechanisms and structural arrangements that can accommodate the coexistence of disparate social and cultural patterns. What has only been touched on in the discussion of the functioning of mediating roles are the problems which arise from a more intricate interpenetration of relatively modern and relatively nonmodern elements than is found in the relations between different, but internally fairly consistent sectors of society. The accommodating patterns of behavior and orientation that evolve under these conditions would explain in part why cyclical migration, village factories, and other similar phenomena are not more disruptive of traditional social life than is frequently observed.

Several generalizations seem possible, however, on the basis of the preceding discussion of segmentation and related forms of subcultural differentiation, mediating roles and their ways of coping with divergent role expectations, and the distribution of strain in the stratification system of modernizing agrarian societies. First, there is every reason to assume that the incidence of such accommodating mechanisms and constellations is quite high. To a large extent they are based on characteristic features of complex agrarian societies which are the most likely candidates for any form of modernization.

Second, these arrangements are effective in limiting contact between disparate structures and in minimizing exposure of the same groups and individuals to divergent sociocultural patterns. In a further "line of defense," they mitigate tensions and strains where contact and "double exposure" do occur. Finally, they contain tension and forestall change by determining the location of strains in the structure of power and influence.

The third comment is more in the nature of a concluding hypothesis rather than a generalization. These accommodating, insulating, and mediating patterns may be effective under a wide variety of circumstances, and they may be stable over long periods of time, but they nevertheless appear to be bound up with special preconditions. Many of them seem incompatible with further advances in modernization and are likely to be undermined by certain critical developments. If maintained by special efforts, they may reduce the flexibility of the total system.

The boundaries of relatively self-contained segmented units may crumble under the impact of such changes as increased internal migration, new patterns of communication and transportation, and the mobilization of the population for armed conflict. Although some related subcultural differentiations of low salience may vanish in this process, many ethnic, religious, and other primordial solidarities will gain in importance and, because sudden increases in contact with others are likely to heighten tension and fuel conflict, mutual toleration on the basis of contextual relativism may turn into an unrestrained aggressive pursuit of the realization of divergent value systems variously associated with different patterns of modernization and tradition. The viability of mediating roles rests on peculiar patterns of power, interethnic sentiment, and/or the terms of exchange on various markets — bases subject to change with further advances of modernization. Finally, the containing effects of the stratification system may be upset if old patterns of authority lose their binding force, if strategic groups experience downward mobility, and if new developments — such as improved communication facilities, widened intellectual horizons, and new forms of cooperation and organization — increase the ability of the lower strata to make their problems felt and to fight for their solution.

CONCLUSIONS: LONG-TERM OUTCOMES

If accommodating and insulating social patterns break down on a large scale, partial modernization is likely to result in strain and conflict. Strains and conflicts will be particularly intense if this breakdown of mediating mechanisms occurs rapidly and simultaneously in different areas. According to the simple equilibration model they will lead to changes in the direction of greater social and cultural consistency, but this is neither a necessary nor a particularly likely outcome. At least as likely are new forms of inconsistency that may or may not stabilize.

Perhaps the most frequent result of an unmediated confrontation of old and new is that both traditional and emergent modern normative orders are undermined, with widespread anomie as a result. Anomic conditions are a fertile ground for radical yearnings and charismatic movements. I have discussed their

frequently regressive components among the conditions that lead to partial modernization. Under favorable conditions, such movements may result in political mobilization systems aiming at rapid modernization. However, though essentially different from the earlier forms of dynastic modernization and from other contemporary patterns, the goals and claims of such mobilization systems typically exceed by far their actual transforming power. Recurrent breakdowns, a waning of the revolutionary *élan*, and compromises with traditional powers and orientations are more likely than the rapid establishment of modern patterns even in these cases.

The conflicts engendered by unmediated inconsistencies of culture and social structure can, as noted above, contribute to more uniform modernization or a reestablishment of older, less rationalized patterns. However, to generalize this possibility implies the assumption that the interests of the major contending parties focus on questions of modernization and that other issues are of secondary importance. If multiple issues are at stake, the lines of antagonism and conflict may crosscut each other so that opponents on one issue turn out to be allies on another. It was the important insight of Georg Simmel and Edward A. Ross that crisscrossing conflicts may result in fairly stable over-all patterns. The transforming power of conflicts partially engendered by developmental inconsistencies would thus be greatly diminished. There are important open problems for empirical analysis in pinpointing the conditions under which modernization fosters these multiple and overlapping patterns of conflict. It seems that certain alignments of "primordial ties" constitute a baseline conducive to such an outcome.

Many conditions typical of late modernization favor a polarization of multiple conflicts along a few lines of cleavage. Industrial class conflict tends to reach a high point after a sizable proportion of the labor force has been concentrated in industrial jobs and severed from traditional orientations and controls and before the industrial division of labor becomes more complex in the process of further development.[37] Religious cleavages as well as ideological and political antagonisms often become associated with class conflicts, as Parsons has argued for the case of Germany;[38] and Seymour M. Lipset has pointed to certain general interrelations between rapid development, the piling up of unresolved issues and the coalescence of different issues in polarized social conflict.[39] Once established, such a polarization of antagonisms can absorb deflected aggressive tendencies from a variety of sources and concentrate them on "the enemy."

Large-scale polarized conflict certainly may set off far-flung social change. Whether it is likely to blast a way towards greater consistency of the societal structure is another question. The very facts of polarization and superimposition of conflict make it difficult to resolve the diverse yet bundled issues. Prolonged hostility and conflict without decisive outcome are under conditions of polarization likely to forge stable solidary subcultures and lasting enmities between conflict groups which tend to survive the original constellation and to become unresponsive to new developments.[40] If the conflicts are accompanied by large-scale violence and yet do not lead to a total dominance of one position, certain issues may be tabooed and certain avenues of development compromised for a long time to come because they are associated with the threat of violent destruction. Quite often, then, we should expect in the wake of polarized conflict new "faults" in the structure of society and culture that are again fairly resistant to strains toward consistency.

In conclusion, I wish to point to a few problems related to the larger consequences of partial modernization, whether contained and buttressed by mediating mechanisms or not. Ralf Dahrendorf has analyzed Imperial and Weimar Germany as a "faulted nation," the explosive potential of which was released in National Socialism.[41] It seems safe to say that partial modernization does not inevitably engender such sinister outcomes, although sudden large-scale confrontations between modern and traditional sectors of society would seem to be one condition in a constellation of factors that can bring about destructive developments of this kind.

Channeling tensions and conflicts into productive social change while avoiding severe institutional disruption appears to be one of the central requirements for sustained development.[42] Comparative analyses of modernization are only beginning to shed light on these problems of long-term societal change. Patterns of partial modernity may under certain circumstances erupt into conflicts and violence not easily contained. On the other hand, some of our earlier considerations have pointed to inconsistent combinations of old and new in the cultural and political core of modernizing societies that may contribute to, may even be a necessary condition for, a successful management of tensions, conflicts, and change. More generally, well-contained and insulated lower levels of rationalization in one sphere of society and culture may support significant advances of rationalization in others.[43] The conditions for modernity as a long-term outcome need by no means coincide with the features of any model of consistent modernity.

If these are uncertain conclusions, they are fitting for an essay that is frankly exploratory. I have advanced several lines of argument which need no summary here. The basic intent was to confront the conception of societies as systems with the fact that processes of modernization very often, if not always, result in fairly stable patterns of coexistence of higher and lower levels of rationalization in the same society. I have sought to develop a number of ideas about the causation of such developmental inconsistencies and about the interrelations that obtain under these conditions between the different spheres.

Searching for a more adequate set of interdependence hypotheses than present societal models will be a long-term and difficult undertaking. If successful, ideal types will be replaced by explicit theoretical statements which should be able to explain both more and less consistent societal structures as well as developments over different spans of time. I think that this is a promising direction for theoretical work. I see the ideas about partial modernization set forth here as theoretical orientations which may contribute to such a development and which in the meantime may aid the understanding of modernization, especially in Latin America, Asia, and Africa.

NOTES

1. The terms are Marion J. Levy's and William G. Sumner's, respectively; see M. J. Levy, Jr., *Modernization and the Structure of Societies* (Princeton; Princeton University Press, 1966), *passim.* and W. G. Sumner, *Folkways* (Boston: Blaisdell, 1940), p. 5f.

2. See, for instance, the characterization of much past research by Wilbert E. Moore, "Social Aspects of Economic Development," R.E.L. Faris (ed.), *Handbook of Modern Sociology* (Chicago: Rand McNally, 1964), p. 883.

It does not seem necessary to list here the long line of conceptual pairs developed by Auguste Comte, Sir Henry S. Maine, Ferdinand Toennies, Emile Durkheim, Robert Redfield, Howard Becker, and others. Less well-known is the critical discussion of these dichotomies, particularly of Toennies' *Gemeinschaft und Gesellschaft.*

Of special theoretical significance are three criticisms that were developed during this debate. (1) The categories designated globally several dimensions of social reality that could be shown to vary relatively independent from each other. This argument appeared first in Max Weber's work and was elaborated in his treatment of different institutionalized patterns of power; it was further developed by Talcott Parsons in his scheme of pattern variables. (2) Although frequently conceived of as pure types representing extreme points on a scale of possibilities, the concepts tended to be used as classificatory terms so that societies could be either of the one or the other character. Such reification, obviously at odds with the crudest empirical evidence, was associated with speculations in the twilight zone between social theory and social metaphysics. (3) Finally, it was shown that no social structure could persist without important elements from both sides of the complex dichotomy. The most recent and the most influential outcome of this critical point is represented by R. F. Bales' and T. Parsons' formulations about four system problems that have to be met by all social systems, more generally by all systems of action, and that require arrangements which can vary in their concrete nature a great deal, which cannot, however, be uniform in terms of either side of the old dichotomy.

The most constructive developments resulting from this discussion are found in the work of Talcott Parsons. Although his basic model of society is built on the assumption of complex equilibrium tendencies or "strains toward consistency," his work also provides starting points for an analysis of the coexistence of inconsistent patterns within the same social system.

3. The most widely noticed study of the Japanese conditions referred to is James C. Abegglen, *The Japanese Factory* (Glencoe, Ill.: The Free Press, 1958). See also Shizuo Matsushima, "Labour Management Relations in Japan," in P. Halmos (ed.), *Japanese Social Studies, Sociological Review,* Monograph No. 10 (1966), pp. 69-81; and Seymour Broadbridge, *Industrial Dualism in Japan* (Chicago: Aldine 1966).

4. See Ralf Dahrendorf, *Society and Democracy in Germany* (Garden City, N.Y.: Doubleday, 1967), p. 46; and Herbert Blumer, "Early Industrialization and the Laboring Class," *Sociological Quarterly,* 1 (January 1960), p. 14.

5. Reinhard Bendix, *Nation-Building and Citizenship* (New York: Wiley, 1964), p. 9 and p. 301.

6. Randall Collins, "A Comparative Approach to Political Sociology," in R. Bendix *et al.* (eds.), *State and Society. A Reader in Comparative Political Sociology* (Boston: Little, Brown, 1968), p. 56, note 34.

7. One of the few meaningful time references actually is involved here, though indirectly. Institutionalization as defined in the text involves internalization of norms and values. It is not necessary to adopt extreme psychoanalytic assumptions to argue that basic value orientations tend to be internalized in childhood. Therefore, institutionalization of basically new patterns tends to be linked with generational changes, though not in a simple fashion.

8. Rationalization in the choice of ends would have more determinate implications for social and cultural structure if one could assume ultimate standards to be invariable and inherent in human nature. Talcott Parsons has shown that the rejection of this assumption, as well as of the related one that ultimate standards are variable at random, was central to the theoretical orientations of the "founding fathers" of modern sociology; see his *The Structure of Social Action* (New York: McGraw-Hill, 1937).

9. See Robert N. Bellah, "Epilogue," in R. N. Bellah (ed.), *Religion and Progress in Modern Asia* (New York: The Free Press, 1965), pp. 169ff.; and Talcott Parsons, *Societies: Evolutionary and Comparative Perspectives* (Englewood Cliffs, N.J.: Prentice-Hall, 1966), Chs. 2 and 7. For related conceptualizations see Karl W. Deutsch, *The Nerves of Government* (New York: The Free Press, 1963), pp. 248ff.; and John Whitney Hall, "Changing Conceptions of the Modernization of Japan," in M. B. Jansen (ed.), *Changing Japanese Attitudes Toward Modernization* (Princeton: Princeton University Press, 1965), pp. 16-41.

Bellah's stipulation that the basic orientations in terms of which increased information is used be relatively stable may be considered as not strictly a component of the definition. It may be conceived of as an empirical condition of the capacity to act in coordinated fashion. In the language of neo-evolutionary theory, it is necessary to have a minimum of coordination and hierarchy among the various selective criteria and retention mechanisms for blind variation to turn into an ordered process of change. It seems that the requisites of physical survival in a changing environment do not result in a clearcut-enough directionality of changes in human societies beyond a certain level of adaptive capacity.

10. Such "ideal" or "pure types" are not arbitrary constructs, but embryonic theories composed of empirical hypotheses. They are embryonic theories because the set of hypotheses presently available does not include all necessary specifications but simply states modal tendencies and compatibilities

qualified in various degrees. On the interpretation of ideal types as incipient theories see Carl G. Hempel, "Problems of Concept and Theory Formation in the Social Sciences," in *Science, Language and Human Rights* (Philadelphia, 1952), pp. 65-86.

11. The contributions of nineteenth-century thought to this model, of Marx and Spencer, of Weber and Durkheim, merely have to be mentioned here. Recent reviews of relevant theory and empirical evidence are George A. Theodorson, "Acceptance of Industrialization and Its Attendant Consequences for the Social Patterns of Non-Western Societies," *American Sociological Review,* 18 (October 1953), pp. 477-484; Joseph A. Kahl, "Some Social Consequences of Industrialization and Urbanization," *Human Organization,* 18 (Summer 1959), pp. 53-74; and Wilbert E. Moore, *The Impact of Industry* (Englewood Cliffs, N. J.: Prentice-Hall, 1965).

Talcott Parsons has made a series of contributions to these problems which include a section entitled, "Institutionalized Rationalization and 'Cultural Lag,'" *The Social System* (Glencoe, Ill.: The Free Press, 1951), pp. 505-520; "Some Principal Characteristics of Industrial Societies," *Structure and Process in Modern Societies* (Glencoe, Ill.: The Free Press, 1960), pp. 132-168; *Societies,* and "Evolutionary Universals in Society," *American Sociological Review,* 29 (June 1964), pp. 339-357. In the latter essay, he defines evolutionary universals as "organizational development(s) sufficiently important to further evolution that, rather than emerging only once, (they are) likely to be 'hit upon' by various systems operating under different conditions" (p. 339). Four of these, "bureaucratic organization of collective goal-attainment, money and market systems, generalized universalistic norms, membership support for policy orientations," are considered characteristic of modern society: "Comparatively, the institutionalization of these four complexes and their interrelations is very uneven. In the broadest frame of reference, however, we may think of them as together constituting the main outline of the structural foundations of modern societies" (pp. 356 and 357).

One example of hypotheses presently under discussion are alternative assertions about the relations between industrialization and the structure of family and kinship; see Sidney M. Greenfield, "Industrialization and the Family in Sociological Theory," *American Journal of Sociology,* 67 (November 1961), pp. 312-322; and William J. Goode, *World Revolution and Family Patterns* (Glencoe, Ill.: The Free Press, 1963).

12. See William J. Goode, "The Protection of the Inept," *American Sociological Review,* 32 (February 1967), pp. 5-19.

13. On "value generalization" see Parsons, *Societies,* p. 23.

14. The most articulate formulations about universal types of problems all social systems have to cope with have come from Parsons and his collaborators in recent years. For a concise outline see Talcott Parsons, "An Outline of the Social System," T. Parsons *et al.* (eds.), *Theories of Society* (New York: The Free Press, 1961), pp. 30-79, esp. 38-41. Gideon Sjoberg, "Contradictory Functional Requirements and Social Systems," *Journal of Conflict Resolution,* 4 (June 1960), pp. 198-208, makes the same basic point; however, he overlooks the central role this idea plays in recent system theory. James C. Davis, "Structural Balance, Mechanical Solidarity, and Interpersonal Relations," in J. Berger *et al.* (eds.), *Sociological Theories in Progress,* Vol. 1 (Boston: Houghton Mifflin, 1966), pp. 74-101, is an important formulation of hypotheses about tendencies toward similarity in elementary social behavior which notes the limits of such "strains toward homogeneity."

15. See Gilbert Kushner *et al., What Accounts for Sociocultural Change? A Propositional Inventory* (Chapel Hill: University of North Carolina Press, 1962); and Felix M. Keesing, *Culture Change: An Analysis and Bibliography of Anthropological Sources to 1952* (Stanford: Stanford University Press, 1953), for a number of generalizations on diffusion and sociocultural change sifted from the anthropological literature. See

also Edward H. Spicer's theoretical summary of a seminar on acculturation: "Types of Contact and Processes of Change," *idem* (ed.), *Perspectives in American Indian Culture Change* (Chicago: University of Chicago Press, 1961), pp. 517-544.

16. See for instance J. H. Boeke, *Economics and Economic Policy of Dual Societies* (New York: Institute of Pacific Relations, 1953) (first published as two separate volumes in 1942 and 1946); and J. S. Furnivall, *Netherlands India: A Study of Plural Economy* (Cambridge: Cambridge University Press, 1939).

17. This insight had a central place in the theoretical orientations of both Durkheim and Weber. Weber accepted the idea that religious orientations are "adjusted to the needs of the community," subject to "social influences, economically and politically determined," but he insisted on two qualifications, first that nonreligious influences are usually "secondary," i.e., mediated by "religious needs" of the community, and second that after its formative period, "once stamped," a religion tends to become less responsive and tends to shape "the life-conduct of very heterogeneous strata." H. H. Gerth and C. W. Mills (eds.), *From Max Weber*, pp. 269f. The two qualifications about the relative autonomy and the relative stability of religious orientations have been emphasized and elaborated both in theoretical and in empirical analyses by Talcott Parsons, Neil J. Smelser, and Robert N. Bellah, among others.

In one interpretation, the relation between Protestantism and the emergence of modern sociocultural patterns provides a clear example for the assertion made in the text. Increasing economic and social differentiation preceded the Protestantic "revolution" by a long time. While Protestantism, especially in its Calvinist forms, established a base for value orientations compatible with further differentiation, Counter-Reformation Catholicism did not; and subsequently differentiation and rationalization of economic and, to a lesser degree, political activities stagnated in the Catholic countries. At the time of the Reformation a crucial threshold had apparently been reached, but "modernization" proceeded for centuries without creating intolerable strains; and when these strains finally reached a critical point it was by no means a foregone conclusion that the religious orientations would "give." See Herbert Luethy, "Once Again—Calvinism and Capitalism," *Encounter* (January 1964), pp. 26-39, and Benjamin Nelson, *The Idea of Usury* (Princeton: Princeton University Press, 1949).

18. On the significance of different basic types of religion for "progress" see Bellah, "Epilogue," *op. cit.*; "Religious Evolution," *American Sociological Review*, 29 (June 1964), pp. 358-374; and "Religious Aspects of Modernization in Turkey and Japan," *American Journal of Sociology*, 64 (July 1958), pp. 1-5.

19. Karl Mannheim, "Das Konservative Denken," *Archiv für Sozialwissenschaft und Sozialpolitik*, 52, pp. 68-142 and 470-495; translated in Karl Mannheim, *Essays on Sociology and Social Psychology* (London and New York: Oxford University Press, 1953). Among more recent discussions see Bert F. Hoselitz, "Tradition and Economic Growth," R. Braibanti and J. J. Spengler (eds.), *Tradition, Values, and Socio-Economic Development* (Durham, N. C.: Duke University Press, 1961), pp. 87f., 99f., and Robert N. Bellah, "Epilogue," *op. cit.* Hoselitz contrasts traditionalist ideologies with other forms of tradition which may be more compatible with economic growth and modernization. Bellah develops a differentiated typology of responses of religious idea systems to modernization.

20. Reinhard Bendix recently emphasized this connection between the process of diffusion and the particular importance of education and the intellectuals; see "Tradition and Modernity Reconsidered," *Comparative Studies in Society and History*, 9 (April 1967), pp. 334f.

21. On the phenomenon of polarization and the conditions of a decline of intermediate positions see Karl Mannheim, "Die Bedeutung der Konkurrenz im Geistigen," in *Verhandlungen des sechsten deutschen Soziologentages* (Tuebingen: 1929),

pp. 35-83; translated in K. Mannheim, *Essays on the Sociology of Knowledge* (London: Oxford University Press, 1952).

Mary Matossian's essay on "Ideologies of Delayed Industrialization," in *Economic Development and Cultural Change*, 6 (1958), pp. 217-228, identifies the same dimensions of orientation but emphasizes the combination of contradictory ideas, which she analyzes in terms of their functions. It should be noted that she concentrates on ideologies that were at least temporarily successful in dominating national policy and in unifying heterogeneous elements of the population of developing societies. See the following discussion of nationalism.

22. See David E. Apter, *The Politics of Modernization* (Chicago: University of Chicago Press, 1965). See also the typology of patterns of industrialization in terms of elites advanced by Clark Kerr *et al.*, *Industrialism and Industrial Man* (Cambridge, Mass.: Harvard University Press, 1960).

23. It appears that in Japan there has been considerable continuity in the relations to the government and the ruling elite from merchant guilds to large industrial combines. The arrangements always facilitated political control. See Harry K. Nishio, *Political Authority Structure and the Development of Entrepreneurship in Japan. 1603-1890*. unpubl. Ph.D. dissertation, Berkeley, University of California, 1966. In Germany the case is complicated by the laissez-faire policies in the early phases of governmental encouragement of economic development. These policies were the developmental techniques of the time, obviously superior to earlier mercantilist techniques which involved the government more directly. Conditions, consequences, and the partially modern, partially traditional aspects of the later policy of encouraging concentration in industry and the formation of cartels cannot be discussed here.

24. Bellah, "Epilogue," *op. cit.*, p. 206.

25. Alvan O'Neil Zarate, *Urban Fertility and Urban Industrialization in Mexico 1940-1960*, unpubl. Ph.D. thesis, Brown University, 1966, pp. 133f.

26. See Hoselitz, *op. cit.*, p. 112; and James J. Berna, "Patterns of Entrepreneurship in South India," in *Economic Development and Cultural Change*, 3 (1959), pp. 343-362.

27. See J. C. Mitchell, *Tribalism and the Plural Society* (London: Oxford University Press, 1960); "Primordial attachments" of this kind involve, of course, very real interests, too, and do not only result in improvised frames of reference for new forms of political behavior:

> This thrusting of a modern political consciousness upon the mass of a still largely unmodernized population does indeed tend to lead to the stimulation and maintenance of a very intense popular interest in the affairs of government. But, as a primordially based "corporate feeling of oneness" remains for many the *fons et origo* of legitimate authority—the meaning of the term "self" in "self-rule"—much of this interest takes the form of an obsessive concern with the relation of one's tribe, region, sect, or whatever to a center of power that, while growing rapidly more active, is not easily either insulated from the web of primordial attachments, as was the remote colonial regime, or assimilated to them as are the workaday authority systems of "little community" [Clifford Geertz, "The Integrative Revolution. Primordial Sentiments and Civil Politics in the New States," in C. Geertz (ed.), *Old Societies and New States* (New York: The Free Press, 1963), p. 120].

28. Melvin M. Tumin, "Competing Status Systems," in Wilbert E. Moore and Arnold S. Feldman (eds.), *Labor Commitment and Social Change in Developing Areas* (New York: Social Science Research Council, 1960), p. 290.

29. Parsons, "An Outline of the Social System," *op. cit.*, p. 45.

30. Wolfram Eberhard, *Conquerors and Rulers: Social Forces in Medieval China* (Leiden: Brill, 1965), here quoted as reprinted in Bendix *et al.* (eds.), *op. cit.*, p. 22.

31. On hierarchies of cybernetic control see Parsons. "An Outline of the Social System," *op. cit.*, and *Societies, Ch. 2*. The

list of principal components of social structure, too, was developed by Parsons and is discussed in the publications referred to. For variants of this classification see Neil J. Smelser, *Theory of Collective Behavior* (New York: The Free Press, 1963), Ch. 2, and Moore, "Social Aspects of Economic Development," *op. cit.*, pp. 890-899.

32. Parsons, *The Social System*, p. 491; see Ch. 11 *passim*. Parsons makes the initiation of re-equilibrating processes part of the definition of strain—a conceptualization I do not intend to follow here.

33. See Geertz, *op. cit.*, *passim*; among the detailed studies Geertz refers to is M. Freedman, "The Growth of Plural Society in Malaya," *Pacific Affairs*, 33 (1960), pp. 158-167. Geertz indicates the meaning of the term "primordial attachment" as

> one that stems from the "givens"—or, more precisely, as culture is inevitably involved in such matters, the assumed "givens"—of social existence: immediate contiguity and kin connections mainly, but beyond them the givenness that stems from being born into a particular religious community, speaking a particular language, or even a dialect of a language, and following particular social practices. (p. 109)

I include status groups because in agrarian societies they are frequently of the same ascriptive primordial character.

34. Clifford Geertz, *The Religion of Java* (New York: The Free Press, 1960), pp. 356 and 373-374. Geertz discusses "contextual relativism" among the factors moderating religious conflict in Java by reducing the tendency toward missionizing. Another illustration for the more general hypothesis is found in the typical patterns of success and failure of communist appeals in many parts of the *Tiers Monde*. For an analysis of the advantages communal and segmental hostilities provide for communism and of the limitations the same pattern imposes, see Donald S. Zagoria, "Communism in Asia," *Commentary*, 39 (February 1965), pp. 53-58, esp. 54-56.

35. See M. Rainer Lepsius, "Immobilismus: das System der sozialen Stagnation in Süditalien," *Jahrbücher für Nationalökonomie und Statistik*, 177 (1965), pp. 304-342. His analysis is at variance with E. C. Banfield's in *The Moral Basis of a Backward Society* (Glencoe, Ill.: The Free Press, 1958). Arguing against Banfield's explanation in terms of value orientations, Lepsius insists on the importance of the labor market conditions.

36. See Parsons, *The Social System*, esp. pp. 297-325; Harry Bredemeier and Richard M. Stephenson, *The Analysis of Social Systems* (New York: Hold Rinehart and Winston, 1960), pp. 147-156; Robert K. Merton, *Social Theory and Social Structure,*

rev. ed. (Glencoe, Ill.: The Free Press, 1957), pp. 371-384; William J. Goode, "A Theory of Role Strain," *American Sociological Review*, 25 (1960), pp. 483-496.

37. See Arnold S. Feldman and Wilbert E. Moore, "Spheres of Commitment. The Society," in Moore and Feldman (eds.), *op. cit.*, pp. 68ff.

38. Talcott Parsons, "Democracy and Social Structure in Pre-Nazi Germany," in *Essays in Sociological Theory*, rev. ed. (Glencoe, Ill.: The Free Press, 1954), pp. 104-123.

39. Seymour M. Lipset, *Political Man* (Garden City, N.Y.: Doubleday, 1960), Chs. 2 and 3.

40. For an analysis of such patterns in German political development see M. Rainer Lepsius, "Parteiensystem und Sozialstruktur: Zum Problem der Demokratisierung der deutschen Gesellschaft," W. Abel *et al.* (eds.), *Wirtschaft, Geschichte und Wirtschaftsgeschichte* (Stuttgart: Fischer, 1966), pp. 371-393; and *Extremer Nationalismus, Strikturbedingungen vor der nationalsozialistischen Machtergreifung* (Stuttgart: Fischer, 1966). See also Guenther Roth, *The Social Democrats in Imperial Germany* (New York: Bedminster, 1963).

41. Dahrendorf, *op. cit.*, Ch. 4 and *passim*.

42. S. N. Eisenstadt has argued this thesis in several publications. See "Modernization and Conditions of Sustained Growth," *World Politics*, 16 (1964), pp. 576-594; also "Breakdowns of Modernization," *Economic Development and Cultural Change*, 22 (1964), pp. 345-367; and *Modernization: Protest and Change* (Englewood Cliffs, N. J.: Prentice-Hall, 1966).

43. I would not go quite so far as Samuel P. Huntington who tentatively states this idea as a general rule of long-term societal change:

> Modernity is thus not all of a piece. The American experience demonstrates conclusively that some institutions and some aspects of a society may become highly modern while other institutions and other aspects retain much of their traditional form and substance. Indeed, this may be a natural state of affairs. In any system some sort of equilibrium or balance must be maintained between change and continuity. Change in some spheres renders unnecessary or impossible change in others. In America the continuity and stability of governmental institutions has permitted the rapid change of society, and the rapid change in society has encouraged continuity and stability in government. The relation between polity and society may well be dialectical rather than complementary [*Political Order in Changing Societies* (New Haven: Yale University Press, 1968), p. 132].

31

MEDICAL EVOLUTION

Renée C. Fox

Through his analysis of modern medical practice, Talcott Parsons has made a pioneering conceptual contribution to the specialized field of medical sociology which, at the same time, has general significance for behavioral science theory. This essay will explore those aspects of his writings that bear on health, illness, and medicine.[1] Its theoretical goal is a two-fold one: to synthesize rather than merely summarize this sector of Parsons' work and to set it down in the broad evolutionary perspective on the structure and dynamics of total societies that has been central to his thinking over the last ten years.[2]

Parsons' analysis of modern medical practice turns around three interrelated ideas. The first is a view of the physician (for Parsons, the ideal-typical medical practitioner) as cast in a role that belongs to the "professional complex,"[3] which he considers a distinctively important characteristic of modern society. The second notion is a breakthrough insight into the fact that illness is not just a biological and/or psychological condition, but that it also constitutes a social role complementary to that of the physician, what Parsons calls the sick role. The third idea links the other two. In spite of the "competence gap"[4] that exists between physician and patient, because one is a trained expert in matters of health and illness and the other is not, they are seen as bound to one another in a semi-collegial relationship. In Parsons' perspective, they form a collectivity based on their joint commitment to the recovery of the sick person and on the solidarity and mutual trust that are both prerequisite to their pursuit of this common goal and a consequence of it.

Parsons regards "the case of modern medical practice" as a particularly vivid exemplification of the interplay of the four subsystems of action—social, cultural, personality, and physical-organic—as they converge on a strategic area in modern society:

> To be sick [is] not only to be in a biological state . . . but requires exemptions from obligations, conditional legitimation, and motivation to accept therapeutic help. It

[can] thus, in part, at least, be classed as a type of deviant behavior . . . socially categorized in a kind of role.[5]

The fact that the relevance of illness is not confined to the non-motivated purely situational aspect of social action greatly increases its significance for the social system. It becomes not merely an "external" danger to be "warded off" but an integral part of the social equilibrium itself. . . . Medical practice . . . is a "mechanism" in the social system for coping with the illness of its members. It involves a set of institutionalized roles . . . "professional" roles, a sub-class of the larger group of occupational role. . . . [It] also involves a specialized relation to certain aspects of the general cultural tradition of modern society. Modern medical practice is organized around the application of scientific knowledge to the problems of illness and health, to the control of "disease." Science is of course a very special kind of cultural phenomenon and a really highly developed scientific level in any field is rare among known cultures, with the modern West in a completely unique position. . . .[6]

The kinds of functional significance that Parsons accords to the health-illness-medical practice complex qualifies it to be defined as one of the major institutions of a modern society, although he himself never conceptualizes it in this way. The over-arching societal importance that he assigns to what we would term the institution of medicine is of two general sorts. The first is primarily social structural and motivational in nature. For Parsons, illness is an "impairment of the individual's capacity for effective performance of social roles and those tasks which are organized subject to role-expectations."[7] It is a form of partially and conditionally legitimated deviance which, when aggregated, can have seriously disruptive consequences for the ongoing of a society. As he points out, the effect of great numbers of persons in a society taking to their beds could, in its passive way, disturb the usual functioning of that social system as much as an insurgent refusal on the part of those same individuals to tend to their daily activities and responsibilities.[8] (Here, he anticipates the "sick-in" as a form of social protest.) Furthermore, he suggests, the exemption, withdrawal and dependence that

773

illness characteristically entails is an especially strategic and threatening form of deviance in the kind of modern industrialized society that emphasizes value-orientations like instrumental activism, achievement, personal responsibility, and independence.[9]

In Parsons' analysis, the second source of medicine's macrosignificance lies in its cultural and, one might say, existential import. Health, illness, and medical practice are integrally associated with what he has variously called "the environment above action," "ultimate reality," and "problems of meaning."[10] Both the experience of illness and the act of caring for the sick, then, are related to the "ultimate conditions" of man's existence that Robert Bellah considers to be the immutable core of religion.[11] Notably, illness and medical practice evoke questions about the "why's" of pain, suffering, the limits of human life and death, and (latently, in a modern society), about their relationship to evil, sin, and injustice.

In this connection, Parsons is keenly aware of the special poignancy of the uncertainty dimension in modern medical practice. As he indicates, the fact that a powerful battery of scientific knowledge and technique is applied to illness and the "deepest human concerns" it arouses does not eliminate uncertainty from medicine. To begin with, by its very nature, science is an open, searching mode of thought, as much an organized way of raising systematic questions and doubts about what are assumed to be established concepts, facts, and methods, as of furthering knowledge and skill. Although medical scientific advance may solve certain problems, it also helps to create and maintain two basic types of uncertainty that affect both medical practitioner and patient.[12] The first kind of uncertainty derives from the hiatuses, limitations, and errors that characterize medical knowledge at any given point in time. The second type of uncertainty results from the paradoxical fact that despite its inadequacies, medical science is so vast and highly developed that no one can totally encompass or perfectly master it.

Parsons' insights into these cultural aspects of medicine are among the most original of his medical sociology formulations. And they are consistent with the critical place that he assigns to the cultural system in his general theory of action. "In the cybernetic sense," he writes, the cultural system "is the highest within the action system" and, as such, a major source of societal evolution and "large-scale change."[13]

The fact that Parsons considers modern medical practice a "case" implies that he views it in a comparative evolutionary framework, as the crystallization of a certain stage of medical development and institutionalization. Occasionally he makes this evolutionary outlook more explicit, either by contrasting some of the attributes of modern medicine with those of earlier phases or by offering analytic speculations on what the health-illness-medicine complex will look like in the future. Thus, for example, he reminds us that:

> . . . the treatment of illness as a problem for applied science [should not] be taken for granted as "common sense." The comparative evidence is overwhelming that illness . . . has been interpreted in supernatural terms, and magical treatment has been considered to be the appropriate method of coping with it. In non-literate societies there is an element of empirical lore which may be considered as proto-scientific. . . . But the prominence of magic in this field is overwhelmingly great. This, however, is by no means confined to non-literate cultures. The examples of traditional China and our own Middle Ages suffice. . . .[14]

In a theoretically based attempt to forecast the direction in which modern medicine can be expected to move, Parsons predicts its growing differentiation in several respects. These include: its progressive "involvement in the nexus of formal [collectivity-oriented] organization"; the continuing "upgrading of the level of science involved in medicine, and with it the . . . increasing participation of scientists who are not themselves medical men"; and "extension of the focus of ultimate [fiduciary] responsibility for the health problems of the society," with the consequence that it will be less exclusively carried by the medical profession. In addition, Parsons foresees a continuing "generalization of the value complex involving health problems [so that] the basic concepts of health, and hence illness [will be applied] to higher levels and broader ranges in the organization of human action systems."[15] In effect, what he has done here is apply his paradigm of evolutionary change by sketching out how he thinks the broader processes of increasing differentiation, complexity, inclusiveness and integration of organization, normative upgrading, and generalization of the value system are affecting the "present complex and rapidly changing situation" of modern medicine.

Taking these statements as clues and jumping-off points, I shall first discuss more fully the key features that Parsons identifies as characteristic of modern medicine. I shall then move back to an earlier stage on the evolutionary spectrum to consider medicine in what Parsons and Bellah would term an advanced primitive or archaic society. I have chosen to consider this phase of medical development not only because it is theoretically suggestive but also because I have had first-hand experience doing research in a developing Central African society which, despite its progressive modernization, still retains many of the sociocultural attributes of the archaic type of society from which it is evolving. My discussion of advanced primitive medicine, then, will be largely drawn from field work I conducted in Zaïre over the period from 1962 to 1967, supplemented by wide reading of English, French, and Belgian anthropological monographs on various African societies.[17] Finally, I shall try to imagine and formulate what the essential features of medicine might be in what we will call a post-modern society.[18] In this context, "post-modern" is merely a descriptive label referring to an evolutionary stage of society that at some historical juncture may develop from a modern type of society. My major empirical referents will be, on the one hand, what I know about the attitudes and values of the "new" medical student now training to be a physician in American medical schools and, on the other, what I consider to be the sociological implications of organ transplantation, taken as an ideal typical example both of present and future clinical medical advance.[19] Whether the medical trends that I discern will actually be institutionalized is not yet clear, and it is still too early to ascertain how continuous and compatible with modern medicine these developments may prove to be.

MODERN MEDICINE

The general framework within which illness is defined and explained in modern society is more ideological than cosmological. Illness is believed to be a "natural" rather than a supernatural happening: a state of disease and dysfunction impersonally caused by microorganisms, inborn metabolic disturbances, or physical or psychic stress. No mythical beings, spirits, or gods are assumed to be at work bringing sickness to bear on particular individuals; nor are persons considered to be motivated or able to use arcane powers to do so. Furthermore, as Parsons indicated, one of the attributes of the sick role in modern society is that the person who falls ill is not supposed to have caused his condition by displeasing the gods, the ancestors, or "significant others" in his social milieu who, as a consequence, magicoreligiously afflict him. Rather, he is regarded as being in a state attributable to factors that not only lie outside his personal control but also outside his moral and religious responsibility. Illness, then, is thought to be a natural part of the human condition, though not in a resigned or even passively accepting sense. It is considered a state that is, but that ideally ought not to be: one that should be interpreted, investigated, treated, controlled, cured, and, beyond that, eliminated.

In the opinion of microbiologist René Dubos, "Complete and lasting freedom from disease . . . is almost incompatible with living . . . a dream remembered from the imaginings of a Garden of Eden."[20] However mythical or utopian it may be, it is nonetheless a fervently espoused goal in modern society, one that is believed possible, as well as desirable, through the advance and application of scientific knowledge and medical technology. Modern medicine is also surrounded by the pervasive conviction that largely as a consequence of medical scientists' research and discoveries, members of the society enjoy a level of health superior to that known to men in bygone aras. Dubos challenges this, deeming it an "illusion" to contend either that general health has improved to this extent, or that the "laboratory scientist's labors" and the "scientific management of . . . body and soul" are that exclusively responsible for whatever progress has been made in this respect.[21] The fact that such assumptions of modern scientific medicine are subject to debate demonstrates, to use Parsonian terms, that the type of orientation it represents contains important evaluative as well as cognitive elements.

Phrased more sociologically and less subjectively, what Dubos calls an illusion can be taken to be an indicator of the fact that the conceptions and beliefs about illness institutionalized by modern medicine are supported by strongly felt cultural commitments to them. Other telling indicators of this at once evaluative and affective commitment can be cited. For example, in modern society, a person's conviction that his illness was caused by evildoers, in the form of supernatural entities or human enemies would not be granted objective credibility, as it would in a primitive society. Rather, it would be more likely to be viewed as a paranoic symptom of mental illness. An individual persuaded that sickness is a visitation of God, an expression of His will that cannot and ought not be dealt with by other than religious means, would be considered an extreme "fundamentalist" and "fatalist," bordering on religious "fanaticism." He would not be judged to be piously exemplary, except by members of a few religious sects, as he might have been in certain kinds of theistically oriented intermediate societies. The labels "mentally ill," "fundamentalist," and "fatalist" invoked in this context imply aberrations from the normatively expected ways of thinking about illness in modern society of sufficient magnitude and import to be classified as deviant.

The modern view of illness as a "natural phenomenon," in Parsons' words, does not mean that, "like the vagaries of the weather," it is regarded as independent of the "motivated interaction of human beings."[22] Rather, influenced by personality psychology and psychiatry, the modern perspective on illness includes the underlying premise that there is "a component of motivatedness in almost all illness":[23] its etiology, meaning, impact, and/or outcome. In this respect, "the most completely 'mental' of mental illnesses . . . various ranges of psychosomatic phenomena . . . [and the most] completely 'somatic' illnesses may be said to form a continuum."[24]

The dissociation of modern conceptions of illness from the machinations of spirits, gods, ancestors, or living relatives is not only a consequence of the degree to which they are shaped by science; it is also correlated with the extent to which medicine is differentiated from kinship, religion, and magic in modern society. As already indicated, the primary agents who define, diagnose, certify, and treat illness in modern society are not magical or religious practitioners or family members. Rather, they are medical professionals, trained to be technically competent in the secular and specialized, though vast, body of scientific knowledge and technique considered appropriate, meaningful, and effective in matters of health and illness. One of the attributes of the medical professional role (which it shares with other professional roles) is the value-orientation that Parsons has formulated as the pattern variable, affective neutrality, which I have renamed "detached concern."[25] The physician and other medical professionals are enjoined to relate to the patient by blending empathy for his person, background, condition, and feelings with sufficient objectivity and dispassion to insure that their clinical judgment will not be distorted or their efficacy impeded by too much emotional involvement with the patient. Physicians recognize that, in spite of the professional socialization they have undergone, an optimum balance of detachment and concern would be very difficult to attain were they to care for members of their family, most especially their spouse, children, parents, or siblings. An informal norm has grown up around this insight in the profession, impelling most physicians to refer close family to other colleagues. A tandem arrangement is thus established, whereby physicians care for other physicians' relatives.[26]

This convention suggests other, more general ways in which family and medical roles are differentiated and, to a certain extent, insulated from one another in modern society. The physical and psychic intimacies that a patient entrusts to a physician differ in significant respects from those he would ordinarily share with members of his family. As Parsons has emphasized, the kind of access to the patient's body granted the physician is a privileged one. "Indeed, some of his contacts, as in the case of a rectal or vaginal examination, would not be permitted to any other person,"[27] even to a husband or wife. The physician also has entrée to confidential information about those aspects of a patient's private life and feelings that are pertinent to his medical condition, information that he would not necessarily disclose to relatives. It would seem that the structure of the medical professional role, as compared with that of a kinship role—most especially, its functional specificity and detached concern—makes it psychologically easier for patients to permit the physician these health-related intimacies. Being treated by a physician who was also a relative would introduce a modicum of diffuseness and affectivity associated with family roles into the doctor-patient relationship. This would be likely either to inhibit the privileged communication between patient and physician or to push it beyond the bounds of what is emotionally tolerable for both parties, as well as medically functional. The fact that the patient is willing to bare himself to a medical practitioner who is not a kinsman or a personal friend is not only related to his confidence in the physician's medical scientific capacities, but also to his impersonal trust in the doctor's commitment to professional norms of privacy and confidentiality.

The degree of segregation between sick and medical professional roles, on the one hand, and kinship roles, on the other, that is institutionalized in modern society is partly related to the structural properties of a modern family. As Parsons and Fox have indicated,[28] this small, conjugal, relatively isolated, close knit, emotionally intense type of family is prone to certain difficulties in dealing with illness. In contrast to the more far-reaching kinship relationships characteristic of an extended family system, emotional attachments to kin in a modern family are almost totally confined to the few relatives who make up the nuclear family. Partly as a consequence, the emotional importance and intensity of these relationships are likely to be so high that the illness of any one of this narrow circle of kin will powerfully affect and, in the psychological sense of the term, threaten all the other members of the family. Individually and collectively, they may easily be thrown into a state of disequilibrium. Under these circumstances, it is probable that a sick person's relatives will overreact to his illness, with the kind of excessive sympathy or inordinate severity that will sociopsychologically impede rather than facilitate his recovery.

The relative differentiation of medicine from kinship in modern society also seems to have the latent function of preventing the psychologically-induced spread of illness within a family unit. To the extent that illness may be said to have a motivational component, the modern family would be particularly vulnerable to this kind of contagion, by virtue of the relatively exclusive and strongly affective way in which its members identify with each other. Furthermore, the sick role, comprising as it does a semilegitimate channel of withdrawal from normal social responsibilities and a basis of eligibility for care by others, is inviting to various family members in patterned, often unconsciously motivated ways. The psychological "temptations" in this regard are systematically related to the structural strains associated with various role constellations in the modern family:

> To the wife-mother, [illness] offers an institutionalized way of reacting to her heavy affective-expressive responsibilities in the family and a compulsively feministic way of [responding] to her exclusion from certain prerogatives and opportunities open to the man. For the husband-father, illness legitimizes respite from the discipline, effort, and dualistic demands of interdependence and autonomy that his occupation [requires] of him. For the child, being moved by the process of socialization along the tension-ridden path toward adulthood, illness provides an escape from increasingly exacting obligations to behave as a mature person. And for the elderly individual, retired from the occupational system, widowed, and with no traditionally assured place in the families established by his children, illness may serve as an opportunity to solicit forcibly their concern and care.[29]

The striking degree to which sickness is cared for in a hospital rather than in the home in modern society is a complex phenomenon, to which numerous factors have contributed. Not the least of these is the need to localize and integrate the complex professional teams and technological facilities that scientific medicine brings to bear on the diagnosis and treatment of illness. In addition, in the light of the susceptibilities and strains of the modern family already discussed, hospitalization has an important social control function. It places the sick person in an extrafamilial setting, where he is less likely to be emotionally reinforced in illness and where the detached concern, specificity, and universalism of the medical staff can provide some motivational leverage for progressively moving him out of the sick role and towards recovery. At the same time, isolating the sick person from members of his family mitigates the emotional strain they are likely to experience in the face of his illness and thus helps them to resist the contagious temptation to take to their own beds in response to the situation.

In modern society, then, illness is significantly disunited structurally, as well as conceptually, from religion, magic, and kinship. It is also differentiated from other types of deviance, such as crime and certain forms of sin, that incur blame or punishment, because the individual engaged in them is judged to have willfully violated important values, norms, or role-obligations. In addition, modern ideas about illness distinguish it from other sorts of human malaise, adversity, or misfortune. (A notable exception to this is death, which is closely linked with the sick role because it is so often preceded by illness.)

Although, as we shall see, these modern conceptions liberate individuals and groups from some of the basic existential and psychological anxieties about the significance of illness to which, for example, members of a primitive society are subject, they nonetheless generate a characteristic form of disquietude of their own. We have said that in all societies health and illness are related to what Parsons has termed "ultimate reality." "But who of us really believes that his own bodily infirmities and the approaching death is a purely natural occurrence, just an insignificant event in the infinite chain of causes?" Bronislaw Malinowski has written. "To the most rational of civilized men health, disease and the threat of death, float in a hazy emotional mist, which seems to become denser and more impenetrable as the fateful forms approach."[30] By disclaiming that the cause and meaning of illness have anything to do with the supernatural or the inherently mysterious, modern medicine provides no legitimation for the occurrence of such problems of meaning and no institutionalized way of dealing with them. Precisely because of its essentially scientific orientation, it only offers explanations for the "hows" of illness; but it does not explicitly recognize, dispel, or answer the questions of "why" that inevitably arise. This phenomenon, a source of structural strain, has considerable significance; for in modern society, there is a progressive tendency for attitudes and behavior patterns once defined as sinful or criminal to be reclassified as sickness.

Paradoxically, the fact that these questions of meaning triggered by the experience of illness fall outside the purview of modern medicine contributes to the development of new forms of magic. Along with the problems of uncertainty and the therapeutic limitations that still characterize the field of medicine, the unanswered "whys" of illness find expression and some degree of symbolic resolution in what might be termed scientific magic. In effect, these are magical attitudes and behaviors patterned in ostensibly medical scientific ways, that help to explain illness and to increase confidence in its positive outcome. Parsons has pointed out that what he calls these "functional equivalents of magic,"[31] or "pseudoscientific elements"[32] are observable among medical professionals, as well as patients and the lay public at large. On the medical practitioners' side of the interaction, he specifically mentioned their inclination to favor the most demonstrably vigorous of alternative ways to treat patients, their accentuate-the-positive tendency to be optimistic about the success of their active intervention, and their non-immunity to jumping on the bandwagon of "fashion change" in medical conceptions and therapies when it occurs.[33] With respect of medicomagical orientations of the public, Parsons cites various forms of health faddism, a continuing, widespread belief in patent medicines and home remedies, and the development and recruitment power of numerous health cults.[34]

In my own sociological observation of modern American medical practice and research over the years, I have been struck by three other scientific magic constellations through which both physicians and patients try to deal with the problems of meaning, uncertainty, and limitation that grave illness and the proximity of death pose for them.[35] The first of these is medical humor, a form of gallows humor, at once counterphobic, impious, defiant, and cathartic. The second is a "game of chance" orientation: in the same spirit of blasphemous hilarity, making wagers on the diagnosis of an illness, the impact of therapy on it, its prognosis and, most audacious of all, whether a patient will live or die. The third pattern might be called a celebration syndrome. It consists of the giving of *rites de passage* parties, in honor of the birthday of a patient or a member of the medical team, to mark the anniversary of an operation or to fete sheer survival. All three of these configurations make ironic commentary on the apparent lack of order, predictability, and sense in the shared predicament of those who fall ill and those who try to care for them. All express protest against what seems capricious, arbitrary, and existentially absurd in this situation. And all make affirmative petitions that the day will come when the illness and death of human beings are more fathomable and more effectively dealt with by the science and practice of medicine.

In an essay on "Death in American Society,"[36] Parsons and Lidz emphasize the extent to which the "enhanced capacity to save and prolong lives . . . achieved by modern medicine" has made it possible to "differentiate the death complex" into two components. The aspects of death "inevitably grounded in the human condition" are distinguished from those which are considered "adventitious" because they are "potentially subject to some kind of human control." Parsons and Lidz contend that the ultimate reality and necessity of death are not handled with "denial" in this type of society, as some would claim. For, death "coming at the completion of a normal life cycle" is not only regarded as natural and inescapable, but also as positively functional in certain biological and sociocultural ways. The nonresignation constituent in the modern cultural orientation towards death, the authors argue, is quite specific. It involves an institutionalized commitment to doing all that can be done to prevent or postpone as many adventitious deaths as possible. This is in keeping with the general pattern of instrumental activism that characterizes modern Western (and particularly American) society.

My own sociology of medicine studies have sensitized me to some of the distinctive ways in which such a cultural perspective may affect the attitudes of physicians and patients towards death. To begin with, partly as a consequence of this orientation and the far-reaching medical scientific advances associated with it, death from illness in childhood, youth, or otherwise prior to old age has been dramatically reduced, in comparison with a pre-modern society. Furthermore, for the reasons I have already analyzed, most serious illness is cared for in a hospital, which is commonly the site where death takes place, rather than in the patient's home. Partly as a result of these social situational factors, the young men and women in a modern society who choose medical careers are likely never to have viewed or even personally experienced the death of a human being. Yet, more than most occupations, the field they have chosen entails the ushering out as well as the ushering in of life and, in the case of physicians, the unique right and responsibility officially to "pronounce" death. In addition, medical students often begin their medical training with such intensive dedication to "combatting" and "winning out" over illness and death that, as one of them put it, "In a way, it's a shock for us to realize that some of our patients are going to die." What is implied here is that a desocialization-resocialization process has to take place for this "realization" to occur, for the medical professional to distinguish between deaths that can and cannot be forestalled, and for him to learn when it is and when it is not appropriate to make "heroic" efforts to "save" a patient. The acceptance of life-threatening illness and all deaths, except those that occur among the elderly, comes hard in a modern society, for medical professionals as well as lay persons. From what I have observed, I would say that even at the end of a long process of professional training many physicians still regard the death of any but their aged patients as a "failure," for which they as doctors are both medically and personally accountable.[37]

If anything, this tendency is reinforced by patients and their families, whose belief in the capacity of modern medicine to combat death and to cure is generally high and who do not have sufficient medical knowledge to be as cognizant of the field's uncertainties and limitations as are medical professionals. This same kind of faith in the actual and incipient powers of medicine, combined with a zealous disinclination to be passive in the face of illness, contributes to the widespread willingness of patients whose diseases elude the present knowledge and skill of modern medicine to serve as human research subjects.[38] Their motivation for doing so has two facets. It actively expresses their hope that through their participation in medical experimentation new insights or treatments may be developed that could directly benefit them. It is also a testimony to their disinterested conviction that, in the words of one patient-subject, it will be "for the good of medical science and the humane benefit of others in the future."[39] The phenomenon of gravely ill patients who seek promise and meaning in the role of a medical research subject is so common that, in the opinion of Dr. Francis D. Moore, "the posture of 'informed consent' in therapeutic innovation" that the physician ideally ought to assume not only involves "trying safely and sanely to explain to a volunteer what is going to be done," but also "the much more difficult task of explaining alternatives to a worried patient who wishes, above all else, to have the experiment carried out on him."[40]

In some respects, it is in this physician-investigator, patient-subject relationship, one of the unique institutionalized characteristics of modern medicine, that Parsons sees the quintessence of the collectivity-orientation both of the sick role and the doctor's role. He attaches great analytic importance to this institutional pattern. In all his writings on medicine in modern society, Parsons has emphasized that this is one of two core characteristics that distinguish professional from nonprofessional occupational roles. (The other singular attribute of a profession that he has stressed is the fact that it entails "high-level and specialized competence" acquired through prolonged training, "grounded in mastery of some part of society's generalized (intellectual) cultural tradition." This training, he points out, is "increasingly. . . acquired in the university, whatever special provisions for *practicum* experience there may also be."[41]) Parsons' formulation of what he means by collectivity-orientation (one of five pattern-variable pairs), how it is institutionalized in the medical case, and what he considers to be its general societal import has evolved over the years. At first, it referred to a type of obligation built into a genre of social roles: concretely, the responsibility of incumbents of professional roles to put the welfare of the client and disinterested service to him before such self-interested goals as maximizing profit, striving for recognition, advancement, and the like. Progressively, however, Parsons has extended his notion, so that it has become more interactive and inclusive. Collectivity-orientation now also refers to certain aspects of the client's relationship to the professional as well as to the collegial dimension of the relationship of professionals to one another.

Parsons maintains that professionals and clients are bindingly interlinked in somewhat the same way that fellow professionals are: by virtue of their joint membership in what he calls a "common solidary collectivity." By this he means that they are mutually engaged in an enterprise that is of high functional significance not only for the particular individuals involved but also for the society at large. And they are reciprocally committed to the values and goals on which this enterprise is based. In turn, especially because there is a competence gap between professionals and lay persons, both the mutuality of their commitment and the viability of their relationship are contingent on the institutionalization of some degree of impersonal as well as personal trust between them. In these several respects, in addition to being collectivity-oriented, the professional-client relationship is a fiduciary one.

Applying these theoretical insights to the case of modern medicine, it can be said that physicians and patients not only work together to ease birth, facilitate normal growth and development, and promote health but also to prevent or relieve illness, deformity, physical and psychological suffering, and to forestall "needless" death. Although the patient is not a full and equal colleague of the physician, Parsons concedes, his active collaboration and trust are necessary to the successful outcome of their common undertaking. Seen in comparative evolutionary perspective, physicians and patients in modern society have a relatively high degree of confidence in each other's commitment, integrity, and competence. At one and the same time, this "draws upon" and contributes to a reservoir of trust in medicine as an institution and, beyond that, a more generalized societal pool of trust. As I shall show, the fiduciary matrix in which modern medicine is dynamically embedded differs considerably from what is characteristic of an advanced primitive or archaic society, where a high level of nontrust is broadly institutionalized.

Parsons does not imply that the situation of modern medicine is so utopian that physicians and patients perfectly live up to their respective role obligations and collectively enjoy a relationship devoid of strain, suspicion, and resentment. In fact, he emphasizes that one of the reasons the institutionalization of a modicum of solidarity and trust in the physician-patient relationship is important is that a "persistent ambivalence . . . exists in public attitudes" towards the professions in general and medicine in particular.[42] As Robert K. Merton and Elinor Barber have suggested, this characteristic ambivalence is both sociological and psychological in nature.[43] It is generated as much by the normatively structured expectations that patients and physicians have of one another and the patterned conditions under which people obtain medical care as by physicianly deviance or malpractice.

Parsons does not gloss over what he regards as

retrogressive traits in the social organization of modern American medicine. There are two sets of these tendencies that he considers strategic: some of the ways in which the medical profession "jealously guards" its independence and autonomy against what it terms lay control[44] and its tenacious adherence to a solo-practice, fee-for-service model. In effect, Parsons predicts that these patterns, which are already incompatible with basic structural and cultural features of a modern society, will prove nonviable in a postmodern society:

> Essentially, we may say, the classical private physician was—and to some degree still is—a kind of "aristocrat" of the occupational world. His *technical* functions had become specialized around the application of scientific knowledge, but his *social status* was a typically diffuse *fiduciary status*. In terms of the general process of structural differentiation which must be regarded as central to the development of industrial societies, this classical private physician must be regarded as a special, probably transitional, role-type. It seems inconceivable that this structural type could resist the pressures to further differentiation which have operated throughout the society.[45]

ARCHAIC MEDICINE

By and large, postprimitive or archaic societies attach general and often central symbolic significance to health and illness. This is related to the fact that the health-illness-medicine complex is tightly interlocked with the predominant institutions of an archaic society—kinship, religion, and magic—which are themselves closely interwebbed. The relative nondifferentiation of archaic medicine, religion, and magic, for example, is nicely illustrated by the fact that in the cultural tradition of numerous Central African societies, no semantic distinction is made between the term for medicines or medications, magicoreligious charms and supernaturally conferred powers such as strength, fecundity, and invulnerability.[46]

In contrast to archaic medicine, modern medicine has its closest links with the institution of science, on the one hand, and the occupational sector of the economy (specifically, the applied professions), on the other. From a comparative evolutionary point of view, it is important to note both that, in archaic society, medicine's most intimate bonds are with different institutions than in modern society and that this relationship is less independent and specialized than in the modern case.

This is not to imply that archaic medicine is devoid of scientific lore and technique. But the characteristic way of thought on which it is premised is more magicoreligious than scientific. It shares with scientific thought at least two fundamental attributes: the

quest for an explanatory theory in a causal context and an interest in classification and taxonomy. However, in a number of crucial respects, archaic medical thought is nonscientific and, in certain regards, incompatible with scientific reasoning.

An "imperious, uncompromising demand for . . . determinism," to use a phrase coined by Claude Lévi-Strauss,[47] is one of the most fundamental characteristics of the cognitive precepts and existential beliefs on which archaic medicine is based. This is consonant with a more general cultural orientation, distinctive to members of this type of society. They are inclined to seek and to find explanations for all that befalls them, awake or asleep, in the realms of the conscious and the unconscious, in life and in death. Most happenings—illness figuring prominently among them—are interpreted either as adverse or felicitous, relatively few experiences are regarded as neutral or without meaning, and virtually none are considered to be fortuitous. They are viewed as being determinatively caused, primarily by supernatural, psychic, and interpersonal forces, within a closed system of thought and belief, whose inner logic is cogent, self-confirming and self-fulfilling. Explanations for events like illness are pre-established, limited in range, and fixed. When evidence contrary to traditional interpretations presents itself, there is a tendency to develop what Evans-Pritchard has termed "secondary elaborations,"[48] that "excuse" or explain away the untoward occurrence and thereby protest established premises. There is no room for the concept of probability in this way of thought, nor for the formal acknowledgement of an ultimate, irreducible degree of uncertainty as an inherent property of man's attempts systematically to understand, explain, and predict physical, biological, social, cultural, and psychological phenomena. Archaic thought and belief is also monistic in nature. It does not distinguish between objective and subjective reality or dissociate ideas from empirical happenings and occasions. Reality is that which is thought and believed, and ideas are "bound to the particular occasions that evoke them."[49]

Essentially, the archaic medical perspective on health and illness is metaphysical. It is the prototypical expression of the "primal world view"[50] that pervades an archaic society, blending supernatural and anthropocentric notions in a particular kind of way. Health signifies that one's life-force is intact and that one is sufficiently in harmony with intersecting social, physical, and supernatural environments both to receive and enjoy the positive values of life and to ward off its dangers, misfortunes, and evils. Illness is the antithesis of health. It is one of the principal negative, discordant, depleting, and potentially tragic experiences of life. In this respect, its dynamics and meaning are not sharply distinguished from those of other major forms of adversity, such as sterility, failure, interpersonal mischance, and death.

In the archaic view, illness is "unnatural." Ideally, it ought not occur, and empirically, it would not, without the intervention of transhuman forces, mediated by human agents who are either intentional or unintentional evildoers. Illness is presumed to be caused by the evil thoughts, feelings, or motives of a significant other person. It may result from feelings of envy, jealousy, resentment, hatred, aggression, destructiveness, or the like on the part of an individual who is not necessarily aware of the fact that he harbors these emotions or that he is deliberately intent on harming the person who is his "victim." (Anthropologists generally use the term "witchcraft" to refer to this kind of secret, unconsciously motivated psychic act.) But it is also possible that illness is due to the conscious and overt malevolent thoughts, feelings, and motives of an individual who has used symbolic, ritualistic means to cause the harm which has occurred. (Anthropologists would call this "sorcery," as distinguished from witchcraft.) In either case, the thoughts and feelings of the malefactor have the capacity to harm, because they are believed to harness the power of one of the numerous kinds of spirits that move back and forth between the spheres of the dead and the living, filling the cosmic space between the Supreme Being or Creator and Man.[51]

In this cosmic outlook, the Supreme Being, the shades of the ancestors, and certain of the spirits are "good." Along with the living members of the kinship descent group to which one belongs, they are primary sources of well-being, protection, and aid. At the same time, it is also true that the universe throbs with dangerous and evil counterpresences. Among the persons in one's entourage most able and likely to cause one harm through their malignant thoughts and feelings are very close kin. "Bewitched" is one of the first anxious hypotheses entertained when things do not go well, in general, and in matters of health, in particular.

Some illnesses, like some deaths, are considered to be independently and nonvindictively caused by the Supreme Being, without the intervention either of spirits or of human beings. For example, the illness and death of very elderly persons, white-haired and toothless, would be likely to be interpreted in this beneficent way, partly because they are not considered unduly premature. But, by and large, illness is regarded as an event that, like a bad and frightening dream, carries a negative message of import that must be deciphered and acted upon, if it is to be healed. In contradistinction to modern medicine, then, archaic medicine is focally concerned with explaining the "why's" as well as the "how's" of illness; and it equates the diagnosed meaning of illness with its etiology and ultimate cure.

As already suggested, a person's kinsmen and tribesmen—those to whom he is related proximately or distantly by blood—are considered to be a fundamental source of both his physical and psychic well being. Each individual is a member of a lineage made up of dead ancestors and of their living descendants. The living and dead of the same lineage constitute a mystic as well as a biological collectivity, on which the health and, beyond that, the very existence of the individual depends. More directly and immediately than the Supreme Being, kinsmen and, especially, the shades of the ancestors are believed to control all the positive values of life. Thus, the individual protects himself against illness (and other forms of misfortune and evil), and maximizes the degree of health he can expect to enjoy by maintaining good relations with his ancestors (caring for their graves, remembering them, observing ancestral norms) and also with his living kin.

Diffuse anxiety about the intentional or inadvertent harm the thoughts and feelings of others may cause, along with the bivalent conception of kinsmen as key sources of danger as well as defense, contributes to the high level of distrust and vigilance implicit in all relationships and activities. However smilingly it may be masked, or politely and skillfully dissembled, this psychocultural state of suspicion and watchfulness is omnipresent in an archaic society. It is fraught with the kind of tension that is generative of psychosomatic, sociosomatic, and psychological disorders that might not otherwise exist. In this sense, it may be said that the cosmic outlook of an archaic society is culturally conducive to the development of certain types of illness.

In an archaic society, as in a modern one, when illness occurs, it is shaped into what might be termed a sick role. However, some of the structural attributes of the archaic sick role systematically differ from those that characterize its modern counterpart. To begin with, an afflicted person in an archaic society more easily claims and is granted exemption from normally required activities and responsibilities than in the modern case. He is not under obligation to try to "carry on" his usual duties in the face of illness, to be emotionally forbearing about it, or to handle it in a relatively individualistic and personalized way. Rather, he is permitted and even expected to react to his state of illness with strong feelings of anxiety and depression, patently and forcibly to express those feelings, and actively to solicit the attention, support, and care of numerous family members, neighbors, and kinlike friends.

This patterned behavior has several functions. It enables the sick person to give vent to emotions that, if hidden, through the medium of witchcraft could not only be injurious to himself, but also to others associated with him. It rallies a group of persons around the patient, whose solidary presence helps to shield him against whatever harmful supernatural forces are at work, at the same time that it provides him with sympathy and succor. Finally, the way that his kin and others with whom he has a close relationship respond to his predicament gives the ill person some indicators to judge whether any of them might be responsible for the fact that this adversity has befallen him. In fact, the failure of a significant member of the solidary group to visit a seriously ill person and to give him both moral and material support would expose him to the suspicion that he is the agent who has caused the sickness.

Given the causal conception of illness in an archaic society, it follows sociologically that the reason for a sickness of any consequence must be personified. In contradistinction to the "it is not his fault" exemption-from-responsibility facet of the sick role as institutionalized in modern society, the etiology and meaning of illness in archaic society must ultimately be explained in terms of "who" invoked it and why. The sick person himself may be "blamed" for causing his illness, usually because he has broken important magicoreligious taboos or failed to live up to certain norms considered crucial by the kinship system or its extended expression in the larger community. Just as frequently, if not more so, culpability for illness is projected onto significant others in the entourage of the patient. This is a specific manifestation of a more general cultural trait. The supernatural and psychic determinism of an archaic society leads to an at once fatalistic and self-protective "it is not my fault" conception of responsibility, coupled with a tendency to reproach designated others for what goes wrong.

When a member of an archaic society feels that he is sick, he is expected to consult an expert in matters of health. He is likely to do so without delay and with a sense of urgency for the existential and psycho-social anxieties that illness evokes in him are not easy for him to withstand. The role of medical practitioner in archaic society is a differentiated one.[52] Its incumbents possess more empirical knowledge about particular diseases than "laymen" and a greater command of medications assumed to heal. But the functions of a medicine man (or woman) are never completely dissociated from those of a magicoreligious specialist. This is because the comprehensive diagnosis and effective cure of an illness always includes the use of mystic rites and charms to identify who has called forth illness, his motives for doing so, and the means that he has used; to exorcise the noxious spirits at work; and to restore the patient to a state of inner and interpersonal harmony consonant with health.

One of the most common and strategic rites enacted in this context is a ceremonial palaver. Typically, not only the patient and the medical practitioner, but also the patient's family and his close acquaintances are involved in such a curative parley. A vigorous, protracted, but highly stylized and tightly structured process of inquiry takes place. This is followed by a confession of wrongdoing, bad feelings, or evil intentions on the part of the patient, the other participants, or both. The ceremony terminates in conciliative and expiatory acts that are supposed to bring about healing. Thus, the way that the sick role is patterned in an archaic society does not only require the patient's active cooperation with the practitioner. It also mobilizes his relatives, neighbors, and friends, obliging them to physically, psychically, and socially participate in a collective effort to make him better. This curative rite classically expresses the interpenetration of health and illness, kinship, religion, and magic characteristic of an archaic society. It is also an important social control mechanism. For it enunciates primary values, taboos and norms of the societal community; it dramatizes the harm that deviating from them can cause; and it brings the patient, his relatives, and close associates together in a renewed state of concord.

When a person's illness does not seem to respond to the medications, charms, and ministrations of a particular practitioner, he will quickly seek the aid of other specialists or remedies presumed to be medically and magically more potent. He is not expected or likely to exhibit the same kind of loyal, trusting commitment to a given medical practitioner that is institutionalized in a modern society. Nor is the practitioner under the same obligation to maintain a continuing fiduciary relation with the patient as in the modern case.

What the sick person typically expects to receive from the practitioner's treatment is an immediate and total cure. This is consistent with at least two attributes of the value and cognitive systems of an archaic society that we have already cited. First, it is believed that because thoughts and feelings have the power to create and transmute reality, a fervently desired state like health ought to and can be made imminently accessible. Second, the cosmic outlook is an absolute, polarized one, an "all or nothing" perspective. There is extreme badness (illness) on the one hand and extreme goodness (health) on the ohter. The two antitheses are symbiotically linked, but there is no mixed zone in between. Thus, it is expected that dispelling the source of evil will automatically induce a wholly beneficent state.

Be this as it may, some illness does prove intractable. When this occurs, the "secondary elaborations" to which we referred earlier are invoked. It is assumed that the malefactor at work causing the sickness is especially powerful, has feigned good will and active collaboration in the healing process, and/or is chronically evil. If he cannot be magically vanquished by the supernatural forces of the practitioners consulted, then in order to preserve the sanctity and safety of the entire community, the most drastic form of punishment will be exercised against him. His physical or social death (ostracism) will be brought about by prescribed magicoreligious means.

One final, additional word might be said about the "death complex," which, in an archaic society, as in all societies, is associated with illness. I have shown that in this type of society, as Parsons and Lidz phrase it, "a concept of 'natural death' seems to be virtually absent," and that "deaths are always thought to be *imposed* by human action, by effects of the sacred 'souls', or by both through the mediation of black magic."[53] I have also indicated that life and death are coterminous, mediated and prevailed over by the ancestors around whom a cultic set of religious observances is organized. Death, then, is no more than a transposition from a village of living kin to one of deceased kin, with whom one has never ceased to communicate. In this respect, it is neither a traumatic nor a transcendental journey. Yet, death is also considered to be one of life's most dreaded, unnatural occurrences. For it brings one into continuing, face-to-face contact with the ancestors: sacred, superkin who have a far greater power to do one harm, as well as good, than any relative in the community of the living. And so, death in an archaic society does not release one from the primal worldview. It is carried to the grave and to the village of the ancestors that lies just beyond it.

POSTMODERN MEDICINE

Any attempt to depict what postmodern medicine will "look like" is a speculative enterprise. Nevertheless, it seems to us that the evolutionary trends suggested by our delineation of archaic and modern stages of medicine, when combined with reflection on strategic changes that contemporaneous medicine is now undergoing, provide reasonable guidelines for venturing certain predictions. As might be expected, various social and cultural attributes of postmodern medicine that we see coming into view appear to be extensions of the evolutionary changes that the comparison of archaic with modern medicine has identified.[54] At the same time, there are indications that other characteristics of postmodern medicine may prove to be discontinuous with certain traits of modern medicine out of which they have grown. Some of these ostensible breaks with modern tendencies are structured reactions against trends that are considered neither desirable nor inevitable.

Others might be called unanticipated consequences of the further development of orientations institutionalized in modern medicine. Although it would be inaccurate to label these two types of discontinuity a "return" to prior stages of medical evolution, in some respects they resemble characteristics of premodern medicine.

In postmodern medicine, the causes of illness are considered to be biological, psychological, and social, rather than religious or magical. In this sense, disease is regarded as a natural phenomenon. However, health and illness are also interpreted in a highly ideological way. The conviction prevails that good health and excellent medical care for all are basic human rights. By and large, anything less than optimal health and care is viewed as a form of deprivation that, ideally, should neither exist nor be tolerated. The fact that such conditions have not been totally eliminated is linked to the various ways in which the society falls short of realizing its ultimate values. Social inequities, injustices, and evils are invoked to explain the persistence of certain types of illness and the emergence of new disorders, as well as to account for imperfections in the system of delivery of medical care. In effect, society is "blamed" for helping to nurture or trigger all but the irreducible minimum of sickness. The same kind of projective mechanism is involved here as in the accusatory singling out of witches and sorcerers such as occurs in an archaic society. What is significantly different is that in a postmodern society an impersonal, collective, secular entity is held causally responsible for illness, whereas in a postprimitive society, specific individuals are identified as magicoreligious vectors of disease.

As in a modern society, illness is differentiated from other forms of misfortune and adversity. At the same time, it is associated with a cluster of what are defined as society-borne evils that are within human capacity to control, reduce, and even to eliminate. Along with poverty, pollution, overpopulation and war, it is believed, illness will yield to a massive quickening of public concern and conscience about the social conditions that foster it, if accompanied by organizational reforms of those political, economic, and professional structures that bear upon it. Thus, in a postmodern society, health and illness are viewed in a conceptual framework that not only invokes generalized social analysis and social criticism but also actively mobilizes energies for purposive, far-reaching social action and change.

Progress in medical scientific knowledge and technique, in tandem with the evolution of social scientific, ethical, and religious thought, make increasingly clear "the distinction between conditions that are really ultimate and those that are alterable."[55] Postmodern medicine has significantly advanced the understanding and control of disease, life, and death. Certain illnesses, like cardiovascular disorders, cancer, and schizophrenia, that virtually came to symbolize the uncertainties and limitations of modern medicine, the inevitable degree of suffering that illness imposes on man, and his ineluctable mortality have been illuminated and subdued by postmodern medicine. Man's life span has also been greatly prolonged. And yet, neither disease nor death has been abolished.

The furtherance of clarification, knowledge, and control, however, has not brought about a serene acceptance of the ultimacy of disease and death. Not only has the development of a more sociologically oriented theory of health and illness increased social activism in this domain, but also age-old philosophical and religious questions are revitalized by what is felt to be the mystery-laden relationship between what now seems to be alterable and what not. Who and what is man? What are the meaning and purpose of his existence? What is life, what is death, and wherein lies the essence of the distinction between them? Why do men fall ill and suffer and die? How should we understand these experiences and behave towards them? This sort of querying is characteristic of postmodern medicine and its practitioners, as well as of its patients. If one accepts the sociological view that preoccupation with such questions of meaning constitutes a religious act, then one might say that in this sense, postmodern medicine is less secular and more sacral than modern medicine.

The sources of this postmodern existential awareness and emphasis are complex. Although the advancement of science and technology has not dispelled all medical uncertainties and limitations, it has increased the sense that human knowledge in this domain (and others) is finite and that mankind may be approaching the outer boundaries of what is knowable. The definition of death institutionalized in postmodern medicine is brain death. Historically, it emerged from a reexamination of what should be considered the most accurate and proper operational criteria of death, precipitated by developments in resuscitative techniques, organ transplantation, and the implantation of artificial organs. The controversy and debate that surrounded this issue not only helped to modify modern medicine's working definition of death as the cessation of breathing and heartbeat; it also fostered an enduring consciousness among medical professionals and lay persons alike that any codified definition of death is to some degree approximate, relative, and arbitrary. The progress in preventing and curing illness and in extending life that characterizes postmodern medicine, viewed within its distinctive societal perspective, has been generative of still other religiophilosophical deliberations. Systematic conjectures regarding the func-

tions of sickness and death have eventuated in teleological notions about the necessary and desirable role that these otherwise tragic experiences play in insuring biological, social, and spiritual renewal.

There is also a general reflectiveness about whether the quality of life to which a suffering, debilitated, or old person will be subject, if reprieved from death by the prowess of postmodern medicine, constitutes an existence that is sufficiently human and meaningful to justify heroic efforts to sustain him. Finally, the participation of many persons in organ transplantation, as donors or recipients, that postmodern medicine has brought to pass has increased awed awareness of how widespread essentially mystic conceptions about the human body and its parts are, and how fundamental. And for all of its sociopsychological complications, the network of giving and receiving that transplantation has established has involved a significant number of people in an act that they experience as transcendent, because they feel that it furthers their self-knowledge, enhances their self-worth, gives them a sense of totality, belief, and commitment, and augments their sense of oneness with humanity.

What I have designated as the entwined existential and societal outlooks of postmodern medicine are also reflected in the structure of the sick role. I have implied that the way of thought about sickness largely exempts the individual from responsibility for having fallen ill. In a nonsick or presick role, he has some obligation to do all that he can to prevent the onslaught of illness. Nonetheless, should he actually become sick, responsibility for his condition will be collectively defined, principally in biosocial and biocosmic terms. The process of getting better not only entails an active, mutually trusting and collaborative effort *à deux* by physician and patient. If the illness is of any consequence, it mobilizes a group of different kinds of medical and health care personnel, who combine specialized knowledge, skills and duties with supple teamwork that is neither hierarchically fixed nor rigidly predetermined.

The physician retains ultimate responsibility and authority in the care of the patient. His singularity in this respect is based on the more extensive medical training he has received than other team members, his executive-managerial skills and functions, and the institutionalized charisma attributed to him by patients, who continue to see him as the symbolic personification of medicine's capacity to help and heal them. But the physician's relationship with his patients and with the various categories of medical personnel who comprise the health team is more egalitarian, elastic, and responsive than is generally true of modern medicine. It is also more affective. Detached concern still is one of the physician's basic role orientations and obligations, particularly with regard to his patients. But in comparison with the physicianly stance institutionalized in modern medicine, the over-all balance between these counterattitudes has shifted somewhat, so that the physician is now enjoined to be more concerned and less detached in his feeling and behavior toward the patient. This is consonant with other reciprocally open and communicative aspects of the postmodern doctor-patient relationship.

A fee-for-service, private physician pattern of practice exists. However, it is not as predominant as variously structured prepaid group practices, on the one hand, and neighborhood health centers, on the other. The hospital looms large on the landscape of postmodern medicine, serving the triple functions of care, teaching, and research. But the prepayment groups and local centers, along with the sociomedical emphasis on prevention of illness, help to provide the facilities and finances as well as the motivation and knowhow to treat many nonsick, presick, and ambulatory sick persons outside the walls of the hospital. In turn, physically and emotionally, this involves the family more in the dynamics of health and illness than in a modern society and insulates them less. Finally, although peer review and control are the chief modes of regulation to which the medical profession is subject, informal and organized lay opinion as well as government pressure and statutes exert significant influence upon it.

CONCLUSION

This schematic presentation of archaic, modern, and postmodern medicine is compatible with the evolutionary perspective shared by Parsons, Bellah, and Eisenstadt: a macrosocietal view of progressive specialization, differentiation, "organic" integration, in the Durkheimian sense of the term, and adaptation. It also parallels Bellah's proposition that at each stage of religious evolution "freedom of personality and society is increased relative to the environing conditions . . . because at each successive stage the relation of man to the conditions of his existence is conceived as more complex, more open, and more subject to change and development."[56] At the same time, my account of the patterned unfolding of medicine highlights the importance of a particular cultural dimension of analysis for a general theory of social evolution. Specifically, I refer here to the complex interrelationships between three aspects of culture that our profile of medical evolution has identified: scientific knowledge and technique, cosmic view, and societal outlook.

Relative to modern and postmodern medicine, archaic medicine is less scientifically developed and more empirical in nature. It is embedded in a general magicoreligious way of thought that is deterministic, closed, monistic, and conducive to existential anxiety, suspicion, and distrust. Illness and death are thought to be products of supernatural powers and evil human intent working in tandem. Although they are apprehensively expected, they are defined as not inevitable. Kinship is regarded as the primary basis of solidarity and safety, in the face of ever-present dangers like sickness. It is also considered a source of individual and collective peril, partly because physical, psychic, and spiritual security are so exclusively dependent upon it.

Modern medicine is scientifically oriented, to the point of formally excluding magical and religious explanations of health, illness, life, and death from its orbit. Questions of meaning generated by the predicament and experience of illness are either silently ignored, latently rather than manifestly acknowledge, or siphoned off to religious specialists. A confident and energetic rationality prevails. It is felt that disease and premature death, like numerous other problems that beset man, will progressively give way to scientific searching, robust, targeted action, and informed, organized care. Impersonal as well as personal trust is institutionalized in many nonkinship relations, albeit accompanied both by social and psychological ambivalence. The doctor-patient relationship is one of the prototypes of this more general societal characteristic. The nonpersonified way in which the causes of illness are conceptualized and their definition as not the fault of the patient, his kin, or those closest to him are consistent with this orientation.

Postmodern medicine is even more advanced scientifically and technologically. Partly as a consequence, it has reached the point where it is equally conscious of its accomplishments and its limitations and defines particular aspects of what it does not know and cannot effectively do as irreducible. This leaves more room for mystery and awe in postmodern medicine than in either archaic or modern medicine. It also means that postmodern medicine is centrally and explicitly concerned with the complex existential as well as ethical issues that develop when a highly evolved science is brought to bear on health and illness, life and death. Postmodern medicine, like archaic medicine, then, has an existential focus, but it is more religious than archaic medicine and less magical. For, it is not so exclusively directed towards the achievement of concrete empirical goals like good health and longevity. Furthermore, the cosmic view that underlies it is less fearful and more trusting. Postmodern medicine is also societally oriented in a sense that differs both from archaic and modern medicine. In contradistinction to modern medicine, postmodern medicine emphasizes the extent to which society is both positively and negatively responsible for health and illness. In comparison with archaic medicine, postmodern medicine makes reference to a broader, more universalistic community than an extended kinship system. It formally recognizes the relationship between the imperfections of society and some illnesses and deaths, and it inveighs against them. But it does so with less apprehension than archaic medicine and with more confidence that a positive equilibrium can be established, in which beneficent forces will outbalance noxious ones. Yet, unlike archaic medicine, it does not have a millennarian vision of ultimate deliverance from disease and death.

The evolutionary relationship among medicine, religion, magic, and ideology, then, is not a simple linear progression. It has its own kind of social and cultural logic and coherence. But it develops in patterned ways that are more complex than a steady advance "from sacred to secular."

NOTES

1. For this essay we have drawn upon the following works, Parsons' principal sociology of medicine writings. Talcott Parsons, "Illness and the Role of the Physician: A Sociological Perspective," in Clyde Kluckhohn, Henry A. Murray and David M. Schneider (eds.), *Personality in Nature, Society and Culture,* 2nd rev. ed. (New York: Alfred Knopf. 1953), pp. 609-617; "The Professions and Social Structure" and "The Motivation of Economic Activities" in T. Parsons, *Essays in Sociological Theory,* rev. ed. (Glencoe, Ill.: The Free Press, 1954), pp. 34-49, 50-68; "Social Structure and Dynamic Process: The Case of Modern Medical Practice," in T. Parsons, *The Social System* (Glencoe, Ill.: The Free Press, 1951), pp. 428-479; T. Parsons and Renée C. Fox, "Illness, Therapy, and the Modern Urban American Family," in E. Gartly Jaco (ed.), *Patients, Physicians and Illness: Sourcebook in Behavioral Science and Medicine* (Glencoe, Ill.: The Free Press, 1958), pp. 234-245 [first published in the *Journal of Social Issues,* 8 (1952)]; T. Parsons, "Definitions of Health and Illness in the Light of American Values and Social Structure," in Jaco (ed.), *op. cit.,* pp. 165-187; "Some Trends of Change in American Society: Their Bearing on Medical Education," in T. Parsons, *Structure and Process in Modern Societies* (Glencoe, Ill.: The Free Press, 1960), pp. 280-294; "Some Reflections on the Problem of Psychosomatic Relationships in Health and Illness," and "Health and Illness," in T. Parsons, *Social Structure and Personality* (Glencoe, Ill.: The Free Press, 1964), pp. 112-126 and 255-358; T. Parsons and Victor M. Lidz, "Death in American Society" in E. Shneidman (ed.), *Essays in Self-Destruction* (New York: Science House, 1967); T. Parsons, "Research with Human Subjects and the 'Professional Complex,'" in *Ethical Aspects of Experimentation with Human Subjects, Daedalus,* 98 (Spring 1969), pp. 325-360; T. Parsons, Renée C. Fox, and Victor M. Lidz, "The 'Gift of Life' and Its Reciprocation," *Social Research,* 39 (1972), pp. 367-415.

2. The published works in which Parsons' thinking on evolution is elaborated are: T. Parsons, "Evolutionary Universals in Society," *American Sociological Review,* 29 (June 1964), pp. 339-357; Robert N. Bellah, "Religious Evolution," *American Sociological Review,* 29 (June 1964), pp. 358-374;

S.N. Eisenstadt, "Social Change, Differentiation and Evolution," *American Sociological Review,* 29 (June 1964), pp. 375-386; T. Parsons, *Societies: Evolutionary and Comparative Perspectives* (Englewood Cliffs: Prentice-Hall, 1966); T. Parsons. *The System of Modern Societies* (Englewood Cliffs, N. J.: Prentice-Hall, Inc., 1971).

3. Parsons, "Research with Human Subjects and the 'Professional Complex,'" *op. cit.,* pp. 330-335.

4. *Ibid.,* p. 336.

5. Parsons, *Social Structure and Personality,* p. 332.

6. Parsons, *The Social System,* pp. 431-432.

7. Parsons, *Social Structure and Personality,* p. 112.

8. Renée C. Fox, "Illness" in David L. Sills (ed.), *International Encyclopedia of the Social Sciences* (New York: Macmillan and The Free Press, 1968), Vol. 7, p. 92.

9. Parsons, *Social Structure and Personality,* pp. 277-291.

10. Parsons, *Societies,* p. 8. "Problems of meaning" is a term that Parsons adopted from Max Weber's writings.

11. Bellah, *op. cit.,* p. 359.

12. Renée C. Fox, "Training for Uncertainty" in Robert K. Merton, George Reader, and Patricia L. Kendall (eds.) *The Student-Physician* (Cambridge: Harvard University Press, 1957), pp. 207-241.

13. Parsons, *Societies,* pp. 9-10.

14. Parsons, *The Social System,* p. 432.

15. Parsons, *Social Structure and Personality,* pp. 342-358.

16. Parsons, *Societies,* pp. 21-24.

17. The most general sociological statement that I have written on the basis of that field work and anthropological reading is an essay entitled, "The Intelligence Behind the Mask: Beliefs and Development in Contemporary Congo," The Eighteenth Conference on Science, Philosophy and Religion, Jewish Theological Seminary of America, New York, N.Y., 1968, unpublished paper.

18. The term "post-modern society" is influenced by Daniel Bell's phrase "post-industrial society," which he coined in his role as Chairman of the Commission on the Year 2000 of the American Academy of Arts and Sciences.

19. I have recently completed a sociological study of organ transplantation and hemodialysis with Judith P. Swazey which has been published as a coauthored book: *The Courage to Fail* (Chicago: The University of Chicago Press, 1974). In my capacity as Professor of Sociology in the Department of Medicine and the Department of Psychiatry, as well as in the Department of Sociology at the University of Pennsylvania, I am also engaged in exploratory research into the socialization of medical students in the 1970's. I bring to these explorations a comparative, historical perspective. For, in the mid-1950's, I was one of the chief field workers associated with the Columbia University Bureau of Applied Social Research studies in the sociology of medical education.

20. René Dubos, *Mirage of Health: Utopias, Progress, and Biological Change* (New York: Harper and Brothers, 1959), pp. 1-2.

21. *Ibid.,* pp. 17-21.

22. Parsons, *The Social System,* p. 430.

23. Parsons, *Social Structure and Personality,* p. 331.

24. *Loc. cit.*

25. I first formulated this concept in a paper that I co-authored with Miriam Massey Johnson in the academic year 1950-1951, when I was still a graduate student in the Department of Social Relations at Harvard University. The paper was written for a seminar conducted by Talcott Parsons, on some of the theoretical ideas with which he was preoccupied in the course of writing *The Social System.* Miriam Johnson and I applied the concept to the medical case. Many years later, I published an essay on the role of training for detached concern in the socialization of medical students. See Harold I. Lief and Renée C. Fox, "Training for Detached Concern in Medical Students," in Harold I. Lief, Victor F. Lief and

Nina R. Lief (eds.) *The Psychological Basis of Medical Practice,* (New York: Harper and Row, 1963), pp. 12-35.

26. It is interesting to note that in this situation a kinship-like courtesy is institutionalized. Generally, physicians do not charge very close relatives of doctors for their medical services. This custom seems to be an extension of another informal professional norm: that of physicians waiving a fee when they take care of each other. The latent function of this professional courtesy seems to be an at-once instrumental and expressive acknowledgement that a physician treating the members of a colleague's family is acting in lieu of their doctor-relative.

27. Parsons, *The Social System,* pp. 451-452.
28. Parsons and Fox, *op. cit.,* pp. 234-245.
29. Fox, "Illness," *op. cit.,* p. 93.
30. Bronislaw Malinowski, "Magic, Science, and Religion" in *Magic, Science and Religion and Other Essays* (Glencoe, Ill.: The Free Press, 1948), p. 15.
31. Parsons, *The Social System,* p. 469.
32. *Ibid.,* p. 466.
33. *Ibid.,* pp. 466-469.
34. *Ibid.,* pp. 432-433.
35. Renée C. Fox, *Experiment Perilous* (Glencoe, Ill.: The Free Press, 1959), pp. 69-113, 139-190, 242-247, and 250-254; and also Renée C. Fox and Judith P. Swazey, *op. cit.,* pp. 62, 87, 100-104, 268, 318, and 320-321.
36. Parsons and Lidz, *op. cit.*
37. In their medical scientific publications, it is not uncommon for physicians to use the noun "failure" as synonymous with the death of a patient.
38. This is especially characteristic of modern American society. See Renée C. Fox, "Some Social and Cultural Factors in American Society Conducive to Medical Research on Human Subjects," *Journal of Clinical Pharmacology and Therapeutics,* 1 (July-August 1960), pp. 433-443.
39. Fox, *Experiment Perilous,* p. 150.
40. Francis D. Moore, "Therapeutic Innovation: Ethical Boundaries in the Initial Clinical Trials of New Drugs and Surgical Procedures," in *Ethical Aspects of Experimentation with Human Subjects, Daedalus,* 98 (Spring 1969), p. 510.
41. Parsons, "Research with Human Subjects and the 'Professional Complex,'" *op. cit.,* p. 122.
42. *Ibid.,* pp. 129-130.
43. Robert K. Merton and Elinor Barber, "Sociological Ambivalence," in Edward A. Tiryakian (ed.), *Sociological Theory, Values and Sociocultural Change: Essays in Honor of Pitirim Sorokin* (New York: The Free Press, 1963), pp. 91-120.
44. Parsons, *The Social System,* p. 470.
45. Parsons, *Social Structure and Personality,* p. 342.
46. For example, in Swahili, the word *dawa* means medicament, charm, and magicoreligious powers; in KiKongo and Lingala, the word *nkisi* has these three meanings.
47. Claude Lévi-Strauss, *The Savage Mind,* George Weidenfeld (tr.) (Chicago: University of Chicago Press, 1966), p. 11.
48. E.E. Evans-Pritchard, *Witchcraft, Oracles and Magic Among the Azande* (Oxford: Oxford University Press, 1937), *passim.*
49. Robin Horton, "African Traditional Thought and Western Science," *Africa,* 37 (April 1967), p. 161.
50. John V. Taylor, *The Primal Vision* (London: SCM Press, 1965), p. 192.
51. In an essay on ethnomedicine, Charles C. Hughes points out that "widespread throughout the world are five basic categories of events or situations which, in folk etiology, are believed responsible for illness: (1) sorcery; (2) breach of taboo; (3) intrusion of a disease-object; (4) intrusion of a disease-causing spirit; and (5) loss of soul." He goes on to say that groups and societies differ in the extent to which they focus on one or a combination of these causes. In many African societies, he states, "the malevolence of sorcerers or witches is especially emphasized." See C.C. Hughes, "Medical Care: Ethnomedicine" in Sills (ed.), *op. cit.,* Vol. 10, p. 88.
52. How differentiated and specialized the role of an archaic medical practitioner is, varies from society to society. As Charles C. Hughes points out,

> Sometimes the specialist's role is a full-time activity, but more frequently it is combined with other principal roles appropriate for the practitioner. In some societies there are more complex social organizations involved than the simple dyadic relationship between healer and patient. Even as the kin and covillagers of the patient may be explicitly involved in the curative process, so too there may be a society of healers, or several societies of healers devoted to diagnosis and cure of various diseases (Hughes, *op. cit.,* p. 91).

53. Parsons and Lidz, *op. cit.,* p. 12.
54. In the body of the text, I shall not describe and analyze the attributes of medicine in the stage of societal evolution that Parsons terms "advanced intermediate." The main characteristics of a society of this type, as he sees it, are "full upper-class literacy and, on the cultural side, what Bellah calls an *historic* religion, one which has broken through to *philosophical* levels of generalization and systematization." Parsons, *Societies,* p. 5 (italics Parsons' own). Within the evolutionary framework that Parsons has elaborated, advanced intermediate society is post-archaic and pre-modern. As traditional China and India are two intermediate societies that he cites, it is interesting to consider the cognitive, social, and cultural traits that Ralph C. Croizier, an expert on medicine in these societies, considers their distinguishing features. In a way that is consistent with Parsons' evolutionary paradigm, Croizier emphasizes the differences between these medical systems and "primitive or folk medicine," as well as "modern scientific medicine," situating Chinese and Indian medicine somewhere between the two. "First," Croizier writes, traditional Chinese and Indian medicine have a

> complex and predominantly rational theoretical basis. Second, it is contained in a large corpus of medical 'classics' of great antiquity. Third, the theoretical principles are intimately related to the dominant cosmological concepts of the society and its cultural values. Fourth, there exists a class of secular medical practitioners who are guardians of the classic medical tradition. This class of physicians stands apart from the common folk medicine practitioners of the society whose practices are often distorted reflections of the high medical tradition. Moreover, in his command of a literary tradition, the physician has pretensions to scholarly standing but suffers from the artisan, or tradesman, associations of practicing medicine as a profession. . . . As for their theoretical principles, both [traditions] may be said to have basically a homeostatic concept of health and disease. Health consists of maintaining a harmony or equilibrium within the human organism and disease is the result of physical or psychic (this allows for moral factors) disturbance of such equilibrium. . . . [R. C. Croizier, "Medicine, Modernization, and Cultural Crisis in China and India," *Comparative Studies in Society and History,* 12 (July 1970), pp. 277-278.]

55. Bellah, *op. cit.,* p. 374.
56. *Loc. cit.*

32

ON HISTORICAL CONTINUITY AND SOCIAL CHANGE IN MODERNIZATION

S. N. Eisenstadt

The study of processes of modernization has provided the social sciences with some of the most fascinating cases for comparative macrosocietal analysis, as well as for the analysis of social change, and has highlighted some of the problems of the relations between these two areas of research.

One of the major problems cutting across these two areas has been that of social and historical continuity or discontinuity of a society. The relative emphasis on discontinuity as against continuity has greatly varied in different stages of studies of modernization, as have the analytical frameworks into which these problems were put. But common to all these frameworks was, of course, the attempt to define in some way the common core of modernity and modernization, on the one hand, and to explain the diversity of various institutional patterns attendant on modernization, on the other.

APPROACHES TO MODERNIZATION

The common core of modernity has been identified in the social sciences literature, as is well known, on two levels: the structural and sociodemographic and the symbolic and structural. The structural and sociodemographic characteristics of modernization were usually defined in terms of growing division of labor, structural differentiations and specialization, social mobilization and the development of free resources.[1]

The symbolic aspects of modernization and their structural implications were mostly defined in terms of the breakdown of traditional legitimation of the social, cultural, and political orders and the concomitant growing mutual impingement of centers and periphery.[2]

In the first stages of the development of the research of modernization, the differences between traditional and modern societies and among various modern or modernizing societies were mostly defined in terms of quantitative differences in the development of basic structural and sociodemographic indices of modernization. At the same time many of these studies have for a long period focused on the problems of the conditions of relatively successful or unsuccessful transition from traditional to modern societies.

This concern with such satisfactory or unsatisfactory conditions of modernization was on the whole closely connected with a great emphasis on a dichotomous conception of the distinction between traditional and modern societies and on the discontinuity, in the history of any society, between its premodern, historical, and modern stages. The historical background of a modern or modernizing society was perceived mostly as relevant to the facility of transition between such discontinuous stages of development. Here the differences between various modern societies—the analysis of which constituted an important focus of comparative research—were very often related to some of the basic respective starting points of processes of modernization in these societies, i.e., whether they started from feudal, urban, caste, or tribal societies, and to the degree of discontinuity between the premodern and the modern settings.[3]

With the accumulation and diversification of research in this field it became apparent that many significant differences between modern or modernizing societies cut across relatively similar levels of structural or sociodemographic development. With the gradual abandonment of the initial implicit assumption found in many of these studies of the over-all convergence of institutional patterns attendant on modernization or industrialization into a direction similar to that of the first modern societies

The author is greatly indebted to Mrs. L. Aran for a very detailed criticism of an earlier draft of this essay.

—Western Europe and the U.S. and later even Russia or Japan—there developed an emphasis on symbolic diversity of modern societies beyond the quantitative differences just mentioned. The recognition of this diversity was often combined with a greater emphasis on the historical and social continuity of the respective societies in their premodern "traditional" and "modern" stages.

Initially such continuity was perceived in terms of persistence of some broad cultural orientations, very often related to or derived from the "culture and personality" or other culturologist approaches —with relatively little relation to the more structural aspects of modern societies.[4] Thus the emphases on historical continuity or discontinuity were, in the study of modernization, to a large degree connected with divergent analytical frameworks. The emphasis on symbolic or on cultural aspects in the study of modern societies was more often coupled with a concern with continuity while the emphasis on structural or sociodemographic aspects was coupled with a concern with discontinuity.

In the following discussion I shall attempt, in a preliminary way, to bring these aspects together within a common analytical framework and to see what new light it may throw on the analysis of problems of social change.

THE CONCEPT OF "CODES"

Starting with the symbolical sphere I shall go beyond an analysis of general cultural orientations and attempt to specify some symbolical modes which have definite institutional derivations and then to analyze some possible relations of such modes to specific structural problems of social organization in general and of modern societies in particular.

It seems to me that a good starting point for the analysis of such symbolic modes with some specific institutional implications may be found in the work of Max Weber and especially in his concept of the *Wirtshaftsethik*,[5] or rather in some broader analytical derivatives of this conception.

As is well known, Weber's *Wirtshaftsethik* neither connotes specific religious injunctions about the proper behaviour in the economic field nor is just a logical derivative of the intellectual contents of the theology or philosophy predominant in a given religion. Rather it connotes a general mode of orientation to a specific institutional sphere and its problems, the evaluation of this sphere in terms of the premises of a given religion or tradition as to the basic problems of the cosmic order and their relations to human and social existence, and the consequent structural and behavioral derivatives of such evaluation.

Thus *Wirtshaftsethik* is a general "formal" orientation, a "deeper structure," a "code." However, unlike many modern structuralists,[6] Weber did not conceive these orientations as a purely "formal" set of signs which organize sets of abstract, symbolic contents only, but rather as a set of orientations toward symbolic, structural, and organizational aspects of the basic problems of human and social existence.

Such orientations connote operational codes which go beyond concrete contents and structures and which, at the same time, may guide the crystallization of types of cultural contents and organizational structures at different stages of social differentiation or "social mobilization."

Although it would be out of place to attempt here an exhaustive list of basic problems around which such codes tend to crystallize, it might be worthwhile to point out some which are of special interest for our analysis.[7]

One such focus or problem around which such codes tend to crystallize is the definition of the relative importance of different dimensions of human existence and of their structural and symbolic implication for the definition of the boundaries of political and cultural collectivities.

A second is the conception of the degree of autonomy or interrelation of the cosmic, cultural, social, and political orders and of their mutual relevance.

A third consists of those codes which tend to define an active or passive attitude towards the possibility of participation in the social and cultural orders and in their formation.

A fourth area consists of the different conceptions of change, of attitudes to change, and of the possibility of an active as against more passive participation in the formation of such changes in the major social and cultural spheres.

A fifth is the basis of legitimation of social order in general and of the relations between the center and periphery in particular. Here the basic distinction is that between the center as a "resource" as against commitment to the center and/or the social order.

All these, as many other codes we shall not analyze here, have indeed several important structural repercussions on the crystallization of different institutional structures which may cut across different stages of structural differentiation. Different constellations of such codes have greatly shaped the cultural and institutional features of different societies both their modern and their premodern stages.

I shall attempt to illustrate the influence of such codes first in the analysis of the parameters of Western European modernity in their relation to the parameters of the Western European premodern social orders, as well as in the respective parameters of traditional and modern social orders in non-Western (European) societies. I shall then attempt to illustrate very briefly some of the differences between the Western European pattern on the one hand and the Russian and—to a lesser degree—the Japanese on the other.

THE IMPACT OF CODES

The modern socio-political order which had developed in Western Europe[8] has been characterized by: (1) a high degree of congruence between the cultural and the political identities of the territorial population, (2) a high level of symbolic and affective commitments to the political and cultural centers and a close relation between these centers and the more primordial dimensions of human existence, (3) a marked emphasis on common politically defined collective goals for all members of the national community, and (4) a relatively autonomous access of broad strata to symbols and centers.[9]

It was in close relation to these features that some of the patterns of participation and protest specific to the European scene developed. The most important of these assumptions was that both the political groups and the more autonomous social forces and elites tend to crystallize in the relatively antithetic autonomous yet complementary "units" or "forces" of "state" and "society" and tend continuously to struggle about their relative importance in the formation and crystallization of the cultural and political center of the nation-state and in the regulation of access to it; that the various processes of structural change and dislocation—which were concomitant with the development of modernization in the periphery—gave rise not only to various concrete problems and demands but also to growing quest for participation in the broader social and political order; and that this quest for participation of the periphery in such social, political, and cultural orders is mostly manifest in the search for access to the respective centers of these orders and societies.

These characteristics of European modernity were very closely related to some of the basic parameters or codes of the preceding European traditions, namely to those of imperial traditions, city-states, and feudal societies. They combined the strong activist orientation of the city-state, the broad and active conception of the political order as actively related to the cosmic or cultural order of many imperial traditions, as well as of the tradition of many of the great religions and the pluralistic elements of the feudal traditions with their emphasis on the autonomous access of the major groups to the basic attributes of the social and cultural order.[10]

These various orientations in the European (especially Western European) traditions have initially developed a social structure which became characterized, to no small degree under the influence of these very orientations, by a relatively high degree of commitment of various groups and strata to the social and cultural orders and a high degree of autonomy in their access to these orders and their respective centers; and the characteristics of this structure have proved to be a fertile ground for a further continuation and expansion of these orientations and codes.

The parameters of traditional as well as modern social and cultural orders beyond Western Europe already have other characteristics. Most of these societies did not share some of the Imperial, city-state, and feudal traditions specific to the European traditional order. Thus, for instance, in the Imperial, European or Asian societies—as in Russia or Japan or China—the pluralistic elements were much weaker than in the feudal or city-state societies. In many other societies—in Southeast Asia, in Africa, and to some degree in Latin America—the forces of (later) modernity impinged on patrimonial systems where the level of commitment to a sociopolitical order was much lower, and in which the active, autonomous relation between the conception of the political and the cosmic order was much weaker, although there existed a closer coalescence between the two.

Their political traditions rarely envisaged the same type of split or dichotomy between State and Society as did the European tradition. They tended more to stress the congruent but often passive relations between the cosmic order on the one hand and the sociopolitical order on the other. Unlike in the Western tradition, the interrelation between the political and the social orders was not envisaged in terms of an antithesis between the entities but more often stated in terms of the coalescence of different functions within the same group or organization, centered around a common focus in the cosmic order.[11]

Thus, for instance in Russia, there did not, on the whole, develop the conceptions either of a relatively autonomous access of the major strata to the political and cultural centers or of the autonomy of the social and cultural order in relation to the political ones. Similarly in Japan there were continuously prevalent the conceptions of the close identity between the cosmic and the political order and of a very high degree of unconditional commitment of broader strata to the center which represented this cosmic-political identity.

For all these reasons, the ways in which the challenge of modernity was perceived by these civilizations, the crises engendered, and the responses to them naturally differed greatly from the respective processes in Europe. Thus in the case of Russia and Japan alike modernity was ushered in under the aegis of the State, the political center was on the whole perceived as the main embodiment of the social order and as the major mediator to the cosmic order, and it was in the center that the definition of the symbols of community was vested.[12]

Accordingly, the demands of the broader groups for access to the center were, on the whole, couched in terms of possible participation in a social and cultural order as defined by the center, or in terms of attempts to overthrow the existing center and establish a new one similar in their basic characteristics, but on the whole these demands were not couched in terms of autonomous access to such order and continuous struggle with the center about the relative influence in the formation of such order.[13]

But did the various codes, as just analyzed, have also some definite structural implications beyond the broad definitions of the parameters of social and cultural orders? In other words, is it possible to identify those loci within the structural nexus of societies in general and of modern societies in particular in which such "qualitative" differences may become more salient, which can therefore also explain structural differences, other than levels of structural differentiation, among various societies in general and modern societies in particular, and which can be related to the various codes analyzed here?

As we have seen above, the initial approaches to historical continuity as well as the definition of various codes we have proposed here heavily focused on some modes of integration of social and cultural orders. It might therefore be most advisable to look for such loci in some aspects of the patterns of integration of the flow of resources which are concomitant with growing differentiation attendant on many processes of change in general and those of modernization in particular. Especially important here seems to be the degree of the relative autonomy of the various societal institutions or organizations in the regulation of the free resources which develop in a society through the processes of structural differentiation.

The possibility of such autonomy is given in the very process of structural differentiation and the development of free resources, but the degree to which such autonomy is in fact actualized is greatly influenced by other factors, especially, as we shall attempt to illustrate by the prevalence of some of the codes just analyzed.

We may start with the analysis of some of these problems in modern social order. Here the breaking up of ascriptive units and the development of free resources have, of course, greatly influenced the nature of flow and interchange of resources among the major institutional sectors of modern societies. They gave rise to growing interrelation between the different types of institutional resources and commodities, together with the growing specialization of their respective organizational frameworks.

One of the most important aspects of this development was, as Parsons has so well analyzed, the development of generalized media of exchange. It is one of his most important contributions to have shown that such generalized media develop not only within the economic structure with its monetary and credit structure but also in the political and societal sectors, with respect to their respective resources and media of exchange, namely power and influence.[14]

The problem of integration of relatively free resources and of highly generalized media of exchange is indeed more salient in modern societies. The development of such generalized media as well as such institutional frameworks as markets and bureaucratic and representative organizations has provided some of the mechanisms which can deal with the integrative problem arising out of the growing structural differentiation as well as out of the impingement of the periphery on the center. But within such relatively similar structural and organizational frameworks there may still develop, in different modern societies, very important differences in the principles or criteria according to which such integration is effected. The relative strength or autonomy of the center against the various institutions in this process of integration is one of such crucial criteria, in modern and traditional societies alike.

In modern and traditional societies alike the differential degree of such autonomy tends to influence many aspects of social structure. But the similarity in this influence on the institutional structure in traditional and modern societies alike can perhaps be most clearly discerned in two major and closely interrelated foci of integration in social systems in general which it has again been Parsons' signal contribution to identify and analyze, namely, in the symbolism and mechanisms of social stratification and in several aspects of the structure of two crucial social groups or categories, the elites and the professions.[15]

The aspects of social stratification and structure of elites and professional groups which are most important from this point of view in traditional and modern societies alike are: (1) the degree of the relative autonomy of such groups with regard to their commitment to a broader social order and to their access to participation in the respective centers of the society and (2) the concomitant degree of status segregation as against broader status association of relatively close occupational and professional groups.[16] The degree of status association or dissociation is in its turn closely related to several aspects of the structure of elites and professional groups in modern societies and of parallel groups in traditional ones.

Thus the elites in different societies may be distinguished according to the degree of association or dissociation among various groups within them and their relations to broader status groups. In some societies these groups tend to be closely associated by virtue of their social origin, style of life, and so on. In others, they tend to develop as separate, almost self-enclosed status groups and are therefore spoken of as dissociated.

Similarly, professional groups may be distinguished according to the degree to which each profession organizes itself internally as an exclusive body with strict apprenticeship requirements and a tendency toward making its positions hereditary and the degree to which the professions as a whole display commitment to a wider social order, real or ideal, as opposed to a commitment that extends no further than fulfilling their respective professional functions.

CONTINUITIES IN CODES: THE RUSSIAN CASE

Next I would like to analyze, if only in a very preliminary and illustrative way, the degree to which some of such broad integrative principles or codes could be found in different stages of the development of the "same" societies and especially in their "premodern" and "modern" stages. I shall attempt to indicate how these similarities and continuities are related to some of the basic codes prevalent in the societies previously analyzed and to illustrate this point by a brief comparative analysis of the system of stratification in the traditional and modern phases of these societies.

In traditional Tsarist and modern Soviet Russia alike the ruling elites tended, for instance, to develop relatively similar policies oriented to several basic aspects of social stratification within these societies.[17] The elites of these societies tended to encourage the segregation of the styles of life and patterns of participation of different local, occupational, and territorial-kinship groups. Closely related to this were the attempts of these elites to minimize the "status" or "class" components of family or kinship group identity and the autonomous standing of the family in the status system.

They also attempted to establish a uniform hierarchy of evaluation of major positions, especially with regard to the access to the center. They aimed at making this hierarchy a relatively steep one — within the center, between it and the periphery, and to some degree also among the peripheral groups. They tended to discourage the development of any countrywide class-consciousness among most groups and strata.

Significantly enough, this was true in Tsarist Russia, even if to a somewhat lesser degree than in Soviet Russia. It is true that the elites had a much higher social standing and a greater control of resources than any other group. Moreover, by virtue of their very proximity to the center, as well as certain survivals of their own semifeudal traditions, they did evince rather more countrywide links than the urban middle classes and the peasantry. Yet even they lacked class-consciousness or an autonomous class organization. Whatever autonomy they had originally managed to save from the pre-absolutist period was shattered by the later rulers.

Similarly they tended to minimize semi-normative styles of life of different strata. Thus they tended to exhibit a smaller emphasis on styles of life and family continuity, a much greater openness towards different new occupational or economic and educational activities, and a greater readiness to approach the modern center, even if only to use it as a basic resource for their own goals.[18]

Similar outcomes of these types of stratificational policies can also be discerned in Soviet Russia, where there is, among different occupational groups, a tendency to social segregation and to emphasis on their own distinct occupational or professional goals.

Such groups tend often to coalesce into relatively closed semi-strata, each stressing its separateness from other such groups, even while stressing similar desiderata and especially using the same basic types of institutional commodities and means of exchange.

The legitimation of the styles of life of each such subgroup tends to be severely controlled by the monopolistic tendencies of the central elite which continuously attempts to limit and to break up any tendencies of any such stratum to transcend its own style of life beyond very limited, parochial scopes or to claim legitimation for its style of life in terms of wider, central values independent of the elite. Accordingly, the central elite tends in these societies to attempt to minimize any tendencies to base such styles of life on differential access to positions through family transmission.

These limits necessarily affect the nature of participation of different status groups in various spheres of social life and of their intercourse. Most groups are here in principle allowed to attempt to participate in different spheres of life, but their success in effecting such participation will greatly depend on their relative standing with regard to the central elite. Relatively common participation is possible in such spheres of life as the ritual-political ones or in communal-sporting activities controlled by the central elite, but it is not possible in the more private spheres of each stratum or in the more central spheres of the elite itself.

These general characteristics of the system of stratification are paralleled by or manifest in some crucial characteristics of the structure of the elites and the professions alike. We find here a high degree of dissociation both between the elite groups themselves and (in most respects) between them and the rest of society, with one elite group always trying to dominate the others.

Under these conditions, most — especially the secondary — elite groups tend to have little in common except their social origins. Moreover, groups in other non-elite positions are prevented by the central ruling elite from exercising final control over access to the resources at their disposal.[19]

Similarly, the professional groups — not unlike the urban guilds of Tsarist times — evince here a very small degree of autonomy or of autonomous commitment to a broader social order, a narrow conception of their technical function together with a high subservience to the state by which they are closely supervised.

Thus in general there tended to develop in traditional and in modern Russia alike a relatively small level of institutional credit or autonomy, although this did not necessarily impede the development of a relatively high degree of technical capacity or structural differentiation.

CONTINUITIES IN WESTERN EUROPE

A similar type of parallelism or continuity in the principles of stratification can be found in Western Europe. The first important characteristic of the "traditional," feudal or absolutist system of stratification of Western Europe[20] was the development of a multiplicity of hierarchies of status and of different patterns of status incongruity, as well as strong tendencies to obliterate the legal distinction between free and servile groups.

The second important characteristic of European strata, closely related to the preceding one, was the existence of a very strong tendency to relatively unified, countrywide strata consciousness and organization. This was especially evident among the higher strata but certainly not absent among the middle and even lower "free" (peasant) strata. The fullest

expression of this tendency can be found in the system of representation as it culminated in the systems of "estates."

The roots of this tendency are to be found in the possibility of political participation or representation of most groups in the center by virtue of their collective identities, as corporate or semicorporate bodies. Hence this country-wide "consciousness" or organization was confined not only to the higher groups but could also be found among the "middle" or lowest free groups and strata.

Third, unlike the Russian case, there tended to develop a close relationship between family and kinship identity, on the one hand, and collective-strata identity, on the other. Family and kinship groups constituted very important channels, not only of orientation to high positions but also of ascriptive transmission of such positions.

Fourth, the degree of access of different groups or strata to the center was not ascriptively fixed but constituted a continuous bone of contention of what one could call "strata conflict," i.e., conflict among different strata as strata about their relative prestige standing in general and about the scope of their participation in the center in particular.

Fifth, again very much unlike the Russian case, each such stratum and especially the "middle" ones (but sometimes also the aristocracy) tended to encompass a great variety of occupational positions and organizations and to link them in some common way of life and in common avenues of access to the center.

These common styles of life of various strata comprised, as we have seen, different types of combination of participation in primordial, kinship-territorial orders as well as in broad universalistic cultural orders, of orientation to the center and participation in it. They were closely connected to various economic occupational activities and to performance of various institutional and occupational tasks.

Some of the principles underlying these characteristics of strata formation in premodern Western European societies can also be discerned in some of the major characteristics in their modern class structure. Here the most salient feature was the relatively small degree of status dissociation among the different relatively "close" occupational positions. In most of these societies varied occupations tended to become encompassed, in the perception of their members, under some such modern broader class categories.

The concrete ways in which various occupations are so combined and the criteria of such combination vary greatly among these societies, but common to all of them is some association closely related to a general perception of the social order in terms of relative approximation of different groups to some common attributes to which all may have some degree of autonomous access. It is such perception of the differentiation of the social order that constitutes the basis for the development of relatively close status relations between occupational groups. Such high degree of association between close occupational groups is manifest in a relatively large extent of common participation in different institutional spheres, as well as a somewhat wider, not purely local or occupational scope of intermarriage. It was also, in modern times, closely connected with the development of countrywide class-consciousness as well as with growing importance of stratificational and class struggle as basic components of perception of the social order on the one hand and of the political process on the other.[21]

Very closely related to this was the structure of intelligentsia elites and professional groups. The major parts of the Western European intelligentsia had two outstanding characteristics: a general lack of exclusiveness in relation to other status groups and a good deal of social and cultural autonomy. The major prototypes of such intelligentsia in the history of Western societies have been the various Protestant groups, to be later followed by more diversified intellectual and professional groups. With the growing differentiation and professionalization of intellectual life, there developed here, on the one hand, a growing proximity of the intelligentsia to professional groups. On the other hand, there could also develop another more oppositional, protest-oriented substream, oriented towards the creation of a new social order,[22] but most of them tended to retain some of the basic characteristics outlined before.

Similarly, these professional groups that developed in these societies were on the whole characterized by some degree of autonomous organization and tended to combine it with commitment to some social and cultural order and public service.

These characteristics of the Western European system of stratification, as well as of the structure of their elites and professional groups, have been in general connected with and testify to a relatively high degree of autonomous credit of various institutions — evident not only in the spheres analyzed but also in such spheres as economics and, above all, in the development of cultural and scientific institutions.

CODE CONTINUITY IN JAPAN

Similar continuity can be found in Japan, where in both in the premodern and the modern society there existed a strong emphasis on the control, by the center, of the status attributes of even the seemingly more autonomous groups — like the feudal lords — and where it was loyalty to the center which served as the ultimate criterion of status.

The structural implications of these orientations were indeed very closely related to or derived from some of the basic codes of Japanese civilization briefly mentioned before and they persisted to a very large degree after the Meiji revolution, influencing greatly the system of stratification that developed there.[23]

The ruling elite of this period, themselves stemming from the secondary aristocracy of the Samurai, not only did away with the political and economic power of the older aristocracy and of most of the Samurai, but even used traditional symbols, especially imperial ones, to legitimize these changes. To replace these traditional groups they created a completely new and far less rigid status system. Nevertheless, the neotraditionalism of the elite placed many limitations on the ability of various social and intellectual groups to develop an autonomous stratum consciousness.

Because of the combination of a relatively strong center and the relative weakness of the autonomous stratum orientation of the groups, the original status configuration that developed in Japan tended to be relatively segregative, based partially on traditional and partially on functional-secular criteria of services to the State.

Hence, the system of stratification that developed in Japan with ongoing urbanization and industrialization was only superficially similar to that of the West. In the first place, it was on the whole the political change instigated by the Meiji ruling elite that formed the pattern taken by the class structure. Second, the political and industrializing elite was urban from the very beginning, but it was very strongly bureaucratized, both in the government and in the large business corporations. Entry to this class was very largely based on formal educational criteria. A similar pattern of bureaucratization developed in the professions. This was especially true of the legal professions, where most members were employed in the state or corporation bureaucracies. Thus the various corporate units, not the local or semiprofessional groups, constituted the major status units of Japanese society.

Thus here also, despite the very high degree of structural differentiation and economic development, modernization was characterized by a very low level of institutional autonomy — whether in the professional, scientific, or status groups. It was only later, beginning with the 1930's, but especially after the Second World War, that new types of class and status orientations, based already to a much greater extent on new perception of the social order, tended haltingly to develop.[24]

STRUCTURAL IMPLICATIONS OF THE CODES

On the basis of the preceding analysis some very tentative hypotheses on the relations between certain codes on the one hand and structural characteristics on the other may be proposed. It may be suggested that the degree of autonomy of major groups in regulating the integrative institutions in these societies and its manifestations in the field of stratification and structure of elites is possibly related, in traditional and modern societies alike, first in the conception of the social, cultural orders and of their interrelation, second in the degree of commitment of various groups, as against an adaptive resource attitude to these orders, and last in the degree of "total" as against "segmental" orientation to goals and social orders prevalent in them.

The more these different orders are perceived as relevant to one another and mutually autonomous the greater is, as in the Western case, the degree of potential institutional autonomy. The more they are subsumed under one of them, as in Russia, or the more they are dissociated from one another, as in many patrimonial societies not discussed here, the smaller will be the degree of such autonomy.

This structural influence of the codes is discernible in different stages of structural development of the same societies, and thus it indicates a degree of continuity in some basic institutional modes which cut across different types of structural differentiation and organization. Moreover, these modes persist also beyond changes of political systems, regimes, and some of the symbols of collective identity.

This does not mean that within any culture or civilization there do not tend to develop changes in such codes. The European illustration itself connotes one such major change, that connected with the transformative effects of the Protestant Ethic — namely, the growth of active participation in the formation of cultural order and a perception of growing interrelation between the social and the cultural order.[25] The Russian case indicates a similar very important change — namely, from a relatively passive to a more much active orientation to nature.

Needless to say, such changes have also important structural implications which we need not, however, analyze here. But even such changes cut across different levels of structural differentiation. Moreover, such changes are not necessarily connected with changes in continuity of political regimes or symbols of collective identity. In some cases the latter may change while the codes persist; in others the political regimes may persist while some codes may change.

CODES AND CHANGE AND CONTINUITY

The preceding analysis indicates that in the study of social change in general and of modernization in particular, and by implication also in any analysis of social systems, we have to differentiate among several levels of social order. It is especially important to differentiate among different symbols of collective identity, political regimes, their centers, and their respective boundary-maintaining mechanisms; among levels and types of structural differentiation and organization; and among the various codes, some of which we have attempted to analyze. Moreover it is necessary to recognize that these levels or components of social orders may indeed change within the "same" society to different degrees or in different ways in various areas of social life.

Here we touch already on one of the most baffling and crucial problems in the analysis of social change — namely, the relation between change of codes and the continuity of social systems and of symbols of cultural traditions, or in more general terms the cybernetics of various aspects of social order in the process of social change. However little we know about this problem, it is indeed clear that it should not be necessarily assumed that one code — as for instance the one which refers to the definition of the basic parameters of human life and of social order and which influences the definition of collective identity — does necessarily have a "higher" cybernetic value than others, i.e., that any change in it necessarily involves all the others in a one-to-one correlation.

In other words, we need not assume that either persistence or change in any one of the codes or many constellation of codes does automatically connote either the persistence or breakdown of the regulative and boundary-maintaining mechanisms within any such systems and/or of the symbols of continuity of collectivity and cultural traditions.

Needless to say these various aspects are not unconnected, but such connection does not imply a one-to-one variation among them. Rather, each of them may greatly influence one another in different ways and through different mechanisms, the investigation of which should constitute an object of systematic sociological research.

Within the range of these problems of special interest in the present context is the problem of who are the carriers of the codes, i.e., how these codes are transmitted or changed. Obviously they cannot be explained in terms of either the basic structural or symbolic "core" of social change in general and of modernization in particular.

In the cases mentioned, the changes in codes have been indeed effected by various revolutionary or transformative elites who then through the family and educational system, on the one hand, and through some restructuring of political coalition and market situation, on the other, attempted to institutionalize such changes.

It may thus perhaps be postulated that similarly the continuity of such codes is carried by the socializing and communicative activities of such elites, who evince special capacity to set up broad orientations, to propound new norms, to articulate various goals, to establish organizational frameworks, and to mobilize the resources necessary for all these purposes.

Indeed, it has already been indicated in other contexts that the development of such "charismatic" or entrepreneurial personalities or groups constitutes perhaps the closest social analogy to "mutation."[26] It is the possibility of such mutation which explains that at any level of differentiation a given social sphere contains not one but several, often competing, possible orientations and potentialities for development.

Here it is important to point out two facts. The first is that such mutations tend also to arise, or persist, to some degree at least, independently of internal structural changes of any single society, and they may greatly be influenced by some aspects. Some of the components and enclaves of such system—related to Parsons' "seed-societies"—may indeed also serve as important reservoirs of such carriers.[27]

Second, the importance of such entrepreneurial activities has, as I have mentioned, already been recognized with regard to the establishment of new symbols of collective identity and boundaries of societal centers on the one hand and various institutional frameworks on the other. Indeed, the more spectacular such elites—like many of the modern revolutionary elites—have attempted both to establish new collectivities with their specific symbols and to develop at least some new codes. But it is not always that these two types of "entrepreneurial" activities have to go together, and here several important questions for further analysis arise.[28]

The first such question is the study of the differences in the conditions of development and patterns of activities of those entrepreneurs which orient themselves mostly to the setting up of new collective symbols, as compared with those who tend mostly to emphasize new codes. Second is the question of the different mechanisms through which each of these respective orientations are institutionalized and transmitted. Third is the analysis of the conditions under which these different types of orientations are transmitted through the same mechanisms as against the conditions under which they are carried by different entrepreneurs and mechanisms.

It seems to me that the answers to these questions may greatly facilitate also the approach to the problem of conditions of differential continuity or change of different aspects or components of social systems.

NOTES

1. See K. Deutsch, "Social Mobilization and Political Development," *American Political Science Review*, 55 (September 1961), pp. 493-515.
2. E. Shils, "The Theory of Mass Society," *Diogenes*, 39 (1963), pp. 45-66; and "Society and Societies," in T. Parsons (ed.), *American Sociology: Perspectives, Problems, Methods* (New York: Basic Books, 1968); and T. Parsons, *The System of Modern Societies* (Englewood Cliffs: Prentice-Hall, 1971).
3. S. N. Eisenstadt, *Modernization: Protest and Change* (Englewood Cliffs: Prentice-Hall, 1966).
4. See for instance, R. Benedict, *The Chrysanthemum and the Sword: Patterns of Japanese Culture* (Boston: Houghton Mifflin, 1946); G. Gorer, *American People: A Study in National Character*, rev. ed., (New York: Norton, 1964).
5. See Max Weber, *The Theory of Social and Economic Organization*, A. M. Henderson and Talcott Parsons, trs., with an introduction by Talcott Parsons (Glencoe: The Free Press, 1964); S. N. Eisenstadt, "Some Reflections on the Significance of Max Weber's Analysis of the Non-European Religions for the Analysis of Non-European Modernity," *Archives des Sociologies des Religions*, no. 32 (1971), pp. 29-52.
6. See, for instance, Claude Levi-Strauss, *Elementary Structures of Kinship* (London: Eyre, 1969); E. Leach, *Levi-Strauss* (London: William Collins, 1970).
7. Eisenstadt, "Some Reflections . . . ," *op. cit.*
8. See introductions to the chapters on City-States, Feudalism, Centralized Empires and Modern Political Systems in S. N. Eisenstadt (ed.), *Political Sociology* (New York: Basic Books, 1970).
9. See on this in greater detail the introduction to the section on modern societies in *ibid*.
10. See for instance, R. Heine-Geldern, "Conceptions of State and Kingship in Southeast Asia," Southeast Asia Program Data Paper, No. 18 (Ithaca: Cornell Univ., April 1956), pp. 1-13.
11. On Tsarist Russia see M. Beloff, "Russia," in A. Goodwin (ed.), *The European Nobility in the Eighteenth Century* (London: Adan & Charles Black, 1953); O. Young, "Russia," in J. O. Lindsay (ed.), *The New Cambridge Modern History*, 44 (1957), pp. 318-38; M. Raeff, *Origins of the Russian Intelligentsia: The Eighteenth Century Nobility* (New York: Harcourt, Brace & World, 1966); J. Blum, *Lord and Peasant in Russia* (Princeton: Princeton University Press, 1961).
On Soviet Russia see: Z. K. Brzezinski, *Ideology and Power in Soviet Politics* (New York: Praeger, 1962); M. Fainsod, *How Russia Is Ruled* (Cambridge: Harvard University Press, 1953).
On Japan see: Robert N. Bellah, "Values and Social Change in Modern Japan," in Eisenstadt (ed.), *op. cit.*; and Thomas C. Smith, "Japan's Aristocratic Revolution," *Yale Review*, 50 (1960-61), pp. 370-83.
12. See Marius B. Jansen (ed.), *Changing Japanese Attitudes Toward Modernization* (Princeton: Princeton University Press, 1965); H. Benda, "Non-Western Intelligentsia as Political Elites," in J. H. Kautsky (ed.), *Political Change in Underdeveloped Countries: Nationalism and Communism* (New York: Wiley, 1962); Carven Blacker; *The Japanese Enlightenment* (Cambridge: Cambridge University Press, 1964); Richard E. Pipes (ed.), *Russian Intelligentsia* (New York: Columbia University Press, 1961); Hugh Seaton Watson, *The Decline of Imperial Russia* (New York: Praeger, 1964); L. Shapiro, *The Communist Party of the Soviet Union* (New York: Random House, 1960).

13. T. Parsons, *Structure and Process in Modern Societies* (Glencoe: The Free Press, 1960).

14. See Parsons' essays on the concepts of power, influence, and value-commitments in T. Parsons, *Politics and Social Structure* (New York: The Free Press, 1969).

15. T. Parsons, "A revised approach to the theory of social stratification," in T. Parsons, *Essays in Sociological Theory* (Glencoe: The Free Press, 1954).

16. This analysis is based on S. N. Eisenstadt, *Social Stratification and Differentiation* (Glenview, Ill.: Scott, Foresman, 1971).

17. See on this in greater detail, S. N. Eisenstadt, "Prestige, Participation and Strata Formation," in J. A. Jackson (ed.), *Sociological Studies* (Cambridge: Cambridge University Press, 1968), pp. 62-103 and the bibliography.

18. On Tsarist Russia see Beloff, "Russia," in Goodwin (ed.), *op. cit.*; Young, "Russia," in Lindsay (ed.), *op. cit.*; Raeff, *op. cit.*, Blum, *op. cit.*

19. On Soviet Russia see Brzezinski, *op. cit.*; Fainsod, *op. cit.*

20. Eisenstadt, "Prestige, Participation and Strata Formation," in Jackson (ed.), *op. cit.*

21. *Ibid.*

22. See Eisenstadt, *Social Stratification and Differentiation.*

23. S. N. Eisenstadt, "The Protestant Ethic Thesis in Analytical and Comparative Framework," in S. N. Eisenstadt (ed.), *The Protestant Ethic and Modernization: A Comparative View* (New York: Basic Books, 1968); Eisenstadt, *Modernization: Protest and Change.*

24. See Smith, *op. cit.*; A. Craig, "Fukazawa Yukucki: The Philosophical Foundations of Meiji Nationalism," in R. E. Ward (ed.), *Political Development of Modern Japan* (Princeton: Princeton University Press, 1968); K. Odaka, "The Middle Classes in Japan," in R. Bendix and S. M. Lipset (eds.), *Class Status and Power* (London: Routledge & Kegan Paul, 1967).

25. See Eisenstadt, "The Protestant Ethic Thesis in Analytical and Comparative Framework," *op. cit.*

26. *Ibid.*

27. T. Parsons, *Societies: Evolutionary and Comparative Perspectives* (Englewood Cliffs: Prentice-Hall, 1966), Ch. 6.

28. S. N. Eisenstadt, "Charisma and Institution Building: Max Weber and Modern Sociology," Introduction to a selection from Weber's works published in the Heritage of Sociology Series (Chicago: University of Chicago Press, 1968).

VI

ORGANIZATIONAL ANALYSIS

INTRODUCTION

Andrew Effrat

The theory of organizations is one of the less-developed aspects of the theory of action. As usual, Parsons has written some insightful and seminal essays in this area,[1] and others have drawn on the theory of action in their work,[2] but compared to other aspects of the theory and to what remains to be done, this area strikes me as one of the more neglected, both theoretically and empirically.

Given this underdevelopment and given Hills' rather good overview of the theory in the next chapter, my main concern in this essay will be to indicate what I regard as some of the important gaps to be filled and work particularly needed now for the development of the theory of organizations within the theory of action framework. Although most of this essay will present a review and critique of the essays in this section, I will be dealing, at least by implication, with needs and inadequacies that characterize the treatment in the theory of organizations in the theory of action in general. Even the summaries of the essays are intended to convey the breadth, concerns, and strategies of the theory.

Many of the comments will, in a sense, be negative, focusing on gaps in the essays, problematic points, and some of the more serious issues of disagreement. This is not intended to undercut what we feel are valuable contributions to the literature but to provide the reader with some alternative perspectives and to continue openly what we hope are fruitful critical dialogues for the field.

As indicated, Hills' first essay provides a very good brief overview and integration of the theory of action of organizations. It maps Parsons' principal conception of the meaning of the concept of organization, the societal function or contribution of organizations, internal functional problems and solutions, structural levels and internal role differentiation, and the various boundary interchanges. It also presents a basic typology of organizations in terms of the AGIL scheme. Further, Hills provides a rather

neat synthesis of much of this material in terms of a four-by-four-by-four figure. In a sense, this figure represents the functional paradigm on three planes — components of social action (values, norms, collectivities, and roles), functional problems (AGIL), and vertical levels of control (where, of course, the technical has primarily A significance; the managerial, G; the institutional, I; and the societal, L).

The thrust of this essay and perhaps its principal contribution is to "demonstrate the possibility of bringing the study of organizations more closely into relation with the study of the structure and functions of society." It does this both by considering the analytical interrelationships between organizations and society and by developing in more detail than heretofore the components of organizations and interchanges among them in a fashion analogous to Parsons' analysis of other, more macrolevel systems, particularly society.

Hills' second essay is an application to the public school of many aspects of the theory of action of organizations presented in his first essay in a fashion rather deliberately parallel to Parsons' essay on mental hospitals. The focus is quite heavily on the prototypical American public school in American society. Hills conceptualizes the public school as a pattern-maintenance organization and maps it primarily in regard to its place as a functionally differentiated subsystem in the broader society, the principal levels of school organization, and the relative coherence of the internal structure and function of schools as L-type organizations. Along the way he manages to touch on and locate in the scheme a number of the major substantive concerns of contemporary education — voucher systems, authority relations in schools, teacher certification and merit pay, the semiprofessional status of teachers, difficulties in reaching ghetto pupils, and so on. Of course, one might have wished for more extended treatments of these and other issues, although given the focus and length of the essay this was no doubt impracticable.

One might also have wished the author to discuss some other important contemporary substantive issues and works in the field. Let me note a few of those as well as some of the theoretical criticisms that might be offered of both of Hills' essays.

One seriously neglected facet is the history and evolution of schools, in regard to both their internal structure and their external relationships to other institutions and organizations. Some particularly important aspects to consider in this regard would be their place in general societal evolution and their consequences for societal adaptive capacity, the emergence of public schools in nineteenth-century America and some of the critiques of its functions,[3] and the contemporary deschooling movement and its implications (perhaps as a next step in structural differentiation).[4] More generally, an analysis of the development of schools or organizations in general in terms of an evolutionary perspective seems quite desirable and remains to be done. This perspective would take into account such issues as patterns of structural differentiation and integration in organizational development, how the development of specialized organizations may contribute to or interfere with the adaptive capacity of society, the pattern of phase movements characterizing organizational development, and the like. (See my introduction to Part V for elaboration.)

A second area concerns the conflicts among competing educational philosophies and how they have influenced educational policy and practice. Relatedly, a third area would be the questions of what is actually learned in schools and how it is learned. Particularly important here are works by Dreeben and Loubser[5] that, among other things, draw out the importance of alternative structural arrangements for learning outcomes. The experimentation with ever more innovative and "open" schools and classrooms would also be important in considering structures and processes in schooling, particularly given the obvious linkage with such notions as open systems and systems with more adaptive capacity in the theory of action in general. Relatedly, it might be observed that the general model (particularly concerning interchanges) is rather "mechanical" as it has been developed thus far. One gets little sense of dynamics and processes, particularly in regard to how elements combine to produce their outcomes.

A fourth relatively untouched area is that of cross-cultural comparisons that would explore the way that different value primacies and structural arrangements influence school structure and process. For example, some of the attributes of schools that Hills deals

with seem related less to the fact that they are L-primacy organizations than to the American value context (e.g., the emphasis on forms of community political input and the treatment of education as in certain respects a community responsibility seem largely a function of an American populist tradition, particularly in light of comparisons with European cases).

More generally, this might call for paying more attention to the content of values, norms, and the like. Thus, instead of treating all L or pattern-maintenance organizations together, one might differentiate among them according to the type or content of the pattern to be maintained (e.g., authoritarian or democratic). Further, it would be useful to pay more systematic attention to the value context of organizations — taking into account the differences in functioning between, say, A organizations in a G or in an L society. These sorts of approaches would build a considerably more systematic cross-cultural perspective into the theory and give considerably greater leverage on the tremendous variation in organizational phenomena across societies.

One final point that is perhaps the most important to be made is that Hills' essays, given their heavy analytical and ideal-typical emphasis, may have conveyed a more "harmonious" and tightly integrated conception of schools and organizations, and indeed societies, than is appropriate to action theory. For example, in the first essay Hills states:

> Because the attainment of an organizational goal is always the performance of a differentiated function for the society, the value system of the organization must be a differentiated, concretely specified version of the societal value system, a differentiation whose direction is determined by the function of the organization for the society. Thus, the values of any organization are a spelling-out of the societal value pattern in the specific context of its principal function. The characteristic features of the organization thus derive from (1) the value pattern of the society, (2) the goal-directedness of the organization, (3) the nature of the function performed by the organization and, as we shall see, (4) the location of the organization in the structural hierarchy.

Clearly this treatment neglects many conditional components as factors in shaping organizations. This point will be taken up in more detail in regard to Dreeben's article, which can be seen as a criticism of precisely these kinds of neglects. Further, this sort of interpretation seriously neglects the kinds of value inconsistencies, incomplete and ambiguous institutionalization, and partial autonomy of different layers of society that are likely to exist in any concrete empirical social system. Further it neglects a whole range of subcultural influences that the theory of action also tries to take into account, such as religious, social class, ethnic, and regional variations. These lines of criticism would seem to be appropriate to a number of points in both essays. Perhaps most seriously it is reflected in the failure of Hills to take seriously the criticisms of schools by many humanistic critics (that I and other theorists of action find quite appropriate) that schools are in many ways oppressive, narrow in their socialization goals, and failing to implement or socialize in regard to many presumed American values.

Dreeben's essay is also concerned with exploring the adequacy of Parsons' approach for organizations in general and public schools in particular. He is particularly concerned with the following questions: Can the theory of action account for the structure and process of particular types of organizations and variations within types? Can it account for why a particular set of organizational arrangements tends to cluster together?

Dreeben reviews some of the principal attributes of American school systems, schools, and processes of schooling, pointing up many variations within these categories. The essay has many fine and insightful points that will be of use to sociologists of education in making obvious and taken-for-granted features of schools sociologically interesting and important.

The main thrust of his analysis is to raise serious questions concerning the adequacy of the theory of action approach — characterized by him as emphasizing (or overemphasizing) the values-goals-functions scheme. Dreeben offers an activities-technology approach as a possibly superior alternative or at least complement to the mainstream of the theory of action.[6] In his analysis, he tries to point up a number of ways in which "schools differ structurally from other organizations and among themselves for reasons that have little or no necessary connection with values" and seem more related to organizational activities, technology, ecology, and history.

I think that Dreeben raises a number of issues that are quite important and central, both to the theory of action on values, goals and functions as explanatory to present and develop the activities aspects will probably bear much fruit. However, I think that there would be a number of serious and instructive disagreements in the interpretation of the theory of action between himself and many theorists of action. Let me just touch on three lines of criticism.

First, Dreeben overstates the reliance of the theory of action on values, goals and functions as explanatory factors. The theory certainly emphasized the importance of values that treats other cultural components as higher in the hierarchy of control (such as existential beliefs), as well as other cultural categories (such as empirical knowledge) as influential. Further,

Parsons and others consider such variables as the nature of interchange media, the level of function, the nature of available technology, degree of organizational formalization, and exigencies of resource acquisition as important in organizational analysis.[7] Thus values, goals and functions are not necessarily the sole or primary determinants in the scheme. One quote from a rather different context might be particularly salient here:

> ... a system of interdependent variables, on the one hand, and of units or parts, on the other, by its nature implies that there is no necessary order of teleological significance in the sources of change. This applies particularly to such old controversies as economic or interest explanations *versus* explanations in terms of ideas or values ... of a set of "factors" *any or all may be sources of change,* whose nature will depend on the ways an initial impetus is propagated through the system by types of dynamic process.[8]

This brings us to the second line of criticism, which is not quite the obverse of the first. Dreeben underappreciates the extent to which technology and activities are incorporated into the scheme. For example, the scheme of technical and managerial levels of organizations that Dreeben seems to regard as being close to an activities model is clearly related to and derivable from an AGIL four-function scheme as indicated in Hills' essay. Perhaps more basically, organizational activities can be seen as aspects of the division of labor in society. Hence, activities tend to be differentiated among organizations in functional terms, at least in part. In a sense, then, the functions and interchange processes that Parsons and others have proposed are very close to or actually a conceptualization of types of tasks and activities.

Further, the theory of action recognizes the influence of technological considerations in the general notion of the hierarchy of conditions and the ways these factors set limits on or influence structure and process. Put somewhat more precisely, informational aspects of technology are conceptualized as part of the cultural system.[9] Material aspects are regarded as heavily dependent on, among other things, the state of informational technology and definitions of what are legitimate uses of resources and personnel. Further, the theory recognizes that "lower-level" (more "specific") and proximate factors can have greater immediate and apparent impact on specific activities, outcomes, and structural forms than the higher-level components.[10] But still one must ask what governs and guides the actions of those lower-level factors.

Third, Dreeben seems to under-appreciate the extent to which normative and functional components enter into his own explanations as, for example, when he discusses teachers' authority positions or important aspects of how teachers process students. For example, the choice of how to relate to children rests not merely on "technical" considerations (or, if it did, this would be a culturally defined and legitimated decision), but also on cultural definitions of what children are thought to be capable of, what they should be taught, what it is inappropriate to do with and to them, how they are best sanctioned, for what purposes they are being processed, and so on.[11] In a sense, this is to suggest that, insofar as we distinguish between activities and functions, it would still seem to be the case that functions, values, and goals are important factors in influencing the selection and development of the activities and technology employed.

These points would also suggest a partial answer to Dreeben's challenge to explain several propositions which he suspects are both true and inexplicable in terms of societal values or functional problems. Although I would not claim a full explanation could be provided by either of these components, I think these types of components are clearly relevant to explicating what society and specific relevant actors would define as legitimate, desirable, and efficacious ways of treating the actors noted in his propositions (students, professional personnel, customers) and hence of accounting for the kinds of activities or performances that are manifested.

Let us deal with the two papers by Ben-David and Bidwell together. Neither was intended to focus on issues in organizational analysis, but I shall be concerned mainly to explore what linkages there may be.

Ben-David's very rich and broad paper is most obviously an exploration of answers to three focal questions concerning the institutionalization of scientific roles and collectivities in modern society: What are the historical roots of scientific professionalism? What are the bases of legitimation of the professional privileges of scientists (especially when other claims to privilege have been rejected)? What have been the consequences of the overextension of scientific professionalism?

Bidwell is primarily concerned to explore aspects of the professional-client relationship (largely of a dyadic sort) in the "helping professions." Among other things, he considers various types of trust, their importance, factors promoting and inhibiting them, and their interactional consequences. One of his main concerns is to point out the apparent appropriateness or "rationality" of various client concerns for affectively-based trust and forms of professional "counter-transference."

However, there are a number of other important issues in both of these papers that are raised or dealt with at least indirectly that can have some payoff for organizational analysis. Given the complexity

and suggestiveness of the analyses, I shall turn this discussion around somewhat and focus on some of the important gaps in the theory of action of organizations to which these papers help sensitize us and provide us with some resources for dealing with them.

One important set of issues that Ben-David's essay raises and addresses in part is that of the history and development or evolution of organizations. Certainly this is one of the more glaring gaps in the explicit discussions of organizations and roles-in-organizations in the theory of action, and conversely, in the theory's analyses of change, which, with a number of important exceptions, have focussed rather heavily at the societal and institutional levels of analysis.

Particularly in considering the change in the nature of universities, Ben-David suggests some of the sources and consequences of the differentiation of roles and organizations out of the more diffuse religious matrix. One particularly interesting but not very developed aspect of his analysis is his suggestions about conflict among competing ideologies, organizational principles, and societal subgroups — notably clergy and more "rationalized" sectors. (This latter point raises an interesting issue in itself — why so many focal conflicts are between more traditional and more rational sectors of society.) Clearly this points to the value of further exploration of the evolutionary processes involved — the sources, how the struggle is conducted, factors influencing outcomes, how the changes could be conceptualized in terms of the interchange scheme, and how and why new roles emerge and become embedded in organizations.

A second area concerns how the generalized media of exchange relate to organizational processes. In a sense, both papers (Bidwell in regard to trust and Ben-David particularly in regard to influence) point to ways that organizations can help (or fail) to regulate the supply of the media, to certify or back its acceptability, and to maintain its "productive" base and its institutionalized value.

Finally, a third set of issues would concern the relationship between bureaucratic organizations and professional roles, or between bureaucratic principles of organization and professional principles. One way the problem might be put is to ask what sort of normative and structural arrangements can be established to faciliate the incorporation within one collectivity of what can be quite conflicting functional needs, types of relationships, and so on.

The solutions that Ben-David suggests have emerged and been effective would certainly call for further analysis but relate to the kinds of mechanisms the theory of action would readily deal with. These solutions include the development of more generalized norms (as in regard to academic freedom) and the differentiation among roles and among organizational levels that create buffers or protective zones within which different principles may operate somewhat more freely. These solutions seem to have meant the modification of both professional and bureaucratic ideal types in actuality. Further, upon closer examination one might not be surprised to find that many actual cases are not necessarily stable or fully institutionalized. This raises the possibility that the tensions we now see in these organizations are part of a transitional stage in the evolution of organizations to more "purely" professional and associational structures along the lines of the trends to associationism that Parsons has discussed.[12]

Relatedly, Bidwell's essay brings out the fundamental pattern variable dilemmas facing teachers and anyone in the helping professions (or perhaps any L-type organization). That is, if one treats clients in a universalistic, affectively neutral fashion then it may be difficult to mobilize the motivational energies necessary to obtain commitment. However, if these are mobilized then it may be difficult to fend off the demands for more particularistic, affective involvement that may interfere with bureaucratic and administrative efficiency. For a variety of reasons explored by Bidwell, some organizational arrangements could conceivably be more effective in dealing with these problems than dyads or other "deorganized" relationships.

In closing, I would like to note one other general and important set of gaps in the work of theorists of action. These are a number of issues in "mainstream" organizational analysis to which the theory of action has hardly addressed itself. Among these issues would be: What is an optimal "span of control," and why? What alternative lines of communication can be conceptualized, and what are their relative advantages? What tensions are likely to arise in staff-line relations, why, and how might they be solved? How might "goal displacement" be prevented? What arrangements can be most effective in dealing with the dilemmas in maximizing both administrative efficiency and participatory democracy? In general, these and other issues could be seen as relating particularly to a structural rather than a functional analysis of organizations—or to attempt to articulate structural and functional analyses even more systematically and extensively than the theory presently does. These issues call for a textured analysis of the alternative structural characteristics, how they fit together, and what their principal consequences are.

So much then for a very brief attempt to touch on a number of the main aspects of the theory of action of organizations, to indicate some of the possible refinements and criticisms that might be offered in regard to the essays that follow, and to map some of the major areas of the theory that still appear to need considerable development. Clearly the theory has only begun to mine this rich area.

NOTES

1. See the following articles by Talcott Parsons: "Suggestions for a Sociological Approach to the Theory of Organization—I," *Administrative Science Quarterly* 1 (1956), pp. 63-85; "Suggestions for a Sociological Approach to the Theory of Organization—II," *Administrative Science Quarterly* 1 (1956), pp. 225-39; "Some Ingredients of a General Theory of Formal Organizations," in Andrew W. Halpin, *Administrative Theory in Education* (Chicago: Midwest Administrative Center, 1958), pp. 40-72; and "The Mental Hospital as a Type of Organization," in Milton Greenblatt *et al.* (eds.), *The Patient and the Mental Hospital* (Glencoe, Ill.: The Free Press, 1963), pp. 108-29.

2. In addition to the essays in this collection, see: Charles E. Bidwell, "Schools as Formal Organizations," in James G. March (ed.), *Handbook of Organizations* (Chicago: Rand-McNally, 1965), pp. 972-1022; Robert Dreeben, *On What Is Learned in Schools* (Reading, Mass.: Addison Wesley, 1968); Amitai Etzioni, *A Comparative Analysis of Complex Organizations* (New York: The Free Press, 1961); Henry A. Landsberger, "Parsons' Theory of Organizations," in Max Black (ed.), *The Social Theories of Talcott Parsons* (Englewood Cliffs, N.J.: Prentice-Hall, 1961), pp. 214-49; and Jan J. Loubser, "The Contribution of Schools to Moral Development: A Working Paper in the Theory of Action," *Interchange* 1 (April 1970), pp. 99-117.

3. See especially Michael B. Katz, *The Irony of Early School Reform* (Cambridge: Harvard University Press, 1968).

4. See Everett Reimer, "An Essay on Alternatives in Education," *Interchange* 2 (1971), pp. 1-35.

5. See Dreeben, *op. cit.,* and Loubser, *op. cit.*

6. Very similar criticisms of Parsons' work are also offered by Landsberger, *op. cit.,* and William Foote Whyte, "Parsons' Theory Applied to Organizations," in Black (ed.), *op. cit.,*

7. See particularly Parsons' article in Halpin, *op. cit.*

8. Talcott Parsons, "An Outline of the Social System," p. 72, in Talcott Parsons *et al.* (eds.), *Theories of Society* (New York: The Free Press, 1961).

9. See the L_a category—empirical knowledge—discussed in, for example, Talcott Parsons, "Culture and the Social System," pp. 963-96, in Parsons *et al.* (eds.), *op. cit.*

10. See, for example, Smelser's scheme representing the components of social action and their interrelationships, in Neil J. Smelser, *Theory of Collective Behavior* (New York: The Free Press, 1963), pp. 23-46. The lower-level components are particularly likely to be of major salience under certain circumstances, for example, when the organization or activity in question is primarily an adaptive or technical one, or when the phenomenon to be explained is of relatively brief duration such as a near-term change.

11. These points, by the way, indicate an area that requires considerably further development—how various existential beliefs (particularly about the nature of social actors and social systems) shape value patterns, organizational arrangements, role expectations, and the like.

12. Talcott Parsons, *The System of Modern Societies* (Englewood Cliffs, N.J.: Prentice-Hall, 1971), p. 116.

33

THE ORGANIZATION AS A COMPONENT IN THE STRUCTURE OF SOCIETY

R. Jean Hills

INTRODUCTION

Major developments in science occur in a variety of forms, one of the most important of which is the integration of two or more relatively independent lines of investigation within a single, more encompassing framework. Newton's great contribution was the development of a single theoretical system which did the work which had until then required two—one for celestial and another for terrestial motion. Maxwell unified electricity, magnetism, and light. Matter and electricity merged in the work of Bohr, and so on. The list could be extended to include many others.

The degree of importance that will be assigned to Parsons' work by historians of science cannot be foretold, but it is clear, at least to the writer, that Parsons has laid the groundwork for the eventual integration of a variety of relatively independent areas of investigation in the social sciences. The purpose of this essay is to discuss one of those integrative contributions, that which provides the basis for the unification of the study of organizations and the study of society.

One might argue that no such unification is necessary, or even possible, as the study of organizations has long been regarded as a part of the study of social structure. That argument can be supported if by "unified" one means that the study of organizations has gone forward under the same general concepts employed in other areas, e.g., anthropology, political science, and sociology. On the other hand, if one means by "unified" that generalizations concerning organizations can be systematically related to generalizations about the structure and functions of society, then even a superficial perusal of the relevant literature will settle the matter. The literature of the field of organizational studies is a welter of information concerning specific properties of specific kinds of organizations. There is available a great

deal of information about industrial organizations, about educational organizations, about prisons, and about hospitals. But, it has not been possible to systematically relate either the characteristic internal structure and functions or the external functions of a given type of organization to those of other types which differ from it. To put it another way, it has not been possible to relate what we know about given types of organization to what we know about other types of organizations, and it has not been possible to relate what we know about variations among organization types to what we know about higher levels of social structure and function.

What is lacking is a conception of society which includes organizations as integral parts. In the space available here we cannot possibly present all the relevant material, but perhaps a useful beginning can be made by examining three aspects of Parsons' work which seem especially relevant: (1) the view of the collectivity as the category of structural components of the social system differentiated with reference to political functions, i.e., the collective pursuit of collective goals, or the performance of social goal-attainment functions; (2) the view of the collectivity as a functionally differentiated subsystem of the more inclusive social system, i.e., as an agency of the performance of a specific differentiated societal function; and (3) the view of the collectivity as a hierarchically differentiated structural subsystem of the social system. Point (1) will be treated in the immediately following section. Points (2) and (3) will be treated separately in subsequent sections.

THE COLLECTIVITY AS A COMPONENT OF SOCIAL STRUCTURE

In contrast to the view of the organization as an organized island in an amorphous environment which one derives from the literature, Parsons proposes that we regard the organization as a component woven systematically into the fabric of society. One aspect of this view is the treatment of the organization as a collectivity, which, in turn, may be regarded as one of four major types of structural components, or subsystems, of the social system. The structure of a social system,

> . . . consists in the patterning of the relations of individuals and may be analysed on four levels of generality so far as its units are concerned: (1) Individuals in roles are organized to form what we call (2) collectivities. Both roles and collectivities, however, are subject to ordering and control by (3) norms which are differentiated according to the functions of these units and to their situations, and by (4) values which define the desirable type of system of relationships.[1]

> These four structural categories—values, norms, collectivities, roles—may be related to our general functional paradigm. Values take primacy in the pattern-maintenance functioning of a social system. Norms are primarily integrative: they regulate the great variety of processes that contribute to the implementation of patterned value commitments. The primary function of the collectivity concerns actual goal attainment on behalf of the social system. Where individuals perform *societally* important functions it is in their capacity as collectivity members. Finally the primary function of the role in the social system is adaptive. This is particularly clear for the category of service, as the capacity to fulfill valued role performances is the most basic generalized adaptive resource of any society, though it must be coordinated with cultural organic and physical resources.[2]

The collectivity, then, is the category of structural components differentiated around the functional problem of goal-attainment, i.e., the attainment and/or maintenance of states of interaction between the system and its environing situation that are relatively desirable from the point of view of the system.[3] Goal-attainment is tied directly to the processes of change in the interrelations between a system and its environing situation. It becomes a problem, or a goal exists, insofar as there arises a discrepancy between the desired states of the system with respect to input-output interchange and the actual or expected states at the inception of action. For the social system as such, i.e., viewed in relation to the other subsystems of the action system—the behavioral organism, the cultural system, and the personality system—the focus of its goal orientation lies in its relation to the personalities of the participating individuals. Its principal concern in that context, therefore, is motivation to contribute what is necessary to the functioning of the system.[4] Thus, from one point of view,

> Collective organization should be regarded as a critical mode of articulating the internal, normative structure of a social system, with its environment, which for

present analytical purposes centers in the personalities of its members. It is a way of integrating the motivation of individuals with the norms of a society.[5]

> In this context, the crucial problem concerns the relations between the exigencies of collective organization for the attainment of goals (which, valued by individuals, are yet defined as a collective concern) and the motivational "interests" of participating individuals.[6]

For any given social system, however, the environing situation is never exhausted by the personality systems of participating members. It includes, among other things, the physical environment, and other social systems. Thus a crucial aspect of the environment of a given societal system consists of other societal systems in the international system. Similarly, for a subsystem of a societal system, e.g., an organization, a prominent aspect of the environing situation with which it interacts consists of other intrasocietal subsystems. Hence, the attainment of a system goal consists in the attainment of states of interaction between the system of reference and some aspect of its intrasocietal environment, e.g., other cognate systems, or its extrasocietal environment. For a given collectivity it may concern relations not only to other collectivities, but also to personalities of individuals, cultural objects, and organic or physical objects. In each of these contexts, changes in the environing situation may bring about a discrepancy between the actual or expected state of system-environment interaction and the desired state.

> Especially for a collectivity continuing in time and holding multiple interests, a particular goal is not isolated; it is part of a system of goals. Any particular goal must, therefore, be fitted into a larger system of goals, according to its rank-order and timing with reference to other goals.[7]

To narrow our subject somewhat, the category of agencies which we customarily term "organizations" may be regarded as a type of collectivity distinguished from other types, such as communities, ascriptive solidarities, and associations, by the primacy of their orientation to the attainment of a specific goal. This places the organization, in one of its aspects, squarely in the polity.

THE POLITICAL ASPECT OF ORGANIZATION

A cryptic note will have to suffice here to characterize the broad features of the polity, the political, or goal-attainment, subsystem of the societal system.[8] Analytically defined, it is that aspect of all social action concerned with the attainment of a collectivity's goals through the production of effective collective action. As noted, it is specifically related to the processes of change in the interrelations between the system, or collectivity, and its environing situation; and its processes are those through which the necessary organization is built up and operated, the goals of action are determined, and the resources requisite to their implementation are mobilized. The production of collective action is, for the polity, parallel to the production of goods and services, for the economy. The value principle of effectiveness, for the polity, as symbolized and measured by power, parallels that of utility as symbolized and measured by money for the economy. Authority, leadership, and regulation are the political parallels of the economic institutions of property, contract, and occupations.

Power is a collectivity's means of effectively mobilizing obligations in the interest of collective goals. For the political subsystem of the collectivity, it is a generalized adaptive facility stabilizing relations with other subsystems. It is generalized in the sense that it is the capacity to make decisions binding on member units independently of specific conditions prescribed in advance either by ascription or prior agreements. It is an adaptive facility in the sense that it permits those bearing political responsibility to cope effectively with contingencies that cannot be anticipated, by imposing previously unspecified situationally adapted obligations.

Essentially, the process is always one of translating generalized expectations into more specific ones. Responsible leadership obviously cannot predict in advance the specific actions that exigencies will require of their collectivity if its generalized effectiveness is to be maintained. Without precise knowledge of situational and environmental conditions, leadership cannot even define the goals which appear to be most attractive in terms of the generalized collective commitments. Hence, it cannot impose situationally adapted obligations on its members far in advance of actual developments. But, lacking knowledge of what goals and means of implementation will be involved in future actions, responsible leadership can use its generalized power to allow for contingencies by holding open freedoms of choice which never emerge in ascriptive conditions, and which are exceedingly awkward to manage in barter conditions. Thus, the user of power can specify political obligations to levels of performance which were left unspecified when the general undertaking began, e.g., in making an employment contract or in giving political support to a leadership element.[9]

The important point for present purposes is the view of the polity, and hence of the organization, as maintaining its power potential through continual interchanges with its environment. In a manner analogous to the business firm, units specializing in political function are dependent on an "income" of power to replace that "spent" or expended through decisions which impose binding obligations. This "income," analogous to that of the firm from consumer spending, takes the form of political support from the constituencies of the political processes which directly affects the leadership's capacity to impose further obligations.

"On the one hand, it 'exports' power in the form of opportunity for effectiveness, and gets in return power in the form of commitment of services. On the other hand, it 'exports' power in the form of policy decisions, and gets in return power in the form of political support."[10]

The preceding identifies two of the three primary external functions of political systems, be they public or private, societal collectivities or subcollectivities. Figure 33-1 abstracts the relevant parts of the general societal interchange system, identifying the other subsystems involved in the several interchanges. Turning directly to the interchanges,

The first concerns the legitimation of collective goals and of the authority and power needed to implement them in terms of the values of the wider social system, not those of its political subsystem. The wider value patterns must be specified as commitments in the context of collective action along the requisite lines and subject to the requisite limitations . . . . Any concrete collectivity depends on fulfillment of these functions, however rudimentary the agencies which implement them may be.

Secondly, a political system is an agency for mobilizing resources from its intrasocietal environment and utilizing them to implement its policies. This is the function of the bureaucratic element within which organization based on hierarchical "line authority" is most clearly differentiated. This principle, however, is sharply modified at the boundary where needed resources or capacities can be brought into the polity only by inducement and can be controlled by authority only through the intervention of influence.

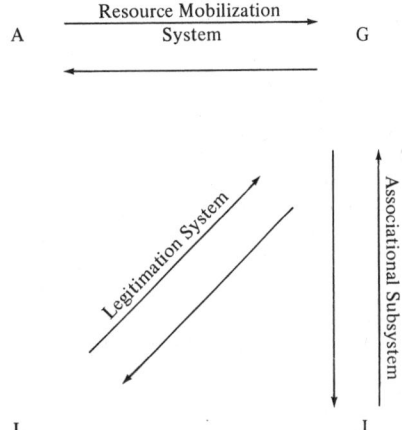

Figure 33-1. The political system in the societal interchange system.

Thirdly, there is the associational subsystem. This mobilizes not implementive resources, but rather constituent support and determination of the policies to be implemented. Such mobilization involves the interplay of power and influence between leadership and membership, the latter having dual roles as constituents and as interest groups.[11]

The typical manufacturing firm provides a convenient illustration. The goals of the firm and the authority and power required to implement them must be legitimized by the values of the societal system. It must mobilize resources from its intrasocietal environment for utilization in the implementation of policies. And, its leadership, its board of directors and top management, must secure support for policies from stockholders which may on occasions become divided into actively opposing interest groups.

To summarize in Parsons' words:

> We have conceived the bureaucratic subsystem to be differentiated primarily in relation to the economic exigencies, namely the procurement and management of the more-or-less fluid resources at the polity's disposal, and the corresponding outputs of political benefits. The critical resources are, first, financial, and, second, the services of individuals and collectivities. In a developed system, physical resources are mediated by these factors. The associative subsystem is differentiated with respect to problems of support, and outputs of policy decision are differentiated with respect to the management of influence inputs and outputs. Finally, the legitimation subsystem is differentiated with respect to relationship between the polity and the general normative structures (value-patterns and legal norms) of the society.[12]

Viewed as a political system, then, the goal output of the organization, whatever its functions may be, is policy decisions; and the state of input-output interchange which constitutes goal-attainment is one in which the relation between systems and environment is supportive of processes within the system.[13]

These external references of structural differentiation relate very closely to internal differentiation. For purposes of the present discussion, however, we need only identify the main lines of internal differentiation. As an organization is by definition a type of collectivity oriented to the attainment of relatively specific goals, there is a special emphasis on the goal-attainment subsystem. This subsystem may be identified as the "leadership subsystem" (see Figure 33-2), flanked on the adaptive side by the "administrative or bureaucratic" subsystem and on the integrative side by the "legislative" subsystem. Finally, the political system as a whole is grounded in, and legitimated by, what may be termed the "constitutional" subsystem. Thus, whether it be formal or informal,

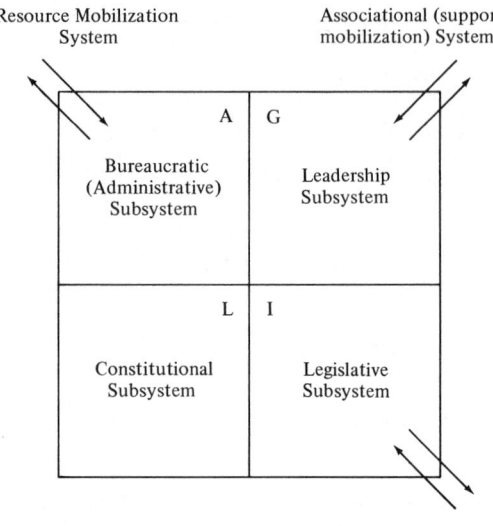

Figure 33-2. Primary internal subsystems of political systems.

every organization, public or private, has its "constitution" or set of norms governing the political functions necessary for its effective operation.

Legitimation, then, functions to define what political organization is for and, hence, to define the nature and scope of the agencies — collectivities and roles — which perform political functions. Correlative with these structural definitions are both authority for implementation of the legitimate responsibilities, and access to power and the conditions of its use. In a sufficiently differentiated polity, we call this the *constitutional system* — with private as well as public collectivities having constitutions more or less formally specified.[14]

In speaking of the internal differentiation of these four primary internal subsystems, even in the brief comments that we have to make about the leadership subsystem, it is well to couch the discussion in terms of functions, rather than in terms of positions, roles, or subcollectivities. The reason for this is that only in the most complex, large-scale organizations would one expect to find concrete organizational positions approximating full differentiation along functional lines. Perhaps it is even better to speak of the leadership, or goal-attainment function, as well as others, as consisting of analytically independent subfunctions which may be concretely identical in terms of location.

The central component of the leadership subsystem, then, is the highest-level executive function which is the locus of "political responsibility," i.e., responsibility for the attainment of collective goals, and the source of "executive policy." The adaptive component of the leadership subsystem is mainly an "executive policy" implementation function. Concretely, in the differentiated case, it takes the form of an executive, or administrative, staff, or cabinet. The integrative component may be identified as a liaison between the executive and legislative subsystems. Finally,

> The relatively "inert" pattern-maintenance subsystem of the leadership system is perhaps best described as the set of commitments of the whole leadership cohort to the values of the political system as a whole, to effectiveness, but effectiveness within the framework of the more general societal value system and its political constitution.[15]

In closing the highly truncated sketch of the political functions of organizations, it may be appropriate to emphasize that we have been concerned only with that analytically (not concretely) independent aspect of organizations which may be conceived as having political primacy, i.e., as facilitating the attainment of collective goals, independent of the content of those goals. Certainly, no claim is made to having presented any new knowledge about organizations, or even to having codified any substantial part of available knowledge. Rather we have focussed on certain commonly held information concerning the resource, support, and legal requirements of organizations and suggested that these may be viewed as boundary processes through which organization, in its political aspect, i.e., from its location in the polity, is linked to the three other primary societal subsystems.

THE ORGANIZATION AS A FUNCTIONALLY DIFFERENTIATED SUBSYSTEM OF THE SOCIAL SYSTEM

The preceding section sketched in broad outline the view of the organization, as "a mechanism by which goals somehow important to a society or to various subsystems of it, are implemented and to some degree defined,"[16] which is linked through its boundary relations with specific points in the structure of society. That is to say, the specialized output of the collectivity was viewed as a specialized input to a specific sector of the societal system which reciprocates with a specialized output constituting a specialized input to the collectivity. The ordering of information begun there can be greatly extended by viewing the organization as functionally differentiated subsystem of the societal system. Thus, whereas the preceding section focussed on the organization as a collectivity, as distinguished from other components of social structure, the present section will focus on given types of collectivities, as distinguished from other types within the category of specific-function collectivities. Again, in the preceding

section we were concerned with the boundary relations characteristic of collectivities as such. Here we are interested in variations in the boundary relations of collectivities and the linkage between these and functional differentiation. The point we wish to emphasize, of course, is that a considerable amount of what is common knowledge about organizations can be organized within the view under consideration.

Boundary Relations of Organizations

Like any action system, the social system of an organization must be analyzed in terms of two sets of processes, "boundary processes," which involve the relations between the organization and its environing situation, and internal processes which involve the structural units of the organization and their relations to one another. We shall have no opportunity to consider the internal structure and processes of organizations in this discussion, but if space permitted the view under consideration would certainly permit us to do so.

The boundary processes of organizations may be discussed under four main headings: (1) legitimation processes, the processes by which the right of the organization to operate is established, and community confidence in it is insured; (2) integrative processes, the processes through which the procedures of the organization are made acceptable to the community at large; (3) disposal processes, the processes involved in dealing with recipients of the organization's output; and (4) procurement processes, the processes of acquiring the facilities necessary for the organization to carry out its functions.

Legitimation

The broad pattern of legitimation is given in the relation between the societal and organizational value systems — the latter, in the integrated case, being a specification of the former to the relevant function in the context of collective action. Legitimation is the positive appraisal of action in terms of shared values, and the system-subsystem relation between societal and organizational values is the primary mechanism involved. The organizational goal is linked with the more general value pattern of the society and is legitimated in terms of the significance of its attainment for the functioning of the superordinate system. Thus, the goal of the mental hospital is linked with the more general values through the valuation of the individual personality and of achievement. It is chiefly because mental illness hinders effective achievement that in American society it is defined as an undesirable state.[17]

Values will, within limits, be acted upon wherever appropriate independent of cost. This is what is implied by the term "commitment." Hence, as a subsystem of the societal value system, the organizational value system defines the societal commitments on which its functioning depends. The operation of an established organization may be conceived as based fundamentally on such a set of commitments. This means that, within limits which vary from organization type to organization type, and from organization to organization within types, the organization has under its control certain societal resources whose supply is not contingent on short-run sanctions. The firm, for example, has at its disposal relatively nondepreciating, non-obsolescing sites, physical facilities, equipment, technical know-how, state of the organization, and human services, access to which is assured as long as it remains in operation. Thus, one may conceive of personnel who would leave the organization only in dire circumstances or in the event of liquidation, and of technical knowledge, readily available experience, and organization of the enterprise which, however dependent on human agents for their implementation, constitute analytically distinct "givens" access to which is unproblematic.

These considerations concern the legitimization of the existence of a type of organization and the specification of the societal commitments on which its functioning depends. But the legitimation of and the specification of commitments for the type does not insure the legitimation of a particular, concrete organization of the type in a particular community. Hence, a more specific problem of legitimation and specification is that of establishing, maintaining, and enhancing a positive community appraisal of the actual functioning organization. That is, it is not only the legitimation of a given type of organization that is at stake but also the legitimation of the actual conduct of a particular organization and the maintenance of an adequate level of commitment to its functioning. Although the legitimation of the goal or function of the organization may be rooted in its linkage with superordinate values, the legitimation of the implementation of that goal by a particular organization in a particular community cannot be assumed to occur automatically. Hence, there will be relatively specific mechanisms designed to insure community confidence in the organization, e.g., securing the sponsorship of elements of the community which have good standing in the community and a reputation for responsibility. Public schools, for example, make rather frequent use of "lay advisory boards" (not to be confused with elected or appointed boards of trustees) whose members tend to be prominent business, professional, and religious leaders in the community. Various activities included under the heading "public relations" also belong here.

Integration

The integration of the organization with its environment involves the maintenance of compatibility between the practices and procedures under which the organization operates and those of other organizations and social units.

> This above all involves adherence to values and patterns of operation which (a) are generalizable beyond the particular organization, or (b) are considered justified by the particular circumstances of the particular case or type of organization.[18]

The underlying problem on a transorganizational level is the definition of the loyalty participants owe to a given organization in ways that fit into the larger system of loyalties which they bear, e.g., to family and to country. Hence, an essential ingredient in organizational operation is the set of rules defining and regulating the limits of commitments to this organization as compared with others in which the same clients, employees, and resource suppliers are involved.

The three primary complexes of rules involved here are the contractual complex, the authority complex, and the universalistic rule complex. The contractual complex, which includes subcomplexes related to relations with providers of human services (employment) providers of fluid funds (investment) and providers of possessions (property), defines the obligations of loyalty that are assumed by providers of these three categories of resources. To insure integration, the parts of the organizational value system regulating these relations must be consonant with those operative in the environment. A particularly important case is that of "professional" personnel who have dual occupational commitments, one to the employing organization and another to the professional group of which they are members.

Similar considerations apply in connection with the authority complex which defines, on a basis broader than that of the particular organization, the ways and extent to which any given actor, individual or collective, can in a given status in the organization bind others by his decisions, and the ways and extent to which his action can be bound by the decisions of others. Both the contractual and authority complexes define in relatively specific ways what is to be expected of the organization and, hence, the conditions under which it will be tolerated or supported by environing systems. "These two institutions define the obligations specific to the role in the particular organization which come into force only so far as the incumbent accepts a relation to the organization."[19]

Finally, the universalistic rule complex defines for the society as a whole, or the transorganizational sectors of it, standards of "good practice." These include rules regulating the use of force, the prohibition of violations of personal freedoms, and fraud. More generally, they set limits on the treatment of human beings and nonhuman resources within which the conduct of the organization must remain. Conformity with social standards of acceptable conduct, as well as with the limits of loyalty specified by the principles of contract and authority, is an essential condition of the smooth functioning of an organization within its environment.

Disposal

For an organization, the primary boundary relation is that of goal attainment. Over this boundary, the organization produces an identifiable output which can be utilized in some way by environing systems. Accordingly, there must be general principles concerning the sorts of goods or services that will be made available, in what quantity and quality, to whom, on what terms. These principles, or rules, are the outcomes of what are ordinarily called policy decisions, an important aspect of which is the integration of, and establishment of priorities among, competing goals. At stake here are questions concerning whether a mental hospital, for example, is to be primarily a therapeutic, custodial, or protective agency, or whether a school is to be primarily an academic or a vocational school.

Procurement

Finally, there will be normative rules governing the adaptive process of the organization, general principles governing the acquisition of facilities, rules which specify the general manner in which financial resources are to be raised, as well as where the primary responsibility resides. In the acquisition of human services, a particularly important category of norm is that providing the basis for remuneration of personnel. Another is that defining the qualifications of personnel. Still another is that setting forth the terms for the continuation or termination of employment.

Because the attainment of an organizational goal is always the performance of a differentiated function for the society, the value system of the organization must be a differentiated, concretely specified version of the societal value system, a differentiation whose direction is determined by the function of the organization for the society. Thus, the values of any organization are a spelling-out of the societal value pattern in the specific context of its principal function. The characteristic features of the organization thus derive from (1) the value pattern of the

society, (2) the goal-directedness of the organization, (3) the nature of the function performed by the organization and, as we shall see (4) the location of the organization in the structural hierarchy.

The American value pattern places primary emphasis on universalistically defined achievement — the rational achievement of ends with minimal specification of what those ends should be. In the absence of goal specification such as would derive from a paramount societal goal, the selection of goals is, within limits, an individual matter; and the primary responsibility is to achieve the goal, whatever the goal may be, in the most rational manner possible. This entails a strong pluralistic emphasis and an indefinite commitment to progress with no particular terminal state in view. Parsons has termed the American pattern "instrumental activism," implying an orientation toward active mastery of the environment in the interest of adaptive capacity, i.e., the capacity to pursue a wide variety of societal and individual goals through the development of generalized resources which are committed in advance to no particular goal.

This is the value base from which all American organizations take their departure. The direction of that departure is determined by the primary function performed by the organization for the society. That is to say,

> . . . organizations may in the first instance be classified in terms of *the type of goal or function* about which they are organized. The same basic classification can be used for goal types which has been used earlier in dealing with the functions of a social system. Thus we may speak of adaptive goals, implementive goals, integrative goals, and pattern-maintenance goals. The reference is always to function in the society as a system.[20]

From this point of view, the principal types of organizations are: (1) organizations oriented to economic production, the type case being the business firm; (2) organizations oriented to political goals, e.g., governmental agencies; (3) organizations oriented to the integration of units in social systems, such as political parties; and (4) organizations oriented to the maintenance and/or creative modification of cultural and motivational components of social systems, e.g., religious and educational organizations.

Economic Organizations

Specified to the level of the business firm the value emphasis becomes the maximization of production at minimum cost — economic rationality. Now if we view the boundary relations of organizations as external functions which have to be solved, then we can see that the solutions to the problem vary according to the function performed by the organization for society. That is, organizations differentiated around the adaptive function for society tend to exhibit different types of solutions to the legitimation, integration, goal-attainment, and adaptation problems than do organizations differentiated around the pattern-maintenance function. The organizational value system stands at top of a normative hierarchy of control, setting the stage for the kinds of solutions most likely in each context.

The societal commitments on which the functioning of the business firm depends may be discussed under four headings (1) cultural, the state of the arts, commonly held technology, intuitive knowledge of market conditions and business experience; (2) social, the organization of the social system in non-economic respects; (3) physical, a given supply of nondepreciating, non-obsolescing physical facilities; and (4) motivational, a set of commitments to productive functions independent of changes in current wage levels. The extent to which these assets are givens, i.e., segregated from the operation price mechanisms or withdrawn from the market, varies from factor to factor and from organization to organization. However, it seems fair to say that the ordinary business firm has relatively few assets that are withdrawn from the market. That is to say, few of a firm's assets are so thoroughly committed to its particular function, or even to the economic function generally, that they cannot be had for a price. Sites, facilities, personnel, and cultural objects, e.g., patents, are highly mobile. It is not uncommon for firms to be liquidated, and for the assets under their control to be placed on the market. The areas in which this tends not to be the case are those to which there is a strong commitment often expressed as a governmental subsidy, as in the case of the family farm.

The boundary relations of the business firm follow relatively directly from the value pattern of economic rationality. In the procurement of resources, the values call for independent self-financing out of the proceeds of sales, remuneration of personnel on a marginal productivity basis, employment contracts that are terminatable at will by both parties (within the limits imposed by higher-order union contracts), and a general emphasis on cost accounting.

In the product disposal relation, goods and services are made available on a full-payment-of-costs basis governed by marginal utility, and the firm must rely on economic inducements and advertising to encourage consumers to become recipients of the organization's output. In other words, the client is free to accept or reject the services and products of the organization, contributes nothing to their production, and does not expect to be consulted in the determination of the nature and price of the product

In the integrative context, economic self-interest is the governing principle. Suppliers of human services, and financial and physical facilities extend loyalty to the firm only within the limits of their own economic self-interest. The employee will not be blamed for quitting for higher wages, and the investor will not be blamed for withdrawing his funds for higher dividends. Organization authority is limited by the right to quit. Finally, formal legitimation tends to take the form of incorporation, licensing, or chartering by a governmental body. Informally, in the case of the particular organization it encompasses a wide area of public relations activities, particularly what is known as "institutional advertising."

In discussing societal commitments it is essential to distinguish between commitment to a societal subsystem, e.g., the economy or polity, on the one hand, and commitment to a particular organization, on the other. At the societal subsystem level, in the American case, the highest level of commitment is accorded to the economic function. However, the level of commitment to any particular organization within the economy is relatively low. Business firms are liquidated and their resources redistributed. In the goal-attainment case the subsystem commitment is considerably less than that of the economy, but the particular organization commitment tends to be greater. Though there are exceptions, particularly in the military, governmental units are liquidated relatively infrequently. City hall is seldom sold and converted to other uses.

Political Organizations

The primacy of the goal-attainment organization's orientation to the attainment of a specific goal, combined with differentiation in the direction of goal-attainment values, yields a primary emphasis on technical effectiveness. That is, the firm and the goal-attainment organization, say, the military organization of the governmental bureau, are similar in the primacy of their orientation to the attainment of a specific goal, but there the similarity stops. For the firm, differentiation from the adaptive sector of the societal value system rules out those goals which can be attained only at the cost of its adaptive capacity, i.e., its solvency. Although financial considerations are never wholly irrelevant, the situation of the goal-attainment organization is very different from that of the firm. Here the emphasis is not on the enhancement of the organization's adaptive capacity through the maximization of production at minimum economic cost but on the enhancement of the goal-attainment capacity through the maximization of production of effective collective action at minimum political cost. Now, all goods and services which might be produced by firms do not have economic value, i.e., utility, or want-satisfying capacity. Hence, utility is a value standard in terms of which the contributions of firms may be evaluated. Utility, of course, is symbolized by monetary price; the higher the utility the higher the monetary value attached to an object. The firm spends money to secure objects of utility, i.e., human, physical, and cultural resources, and then combines them in ways which in successful cases, add utility. In order to succeed the firm must produce goods or services which have greater utility, as measured by monetary value, than the resources combined to create them. That is, the return of money from the sale of products must, in the long run, cover all the costs of operation, including of course interest on investments.

In the goal attainment case, the output is collective action. But, just as not all economic outputs add utility to the factors of production, not all collective actions add value to the factors combined to produce them. The relevant value principle, parallel to utility in the economic case, is effectiveness. It is a standard in terms of which both the contributions of the organization and the resources it utilizes may be evaluated. The goal-attainment organization spends power to secure the resources required to produce action in the interest of collective goal attainment. In the successful case the resources are combined in ways that yield collective action which is more effective, i.e., gets better results, than could have been gotten had they not been combined.

Insofar as the organization adds effectiveness through the combinatorial process, it receives a return of power greater than that expended in securing the resources utilized, hence, its value system may be termed political rationality.[21] This means that the successful goal-attainment organization will produce only those outputs which do not entail expenditures of power for resources greater than the power income they yield. Thus, a governmental agency would not knowingly impose through its decision-making powers, binding obligations necessary to produce collective action which was expected in advance to get no better results in relation to valued ends than independent individual action. To do so would be to incur a loss of power, i.e., a loss of capacity to secure the performance of binding obligations in the interest of collective goals.

In the case of the business firm, the standard of successful utilization of the monetary medium is the maintenance of a positive balance between income and expenditures, i.e., solvency. The parallel standard in organizations having goal-attainment primacy is sovereignty, or success. In these terms, the organization is sovereign insofar as it maintains the authority of its offices and attracts services and support without depending on political subsidy.

Units failing to maintain sovereignty must obtain inputs of power in addition to the "proceeds" of their own operations, or they must forego some of their capacity to command binding political obligations.[22]

The normative standard sovereignty applies in some measure to all collectivities, but it applies with particular force in the case of the collectivity with goal-attainment primacy.

In the light of this discussion it becomes clear that the business firm is in its aspect as a collectivity in our technical sense, the case where the two standards of success and solvency coincide. The firm uses its power income primarily to maintain or increase its productivity and, as a measure of this, its money income. A surplus of power will therefore in general be exchanged for enhancement of its control of economic productivity. For a collectivity specialized in political function the primary criterion of success would be given in its power position, relative that is to other collectivities. Here there is the special problem of the meaning of the term power position. I interpret it as relative to other collectivities in a competitive system, not as a position in an internal hierarchy of power.[23]

The boundary relations of the goal-attainment organization follow directly from the preceding value pattern. Goal-attainment organizations typically earn no income whatever in the usual sense. Financing is dependent on grants by public authority out of funds secured through taxation. Grants may be made on the basis of authoritative allocation or legislative apportionment, or both. In the extreme case of the military organization, emergency conditions call for the procurement of personnel through conscription. Even the volunteer must sign up for a specified term and cannot terminate the relation prior to the expiration of that term. Remuneration of personnel is far removed from marginal productivity and is based primarily on rank with special provision for hazardous duty.

Non-military governmental agencies differ from this pattern in some respects, but exhibit the same general pattern. The goal of the government bureau, e.g., the Bureau of Internal Revenue, is to implement specific public policies, i.e., to secure the performance of binding obligations by taxpayers. Thus, where the goal for a business firm involves the establishment of a relation between the firm and consumers of its product, the goal for the bureau involves the establishment of a relation between the bureau and taxpayers. Here another highly important difference between the two types of organization may be seen. Whereas the customer of the business firm is free to enter or not to enter into a relation with the firm, according to his self-interest, the object of the governmental bureau's goal relation is not. The taxpayer is not free to decline in the way that the customer is. The taxpayer must accept the product of the governmental bureau whether he likes it or not, or suffer the consequences.

In the integrative boundary context, parallel differences can be seen. Here the particular emphasis on sovereignty comes into play in that it is critical that the binding obligations undertaken by the organization be balanced by equally binding inputs of commitments to perform services, either in a status within the organization or for the organization on a contractual basis. Thus in the military organization the "employee" does not have the right to quit at any time, and the concept of "conflict of interest" is prominent in most governmental agencies. The individual must not be in a position to profit financially from his involvement in the making and implementation of public policy. The concepts of "duty" and "service" are heavily emphasized, in some cases entailing personal sacrifices. The businessman, called upon to serve in government, has a duty to serve though it may involve substantial financial sacrifices. The demands of loyalty greatly exceed the limits of economic self-interest, thus justifying in nearly all governmental positions, especially in key posts, elaborate security checks and clearances. In the recruitment of personnel the business firm is concerned about the capacity of potential employees to add utility to the product, hence the concept of marginal productivity. In the goal-attainment case, the organization is concerned about the capacity of potential employees to add effectiveness to the product, i.e., to add to the effectiveness with which the relevant policies are implemented. As the organization is an agency of the societal community, implementing decisions arrived at by collective decision-making organs, loyalty to that community is a crucial ingredient of effectiveness.

Integrative Organizations

In the integrative type of organization, primarily the associative type of collectivity, e.g., the interest group or political party, the value principle parallel to utility in the adaptive case and to effectiveness in the goal-attainment case is solidarity in the sense of ". . . maintaining the complementarity of units making qualitatively differentiated functional contributions to the society as a system."[24]

> Solidarity is a state of "cohesion" of a social system which includes both resistance to centrifugal forces, such as "factionalism," which tend to divide and fragment it, and the promotion of positive coordination among the segmented and differentiated parts.[25]

> A social system then possesses solidarity in proportion as its members are committed to common interests through which discrete unit interests can be integrated

and the justification of conflict resolution and subordination can be defined and implemented.[26]

The category of symbol which serves as a medium of exchange and as a measure of value parallel to money and power is influence. Here, influence is defined as the generalized medium of persuasion, of securing consent to opinions, beliefs, policies, or objectives.

The intrinsic persuaders, or "consent getters," parallel to intrinsic "want satisfiers," or utilities of economic action, are intrinsically convincing information, i.e., "facts" and declarations of firm intentions to act in ways favoring particularistic interests. Influence as a symbolic medium and measure of value, however, must be generalized beyond these intrinsic levels which are analogous to economic and political barter. As a generalized medium, influence depends not on the intrinsic features of the message, the convincingness of the "facts" or the statement of intention, but on the prestige, or reputation, of the source.

> If the declaration of specific intentions, the effect of which is to establish solidarity in some kind of "coalition" with the object of persuasion, as the barter prototype of the exercise of influence, the medium itself operates at a higher level of generality, not the declaration of specific intentions, but rather of support for the more general "objectives" of the object of persuasion. Here the essential point is the establishment of solidarity and a contribution to its operation without specifying just *what* goals or interests are to be actively supported. . . .[27]

The wielder of influence secures consent from the object of influence by supporting the general objective or interest of the latter, which, in turn, is to establish a bond of solidarity between them. Hence, solidarity is a state of consensus, i.e., acceptance on the part of the members of a collectivity of their belonging together in the sense of sharing, over a certain range, common interests, interests which are defined both by type and by considerations of time.[28]

Integrative organizations (and associations) spend influence through persuading holders of resources that the organization will, in future situations, act in ways that are in line with the general objectives of the objects of persuasion. Those resources are then combined, in the successful case, in ways that yield a greater income of influence than that expended for the resources. Thus an interest group may be successful in persuading political decision-makers to support policies advocated by the group, utilizing that input along with others to produce an output (in this case a relation between the association and a functionally differentiated unit) having greater value on a scale of solidarity than the resource utilized to achieve it.

The solidarity value of the outcome is symbolized

by influence, and the successful outcome yields more influence than that expended on its production. Now, the firm engages in transactions over its goal-attainment boundary in which it attempts to secure money payments from consumers in exchange for goods and services. The consumer, of course, always has the option of deciding that the price is too high, either because he can get the same commodity elsewhere for less or because it entails too great a sacrifice in terms of other things he wishes to buy. If for either reason a sufficient number of consumers elect not to buy, then the firm's monetary return is less than the cost of production, and it is threatened with insolvency and possible bankruptcy. Similarly, the integrative organization engages in transactions over its goal-attainment boundary in which it exchanges political support in return for influence in the form of leadership responsibility. The "purchaser" of support must persuade the collectivity that the objectives for which he is willing to assume responsibility correspond to those sought by producing collectivity and that the shift in benefits and burdens implied by the pursuit of those objectives are fair.

In the prototypical case, political party leadership elements, which tend to be candidates for office, must "purchase" votes by establishing among party members, and others as well, the expectation that in future situations the leader will act in ways relatively acceptable to them, not in terms of specified commitments but in terms of general objectives. The standard of success which parallels solvency in economic action is "consensus." That is to say, the political party or interest group is successful in proportion as it mobilizes support without the utilization of power, money, patronage, or other forms of inducement. In order to constitute a contribution to the solidarity of the societal system, members of the group must be persuaded, not coerced or induced, to vote for candidates and policies. In a highly developed system the unit's capacity to make further contributions to solidarity is directly affected by its level of consensus. Thus, just as the firm must evaluate alternative courses of action, both with respect to resource procurement and products to be supplied in terms of their effect on solvency, so must the integrative organization evaluate potential resources and products in terms of their effects on consensus. Among the resources required for the "production" of solidarity are policy decisions secured from the polity and commitments to association from the pattern-maintenance subsystem.

Just as firms pay wages to secure control of labor as a factor of production so, we may suggest, in particularly important contexts holders of value-commitments "pay" [the integrative organization] for the privilege of association with others in the implementation of their commit-ments. This means that they "give" commitments to the association of reference, which become "assets" to that association, both collectively and for its members individually. The association is in a stronger position for the implementation of the value held in common by its members, by virtue of the fact that those who join it have "given" their commitments to it. For the "joiners" then, the commitments have been "spent" in the sense that they have in a degree relinquished control of them. They have come to be bound by obligations of loyalty to the associational collectivity which they have joined.[29]

The critical point in the present context is the possibility that, in securing either commitments to membership, or policy decisions, the association may pay too high a price in terms of its own consensus, thus jeopardizing its capacity to mobilize support. On the one hand, ". . . in unity there is strength in that the assembled commitments of a plurality of associated units have a greater impact than if they were implemented only unitwise with the possibility of fragmentation and dissipation of effect."[30] On the other hand, in plurality there is diversity, in that the more inclusive association must accommodate to a greater range of interests, with the possibility of diminished consensus.

Resource procurement in the integrative case, then, tends to be based neither on the sale of products nor on grants from public authority, but on voluntary contributions. At the goal-attainment boundary, recipients of the output of the organization become in some sense members of the service supplying collectivity, and those services are available to some degree on a no-financial-cost basis to all who are willing to adhere to organizational policies. The formal bureaucratic organization which most nearly approximates this pattern is the hospital. Sociologically, the sick role is a deviant role; and the function of the hospital is to restore the deviant to conformity with role expectations. Financing is typically a mixture of income derived from services, taxation, and voluntary contributions.

Medical treatment is generally regarded as a right of all members of the society, regardless of their ability to pay. Services thus tend to be made available to recipients on terms consonant with their ability to pay. The patient clearly becomes a partial, temporary member of the hospital and is expected to do all he can to speed his own recovery. Although not compulsory in the sense that paying taxes is compulsory, there is a clear and widely accepted obligation on the part of the sick person to seek and accept medical assistance. Whether or not the individual seeks medical treatment is not a matter on which the society at large is indifferent.

In the integrative context the loyalty of both the hospital and the patient extends well beyond economic self-interest. On the one hand, patients are not to shop around for "medical bargains," On the other hand the guiding norm for the physician and the hospital is the welfare of the patient. The authority of the integrative organization in relation to those on whom its functions are performed is very different from that of the goal-attainment organization. In the former neither the recipient of action nor his family have any choice in the matter. In the latter the recipient may have a choice, and even when he is considered incapable of making a choice the family must be consulted. The authority of the hospital is clearly limited also by the right of the patient to leave the hospital at a time of his own choosing, whether or not he has been officially discharged. In such cases, however, the hospital is relieved of responsibility for the patient's health.

Pattern-Maintenance Organizations

The same basic paradigm may be applied to the pattern-maintenance organization, of which the church and the educational organization are appropriate examples. Parsons has suggested that the relative level of commitment to pattern-maintenance functions is, in American society, second only to adaptation. Whatever the case may be on the societal subsystem level, at the level of particular organizations commitments are particularly prominent in the functioning of pattern-maintenance organizations. Churches, for example, have relatively unconditional access to land, physical facilities, and human services. Church property and income is excluded from taxation, it is seldom for sale or even for hire, and monetary remuneration is relatively insignificant as a factor in securing and retaining the services of the clergy.

Running a close second behind the church is the educational organization. The university, for example, has relatively permanent access to sites which are, in economic terms, extremely valuable but which are simply not for sale. Regardless of how well or how poorly the university functions, access to these and other resources is assured. Trustees may be removed from office, administrative appointments may be terminated, and faculty members may be replaced, but the liquidation of a university is almost unthinkable. The procurement and retention of human services is more dependent on monetary factors than in the church, but, other factors being equal, considerably less than in other occupational sectors.

The values of the educational organization are differentiated from those of the society in the direction of pattern maintenance. Pattern maintenance, as the term suggests, refers to the maintenance and creative modification of the pattern of the elements of the system. Because, in Parsons' view, the structure of social systems consists in institutionalized patterns of symbolic culture, the fundamental processes involved here are the maintenance and creative modification of the cultural tradition and the development, maintenance, and modification of motivational commitments to those patterns. The educational organization, e.g., the university, is a socializing agency concerned with the development in students of the commitments and capacities required for future role performance, a research and scholarship center contributing to the modification of the cultural tradition, and far less often and probably only indirectly, an agency of moral leadership. The risks involved in attempts by universities to exercise moral leadership are apparent in the evident withdrawal of support by legislative and alumni bodies in those cases where the university is suspected of being too radical or too permissive. On the other hand, some universities seem to be having some success in extending commitments to include a moral obligation to educate the youth of minority groups, particularly those who could not qualify for admission under standard procedures.

This leads directly into a consideration of the value principle to which pattern-maintenance action is subject. Corresponding to utility in the economic case, effectiveness for the polity, and solidarity in the integrative context is integrity in the pattern-maintenance context. That is, the output of the pattern-maintenance organization is evaluated in terms of its contribution to the maintenance of the integrity of the value pattern of the societal system.

The generalized measure of value and symbol of integrity operating in the context of pattern-maintenance is generalized commitments. Generalized commitment may be defined as the capacity to effect or secure the implementation of values on the basis of credible promises.

> Its messages are essentially assertions of commitment to the relevant value pattern which may take the form of elements implicit in acts pointing toward implementation, such as promises, which we often explicitly call commitments, to undertake certain specified obligations.[31]

In the same way that influence is based on the prestige or reputation of the message source, the capacity to secure implementation of values on the basis of commitments is based on moral authority. Moral authority, in turn, is acquired through a reputation for integrity of commitments. This leads directly to "pattern-consistency," the normative standard regulating the use of commitments parallel to solvency in economic action. In the pattern-maintenance case the concern is consistency of action with commitments. The pattern-maintenance unit which fails to "honor" its commitments runs the risk of exhausting its supply. Failure to "come through" on commitments, on the strength of which other units have made resources available, leads to the impairment of capacity to secure additional resources on the basis of further commitments.

Thus, the pattern-maintenance organization "spends" generalized commitments to secure control of the resources required for its operation. From the point of view of those who supply resources, this is an exchange of value implementation on their part in exchange for generalized commitments from the organization. The implication of the term "generalized" in this context is that the values which the organization commits itself to implement are not specified in detail in advance. The organization is presumed to possess sufficient commitment at generalized levels so that the specific values implemented will be consistent with the relevant value pattern. This freedom of the unit to make its own judgments about the legitimacy of the more detailed implementive action is a crucial dimension of the generalization of value commitments in the social system, and the basis of "moral leadership."

Units operating in the context of commitments tend, on the one hand, to function as guardians of the integrity of the value pattern, but they may, on the other hand, utilize the commitments at their disposal to engage in innovative extension of commitments and implementation in the same way that political leaders utilize the grant of power deposited with them through the electoral process to undertake lines of collective action for which there has been no prior authorization. Just as political leadership can make a net addition to the amount of power in circulation and, correspondingly, to collective effectiveness, moral leadership can make a net addition to the generalized commitments and to the integrity of the value pattern. Similarly, funds on deposit in banks provide the basis, through investment, for economic innovators to reorganize the production system in ways that yield an increase in total productivity.

In all three cases, innovative extension, to be successful, must yield a net increase in the level of value implementation, i.e., utility, effectiveness, or integrity. Failing in this, the extension is inflationary.

In the context of pattern-maintenance action, then, pattern consistency requires that action of the unit be consistent with the implicit and explicit commitments of the unit. Failure to "honor" such commitments, either in routine or innovative contexts, calls into question the integrity of the unit's commitments with the consequence that trust in its future commitments, as well as those already in force, is lessened.

Thus, the organization "spends" generalized commitments to secure control of the resources required for its operation, it produces value-implementive action and, insofar as the value implementation produced contributes to the integrity of the system, receives a return of generalized commitments. The key criterion of success in this case is "pattern-consistency." In the economic case solvency requires the selection of resources on the basis of their contribution to the utility of the product; in the case of human services, their productivity. In the pattern-maintenance case, the problem is one of selecting resources on the basis of their contribution to the value of the product on a scale of integrity. In the case of human services, it is a question of the extent to which their actions can be expected to contribute to value-implementive action consistent with the values of the larger system. Hence, in the United States, one does not employ an avowed communist to teach, even in a university, without raising questions about the organization's integrity of commitment.

As in the case of other types of organizations, the principal boundary relations of the educational organization follow from its value pattern and goals. In the procurement of resources, the value pattern of the university, for example, calls for the payment of the cost of operations partly through tuition fees, partly through voluntary contributions and increasingly through taxation. Financing higher education on a basis of full payment of cost of services would mean that only the wealthy minority could attend, a condition clearly incompatible with the value pattern. The high valuation of achievement leads logically to a similarly high valuation of the conditions and factors on which it is contingent—health, education, freedom, and opportunity. Limiting access to a small privileged class would obviously deny opportunities for high-level achievements and the rewards associated with them to the vast majority of persons. Moreover, "pay its own way" financing tends to emphasize the short-run utility of services at the expense of long-run benefits and services whose principal value is on a scale of utility.

Although these components are far from trivial, the primary contributions of the university—socialization in the higher levels of and the creative modification of the cultural system—are not direct contributions to utility. That is to say, they are contributions first to the maintenance and enhancement of the integrity of the system value pattern and secondarily to the utility of available resources. A university required to pay its own way out of proceeds of "sales," and to serve more than a wealthy elite, would, in all probability, be forced to abandon all socialization and culture modification (research and scholarship) goals other than those having short-run utility, thus becoming a high-level trade school and applied research center. Such an outcome, in turn, if not compensated for by the emergence of functional equivalents, would constitute the loss of contributions essential to the maintenance and enhancement of the value pattern.

Personnel remuneration does not reflect contribution to production, i.e., payment on the basis of what services are worth in marginal productivity terms, as in the business firm. It is calculated on the basis of a concept of "just price" and supplemented with the security provided by tenure. The employee renounces the possible financial advantages of a business career, and an element of self-sacrifice is expected.

In the product-disposal relation, services tend to be made available on a partial payment basis, heavily supplemented by scholarships. The primary criterion of admission to the university has tended to be demonstrated preparedness to benefit from advanced education. Although monetary considerations weigh heavily in the majority of admissions at particular universities, scholarships, loans, and other provisions enable most of those who have the desire and a reasonable degree of preparation to secure admission to some university or college, albeit not necessarily the one of their choice. The most recent development in this area is the increasing tendency to admit at least some persons on the basis of "capacity to benefit" from higher education whether "prepared" or not. Despite these and other marginal modifications, it seems fair to say that the primary criterion is completion of earlier stages of education with a level of achievement sufficiently high to make success likely. Discontinuation of the relation with, or membership in, the university is wholly voluntary (excluding parental interference). The student may withdraw at any time. Continuation of the relation, however, is contingent on meeting minimum university requirements. The university retains the right to terminate the relation under certain conditions, the most prominent of which is "failure" on the part of the student to do his part in bringing about his education. Education requires that the student play an active contributory role in the process and the university tends not to be held responsible in those cases in which the student "fails" to cooperate actively.

The preceding discussion highlights another aspect of the university-recipient relation — one, incidentally, from which there are increasingly frequent deviations. The pattern has been one in which the right to determine what kinds of educational services be made available to whom, in what quantity and quality, and on what terms, rested primarily in the hands of the university faculty, subject to review by higher-level agencies. Certainly one of the most prominent aspects of current campus activity is the widespread, vocal, and increasingly successful demand on the part of students that they have either an opportunity to exercise influence in relation to decision makers or the right to participate in the decision-making process.

Unlike the commercial case in which disposal is often a quick "selling" transaction and unlike the disposal relation between a governmental agency with a mandate to secure compliance with authoritative decisions, the disposal relation in education necessarily entails a long, continuing association between the client and a succession of teachers. The student is formally admitted to the university and becomes a member of it. In the broad "socialization" sense of the term, one does not "buy" education any more than one "buys" religion. Instruction leading to the acquisition of knowledge and skill can be obtained commercially, as witness secretarial, electronic, and various technical schools. Doubtless even reading, writing, and arithmetic skills can be provided commercially, but the development of motivational commitments to both broad societal values and role performance and the development of capacities to behave responsibly require the establishment of a bond of solidarity between recipient and supplier that is incompatible with the fully commercialized relationship.

In the integrative context the case of the university is similar to that of other organizations in which operative personnel are highly trained specialists. This has implications for the limits of loyalty of personnel to the organization and for the patterns of authority under which the organization operates. Thus, the sphere of autonomy of the university faculty members tends to be far greater than that of comparably qualified personnel in other types of organizations. The authority of administrative personnel is further limited by the institutions of tenure and academic freedom and, of course, by the right of employees to terminate the contract of employment at will. Although economic rationality is not the primary integrative principle, no stigma is attached to accepting higher salaried positions. At the same time

> . . . a readiness to consider offers of new appointments in other universities need not be a function *only* of seeking personal advantage, such as higher salary, but may involve better *opportunity* to implement one's academic value commitments. To put loyalty to one's current university too highly above readiness to utilize such opportunities might imply relative weakness in commitment to the relevant values.[32]

Finally, the legitimation boundary is a particularly

crucial one for the pattern-maintenance organization. The university, for example, does not itself engage in economic production; it does not contribute directly, except in the context of its own goals, to the effectiveness of collective action; it does not contribute directly to the integration of the interests of its members relative to particular foci of concern. As it does not pay its own way, is not vital for short-run collective effectiveness, and does not appeal to particular interests, it must rely more heavily than other types of organizations on the legitimation of its goals by demonstrating their congruence with higher-order values. Put another way, the set of societal commitments on which the functioning of the university depends is far heavier in relation to its total resource needs than is the case for most other organizations. Possible exceptions are religious organizations and public schools. Heavy reliance on commitments which are contingent on legitimation rather than on short-run sanctions is, in the main, a source of organizational stability. The insulation of resource supply from short-run sanctions means that the university tends to be one of the last organizations to benefit in times of prosperity and one of the last to suffer in times of recession. The contingent relation between legitimation and commitments may, however, be a source of instability. The university's role in the creative modification of the cultural tradition, as well as the activities of both faculty and students, provide relatively frequent opportunities for members of the larger community to question the legitimation of university goals. Students themselves, along with off-campus associates, raise this issue in questions concerning the legitimacy of defense-related research. A more prominent example is the apparently widespread public reaction to the activities of "radical" students and faculty members.

To summarize and conclude this section we may note that a more complete classification of organizations would use this initial categorization as a point of departure for further differentiation. That is, within the category of economically oriented organizations, subsequent classification would be based on the function performed for the economy. Within the economy one would differentiate organizations oriented to the adaptive implementive, integrative, and pattern-maintenance goals of the economy. In the preceding discussion we considered only the four primary organizations.

Although our discussion falls far short of an adequate characterization of the range of variation among organization types, perhaps enough has been said to support the contention that the boundary relations of organizations are modified sharply and relatively systematically as a consequence of the functional content of the organization. Or, to put the matter another way, the theoretically based taxonomy of organization just outlined has the merit of ordering the entities classified in such a way that they fall into groups, or families, exhibiting similar characteristics. In this respect, it serves in the same manner as does the periodic table in chemistry or the taxonomy of life in biology. Figure 33-3 summarizes the main points we have outlined.

LEVELS OF ORGANIZATION OF SOCIAL STRUCTURES

In the preceding sections we considered in some detail two aspects of Parsons' theory which contribute to the integration of the field of organizational studies, on the one hand, and the study of society, on the other. The first was the view of the organization as the structural component of the social system differentiated from other structural components with reference to the collective pursuit of collective goals or, more broadly, the political function. The second was the view of organizations as linked to their intrasocietal environments through boundary relations, variations in which are organizable under the view of organizations as being located in one of four primary functional subsystems of the societal system. The picture that emerges in both of these cases is one which might be likened to a laterally diferentiated plane surface—a terrain with horizontal variation but with no dimension of elevation. Collectivities were seen to be differentiated from values, norms, and roles in terms of their location in a two-dimensional functional space. Moreover, collectivities were seen to be differentiated from one another in terms of their location in the same two-dimensional functional space.

Clearly, something is missing in this picture, and it is precisely that missing element that we wish to consider in this section. We may begin by noting that no complex, open system, certainly no action system, is structured only on a "flat" basis. Life processes, whether we consider relations between such structures and processes as physiological, psychological, or social or relations between structures and processes within any one of those broad areas, we find hierarchies of levels of organization and control. Given the proposition that the structure of social systems consists in institutionalized patterns of normative culture, it follows that the structural components of social systems must constitute such a hierarchy. This, of course, is a central feature of the theory of action.

In Parsons' terms:

> . . . the structural analysis of complex social systems

requires discrimination not only of functional "types" of structure, but also of *levels* of organization.[33]

Parsons proposes:

> . . . a scheme of four levels of structural organization which need to be carefully and systematically distinguished from one another and yet related to one another for purposes of structural analysis. These I call the "primary" or "technical" level of organization, the "managerial" level, the "institutional" level, and the "societal" level.[34]

As a matter of making our analytical procedure explicit, it may be pointed out that this is the third application of the four functional problem schema. The first application identified values, norms, collectivities, and roles respectively as the L, I, G, and A components of social structure. The second identified pattern maintenance, societal community, polity, and economy respectively as the L, I, G, and A functional subsystems of the societal system within which collectivities could be classified. The third application identifies the societal, institutional managerial, and technical levels respectively as the L, I, G, and A levels of societal organization.

It is important to keep in mind here that the components of social structure are roles, collectivities, norms, and values, i.e., institutionalized patterns of normative culture. The assertion that the analysis of complex social systems requires discrimination not only of functional types but also of levels of structure means that roles, collectivities, norms, and values tend to become differentiated not only along functional lines but also along hierarchical lines.

There are four main respects in which the levels constitute a hierarchy: (1) the generality of the normative patterns governing levels increases at each level. At the lowest levels the patterns apply to special categories of units while at the highest they apply to the entire society. (2) Decisions made at each successive level bind larger and larger sectors of the society. Decisions made within a family are binding on relatively few persons while those made by the top management of a business firm are binding on many. (3) The facilities utilized become increasingly general at each level in the hierarchy. Lower levels tend to utilize facilities specifically adapted to their uses but not widely transferable, e.g., physical objects. Higher levels utilize facilities which command a greater range of materials, as in the example of money. At still higher levels, the monetary system itself is subject to control and regulation. (4) The extensiveness of the range of solidarity increases at each level. The range of solidarity in a family unit is relatively restricted, while in occupational organizations, communities, and the national community it is progressively greater.

We may, then, think of a technical or primary level of system organization at which interacting units constitute a social system confronted on its own level by the four system problems.

A "technical" or "primary" social system typically is a unit in a differentiated system and as such produces an output of significance to other units and to the society as a whole. It is also, of course, itself the recipient of inputs from other primary subsystems. This is true at other levels of organizations, but it is essential to differentiate

	L — Primacy	I — Primacy	G — Primacy	A — Primacy
			— Primacy —	
Example	University	Political party	Governmental body	Business firm
Function	Maintenance of the pattern of the system	System integration	Attainment of collective goals	Creation of generalized resources
Value principle	Integrity	Solidarity	Effectiveness	Utility
Symbolic medium and measure of value	Generalized commitments	Influence	Power	Money
Standard of successful use of media	Pattern consistency	Consensus	Success or sovereignty	Solvency
Goal output	Maintenance or creative modification of motivational or cultural components	Integration of units in social systems	Implementation of authoritative decisions	Commodities

Figure 33-3. Functional types of organization.

the input and output categories which are relevant at the different levels. I may distinguish four categories of primary level output as follows: (1) physical production in the economic sense, i.e., of commodities; (2) administrative implementation of authoritative decisions; (3) integration of units in social systems; and (4) maintenance of creative modification of motivational or cultural components of the social system (properties of units).[35]

These four primary-level outputs clearly correspond to the four functionally differentiated subsystems discussed elsewhere in this volume. Physical production, decision implementation, unit integration, and maintenance and modification of motivational and cultural components respectively are the technical level outputs of the adaptive, goal-attainment, integrative, and pattern-maintenance subsystems.

In each of the four functionally differentiated subsystems of the societal system—the adaptive, goal-attainment, integrative, and pattern-maintenance—there are technical functions to be performed. In the pattern-maintenance case, a variety of units produce a variety of specific outputs, all of which fit the category of maintenance or creative modification of motivational or cultural components of the social system. Thus the output of the family, the school classroom, the university department, and the parish church are comparable in the same sense that automobiles, furniture clothing, and food are commodities.

To return to the technical, or primary, level of social organization.

> The crucial point in the involvement of individuals with one another in cooperative activities which involve physical presence, at least part of the time, and direct cooperation in physical manipulations of the environment, whether the manipulation be primarily "technological" or "symbolic" or communicative. It is through such processes that physical production is carried out, however ramified the relations of the subsystems involved may be. The care and feeding of children (and of husbands) belongs in the same basic category, as does presence around the same committee table.[36]

The primary set of problems to which the technical-level social system is concerned is that imposed by the nature of the technical task — the objects, material, human, or cultural, which must be processed. But technical subsystems cannot subsist independently in a differentiated society. Where resources are sufficiently mobile and are not immediately and automatically available, technical levels of organization face a set of problems concerning the management and regulation of input and output exchanges which become the foci for the managerial level of societal organization.

In simple cases, the solution of these problems need not lead to the emergence of distinct roles or collectivities, but with increasing mobility of resources there is a strong tendency to develop more or less fully differentiated roles and collectivities which specialize in (1) the mediation of relations to the recipients of the output of the technical level, (2) the procurement of facilities necessary for performing the function, and (3) the control or supervision of technical-level operations. The central aspect of the mediation of relations with recipients of the output is decisions concerning what and how much to produce, in what quality, for whom, and on what terms, financial or otherwise. Together, these constitute the disposal function. The procurement function, deals with the financial, material, and personnel resources necessary for implementing technical functions.

> . . . in a school system teachers have to be especially appointed and allocated to teach particular classes. Moreover, classrooms have to be provided. The teacher does not automatically control adequate facilities for performing the function. Furthermore . . . what should be taught in what schools to what children is by no means automatically given. In a complex division of labor, both the resources necessary for performing technical functions and the relations to the population elements on whose behalf the functions are performed have become problematical. Resources are made available by special arrangements; they are not simply "given" in the nature of the context of the function. And who shall be the beneficiary of what "product" or "service" on what terms is problematical.[37]

Technical levels of organization, then, come to be controlled and serviced by differentiated role and collectivity structures whose functions are qualitatively different from those of the technical level and whose external responsibilities concern the relation between the organization and the system of market relations in the dual context of procurement and disposal. In terms of the relevant functional subsystem as a whole, market mechanisms and decisions are ways in which managerial agencies control technical processes through specification of goals, through provision of the requisite facilities, and through more or less direct supervision.

Performance of these external functions may be conceived as the management of the organization's adaptive and goal-attainment boundary relations. The organization is conceived as oriented to the attainment of a specific goal which is, from the point of view of the larger system of which it is a functionally differentiated part, a specialized or differentiated function, or contribution. Thus, in the attainment of the goal, the organization "produces" an identifiable something, an output, which is, for some other system, an input, a contribution to its functioning. The four broad categories of technical-level output have been outlined. In each of these cases there is a set of consequences of the processes which go on within the organization which "make a difference" to the functioning of some other subsystem of the society.

The availability of the organization's output to the recipient unit must be subject to some sort of terms of exchange.

> Thus in the familiar case the economic producer "sells" his product for a money price which in turn serves as a médium for procuring the factors of production, most directly labor services, necessary for further stages of the productive processes. It is thus assumed in the case of all organizations there is something analogous to a "market" for the output which constitutes the attainment of its goal (what Chester I. Barnard calls "organization purpose); and that directly, and perhaps also indirectly, there is some kind of exchange of this for entities which (as inputs to it) are important means for the organization to carry out its function in the larger system. The exchange of output for input at the boundary defined by the attainment of the goal of an organization need not be the only important boundary exchange of the organization as a system. It is, however, the one most directly involved in defining the primary characteristics of the organization.[38]

The relations between the technical and managerial levels of organization have been characterized above as relatively continuous in that complex technical functions are performed by suborganizations controlled and serviced by higher-order organizations. Although this is correct as far as it goes, it does not go far enough. To a considerable extent, decisions made at the managerial level do control the operations of the technical level. The technical level of the business firm does not just produce goods apart from questions of whether there is a demand for the goods, on what terms they will be made available, who will do the work, and where the materials will come from. Questions of this sort must obviously take precedence over technical, operational questions. But, given the definition of the broad technical task to be performed, the scale of operations, and policies concerning employment and purchasing, a break in the continuity of the relation occurs.

> This is essentially because the people "lower down" typically must exercise types of competence and shoulder responsibilities which cannot be regarded as simply "delegated" by their "superiors." This again is because the *functions* at each level are qualitatively different, those at the second level are not simply "lower-order" spelling-out of the "top" level functions.[39]

As in any case of functional differentiation, this means that managerial-level personnel are typically only partially competent to plan and supervise the execution of technical operations. Hence, they must recognize an independent technical basis for lower-level personnel to perform their functions in ways

which, in their own technical judgment, seems desirable. Particularly at high levels of technical competence, technical-level personnel can be held accountable for the results of their decisions but not "dictated" to with respect to the technical procedures by which they get their results.

Thus, between these two levels there is a break which is partly qualitative. Managerial functions are not simply higher-order technical functions but qualitatively different in the sense that they deal with different categories of inputs and outputs and hence require different kinds of competence. Technical personnel are seldom, if ever, the equals of managerial personnel in terms of competence in performing market and allocative functions, i.e., in assuming managerial responsibility.

The question which now arises is, what is the nature of the managerial output and input interchange which sets it apart from the technical level. The technical-level input-output interchange in the case of the organization with economic primacy involves an exchange of goods and/or services for money payments. In the case of the hospital it involves an exchange of medical services for cooperative effort toward recovery and, in most cases partial payment of costs. Similarly, in the goal attainment sector there is an exchange of implementation of authoritative decisions for necessary cooperation or compliance. The qualitatively different output of the managerial level which makes it more than simply a facilitator of technical processes is, in each case, a contribution to the generalized capacity of the society to perform the relevant category of function effectively. Put another way, it is a contribution to the society's level of effectiveness in achieving the relevant type of goal. Through organizing technical processes and adapting them to conditions in the community in the sense of deciding what kind, quality, and quantity, of products to make available, the managerial system creates a generalized disposable capacity which increases the level of community or societal effectiveness in the relevant functional area. In the economic case this takes the form of an output of wage payments which increases the generally disposable purchasing power of the community. This constitutes a genuine generalization of facilities, a contribution to the community's level of economic effectiveness, produced as a consequence of decisions of the kind outlined. These decisions are the result of ideas and plans on the part of the managerial level and of the consumer "demand" in the community for the relevant output.

The corresponding input from the community is support for the function of the organization, in the economic case, a share of the performance capacity of the community, i.e., labor power. In the goal-attainment context, the lower-level exchange is, as noted, implementation of authoritative decisions for compliance motivated by interest demands. At the managerial level "assumption of leadership responsibility" as a contribution to the general level of political effectiveness is exchanged for generalized political support, generalized in the sense that it is not tied to specific issues. In the integrative subsystem, which is the source of political support, the managerial contribution to the level of integrative effectiveness is precisely the generalized support just identified.

The input-output interchanges previously discussed relate both the technical and the managerial levels to the corresponding levels of organization external to the organization of reference, i.e., technical levels exchange with technical levels, and managerial levels exchange with managerial levels.

But those "lateral" external relations do not exhaust the "external" problem foci of a managerial system. The organization which consists of both technical and managerial suborganizations never operates subject only to the exigencies of disposal and procurement from other agencies (which stand on an approximately equal level) as "customers" or as sources of supply. There is always a superior agency with which the organization articulates.[40]

Essentially, this means that just as a technical organization (at a sufficiently high level of the division of labor) is controlled and "serviced" by a managerial organization, so, in turn, is the managerial organization controlled by the "institutional" structure and agencies of the community."[41]

These institutional structures and agencies take a variety of forms. In the simplest cases they do not involve distinct agencies at either the role or collectivity level at all; e.g., in the "ideal" case of a "free enterprise" economy such processes take place without any direct decision making at levels of organization higher than the managerial. In such instances the managerial system, and through it the technical system, is subject to formally codified legal statutes and informally accepted standards of good practice which are invoked only when deviance is suspected. In other instances a formally organized agency, e.g., a board of trustees or directors supervises the managerial organization on a continuous basis. Such boards constitute what may be termed the institutional level of organization of society.

Fiduciary boards in turn have certain supervisory responsibilities and prerogatives over the managerial organizations they control. What they give to such organizations may be said to consist mainly in what may be called "legitimation" and a certain kind of "support." The essential point is that the position of a managerial organization in the community is problematical, the more so the larger it is and the more it has become differentiated from ascriptive solidarities such as those of kinship. The role of the fiduciary board in this context is not so much to tell the executives what to do—that is, to exercise "line authority" over them—as to define broad limits of what they may *legitimately* do and give them relatively broad community support in doing it.[42]

It is for this reason, above all, that such boards are generally made up only partly of "professionals" in the field of operation.

In relation to the managerial level, then, the institutional level serves as a higher-level supervisory and control agency and as a source of legitimation and support which management cannot secure through its relations with recipients of the organization's product. It is also clear that where financial resources must be raised in order to finance the organization's operation, that responsibility generally either rests at the institutional level or, in the case of tax-supported functions, at higher levels in the organization of society.

At this point an important reminder may be appropriate. The functions and levels of organization are analytically independent and distinct. Concretely they may overlap to a considerable degree. For example, the highest-level executive in a managerial system usually has a key role in money-raising activities. The money-raising function, however, is an institutional function. Here the executive participates in two adjoining systems and hence may be said to occupy an interstitial role.

As in the case of the managerial level, an institutional level has not only vertical relations with the level below it, for which it takes some supervisory responsibility, but also lateral relations with the community and vertical relations with levels above it. In the lateral context the primary functions of the institutional level center around the integration of the higher-order system within which the function at the managerial level is placed.

Its role is to mediate between the claims of this function on community resources and legitimation, and the exigencies of effective performance of the function on the "lower" levels.[43]

The fiduciary board is the focus of the "political" problem of determining the community's commitments to the relevant function, in relation to other competing demands on its total resources. The questions involved are "What is the value of the function which the organization subserves?" "What is the position of the organization's function in the community and society?"

A striking example is the business corporation's policy on what proportion of income will be distributed in dividends and what proportion will be "ploughed back" into the company. This is a decision between two alternative uses of functional resources, consumption or economic investment.[44]

Similarly, with respect to education or health, decisions have to be made about the place of these functions in the community as a whole and the cost, in the sense of withdrawing mobile resources from other functions, of maintaining them at a given level. Financial resources play a prominent part in all these allocative decisions but by no means stand alone. Expression of positive valuation, organizational authorization, and support on other essential factors.[45]

The financial aspect (the procurement function) of institutional level operation has been mentioned. This is a prominent problem — the more so, the greater the departure from the economic case in which operations are financed out of the proceeds of sales. Other crucial inputs are power and performance capacities.

> The board must have the primary concern for the position of the *category* of organization for which it is responsible within the power system of the community as a whole.[46]

> The essential point is the "subsumption" of the organization's goals under the more generalized goal structure of the still higher level social structure and therefore the explicit or implicit "authorization" to embark on the organizational activities in question and to "take them seriously" to the degree to which that is done. A very important aspect of what is sometimes called the struggle for power in a society consists in this competition for support and authorization among the many different organized interests of the society.[47]

It is important to note that the fiduciary board is only one type of organization at this level.

> . . . it is the type which is most directly concerned with supervisory and supportive functions with respect to a specific managerial-technical complex. But there is a whole range of others with a fiduciary primacy. In the financial field, for example, a good deal of banking and insurance falls into this category, as do school boards and voluntary associations which promote various "good causes." Vis-à-vis the societal level, these often take on the character of "pressure groups," but it is important to look at them in terms of the nature of the "interests" they represent.[48]

> The Catholic church is an interest group par excellence, as is the National Association of Manufacturers. The point is that there is a problem of allocating power to *all* significant organized units in the society. The assertion and mediation of the claims of this interest necessarily focus at what I have called the institutional level.[49]

The relations discussed here relate to the resource mobilization and support system referred to in the first major section of this paper. On the one hand, banks and insurance companies, through their capacities as lending agencies, are in this sense elements of the polity which export power in the form of "opportunity for effectiveness" and get in return power in

the form of "commitment of services." The power aspect of a loan is a grant of opportunity through which the recipient can make an otherwise unavailable increment to the relevant category of productivity. On the other hand, school boards, and boards of directors, in their capacity as elements of the polity, export power in the form of policy decisions in return for political support from constituencies, among which are interest groups which serve as support mobilizers. From this point of view, one of the principal differences among functionally differentiated types of organizations is what they do with their incomes of power. The business firm, for example, uses its power income primarily to maintain or increase its productivity.

> The organization, through its executive officers, "spends" power in making commitments for the utilization of the resources it controls, the implementation of which is to be carried out by employed persons. From the point of view of these persons, however, this arrangement constitutes a receipt of power. They receive "authorization" to operate within the organization effectively in making their contribution to its functioning. The input of power, which to some extent balances this output, is derived from the commitments of employed personnel to performance of services within the framework of roles in the organization.[50]

The expenditure of power may thus increase productivity, hence monetary income, and hence, through money, control of an increased share of economic productivity. The interest group, on the other hand, spends its power to increase its capacity to influence public policy decisions.

What has been said about power can be extended to performance capacity, or labor power. This too is a generalized resource which must be allocated among different functions in the society. Fiduciary boards and organizations must be concerned with the extent to which their specific organization, as well as the general type, has access to the quality and quantity of performance capacity which is essential to the proper performance of functions. Discrepancies between salary levels in a given functional context and competing contexts may be a serious threat to the given area's and specific organization's access to essential performance capacities.

Finally, the institutional level, as well as the technical and managerial levels, has connections upward with a higher level of organization, the societal. Government at the national level is the most conspicuous aspect of organization at this level. The relations between the institutional and societal levels fall primarily in the area of legitimation and support. The context in which these relations are most conspicuous is where the function in question is held to be a public or political responsibility and the organization responsible is made an integral part of the governmental structure itself. Here, both responsibility and legitimation is sharply focussed from local to national levels of government.

So long as the responsibility is accepted as a *public* responsibility, there is an obligation on government to "do justice" to the exigencies of discharging it effectively. From this case, there is a shading off to the ideal type of laissez faire sectors of economic organization, where public responsibility is confined to protecting the freedom to produce for the market and reap the rewards, setting up the necessary regulatory system of legal rules, etc.[51]

In addition to having certain regulatory and supportive functions in relation to all the lower levels of organization, national government is also the prime agency in dealing with the situation external to the society, particularly in relation to comparable national units.

A reasonable conclusion to be drawn from the second section of this paper is that the only significant variations among organizations are between functionally differentiated types. Or, to put it negatively, there are no significant within-functional-type variations. Given the fact that, within the action frame of reference, the structure of social systems consists in patterns of institutionalized normative culture, this means that there are no within-type variations in values, norms, collectivities, or roles.

As the immediately preceding discussion has shown, there are sound theoretical and empirical grounds for rejecting that conclusion. Figure 33-4 summarizes the discussion in schematic form. Collectivities are differentiated not only by function but also by level in the hierarchical structure of society. The same may be said of values, norms and roles. Thus, we may discriminate among technical, managerial, institutional, and societal roles, collectivities, norms, and values, relevant to adaptation, goal-attainment, integration, and pattern maintenance. Our primary concern however, is collectivities. Hence Figure 33-5 defines sixteen categories of collectivities—technical, managerial, institutional, and societal—within each of four areas of functional primacy—adaptation, goal-attainment, integration, and pattern maintenance. Each level within each functional area may involve a collectivity, a system with its own boundary relations and internal structure and processes, qualitatively different from, yet systematically articulated with both adjacent levels in the hierarchy and cognate levels in environing hierarchies. Each is subject, on its own level, to the four system problems and engages in an interchange of inputs and outputs across breaks between levels within the hierarchy and across lateral boundaries.

From this point of view, the discussion in the second section dealt indiscriminately with multiple levels, obscuring thereby within-type differences. Although

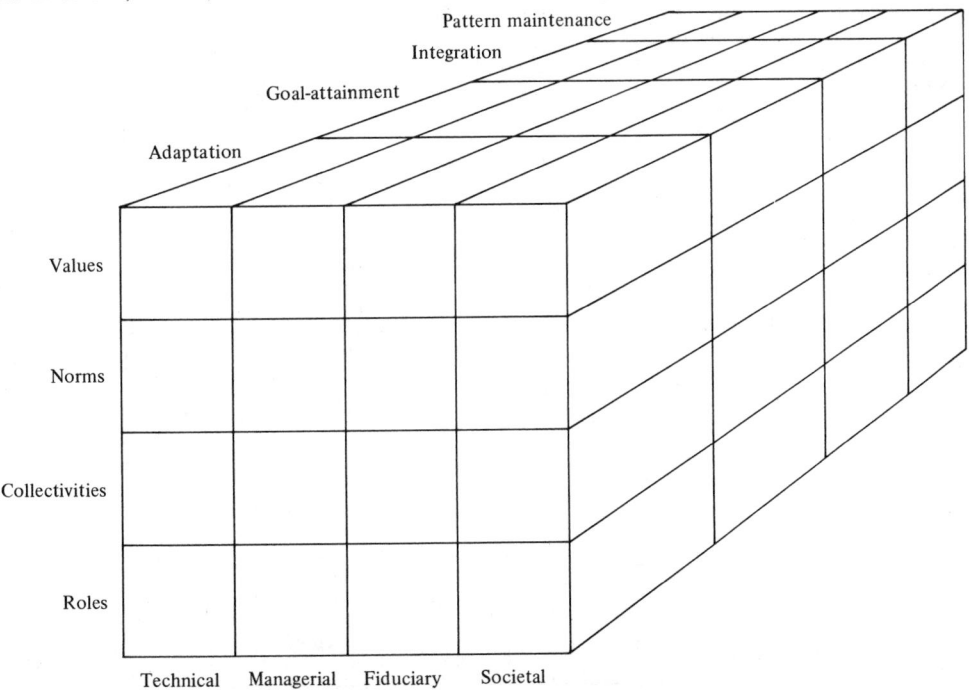

Figure 33-4. Categories of social structure.

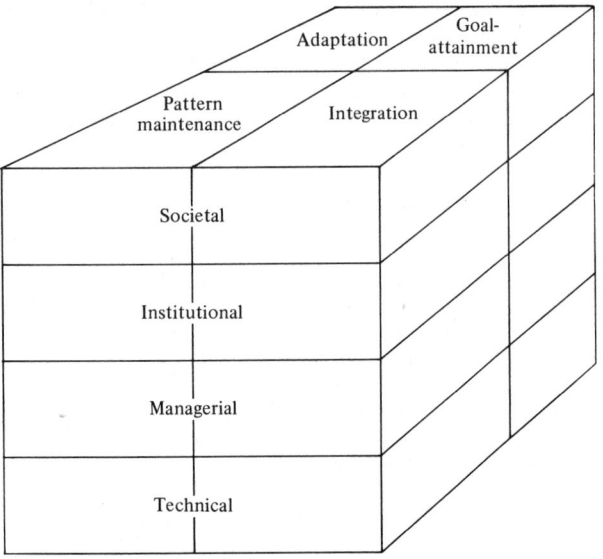

Figure 33-5. Categories of collectivities.

space does not permit a thorough discussion, we may note several prominent cases. Within the economic category, for example, remuneration of personnel on a basis approximating marginal productivity applies only at the technical level. Executive or managerial remuneration is based on responsibility; of course, personnel at the institutional level seldom receive more than token payments, if that. In the goal-attainment or disposal context, the exchange of commodities for money payments is a transaction

between technical levels, mediated of course by the managerial level. This discussion of differences between levels in procurement patterns can, incidentally, be related to the category of norms in Figure 33-3. Speaking directly to Figure 33-5 now, it is clear that distinct collectivity structures can be identified at each level in each functional area, as in Figure 33-6. Space and time permitting, we could codify a considerable amount of information concerning differences in the relations between levels in each functional area, and differences between the lateral relations of given levels in the several functional areas. A brief beginning in this direction was made in preceding pages, but much remains to be said. For example, in integrative and pattern-maintenance areas, such as education and health services, a prior relationship to the recipient of services must be established before technical operations can be undertaken. Teaching presupposes students in the school, and surgery or therapy presupposes patients in the hospital. In such cases the recipient of services must become at least a temporary member, in some cases a long-standing member, of the service-providing organization; and securing his active cooperation is commonly a condition of successful performance of technical functions. Here the necessity of establishing a prior relation with and securing cooperation from recipients of services modifies the relation between technical and managerial personnel in the direction of strengthening the former's position vis-à-vis the latter. Technical personnel are in a position to insist on the conditions they think essential to secure the cooperation required to do their job

Hierarchical Level		Functional Type			
		Pattern maintenance	Integration	Goal-attainment	Adaptation
	Societal	Office of Education	Dept. of Health	Dept. of Urban Affairs, National administration	Dept. of Commerce
	Institutional	Board of Trustees, Assn. of Univ. Professors	Board of Directors, Medical Assn.	City Council, Taxpayers Assn., Political party	Board of Directors, A.M.A.
	Managerial	Administration	Administration	Bureau, Administration	firm
	Technical	University faculty	Hospital staff	Municipal Bureau, Bureau of Internal Revenue	plant

Figure 33-6. Categories of collectivities by functional type and hierarchical level.

adequately. Hence the degree of control exerted by managerial personnel over technical process tends to be less in these areas than in others.

Some attention was given in the preceding discussion to differences between levels and across functional areas in inputs and outputs. This could be extended across the board. On completion of this codification task, one would have filled in the cells of the 64 cells of Figure 33-4. A more important consideration for present purposes at least, is the clarification of an element of distortion in Figure 33-5. This figure serves well enough as a taxonomy of organizations by type and level, but it does not serve at all well as a representation of the linkage between levels. The implication of Figure 33-5 is that a "full-blown" technical system, i.e., one characterized by A, G, I, and L subsystems, has superimposed on it a managerial system with similar characteristics, followed in turn by institutional and societal systems. A more adequate representation of the linkage between levels is provided by Figure 33-7.

The general principle is one of articulated layers of L-I (pattern maintenance-integration) and A-G (adaptation-goal attainment) pairs in a series to form a continuous hierarchy. The A and G components of a managerial system articulate with the L and I components of a technical system to form the system which we ordinarily term the organization. The absence of horizontal arrows to and from the technical level reflects the "fact" that its relation to the environment is mediated through the managerial system. The identification of the institutional level with the L-I pair above the managerial reflects the integrative-legitimation emphases of that level. It also reflects the fact that the adaptive and goal-attainment adjustments relevant to the maintenance of the institutional level are made at the managerial level. That is to say, the managerial level serves as the adaptive and goal-attainment component for two systems, the technical and the institutional.

CONCLUSION

This essay has been designed to demonstrate the possibility of bringing the study of organizations more closely into relation with the study of the structure and functions of society. The attack has been couched entirely in terms of the theory of action as the writer interprets that body of thought; and the basic approach has been to begin with a systematically articulated conception of society as a social system which includes the organization as a structural element. Three aspects of the theory of action were singled out for examination in terms of their relevance to the study of organizations. First the organization was viewed as the structural component of the societal system differentiated with reference to political functions, i.e., the collective pursuit of collective goals. In that context it was seen to have features in common with political systems of a broader variety, notably linkages with their intrasocietal environments through resource mobilization, support mobilization, and legitimation systems. Second, the organization was viewed as a subsystem linked to the more inclusive social system through boundary relations which vary systematically as a consequence of the function performed. Finally, the organization of "common sense" was dismantled and reassembled in the view of four levels of structural organization of social systems. In this context, the organization was viewed as related directly into the intrasocietal environment through lateral and vertical input-output interchanges.

Although no systematic attempt has been made to survey the relevant research literature, our contention has been that, given the level of generality in which the analysis was couched, the view presented gives order and coherence to a great deal of what

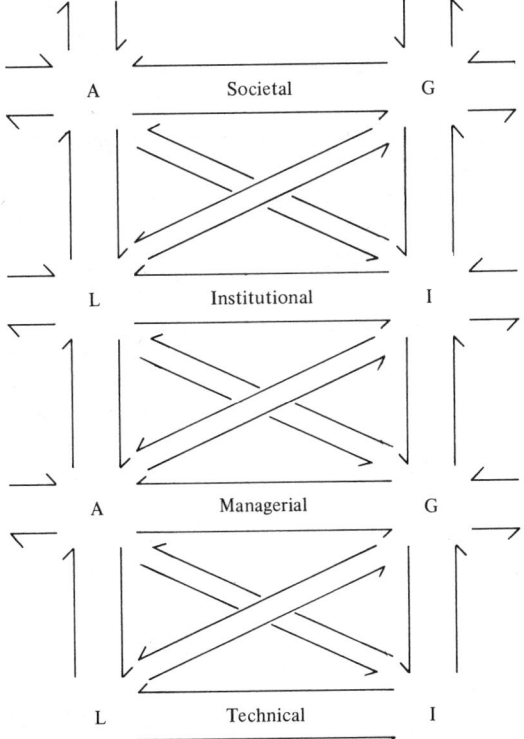

Figure 33-7. Distribution of levels in a hierarchical system.

is now known about the subject matter under consideration.

NOTES

1. Talcott Parsons, "An Approach to the Sociology of Knowledge," in T. Parsons, *Sociological Theory and Modern Society* (New York: The Free Press 1967), p. 141.

2. Talcott Parsons, *Societies: Evolutionary and Comparative Perspectives* (Englewood Cliffs: Prentice-Hall, 1966), p. 19.

3. Talcott Parsons, "An Outline of the Social System," in Talcott Parsons, *et al.* (eds.), *Theories of Society* (New York: The Free Press, 1961), p. 47.

4. *Ibid.*, p. 39.

5. Talcott Parsons, "Components and Types of Formal Organization," in Preston P. Le Breton (ed.), *Comparative Administrative Theory* (Seattle: University of Washington Press, 1968), p. 13.

6. *Loc. cit.*

7. Talcott Parsons, "The Political Aspect of Social Structure and Process," in David Easton (ed.), *Varieties of Political Theory* (Englewood Cliffs: Prentice-Hall, 1966), p. 72.

8. For detailed discussions, see Talcott Parsons, "The Political Aspect of Social Structure and Process," in David Easton (ed.), *Varieties of Political Theory* (Englewood Cliffs: Prentice-Hall, 1966), pp. 71-112 and "On the Concept of Political Power," *Proceedings of the American Philosophical Society*, 107 (1963), pp. 232-62.

9. Parsons, "The Political Aspect of Social Structure and Process, "*op. cit.*, p. 97.

10. *Ibid.*, p. 98.

11. *Ibid.*, p. 93.

12. *Ibid.*, p. 96.

13. A more detailed discussion would indicate that the interchange is a double one, mediated by symbolic media. It is analogous to the interchange of labor capacity for commodities between economic units and consumers, mediated by money in the form of wage payments and consumer spending.

14. Parsons, "The Political Aspect of Social Structure and Process," *op. cit.*, p. 82.

15. *Ibid.*, p. 95.

16. Talcott Parsons, *Structure and Process in Modern Societies*, Glencoe: The Free Press, 1960), p. 63.

17. Talcott Parsons, "The Mental Hospital as a Type of Organization," in Milton Greenblatt, et al. (eds.), *The Patient and the Mental Hospita* (New York: The Free Press, 1963), p. 112.

18. *Ibid.*, p. 120.

19. Parsons, *Structure and Process in Modern Societies*, p.40.

20. *Ibid.*, p. 45.

21. At the technical level of the polity, that of the decision implementing bureau or administrative agency, the value emphasis is effective implementation of the mandate through securing compliance. This corresponds to the economic organization in which "economic rationality" is a focal concern for the managerial levels but not the technical level. In the context of government the term "organization" must include the legislative level as well as the executive and bureaucratic.

22. Parsons, "The Political Aspect of Social Structure and Process," *op. cit.*, p. 99.

23. Talcott Parsons, "On the Concept of Political Power," in Parsons, *Sociological Theory and Modern Society*, pp. 297-354 at p. 338.

24. Talcott Parsons, "On the Concept of Value Commitments," *Sociological Inquiry*, 38 (Spring, 1968), p. 140.

25. *Loc. cit.*

26. Parsons, "On the Concept of Political Power," *op. cit.*, p. 328.

27. Parsons, "The Political Aspect of Social Structure and Process," *op. cit.*, p. 90.

28. Parsons, "On the Concept of Political Power," *op. cit.*, p. 328.

29. Parsons, "On the Concept of Value Commitments," *op. cit.*, p. 149.

30. *Loc. cit.*

31. *Ibid.*, p. 148.

32. *Ibid.*, p. 152.

33. Talcott Parsons, "General Theory in Sociology," in Robert K. Merton, *et al.* (eds.), *Sociology Today* (New York: Basic Books, 1959), p. 16.

34. *Ibid.*, pp. 4-5.

35. *Ibid.*, pp. 10-11.

36. *Ibid.*, p. 10.

37. Parsons, *Structure and Process in Modern Societies*, p. 61.

38. *Ibid.*, p. 18.

39. *Ibid.*, pp. 65-66.

40. *Ibid.*, p. 63.

41. *Ibid.*, p. 64.

42. Parsons, "General Theory in Sociology," *op. cit.*, p. 14.

43. Parsons, *Structure and Process in Modern Society*, p. 89.

44. *Ibid.*, p. 40.

45. Parsons, "*General Theory in Sociology,*" p. 15.

46. Parsons, *Structure and Process in Modern Society*, p. 91.

47. *Ibid.*, p. 90.

48. Parsons, "General Theory in Sociology," *loc. cit.*

49. Parsons, *Structure and Process in Modern Society, loc. cit.*

50. Talcott Parsons, "Some Reflections on the Place of Force in Social Process," in Harry Eckstein, (ed.), *Internal War: Basic Problems and Approaches* (New York: The Free Press, 1964). p. 50.

51. Parsons, *Structure and Process in Modern Societies*, p. 93.

34

THE PUBLIC SCHOOL AS A TYPE OF ORGANIZATION

R. Jean Hills

INTRODUCTION

This essay has been conceived as a sequel to the preceding chapter, "The Organization as a Component in the Structure of Society." It is intended as a direct application of the analytical framework explicated there to a particular category of organizations, that referred to as the public school. The format of the present essay will follow closely that of the more general analysis. We shall first consider the political functions of the public school in the special sense of that term used in the last chapter. We shall then treat the public school as a functionally differentiated subsystem linked to a more inclusive social system through sets of boundary relations. Here our concern will be to detail these relations and to contrast them with those of other types of organizations. Finally, we shall consider the matter of levels of organization in education with particular attention to the location of the public school in the hierarchy of levels. In this context we shall introduce considerations on the internal structure and functions of the public school not treated explicitly in the first paper.

Before addressing ourselves to those tasks, however, it seems advisable to make explicit the nature of the enterprise being undertaken here. The nature of the enterprise is a consequence of the relation between theoretical systems, on the one hand, and "what's out there," on the other. A theoretical system is a set of logically interrelated propositions of empirical reference. An empirical system, on the other hand, is a set of contingent relations among observable phenomena. Any given empirical system is always embedded in a concrete situation which is, to that system, an environment or set of environments. Put the other way around, no empirical system is a total concrete entity. Rather, it is a set of properties of the concrete entity or entities, which is treated, for certain purposes and under certain conditions, as amenable to independent examination.

When empirical systems are relatively closed, few problems arise in the context of applying theoretical systems to them. Thus, the fact that the Newtonian theoretical system treats the earth as a particle with a given mass, location in space, and velocity and completely ignores its other characteristics creates no particular difficulties. On the other hand, when the systems of concern are open and can at best be regarded as analytically independent subsystems of a more inclusive system, real difficulties arise. The situation is difficult enough when application is attempted with full awareness of the fact that the theoretical system was never intended to apply to a total concrete entity or some part of the observable world in its concrete wholeness, but to an analytically independent (and in principle, under specifiable parametric conditions, empirically independent) subsystem. It is impossibly difficult, and perhaps fruitless, when application is made in the expectation that somehow all that can be said about concrete entities will be said.

The analysis of an organization as a social system, then, is not the conceptual interpretation of any concretely complete category of behavioral phenomena. The social system, as a theoretical system, is only one of four such theoretical systems — the other three being the behavioral organism system, the psychological system, and the cultural system — all of which are abstractions from the same concrete phenomena. Social system theory is thus a conceptual system which deals with a restricted set of variables and their interrelations, subject to parametric conditions which are the values of the other variables operating in environing systems, e.g., the psychological systems of concrete persons.

THE PUBLIC SCHOOL AS AN ELEMENT OF THE POLITICAL SYSTEM

In its aspect as a member of the category of structural components of the societal system differentiated with reference to the goal-attainment function, the public school — or any organization, for that matter — may be regarded as an element of the political subsystem of the society. That is to say, it may be regarded as a mechanism through which states of interaction between the societal system and its environing situation that are desirable from the point of view of that system are to some degree defined and the resources requisite to their attainment are mobilized and utilized. What states of interaction between the system and its environing situation are desirable from the point of view of the system as a function of value commitments? If the conditions of the implementation of those commitments were stable, and if there were no changes in the environing situation, then goal attainment would not be a problem. The implementation of value commitments could be wholly routinized. But, the environing systems of the societal system (the cultural system, the behavioral organism and personality systems of participating individuals, the physical environment, and cognate societal systems) undergo constant change such that a relation between one or more of them and the system considered desirable in terms of commitments cannot be presumed to remain stable. Environmental changes disturb states of input-output interchange that fulfill the internal needs of the system, necessitating adjustments within the limits imposed by institutionalized value commitments. This is what is meant by saying that goal attainment is tied directly to interrelations between a system and its environing situation.

As an element of the organization of the societal system oriented to the attainment of collective goals, the public school is subject to the three sets of exigencies outlined in the companion essay, those of legitimation, resource mobilization, and support mobilization. Each of these will be considered in turn.

Legitimation of the Public School

Legitimation functions to define what political organization is for and, hence, to define the nature and scope of the agencies (collectivities and roles) which perform political functions.

> Correlative with these structural definitions are both authority for the implementation of legitimate responsibilities, and access to power and the conditions of its use. In a sufficiently differentiated polity, we call this *the constitutional system* — with private as well as public

collectivities having constitutions more or less formally specified.[1]

Formally specified constitutions for public schools are found in the legal statutes of the several states (the Public Schools Act, in British Columbia) which provide not only for the establishment of school districts but also broad definitions of the nature of their responsibilities, definitions of their structure, i.e., of the principal subcollectivities and roles, and specification of the authority for the implementation of responsibilities, as well as access to power and the conditions of its use. Consistent with the low priority assigned to collective effectiveness in the societal value system, the emphasis in the United States has been on the autonomy of the local district rather than on subordination to wider collective interests. Although wide variations among the several states may be seen, the predominant pattern has concentrated authority in the local school board, with state agencies retaining important regulatory rights, including the right to amend the "constitutions," e.g., in school district reorganization. Both these levels, of course, are subject to the provisions of the federal constitution as interpreted by judicial agencies, a relation made highly visible in the context of racial integration. In other contexts the trend of judicial interpretation has been to restrict the "arbitrary" powers of school officials vis-a-vis students and parents.

Resource Mobilization

The legitimation of the political functions of the public school is an aspect of the relation between that agency, as an element of the polity, on the one hand, and the institutionalized value pattern and the agencies bearing primary responsibility for it, on the other hand. Resource mobilization, however, relates elements of the polity to elements of the economy through a system of interchanges.

In one of these interchanges a share of the productivity of the economy is made available to elements of the polity. As the money in circulation represents the productivity of the economy, ultimately in the form of goods and services, the monetary resources of an element of the polity, e.g., an organization, whether acquired through earnings, taxation, or voluntary contributions, may be conceived as an input of generalized control of productivity which may be converted as desired into the particular goods and services needed. Thus, the monetary funds available to the organization, conceived as a generalized input of control of productivity from the economy, may be converted into "real assets" through the process of inducing an individual to accept employment or the process of purchasing commodities. To induce a prospective employee to enter into a contract of employment, however, is not merely a matter of converting generalized control of productivity into specific facilities. In addition, it constitutes an output of power in the form of "opportunity for effectiveness" from the relevant element of the polity to the relevant element of the economy (in this case the individual in his occupational role). What the individual receives is authorization to operate within the organization to make a contribution more effectively than working on his own would allow. An aspect of this authorization, of course, is the settlement of the employee's position in the organization's internal hierarchy of authority and power, a matter ordinarily referred to as the delegation of power.

An inherent aspect of power systems, however, is the necessity for balancing expenditures of power through delegation by an income of power in the form of consent to accept organizational authority. That is to say, the input of power which to some extent balances outputs in the form of "opportunity" is derived from the commitments of employed personnel to the performance of services within the framework of roles in the organization.

> In return for this opportunity, the employee typically gives the collectivity rights to control his actions in the context of employment. The critical element to the collectivity is the right to insure with binding power that his action contributes effectively to collective goal-attainment. A primary source of the power which the collectivity's leadership uses and allocates through the hierarchy of authority is the aggregate of commitments to service made by units who have accepted employment in the collectivity. Such commitments are initially generalized defined only by the terms of the "job"; over time, they are continually specified to the many particular tasks undertaken and performed as occasions arise.[2]

The final aspect of the set of interchanges under discussion is an output from the element of the polity in return for the commitment of services. This is the allocation of fluid resources to the purveyors of services as facilities essential to the performance of their obligations. In the general case fluid resources take the form of monetary funds, either placed at the disposal of the performer's role through budgetary allocation or spent by higher echelons for the benefit of his role.

Most of what may be said of the public school in this context is relatively commonplace. Its control of a share of the productivity of the economy derives almost exclusively from taxation, and the allocation of fluid resources is a relatively straightforward budgetary process. Only in the context of opportunity for effectiveness and commitment of services does it appear much of interest can be said. Over a period of time two developments have been set in motion, neither of which has run its course and both of which place limits on the collectivity's capacity to control the actions of teachers in the context of employment. One of these is the increasing reliance of teachers on collective action in the negotiation of the conditions of employment, which are by no means limited to the matter of monetary remuneration. The other is the widespread educational upgrading of the teaching force. Whatever may be said about the difficult question of teaching competence *per se,* there is no doubt at all that teachers have become increasingly well grounded in the subject matter of their teaching fields and in the methodology of teaching. To a greater degree than in the past, then, the teacher is a technical specialist whose competence is not likely to be matched by that of his organizational superiors and who can, and increasingly does, demand freedom from intervention within his sphere of competence. The common outcome of these two developments is a decrease in the willingness of teachers to grant public school officials the right to control their actions in the context of employment.

The sphere of competence within which teachers can effectively lay claim to some degree of autonomy does not, however, include the selection of educational objectives to be sought. Recent events in both Canada and the United States emphasize this point. In Canada a few days prior to this writing, the government of the Province of British Columbia issued an order in council requiring the removal from public schools and university classrooms of any teachers expressing support for the policies of the Federation de Liberation du Quebec or advocating the overthrow of democratically elected governments by violent means. In the United States, perhaps the most recent and visible demonstration of such limitation has focused on the question of "sex education."

Support Mobilization

Because it has been more a question of school district policy than of individual teacher autonomy, the sex-education controversy provides a convenient point at which to shift to a discussion of the final set of political processes, those of support mobilization. The interchange here is conceived as follows:

> The circulation of power between polity and integrative system I conceive to consist in binding policy decisions on the one hand, which is a primary factor in the integration process, and political support on the other, which is a primary output of the integrative process. Support is exchanged by a "public" or constituency, for the assumption of leadership responsibility, through a process of persuading those in a position to give binding support that it is advisable to do so in the

particular instance—through the use of influence or some less generalized means of persuasion. In the other political "market" *vis-à-vis* the integrative system, policy decisions are given in response to interest-demands . . . . This is to say that interest groups . . . attempt to persuade those who hold authority in the relevant collectivity that they should indeed commit the collectivity to the policies the influence wielders want.[3]

Unlike the typical business firm in which the constituents of the political process have the relatively passive role of stockholders and in which their leaders, the board of directors, are often almost assimilated into the top management, the constituents or publics which constitute the source of demands for policy decisions are various kinds of interest groups. Some of these are relatively permanent associational collectivities, e.g., the American Legion, taxpayers' associations, the teachers' association. Others come into being around particular policy issues and disband once the relevant issues are settled. Although education is idealized as an area that should be removed from politics, it is obviously highly political in the present sense of the term. In those areas in which the office of school trustee is elective, candidates campaign actively on the basis of current issues, soliciting electoral support which, for the successful candidate, constitutes a grant of power.

> Election to office is a power input to the leadership of the polity, enabling it to exercise or spend power in making policy decisions which commit collective resources to specific uses and in delegating opportunity for effectiveness to members of the administrative system.[4]

Both these interchanges between the public school and its constituencies have tended in the past to be relatively "invisible" except in times of controversy. For the most part, school board elections were quiet affairs which attracted little public interest and in which no more than 15% to 20% of eligible voters participated. Similarly, the policy decision—interest demand market tended to be characterized by a limited amount of competition among constituencies. Currently, both interchanges are highly visible. Issues arising from the Supreme Court decision concerning racial integration, e.g., bussing students; from the concern over lack of success in educating the "disadvantaged"; from particular curricular innovations, e.g., sex education; and so on have become the basis for the mobilization of constituent support and for the initiation of interest demands. Perhaps the most remarkable development of all is the extent to which, at least at the secondary school level, the direct recipients of educational services, the students, have become constituents of the process.

We might summarize this discussion of the political

aspect of the public school by observing that, although the political aspect of the process has, by definition, always been present, recent years have seen the more active politicization of education. In two of the three interchanges discussed, the equilibrium of past years has been upset and a new balance has not yet emerged.

THE SCHOOL AS A FUNCTIONALLY DIFFERENTIATED SUBSYSTEM OF THE SOCIAL SYSTEM

The Primary Function of the School

Given the proposition that the structure of the social system consists in institutionalized cultural patterns, then the necessity of internalizing those patterns in each oncoming generation is second in functional importance to the maintenance of adult levels of that culture. It is this cultural-motivational imperative that underlies the functioning of the public school as a functionally differentiated subsystem of the social system. Hence, the public school parallel to the production of one or more categories of commodities as the goal-output of the organization oriented to economic production is the development of one or more categories of commitments and capacities required for the implementation of values in future role-performances. Indirectly, this is a contribution to value-implementation, a category of output which, like the production of commodities, is regulated by a value standard and facilitated by a symbolic medium of exchange and measure of value. In the case of economic production the value standard is utility, and the medium of exchange and measure of value on a scale of utility is money. The parallel value standard in the case of value implementation is integrity (of the value pattern), and the symbolic medium of exchange and measure of value on a scale of integrity is commitments.

In economic action the cost of resources that undergo combination in the process of production and the actual or prospective value of outputs are measured in monetary terms. In the context of value-implementation, the cost of resources and the value of outputs are measured in terms of commitments. Commitment as a medium of exchange has been defined as generalized capacity and credible promises to effect the implementation of values.

> Its message are essentially assertions of commitment to the relevant value pattern which may take the form of elements implicit in acts pointing toward implementation, such as promises, which we often explicitly call commitments to undertake certain specified obligations.[5]

Moral authority, the basis of commitments, is earned through a reputation for integrity of commitments.

The school, then, secures resources through implicit and explicit expenditures of commitments, commitments to cultural values. The school is explicitly committed, in the terms of its legitimation, to teach students to believe, feel, and value within the framework of the paramount cultural pattern. This means that a variety of school activities, such as the teaching of history, social studies, and literature, as well as many informal discussions, must be handled in the "proper" way. In the extreme case, the school must even perpetuate or avoid contradicting erroneous, or at least very questionable, empirical beliefs. Witness the belief in the inferiority of the Negro and the rejection of the theory of evolution. The number of occasions on which schools come under fire for violating community value commitments would seem to exceed by far those on which they are criticized for failure to develop knowledge or skill. The wrong book in literature class, the wrong comment in history, or the "ill-advised" digression in biology may be a source of real concern in the community. This is a consequence of the primacy of the value standard integrity. Above all, the smooth functioning of the school requires that the quality of attitude, the values, expressed by the action of school personnel be contributions to value implementive action having a high value on a scale of integrity. That there are local variations in cultural patterns is reasonably obvious. What is consistent with the pattern in a high-income suburb may not be consistent with the pattern in an industrial community, and what is consistent with the pattern in California may not be consistent with the pattern in Idaho.

Societal Commitments

Whatever the nature of the detailed elements of the pattern, values will be acted upon, within limits, wherever appropriate independent of cost. This is what is implied by the term commitment. As the organizational value system is a subsystem of the societal value system, it defines the societal commitments on which the functioning of the organization depends. The operation of any organization may be conceived as based fundamentally on such a set of commitments. This means that, within limits which vary from organization type to organization type and from organization to organization within a given type, the organization has under its control certain societal resources access to which is not contingent on short-run sanctions. The business firm, for example, has relatively unconditional access to nondepreciating, non-obsolescing sites, physical facilities, and equipment, to commonly held technical knowledge, organizational knowhow, and to certain human services. In the latter case, one may conceive of personnel who would leave the organization only in dire circumstances and of technical knowledge, accumulated organizational experience, access to which is unproblematic.

Commitment factors are probably most visible in the religious organization. Churches have relatively unconditional access to land, physical facilities, and human services. Church property and income is exempt from taxation, it is seldom for sale, or even for hire, and monetary remuneration is a relatively insignificant factor in securing and retaining human services. The school follows closely behind the church in the prominence of commitments. The school system of a given community, for example, has relatively permanent access to sites which may be, in economic terms, extremely valuable, but which are not for sale so long as there is educational use for them. Regardless of how well or how poorly the school functions, access to these and other resources—not the least of which is students—is assured. Trustees may be voted out of office, administrative appointments may be terminated and teachers may be replaced, but school systems are never liquidated. The procurement and retention of human services is more dependent on monetary sanctions than in the church, but considerably less so than in other occupations.

The Goals of the School

There are numerous ways of formulating the goal of the public school, but all mean essentially the same thing. From one point of view the primary goal can be said to be the socialization of youth in the cultural tradition of the society, with particular, but by no means exclusive, emphasis on the cognitive elements. Another way of saying much the same thing is to speak of the goal as the training of individual persons to be motivationally and technically adequate for performance in adult roles. Still another is to say that the goal is the development of the character, knowledge, and skill levels of pupils. Whatever the wording, the development of motivational commitments and capacities is involved.

> Commitments may be broken down . . . into two components: commitments to the implementation of the broad *values* of society, and commitment to a specific type of role within the structure of society. Thus a person in a relatively humble occupation may be a "solid citizen" in the sense of commitment to honest work in that occupation, without an intensive and sophisticated concern with the implementation of society's higher-level values. . . .
>
> Capacities can also be broken down into two components, the first being competence or the skill to perform the tasks involved in the individual's roles, and the second being "role-responsibility" or the capacity to live up to other people's expectations of the inter-personal

behavior appropriate to these roles. Thus a mechanic as well as a doctor needs to have not only the basic "skills of his trade," but also the ability to behave responsibly toward those people with whom he is brought into contact in his work.[6]

The goal of the public school can be more precisely defined in terms of a complex of responsibilities vis-à-vis the students entrusted to its care. Although their number is extensive, they cluster under four main categories, with a good deal of overlapping between categories: (1) custody, (2) protection, (3) socialization in the role of student, and (4) socialization for subsequent roles. The custodial responsibility is simply that of "meeting the needs" or "taking care" of the student. In the early years of the elementary school, this involves such mundane matters as seeing children are properly dressed (both in the sense of wearing the clothes they have and in the sense of having clothes to wear), seeing that they receive minimally adequate dental and medical treatment, and so on. This tends to be a low-priority goal legitimated in terms of the significance of its attainment for the primary educational goal.

The protective goal covers a range of responsibilities, beginning with protection against physical harm resulting from the students' own actions or the actions of other students. Included here responsibilities for supervision of playgrounds, athletic and physical education activities, laboratories, and the maintenance of internal order. Somewhat less routine are the responsibilities for seeing that students are not exposed to intellectual and social experiences with which they cannot cope, that they do not make decisions which jeopardize their educational and/or occupational futures. Much of guidance activity fits into this category.

Socialization in the role of student is a critical goal in those instances in which that task has not been well-initiated in the home. Before anything worthy of being called "the development of commitments and capacities" can be undertaken, it is necessary to make the student a member of the organization. The student is a nominal member by virtue of having been formally admitted to the school, but this is far from sufficient. What is required for best results is membership in the sense of internalizing the school's values and accepting its goals. Although there are legitimate mitigating circumstances, the school is held responsible for seeing that the students accept the idea that they should be in school, that they appreciate the importance of securing an education, and that they cooperate actively in the educational process. In these respects the school is comparable to the mental hospital, where therapeutic goals simply cannot be achieved unless the patient accepts the idea that his condition is justifiably defined as mental illness, regards recovery as desirable, and cooperates by doing his part toward recovery.

Education too is cooperative work. The positive contribution of the student is an essential ingredient, and success with those students for whom the school represents a prison from which to escape at the earliest possible moment is extremely unlikely. Schools utilize a variety of means of socializing students in role and maintaining their interest in school. Classrooms are made comfortable and attractive. Social activities, athletic events, and special interest clubs of various sorts are standard features of the secondary school.

The fourth, and generally primary, goal of the school is socialization in the broader sense of the development of the commitments and capacities that are prerequisites for performance in adult roles. Protective, custodial, and student role-socialization goals tend to be legitimated in terms of the significance of their attainment for the broad socialization goals of the school. Included here are the complexes of teaching and learning activities designed to lead to the development of the character, knowledge, and skill levels of students. Ideally, every student should achieve a level of development consistent with his potential, with those exhibiting higher levels of motivational and academic potential being prepared for college entrance. The minimum desirable level in any case, however, is the achievement of the motivational and technical capacity to fulfill the requirements of a wide variety of roles, such as those of wage earner, responsible citizen, wife, and husband.

These four subgoals of the more general goal of developing the commitments and capacities which are essential prerequisites of future role performance provide a basis for analysing the functions of the school vis-à-vis students. Different types of students tend to require different types of protective, custodial, student role-socialization, and broad socialization measures; and different types of student populations tend to require different balances of emphasis, or orders of priority, among subgoals. Given a student population that is difficult to socialize, then protection becomes a high-priority goal. Quite generally, the problem of achieving a proper balance among subgoals is a major policy issue for the school.

Boundary Relations of the Public School

The boundary relations of the public school may be discussed under the same four headings identified in the preceding paper. These were: (1) the legitimation function, the legitimation of the operation of the organization in the community; (2) the integrative function, the integration of the organization into the community in which it operates; (3) the goal-ouput disposal function, the disposition of the organization's goal-output; and (4) the resource procurement function, the acquisition of the resources required to carry out the organization's function.

Legitimation

The broad pattern of legitimation is given in the relation between the societal and organizational value systems, the latter, in the integrated case, being a specification of the former to the relevant functional context. Legitimation is a matter of answering the question, "Why should there be schools, with given powers, and given limitations?" It involves the invocation of higher-level values in the sense that those higher-level values provide reasons with which to answer the question. Hence, the system-subsystem relation between societal and organizational values is the primary mechanism involved. The organization goal is linked with the more general value pattern of the society and is legitimated in terms of the significance of its attainment for the functioning of the superordinate system. Thus, the goal of the school is linked with the more general values through the valuation of the individual personality and of achievement. It is chiefly because education facilitates effective achievement that in American society it is defined as a desirable process.

These considerations concern the legitimization of the existence of a type of organization and the specification of the societal commitments on which its functioning depends. But the legitimation of the type does not insure the legitimation of a particular, concrete organization of the type in a particular community. Hence, a more specific problem of legitimation is that of establishing, maintaining, and enhancing a positive community appraisal of the actual functioning organization. That is, it is not only the legitimation of a given type of organization that is at stake, but also the legitimation of the actual conduct of a particular organization and the maintenance of an adequate level of commitment to its functioning. Although the legitimation of the goal or function of the organization may be through its linkage with superordinate values, the legitimation of the implementation of that goal by a particular organization in a particular community cannot be assumed to occur automatically. Hence, there are relatively specific mechanisms designed to insure confidence on the part of the community that the organization is in fact making the contribution that it is supposed to make, e.g., securing the sponsorship of elements of the community which have good standing in the community and a reputation for responsibility. Public schools make rather frequent use of "lay advisory boards" whose members tend to be prominent business, professional, and religious leaders in the community. Various activities included under the heading of "public relations" also belong here, but the principal mechanism is probably the association of reputable community members with the school in their capacities as trustees.

Integration

The integration of the organization with its environment involves the maintenance of compatibility between the practices and procedures under which the organization operates and those of other organizations and social units.

> This above all involves adherence to values and patterns of operation which (a) are generalizable beyond the particular organization, (b) are considered justified by the particular circumstances of the particular case or type of organization.[7]

The underlying problem on a transorganizational level is the definition of the loyalty participants owe to a given organization in ways that fit into the larger system of loyalties which they bear, to family, to country, and so on. Hence, an essential ingredient in organizational operation is the set of rules defining and regulating the limits of obligations to this organization as compared with others in which the same clients, employees, and resource suppliers are involved.

The three primary complexes of rules involved here are the contractual complex, the authority complex, and the universalistic rule complex. The contractual complex, which includes subcomplexes related to relations with providers of human services (employment), providers of fluid funds (investment), and providers of possessions (property), defines the obligations of loyalty that are assumed by providers of these categories of resources and the nature and extent of the responsibility of the community for the education of children and youth. On the other side, it defines the categories of personnel who are competent to carry on this function and their status in the community. In addition, it specifies the standards of training and competence required for various categories of personnel. To insure integration, the contractual pattern of the organization must be consonant with those governing this category of organization and those operative in the environment. A particularly important case is that of "professional" personnel who have dual occupational commitments, one to the employing organization and another to the professional group of which they are members.

Several outstanding features of the school may be noted here. First, the local community bears the primary burden of responsibility for the provision of education. There is an increasing tendency to shift the financial burden to higher levels of government, but this seems less a matter of shifting responsibility than of recognizing limitations and of equalizing opportunities. More than any other function — medical services, law enforcement, fire protection — education is a community responsibility.

Second, the single category of personnel considered competent to carry out educational functions is that of persons holding valid certificates issued by a state department of education. Standards of training, typically expressed in terms of numbers and distribution of course credits, are also set by the state agency. The emphasis on the distribution of courses is particularly noteworthy, because it excludes large numbers of persons holding degrees who are presumably competent in terms of subject matter but have not received training as teachers. The fact that this requirement is omitted at post-secondary levels of education without disastrous effects suggests that certification based on teacher training is to a considerable extent a certification of commitment. This suggestion seems reasonable in view of the teachers' status in the community. Although the teacher is not regarded as having an outstanding degree of specialized technical competence which sets him apart from the reasonably well-educated layman, he is regarded as a "solid citizen," a preferred insurance and credit risk. Although the status of teacher may be relatively low in prestige and influence, it is relatively high in moral authority and commitments.

Similar considerations apply in connection with the authority complex which defines, on a basis broader than that of the particular organization, the ways and extent to which any given actor, individual or collective, can in a given status in the organization bind others by his decisions and the ways and extent to which his action can be bound by the decisions of others. Both the contractual and authority complexes define in relatively specific ways what is to be expected of the organization and hence the conditions under which it will be tolerated or supported by environing systems. These two institutions define the obligations specific to the role in the particular organization which come into force only so far as the incumbent accepts a relation to the organization.

The principal relations regulated by the authority complex are those between the organization and the recipients of its services and between the organization and the operative personnel. The determination patterns of authority operative in these contexts can never be the sole jurisdiction of the school itself. Such patterns must be compatible with those governing that category of organization and the surrounding community as well. This is particularly critical in

relation to legitimation and community support because the recipient of services is compelled to accept those services whether he or his family wishes it or not and because the duration of the students' exposure to those services is relatively long. The student, of course, is a member of both the school and the family. Though the family's consent is not required for enrollment, it does retain a legitimate concern about what happens to the student during school hours. Hence, the relations between teachers and other school personnel, on the one hand, and students, on the other, need to be institutionally regulated on a basis broader than the particular organization.

The patterns here are neither completely uniform from community to community nor completely stable through time. The teacher and the school have tended to stand in *loco parentis* vis-à-vis the student, but this has been modified, both informally and in some cases legally, to exclude physical punishment. The trend over time has been a gradual reduction of both the scope of the authority of the school and the severity of the sanctions it may employ. Court decisions have modified considerably the once-unquestioned right of school board to adopt whatever rules were deemed essential to the administration of the school.

Finally, the universalistic rule complex defines for the society as a whole, or for transorganizational sectors of it, standards of "good practices." These include rules regulating the use of force, the prohibition of violations of personal freedoms, and fraud. More generally, they set limits in the treatment of human beings and nonhuman resources within which the conduct of the organization must remain. Conformity with social standards of acceptable conduct, as well as within the limits of loyalty specified by the principles of contract and authority, is an essential condition of the smooth functioning of an organization within its environment.

Disposal

For an organization, the primary boundary relation is that of goal attainment. Over this boundary, the organization produces an identifiable output which can be utilized in some way by environing systems. Accordingly, there must be general principles concerning the sorts of goods or services that will be made available, in what quantity and quality, to whom, on what terms. These principles, or rules, are the outcomes of what are ordinarily called policy decisions, an important aspect of which is the integration of and establishment of priorities among competing goals. At stake here are questions concerning whether the school is to be primarily a socialization or a protective agency and, more specifically, what to teach to what categories of pupils, at what cost to the taxpayer. It is in these areas that the value principle "integrity" and the coordinative standard "pattern consistency" bear most heavily on the operation of the school. As noted, through contributions to the development of commitments and capacities on the part of students, the output of the school is value-implementive action in a wide variety of functional contexts and at a variety of levels in the structural hierarchy. The school does not simply socialize all students subject to its influence in a standard set of commitments and capacities. It performs a genuine allocative function as well in the sense that one of the consequences of its operation is contributing to the process of sorting students along two major dimensions: (1) the kind of values to be implemented, i.e., economic, political, integrative, and (2) the level of responsibility at which those values are implemented, e.g., the technical level, managerial level, or institutional level.

Despite the wide variety of commitments and capacities that may be relevant to future role performances and despite the impossibility of knowing in advance just which commitments and (more especially) capacities will in fact be contributions to integrity, the value principle of integrity still applies in those areas which are seen as contributing nothing to the implementation of values in any conceivable circumstances or as undermining those values. In the one category fall those elements of school programs, often referred to as "fads and frills," which are the first to be abandoned when financial considerations weigh heavily. In the second fall those elements that can be construed as bordering on the "un-American," the disloyal, and the immoral. Whatever else may be said about the public school, it seems clear that the primary criterion for the assessment of its proximate goal-outputs is integrity. While a considerable amount of doubt about the ultimate relevance of school programs to subsequent value implementation may be tolerated, programs and activities that appear to lead toward the implementation of opposing values will not.

The application of the value principle of integrity leads to a curious kind of "structured strain" for the school. On the one hand, knowledge and skill are clearly facilitators of value implementation in a variety of contexts. On the other hand, the very knowledge and skill that in some sense facilitates value implementation is at least believed to subvert commitment to the very values for which they might have implementive relevance. Thus sex education, which might, on the one hand, be conceived to facilitate the implementation of values in the family

setting, is, on the other hand, regarded as a threat to moral standards.

In the context of relations with recipients of services the school shares certain of the characteristics of agencies providing medical and legal services. The most noteworthy is the admission of the direct recipient of services to membership in the service-providing organization and the "joint product" nature of the outcome. Students do not simply purchase a certain amount and kind of education, as though it were a commodity; and they do not simply make an appointment with the teacher, as though seeking medical advice. The student is formally enrolled, or admitted to membership, in the school. Whatever the outcome of the relation, it is the joint product of the efforts, or lack thereof, of the school, the student, and the student's family. Both the student and the family contribute significantly to the realization of educational goals; in a sense, the former occupies simultaneously the roles of employee and customer. The student is, of course, "paid" for his services with grades, approval, and a variety of privileges and honors. Those who do well in school tend to receive more recognition, more privileges, and higher honors than those who do less well, despite some emphasis on the scaling of recognition to ability.

"Doing well" in school, however, means far more than simply "getting one's lessons."[8] It includes participating willingly, cooperating with instructional and administrative personnel, observing the rules of the game concerning lessons (doing one's own work), observing rules of proper conduct, and all that was once included under the heading of "deportment." Thus, although the school is a specific function organization, concerned only with education and not with economic production, the maintenance of political order, or social control, it is concerned with diffuse aspects of the student's character. Although it is not the case that the school is concerned with the total personality structure (as in the case of the mental hospital), neither is it the case that it is concerned solely with cognitive development. Motivational and technical adequacy are equally legitimate concerns of the school.

In addition to the similarities between the school and the just-mentioned agencies, there are several distinct contrasts. Consider the case of medical service. Admission to the hospital is based on need in the sense of being ill, and the patient is discharged on recovery, or when all that can be done has been done. However, with several very important exceptions, it is the patient himself, or his family, who decides to enter the hospital. Moreover, the patient can leave the hospital without being formally discharged. In doing so he relieves the hospital of any responsibility for the consequences but, with exceptions to be noted, he cannot be compelled to remain. The exceptions, of course, are those cases of mental illness or contagious disease in which it is in the public interest for the patient to be confined. In those cases, commitment to a mental institution or quarantine may be mandatory, the patient being eligible for discharge only when he is no longer a threat to public safety or health.

The similarity between these two cases and the school is striking. Neither the student nor his family have anything to say about admission to some school. Although they may determine which school by changing residence or by paying tuition, the student must be enrolled in some school or be receiving a comparable education. Nor do they have anything to say about the termination of the relation. The student is committed to the school, and his release cannot be effected until a certain level of attainment or a certain age is reached. Although the nature of the threat is different in each case, the potentially violent mental patient, the carrier of a contagious disease, the criminal, and the uneducated are threats to the public interest; and hence they are compelled to accept membership in the appropriate organization. If education were strictly, or even primarily, a matter of "meeting the needs," providing for the "self-actualization," or "developing the potential" of students in some "value-free" sense, this would not be so. But education is, above all, geared to meet the needs of the society for structural stability and orderly change. As the structure of a society consists in institutionalized patterns of normative culture, it is essential that each succeeding generation acquire the requisite commitments as well as the capacities.

Procurement

Finally, there are normative rules governing the adaptive process of the organization, general principles governing the acquisition of facilities and rules which specify the general manner in which financial resources are to be raised as well as where the primary responsibility resides. In the acquisition of human services, a particularly important category of norm is that providing the basis for remuneration of personnel. Another is that defining the qualification of personnel. Still another is that setting forth the terms of the continuation or termination of employment.

The characteristics of the school in this context follow from the general nature of education. Because education is heavily laden with public interest, ability to pay cannot be a criterion of admission. Financial resources must be raised from sources other than payments by recipients of services. With marginal exceptions, e.g., nonresident tuition payments, the total income of the school is derived from tax funds. Through this mechanism the cost of education is made a public burden, a burden born by all tax-payers whether or not they receive direct benefits, i.e., whether or not they have or have had children in school.

Although there are others, the two key categories of personnel to be considered under the heading "the acquisition of human services" are teachers and administrators. As nearly all administrators are recruited from the ranks of teachers, we shall consider teachers first. Extenuating circumstances and local conditions produce a variety of exceptions, but the clear pattern is one in which only those with "proper" training are permitted to teach. What constitutes proper training for a given role is ordinarily determined by a state department of education, but the detailed assessment of the extent to which standards have been met is a part of the training process itself. The certifying agency does not conduct an independent assessment of the candidates' qualifications but merely establishes that the proper numbers and kinds of courses have been taken. The training agency itself assumes responsibility for the assessment of adequacy in terms of course content, and there is no parallel of the independently administered bar or medical board examination.

The fact that the detailed assessment of qualifications is performed by the training agency and the parallel fact that the occupational group has little to say about the admission of persons to the practice of teaching suggest that this process is not the strict analogy to admission to the practice of law and medicine that it is sometimes assumed to be. The latter are regarded as procedures by which new members are admitted to a professional group, and teaching is held to be a profession. Without entering directly into the debate concerning the status of teaching, it may be pointed out that a distinguishing feature of such fields as law and medicine is the independent trusteeship of the occupational group of an important part of the cultural tradition of the society. The typical member of the occupational group is trained in that tradition, usually by means of a formally organized educational process; and only those properly trained are considered capable of engaging in the activities of the occupation and in the creative modification of the relevant part of cultural tradition. Moreover, only those with proper training are considered qualified to give authoritative interpretations of that part of the cultural tradition. Finally, a substantial proportion of the members of the group is ordinarily concerned with the practical application of the tradition to a variety of situations in which it is useful to persons outside the group itself. The practitioner is thus a "technical expert" by virtue of his mastery of a part of the cultural tradition and the skills of its use.[9]

Clearly, it is the independent trusteeship of an important part of the cultural tradition and the skills of its application that gives certain occupational groups special privileges, among which are the right to determine, or participate heavily in the determination of, what constitutes proper training, the right to assess the degree to which candidates have met standards of proper training, the right to disqualify persons for practice in the field, and the right to provide authoritative interpretations of the relevant part of the cultural tradition. Whatever the reality of the situation may be, it seems clear that teachers are not generally regarded as holding an independent trusteeship of any important part of the cultural tradition of the society. The cultural tradition in which the teacher is trained is, for the most part, the same tradition in which the ordinary college-educated member of the society is trained. The teacher may be more thoroughly trained in specific subject matter areas than the layman, but he is far from holding an independent trusteeship and is seldom regarded as uniquely qualified to give authoritative interpretations of the tradition. Nor is the teacher concerned with the practical application of the tradition. Hence, he cannot be regarded as a "technical expert" by virtue of his mastery of the tradition and the skills of its use.

The reference made to "the practical application of the tradition" suggests that the cultural tradition for which teaching may hold an independent trusteeship is that which concerns the processes of education themselves. Again, whatever the reality of the situation, the teacher is not generally regarded as uniquely qualified to make either authoritative interpretations or practical applications of a part of the cultural tradition. The scope of the cultural tradition dealing specifically with education is not great enough for those who master it and the skills of its application to be accorded the status of either "authoritative interpreter" or "technical expert." (The frequency with which "lay" patrons of the schools challenge the "professionals" on matters of method is ample evidence for this assertion.) Hence, the certification of teachers is far more a matter of an agency of the society certifying an acceptable degree of mastery of the paramount cultural tradition than it is a matter of the holders of an independent trusteeship of a part of that tradition certifying mastery of that part and the skills of its application. The latter emphasis, however, has become more prominent in recent years and, with the increased emphasis on research, seems certain to become increasingly prominent, in the context of teacher certification.

The remuneration of teachers forms part of this consistent pattern. Salaries tend to be tied closely to level of training and years of service, all persons in a given training and service category receiving the same salary. Numerous attempts have been made to establish "merit" pay plans in which salary level is linked directly to level of technical competence, but none seems to have survived over an extended period of time. Perhaps the most important reason for this is the fact that "technical competence" is an evaluative standard emphasizing level of knowledge and skill in its application. The doctor is obviously more competent in the treatment of illness than his lay patient, and the teacher is obviously more competent in interpreting his academic specialty than his student. In the case of the teacher, however, the cultural tradition that he transmits and interprets is distinctly different from that which he applies. As noted, that which he applies is insufficiently developed to provide a firm basis for evaluation. A second contributing factor is the fact that "doing well as a teacher" is very similar to "doing well in school" for the student. Both consist in performing in accordance with a complex set of normative standards, only part of which concern knowledge and its application.

A final feature of the market for teaching services, which distinguishes it both from the administrative case and that of a variety of other organizations, is the institution of tenure. Tenure has been interpreted

> ... as a symbol of moral approval which "compensates" the risk involved in commitment to an occupational role which cannot be supported directly from the proceeds of production, it justifies confidence in entrusting the [economic] security of the [employee's] household not primarily to the "market" but to those agencies responsible for "nonproductive" functions.[10]

As noted, personnel for administrative roles tend to be recruited almost exclusively from the ranks of teachers and, with the exception of elementary school principals and certain supervisory roles, from among males. How much having been a teacher contributes to the administrator's performance in a strictly administrative capacity is open to question, but it very likely is a source of teacher confidence in the administration. A principal concern of teachers is the threat of the corruption of educational goals and standards by economic and political pressures. From their point of view, decisions are all too frequently made with economic and political considerations in mind, rather than educational, and it is probably the rare administrator who has not on some occasion been accused of being motivated by "political" considerations.

The status of the administrative group with respect to an independent trusteeship of an important part of the cultural tradition is at least as ambiguous as that of teachers. Until relatively recently, the cultural tradition of educational administration consisted primarily of the content of such subject areas as "school law," "school finance," "the organization of education," "the supervision of instruction," and "school public relations." With the exception of those areas governed by legal statutes or levels of administrative jurisdiction higher than the local district, the content of these areas tended to be a combination of commonsense knowledge and empirical beliefs based on practical experience, ideological positions, and conceptions of the desirable. Since the early 1950's, however, training programs have placed increasing emphasis on social and behavioral science materials. At the present time it is probably the rare program that does not include a course in "administrative theory" or "organization theory," and many include such courses as the "politics of education" and the "economics of education." None of this, of course, gives administrators an independent trusteeship of an important part of the cultural tradition. Moreover, few would maintain vigorously that the trained administrator is prepared either to provide authoritative interpretations or make skilled application. Most of the materials in question can be characterized as general conceptions or paradigms and hence are not directly applicable to concrete situations.

Although there is no data at hand to confirm or refute the point, casual observation would indicate that the typical individual's first administrative post is held in a district in which he was formerly a teacher. Only rarely does it seem that a teacher secures administrative training and then receives an administrative appointment in a district other than that in which he was teaching. In spite of this, however, it is not uncommon for "unsponsored" teachers to pursue and complete administrator-training programs, and it seems likely that there is a considerable number of persons now teaching who possess the formal qualifications for appointment to administrative positions. If the facts of the case are as outlined here, then two implications follow. First, the effective screening of persons for administrative roles occurs in the schools themselves before training is undertaken. This differs markedly from some other fields in which the candidate for a position requires no prior association with an organization to secure an initial administrative appointment and can be reasonably confident that possession of the proper formal qualifications will gain him an appointment. Second, the informal qualifications emphasized by those who sponsor teachers for an administrative appointment are more effective determinants of who does and does not secure an administrative position than are the formal qualifications established by training and certifying agencies. These comments, of course,

apply only in connection with the initial administrative appointment. Having gained an initial appointment and some administrative experience the individual is then in a position to move into the open market for administrative services where the sponsorship of respected professors of administration plays a key part.

Salary levels for administrative personnel tend to be somewhat higher than those of teachers with comparable levels of training and experience. To some extent the additional remuneration reflects a longer contractual period, administrators ordinarily being on duty from four to twelve weeks during summer months when teachers are not. Its primary significance, however, is as a symbol of the responsibility borne by the administrator for collective goal attainment and as compensation for the added risk entailed by foregoing the protection of the institution of tenure.

LEVELS OF EDUCATIONAL ORGANIZATION

The companion chapter outlined in some detail the conception of levels of organization of social structure. We shall not replicate that discussion here, but rather move directly to a consideration of levels of organization in education. Our discussion here draws heavily on Parsons' own discussion of the same subject.[11]

The emergence of levels of organization is a function of the division of labor in society. If we regard the actual process of teaching as the technical level of function in education, then in an area in which parents teach their own children no functional problems beyond the technical need arise, and no special technical organization is required. As soon as this technical function comes to be differentiated from the family, however, problems arise which are not in themselves technical. Teachers must be recruited, appointed, allocated to classrooms, paid, supplied with materials, and given directions concerning what to teach to what categories of children, on what terms. In a relatively small, simple village or rural school, these problems may be handled jointly by a full-time teacher designated "head teacher" and a board of trustees, but in a school system of any size the emergence of a distinct level of organization focussing on some of these problems seems inevitable. Insofar as teachers remain primarily oriented to the exigencies imposed by the technical task, and as long as the role of trustee remains a non-occupational role, no other alternative seems feasible.

The emergence of administrative functions, then,

is a consequence of the division of labor in society, and the development of an administrative level of organization (in the sense of distinct roles and collectivities) is a function of increasing complexity. A technical system simply cannot subsist alone in a differentiated society, and a technical system controlled and serviced by an institutional system (e.g., a board of trustees) simply cannot subsist alone in a complex society. As in the case of the business firm, the hospital, or the university, in the public school there tends to be an administration concerned not with the conduct of classes but with: (1) the mediation of the relations of the technical level to recipients of its products; (2) the procurement and distribution of materials, equipment, and personnel; and (3) the control and supervision of technical operations.

In the public school the mediation of relations with recipients of technical level outputs most directly concerns what to teach and what other services are to be provided to what categories of students. (As we shall see, to identify these as administrative functions is not to assert that they are performed exclusively by administrative personnel.) The procurement function is too straightforward a matter to require comment beyond noting that it is never a matter of administrative personnel simply deciding what resources are required and then making them available to teaching personnel. Given the variety of specific technical tasks involved, and the even wider variety of resource options, administrative personnel must rely on informed technical opinion in the performance of the procurement function. This may involve taking teachers into the decision-making process, or it may involve the utilization of area specialists in "staff" positions at the administrative level. Either way it is clear that such matters cannot be handled satisfactorily through unilateral administrative action.

Similar considerations apply in the context of direct supervision of technical operations. On the one hand, administrative personnel are held responsible for the supervision of teaching personnel in the sense of observing the work of teachers and making recommendations concerning contract renewal. On the other hand, few administrators have sufficient competence or time to provide detailed supervision in the sense of scrutinizing the work of teachers, identifying unsatisfactory practices, and seeing to the elimination of those practices. Still less do they have either the time or the competence to keep abreast of new developments in all fields and see to their utilization by teachers. At best, direct administrative supervision in the public schools is a matter of identifying and eliminating the grossly unsatisfactory teacher.

The most visible aspect of the institutional level of organization in education, the institutional structure and agencies of the community, is the school board. In the "primitive" situation in which the education function is not differentiated from the family, problems concerning the mobilization of community support for policy decisions, the legitimation of the function, the financing of the function, and the integration of the demands of this function with those of other competing functions do not arise. As long as education remains the concern of each individual family, there is no collective organization devoted to that specific function. Moreover, as long as there is no collective process, there is no need to mobilize community resources to support these processes, and no need to mobilize power to define and implement policies. Once the technical function does become differentiated from the family, i.e., once education becomes a collective goal, and once an organization is created for the pursuit of the goal, then whether or not an administrative level of organization has evolved, policies must be set, the resources requisite to their implementation must be secured, the power required for effective collective action must be mobilized, and the commitment of the community to this function in proportion to competing commitments must be settled. Given the inherent possibility of competing demands from constituents of the collective process, competing demands on limited resources, and the lack of immediate access to facilities, some mechanism for the orderly solution of these problems must be devised. The elected or appointed board of trustees is only one possible solution but, given a pluralistic, democratic approach to collective action, a logical one. From this point of view, the electoral process through which trustees secure their offices is a set of procedural rules specifying the amount of community support that must be mobilized in order for a general objective to be made binding on the community. In the case of appointed boards, the mechanism simply operates at a higher level.

With the emergence of a distinct managerial system, the principal functions of the institutional system, i.e., the institutional structure and agencies of the community, come to be: (1) providing for the control of the managerial level, and through it, the technical level; (2) providing legitimation for the managerial level; (3) providing support for the managerial level; (4) providing for the raising of funds to finance the function of the organization; and (5) providing for the integration of the organization into the higher-order system of the community.

Control of the managerial level is accomplished in one or more of three principal ways. First, there are generalized normative standards, valid throughout the community, either formally codified in legal statutes or included in "standards of good practice." Here no specific agency need have primary responsibility for surveillance and enforcement. Control tends to be exercised in cases of suspected violation by law enforcement agencies, by public opinion—perhaps through news media—or by litigation in the courts. All of these tend to occur in relation to the public school, even though there is an agency having primary responsibility for surveillance and enforcement. Law enforcement agencies intervene in cases in which charges are brought, e.g., in misappropriation of funds. News media, interest groups, and professional associations call attention to instances of suspected malpractice.

The second type of control mechanism is a formally established agency, or collectivity, which exercises surveillance and control over the managerial system, e.g., the school board. The third is that which links the managerial level directly into a structure of public authority at some level. In the case of the public school this tends to be the state department of education which has both service and control functions vis-à-vis school districts.

All three types of controls just outlined are involved in the legitimation of the school. Generalized norms of both the legal and the uncodified varieties establish the right of the organization to operate, to command resources and support, and to subject clients to discipline. Boards of trustees spell out the limits of what managerial and technical personnel may legitimately do in areas for which legal statutes and standards of good practice do not provide adequate or appropriate coverage. Institutional structures legitimate implementive action, and when the conditions of implementive action are undergoing rapid change there is a continuing need for the reevaluation of the legitimacy of different modes and aspects of implementation. In one of its aspects the board of trustees is a mechanism for speeding up the "legitimation adjustment" process.

In part, the maintenance of community support for the school is a matter of school personnel adhering to the generalized normative standards previously identified, i.e., of insuring that its procedures are made acceptable to the community at large. Such standards define the conditions under which the operation of the school will be tolerated and supported in the community. As in the case of legitimation, however, changing conditions make standards that were appropriate at one point in time inappropriate at another. Successful performance of functions at both the technical and administrative levels requires the reexamination and modification of the normative standards regulating the operation of the school. The modification of such standards, however, poses problems in the maintenance of community support

which are met by the board of education in its representative capacity. In one of its functional aspects then, the school board is a mechanism for maintaining support despite what, under other circumstances, might be viewed as violations of established normative patterns. This is not to suggest that any given board is always successful. Constituents of the educational processes do repudiate the policies of their elected (or appointed) representatives, but this simply indicates failure to win support for the policies in question.

Similar comments can be made in the context of providing the financial resources required for the performance of technical and managerial functions. In a very simple situation a set of prescriptions concerning procedures through which the resources required for the performance of educational functions may work over an extended period of time. But in a complex money and market economy any given set of provisions seldom retains its suitability over more than a short period. Hence, these too must be reexamined and revised. Although boards of education play a considerable part in the process, it tends to be within limits imposed by state-wide legislation. Moreover, there has, over a period of years, been a trend in the direction of shifting responsibility for providing financial resources to higher levels of organization. The most obvious development in this context has been the rather recent heavy involvement of the federal government.

Finally, the principle function of the institutional level of organization in its lateral relations is to contribute to the integration of the community in the sense of determining the place of the educational function in the community and the cost, in terms of withdrawing resources from other functions, of maintaining it at a given level. Again, in the simple situation, the determination of the community's evaluation of the educative function and the determination of the proportion of resources to be devoted to it in comparison to and in competition with other functions is relatively unproblematic. In any case fluid resources and political support are scarce resources for which there is keen competition, but when these resources are highly mobile some device must be provided for keeping the system from getting too far out of balance. On the one hand, there is the problem of seeing that the educational enterprise has sufficient command of financial, human, and material resources, as well as legitimation and support, to perform its functions. On the other hand, the allocation of any of these to education constitutes a sacrifice in gains that might be had in other functional areas, e.g., health services, consumption, transportation, etc. Thus, the board mediates between the needs and claims of the school on the one hand, and the exigencies of scarce resources on the other. Technical and administrative personnel in education, as in any area, tend to see theirs as the top priority function and would in all probability, if left uncontrolled, place demands on community resources that resulted in intolerable deprivations in other areas. The principle output of the institutional level then, may be identified as a contribution to the integration of the higher-order system within which the function at the managerial level operates.

The parallel goal-output at the technical level, which is primarily an input to the household, ". . . is change in the character, knowledge and skill levels of individual pupils."[12] The role of the teacher is to educate in exactly that sense. The parallel at the managerial level can best be seen through the analogy of the business firm. There, the output of commodities is primarily the contribution of the technical system. The corresponding input is consumer demand, i.e., money payments for commodities. Although there is a widespread tendency to view the administrative level as nothing more than a facilitator of technical processes, there is another output for which it has primary responsibility. This is the second part of the interchange between the economy and the household which, in addition to the exchange of commodities for money, includes the exchange of wage payments for labor capacity. In return for wage payments the firm is allocated a share of the community's performance, or labor, capacity. Wage payments, however, are not only a means of securing control of labor capacity. They also constitute a contribution to the pool of purchasing power in the community.

> The firm "makes money" in a double sense; it is the recipient of proceeds of sales, but it also contributes to the flow of commodities and to the community's purchasing power. This is the main mechanism for the *generalization* of facilities, for increasing the community's level of economic effectiveness.[13]
> . . . the main point here is that the output of purchasing power is not merely an "instrumentality" for purchasing labor; it is an essential part of the functional *contribution* of the firm, and of course the same is true on the consumer's side.[14]

The function of the firm, i.e., the administrative level, is not the technical function of producing commodities but that of organizing the productive process to make it as effective as possible, thereby contributing to the generalized capacity of the society to perform economic functions. It is a contribution, through organization, to the community's level of economic effectiveness. The economic effectiveness of a community, i.e., its capacity to perform economic functions, or wealth, is not determined by the aggregate of physical commodities.

It includes an element of generalized disposability based on allocation relative to need. Through such decisions as what to produce, in what quantity and quality, for what market, on what terms, the managerial level enhances the generality of facilities. It is only through allocating resources (which include labor services) relative to need that contributions to purchasing power can be made.

The parallel in the case of the school may be outlined as follows: The technical level exchange involves an output of "change in the character, knowledge and skill levels" of individual pupils to the family household by active participation and cooperation—without which the relevant changes could not be brought about. Both the student and his family have a positive, contributory role in the educational processes. The student cannot be a passive, inert object on which teachers work or a receptacle into which character, knowledge, and skill is poured. And the family cannot be actively opposed to or even indifferent to what happens at school. At the administrative level the parallel of the firm's contribution to economic effectiveness through increasing purchasing power may be seen as a contribution to the community's generalized disposable performance capacity. Through organizing technical educational processes to make them as effective as possible, the managerial system contributes to the society's generalized performance capacity, i.e., that which is disposable through the labor market. Through such decisions as what to teach to what categories of pupils and through the formulation and implementation of educational policies, the managerial level influences the pool of generalized, disposable performance capacity.

In the same way that the wealth of a community is not a simple aggregate of physical commodities, but a function of the generalized disposability of facilities, the capacity of a community to get valued things done, i.e., its performance capacity, is not an aggregate of individual character traits, knowledge, and skills but a function of the level of disposability of performance capacities achieved by adapting technical education processes to the demand for trained performance capacities in the community. Failure on the part of the firm to adapt technical production processes to community conditions means that it does not make money through the sale of commodities. That, in turn, means that it cannot continue to make wage payments which constitute both an instrumentality in securing labor services and a contribution to economic effectiveness. In the same way, failure on the part of administrative personnel in the school to adapt technical education processes to community demands means that it does not secure cooperation from students and families. This failure, in turn, means that the school cannot continue as effectively as it might to produce generalized performance capacities. The similarities and differences between the firm and the school outlined here can be represented schematically as in Figure 34-1.

It seems possible at this point to link one of the most problematic features of public school operation to imbalances in the school-household interchange outlined above. The feature referred to is the widely discussed "failure" on the part of the urban school system to "reach" the children of the ghetto. Phrasing the problem in those terms seems to obscure rather than to illuminate matters. A more useful approach would appear to see the situation as the analog of deflation in the economic context. There, oversaving on the part of consumers (principally, but not only, households) leads to lower income for firms, lower rates of production, lower contributions to purchasing power, and lower commitment of labor capacity. The same result follows from undercommitment to, or lack of initiative in, the production of commodities on the part of firms, i.e., failure to adapt production processes to conditions of demand or to anticipate demands.

In the educational context the parallel of oversaving is unwillingness to participate actively and cooperatively in the educational process, leading to a failure to produce changes in character, knowledge, and skill levels. Failures at this level are reflected at the level of generalized performance capacity, which leads to reduced support for education as a function. Again, precisely the same result obtains

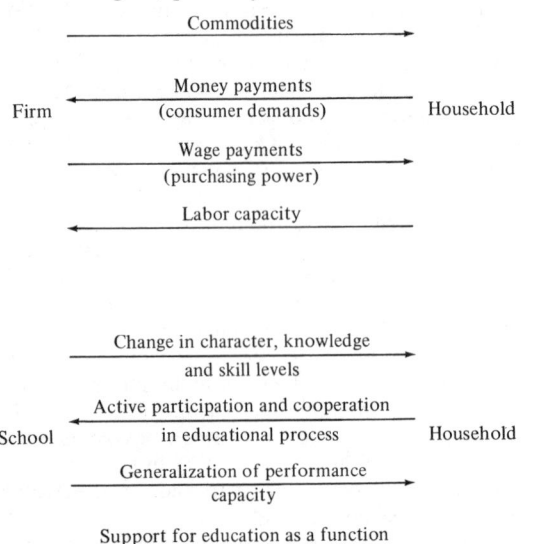

Figure 34-1. Comparison of firm-household and school-household interchanges.

from undercommitment to, or lack of initiative in, the adaptation of educational processes to conditions in the community by administrative personnel. Here the failure is one of allocation relative to need or demand for trained performance capacity in the community. The relevant demands here are those of direct clients of the school, i.e., families and interest groups that are oriented to educational goals. Given this analysis, proposed voucher systems which would permit the student and his family to select among schools which are dependent on the consumer's voucher for fluid resources would seem to hold some promise for encouraging greater adaptation of technical processes to community conditions, i.e., allocation relative to need. As a possible means of correcting the postulated deflationary situation, it certainly appears more promising than attempts to secure higher levels of participation and cooperation from students' families, which is the analog of stimulating consumer demand.

We noted that the board of education has a major responsibility for the procurement of financial resources and that there is a strong tendency to shunt that responsibility to higher levels of organization. We have no figures at hand, but there seems little doubt that the proportion of financial support for education raised at the state level has increased steadily in the past decade. Other prominent aspects of the resource procurement function at the institutional level concern personnel, not at the level of making specific appointments but at the level of insuring, through salary policies, access to adequate human resources.

Despite the implicit constitutional allocation of educational responsibilities to the several states and despite the long tradition of local district autonomy, educational organization at the societal level is not a new phenomenon. It dates back to the earliest days of the republic. What is new is the degree to which the welfare of society, rather than that of local communities and states, is now thought to be at stake in education, and the degree to which major responsibility for educational effectiveness has come to be institutionalized at the societal level. Evidence of this may be seen not only in the increasing involvement of the federal government in financing education but also in the fact that educational policies now have a prominent place in party platforms and are explicit campaign issues. One of the safest predictions that one can make about public education is that it will become more highly organized at the societal level.

The preceding discussion of levels of organization may be represented schematically as in Figure 34-2. Far from all of Figure 34-2 has been covered, but the main relations and interchanges among levels have

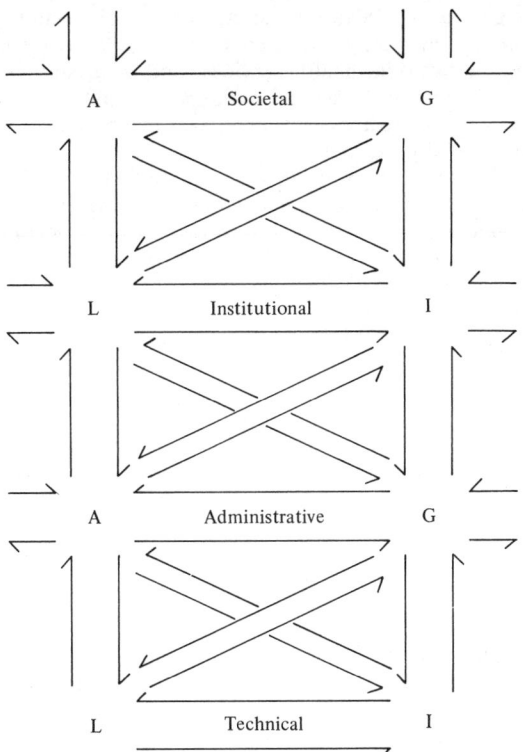

Figure 34-2. Articulation of levels of organization in education.

been touched upon. The system consists of articulated layers of L-I and A-G pairs in a series to form a continuous hierarchy. The A and G components of the administrative system articulate with the L and I components of the technical system to form what is most frequently identified as the "school system."

INTERNAL STRUCTURE AND FUNCTION OF THE SCHOOL

The transition from the discussion just presented to a consideration of the internal structure and functions of the school can be made by linking the hierarchically differentiated structure portrayed in Figure 34-2 with functionally differentiated subsystems. At one level of analysis, organizations are social systems in their own right. As such, they are subject to the four system problems, or functional imperatives, which may be outlined as follows. Given the proposition that the value system of the school is a subvalue system of the value system of the wider community and given the further proposition that values are commitments to action which will, within

limits, be acted upon whenever appropriate independent of cost, then it follows that the value system of a particular school constitutes a set of community-societal commitments to its functioning. Concretely, these commitments constitute a set of givens on which the functioning of the organization depends. This means that, within limits, the school has under its control certain societal resources access to which is not contingent on short-run sanctions. Like the business firm which has noncontingent access to sites, physical facilities, commonly held technology and knowledge, and human services, the school has noncontingent access to sites, premises, physical facilities, commonly held technical lore and knowledge of both educational and organizational matters, and human services. Thus, one may conceive of personnel who would leave the organization only in dire circumstances, and, more generally, of a component of all human services made available on value grounds alone (in education a component significantly higher than are most other areas). One may also conceive of readily and freely available knowledge of education and of organization for education, which, however dependent on human agents for their implementation, are analytically distinct components access to which is unproblematic.

Because the primary focus of the value system of the school is the definition of its goal, the implementation of the motivational, or human service, component of the set of commitments constitutes the direct implementation of the goal. Moreover, to the extent that value commitments are implemented, by definition, the pattern of the system is maintained. Goal-attainment for a collectivity, however, consists in the maintenance of a relatively optimal relation between the collectivity and some aspect of its intrasocietal or extrasocietal situation, e.g., other collectivities and agencies which are recipients of its output. If wants relative to that output, the set of underlying commitments, and the conditions of implementation of commitments were completely stable, then educational processes could be completely routinized.

In the actual case, none of these conditions obtains. Wants relative to the output of the school change, the conditions of implementation change, e.g., new knowledge of educational and organizational processes become available, and motivational commitments are by no means stable. Hence, relative to the set of value commitments underlying organizational functioning, a set of organizational processes and structures differentiates around. the problem of accommodating to these changing conditions. This is the goal attainment subsystem, the primary function of which is the mobilization of collective action to maintain an optimal system-environment relation.

The adaptive subsystem of the school is concerned with the management of resources. The primary problem is the maintenance and improvement of the patterns of organization and allocation necessary to provide the facility base for the performance of operative functions.

The integrative subsystem of the school specializes in the maintenance of complementarity among units making qualitatively different functional contributions to the system as a whole. Put in other terms, the problem is one of maintaining a state of cohesion which resists centrifugal and divisive tendencies and promotes positive coordination among the segmented and differentiated parts.

These four primary organizational subsystems may be linked with the A, G, I, and L components in Figure 34-2, which together constitute the administrative and technical levels of organization (see Figure 34-3).

The pattern-maintenance subsystem, then, is that complex of interactive relationships differentiated with reference to direct implementation of value commitments. In the firm, this is the technical production system; in the mental hospital, it is the treatment system; and in the school, it is the instructional system. In each case these fundamental goal-implementation processes exercise control over numerous other organizational processes, setting the limits within which goal-attainment adjustments must be made if the system is to retain its identity. The amount and nature of control exercised, of course, depends on the character of the technical activities themselves, particularly the sorts of "materials" upon which they are performed and on the degree of expert knowledge required to perform them. In the case of physical production, complex technological devices may be required; but it is not necessary to secure the cooperation of the raw materials upon which technical operations are performed. Neither is it necessary to get the consent of the finished product in order to dispose of it to users outside the organization. In those instances in which technical operations are performed on human individuals, e.g., education, health services, and legal services, the necessity to secure cooperation and consent imposes special constraints on nontechnical organizational processes.

Whatever the nature of the technical processes, once operating on a satisfactory basis they may be conceived, for analytical purposes, to have become more or less routinized. This is not an assumption of empirical stability. It is an assumption to the effect that if wants relative to technical outputs were stable, if the conditions of their production were determined by the "givens," then once an allocation of organizational resources relative to those wants had been established no change would occur. The fact is, of course, that changes do occur, both in the context of wants relative to technical outputs and in the context of the conditions of implementation. Any complex organization continuing in time holds multiple interests such that it has not a goal, but a system of goals ordered in terms of priority. Environmental changes require the reordering of priorities, and the reordering of priorities requires the reallocation of resources. Such decisions, in turn, bear unevenly on different groups within the organization posing threats to the loyal cooperation of personnel. If the organization is to be reasonably successful, these threats must be met with measures which insure a sufficient degree of support for current commitments.

Functional Differentiation in the School

Two principle sets of considerations will concern us in the discussion of internal structure and processes which follows. One is the identification of the four primary functionally differentiated subsystems of the school and the characterization of each in terms of its orientation, evaluative standard, institutionalized norms and medium. The other is the processes of interchange among these functionally differentiated subsystems of the social system of the school. In the first context, each of the subsystems of the school may, in a manner analogous to the societal system, i.e., the economy or the polity, be conceived as characterized by a primary orientation, a primary goal, a primary value standard, a primary set of normative rules regulating the pursuit of the goal, and a primary symbolic medium and measure of value.

As the value system of any specific-function collectivity always gives first priority to the goal-attainment function, the value standards in terms of which subsystem outputs are assessed are all differentiated versions of the general value standard of effectiveness. Moreover, the normative standards regulating the

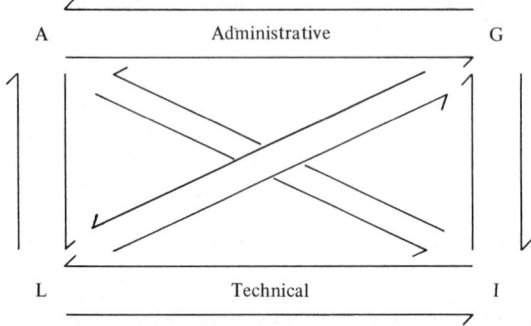

Figure 34-3. Internal structure and functions of the school.

pursuit of subsystem goals are all aspects of the institutions of authority, leadership, and regulation; and the media utilized by subsystems to facilitate their operation are all forms of power. Thus, the central process of organization, in its internal aspects, is the mobilization of power for the attainment of collective goals, and the central structural feature is the institution of authority.

Turning now to the principal characteristics of the functionally differentiated subsystems, we may begin by noting that the primary reference in the orientation of the pattern-maintenance unit is not the relation between the system and its environment, but the internal states and properties of the system, and not the consummatory relations among units within the system but the instrumentally significant resources of the units. For the unit with pattern-maintenance primacy the emphasis is on the implementation of morally binding obligations independent of their system-environment or subsystem consequences. In less technical terms the primary concern of the teacher is the implementation and maintenance of commitments, i.e., the maintenance and expression of an orientation independent of its implications for the external relations of the school or the relations among subsystems within the school. Teachers thus tend to view any concessions to parents or to community interests as a compromise of educational values. Administrators who make such concessions tend to be viewed as having "sold out," to have compromised educational values in the interest of personal safety or aspirations. One of the most severe criticisms a teacher can direct at an administrator is that he is "politically motivated"; that he hasn't the intestinal fortitude to stand on his convictions regardless of personal cost. The same concern is at the root of a second frequent criticism, that of giving "economic" considerations priority over educational.

The primary goal-output of the teacher is action implementing value commitments, specifically change in the character, knowledge, and skill levels of students; and the worth of such outputs is measured in terms of their value on a scale of effectiveness in the maintenance of the integrity of the school system value pattern. Given the proposition that the value system of an organization is concerned primarily with the definition of organizational goals, the value standard becomes effectiveness in the maintenance of the integrity of system goals. Thus, teachers may be highly productive in bringing about changes in the character, knowledge, and skill levels of students, but productivity as such is not automatically a contribution to the effective maintenance of the integrity of system goals. Conversely, changes proposed by administrative personnel may hold high promise for increased effectiveness in producing changes in character, knowledge and skill levels, but if they are perceived as violations of the integrity system, goals are not accepted readily. The assessment of teacher effectiveness, then, is never purely a matter of determining the effectiveness with which changes in character, knowledge, and skills are brought about. It includes a heavy emphasis on the value of those changes on a scale of integrity. Hence, a teacher who is extremely effective in bringing about changes in character, knowledge, and skills may be ineffective from the point of view of contributing to the maintenance of the integrity of the value pattern, i.e., of organizational goals. In one sense there is no fundamental difference between this emphasis and the corresponding emphasis at the operative level in the economic organization. There the organizational goal-orientation may be the production of a category of commodities, and the orientation of the operative level is the direct implementation and maintenance of that goal. The assessment of the operative member is in terms of his effectiveness in producing commodities not as such but those of relevance to this particular organization. An extremely important difference, however, is that the output of the firm is assessed in terms of its value on a scale of utility, and the criterion of satisfactory contribution to the value utility is solvency. The output of the school, on the other hand, is assessed in terms of its value on a scale integrity, i.e., as a contribution to the maintenance of the integrity of the value pattern of the larger system; and the standard of successful contribution to integrity is pattern-consistency in the sense of consistency between commitments and action. Thus, whereas rationality in the economic context calls for the selection and retention of personnel and practices which maximize solvency, i.e., minimize costs, rationality in the school calls for the selection and retention of practices and personnel which maximize pattern consistency in the sense of fulfilling in action the commitment of the school to superordinate values.

In our view it is this characteristic of the school, more than any other, which accounts for a number of frequently cited inadequacies of the school. Among these are inefficiency, failure to reward personnel in accordance with merit, lack of emphasis on the development and adoption of improved practices, slowness with which curricular changes are made, and so on. It would also seem to account, at least in part, for one of the most severely criticized shortcomings of city school systems, that of failing to succeed in educating those who have come to be termed the culturally deprived or disadvantaged. The problem would seem to be that success with such students requires the teacher to behave in ways that violate commitments to the paramount value pattern. Success in such cases would seem to require a far greater emphasis on therapy than either present personnel or conditions permit.

The medium of exchange and symbol value operating in this context is technical power, i.e., that which is based on functional specialization. From the point of view of the employee, appointment to a position in an organization constitutes a receipt of power. He receives authorization to operate within the organization and in the assignment of his functions is allocated responsibilities to make decisions. Termination of employment constitutes a withdrawal of power, and demotion a reduction of power. There are, however, mechanisms for increasing and decreasing grants of power more subtle than these, e.g., a teacher who has demonstrated his capacity to effectively maintain the integrity of organizational goals is rarely subjected to supervision.

Finally, the institutional patterns governing the pursuit of the goals of pattern-maintenance units are concerned primarily with the definition and limitation of authority. From one point of view, teaching is primarily a decision-making process. The teacher is the institutionally defined superior of the student, and it is through making and enforcing decisions concerning work to be done, standards of work and conduct to be met, materials and methods to be used, and sanctions to be allocated that the custodial, protective, socialization-in-role, and broader socialization goals of the school are implemented. Given compulsory school attendance and the relative vulnerability of the student, it is essential that the exercise of the teacher's authority be institutionally regulated.

As noted in a previous section, institutions are derivations from more general conceptions of the desirable which are integrated in the concrete action of the units of a system in their interaction with each other through the definition of role expectations and the organization of motivation. They define what are felt to be, in a given system, proper, legitimate, or expected modes of action, or of social relationship, e.g., teacher-student, teacher-principal.

> Institutions are those patterns which define the essentials of the legitimately expected behavior of persons insofar as they perform structurally relevant roles in the social system. There are, of course, many degrees of conformity, or the lack of it, but a pattern is institutionalized only insofar as at least a minimum degree of conformity is expected — thus its absence is treated with sanctions at least of strong disapproval — and a sufficient degree of conformity on the part of a sufficient proportion of the relevant population exists so that this pattern defines the dominant structural outline of the relevant system of concrete social relationships.[15]

The primary institutional patterns governing the pursuit of technical goals in the school, then, can be said to be those which define what are felt to be proper, legitimate or expected modes of decision-making and decision-enforcing behavior. These patterns define legitimate and illegitimate modes of action in pursuit of the goal of preserving the integrity of the value system which specifies the goal of the school. Institutional patterns, however, are not arbitrarily specified definitions of legitimate and illegitimate modes of action, they are derivations from the value pattern that spell out the implications of that pattern for concrete social relationships. Just as in the value system economic rationality is institutionalized in the authority, or right, of business managers to introduce technological changes which reduce production costs, the value system of the school is institutionalized in the right of the teacher to decide (within limits) what constitutes proper conduct within his classroom, and to enforce those standards with sanctions. Given the value principle of integrity as the standard in terms of which educational outputs are evaluated, and given commitments as the means of defining the costs of "production" and the value of outputs, the personnel directly responsible for value implementations must have, in the school setting, authority very much like that of the parent.

The increasing emphasis on the socialization goals of the school, however, has resulted over a period of time in the institutionalization of an expectation that the authority of the teacher will be wielded in a less and less autocratic manner. Socializing the student in the values of the school and securing his acceptance of the role of student and his active cooperation in the achievement of instructional goals requires that the decisions of teachers be regarded as fair by the student.

A complication in institutional patterns is introduced by the fact that teaching is at least a semi-profession. Though there may be some question about the extent of the body of empirical knowledge for which teachers have an independent trusteeship, there is little doubt that there is some, and no doubt at all that there is a more or less well-defined set of ethical ideals which have implications for institutional patterns. The relevant institutions concern not only teacher-student relations, but teacher-teacher and teacher-administrator relations as well. For the most part the norms are informal and the professional group has little sanctioning power, probably because the empirical knowledge component of the trusteeship is insufficient to warrant the institutionalization of the teacher as the sole competent expert with respect to matters of good educational practice, and hence with respect to malpractice. Much the same point would seem to apply in the teacher-administrator relation. As the teacher, though admittedly more competent in specific areas than the administrator, is not defined as the sole competent expert on educational matters, he cannot be regarded as the sole competent expert concerning the functions of administration in relation to the facilitation of the effective functioning of the technical staff. Hence, the teacher is far more the subject of administrative authority than is the physician in the hospital or the psychiatrist in the mental hospital.

In the context of teacher-teacher relations the most visible norms have to do with interfering with the work and with "undermining" the authority of others. The norms prohibit open criticism of teachers by teachers and, generally, the "airing of dirty linen in public."

The primary reference in the orientation of the adaptive subsystem of the school differs from that of the pattern-maintenance subsystem in that it is to the relation between the system and its environment. The two are similar, however, in the instrumental emphasis. Here the emphasis is not on the implementation of system commitments but on the enhancement of the instrumental capacities of the system. Adaptation consists in maximizing the supply of generalized facilities available to the system, generalized in the sense that they can be utilized in the facilitation of the attainment of a wide variety of system and subsystem goals. As the primary, generalized facility for organizations is fluid funds, this is primarily a problem of securing such funds and insuring their efficient use.

The primary goal-output of the adaptive subsystem is the flow of facilities for the performance of technical functions, and the value standard in terms of which that output is assessed its effectiveness in maximizing the utility of resources, i.e., economic efficiency. The emphasis on efficiency yields such common tendencies as those toward standardization of materials and centralization of purchasing that are characteristic of procurement departments in large school systems. But it does not end there. One of the principal resources of organizations is the human services available to it, and one of the principal concerns in the conservation of resources is the deployment of personnel in a manner which yields maximum utilization of their services. Hence, there is an allocative aspect of resource management which pertains directly to personnel and their organization. This allocative aspect of the problem can be seen most clearly in the context of designing a new organization. Here it is clear that a basic set of organizational questions concern specification of the functions essential to the implementation of organizational values, the linkages between those functions, and the allocation of those functions to personnel and suborganizations. In simplest terms, this is a matter of deciding what must be done, in what order, by whom. Hence, the allocative organization is the system's basic plan for achieving its objectives. In the school, the adaptive emphasis on

efficient human resource utilization can be seen in the current interest in "differentiated staffing," in the recurring interest in "merit pay" plans, and in such historical trends as those identified by Callahan.[16] As noted, one of the basic sources of dissatisfaction among teachers is what is, from their point of view, the tendency of administrative personnel to sacrifice value implementation to efficiency.

As seen earlier, underlying the allocative organization is a conception of the activities and resources required for value implementation. The maintenance of the allocative pattern, then, encompasses what is commonly termed "supervision," i.e., seeing that human, material, and financial resources are utilized in the manner intended. Perhaps the more general term administration, defined as the processes designed to bring persons and collectivities and categories of them to fulfill the obligations imposed by legitimate authority, is more appropriate.

Again, the symbolic medium of exchange and measure of value is power, and the norms governing the pursuit of administrative goals concern allocative authority. The price of participation in a system of collective action is acceptance of the organization's authority system, and the allocative category of authority includes the right to allocate responsibilities, to allocate physical and financial resources, and to administer in the sense of seeing that the obligations imposed by the allocative decisions of legitimate authorities are implemented.

The main burden of the administrative or supervisory aspect of the resource-management function in the school falls on lower-level administrators, particularly principals and to some extent department heads. Unlike university department heads and deans, public school administrative personnel have the right to supervise the work of the classroom teachers and to hold them responsible not only for fulfilling their assigned tasks but also for fulfilling them in the proper manner. Teaching has not reached a level of professionalization at which the technical expert can be held accountable for the results he gets, but not the methods by which they are gotten. Supervision tends to be relatively close during an initial probationary period but infrequent thereafter except in cases of actual or suspected deviance.

The primary reference to the orientation of the goal-attainment subsystem of the school is the consummatory side of the system-environment relation. Goal attainment concerns the maintenance of states of interaction between the system and its environment which are desirable from the point of view of the internal needs of the system and, hence, is related directly to changing environmental conditions. The particularly important aspect of the environment in this context is the market for the disposal of the product; in this case the members of the community who are the direct clients of the school, e.g., families and interest groups oriented to educational goals. The problem then, is primarily one of mobilizing the resources of the system in the interest of establishing, maintaining, and re-establishing the optimum relation between system and environment. The primary goal-output of the goal-attainment subsystem is collective action in the interest of effecting the measures required to maintain an optimal relation to the environment, and the standard for assessing the value of outputs is effectiveness in the implementation of external commitments, i.e., policy decisions. For want of a better term, the category of authority regulating the pursuit of such goals may be called "executive" authority. Concretely, the personnel involved here are top-level administrators, the superintendent, his immediate subordinates and administrative staff, sometimes constituting an administrative cabinet. The responsible executive and his staff are, of course, subject to the control of the institutional structures and agencies of the community, particularly the board of education, but they are seldom passive administrators of the clearly delineated policies of the governing board.

Finally, the primary reference in the orientation of the integrative subsystem is the consummatory relations among the subsystems constituting the social system of the school. Its primary function is the maintenance of positive coordination among the differentiated and segmented parts of the system, particularly the pattern-maintenance, adaptive, and goal-attainment subsystems. Its primary goal-output is support for policy commitments, and the standard of value for judging the worth of such outputs is effectiveness in the coordination of activities in the sense of maintaining complementarity among units making qualitatively differentiated contributions to the functioning of the system. The relevant authority pattern may be termed "coordinative" authority.

The problem in the school, as in any organization, is that the requisite degree of complementarity between functionally differentiated subsystems, each regulated by a different value standard, cannot be presumed to be given. On the one hand relations between the technical and policy implementation subsystems may be strained by the fact that policy commitments have consequences which bear unevenly on different groups and suborganizations or which are perceived as violations of the integrity of the value pattern. Seeing that the relative burdens and benefits received as a consequence of policy commitments do not get too far out of line with what is considered fair and just and that value integrity is not seriously compromised is a condition of the maintenance of support for those commitments. On the other hand, new policy commitments often require new combinations of facilities or new patterns of resource allocation, which cannot be expected to occur automatically. It is always possible, indeed likely if special measures are not taken, that the several functionally differentiated subsystems will get "out of phase" with one another. Hence, seeing that facilities match implementation needs is a condition of smooth organizational functioning. In simplest terms, then, the function of the integrative subsystem is to coordinate the activities of the technical, administrative, and leadership subsystems, a primary aspect of which is the mobilization for policy decisions.

Input-Output Interchanges in the School

The second set of processes to be considered in the context of the internal structure and functions of the school has to do with the processes of input-output interchange among functionally differentiated subsystems.

The respective emphases of the adaptive, goal-attainment, integrative, and pattern-maintenance subsystems are the maintenance and improvement of the patterns of allocation and organization necessary to provide the facility base for the performance of technical functions, spelling out the implications of policy commitments, enlisting the loyal cooperation of personnel, and the direct implementation of value commitments, i.e., technical processing. Henceforth we shall refer to these as the facility-maintenance, policy implementation, coordinative, and technical subsystems. These internal functions, and the associated internal interchange processes, are not identical with concrete suborganizations or individual roles as commonly defined, i.e., teacher, principal, or superintendent. Whether these functions, roles in the analytical sense, are coterminous with the activities of concrete individuals and organizational subdivisions is a function of the division of labor within the organization.

Each of the four primary subsystems just identified is conceived as subject to the four system problems and itself internally differentiated. Each operates on the basis of a subset of value commitments, a subsystem of the organizational value system. Each has its own adaptive, goal-attainment, and integrative problems. Figure 34-4 identifies the pattern of interchanges among functionally differentiated subsystems. If we adopt, for purposes of the present discussion, the notation system SA, SG, SI, and SL to refer respectively to the facility maintenance, policy implementation, coordinative, and technical subsystems of the school and SAa, SAg, SAi, and

SA1 as the paradigm for referring respectively to the four subsystems of any primary subsystem, then the full set of interchange relationships is as follows:

$$
\begin{array}{ccc}
SAg & \longleftrightarrow & SLg \\
SAa & \longleftrightarrow & SGa \\
SAi & \longleftrightarrow & SIi \\
SGg & \longleftrightarrow & SIg \\
SGi & \longleftrightarrow & SLi \\
SIa & \longleftrightarrow & SLa
\end{array}
$$

The general nature of these interchanges is determined by the subsystems involved. In the SAg — SLg interchange it is the goal-attainment subsystems of the allocative and technical systems, hence, this is a mutual exchange of goal-outputs. The same applies to the SGg — SIg interchange. The SAa — SGa interchange links the adaptive subsystems of the facility maintenance and policy implementation systems, indicating an exchange of adaptive facilities. The

SLa — SIa interchange shares that characteristic. Finally, the SAi — SIi interchange couples the integrative subsystems of the allocative and support mobilization systems in a mutual exchange of resources required for subsystem integration. The specific content of these interchanges is far from obvious. In what follows we shall rely on the sketchy discussion provided by Parsons, the logic of the paradigm itself, and anecdotal evidence. The result will be far from satisfactory, but a beginning may be made.

We have located the basic value-implementation functions in the pattern-maintenance subsystem of the school. In essence, this is a problem of the maintenance and/or enhancement of a level of value implementation in accordance with a level of facilities. For the individual teachers, this means the maintenance or enhancement of a given "teaching style" in accordance with a given facility level. Teaching styles require, in a manner analogous to family life

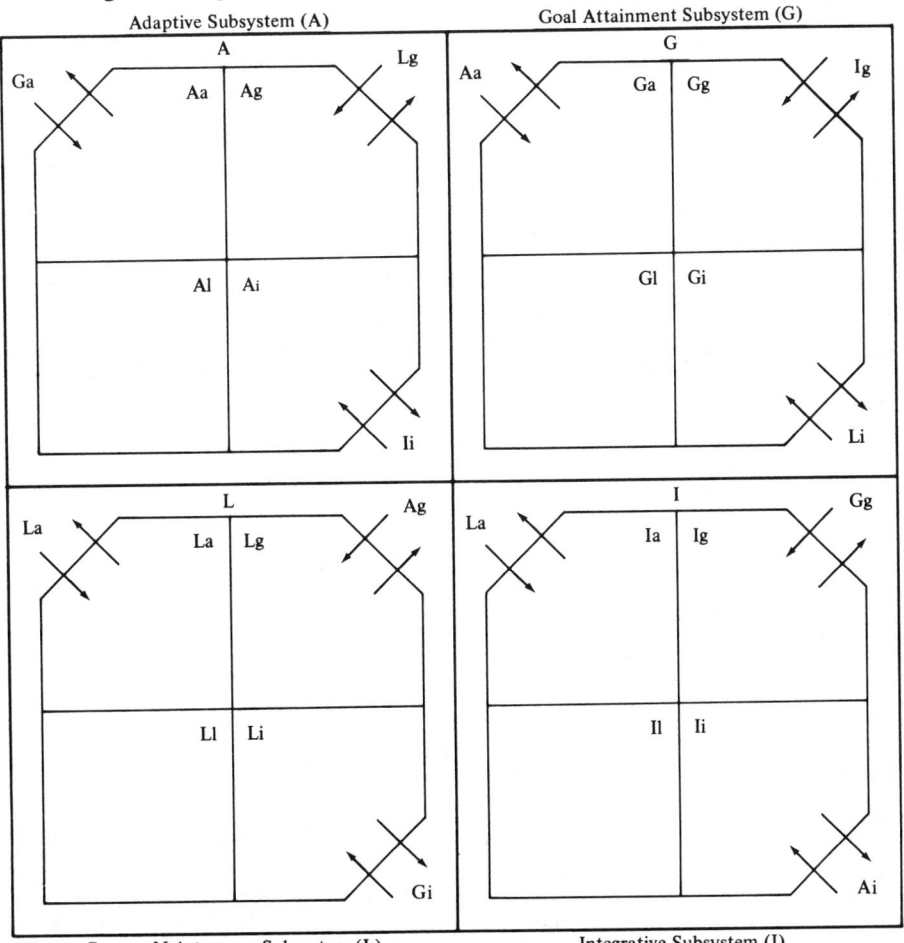

Figure 34-4.   In put-output interchanges within the social system.

styles, concrete premises in which everyday technical functions are performed, providing classroom equipment, books, supplies, and other instructional materials.

We have used the term teaching style quite deliberately, for as Jackson has noted, "They [teachers] are interested . . . in stylistic qualities of their own performance as much as in whether specific goals were reached and specific objectives attained."[17] As Jackson further points out, the "rational achievement" model simply does not describe the behavior of the classroom teacher. Moreover,

> The teacher's concern with the here-and-now and her emotional attachment to her world was often accompanied in her conversations by an accepting attitude toward educational conditions as they now exist. Interest in educational change was usually mild and typically was restricted to ideas about how to rearrange her room or how to regroup her students — *how to work better with the education "givens,"* in other words. Rarely, if ever, was there talk of need for broad or dramatic educational reforms, even though the interviews provided ample opportunity to discuss these matters.[18]

Concretely the problems encountered in the technical system are primarily those of effectively maintaining the ongoing activities of the classroom. As noted, this is seldom a matter of rationally selecting the means best suited to the attainment of instructional objectives. Again, Jackson's comments are instructive.

> Teachers, particularly in the lower grades, seem to be more activity-oriented than learning-oriented. That is, they commonly decide on a set of activities which they believe will have a desirable outcome and then focus their energies on achieving and maintaining student involvement in those activities. Learning is important, to be sure, but when the teacher is actually interacting with his students it is at the periphery of his attention, rather than at the focus of his vision.[19]

In some ways, the teacher's concern with the learning of his students is similar to a mother's concern with the nutrition of her children. Most mothers surely desire their children to develop healthy and strong bodies and they understand the general relationship between the quality of food they provide and the status of their child's health. But in planning their meals the nutritional value of the foods they use is thought of if at all, in the very broadest terms. Many other variables, such as cost, convenience, esthetic quality, and idiosyncratic taste play a part in the selection of and preparation of the family diet. Because of the adaptiveness of humans, in most cases the result is a healthy family.

Like mothers, teachers have responsibility for definite aspects of their students' growth, They too understand the overall relationship between their daily activities and the achievement of educational ends. But in their moment-by-moment decisions the details of this relationship, the process of learning per se, is not uppermost in their minds.

Rather, they seem to be guided by certain rule-of-thumb considerations that are constantly being modified by the specifics of each classroom situation. The result, if we can believe achievement test scores and other indicators of academic attainment, is "normal" educational growth for most students.[20]

The more specific goal of the technical subsystem of the school, then, can be identified as the maintenance of an optimum rate of change in the character, knowledge, and skill levels of students, and the primary situational exigencies to which the teacher must adapt are those presented by the personalities and levels of development of the students themselves.

The generalized adaptive facilities underlying the realization of technical goals, and the capacity of the technical system to meet unforeseen contingencies are knowledge and skills of operative personnel. A major source of differences in the internal structure of organizations can be located in the varying levels of technical skill and knowledge required for operative performance. As Jackson so aptly points out, the knowledge the teacher brings to bear, apart from his knowledge of subject matter, is largely intuitive. Teachers have a

> tendency to approach educational affairs intuitively rather than rationally. When called on to justify their professional decisions, for example, my informants often declared that their classroom behavior was based more on impulse than on reflection and thought. In other words, they were more likely to defend themselves by pointing out that a particular course of action *felt* like the right thing to do, rather than by claiming that they *knew* it to be right. As the structure of a teaching session or of a class day unfolds, the teacher frequently behaves like a musician without a score. He ad-libs.[21]

> Rarely if ever, did they turn to evidence beyond their own personal experience to justify their professional preferences.[22]

This heavy reliance on intuition in classroom teaching means that the teacher's primary claim to autonomy has to be based primarily on "closeness to the problems" and on experience rather than on specialized technical competence. Given the fact that administrators have had a number of years of "successful" teaching experience and relatively unlimited opportunity to observe a wide variety of classrooms, plus the fact that intuition is impossible to defend rationally, the teacher tends not to be viewed as the sole expert on instructional matters.

Finally, the integration of the technical subsystem concerns the organization of instructional roles. Much of the current emphasis on innovation is directed here. Such practices as team-teaching and open-area schools are basically attempts to reorganize the technical subsystem of the school.

The results of technical performance, the goal-output of the technical system, analogous to the output of labor capacity by the household at the societal level, is exchanged for the goal-output of facility maintenance subsystem. The facility main- tenance function concerns not only the maintenance of an adequate facility base for the performance of technical functions but also the maintenance and improvement of the patterns of allocation and organization necessary to provide that facility base. This

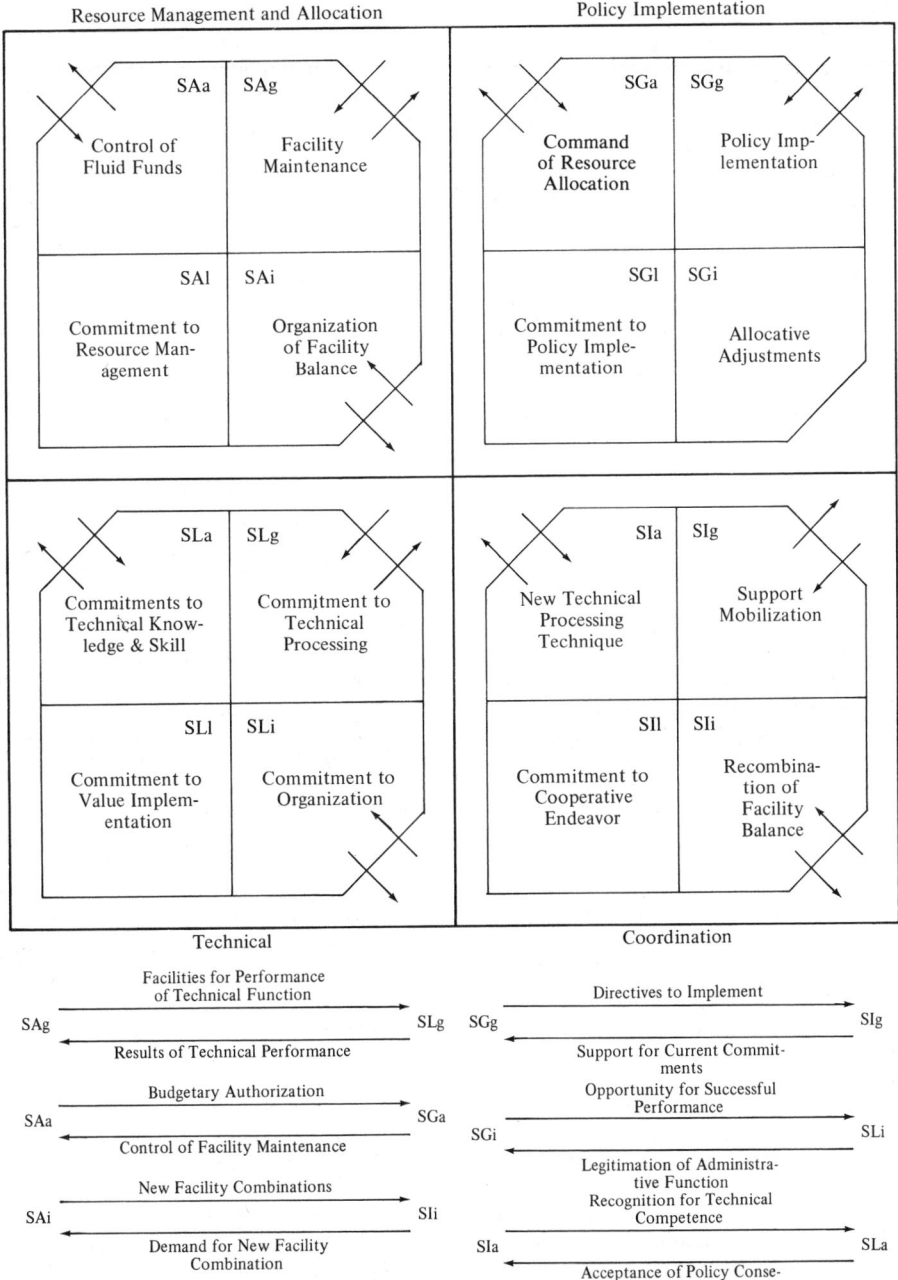

Figure 34-5. Internal structure and process of organization.

includes responsibility for the allocative organization through which resources are channelled and distributed within the organization. The term "facilities" must be understood more broadly than physical resources. It includes the allocation of responsibilities, authority, and of the financial and physical means for carrying out responsibilities.

In an established organization the allocative organization is more or less stabilized, and the facility-maintenance function focuses primarily on (1) maintaining an adequate flow of facilities, materials to be processed, and replacement personnel; (2) the organization and supervision of auxiliary personnel; and (3) supervision, i.e., insuring that suborganizations and personnel carry out their assigned responsibilities.

What is provided as the output of the facility maintenance system, then, is not a stream of discrete bits and pieces of needed resources, but a particular, more-or-less integrated combination of resource components and the supervision of their utilization. The integrative problem of the facility maintenance system centers around the maintenance of an appropriate balance among resource factors, e.g., responsibility and authority, human and financial resources, and task assignment. Financial resources secured through procurement channels constitute the primary adaptive facilities on which the facility maintenance subsystem depends. Fluid kinds are generally disposable resources enabling the system to meet, or to adapt to, unforeseen situational contingencies. The principal source of such contingencies is the changing implementation needs of the policy implementation subsystem. The primary function of the latter is to spell out, authorize, and enforce the measures required to implement external commitments, i.e., policy commitments to constituents of the educational processes. Its adaptive need is primarily to insure that the accumulation of facilities and their allocation proceeds selectively, in accordance with policy implementation needs. The central mechanism here seems to be the budget. The facility maintenance subsystem may be conceived as controlling the fluid funds available to the organization. Through the process of budgeting, it selectively accumulates and allocates facilities in accordance with current policy implementation needs, thus providing the policy implementation subsystem with an input of "control of facility allocation" which meets its adaptive needs. The counter-input, from the policy implementation subsystem to the facility maintenance subsystem would seem to be budgetary approval, i.e., authorization to utilize fluid funds in the manner specified.

As suggested, the focal concern of the policy implementation system is the question of how, on a general level, to implement commitments undertaken in the policy-decision-political support interchange at the organization-environment boundary. The output of binding directives to implement requires the spelling out of the internal implications of policy commitments. The adaptive needs of the policy implementation subsystem articulate with the allocative organization's need for the fluid funds. To effectively implement policy commitments, the implementation subsystem must have command of resource allocation. The required control is inherent in the budgetary process. The actual processes of "budget building" may begin with the specification of needs by operative units and suborganizations, but final approval, or authorization, typically is a decision reserved for the board of trustees and in some cases requiring a public hearing. Budgetary authorization constitutes a "go-ahead" signal to the facility maintenance subsystem, a signal to proceed with further facility processing. The exchange can be conceived, then, as the mutual enhancement of adaptive capacities — authorization in return for control of facility allocation.

The SGg-SIg linkage involves an exchange of directives to implement, spelling out the implications of policy decisions, for support for current commitments mobilized within the coordinative subsystem. Policy decisions have consequences which bear unevenly on groups within the organization, and this unevenness is the primary source of the integrative problem of organizations. The emphasis here is on securing support for current policy commitments in spite of differential consequences in terms of relative rewards and burdens. Groups and individuals within the organization must be persuaded that the consequences of such decisions correspond to norms of fairness and of authority. The critical situational exigency to which the coordinative subsystem must adapt is the degree of commitment of operative personnel to technical knowledge and skill. This has a direct bearing on the willingness of personnel to accept the consequences of policy decisions. The problem is readily apparent when operative personnel are "high-level" professionals, in which case the organizational authority pattern must give adequate recognition to their technical competence, right to autonomy, and integrity. The exchange between SIa and SLa, then, can be conceived as an exchange of recognition of technical competence for acceptance of the consequences of policy decisions, the former fulfilling the adaptive needs of the technical subsystem, the latter fulfilling the same need of the coordinative subsystem by providing an essential ingredient in the process of mobilizing support.

What of the SAi-SIi interchange? According to the paradigm this is a mutual exchange of factors essential to subsystem integration. We noted that the primary integrative problem of the allocative system concerned the maintenance of suitable balance among the resource factors constituting the facility base. Hence the input from SIi may be identified as directives to alter the resource balance. This may be seen as an input of organization to the facility maintenance subsystem. Disorganization in this subsystem arises from disproportion in the balance of resources, e.g., disproportion between responsibility and authority, between responsibility and access to funds. The counter-input from SAi is new combinations of resource factors. The significance of this input is integrative insofar as resource allocation patterns symbolize the location of units relative to each other in the stratification system. Within organizations a critical aspect of this is insuring that the pattern of allocation of authority and responsibility provides adequate symbolic recognition to the special technical competence of highly trained personnel.

The final interchange, that between SLi and SGi has to do primarily with the legitimation of the powers and authority of the administration, on the one hand, and insuring opportunity for successful technical performance, on the other.

> This legitimation cannot be directly derived from the individual technical competence and moral integrity of the administrative personnel, since their direct functions are not as such operative. The primary focus of legitimation must be in recognition of the exigencies which make organization necessary so that its cost is justified. On the other side, within the framework of an established organization, the administration takes responsibility for adjusting the allocation of responsibilities among the operative groups.[23]

> What is required here is to earn the "confidence" of the operating personnel through insuring opportunity for successful achievement. This is a higher order basis for securing the loyal cooperation of the organization than that involved in support for policy decisions in the usual sense. I am discriminating two different factors in what is often called "satisfaction" of personnel with the administration. On the one hand there is the problem of support for the current commitments which have varying consequences for different elements within the organization. Here the emphasis is on the *relative* burdens and rewards received as a consequence of such decisions. The other component is the shared attitudes of legitimation of the over-all conduct of the administrative function, not taken in distributive terms.[24]

Legitimation functions to define what leadership organization is for, and hence, the nature and scope of the agencies and roles which perform these functions. The central concern here is not the allocation of authorization and responsibilities among personnel and suborganizations, and not the adjustment or recombination of these factors seen in distributive terms, but the definition of the leadership function itself, vis-à-vis the technical processing system. The input of legitimation from SLi, in defining the functions of leadership elements, contributes to the integration of SGi. At the same time, the definition of the purposes of leadership by elements of SLi concerned with the direct implementation of basic values, insures that these functions are defined (though not necessarily performed) in such a way as to contribute to the successful achievement of technical goals. Within the framework of an established definition of leadership function, managerial personnel have the responsibility for the allocation of resource factors. But this leaves open the question of the definition of the leadership function itself, which is the focal concern of SGi. This adjustment in the allocation of responsibilities in accordance with the definition of functions is the source of the counter-input of opportunity for successful technical achievement to SLi. In the mental hospital, for example, the psychiatrist is regarded as the expert in the diagnosis and treatment of mental illness, and hence the expert in the functions of hospital organization and administration insofar as these facilitate effective performance of the therapeutic function.

As noted in a previous section, legitimation of authority imposes on the legitimated authorities responsibility for the successful implementation of values. Success in the implementation of its mandate is the normative standard guiding political action analogous to solvency in the economy. Success in this sense entails the maintenance of the authority of the organization's offices without depending on external sources of power. The most prominent current example of unsuccessful administration may be seen in universities which have had to rely heavily on "political subsidies" to maintain the authority of their offices. In the public school, the most visible evidence of difficulty in this exchange is the complaint of teachers that administrative personnel fail to "back them up" in matters concerning the discipline of students.

CONCLUSION

This paper represents an attempt to make direct application of a general analytical framework to a particular kind of organization, the public school. It is, like the paper after which it was partially patterned,[25] more in the nature of a prolegomenon than of a full, satisfactory analysis of the school as a type of organization. To paraphrase Parsons' concluding comments in that paper, attempts to go farther, in the direction begun here, will have to aim at locating the relationship of the school, in terms of both its external functions and its internal structure and functions, to other types of organizations. This locating is not in terms of specific points, but rather in terms of ranges within which the relevant features of the school can be expected to fit in relation to other types of organizations. Why the school should fall within a given range and differ from other types of organization must then be related to the nature of its functions, to the types of students it must deal with and how, to the types of personnel it employs, to the modes of its financial support, to its "public relations," and to the many internal exigencies of the sort we have attempted to outline.

Above all, it is to be emphasized that an understanding of the school is heavily dependent on the extent to which the peculiarities of the school as an organization can be systematically related to those of other types of organization which differ from it. This cannot be derived from the study of schools alone, but only from its place in the comparative study of the whole range of types of organization.[26]

NOTES

1. Talcott Parsons, "The Political Aspect of Social Structure and Process," in David Easton (ed.), *Varieties of Political Theory* (Englewood Cliffs: Prentice-Hall, 1966), p. 82.

2. *Ibid.*, p. 78.

3. Talcott Parsons, "On the Concept of Political Power," in T. Parsons, *Sociological Theory and Modern Society* (New York: The Free Press, 1967), pp. 297-354 at p. 323f.

4. Parsons, "The Political Aspect of Social Structure and Process," *op. cit.*, p. 84.

5. Talcott Parsons, "On the Concept of Value Commitments," *Sociological Inquiry* 38 (Spring), p. 148.

6. Talcott Parsons, *Social Structure and Personality* (Glencoe: The Free Press, 1964), p. 130.

7. Talcott Parsons, "The Mental Hospital as a Type of Organization," in Milton Greenblatt *et al.* (eds.). *The Patient and the Mental Hospital* (New York: The Free Press, 1963), p. 120.

8. Philip W. Jackson, *Life in Classrooms* (New York: Holt, Rinehart, and Winston, 1968).

9. Talcott Parsons, *Essays in Sociological Theory* (revised edition) (Glencoe: The Free Press, 1954), p. 372.

10. Talcott Parsons and Neil J. Smelser, *Economy and Society* (New York: The Free Press, 1965), p. 155.

11. Talcott Parsons, *Structure and Process in Modern Societies* (New York: The Free Press, 1960), Chapter II. Also, T. Parsons, "General Theory in Sociology," in R. K. Merton, *et al.* (eds.), *Sociology Today* (New York: Basic Books, 1959).

12. Parsons, *Structure and Process in Modern Society*, p. 76.

13. *Ibid.*, p. 75.

14. *Loc. cit.*

15. Parsons, *Essays in Sociological Theory*, p. 239.

16. Raymond E. Callahan, *Education and the Cult of Efficiency* (Chicago: University of Chicago Press, 1962).

17. Jackson, *op. cit.*, p. 167-68.

18. *Ibid.*, p. 148.

19. *Ibid.*, p. 162.

20. *Ibid.*, pp. 163-64.

21. *Ibid.*, p. 145.

22. *Ibid.*, p. 146.

23. Parsons, "The Mental Hospital . . .," *op. cit.*, p. 124.

24. *Ibid.*, pp. 126-27.

25. Parts of this essay follow closely the format of *ibid.*

26. *Ibid.*, pp. 128-29.

35

THE ORGANIZATIONAL STRUCTURE OF SCHOOLS AND SCHOOL SYSTEMS

Robert Dreeben

Talcott Parsons, in several of his most intriguing theoretical papers, has concerned himself with the nature of large-scale organizations. Two of these papers,[1] general in character, develop a scheme designed to account for structural variation between and within organizations; three others[2] illuminate the peculiarities of specific organizations (mental hospitals, schools, and universities) according to the general scheme proposed in the first two. These writings scarcely exhaust Parsons' thinking about organizations; one finds many references to them throughout his work on the general theory of action. They do, however, represent his explicitly formulated position.

My aim in this essay is to confront a set of theoretical ideas with certain concrete social phenomena, specifically, Parsons' formulation of large-scale organization and the social properties of American public schools and school systems. I begin by treating schools from three perspectives. The first two are conventionally organizational: What are the structural properties of schools and of school systems? The third is processual, but with implications for structure: What is the character of schooling? I follow by juxtaposing the structural analysis with Parsons' formulation.

My discussion of schools, school systems,[3] and schooling is empirical, though crudely so because it relies on rough and ready observation; the literature on school organization contains hardly any propositions in quantitative form. Description, however, reveals organizational patterns that may be accounted for by Parsons' formulation, possibly by alternatives, and perhaps by both.

I wish to thank C. Arnold Anderson, Charles E. Bidwell, Philip J. Foster, Victor Lidz, and Jan J. Loubser for their helpful comments.

SCHOOL ORGANIZATION AND SCHOOLING

An analysis of social organization must start with description, and selective description at that. To set the record straight, let me acknowledge at the outset that some of my observations and some of the distinctions I draw have their roots in Parsons' work; others, of course, have different origins.

School Systems

Public education in the United States falls under the political jurisdiction of state governments. Although Congress enacts legislation affecting educational policy in the states, and the U.S. Office of Education as part of the Executive Branch concerns itself with the administration of such policies, there is no national ministry. Although state governments serve legislative and regulatory functions of a general sort and finance a substantial part of the educational enterprise within their boundaries, municipalities usually constitute the most immediate political units within which public educational activities are carried on. A school system, comprised of a school board, an administration, and one or more schools, is an educational apparatus operating within political units smaller than states.

The governance of school systems is most difficult to identify because organizational charts and even widely accepted formulations about the nature of authority provide few clues as to where the power to make binding decisions resides. Conventionally, school boards are empowered by state laws to make binding decisions in matters of general educational policy; school superintendents, in their executive capacities as hired functionaries of the board, supposedly hold responsibility for effecting policy.

Perhaps that arrangement exists somewhere, but to formulate the problem of governance in those terms does injustice to the complexity and variety of educational reality.

Consider the case of salary policy. Policy making in this area involved organizational functions at two levels (in Parsons' terms): at the institutional level,[4] where the issue is mobilizing community resources in the interest of accomplishing organizational goals, and the managerial level, where the issue is the distribution of resources according to internal priorities. Empirically, according to the findings of Alan Rosenthal in his study of five city systems, the mayor's power predominates in two cities, the school board's in three, and the superintendent's in two.[5] Obviously, there is overlap in some cities: more than one locus of power. Clearly, there is no simple correspondence between organizational function and functionary; in fact, to the extent that mayors are involved, policy making extends beyond the conventional boundaries of the school. In other policy areas besides salary, the loci of governance vary from city to city and according to historical circumstances and do not necessarily reside in any one place within any one city.

Why should there be such variation? One reason is the constitution of the school board. Some boards are appointed, others elected; all boards with the power to tax are elected, not all elected boards have the power to tax. A second reason pertains to the fiscal policies of cities, particularly whether binding power in matters of school finance rests with a mayor or city council (*de facto* or *de jure*), or whether a school board holds such power in its own right. The superintendent's power will vary according to statutory limitations, tradition, and his own political astuteness.

A third reason pertains to the variety and peculiarity of relationships between school boards and superintendents, particularly in the area of authority. School boards almost invariably consist of laymen; their claim to legitimacy derives either from appointment or election. The superintendent is hired by the board, and in that sense he is subordinate; but the legitimacy of his power as an executive derives from his expertness in matters educational, and in that sense, the board is subordinate. At the highest level, the power to govern a school system is borne of conflicting principles of legitimacy; accordingly, we should expect that the governance of school systems depends either on the nature of the resolution of conflicting principles or on the nature of the running warfare — not to mention the actual involvement of political figures in municipal government and of administrators farther down the line.

In the nature of the case, we can only establish that schoolmen will address certain organizational issues: The acquisition and allocation of resources, the mediation of conflicting community interests, and the formulation of educational policy. Which individuals and which organized bodies actually address these issues and with what outcomes vary with political and historical circumstances and with the capacities and interests of the individuals involved.

In most respects, school systems are bureaucratic organizations (in the Weberian sense), at least if schools are regarded (for the moment) as undifferentiated operating units, that is, the managerial component is organized largely on bureaucratic principles. Systems vary in terms of where policy decisions are made, but they are made and effected largely through an administrative apparatus. The primary administrative problem is to assure that systemwide policies pertaining to curriculum, supervision, teacher transfer, recruitment, promotion, and the like are carried out in each school. Accordingly, one typically finds a hierarchy of positions ranging between the superintendency and the principalship but with variations in the nature of the hierarchy. The levels of deputy, associate, and assistant superintendent can be organized territorially, functionally, according to school level, or some combination of these. Higher-level administrators usually have a broader scope of responsibilities than their lower-level counterparts and customarily have powers of veto and review. Administrators are salaried employees, and their promotion follows a variety of principles: competence (always difficult to evaluate for persons in managerial positions), loyalty, seniority, and "politics" (including religious and ethnic considerations, payment for past dirty work performed, and favoritism).

Although the apparatus is bureaucratic, and the more conventional and routine decisions are made within the confines of this hierarchical arrangement, the actual distribution of power is frequently quasifeudal rather than bureaucratic (quasifeudal in a metaphorical rather than in a literal sense, referring to the prevalence of protected corporate domains). For example, in some systems, a formal association of school principals may wield extraordinary power not only in standard policy questions but particularly when issues arise that touch their interests directly (such as redrawing school-district boundaries or changing the grade composition of schools).[6]

Observers of large-scale organizations, finding two distinct organizational patterns prevailing simultaneously in the same setting, have customarily called one formal, the other informal, treating the latter either as an unexpected excrescence of the former or as serving a "necessary" function for the former's existence. The assumption underlying the distinction is that social reality consists of two parts: a structural component (usually ideal-typical in conception) and a human component (usually somewhat devious in nature). Alternatively, why not accept the simultaneous presence of several structural forms as empirical fact and inquire into their origins? Doing so certainly does not negate the importance of the human component but rather puts it in the context of each structural arrangement.

Bureaucracy, as an administrative arrangement, is characteristically associated with the performance of routine, standarized activities in large-scale organizations. No surprise, then, to find school systems organized (at least partially) along bureaucratic lines, as one of the main tasks in running them is to assure that certain rules, regulations, and policies are followed uniformly in all schools. Among these are matters of salary, recruitment, building maintenance, land acquisition, and the establishment and enforcement of minimum standards of school operation. (This is not to imply, of course, that what is supposed to be bureaucratically uniform has not, on occasion, been found to be irregular, if not corrupt.)

Many facets of school system operation, however, are far from routine. Schools, for example, serve both neighborhood and larger territorial constituencies; because these regional areas differ in social composition and in the kinds of problems they pose for school operation, they cannot be treated administratively as indistinguishable units. Only at its peril can a system administration ignore the diverse pressures originating in particular schools and school districts. Largely because school systems are frequently organized politically at the municipal level and because much of their financing comes from locally collected taxes (not to mention the American ideology that supports the local control of schools), parents and more or less highly organized citizen groups make their wishes known at all levels of the school system, from the individual teacher to the school board. The tradition of parental access has deep roots, but only recently has there developed a movement in large cities for direct parental participation and control both in running particular schools and in management at the district level. In short, the diversity of schools and of parental interests create problems for which bureaucratic responses are hardly adequate.

Within school systems, one finds groups organized around occupational interests: associations of teachers (union and NEA affiliates), and associations of administrators (based on school level, especially in the case of principals; around common problems; and around vested interests including the residues of past wars won and lost and the anticipated gains and losses, real and imagined from future contingencies). One also finds organized groups, particularly of teachers, administrators, and citizens, not strictly

part of any school system, whose reason for existence is the mobilization of sentiment around school-related issues. Most important conceptually is the fact that the functioning of school systems cannot be adequately understood without taking these groups into account. The teacher qua union member is both an employee and a constituent of an interpenetrating organization; similarly, a private citizen may be both a client of a school system (a parent, or even more remotely a taxpayer) and a member of a voluntary association that mobilizes community sentiment around some educational issue.

Some of these interest groups are transitory, others stable and enduring. Their interests are served and threatened by a variety of issues; and as issues shift, so do the alliances and cleavages. The existence of these more or less permanent groups and the quasi-feudal characteristics of the administration make the school system very much a mixed case, at best misleadingly characterized by the term "bureaucracy" in its technical meaning.

It is misleading, I contend, to view the structure of school systems as essentially bureaucratic but modified by manifestations of informal organization or the willfulness of human nature. Rather, we find a structure whose design is more readily understood in terms of a variety of forces: the nature of administrative tasks (routine and nonroutine); the geographical dispersion of individual schools with their peculiar districts, problems, and constituencies; the character of urban politics; the presence of organized groups within, without, and crosscutting the legally defined boundaries of the system; and an environmental setting in which new issues arise and old ones persist, issues to which the system must be responsive. Given this variety of environmental forces, it would be surprising to find that school systems could be classified within a single organizational category. And for the same reasons that school systems cannot be easily categorized, they resist ready classification into Parsons' organizational types basically because those types were not derived in a way that takes explicit account of history, environment, and issues.

Schools

Though clearly components of school systems, schools are sufficiently distinct and variable organizationally to be treated separately. Whereas school systems contain primarily the managerial and institutional levels of organization, schools for the most part represent the technical level[7] in that they are designed for instructional activities. In broad outline, schools are distinguished according to level (elementary, junior high, and senior high); they are staffed by teachers who instruct batches of pupils in age-graded, self-contained classrooms, although exceptions exist to that predominant pattern; managerial responsibilities are assumed by principals (often with the aid of managerial subordinates) whose assigned tasks are to effect systemwide policies within the school and to supervise the work of teachers. These are the most visible organizational properties; they constitute modal patterns, and the existence of different arrangements must be acknowledged, though they do not predominate.

The one dimension of organization on which schools manifest the greatest structural difference is level. To simplify comparison, consider elementary and secondary schools rather than the familiar three-level distinction. Secondary schools are larger on the average, departmentalized according to subject matter, and differentiated in that guidance and other auxiliary functions are hierarchically distinct from the instructional one and in that pupils are "tracked" or "streamed" roughly according to level of achievement. The hierarchy tends to be more complex, as one or more echelons of administrators separate teachers from principals. Teachers instruct about 160 pupils per day on the average, they specialize according to subject, and men and women are employed in about equal numbers.

Elementary schools are smaller, much less departmentalized, and less differentiated. They lack a formal system of tracking, but classrooms are frequently tracked informally and less rigidly. Except in the largest schools, principals seldom have assistants; the administrative hierarchy tends to be flat. An overwhelming proportion of teachers are women, and men teach mainly in the upper grades. Average teaching loads run about 30, but the nature of the load differs from that of secondary teachers. Each teacher instructs the same group of children for the better part of every day,[8] and at the secondary level, each teacher faces a sequence of different classes, each of about 30 pupils. The intensity and frequency of contact between teachers and pupils, therefore, differs markedly at the two levels primarily because elementary teachers and their pupils remain together for most of each school day.

However familiar this description of school structure, it provokes a number of general sociological questions, among them the problem of how individuals are affiliated with an organization, a problem that Parsons treats in the context of "contract." Hiring is perhaps the most common means of affiliation and entails an exchange of specified performance for agreed-upon remuneration. It is but one of a class of affiliative devices that includes partnership, slavery, indenture, patronage (in the sense of a patron subsidizing the creative activities of an individual),

conscription, and privilege (as it applies to a physician's right to treat hospitalized patients), and various forms of "clienthood." All of these arrangements involve an exchange of one kind or another, but they differ in the nature and scope of untrammelled activity permitted to the organization member.

Slavery and indenture are the most coercive and restrictive; hiring probably comes next. To put it somewhat cynically, the principle of hiring is that he "who pays the piper calls the tune." The contract, of course, can be violated by either party; but when it is in force, an employee accepts an obligation to follow orders pertaining to what he has agreed to do and to how he does it and to accept supervision of his activities. By and large, one finds hiring in those organizations (or sections of them) designed for the performance of routine, standardized activities by substantial numbers of blue-collar, clerical, and sales workers; that is, in organizations resembling Weber's model of monocratic bureaucracy. But schools do not fit this model very well, one reason being the mode of pupil affiliation.

Mandatory school attendance is the rule for children between the ages of six and 16, which makes them conscripts. Some pupils obviously enjoy doing what they are legally required to do; others find it onerous at best, alien and threatening at worst. In hiring adults, the terms of the contractual agreement are settled prior to gaining organizational membership. In conscripting children, by contrast, membership is established first, and the subsequent settlement of terms becomes one of the organization's primary tasks, particularly in the early elementary grades. In fact, "negotiations" can be prolonged over an extended period of time, and in some cases a settled "contract" is never agreed upon. When hiring is the mode of organizational affiliation, the emerging problems mainly concern contract violations and can be dealt with through the machinery of bureaucratic administration. Problems arising from conscriptive affiliation cannot be similarly handled. Although teachers are hired explicitly as instructors, a substantial portion of their time and energy, particularly in the lower grades, must be devoted to gaining the allegiance of pupils on terms acceptable to the school regime. The obligation to perform that task is taken for granted at the time of hiring and not explicitly included among the terms of the teacher's employment contract;[9] that a teacher will maintain "discipline" is tacitly assumed.

From the affiliative point of view, it would be a gross distortion to describe the structural properties of schools as bureaucratic; moreover, schools do not resemble universities, hospitals. or prisons in structure every though these organizations also take their "clients" in as members. No single term exists to describe in summary fashion the structure of schools; the important point is that the hierarchy from the level of teacher to that of principal is largely bureaucratic, but the classroom hierarchy definitely is not. Again, we have no simple term to characterize the properties of classrooms—the residual "non-bureaucratic" will not do. Accordingly, an adequate structural analysis requires further description, particularly of teaching activities and the authority structure of schools.

Teaching activities at all levels take place in classrooms usually consisting of one teacher and an aggregate of pupils. Teachers set tasks for pupils to perform and judge the results according to quality. Methods of instruction vary and include the assignment of written work, class discussion, recitation, lecturing, putting pupils to work on long-term projects, helping them on a one-to-one basis, and the like; these activities are staples of the teacher's trade. But in addition, teachers must perform certain tasks deriving not from their employment contract (as do those mentioned above) but rather from two structural properties of classrooms: the aggregate character of the student body and the problematic nature of pupil membership.

Thirty or more young children or adolescents occupying one room for a half hour or more spells potential trouble. How does one "preside over" such a gathering and at the same time keep everyone productively occupied so that the stated aims of instruction materialize? It takes only one troublemaker to bring a class to its knees; but even if we ignore the seamy side, how does a teacher instruct in a setting that includes members possessing different interests, motivations, and capacities? Contingencies arise unpredictably—a few children have a great deal of difficulty with an assignment, a bright question that forces the teacher to choose between following a planned lesson or an interesting digression, the onset of widespread boredom, an episode of cheating, an epidemic of note-passing, and noise? "Delay, denial, interruption, and social distraction," according to Philip Jackson, are four, very real "unpublicized features of school life."[10]

Given the social and psychological diversity of pupils in a classroom, teachers are constantly confronted with a dilemma of responsibilities—to the class as a social unit and to each member as a unique individual. A teacher is held responsible for covering a certain portion of the curriculum and for maintaining order and is conventionally expected to treat pupils fairly, avoid favoritism, and grade according to universalistic standards. At the same time, a teacher is enjoined ideologically to recognize "individual differences," give extra attention and even inflated grades (at times) to the pupil whose work is poor but

who tries hard, punish less severely when there is reason to believe that stronger sanctions might have harmful effects, and the like. The teacher's dilemma is particularly sharp because the classroom is a public place and his conduct is visible to everyone; there are few opportunities to deal with "clients" one at a time and in private, a luxury characteristic of medical and legal practice.

How does a teacher deal with these problems of instruction and classroom management? We don't really know. But not knowing is a confession of ignorance only in part; it is also an acknowledgement that the prevailing technology of teaching—a set of procedures for achieving explicit goals—is still poorly codified. Over time, teachers develop rules of thumb based on their own experience and on conversations with colleagues: strategies for gaining attention, for getting quiet, for isolating difficult pupils, for stimulating interest; they may learn how to use humor, change the tempo of activity, switch from one task to another, bring a diffident pupil into the mainstream of events, and the like. For the most part, these strategies remain "tricks of the trade" and have yet to become—if they ever do—well-formulated techniques designed to cope with the exigencies of classroom life under specifiable conditions. Little in the current technology of teaching compares, for example, with the physician's use of differential diagnosis or the lawyer's use of the rules of evidence. As Dan Lortie has observed, the state of the art remains highly personalized and noncumulative, characteristics of the work reflected in the occupational language of teachers. "The absence of a refined technical culture," he states,

> is evident in the talk of elementary school teachers. Analysis of long, somewhat "open" interviews with teachers reveals little by way of a special rhetoric to delineate the essence of their daily grappling with interpersonal and learning problems. . . . Where trade jargon is used, it is frequently characterized by various meanings among different speakers (e.g., "growth" is advanced performance on achievement tests for one, the overcoming of shyness for another). Isolation and evanescence seem to have had the expected effects.[11]

The same, I might add, is true of secondary teachers.

Teaching activities that derive from the collective nature of classrooms do not fit any neat scheme of organizational classification; yet they do possess certain characteristic properties. Explicit job content (curriculum and methods) is defined to some extent by administrative superiors, but the subordination of teachers in the usual bureaucratic sense varies greatly within and between schools. Even when activities are clearly specified, the privacy of classrooms provides opportunities for the expression of different personal teaching styles. The work tends to be technologically unsophisticated (in terms of means-ends linkages) because the intended outcomes are intangible and difficult to locate in time and because teachers have been wont to develop the skills of their trade more through personal experience and individual reflection than through occupationwide means of communication and research. This is less true at the secondary level, where teachers' mastery of subject matter is part of their technology, than at the elementary level; but the classroom "management" component of the technology tends to be uncodified at each level. Because pupils vary so much in their interests and capacities and because classroom events are so vulnerable to unpredictable interruption, a teacher's energy and attention are drawn strongly to the immediate situation. Jackson has captured this facet of the work most precisely:

> The *immediacy* of classroom events is something that anyone who has ever been in charge of a roomful of students can never forget. There is a here-and-now urgency and a spontaneous quality that brings excitement and variety to the teacher's work, though it also may contribute to the fatigue he feels at the end of the day.
>
> Although a teacher might be thought of as being chiefly concerned with cognitive reorganization—with producing invisible changes within the student—this select group of teachers [interviewed by Jackson] did not rely very much on pious hopes of reaping an "unseen harvest." One aspect of this immediacy particularly evident in the reports of our teachers was the extent to which they used fleeting behavioral cues to tell them how well they were doing their jobs.[12]

The aggregate character of classrooms and its implication for the work of teachers is one aspect of classroom structure; settling the terms of pupil membership is another.

Few service organizations entail client membership, but among those that do, it is invariably problematic. In general hospitals, for example, patient "membership" can be traumatic, but three conditions ease the settlement of terms, however painful the consequences; the patient's vulnerability, the attending physician's expertise, and the hospital's coerciveness. Schools pose a more difficult problem: pupils are anything but vulnerable, and in the aggregate they have considerable power; the teacher's technical expertise is far less widely acknowledged than the physician's; and the school's coercive resources are fragile compared to those of the hospital. Schools, moreover, require much more active voluntary participation by their client members.[13]

Most simply, the problem of settling the terms of membership boils down to getting children to like school or at least to accept the prevailing rules of the game. The nature of the problem varies according to school level. For most children, elementary school represents the first prolonged and serious foray outside the household; serious because school and family settings conflict in their definitions of appropriate conduct and because children spend a great deal of time in school engaged in potentially threatening activities without the customary support available in many families. Although the transition from family to school entails several conditions producing personal stress, one of the most important is the system of grading, the systematic evaluation of all children according to how well they perform common tasks. Young children particularly can be unclear about whether a grade represents a judgment of a specific task only or whether it also pertains to them as persons. Although not all parents treat their children with respect and affection, the family provides better opportunities than the classroom for supporting a child's sense of self-esteem. Parents are freer than teachers to attend to the individuality of their children, and parenthood does not typically involve the systematic and repetitive setting and evaluating of tasks.

Elsewhere I have described one of the critical tasks of the elementary teacher as establishing a sense of goodwill among pupils.[14] When a regime operates according to achievement criteria, poor performance and failure are inherent outcomes for some members (when a range of capacities is represented). As in addition school work and attendance can be onerous and taxing, settling the terms of membership is problematic. How can a teacher induce willing participation in school and acceptance of its rules when adherence to those rules can create unpleasant and often threatening personal consequences? One way, clearly, lies in attempting to create a sense of diffuse positive attachment to the school, to convey to pupils that school can be pleasurable or at least pleasurable enough.

In conventional sociological terms, settling the terms of membership is actually a problem of establishing the noncontractual elements of contract. In forming contractual agreements (e.g., in commercial transactions or labor agreements), two parties take the noncontractual elements for granted; only the terms of exchange remain problematic. In school membership, the contractual terms (the performance-grade exchange) must be settled, but so must the nature of the institutional arrangement (the noncontractual element) in which the relationships between pupils and teachers and between pupils and the school are established. For the school regime to operate, at least a substantial number of pupils must learn to accept a social arrangement with its associated norms such that the exchange of performance for grades is accepted as legitimate. The problem of legitimacy is particularly acute for pupils who do poorly; Why should they accept the rules of a game that relentlessly make them losers?

High schools operate on the assumption that pupils already accept the noncontractual elements (whether or not they actually do). Pupils may disagree with a grade, or parents may become distraught if they think their child's work has been underrated, but the system of grading is not typically questioned. Dropping out, passively withdrawing from activities, vandalizing school property, or assaulting teachers, however, may all represent different ways of attacking the legitimacy of the school regime.

How teachers create good will, get children to like school, and accept the rules of the game when the rules work to their detriment remain matters of conjecture. Certainly the activities involved have never been formulated in technological terms. The principle underlying these activities, however, appears to be that of expressing gratuitous and pleasurable sentiment: smiling, friendly greeting, encouraging, showing interest and concern, and the like. General demeanor, affective and universalistic in character, seems better suited to fostering pupil's allegiance to the school and the enterprise of schooling than quid pro quo exchange (the principle underlying the performance-grade contract) because its expression does not create winners and losers.

Although schools are organized around achievement-based activities, the work of teachers—particularly at the elementary level—cannot be focused narrowly on those activities primarily because the task of including pupils as willing, actively participating members would be undermined. Both the collective nature of classroom composition and the need to settle the terms of pupil membership militate against the bureaucratization of classrooms. Accordingly, any analysis of structure must take account of the variety of organizational forms characteristic of schools. For this reason, some of the recently developed schemes for comparing organizations do not work very well. The Blau-Scott "*cui bono*" formulation[15] (which classifies schools as service organizations), and the Etzioni "compliance structure" formulation[16] (which classifies schools primarily as normative organizations), for example, cannot readily handle structural variation within schools, that variation being one of their defining properties, because both schemes treat organizations as clearcut structural types, not as complex mixtures of such types. (Parsons' formulation poses a more complex problem to be discussed later.)

The description of school organization has so far included a discussion of affiliation and teacher activities; regarding the latter. I have passed over questions of classroom management that can be treated more appropriately in the context of authority. To round out this brief discussion of school organization, I turn to the nature of authority relationships.

On a conventional organizational chart, a school takes the form of a pyramidal bureaucracy; even the formal responsibilities of the members fit the bureaucratic model. But from what we already know about schools, a chart amounts to a graphic misrepresentation. The principal occupies the top managerial post; the nature and scope of his authority, however, is anomalous. He cannot hire and fire, though he can influence hiring and firing through his superiors. He can discipline pupils, but only with considerable difficulty can he have them transferred out of his school. Seldom does a principal give teachers direct orders about how and what to teach. He has little power in determining the size of his budget but can usually exercise substantial control over its allocation.

The principal's authority is paramount in two areas: the allocation of internal resources and supervision. In addition to disbursing funds, his authority extends to the assignment of teachers, a matter of considerable importance for school operation because the principal can to some degree match the "difficulty" of classes with the competence of teachers, assure equity of teaching loads, and (with caution) "punish" teachers by assigning them difficult classes to manage. As supervisor, the principal has the right to enter classrooms, observe the proceedings, offer criticism and help, evaluate teacher performance, and recommend teachers for tenure and promotion. However, according to interviews held with some 500 principals in 41 large American cities as part of the National Principalship Study,[17] most claim that although supervision (classroom visitation) has very high priority among the various facets of their work, they seldom have the time (or inclination?) to get into classrooms. In short, though the exercise of supervisory authority is one of the prerogatives of their office, principals characteristically find that the exigencies of the job—program planning, meeting with parents and groups in the community, advertising and defending the school's program, recruiting, and the like—keep them from exercising it.

Some sociologists follow Weber and Barnard in viewing authority in the context of relationships entailing orders and compliance. While that formulation applies most appropriately where hierarchical superiors are held responsible for the work of their subordinates and where the work of subordinates involves standardized activities, repetitive in nature, it applies poorly to the principalship for several reasons: Teachers have a modest though sufficient claim to professional status (and at the high school level a subject mastery not shared by the principal) so that principals rely on their (teachers') individual competence and judgment; classrooms (particularly in large schools) are sufficiently numerous and spatially isolated to inhibit steady surveillance, and principals cannot realistically keep abreast of the distinctive flow of events in each of them. Both occupational and ecological conditions, then, make it difficult and inappropriate for a principal to exercise authority on a command-compliance basis.

A teacher's position of authority in the classroom differs markedly from that of a principal vis-à-vis teachers. The rights to make assignments and to discipline children to keep order inhere in the position; but gaining compliance is problematic for reasons discussed earlier. When most pupils are motivated to do their schoolwork, the exercise of authority presents no great problems. When disruptions occur, however, the teacher must establish order in a collective, public situation, armed with only a narrow range of sanctions. It is virtually impossible to force a child to learn; accordingly, a teacher must rely substantially on the motivation pupils bring to school and on their acceptance of the school's conventional sanctions—grades and praise—the efficacy of which cannot be taken for granted.

As far as classroom management is concerned, the teacher's repertoire of sanctions is limited; moreover, the rewards and punishments that work with some pupils can prove ineffective with others. Yet the teacher must be even-handed lest he be accused of favoritism and thereby have his authority undermined. Corporal punishment is proscribed in most school systems (though used surreptitiously); teachers admonish and insult, send pupils out of the room or to the principal's office, keep them after school, send for their parents, and the like. Except perhaps in the eyes of those pupils who are already committed to school, these sanctions are hardly awesome. The teacher's main dilemmas are to avoid diminishing returns and to assure that rewards are rewarding and punishments punishing. Given the weakness of the conventional sanctions, teachers must rely on personal resources to gain the good will and respect of pupils, for without them, the available sanctions do not amount to much, especially as pupils must attend school.

We have no clear descriptive term for the type of authority exercised in classrooms even though the hierarchical arrangement is readily identified with teachers occupying the legally constituted superordinate position. Clearly, the situation conforms neither to the bureaucratic nor to the professional models.[18] Rather, the nature of the teacher's authority emerges from the situation of conscripted pupils aggregated in classrooms, weak formal sanctions, and problematic terms of pupil membership. But if the nature of school authority is situationally determined, then logical consistency enjoins us to regard bureaucratic and professional authority as situational as well.

Perhaps the clearest way to delineate the authority structure of schools is in terms of zones or domains,[19] as Lortie has suggested; that is, the bailiwick, rather than the more frequently discussed hierarchy or professional elite, is the basic unit of authority. Questions of finance, budget, and hiring are clearly the responsibility of administrators, while those of classroom management and methods of instruction fall within the domain of teachers; other issues cross domains and may or may not precipitate conflicts depending on whether contradictory interests are involved. This is not to say that bureaucratic and professional elements are absent: a policy for taking attendance, for example, is likely to be passed down the line as an "order" and administered bureaucratically; decisions about how best to teach chemistry are left to teachers with professional competence in that subject. But the zoning pattern predominates, a reflection of the facts that teaching activities are too diffuse and varied to be governed by specific directives (hence, schools differ in structure from insurance companies), and that the prevailing technology is not sufficiently developed to support an autonomous professional contingent (hence, schools do not resemble general hospitals).

Schooling

Schools are agencies of socialization, which means that individuals who pass through them are exposed to their internal environment and are expected as a result to possess different psychological capacities at the end than when they entered. Schools, in fact, are one of a number of organizations and nonorganizational settings explicitly designed to effect changes in people (whether or not they actually succeed): mental hospitals, colleges, prisons, and churches, among the organizations; among the "settings," with definite structural properties, one finds psychotherapy, brainwashing, and religious conversion. Despite their diversity and obvious differences in goals, all have characteristics in common, or at least can be compared on the same set of dimensions: the social position of the individuals subject to change, the forces of psychological leverage, and an agent(s) of change who occupies two social positions. The process of change usually requires that the subject relinquish or modify some pattern of conduct and/or mode of psychological functioning (one that is either gratifying or difficult to give up even if not gratifying) and acquire some new mode of conduct or functioning deemed desirable by the agency or by conventional mores. Raising children in a family is an obvious case in point.

Pupils, college students, prisoners, mental patients (hospitalized and ambulatory), parishioners, victims of brainwashing, and candidates for conversion all have two social circumstances in common: Their status is low (sometimes debasing) compared to that of the agent working on them, and their position can afford them a view of "better" (at least different) things ahead. The basis of their subordination may differ according to the agent's claim to superordination: Based, for example, on expertise, coercion, hierarchical position, or charisma; the subordinate's room may be uncomfortable, but still the room has a view.

Although the forms of leverage vary widely, they have one characteristic in common: either by design or by accident, they arouse powerful emotion. This is not surprising when the subject has a strong investment in the psychological status quo from which the agent's task is to "pry him loose." In schools, leverage takes the form of threats to pupils' self-respect and is derived from the demand that he perform in public and subject himself to public evaluation by teachers and peers. Other forms of leverage can readily be matched with their corresponding settings: anxiety over grades with one's occupational prospects hanging in the balance, withdrawal of affection in relationships of dependency, transference, terror, coercion and the deprivation of human and civil rights, tyranny,[20] the deliberate arousal of emotional frenzy over the state of one's soul, and deracination.[21] Although life without emotion would scarcely be bearable, prolonged states of highly intense emotion (particularly unpleasant ones) are exceedingly painful; and one need not subscribe to any naïve version of the law of effect to contend that people will attempt to regain a sense of emotional equanimity. The problem confronting the socializing agent is to harness the desire for equanimity to some new state of psychological affairs: accepting the rules of a school regime and the desire to achieve, regaining "mental health," creating a loyal Maoist, returning a criminal to the straight and narrow, gaining a new defender of the faith, or whatever.

The explicit aim of most socializing agencies is to turn their members out as changed persons; one purpose of membership in the agency (or in the relationship) is the termination of membership. We look askance at the overly dependent child, the professional patient, the "academic bum," and the recidivist. But what are the social and psychological linkages between the subject's present state and a different, future state? Perhaps the main one is an agent who has strong social ties both with the subject and in some outside social setting in which the subject currently lacks but will subsequently attain membership. A father is a case in point, as family member (with a close relationship to a young son) and as occupational participant (which the son some day will become). Compare, however, the difficulty a jailer has in establishing a close relationship to a prisoner (though the jailer has ties with the conventional world beyond the walls); and so with the Chinese soldier and the American P.O.W. Note also the overprotective parent with close ties to a child but unable to "let go." The agent's position is delicate in that he must maintain an identity outside the bounds of his relationship with the subject, yet maintain a relationship with the subject without appearing alien as a consequence.

Schooling fits this model of socialization rather closely: the pupil's status is low and can afford him a glimpse of better prospects; the authority of the teacher and the pupil's exposure to public judgment provide bases for leverage; and the teacher occupies a position both as a classroom member and as an adult occupational participant. But we must treat this argument with caution. For many pupils, the view out of the classroom is far from promising, and to that extent they find little to work for; the efficacy of the "leverage" depends on the teacher's success in establishing the legitimacy of the school regime; and some teachers maintain a posture of aloofness so that they are in the classroom but not of it — three points of potential weakness in a socializing agency.

Schools and school systems pose a good test for any general formulation of organizational structure primarily because they contain a variety of structural forms. I turn, then, to the questions of whether Parsons' formulation of organizational structure can account for variations in school organization and whether other formulations need to be introduced. The critical question is whether Parsons' scheme, containing a classification of organizations based on value-derived functional problems characteristic of all social systems, can deal adequately with structural variation within organizational types and organizational variation not based on values.

PARSONS' FORMULATIONS

I have deliberately referred to formulations in the title of this section, not to a single formulation, because Parsons' two theoretical papers are strikingly distinct (though not contradictory).[22] Although he explicitly devotes the "Theory of Organizations" paper to values and institutions and the "Formal

Organization" paper to collectivities and roles, all presumably part of the same conceptual apparatus, he actually propounds two very different strategies for the analysis of organizational structure. The first is characteristic of Parsons' work:

> On what has just been called the cultural-institutional level, a minimal description of an organization will have to include an outline of the system of values which defines its functions and of the main institutional patterns which spell out these values in the more concrete functional context of goal-attainment itself, adaptation to the situation, and integration of the system.
>
> *The main point of reference for analyzing the structure of any social system is its value pattern.* [23]

The second is not as uniquely Parsons':

> I would like to suggest a way of breaking down the hierarchical aspect of a system of organization. . . . I make this breakdown according to three references of function or responsibility, which become most clearly marked in terms of the external references of the organization to its setting or to the next higher order in the hierarchy. These three may be called, respectively, the "technical" system, the "managerial" system, and the "community" or "institutional" system. [24]

The main difference between the two approaches is that the first is stated in terms of societal values, the second in terms of organizational activities characteristic of different organizational levels. The central question is whether variation in structure can be more readily explained in terms of values, activities, or a combination of the two.

The Values-Goals-Functions Scheme

From the perspective of societal values, organizations are social systems that serve goal-attainment functions; on the basis of values, in other words, one can distinguish social systems according to the functions they serve for personality, cultural, and other social systems. [25] Organizations, like societies, are also social systems; hence, by definition, they can be distinguished by type in terms of the four-fold AGIL scheme of functions and system problems. In societal terms, then, schools serve a G function because they are organizations, for as Henry Landsberger reminds us: "To be classed as an organization, a group merely needs to act 'as if' it were goal oriented, by *actually affecting another system.*" [26] At the organizational (rather than the societal) level, however, schools are of the L type because they socialize individuals; that is, change their psychological capacities so that they can conduct themselves appropriately in other social systems. Note, moreover, that this discussion and Parsons' (as indicated by the titles and substance of his papers) deal with theory at the level of organizations, not at that of societies. Whether

the same theoretical content will serve at both levels is debatable.

In general, Parson's scheme is predicated on the propositions that social systems, extending from the level of personality to that of culture, are interleaved and that values constitute the crucial linkages between levels. He formulates these linkages in terms of "cybernetic control" in which the order of functional priority is L-I-G-A. All social systems, then, at any level, have the same set of functional problems, the primary one being the "input" of values. Landsberger summarizes Parsons' argument for the case of schools:

> Culture for a lower order system consists, then, among other ingredients, of the values of the next larger social system. This constitutes "the legitimation of" [the organization's] place or "role" in the superordinate system. . . . Such legitimation . . . enables the organization, when faced with outside pressures, to assert the primacy of its goal over other possible goals. For example, an educational organization can assert the primacy of producing educated citizens over creating good will in the community (I) and over the production of facilities and the making of a profit (A). Functions cannot be accomplished . . . unless culture values recognize the goal to be a legitimate one. [27]

Schools as organizations, in short, "specialize" in pattern-maintenance functions (i.e., in terms of their contribution to other systems), and that specialization is legitimized according to the values of some higher-order system. Type of organizational structure, moreover, is related to function:

> Organizations may in the first instance be classified in terms of the *type of goal or function* about which they are organized. The same basic classification can be used for goal types which has been used earlier in dealing with the function of a social system. Thus, we may speak of adaptive goals, implementive goals, integrative goals, and pattern-maintenance goals. The reference is always to function in the *society* as a system. [28]

Although he does not say so explicitly, it is abundantly clear from his examples that by classifying organizations according to goals-functions, Parsons has distinguished them structurally; organizational structure, in short, varies with organizational goals. [29]

The Organizational Activities Scheme

Parsons' "Formal Organization" paper differs from his "Theory of Organizations" paper in that it contains few references to values (as that concept is used in the latter); in fact, the paper could have been written had the theory of action never been developed, despite the fact that the distinctions made in the paper in no way contradict or distort the theory. Even the concept of function is used more conventionally to refer to responsibility or task.[30] The central argument questions the commonly held notion that organizational operation consists of the narrowing specification of orders as they are passed down the line. Parsons contends that organizational activities are of three types — technical, managerial, and institutional — each primarily characteristic of a particular organizational level. The hierarchy, in other words, is discontinuous, and organizational levels should be distinguished according to jurisdictions over particular kinds of decisions and activities.

> I have emphasized these *three* different levels of the organization hierarchy because at each of the two points of articulation between them we find a qualitative break in the simple continuity of "line" authority. School boards, boards of directors, or trustees and political superiors do not . . . simply tell people at the next level down "what to do." This is essentially because the people "lower down" typically must exercise *types of competence* and shoulder *responsibilities* which cannot be regarded as simply "delegated" by their "superiors." This again is because the *functions* at each level are qualitatively different; . . . .[31]

The phrase, "types of competence," though buried in the quotation gives the "Formal Organization" paper its unique emphasis; it calls attention to what men do as an important consideration in the comparative analysis of organizations.

The contrast between the "values" and "activities" schemes can be illustrated, for example, by specific reference to the problem of procurement.

> Using the value system as the main point of reference, the discussion of [the institutional] structure can be divided into three main headings. The primary adaptive exigencies of an organization concern the procurement of the resources necessary for it to attain its goal or carry out its function; hence one major field of institutionalization concerns the modes of procurement of these resources.[32]

In effect, this says that in considering the procurement function of any organization, one should take the question of legitimation into account — a contention in the concept of values. (The statement obviously cannot be given the empirical meaning that all modes of procurement are legitimate.)

Procurement, according to the activities scheme, occurs at both the technical and managerial levels; but the important point is to note the different kinds of statements made about it. Parsons distinguishes between the procurement of physical objects (whose motivations need not be taken into account) and human or social ones. "The important point . . .," he states, in referring to the technical level,

> is that the second case, where the object is a "social" object, necessitates a special link at the managerial level

between the technological process and the disposal process. In the physical case the technical production process can be completed, and then, quite independently, those responsible for sales can take over; the customer need have no relation at all to the technical production process. . . .

> In the case of the social object, however, a prior relation to the recipient or beneficiary of the "service" is a prerequisite for undertaking the technical process at all.[33]

The procurement function at the managerial level concerns the linkage between an organization and its external markets for resources. Consider Parsons' treatment of personnel procurement:

> The farther the function of an organization moves away from the production of commodities for a market, the more the pattern of employment and remuneration of "operatives" tends to move away from the "marginal productivity" standard. The largest-scale example of a very different type is provided by the civilian operative employees of governmental agencies. Here two patterns are particularly conspicuous, namely, the seniority principle and the institutionalization of tenure.[34]

Note that each of the last two quotations contain empirical generalizations describing variations in organizational structure. The first says that the *nature of the linkage* between the technical and managerial levels varies with the nature of the "raw material" (physical or human); the second specifies the nature of variation in managerial operation. Thus, when organizational activities at the technical level involve working on physical materials to transform them into commodities for sale on a market, managerial decisions concerning the procurement of labor follow the principle of marginal productivity (usually involving affiliation by means of hiring). With different kinds of technical activities, one finds different modes of affiliation.

An interesting aspect of these propositions is that they do not derive from a premise about the primacy of values, but rather about the nature of raw materials, that is, one does not arrive at them by first postulating the "system of values which defines [an organization's] functions." At the same time, they neither deny the importance of values — as Parsons indicates, both the technical and managerial functions are institutionalized — nor do they undermine a functional scheme that links the elements of an organization to each other, to the system as a whole, and to sectors of the external environment.

The Elements of Organizational Structure

Parsons' formulation raises two critical issues for the structural analysis of organizations. First, if organizational structures can be distinguished according to function (in terms of the AGIL scheme), should not all organizations serving pattern-maintenance functions, for example, resemble each other structurally? Within this functional category, Parsons includes organizations "with primarily 'cultural,' 'educational,' and 'expressive' functions:"[35] churches and schools, and presumably universities, scientific research institutes, theaters, symphony orchestras, museums and art galleries, and learned societies. Not only do they all differ markedly in structure, but some, like universities, resemble general hospitals (I) more closely than they resemble schools.

Second, the formulation leaves the concept "situation" unconceptualized. Return for a moment to the quotation cited in footnote 23: here Parsons refers to institutional patterns spelling out values in concrete functional contexts, including "adaptation to the situation." Certain aspects of "the situation" are conceptualized: given system A (an organization, for example), systems B . . . N, which have boundary exchanges with A, are part of A's situation. But A's ecology, history, some of its raw materials (note the human-physical distinction discussed earlier), and technology, all part of the situation and all noted earlier in the structural description of schools, cannot be treated as social (or personal) systems and hence, remain residual to the value formulation. The question of technology is particularly important, as Landsberger has indicated:

> The aspect of organization not adequately covered . . . is that of technology. Despite repeated references to the fact that among the adaptive problems of organizations are requirements to adapt to "technological exigencies" and despite references to the effect on the organization of the nature of its goal, Parsons' theoretical system cannot systematically handle the influence of technology on organizational relationships.[36]

Landsberger's criticism might be too harsh; for while the values-goals-functions scheme cannot handle technology (or treats it residually), the activities scheme can — and does to some extent. The problem is that Parsons has not tied the two schemes together. Moreover, though he deals with organizations in terms of the general theory of action, with values as the central principle, he actually accounts for variations in structure, albeit by elliptical argument, in terms of activities, raw materials, and technological exigencies; and ironically, it is precisely those considerations that would enable him to avoid including structurally diverse organizations in the same category.

Any formulation designed to account for structural variation in organizations must be able to provide a reason why the following propositions (illustrated by accompanying examples) are true:

> A good organization for the physical production of goods at the technical level would inevitably be a bad one for the educational process. . . .
>
> No organization dependent on *highly trained professional personnel* can employ them typically on the basis of a *marginal productivity,* terminable-at-will contract of employment. Or, on the other side, the organization which *produces commodities for a market* must be very different in structure from the residential college which *takes its "customers" into a special type of membership status.*[37]

I strongly suspect that these contentions are empirically correct, and at the same time that the relationships they specify cannot be explained either in terms of societal values or by reference to functional problems at whatever system level. My skepticism is based on the logic of Parsons' scheme itself. If there is variation within A, G, I, and L types of organizations, should not this variation be explainable in terms of the same AGIL scheme specified one level down in generality? True, Parsons identifies subsystems of particular organizations in terms of this scheme, but that is not necessarily the same as explaining variation within types. Are schools, for example, a G-type of pattern-maintenance organization while museums are an L-type, and more importantly, can the structural differences between schools and museums be attributed to the G and L functions they serve within the pattern-maintenance rubric? I see little justification for making these distinctions (and little evidence supporting them), yet the "nesting" quality of Parsons' scheme would suggest making them.

Alternatively, why should we not take the empirical substance of the quoted statements and ask, for example: What is there about taking "customers into a special type of membership status" that puts limits on other structural properties of those organizations that extend "membership" to their customers? We might also inquire into the characteristics of those customers, for as we know, elementary and secondary schools differ structurally and each takes in different kinds of customers as members.[38]

Consider Parsons' analysis of universities — like schools, pattern-maintenance organizations. In analytical terms, the input from a higher system level into the pattern-maintenance sector (the values determining organizational goals) is two-fold: socialization and research (i.e., inculcation into the modification of the cultural tradition). The adaptive problems of acquiring personnel and financial resources are dealt with on a "just price" basis; and by a combination of fee-for-service, voluntary contribution, and taxation basis; respectively. The operative code (A), because university faculties are staffed by technical experts in a variety of disciplines, fits the "company of equals" rather than the "line" model. The integrative problem, particularly with respect to authority, is "solved" by means of restricting the power of the administration and by defending academic freedom (largely through tenured employment).[39] Parsons' analysis of the university is designed to be illustrative, not exhaustively explanatory. But two questions remain: Why should one organization differ from another (universities and schools), and why should the structural characteristics of any organization cluster as they do?

It is my contention that Parsons' propositions about organizational variation are in fact based not on the premise of value primacy but on empirical observation and on a set of implicit conceptions of structural constraints: ideas about what kinds of social phenomena can exist together simultaneously and what kinds are mutually disruptive. His propositions at the organizational level, in other words, do not really derive from the AGIL scheme. The scheme actually tells us where to look for some problematic issues, primarily those having a normative component; it does not, however, delineate different clusters of structural properties especially within functional types. Nor does the AGIL scheme tell us why a collegial form of association is "consistent" with independent, professional work activities, or why these activities are "inconsistent" with a marginal productivity form of remuneration.

Consider, however, certain occupations, the work of whose members entails independent, discretionary, original, or creative activities in organizational settings: law, medicine, architecture, university teaching and research, and the like. In each case, one finds reasonably strong collegial ties among practitioners (a characteristic of the occupation, not of the organizational setting), affiliation by means other than or in addition to hiring (e.g., partnership, privilege, patronage), and remuneration not based on the marginal productivity principle (e.g., fee for service). Collegiality, I contend, derives more from the fact that the work activities in these occupations depend on the development and diffusion of knowledge necessary to maintain a viable technology (one that can gain the confidence of a consuming public and that works) than it does from any organizational values or goals; that is, diffusion will not occur unless men either get together or communicate. As for affiliation and remuneration, hiring and salaried employment in each case entail obligations to hierarchical superiors that would be potentially inimical to the exercise of professional judgment, loyalty to clients, and free inquiry. That is, these obligations to administrators could interfere with the performance of the work. It is interesting to note, in this connection, that law firms hire their most junior members, that is, those whose early employment actually constitutes the advanced stage of their training.[40] Similarly, medical internes and residents are hired

(or paid a stipend, indicative of their status as students), as are physicians who do most of their work for insurance companies. In these cases of hiring, the practice of neophytes is directed by superiors, or occupational practice is largely routine.

How, then, shall we view organizational goals? Goals, in fact, represent general criteria for specifying which activities among available alternatives shall be performed within the organizational setting. In professional organizations, the nature of these activities is defined by occupations; accordingly, one finds empirically that organizational structures have developed as reasonably hospitable settings for the performance of these activities. The indeterminacy of the connection between goals and structure, moreover, is clearly illustrated in those industrial organizations (A) where the product can be manufactured through the application of more than one technology (hence, the engagement of workers in different kinds of activities). Mass production industries, for example, differ structurally from those designed for custom production even though both turn out an identical product;[41] and different manufacturing industries—automobiles, ships, petrochemicals, steel, television sets, houses, among others—vary structurally according to the characteristics of the labor force, exigencies associated with batch or unit production, seasonality of work, geographical dispersion, among other considerations.[42]

One major determinant of organizational structure—and perhaps the major one—is the nature of technology and the work activities associated with it. Viewing structural variation in technological terms not only allows an understanding of why organizations with the same goals differ, it also does justice to their historical development. Organizations, after all, are founded to produce specific things or provide specific services in specific ways and are constrained by the available supply of labor and raw materials (both in quality and quantity) and by the efficacy of prevailing technologies. As more than one of these means of production is likely to be subsumable under any given goal, one would expect that organizational structure would vary with the nature of these means rather than with goals.[43]

This formulation in no way denies the viability of a functional interpretation because it still leaves open the question of how the parts of an organization are related to each other and how an organization is related to its external environment—both questions that must be conceptualized. Neither does it downgrade the importance of social values, because organizational activities and the social relationships among men at work must still be viewed in terms of their sources of legitimacy. The formulation does imply, however, that one does not look to values to account for variations in organizational structure.

THE STRUCTURAL PROPERTIES OF SCHOOLS

Because it is important to understand the functional connection between one social system and another, and among social, personality, and cultural systems, that does not necessarily mean the most useful way to account for variation in organizational structure is to identify organizations according to function. If Parsons' initial conception — "As a formal analytical point of reference, *primacy of orientation to the attainment of a specific goal* is used as the defining characteristic of an organization *which distinguishes it from other types of social systems*"[44] — is correct (and I think it is), then the next analytical step is to conceptualize the terms "attainment" and "goal," not to proceed to the analysis of goal attainment at the institutional level. In actuality his formulation leads to the consideration of technology: the nature of men's activities once goals have been specified in terms of what men can work on. Charles Perrow's formulation makes this point with great clarity: "First, technology, or the work done in organizations, is considered the defining characteristic of organizations."[45] And I would contend that this statement is almost equivalent in meaning to that of Parsons. Perrow continues:

> By technology is meant the actions that an individual performs upon an object, with or without the aid of tools or mechanical devices, in order to make some change in that object. The object, or "raw material," may be a living being, human or otherwise, a symbol or an inanimate object.[46]

By implication:

> We cannot expect a particular relationship found in one organization to be found in another unless we know these organizations are in fact similar with respect to their technology. . . . Less obvious, however, is the point that types of organization — in terms of their function in society — will vary as much within each type as between types. Thus, some schools, hospitals, banks and steel companies may have more in common, because of their routine character, than routine and non-routine schools. . . .[47]

We should not then accept Parsons' terms like "primacy" or "the defining characteristic" too literally, as if they referred to sole considerations.

In the case of schools and school systems (and undoubtedly in other organizations as well) several considerations must assume importance for an adequate structural analysis: (1) how occupational groups (i.e., the collective embodiments of teaching technology) are affiliated, (2) the existence of state, municipal, and other jurisdictions of political control (a short-range and probably long-range given), and

(3) architecturally determined ecology — in addition to the character of teaching technology itself. These three considerations are critical, first because they cannot be derived either from the nature of technology or from values and second because they all affect the structural properties of schools and school systems.

Four properties of schools and teaching, I contend, are the main determinants of their organizational structure: (1) the "soft," uncodified, human relations technology of teaching activities; (2) pupil conscription; (3) the classroom as the basic ecological unit; and (4) the weak occupational community of teachers. It is widely acknowledged that one finds bureaucratic forms of structure (conduct governed by rules through hierarchically arranged positions) when workers are engaged in routine, repetitive activities. However, when work requires originality, unfettered professional judgment, or creativity, and workers have the support of a strong occupational community (whose strength is centered as much on the maintenance of high work standards as it is on economic well-being), then one is unlikely to find bureaucratic forms of administration.

The imperious demands of classroom pressures, the absorption of teachers' attention in events occurring in the classroom, the mandatory attendance of pupils, and the uncodified nature of their technology all militate against the control of their conduct by bureaucratic means: reliance on rules and orders. The situation is clearly described by Lortie:

> Self-contained classrooms are small universes of control with the teacher in command; administrators refer, ambivalently, to the "closed door" which the teacher can put between herself and administrative surveillance. Another impediment to close control lies in the relative indivisibility of the teacher's tasks. How does one subdivide a warm and empathic relationship established between teacher and class? . . . As teachers spend almost all their school time in the presence of their students, there are few occasions for superordinates to direct teachers without incurring the risk of embarrassing a "subordinate line officer."
>
> The relatively unrationalized nature of teaching technique also restricts initiation by administrative superiors. There are few settled matters in pedagogy. If greater agreement prevailed, superiors could, through mastery of that consensus, assert the right to prescribe for subordinates.[48]

Moreover, the softness of the technology and the weakness of the occupational community (a condition not unrelated to the undeveloped state of the technology) in advancing and protecting that technology provide little impetus to change the hierarchical nature of school structure. The hierarchy, in other words, cannot readily serve as a mechanism for the administrative control over the work through rules.

Two additional questions about school and school system structure remain unexplained: Why are hierarchical arrangements so conspicuous if they are not highly instrumental in the control of work? And why the quasifeudal characteristics of school organization? First, schools and school systems do not operate free of rules; it is only that many central work activities of classroom teachers are difficult to specify and control by means of rules. But as I have indicated earlier, other facets of organizational operation do entail standard, routine procedures; and their performance is highly consistent with bureaucratic administration. Second, schools are publicly controlled agencies, recipients and spenders of tax revenue. Whenever this is the case, one will find mechanisms designed for regular surveillance (such as bureaucratic administration) simply to meet demands for public accountability, whether or not the means of control and surveillance are actually appropriate to the nature of the work. Finally, quasifeudal administrative structures are likely to arise when enough members of an organization have interests and problems in common to support collective association (e.g., school principals), when the distinctiveness of administrative tasks define organizational domains, and when contact with various outside constituencies defines and distinguishes administrators; interests.

Accordingly, the technical, managerial, and institutional ingredients of Parsons' scheme, as well as a variety of nonnormative elements of organizations, leads us much closer to a structural analysis of schools and school systems than does the theory of social action based on the primacy of values. Knowing what men do and in what organizational locations, in other words, tells us more about how organizations are put together than knowing what societal functions organizations serve.

EPILOGUE

It is useful to distinguish social systems whose value primacy is goal attainment (organizations) from those whose primacy is not. The distinction, one should remember, and the functionalist theory that underlies it, are definitional, not empirical. It does not follow, however, that a distinction useful at one level of analysis is necessarily useful at another. Accordingly, the question of whether organizational variation can be understood using the same framework applicable to societies can be settled more readily by studying organizations and societies rather than by applying criteria of logical parallelism. Moreover, even if variations in social systems at all levels yield to functional formulations, that does not

necessarily mean that the content of functional categories must remain the same at each level.

My descriptive statements about schools, school systems, and schooling in no way undermine the tenability of functional formulations. (Neither do they necessarily support them.) They do, however, call into question—not refute—functional statements based primarily (solely?) on values simply because schools differ structurally from other organizations and among themselves for reasons that have little or no necessary connection with values. My own bias is that the literature provides more support for a technological interpretation than one based on values. The case, however, is by no means airtight; it does appear tight enough, though, that any attempt to account for variation in organizational structure should include technology, work activities, ecology, and history at least on a par with values.

The theoretical question that the analysis of schools opens up is whether organizational variation is best understood in terms of a functional explanation or in terms of one based on categories with sociological content: activities, technology, affiliation, values, and the like. Admittedly, I have argued the latter case— but not against the former. The two modes of interpretation actually talk past one another; they do not address the same questions. The functional scheme, it seems to me, speaks to questions concerning the logic of relationships between social systems; among personality, social, and cultural systems; and between the parts of a system and the whole. It deals with questions of how we know that some social process or structure does or does not serve a particular function for some system, or whether it contributes to the solution of a system problem. In short, functional analysis concerns logical relations of necessity (if non-A, then non-B) and sufficiency (if A, then B). It pertains to what we mean by saying that a phenomenon or system remains stable or changes and to how we establish the connection between stability, change, and the conditions related to them.

The activities-technology formulation pertains to the content of the A's and B's, that is, what phenomena are empirically related to what other phenomena, within social systems and between them, at the same and at different levels. Parsons' papers on organizations, in fact, indicate the distinction between the two types of formulation; in accounting for variation in types of organizations, he relies on observations and shows empirically what structures and processes tend to cluster. The functional scheme permits one to move from one level of analysis to another, over the "boundaries" in "interchanges." Values, I contend, have no inherent connection to the functional scheme; they are data applicable to organizations and to other social units or phenomena.

In sum, I take the position that functional propositions are neutral with respect to the substantive content (such as values) of relationships being analyzed; it is a mode of inquiry, a design for asking questions. It becomes useful when applied to empirical data, not when identified with data. Values, then, have no more or no less importance to a theory of organizations than do any other kind of substantive data; and hence, as far as organizational properties are concerned, there is no reason to attribute special importance to any set of characteristics except as empirical investigation shows one or more sets to have greater explanatory power. As far as the four system problems as they pertain to organizations are concerned, one does not need to posit values to derive them; they stand on their own as strong and as vulnerable as any other set of axioms. And in addressing the Hobbesian problem of order in societies, we are not yet able to state with certainty whether values have the status of an axiom, nor have we yet succeeded in establishing their explanatory primacy empirically.

NOTES

1. Talcott Parsons, "Suggestions for a Sociological Approach to the Theory of Organizations—I," *Administrative Science Quarterly,* 1 (1956), pp. 63-85; Talcott Parsons, "Suggestions for a Sociological Approach to the Theory of Organizations—II," in Talcott Parsons, *Structure and Process in Modern Societies* (New York: The Free Press, 1960), pp. 16-58. Talcott Parsons, "Some Ingredients of a General Theory of Formal Organization," in *Structure and Process in Modern Societies,* pp. 59-96.

2. Talcott Parsons, "The Mental Hospital as a Type of Organization," in Milton Greenblatt, Daniel J. Levinson, and Richard H. Williams (eds.), *The Patient and the Mental Hospital* (Glencoe, Ill.: The Free Press, 1957), pp. 108-129; Talcott Parsons, "The School Class as a Social System: Some of Its Functions in American Society," *Harvard Educational Review,* 29 (1959), pp. 297-318; and Talcott Parsons and Gerald M. Platt, "The American Academic Profession," unpublished ms., 1968.

3. The term "systems" here refers to school systems in the ordinary sense of that phrase, not to systems in any sociologically technical sense.

4. Parsons, "Some Ingredients of a General Theory of Formal Organization," *op. cit.,* pp. 63-65, 61.

5. Alan Rosenthal, *Pedagogues and Power: Teacher Groups in School Politics* (Syracuse: Syracuse University Press, 1969), p. 128.

6. For a case in point, see David Rogers, *110 Livingston Street* (New York: Random House, 1968).

7. Parsons, "Some Ingredients of a General Theory of Formal Organization," *op. cit.,* pp. 60-65.

8. With the advent of team teaching, many though hardly a majority of elementary schools have become somewhat departmentalized. Elementary teachers, however, still remain identified with a grade level rather than with a subject area like their secondary counterparts.

9. Parsons has dealt at length with the problems of organizations that include their clients as members as distinct from those that deal with clients at arm's length and from those that process physical objects. See "Some Ingredients of a

General Theory of Formal Organization," *op. cit.,* pp. 70-73; and "The Mental Hospital as a Type of Organization," *op. cit.*

10. Philip W. Jackson, *Life in Classrooms* (New York: Holt, Rinehart, and Winston, 1968), p. 17.

11. Dan C. Lortie, "The Balance of Control and Autonomy in Elementary School Teaching," in Amitai Etzioni (ed.), *The Semi-Professions and Their Organization* (New York: The Free Press, 1969), p. 29.

12. Jackson, *op. cit.,* pp. 119-120.

13. One should not underestimate the importance of voluntary "participation," if only willing compliance, on the part of general hospital patients. In mental hospitals, the expectation that patients will "work" at getting well has been widely reported, by Parsons and others.

14. Robert Dreeben, *On What Is Learned in School* (Reading, Mass.: Addison-Wesley Publishing, 1968), p. 37.

15. Peter M. Blau and W. Richard Scott, *Formal Organizations* (San Francisco: Chandler Publishing Co., 1962), pp. 45-57.

16. Amitai Etzioni, *A Comparative Analysis of Complex Organizations,* revised and enlarged edition (New York: The Free Press, 1975), pp. 3-67.

17. The National Principalship Study was directed by Neal Gross at the Harvard Graduate School of Education and sponsored by the Cooperative Research Program of the U.S. Office of Education. The interview findings referred to are unpublished.

18. For a discussion of the latter, see Parsons and Platt, *op. cit.,* and Etzioni, *op. cit.*

19. See Lortie, *op. cit.,* pp. 10-15.

20. Newcomb's classic investigation of political attitude change at Bennington College has traditionally been regarded as a reference group study. It can just as well be viewed as a study in the tyranny of the majority and of an elite. Where in that college climate was a student likely to find support for other than pro-New Deal political views? See Theodore M. Newcomb, *Personality and Social Change* (New York: Dryden Press, 1943).

21. The mechanisms of leverage are discussed, directly or indirectly, in the following additional works: Edgar H. Schein, "The Chinese Indoctrination Program for Prisoners of War," *Psychiatry,* 19 (1956), pp. 149-172; Robert K. Merton and Alice S. Kitt, "Contributions to the Theory of Reference Group Behavior," in Robert K. Merton and Paul F. Lazarsfeld (eds.), *Continuities in Social Research: Studies in the Scope and Method of "The American Soldier"* (Glencoe, Ill.: The Free Press, 1950), pp. 95-99; Gresham Sykes, *The Society of Captives* (Princeton: Princeton University Press, 1958), pp. 63-83; Frieda Fromm-Reichmann, *Principles of Intensive Psychotherapy* (Chicago: University of Chicago Press, 1950), pp. 97-107; Dreeben, *op. cit.,* pp. 35-39.

22. See footnote 1.

23. Parsons, "Suggestions for a Sociological Approach to the Theory of Organizations," *op. cit.,* p 20 (my italics).

24. Parsons, "Some Ingredients of a General Theory of Formal Organization," *op. cit.,* p. 60.

25. I assume the reader's familiarity with Parsons' scheme of functional problems; accordingly, I shall refer to it but not describe it. For the most useful summary statements, see Talcott Parsons, "An Outline of the Social System," in Talcott Parsons, Edward Shils, Kaspar D. Naegele, and Jesse R. Pitts (eds.), *Theories of Society,* (New York: The Free Press, 1961), pp. 30-79; and Edward C. Devereux, "Parsons' Sociological Theory," in Max Black (ed.), *The Social Theories of Talcott Parsons* (Englewood Cliffs: Prentice-Hall, 1961), pp. 1-63.

26. Henry A. Landsberger, "Parsons' Theory of Organizations," in Black (ed.), *op. cit.,* p. 223 (my italics).

27. *Ibid.,* p. 228.

28. Parsons, "Suggestions for a Sociological Approach to the Theory of Organizations," *op. cit.,* pp. 45, 44-58.

29. Oddly enough, Parsons does not distinguish between goal and function distinctly. For example: "An organization is a system which, as the attainment of its *goal,* 'produces' an identifiable something which can be utilized in some way by another system. . . . In . . . an educational organization [the *out*-put (function)] may be a certain type of 'trained capacity'. . . ." Parsons, "Suggestions for a Sociological Approach to the Theory of Organizations," *op. cit.,* p. 17 (my italics). The goal of an educational organization is not to produce trained capacity, though its function certainly is.

30. Parsons, "Some Ingredients of a General Theory of Formal Organizations," *op. cit.,* p. 60.

31. *Ibid.,* pp. 65-66 ("types of competence," my italics; other italics are in the text).

32. Parsons, "Suggestions for a Sociological Approach to the Theory of Organizations," *op. cit.,* p. 22.

33. Parsons, "Some Ingredients of a General Theory of Formal Organization," *op. cit.,* pp. 70-71.

34. *Ibid.,* p. 81.

35. Parsons, "Suggestions for a Sociological Approach to the Theory of Organizations," *op. cit.,* p. 46. Kinship units serve pattern-maintenance functions, but they are not organizations in any conventional sense, as Parsons makes abundantly clear.

36. Landsberger, *op. cit.,* p. 228.

37. Parsons, "Some Ingredients of a General Theory of Formal Organization," *op. cit.,* pp. 94, 95 (my italics).

38. See Parsons, "The School Class as a Social System," *op. cit.,* and also the discussion of school level earlier in this paper. It is noteworth that mental hospitals, which also take their clients in as members, differ structurally according to the characteristics of patients (particularly with respect to the nature of the illness and the problems it poses). Parsons' analysis of mental hospitals ("The Mental Hospital as a Type of Organization," *op. cit.*) is based almost entirely on the work of Alfred H. Stanton and Morris S. Schwartz, *The Mental Hospital* (New York: Basic Books, 1954), a study of a hospital that mainly provides active treatment for acutely ill schizophrenics. Ivan Belknap, in *Human Problems of a State Mental Hospital* (New York: McGraw-Hill, 1956), deals with a custodial hospital designed for "treating" chronic and somatic illness; and Robert N. Rapoport, in *Community as Doctor* (London: Tavistock Publications, 1960), is concerned with a hospital for actively treating personality disorders. All three hospitals differ markedly in structure; and in each case, the properties of organizational structure can be readily traced to differences in the characteristics of patients and the problems they create for treatment and care.

39. Parsons, "Suggestions for a Sociological Approach to the Theory of Organizations," *op. cit.,* pp. 47-56. Note that Parsons contrasts business firms, military organizations, and universities and attempts to explain their respective structural differences according to the AGIL scheme.

40. Erwin O. Smigel, *The Wall Street Lawyer* (New York: The Free Press of Glencoe, 1964), pp. 72-112.

41. Philip Selznick, *Leadership in Administration* (Evanston, Ill.: Row, Peterson, 1957), pp. 53-54.

42. Arthur L. Stinchcombe, "Bureaucratic and Craft Administration of Production: A Comparative Study," *Administrative Science Quarterly,* 4 (1959), pp. 168-187; Joan Woodward, *Management and Technology* (London: Her Majesty's Stationery Office, 1958); and Joan Woodward, *Industrial Organization: Theory and Practice* (London: Oxford University Press, 1965), pp. 50-67; and Alvin W. Gouldner, *Patterns of Industrial Bureaucracy* (Glencoe, Ill.: The Free Press, 1954).

43. For a general analysis of organizational structure based on the nature of environments and technologies, see James D. Thompson, *Organizations in Action* (New York: McGraw-Hill, 1967). On the founding of organizations, see Arthur L. Stinchcombe, "Social Structure and Organizations," in James G. March (ed.), *Handbook of Organizations* (Chicago: Rand McNally, 1965), pp. 153-164.

44. Parsons, "Suggestions for a Sociological Approach to the Theory of Organizations," *op. cit.,* p. 17.

45. Charles Perrow, "A Framework for the Comparative Analysis of Organizations," *American Sociological Review,* 32 (1967), p. 194.

46. *Ibid.,* p. 195.

47. *Ibid.,* p. 203.

48. Lortie, *op. cit.,* p. 9.

36

SCIENCE AS A PROFESSION AND SCIENTIFIC PROFESSIONALISM

Joseph Ben-David

Until the beginning of the nineteenth century science, like literature and politics, was practiced by amateurs. It was not considered as a career but as something done for its own sake. Achievements were attributed to personal gift, and little consideration was given to other conditions of scientific work. Throughout the nineteenth century science became a career in one country after another. Would-be scientists were trained in a fairly standard fashion, and scientific research became organized according to accepted routines.[1] The new career assumed the characteristics of the traditional learned professions of law, medicine and theology.

Although it is often difficult to decide whether a given occupation should or should not be classified as a profession, it is possible to list a set of characteristics associated with the term to serve as the criteria of classification.[2]

These criteria are as follows:

1. Higher educational qualification as a prerequisite to entry to an occupation.
2. Monopoly rights over the performance of certain functions (such as treating patients, signing blueprints of construction projects).
3. A measure of control of admission into the occupation, as a means of maintaining its standards and status.
4. Formal or informal authority of the professional community over the conduct of its members; a reluctance to admit lay interference in the affairs of the profession, and regulation of the competition among the members of the profession.

Although tendencies of this sort exist among other occupations too, they are considered as legitimate only among professions. Thus the regulation of competition among doctors is enforced by law in the U.S. (which grants all kinds of rights in this respect to local medical associations), but the same thing is considered illegitimate or actually criminal if it is done by businessmen and industrialists and is regarded as an economically harsh extortion if it is enforced by trade unions.

5. Limitations on the contractual obligations of the professional towards his client or employer. The patient cannot order a certain kind of treatment from his doctor, university teachers demand academic freedom to teach the way they want and to some extent what they want, and there usually is a limitation of the lay supervisory authority over professionals in industrial and service organizations.[3]

These are not present to the same extent in all the occupations considered as professions. Characteristics 1, 2, and 5 are probably present in all of them, while the rest are less general. There is, however, a view that these characteristics go together and that they are prerequisites for the performance of work which requires learning (professionalism). Occupations which possess these characteristics are considered more prestigeful than others. They are supposed to confer a superior moral quality to an occupation, such as income from landownership used to confer in the past. As a result there has been a tendency among different occupational groups to "professionalize" themselves by assuming these characteristics.

These characteristics are reminiscent of the privileges of medieval guilds and eighteenth-century

I am indebted to Professors Shmuel Eisenstadt and Morris Janowitz for their comments and suggestions and to the Center for Organizational Studies of the Department of Sociology, the University of Chicago, for its support of this study.

estates, and the connections between present-day professionalism and those earlier antecedents can often be historically traced. The existence of such "survivals" in present day societies which are opposed to status privileges as well as to economic monopolies presents a problem which has been widely discussed in the sociological and economic literature.[4]

The existence of privilege is a basic problem of every kind of social order. Privilege is nowhere accepted as a matter of course. In traditional societies the tendency had been to justify its existence after the event, but in modern society privilege is rarely accepted as legitimate. In view of this professionalism — which has become as typical an institution for the conferral of social privilege and economic monopoly on occupational groups as the conferral of corporate privileges on selected occupational and local groups used to be under the old régime — requires an explanation. How did it occur that such an institution was not only accepted as legitimate, but also became one of the most rapidly growing social phenomena in this century?

The answer usually given to this question is that professions are treated as exceptions in the present day occupational structure because (1) their practice requires highly specialized training and (2) their orientation to service, or collectivity orientation in Parsons' terms. Highly specialized training makes the supervision of professional work by nonprofessional bureaucratic superiors of clients particularly difficult; service-orientation — that is the belief that professionals can be trusted to act towards commonly accepted goals in their professional work — makes such supervision less necessary than in other occupations.[5] Hence the tendency to leave the supervision of professional conduct to the professional associations which draw up codes of ethics and establish committees for their enforcement.

The difficulty with this explanation is that it fits perfectly only medicine and perhaps law. In both of these cases, however, there is in addition to specialized technical training, and service-orientation, as Parsons showed, also a rather specialized kind of personal trust.[6] Furthermore, both of these are traditional professions which inherited their present privileges from the old régime of guilds and estates. Although this makes them particularly apt models for other would-be professions, it probably makes them less than ideal cases for studying the more general phenomenon of modern professionalism.

On the other hand there are a number of reasons for considering the study of science as a profession as an important step towards the understanding of the distinct characteristics of present-day professionalism. Lately science has been a serious and successful competitor to the older professions of law and medicine in prestige as well as professional autonomy. In rankings of occupational prestige in the U.S. "scientist" rose from rank 8 in 1947 to rank 3.5 in 1963, and "nuclear physicist" went up from rank 18 to 3.5. In 1963 scientific occupations (nuclear physicists, scientists, and government scientists) constituted three of the six most prestigeful occupations in the U.S.; in 1947 there was not even one scientific occupation in this top category.[7] This was accompanied by a great increase of professional autonomy among university as well as industrial scientists.[8]

In addition, the scientific profession has become the gatekeeper of professionalism in general. The training of all the professions, including law and medicine, has been performed to a growing extent by professional scientists or scholars working at universities and other institutions of higher learning and research, rather than by practitioners, since the early nineteenth century. The institution of a university training program leading to a degree and combined with research is usually accepted as the main justification for the granting of professional privileges to the members of an occupation. Thus since the nineteenth century it has been possible to speak of a new kind of "scientific professionalism."[9]

The circumstance further enhances the relative autonomy of science as compared to other professions. It is now the only profession which maintains its exclusive privilege to train and license candidates for practice. All the other professions have either ceded this right to the universities, that is, to professional scientists and scholars (the term "scientist," as in German, will be used subsequently in a sense which includes also scholars using the scientific method) or, at least, have come to share it with scientists.

There is still a further sense in which the scientific profession is more privileged than the others. Law and medicine are supposed to supervise the ethical conduct of their members through formal arrangements of self-policing and internal judicature. Scientific societies or self-governing faculties, however, have usually no such formal arrangements. This seems to indicate that in some way scientists are more trusted than the members of other professions.

Finally, science is a typically modern profession. It emerged as an amateur activity in the seventeenth century and became a profession only in the nineteenth and twentieth centuries. Thus there can be no question here of a survival of old patterns. If the autonomy of the scientists is considered as legitimate in present-day society, then the reasons for this legitimation cannot be explained as the continued recognition of acquired customary privilege.

In order to explain how professional science acquired these privileges, I shall first sketch briefly the rise of science as a profession. The main purpose of this history is to show that, indeed, in this case there does not exist a historical continuity between earlier corporate privileges and present-day professionalism. Subsequently an attempt will be made to explain what was the new basis of legitimation of the professional privileges of scientists and why this new basis was accepted as consistent with the universalistic values of modern societies while other privileges were rejected. Finally it will be shown that the rationale on which scientific professionalism is based has been extended beyond the limits of its validity and that this gave rise to certain problems which became acute during the last decade.

THE RISE OF SCIENTIFIC PROFESSIONALISM

The universities where science was first professionalized have been in existence since the Middle Ages. But there is little continuity between the scientific profession today and the professional scholars who worked at the universities in the Middle Ages or even as late as the eighteenth century. Modern science started largely outside the universities by independent people at times loosely organized into "Academies." The universities ruled by scholastic theologians and philosophers and/or by humanistic scholars were usually inhospitable to science, scientists, and scientistic philosophers. In Italy, England, and France, which were the successive centers of scientific activity between the sixteenth and the early nineteenth centuries, scientists did not usually work at universities. And when under the French Revolution educational policy came under the influence of scientists and scientistic philosophers, they welcomed the abolishment of the universities alongside all the other guilds and their eventual replacement by a set of bureaucratically supervised specialized vocational schools.[10]

Thus there was nothing in the development of scientific work until the end of the eighteenth century to indicate that scientific research would become one of the learned professions, alongside law, medicine, and theology (or replacing theology). Rather, it appeared that science would become an element in the training and practice of many technological occupations possessing no particular privileges and not bound to any particular organization and that eventually the old professions would also drop their privileges and particular organizations.

The turn to professionalism came about as an unintended consequence of the general philosophical function of science. Intellectuals who regarded science as the spearhead of an open-ended innovative culture had been in a state of chronic conflict with the representatives of traditional culture, especially the clergy. Control of education, the key to the transmission of culture, was the principal issue of the conflict.[11] Starting with the French Revolution, the conflict was decided everywhere in favor of the innovative scientistic movement. In one country after another the new type of intellectuals, philosophers, scientists, and scientific scholars succeeded in the abolition of church control in higher and eventually also in other levels of education. Scientific authority was to a great extent substituted for the religious one, as the dominant type of intellectual authority in present-day societies.

This did not immediately lead to professionalization. There emerged ideas about turning scientists into a new type of priesthood, and scientists and scientistic philosophers played a central role in devising and running the new system of education established in France between 1794-1804. But this did not involve attempts at turning scientific research into a profession. Research and discovery were not considered as a service to be paid for or as a career to prepare for. They were charismatic acts for which some scientists were rewarded after the event, but not work in the economic sense of the word. Besides, the spirit of the scientific community was opposed to any formalization of authority and to any identification of science with particular groups and institutions. Discovery was an individual achievement that belonged to the whole of mankind. The scientist had to be, therefore, completely independent in his research, accountable not to anyone but to the judgement of the competents, irrespective of who those competents were, where they lived, and what was the source of their income.

Indeed in France scientists did not assume the privileges of the clergy whose educational functions they inherited. They did not object to the new educational institutions where teachers at all levels were to be employees of a state bureaucracy carrying out the missions imposed on them by the employer as all the other civil servants. Research was still completely free, since whether done by teachers or others, it was done privately and in complete freedom.[12]

But in Germany, where the polity was authoritarian and hierarchic throughout the nineteenth century and where the social classes which could afford the time and money required for research were small, the scientists and the new type of philosophers and scholars needed both the income and the privileges of the university as conditions to do research and to teach and publish freely.[13] This posed a dilemma for the reformers of the German university. They realized, not less than their French counterparts, that scientific discovery could be nurtured only under conditions of complete freedom of the creative individual and the application of completely universalistic standards. They were well aware that it would not be easy to secure such conditions at the universities, which tended to act as conservative guilds and were prone to put the honor and the interest of their members before those of science.[14]

The university could be adopted as the principal seat for scientific research only with important reservations. These were embodied in a set of principles known as "academic freedom." First of all the university was secularized and declared a purely scientific institution where teaching and research were not subject to any external control, only to the discipline inherent in the scientific method. Although employed and paid by the state, the academic teacher was supposed to be as free as any private individual in his research and teaching. The arrangements devised for this end were the institutions of corporate self-government, tenure, formal freedom of teaching of the academic teachers (in Germany there was also far-reaching freedom for the students to choose their courses and to transfer credits), and the *Privatdozentur* which made it possible for the university to confer the right of teaching (*venia legendi*) on those who qualified themselves for it through an advanced thesis based on original research *(Habilitationsschrift)*, even if they were not given salaried positions as professors.

These arrangements were still not an attempt at the creation of a new scientific profession. Their main purpose was to make scientific work possible for a small group of highly selected individuals by using an existing institution, the university, for the provision of the resources necessary for the purpose, and to use the same institution for the purpose of extending the influence of the scientific spirit (defined in the terms of idealistic philosophies) in Germany. Professorship was still conceived as an intellectual élite position and not as an occupation, and the *Privatdozent* was not a salaried position but merely a recognition of scientific qualification. Research was to remain free and private, one was paid only for teaching, and the highest teaching posts were reserved as prizes for outstanding researchers.

In spite of this attempt to preserve the non-occupational charismatic character of scientific research, scientists came to regard their work as a career and not only an inner calling. As the institutional arrangements did not take into account

this development, there arose tensions and difficulties in the German universities by the end of the nineteenth century.[15] In spite of all this, the German model of academic science became dominant, and was diffused to most other countries, as well as to nonuniversity research establishments after these emerged, starting from the 1880's.[16]

The diffusion of the German model consisted of two parts: (1) the diffusion of the actual arrangements of the German university and (2) the diffusion of the ideas of academic freedom. The diffusion of the arrangements was caused by historical circumstances. About the middle of the nineteenth century Germany was the only country which possessed a system of advanced scientific research and training. On the whole this was much more effective than the amateur science of other countries. Scientists from all over the world went therefore to Germany for advanced studies. As foreigners, and in many cases privileged ones, they were unaware of the difficulties of the academic career in Germany, and as they went to the best places, they were also rarely aware of the rigid conservativeness of other parts of the system. Hence they tended to believe that the German model was the best possible one.

Nevertheless, in actual fact the adoption of the German patterns led to quite different results in different places. In some of the countries of Central and Eastern Europe, universities became actually parts of the German system with titles and usages more or less precisely corresponding to those prevailing in Germany and with German serving as the main language of scientific publication. The imitation of the German system was almost as slavish in far-away Japan, at least in the imperial universities. In Britain and France the imitation was much more selective, and in the U.S. the pattern was considerably reformed. In that country science became professionalized not only in fact, but also in principle. The introduction of the Ph.D. training program was a decisive departure from the charismatic conception of the scientific role which—at least in theory—had been maintained everywhere in Europe. The new degree was an official admission of the fact that scientific research was a vocation that one could be trained for, as for any other profession, and not a charismatic gift which could be recognized only after the event.[17] This is not to say that there was no charismatic element left in the scientific role, but this is true also of other occupational roles.

This explicit professionalization of the scientific role was accompanied by important changes in the organization of scientific work at the universities and elsewhere. The administration of academic affairs in the U.S. was vested not in self-governing corporations but in formal office-holders. Indeed participatory academic self-government had never been complete even in Europe, and it became more a slogan than a reality after the end of the last century when the great increase of nonprofessorial scientific employees at the universities began. In the U.S., however, the principle was never introduced. The university corporation there never became a guild of professors but was a legal entity governed by a board and administered by career executives.[18]

This change has considerably decreased the gap between academic and nonacademic scientists. It also eliminated the ambiguity in the professional status of the junior scientific workers in large research teams and organizations. The fact that their autonomy was curtailed to some extent in these positions did not imply a denial of their professional status as scientists. They were on the same career line as their superiors. This eliminated many of the problems which arose in Germany as a result of the *de facto* but not *de jure* professionalization of science.

The "autonomy" of some scientists was also modified in the sense that many of them worked in applied fields, where the choice of problems was determined by economic, military, and political rather than intrinsically scientific considerations. Since World War II all these changes have become diffused to the whole world and have increasingly professionalized the previously charismatic conception of the scientific role everywhere.

As opposed to these changes in the concrete arrangements of scientific work, the principles of academic freedom remained unchanged and became actually the main contents of the prevailing professional ethics of scientists in general. In this respect there has been a complete continuity of tradition from Wilhelm Humboldt up to the present day, according to which scientists should have tenure and autonomy to pursue their own interests. They should also be free to publish and teach, and, if working in organizations, they should not be subject to bureaucratic control.[19] Although in many countries nonacademic scientists outweigh in numbers the academic ones, scientists working in the former kind of frameworks (industrial firms, governmental organizations) demand privileges of "academic freedom."[20]

Thus the transformation of scientific research into an occupational career branching widely into industrial production and public and private services, and the actual changes in the patterns of scientific work which accompanied it, did not alter the ideas about the proper definition of the scientist's role and the organization of research. These are still conceived in the same terms as they were early in the nineteenth century when they were formulated for the purpose of adjusting the structure and usages of the traditional university corporations to the needs of charismatically conceived research.

AN INTERPRETATION: EVOLUTION OF SOCIAL STRUCTURES AND CONSTANCY OF CULTURAL VALUES

One interpretation of this development would be evolutionary. The social structures within which scientific activity has taken place since the seventeenth century were not designed specifically for the pursuit of science but were chosen one after the other because they suited the purpose and the interests of successive generations of scientists working under changing conditions. Those structures which scientists found most congenial, namely the French type of Academy in the eighteenth century, the German type of university and professorship in the nineteenth century and the U.S. type of university, research institute and professional science in the twentieth century, were "selected" out, imitated, adapted to circumstances, and diffused all over the world.

It could also be argued that this process was guided by a search for privilege, as all these structures implied high social status and a measure of monopoly. The principles of academic freedom would then be interpreted as a rationalization, or justification of privilege, a so-called ideology in the abusive sense of the word that implies a distortion or falsification of reality. The circumstance that these principles remained unchanged amid so many changes in the social structure of scientific work could be considered as a partial evidence for this interpretation; structures had to change under the pressure of reality, but privilege and its justification remained constant.

But this interpretation would not account for the acceptance of privilege as legitimate by societies which have successfully fought and abolished privileges in other fields. Furthermore this interpretation is not consistent with the fact that the successive social structures of scientific work have led to an acceleration, rather than a deceleration, of scientific growth. Had the purpose of the changes been to protect and increase privileges then scientific interests would have been sacrificed. Indeed this happened on several occasions; in the Royal Society of London during the eighteenth century, in the French system of higher education in the nineteenth century, and in the German universities at the turn of this century. Had the long-run process of the selection of social structures been determined by the selfish interests of scientists in social privilege, then these privileged structures would have prevailed, in spite of their disadvantages from the point of view of the needs of research. But, instead, there arose new structures, usually in other countries, which suited the scientific purpose better, and they eventually became dominant.

This shows that privilege could not have been the only, or even the primary, guiding principle in the evolution of the structures of science leading to the rise of professional science. Whether or not it was also consistent with privilege, that evolution was consistent with scientific growth.[21]

Instead of interpreting, therefore, the unchanging persistence of the principles of academic freedom as a rationalization of privilege, I suggest to interpret it as somehow connected with this cybernetic function of selecting the social structures of science in a way consistent with the intrinsic goals of science. This, of course, has been the ostensible rationale of these principles for the scientists, and I propose to make this ostensible rationale the basis of the present interpretation, rather than exposing it as a so-called ideological justification of privilege.

At the time when these principles were formulated (when the University of Berlin was established in 1809), the principles of academic freedom served the purpose of asserting the continuity of the academic community with the informal community of amateur scientists and scholars of the eighteenth century. Although academic scientists were now employees of the state, these principles announced that their research and teaching were to remain as free and private as they had ever been. Anyone was to have a chance to prove oneself through writing a *Habilitationsschrift* and thus obtaining the right to lecture (*venia legendi*), and no lay authority could deprive him of this right or of the professorship, once obtained.

When it turned out that the German arrangements did not work satisfactorily and they were replaced as the dominant structure by the U.S. type of professional science, the principles of academic freedom still continued to serve the same purpose of asserting the continuity of scientific work in its new structures with science as pursued in the scientific communities of the founding fathers of European science.

However, instead of a device for keeping research private and apart from the formal organization of the university, academic freedom was now used as a guide for the proper organization of scientific work. It having been realized that science was to become more and more professionalized and organized, an attempt was made to create a new type of professional organization based on collegiality and modeled on the informal structure of the amateur scientific community.

Thus arose the university department which became increasingly a participatory democracy, the professional scientific societies where all qualified members were equal, the democratic election of editors for the most important scientific journals by these societies, and the insistence on impersonal and universalistic refereeing of papers. All of these arrangements are in sharp contrast to those which had prevailed in the European centers of learning up until World War II. Still they are designed to serve in a different way the same purpose as the nineteenth century arrangements were meant to serve, namely, to ensure the freedom and spontaneity of scientific work. But while in the nineteenth century freedom and spontaneity were thought as synonymous with privacy and informality, now it is believed that organizations and associations, if properly conceived, can also become free and spontaneous.

According to this interpretation the principles of academic freedom have served the simple purpose of evaluation of existing or planned scientific institutions. If the principles have remained constant this was because they were considered as implied in the acceptance of the scientific pursuit of truth as a social value which has been a constant characteristic of Western society since the seventeenth century. The principles of academic freedom can, therefore, be regarded as part of an ideology in the nonabusive sense as defined by Talcott Parsons as the evaluation of social situations in the light of certain values held in common by a collectivity.[22]

THE RATIONALE OF ACADEMIC FREEDOM: THE SELF-REGULATION OF SCIENCE

Assuming that the principles of academic freedom have been considered by the scientists as valid criteria for the evaluation of the suitability for science of different social structures, it remains to be seen what was the rationale of this belief. Why have scientists believed that the optimal organization of research is that which excludes all formal authority[23] in the supervision of research, either by making the research completely private or by organizing it on a completely collegial basis.

This rationale has been spelled out in the conception of the "scientific community." Science is viewed as an informal network of communication and evaluation which is capable of regulating itself (provided, of course, that there is a prior consensus about the value of science as an end in its own right). The rationale of viewing science this way originated in the amateur science of the past. I shall, therefore, start with the description of the distinguishing characteristics of the scientific community of the seventeenth and eighteenth centuries and show how these characteristics made it plausible to conceive of this as a self-regulating mechanism.

1. Earlier intellectual communities had to protect their integrity by a sectarian way of life, rituals, and very often also, especially in religion and moral philosophy, by political coercion. The scientific community did not require all this. The specificity and interpersonal objectivity of scientific knowledge welded scientists from all over the world into consensual groups which were capable of restricting deviance without resource to coercion.[24]

2. The criterion of experimental test provided a plausible claim that scientific knowledge would be ultimately useful and that the scientific method was of general value in deciding what worked in any practical field. Previous kinds of learning had in most cases only purely cognitive, aesthetic, or religious-moral value. In the few cases where intellectual traditions had practical applications, such as in medicine, law, and technology, the traditions were very specific and of limited generalizability. Science, on the other hand, had in principle unlimited applications and its method was transferable to any practical problem of an instrumental kind.

3. The organizations of science, namely the academies were different from the guilds or from religious organizations in the sense that they did not possess formal hierarchies and executive or legislative powers. They functioned in accordance with the novel nature of science. As scientific truth spoke for itself through the experiment, it is perhaps surprising that there arose any formal organizations at all. They did arise, nevertheless, as in order to grasp its truth one had to know the language of science. This knowledge of "language" by a group of people and its accessibility to all who were able enough to learn it were conditions without which the claim for objectivity (and therefore for the autonomy) of science could not have been substantiated. Thus while the scientific ethos claimed complete freedom for the individual scientist, the granting of this freedom required the existence of a publicly identifiable community of scientists. Only the assurance that there was such a community, capable of criticizing and evaluating the discoveries and open to all who were competent, could provide a basis of legitimacy for the new intellectual role of the scientist. Hence, the need for a publicly recognized organization. This organization did not claim doctrinal authority, or formal powers of control. It had no formalized hierarchy, nor formal means of enforcement of decisions. It acted like an informal community uniting all those who were competent and "knew the language." What lent to such organizations as the Royal Society or the Académie des Sciences their authority was the spontaneous recognition of the scientists all over the world that these organizations represented a universalistically valid scientific judgement. Without this recognition no royal charter could have lent them any influence.

The organization, therefore, did not serve the purpose of coordinating division of labor, of controlling by formal authority individual deviance, or protecting economic interests. Its function was merely to attest to the public nature of science as an intellectual pursuit equal in dignity and equal or superior in its validity to traditional intellectual pursuits. Scientists could know that although they were not understood they were appreciated by society, and "society" could rest assured that although scientists were free to do what they wished and as they wished the results of their activities were in fact under public control.

The purpose or the function of these arrangements was cultural: to make possible the public pursuit of science in a way which was consistent with its needs as an innovative intellectual activity with unpredictable effects. The social conditions and value premises which induced people to accept and approve such a potentially subversive activity have been described elsewhere.[25] England, where the crucial first step was taken, was a society interested in change and willing to put up with a degree of religious pluralism. Thus it welcomed the emergence of experimental science as a method capable of combining intellectual freedom and autonomy with self-regulation and strict intellectual discipline and responsibility. Scientists were publicly recognized and honored as new types of intellectuals equivalent or superior to traditional scholars after they have proved themselves capable of arriving at consensus and discipline through the application of experimental and mathematical methods, without recourse to persuasion or coercion. The institutionalization of this self-regulatory mechanism in science accomplished in cognitive culture what the institutionalization of the two other self-regulatory mechanisms of modern society, namely free elections and the free market, accomplished in the polity and the economy. It made possible continuous growth and permanent change in cognitive culture and, as a result, in all human activity making use of knowledge; and it created a sense of mastery over the mysteries of nature, replacing in these areas the warring and coercive religions and intolerant philosophical sects. It should be noted that out of the three self-regulatory mechanisms of modern society science was the first to be institutionalized and widely diffused and that it is still the only self-regulatory social mechanism allowed in many a present-day society.

SCIENTIFIC SELF-REGULATION AND THE PROFESSIONALIZATION OF SCIENCE

Originally the self-regulation of science had nothing to do with the allocation of economic resources and rewards. The function of the self-regulatory mechanism was to abolish or rather to make superfluous formal authority in cognitive culture. It seemed to reconcile complete freedom from constituted authority with strict intellectual discipline and responsibility, because the scientific method was supposed to lead to the inexorable detection and elimination of falsehood and error.

The emergence of salaried careers and bureaucratic organizations in science during the nineteenth century created a new situation. It was one thing to rely on the informal mechanisms of the scientific community for telling good from bad science, and another thing to rely on those mechanisms to decide which scientists should get how much for what, what should be their conditions of work, or how to determine the amount to be spent by society on science in general as compared to health, education, goods, and other things. Of course, had science been supported from private funds, this latter problem would not have arisen, as different decisions would have been taken by individuals according to their personal tastes. However, as support for science has come overwhelmingly from public funds, the question of priorities could not be avoided.

Indeed, this last question has not been avoided. How much should be spent on science and on what basis should funds for science be allocated have been much-discussed questions (even though the discussions were not conclusive). But the question of allocation within science and the organization of scientific work has been left to a large extent to the scientific community. Appointments to academic positions or to positions in basic research in general, the adjudication of applications for research grants, and the distribution of basic research funds have usually been left in most of the scientifically important countries in the hands of committees representing, or at least said to be representing, the scientific community rather than the public. And scientific organizations have been as a rule self-governing. The rationale of this privileged treatment of the scientific profession has been as follows.

1. It has been assumed that the effectivity of the scientific method in securing consensus among scientists is not altered by professionalization. What is and what is not a soluble problem is known by every competent scientist, and mistakes are rapidly detected by experiment, observation, and logical analysis. There is, therefore, no need to control the allocation of resources for science. The efforts will go anyway in the directions which are most promising. Accordingly there is also no need to coordinate efforts by authoritative decisions, as the limited range of soluble problems ensures that the individual efforts will fit together. There is, as a matter of fact, a great deal of evidence for the existence of such unplanned coordination from independent multiple discoveries, as well as the spontaneous emergence of "schools" around creative people.[26] Hence the organization of professional science should not present more of a problem than the organization of amateur scientific work. The scientific community can be granted economic means and left all its freedom and autonomy. It will organize itself optimally irrespective of whether the researchers are amateurs or professionals.

2. This would still not eliminate all invidious privilege from science. Scientists enjoy freedom such as no other worker does. Like erstwhile priests or mandarins, they are exempt from the control of the market, as well as from political-bureaucratic discipline, to an extent that no other present-day occupational group is.

There is, however, an important difference between science, on the one hand, and the traditional intellectual roles, on the other. The authority of the latter was either personal (charismatic), deriving from superior mental and moral endowment, or institutional, deriving from officially vested coercive authority. Both implied a diffuse and, therefore, invidious superiority to others. The authority of the scientists, although it also contains personal and institutional elements, is based on universally accepted and valid criteria. Neither personal charisma nor office, but the mathematical proof and the experimental test are the basis of whatever authority they possess. That authority is specific and cannot be legitimately extended to anything beyond what has been proved or tested. Hence, however great their authority is compared to that of others, it does not, in principle, involve anything which establishes a generalized inequality between scientists and others.

3. There is also a more intrinsic relationship between service and reward in the case of science than in that of priesthood. Because priests and mandarins performed nonproductive services, their relatively high rewards implied an intrinsically higher evaluation of religious than of other kinds of human activity. Science, however, is assumed to have short

or long term industrial utility, in addition to having immediate cognitive value. Furthermore, this utility is directly related to the cognitive value of science. What makes a scientific discovery true, is also a necessary condition of its usefulness. Clark Maxwell's theory of electromagnetic waves proved useful for the development of wireless transmission, because it was a good theory. Thus although the aim of the pure scientist is to discover truth and not to be of other service, he can be regarded as part of the productive system. The total amount of funds allocated for research is presumably related to this productive function of science. The exemption of the scientists from bureaucratic control and economic competition is, therefore, not a benefit accorded to them as the members of a group performing a privileged function but an instrumental requirement of a certain kind of work which is as much subject to the impersonal discipline of achievement as any other.

4. Finally, the closure of the scientific organizations which manifests itself in requirements for formal qualification and self-governing arrangements is not conceived as a contradiction to any principle of universalism. Guilds of all kinds distantiated themselves from others on the basis of economic and/or political interests and then used legal, ideological, and social devices to protect their particularistic privileges. But the primary basis of solidarity for academic and other scientific communities has been the existence of a common intellectual interest and competence.[27]

Thus associations of businessmen, artisans, and workers have little content intrinsically related to the work of the members of these different occupations. The aim of the associations is protection of special interests and the attainment of special advantages. Associations of scientists may be just as selfish in respect of group interests as any other association. But in addition and usually prior to the protection of economic interests, they also have a substantial amount of intrinsically intellectual interests in common. Therefore, associations of businessmen or workers only make sense in a context of economic conflict between groups unwilling to submit to universalistic standards of economic allocations. Associations of nuclear physicists or molecular biologists can exist on a purely scientific basis. The exclusiveness of trade associations is rooted in economic discrimination and makes no other sense. The exclusiveness of scientific groups can be justified on the basis of competence, and it serves a useful purpose of identification and channeling communication quite irrespective of economic interests.

To sum up, professional science which insists on arrangements of "academic freedom" is a peculiar and new kind of social development. As all other professionalism it is a set of monopolistic privileges as well as a genuine community formation based on shared cognitive values and norms which are spontaneously adhered to. But unlike the older professions whose privileges were based on particularistic relationships between classes and corporations and on invidious evaluations of the diffuse quality of the calling and the way of life of the professional person, scientists were valued as producers whose services are measured by universalistic standards of specific achievement. This justified the special freedom and autonomy granted to scientists. Their exemption from political-bureaucratic controls and the competitive market was not conceived of as a generalized privilege granted to a status group but as specific authority granted to an expert group possessing special qualifications in a limited field which was effectively controlled anyway by the self-regulatory mechanism of science.

It is also possible to explain now the question of how the introduction and/or extension of the scientific training for the professions at the universities reversed the early nineteenth-century trend of the abolition of professional privileges and lent a new legitimacy to professionalism in general. The substitution of science for professional lore and general humanistic education as the basis of professional practice appeared as a sufficient safeguard against the emergence of particularistic privilege. Scientific training and research at the universities in the fields of the practicing professions appeared to subject the latter to the self-regulation of science.

This assumption, coupled with the idea of the unlimited applicability of science, made possible the extension of the new scientific professionalism to an ever-growing number of occupations. Organized groups of people engaged in a variety of endeavors tried to and often actually did gain professional privileges as a result of the establishment of university degree courses and the institution of research in their general field.

This development provides an interesting contrast to the "routinization of charisma" described by Max Weber as characteristic of religious and political movements when success transforms them into stable institutions. In religion (as well as in politics) institutionalization leads to a decrease in the scope of the applications of the religious principles and usages. In the charismatic and informal religious community (the "sect") religion is considered relevant in every situation and applicable to every social role. But when religion is institutionalized, its scope becomes defined and limited, and its practice, apart from specific occasions and situations, becomes the speciality of priests. Routinization in religion leads through division of labor to "secularization," i.e., to a diminishing application of religious considerations to other fields of human endeavor.

In science the process has been reversed. Routinization and division of labor occurred here too. The informal communities of scientists for whom knowledge was an end in itself and who adhered spontaneously to the mental and moral discipline of the scientific method and such usages as publication of results and recognition of the achievements of others without bias and prejudice gave place to formal organizations and regular careers.[28] But this division of labor did not place a limit to the scope of the applications of science. To the contrary, it extended this scope by giving rise to an ever-increasing application of science to all kinds of work and a concomitant increase of occupations modeling themselves on the scientific profession.

This interpretation explains the existence of professional privileges of scientists and is, probably, an important part of the explanation of modern professionalism in general. The claims of science, and of scientific professions in general, for academic freedom or professional autonomy were legitimized, because they had a basis in the self-regulatory mechanism of science. This is, however, not to say that in all the cases where such claims were made, there really was effective self-regulation. Like other social mechanisms, the application of this one is also limited by a variety of conditions. Some of these may be evident; others may have to be discovered through trial and error. An attempt will be made now to explore these limitations of self-regulation in science.

PROBLEMS AND FALLACIES OF SCIENTIFIC PROFESSIONALISM

The plausibility of these assumptions is, however, only apparent. As has been pointed out, self-governing communities of academic scientists did not always adhere to the strict standards of science, but developed vested interests of their own. Elsewhere, I have shown that effective self-regulation (i.e., in accordance with the standards of science) in professional science occurred only under special cicumstances where universities competed with each other in an open market for talent and was not an automatic result of academic freedom and self-government.[29] Indeed it is difficult to conceive how the distribution of funds and formal authority could be governed by the same mechanism as the distribution of information, criticism, and appreciation.

There exists a fairly effective network of publication and communication for the latter. It makes therefore sense to refer to an informal community of chemists or physicists, in every country or even on a worldwide scale as the framework within which this exchange of communication takes place.[30] But money, positions, and other resources are not awarded by this community but by government departments, foundations, academies, donors, universities, institutions, and firms. One may wish that these organizations should act in accordance with the currents of ideas and wishes which can be discerned in the scientific community. But these currents do not translate themselves automatically into mechanisms for the allocation of funds.

To mention only some of the difficulties, the allocation of resources is a national affair, while scientific communication and evaluation take place on a worldwide scene. There is also a great deal of difference between the flexibility of scientific communication and that of the allocation of funds. As has been shown by studies of scientific citations, the currents of scientific opinion change very rapidly, and the patterns of communication reflect correctly the changing research front.[31] Allocation of resources is unlikely to reflect this front as truthfully and rapidly as communication. Funds invested in buildings and equipment determine the place and thereby the personnel of research for decades ahead. There have to be, therefore, special mechanisms apart from the informal workings of the scientific community to make possible a measure of flexibility.

Furthermore, one of the principal problems of allocation is that which concerns the distribution of funds for different fields. For this purpose the scientific community cannot serve as a guide, as effective communication and evaluation take place within each field but not between the different fields. It is, therefore, meaningless to say that the allocation of funds for different fields should take place according to the relative importance attached to them by the scientific community, because there is no effective informal general scientific community for making comparisons between fields.

Finally, the whole idea of relying on the informal processes of the scientific community for decisions concerning what research and which researcher are worth supporting rests on the assumption that science can be unequivocally distinguished from technology. As a matter of fact, however, only the scientific and the technological purposes are distinguishable: the purpose of science is to augment knowledge and that of technology is to create wealth and welfare. But the means to attain these two ends are often overlapping, so that much scientific work also serves technological purposes. For instance, all research done in schools of engineering, medicine, or agriculture is supposed to be related somehow to a technological purpose. In fact the very existence of scientific research in such schools introduces a technological bias in the allocation of funds for research. These fields which are not included in the curricula of professional schools are supported only on the basis of their intrinsic scientific value (however this value is established), while those included in professional curricula receive additional support on ultimately technological grounds. As technological allocation is a matter of social choice, it is not justified or useful to entrust the decisions concerning this to the scientific community.

Because all these problems are well known and have been discussed in the literature before, I shall not go here into further details. There are, however, problems of a more strictly sociological character which seem to have been overlooked so far. These concern the self-regulation not only of the professional but also of the amateur scientific community.

BREAKDOWNS OF SCIENTIFIC SELF-REGULATION

It appears that the scope of self-regulation is narrower than usually assumed. It is most effective in experimental science, where it was originally conceived. There complete freedom and spontaneity of the individual has usually been consistent with "discipline" and responsibility, as the interpersonal validity of the criteria by which achievement is evaluated is so high that deviance is almost impossible. As a result there seems to be little motivation to deviate. Experimental scientists are professionally the most righteous of all intellectual communities. There is, furthermore, relative to other intellectual endeavors, a very great deal of consensus among experimental scientists concerning the goals of research. They agree more about what is and what is not a worthwhile question to investigate, and their work is usually much more closely related to (at times actually coordinated with) that of their colleagues than in other fields. This consensus, however, is not the result of the scientific method but of the built-in constraints of experimental work. The possibilities of experimental work are limited by instrumentation, and the work is so laborious and detailed that the efforts of the individual scientist make sense only within an advanced division of labor. On the one hand, this creates great disincentive to those who might be inclined to go it alone, and on the

other hand, it ensures that those who still go their own individual ways will be left alone only if unsuccessful. If they make valuable discoveries they will promptly attract a community to the new field of research, as the reward potential (that is, the chance of making discoveries) in a new field is much higher than in older ones.

But even in this extreme and unique case there are exceptions. The working of the scientific community will be perfect only as long as there are worthwhile discoveries to evaluate, assimilate, and develop. But there is no mechanism which can ensure that there will always be new discoveries, as — in contrast to testing them — there is no method for making discoveries. Thus, as has been shown by Thomas Kuhn, scientific communities can arrive at situations of *anomie*, when there is a theoretical impasse which makes advance impossible (Kuhn did not use the term anomie, but this is exactly what he described).[32]

There is also no mechanism, except the constraints of experimental work, which ensures consensus. This problem has been described by Hagstrom in relation to pure mathematics. Even where this produces valid and theoretically important results, there is always a danger of research falling apart into a large number of disconnected enterprises. Not subject to the limitations of natural events and experimental tools which establish a commonly accepted range of worthwhile enquiries among empirical scientists, the mathematical community does not possess any inherent characteristics to ensure its cohesion and the interrelation of its activities. This situation can apparently lead to a breakdown of the control mechanism, feelings of worthlessness, and perhaps intellectual stagnation.[33]

These are implicitly or, in the case of Hagstrom, explicitly, situations of anomie. That described by Kuhn is a case of the type of anomie originally described by Merton where institutionalized means are inadequate to attain institutionalized ends, as the best experiments will not yield interesting results without the existence of good theories. The case of mathematics, on the other hand, as told by Hagstrom is a classic case of Durkheimian anomie, where there is a breakdown of the social mechanism establishing goals due to the absence of social conventions or other constraints concerning the choice of goals.[34]

In principle there is no solution to these problems. The self-regulating mechanism of science cannot ensure the continued production of new ideas, nor, in the absence of external criteria of relevance which exist only in the empirical sciences, can it establish a consensus about which goals are worthwhile to explore. It is true that so far there was always a way out. Mathematics was from time to time revitalized by turning to "applied" problems (that is, to the solution of theoretical problems arising out of empirical science), and the exhaustion of theory has never occurred in all the fields of science at one and the same time. The blocking of advance of science at one front has not prevented it from advancing at the same time on others and of removing the obstacles by eventually outflanking them. But (1) there is no assurance that this will be the case also in the future; and (2) the fact that *anomie* did not destroy the scientific enterprise so far depended on an empirical condition, namely, that people did not lose their belief in the value and possibilities of the acquisition of further knowledge as a result of *anomie*. The continuation of this belief is, of course, also not a part of the self-regulating mechanisms of science. There may come a stage when disappointment with science will lead to the loss of its charisma. The continually accelerating rate of investment of resources in research is, in fact, likely to bring about such a situation, by arriving at a stage of diminishing returns. This is particularly likely to happen, if investment in research is not matched by investment in education.

In field of professional learning other than natural science and mathematics, the self-regulatory mechanism of empirical and logical validation has worked much less satisfactorialy. In historiography, the study of literature and art, and in most fields of social science there has been more often a state of *anomie* than consensus. Partly because of the inadequacy of the methods of inquiry and partly because of the virtually unlimited range of valid questions which can be asked in these fields, there has been a frantic search for originality and innovation, which at times have been attained by intellectually illegitimate means. This type of innovation not only led to crises within the intellectual communities concerned but also affected social life in general by fomenting ideological conflict for its own sake.

Thus the self-regulation of the scientific community is effective only within limits. Within those limits, established by the range and methods of experimental science, self-regulation has worked so far without serious breakdowns. But keeping within these limits and refraining from extending the applications of the scientific method in illegitimate and deceptive ways can only be achieved through moral decision and commitment. As in the free market or in democracy. self-regulation works only under conditions of such moral commitment. It is possible to hypothesize that arrangements which provide the greatest freedom of individual scientists or the greatest degree of self-government to scientific organizations are optimal for the purpose of creating or strengthening a moral commitment to scientific values. But this will be a hypothesis which has to be tested empirically and not a logically determined principle.

INVIDIOUS PRIVILEGE AND CLASS CONFLICT IN SCIENTIFIC PROFESSIONALISM

The final problem to be dealt with is that of invidious privilege. As has been pointed out, one of the justifications of scientific as compared to traditional professionalism was that in the former professional autonomy and freedom did not constitute invidious privileges but only prerequisites, or means, necessary for research work. As long as scientists were uninvolved in class or national conflict, this assumption was rarely questioned. Recently, however, this situation has been changing due to the changing context of the involvement of scientists in technological development and higher education. Until World War II, the association of scientists with technological work was a relatively unimportant matter. Furthermore, the majority of technological purposes thus served were generally agreed on and were considered as socially useful. Since the Second World War, however, the situation has changed as, in addition to the frightening military technology, a great many civilian technologies have also turned out to be potentially harmful and controversial.

Thus physicists conducting inquiries in the structure of the atomic nucleus during the 1920's and the 1930's could completely devote themselves to their scientific curiosity without thinking about consequences. By 1942 some of them were part and parcel of the most powerful military enterprise in the history of mankind and shared moral responsibility for decisions affecting the lives of everybody.

A similar transformation took place in the social position of scientists as educators. The university has been a channel of social ascent since its emergence in the Middle Ages. But, at least in the advanced countries, it was not a very decisive channel. The professions for which higher educational training was required constituted only a small fraction of the labor force, and it was assumed that in these cases higher educational training was instrumentally necessary. The requirement did not appear, therefore, as unreasonable in any sense.

This was not quite the case with the requirement of university education for civil service and, in some countries, for political careers. The legal or (in Britain) classical education required for these had little intrinsic connection with the job of the future civil servant or politician. But in the nineteenth century the requirement of university training for entrance into the civil service was a great advance towards social justice and equality, as compared to the situation where entrance depended on noble birth, connections, bribe, or the sale of office.[35] It could also be argued that university studies were to some extent instrumentally relevant for the civil servant. This was certainly true in places where legal education was required. But even in England, where the custom was to study classics, the discipline to think, argue, and write clearly and systematically, which these studies were supposed to foster, was a valuable asset for the civil servant.

Nevertheless, the invidious position of the university as a gatekeeper of social mobility became evident at an early stage in connection with this function. In the more backward countries of Eastern Europe, and elsewhere, where civil service careers were the most important channel of upward mobility for the lower middle classes, there was an influx of unqualified and poorly motivated students who were frustrated by their studies. When their expectations for social mobility were also disappointed, they adopted anti-intellectual and antiscientific ideas and world views as part of their resentment towards the university studies which did not produce for them the expected results.[36]

In the West, where there were plenty of other channels, those who went to the universities were either the scholarly type who enjoyed it or the rich who were not dependent for their future careers on the success in their studies.

Nowadays, however, universities have become the most important allocative mechanism for practically all the desirable occupations in modern societies. This has placed an enormous power in the hands of the universities and their teachers. They have become the gatekeepers of the central channel of social ascent and descent and are, therefore, the obvious target of generational conflict and class envy.

Furthermore, the circumstance that now half of the appropriate age group in the U.S. enters college implies that college study has become an increasingly necessary but decreasingly sufficient condition of entry into desirable occupations. This means that college, and presumably all that it stands for, can offer few rewards but can present a serious threat to young people.

All this creates a powerful motivation to deny the legitimacy of the professional autonomy of scientists, or else it gives rise to demands for a share in these privileges by all kinds of scientifically unqualified groups. By drawing one-sided attention to the problematic aspects of scientific autonomy,[37] these trends threaten the moral commitment to the values of science and "cognitive rationality."

CONCLUSION

It has been suggested that the legitimacy of the professional privileges of scientists — and probably of the scientific professions in general — is based on the self-regulatory mechanisms of the informal scientific community. But these privileges have been in many instances extended beyond the limits of effective self-regulation. This overextension gave rise to situations of anomie.

Furthermore, it has been shown that since World War II scientists have acquired a great deal of invidious power, mainly as a result of the key role of the universities in occupational placement and the dangers to human survival presented by the misuse of some science-based technologies. This has probably contributed a great deal to the rise of antiscientific sentiments and doubts about cognitive rationality as a social value.

The main threat to science derives from a combination of envy and anomie. As more and more young people, who have no commitment to science, realize that their future depends on their studies in scientific subjects, there are growing claims on their part to share in the privileges of academic freedom. Claims for such a share are based on any kind of connection to the university (students, past students, would-be students, workers of the university, or anyone who suffered real or imaginary injustices from the university, or the so-called system or establishment of which the university is a part), and may be made for any kind of political or other nonscientific activity. The resulting class envy which engulfs the university creates a pressure for an overextension of the privileges of academic freedom to scientifically unqualified groups engaged in activities which do not even claim to be regulated by the self-correcting mechanism which is the basis of the legitimacy of academic freedom. This has given rise to widespread anomie and disillusionment with science and rationality in general.

NOTES

1. As will be seen, this process had certain analogies to but was not identical with the "routinization of the charisma" described by Max Weber concerning the transformation of religious and political movements. See H. H. Gerth and C. W. Mills, *From Max Weber* (London: Routledge and Kegan Paul, 1947), p. 297.

2. The most comprehensive survey of the development of the professions in any country is Alexander M. Carr-Saunders and P. A. Wilson, *The Professions* (Oxford: Humanities Press 1933); for a recent survey of the sociology of the field see Howard M. Vollmer and Donald L. Mills (eds.), *Professionalization* (Englewood Cliffs, N.J.: Prentice-Hall, 1966). The relationship between science, universities, and modern professionalism

(to be referred to in this paper as scientific professionalism) has been analyzed systematically by Talcott Parsons. See especially *The Social System* (Glencoe, Ill.: The Free Press, 1951), pp. 326-479; "Unity and Diversity in the Modern Intellectual Disciplines," *Daedalus*, 94 (1965), pp. 39-65; "Professions," in David L. Sills (ed.), *International Encyclopedia of the Social Sciences* (New York: Macmillan and The Free Press, 1968), Vol. 12, pp. 536-547; and Talcott Parsons and Gerald M. Platt, "Considerations on the American Academic System," *Minerva*, 6 (1968), pp. 497-523.

3. See Joseph Ben-David and Randall Collins, "A Comparative Study of Academic Freedom and Student Politics," in S. M. Lipset (ed.), *Student Politics* (New York: Basic Books, 1967), pp. 148-195.

4. See D. Garceau, *Political Life of the American Medical Association* (Cambridge, Mass.: 1941); Milton Friedman and Simon Kuznets, *Income From Independent Professional Practice* (New York: Columbia University Press, 1945); Hyde and Wolff, "The American Medical Association: Power, Purpose and Politics in Organized Medicine," *Yale Law Journal*, 63 (1953-54), pp. 38-1022; and Reuben A. Kessel, "Price Discrimination in Medicine," *The Journal of Law and Economics*, 1 (1958), pp. 20-53.

5. See T. H. Marshall, "The Recent History of Professionalism in Relation to Social Structure and Social Policy," in his *Citizenship and Social Class* (Cambridge: Cambridge University Press, 1950), pp. 128-155; and William J. Goode, "Professions and Non-Professions," in Vollmer and Mills (eds.), *op. cit.*, pp. 34-43.

6. See Talcott Parsons, *The Social System*, pp. 428-479, and "A Sociologist Looks at the Legal Profession," in his *Essays in Sociological Theory*, revised edition (Glencoe, Ill.: The Free Press, 1954), pp. 370-385.

7. See Robert W. Hodge, Paul M. Siegel, and Peter H. Rossi, "Occupational Prestige in the United States: 1925-1963," in R. Bendix and S. M. Lipset (eds.), *Class, Status and Power*, second edition (New York: The Free Press, 1966), p. 324.

8. See William Kornhauser, *Scientists in Industry* (Berkeley: University of California Press, 1962); Simon Marcson, *The Scientist in American Industry: Some Organizational Determinants of Manpower Utilization* (Princeton: Industrial Relations Section, Princeton University, 1960).

9. See T. H. Marshall, *Citizenship and Social Class*, pp. 151-152. In England scientific training did not initially imply training at a university. But this was due to the deficiencies of the old English universities, and the demand for their reform and for the establishment of new kinds of universities was based on the demand for scientific training for the professions. See W. J. Reader, *Professional Men: The Rise of the Professional Classes in Nineteenth Century England* (New York: Basic Books, 1966), pp. 71-72, 127-145. For a systematic exposition of the relationship between science and present-day professionalism and of the place of "cognitive rationality" in the social structure of the U.S., see Parsons and Platt, *op. cit.*

10. See Joseph Ben-David, "The Rise and Decline of France as a Scientific Centre," *Minerva*, 8 (April 1970), pp. 160-179.

11. See F. A. Hayek, *The Counterrevolution of Science* (New York: The Free Press of Glencoe, 1955), pp. 94-116; and George Lefebvre, *The French Revolution: Vol. II: from 1793 to 1799* (London: Routledge and Kegan Paul, 1864), pp. 297-303.

12. See Maurice Crosland, *The Society of Arcueil: A View of French Science at the Time of Napoleon I* (London: Heinemann, 1967), pp. 1-5, 70, 151-179, about the way research was conducted in France under Napoleon, and Ben-David, *op. cit.*

13. See Joseph Ben-David and Awraham Zloczower, "Universities and Academic Systems in Modern Society," *European Journal of Sociology*, 3 (1962), pp. 45-48.

14. See Eric Ashby, "The Future of the Nineteenth Century Idea of a University," *Minerva*, 6 (Autumn 1967), pp. 3-17; and "University Reform in Germany," *Minerva*, 8 (April 1970), pp. 242-267.

15. See Alexander Busch, *Geschichte des Privatdozenten* (Stuttgart: Enke, 1959).

16. See Abraham Flexner, *Universities: American, English, German* (New York: Oxford University Press, 1930).

17. See Joseph Ben-David, "The Universities and the Growth of Science in Germany and the United States," *Minerva*, 7 (Autumn-Winter 1968-69), pp. 6-13.

18. *Ibid.*, pp. 19-21, and Burton R. Clark, "Organizational Adaptation to Professionals," in Vollmer and Mills, *op. cit.*, pp. 283-291.

19. See Ashby, *op. cit.*; Flexner, *op. cit.*; and Parsons and Platt, *op. cit.*

20. See S. Marcson, *op. cit.*; and Bernard Barber, *Science and the Social Order* (New York: Collier Books, 1962), pp. 152-155.

21. Indeed, the application of any evolutionary model to society can only be made with important qualifications. Unlike in biological evolution where the purpose of survival is given, in social evolution the purpose has to be culturally defined. Thus "suitability to the scientists" is not an equivocally defined criterion. Suitability may be due to material or social advantages, or in other words simple privilege, or to conditions conducive to scientific creativity and productivity. In order to explain, therefore, that actually the evolutionary process has resulted in the selection of structures increasingly suitable from the point of the furtherance of scientific creativity and productivity, there had to exist a precondition. Those who made the selection had to adhere most of the time to the same purpose and to apply to their selection the criteria of scientific creativity and productivity.

22. See Parsons, *The Social System*, p. 349.

23. The emphasis is on formal authority. Informal charismatic authority is not excluded.

24. See Margary Purver, *The Royal Society: Concept and Creation* (London: Routledge and Kegan Paul, 1967), pp. 63-100.

25. See Joseph Ben-David, "The Scientific Role: The Conditions of Its Emergence in Europe," *Minerva*, 4 (Autumn 1965), pp. 15-54.

26. See Michael Polanyi, *The Logic of Liberty* (London: Routledge and Kegan Paul, 1951), pp. 32-90, about self-regulation in general; Robert K. Merton, "Singletons and Multiples in Scientific Discovery," *Proceedings of the American Philosophical Society*, 105 (October 1961), pp. 470-486, about the prevalence of independent multiple discoveries; Stephen Cole and Jonathan Cole, "Scientific Output and Recognition: A Study in the Operation of the Reward System in Science," *American Sociological Review*, 32 (June 1967), pp. 370-390; and Stephen Cole and Jonathan Cole, "Visibility and the Structural Bases of Awareness of Scientific Research," *American Sociological Review*, 33 (June 1968), pp. 397-413. about the effectiveness of scientific evaluation.

27. Priests and mandarins have also justified their privileges on similar grounds. But in their case it is impossible to eliminate particularism, as religious or philosophical systems are arbitrary in a sense in which scientific ones are not.

28. On the norms of the scientific community see Robert K. Merton, "Science and the Social Order" and "Science and Democratic Social Structure," in his *Social Theory and Social Structure*, revised edition (Glencoe, Ill.: The Free Press, 1957), pp. 537-561; Barber, *op. cit.*, pp. 122-142; and Norman

Storer, *The Social System of Science* (New York: Holt, Rinehart and Winston, 1966), pp. 75-98.

29. See Ben-David and Zloczower, *op. cit.*

30. See W. Hagstrom, *The Scientific Community* (New York: Basic Books, 1965).

31. See Cole and Cole, *op. cit.* (1967 and 1968).

32. Thomas Kuhn, *The Structure of Scientific Revolutions* (Chicago: University of Chicago Press, 1962).

33. Hagstrom, *op. cit.,* pp. 226-236.

34. Robert K. Merton, "Social Structure and Anomie," in his *Social Theory and Social Structure,* pp. 131-194; E. Durkheim, *Suicide, A Study in Sociology,* John A. Spaulding and George Simpson trs., edited and with an Introduction by George Simpson (New York: The Free Press, 1951), pp. 241-276.

35. See Reader, *op. cit.,* pp. 73-84.

36. See Walter Kotschinig, *Unemployment in the Learned Professions* (London: Oxford University Press, 1937); Joseph Ben-David, "Professions in the Class System of Present-day Societies," *Currect Sociology,* 12 (1963-64), pp. 156-277.

37. See Alvin M. Weinberg, "Scientific Choice and the Scientific Muckrakers," *Minerva,* 7 (Autumn-Winter 1968-69), pp. 52-63, for a survey of some of the literature critical of science and the problems which it poses. For a case of disillusionment with cognitive rationality, see Hilary Rose and Steven Rose, *Science and Society* (London: Allen Lane, 1969), pp. 253-261.

37

THE STRUCTURE OF PROFESSIONAL HELP

Charles E. Bidwell

Talcott Parsons has observed that the professions are found in their most fully-developed form in modern Western societies, a development that has been fostered by:

1. values conducive to rational thought and empirical investigation;
2. the institutionalization of science as a system of specialized occupational, indeed professional, roles, especially in the universities; and
3. the application of scientific knowledge to the solution of the practical problems of the society through another set of occupational roles, the professional fields of applied science.[1]

Parsons also has indicated that there are certain dilemmas and uncertainties surrounding the development of science and of the professions as fields of scientific application, namely:

1. conflict between the open-ended quality of scientific investigation and the limited orientation to specific problems characteristic of the "practical man" and the realm of practical action;
2. a "communication gap" between the expert and the layman, resulting in uncertainty over the locus of control of scientific application;
3. the indeterminacy of the use of scientific knowledge for practical purposes, given limits to knowledge or imperfect control over the parameters of the area of practical action; and
4. tensions between science and other bases, such as religious charisma, for the legitimation of authoritative or "leadership" roles.

Nonetheless, Parsons has found in modern societies a secular trend toward the primacy of science and the professions, just as he has seen in belief systems a trend to rationality.[2]

This aspect of Parsons' writings on the professions anticipates much later work on the place of the professions in society[3] and helps us to understand current controversies in the United States over access to control of professional services and over the goals that are to govern these services (for example, "community control" of medical service or of schools). However, the core of Parsons' study of the professions in the professional-client dyad, the immediate cultural and social structures in which help is given and received. He has been concerned especially with the ways in which these structures set conditions to the realization of the goal of applying scientific knowledge and scientific analysis and judgment to the concrete practical problems that confront individuals during their conduct in society. That is, his main interest has been in what now often are called the "helping professions" and with their functions as agents of help for persons, in contrast to their actual or potential involvement in the solution of problems at a higher level of social aggregation (e.g., community medicine or the formation of public policy).[4] More specifically, Parsons' concern has been for the helping professions as agents of social control, with the mechanisms through which they maintain social equilibrium by restoring persons in deviant roles (their clients) to the enactment of fully legitimate roles. He has taken medical practice as the type case of social control through professional help.

It is probably true that there is now underway a secular trend toward the organization of fairly large-scale structures for the application of knowledge to societal problems and toward the engagement of the professions with collectivities as "clients." Nonetheless, the professional-client dyad remains a primary mode for giving help, even in organizations or programs of broader social range, and analysis of this dyad retains its significance.[5]

In this essay, therefore, I shall review Parsons on the professional-client dyad as it occurs in the helping professions and especially in medicine. Among

Much in this essay has been stimulated by participation in the Faculty Seminar on the Comparative Study of Professions at the University of Chicago. In the spring of 1971, Talcott Parsons was a valued member of this seminar.

these professions, we can see clearly the bearing on professional-client relations of social and cultural factors affecting human conduct. In this review, I shall consider several points at which I believe Parsons' analysis is too narrow and requires revision. Especially I shall argue that the question of trust, or client confidence, in the helping professions and their practitioners has a place even more central than Parsons gives to it. I shall discuss types of client trust and certain of the antecedents and consequences of each in professional-client relations. I shall try to show that issues of trust reveal certain instrumental goals and rationally-grounded patterns of conduct among clients that are rather different from the elements of the nonrational and expressive to which Parsons gives much attention (though their effects on the professional-client relation are often similar).

I hope that it will become clear that these goals and patterns of conduct are not essentially different from those generally characteristic of social relations in which trust is of paramount importance, especially those in which occupational specialization gives to the recipient of goods or services the disadvantage of lack of knowledge. In this sense, I shall try to show that problems centered on the client's social deviance and on the helping professions as agents of social control, although often important in the practice of the helping professions, do not define its essential quality.

I shall also discuss ways in which a view of the social organization of professional help that extends beyond the professional-client dyad sheds light on the conduct of both professional and client in the helping relation, again focussing the discussion on the issue of trust.

PARSONS ON DEVIANCE, SOCIAL CONTROL, AND MEDICAL PRACTICE

Deviance and social control are described by Parsons[6] as ubiquitous social phenomena. We must detour through his views on deviance and social control before we can discuss his analysis of medicine.

Deviance is a disruption of social equilibrium that results from certain "strains" encountered by actors (e.g., unexpected responses of alter to ego's self-definedly appropriate acts or one or another variety of role conflict). These strains lessen ego's motivation to conform to norms shared by ego and alter and foster tendencies toward disruptive activity. Of especial importance is the idea of the "vicious circle of deviance," in which the initiating strain promotes in ego a tendency to expect of alter and to evoke from alter responses that confirm or reinforce the strain. This process locks ego into the deviant pattern as he develops an emotional investment

in his deviance, a process, as Parsons notes, substantially like the "secondary gain" to be derived from neurotic behavior.

Deviance in Parsons' analysis is not the only possible reaction by an actor to strain. As deviance is a disruption of patterned norm-conformity in personal conduct, one possible solution to strain is relearning of norms and patterns of action, or alterations of value commitments or affective attachments to others. The actor may find it possible to tolerate ambiguity, or the social structure may permit the segregation of patterns of conduct in a way that reduces the strain to tolerable proportions. Thus deviance arises when these solutions are not possible without the action of some mechanism of social control.

These mechanisms are of three basic kinds:

1. support, the reduction of strain-induced anxiety through persistent solidary relations with other persons in the "normal" sector of the social system;
2. permissiveness, an expectation that persons under strain will not fully comply with the norms shared in this sector; and
3. restrictiveness of reciprocation, a refusal by alter to engage in a reciprocal exchange of interaction built on ego's definition of their relation (e.g., hostility, attempts at dominance, or scrupulous norm-adherence).

Together, these mechanisms of social control prevent the relation between ego and alter from taking on those characteristics which foster the vicious circle of deviance. Moreover, Parsons is careful to point out that their effectiveness rests fundamentally on the allocation to ego of rewards derived from the social relation ("alter's attitudes of love, approval, and esteem"), rewards that may be manipulated deliberately by alter or that may be less self-consciously involved in the interaction.[7]

In most social systems one finds certain strains of unusual quality or severity, to which "minor" or ubiquitous control mechanisms are inadequate. Differentiated social structures arise specifically to control deviance generated by these strains. These specialized structures are of several types. Magic and ritual are structures of this kind, and especially important among them are what Parsons calls "secondary institutions," such as youth culture, which provide the three basic mechanisms of social control while containing potentially deviant persons or groups within a framework of institutionalized values.

Now we come to the helping professions. Given the primacy of occupations in modern societies and as well a tendency toward strain and deviance resulting from the complexity and loose integration of these societies, one finds in them a range of occupations and attendant social structures specialized with respect to the control of certain forms of pervasive but unusual deviance (e.g., police, lawyers, courts, and prisons, or physicians, nurses, hospitals, and clinics). These occupations act as agents of social control through the use of technical procedures that involve the three basic control mechanisms. In addition, specialization of client as well as professional roles serves to isolate deviant actors from nondeviants (limiting their influence as sources of legitimation of the latent deviant motives of the nondeviants) and in some cases also isolating the deviant from fellow-deviants, thus reducing the chances of his gaining legitimation for his deviant motives and acts.

The primary question for Parsons in the analysis of medicine as exemplifying the practice of the helping professions is to show how their values, role structures, and belief systems serve the social control function, that is, how and with respect to what range of deviant phenomena they permit the operation of the mechanisms of support, permissiveness, and restricted reciprocation.

Illness, Parsons argues, is problematic for the social system in two ways. It incapacitates persons for role performance, but it also involves issues of motivation in regard to exposure to injury or infection, "psychosomatic" disorders, mental illness, and so on. Thus illness is not simply an aspect of the "situation" of the social system, "an external danger to be 'warded off,'" but an integral part of the social equilibrium itself."[8]

Medical treatment, therefore, involves the motivational and social structural, as well as the somatic, components of illness. The institutionalization of science and its application in modern societies provide powerful means for rational treatment of illness as both a biological and a motivational and relational phenomenon.[9]

The physician, then, is an applied scientist. His role is achieved and its enactment judged principally by standards of technical competence. Selection for the role of physician and the context of its enactment are to a high degree segregated from the other bases of social status. It is specialized not only in its technique (knowledge application) but also in the employment of this technique for the solution of a delimited range of practical problems. The physician's relation to his patient (his diagnosis, whether he will accept the patient, how he treats him) is determined by the classificatory principles of medical knowledge and rules of medical procedure, rather than by any other relational criterion (e.g., kinship). In common with the predominant patterns of occupational roles in modern societies, that of the physician is universalistic, functionally specific, and affectively neutral.

Unlike the role of the businessman, however, it is collectivity-oriented rather than self-oriented. Collectivity orientation is important especially with reference to the physician's authority. In Parsons' analysis, the physician's authority is viewed under two aspects, although he does not always distinguish clearly between them.

The first aspect is a generalized "authority" of physicians as professionals or as applied scientists. They are incumbents of one of a set of leadership roles in modern societies that can make "binding commitments" for the society or certain of its subsectors by virtue of a legitimacy grounded in popular belief in the value of science and in the social utility or gain to social welfare of its practical applications. In this sense the physician, like the pure scientist, is "an authority." From his standing as an authority derives a special set of obligations defined prominently in the "ideology" or belief system of the profession. Central are the obligations "to put the 'welfare of the patient' above his personal interests" and to regard "'commercialism' as the most serious and insidious evil with which [he] has to contend."[10] Collectivity orientation, then, is more a matter of the institutionalized values and shared beliefs characteristic of medical practice than of any distinctive motivation on the part of physicians.

The second aspect is the more limited authority that every physician has to some degree with respect to each of his patients. This authority is grounded in part in the authoritativeness of his role (in the sense just discussed), in part in the specific manifestation of his broader collectivity-orientation as a concern for the welfare of each patient whom he accepts, and in part in his specialized competence and qualification thereby to make judgments with respect to the patient's medical problem (i.e., the physician's responsibility for the "management of the case"). The degree of authority that inheres in a discrete professional-client relation is indicated by the patient's willingness to follow "doctor's orders." As we shall see, the physician's authority with respect to a patient requires further some minimum level of patient confidence or trust that the physician will in fact put the patient's welfare before his own interests, which in turn allows the physician some degree of confidence that the patient will be cooperative.

Thus the collectivity-orientation of the physician is both to the society and to the "treatment collectivity." To maintain this distinction, from the standpoint of the professional-client dyad, I shall refer to a physician's, or more generally a professional's, broader societal authority as "authoritativeness," that is, as an attribute imputed to professional practitioners by virtue of their occupational statuses. I shall refer to his limited authority within the professional-client relation simply as "authority," that is, as the capacity of a practitioner to gain client compliance with his expectations for client conduct within the context of the treatment or service relation.

It is important to note that in his discussion of medical practice Parsons (and I shall follow him in this) uses the term "authority" with some latitude. A narrower definition of authority as, say, legitimated by official or legal rules shows how tenuous is most of a physician's (or more generally, any professional's) authority. Aside from a few legal mechanisms (such as obtaining a patient's or patient-surrogate's consent to surgical procedures) or the ultimate sanction of "dropping" a patient, the physician's authority is primarily a matter of power in the form of influence — a matter of his ability to persuade or induce the patient to "do his part."

Parsons sees entry into the patient role as an explicit submission to the physician's authority. But he also shows very clearly that patients can be rebellious, recalcitrant, or excessively compliant and dependent. The patient has the ultimate option, as does his physician, of ending their relationship. But within this relation, the patient's compliance is problematic and is substantially dependent on his trust in his physician. I shall try to show certain critical connections between the authoritativeness of a professional, client trust in him, and his authority — as these connections have been viewed by Parsons and as his views may be revised and extended.

The role of the patient is, in Parsons' view, strictly complementary to that of the physician insofar as its institutionalized definition is concerned. First, especially because of its motivational components, it is appropriate to view sickness as a social role, rather than as a "state of fact" for the actor, the incidence of illness as an aspect of social structure rather than of the "situation" of the social system. Second, illness constitutes an important strain for the social system by virtue of the incapacity of members to enact their normal social roles, while it creates strains for ego as he is unable to meet the responsibilities that these roles entail or to perform to expected standards.[11] Incapacity in illness involves important questions of ego's motivation, both with respect to having become ill (seen most clearly in mental illness but an aspect of apparently somatic disorders as well) and with respect to recovery. Thus it is appropriate to view the sick role as a deviant role.[12]

Third, the sick role involves exemption from normal responsibilities, varying with "the nature and severity of the illness." It is deviance of the passive-alienative" type.[13] To gain this exemption requires legitimation by some external agent — perhaps a member or members of his personal circle or the physician himself.[14]

Fourth, "the sick person cannot be expected by pulling himself together to get well by an act of decision or will. In this sense also he is exempted from responsibility—he is in a condition that must be taken care of."[15]

As the third and fourth points indicate, illness gains its legitimacy from the nondeviant sector of the social system. It is a role that is partly deviant and partly not. Thus the sick person is in a position to accept help from nondeviant sources — his personal circle and his doctor. The legitimacy of sickness, in other words, is "conditional" or "relative." It is defined as temporary. But in a modern society receiving help occurs through the intervention of "*technically competent* help, namely, in the most usual case, that of a physician," with whom one must cooperate in the process of getting well. In this way in modern societies the sick role characteristically entails the patient role. The responsibilities of the patient role, coupled with the expectation held in the personal circle of the patient that he will try to get well through appropriate means, counteract such secondary gains of sickness as exemption from normal responsibilities.

This chain of reasoning leads Parsons to conclude that sickness is achieved, at least in the sense that other aspects of status do not primarily determine recruitment to it. (Like many achieved roles, however, ascriptive factors affect what and how much achievement occurs; note, for example, the substantial evidence of effects of social class on the etiology of a variety of illnesses.) The sick role is universalistic in that "classificatory" or generally objective criteria affect whether one is said to be sick and later diagnosis of the illness. It is functionally specific in that it is limited to questions of health and its manifestations, other aspects of ego's social relations, such as his business dealings, presumably entering only as they may be sources of strain. It is affectively neutral, since the effort at recovery is focussed on the "objective problem" of recovery, though emotional ties to others and psychological disturbance may affect the nature and resolution of the problem.

Moreover, the sick role is collectivity-oriented. This point, I think, is especially significant in Parsons' presentation of the doctor-patient dyad. Here, as in Parsons' discussion of the physician's role, collectivity-orientation has two aspects. First, the sick person, with respect to the broader society, has a responsibility to "try to get well." Second, this broader responsibility is most immediate and palpable in his relations with specific alters — his "personal circle" especially, and upon becoming a patient, his physician. The doctor's societal responsibility is manifested in his concern for the welfare of each of his patients individually, that of the patient in willingness "to do his part" to cooperate with his doctor.

The reciprocal collectivity-orientation of the physician-patient relation implies that there is a mutual relation of trust between doctor and patient. That is, the doctor can be confident that the patient will co-operate, while the patient can be confident that the doctor has placed the patient's welfare to the fore. Here Parsons finds the main grounding of the doctor's authority. The patient is to follow his physician's "orders," requests, or advice, and no other's. He is not to "shop around," must request consultations through his "own" physician, and so on. If he does not find his physician to his liking, he can leave one doctor and go to another, but by contrast "in the ideal type of commercial relationship one is not A's customer to the exclusion of other sources of supply for the same needs."[17]

Of course the physician also can drop a patient who violates the norms of collectivity-orientation. But within an ongoing therapeutic relationship, the effectiveness of the physician's work rests on his authority (i.e., for the most part, on his influence); it requires a patient who will cooperate — therefore a patient with at least a modicum of trust in the physician.[18]

The doctor-patient relation, therefore, is solidary. This solidarity points up the centrality to medical therapy of problems of patient motivation that are implicated in the social structural aspect of illness. One might add that in certain professions concerned less with "help" in the sense of intervention in the motives and conduct of clients, more with the application of science to "technical" problems, client-professional solidarity is less evident, and these relations tend toward the contractual. They have little to do with support, permissiveness, and restricted reciprocation. But, because health problems do involve the client's response to strain, Parsons argues, they call for the basic social control mechanisms. These mechanisms, moreover, can operate effectively only within a solidary social relation in which the professional's response to client conduct is a central means of therapy.

Parsons also sees as a major component of the situation of medical practice the isolation of the patient from other sick-role deviants. In becoming a patient the sick-role incumbent is cut off from interaction with others who are sick, as the sources for the legitimation of his partial deviance are the physician and the personal circle. Not only is the patient in this way placed within a *cordon sanitaire* as an instigator of deviance in others (the circle and the physician aside), he can obtain supportive responses to his conduct, essential to self-esteem, only from the circle and especially from his doctor who is the final authoritative arbiter of the legitimacy of his role situation.[19]

As we have seen, in Parsons' analysis the solidarity of the doctor-patient relation is substantially a product of the patient's confidence in his doctor—his trust that the doctor is doing his best for him, that he has his welfare at heart. Here the patient's beliefs enter. It is not pushing Parsons' ideas very far to suggest that these beliefs constitute a self-oriented view of the physician's collectivity-orientation. That is, it is not for most patients the physician's generalized altruism, but that he is "concerned about me" that is crucial. Here is a major strain which Parsons argues is endemic to the situation of medical practice over and above the strains of the sick role itself. The layman-patient cannot make a completely rational selection of a physician, though he may have some knowledgeable basis for doing so. But the definition of the sick role demands that he become someone's patient.

How, then, can confidence in the physician emerge? Partly, Parsons suggests, it is generated by the physician's status as an "authority" (his authoritativeness) and the attendant symbols of this status, given a pervasive modern belief in the efficacy of science. Partly it comes from the physician's careful observance of the norms that specify collectivity-orientation (restraint in advertising, in the discussion of fees, and so on). In addition certain nonrational beliefs of the patient bolster confidence, in particular the belief that one's physician, whoever he may be, is the "best in town." And of course, the obligation of the sick role that one will try to recover reinforces the tendency to cooperate and trust one's authoritative helper.

These phenomena tend to generate and strengthen confidence, but there remains nonetheless a certain anxiety about the physician, an ambivalence borne of lack of expertness to judge the physicians' reputation and performance and of popular uneasiness about the utility of science and about the nature of its contribution to human welfare.

In any event, the solidarity of the physician-patient relation is essential for the social control of sickness, that is, for the operation of the basic mechanisms of support, permissiveness and restricted reciprocation — in Parsons' eyes, the central components of the "art of medicine." The solidarity of the relation between patient and physician generates support for the patient because, in the context of their interaction, the physician's approval of the patient's conduct becomes of paramount importance along with the love, esteem, and approval forthcoming in interaction with members of the patient's personal circle. When we consider the mechanisms of permissiveness and restricted reciprocation, we see further strains in the interaction of doctor and patient. These center especially on the phenomena of transference and counter transference, which Parsons believes to be centrally involved in all medical practice.

Permissiveness enters the relation, says Parsons, primarily in the sense that the patient cannot be held directly accountable by the physician for his illness or for certain things that he says or does because he is sick. But as is the case generally in the social control process, permissiveness is always limited by the doctor's refusal to reciprocate the full range of sentiments and conduct that the patient comes to expect of him. That is, the anxiety induced by the strain of being in the sick role itself, which of course will vary with the nature and seriousness of the specific disorder, generates emotional pressures from the patient on the physician. These are pressures toward a fuller legitimation of the patient's deviance than the physician can give and, more generally through the transference phenomenon, toward the assimilation of the physician to a particularistic and affective relation with the patient (e.g., to be a friend who can be loved or hated).

There are strains on the physician, too, Parsons argues. Some of these come from the indeterminacy or limitations of his knowledge and the accuracy of judgment possible in the specific medical case. The physician also will experience inevitable affective reactions to each of his patients, however strong his professional orientation. Moreover, the physician must be granted a certain range of permissiveness by the patient — access to the patient's body or mind in ways that under other circumstances would violate strong, widely shared norms of privacy. Even though these acts by the physician may be clearly legitimate as means toward specific goals of treatment, nonetheless they are likely to provoke resistance in the patient that is expressed in the transference. In addition, these "violations of privacy" may move the physician toward particularistic and affective involvements with the patient, which the physician must control in himself.

The demands that the physician makes on the patient for self-revelation (physical or psychical) and in addition the inconvenience or suffering that the patient likely will be asked to endure in the course of treatment can be borne by the patient according to the measure of his trust in his doctor — his confidence that his own welfare is at issue. But the foregoing argument suggests that trust with respect to the physician's competence is instable not only because of the patient's lack of technical expertness to judge the physician but also because of transference. Trust within the functionally specific limits of the treatment situation is pressed toward the more diffuse trust of friendship or love and may easily be transmitted into the distrust of hate or antagonism. Moreover, trust arising from a diffuse relation ceases to center on competence and thus erodes the patient's belief in the physician's authoritativeness. The physician's authority then is undermined, with respect to his ultimate sanction of terminating the relation and his capability to restrict reciprocation of the patient's conduct. Undermined, too, is his ability to foster recovery by selectively rewarding the patient's efforts to abandon the sick role.

For these reasons the physician cannot become the friend or lover, cannot probe more deeply or broadly into the body or mind of the patient than the diagnosis requires, and must resist his own tendency toward countertransference. In point of fact, if the relation of physician to patient becomes particularistic and affective, the physician acts to foster rather than break the vicious circle of deviance, as he can neither restrict his reciprocation of the patient's conduct nor judge how the nature or timing of reciprocation best will serve the patient's welfare. In addition, Parsons notes as one aspect of the motivational impairment of sickness a lessened capacity to trust. The resulting distrust is projected onto the physician in the transference. Here the physician's collectivity-orientation, in the shape of prime concern for his patient's welfare, is of great importance "to counteract these transference tendencies in the patient [and] thus to set up a discrepancy between his neurotic expectations and reality which is as difficult as possible for him to avoid understanding."[20] I shall argue, however, that client tendencies toward distrust can be seen in large part as rational, rather than neurotic, phenomena.

In view of these strains in the relation of physician and patient, the physician must, as Parsons puts it, have "' an Archimedean place to stand" outside the reciprocities of ordinary social intercourse."[21] This "place to stand" is provided primarily by the functional specificity and affective neutrality of the physician's role. His value commitments and the definition of his role, in short, bind him to disinterestedness and the narrowing of his concern for the patient to those matters about which he is competent. Parsons also notes how these values are expressed and reinforced by various structural mechanisms in the interaction of patient and doctor for segregating the treatment situation from other social situations in which they could become engaged: the office or ward visit, the presence of the nurse in the case of cross-sex treatment, and so on.[22]

SOME COMMENTS ON THE HELPING PROFESSIONS

I would add to Parsons' discussion of the physician's value commitments and of the structurally restricted setting of medical practice that these phenomena will reinforce the patient's belief in the doctor's altruism, authoritativeness, and skill, provided that this belief is grounded initially in a generalized acceptance of the fact that physicians as a social category have these traits. (This would be equally true, I should think, of the other helping professions.) Parsons, recall, argues that such generalized beliefs are present in modern societies, concomitants of the institutionalization of "basic" and applied science. But given a widespread ambivalence of beliefs about science, certain factors in the social organization of modern societies — especially variation in the distribution of education, in the integration of persons or groups into the "central" cultural and political systems, and in their standing of relative advantage or disadvantage in the distribution of valued services from the helping professions themselves — may tip the balance for some population sectors away from favorable beliefs toward a more negative view of the altruism, authority claims (both societal, to authoritativeness, and in concrete service situations), and even the narrower technical skills of scientists and practitioners. Under these circumstances, professional values, norms, and symbols defining the relation of professional and client as one of disinterestedness and specialization may reinforce the client's belief that the professional is less oriented to the collectivity than to self-interest, more a technician (and not necessarily a good one) than a helper.

If so, the relation of client and professional becomes not solidary but antagonistic, marked by distrust, rather than confidence. Remember that the patient's (and I would say more broadly the client's) view of the professional's collectivity-orientation, as evidenced by his conduct and apparent motives, with rare exceptions will be couched primarily in terms of the patient's or client's own problems, needs, and welfare, much less in terms of broader values or categories of social relationship. It will be self-oriented rather than altruistic. If the physician (or other professional) seems to be unconcerned and distant, to be manipulative rather than responsive, and to be acting in these ways for a healthy fee, then there is no more ground to trust him than for a customer to trust a garage mechanic who finds disorders in the customer's car that he never suspected existed.

One can approach the question of client trust in more general terms by describing the professional-client relation, at least in the helping professions, as one of asymmetrical solidarity.[23] The client is characterized by withdrawal from fully normal social participation; he is not competent to help himself or to judge the help that he receives. The professional, on the other hand, is a full social participant, he is expert, and he is the final arbiter not only of the client's condition but of the quality and appropriateness of the help that he himself offers.[24] Moreover, the client's efforts to build symmetry into the relation, that is, to shift its ground to a basis that he can manipulate toward affectivity and particularism, must be rebuffed.

These conditions, other things being equal, should foster either client resistance or rebellion, or, by virtue of "secondary gains" from the passive dependence that structural asymmetry entails, a superficial compliance with "doctor's orders" that masks an effort to prolong dependence. However, trust in the professional in the former case makes the dependence tolerable, and perhaps fully acceptable; in the latter case it reduces the secondary gain to the extent that it reinforces the functional specificity and affective neutrality of the professional-client relation.

Here it is essential to draw a distinction that is implicit in Parsons' discussion of medical practice. This distinction has to do with the basis or grounding of trust: in the one case, belief in the competence of a specialist to solve a problem; in the other, confidence arising out of an affective tie. The former reflects the primacy of ego's instrumental concerns and occurs most frequently in social relations of the universalistic, functionally specific, and affectively neutral kind. It also centers primarily on evaluation of alter's achievements, that is, those relations of which, as Parsons says, the occupational are the type case. The latter has a much clearer expressive component, although it may, of course, be the basis for instrumental action. It is most common in particularistic, diffuse, and affective relations, with ascribed roles providing both a fostering condition for the occurrence of such relations and independently a basis for trust of this second kind.

One can go further and suggest two principal varieties of "trust-in-the-specialist." On the one hand is trust arising in relations in which ego is competent himself to judge alter's specialist performance. Such trust is highly contingent, as it depends on continuing "expert" surveillance of alter's achievements within the relation and approaches a contractual form (as in the hiring by a corporate legal counsel of an outside lawyer or law firm). Because such relations of trust are structurally symmetrical, they are not subject to the strains that Parsons describes for the physician-patient relation.

On the other hand are the asymmetrical relations that we have been discussing, in which ego is not competent to judge alter's performance and in which alter is acknowledged by ego on less than fully rational grounds to be an authority. The obligation to cooperate can be seen to derive from the inability of ego to make a rational decision about whom among the specialists to trust. Thus the client's willingness to grant authority primarily or exclusively to a given professional can be treated as a solution to the problem of whom to trust. Having no readily apparent basis for the comparative evaluation of professionals, and thus for the decision to receive different services from different specialists according to the likely effectiveness of each of these services, the client "gives himself over" to one among them who then acts as a presumptively more knowledgeable surrogate in decisions about what services to provide and, indeed, what other professionals to involve in the case (e.g., medical consultants). To "shop around" would simply raise the insoluble problem of whom to trust all over again. This is not to say that no client "shops around," but it is noteworthy that "shopping around" most often takes the form of a search for a more secure affective bond (e.g., a better "bedside manner") or for an authority easier to endure (e.g., a doctor who will ask less of the patient or who will be more permissive). The search simply may continue until the client "gets better" willy-nilly. It is not often a search for service that is acceptable on the basis of informed technical judgement.

The strength of trust in asymmetrical relations and the consequent willingness to cooperate without serious reservation are, of course, as Parsons argues, influenced by the degree to which ego believes in the generalized legitimacy of alter's role and in the viability of alter's collectivity-orientation, and also by the various structural and evaluative phenomena that he describes. But I would argue that such trust is endemically unstable relative to either trust in a fellow expert or affectively-based trust.

It is interesting that in the absence of a fully rational basis of choice, laymen are not very systematic in the selection of professional helpers; whether "shopping around" or not, they tend not to follow whatever evidence of competence may be available. Instead they are very likely to take the advice of friends and neighbors, as Parsons notes, and moreover, as I have suggested with respect to "shopping around," to attend especially to information about the "personal qualities" of the professional, for example, whether he is "nice," "sympathetic," or prompt with his appointments. This phenomenon no doubt indicates in part a search for evidence of concern for clients' welfare and in part problems of the client that are not directly pertinent to the nature of the service received (e.g., conserving the client's time). But I think that it also involves an effort to find a relatively stable affective basis for trust, both in the qualities of the professional and in a substitution for the uncertain prospect of a trustworthy professional of a relatively secure affective bond with someone in the client's "personal circle." One may be more sure of the "good intentions" of a friend than of the less palpable motives of, say, a doctor or lawyer.

Whatever the strength of belief in the professional's authoritativeness, of the client's dependency needs, or of culturally defined obligations to cooperate, in the absence of fully rational grounding for the choice of a trustworthy specialist there is no clear evidence

to the client that his cooperation will result in the attainment of his own instrumental goal (to get well, to win his case at law, to firm up a shaky marriage, and so on). Thus we arrive from a somewhat different perspective at Parsons' conclusion that patients', or more generally client's', anxieties and resistances arise substantially from strains generated by inability either to help one's self or to know what one is about in selecting a helper. [25]

The pressure toward what I have called "affectively based trust" can be seen as a rational attempt by the client to ground his trust in a way that frees him to cooperate in the reasonable expectation of reaching his instrumental objective. I have noted that from the standpoint of the client, the solidarity of his relation with a helping professional is substantially self-interested. Thus it is the rare patient who will submit without serious reservation to experimental treatment when he believes conventional therapy to have a good chance of success.

Now it is precisely affectively based trust that provides the strongest expectation by ego that alter will put ego's interests to the fore. That is, by symbolizing the noncontingent solidarity of the relation such trust suggests that alter will do his best for ego (on ego's terms), whatever the stakes and whatever the situation. So, the expressive nature of affectively based trust provides a realistic expectation that ego's problem will be solved with alter's help, or more generally that ego will be "ahead of the game" by cooperating with alter. Although I do not mean to deny that pressures toward particularism, affectivity, and diffuseness are in part transference phenomena, I would suggest that perfectly rational elements, centered on the stabilization of ego's trust in alter, are also a major source of these pressures. It is of course true that a helping professional must resist such pressure in the client's long-run best interests, though I shall suggest that the social organization of the practice of helping professions under certain conditions may make this resistance difficult.

If trust in the specialist, in relations of lay dependence on expert help, is inherently unstable, we must search for those conditions in the structure of the professional-client relation that strengthen it sufficiently to make such dependence tolerable for the client, to reduce the uncertainties of inability to know clearly whether his interests are being served, and thus to reduce resistance and chances of client rebelliousness while at the same time reducing the secondary gains of passive dependence by making possible effective restricted reciprocation on the part of the professional. One of the main conditions clearly is a strong client belief in the altruism of science and the professions and in the practical utility of its application, probably further reinforced if these beliefs are widely shared in the circles and subculture from which the client comes. Another is, as Parsons says, the symbolization in the situation of professional practice of the professional's competence and concern for client welfare. Finally, the severity of the problem that the client presents will have a stabilizing effect — the worse the problem, the more likely is the client to run the risk of accepting a professional's help.

I believe in addition that to the extent that the professional can make clear to the client that the treatment or service to be given is a rational means of help, in view of the client's circumstances — that it has high instrumental value in the client's own case — trust in the specialist will be strengthened. This may occur partly through explicit, more or less detailed explanation and partly by indirection through the specification, in the client's mind, of expert competence and authoritativeness in general to the concrete acts of the expert. It may also be possible for the professional to rely on "common knowledge" about what is "done" in the professional role.

These comments suggest that the opportunities for relatively stable trust in the specialist will be greater among clients of at least middle social class, who are at once likely to be sophisticated about and favorably inclined toward science and specialism and able to afford more intensive forms of professional-to-client service in which the connection between help and the client's well-being can be made manifest. If so, client resistance or rebellion or persistent passive dependence and the strongest pressures toward affective trust should occur among clients of lower social class. These are also the clients who are apt to receive more routinized forms of service, in which professional concern for individual client welfare is not always readily apparent.

Is there any reason why Parsons' analysis and my own further comments on trust should be limited to one or a few of the helping professions, or even to those of the helping professions concerned mainly with social control, with deviance and its remedy? Can they not be applied as well in their essential elements to professions concerned mainly with socialization, that is, to the various teaching occupations? Note here that each of the helping professions — in addition to medicine, the other health professions, the law, teaching, social work, and the ministry in particular — despite marked differences of technique and relation to a scientific field of application, is concerned more or less centrally with the motivation of human conduct.[26] As such, the helping professions alike share the main attributes that Parsons notes for medicine.

I assume that there would be little disagreement with the following assertions. The helping professions generally are characterized by an achievement orientation and by universalism, functional specificity,

affective neutrality, and, at least relative to the spectrum of occupations, a marked collectivity-orientation. Each deals with an inexpert clientele, one that confronts problems that reflect inability to meet "normal" role expectations (either current or prospective). Moreover, these problems carry the more or less clear social definition that expert help is required, that they are beyond the resources of ego or others with whom he usually interacts to solve.

If these assertions hold, I would predict that in the practice of each of the helping professions arise the issues of client trust that I have outlined, with their attendant phenomena of client ambivalence, resistance, and anxiety and that these in turn require the professional to find an "Archimedean place to stand," beyond client pressures toward affective trust. And indeed in each of these professions is found a substantial lore about "handling clients," apart from the scientific knowledge-base of the profession, that corresponds to the "art of medicine."

There is, of course, a great range of variation in the degree to which the helping professions display these traits, and I believe that one of its main sources is the degree to which clients' problems are defined socially as deviant, the degree to which the client is in a deviant role. If a deviant role is at issue (e.g., the forms of illness that the doctor or psychotherapist treats or problems of juvenile law-breaking that may confront the social worker), the normal role relations of the client are thoroughly disrupted. If, as Parsons argues, under these circumstances substantial commitments to these relationships are retained, a client's investment in his "recovery" will be substantial and his sense of inability to judge rationally the quality of the help he is getting will be acute. Therefore he will be strongly impelled toward affectively based trust in the professional.[27]

However, the problems of the client are not always so acute, either because they constitute disruptions of role performance that do not entail a legitimate, mandatory withdrawal from the role (family trouble, for example, that may be brought to a social worker) or are seen as disabling or aggravating without involving more than a very temporary disturbance of one's usual social relations (e.g., a toothache). Although the former is a problem of social deviance, and the latter may have some motivational components (a tendency, for instance, to eat too many sweets), in the absence of a social definition of the trouble as extremely serious, the issue for the client is more clearly instrumental than in the socially critical case, his cooperation more voluntary than obligatory, and his trust more likely to be fairly stable trust in the specialist. Thus, the specialist's competence is of relatively less moment, anxiety over the problem at issue less acute, and the consequences of terminating the relation, or of seeking another professional if the present one proves unsatisfactory, are less costly than in the case of more explicitly deviant client problems.

It follows that in these professional-client relations the client's tendency to convert the basis of trust from the competence or authoritativeness of the expert to affectivity and the basis of cooperation from the legitimacy of the professional's authority to a diffuse and particularistic solidarity will be relatively weak, so that the criterion of trust remains the quality of professional help in whatever way the client is able to evaluate it. Nonetheless, as this evaluation is based on the client's own inexpert definition of his problem, the professional may find it difficult to gain the client's cooperation in certain matters that in the professional's judgment are important.

When the client's motives are central to the diagnosed problem (as is usually the case in social work, for example), the resulting strain on the professional may press him toward an affective relation with the client. In the absence of strong commitments to a professional ethic that specifies affective neutrality and stresses the societal aspect of collectivity-orientation, the professional may either succumb or avoid the personal costs of emotional involvement with the client by an impersonal facade of "bureaucratic," routine treatment. The impersonal facade is likely to produce still lower levels of client cooperation and further "bureaucratic" treatment, the relation perhaps terminating with little help ever forthcoming. The result, in short, is either a "vicious circle of deviance" or a "vicious circle of indifference" on the part of the professional.

If the client's motives are not much involved in the problem that he presents, as in a great deal of dental practice, for example, the professional's line of response is simpler. Because his is a "tinkering trade," centered on technical applications to "fix up" the client whatever the source of his trouble, the professional is likely simply to point out how the client might avoid such troubles in the future, show him the costs of failure to follow these suggestions, and then let the matter drop. The client's welfare is at issue, but not in a way that is critical for him or for the society. The welfare obligation is met when the technical job is done well and the advice given clearly. This is not to say that the professional in such instances may not try hard to alter or selectively reinforce his client's motives, but that these efforts are less crucial to maintaining the helping relation. A dentist, for example, may be disappointed in a patient who stubbornly persists in an improper diet or who will not brush his teeth correctly, but he rarely drops the patient, as a physician more often does with one who is very recalcitrant. The dentist is likely simply to shake his head and fill the cavities.

AFFECTIVELY BASED TRUST

In the remainder of this essay, I shall center my comments for the most part on those professional-client relations in which the client's problem is more socially critical and in which the client experiences pressures toward affective trust. In such relations these pressures are endemic, as a result of the several factors that I have reviewed — ambiguities surrounding the professional's authoritativeness and commitment to client welfare, the anxieties engendered by the client's helplessness, and so on. If the professional and client can find some viable basis for the client's trust in the specialist, the functionally specific solidarity of disinterested help and cooperativeness will be sufficient to overcome this tendency. When no such basis can be found, pressure on the client toward affective trust becomes very strong, and the functionally specific solidarity of the professional-client relation will be weakened seriously or destroyed. Before this point is reached, there likely will have occurred a series of attempts to ground the client's trust in the specialist, given evident client distrust or uncooperativeness. The nature of these attempts, of course, will depend on the client's problem, the traits of the client, and the social organization of the setting for professional help — sources of variation that I have no space here to explore. To provide only a few examples, they may include an appeal to the client's self-interest by making more clear the instrumental value for him of the professional's own conduct and expectations for his client (appeals of greater or lesser clarity and logic — ranging in medical practice from "If you don't do as I ask you won't get well" to a detailed explanation of the effects of therapeutic procedure), an appeal to "science" or to the opinion of consultants to bolster the professional's authoritativeness, attempts to reinforce the client's collectivity-orientation (his obligation to himself, to the society, or to his family or others in his personal circle), reliance on a more imperative authority in lieu of persuasion, or threatened termination of the relationship.

In effect, confronted by a breakdown of client trust in the specialist, the professional is forced to spend more and more precious influence resources, first in an effort to rebuild this trust and, if this effort fails, to shift the basis of their relation to a form that is more coercive (e.g., imperative control or the threat of termination). At this point, I believe, because the professional has only limited means of coercion and because the use of these means is likely to foster increased distrust and a drastic decline of the client's cooperativeness, more active client rebellion, or, indeed, loss of the client, pressure on the professional toward affectivity and particularism becomes quite strong. I have noted similar pressures in the case of professionals serving less critically disabled clients, arising when professional and client definitions of the service need diverge. Failures of professional authority, whatever their origins, tend toward the professional's use of affective incentives for client cooperation.

The strength of these pressures toward affectivity and particularism will vary with the costs to the professional of failure to help the client or loss of the client—in income or reputation, for example. Another cost, resulting from inability to "do something" for the client, whether technically justified or not and whatever the client's conduct in their relationship, is a sign of an already-emerging affective tie to the client. As I have noted, if the professional's commitment to client welfare is weak, or if the professional's clientele is a more or less captive population, the tendency toward the "impersonal facade" will be quite strong, in part as a solution to the costs of affectivity and in part because captive clients may also be served by captive professionals (for example, under conditions of regularized professional-to-client assignment). Otherwise in the face of failures of a client's trust in the specialist, affective involvement with the client will be hard for the professional to resist.

The Example of Teaching

My list of helping professions included teaching. Teaching, of course, is an instrument primarily of socialization rather than of social control. Yet Parsons has viewed socialization and social control as closely linked, in process characteristics as well as in their central functional significance for social equilibrium. I believe that Parsons' analysis of professional practice applies as well to teaching as it does to those helping professions concerned with social control. Indeed many of the characteristics and strains that Parsons has described for medical practice have been observed in the classroom.[28] There are in point of fact marked similarities between the roles of patient, as described by Parsons, and of student. These similarities make clear the sources of the student's dependence on teachers and schools.

Corresponding to the sick role is a rather less well-institutionalized role that we may call the role of the novice. To be sure novices, whatever their ages, unlike the sick or incumbents of other deviant roles, must be prepared for a prospective role rather than returned to fulfillment of role responsibilities. Nonetheless, novices, too, are incapacitated with respect to some "normal" range of role enactment, albeit as a function of age-grading, age-linked competence,

or simple lack of training. Moreover their incapacity is defined as something they "cannot help" or "could not have helped," but also as temporary—to be remedied by effort and a desire to learn. Thus motivational issues are central. The role of novice carries the expectation of deferred (i.e., temporally segregated) role enactment, but also the obligation to seek help in preparing for the prospective role.

Further, teaching has long been a specialized occupation in Western societies, and the role of the novice with relatively few exceptions entails the role of student. Help is to be sought from a teacher by going to school, with the concomitant obligation to be taught and to cooperate with the teacher by trying to learn. Of course, associated with studenthood and schooling, except at their very lowest and at their higher levels, is the secondary institution of youth culture, which provides for a partial segregation of students from adult society.

One principal task for the teacher is to maintain in his students a level of motivation to perform as a student that is sufficient to whatever degree of academic achievement the teacher has set as appropriate (whether for the student individually or for the class in general). At the same time there is, often latent in the teacher's work with his students, an effort to foster their commitment to the role or roles for which they are being prepared, and with this commitment appropriate values and beliefs. This "moral" content of teaching is quite apparent in elementary schools, with their stress on the development of student character and citizenship, but it is present to a degree in all forms of teaching.

I believe that fundamental to this motivational issue is the degree to which the student wants to learn the role — the strength of his anticipatory commitment to it. The teacher must work to reinforce this commitment, refine it, and give it a "realistic" grounding in accurate knowledge of the way in which the role is defined and of the social situations in which it is enacted. His work in this respect and in all aspects of his teaching is hard if students are indifferent to their presumptive social destinations, harder still if they actively resist them. And the student's anticipatory role commitments are strongly influenced, I shall suggest, by their ages and certain other criteria for recruitment to the student role.

In addition, students, like all clients of the helping professions, will be ambivalent toward assuming their destined roles. For one thing, there are anxieties about eventual mastery of role requirements, about how well they will do once school is finished or training completed. Clearly one of the several functions of testing and grading is to give to the student some assurance about his progress toward competence (or to provide a "realistic" or objective basis for "cooling-out" the student). As a means of reassurance, however, the effectiveness of grades or test scores is positively related to the level of the student's commitment to the prospective role; as justification for cooling him out, it is negatively related to such role commitment.

Moreover there are notable secondary gains from being a student. It is a fully legitimate role, as least until age-grade definitions point to a disparity between adulthood and studenthood, that insulates the student from the rigors of full-fledged social participation; it is likely to involve the student in rewarding solidary relations with peers; and if the student is doing reasonably well, his studies themselves bring a variety of rewards, some intrinsic to growing mastery of the subject-matter, others extrinsic, such as grades or approval of teacher or peer.

One of the functions of school-leaving ages and of age-grade promotion through the levels of a school system is to define points at which studenthood ceases first to be mandatory (the leaving age) and subsequently to be legitimate. Awarding degrees is an example of a defined boundary of legitimate studenthood; colleges normally do not allow students to begin again a course of study formally completed. Age-grade expectations have similar consequences. But most markedly in the upper reaches of an educational system, the legitimation of studenthood often is unclear, principally as a correlate of the extent of formal temporal structure in the student's program. Thus medical or law schools can specify when the degree is to be awarded and the student role terminated. In arts and sciences graduate schools, this specification is more difficult, and an endemic problem in these schools is the student "who could get on with his work if only he'd stop fooling around."

Now, what are the strains encountered by teachers given these attributes of schooling? Like other professional roles, teaching roles are defined more or less in terms of universalism, affective neutrality, functional specificity, and collectivity-orientation. (There are certain variations across the teaching roles in the salience of universalism, affective neutrality and functional specificity, to be discussed in a moment.) These attributes of the teacher's role are essential to his dispassionate judgment, his ability to reward students objectively (i.e., with respect to mastery of the role for which they are being prepared), and his restricted reciprocation of student conduct and selective approval of academic performance in the light of his judgment about progress toward mastery — mastery here in the sense of learning skills and knowledge and, as well, of developing moral orientations and beliefs.

This is not to say that all students are to be treated alike, but judgments about "individual differences" must be made in the light of more generalized

standards: What each student can be expected to accomplish is a matter of his abilities and motives viewed with respect to a general formulation of the nature and levels of student conduct and achievement. These standards are dictated by the requirements of the role destination and thus can be more or less flexible according to the degree of permissiveness, the latitude for variable performance, in the definition of the prospective role.

Here the age-grade of the teacher's students becomes a central variable in the analysis of teaching. Very young children, as Parsons has said, enter school with diffuse commitments to the student role and to the school itself.[29] The question of their adult destinations is opaque, of little concern and an object of little knowledge. Indeed to begin school, to become a student, is for these children an important attainment in itself. In my terms, children begin schooling on the basis of affective trust; and Parsons has pointed out the ways in which the primary school teacher, usually a woman, is a maternal surrogate for her charges. Moreover, the adult roles on which the early years of schooling center are broadly defined, with wide latitude for individual variability in their enactment. The minimal competences and motives requisite for citizenship, in fact, set much of the early school curriculum.

As a result, the teacher of young children confronts neither very intensive nor very pervasive problems of student trust, while she can be quite free about the expression of positive affect. That is, the primary school class is especially centered on support and is relatively permissive. Considerable individual variation in student conduct is tolerable, so long as it is not excessively disruptive of classroom order. But such variability has less salience than at higher pupil age-grade levels as an indicator of academic achievement. The issue of restricted reciprocation is usually concerned mainly with student compliance with the requirements of order and with teaching the child to respond to school grades and marks, even though they are extrinsic to the subject-matter being studied. The child is taught that they are rewarding in themselves.[30] The bond of affective trust between child and teacher, as an aspect of a quasifamilial solidarity, gives to the teacher a pervasive moral authority that imbues the marks he assigns, early in conjunction with judicious allocation of approval, with a strongly expressive quality as symbols of the affective solidarity of the teacher-pupil dyad.[31]

Teaching students to value marks is important analytically in two ways. First, it points to the significance for the practice of the helping professions of client socialization to the client role. In most cases in modern societies adult clients have already learned these roles, often vicariously. When such learning has not occurred, however, the need to teach one's clients how to act as clients, what the norms, rights, and obligations are, is a powerful force for particularism and affectivity in the relation.[32] If the client is unequipped to accept the authoritativeness of or grant authority to an expert, to trust the specialist, and thus to be confident of his concern for his client's best interests, the one basis for trust is the affective bond. Professionals may be forced to succumb for the time so that they may be teachers of novice clients, or they may lapse into the indifference of a service routine if the outcome for the client is of little concern, that is, if the norms specifying collectivity-orientation are poorly enforced or weakly held. But for the teacher of young children this aspect of teaching is an expected part of the teaching task and is manageable without strain because the relation with students is defined as having a significant component of affectivity and as relatively diffuse.

Second, teaching young children to value marks is important because the school's marking system is a major structural defense against pressures toward affectivity and particularism later in the school grades. In the upper grades of elementary school, still more in high school and college, adult roles are proximate, achievement standards for students more salient and universalistic, the curriculum more differentiated with respect to distinctive adult roles and status groups.[33] Students are more knowledgeable about what they want from school; they begin to make instrumentally oriented judgments about the value of the schooling that they receive.

By the time students reach the upper elementary school grades, the basis for their trust in teachers has begun to shift from affectivity to trust in the specialist, a process substantially completed by high school. The teacher's authority now is less the diffuse moral authority of familistic solidarity, more that of the subject-matter specialist and instructional technician. Instrumental goals become more salient for students, questions of what and how much to learn, for example. However flawed, student evaluations of teachers become increasingly matters of "how good" they are — how much they know of the subject, how well organized are their presentations, how effective they are at discipline, and the like. Elements of affectivity and expressiveness are still present, but they are muted.[34] Moreover, students have learned about the teacher's own role responsibilities, not only with respect to subject-matter command but also "even-handedness," "fairness," and steady judgment.

Given the inherent motivational ambivalence of studenthood and the fact that students now make instrumental decisions about their schooling (to say nothing of the effect on their own values and beliefs of similar decisions by their parents and peers), the teacher cannot readily assume that motivations in the student role will be forthcoming or that students are acquiring the anticipatory commitments to prospective adult roles that the teacher hopes to develop.

Furthermore, the teacher's role below the college level is less fully institutionalized as "scientific" than are most of the professional fields — school-teaching is not usually considered a "learned profession" and as an occupation ranks fairly low in prestige. Compared with, say, the physician, the teacher is more vulnerable to student and parent values or beliefs about schooling and to the vagaries of lay adult and student judgments of teaching skill, while he commands in point of fact a less thoroughly developed technique and body of knowledge. He is less an "authority," is less authoritative. Indeed, the absence of a developed knowledge base and technique, at least with respect to the means of teaching if not its content, in college and university as in lower schools, undoubtedly makes teacher conduct relatively variable and idiosyncratic and in this sense too more open to lay judgment.

As a result there is in greater or lesser measure in any school class above the primary grades a pressure on teachers to employ affectivity (friendship, comradeship, and the like) as a means of motivating students to work at least to the minimum achievement standard and to be relatively decorous in class. If students will not work or "behave" for love of the material respect for the teacher (that is, trust in him as a specialist), or instrumental gain (built on nascent adult role commitments), perhaps they will work or conduct themselves properly for a teacher whom they like or love or for a teacher whom they fear or hate.

Also to be taken into account are the secondary gains of studenthood, which center very largely on the solidarity and concomitant social support of the student peer group. These gains, the pervasive tendency of student groups to develop "output norms" defining maximum performance (to safeguard peer solidarity in a competitive situation), and students' anxieties about their own performance and competence combine to produce rather intense student "transference" — often as a collective attempt to coopt the teacher to quasimembership in the classroom peer society or at least to achieve a negotiated settlement of performance standards.[35]

Thus the teacher may lose his students' commitment to studenthood and fail to develop in them satisfactory anticipatory adult role commitments if his conduct stresses universalistic evaluation of student achievement and contingent reward and restricted reciprocation. Yet he may lose control of his students' motivation as students if he relies primarily on affect to gain their trust.

If students have learned to value teachers' marks,

which can be allocated with explicit reference to "objective standards," these rewards are a means of maintaining student motivation that is separated structurally from other aspects of the teacher's relations with his students. He can be a "friend," but retreat to the objectivity of the standard, which my be "out of his hands" at crucial motivational points in the work of the class. This is always an uneasy arrangement, as the teacher's "sincerity" may be placed in doubt by discrepancies between daily friendliness and the differential allocation of grades. The value and objectivity of the grade may be eroded if it does not appear to be assigned without prejudice. Moreover, students who value grades highly may be especially tempted to negotiate with teachers about the achievement standards to which marks correspond, unless in learning the student role the student has developed a belief in the close correspondence between the mark and what is "really learned."

Conclusion

The foregoing comments on teaching, I hope, show the general applicability of a somewhat modified Parsonian approach to the practice of the helping professions. Several conclusions can be drawn from this and the earlier discussion.

First, while the cooperativeness of the client may always be problematic, its contingent quality is not only a matter of secondary gain and transference phenomena that arise from anxiety centered on the social definition of the need for help. It is a matter also of more strictly instrumental considerations. These considerations involve the value of the help received as determined by the client's own lay standards, standards that may derive from the client's goals in seeking help or from secondary gains derived from the helping relation, if the client was voluntarily recruited.[36]

Second, when a client is oriented primarily to instrumental goals, his trust in the professional derives mainly from the professional's specialist standing and to the degree that this standing is authoritative. it is more or less sufficient to sustain cooperation, though I have suggested that in the absence of fully rational grounds for choosing a professional there is always some pressure toward affective trust. If the professional's standing is less than authoritative, by virtue of the prestige of his occupation, its mixed "scientific" grounding, or evidence in the course of the helping relation of lack of skill or knowledge, trust in the specialist will be weak. Then if the social expectation of client cooperativeness is very clear or if there are no viable alternatives for help and if the client's presenting problem clearly

calls for help, he is likely to search for a more valid basis of trust—an affective tie to the professional.

He may, on the other hand, "shop around." But Parsons has shown how great a violation this is of norms defining collectivity-orientation in the professional-client relation, norms widely shared by professionals and probably by the larger proportion of clients as well. If the client does "shop around" he runs the risk of cutting himself off from any help except from marginal practitioners, if his case is dropped by the professional with whom he began and is not accepted by others in the absence of an appropriate referral. In addition, I have suggested that the client's lay ignorance and his uncertainty about whom to trust as a specialist are likely to make "shopping around" at least as problematic as receiving service from only one professional. So the norms of client collectivity-orientation are strongly reinforced by both the actions of "reputable" practitioners and by the very circumstances of client inexpertness and anxiety that leave the professional's authority open to question. It then may be for the client the line of least resistance to try to find a more acceptable and stable basis for cooperation with the professional—the affective bond that implies noncontingent acceptance by the professional of the client's conduct and assures him that his own best interests are indeed of prime mutual concern in their relationship.

Thus transference and the pressure to particularism can arise independently of more strictly psychodynamic processes or the effort to gain full legitimacy for a socially marginal or deviant status. That is, the client-professional relation in part can be viewed as an exchange of service and cooperation, in which cooperation is contingent on the value assigned to the service by the client. If the client can find no basis for trust in the professional, he may either terminate the relation with the professional or become recalcitrant or rebellious.

When the client's orientation to the professional-client relation is primarily expressive, trust derives from an affective tie to the professional (though his authoritativeness and his demonstrated competence may influence the strength and the nature of this tie). Cooperation *per se* is not likely to be problematic. But whether this cooperation facilitates the provision of effective help depends on the degree to which support and permissiveness or restricted reciprocation are at issue in the professional's work with his client.

Third, it follows that the client's motivation is at issue not only with respect to the attainment of or a return to a "normal" adult role, but also with respect to conduct as a client. Variation in the nature ("specialist" or affective) and amount of client-held trust sets powerful conditions to the formation and durability of motivation to enact the client role.

Fourth, persistent failures of client trust, whatever its nature, create for the professional a tendency toward affectivity and particularism in an effort to strengthen the client's motivation to cooperate (though under certain conditions that I have described this tendency may be deflected into the "impersonal facade" of routinized service). This tendency always is counterproductive in situations in which the help to be provided demands of the client preparation for or resumption of a specialized role or achievement to a universalistic standard. Indeed under these conditions of professional help, a particularistic, affective relation to a client will weaken rather than strengthen the professional's ability to influence the client toward conduct appropriate to the presumptive role destination. That is, the professional loses his ability to restrictively reciprocate or selectively reward client conduct. Thus the tendency is toward reinforcement of the vicious circle of deviance, or in the case of teaching, toward a protracted studenthood and inadequate preparation, both moral and technical, for the student's prospective role. Thus it is not entirely clarifying to view the professional's tendency toward affectivity and particularism as in the main "countertransference."

SOCIAL ORGANIZATIONAL FACTORS

Variation in the nature and degree of client trust and the consequent problems of professional help, however, are matters not only of the foregoing attributes of the client-professional dyad but also of the social organization of the practice of these professions. I have space here only to illustrate briefly the consequences of social organizational factors for the problem of client trust and will discuss two dimensions of social organization, implicit in many of my earlier comments: the recruitment base of the client role and the structure of the client collectivity.

Client Recruitment

With respect to client recruitment, we can distinguish two main forms: voluntary and involuntary. Voluntary recruitment occurs when the potential client's own initiative (self-definition as in need of expert help) is the prime motive force. Involuntary recruitment refers to the action of a third party, first in defining ego as in need of expert help and second in selecting the helping agent.[37]

Involuntary recruitment may be subdivided according to the relation between the potential client and the third party and according to the principle on which the latter acts. On the one hand are those particularistic relations (e.g., involving members of a "personal circle") in which some form of affective bond — love, concern, or hostility, for example — both motivates and, at least when the bond is positive, justifies the third party's intervention and in which the professional is selected primarily out of concern to find a helping agent best able to handle the distinctive problem that the potential client presents (though, most clearly in the case of a negative bond, this concern may be more self-interested than altruistic). On the other are universalistic relations (as between a government and its citizens), in which the identification of potential clients is based on the criterion of "common welfare," and assignment of clients to professionals is according to a general rule. A family members' referral of a minor or incompetent to a physician is an example of particularistic involuntary recruitment; mandatory schooling or the isolation of persons with communicable diseases in which client-allocation is based on a domiciliary criterion (e.g., the catchment area of a local school or isolation hospital) are examples of universalistic involuntary recruitment.

Other things being equal, voluntary client recruitment is most favorable to the formation of trust-in-the-specialist and fosters a relatively uneventful relation of cooperation between client and professional. The authoritativeness of the professional and his reputation for competence are likely to have been especially important in client self-recruitment. Moreover, the client has clear instrumental goals and believes that the professional specialist will help him to attain them.

Nonetheless in recent years it has become clear, for example, to graduate and professional school faculties, that voluntary recruitment does not inevitably bring with it a complementary definition by client and professional of the service to be received and given. Despite voluntary recruitment there may be an erosion of trust in the specialist, in the present example resulting from a decline among the educated classes of Western society of belief in the legitimacy and primacy of science and scientific roles. And the case of contemporary undergraduate colleges shows that formally voluntary recruitment may contain strong involuntary elements because there is no attractive alternative to the client role (in this case a restricted choice that has resulted from changes in the labor force, for example, educational upgrading of occupations, from altered popular conceptions concerning the "right" to a college education, and in the United States from the military draft)[38] Thus it is impossible to disentangle recruitment to professional service and the formation of client trust in specific situations of professional practice from broad macrosocial phenomena.

Involuntary recruitment presents uniformly unfavorable conditions for the formation of trust in the specialist. The client had in the first place no desire to be a client; he is acutely anxious about being defined as "helpless," and not having selected the professional he is at the least unsure of the professional's skill or "good intentions." Lack of client motivation to enact the client role, resulting from these factors, presses the professional toward affectivity, while the client himself, to make his situation more comprehensible, tolerable, and manipulable, also seeks to establish an affective, particularistic relation with the professional. This is a situation that is especially prone to a "vicious circle of deviance" in the professional role.

Note that the affectivity of the relation may be negative as well as positive, leading to client hostility or rebellion, especially when the authority of the professional is not fully legitimated. Note also that professionals dealing with clients they cannot themselves easily reject may be especially prone to a negative "countertransference." This point derives from differences in the consequences for the professional-client relation of involuntary recruitment of the particularistic and universalistic types. The latter is especially prone to client distrust in the professional that leads to hostility and rebellion and to negative professional countertransference, for the universalistic criterion of client allocation bears as much on the professional as on the client. I should guess that in these relations the professional's main defense against affectivity and particularistic involvement with his clients is "bureaucratic" routine and indifference, fostered by both his own inability to select clients and the fact that they come to him via a routine procedure. This, then, is a situation especially prone to the "vicious circle of indifference."

These phenomena are especially evident in attempts to provide professional help (medical, educational, social service, or counselling, for example) to the inmates of prisons. In the prison setting, the conditions favoring negative affect in the professional-client relation are all strongly present. Indeed, this example may be the limiting case of a more general phenomenon. Professional help, to the extent that it involves restricted reciprocation or discomfort or inconvenience, is characterized by a moral regulation of the client's conduct that, I believe, is always difficult for the client to bear and may be very nearly intolerable if the client cannot see how his own interests are served thereby. The basis of the functionally specific professional-client relation, the reciprocal obligations of welfare concern

and cooperation, then is contradicted by the client's self-interest, and such solidarity is highly problematic. But if the client role has been entered under duress, as the result of involuntary recruitment unsupported by a positive social bond to the third party, the professional in most cases will be seen as opposed or at best indifferent to the client's interests, and the diffuse solidarity generated by a positive affective tie also is not likely to emerge. Under these conditions, with the realization of self-interest blocked by the necessity to submit to a seemingly malevolent moral regulation, a Durkheimian fatalism may set in for the client rather quickly. Although this state of mind may lead to passive submission or even overdependence, it may also foster active rebellion or recalcitrance, at least with respect to a return to "normal" role responsibilities to which the client presumably retains a partial commitment. The conditions influencing these modes of response—aspects of the client's personality, the possible existence of a negatively oriented client subculture, or the degree to which the client is subordinated to repressive control in roles linked in some way to the client role (as in the case of inmate-clients)—are beyond the scope of this paper.

When recruitment is involuntary but particularistic, the professional may be able to rely on the solidary incentives toward client cooperation provided by the members of the client's personal circle and to enlist them as a justification for his own dispassionate judgment and restricted reciprocation of the client's conduct. But he can do so only when the client's affective ties to the personal circle are positive. If instead they are negative, especially if they involve a high level of aggression or hostility, the professional's task is exceptionally difficult, as the client's sentiments are likely to generalize from the members of his circle who "did this" to him, to their seeming professional ally.

The Structure of the Client-Collectivity

In what ways does the structure of client-collectivities affect the solidarity of the professional-client relations?[39] I shall consider two forms of practice of the helping professions that differ from the discrete professional-client relation in that they involve client groups in some way in the service or treatment situation. On the one hand are those client groupings that are ancillary to the provision of service and exist primarily for the sake of administrative or logistical efficiency. By bringing clients together into one organizational location, economies of scale permit professional help beyond the financial or organizational reach of the isolated professional (e.g., the ward of a general hospital). In these situations, professional service still is provided for the most part on a person-to-person basis.

On the other are groupings that are intrinsic elements of the structure of client-serving interaction. The professional deals with clients as a group. Even when he interacts with one or a few of the group's members, the interaction is directly visible to other members, and it is a part of the temporal and social organization of the group's activities. In fact, these settings can be regarded as collectivities stratified primarily with respect to the professional or client status of their members. Although such groupings at one time may have been dictated by efficiency criteria (e.g., the organization of schools as classroom units), it is interesting that the collective properties of the group usually come to be regarded as resources for professional service and, contrariwise, as problems central to the professional's work (viz., the debate among educators over the merits of "homogeneous" or "heterogeneous" classes). At times such groups are established initially for the sake of presumed gains to the effectiveness of professional help, the "therapeutic community," for example.

What are the consequences of these variable properties of the social organization of the practice of the helping professions for client trust and the solidary quality of professional-client interaction? First, the client-serving organization (the hospital or school, for example) can itself be an object of client trust to the degree that it is viewed by clients as centered on client-welfare goals, as enforcing on its client members status-demeaning or status-enhancing actions or roles, as being an organizational manifestation of "scientific" endeavor or at least of service efficiency, or as raising or lowering the costs of service. It can be, in point of fact, the object of greater or lesser degrees of trust of either an instrumental or an expressive kind. Thus, for example, adult patients tend to make most of the foregoing judgments of hospitals, and I have suggested that for young children the simple fact that they are "ready for school" in itself is an event of substantial expressive significance. The main point is that the nature and level of the client's trust in the service organization (as instrumentally or expressively grounded) tends to devolve on members of its staff (as trust in the specialist or as affective trust), at least for a while independently of their own attributes or performance.

The timing of events in the course of professional service also is important. If the client is referred to the service organization by a professional with whom a level of trust already has been established, that level

of trust then will tend to devolve on the organization, as in the usual pattern of private medical practice. The reverse is likely to occur if recruitment to the client role takes place initially through the service organization, as in the case of "charity" hospitals. Here the staff are largely unknown quantities and are usually assigned to clients, so that client beliefs about the service organization are paramount in the establishment of trust.

Moreover, initial experiences with the organization —whether they are relatively pleasant or unpleasant, whether they conflict with or reinforce the client's own conception of worth and need, and whether they confirm his ideas about the operation of a "professional" enterprise—will affect subsequent levels of trust in the organization. Consider, for example, the consequences for a patient's trust of entering a hospital via an overburdened emergency room or through the admitting office on the referral of a personal physician.

Second, the existence of a client collectivity, whatever its other properties, means that while clients may be insulated from contact with groups and persons outside the client-serving organization, they often are not insulated from one another. In a hospital, "critical" or infectious or contagious cases may be entirely isolated; other patients who are in private rooms or who are immobilized by disease or "doctor's orders" are isolated nearly as much. Patients or other kinds of client-members (e.g., boarding-school students) who can move about, but mainly in the relatively narrow confines of an organizational location, especially those who are served or treated in groups, are very much in interaction; the moral density of the client society is high. Especially if they are client-members for long periods of time, they are likely to develop solidary relations among themselves (e.g., clients in boarding schools, nursing homes, or wards for chronic or lingering terminal illnesses).

It is not only that such settings increase the "secondary gains" of a client role. More or less stable client societies present clients with common problems of client status (e.g., recovery from the same or similar illnesses, mastering the same curriculm, or dealing with the same staff members). Most notably if the service units of a client-serving organization are specialized according to such social categories as the age or sex of the client or with respect to the service to be given, these societies are prone to the development of client subcultures that define shared solutions to common client problems. Client subcultures are likely to include a definition of the service need, evaluations of staff and specification of effective ways of "dealing with them" (getting what the clients want—either in the form of service or escape from "unwarranted" demands or routines), and "output norms" that define acceptable limits of client cooperation.

Factors affecting confidence in the organization or the trustworthiness of staff members will influence the degree to which client subcultures foster client cooperation; but given the ambivalence of client status, the inexpertness of clients in the professional field, and the anxieties that seeking help engenders, these subcultures will inevitably contain significant elements promoting skepticism and resistance. As such they pose often severe problems for the professional staff, especially as the dispassionate professional stance and the more or less apparent manipulativeness of restricted reciprocation tend to reinforce these organizationally "negative" aspects of client subcultures. One means of breaking client solidarity is the formation of particularistic, affective relations with clients — yet another force for the "deprofessionalization" of professional-client interaction.

Third, in many service organizations (lower schools being a notable exception), clients interact with several staff members. The existence of a visible staff collectivity has numerous consequences for client trust. For example, especially if several of the staff share the same specialty, the client can make comparative evaluations of competence and of supportiveness and set his level of trust, either trust in the specialist or affective trust, accordingly. But the presence of nonprofessionals with whom clients interact or of subprofessionals or professionals of varied occupational or organizational status, with correspondingly differentiated levels of responsibility for the "management of the case," may provide at the lower ranks opportunities to provide high levels of support and permissiveness and relatively unrestricted reciprocation of client conduct, freeing more senior staff of pressures toward particularistic, affective solidarity. Nurses and school janitors appear often to perform this function.[40]

Fourth, if the professionals and the client group form a collectivity, as in the school classroom, the provision of service takes on certain distinctive characteristics. The professional's conduct is a public matter within the collectivity. Client-defined inequities of treatment can become central issues of common client concern. This fact may move the professional toward "even-handedness," but the criterion of equity involved is specific to the collectivity and its observance may violate broader universalistic principles of technical performance and thus violate the professional's commitment to collectivity-orientation. This strain may, for example, underlie teachers' problems in "teaching to a standard" while observing pupils' "individual differences," a strain that, of course, is exacerbated by marked variations of pupil motivation to cooperate and wide variations in their abilities to enact the client role.

Client conduct during helping interaction also is public, and client subcultures thus are strongly binding, as their norms are readily enforced by client-peers. At the same time client ambivalence, on occasion reinforced by more explicit forms of resistance, is likely to result in disorderly or disruptive conduct by individual clients that makes effective work in a group setting difficult and is likely to spread among the clients. This phenomenon, most frequent where client trust is relatively low, tends to give order-keeping primacy over service-giving. It is especially a problem in settings in which the staff is relatively unstratified and there are no subprofessionals to whom order-keeping can be delegated.

Finally note that shared professional-client group membership gives to clients certain distinctive sanctions, often very effective, over professional conduct. Disorder is prime among these sanctions, as is collective client failure to cooperate more directly in the service relationship. As a result, professionals in such settings, much like first-line managers in industry, cannot safely exceed levels of demand on their "client-subordinates" specified by the output norms of the client subculture or depart too far in the service given from collective client definitions of client needs. Teachers, for example, often dignify this issue by speaking of "starting where the student is." In short, in such settings client trust in the specialist is contingent not only on the professional's personal traits and technical performance, but on his conduct as a group member—conduct that often must depart from his own best judgment. This attribute of certain collective settings for professional help makes it especially possible for clients to coopt professionals to a particularistic professional-client relation.

POSTSCRIPT

In the foregoing pages, I have tried to show how Parsons' analysis of medical practice, with certain revisions, helps us to understand the more general case of the practice of the helping professions. The discussion has been limited primarily to professional-client interaction. Nonetheless, an important aspect of the development of modern societies is the emergence, though at differing rates, of the major areas of professional help as "welfare goods." Historically the process has been most advanced in the case of education; now health care is an area rapidly catching up.

The concept of professional help as a welfare

good implies that professional service of one kind or another becomes a matter of political debate and public policy, the provision of service an object of deliberate public planning, and the allocation and quality of service to population groups joint public issues of high importance.

Under these circumstances decisions about who is to be a client are less a matter of the definition of individual status in respect to "unusual" personal circumstances, more a matter of the accessibility to broad population groups or categories of a service that they must or may receive. It is not then possible to rely on a series of discrete choices by persons or their surrogates among available professionals; and the political processes through which decisions are made about the quality and allocation of professional help, along with the social arrangements for the provision and distribution of professional service, emerge as major areas for sociological analysis. These trends are indicated by increasing concern for the "delivery" of service in contrast to the quality of professional technique or help for individual clients.

Confidence in the professions in this context can be seen as a matter of collective structures of values and beliefs, interacting with the processes and results of political decision-making. The distribution, for example, of popular and elite beliefs about effective modes of help ("applied science" or something else) in relation to the distribution of political power is an important variable in studying professional help as a welfare good. So, too, is the tendency for access to services and for means of lay control over such help to become elements of broader political processes, as in the spread of local community boards of control among helping organizations — an apparatus that may be accepted by professional groups and their allies as, in part, a way to build client (or clientele) confidence in the profession and helping organization (though a confidence grounded more in such political factors as interest-representation than in belief in the altruism or authoritativeness of professional helpers).

If it remains true that concrete acts of professional service will continue to involve intimate forms of social interaction, research on professional help must attend not only to these phenomena in themselves, but also to their consequences for the organization of the helping professions and of the settings in which help is provided and for the nature of professional-client interaction within these settings. The solidarity of such interaction and its bases will remain as significant variables, but now within the context of structures and meanings derived from the social definition of access to professional help as an aspect of citizenship.

NOTES

1. See especially Talcott Parsons, *Essays in Sociological Theory* (Glencoe, Illinois: The Free Press, 1954), Ch. 8, and Talcott Parsons, *The Social System* (Glencoe, Ill.: The Free Press, 1951), Ch. 8.
2. Parsons, *The Social System*, p. 352.
3. For example, see Joseph Ben-David, "Professions and Professionalization," Center for Social Organization Studies, Department of Sociology, University of Chicago, multilith.
4. The term "helping profession" never has been defined adequately. I shall define the helping professions as those in which a service is provided to a clientele, the service having as a central, though not sole or necessarily primary, component modification of the client's motivation to enact a legitimate social role.
5. It is not at all clear that medicine remains the typical case of professional practice in contemporary Western societies, given accelerated professionalization of occupations and the emergence of large-scale organizations for professional service. Parsons, in a recent essay that ranges more widely and comparatively across the professions, alludes to these issues. See T. Parsons, "Professions," in D. Sills (ed.), *International Encyclopedia of the Social Sciences* (New York: Macmillan and The Free Press, 1968), Vol. 12, pp. 536-547. However, his discussion of medical practice retains a central place for students of the professional-to-client helping relation.
6. Parsons, *The Social System*, Ch. 7.
7. *Ibid.*, p. 301.
8. *Ibid.*, p. 431.
9. Nonetheless, as the institutionalization of science is surrounded by a penumbra of popular doubt and uncertainty, while the application of scientific knowledge to practical problems always contains a certain element of indeterminacy, supernatural and magical orientations to illness persist in the West, even among physicians.
10. *Ibid.*, p. 435. As Parsons notes, these beliefs are widely shared among the professions (and indeed are not absent in many other occupations), but he regards medicine and the clergy as especially exemplary.
11. By 1963 Parsons was arguing that the personal strain for ego centers, at least in the United States, on his inability to achieve. In a 1963 paper, Parsons also noted a trend in medical perspectives on illness "from the emphasis on purely external pathogenic agents through the emphasis on the internal organic aspect of illness, to that of motivated personality factors which has entailed increasing importance of the patient's willing cooperation in the therapeutic process." Thus the issue of patient trust has gained salience with change in physicians' conceptions of illness and treatment. See T. Parsons, "Social Change and Medical Organization: A Sociological Perspective," *Annals of the American Academy of Political and Social Science*, 346 (March 1963), esp. pp. 22-25.
12. Indeed a person's sickness constitutes a condition of strain for those others tied to him by ascriptive or affective bonds — his "personal circle" of kin and close friends. Their reactions to his illness, as well as his illness itself, will elicit some form of social control.
13. Parsons, *The Social System*, p. 436. This attribute of the sick role refers to the role's characteristic mode of social orientation. With respect to the genesis of sickness, it can be regarded as "adaptive deviance," that is, ego's lack of resources to achieve or meet role responsibilities. Though this view of the sick role is implicit in Parsons' *Annals, op. cit.*, essay, it is most fully developed by Jesse Pitts, "Introduction," *Theories of Society* (New York: The Free Press, 1961), T. Parsons, E. Shils, K. Naegele, and J. Pitts (eds.) pp. 701-702, as part of an application of Parsons' AGIL formulation to the personality.
14. Of course, not all sickness is legitimated, for example,

the "crock" or the malingerer. It would be interesting to speculate on conditions affecting the scope of legitimation for roughly comparable presenting problems — for example, in the case of medical practice, the degree of formalization of diagnostic procedures, the dependence of the physician on fees (or on this patient's fee), discrepancies as between the social status of physician and patient, the degree of voluntarism or binding obligation in the patient's "normal" array of roles (e.g., the military or prison setting), the degree to which the physician is aware of conditions of "secondary gain" for the patient (see later discussion), or beliefs that patients from certain social origins or roles may not be willing to fulfill social expectations (e.g., soldiers, workers, or students).

15. Parsons, *The Social System*, p. 437.

16. *Ibid.*, p. 437.

17. *Ibid.*, p. 465.

18. The attributes of the sick role and of the doctor-patient relation undoubtedly vary with societal values. Parsons implies this in his *Annals* article (*op. cit.*), and the idea is further developed by Pitts (*op. cit.* pp. 704-705). But neither Parsons nor Pitts carries forward the cross-societal comparison of the sick role or physician-patient relation in a systematic way. There is no space in this essay to so do, and in any event I believe that my more general conclusions regarding professional relations will obtain for any modern society.

19. Parsons is not, I believe, suggesting that the patient role always isolates the patient ecologically, but that even in collective treatment situations, such as hospital work, the dyadic relation to one's doctor remains paramount. Nonetheless, as I shall try to demonstrate, situations of professional help that involve client collectivities often present great problems for effecting the isolation of the client. See Renée Fox, *Experiment Perilous* (New York: The Free Press, 1959). At times the client collectivity is itself the "object" of the professional's work.

20. Parsons, *The Social System*, p. 465.

21. *Ibid.*, p. 461.

22. The foregoing review of Parsons' analysis of medical practice, as it is centered on the doctor-patient relation deals with a form of practice that in the United States has been characteristic especially of traditional "private practice." In his *Annals* article (*op. cit.*), Parsons notes that the solidary qualities of the physician-patient relation have been fostered by the "nonbureaucratic" aspect of private practice, in which the primacy of the patient's welfare can be made very evident. He asks whether this solidarity may be affected by "modern" forms of medical practice, especially as these are marked by an intensive division of therapeutic labor, the "bureaucratic" setting of hospital treatment, and forms of payment alternative to the fee for service. Unfortunately he does not try to answer this question, but I shall turn shortly to a few of the factors in "modern" professional practice as they may affect client trust.

23. Trust, in general terms, may be defined as confidence in the good intentions of alter when his conduct cannot itself be predicted within error limits acceptable to ego.

24. Indeed Parsons notes that colleague controls on doctors must be informal and loose to provide the flexible range of judgment necessary for differentiated treatment of cases and to prevent a bureaucratized rigidity that in fact would not serve patient welfare. Thus the patient, except in a more obvious instance of malpractice, has no court of last resort.

25. It may be that as both bureaucratization and the professionalization of occupations increase in contemporary societies and as the incidence of contact with such organizations and occupations spreads across populations, effective socialization to the client role (in the sense of certain generalized predispositions, especially toward universalism, affective neutrality, and functional specificity, as well as preparation more directly for the enactment of client roles) will characterize these populations. Such predispositions have been noted as typifying the

"modern man," but I have followed Parsons in arguing that there are important sources of ambivalence toward professional help, centered especially on the tension between the lay client's self-interest and his collectivity-orientation, which I believe persist despite the "modernization" of societies or of the values and beliefs of their members. Nonetheless, these aspects of modernization may tend to reduce anxieties about professional help and may increase willingness to trust specialists despite lay ignorance. If so, this tendency will work against the phenomena that I have been describing.

26. I have included the ministry as a "scientific field" despite its distinctive function of mediating between the sacred and profane. Among the Protestant and Jewish clergy, especially, one finds growing areas of scientific application: counselling, certain kinds of therapy, and the like. Its position is not entirely clear with respect to a definition of the professions as applied sciences, however. The law is a peculiar and interesting case. It demands a high level of specialized training that is based upon the rational investigation, analysis, and codification of legal procedures, doctrines, and precedents. In this sense, it may be considered "scientific." But the legal specialties are highly varied in the degree to which they provide help as I have defined it, that is, assist clients with problems centered on their motivational capacities to enact legitimate social roles. The provision of help certainly characterizes criminal or divorce law and may perhaps be stretched to include such fields as taxation, but what of admiralty or patent law, for example? In these and similar areas of legal practice the lawyer may assist the client to define his rights and liabilities and thus be involved in a helping relation. On the other hand, many of a lawyer's services are more narrowly technical, as in safeguarding the transfer of property, or may be concerned mainly with channeling the client's conduct in relatively "safe" directions or in representing the client to others (e.g., legislative lobbying) without much concern for his motives. Indeed one might argue that to the extent that the client's conduct involves deviance, the lawyer is supportive and permissive and at the same time rather fully reciprocates the client's conduct, so that he fosters the vicious circle of deviance while protecting the deviant from social control — viz., the popular reputation of the "shyster," or, at the other end of the prestige scale, the "Philadelphia lawyer." There are to be sure similar elements in all professions, but they are unusually clear in legal practice. Relatively few physicians seek to "protect" patients from recovery, although some private physicians, for example, may cater to hypochondriacs for the sake of the fees they can pay. Another issue is the case of practitioners of helping professions whose services are largely or entirely to colleagues, the pathologist for instance. Their services occur in a symmetrical relation, but of a special colleague-to-colleague kind. To simplify matters, I must ignore these fascinating complications presented by the varieties of legal and other professional practice.

27. Here I assume a clientele that is voluntarily recruited. This is not always the case, with additional problems for trust that I shall discuss later.

28. See, for example, Willard Waller, *The Sociology of Teaching* (New York: Wiley, 1932); C. Wayne Gordon, *The Social System of the High School* (Glencoe; The Free Press, 1957); Jules Henry, "Docility; On Giving the Teacher What She Wants," *Journal of Social Issues*, 11 (1955), pp. 33-41.

29. T. Parsons, "The School Class as a Social System," *Harvard Educational Review*, 29 (1959), pp. 297-318.

30. Parsons, "The School Class as a Social System," *op. cit*; Robert Dreeben, *On What Is Learned in School* (Reading, Mass.; Addison-Wesley, 1968), pp. 34-35.

31. On expressive components of teaching, discussed with respect to higher school levels, see Parsons, *The Social System*, pp. 240-242.

32. Elihu Katz and S. N. Eisenstadt, "Some Sociological

Observations on the Response of Israeli Organizations to New Immigrants," *Administrative Science Quarterly*, 5 (1960), pp. 113-133.

33. See especially Parsons, "The School Class as a Social System," *op. cit.*

34. This is not to say that in other respects affective elements may not be of great significance at these levels of schooling. For example, the greater salience and specificity of role destinations may imbue a teacher with a focussed but intense quality as a moral exemplar or role model (a phenomenon related to the "respect" for the teacher of which Parsons speaks). Thus higher levels of schooling may have greater affective impact on students' identities, through means that in point of fact would be considered somewhat out of place in the lower grades.

35. See Gordon, *op. cit.*; Waller, *op. cit.*

36. As Parsons notes, voluntary and involuntary elements are mixed in the recruitment process — for example, the person who satisfies his "personal circle" by seeing a doctor or the primary school pupil for whom schooling is both mandatory and evidence of age-grade attainment.

37. There are also three principal mixed types of client recruitment. First, recruitment to the client role may be mandatory, but selection of the helping agent is left to the client or to a client-surrogate (e.g., voucher systems of education or private elementary and secondary education). Second, the potential client may realize his need for help but for reasons reviewed earlier resist making this need explicit by becoming a client. Here the "personal circle" may act to "tip the balance" (partic-ularistic influence) or the availability of nonmandatory service on a universalistic principle may help him decide to become a client (e.g., public health clinics, family guidance centers, or hospital emergency rooms). Third, the client may select freely a client-serving organization, but the organization assigns him to those member or members of its professional staff who will deliver the help. This third mixed type, of course, is limited to professional help offered by organizations and parallels the first type in the sense that the helping agent, the client-serving organization, acts as a surrogate for the client in selecting the specific professional helpers (e.g., voluntary admission to a hospital as a "charity" patient). I shall discuss later some of its implications for client trust.

38. Note the parallel to the constraints of a "formally free" labor market [Max Weber, *The Theory of Social and Economic Organizations*, Talcott Parsons (tr.), (New York: Oxford University Press, 1947), pp. 235-236] a market that despite the absence of "appropriation" may be highly alienating for individual workers.

39. I shall be able to discuss only collectivities of clients, although the social organization of the professional collegium is another topic of equal significance.

40. It also is possible that the professional staff will be in conflict over the treatment of a case or divided in other ways of which clients become aware. Such conflicts seem likely to erode client trust in the staff members, as specialists, though they may foster affective trust in those staff members perceived by the clients as "on their side."

INDEX

A

Abilities, 249
Abstraction, 3, 50, 63–65, 170, 423
Accommodation, 211–15, 221
Achievement norms, 407–409, 758, 774, 811
Action, 125, 152, 170, 202, 248, 290–91, 451–52, 510, 515–18, 523–27n., 536–37
    components of, 4–8, 241–42
    levels of, 8–9, 16, 22n.
    process, 117
    social, 4
    system of, 5, 183, 203, 241–43
Action theory
    criticisms of, 3–7, 10, 15–19, 35, 197, 258, 273, 297–300, 355, 642–48, 676, 802, 866–69
    epistemology, 3, 27, 39–44
    frame of reference, 4–5, 139, 278
    fundamental duality, 5, 91, 93, 108–109
    metaphysical foundations, 33, 39–44, 90–122
    methodology, 51–56, 296
Activities, 802, 861, 866–71
Actor, 4, 7, 33, 106, 130, 133
Actor-situation duality, 10, 13
Adams, R. N., 432
Adaptation, 210–12
Adaptive capacity, 669–71, 737
Adaptive function, 132–33, 471
Adaptive upgrading, 214, 456
Adolescence, 377, 407–14, 438, 442
Advertising, 618
Affect, 10, 131, 148, 154, 165, 201–202, 217, 343, 616–17, 899–902
Affinal bond, 420–21, 425–28
Age, 332, 900
AGIL scheme: see Four-function paradigm
Agrarian societies, 746, 764–66
Alexander, H. B., 285, 288, 359
Alienation, 19, 300, 303–306, 323, 346, 368, 372, 574, 634, 723, 746, 750
Allport, Gordon W., 357
Almond, Gabriel, 369, 454, 725
Altick, R. D., 631

Ambivalence, 372, 375
Analytical aspects, 3, 39–40, 49, 105, 280, 423
Analytical realism, 3, 27–28, 33, 39, 260
Anderson, A. R., 182
Angell, Robert C., 719–24
Anomie, 300, 303, 314, 762, 768–69, 884–86
Approval, 345
Apter, David, 762
Aquinas, T., 287
Archaic societies, 271, 513, 774, 780
Archimedes, 26
Arendt, Hannah, 288, 601
Aristotle, 32, 37, 102, 283, 288, 513
Art, 132, 152, 159, 168, 176, 228, 265, 267, 520
Ascetic, 305
Ashby, W. R., 508
Ascription, 465, 671–72, 744
Aspirations, 324–25, 391–406, 410
Assimilation, 211–15, 221
Associationism, 367
Atkinson, J. W., 400
Attitude, 357–59
Audiences, 741
Ault, P. M., 633
Authoritarianism, 370, 379–81
Authority, 322, 329, 332, 342, 810, 816, 830, 836, 848, 855, 863–64, 891–92

B

Bacon, Francis, 38, 41–42, 44, 298
Bales, R. F., 42, 122, 321–22, 332, 380, 432–37, 673
Banking, 254–55, 466, 645; see also Media of exchange
Barber, Elinor, 779
Barnard, Chester I., 822, 863
Barter, 9, 256, 457, 646–47
BASE model, 133
Baum, Rainer C., 26–34, 400–401, 448–69, 533–56, 579–608
Beatles, 380, 546
Behavior, 170
Behavioral organism, 7, 22n., 132, 155, 160, 195, 395

The editors gratefully acknowledge the assistance of Mr. Ed Herberg in the preparation of much of this index as well as the help of Ms. Sheila Nilsson and Ms. Eileen Swinton.

Behavioral system, 132–33, 147, 203–204, 213–15, 441–44
Behaviorism, 66–67, 198, 396–97
Beliefs, 126, 147
Bellah, Robert N., 212, 272, 535–37, 580, 674–76, 695, 706, 749, 758, 763, 774, 785
Ben-David, Joseph, 803, 874–88
Bendix, Reinhard, 745, 757
Beneviste, E., 543
Benitez, J. C., 360
Bentham, Jeremy, 300
Berelson, Bernard, 648–50
Berger, Bennett, 377
Berger, Gaston, 285, 290
Berle, A. A., 650
Bidwell, Charles E., 803–804, 889–909
Biehl, K., 453
Biological organism, 203
Blau, Peter, 863
Blumer, Herbert, 66, 515, 756
Body image, 385
Bohr, Niels, 36
Boorstin, D., 615
Bourricaud, François, 460, 557–78
Braithwaite, R. B., 47, 56
Brecht, B., 347
Broom, L., 357
Brown, Roger, 152
Buber, Martin, 290
Burckhardt, J., 304
Bureaucracy, 570, 573, 758, 803, 808, 858, 863
Burke, Kenneth, 152, 273–74, 295

C

Cancian, Francesca M., 47, 324–25, 354–66
Capital, 691
Capitalism, 296–97, 305–306, 483
Cartwright, Bliss C., 467, 639–60
Cassirer, Ernst, 152, 171, 266, 281
Cathexis, 42, 99–104, 130, 164, 373
Cazeneuve, Jean, 632
Center and periphery, 571, 575–76, 727, 739–41, 788–93
Centralization, 261
Change, 15–18, 29–30, 55, 69–71, 117, 126, 404, 450, 459–60, 541, 551, 563, 596–97, 604, 662–712, 795, 876; *see also* Differentiation, Evolution

Charisma, 372, 376n., 379, 466, 478, 500n., 706, 796, 882, 885
Chicago school, 79
China, 459
Chombart de Lauwe, P., 392–94, 397
Chomsky, N., 139, 155, 175
Church, 816, 833
Cicourel, Aaron V., 139
Class, 297, 299, 885
Code, 137, 140, 144, 252, 256, 444, 461, 475, 498n., 520, 589, 599–601, 640, 789–97
Cognitive rationality, 335, 345
Cognitive systems, 266
Coleman, J., 409–12, 647
Collective behavior, 368–69, 378, 382
Collective consciousness, 310, 371
Collective representations, 146, 148
Collectivities, 8–9, 451, 805–806
Collins, Randall, 757
Colonialism, 760
Commitments: *see* Value commitments
Commonsense, 26–28
Commune movement, 413
Communication, 137, 286, 511, 534, 540–56, 616, 724
Community, 298–99
Competition, 626, 677
Complexity, 262
Complexity (or contingency) reduction, 5, 11, 251–52, 508–24, 535, 539–50, 584, 592
Comte, Auguste, 84, 558, 681, 686
Concrete structures, 451
Conflation, 582, 587, 591–92, 601–606
Conflict, 4, 16–18, 129, 145, 297, 355, 671, 677, 747, 757, 765–69
Conflict theory, 558, 560, 684–85
Consciousness, 103
Consensus, 464, 576, 725, 739, 744, 815
Conservative bias, 18–19
Consummatory passivism, 323
Contract, 299, 301, 810, 860–62
Cooley, C. H., 510, 616–17
Coordinative standards, 14
Cottle, Thomas J., 321–23, 328–53
Cowley, M., 377
Creativity, 394
Crisis, 575
Cross, H. L., 628
Crozier, M., 573–74
Cultural system, 7, 22n., 119–20, 126–27, 147, 169, 284, 291, 395, 626
definition of, 182, 266

HETERICK MEMORIAL LIBRARY
301.01 E96 v.2
/Explorations in general theory in socia   onuu

3 5111 00152 2964